The Human Odyssey

LIFE-SPAN DEVELOPMENT

The Human Odyssey

LIFE-SPAN DEVELOPMENT

PAUL S. KAPLAN
Suffolk County Community College

WEST PUBLISHING COMPANY
St. Paul   New York   Los Angeles   San Francisco

To My Wife
Leslie Rochelle Kaplan
My Life's Companion
From Courtship to Future Golden Years

Copyediting Peggy Hoover
Design Diane Beasley
Illustrations Rolin Graphics, Cyndie Clark-Huegel
Composition Parkwood Composition Service, Inc.
Cover Design David J. Farr, Imagesmythe, Inc.
Cover Art Claude Monet, *Wild Poppies*, 1873, Louvre
Museum, Paris. Photographie Bulloz, Paris.

Library of Congress Cataloging-in-Publication Data
Kaplan, Paul S.
  The human odyssey.
  Includes index.
  1. Human growth. I. Title.
QP84.K36 1988   155.2   87-29441
ISBN 0-314-62539-9

Acknowledgments

Page 7, quotation. From *Cradles of Eminence*, by V. Goertzel and M. G. Goertzel. Copyright © 1962 by Little, Brown and Company. Reprinted by permission.

Page 18, Table 1.2. From "Practical Parenting with Piaget," by J. Thibault and J. McKee in *Young Children*, November 1982, by permission of the author.

Page 29, Fig. 1.1. From "Cross-Sectional Studies of Personality in a National Sample 2—Stability in Neuroticism, Extraversion, Openness" by Paul T. Costa et al. In *Psychology and Aging*, June 1986, 148. Copyright © The American Psychological Association. Used by permission of the author and the American Psychological Association.

Pages 52–53, Table 2.1. From "The Origin of Personality," by A. Thomas, S. Chess and H. G. Birch. Copyright © 1970 by Scientific American, Inc. All rights reserved.

Page 66, Table 3.1. Reprinted by permission from *Infancy—Infant, Family, and Society*, by A. Fogel. Copyright © 1984 by West Publishing Company. All rights reserved.

Page 68, Table 3.2. Reprinted by permission from *Human Intimacy*, by F. Cox. Copyright © 1984 by West Publishing Company. All rights reserved.

Page 74, Fig. 3.1. From *Before We Are Born*, 2nd Edition, by K. L. Moore, Philadelphia, W. B. Saunders Company, 1983. Used by permission of the author and publisher.

Page 76, Fig. 3.2. Reprinted by permission from *Understanding Nutrition*, by E. N. Whitney and E. M. N. Hamilton. Copyright © 1984 by West Publishing Company. All rights reserved.

Page 93, Fig. 4.1. From "The Origin of Form Perception," by R. L. Fantz. Copyright © 1961 by Scientific American. All rights reserved.

Page 100, Table 4.1. Reprinted by permission from *Introduction to Child Development*, 2nd Edition, by J. P. Dworetsky. Copyright © 1984 by West Publishing Company. All rights reserved.

Pages 106–7, Fig. 4.3. From *The First Two Years: A Study of Twenty-Five Babies*, by M. M. Shirley. Copyright © 1933, University of Minnesota. Original edition published by University of Minnesota Press, Minneapolis, Minnesota.

Page 110, Fig. 4.4. Reprinted by permission from *Understanding Nutrition*, 3rd Edition, by E. N. Whitney and E. M. N. Hamilton. Copyright © 1984 by West Publishing Company. All rights reserved.

Page 130, Table 5.2. From "Socioemotional Development," by L. A. Sroufe. In *Handbook of Infant Development*, J. Osofsky, ed. Copyright © 1979 by John Wiley & Sons, Inc. Reprinted by permission of John Wiley & Sons, Inc.

Page 138, Table 5.3. From *Infant Day Care: Toward a More Human Environment*, by A. L. Jacobson. Copyright © 1978 National Association for the Education of Young Children. All rights reserved.

(Continued following subject index)

CONTENTS IN BRIEF

(continued on next page)

C O N T E N T S

PART TWO

Infancy and Toddlerhood

PART THREE

Early Childhood

PART FOUR

Middle Childhood

PART   FIVE

Adolescence

PART SIX

Early Adulthood

PART SEVEN

Middle Adulthood

Later Adulthood

Sometimes a relatively simple idea has tremendous implications. Life-span development is such an idea. The life-span perspective forces us to look at development from a unique perspective. No longer can we simply equate development with growth, learning with childhood. We must take a longer view and look at the cumulative factors that affect people's lives from infancy through later maturity.

This book was written in the hope of offering students and professors a text that contains a balance of research, theoretical clarity, practical application, and objective and extensive coverage of current issues. Life-span development is an exciting, evolving field; I hope this text will convey some of that excitement and help you understand the directions in which the field is going.

Over the past two decades, the amount of research in life-span development has increased markedly and this text presents the modern scientific research in the field. The research in development is interdisciplinary in nature and research studies performed around the world by professionals representing such fields as psychology, education, health care and medicine, nutrition, and many others add greatly to our understanding of development. At the same time, in writing this text I have tried not to lose sight of the subjective experience of the individual who is negotiating the challenges of a particular period of life.

Sometimes the public believes that we have all the answers, that one theoretical view is somehow completely superior in all areas to another, or that there is complete agreement on issues. In order to remedy this, I have indicated where we have some of the answers and where there is basic controversy, demonstrated the strengths and weaknesses of various theoretical approaches, and presented issues as issues, noting why controversy exists and offering a number of different views of the issue in question. I have also tried to show how research results can help us with practical concerns. There are a number of new and exciting areas in life-span development such as the new research showing how family relationships change throughout childhood, adolescence, and adulthood and this research is evaluated from both the child's and parent's point of view.

This text also utilizes a wider perspective emphasizing the participation of the individual in his or her own development. This is seen in two ways. First, there is the popular reciprocal interaction view that notes that the individual affects the environment as well as the environment affecting the individual. No longer do we look just at how parents affect their children; we also examine how children affect their parents. No longer do we look only at how a manager affects his or her workers; we consider how workers affect their total environment. Second, there is the element of choice. Voluntary decision is seen as an important factor in development. Choice is found in childhood but becomes even more important as we look at life-span development and adulthood. An adult confronts many choices in the areas of marriage, family, and basic life-style and each choice leads to a different path. Today the number of choices available is greater than at any other time in history.

This text offers a number of special features that I hope will be helpful to the professor and the student. **Pedagogical features.** Each chapter begins with a *true-false motivational quiz*. The questions are repeated following the paragraphs in the body of the text where the answers can be found. An answer box is placed at the end of each chapter. Another feature is the *cross-cultural current*. Recently, there has been increasing interest in cross-cultural research and I have tried to include a great deal of this in the body of the text. However, in order to show the many challenges of conducting such research, I have used the cross-cultural current feature to describe some research studies in greater detail. These cross-cultural currents demonstrate how such research can aid us in better understanding the issues and concepts in life-span development. In addition, all *key terms* are presented in boldface and defined in a boxed *running glossary* which appears on the same page as the terms. A point by point *summary* can be found at the end of each chapter, and a *glossary* is presented at the end of the text.

Content. All texts in life-span development cover the basics and this text does so as well. However, I have found that many of the most interesting current and challenging topics and issues, especially those concerning adulthood, are often slighted or presented in a quick box that often makes them seem as if they are not connected with the main stream of developmental concerns. In this text, the important issues and interesting topics are dealt with within the body of the text and are not relegated to second-class status as boxes. For example, nutrition across the life span, bilingualism, day care, exercise, child abuse including psychological abuse, adjustment to retirement, nursing home care, mid-life questioning, mainstreaming for exceptional children, memory in later years, job satisfaction throughout life, the empty nest stage, the elderly driver, and many more topics are presented along with the current research surrounding them and without preaching. Many issues and topics that in a child development text are seen only from the child's viewpoint must in a life-span text be viewed from multiple perspectives. For example, divorce, stepparenting, and the changing nature of child-parent relationships throughout life are just some of the issues that must be looked at from both sides. In addition, the major theoretical approaches are discussed, evaluated, and updated. For example, the information-processing approach is covered throughout the text and many new theories of adulthood are presented. I have also tried to show the main points of agreement and disagreement as well as how theory is basically a useful tool.

Organization. This text is organized using the chronological and ages and stages approach with two variations and allows for a great deal of flexibility. Two special chapters covering language development and theories of adulthood are presented. Many professors prefer a separate chapter on language development because the topic raises so many fascinating questions and it is easier to focus on this important area if the material is given chapter-wide treatment. The theories of adulthood chapter was placed just before the chapters covering adulthood because we have few life-span theories. Most theories either cover childhood or begin in late adolescence or early adulthood. The placement of the chapter here allows for maximum flexibility.

Tables, figures, and appendices. Great care and attention have been given to the tables and figures throughout

the text. Many of the tables are summaries of material that will be helpful to students. The figures graphically present the material in a way that makes comparisons easier to comprehend. Some of the tables such as those covering genetic diseases, theorists, and height and weight have been placed in the Appendix to make them readily available for reference.

Examples and practical application. This text offers many examples and applications. The examples are an integral part of the text and the applications indicate how the principles of human development may be used to understand and predict behavior.

Instructors manual, test bank, and study guide with action/reaction exercises. An instructors manual with a test bank is available as well as a study guide written by Michael Jaffe of Kean College as part of the instructional package. The *Study Guide* and *Instructor's Manual* contain a number of useful exercises and material that complements the text. In addition, each contains a number of *action/reaction* features. These features present cases that illustrate various practical situations and problems and contain questions for thought and discussion.

A great many people are involved in the process of developing and writing a text. I wish to thank Peter Marshall, Mark Jacobsen, Maralene Bates, Laura Mezner, Jane Bacon and so many other people at West Publishing Company whose professionalism, expertise, understanding, and encouragement made this book possible. I also wish to thank Dr. Everett Waters of the State University of New York at Stony Brook for helping me better understand some of the current controversies in the field, Dr. Jaime Colomé of California Polytechnic and State University for his help with the genetics table in the Appendix, and Professor Sandra Kreeger of Suffolk County Community College for her help in clarifying some of the issues. I have been fortunate to receive valuable assistance in those areas that deal with medical and health concerns from Dr. Stanley Tyler, a dedicated and knowledgeable physician who has always been ready to help. In addition, it is often necessary to locate difficult sources and I would like to thank David Quinn and Joyce Malik of the Suffolk County Community College Western Campus Library for their help in this regard. Constructive criticism is an indispensible part of writing the text and I have been fortunate to receive feedback from a number of professionals. I would like to express my personal gratitude to the following members of the academic community:

Felice Green, University of N. Alabama
David Geary, University of Texas-El Paso
Peggy Pearl, SW Missouri State University
George Holden, University of Texas-Austin
John Klein, Castleton State College
Ronald Mullis, North Dakota State University-Main
Francis Terrell, North Texas State University
Sandy Fiske, Onandaga Community College
Terrence Luce, University of Tulsa
Murray Krantz, Florida State University
Sharon Nelson-LeGall, University of Pittsburgh
Suzanne Waller, University of Wisconsin-Milwaukee
Craig Campbell, Weber State College

Virgil Christensen, Mankato State University
Stephen S. Coccia, Orange County Community College
W. F. Steinman, Jamestown College
Robert McLaren, California State University-Fullerton
Harriett Wall, University of Michigan-Flint
Shirley Breeden, Grossmont Community College
Don Stanley, North Harris Community College
Paula Avioli, Kean College
Betty Lorch, University of Kentucky-Lexington
Jim Brown, San Diego State University

Writing a book is indeed a family affair and I would like to thank my wife, to whom this book is dedicated, and my children Stacey, Amy, Jodi, and Laurie for their understanding and patience during the process of writing this text.

PART ONE

Foundations

The Challenge of
Human Development

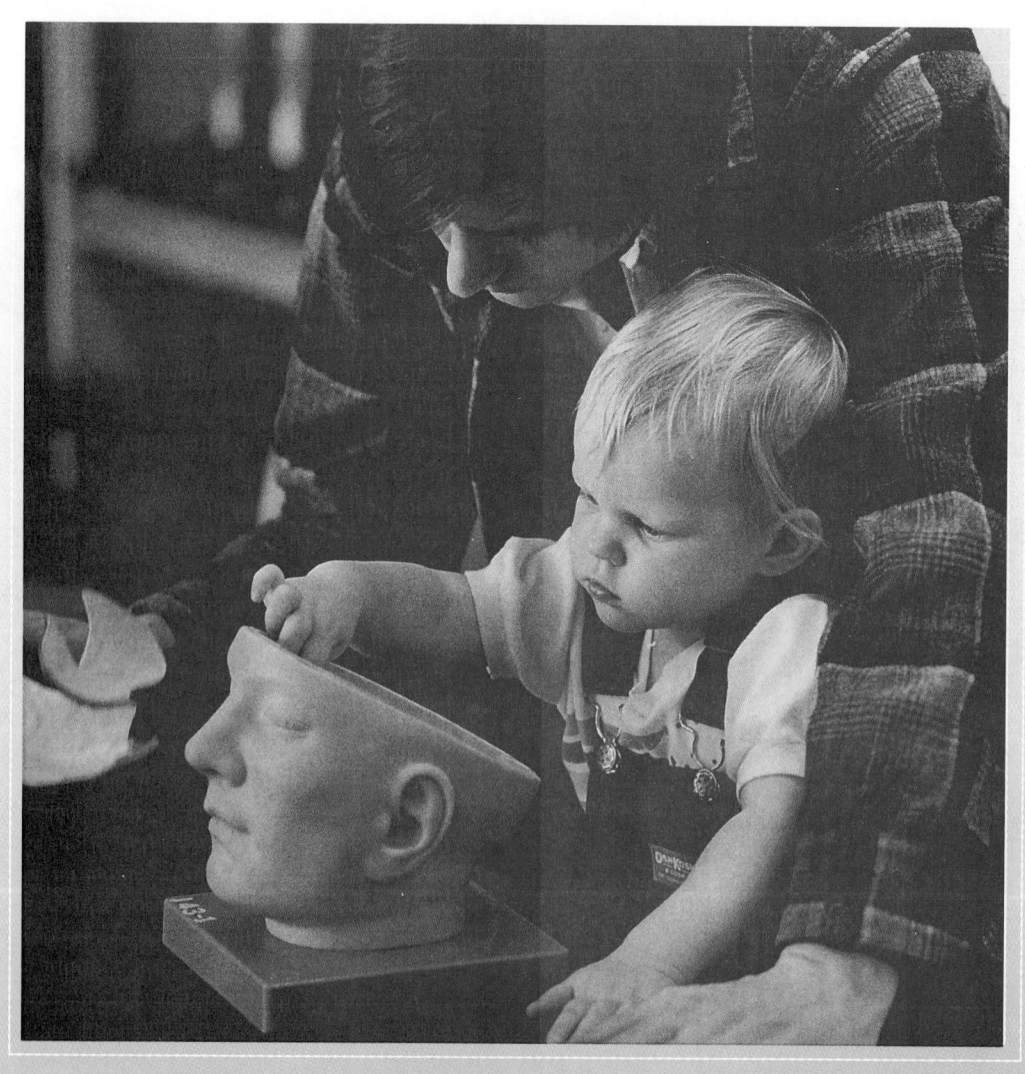

❖

Are the Following Statements True or False?

Try the True-False Quiz below. See if your answers correspond to the information in this chapter. Each question is repeated after the paragraph in which the answer can be found. The True-False Answer Box at the end of the chapter lists the complete answers.

_____ 1. Children's understanding of friendship remains remarkably stable between early childhood and late adolescence.

_____ 2. Older adults are more likely than younger people to be cautious and to value accuracy over speed when presented with a problem to solve.

_____ 3. Studies show that terrorists' childhood experiences are marked by hopefulness and a surprising lack of anger.

_____ 4. The consequences of a poor early environment are permanent and cannot be overcome.

_____ 5. About one in every five children today grows up in a single-parent family.

_____ 6. Freud believed that children under the age of ten experience sexual urges comparable to adult sexuality.

_____ 7. It is dangerous for a small and vulnerable toddler to develop a sense of autonomy.

_____ 8. There are many qualitative differences in the ways young children and adults reason.

_____ 9. School-age children have difficulty understanding political cartoons and proverbs.

_____10. Observation is not a valid tool for conducting research.

_____11. Two traits that seem to be stable in adulthood are extroversion and openness.

_____12. Most psychological experiments cause no physical or psychological harm to the people who participate in them.

The Continuous Process of Development

Write down five ways in which you have changed in the last ten years. Think about it for a moment. Are you as aggressive as you were ten years ago? Have your political and religious attitudes and values changed? What about your goals in life? If you have trouble with this task, ask some people who know you well and check your perceptions with theirs.

Now consider the future. How do you think you will change in the next ten years, twenty years, or thirty years? To answer these questions, think about the kind of lifestyle you would like in the future, what psychologists call the "dream." Consider also the lives of people who are ten, twenty, or thirty years older than you. How do their concerns and activities differ from what yours are now?

By performing this little task, you will come to realize that development continues throughout the adult years and that different challenges and concerns arise in each stage of life. **Life-Span Developmental Psychology** is concerned with describing, explaining, and at times modifying the changes that occur over the entire life span, from cradle to grave (Baltes et al., 1980). It seeks to discover how organisms change quantitatively and qualitatively over time. This does not mean that people change so much that there is no continuity. As we shall see, there is considerable stability over time in some areas. Although you may change a great deal between adolescence and middle adulthood, you are still somehow the same person. In this text, we shall be looking at both change and stability throughout the life span.

The Nature of Change

Developmental psychologists catalog changes into two distinct categories—quantitative change and qualitative change (Appelbaum and McCall, 1983). Some changes are both qualitative and quantitative.

Quantitative Change

If we could chart the number of hairs on a person's head, we would see an increase from birth through adolescence

life-span developmental psychology The study of human development that is concerned with describing, explaining, and at times modifying the changes that occur over the entire life span.

and then a slow decline. The same might be said for teeth. Our teeth come in until we have all our baby teeth; then we begin to lose them and get permanent teeth. We stay with that set until in late adulthood we may slowly begin to lose teeth. Height and weight also fit into this category. Any changes that involve an in-

The changes that occur during infancy and toddlerhood are dramatic and easy to see.

crease or decrease in some characteristic are **quantitative.** Such changes are usually quantified easily—for example, in terms of inches or pounds.

Qualitative Change

Qualitative change is different. Try this experiment. Cut out sixteen pictures from various magazines. Make certain that four pictures show food, four show pieces of furniture, four show toys, and four show items of clothing. Ask children of various ages first to look at all the pictures and then try to recall as many pictures as they can, after a minute or two of study. As you would expect, the older children will remember more of the items than the younger children will (Brown et al., 1983). This is basically a quantitative change in ability to recall information. But if you had observed them studying the pictures, you would have noticed a qualitative change in the strategies they used to help them remember the items (Kail and Hagen, 1982). Younger children do not make use of the categories, while older children do (Furth and Milgram, 1973).

Qualitative changes involve changes in process or function. For example, a child's understanding of and practice of friendship changes as the child grows (Selman, 1981). Until about age four, friendship is defined by physical proximity or by a desire to play with another child's toys. Between the ages of four and nine, children engage in one-way friendships—friendships in which they do not practice the give-and-take that characterizes later friendships. Elementary school children adopt the idea of give-and-take in friendship, but they are motivated by self-interest, not mutuality. Somewhere between the ages of nine and fifteen, children begin to share feelings as well as material things. These friendships, though, are limited by jealousy and exclusivity and are punctuated by frequent disagreements and hurt feelings when the children interact. The final stage, where friendship involves mutuality and trust, is seldom reached before age twelve.

True or False Children's understanding of friendship remains remarkably stable between early childhood and late adolescence.

quantitative changes Changes that can be considered solely in terms of increases or decreases, such as changes in height or weight.

qualitative changes Changes in process or function.

Qualitative changes occur throughout the life cycle. For instance, older adults may solve certain types of problems differently from younger people. In general, older people are more likely to be cautious, to value accuracy over speed, and to stay with a strategy longer once they adopt it than young adults (Botwinick, 1984; Salthouse, 1982). What is important here is that older adults approach the problem-solving process differently, not that they solve more or fewer problems correctly. Because people approach problems or think differently does not mean that one way of problem-solving is necessarily better than another. Differences do not necessarily mean deficits.

True or False Older adults are more likely than younger people to be cautious and to value accuracy over speed when presented with a problem to solve.

Basic Themes in Life-Span Development

The study of life-span development is based on a number of themes that will be developed throughout this text (see Featherman, 1983).

Developmental Changes Occur over the Entire Life Span

Many people believe that development is synonymous with growth and therefore ignore the idea that development continues over the life span. However, in the last twenty years the entire concept of life-span development has gained momentum, and it continues to thrive. Many books about development in adulthood have made the best-seller list, and courses in life-span development as well as adulthood are becoming popular in colleges.

Developmental Changes Are Influenced by Many Biological, Social, Psychological, Physical, and Cultural Factors

The days when psychologists said that certain developmental events were due to biological changes and others solely to environmental changes and learning are over. There are indeed some areas in development, like growth, that are determined mostly but not entirely by one's genetic endowment, and other areas, like balancing a checkbook, that are affected mostly by learning. However, usually both genetic and environmental determinants are important in understanding behavior.

Maturation. The unfolding of an individual's unique genetic plan is known as **maturation** (Hottinger, 1980). Maturation largely explains such things as the time a child's teeth erupt, the time an adolescent girl first menstruates, and the physical aging process. The maturational process depends most strongly on the individual's genetic master plan. This master plan, which functions as a timetable of sorts, largely (but not entirely) determines when certain events will occur. The genetic master plan may also place limits on the speed of progress. For example, before a baby can walk, he or she must have the necessary strength and balance, which are determined largely by maturation (Stewart, 1980). A child is ready to walk only after this prerequisite is met. However, the environment must be taken into consideration too, because nutrition and experience are important as well (Bower, 1977). Infants need opportunities to practice their skills. Most of the time, it is not too difficult to provide these basic experiences.

The same is true of the aging process. The aging process itself is thought to be under genetic control (Schneider, 1978). But people who take good care of themselves show fewer signs of aging (Botwinick, 1984). People who get little exercise, eat a diet rich in fat, drink alcohol immoderately, believe exercise stops at adolescence, and do not get proper rest are likely to show signs of aging much earlier than people who have better health habits.

Learning and experience. The maturation process proceeds in much the same way for people in all cultures. Unlike the learning process, whose course is determined largely by external events, maturation is determined largely by internal signals. Any relatively permanent changes in behavior caused by interaction with the environment

> **maturation** A term used to describe changes that are due to the unfolding of an individual's genetic plan. These changes are relatively immune to environmental influence.
>
> **learning** Relatively permanent changes in behavior due to interaction with the environment.

are due to **learning.** By definition, such changes cannot be the result of maturation (Rachlin, 1976). When a child recites the alphabet or imitates a brother's fear of spiders, or when an adult plays one way with a son and a different way with a daughter, learning has occurred.

A person's understanding of sex roles, morality, and problem-solving are dependent on learning, but we cannot see learning. We can only infer from behavioral change that learning has taken place. A person who couldn't balance a checkbook a week ago but can now is said to have learned.

In contrast to maturation, learning is extremely dependent on the environment. Children learn what they see and experience. Children whose parents habitually fight, scream at their children, and encourage them to be aggressive will learn to be aggressive. These children may grow up to interact with their spouses the same way, and perhaps even raise their children in a similar manner. Children who are abused or neglected often abuse and neglect their own offspring (Galston, 1975).

Parents are not the only influence on their children. As children's social world expands, peers, teachers, friends, colleagues at work, supervisors, television, and a host of other environmental influences affect what they learn. When Patterson and colleagues (1967) observed children in nursery school, they found that when preschoolers' aggressive acts got them what they wanted from another person, the aggressor was more likely to attack that victim again. Some children who were at first passive began to fight back, and if they were successful some of them began to initiate aggression too.

The Factors That Determine Development Express Themselves Cumulatively

There is a proverb that says the child is the father of the man. There is some truth to that. Early experience is important. Children who do not receive enough emotional care may show abnormal behavior patterns that

Skills like walking depend greatly upon maturation. However, the child also requires an opportunity to practice this skill.

limit later social and emotional functioning (Rutter, 1979). Indeed, the psychological makeup of terrorists has been linked to their experiences in childhood involving hopelessness and rage and a lack of nonviolent role models; the only effective role models terrorists had belonged to terrorist groups. In addition, about half the terrorists studied described a life-threatening childhood illness that few in their culture survive. This led them to deny the risk of death in adulthood (see Goleman, 1986a). Other studies found that aggression as well as altruism can be traced to childhood influences (Hornstein, 1976). Physical problems in the elderly may be related to childhood experiences. The earliest stages of hardening of the arteries are seen in teenagers who have high plasma cholesterol levels. It seems that all we have to do is look at factors in childhood to explain adult behavior.

True or False Studies show that terrorists' childhood experiences are marked by hopefulness and a surprising lack of anger.

But consider these two cases:

Boy, senior year secondary school, has obtained certificate from physician stating that nervous breakdown makes it necessary for him to leave school for six months. Boy not a good all-around student; has no friends—teachers find him a problem—spoke late—father ashamed of son's lack of athletic ability—poor adjustment to school. Boy has odd mannerisms, makes up own religion, chants hymns to himself—parents regard him as "different."

Girl, age sixteen, orphaned, willed to custody of grandmother by mother, who was separated from alcoholic husband, now deceased. Mother rejected the homely child, who has been proven to lie and to steal sweets. Swallowed penny to attract attention at five. Father was fond of child. Child lived in fantasy as the mistress of father's household for years. Four young uncles and aunts in household cannot be managed by the grandmother, who is widowed. Young uncle drinks; has left home without telling the grandmother his destination. Aunt, emotional over love affairs, locks self in room. Grandmother resolves to be more strict with granddaughter since she fears she has failed with own children. Dresses granddaughter oddly. Refused to let her have playmates, put her in braces to keep back straight. Did not send her to grade school. Aunt on paternal side of family crippled; uncle asthmatic. (Goertzel and Goertzel, 1962, p. xiii)

These descriptions of the early environments of two children would make it difficult for you to give a positive prognosis for their later adjustment or accomplishments in life. But the first case describes Albert Einstein, and the second describes the early life of Eleanor Roosevelt, wife of President Franklin D. Roosevelt and a powerful figure in her own right. So it is apparently not so easy to make sweeping generalizations and predictions based on early childhood data.

Early experiences are important, but later experience can compensate at least partially for poor early experiences. Children raised under very poor conditions are often retarded in many areas of development, but with extra care and attention the effects of that environment can be compensated for, to some degree (Clarke and Clarke, 1976). A study of children whose early environment was very poor found that they improved greatly when they were adopted later in childhood (Kadushin, 1976). In another study, children were observed in a mountainous, isolated area of Guatemala (Kagan, 1976; Kagan and Klein, 1973). The researchers described the infants as silent and pathetic, and the three-year-olds as passive, quiet, and timid. The eleven-year-olds, how-

The case of Albert Einstein demonstrates how difficult it can be to make predictions for people based on early childhood experiences.

ever, were active, happy, and intellectually competent. These children were restricted in infancy, and adult-child interaction was minimal, but this all changed in the second year of life. When the children began to walk, their social world expanded greatly to include other children, domestic animals, and other adults. In middle childhood they were required to do chores and care for younger siblings. When a number of culture-free tests, such as tests involving memory and perception were administered to these children, the researchers found that by age ten these Guatemalan children were just as capable as American children. The effects of early experience, then, can be modified by later experience.

True or False The consequences of a poor early environment are permanent and cannot be overcome.

Psychologists often focus on early experience because most children who have a poor start continue to be

victims of a poor environment throughout childhood and adolescence, resulting in poor interpersonal relationships in adulthood. If children enter school already behind in certain important skills and nothing is done to help them catch up and achieve, they may fall further behind and never fulfill their potential. This may affect vocational opportunities, the nature of their social world, and their interests in adulthood. In other words, often early childhood experience seems so important because there is no change in the environment in later childhood. Where a positive change does occur, better outcomes are the rule. Of course, prevention is easier and superior to remediation, and it is best to create a good early environment for children instead of trying to reverse the problems caused by poor early experience.

The Challenges People Face as They Develop Are Somewhat Predictable

People face certain challenges during certain periods of their lives. The two-year-old begins the task of becoming toilet-trained, the six-year-old must cope with school, the thirteen-year-old with puberty, the young adult with occupational considerations and marital questions, the middle-aged person with the loss of parents, and older adults with retirement and chronic illness. Such challenges are roughly related to age, but they need not be. A young adult may lose a parent, and a child may suffer a chronic illness.

People Are Affected by the Historical Time in Which They Live

The generation of the 1960s and 1970s was greatly affected by the Vietnam War; the present generation views that war as history. The present generation is used to computers; older people are not. This effect of growing up in a particular time period is known as the **cohort effect.** Look at the differences between generations. Twenty-five years ago, one child in ten grew up in a single-parent household, but currently it is somewhat more than one in five (U.S. Bureau of the Census, 1986). The present generation is better educated than any generation before. Events that occur at one point in time—such as economic depressions, epidemics, and revolutions—affect people's lives greatly (Baltes et al., 1980). People in the same generation share common experiences (Bronfenbrenner and Crouter, 1983). Older people talk about the Great Depression, younger adults speak of the 15 percent inflation rate in the early 1980s. Whenever one is comparing people of different ages, the cohort effect must be taken into account.

True or False About one in every five children today grows up in a single-parent family.

Individual Factors Cannot Be Ignored

Even if you are the same age as your friend and therefore grew up in the same historical period, there are differences between you. You have had different personal experiences. The death of a parent at an early age, divorce, winning the lottery, and severe illness and unemployment are examples of significant events that occur in the lives of some people and are relatively unpredictable. In developmental psychology, we take these events, as well as a person's subjective experience, into consideration.

Intervention Can Be as Effective with Older People as It Is with Younger People

Older people can be taught to solve problems in new ways and can be helped to improve their performance, even on intelligence tests (Denney, 1982). We also know that we can teach older workers new skills. But people usually think of intervention in terms of the younger person, particularly the child. Special programs are designed to stimulate premature infants to enable them to function better in life (Rice, 1977). Preschool programs are designed so children can improve their skills and succeed later in their school years (Lazar et al., 1982). But the common belief that older people cannot learn new skills keeps us from working with middle-aged and elderly people to help them change. This is unfortunate, because there is ample evidence that adults remain malleable throughout life (Featherman, 1983).

Focus on Stability

So far we have been looking at change, but what of stability? Some patterns, such as personality traits, are

quite stable in adult[   ] dren who showed te[   ] of age were later ju[   ] irritable, and moody t[   ] et al., 1987). Becaus[   ] bility is sometimes d[   ] personality structure [   ] if we examine the inte[   ] uli, we find an interes[   ] may cry loudly at the [   ] laugh hard when a par[   ] to greet his father and [   ] laughing hard at five years, and tear up an entire page of homework if one mistake is made, or slam the door of his room when teased by his younger brother, at ten years (see Thomas et al., 1970). We would hardly expect a ten-year-old to show the same behavior as a one-year-old, even though the same structure—in this case, intensity—underlies all these behaviors and is relatively stable.

Theories of Development

Developmental psychologists have constructed a number of theoretical approaches to help us understand stability and change, but few of these approaches can be considered life-span theories. Many explore development only until late adolescence, ignoring the changes that occur in adulthood. Others begin their analysis of development in adulthood. Theories that deal mostly with childhood will be presented here, while theories that deal strictly with adulthood will be covered in Chapter 13.

Stage and Nonstage Theories

Do people develop in an orderly sequence of stages, or does development occur in a more continuous manner, without definite boundaries? Basically, developmental theories can be divided into two categories: stage theories and nonstage theories. Stage theories present development in terms of age-related periods in which people are faced with particular problems and have specific abilities. These theories see development as occurring in a stage-like sequence. Progression from stage to stage occurs in an invariant order, and new skills develop from skills acquired in previous stages. Each person progresses through the same stages and cannot skip a stage, but people may enter or leave a particular stage at different times, so it is incorrect to simply equate ages and stages. The ages

...s text are nothing more than av-
...and should not be thought of as ab-
...stage theories—Freud's psychoanalytic
...son's psychosocial theory, and Piaget's theory
...tive development—will be described here.

Freud's Psychoanalytic Theory

Most people have an opinion about Freud's theory. Usually, they are either fascinated by it or reject it out of
hand. But if you ask people what Freud said, many do
not understand it well at all. The following major elements comprise psychoanalytic theory.

Levels of Consciousness

Freud (1933, 1923, 1900) posited three levels of awareness. The **conscious** involves one's immediate awareness
and comprises only a small portion of the total mind.
The **preconscious** comprises memories that can easily
become conscious. For example, you may remember the
correct answers to the questions on an exam only after
the test is over (Kline, 1972). Finally, some memories—
as well as certain impulses and wishes—that are unacceptable to a person because they run counter to society's
standards are stored in the **unconscious,** the portion of

the mind that is beyond normal awareness. The unconscious may manifest itself in many ways—for instance,
through dreams and slips of the tongue.

Freud (1933) believed that behavior could be caused
and maintained by early experiences that had apparently
been forgotten. These experiences, which are stored in
the unconscious, are beyond normal awareness but can
still have a profound effect on behavior. For instance, a
person may experience sexual difficulties in marriage because of traumatic sexual experiences in childhood that
the individual no longer remembers (DiCaprio, 1983).

Freud insisted that we may not be aware of our true
motives and wishes, probably because they are unacceptable to us or because society forbids us to gratify
them. If a child who is angry at her mother kicks a

*The great depression of the 1930's affected an entire generation of people. The effect of growing
up in a particular time, called the cohort effect, must be taken into consideration when looking at
how generations differ from one another.*

younger sibling instead—a situation referred to as **displacement**—the child will refuse to admit to feelings of hostility toward her mother. The child is not lying, but is unaware of those feelings.

The Constructs of the Mind

Freud (1923, 1940) explained the workings of the mind using three constructs: the id, the ego, and the superego. The **id** is the source of all wishes and desires. It is unconscious and exists at birth. The id wants what it wants when it wants it and cannot tolerate delay. It functions through the **primary process,** which entails instant gratification for every wish and desire, and avoidance of pain and tension. In this sense, the infant is complete id.

Within the first year, the **ego** begins to develop. Some needs, such as hunger, can be satisfied only by interaction with the real world. The ego, which is partly conscious, operates through the **secondary** or **reality process.** It is responsible for dealing with reality and for satisfying the needs and desires of the id in a socially appropriate manner. Whereas the id knows only its subjective reality (I want), the ego must also understand the world outside the mind and the self. As the child grows and matures, the ego becomes stronger, becoming able to delay gratification and to balance the desires of the id with the restraints of the third construct, the superego.

The **superego** is analogous to the conscience. It contains the principles gathered from interacting with others in society and serves to regulate behavior. The superego compares your behavior to your **ego-ideal**— that is, what you think you should be like. The superego is perfectionistic, seeking to inhibit the id's antisocial desires and causing an individual to experience guilt when transgressing, or even considering a misdeed. The ego must mediate between the desires of the id, society's prohibitions, and the weight of superego constraint. Life is a compromise, and proper adjustment is a matter of maintaining a delicate balance.

Defense Mechanisms

The ego has a difficult job. It must satisfy the organism's needs, adhere to socially acceptable behavior, and not violate the built-in conscience—the superego. It is sometimes overwhelmed, and when that occurs the resulting tension is experienced as anxiety. If the anxiety becomes too great, the ego may defend itself by using a protective

displacement The process by which an emotion is transferred from one object or person to another more acceptable substitute.

id In Freudian theory, the portion of the mind that serves as the depository for wishes and desires.

primary process The process by which the id seeks to gratify its desires.

ego In Freudian theory, the part of the mind that mediates between the real world and the desires of the id.

secondary or reality process The process by which the ego satisfies the organism's needs in a socially appropriate manner.

superego In Freudian theory, the part of the mind that includes a set of principles, violation of which leads to feelings of guilt.

ego ideal The individual's positive and desirable standards of behavior.

defense mechanism A behavior that serves to relieve or reduce feelings of anxiety or emotional conflict.

eros In Freudian theory, the positive, constructive sex instinct.

maneuver called a defense mechanism. A **defense mechanism** is an automatic and unconscious process that serves to relieve or reduce feelings of anxiety or emotional conflict (Laughlin, 1970). For example, in the defense mechanism known as projection, feelings that are unacceptable to oneself are transferred to someone else. In such a case, a child who is angry at his mother for not driving him to the ballgame might ask her why she was angry at him, instead of saying he is angry at her. Table 1.1 shows common defense mechanisms.

The Psychosexual Stages

One of Freud's most challenging concepts is that of infantile and childhood sexuality, the idea that infants and children experience sexual feelings (Noam et al., 1982). But, Freud did not believe that young children experienced adult sexual feelings. His idea of sexuality resembles what we might consider sensuality and pleasure. Freud saw life as the unfolding of the sexual instinct called **eros.** The energy emanating from eros is known as the **libido,** which attaches itself to different portions of the body as the child matures. This is the basis for Freud's theory of development, which involves a description of the **psychosexual stages.** Freud (1933) stressed the importance of early experience in the formation of personality, and he focused attention on early parent-child interactions as determinants of later personality traits.

True or False   Freud believed that children under the age of ten experience sexual urges comparable to adult sexuality.

The oral stage.   At birth, the infant gets pleasure from sucking and then later from biting. During this oral stage, the child's need for oral experiences takes precedence

libido   In Freudian theory, the energy emanating from the sex instinct.

psychosexual stages   Stages in Freud's developmental theory.

over other needs. If a child is either frustrated or overly stimulated, the child may become fixated, that is a part of the child remains in the previous stage of psychosexual development, and development is partially arrested (Eidelberg, 1968). But this does not mean the child does not progress to the next step. Rather, the child's personality shows some characteristics of this fixation. According to Freud, fixation at this stage, if it involves

T A B L E 1.1

Defense Mechanisms

Defense mechanisms are used to reduce or eliminate unpleasant feelings such as anxiety or emotional conflict. This table shows some of the more prominent mechanisms.

Defense Mechanism	Description	Example
Rationalization	Making up plausible but inaccurate excuses to explain some behavior.	A student who is getting poor grades in school explains it away by telling you, "It's what you learn, not your grades, that are important" or "Schools teach nothing useful anyway."
Denial	A person refuses to believe something has occurred.	A person refuses to believe that someone has died.
Compensation	Making up for a real or imaginary deficiency by putting effort into a similar area (direct compensation) or into a different area (indirect compensation).	An unathletic person who feels physically inferior may buy body-building equipment and work out until he is a first-class weight lifter (direct compensation), or put his efforts into schoolwork to become the best student he can (indirect compensation).
Reaction Formation	An individual experiences feelings that are unacceptable to him or her and so acts in a manner that is contrary to those feelings.	A junior high school girl who likes a boy may act very rude or even hit him to "prove" to her friends that she doesn't really like him.
Projection	Feelings that are unacceptable to oneself are transferred to someone else.	A child who feels angry at his mother for not driving him to the ball game asks her, "Why are you angry at me?" instead of telling her he is angry at her.
Regression	Returning to a time in life that was more comfortable.	A 3-year-old girl who is talking and toilet-trained begins to talk baby talk and wet her pants after a baby brother is brought home from the hospital.
Repression	Memories are barred from consciousness so they no longer bother a person.	A person who accidentally struck another with his bat during a baseball game cannot remember the incident.
Displacement	The transfer of feelings from one person or object to another.	A child is angry at her father but yells at her sister.
Rechannelization (Sublimation)	Unacceptable impulses are rechanneled into socially appropriate pursuits.	An aggressive person learns to express himself through sports or music.

sucking, may lead to gullibility—accepting anything that is presented (Hall and Lindzey, 1957)—being dependent and inactive, and believing that others will provide the comforts of life for him (Kline, 1972). Freud also noted an intense concentration on such oral activities as eating and drinking in orally fixated individuals. Fixation at the biting stage may result in a sarcastic or "biting" personality that is often in conflict with others.

The anal stage. At about eighteen months of age, the muscles responsible for elimination mature to the extent where some control is possible. The libido becomes attached to the anal cavity from that age to about age three, and this coincides with attempts to toilet-train the child. The anal stage can be divided into the anal-expulsive and anal-retentive substages. In the first substage, the child gains pleasure from expelling the body's waste products. In the second, gratification is obtained from withholding them. If parents create a situation in which a power struggle rages over bowel and bladder control, an anal-retentive character may result. In that case, the child will gain satisfaction from holding back feces and may show such character traits as miserliness, obstinacy, and incredible orderliness and neatness. If, on the other hand, the child relents and gives feces, especially at inappropriate times, such anal-expulsive traits as cruelty and messiness result.

The phallic stage. At about the age of four, the libido becomes attached to the genital organs—the penis in males and the clitoris in females. There is no difference in the development of males or females in the oral or anal stages, but in the phallic stage the experiences of boys and girls differ greatly.

According to Freud, the child experiences the **Oedipus complex** during this stage. The young male experiences sexual feelings toward his mother and views his father as a rival for the mother's affections. The child's sexual attachment to the mother is defined by exclusivity and jealousy (Mullahy, 1948). Unconsciously, the child wants to take the father's place but is caught between his respect and positive feelings for his father and his jealousy and hostility toward him. At the same time, the child realizes he is at a great disadvantage in competing with his father because of the differences in size, and he fears his father will discover his desires and castrate him. He experiences castration anxiety. The young boy resolves this dilemma of wanting his mother but fearing

Oedipus complex. The conflict during the phallic stage in which a boy experiences sexual feelings toward his mother and wishes to do away with his father.

the father's retribution by identifying with his father and repressing—that is, burying—the feelings toward his mother deep in the unconscious.

In the case of the female the situation is more complicated, the Freud admitted there was not enough known about this subject (Mullahy, 1948). Nevertheless, he did posit a type of Oedipal situation (often called the Electra complex) for young girls. The young girl is first attached to her mother, but she turns her affection and attention to her father when she realizes she does not have a penis. She blames her mother for this situation and wishes to take her mother's place in her father's affection. This gives rise to "penis envy" and a desire to possess the male organ. Because castration is no threat to her, the resolution of the Electra complex is not as important or severe as in males. Instead of simply repressing her feelings toward her mother, a girl identifies with her mother and continues to build on the relationship she established before the phallic stage (Chodorow, 1981).

Problems in the phallic stage lead to a variety of disturbances in personality. For example, when the resolution of the Oedipal conflict is not positive, a boy will resent his father and generalize this resentment to authority figures later in life (Nye, 1975). A number of sexual problems also date from difficulties in this stage.

The latency stage. The phallic stage ends with the resolution of the Oedipal situation. The child then enters the latency stage. From about age six up to puberty, the child's sexuality lies dormant. Since the boy has identified with his father, he tends to imitate him at every turn. Boys have also repressed their feelings toward their mothers, but because they are so young this repression generalizes to all females. Thus, eight-year-old boys are likely to stay apart from eight-year-old girls. The resolution of the Electra situation is less abrupt in females, so there is not so much of this behavior with girls. Girls do show this aversion to boys, but usually on a much less intense level.

The genital stage. The emergence of puberty, with its hormonal changes and sexual arousal, throws the child out of latency stage and into the genital stage. The young adolescent boy turns his attention to a girlfriend, while the young adolescent female seeks a boyfriend. This is the beginning of mature adult sexuality.

Evaluation of Freud's Theory

Freud's emphasis on the importance of early interaction between parent and child has been largely accepted by psychologists, although few now believe that the marks and injuries suffered in childhood are necessarily permanent. In addition, some of Freud's concepts concerning the unconscious and defense mechanisms have allowed psychologists to obtain new understandings of behaviors that in the past were incomprehensible. Freud's idea that sexuality begins early in life is also challenging, but most psychologists disagree with his emphasis on sexuality.

On the other hand, psychoanalytic theory was formulated on the basis of Freud's clinical experiences (Cairns, 1983). His patients were troubled, and his theory may have more to say about abnormal development than normal development. It may be a mistake to base our ideas about normal development and child-rearing on clinical experiences with emotionally disturbed people. In addition, Freud's formulations are difficult to test empirically (Baldwin, 1967).

Erikson's Psychosocial Theory

Of all Freud's followers, Erik Erikson has had the greatest influence on developmental psychology. His theory is also one of the few theories that cover the entire life span, and it has become a popular way to view human development.

The Psychosocial Stages

Erikson (1963) argued that human beings develop according to a preset plan called the **epigenetic principle.** This principle consists of two main elements. First, personality develops according to predetermined steps that are maturationally set. Second, society is structured in a way that invites and encourages the challenges that arise at these particular times. Each individual proceeds through eight stages of development from cradle to grave. Each stage presents the individual with a crisis. If a particular crisis is handled well, the outcome is positive.

epigenetic principle The preset developmental plan in Erikson's theory consisting of two elements: that personality develops according to maturationally determined steps and that each society is structured to encourage challenges that arise during these times.

If it is not handled well, the outcome is negative. Few people emerge from a particular stage with an entirely positive or negative outcome. In fact, Erikson argues that a healthy balance must be struck between the two poles, although the outcome should tend toward the positive side of the scale. People can reexperience these crises during a life change, but by and large the crises take place at particular times in life. The resolution of one stage lays the foundation for negotiating the challenges of the next.

Erik Erikson's psychosocial theory was one of the first truly life-span theories, beginning its analysis in infancy and progressing through old age.

Trust vs. mistrust. The positive outcome of the stage of infancy is a sense of trust. If children are cared for in a warm, caring manner, they are apt to trust the environment and develop a feeling that they live among friends. If the parents are anxious, angry, or incapable of meeting a child's needs, the child may develop a sense of mistrust. Trust is the cornerstone of the child's attitude toward life.

Autonomy vs. shame or doubt. Two- and three-year-olds are no longer completely dependent on adults. Toddlers practice their new physical skills and develop a positive sense of autonomy. They learn that they are persons in their own right. If children of this age are either not allowed to do the things they can do, or are pushed into doing something for which they are not ready, they may develop a sense of shame or doubt about their own abilities and fail to develop self-confidence. Parents can help a child acquire a sense of autonomy if they encourage children to do what they can do for themselves.

True or False It is dangerous for a small and vulnerable toddler to develop a sense of autonomy.

Initiative vs. guilt. By the time children reach about four years of age, they can begin to formulate a plan of action and carry it through. The positive outcome of this stage is a sense of initiative, a sense that one's desires and actions are basically sound. If parents encourage children of this age to form their own ideas, the children will develop a sense of initiative. If a child is punished for expressing his or her own desires and plans, the child develops a sense of guilt, which leads to fear and a lack of assertiveness.

Industry vs. inferiority. During middle childhood, children must learn the academic skills of reading, writing, and math, as well as social skills. If a child succeeds in acquiring these new skills and if the accomplishments are valued by others, the child develops a sense of industry. But children who are constantly compared with others and come up a distinct second may develop a sense of inferiority.

Identity vs. role confusion. During adolescence, children must decide on their vocational and personal future and develop a sense of who they are and where they belong. The adolescent who develops a solid sense of identity formulates a satisfying plan and gains a sense of

security. Adolescents who do not develop this sense of identity may develop role confusion, a sense of aimlessness and being adrift without an anchor or plan.

The final three stages. Erikson's final three stages will be discussed in Chapter 13 with other perspectives on adulthood. Briefly, Erikson sees the positive outcome of early adulthood as the attainment of intimacy, while a person who is fearful or who chooses not to enter into close interpersonal relationships may develop a sense of isolation. In middle age, people must find a way to remain productive and to help others. This positive outcome Erikson called generativity, the negative outcome and danger being a feeling of stagnation. Finally, in old age people must develop a positive sense of pride about their accomplishments in life, which Erikson called ego integrity. If, on the other hand, all they see is missed opportunities, they may become depressed and bitter, developing a sense of despair.

Evaluation of Erikson's Theory

Erikson's theory is clear and easy to understand and serves as an excellent introduction to the general concerns of people at different ages. His vision of development as continuing throughout life is one that is now well accepted. In addition, Erikson's theory is far more optimistic and less biologically deterministic than Freud's. Finally, Erikson's conception of identity has become the cornerstone for understanding adolescence.

Criticisms of Erikson's theory follow those directed at Freud's theory. Erikson's theory is difficult to test experimentally. There is some support for Erikson's concept of identity (Hjelle and Ziegler, 1976), but little research has been done on the other stages. In addition, Erikson's theory is rather general and global, and some psychologists doubt that all his stages exist (Thomas, 1979). Despite these criticisms, Erikson's theory offers a convenient way to view development throughout the life span.

Piaget's Theory of Cognitive Development

Children are not little adults. Perhaps you shrug your shoulders at this rather banal statement, but for years most people did not really understand that children think and deal with problems differently from adults. They saw children's mistakes as signs of stubbornness against growing up. Jean Piaget devoted his adult life to studying the cognitive (intellectual) development of children, including how they think and how they develop their notions of time, space, math, and reality. Much of his work is sweeping and monumental in scope, and his is the most complete theory of cognitive development available today.

How Children Develop

According to Piaget, development involves continuous alteration and reorganization of the ways in which we deal with the environment (Piaget, 1970). Development is defined by four principal factors: maturation, experience, social transmission, and the process of equilibration. We have already discussed maturation—the gradual unfolding of the genetic plan for life. Experience involves the active interaction of the child with the environment. Social transmission refers to the information and customs that are transmitted from parents and other people in the environment to the child. We can consider this the educational function in the broad sense. Finally, the process of equilibration defines development. **Equilibration** is the process by which children seek a balance between what they know and what they are experiencing. When they are faced with information that calls for a new and different analysis or activity, children enter a state of disequilibrium. When this occurs, they must change the way they deal with the information and establish a new, more stable state of equilibrium. In this way children progress from a very limited ability to deal with new experiences to a more mature, sophisticated level of cognitive functioning. To Piaget, children are not simply passive receivers of stimulation. Children actively interact with the environment, and their active experiences impel them to new heights in cognitive functioning and action.

Piagetian Concepts and Processes

As children develop, they perceive and deal with the world in more sophisticated ways. Piaget uses the term **scheme** to describe an organized system of actions and thoughts useful for dealing with the environment that can be generalized to many situations (Piaget, 1952). For instance, the infant given a block may place it in her mouth and suck on it. This is the sucking scheme.

equilibration In Piagetian theory, the process by which children seek a balance between what they know and what they are experiencing.

scheme A method of dealing with the environment that can be generalized to many situations.

assimilation The process by which information is altered to fit into one's already existing structures.

When given other items, she may do the same. The infant is also master of other schemes, including looking, listening, grasping, hitting, and pushing. Schemes are tools for learning about the world, and they become more involved as the child matures and new schemes are developed. For instance, the child may first look at the block and bang it against the side of the crib. Later she may coordinate schemes—picking up the block, examining it, and placing it on top of another (a building scheme). Thus, two independent schemes become reorganized into a superordinate scheme that allows the child to adapt more easily to the environment.

Adaptation

Every being must adapt to its environment in order to survive. Adaptation can be understood in terms of adjustment. As the forces in the environment change, so must the individual's ability to deal with them. Adaptation involves two complementary processes: assimilation and accommodation.

Assimilation. In the process of **assimilation,** input is filtered or modified to fit already existing structures (Piaget and Inhelder, 1969). When we assimilate something, we alter the form of an incoming stimulus to adapt it to our already existing actions or structures (Piaget, 1983). If a child sees an odd-shaped piece of paper and uses it as an airplane, he has assimilated the paper into his structure and knowledge of an airplane. A child may bang a rattle against the side of the crib, but when given another toy—perhaps a plastic block—she will assimilate it by banging it against the crib too.

Accommodation. The process that involves modifying internal existing schemes to meet the requirements of new experience is called **accommodation** (Piaget and Inhelder, 1969; Salkind, 1981). When we accommodate, we create new schemes or modify old ones. For example, a child may be very good at using a one-handed pickup scheme—that is, lifting an item with one hand—but when faced with a beach ball the child must accommodate and use a two-handed pickup scheme.

Assimilation and accommodation work together. Suppose you are riding in a car with a young child and she points to a large Cadillac and says "Car." "That's right," you remark as you continue driving. She then spots a rusty old Volkswagen beetle and says "Car." You are impressed. After all, even though the Cadillac and the Volkswagen are noticeably different, the child understands that they are both cars—an example of assimilation. As you drive on, the child points to a large truck and says "Car." You correct her saying, "No, that is a truck." After a while the child points out a few more examples of trucks. She has accommodated. Now she has separated her concept of a car from that of a truck.

Jean Piaget conducted research by presenting children of varying ages with problems to solve, then noting how they approached them and the nature of their mistakes.

> **accommodation**   The process by which one's existing structures are altered to fit new information.

In this way, using assimilation and accommodation, the child begins to understand the world.

The Stages of Cognitive Development

Piaget (1954) argued that children's cognitive development can be viewed as occurring in a sequence of four stages (see Table 1.2). Each stage represents a qualitative advance in the child's ability to solve problems and understand the world.

The sensorimotor stage.   Between birth and about two years of age (remember, the ages are merely guidelines), infants progress through the sensorimotor stage. They investigate their world using the senses (vision, hearing, etc.) and motor activity. They develop object permanence, the understanding that objects and people do not disappear merely because they are out of sight. Very young infants believe that when a parent leaves the room the parent has disappeared. Older infants with some idea of object permanence know this is not so. The child's abilities in this stage are limited by an inability to use language or symbols—things that stand for other things. Children must experience everything directly through their senses and through feedback from motor activities. Intelligence during this period involves organized systems or schemes of actions and behaviors that become increasingly complex and coordinated.

The preoperational stage.   From about age two through age seven, children negotiate the preoperational stage. Now the child can use one thing to represent another—for instance, a piece of wood to symbolize a boat. Children also use language, and this allows them to go beyond their own direct experience, opening up a new world. But their understanding of the world is limited. Children often believe that inanimate objects are alive, that stuffed animals have a life of their own, for example. They are also egocentric, believing that everybody sees a situation the way they do. Seeing father tired, the child may bring him her favorite toy. Since it makes her happy, she presumes it will make daddy happy too. Preschoolers also do not understand conservation, the idea that the quan-

TABLE 1.2

Highlights of Piaget's Stages of Development

According to Jean Piaget, children progress through four stages in their cognitive development—sensorimotor, preoperational, concrete operational, and formal operational (column one). The indented material under the sensorimotor stage represents the six substages of the first stage of cognitive development. The second column indicates the type of behavior commonly found in children negotiating a particular stage, while the third column notes activities that can optimize the child's cognitive development. Remember, the ages are simply guidelines and are not absolute.

Stage	Child's Activity	Adult's Activity
Sensorimotor (birth to 2 years)		
Reflex activity (birth to 1 month)	Refines innate responses	Respond to and stimulate the child's senses (sight, sound, taste, touch, and smell)
Primary circular reactions (1 to 4 months)	Repeats and refines actions that once occurred by chance	Stimulate the senses through objects the child can interact with—rattles, bells, or mobiles
Secondary circular reactions (4 to 8 months)	Manipulates objects Repeats actions by choice Develops object permanence	Provide toys to handle with various shapes, textures, and colors Partially hide a toy while child watches
Coordination of secondary reactions (8 to 12 months)	Combines previous activities for new results Imitation begins	Provide toys: familiar dolls, balls, or blocks Encourage imitation
Tertiary circular reactions (12 to 18 months)	Experiments with objects to discover new uses Locates an object with eyes and tracks it	Provide experience with water, sand, textures Include toys that can be manipulated to turn, nest, roll, open or close
Invention through mental combination (18 to 24 months)	Practices deferred imitation Applies old skills in new situations	Provide opportunities to apply old skills to new experiences Provide peer contact and interaction
Preoperational (2 to 7 years)	Language appears Imaginative play, deferred imitation, and egocentrism prevalent Can complete simple operations, but cannot explain why	Provide dolls, cars, blocks, crayons, paste, paper, scissors, books, musical instruments, etc. Communicate at child's level or above Provide informal experience with liquid, mass, and length Encourage decision-making (red shirt or yellow, apple or orange, bath before dinner or after)
Concrete operational (7 to 11 years)	Applies simple logic to arrive at conclusions Reasons deductively Performs simple operations with physical objects Conserves	Provide opportunity to pursue areas of interest Use questions to understand child's reasoning processes but do not question too much
Formal operational (11 to 15 years)	Reasons abstractly Solves problems through inductive reasoning Employs logical thought	Propose hypothetical problems for child to solve Discuss ethical questions Encourage personal decision-making and problem-solving

Source: Thibault and McKee, 1982.

tity of something may remain the same despite changes in its appearance. For instance, preschoolers often do not understand that a short cup and a tall glass can hold the same amount of liquid.

True or False There are many qualitative differences in the ways young children and adults reason.

The concrete operational stage. Children from about age seven to age twelve progress through the stage of concrete operations. In this stage, many of the preoperational deficiencies are slowly overcome, and children become less egocentric and begin to understand conservation. The child still has difficulty, though, with abstract terms such as freedom or liberty, but can understand things concretely. A saying like "You can lead a horse to water, but you can't make it drink" is often met with a questioning frown and they have difficulty understanding political cartoons. In short, children in this stage understand the world only on a concrete, tangible level.

True or False School-age children have difficulty understanding political cartoons and proverbs.

The formal operational stage. During adolescence, children enter the stage of formal operations. They now develop the ability to test hypotheses in a mature, scientific manner and can understand and communicate their positions on complex ethical issues that demand an ability to use abstractions. They can also think about thinking—that is, they become aware of the process by which they came to hold a particular opinion.

Evaluation of Piaget's Theory

Piaget's studies exploring how children think, reason, and solve problems allow us to understand how a child progresses cognitively from infancy through adolescence. We now have a valuable map that shows the sequence of stages children progress through to finally attain adult reasoning. Piaget's conception of the child as a searching being actively attempting to understand the world is also valuable. It implies that children should be encouraged to discover and to experience, that they are active agents in their own development, both shaping and being shaped by their environment.

Critics of Piaget's theory argue that he underestimated the influence of learning on intellectual development. In addition, there is evidence both for and against the idea that children progress through a series of stages in

cognitive development (Flavell, 1982). Some Piagetian concepts, such as egocentrism, have come under fire as well. For example, Flavell (1975) showed children in the preoperational stage a number of proposed gifts for their fathers and asked these children to choose the appropriate gift. Most of the children chose the appropriate gift, demonstrating that they are able to take the point of view of others when they have had experience in a particular activity. The nature of the experimental task and the past learning experiences of the child may be more important than Piaget realized.

The theories formulated by Freud, Erikson, and Piaget are all *stage theories*. Although developmental specialists are partial to stage theories, other approaches can be useful too. Three such nonstage theories will be discussed here. The first, information-processing, looks deeply into the cognitive roots of our abilities. Two others—the behavioral approach and social-learning theory—emphasize the importance of learning.

The Information-Processing Approach

If a speaker announced "How you ask your question partly determines the answer you receive from another person," you wouldn't see this as a startling breakthrough. After all, put a question to a person in a certain way, and you may receive a blank stare in return. Perhaps your question was not phrased in a way the person could understand. Were the words too difficult? Did the individual understand what you were referring to? Could he or she process the words quickly enough? Could the person's memory be at fault?

A Focus on Underlying Processes

Information-processing specialists investigate the way people take in information, process it, and act on it. Such factors as attention, perception, and memory, the mediating processes by which people do something to the information in their mind, and their response system are important.

These scientists often use the computer as an analogy to the workings of the human mind, but this does not mean they see human beings as computers or robots. The computer analogy helps us understand how people solve problems and use information. What we type into the computer, called the "input," is roughly analogous to information we gather from the environment through our senses. Some operations are performed on the in-

As the childhood years go by, the year to year changes are more difficult to describe but, nevertheless, are still occurring.

formation according to the program, and the information is encoded and stored so that it can be retrieved. We must go through some processes in our minds that enable us to attend to a particular stimulus, organize it, and remember it so we can use it in the future. The information that is retrieved and used if the proper command is given could be considered "output." In the human being, the output could be some motor activity, such as moving the right arm to catch a baseball, or a verbal response, as when you come up with the answer to a math problem. Finally, an individual receives feedback—information noting whether the answer or movement was effective. Just as the title of a computer program gives some clue about what the general results of the program will be, human beings may have an upper executive plan that coordinates the activities described above and guides purposeful behavior. Information-processing theorists are interested in following the information through the system in order to learn how it is encoded, processed, and retrieved (Sternberg, 1985; Kail and Hagen,

1982). Thus, they look at cognition on a very detailed level, investigating the processes of perception, attention, representation, memory, and finally retrieval.

In one study that used an information-processing approach, elderly people and university students with similar verbal abilities and educational experience were required to listen to a speaker lecturing at different rates of speed and using sentences of varying complexity and to recall the statements the speaker made (Stine et al., 1986). Although older adults showed more of a decline in recall when the speech rate was increased, varying the complexity did not lead to any significant differences between older and younger people. The experimenters suggest that in the elderly some operations—such as decoding auditory signals and encoding them into working memory—become less efficient with age, but that other operations, such as integrating propositions and relating what is said to world knowledge, do not show these declines. Perhaps this is because the greater experience older people have allows for alternative ways of processing information. The nature of these different strategies are yet to be identified. Perhaps speakers trying to communicate with an elderly audience should be more aware of their rate of speaking but need not reduce the complexity of their arguments.

Evaluation of Information-Processing

The information-processing approach allows us to delve more deeply into the same kinds of phenomena that interested Piaget. As we shall see throughout this text, the Piagetian and information-processing viewpoints can complement each other and give us new ways to analyze a person's cognitive growth and development.

However, this perspective is so new that it is difficult to analyze it critically. A number of models have been advanced to account for the numerous subprocesses—such as encoding, memory, and retrieval—involved in processing information. No one yet knows how far the computer analogy can be taken, or whether the mind will yield to the step-by-step analysis of subprocesses vital to the usefulness of this viewpoint. Although the perspective is interesting, much work remains before we can judge its value.

The Behavioral Approach

Give me a dozen healthy infants, well-formed, and my own specified world to bring them up in, and I'll guarantee to take any one at random and train him to become any type of specialist I might select—doctor, lawyer, merchant, chief, and yes, even beggar-man and thief, regardless of his talents, penchants, abilities, vocation and the race of his ancestors (Watson, 1930).

This passage was taken from the writings of John Watson, a psychologist who changed the history of psychology. Watson argued that psychologists should study only observable behavior and ruled out studying mental processes like thinking.

Processes of Learning

Behaviorists argue that the environment determines behavior and that if the environment changes, behavior is altered. Behaviorists such as Watson and, later, B. F. Skinner explain behavior in terms of the processes of learning, including classical and operant conditioning.

Classical conditioning. The process of **classical conditioning** involves pairing a neutral stimulus with a stimulus that elicits a particular response until the stimulus that was originally neutral elicits the response (Reese and Lipsett, 1970). For instance, suppose every time Ken is taken to the doctor he experiences some sort of pain—often an injection. After a while, just seeing the doctor will be enough to cause Ken to cry. The sight of the doctor was probably neutral at first, but when paired with discomfort or pain it eventually elicits crying. Now whenever Ken sees the doctor he may cry. To understand classical conditioning, some definitions are necessary. An **unconditioned stimulus** is the stimulus that elicits the response prior to the conditioning. In this case, the shot is the unconditioned stimulus because it caused the crying response before the conditioning took place. The **unconditioned response** is the response to the unconditioned stimulus. The child's crying after receiving a shot is the unconditioned response. The **conditioned stimulus** is the previously neutral stimulus that acquires the ability to elicit a response when it is associated with an unconditioned stimulus. In this case, the doctor is a conditioned stimulus. Only when his presence was paired with the shot did it cause Ken to cry. Finally, the **conditioned response** is the learned response that becomes attached to the conditioned stimulus. In this case it is the child's behavior of crying when he sees the doctor.

Ken may also exhibit this response with a number of different people who look similar. This is called **stimulus generalization.** Experience will teach Ken to differentiate

classical conditioning A learning process in which a neutral stimulus is paired with a stimulus that elicits a response until the originally neutral stimulus elicits that response.

unconditioned stimulus The stimulus that elicits the response prior to conditioning.

unconditioned response The response to the unconditioned stimulus.

conditioned stimulus The stimulus that is neutral before conditioning and after being paired with the unconditioned stimulus will elicit the desired response by itself.

conditioned response The learned response to the conditioned stimulus.

stimulus generalization The tendency of an organism that has learned to associate a certain behavior with a particular stimulus to show this behavior when confronted with similar stimuli.

discrimination The process by which a person learns to differentiate among stimuli.

extinction The weakening and disappearance of a learned response.

operant conditioning The learning process in which behavior is governed by its consequences.

between the doctor and men of similar appearance. When this occurs, Ken has learned to **discriminate** between the people. He will then cry when he sees the doctor, but not when he sees other men. Will Ken's fear ever end, or will he always cry in the doctor's office? Perhaps after many experiences in which a visit to the doctor does not mean experiencing pain, the response will be **extinguished**—that is, Ken will no longer respond to the situation with crying.

Classical conditioning is especially useful for understanding emotional response, such as your response to the voice of your boss or your lover. The voice of your boss may have been neutral, but when paired with constant criticism it may cause you to feel anxious every time you hear him speak. In the same way, your lover's voice may elicit positive feelings of tenderness.

Operant conditioning. In **operant conditioning**, behavior is followed by some event that increases or decreases the frequency of that behavior. If the event increases the likelihood that the behavior will recur, the action is said to be **reinforced.** In operant conditioning, then, behavior is governed by its consequences. Suppose you stay late at work helping the boss with some project and you find with your paycheck an extra twenty dollars. You've been reinforced for the behavior, and chances are you would do it again. But reinforcement need not be tangible; attention and praise can be and often are effective reinforcers.

As with classical conditioning, generalization and discrimination are important concepts and explain many behaviors. If Patrick is reinforced for being aggressive by getting what he wants, he will show this behavior in many contexts. He begins by taking toys away from a younger brother and then generalizes this behavior to peers in school. But soon Patrick learns when this will work and when it will be counterproductive. He must learn to discriminate. Using profanity with friends may be acceptable, but it is not appropriate in front of grandma. Aggressiveness may help him get his way with some peers during childhood, but it is not effective in early adulthood when he is trying to talk his way out of a speeding ticket.

Notice that the behavioral perspective emphasizes the past history of the organism, the stimuli in the present environment, and the reinforcements available. No mention is made of what occurs within the mind—of thought processes or of memory.

Reciprocal Interaction

We both affect and are affected by the people around us. Spend some time observing the interactions between a parent and an infant. Perhaps the parent hugs the baby, who responds with a smile. The parent then says something to the baby, who reacts with a vocalization. The baby's vocalization brings a string of verbal praise from the parent. For years, psychologists have looked at the caregiver-child relationship in terms of what the mother or father did to the child, but the effect of the child on the parents was rarely considered. Today child development specialists look at how each affects the other.

In the above example, the actions of both parties served as responses and stimuli, which promoted new actions. The baby's smile stimulated the parent to speak to the child, and this in turn stimulated the baby to

> **reinforcement** An event that increases the likelihood that the behavior that preceded it will reoccur.
>
> **reciprocal interactions** The process by which an organism constantly affects and is affected by the environment.

vocalize. The interaction proceeded rapidly, with both parties affecting the behavior of the other. We can best understand behavior by looking at the **reciprocal interactions** between the parties. The system is bi-directional, with information flowing both from one party to the other and back again (Bell, 1979; 1968). Any analysis of behavior, then, must consider the effect each party

People are very familiar with the changes and challenges that face adolescents.

has on the other. Reciprocal interaction is an approach that will be used more and more in the future.

Evaluation of Behavior Theory

The behavioral view is valuable in pinpointing the importance of the environment. Even those who criticize behaviorism usually acknowledge that the environment has a tremendous effect on behavior (Rogers, 1980). The question is whether the environment has total control or whether internal, cognitive factors—such as thinking and information-processing abilities—must be taken into account to understand the organism better.

The most common criticism of the behavioral view of human development is that it is too mechanical. The approach makes human beings seem too predictable. In addition, the avoidance of such concepts as consciousness, thinking, and subjective experience is a problem. It is doubtful that all human development can be understood on the basis of the principles of learning.

Social-Learning Theory

People learn by observing and imitating others. Imitation is so common that we may not fully appreciate its importance. Social-learning theory investigates the process of imitation and observation-learning (Bandura, 1986).

What and How We Imitate

Imitation can be seen in many behaviors. People can learn to be aggressive or altruistic through observing respected models engage in these behaviors (Mussen and Eisenberg-Berg, 1977). People also learn partly through observation how males and females are expected to act within a particular culture (Bandura, 1986). Sometimes, children imitate exactly the gestures and words they see and hear, as when one little girl of two pointed as if lecturing and called out to her sister, "Darn it, you better do that," an exact imitation of the way her mother would do it.

However, imitation is not always so exact. You may watch Jimmy Connors or Chris Evert play tennis and try to imitate their play, yet you will be limited by your physical ability. We adapt what we see in a creative way that mirrors our own understanding of the situation and our abilities. At times we learn general principles when

watching others. When children watched a model expound on ways to use a cardboard box creatively as a house or hat and were asked to suggest uses for a tin can, these children showed more creativity but did not use the model's ideas. What they learned was that creativity was acceptable (Navarick, 1979).

Observation-learning is governed by four processes. First, the person must attend to the behavior of the model. Second, the material must be remembered. Third, the behavior is then produced in a particular setting and is rarely an exact pattern of what we observed. Finally some reinforcement must be available. Reinforcement provides us with information about what may happen in the future if we perform a particular action. It may also motivate us. We remember the consequences of the act and later use this information to attain our own ends. We do not have to experience the reinforcement personally. We can learn by watching others.

Evaluation of Social-Learning Theory

Social-learning theory reminds us that imitation and observation-learning are important in determining behavior. It helps us understand the genesis of many behaviors, from being charitable to being aggressive (Bandura and Walters, 1963). However, it is not without limitations. In the realm of human development, the theory seems to lack a developmental framework (Cairns, 1979), although some attempt is being made in that direction. The process of imitation is described in terms that give little consideration to maturation or to the differences between the imitative behavior of a child or a middle-aged adult (Thomas, 1979). So although social-learning theory explains some behaviors well, it has difficulty with age-related developmental changes.

Discovery: Research in Human Development

Theories often stimulate research. Research in human development offers the best of two worlds: the excitement of journeying into the unknown, and the structure of an established scientific discipline. While the excitement keeps researchers motivated, the discipline allows them to contribute to a larger body of knowledge. Researchers can adopt a number of strategies or methods. Each strategy has its own strengths and weaknesses, but each can contribute to our knowledge of human development.

Naturalistic Observation

Although observation is the key to most strategies, there are times when a researcher will simply observe events as they occur in the native environment. In this method, called **naturalistic observation,** the researcher only observes and does not interfere. For example, Bronstein (1984) conducted research into how fathers and mothers in Mexico play with their children, and then compared it to the way American parents interact with their offspring. She arranged for observers to watch and tape-record Mexican mothers and fathers interacting with their children. After entering the home, the observer sat in a corner taking notes and recording the session. The results? Fathers were found to be more playful with their children than mothers. Mothers were more nurturant regarding their children's immediate physical needs. In addition, while mothers tended to treat sons and daughters fairly equally, fathers were more likely to treat sons and daughters differently. Fathers reprimanded sons more than daughters, and they were more intellectually involved with their sons. Bronstein noted this pattern in many similar studies conducted in the United States.

> **naturalistic observation** A method of research in which the researcher observes organisms in their natural habitat.

Naturalistic observation is a valuable tool, but it presents us with problems. First, observers may disagree about what they have seen. To counter this problem, it sometimes helps to videotape the events being studied. Second, observers themselves may influence a subject. Would you act the same way if someone was watching you? The very presence of an adult sitting in a classroom or watching parents play with their children may cause the subjects to act differently. For this reason, observers must blend into the background as much as possible. Third, naturalistic observation cannot tell us anything about cause and effect. From the above experiment, we can make no statement about *why* fathers treat sons and daughters differently. We cannot say whether it is some behavior in sons that causes fathers to act differently, or whether some personal factor in fathers is the cause of the differential treatment.

The period of young adulthood brings a number of important changes and many choices—especially in the areas of family and work.

True or False Observation is not a valid tool for conducting research.

Case Studies

What if you wanted to know how a working woman with a large family spends her day? Perhaps you could follow the woman around, noting all her activities. A researcher following the progress of a subject over an extended period of time is conducting a **case study** (Harrison, 1979). Seeking to identify patterns, the researcher painstakingly records the person's behavior and examines all background information available. In some cases, psychological testing is performed.

Case studies often yield interesting insights into a particular situation. For example, Giancotti and Vinci (1986) describe the case of a very depressed five-year-old. They tell about their first contact in a pediatric ward when the child was very agitated, showing jerking movements and telling his parents that "things were going to get him." They describe the background of the child, which was obtained through interviews and medical records, and record their observations and the results of psychological testing. Finally, the play and verbal therapy is described and the child's improvement is noted. In another case, Ransom and colleagues (1979) describe the case of a thirteen-year-old as her family situation changes from a single-parent family (living with the father) through the marriage of her father and the adjustment period following the remarriage.

The case-study approach yields a great deal of information about a subject. We know much about the depressed five-year-old boy and the problems the thirteen-year-old girl experienced when her father remarried. But the case-study method has its limitations. One can never be certain that the person being studied is similar to other people who are the same age or who have a particular condition. Therefore, it is necessary to do many case studies in order to demonstrate a common behav-

A new evaluation of middle age views it as a time of opportunity and challenge.

ioral pattern, and such studies by their very nature are time-consuming and expensive.

The Survey Method

What if you wanted to find out how satisfied 3,000 factory workers were with their jobs, or how older people felt about being grandparents? In these cases you would probably use a **survey** or interview method. In a survey, researchers ask a number of people questions about their own behavior or attitudes, or that of someone else; then answers are tabulated and reported. For example, in one study 177 grandmothers and 105 grandfathers were asked to complete mail questionnaires concerning their role as grandparents. Grandmothers were significantly more satisfied with their role than grandfathers were (Thomas, 1986). Sometimes surveys deal with more intimate questions, such as sexual behavior and attitudes (Roche, 1986).

Questionnaires and interviews are valuable, but they have their limitations. For example, in the above study it is difficult to be certain that the group of grandparents who received the questionnaires and filled them out were representative of grandparents across the nation. The researchers might be able to generalize their findings to this community but not any further. Second, you cannot be certain that respondents are telling you truthfully how they feel or act. Third, in many surveys, questionnaires sent out to people are not all returned. Those who refuse to participate in a survey may be different in some way from those who do answer, making interpretation of the data more difficult. Last, it is not easy to construct a fair and unbiased questionnaire. The researcher must be careful about how the questions are worded. For example, imagine being asked questions concerning how you discipline or punish your child. If a question asks "How often do you spank you child?" you might answer one way, but if the question asks "How often do you beat your child?" you would probably answer that quite differently.

People hold many stereotypes about the changes in the physical and intellectual abilities of the elderly. Many of these stereotypes are being challenged and a new, more positive view of the elderly's abilities is emerging.

clinical method A method of studying children that relies on both observation and individual questioning.

experimental method A research strategy using controls that allows the researcher to discover cause-and-effect relationships.

The Clinical Method

The **clinical method** was pioneered by Jean Piaget. In this method, the researcher presents the subject with a verbal or physical task and both observes the person tackling the challenge and asks the subject questions about it. For example, Piaget took two balls of clay and made certain the child agreed they were equal in mass. Next he rolled one ball of clay into a long, thin "worm" and then asked the child which had more clay. Piaget found that most children younger than age seven believed the worm contained more clay because it was longer (Piaget, 1967). Piaget would then question the child to determine why the child believed the worm was more.

The clinical method combines the observation approach and the interview approach. Researchers using this method sometimes use different questions with different children as the need arises. In this way the method differs from the standard interview or survey method, in which the questions asked are the same.

The clinical method is remarkable in its flexibility and the freedom it gives the researcher. It does have its drawbacks, the most important of which involves a lack of standardization. Because the questions are not standardized, we depend on the researcher to ask the right questions and not lead the subject to give a particular answer because that is what the researcher wants to hear. In addition, interpretations are more variable.

The Experimental Method

Often the only way to answer an important research question is to conduct a controlled **experiment.** To do this, the researcher controls the situation as much as possible, manipulating one or two elements of the environment. To illustrate, let's look at how three researchers tried to discover which methods of helping low-birth-weight babies develop normally were best.

It has long been known that low-birth-weight infants show many biological and psychological disabilities. Many studies have shown that early intervention that provides extra stimulation for these babies is somewhat effective in helping them, although long-term effects either have not been adequately studied or have been inconclusive. The researchers decided to focus on interventions with parents. Their sample consisted of 59 premature infants and 24 full-term cases. The premature infants were randomly assigned to one of three groups. In the parent-infant intervention group the objective was to improve the quality of the interaction between child and parent, and parents were helped to become more sensitive to their child's signals, including body movement and eye contact. In the second group—called the developmental-programming intervention group—parents were helped to assess the child's level of functioning, and an individualized program was designed for the parents to foster development in cognition, communication, and gross and fine motor skills. A third group was a control group of premature infants whose parents received no training. In addition, another control group consisting of full-term infants who also received no instruction was used. A **control group** is a group that does not receive the treatment (Wood, 1974). The performance of the treatment group is compared to that of the control group to assess the effect of the treatment.

All the infants in the study were assessed for sixteen months by trained professionals who did not know which infants belonged in which group. Measures of infant mental and physical growth, the quality of the home, and videotaped parent-child interactions were used to compare each group with the other groups. The results showed that both intervention strategies were successful in producing great improvement in the home environment—some behavioral changes in mother-infant interactions and modest changes in infant cognitive development. Group one, the parent-infant intervention group, was somewhat more successful than group two in facilitating change. The researchers concluded that home intervention can be an effective aid for improving the functioning of premature infants (Barrera et al., 1986).

The elements of an experiment that are manipulated are called the **independent variables.** In this case, only one independent variable was used—the type of treatment program. Some parents were involved in one type of treatment, others were involved in a different program. The factors that are measured are called **dependent**

> **control group** The group in an experiment that does not receive any treatment.
>
> **independent variables** The factors in a study that will be manipulated by the researcher.
>
> **dependent variables** The factors in a study that will be measured by the researcher.
>
> **correlation** A term denoting a relationship between two variables.

variables. In this case, they included measures of parent-child interaction, the child's motor and mental progress, and the home environment.

Experimental studies are often difficult to conduct because the researcher must exercise great control over the environment. However, the effort is often worth the extra trouble because only experimental studies can demonstrate cause-and-effect relationships.

Correlations

Often researchers involved in collecting and analyzing data seek to discover the relationships between two elements in the environment. For instance, there is a relationship between scores on intelligence tests and school achievement. Higher intelligence scores are related to higher achievement levels in school.

Psychologists use the term **correlation** to describe such a relationship. A correlation may be positive, negative, or zero. A positive correlation indicates that relatively large scores on one factor are associated with large scores on another, and relatively small scores on one factor are associated with small scores on another. As intelligence increases, so does academic achievement. A perfect positive correction is expressed as +1.00. A zero correlation indicates there is no relationship between the two factors. A negative correlation indicates that relatively large scores on one factor are related to relatively small scores on another. A perfect negative correlation is expressed −1.00. In adulthood, there may be a negative relationship (but not a perfectly negative relationship) between age and muscular strength. As a person negotiates early, middle, and late adulthood, his muscular strength ebbs (Wright, 1976).

But correlations are usually far from perfect. The correlation between scores on an intelligence test and achievement in school hovers at about +.60, which is high but not anywhere near perfect. Other factors besides intelligence, such as motivation and perseverance, are involved in school success. In addition, correlations do not indicate cause and effect. For instance, there is a positive correlation between the number of hours children watch television and their acquisition of traditional and stereotyped sex roles (Freuh and McGhee, 1975). This does not mean that watching television causes children to acquire such ideas, for other factors may enter the picture. Perhaps children who already have stereotyped ideas about the appropriate conduct of males and females watch more television for some reason. The important facts to remember about a correlation is that it tells us that a relationship exists, the direction of the relationship (whether it is positive or negative), and the magnitude of that relationship. It does not establish cause and effect.

Cross-Sectional and Longitudinal Studies

Developmental research is often concerned with measuring change over time. We may be interested in discovering how people of various ages approach problems, or how their personalities change or remain the same over time. You could find groups of people of various ages and administer a battery of psychological tests to them and measure aspects of their personalities. This is an example of a **cross-sectional** design. On the other hand, you could begin with a group of twenty-four-year-olds and measure their personalities, and then wait four years and measure this same group's personalities again, and then wait another four years and do it a third time, and so on. This is an example of a **longitudinal** design. Both methods are popular, and each has advantages and disadvantages.

Cross-sectional studies are easier to conduct. Groups of different-aged subjects are tested at the same time and the results are compared. Costa and his colleagues used this method to measure the traits of extroversion, openness, and neuroticism (a measure of emotional instability, depression, and anxiety) in more than 10,000 people of different ages (Costa et al., 1986; Costa and McCrae, 1986). The average scores on these three measures for men and women are shown in Figure 1.1. Notice how stable the scores are over the adult years. The researchers concluded that personality seems to be predominantly stable in adulthood.

cross-sectional study A research design in which subjects of different ages are studied to obtain information about changes in some variable.

longitudinal study A research design in which subjects are followed over an extended period of time to note developmental changes in some variable.

True or False Two traits that seem to be stable in adulthood are extroversion and openness.

Cross-sectional studies are useful, but they have limitations. It is difficult to understand the growth and decline of any attribute over an extended period of time, because the same people are not being followed (Nunnally, 1982). In addition, when comparing subjects who differ significantly in age, the effect of growing up in a different generation—the cohort effect—must be taken into account.

Longitudinal studies are more difficult to execute than cross-sectional studies. Subjects must be followed over some period of time and retested at stated intervals (Schaie and Hertzog, 1982). However, they allow us to identify changes in subjects over time. Such questions as "Do obese children become obese adults?" and "Do aggressive teens remain aggressive during adulthood?" can best be studied using longitudinal research designs. In 1968, Spivack and colleagues (1986) asked fifty-six kindergarten teachers from twenty-nine schools to rate their students in adjustment and behavior. As these children progressed through elementary school, their other teachers were periodically asked for assessments as well. There was a significant relationship between the teacher ratings and official police contact with these children between the ages of six and seventeen. In other words, early classroom misbehavior and maladjustment predicted later misconduct both inside and outside the school. This suggests the existence of a high-risk population that might be easily identified in childhood. Some intervention may prove helpful in preventing these children from becoming troublesome adolescents.

Longitudinal studies also have practical limitations. They are more time-consuming, and maintaining contact with subjects over a long period of time is difficult. Some subjects move away, other simply do not return for follow-up interviews or do not return their question-

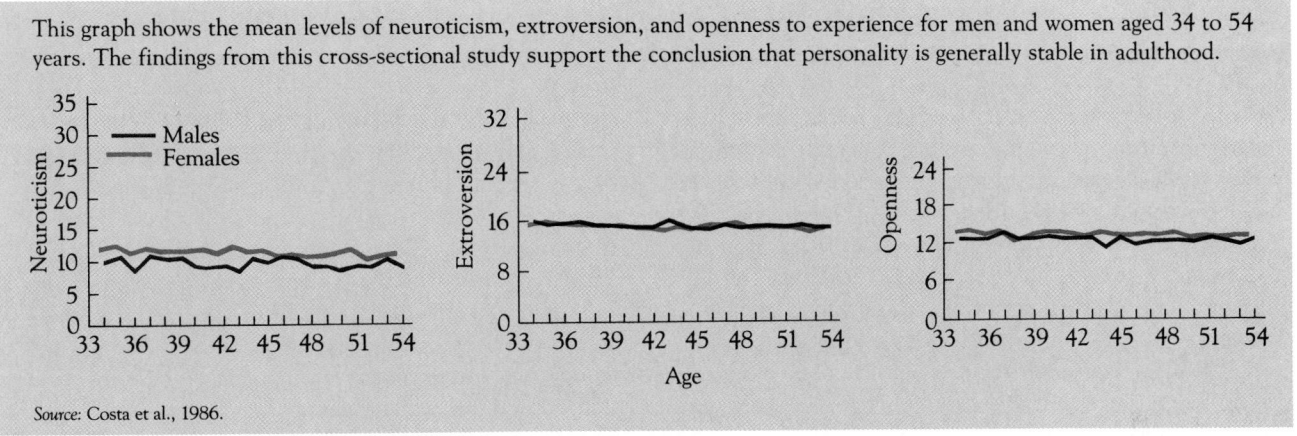

FIGURE 1.1

Stability of Personality in Adulthood

This graph shows the mean levels of neuroticism, extroversion, and openness to experience for men and women aged 34 to 54 years. The findings from this cross-sectional study support the conclusion that personality is generally stable in adulthood.

Source: Costa et al., 1986.

naires, leaving the researcher with incomplete data. It is difficult to determine whether those who drop out differ from those who remain throughout the study. Another problem is the effect of practice and retesting in some longitudinal studies (Blank, 1982). Let's say you want to measure the changes in intelligence over the years. If you use the same or a very similar test, people might become testwise and show an improvement simply as a result of practice. On the other hand, using different measures may create problems, because one measure may not be directly comparable to another. As in the cross-sectional approach, the cohort effect should be taken into account (Birren et al., 1981). Longitudinal studies performed thirty years ago are interesting, but they may be confounded by specific generational differences and may have to be updated.

Researchers are constantly looking for ways to improve their experiments. Some have suggested mixed models that have both longitudinal and cross-sectional components. For example, one could look at the political opinions of ten-year-olds and fifteen-year-olds and test subjects in both groups every year for four years.

Cross-Cultural Research

As you see, no research method is perfect, and each has advantages and disadvantages. We have assumed, though, that the researcher is performing the research in his or her own cultural setting, with no language difficulties,

but this may not be true. More and more research is being done in other cultures. Conducting research in different cultures presents new problems and opportunities. Even executing research studies in one's own nation on subgroups or minorities whose culture may differ can be difficult. Cross-cultural studies are important and valuable if we are to extend our understanding of human development past our own borders (see the Cross-Cultural Current on page 30). Some researchers even argue that unless we look at other cultures it is not possible to make any serious systematic attempt to understand human behavior and development, perhaps because our own cultural biases get in the way (Heron and Kroeger, 1981).

Cross-cultural studies yield many benefits. They help us extend and test theoretical approaches. For instance, Piaget believes that the sequences of cognitive development are invariant—that is, children progress from stage one to stage two to stage three in order, without regressing or skipping any stages. Most cross-cultural studies confirm this part of Piaget's theory (see Dasen and Heron, 1981).

Sometimes cross-cultural studies can help us separate one variable from another (Triandis and Brislin, 1984). Let us say we find cancer rates very high in one part of the world and lower in another. We want to know whether this is due to some genetic difference or to some factor in the environment, perhaps diet. One way to determine this is to follow people from this low-cancer-rate area who move to the United States and see what happens

A Case of Misunderstanding

As a Vietnamese woman comes into the doctor's office accompanied by her one-year-old daughter, the physician rises and through an interpreter asks what ails her. They both sit down. The doctor takes a relaxed position, sitting with his legs crossed, and smiles at the woman. To put her at ease, he compliments the woman on her beautiful child, then continues asking about her symptoms.

It sounds simple and efficient, but the doctor has made so many mistakes and insulted the client so badly that his effectiveness may well be compromised.

Since 1975, more than 750,000 refugees from Southeast Asia have resettled in the United States. As with all new minorities, their culture is misunderstood by many well-meaning professionals who are responsible for providing them with vital services.

The doctor innocently believed he was acting correctly when he asked about symptoms, complimented the child, and sat in a relaxed position. But all three can cause problems. First, among southeast Asians it is considered impolite to ask direct questions immediately. People first make small talk, asking about the entire family and the like, before getting down to business. Second, complimenting a child on her beauty or health may be a problem if the parents come from a rural village in their home country. They may fear that a lurking evil

spirit will hear the praise and take the child away. In some villages, children are not named until two years of age because giving the child a beautiful name may draw the jealous attention of the evil spirit. Third, if the patient is Laotian, crossing one's legs and allowing a toe to point toward the patient is considered an insult.

This brings up another problem. We tend to characterize all people who come from Southeast Asia as one group, but this is incorrect. Language, customs, and traditions differ widely among the Vietnamese, Cambodians, Laotians, and Thais. In one incident, a doctor, Marianne Felice, asked a Vietnamese interpreter to talk to a Laotian youth. The Vietnamese interpreter "indignantly" announced that he was Vietnamese and "stormed away." Later she was told that if she had asked the Vietnamese interpreter to translate for a Cambodian patient it would have been worse, because these two countries have been at war for centuries.

Appreciating the differences between these groups is crucial to understanding the behavior of people who come from the diverse cultures. For example, in Thailand when a person is angry at another he does not show it directly. Instead, he may turn toward another object or person and scold it or him. A doctor must then understand that the angry words directed toward a dog or a child in his presence may actually be directed at him.

to their cancer rate. If it increases significantly, we can presume that some environmental factor is involved and look for it.

Cross-cultural research also allows researchers to discover how people from other cultures handle their problems and develop. For example, a study of how Japanese and American mothers handle certain daily problems showed an interesting difference (Hess et al., 1986). Japanese mothers were more likely to appeal to feelings—for example, asking children "How do you think I will feel if you don't eat those vegetables?" while American mothers were more likely to use appeals to authority or power, such as "I told you to eat those vegetables."

Cross-cultural research also widens our perspective and may serve to increase understanding between people and

to reduce prejudice. We sometimes think that the way things are in our own country is the way they are throughout the world. But research on competition and cooperation, aggression, fathering, education, and gender differences and stereotypes have shown that this is not true (Adler, 1982).

Cross-cultural research presents unique problems, though. Accurate translation is one problem. Devising measuring instruments that can be used across cultures is another. The most serious problem, however, is that a concept may have one meaning in one culture and another in a different culture. For example, achievement in the United States is an individualistic concept, while in some South Pacific islands it has meaning in a group context, where achievements can be shared for the mu-

3. Changes that are relatively immune to environmental influences and are caused by the unfolding of the individual's unique genetic plan are considered maturational in nature.

4. Any relatively permanent change in behavior that can be attributed to interactions with the environment is due to learning.

5. Early childhood experiences have a profound influence on later development and behavior. However, the effects of a poor early environment can be remedied, at least to some extent, by improving the environment.

6. The effect of belonging to a particular generation is known as the cohort effect. Epidemics, depression, technological change, and revolutions may have an important effect on the development of a particular generation.

7. Freud's psychoanalytic theory emphasizes the importance of the early parent-child relationship. Freud argued that children progress through five psychosexual stages that involve the unfolding of the sexual instinct. Some of his concepts, such as unconscious motivation, defense mechanisms, stage development, and infantile and child sexuality, are of interest. Psychoanalytic theory has been criticized because it is difficult to test, considers sexuality the prime motivation, and emphasizes deviancy.

8. Erikson argued that people proceed through eight stages from cradle to grave and that each stage presents people with different tasks. If a task is successfully negotiated, there is a positive outcome. If not, there is a negative outcome. Erikson's theory provides a good framework for viewing human development and sees development as continuing throughout the life span. It has been criticized for being too broad and too general and difficult to explore experimentally.

9. Piaget investigated the cognitive, or intellectual, development of the child. He noted that children do not think like adults, and he described four stages through which children pass between birth and adolescence. Piaget's theory is noted for its description of the sequence of steps children negotiate in order to develop an adult understanding of math, time, space, causality,

and a number of other concepts. Piaget also viewed the child as actively involved with the environment and stressed the importance of discovery. His theory has been criticized for underestimating the importance of formal learning.

10. Information-processing theory focuses on the way people take in information, process it, and finally act on it. Such factors as attention, perception, and memory are investigated. It is a noteworthy approach because it can yield specific information about how a person solves a particular problem. However, it is not as well developed as other theoretical approaches, and only additional experimentation will determine how useful it will be.

11. Learning theorists or behaviorists do not emphasize the concept of stages but stress the importance of classical conditioning and operant conditioning. Social learning theorists emphasize the importance of imitation to the understanding of behavior. These approaches are noteworthy because they emphasize the importance of the person's environment in determining behavior. The behavioral perspective has been criticized for being too mechanical and not adequately taking consciousness and thought processes into consideration. These approaches also seem to lack a developmental framework as well.

12. When investigating any relationships, developmental psychologists emphasize reciprocal interaction—that is, they look at how people both affect and are affected by each other.

13. Developmental psychologists can use many research methods. In naturalistic observation, the researcher carefully observes and records what occurs in the natural environment. The case-study method involves carefully observing and testing a subject for a substantial period of time and collecting as much information as possible. Researchers using the survey method question a number of people, then tabulate and analyze their data. The clinical method combines careful observation and questioning. A person may be presented with a problem, and a researcher observes how the subject handles it and may ask questions about the subject's perception of the

challenge. Researchers using the experimental method control the environment, allowing only the desired variables to change. Such experiments may demonstrate cause and effect. Researchers may also attempt to discover correlations or relationships between variables. These relationships show the extent to which one factor is related to another. They do not show cause and effect.

14. In cross-sectional studies, people from various age- groups are tested at a particular time. In a longitudinal study, a single group of people is tested at certain intervals. Mixed research designs, which combine features of both, are also in use today.

15. Most psychological studies cause no physical or psychological harm to their subjects. Two of the most common ethical problems involve consent and deception.

--------- *Answers to True or False Statements* ---------

1. *False*   Correct statement: Children's ideas about friendship change greatly as they negotiate childhood and adolescence.

2. *True*   Older people are more cautious and do value accuracy over speed.

3. *False*   Correct statement: The childhood experiences of terrorists are filled with hopelessness and rage.

4. *False*   Correct statement: If the environment is suitably changed, even the effects of a poor early environment can be reduced.

5. *True*   About one in five children grows up in a single-parent household.

6. *False*   Correct statement: Freud defined sexuality in a broad sense akin to sensuality and did not believe that young children experienced adult sexual feelings.

7. *False*   Correct statement: Developing a sense of autonomy is an important outcome of the toddler stage.

8. *True*   There are many impressive qualitative differences between how young children and adults reason.

9. *True*   School-age children experience difficulty understanding political cartoons and proverbs, which require the ability to deal with abstract concepts.

10. *False*   Correct statement: Observation is a valid tool for conducting research.

11. *True*   Extroversion and openness are two personality traits that appear to be stable in adulthood.

12. *True*   Potentially dangerous psychological experiments are very few.

Genetic Influence
Across the Life Span

Are the Following Statements True or False?

Try the True-False Quiz below. See if your answers correspond to the information in this chapter. Each question is repeated after the paragraph in which the answer can be found. The True-False Answer Box at the end of the chapter lists the complete answers.

_____ 1. All animal species, including human beings, have the same number of chromosomes: forty-six.

_____ 2. Fraternal twins are no more genetically alike than any other pair of siblings.

_____ 3. If a family consists of five female children, the chances are quite small that their sixth child will be a boy.

_____ 4. The serious genetic disorder cystic fibrosis can be cured through massive doses of vitamins.

_____ 5. If neither mother nor father shows a particular trait, it can still show itself in their offspring.

_____ 6. Color blindness is found mostly in males.

_____ 7. At the present time, all medical science can do for children suffering from genetic diseases is make them more comfortable.

_____ 8. Down's Syndrome—or mongolism, as it used to be called—is caused by an extra chromosome.

_____ 9. Schizophrenia, like cystic fibrosis or Tay-Sachs disease, is transmitted directly from parent to child.

_____10. Intelligence scores can be modified through a program of intense training.

_____11. Genetic influences are more widespread and important in childhood than in adulthood.

_____12. Genetic counselors must often make decisions for their clients concerning marriage and childbearing.

The Strange Case of Twins

The "Jim" twins were a fascinating pair. Separated at four weeks of age, they finally met thirty-nine years later. The similarities between them were incredible. Besides their appearance, both had taken law-enforcement training and served as deputy sheriffs. Both men owned Chevrolets and vacationed in Florida. Both married and divorced women named Linda and remarried women named Betty. Even their dogs shared the same name—Toy.

Another set of twins separated shortly after birth were named Raymond and Richard. Raymond was adopted into a home of a rich doctor in the same town, while Richard was adopted by a family that was always on the brink of financial disaster. Ray had every advantage and never experienced poverty. Richard's father never worked, and the family never lived in one place for any length of time. Richard learned to do things for himself. Though they came from different backgrounds, their IQ scores were almost identical, and their character and emotional stability were as alike as if they had been raised together (McBroom, 1980).

Perhaps the most famous and unusual case involves identical twins Oscar Stohr and Jack Yufe, who were separated shortly after birth and did not meet for forty-seven years. Oscar was taken to Germany by his mother and became a Nazi. His brother Jack was raised by his father as a Jew in the Caribbean and spent some time working on a communal farm in Israel. The similarities were obvious from the moment they met. Both sported wire-rimmed glasses and mustaches, and they shared a number of food preferences. But some of the similarities seem to defy explanation. They both always flushed the toilet before using it and read magazines from the back to the front. They showed remarkable similarities in temperament too.

Can these unusual similarities be explained as mere coincidences? This is a matter of dispute. As more twin pairs who have been raised apart are found and tested, such similarities become more difficult to dismiss as statistical accidents. Perhaps genetic endowment plays a larger role in the development of personality and behavior than we thought.

But not all twins reared apart manifest such similarities. In fact, Raymond and Richard differed somewhat

> **gene**   The basic unit of heredity.
>
> **chromosomes**   Rod-shaped structures that carry genes.
>
> **gametes**   The scientific term for the sex cells.

in temperament. Richard was more aggressive, probably because he had been protected less and needed to develop a greater sense of self-reliance. So experience is also important in the development of personality and behavior. In addition, while twins reared apart who show striking similarities are constantly hounded by the news media, those who do not are often lost in the shuffle. Not all identical twins, who share the same genetic endowment, show such similarities, and the lives of many sets of identical twins differ greatly from each other (Ainslie, 1985).

The extent to which genetic endowment affects development and behavior is a controversial question. In this chapter we shall look at the mechanisms of inheritance and the diverse areas in which genetics seems to have some effect on our lives. Finally, we will look briefly at some of the great advances in genetics and the nature of the choices the new knowledge and technology has given us.

How We Inherit

At the moment of conception, when the male's sperm penetrates the female's egg cell, our genetic endowment is set. Genetic individuality is assured by nature itself.

Genes and Chromosomes

The basic unit of heredity is the **gene,** which is composed of deoxyribonucleic acid (DNA). Genes are carried on rod-shaped structures of various sizes called **chromosomes** (Pai, 1974). Each animal species has its own number of chromosomes. The normal human being has a complement of forty-six chromosomes, or twenty-three pairs. The same forty-six chromosomes are found in every cell of the body except the **gametes,** or sex cells. In a process called **meiosis,** the sex cells divide to form two cells containing twenty-three chromosomes. This allows human beings to maintain the same complement of forty-six chromosomes from generation to generation. But these cells do not have to split right down the middle. Their splitting is more random. Which chromosome ends up in which of the split cells is a matter of chance. There are more than 8 million possibilities in this process alone.

True or False All animal species, including human beings, have the same number of chromosomes: forty-six.

This is not the end of the story. During the process of meiosis, some of the genetic material on one chromosome may be exchanged with the material from another. This exchange, called **crossing over,** further complicates the situation, ensuring more individuality (Kowles, 1985). When crossing over is taken into consideration, the chances that any two individuals are genetically identical are practically zero. Although human beings share a common species inheritance, each person is also genetically unique. The only exception is identical, or **monozygotic,** twins, who share the same genetic composition. Fraternal, or **dizygotic,** twins develop from two different eggs and two different sperm and are no more genetically alike than any other pair of siblings.

meiosis The process by which sex cells divide to form two cells, each containing twenty-three chromosomes.

crossing over The process occurring during meiosis in which genetic material on one chromosome is exchanged with material from the other.

monozygotic (identical) twins Twins who develop from one fertilized egg and have an identical genetic structure.

dizygotic (fraternal) twins Twins who develop from two fertilized eggs and are no more genetically similar than any other sibling pair.

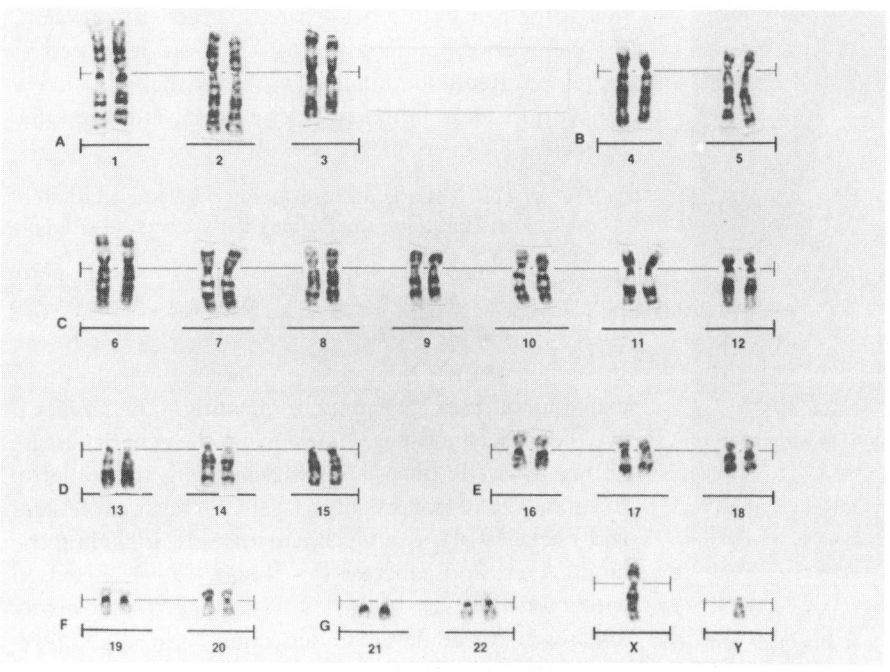

Genes are carried on chromosomes. Each normal human being has 23 pairs of chromosomes.

True or False   Fraternal twins are no more genetically alike than any other pair of siblings.

The randomness of conception is impressive. The average man's semen contains between 50 million and 125 million sperm for each cubic centimeter of ejaculate (Rosen and Rosen, 1981). Only one sperm is necessary for conception. While sperm are continually being produced in the testicles of the male, females are born with a full complement of egg cells. The average female infant comes into this world carrying approximately 2 million eggs. About 25,000 are usable when the young girl reaches puberty, although she will probably use only about 350 throughout her reproductive life (Smith and Neisworth, 1975).

Identical twins share precisely the same genetic makeup while fraternal twins are no more genetically alike than any other pair of siblings.

sex chromosomes   The twenty-third pair of chromosomes, which determines the gender of the organism.

cystic fibrosis   A severe genetic disease marked by digestive and respiratory problems.

The Sex Chromosomes

Twenty-two of the twenty-three pairs of chromosomes look identical, but the twenty-third pair is different. These chromosomes, called the **sex chromosomes,** are responsible for determining the gender of the offspring. There are two types: the X chromosome and the Y chromosome. The genetic composition of a male is XY, while females have two X chromosomes. If during conception a sperm carrying the X chromosome penetrates the egg's membrane, the offspring will be female. If a sperm carrying the Y chromosome penetrates, the child will be male. It is the male, then, that determines the gender of the child. Figure 2.1 shows the chances are fifty-fifty that the offspring will be a male.

The chances are the same for each conception. Even if you have seven boys, the chances are still fifty-fifty that you will have a girl next. Many people fail to understand this basic point, and it is true for all inherited characteristics as well. Some people incorrectly believe that if their first child has a particular genetic problem, the chances of having a normal child are increased or decreased. Reproduction does not work that way. Every conception starts from square one again, and the same odds exist for every pregnancy.

True or False   If a family consists of five female children, the chances are quite small that their sixth child will be a boy.

Dominant and Recessive Traits

If neither you nor your spouse shows a particular trait, can you still pass it on to your offspring? The answer is yes. To understand this, let us look at the genetic disease known as **cystic fibrosis.** Cystic fibrosis is a disorder of the glands that produce mucus, saliva, and sweat (Apgar and Beck, 1974). It affects many organs, including the lungs, liver, and pancreas (Fischman, 1979). A person with cystic fibrosis has a low resistance to respiratory diseases and a tendency to dehydrate because of an excessive amount of salt in the sweat.

FIGURE 2.1

Determination of Sex

The child's mother can contribute only an X chromosome while the child's father can contribute an X or a Y. Statistically, 50 percent of the conceptions will produce males, and 50 percent will produce females. However, other factors, such as conditions in the vagina, influence whether the X- or Y-carrying sperm will reach and penetrate the egg.

FATHER

	X	Y
X	XX	XY
X	XX	XY

MOTHER

recessive traits Traits that require the presence of two genes.

dominant traits Traits that require the presence of only one gene.

genotype The genetic configuration of the individual.

phenotype The observable characteristics of the organism.

carrier A person who possesses a particular gene or group of genes for a trait, who does not show the trait but can pass it on to his or her offspring.

New antibiotics have increased the life span of individuals with this disorder. Between 70 and 80 percent survive to at least age twenty if the disease is discovered early and excellent medical treatment is received. Treatment must be continuous, and hospitalization during periods of crisis can be expected. At this point, there is no cure. Even with excellent care, the disease often worsens. Cystic fibrosis is responsible for more deaths than any other genetic disease in the United States today (Berdine and Blackhurst, 1985).

True or False The serious genetic disorder cystic fibrosis can be cured through massive doses of vitamins.

Cystic fibrosis is caused by a defective pair of genes, and it manifests itself only when both parents transmit the defective gene to their child. Any trait that requires that two genes be present is called **recessive.** If only one gene is required for the trait or characteristic to be shown, it is called **dominant.**

Cystic fibrosis is a recessive disorder. In other words, two genes—one from the mother and one from the father—are required. Let's say that the father has two normal genes and the mother has two normal genes as shown in Figure 2.2(a). It is impossible for their children to have cystic fibrosis. If both parents have cystic fibrosis, then, as shown in Figure 2.2(b), all their children will have the disorder—assuming the parents survive to have children. Of course, the chances of two cystic fibrosis sufferers marrying is very low.

But what if both parents carry one gene for cystic fibrosis? To understand these possibilities, two new terms must be introduced: genotype and phenotype. The **genotype** of a person refers to the specific composition of that person's genes. It is a description of the "kinds of genes possessed, regardless of whether they are expressed" (Sutton, 1980, p. 11). Both the mother's and the father's genotype in Figure 2.2(c) include one gene for cystic fibrosis and one gene for normal functioning. The **phenotype** refers to the "observable characteristics of an individual" (Sutton, 1980, p. 11). In our case, because cystic fibrosis is a recessive trait and requires two genes, neither the father nor the mother shows symptoms of the disorder and their phenotype is normal. However, they can pass it on to their offspring. Both parents then are **carriers,** they do not show the disorder but they can pass it on to their offspring. When both the mother and the father each carry the gene for cystic fibrosis the chances are 25 percent that an offspring will have the disease, 50 percent that the child will be a carrier, and 25 percent that the child will not have the disorder nor be a carrier.

In the condition in which only one parent carries one gene for cystic fibrosis as in Figure 2.2(d), their offspring cannot have the disorder but there is a 50 percent chance that any offspring will be a carrier.

Transmission of a Recessive Trait: Cystic Fibrosis

(a) When Neither Parent Carries the Gene

Neither parent carries the gene. It is impossible for any offspring to suffer from the disorder.

FATHER

	Normal gene	Normal gene
Normal gene	Normal gene Normal gene	Normal gene Normal gene
MOTHER		
Normal gene	Normal gene Normal gene	Normal gene Normal gene

(a)

(b) When Both Parents Have the Disorder

All offspring will have the disorder. The chances of two people with the disorder marrying are extremely remote.

FATHER

	Cystic Fibrosis	Cystic Fibrosis
Cystic Fibrosis	Cystic Fibrosis Cystic Fibrosis	Cystic Fibrosis Cystic Fibrosis
MOTHER		
Cystic Fibrosis	Cystic Fibrosis Cystic Fibrosis	Cystic Fibrosis Cystic Fibrosis

(b)

(c) When Each Parent Carries One Gene

When both the mother and the father carry the gene for Cystic Fibrosis, the chances are 25 percent that an offspring will have the disease (Cystic Fibrosis-Cystic Fibrosis) 50 percent that the child will be a carrier (Cystic Fibrosis-Normal), and 25 percent that the child will not have the disorder nor be a carrier.

FATHER

	Normal gene	Cystic Fibrosis
Normal gene	Normal gene Normal gene	Normal gene Cystic Fibrosis
MOTHER		
Cystic Fibrosis	Cystic Fibrosis Normal gene	Cystic Fibrosis Cystic Fibrosis

(c)

(d) When One Parent Carries One Gene

When either the mother or the father (as in this case) carries the gene, there is a 50 percent chance that any offspring will be a carrier. Since the Cystic Fibrosis disorder is recessive, none of their children will actually have the disorder.

FATHER

	Cystic Fibrosis	Normal gene
Normal gene	Normal gene Cystic Fibrosis	Normal gene Normal gene
MOTHER		
Normal gene	Normal gene Cystic Fibrosis	Normal gene Normal gene

(d)

Note: Some other genetic diseases such as Tay Sachs Disease and Phenylketonuria are transmitted in the same way as Cystic Fibrosis.

True or False If neither mother nor father shows a particular trait, it can still show itself in their offspring.

Some traits are dominant—that is, they require only one gene for the trait to show. Take the example of freckles. What if both parents have a gene for freckles, as in Figure 2.3(a)? If the offspring inherits two genes for freckles, then the child will show freckles (see frame 1). At the same time, if the child inherits two genes for no freckles, the youngster will not have freckles (see frame 4). But what if one parent passes on a gene for freckles but the gene from the other parent is for no freckles? Because freckles is a dominant trait and no freckles is recessive, the child will show freckles (see frames 2 and 3).

Polygenic Inheritance

If the relationship between genetics and behavior was always so simple, predicting traits would be easy. But genetic transmission is not always so direct, and com-

polygenic (multigenic) inheritance Characteristics influenced by more than one pair of genes.

multifactorial inheritance Traits influenced both by genes and by the environment.

paratively few human traits are transmitted through simple dominance and recessiveness. In addition, cystic fibrosis and freckles are caused exclusively by a person's genotype. The effect of the environment on one's genetic endowment has not been mentioned. In the real world, the relationship between genotype and phenotype is more complicated (Scarr and Kidd, 1983). Simple models of prediction soon break down as we consider characteristics that are determined by many gene pairs and are affected by the environment.

When a characteristic is influenced by more than one pair of genes, the mechanism of inheritance is **polygenic,** or **multigenic.** The term **multifactorial** describes a trait

---

FIGURE 2.3

Transmission of a Dominant Trait: Freckles

(a) When Both Parents Have One Gene for Freckles

When both parents carry one gene for freckles, there is a 25 percent chance that a child will have two genes for freckles and thus have freckles. There is a 50 percent chance that a child will carry one gene for freckles, and, since this is a dominant trait, have freckles. There is only a 25 percent chance that a child will not have a gene for freckles and so will not have freckles:

FATHER

	Freckles	No Freckles
Freckles (MOTHER)	1 — Freckles / Freckles	3 — Freckles / No Freckles
No Freckles (MOTHER)	2 — No Freckles / Freckles	4 — No Freckles / No Freckles

(a)

(b) When One Parent Has One Gene for Freckles

When one parent has one gene for freckles, there is a 50 percent chance that the child will have freckles:

FATHER

	Freckles	No Freckles
No Freckles (MOTHER)	Freckles / No Freckles	No Freckles / No Freckles
No Freckles (MOTHER)	Freckles / No Freckles	No Freckles / No Freckles

(b)

that is both polygenic and influenced by the environment. The terms polygenic, multigenic, and multifactorial are often used interchangeably. Skin color is a polygenic trait. A number of gene pairs are responsible for it (Mange and Mange, 1980), but the environment also influences the phenotype. If you have light skin and spend time in the sun, you tan; your genotype has not changed, but your outward appearance, or phenotype, has.

Another example is height. Although adult stature is greatly affected by an individual's genes, the environment also plays a part. Nutrition and health are two prime environmental factors. Japanese teenagers are taller than their parents because their health and nutrition have improved (Curtis, 1975). Even the emotional environment affects growth, because if influences the secretion of growth hormones. Cases of stunted growth occurred in some orphanages where children's psychological needs for love, tenderness, and contact were not met, even if the children were adequately fed (Gardner, 1972). Such a condition is called **psychosocial dwarfism.** The environment, then, can make a contribution even in determination of a trait that is influenced largely by genetic factors.

Sex-Linked Traits

Up to this point we have looked at traits that are determined by genes on the first twenty-two pairs of chromosomes. The twenty-third pair presents us with a special case. A female has two X chromosomes, while a male has an X and a Y. The X chromosome is three times as large as the Y. It contains many more genes, and many of the genes found on the X chromosome do not exist at all on the Y. This has profound consequences for males.

Consider what might happen if a female has one defective recessive gene and one dominant normal gene on the twenty-third chromosome. Let us also assume that these genes are found only on the X chromosome, not on the Y. The female would not show the effects of the recessive gene because she has a gene for normal functioning to counter it. But what if she had children? She could pass on both her normal gene and the abnormal gene—but unlike our previous cases, the child's gender becomes crucial.

Look at Figure 2.4. Notice that if the mother contributes a normal X and her husband contributes a normal X, as in Frame 1, the child will be a female who will

psychosocial dwarfism A condition in which a child's small stature and lack of growth is due to psychological or emotional causes.

sex-linked traits Traits inherited through genes found on the sex chromosomes.

show no signs of the disease and who will not pass it on to her offspring. If the mother contributes an abnormal X chromosome and her husband contributes a normal X, the child will be a female who will show no signs of the disease but who will be a carrier like her mother (see Frame 2).

But what if the child is male? If the mother contributes her normal X and her husband contributes his Y, as shown in Frame 3, the offspring will be a male who will neither show any signs of the disorder nor be able to pass it on. In this case, because the X is normal there is no need to be concerned. But if the mother transmits the defective X chromosome and the father a Y, the resulting male offspring will show signs of the disorder and may pass it on to the next generation (Frame 4). The defective gene on the X has no corresponding normal gene

FIGURE 2.4

Sex-Linked Inheritance

In sex-linked traits, females may carry the defective gene but do not develop the disorder.

FATHER

	X^n	Y^0
MOTHER X^n	1 $X^n \; X^n$	3 $X^n \; Y^0$
X^d	2 $X^d \; X^n$	4 $X^d \; Y^0$

n = normal
d = gene for a disorder — e.g., hemophilia or color blindness.

on the Y to counter it, so the defective gene on the X is in a position to show itself. **Sex-linked traits** involve female carriers, but it is the male who inherits the trait.

There is a considerable amount of interest in sex-linked traits today. Among the proven sex-linked traits are hemophilia and color blindness (Fuller and Thompson, 1978). Both hemophilia (a severe blood disease involving a deficiency in the blood's ability to clot) and color blindness are determined by defective genes found on the X chromosome. Because a female has two X chromosomes, her chances of being a hemophiliac are negligible. She is also much less likely to become color blind. Another possible sex-linked characteristic is spatial perception, which involves the ability to "visualize three-dimensional objects on the basis of a two-dimensional picture and to do mental rotations and other manipulations on them" (Hyde, 1985, p. 187). Superior spatial ability is correlated with higher mathematical ability (Richmond-Abbott, 1983). The male advantage in this ability may be at least partly explained by sex-linked inheritance, although the evidence is not unanimous in this regard and environmental factors may also be important (Linn and Petersen, 1985). Spatial perception is not an ability that one either has or does not have. It is present in everyone to varying degrees, and it can be improved through training.

True or False   Color blindness is found mostly in males.

Could some of the other differences between males and females be genetically determined? Perhaps the fact that women normally outlive men can be explained by genetic endowment (Kermis, 1984). Psychologists differ sharply on such questions. Except for some genetic diseases and physical traits, the interaction of genes with the environment is crucial to understanding the end product. Still, the possibility of explaining some sex differences using the mechanism of sex-linked genetic transmission is tempting.

Sex-Limited Inheritance

Why do many men become bald while most women do not? You might think it was a sex-linked trait, inherited the same way as color blindness. But this is not so. Pattern baldness, in which men lose hair from the top of their head but not from the sides, is a **sex-limited trait.** Some genes are expressed only in one sex because of different hormonal environments. The gene for baldness expresses itself in males because of the relatively

sex-limited trait   A trait—for example, male pattern baldness—that manifests itself in certain hormonal climates but not in others.

high levels of androgens (male sex hormones) found in males but not in females. Females with this trait will show some thinning of the hair in later life, but not baldness.

What We Inherit

Although our genetic endowment is fixed at conception, genetic influences are with us throughout the life span. Our genetic endowment affects us in such areas as physical characteristics, disease, personality, rate of maturation, and intelligence.

Male pattern baldness is a sex-limited trait. The trait is expressed only in males because of the high levels of androgens found in males.

Genetic Influences on Physical Characteristics

The most striking genetic influence involves physical appearance. Hair and skin color, the shape of the nose, and a thousand other physical characteristics are directly influenced by genes. Even weight may have a genetic basis (see the Cross-Cultural Current on page 47).

If we are genetically unique, why do we still look like some other family members? To answer this question, try the following exercise. The next time you're in class, ask yourself how you recognized the person coming in the door as John, Ted, or Frank. You probably used body build and facial features as recognition aids. In this regard, some physical features are more important than others. These features are only a very few of the physical characteristics present in an individual, but for identification purposes they are crucial.

Another reason for familial similarity involves limitations in our gene pools (the total pool of genes in a population). Consider the number of different nose shapes and eye colors that any individual might inherit. The variety is impressive, but there may be only a small number of nose shapes or eye colors in a person's gene pool. When we say that two siblings (who are not identical twins) look alike, we are judging them on the basis of a very small number of physical traits whose variety is limited by their gene pool. We ignore their unique genetic endowment, which may be responsible for physical features that are not as useful for recognition purposes.

Most physical features are trivial, biologically speaking. The color of a person's skin or whether one is a little overweight (being grossly overweight is related to increased susceptibility to certain illnesses) makes very little difference from the point of view of biological functioning or intellectual ability. However, these and many other physical characteristics may or may not be valued by the society in which a person lives. Let's look at weight. Today, thin is "in," but that was not always the case. At one time, to be a bit overweight was fashionable and showed you had sufficient food. Today obese people suffer from discrimination both in the workplace and in social interactions. The same analysis is true of skin color, which is biologically trivial but may be socially important. Any discussion of a physical characteristic, then, must be investigated from both a biological viewpoint (does it lead to some advantage or disadvantage in functioning?), and a social perspective (how is that trait evaluated by the family and society?).

Huntington's Chorea A dominant and fatal genetic disorder affecting the central nervous system.

Tay-Sachs disease A fatal genetic disease found most often in Jews who can trace their ancestry back to Eastern Europe.

Genetic Influences and Disease

The March of Dimes Birth Defects Foundation (1980) has cataloged 1,117 confirmed or suspected recessive disorders and 1,489 confirmed or suspected dominant genetic disorders. There are also more than 200 sex-linked genetic disorders transmitted through the X chromosome. More will probably be added to this list. Many of these diseases are rare, and some show great variability in the severity of their symptoms. The major genetic and chromosomal disorders can be found in Appendix Table 1.

Huntington's chorea: A rare genetic disease of adults. One rare genetic disease, known as **Huntington's Chorea,** affects the central nervous system. Onset is typically in early middle age, after the prime childbearing years. The average age of onset is thirty-five, but variation occurs. The individual suffers from progressive mental deterioration and pronounced involuntary muscle movements. Well-known folksinger Woody Guthrie died from this disease.

If an individual has the gene for this disease, which is dominant, and marries someone who has a normal genotype, there is a 50 percent chance of transmitting the disease gene to offspring (see Figure 2.5). If you had Huntington's Chorea in your family background, you would probably want to know whether you carry the gene. Today a new test is available that can determine whether a person has the gene and therefore help people plan their lives accordingly.

Tay-Sachs disease: Hope through research. Some genetic diseases are more likely to be found in one group of people than another. For example, **Tay-Sachs disease** is most common among Jews whose ancestors came from Central and Eastern Europe. It is a recessive disorder and is transmitted the same way as cystic fibrosis. Infants born with the disease seem normal at birth, but after about six months their progress slows. The disease involves an inborn error in metabolism. The infant's body stores an excessive amount of a material called glycolipid

Is There a Genetic Basis for Obesity?

When you see obese children walking with their obese parents, do you ever wonder whether their weight problem is due to genetic factors or environmental factors—or both? We cannot conclude that just because obese parents tend to have obese children genetics has anything to do with it. Children learn eating habits from their parents. In the past, most psychologists have emphasized the environmental factors that lead to obesity, such as eating habits and lack of exercise. But the possibility remains that there is a genetic basis for obesity. How can this be researched?

One way to discover whether genetic factors are involved in obesity would be to look at adoption studies. Let's say that a child is adopted very early in life. Years later we can compare the child's body mass to that of his or her adoptive parents and biological parents to determine how closely the child resembles each set of parents. If we did this in hundreds of cases, we would have some interesting and valuable information. Unfortunately, however, getting such information about adopted children's biological parents is very difficult in most countries.

But this type of information is available in Denmark from the Danish Adoption Register, which contains the official records of every nonfamilial adoption granted in Denmark. A great deal of information is available, and about 94 percent of the biological mothers and 77 percent of the biological fathers are identified.

Albert Stunkard and his colleagues found information about more than 5,000 adoptees and sent them a general health questionnaire that included items concerning height and weight. More than 3,500 people returned the questionnaires. The researchers derived a body-mass index from the reported weights and heights of the adoptees by dividing weight in kilograms by the square of the height in meters. These values were then placed into four categories: thin, medium, overweight, and obese. The same information was obtained from biological and adoptive parents.

You may point out that some subjectivity might have entered the picture because heights and weights were self-reported. However, the authors performed two earlier studies in the United States and Denmark in which they compared self-reported weights and heights with actual measured weights and heights and found self-reported figures to be quite accurate.

The results showed a "clear relation between adoptee weight class (thin, medium, overweight, and obese) and the body-mass index of the biologic parents: there was no apparent relation between adoptee weight class and the body-mass index of the adoptive parents" (p. 194). In other words, a clear genetic basis for weight was found. It is just as important that the genetic influences found in this study were not confined only to the obese but were also present across the whole range of body weights, from very thin to very fat.

The researchers are quick to point out that this does not mean obesity is inherited the same way eye color is. The fact that a genetic influence exists tells us nothing about the interactions between this hereditary component and environmental factors, such as cultural traditions and attitudes toward eating. The genetic predisposition may well be affected by environmental factors. In addition, it is possible that environmental circumstances, such as famine, could prevent the phenotypical expression of this genetic trait. This study in Denmark describes the outcome of gene-environment interactions in an advanced Western society that has an abundance of food.

The problem with a study like this is that people who are obese might misinterpret the results and say, "You see, obesity is genetic," and give up trying to lose weight. This is unfortunate, for the study says nothing about the effectiveness of environmental programs, such as restricting caloric intake or exercising moderately in an effort to control weight. In addition, there is abundant evidence that nongenetic factors are also important determinants of the amount of body fat. The fact remains, however, that if the results of this study are correct we must appreciate the genetic basis for weight and perhaps, as the authors suggest, target programs to prevent obesity at children who are at risk for the problem.

Source: Stunkard, A. J., et al. An Adoption Study of Human Obesity. *New England Journal of Medicine,* January 23, 1986, *314,* 193–197.

FIGURE 2.5

Genetic Transmission of Huntington's Chorea

If one parent has the gene for Huntington's Chorea, a dominant trait, there is a 50 percent chance that the offspring will inherit the condition, which in the case of this particular disorder shows itself in middle adulthood.

FATHER

	Normal gene	Huntington's Chorea gene
MOTHER Normal gene	Normal gene Normal gene	Normal gene Huntington's Chorea gene
Normal gene	Normal gene Normal gene	Normal gene Huntington's Chorea gene

amniocentesis A procedure in which fluid is taken from a pregnant woman's uterus to check fetal cells for genetic and chromosomal abnormalities.

phenylketonuria (PKU) A recessive genetic disorder marked by inability to digest a particular protein. If the disorder is not treated, it leads to mental retardation.

in the cells of the nervous system. This causes these cells to swell, rupture, and finally die. As more and more nerve cells die, the baby loses motor abilities and finally becomes retarded. The disease is incurable. At the age of two or three, the child dies. Many other diseases show a greater incidence in certain ethnic groups. For example, Italians are most likely to suffer from thalassemia (a blood disease) and phenylketonuria (an inability to digest a particular protein which if left untreated may result in mental retardation) is more common among North Europeans.

A simple test can tell whether one is a carrier for Tay-Sachs. Blood is taken from the fingertip or vein, and the amount of a certain enzyme that breaks down the fatty substances in the nerve cells is measured. People who are carriers will have half as much of the enzyme as noncarriers, although this is enough for a carrier's needs and carriers never show any signs of the disease (March of Dimes, 1984). What if both parents are carriers? As in the case of cystic fibrosis, there is a 25 percent chance that each offspring will have the disorder. However, the presence of the genetic disorder in the unborn can be

identified through **amniocentesis,** a procedure whereby during pregnancy fluid is removed from the amniotic sac and fetal cells that have been discarded are examined for genetic defects. (The procedure is useful in detecting a number of other genetic disorders as well.) Current research is attempting to find a way to supply the brain with substitutes that will break down these fatty substances. Researchers are also looking into methods of transplanting genes from normal cells into defective cells in order to manufacture the chemical.

Phenylketonuria: A success story. Studying genetic disorders can be depressing, especially if you consider Huntington's Chorea or Tay-Sachs disease. But research has made tremendous strides in treating a number of genetic diseases. Perhaps the greatest success story involves the strange case of **phenylketonuria,** known as **PKU.**

PKU is a rare disorder occurring in approximately one in 10,000 births (Rainer, 1972). It involves an inability to digest a particular protein called phenylalanine. If left untreated, brain damage leading to retardation results. Phenylalanine is found in all protein-rich foods, including fish, meats, poultry, eggs, milk, and bread products (Schild, 1979). It is also found in some soft drinks, and now many of these are labeled. The disease is treated by prescribing a diet that is low in phenylalanine. Special preparations are required to meet the child's protein needs. The preventive treatment is very successful (Carter, 1970). Today a blood test to determine whether a newborn baby has PKU is usually given the day the baby is scheduled to be discharged from the hospital.

Three important points about PKU should be kept in mind. First, it is an example of a genetic disease that can be successfully treated. Second, the ravages of the disease do not occur unless it is triggered by the environment. If every individual in a particular culture were to receive a diet low in the offending substance, the disease would never show itself. PKU illustrates how important the environment can be in the emergence and treatment of genetic disorders. Third, the difficulty of keeping children on the regimen should be noted (Reed, 1975). Imagine having to keep a child on an extremely strict diet for years. During late middle childhood, the diet may be relaxed or even abandoned. However, in a recent study children with PKU who abandoned the diet at different ages were assessed for both intelligence and achievement. The findings showed that the earlier a child was allowed off the diet, the more the child's intellectual abilities were negatively affected. The greatest deficiencies were found in children whose dietary restrictions were ended before age six. The authors suggest that even after the age of eight children should be kept on a restricted diet (Holtzman et al., 1986). Women who have PKU should consult a doctor about their diet before and during pregnancy.

True or False   At the present time, all medical science can do for children suffering from genetic diseases is make them more comfortable.

Sickle cell anemia: What to do with our knowledge.   Children who suffer from **sickle cell anemia,** an inherited defect in the structure of red blood cells, experience considerable pain, especially during periods of physical exertion or low oxygen. Although most victims live normal lives, severe cases may have heart and kidney problems (Fogel, 1984). Periods of crisis requiring hos-

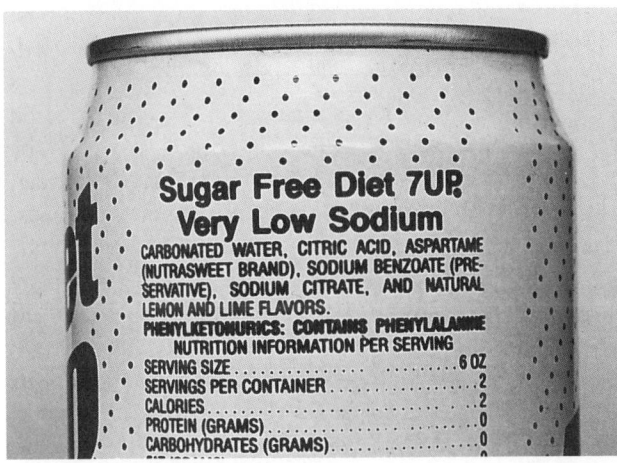

Children with phenylketonuria cannot tolerate anything that contains phenylalanine. Some beverages are labeled for them. For those of us who do not have this disorder, this protein causes us no problem at all.

sickle cell anemia   An inherited defect in the structure of red blood cells found mostly in blacks and Latins.

pitalization are not unusual. Resistance to disease is decreased, and the health of the child is usually poor.

Approximately one in ten American blacks is a carrier, and whether one is a carrier can be determined by a simple blood test. On the average, one marriage out of every 100 between American blacks has the potential for producing a child who will suffer from sickle cell anemia. At present, antibiotics and improved medical treatment can help alleviate the symptoms, but some who have severe cases of the disease die in childhood.

Because the detection process is relatively simple and the gene is rather common, some authorities have suggested that mandatory mass genetic screening be instituted. But this raises ethical problems (Shaw, 1976). For example, some people point out that such screening would be aimed principally at a minority group and see something sinister in this. It should be noted that Latin populations are also at risk for the disorder, although the rates for Latins are lower than for blacks in the United States. Aside from the racial issue, how ethical is it to coerce someone into taking a test? Do people have the right not to know whether they are carrying a "genetic defect?"

One way to sidestep the issue is to recommend the test but not require it. However, recommendations from the government can easily turn into quasi-requirements. Insurance companies and potential employers may learn that an individual is a carrier and increase premiums or refuse that person employment. Any mass screening program must deal with such problems. But no one argues against educational programs about the nature and transmission of these diseases. All populations at risk for genetic diseases should be educated about them. In this way, each person can decide whether he or she wants to submit to a carrier-detection test.

Chromosomal Abnormalities

Some inherited diseases are due to chromosomal abnormalities—that is, abnormalities caused by too few or too many chromosomes rather than by a defect in one or more genes carried on the chromosome. The most important of these diseases are Down's Syndrome, Kline-felter's Syndrome, and Turner's Syndrome.

Down's Syndrome. Some of you know what it's like to look forward to the birth of your child with eagerness and anticipation, a child with whom to share your world and your life, and then to be told after the birth that your hopes and expectations have just been shattered by some chromosomal accident. It is a grief process, because there is real grief over the loss of the child you expected and grief over the devastation of your dreams and hopes (Martz, 1964, pp. 34–35, quoted in Kirk and Gallagher, 1979).

These are the thoughts of a parent who has just been told that his child has **Down's Syndrome**—or mongolism, as it used to be called—the most common chromosomal disorder. Down's Syndrome occurs approximately once in every 600 births and is the result of an extra chromosome on the twenty-first pair. The child has forty-seven chromosomes instead of the normal forty-six. The frequency of the disorder increases with the age

> **Down's Syndrome (mongolism)** A disorder caused by the presence of an extra chromosome, leading to a distinct physical appearance and mental retardation.

of the mother. Between age twenty and twenty-five the risk is one in 1,000 while it is about one in sixty or so at age thirty-five. The frequency rises sharply after the mother reaches the age of about thirty-five (Kowles, 1985). The disorder is also linked to the father. Problems in cell division in the sperm are the cause in an estimated 20 to 25 percent of the cases (Abroms and Bennett, 1980), and there is ample evidence that the disorder is more common when the father is under the age of twenty or over fifty-five (Arehart-Treichel, 1979). Of course, this data is correlational and does not demonstrate cause and effect, and no single accepted explanation for this correlation has been advanced.

True or False Down's Syndrome—or mongolism, as it used to be called—is caused by an extra chromosome.

Children suffering from Down's Syndrome have a distinctive appearance and are mentally retarded.

Most children who suffer from Down's Syndrome are identified either at birth or shortly after by their physical appearance (Hirsch, 1979). Unusual physical features include folds of skin over the eyes (which gave the disorder its original name), short digits, a flat face, a protruding tongue, and a harsh voice (Sue et al., 1981). Mental retardation is associated with Down's Syndrome, most children scoring somewhere between 30 and 50 on intelligence tests (Crandall and Tarjan, 1976), although the degree of retardation can vary.

Down's Syndrome youngsters show the same developmental milestones as normal children, but at a much-delayed pace. This includes smiling and laughing, eye contact during play, self-recognition, some attachment behaviors, and symbolic play. Sometimes qualitative differences in development between Down's Syndrome children and normal youngsters have been noted. In one study, the quality of Down's Syndrome infants' emotional reaction to being separated from their primary caregivers was compared with that of normal infants. Down's Syndrome children showed less-intense separation distress, they took longer to show it, and they exhibited a diminished range of emotions (Thompson et al., 1985). Children with this disorder have a reputation for being lovable, cheerful, and easy to work with, although this is not always true (Bridges and Cicchetti, 1982). While years ago most children with Down's Syndrome were institutionalized immediately after birth, this is not the case today. Many of these children are now raised at home, which is usually beneficial to the child. Many are still institutionalized later, however, when their families become unable to care for them (Reed, 1975). An alternative to institutionalization is the group home, in which they can live with others outside the family with support, affection, and supervision.

Not long ago the life expectancy for Down's Syndrome children was ten years or less. Congenital heart problems are common, and resistance to disease is low. Medical advances have substantially increased the life span of these children. If they survive the first few years, their death rates are about the same as the general population until age forty, after which they are more susceptible to diseases that are related to old age.

Sex-linked chromosomal disorders. Down's Syndrome is not the only chromosomal abnormality. Two of the more common chromosomal disorders are caused by problems that occur on the sex chromosomes. In

schizophrenia A severe mental disorder characterized by one or more of the following symptoms: delusions, hallucinations, disordered and illogical thinking, social withdrawal, inappropriate emotional responses, and bizarre behavior.

Klinefelter's Syndrome, the male receives at least one more X chromosome than he should, thus creating an XXY genotype. This is found in approximately one in 600 male births. Children afflicted with the disorder have small sex organs and are sterile, and many, though not all, are mentally retarded.

Turner's Syndrome is caused by lack of an X chromosome. The genotype is expressed as XO. These females are sterile, short, and do not mature normally. They often require estrogen treatments to attain adult stature. Though they often have specific learning problems, they are not usually mentally retarded (Kalat, 1980). They perform poorly on spatial, attention, and short-term memory tasks and show more difficulty accurately discriminating facial expressions. This last deficit may be the basis of some of their frequent problems in social relationships (McCauley et al., 1987). Turner's Syndrome appears in about one out of every 2,000 female births (Sutton, 1980).

Predispositions to Disorders: Schizophrenia

Not all disorders with a genetic base are transmitted directly. Sometimes a predisposition to a disorder, rather than the disease itself, is passed from parents to children. This is the case with schizophrenia.

True or False Schizophrenia, like cystic fibrosis or Tay-Sachs disease, is transmitted directly from parent to child.

Schizophrenia is the term for a group of mental disorders characterized by one or more of the following symptoms: delusions, hallucinations, disordered and illogical thinking, social withdrawal, inappropriate emotional responses, and bizarre behavior. About 25 percent of the first time admissions to mental hospitals are diagnosed as schizophrenic, and about 50 percent of the residents of mental hospitals at any one time suffer from the disorder. It is a major international health problem.

A number of twin studies suggest that there is a genetic base for schizophrenia (McBroom, 1980). If an identical

TABLE 2.1

Measuring Children's Temperament

Alexander Thomas, Stella Chess, and Herbert Birch found the majority of children could be classified as "easy," "slow to warm up," or "difficult" according to how they rate in key categories on a 9-point personality index that are shown in color.

Type of Child	Activity Level	Rhythmicity	Distractibility	Approach-Withdrawal
	The proportion of active periods to inactive ones	Regularity of hunger, excretion, sleep, and wakefulness	The degree to which extraneous stimuli alter behavior	The response to a new object or person
"Easy"	Varies	Very regular	Varies	Positive approach
"Slow to Warm Up"	Low to moderate	Varies	Varies	Initial withdrawal
"Difficult"	Varies	Irregular	Varies	Withdrawal

twin is schizophrenic, his or her twin is fifty times more likely to become schizophrenic than any other individual in the general population (Altrocchi, 1980). But identical twins share a common environment as well as a common genotype. To control for environmental differences, a number of studies have compared identical, or monozygotic, twins (who develop from one sperm and one egg cell), to fraternal, or dizygotic twins (who develop from two different sperm and egg cells). Fraternal twins are no more genetically similar than any pair of siblings. If there is a substantial genetic component, we would expect that if an identical twin became schizophrenic the other would have an excellent chance of suffering from the disorder too. We would expect that with fraternal twins in which one becomes schizophrenic, the other twin would have a greater chance than the average person on the street of also suffering from the condition, because these twins have about half their genes in common. However, their risk would not be as great as identical twins, who share all their genes in common.

These hypotheses are confirmed by the research in the field. The risk for identical twins in which one becomes schizophrenic is three to six times as great as that for fraternal twins in which one shows signs of the disorder (Rosenthal, 1970). The degree of similarity between twins is called the **concordance rate.** It approaches 50 percent for identical twins and 9 percent for fraternal twins, when one of the twins has schizophrenia (Gottesman and Shields, 1972). Studies comparing identical twins separated at birth and raised in different homes have also found this 50 percent concordance rate when

one twin was diagnosed as schizophrenic (Gottesman, 1978). This concordance rate is less than perfect, which means that factors other than genetic considerations are also associated with the development of schizophrenia.

There is little doubt that a significant genetic component underlies the disorder (Scarr and Kidd, 1983; Weisfeld, 1982), but there is also a strong environmental component. What appears to be transmitted is not the disease itself but rather a tendency, or predisposition, to acquire the disorder. In other words, all environmental factors being equal, an individual with a family history of schizophrenia is at greater risk for the disease than someone with no family history of schizophrenia. At the same time, prenatal, birth, and psychosocial factors are important too. For example, some prenatal insults leading to brain abnormalities, lack of oxygen to the brain, and birth trauma, some cognitive deficits, and chaotic family situations with communication problems may be implicated (Mirsky and Duncan, 1986). Genetic factors may make an individual more vulnerable, but other factors can be important as well.

Studies indicate that other severe psychological disturbances may have a genetic base. Researchers at the University of London found that genetic factors may

concordance rate The degree of similarity between twins on any particular trait.

temperament A group of characteristics reflecting an individual's way of responding to the environment and thought to be genetic.

Adaptability	Attention Span and Persistence	Intensity of Reaction	Threshold of Responsiveness	Quality of Mood
The ease with which a child adapts to changes in his environment	The amount of time devoted to an activity, and the effect of distraction on the activity	The energy of response, regardless of its quality or direction	The intensity of stimulation required to evoke a discernible response	The amount of friendly, pleasant, joyful behavior as contrasted with unpleasant, unfriendly behavior
Very adaptable	High or low	Low or mild	High or low	Positive
Slowly adaptable	High or low	Mild	High or low	Slightly negative
Slowly adaptable	High or low	Intense	High or low	Negative

Source: Thomas et al., 1970.

underlie manic depression, usually called a bipolar disorder, which is characterized by intense mood shifts between euphoria and profound depression (Hodgkinson et al., 1987). In addition, some research indicates that a genetic factor may be implicated in Alzheimer's Disease, a disease in later life marked by mental deterioration which will be discussed in Chapter 18 (St. George-Hyslip et al., 1987; Tanzi et al., 1987).

Genetic Influences on Personality and Behavior

Does genetic endowment affect personality, or our orientation to the world, known as our temperament? This is a controversial area. Although no one claims complete genetic control, many psychologists today believe that genetic factors contribute to temperament and personality.

Temperament. Each child is born with a **temperament,** an "individual style of responding to the environment" (Thomas et al., 1970, p. 2). Thomas and his colleagues found nine behavior patterns that comprise a child's temperament (see Table 2.1). They include (1) the level and extent of motor activity, (2) the degree of regularity of such functions as eating and sleeping, (3) distractibility when there are changes in the environment, (4) response to new objects or people, (5) adaptability to changes in the environment, (6) persistence, (7) intensity of responses, (8) sensitivity to stimuli, and (9) general disposition.

These researchers found that the majority of children fit into one of three general types. "Easy" children are born that way. These children are happy, flexible, and regular. They get along well with almost everyone and present few problems for parents or teachers. "Difficult children," on the other hand, are intense, demanding, inflexible, irregular, and cry a great deal. They may present parents and teachers with many challenges. The third category, "slow to warm up" children, do not respond well to changes in their environment, but their reactions are not intense. They exhibit a low activity level and have a tendency to withdraw from new stimuli. Approximately 40 percent of the subjects in the study by Thomas and his colleagues could be characterized as "easy," about 10 percent at "difficult," and another 15 percent as "slow to warm up." The remaining 35 percent could not be placed in any of these categories because they showed a mixture of behaviors.

A child's temperament can affect the relationship between parents and their children. A child is fortunate if his or her inborn temperament meshes with the parents' abilities and styles. The "difficult" child thrives in a structured, understanding environment, but not in an inconsistent, intolerant home. The "slow to warm up" child does best if the parents understand the child's need for time to adjust to new situations. If they do not, the parents may only intensify the child's natural tendency to withdraw. In fact, Thomas urges parents to work with their child's temperament rather than try to change it. For example, if a child is slow to warm up, parents and teachers should allow the child to warm up to the environment at the child's own pace. Gentle encouragement is best. If the child is "difficult," they advise parents to be very consistent and objective in their handling of the child. Teachers should realize that "difficult" children do poorly in nonstructured, permissive situations and may be easily frustrated by tasks they cannot handle immediately. Firmness and patience are required. "Easy" children may also face problems related to temperament. Sometimes they are unable to resolve conflicts between their own desires and the demands of others.

The temperament of the child also affects how parents see themselves and their role as parents. Parents who have a child who is rated "difficult" are more likely to believe that the child's behavior is not under their control, while mothers of "easy" infants are more likely to believe in their ability to control their child's behavior (Sirignano and Lachman, 1985). Notice that this is a further application of the concept of bi-directionality discussed in Chapter 1.

Temperament is relatively stable in infancy (Matheny et al., 1985). As children mature, temperament may remain stable, but the qualities that comprise temperament may manifest themselves differently. For example, at age two months a child who is easily distractible will stop crying for food if rocked, and at two years will stop a tantrum if another activity is suggested. The underlying characteristic of distractibility is present, but with age different behaviors will be shown.

Even though temperament appears to have a genetic basis (Goldsmith and Gottesman, 1981), there is evidence that behavioral orientations may be affected by parenting practices and attitudes. In other words, the child's interactions with the environment may encourage or discourage a specific behavior related to temperament. In a study of infant temperament in three African societies, de Vries and Sameroff (1984) attributed specific differences in temperament to each culture's child-rearing practices and parenting orientations. For example, mothers of infants in the Digo culture are not very concerned with time and are more likely to respond to a child's immediate needs. There is little emphasis on how long a child should sleep or the time a child should be fed. Perhaps as a result of this caregiving pattern, Digo infants were rated less regular than infants in the other two African cultures. A child's temperament, then, may also be influenced by environmental factors, including child-rearing practices.

Some factors that comprise temperament are related to later personality. Studies have linked temperamental characteristics at age three or so with later Type A behavior patterns, which involve aggressiveness, easy arousal, impatience, a sense of time urgency, achievement striving, and other characteristics related to heart disease in adults. Different elements of temperament are related to different characteristics of the Type A personality pattern. For instance, high adaptability, a negative mood, and low rhythmicity during early childhood are related to the achievement-striving, driven personality that is part of the Type A pattern. Children with a low sensory threshold, low persistence, and low adaptability are likely to show the character trait of impatience, which is another personality trait indicative of the Type A personality pattern (Steinberg, 1985). The results of this research and other studies that relate temperament to later characteristics must be interpreted cautiously. This data is correlational and does not show cause and effect. In addition, because studies like this use parental reports, subjectivity may be a factor; parents may see what they want to see.

It would be wrong to give the impression that Thomas' conception of temperament is accepted totally by all psychologists. In one recent roundtable discussion with four eminent psychologists, it became obvious that there was agreement on some points and not on others (Goldsmith et al., 1987). Psychologists agree that temperament reflects behavioral tendencies, has biological underpinnings, and is easiest to see directly in infancy, but that it becomes more complex as the child matures. They disagree on just how much of an infant's behavior should be considered as emanating from temperament, on the nature of the specific components that comprise temperament, and on whether the term "difficult child" should be used at all, because of its negative connotation (Goldsmith et al., 1987). Despite these differences, the concept of temperament is useful in understanding the factors that underlie a child's tendency to react to certain stimuli in characteristic ways.

Behavioral traits. "Well, she's got her mother's looks, but she took her father's temper" (Wells, 1980, p. 88). How many times have you heard variations of that statement? If your parents are friendly and affectionate, will you be the same? Is extroversion (being outgoing) or introversion (being directed inward) an inherited predisposition? There is evidence that a genetic component underlies this personality dimension (Vandenberg, 1967). Such traits as sociability, emotionality, and activity level also have underlying genetic components (Daniels and Plomin, 1985; Goldsmith, 1983), as do authoritarianism and rigidity (Rose and Ditto, 1983). The tremendous influence of the environment on personality is obvious, but a genetic basis for various personality traits may exist.

Just how would genes affect behavior? There are no genes specifically for behavior, but genes can exert their influence through enzymes, hormones, and neurological factors that in turn can influence behavior (Gottesman, 1966). In other words, genes influence an individual's physiology, which in turn affects behavior.

Maturation Rate

It is no secret that children develop at their own rate. The maturation rate reflects their unique genetic master plan. Such activities as standing, crawling, walking, and talking are largely, but not exclusively, dependent on one's genetic endowment (Mischel, 1976).

Statistics can show that the "average" child walks or talks at a particular age, but it is important to recognize that within the broad "normal" range some children develop faster than others. There may be serious consequences from pushing a child to do something before that child is ready. The concept of **readiness** implies that there is a point in development when a person has the skills necessary to master a particular task. When parents and teachers do not understand this, problems can result. For instance, if a child who does not understand the concept of "number" is forced by parents to try to add two numbers, that child is destined to fail. The child becomes frustrated. Because an understanding of numbers is essential to success in learning how to add, bitter and unnecessary failure results. Repetition of such experiences may lead to a lack of self-confidence. The same argument may hold for any physical or mental challenge.

Intelligence

Is intelligence partly inherited? The issue of genetics and intelligence is fraught with controversy. The problem begins with the very definition of intelligence, for which there is no single, accepted definition. Various definitions will be discussed in Chapter 9. Most studies in the area of genetics examine the genetic contribution to intelligence as indicated by performance on standardized intelligence tests. Is such intelligence partially inherited? If your answer is yes, what percentage of the "trait" would you guess genetically determined? The existence of a genetic component in intelligence is well accepted, but

readiness The point in development at which a child has the necessary skills to master a new challenge.

heritability A term used to describe how much of the variation seen in any particular trait within a population is due to genetic endowment.

anyone who offers a numerical figure is likely to be criticized. Some authorities claim it is impossible to estimate this figure.

The term **heritability** is used to refer to how much of the variation we see in people from a given population on a particular characteristic—such as intelligence—is due to genetic endowment. Some claim we cannot estimate the heritability figure for human traits because we cannot control the environment (Feldman and Lewontin, 1975). After all, people with similar levels of intelligence tend to establish similar environments. Highly intelligent people create more stimulating environments than less-intelligent people. In addition, heritability studies are based not on individuals but on populations, and one must know a great deal about the population and the trait he is measuring in order to understand the meaning of these figures. For example, the heritability figure for a group's ability to sing passably is probably low because practice, persistence, training, and motivation—all of which are environmental factors—are most important. However, these factors do not account for the vocal qualities of some great singers. Almost any child might be able to learn how to sing, but not every child can become a great vocalist, no matter how much training is received. The heritability index would be different for the group of passable singers and for our group of great vocalists. Despite the problems in interpreting heritability figures, some interesting research has been done in the area.

The more closely two people are related, the more likely they are to have similar intelligence levels. The correlation between identical twins reared together is +.87; for identical twins reared apart it is +.75, for siblings reared together it is +.55, and for parents and their offspring generally it is +.50. Correlations for intelligence scores between first cousins is approximately +.26, and for unrelated children reared together it is +.23 (Erlenmeyer-Kimling and Jarvik, 1963). A more recent review of the literature concludes that the figures are a bit lower but shows the same general pattern (Bouchard and McGue, 1981).

None of these correlations is perfect, although some are high. Genetic influence on intelligence is indicated, but the genetic explanation falls far short of explaining all the differences in intelligence between people. An understanding of environmental factors is needed to accomplish that. Such correlations may also be interpreted to show environmental influence. The closer the relationship between two people, the greater the chance they were raised in a similar environment.

Figures for heritability vary widely. Jencks (1972) argues that genetic factors are responsible for about half the variation in intelligence we see among people. Others have offered higher or lower figures. Jensen (1969) argues that it approaches 80 percent, while Kamin (1974), who thoroughly criticizes the studies purporting to demonstrate the heritability of intelligence, places the figure at a much lower level. While older studies have ascribed as much as 80 percent of intelligence to genetic factors, newer studies yield values closer to 50 percent (Plomin and DeFries, 1980). This would ascribe approximately half to genetic factors and the other half to environmental factors. Any heritability figure should be interpreted cautiously. Problems in defining what we really mean by intelligence, and difficulties in research design, combine to provide ammunition for both sides (Walker and Emory, 1985; Horn, 1985). In addition, most psychologists today accept the fact that an important environmental element underlies intelligence, since none of the correlations in the data noted previously is perfect (Willerman, 1979). No matter which estimate of heritability one uses, both environmental and genetic factors are involved in determining intelligence (Scarr and Kidd, 1983).

The question of modifying intelligence. If a significant genetic component underlies intelligence, to what extent can intelligence be modified through environmental methods, such as education or special training programs? A number of studies show that intelligence scores can be modified, but one by Skeels (1966) stands out. In the 1930s, Skeels was working in a bleak orphanage where the children received little attention and were subjected to a rigid schedule. The environment was depressing, and there were no toys. Skeels took a special interest in two girls who spent most of their time rocking back and forth in bed. These two girls were later trans-

ferred to a mental institution, where they came under the influence of an older, retarded woman who showered them with attention. Their behavior changed, and they became much more responsive.

Skeels decided to find out more about this phenomenon. A number of children were removed from the sterile setting of the orphanage and allowed to live with older retardates in a better environment. The intelligence scores of these children improved an average of 29 points, and one child's score actually rose by more than 50 points. The group that stayed in the depressing environment of the orphanage was found to have even lower intelligence scores than when the study had begun.

Most psychologists today conclude that a change in environment accounts for improvement in intelligence, although the methodology used to arrive at this conclusion has been severely criticized (Longstreth, 1981). Some creative programs have successfully increased the intelligence scores of certain groups significantly. For example, Israel has had considerable success in narrowing, sometimes even eliminating, the differences in intelli-

Children's environment affects their development. Studies indicate that if the environment of children like these was improved, many aspects of their development, including their intelligence, would be enhanced.

gence that were present among many of the diverse groups who settled there. Through an intensive program of enrichment, these differences tend to disappear (Smilansky, cited in Reed, 1975). This malleability does not stop in childhood, or even in adolescence. Adults who are placed in spirited, challenging environments tend to show high intellectual functioning, while those who find themselves in deadening environments do not show such functioning.

The genetic influence on intelligence does not limit its malleability (Scarr-Salapatek, 1975). Instead, the genetic factor affects the elasticity of intelligence. Few would argue that any enrichment program could turn a person of below-average intelligence into a genius, but a radical change for the better in the environment would probably have a significant impact on that person's intelligence scores.

Genes, intelligence, and race. In 1969 the heredity vs. environment question took a different turn. In a long, detailed study Jensen (1969) argued that differences in intelligence scores between racial groups were due primarily to genetic rather than environmental factors. Three major points were advanced by Jensen: (1) Intelligence tests can measure general ability, (2) individual differences in intelligence can be attributed mostly to genetic considerations, and (3) educational programs have been ineffective in increasing intelligence test scores (Loehlin et al., 1975). Each of these points is controversial.

Because the background and motivation of the child taking an intelligence test is so important, considerable controversy exists concerning the validity of intelligence tests. Jensen's second point—that most of the differences in intelligence can be attributed to genetic considerations—is not accepted by many experts in the field. Although most agree that genetic factors influence intelligence, the significance and magnitude of this contribution is debatable. Jensen's third point, concerning the ineffectiveness of programs that attempt to increase intelligence scores, depends on how soon the intelligence test is administered after the enrichment program has ended and on the extent to which a permanent change in the environment is made.

If these had been Jensen's only points, they would have attracted some attention, but he also suggested that differences between Caucasians and blacks in intelligence test scores were due to genetic differences—and

that caused a a great outcry. Jensen did not deny the importance of environmental factors, but he did relegate them to a distinctly second-place position in favor of genetic factors.

Although few authorities deny that significant differences exist between blacks and Caucasians in intelligence test scores, this does not indicate anything about what causes the differences. Many minorities in the United States, including blacks, suffer from a steady diet of unequal opportunity, poverty, poor housing, and poor health care. These significant environmental factors have a great effect on intelligence scores.

Jensen's assertion that the heritability of intelligence was as high as 80 percent was denounced at once. Many researchers accept much lower figures (Gardner, 1983). Even those who argue for a substantial heritability figure do not relate it to an individual's ethnicity or race. In addition, these heritability figures are often computed within Caucasian populations, and their usefulness in comparing intelligence scores between races is dubious at best.

Jensen's argument that programs designed to improve the intelligence scores of children with below-average scores have failed may be based on a faulty assumption. We now have evidence that these programs can increase children's scores, although not all the effects are long-lasting (Lazar and Darlington, 1982). Lack of permanence may be the result of failure to improve the environment to which these children return after the programs end. Even so, programs like Project Head Start, which will be discussed in Chapter 7, have been successful in other ways. For example, participants in Head Start programs are less likely to be placed in special-education classes, are apt to show superiority on achievement tests in high school, and are less likely to be left back. The children who benefit most are children from single-parent families, children who have low intelligence scores prior to participating in the program, or children whose mothers had less than a tenth-grade education (Scarr and Weinberg, 1986). In addition, even if some programs have not lived up to the long-term expectations of their designers—that of increasing intelligence scores—it does not mean that better-planned and better-executed programs must fail. There is a major difference between cannot and did not.

True or False Intelligence scores can be modified through a program of intense training.

It is impossible to describe the heritability of any characteristic, including intelligence, without first specifying the child's environment. This point was demonstrated by Whitten and Kagan (1969). Most people would agree that there is a significant genetic influence on height. Children from rural areas of South America are often much shorter than children who come from urban areas, but these differences are due not to genetic differences but to disease and improper diet. The farther you travel from the major cities, the worse the medical care becomes. Over the past twenty years, however, dietary improvement and the extension of medical services into these rural areas have altered the situation. The differences in height between rural and urban children are much less now than in the past.

If the heights of all the children in a suburban elementary school were tabulated, you might reasonably attribute most of the differences to heredity (if we could state that nutrition, health care, and other environmental factors were about equal). Only when environments are similar can we begin to suggest that differences in a particular trait may be substantially due to genetic considerations. The same argument could be made for intelligence. Only when we equalize environmental factors, such as health care, nutrition, opportunity, and housing, can we give heritability figures that make sense. Otherwise, such comparisons are misleading.

Genetics Across the Life Span

Genetic effects can be seen across the entire life span. It is incorrect to think of genetics as something that affects the child more than the adult. In every area of interest we see its continuing effects. The process of aging, which will be described in Chapter 18, is certainly under genetic control, even though there are many theories of how and why we age (Schneider, 1978). Some disorders, such as schizophrenia, involve inherited predispositions that normally show themselves in early adulthood. Intelligence is a quality that is important throughout life, and as we have seen, it is partly due to genetic endowment. In the realm of personality, such traits as extroversion and neuroticism (emotional instability) have a genetic base. It is safe to conclude that genetics affects almost every area of development in some way and that it is as important when looking at adulthood as it is in examining the development of children.

True or False Genetic influences are more widespread and important in childhood than in adulthood.

Genetic Counseling: The Frontiers of Knowledge

Would it be useful if we could reliably determine whether our offspring would suffer from a genetic disorder or would be at risk through a predisposition to some problem? Today in some cases this is a reality.

In many university clinics, professionals trained in genetics are able to help people determine such risks. These genetic counselors help people by (1) diagnosing and describing particular disorders, (2) calculating the probabilities that a disorder will be transmitted to offspring, (3) helping people reach a decision based on genetic information as well as on ethical, religious, and cultural concerns, and (4) describing the treatment and resources available to those seeking such information (Sperber, 1976). On the surface this seems to present few problems, but appearances are deceiving. In reality, genetic counseling is fraught with complicated ethical and practical problems that are quite difficult to solve.

For example, will those seeking the information understand it and remember it? Sibinga and Friedman (1971) reported that only a small percentage of their sample adequately understood the facts communicated to them about PKU. It was their emotional reaction to what they had been told—not their intelligence level—that interfered with their understanding. In another study, only 35 percent of a sample of people who were told their children carried a dangerous recessive gene but would develop normally because they were carriers appeared for counseling. Many who did appear did not remember the counseling experience three to eight months later, although they remembered they had been told their children were normal (Grossman et al., 1985). There are also problems in communicating information about particular defects to parents who are emotionally involved (Walzer et al., 1976). People often use defenses to deny or reject such information (Sperber, 1976). The realization that something is "wrong" with their genes, that they might carry a "defect," can be alarming and can change a person's life. Genetic counselors must be certain their clients understand what they are being told. It is also their duty to help clients deal with emotional reactions to the information (Walzer et al., 1976).

Today, people concerned about a particular genetic problem receive counseling aimed at helping them understand the probability of transmitting a disorder to their offspring.

Most people who seek genetic counseling are faced with some kind of decision. A family with one child who has suffered from a genetic difficulty may have to decide whether to have other children. Others may have to decide whether they should even begin a family. Still others may be forced to decide whether to terminate a pregnancy based on laboratory tests showing that the unborn child has some serious genetic defect—certainly a controversial question. Previous generations did not have the information needed to make such decisions, but success with such diseases as PKU have provided an incentive for more screening to take place in the future (Nyhan, 1986). With the expansion of such programs and the increasing number of inherited disorders that can be detected during the prenatal stage, the number of people faced with such decisions will dramatically increase. Can genetic counselors help people make decisions without allowing their own biases to influence their clients? After all, anyone in the position of a counselor has a great deal of standing and therefore power. A counselor must be careful to explain the facts in terms that will not affect the decision itself. Yet, because helping people deal with their feelings is one of a counselor's tasks, counselors are in a difficult position. People often

ask them what they should do—a question genetic counselors cannot answer. Genetic counselors may influence these decisions inadvertently, however, by the way they provide the information (Lappe and Brody, 1976). If genetic counseling is used correctly, it can ease people's minds. People can leave genetic counseling knowing they are armed with the information that will allow them to make difficult decisions more rationally.

True or False Genetic counselors must often make decisions for their clients concerning marriage and childbearing.

Heredity and Environment Reconsidered

Genetic factors are important to any understanding of development. Heredity influences just about every important area of development all through life. Yet the nature of these influences is greatly misunderstood. With the exception of a few major genetic diseases, one cannot understand genetic influences without also specifying the nature of the environment in which these influences are operating. Heredity and environment interact and complement each other; it is impossible to speak of one in the absence of the other. Our genetic endowment allows us to take a number of different paths through life, but it is the environment that determines which path we actually choose.

Some people yearn for the "good old days," when general statements about what is inherited and what is not could be made. Things were certainly simpler then, even if they were almost always incorrect. The modern view of the nature-nurture controversy is certainly more complicated, and it precludes making simple, grandiose statements about heredity causing one thing and environment affecting another. However, it also gives us the opportunity to marvel once again at the complicated process by which a tiny, one-cell fertilized egg develops into a person, who then, guided by both genetic endowment and environmental factors, can fulfill his or her great human promise.

Summary
---

1. The basic units of heredity are genes, which are carried on chromosomes. Human beings have twenty-three pairs of chromosomes. In the sex cells, however, the chromosome pair splits, so that each sex cell contains twenty-three chromosomes. The twenty-three chromosomes found in both the egg and the sperm cells combine during fertilization to maintain the same forty-six chromosomes found in normal human beings.

2. Each person is genetically unique. The only exception is identical, or monozygotic, twins, who share the same genetic composition. Fraternal, or dizygotic, twins are no more genetically similar than any other pair of siblings.

3. The first twenty-two pairs of chromosomes appear to be alike, but the twenty-third pair—the sex chromosomes—is different. A female has two X chromosomes, while a male has an X and a Y. The male determines the sex of the offspring, because he can contribute an X or a Y while the female contributes only an X. The chances are always fifty-fifty that an offspring will be a male or a female.

4. A trait that is shown if only one gene for it is present is called dominant. Any trait that requires two genes to show itself is called recessive. The term genotype describes the genetic composition of the individual, while the term phenotype refers to observable characteristics. A person's phenotype and genotype may be different.

5. When a particular characteristic is influenced by many genes, we consider the mechanism of transmission to be polygenic, multigenic, or multifactorial. The word multifactorial is sometimes used to denote characteristics influenced by a number of genes as well as by the environment.

6. Some traits, such as hemophilia and color blindness, are considered sex-linked because they are carried on the X chromosome and are much more likely to be shown in males than in females. Other traits, such as patterned baldness, are sex-limited in that they show themselves in a particular hormonal environment.

7. Genetic endowment affects our physical characteristics. Because people value some traits more than others, certain traits become socially important even if they are biologically trivial.

8. A number of genetic diseases have been discovered, including cystic fibrosis, Tay-Sachs disease, phenylketonuria, Huntington's Chorea, and sickle cell anemia.

9. The most common chromosomal abnormality is called Down's Syndrome. Children with this disorder are usually retarded and have a number of distinctive physical attributes.

10. There is a significant genetic component in schizophrenia. However, what is transmitted is not the disease itself, but rather a tendency or a predisposition to suffer from the disease, given a particular environment.

11. Our genetic endowment influences personality, probably by affecting biological functioning. Human beings are born with a temperament, an individual way of responding to the environment. A number of personality traits, such as extroversion, sociability, and activity level, appear to have a genetic basis.

12. Genetic factors are also important in determining a child's rate of development.

13. There appears to be a genetic basis for intelligence, although there is much dispute over the heritability figure. No matter what figure is used, however, an individual's environment greatly affects how genes for intelligence will be shown. Educational programs can raise the intelligence scores of children.

14. Genetic factors are just as important in adulthood as they are in childhood.

15. Genetic counseling offers couples an opportunity to find out more about their genetic background and the likelihood of their having a child with a certain disorder.

16. Heredity and environment interact in many subtle ways. We cannot speak of one in the absence of the other. Throughout life there are many genetically possible paths, but it is the environment that determines which path an individual takes. We must consider both if we are to understand fully how people fulfill their human potential.

Answers to True or False Statements

1. *False* Correct statement: Each species has its own number of chromosomes.

2. *True* Fraternal twins develop from two separate sperm and two separate egg cells and are no more genetically alike than any other pair of siblings.

3. *False* Correct statement: The odds stay the same for each conception.

4. *False* Correct statement: At the present time there is no cure for cystic fibrosis.

5. *True* If both parents carry a recessive trait, it may show itself in their offspring.

6. *True* Color blindness is a sex-linked trait that is carried by females but affects mostly their male offspring.

7. *False* Correct statement: This is an overly pessimistic view, as the success in treating phenylketonuria shows.

8. *True* Down's Syndrome is caused by an extra chromosome on the twenty-first pair, making a total of forty-seven instead of the normal forty-six.

9. *False* Correct statement: What is transmitted is apparently a predisposition to the disorder, not the disorder itself.

10. *True* Some efforts to increase intelligence scores have been successful, although questions surround the permanence of the change.

11. *False* Correct statement: Genetic influences are as important in adulthood as they are in childhood.

12. *False* Correct statement: Genetic counselors offer information that allows their clients to make an informed, personal decision.

Prenatal Development
and Birth

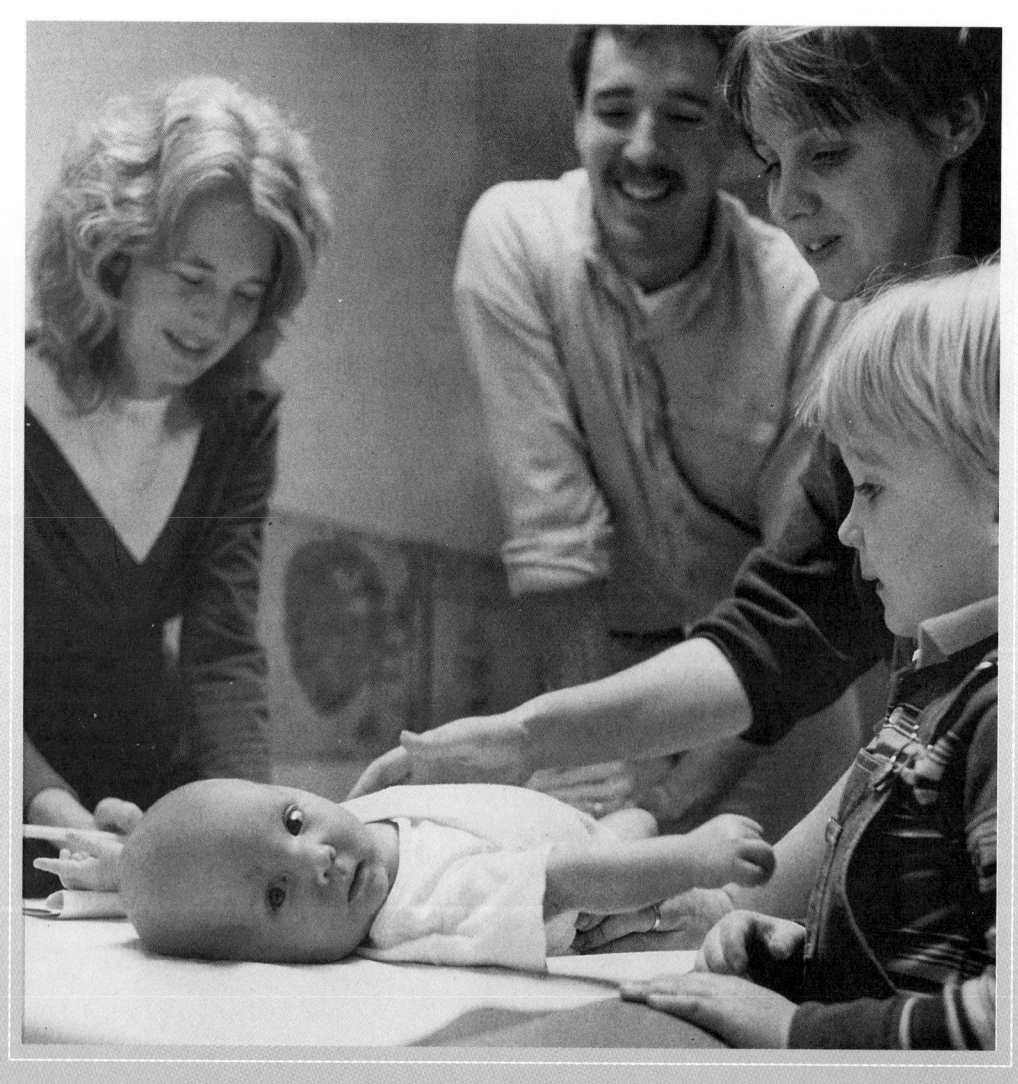

Are the Following Statements True or False?

Try the True-False Quiz below. See if your answers correspond to the information in this chapter. Each question is repeated after the paragraph in which the answer can be found. The True-False Answer Box at the end of the chapter lists the complete answers.

_____ 1. The first organ to function during the prenatal period is the liver.

_____ 2. The placenta stops all foreign substances from entering the bloodstream of the fetus.

_____ 3. Smoking during pregnancy has been linked to increased weight gain in infants.

_____ 4. Most evidence on the effects of caffeine on the fetus show that even one cup of coffee a day can be quite injurious to the unborn child.

_____ 5. Pregnant women who carry the AIDS virus cannot transmit it to their unborn child during the prenatal stage.

_____ 6. Some 70 percent of all birth defects are caused by prenatal insults rather than genetic disorders.

_____ 7. The number of women bearing children after age thirty-five has increased greatly in the past decade.

_____ 8. Severe malnutrition during pregnancy leads to a condition in which the infant has fewer brain cells.

_____ 9. Cesarean births have decreased in the past twenty years, as doctors have come to appreciate the medical risks to the mother and child.

_____10. Premature infants are no more at risk for developmental problems than normal infants.

_____11. Boys are more neurologically mature at birth than girls.

_____12. The United States has the second-lowest infant mortality rate in the free world.

A Prenatal Dilemma

Almost every day the newspapers announce that another substance is harmful to the unborn child. This worries Ellen and Tom, who are expecting their first baby in about seven months. Friends and relatives offer all kinds of advice about what Ellen should do and what she should avoid during the pregnancy. With each newspaper story they all become more concerned and confused. Like all expectant parents, Ellen and Tom want a happy and healthy baby, but they're afraid something will go wrong. How realistic are their fears?

Prenatal Development

An appreciation of the complexity of the prenatal stage begins with some understanding of prenatal development. Development before birth is divided into four main stages: conception, the germinal stage, the embryonic stage, and the fetal stage.

zygote   A fertilized egg.

Conception

During ovulation, one egg is allowed to pass into a fallopian tube, where it is exposed to any sperm that are present. Although many sperm may surround the egg cell, only one will penetrate its outer wall. At this moment of conception, the mother's egg cell is fertilized by the father's sperm. When this occurs, there is a rearrangement and exchange of genetic material, and the genetic endowment of the new being is set for life. This fertilized egg, or **zygote,** continues to travel down the tube into the uterus, or womb.

In some cases two eggs may pass into the fallopian tubes and be fertilized by two different sperm. The result is fraternal, or dizygotic, twins—two separately developing organisms that are no more genetically similar than

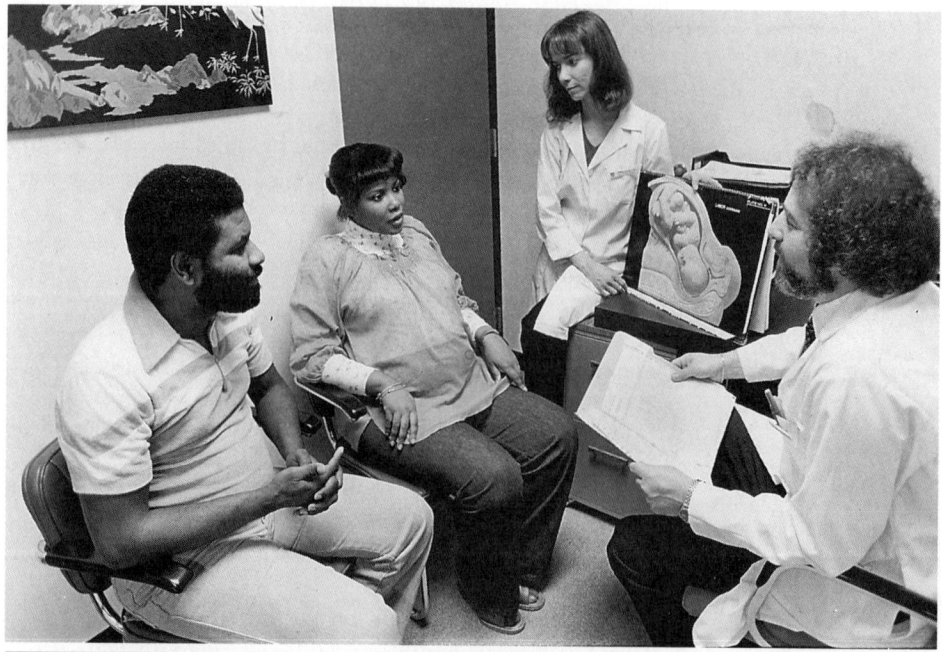

Young couples are warned against so many things during a pregnancy that they often are confused as to just what has been demonstrated by science to be really dangerous to the unborn child.

any pair of siblings. Identical, or monozygotic, twins develop from a single egg and a single sperm. A cell division takes place very early in development, and these twins have an identical genetic makeup. Those rare cases in which the division into two separate zygotes is incomplete result in twins joined together, or Siamese twins.

The Germinal Stage

It takes anywhere from a week to ten days or so for the fertilized egg to embed itself in the lining of the uterus. During this period, called the **germinal stage,** the fertilized egg divides again and again and begins the process of specialization that results in the formation of its organs. On the second day, about thirty hours after fertilization, the cell divides into two new cells (Singer and Hilgard, 1978). At sixty hours the two cells divide to become four cells (Curtis, 1975). This division continues until, at the end of the first week, more than 100 cells are present.

On the fifth day after conception, the cells rearrange to form a cavity. The hollow ball of cells is now called a **blastocyst** (Balinsky, 1970). The majority of cells are found in the outer layer, called a trophoblast, while the smaller number are found in the inner layer, called the inner cell mass. The outer layer will become structures that enable the embryo to survive, including the yolk sac, the allantois, the amnion, and the chorion. The yolk sac produces blood cells until the developing organism can do so on its own, at which time it disappears. The allantois forms the umbilical cord and the blood vessels in the placenta. The amnion eventually envelops the organism, holding the amniotic fluid, which protects the organism. The chorion becomes the lining of the placenta. The inner cell mass becomes the embryo.

Survival of the fertilized egg depends on its ability to burrow into the lining of the mother's uterus and obtain nourishment from her system. This process is called **implantation.** It does this by secreting digestive enzymes that allow the blastocyst to embed itself in the maternal tissues. It now develops the ability to feed off its host.

At about seven or eight days, the inner cell mass has differentiated into two distinct layers: the ectoderm and the endoderm. The ectoderm will develop into the organism's external coverings—including the skin, hair,

germinal stage The earliest stage of prenatal development, lasting from conception to about two weeks.

blastocyst The stage of development in which the organism consists of layers of cells around a central cavity forming a hollow sphere.

implantation The process by which the fertilized egg burrows into the lining of the mother's uterus and obtains nourishment from her system.

embryonic stage The stage of prenatal development, from about two weeks and to about eight weeks, when bone cells begin to replace cartilage.

sense organs, and nervous system. The endoderm becomes the digestive system, the respiratory system, and the glands. At about the sixteenth day, another layer, the mesoderm, appears between the ectoderm and endoderm and develops into the muscles, the connective tissues, and the circulatory and excretory systems.

As development continues, the amnion swells and covers the developing organism. The trophoblast develops projections, or villi, which penetrate the uterine wall, allowing the developing organism to get nutrients more efficiently. The villi on one side organize into the placenta, which is connected to the developing organism by the umbilical cord. The placenta delivers nutrients, removes wastes, and helps combat infection. The germ cell at the end of the first two weeks of life measures about 1/175 of an inch (Annis, 1978).

The Embryonic Stage

The **embryonic stage** begins at two weeks and ends at about eight weeks after conception, when the bone cells appear. At two weeks the tiny mass has just begun to depend on the mother for everything. It is hardly recognizable as a human being. Six weeks later, 95 percent of the body parts will be present (Annis, 1978). During the embryonic period, changes occur at a breathtaking pace. Each system's development follows a certain sequence. At day 31 the shoulders, arms, and hands develop; on day 33 the fingers develop; and on day 34

through day 36, the thumb is completed. Now the organs
form and begin to function in a primitive manner. The
first organ to function is the heart, which circulates the
blood to the placenta and throughout the developing
body. The circulatory system of the embryo is completely
separate from the mother's, and no exchange of blood
occurs. All exchanges of nutrients and oxygen occur by
diffusion. By the end of the first month, the ears, nose
and mouth begin to form, and arms and legs make their
appearance as buds. Fingers and toes become defined.
Internal organs are now rapidly developing. During this
time of extremely rapid growth, the organism is most
vulnerable to environmental insult. The embryo is now
capable of some primitive behavioral reactions. Reflex
action occurs as early as the middle of the seventh week
and the beginning of the eighth. If the mouth is stimulated, the embryo flexes its neck to the other side (see
Table 3.1).

True or False   The first organ to function during the prenatal period is the liver.

The Fetal Stage

During the last seven months of development, the **fetal
stage,** the fetus grows and develops at a tremendous rate.
At the beginning of the third month, the average fetus
is 1¼ inches long and weighs less than one-third of an
ounce. By the end of the third month it is 3 inches long
and weighs 1 ounce. Hormonal action during this third
month causes the genitals to become defined. If the male
hormone, testosterone, is secreted into the fetal system,
it causes the development of male genitalia. During this
third month, the major organs are completed, bones
begin to appear, and muscles develop. The fetus now
moves, kicks its legs, swallows the amniotic fluid and
digests it, and removes waste products through urination.

During the fourth month, the fetus continues to grow
at a great rate. By the end of this month it is 6 inches
long and weighs 6 ounces. As it grows, it develops internally. By the fifth month, the fetus sleeps and wakes
at regular intervals, and some reflexes such as hiccuping
and swallowing have developed (Fitzgerald et al., 1982).

The fetus cries and may suck a thumb. At this point,
the fetal movements are likely to be felt by the mother,
though some mothers experience movement earlier. This
is known as quickening. During the sixth month, the
fetus attains a weight of about 2 pounds and a length of
about 14 inches. The facial features are clearly evident,
and the fetus can make a fist.

During the last three prenatal months, the fetus gains
a layer of fat that will help keep the infant warm after
birth. By the end of the twenty-eighth week, the fetus
measures about 17 inches and weighs about 3 pounds.

T A B L E 3.1

Chronology of Fetal Behavior

As they develop in the womb, unborn infants show more
and more complex behavior.

Age (weeks)	Behavior
8	Stroking mouth region produces flexion of upper torso and neck and extension of arms at the shoulder.
9	Some spontaneous movements. More of the whole body responds when mouth is stroked.
10½	Stroking palms of hands leads to partial closing of the fingers.
11	Other parts of face and arms become sensitive.
11½	Sensitive area spreads to upper chest.
12½	Specific reflexes appear: lip closure, swallowing, Babinski, squinting.
14	Entire body is sensitive, with more specific reflexes, such as rooting, grasping, finger-closing.
15	Can maintain closure of the fingers (grasp) with muscle-tightening, muscle-strengthening.
16–18	Defined periods of activity and rest begin.
19	Chest contractions begin but are not sustained. Grasping with hand appears.
25	Respiration is sustained for up to 24 hours. Eyelids open spontaneously, eye movements occur and Moro reflex appears.
27 to birth	Few new responses appear, except for sucking at 29 weeks. Rhythmic brain waves appear. After this age it becomes less easy to elicit reflexes in the fetus up until the time of birth.

Source: Adapted from Hooker, 1952; Trevarthen, 1973.

Seven months is considered the age of viability, because the fetus has a reasonable chance for survival if born at this time. This is misleading, however, for there is considerable individual variation in weight, health, and developmental readiness. Some seven-month-old fetuses are more ready for an independent existence than others.

During the last two prenatal months, the fetus gains about half a pound a week. Its heretofore red, wrinkled appearance disappears somewhat as it puts on weight. The development of the lungs is especially important during these last months. The entire process of prenatal development (summarized in Table 3.2) proceeds without any need for conscious maternal intervention. It is directed by genetic forces that we are only just beginning to understand. However, the fetus is also affected by the environment.

Developmental Myths

People used to believe that everything a woman did could have an effect on the unborn infant. Unusual occurrences in a pregnant woman's daily life were thought to influence the personality and physical well-being of the child. For instance, if a rabbit crossed her path, some believed the child would be born with a harelip (Annis, 1978). If she ate or squashed strawberries, it was said to lead to a strawberry-shaped birthmark. This belief in total environmental control was replaced by the idea that nothing the mother did really mattered. The placenta was viewed as a barrier that did not allow any dangerous elements into the infant's environment and rendered various poisons harmless.

Today we know that neither viewpoint is correct. The placenta is far from being a total barrier. It allows a number of substances to pass into the system of the fetus. On the other hand, although we no longer believe the superstitions about strawberries and rabbits, we know that the environment greatly affects the health of the fetus.

True or False The placenta stops all foreign substances from entering the bloodstream of the fetus.

Threats to the Developing Organism

So many things have been linked to birth defects that it is difficult to know just what is safe. Although a number of drugs, illnesses, and chemicals have been linked to birth defects, most infants are born free from defects. Any agent that causes a birth defect is called a **teratogen,** and the number of known or suspected teratogens has increased substantially in the past decade or so. The effects of these agents depend upon the type of agent, the dosage, and the genetic characteristics of the fetus. The time at which the fetus is exposed is also important, because some drugs are more likely to produce birth defects if they are ingested during a certain time during the pregnancy. Two problems in interpretation of this research on teratogens should be noted. First, some of it is based upon animal experimentation and although the animal model is useful here (Vorhees and Mullnow, 1987), any cross-species comparisons should be made with care. Second, much of the data relating teratogens to human birth defects is correlational because we cannot experimentally expose pregnant women to particular teratogens and conduct controlled experiments. So when a correlation between ingestion of a drug and birth defects occurs, it is difficult to isolate confounding variables such as diet, exercise, anxiety, and the mother's ingestion of other drugs.

teratogen Any agent that causes birth defects.

Medication

The most famous case of a medication causing birth defects involves the drug thalidomide, which was widely used in Europe as a treatment for morning sickness. A vast number of infants, estimated at over 10,000, were born without limbs or with extremities that were grossly underdeveloped. Relatively few American women took the drug because it was never approved by the Food and Drug Administration.

Other medications have been linked to birth defects, and the research findings on others are contradictory. Tetracycline, a commonly prescribed antibiotic, has been linked to permanent discoloration of the teeth and defective bone growth (March of Dimes, 1983B). While some antibiotics seem safe, our knowledge of most is limited (Knothe and Dette, 1985). The contraceptive pill, if taken right before or during pregnancy, can cause such birth defects as congenital heart disease and other structural abnormalities (U.S. Department of Health and

TABLE 3.2

Summary of Prenatal Development

Prenatal development is orderly and predictable.

Time Elapsed	Embryonic or Fetal Characteristics	Time Elapsed	Embryonic or Fetal Characteristics
4 weeks 1 month	¼–½ inch long Head is one-third of embryo Brain has lobes, and rudimentary nervous system appears as hollow tube Heart begins to beat Blood vessels form and blood flows through them Simple kidneys, liver, and digestive tract appear Rudiments of eyes, ears, and nose appear Small tail	4 months	4 ounces in weight Body now growing faster than head Skin on hands and feet forms individual patterns Eyebrows and head hair begin to show Fine, downylike hair (lanugo) covers body Movements may now be felt
8 weeks 2 months	2 inches long ⅟₃₀ of an ounce in weight Human face with eyes, ears, nose, lips, tongue Arms have pawlike hands Almost all internal organs begin to develop Brain coordinates functioning of other organs Heart beats steadily and blood circulates Complete cartilage skeleton, beginning to be replaced by bone Tail beginning to be absorbed Now called a fetus Sex organs begin to differentiate	20 weeks 5 months	10–12 inches long 8–16 ounces in weight Skeleton hardens Nails form on fingers and toes Skin covered with cheesy wax Heartbeat now loud enough to be heard with stethoscope Muscles are stronger Definite strong kicking and turning Can be startled by noises
12 weeks 3 months	3 inches long 1 ounce in weight Begins to be active Number of nerve-muscle connections almost triples Sucking reflex begins to appear Can swallow and may even breathe Eyelids fused shut (will stay shut until the sixth month), but eyes are sensitive to light Internal organs begin to function	24 weeks 6 months	12–14 inches long 1½ pounds in weight Can open and close eyelids Grows eyelashes Much more active, exercising muscles May suck thumb May be able to breathe if born prematurely
16 weeks	6–7 inches long	28 weeks 7 months	15 inches long 2½ pounds in weight Begins to develop fatty tissue Internal organs (especially respiratory and digestive) still developing Has fair chance of survival if born now
		32 weeks 8 months	16½ inches long 4 pounds in weight Fatty layer complete
		38 weeks 9 months	Birth 19–20 inches long 6–8 pounds in weight (average) 95 percent of full-term babies born alive in the United States will survive

Source: Adapted from Cox, 1984.

Human Services, 1981a). That is why many doctors recommend that a woman who wants to become pregnant stop taking the pill some months before she plans to get pregnant. Scientists are also concerned about the possible effects that such commonly prescribed prescription drugs as Valium and Librium may have on the unborn child. A large study called the Collaborative Perinatal Project concluded that these "minor tranquilizers" have been linked to the incidence of cleft palate, a birth defect affecting the formation of the roof of the mouth. However, evidence is mixed, and another study did not find this pattern (Rosenberg et al., 1983). With such contradictory research, it is difficult to sort out which drugs are safe and which are not.

Most of these drugs cause a defect that is noticeable at birth. One drug that does not fit this pattern is diethylstilbestrol, better known as DES. From the 1940s through 1971, DES was widely administered to about one million pregnant women who had a history of diabetes or who were apt to have miscarriages (Planned Parenthood, 1979). At first there seemed to be little cause for concern; children born to these women were healthy infants. But in 1971, Dr. Arthur Herbst discovered a link between prenatal administration of DES and eight cases of a kind of cervical cancer usually found only in women over age fifty. The chances of a DES daughter getting cervical cancer is about one or two in every 1,000 (Orenberg, 1981), but many DES daughters do suffer from genital-tract abnormalities. All women whose mothers took the drug should be watched carefully by their doctors. DES sons may also be affected by the drug. They sometimes suffer genital-tract abnormalities and benign cysts that require attention from a urologist (N.Y.S. Department of Health, 1979). Recent evidence also indicates that mothers who took DES run a risk of developing breast cancer about twenty years later (Herbst, 1984). The DES story demonstrates that the effects of drugs taken during the prenatal stage may not show up for some time.

Drugs: Legal and Illegal

Most drugs taken during pregnancy are not prescribed by doctors. They are available either legally, as in the case of nicotine and alcohol, or illegally, as with narcotics.

Smoking. In the United States, about 40 percent of pregnant women smoke (March of Dimes, 1985), making

---

fetal alcohol syndrome A number of characteristics—including retardation, facial abnormalities, growth defects, and poor coordination—caused by maternal alcohol consumption.

---

nicotine one of the drugs most commonly taken by women during pregnancy. Nicotine causes a rise in heart rate, blood pressure, and respiration and constricts the flow of blood. The amount of oxygen the fetus receives is reduced (Martin, 1976). Although the effects of nicotine are dose-related, smokers are twice as likely as nonsmokers to have low-birth-weight babies (Fielding, 1985). The infants of smokers weigh an average of 200 grams (about half a pound) less than infants of nonsmokers (U.S. Department of Health, Education, and Welfare, 1979). Smoking has been related to prematurity (Leavitt, 1974) and to an increased number of fetal deaths (McIntosh, 1984). Other research suggests that the decrease in oxygen may lead to brain abnormalities and cleft palate (Stechler and Halton, 1982).

True or False Smoking during pregnancy has been linked to increased weight gain in infants.

Injurious long-term effects from maternal smoking have also been noted. A major study found that at seven years of age children of smokers had lower reading ability and demonstrated more problems with social adjustment than children of nonsmokers (Davies et al., 1972). Another study found a positive correlation between smoking during pregnancy and hyperactivity, low achievement, and minimal neurological dysfunction (Landesman-Dwyer and Emanuel, 1979). Maternal smoking during pregnancy has also been linked to poor attention span in the offspring during the preschool years (Streissguth et al., 1984). One hopeful sign comes from a study that found that mothers who were light smokers and who had stopped smoking prior to the fourth month of pregnancy reduced their risk of having low-birth-weight infants (Butler et al., 1972). Research demonstrates not only a clear danger to the developing fetus but also the possibility that the child's growth and intelligence will be adversely affected (U.S. Department of Health and Human Services, 1981b).

Alcohol. Alcohol is another hazard to the unborn infant. The children of alcoholic mothers may suffer from **fetal alcohol syndrome,** a distinct pattern of abnormal, retarded development. These children are shorter and lighter than other children, and their growth and development is slow. They show a number of cranial and facial abnormalities, heart defects, poor motor development and coordination, and they tend to be retarded (Furey, 1982; Streissguth, 1977). The mortality rate for these children is also higher than average (Jones et al., 1974). The damage caused by alcohol appears to be permanent. Even when children of alcoholic mothers are raised in an improved environment, they continue to lag behind, both in physical growth and in intellectual development (Hanson et al., 1976).

Most women are not alcoholics, and people generally consider the negative consequences of drinking something that happens to other people. However, even moderate drinking can affect the unborn child (Streissguth, 1977). The fetus is sensitive to alcohol, especially in the last trimester when brain growth is great (Stechler and Halton, 1982). In a sample of seventy-four moderate drinkers who drank 2 ounces of 100-proof alcohol each day before and during their pregnancies, Hanson (1978) found that about 12 percent of their offspring showed one or more of the characteristics of fetal alcohol syndrome. The effects of alcohol seem to be dose-related, with lower doses resulting in some but not all of the

Studies show that smoking during pregnancy presents a danger to the unborn child.

characteristics of the syndrome (Clarren and Smith, 1978). A woman consuming about 2 ounces of 100-proof whiskey or one or two cans of beer a day has about a 10 percent chance of visibly damaging her baby. Consuming a six-pack or 10 ounces of whiskey a day leads to a 50 percent chance of damaging the unborn child (*Science News*, March 26, 1977). These figures refer only to the gross abnormalities noted above, not to damage that may not reveal itself in years to come. Although very small amounts of alcohol may not produce birth defects, as little as one drink a day increases the risk of miscarriage during the middle months of pregnancy (Kline et al., 1980; Harlap and Shiono, 1980), and decreased fetal growth (Mills et al., 1984).

Commonly used illegal drugs. The infants of heroin addicts are born addicted to heroin and must go through withdrawal (Brazelton, 1970). They often show disturbances in activity level, attention span, and sleep patterns (Householder et al., 1982). Because these infants are usually premature and very small, this is sometimes a life-or-death situation.

Although no one knows exactly how many pregnant women have used cocaine, it can be assumed that a fairly large number do. We know that cocaine constricts the blood vessels in the placenta, decreasing blood flow to the fetus, and increases uterine contractions. In cocaine users, there is an increase in spontaneous abortions and an increased risk of malformation of the fetus. Infants also show deficits in their ability to interact with others and poor responses to stimuli (Chasoff et al, 1985).

Some research shows that marijuana use leads to fetal abnormalities and lack of fetal growth in animals (Annis, 1978). Evidence with human beings is still controversial, and scientists still do not understand the full effects that marijuana, angel dust, hashish, and other psychoactive drugs have on the fetus (March of Dimes, 1983). Studies of LSD are difficult to perform because most users take other drugs too. However, some evidence indicates a relationship between LSD and congenital malformations (Apgar and Beck, 1974). A very high rate of spontaneous abortions and neurological defects has also been noted (Trulson, 1985).

Over-the-counter drugs. The status of many commonly taken drugs is still controversial. For example, there is some evidence that high doses of caffeine increase the frequency of birth defects in animals (March of Dimes, 1983b). Most recent evidence has failed to link *moderate* caffeine intake reliably to birth defects (University of California, 1985), but high caffeine intake (four or more cups of coffee a day) should be avoided (March of Dimes, 1985).

True or False Most evidence on the effects of caffeine on the fetus show that even one cup of coffee a day can be quite injurious to the unborn child.

Aspirin has been shown to cause damage to the unborn in animal studies (Stechler and Halton, 1982), but in human beings the main finding is that aspirin, if taken excessively in the late months of pregnancy, may adversely affect blood-clotting in both mother and baby (March of Dimes, 1983b).

Disease

Our society has been spared the terrible epidemics of the past. We are not concerned about smallpox or polio. But certain infections are of great concern today.

Rubella. Rubella is the best known of the harmful viral infections. Commonly called German Measles, it is a very mild disorder in adults. Yet the effects of the rubella virus on the developing embryo can be very serious. In the epidemic of 1964–1965, about 50,000 babies were affected. Many died, while others suffered injuries of varying degrees, for instance, eye and ear damage, congenital heart disease, and central nervous system damage (Rugh and Shettles, 1971). The effects of the disease on the unborn fetus is greatest in the first eight weeks of pregnancy (Taina et al., 1985), although infection in the second trimester may also cause fetal damage. But the disease may persist throughout the prenatal and neonatal periods, and the eye damage may continue even after birth. With the advent of a vaccine that prevents rubella, epidemics should become a thing of the past. Unfortunately, though, not every child is being protected, and isolated cases of rubella-induced defects still occur. Although women who do not show immunities in the blood may be immunized, pregnant women should not be vaccinated, because there is a danger that the vaccination itself, which consists of the weakened rubella virus, might injure the unborn infant.

Venereal disease. In recent years, increased attention has been paid to the effects that AIDS, herpes, syphilis,

AIDS (Acquired Immune Deficiency Syndrome) A fatal disorder affecting the immunological system, leading to inability to fight off disease.

and gonorrhea have on the unborn. Evidence is great that such diseases, which are usually transmitted during sexual intercourse, pose significant dangers to the unborn child (Mascola et al., 1984; Knox, 1984).

AIDS, or **Acquired Immune Deficiency Syndrome,** is a fatal disease affecting the immunological system and leading to an inability to fight off disease. It is caused by a virus that can pass through the placenta and infect the infant (Pinching and Jeffries, 1985). The chance that an infected mother will transmit the virus is about 50 percent (Sande, 1986). Not everyone who carries the virus will contract the disease, but infants infected with the virus are more likely than adults to develop it (Sande, 1986). Pregnancy itself may increase the risk that a mother who has the virus but has not developed AIDS may develop the disease (Pinching and Jeffries, 1985).

True or False Pregnant women who carry the AIDS virus cannot transmit it to their unborn child during the prenatal stage.

Women who have herpes may transmit it to the baby during the birth process. If the herpes virus reaches the organs or brain, the prognosis is not good and more than half may die (Corey and Spear, 1986). Antiviral treatment reduces the mortality rate, but impairment is still common (Stagno and Whitely, 1985). In order to prevent the spread of the disease, doctors often check for lesions in the birth canal and may recommend a cesarean section.

Many women who have gonorrhea are not aware of it because they may not show any outward symptoms. Fetuses exposed to gonorrhea are often premature and blind. The standard practice of placing a solution of silver nitrate* in infants' eyes at birth is to protect against blindness in case the mother does have gonorrhea. Antibiotics can treat gonorrhea successfully.

Syphilis in the expectant mother can cause a number of defects in the infant—bone and facial deformities, nerve deafness, and even fetal death. If the pregnant

*In many hospitals erythromycin or tetracycline may be used. Erythromycin combats chlamydia, an infection which also can cause blindness in newborn infants (Simkin et al., 1984).

woman receives treatment by the sixteenth week of pregnancy, the fetus may not be infected (Cave, 1973). After that time, certain tissues that protect the infant break down, and the chances the fetus will be infected increase dramatically (Thompson and Grusec, 1970). However, prompt treatment even after this time will often prevent damage.

Pollution and Radiation

Pollution and radiation can also affect the unborn child adversely and are therefore causes for concern. Mercury has been linked to severe malformations (Stechler and Halton, 1982). In Japan, a number of mothers who had eaten fish laden with mercury during their pregnancies gave birth to extremely disabled children who suffered from cerebral palsy and physical defects (Miller, 1974). And PCB, a contaminant sometimes found in water and fish, can cause immature motor responses as well as other behavioral abnormalities (Jacobson et al., 1984).

The Mother's Medical Condition

While noting some of the dangers present in the environment, we should not forget the mother's medical condition. For example, about 6 to 8 percent of all pregnant women suffer from hypertension, which is related to poor fetal growth, increased perinatal death, and many neurological and developmental problems. Diabetes is also related to many birth defects. These disorders are dangerous to the mother as well. As with so many other maternal medical conditions, competent medical advice and prompt treatment may improve the chances of delivering a healthy child and safeguarding the mother's health.

The Rh Factor

Perhaps the most famous maternal factor affecting the unborn child is the Rh factor. The **Rh factor** is a particular red-blood-cell antigen found in most human beings. About 85 percent of all Caucasians, 93 percent of blacks, and 100 percent of all Asian people, Native Americans, and Eskimo people possess the antigen—that is, they are Rh positive (Stevenson, 1973).

In about 13 percent of the Caucasian unions, the woman is Rh negative and the man is Rh positive. In such a situation, the baby may be Rh positive, and then

Rh factor An antibody often, but not always, found in human beings.

a problem can arise: The mother's body reacts to the Rh-positive antigen in the fetus as it would to an invading germ or virus. Because the blood of the fetus does not mix with that of the mother during pregnancy, she is not likely to manufacture antibodies that might injure the fetus. However, some fetal blood cells do cross the placenta during the birth, especially if it is long and difficult. This causes the mother to manufacture the antibodies. Since the first child of these parents is not likely to be exposed to many of these antibodies, the infant's chances of survival are good. But once these antibodies are manufactured, they tend to remain in the mother's body. The mother also becomes more sensitized to this factor in later pregnancies. During the next pregnancy, the fetus may be exposed to the mother's antibodies, which cross the placenta and destroy the red blood cells of the fetus (Ortho Diagnostic Systems, 1981). In each successive pregnancy the risk to the fetus becomes greater and greater, until the chance that a child will be born healthy is quite low.

Since 1968, a preventive vaccine for Rh problems has been available. Within seventy-two hours after each birth, miscarriage, or abortion, a shot of the vaccine RhoGAM is administered to block the production of these antibodies. Before this vaccine was available, 10,000 babies died every year, and 20,000 were born with severe birth defects from Rh disease (Apgar and Beck, 1974). Now there is no reason for this to occur.

Preventing Birth Defects

Walk into almost any clinic or doctor's office and you will see pamphlets advising women what to do and what not to do during pregnancy. In Chapter 2, we looked at some of the major genetic diseases. Compared with the possibility that a fetus will be injured during the prenatal period, the chance of bearing a child with a genetic deformity is slight. Genetic factors account for only 20 percent of infant defects; chromosomal abnormalities add another 10 percent to the picture. The remaining 70 percent of infant defects are caused by drugs, pollution, diseases, and other environmental insults that occur during the prenatal stage (Martin, 1976). Yet, despite all the information available, thousands of babies are born each year with birth defects or die unnecessarily. Why is it so difficult to prevent birth defects?

True or False   Some 70 percent of all birth defects are caused by prenatal insults rather than genetic disorders.

The main reason is ignorance. Some women do not adequately understand the dangers in the environment. The poor and the young are most at risk. The poor have a higher infant mortality rate and a greater number of prenatally caused infant problems (Birch and Gussow, 1970). They are more often undernourished or malnourished, undereducated, and exposed to a number of teratogens. Inadequate prenatal care is a great problem. Many young women do not see a doctor regularly. One study conducted in a poor, urban area found that 30 percent of pregnant teens under the age of seventeen, 22 percent of the seventeen- to nineteen-year-olds, and 18 percent of the twenty- to thirty-year-olds failed to see a doctor for prenatal care until the third trimester of their pregnancies. About 4 percent of the teens received no prenatal care at all (Hutchins et al., 1979). It is difficult to get the information across to pregnant teens and to motivate them to change their health habits.

Another reason it is difficult to prevent birth defects is that the first three months of pregnancy seem to be the most sensitive to environmental insult. But in the earliest months of pregnancy, a woman may not know she is pregnant and may expose the unborn infant to such an insult. By the time she is aware she is pregnant, the critical period may have passed and the damage may already have been done. The systems of the fetus are developing rapidly during these earliest months, and the system that is developing most rapidly at the time of insult is the one that will be affected by a drug or virus as shown in Figure 3.1. The period during which a particular event has its greatest impact is known as the **critical period.** If an insult occurs at this point, considerable damage may be done. For instance, if a mother contracts rubella in the first four weeks of pregnancy, the chance of the baby's being born with one or more defects

is about 50 percent. This drops to about 17 percent in the third month and is much lower after the third month (Rhodes, 1961). There are similar critical periods for some drugs, including thalidomide (Lenz, 1966).

In addition, many people choose not to believe facts that run counter to their own experiences. Whenever I discuss the dangers of drinking or smoking, some of my students refuse to believe it. After all, some of their friends are smokers and their babies turned out healthy. Most drugs or environmental pollutants do not act as radically as thalidomide. They act in tandem with other environmental insults to produce their effects. Thus, the causal linkage is more difficult to discover, and many simply refuse to believe it. Perhaps the best way to see the effects of smoking and some types of pollution on the fetus is to say that these increase the chances that a problem may develop.

Finally, people have difficulty relating events that occur during pregnancy to the outcome. The time lag involved makes the connection difficult.

Five Modern-Day Issues

As people learn more about the prenatal period, new issues are raised and old issues are perceived differently. Five such issues are especially current: (1) the relationship between the age of the mother and the health of the fetus, (2) maternal nutrition during pregnancy, (3) emotional stress during pregnancy, (4) the father's responsibilities during pregnancy, and (5) the effect of new technology—such as fetal monitoring, amniocentesis, and chorionic biopsies—on mother and child.

The Age of the Mother

Ellen is thirty-four years old now. She readily admits that it wasn't easy to wait while all her friends were having babies, but she and Tom decided they wanted to be financially settled before starting their family. Ellen and Tom are part of a growing movement, especially among professionals, to wait before starting a family. The years between twenty and thirty are the safest for childbearing. As women age, the incidence of high blood pressure and delivery complications increases (Stevenson, 1973). Later parenting may also present social problems. It can be difficult for parents in their late fifties or sixties to guide adolescents. And the older parent is at a greater risk for personal injury, incapacitating illness, and death. Still,

FIGURE 3.1

Critical Periods in Prenatal Development

The dark color shows the time during which that particular organ is at greatest risk. • Indicates common site of action of teratogen.

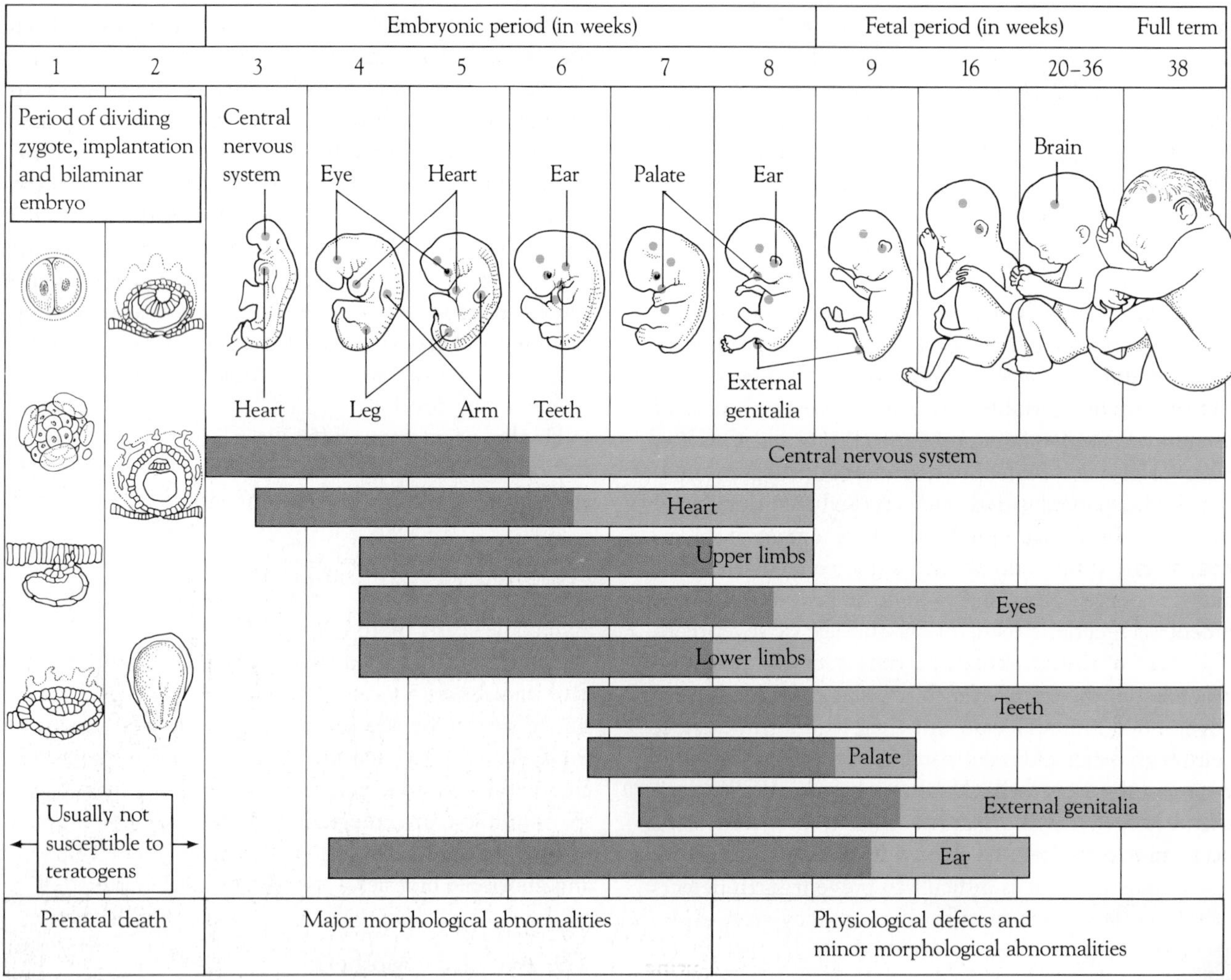

		Embryonic period (in weeks)						Fetal period (in weeks)			Full term
1	2	3	4	5	6	7	8	9	16	20–36	38

Period of dividing zygote, implantation and bilaminar embryo

Usually not susceptible to teratogens

Central nervous system

Eye Heart Ear Palate Ear

Brain

Heart Leg Arm Teeth

External genitalia

Central nervous system

Heart

Upper limbs

Eyes

Lower limbs

Teeth

Palate

External genitalia

Ear

Prenatal death	Major morphological abnormalities	Physiological defects and minor morphological abnormalities

Source: Moore, 1983

an increasing number of people are choosing to start their families in their thirties.

Since the middle 1970s, the birth rate for women above the age of thirty has been growing steadily, increasing over 25 percent. In 1985, mothers over 30 years accounted for one in four births (National Center for Health Statistics, 1987). A significant increase is found for both the 30–34-year-old age group and the 35–39-year-old age group (National Center for Clinical Infant Programs, 1986). Many of these couples have postponed having children for economic and career reasons. While the physical risks are greater, the availability of modern diagnostic procedures, such as amniocentesis and better prenatal care, reduces the risk somewhat. If there is no evidence of chronic disease, the outlook for the intelligent mother entering the world of parenting in her thirties is quite good (Goldstein, 1980).

True or False   The number of women bearing children after age thirty-five has increased greatly in the past decade.

On the other extreme, in 1985 there were 10,220 births to women under the age of 15 years and 467,485 births to women between the ages of 15 and 19 (National Center for Health Statistics, 1987). The teenage birth rate has remained relatively stable since 1976 and is lower than it was in the 1950s. However, the 1950s was a time of early marriage and only 15 percent of teenagers giving birth were unmarried. Today, more than 50 percent of these teenage mothers are unmarried and the birthrate for unmarried teens rose 14 percent from 1980 to 1985 following an increase of 18 percent in the 1970s. About 96 percent of all adolescents who give birth intend to raise their babies (National Center for Clinical Infant Programs, 1986). The formidable social, economic, and familial problems of these young parents will be discussed in Chapter 11. Here, we are mostly interested in health related issues.

Pregnant teens belong to the group at highest risk both for birth complications and for fetal abnormalities (Fogel, 1984). Adolescent mothers suffer the greatest number of prenatal and postnatal problems. This high rate of complications may be explained by the relationship between adolescent pregnancy and such factors as low socioeconomic status, poor education, and poor health care. Out of fear, ignorance, or the desire to deny the pregnancy, many teens do not seek prenatal care until late in the pregnancy. This leads to an increased rate of premature birth and fetal deaths (Hutchins et al, 1979).

The combination of youth, poverty, lack of knowledge, poor nutritional habits, poor health care, drug usage, and lack of motivation to heed warnings is difficult to combat. Teenage pregnancy is part of a larger social and economic problem that must be approached educationally and medically. This may be nowhere more clear than in the case of maternal nutrition.

Maternal Nutrition

Here are a few misconceptions about nutrition during pregnancy:

Eat whatever you want—you're eating for two.
The baby has first call on all nutrients.
The more vitamins you take, the better.
If you are overweight, you should try not to gain any weight during pregnancy.
There's no reason you can't go on a diet during a normal pregnancy.
Every baby costs the mother another tooth.
The brain is the last part of the baby's body to be hurt if the mother is malnourished.

Each of these statements is false, yet many people believe them. The finding that chronic malnutrition dur-

ing the prenatal stage leads to an irreversible condition in which the infant has fewer brain cells—as much as 20 percent fewer than the normal infant (Winick, 1976)—did much to spur interest in this area. Malnutrition is related to fetal deformities and impaired physical and intellectual development. Mental retardation, low birth weight, cerebral palsy, and increased susceptibility to disease have been traced to malnourishment during pregnancy (Annis, 1978). Infants who were malnourished during the prenatal stage show abnormal behavior patterns, such as withdrawal and irritability (Birch, 1971). The significant correlation between nutritional status and prematurity is especially troublesome because extremely underweight infants are at risk for a variety of developmental problems (Ricciuti, 1980).

True or False Severe malnutrition during pregnancy leads to a condition in which the infant has fewer brain cells.

Nutrition during pregnancy is crucial to the health of the child, but the mother's nutritional history before

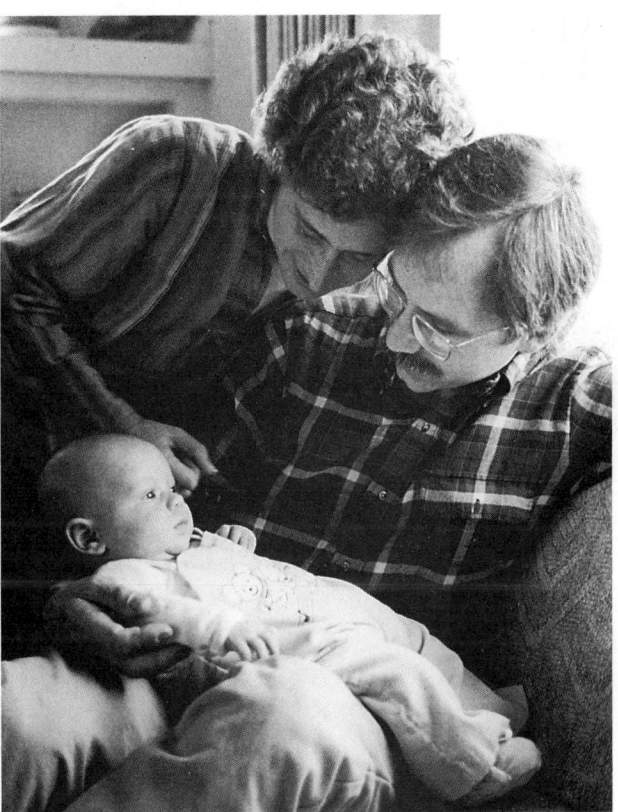

Many couples are deciding to wait to have their first child. Although the risks are somewhat greater, with good prenatal care, most women can give birth to healthy children.

pregnancy is important too (Abel and Clark, 1979). She may have suffered from nutritional problems that affect her own physical development and health, reducing her ability to bear a healthy child. All these factors—past and present nutritional status, prematurity, and infant mortality—are related to poverty and lack of education.

The effects of severe malnutrition on the fetus are well established, but what is the effect of lesser degrees of malnutrition? While severe malnutrition is relatively rare in the United States, many American mothers, especially young pregnant women, suffer from some form of malnutrition involving vitamin and mineral deficiencies or even protein deficiencies (Eichorn, 1979).

Specific nutritional inadequacies in the expectant mother do cause certain fetal problems. For example, lack of iodine leads to physical deformities and mental retardation. Deficiencies in vitamin B_6 are related to convulsions and neurological damage (Dakshinamurti and Stephens, 1969). Inadequate supplies of vitamin C cause skeletal deformities (Annis, 1978). We do not know how

much deficiency is required to cause a particular problem. A small deficiency may cause subclinical problems that can reduce the infant's ability in a specific area, such as the ability to fight off infection. In addition, nutritional deficiencies can combine with other factors, such as drugs or disease, to produce a fetal abnormality. The best advice is to eat nutritious foods and ask a doctor's opinion on nutritional issues. Figure 3.2 compares the nutritional needs of pregnant and nonpregnant women.

Stress During Pregnancy

From the beginning of her pregnancy, Ellen encountered more stress than usual. She became responsible for her elderly parents when they could no longer live in their home. Then, in her third month of pregnancy, her father suffered a stroke that left him partially paralyzed. Her mother became depressed and had difficulty taking care of Ellen's father. Tom's new job required a great deal of traveling, and the company Ellen worked for went through

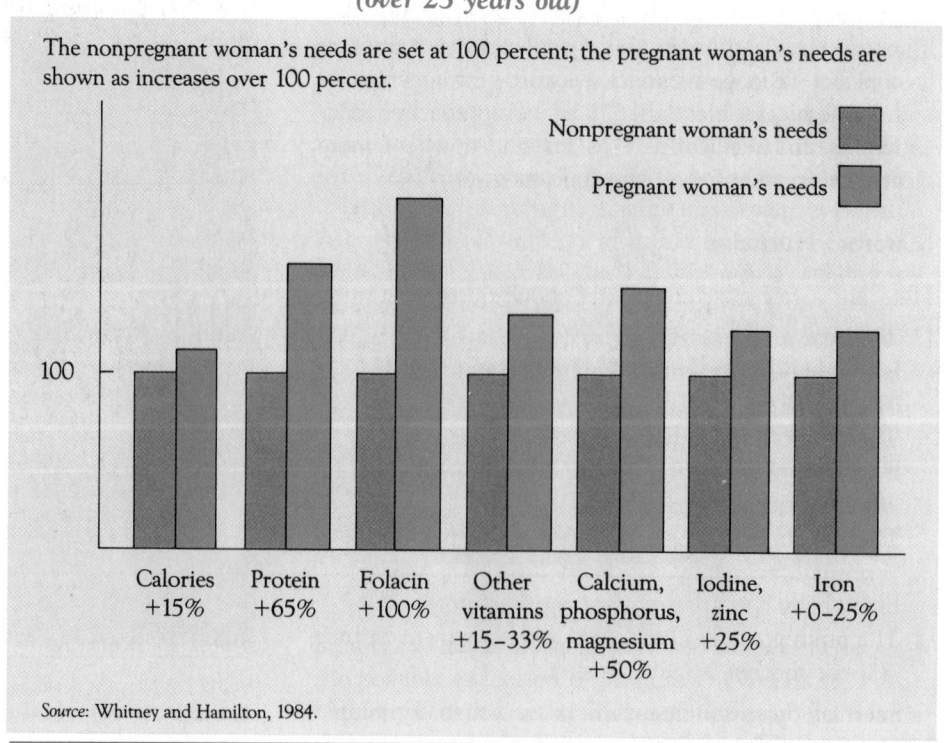

FIGURE 3.2

Nutritional Needs of Pregnant and Nonpregnant Women (over 23 years old)

The nonpregnant woman's needs are set at 100 percent; the pregnant woman's needs are shown as increases over 100 percent.

Nonpregnant woman's needs

Pregnant woman's needs

100

Calories +15% Protein +65% Folacin +100% Other vitamins +15–33% Calcium, phosphorus, magnesium +50% Iodine, zinc +25% Iron +0–25%

Source: Whitney and Hamilton, 1984.

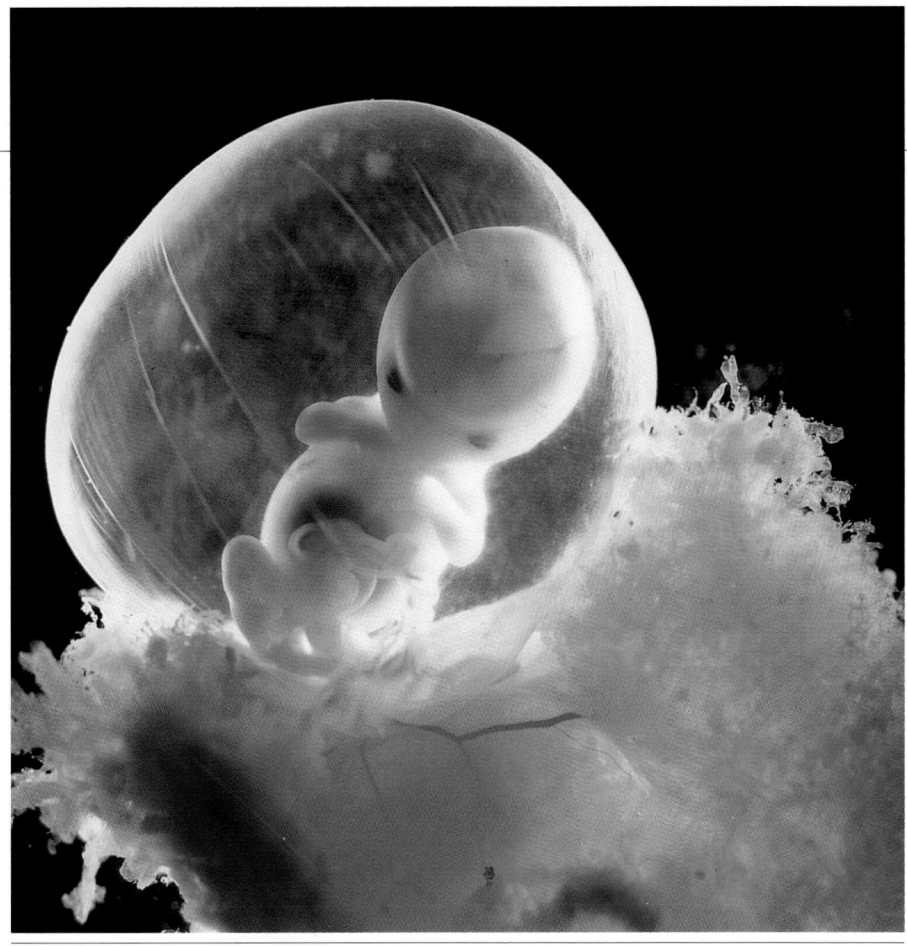

Prenatal Development

When a child is born, we in the Western world begin to count the infant's age from that date. By that time, however, the child has already spent nine months developing in the womb. We understand the sequence of changes through which the unborn child progresses within the womb, but we do not fully understand the mechanisms that cause these changes.

During the germinal stage—the first ten days to two weeks following conception—the fertilized ovum splits many times as it travels down the fallopian tube to the womb. It then burrows into the lining of the uterus. From the second through the eighth week, the embryo (as it now is called) develops very rapidly. As is shown in these pictures, this is a time of tremendous growth and development. During the long fetal stage, lasting from the third month until birth, each system develops and is refined in preparation for independent existence. These astounding pictures allow us once again to marvel at the process by which a fertilized egg develops into an infant ready to begin life outside the womb.

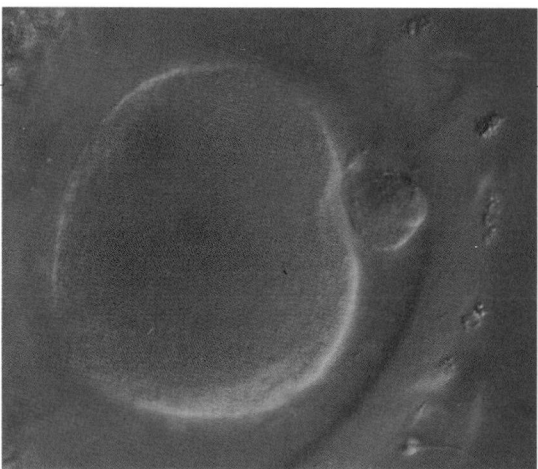

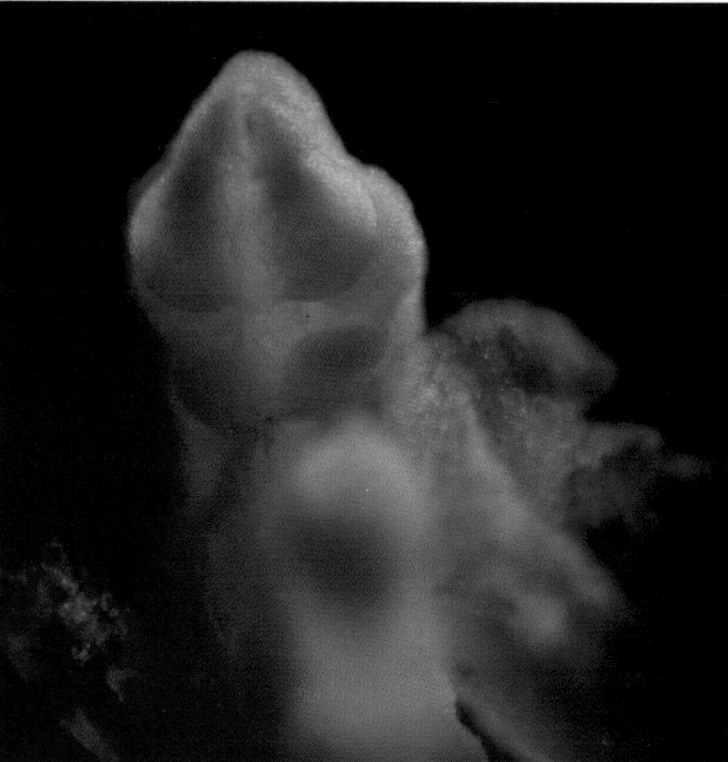

(Above left) The fertilized ovum has divided for the first time. The chromosomes from the father and mother have united and the genetic composition of the new life is fixed. Cell division starts at once, and the developing cluster of cells moves slowly down the fallopian tube toward the uterus.

(Above right) At 26 days, 3 mm (.12 inch). The hole in the middle of the forehead is the front opening of the neural tube which is just about to close, and the arch of the lower jaw is joined just below the pale mouth opening. The cheeks begin to form. Eyes are still missing. The bulging below the chin in the foreground is the heart, which started to beat a few days earlier.

Five weeks old and two-fifths of an inch long. The major divisions of the brain can be seen as well as an eye, the hands, the arms, and a long tail. The upper part of the body develops more rapidly than the lower one—development takes place from the top down.

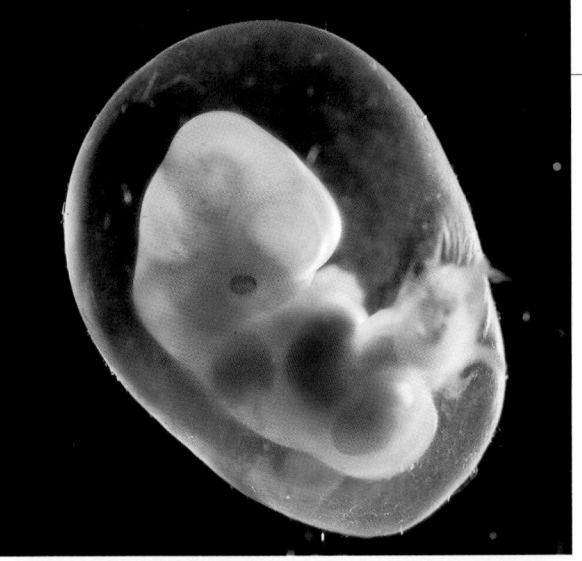

Six weeks old and three-fifths of an inch long. The embryo rests securely in its shock-absorbing amniotic sac. The heart beats rapidly. The brain is growing and the eyes are taking shape. The dark red swelling at the level of the stomach is the liver. The external ears are developing from skin folds.

At eight weeks, 4 cm (1.6 inches), the developing individual is no longer an embryo, but a fetus. Everything that will be found in the fully developed human being has now been established. The fetal stage is a period of growth and perfection of detail. The heart has been beating for a month and the muscles have just begun their first exercises.

(Below) The fetus in the third month. There is never any exchange of blood between mother and fetus. All exchanges of nutrients and oxygen occur by diffusion.

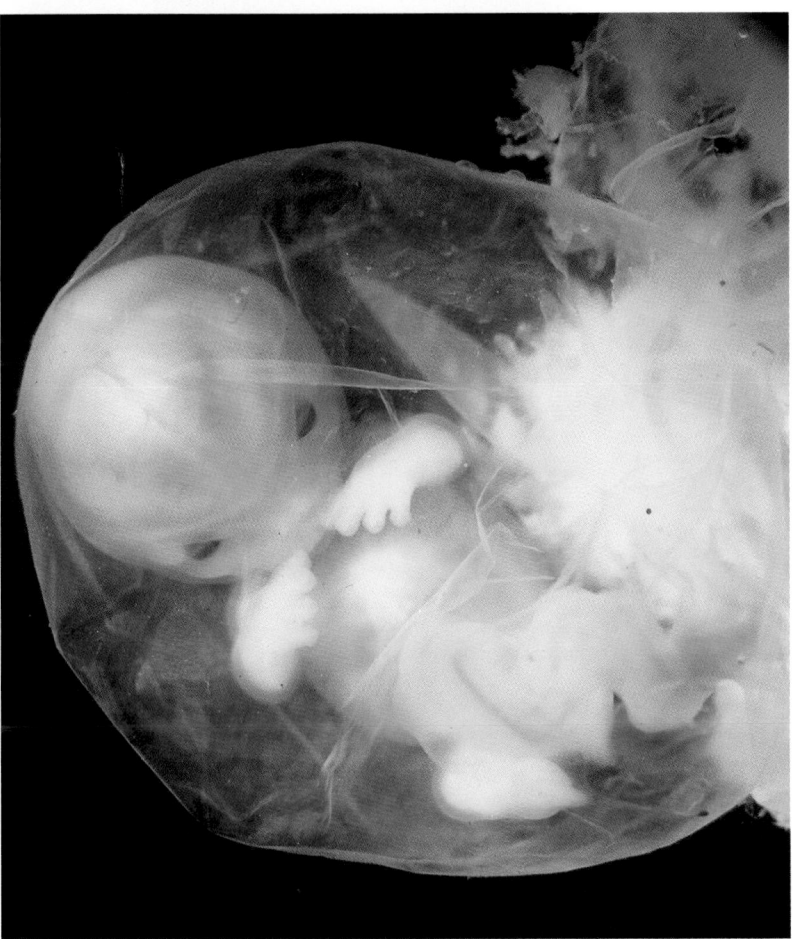

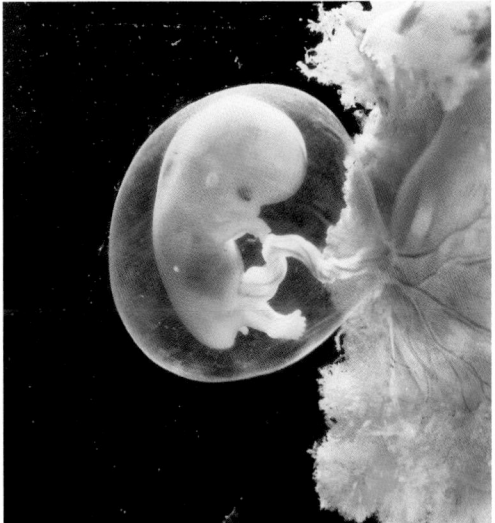

At four and one-half months, about 18 cm (just over 7 inches). When the thumb comes close to the mouth, the head may turn, and lips and tongue begin their sucking motions— a reflex for survival.

(Below) With specially manufactured equipment—a super-wide-angle lens with an ultrashort focal length—the whole fetus is photographed within the amniotic sac. This little girl is just over five months old and roughly 25 cm (10 inches) long.

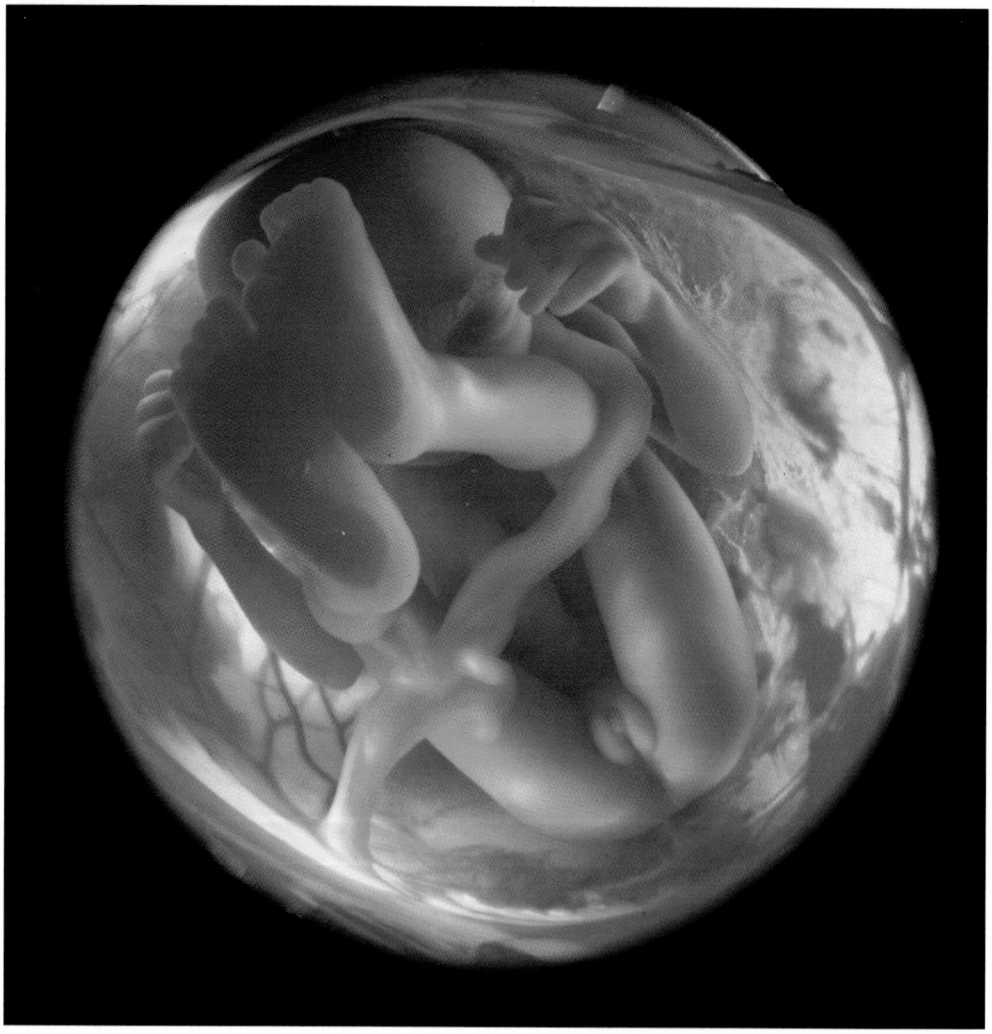

a period of great turmoil, causing even more stress for her. Will the stress affect the baby?

So many factors confound the situation that this is a difficult question to answer. Depressed and anxious, Ellen probably cannot eat or sleep well. In addition, the stress may continue after the baby's birth, making it difficult to separate prenatal factors from postnatal factors when trying to determine what caused the problem.

Some studies have related continuous stress during pregnancy to the birth of infants who are irritable, squirming, and generally more difficult to care for (Stechler and Halton, 1982; Sontag, 1944; 1941). These babies do not feed as well, and they cry more than infants whose mothers have not been under stress (Copans, 1974). The mechanism by which stress leads to these problems is not entirely understood. Stress increases the production of hormones, particularly adrenalin and cortisone compounds, that may cause such reactions (Affonso, 1979). There is also a relationship between anxiety and physical problems in pregnancy. The more stress a woman is under, the greater the chances of complications during pregnancy and delivery (Gorsuch and Key, 1974).

The Father's Role

After noting the many maternal behaviors that affect the fetus, students often complain that the child's father seems to get away with everything during the prenatal stage. To some extent this is true, since a father's drinking, drug-taking and stressful experiences do not directly affect the fetus. If we look a bit deeper, however, his behavior and experiences also affect the pregnancy and the subsequent health of the fetus.

Paternal drug-taking prior to pregnancy may affect the father's genes and in turn directly affect the child. Aside from this, Tom's behavior influences Ellen's actions. If women heed the warnings about drinking, smoking, and drug-taking, they will increase their chances of

giving birth to a healthy child, but if the father is indulging, the mother will find it more difficult to refrain from such behavior. In addition, the mother's need for emotional support places a responsibility on the father. He can help reduce the stress and anxiety experienced by the mother. A father's willingness to understand the expectant mother's special needs for support and assistance can help her through this unique time in their lives.

Technology, Pregnancy, and Birth

Ellen's prenatal care was very different from her mother's. Because Ellen was thirty-five, her doctor had advised her to undergo amniocentesis during her fourteenth week of pregnancy to determine whether the fetus had Down's Syndrome.

During this process the doctor also took a **sonogram,** in which sound waves are used to produce a picture of the fetus (Clark, 1979). Many women undergo sonography to determine the gestational age of the child or to determine whether they are carrying twins. Ultrasound, as it is called, has been used to diagnose a number of rare but important fetal defects and is combined with other techniques to discover cardiac problems in the fetus (Chervenak et al., 1986).

When Ellen entered labor, her contractions and the condition of the fetus were constantly monitored with a fetal monitor. This device tells the doctor how the fetus is reacting to maternal contractions and gives an early indication of any fetal distress (Greenlund et al., 1985).

New procedures that can improve both the diagnosis and the treatment of fetal problems are now being developed. In one procedure, called **chorionic villus sampling,** cells are obtained from the chorion during the eighth to twelfth weeks of pregnancy and checked for genetic problems. This is considerably earlier than these problems could have been found through amniocentesis, and the process of analyzing the fluid takes less time (Chervenak et al., 1986).

In some cases, when a structural problem is found—perhaps through the use of ultrasound—it can be treated. For example, in a life-saving operation a twenty-three-week-old fetus was surgically removed from his mother's womb and an operation was performed to correct a blocked urinary tract. He was then returned to the womb (Blackeslee, 1986). In another example, a small valve was implanted in the skull of a fetus that suffered from water

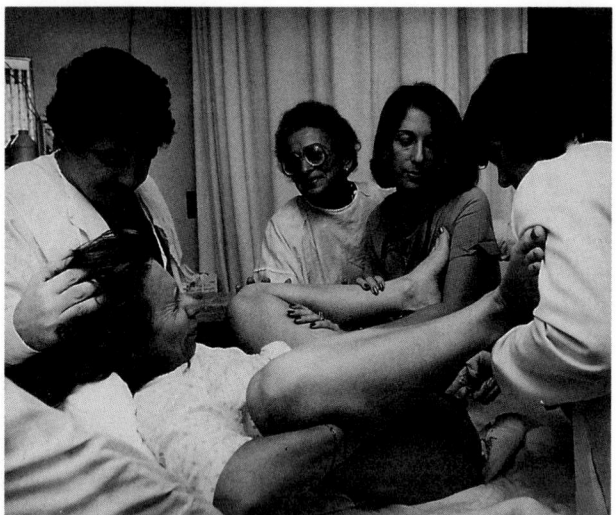

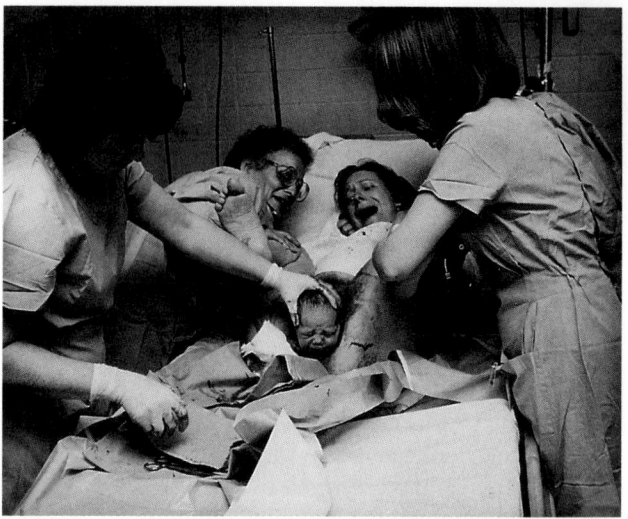

In the delivery of a child, after the cervix is fully dilated the mother is encouraged to push. Normally, the baby's head emerges first, followed by the body. Moments after the birth, the mother has the opportunity to hold her child. Notice that in this case, the woman's husband and mother, as well as a midwife, are attending and that the birth is taking place in a homelike atmosphere.

dilation The first stage of labor, in which the uterus contracts and the cervix flattens and dilates to allow the fetus to pass.

labor A term used to describe the general process of expelling the fetus from the mother's womb.

on the brain to drain away the fluid, allowing him to develop normally (Volpe, 1984).

But each of these procedures has dangers. Some claim that fetal monitoring leads to unnecessary cesarean sections. The long-term effect of sonograms is still a question, although recent studies did not find any increased cancer risk, at least through age six (Wilson and Waterhouse, 1984); there is still need for more research after this age. Amniocentesis is not a risk-free procedure either, and some complications do occur in a small minority of cases (Clark, 1979). Fetal surgery is risky too, and we do not yet know which fetuses will benefit and which will not. Despite these problems, it is clear that technology will continue to give us options that were only dreamed of just a few years ago and that will greatly affect how the woman and her unborn child are treated during the prenatal period and birth.

Birth

Before birth, the average infant spends about 266 days, counting from conception, or about 280 days, counting after the beginning of the last menstrual period, developing in the womb (Curtis, 1975). Unlike other socie-

ties, young people in the United States have little experience with birth. A century ago, most women gave birth at home, but today the overwhelming majority of births take place in hospitals. The dynamics of birth are rarely taught in high school, and young parents may be ignorant of the basic factors surrounding the event.

The Three Stages of the Birth Process

The birth process is divided into three stages (U.S. Department of Health and Human Services, 1983). During the first, or **dilation,** stage the uterus contracts and the cervix flattens and dilates in order to allow the fetus to pass through. The general term **labor** describes this process. This stage can last from about two to sixteen hours, or even longer; it tends to be longer with the first child. When the contractions start, they usually come at approximately 15- to 20-minute intervals and are generally mild. As they continue, they become stronger and more regular. Near the end of this stage, there is a shift in the nature of the contractions. They become more difficult, last longer, and are more frequent. This period, lasting

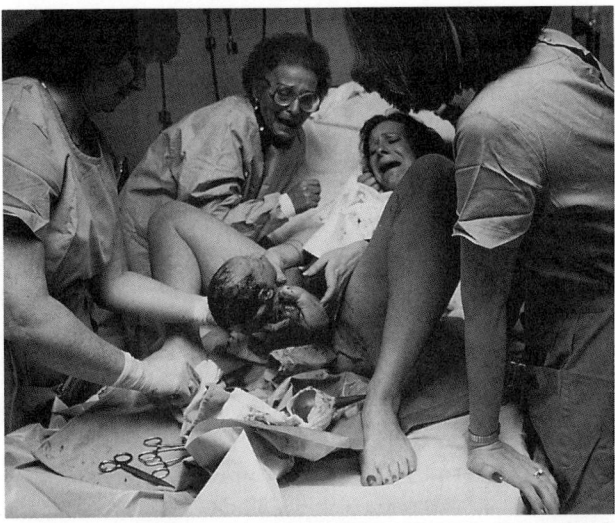 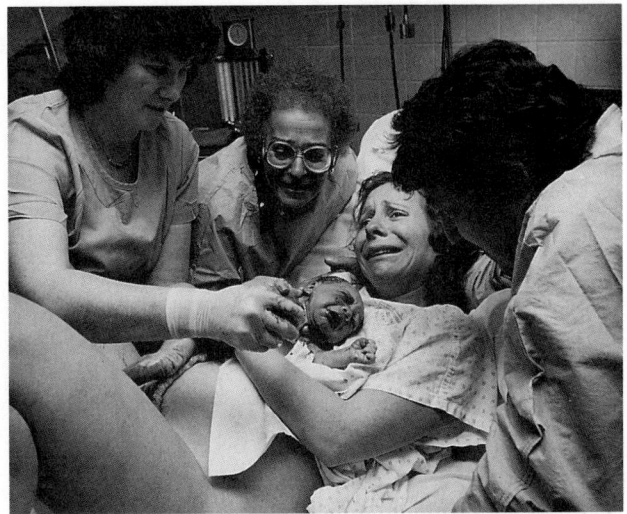

about an hour, is called **transition** and is the most difficult time of labor for many women (Tucker and Bing, 1975). By the end of this stage, the cervix is open about 10 centimeters, and contractions are occurring every minute or so.

The second stage of birth involves the actual delivery of the baby. This **expulsion** stage is variable and lasts anywhere from 2 to 60 minutes. The baby's head appears, an event referred to as **crowning.** The rest of the body soon follows.

The third stage of the birth process involves the **delivery of the placenta,** or afterbirth. During this stage, mild contractions continue for some time. They help reduce the blood flow to the uterus and reduce the uterus to its normal size.

Cesarean Birth

The doctor may advise that the baby be removed surgically through the wall of the abdomen and uterus if problems in the birth process are expected. This is major surgery that typically involves a longer hospital stay (often five days, as opposed to three or fewer for a vaginal delivery). **Cesarean section,** as this type of birth is called, has become much more common in the last two decades (Gleicher, 1984). Before 1965, cesarean sections were performed in about 2 to 5 percent of all births. In 1983 the rate approached 20 percent (Obstetrical and Gynecological Survey, 1986).

A number of explanations for the dramatic increase in cesarean sections have been advanced. The safety of

transition   A period late in labor in which the contractions become more difficult.

expulsion   The second stage of birth, involving the actual delivery of the fetus.

crowning   The point in labor at which the baby's head appears.

delivery of the placenta   The third and last stage of birth, in which the placenta is delivered.

cesarean section   The birth procedure by which the fetus is surgically delivered through the abdominal wall and uterus.

the operation has improved markedly. The fetal mortality rate from cesareans is less than one-third of that reported in the 1950s (Bottoms et al. 1980), although it is still higher in cesarean deliveries than in vaginal deliveries. Other policies that have led to this increase include the practice of repeat cesarean sections on women who have already had one, the increased threat of malpractice suits, and an increase in the number of problems that now indicate the need for a section (Young, 1982). Fetal monitors can alert a doctor to a possible problem early in labor, and the doctor may then opt to practice a conservative, defensive style of medicine rather than risk a possibly difficult vaginal delivery. The increase in cesarean sections has been a controversial issue in recent years. The number of sections may be reduced by not automatically giving pregnant women repeat sections if

Birth in the Peruvian Andes

The human community is spread out over a very diverse geographical area. Some people live in temperate climates, others live in very hot or very cold climates. Some live on or near sea level, others live at high altitudes. Women have been carrying unborn children and giving birth under so many diverse conditions that it is easy to overlook the importance of some geographical element—for instance, altitude—on the unborn infant's development and health.

It would seem reasonable that somehow the childbearing apparatus that has the responsibility for protecting and encouraging development would adapt to changing environmental conditions. Indeed, studies have shown structural differences with increasing altitude. In higher altitudes, placentas are heavier, have a larger total area of capillary surface, and show a number of other differences. But do these factors actually protect the infant from the effects of the thinner air, and are there any differences between infants born at sea level and those born in the high mountains?

To determine whether differences exist, Carmen Saco-Pollitt compared infants born in the mining center of Cerro de Pasco in the Peruvian Andes, situated at about 14,000 feet high, with those born in a medical hospital in Lima, Peru, which is only about 490 feet above sea level. Cerro de Pasco was chosen not only for its altitude but also for its excellent hospital. In order to say that the altitude could be the cause of any differences, all other variables need to be controlled, and medical treatment is certainly one important variable.

Infants, mothers, and fathers from both Lima and Cerro de Pasco were matched on as may variables as possible. Each infant had to be healthy and could not be premature. Mothers had to have lived in their region for at least five years, and their labors had to be similar. Both samples were matched for father's and mother's education and for father's occupation.

The infants were examined twice, once when they were between 24 and 36 hours old, and again when they were between 48 and 60 hours old. These examinations involved measurements of body weight, length, head circumference, and arm circumference, as well as other physical elements. In addition, the Brazelton Neonatal Behavioral Assessment Scale, which assesses an infant's reflexes and sensory and behavioral abilities, was administered to all the infants.

The infants born in Lima (near sea level) were heavier, longer, and had a larger arm circumference than those born at higher altitude. The groups did not differ in head circumference. The behavioral data was also significant. The infants from Cerro de Pasco were less likely to be attentive to stimuli, less likely to orient to visual and auditory stimuli, not as responsive to being held, less active, showed less muscle tone, made more jerky movements, and were less likely to keep their heads up while being moved from a lying position to a sitting position. Some of these differences were not found in the second examination, but generally the infants in Lima were more mature behaviorally than those in Cerro de Pasco.

There were, then, significant physical and behavioral differences between the Cerro de Pasco infants and the Lima infants. The hypothesis that the intrauterine environment of the pregnant mother effectively protects the fetus from the adverse effects of high altitude is not in keeping with the facts. The descriptions of the infants from Cerro de Pasco are similar to those reported for full-term underweight infants or infants born to undernourished mothers—infants that are considered at risk for a number of developmental disabilities. It could be that infants developing at a high altitude are also at risk for these disabilities. Some adaptive mechanisms, such as enlarged lung volume, have been found in young children living at very high altitudes, but more research is needed on these mechanisms. It should be kept in mind that Cerro de Pasco is located at an unusually high altitude and that the problems associated with this extreme altitude may not be present at more moderate altitudes.

It is clear, however, that the altitude at which unborn children develop can affect them. Only future research can determine whether other "natural" environmental factors also affect the physical stature and developmental abilities of newborn infants.

Source: Saco-Pollitt, C. Birth in the Peruvian Andes: Physical and Behavioral Consequences in the Neonate. *Child Development,* 1981, *52,* 839–846.

the reason for the original cesarean is no longer present (Nielsen, 1986).

True or False Cesarean births have decreased in the past twenty years, as doctors have come to appreciate the medical risks to the mother and child.

Obstetrical Medication

In the United States, obstetrical medication is administered almost routinely to women in labor. About 95 percent of all deliveries utilize drugs to control pain during labor. Medicated infants are more sluggish than and not as alert as nonmedicated infants (Brackbill, 1982; 1979). However, the question of the longer-term effects of medication is more complicated.

A leading critic in this area, Yvonne Brackbill claims that obstetrical medication affects the development of a child's gross motor abilities, limiting the rate of progress in the areas of sitting, standing, and walking. She claims that such medication also retards the development of language and cognitive skills and that these deficits are especially obvious when these children are given challenging tasks. These drugs also make the baby more difficult to comfort when crying, and such babies tend to eat less and gain less weight. While the sluggishness of medicated infants is real, the question of longer-term deficits is controversial. Some studies find few differences in infant behavior due to medication (Stechler and Halton, 1982; Murray et al., 1981). Others argue that there are behavioral differences (Lester et al., 1982).

Obstetrical medication may affect the infant-mother relationship as well, thereby possibly accounting for some of the proposed longer-term effects. Attempts of a caregiver to stimulate an infant who is less alert and more lethargic may be quite frustrating for both and contribute to problems in the relationship that may continue even after the full effects of the medication have worn off.

The effects of such medication depend on the type of drug, the time of administration, the dosage, and a number of individual factors that are not well understood. Some studies that found no effect of drugs on infants' later behavior used samples that were given light doses of medication (Stechler and Halton, 1982). Perhaps the standard practice should be to limit the dosage and number of drugs used to that required by the individual patient and to avoid overmedicating both mother and infant.

Alternative Methods of Birth

Not too many years ago, both parents were often robbed of the experience of birth. It was standard practice for mothers to be heavily medicated and separated from their infants for quite some time after birth, and for fathers to

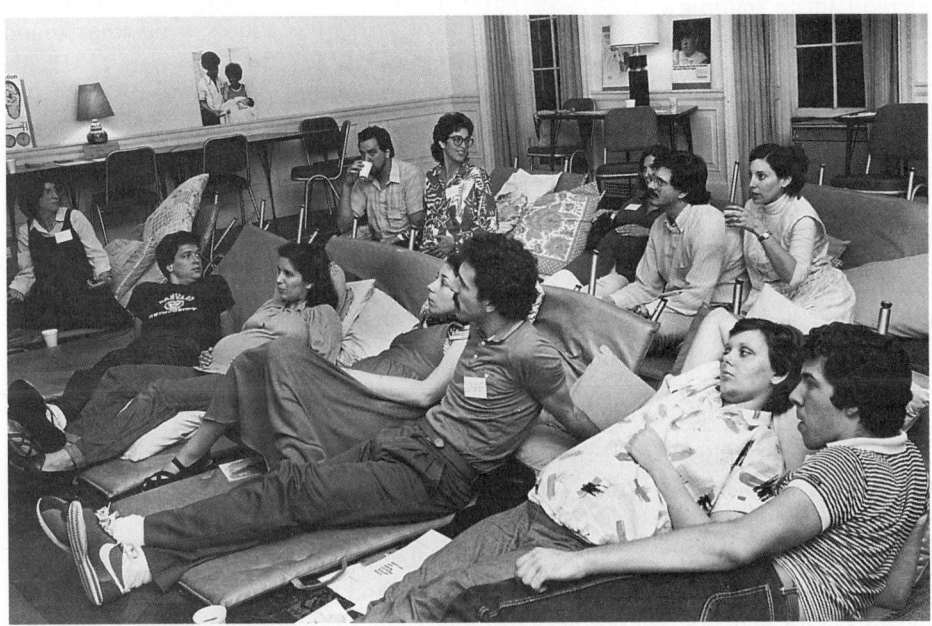

In this prepared childbirth class, both mothers and fathers are getting ready for the experience of the birth of their child, as well as learning how to reduce the discomfort and pain of labor.

be prevented from participating in the birth process and forced to wait outside. Even visitation hours for family members were restricted. Today, however, a revolution has occurred, and many parents are now able to choose to participate actively in alternative methods of birth. One method, developed by Fernand Lamaze, concentrates on the experience of the parents during the birth process. Another method, formulated by Frederick Leboyer, emphasizes the importance of the infant's birth experience.

The Lamaze method. The most popular alternative birthing method was developed by Fernand Lamaze and is known as the **Lamaze method.** Lamaze advocated not only the father's presence but also his active participation in the birth process (Lamaze, 1970). Women are taught specific techniques for managing their discomfort, which reduces the need for painkillers. Relaxation techniques, breathing methods for the various stages of labor, and a number of other procedures help reduce the pain. Finally, the importance of experiencing the birth and of sharing an emotional experience is emphasized.

Lamaze procedures accomplish their goals. They reduce the amount of medication required, and women giving birth using Lamaze techniques report less discomfort and a more positive attitude toward the process (Cogan, 1980). This does not mean that women feel no discomfort, although they do report experiencing less pain than women who do not undergo Lamaze training (Melzack, 1984). They also require fewer painkillers (Charles et al., 1978). The benefits for the father are also great. In one study, the father's participation in birth was related to the father's attachment to the infant (Peterson et al., 1979). These researchers advocate better prenatal education for the father and structuring the birth and home environment to encourage active participation by the father.

The Leboyer method. A different tack was taken by Frederick Leboyer (1975), who emphasizes the experience of the infant in what has come to be known as the **Leboyer method** of childbirth. Leboyer argues that the cries and shrieks of the newborn need not occur. They result from a kind of torture—the traumatic removal from a warm, dark, quiet supportive environment to a cold, bright, noisy one filled with need. He argues that the baby feels everything and truly experiences the birth process, and that what is easiest for the doctor may not be best for the baby. Among other things, Leboyer ad-

Lamaze method   A method of prepared childbirth that requires active participation by both parents.

Leboyer method   A method of childbirth emphasizing the importance of the birth experience for the child and encouraging such practices as dim light, low voices, delay in cutting the umbilical cord, a bath, and a massage.

vocates using dimmed lights and whispering in the delivery room, placing the infant on the mother's abdomen after birth, waiting a few minutes before cutting the umbilical cord, providing a bath in which the father plays a leading role, and having both parents massage the infant. He also notes the importance of preparation for childbirth.

Leboyer's theories have not been met with overwhelming medical support. Some disagree with specific procedures, such as dimming the lights, but the main difficulty involves the lack of scientific evidence presented by Leboyer and his supporters to demonstrate the practical value of such procedures. His supporters tend to stress the experiential value of the method and to base their cases on the theory that the first moments of life are more important both for parents and for the child than was first thought (Berezin, 1980). Leboyer himself uses his clinical experiences and theoretical clarity as arguments in favor of his procedures. One study found that babies born by the Leboyer method were physically and behaviorally more advanced than would otherwise have been expected (Trotter, 1975), but this study lacked adequate controls.

An excellent controlled study was performed at the McMaster University Medical Center in Ontario. Women matched for social class and number of prior pregnancies were randomly assigned to either a Leboyer group or a non-Leboyer group. All Leboyer procedures were carefully followed with the Leboyer group. For the control group, standard medical practices were used. In both groups, mothers and fathers actively participated in the birth process, and gentle handling—a norm at this hospital—was given to all infants.

The results showed no significant advantages for the Leboyer method. The researchers stated, "The infants born by Leboyer method were neither more responsive nor less irritable than the control infants during the neonatal period, nor were there any differences in infant temperament or development at eight months of age" (Nelson et al., 1980, p. 659). Mothers' perceptions of the two deliveries did not differ either. The only reported difference was that "mothers in the Leboyer group were more likely to attribute differences in the behavior of their infants to the delivery experience" (p. 659). The researchers also reported that fears that there would be a greater danger to both infants and mothers were not supported by the study.

The reason for this lack of significant advantages can perhaps be found in the nature of the control group. In this hospital, even without the use of Leboyer's methods, the delivery and postnatal care was gentle. Hospital procedures encouraged participation by both parents and early parent-child interaction. It may well be that the group being compared with the Leboyer sample makes

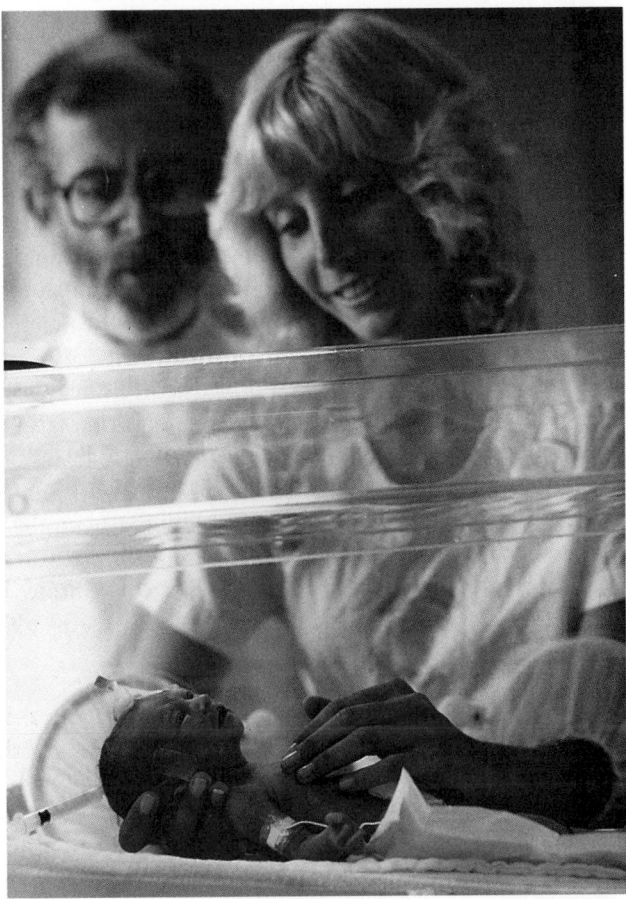

Many premature infants spend their early infancy in the hospital attached to life-sustaining machinery. Today, scientists are concerned with the psychological development as well as the physical development of premature infants.

anoxia A condition in which the infant does not receive a sufficient supply of oxygen.

premature infants Infants weighing less than 5½ pounds or born less than thirty-seven weeks after conception.

all the difference. Comparing Leboyer babies to a highly medicated, roughly treated, parental-separated sample may be unfair, because hospital procedures are changing in the direction of greater family participation and gentler birth. In the last analysis, the details of Leboyer's method may be less important than the humanistic attitudes and approach to birth that he advocates (Young, 1982).

Complications of Birth

Most pregnancies and deliveries are normal, but problems sometimes occur. Such problems as anoxia and prematurity may have serious consequences later in life.

Anoxia

A deficiency in the oxygen supply reaching the baby, **anoxia,** is the most common cause of brain damage. Such damage may be inflicted either during the birth process or for some time during the prenatal period, when the placenta is detached or infected. Anoxia may lead to a number of birth defects, including cognitive and behavioral problems (Wenar, 1982). Except for the more extreme cases, however, making predictions about the future development of anoxic children is difficult. Some anoxic children compare well with peers who did not suffer any anoxia. Anoxia increases the risk for developmental disability in both the cognitive and behavioral areas, but many anoxic children develop normally and show little difference from their peers when they enter school (Wenar, 1982). The quality of care may be most important (Sameroff and Chandler, 1975). The better the care, the less likely mild and moderately anoxic children are to develop these disabilities.

Prematurity: Born at Risk

The greatest threat to an infant's survival is prematurity. A **premature** infant can be defined in terms of birth weight or the length of the gestation period. Currently, a baby weighing less than 2,500 grams (about 5½ pounds) or one who has been born less than thirty-seven weeks after conception is considered premature. Generally, low-birth-weight infants are categorized into two groups. In the first group are infants born below the weight we would expect for their gestational age. Some of these babies are born at their normal term, others are born earlier. These infants are called **small-for-date** babies. The other group involves what are called **preterm** infants, those whose birth weights are appropriate for their gestational age but who are born at thirty-seven or fewer weeks after conception (Kopp and Parmellee, 1979).

Premature infants are "at risk" for a number of physical and intellectual deficits during childhood (Lawson et al., 1984). Children who are premature are more likely to show intellectual problems and learning difficulties than children who are not premature, and they are more likely later to be in classes for the retarded (Caputo and Mandell, 1970). Such children are also at risk for developing a number of social problems, being especially prone to hyperactivity. Many show neurological problems (Drillien, 1964). In addition, premature infants are more likely to die during the first month of life, accounting for about half of all the deaths that occur during this time (Fitzgerald et al., 1982).

True or False Premature infants are no more at risk for developmental problems than normal infants.

Of course, not all premature infants have such long-term problems. Some grow up to be superior children and function well as adults. A variety of outcomes are possible, depending on the size and gestation age of the infant and on subsequent care and upbringing. The lower the birth weight and the shorter the gestation period, the more potentially serious are the consequences (DeHirsch et al., 1966).

Premature infants are at risk because many diseased or genetically abnormal infants are born early, but also because the premature infant is likely to be born into a disadvantaged environment (Scarr-Salapatek and Williams, 1973). While prematurity is found in every socioeconomic group, it is far more common in women living in poverty (Kopp, 1983). Although we do not know the reasons for most premature births, a number of factors have been implicated, including the mother's health and nutrition prior to pregnancy, the mother's age and weight, her weight gain during pregnancy, her

small-for-date infants Infants born below the weight expected for their gestational age.

preterm infants Infants born before thirty-seven weeks of gestation.

retrolental fibroplasia A disorder involving blindness caused by an oversupply of oxygen administered usually to premature infants.

use of drugs, uterine problems and lack of prenatal care (Kopp and Parmellee, 1979). Smoking during pregnancy doubles the chance of a woman's having a small-for-date infant (Ounsted et al., 1985). These factors correlate with social class. For instance, the poor are less likely to eat nutritious food during pregnancy and are much less likely to avail themselves of prenatal care, and their health is likely to be worse. No wonder these children are at a double risk. They are more vulnerable at birth and more likely to be exposed to a poor environment afterward.

Years ago, severely premature infants were fed a very weak formula and placed in oxygen-rich environments. However, too rich an oxygen supply led to **retrolental fibroplasia,** a disorder that causes blindness. Lack of proper nourishment led to developmental problems. Today we have effective tube-feeding techniques and sophisticated machinery that monitors the infant's vital signs. We are also aware that it is important that these children be stimulated. The effects of a deadening, nonstimulating hospital environment must be reduced. A number of studies have shown that extra rocking and tactile stimulation are highly effective in improving the neurological, motor, and psychological development of premature infants. Premature infants who are stimulated are healthier, gain more weight, and develop better physically and mentally (Rice, 1977; Solkoff et al., 1969).

After the Birth

By the end of its normal period of prenatal development, the average American male infant weighs approximately 7½ pounds and measures approximately 20 inches. The average female weighs slightly less, about 7 pounds, but appearances can be deceiving. In reality, the average female is more ready for life. She is about four weeks more mature, as measured by skeletal age (Annis, 1978) and is more neurologically advanced.

True or False Boys are more neurologically mature at birth than girls.

Hospitals have instituted specific procedures to measure the physical functioning and the capacity for independent survival of newborn infants. For example, infants may be evaluated using a rating system called the **Apgar Scoring System** (Apgar, 1953). This system measures five physical characteristics: heart rate, respiration, reflex response, muscle tone, and color (see Table 3.3). The neonate is given a score of 0, 1, or 2 for each item according to specific criteria. For instance, if the newborn has a heart rate of 100 to 140 beats a minute, the infant receives a score of 2; for 100 beats a minute or below, a score of one is noted; and if there is no discernible heartbeat, a 0 is given (Self and Horowitz, 1979). The lower the Apgar score, the greater the chance of behavior problems or infant death (Apgar et al. 1958). Some studies even suggest that there are differences between infants who have received scores of 7, 8, and 9 and those with a perfect 10. Infants with a perfect Apgar score show more mature patterns of attention to stimuli than infants with good but not perfect scores (Lewis et al., 1967). Infants who receive a score of less than 7 need additional watching and care. The Apgar score can alert those responsible for the infant's care to a possible problem.

A more complex assessment for infants is the **Brazelton Neonatal Behavior Scale**, which provides infor-

> **Apgar Scoring System** A relatively simple system that gives a gross measure of infant survivability.
>
> **Brazelton Neonatal Behavior Scale** An involved system for evaluating an infant's reflexes and sensory and behavioral abilities.

mation concerning reflexes and a variety of infant behaviors (Jacobson et al., 1984). Among the behavioral items are measures of responsiveness to visual stimuli, reactions to a bell and a pinprick, and the quality and duration of the infant's alertness and motor activity (Lester et al., 1982). The scale is a diagnostic tool, but it has also been used to research cross-cultural differences among infants.

Hope and Frustration

The study of prenatal development and birth is both hopeful and frustrating. We know so much about preventing birth defects, yet every day we observe pregnant women drinking, smoking, eating improperly, and not availing themselves of proper prenatal care. Even though we know how to minimize deficits that all too often follow the premature infant through life, relatively few hospitals have excellent postnatal wards where the child's total needs are taken into account. And while many teenagers are giving birth, efforts to teach these young parents about the specific needs of their infants remain

---

T A B L E   3.3

The Apgar Scoring System

The Apgar Rating System is a relatively simple scale used to rate newborns. Each child is rated on the five behaviors indicated below. If the total score is greater than 7, no immediate threat to survival exists. If the score is lower than 4, the infant is presently in critical condition. Any score lower than 7 is cause for great concern.

Area	*Score*		
	0	*1*	*2*
Heart rate	Absent	Slow (< 100)	Rapid (> 100)
Respiration	Absent	Irregular	Good, infant crying
Muscle tone	Flaccid	Weak	Strong, well flexed
Color	Blue, pale	Body pink, extremities blue	All pink
Reflex irritability:			
Nasal tickle	No response	Grimace	Cough, sneeze
Heel prick	No response	Mild response	Foot withdrawal, cry

Source: Apgar, 1953.

TABLE 3.4

Comparison of Infant Mortality Rates

As this table shows, a number of other developed countries have lower infant mortality rates than the United States. The rates for underdeveloped nations are much higher. All data is for 1984 unless otherwise indicated.

Country	Death Rate
Japan	6.2
Sweden	6.3
Switzerland	7.7
Denmark	7.7
Norway	7.9
Netherlands	8.3
Canada	8.5*
France	9.0*
Australia	9.6*
Ireland	9.8
United Kingdom	10.2*
United States	10.4
Austria	11.5
Italy	11.6
New Zealand	12.5
Greece	14.1

*1983 data

Source: United Nations, 1986

inadequate (Counseling and Personnel Services Clearinghouse, 1982). We have some answers to our problems, but improving programs to serve the needs of families during this important time of their lives is expensive. We pay for these failures in the years to come, because problems that develop at this stage often lead to psychological, social, and medical problems later that we will be forced to deal with. Professionals who decry efforts in the area of prenatal and perinatal education and medical attention are supported by data (see Table 3.4) showing that many other developed countries have lower infant mortality rates than the United States.

True or False The United States has the second-lowest infant mortality rate in the free world.

But what does all this mean to Ellen and Tom, who are expecting their first child? Our increasing knowledge allows them to make important decisions during pregnancy about what to avoid. Although there are no guarantees that the baby will be born healthy, they now have the information they need to improve their chances of having a healthy infant. They are also more aware of the alternative methods of birth and the choices available to them. For these parents, the new medical knowledge and advances mean their infant has a better chance of being born free of defects and developing normally in the years to come.

Summary

1. Fertilization occurs when a sperm cell penetrates an egg cell. Monozygotic (identical) twins develop from a single fertilized egg. Dizygotic (fraternal) twins form when two egg cells are fertilized by two sperm cells.

2. During the germinal stage, the fertilized egg travels down a fallopian tube and embeds itself in the womb. The embryonic stage, which lasts from two to eight weeks, is a time of rapid development. The heart starts to beat, and 95 percent of the body systems are present. During the fetal stage, which begins when bone cells make their appearance at about two months and lasts until birth, the developing organism continues to develop internally and put on weight.

3. The unborn child may be adversely affected by many environmental factors, including various medications, over-the-counter drugs, and such illegal drugs as narcotics.

4. Smoking during pregnancy is linked to low-birth-weight babies, prematurity, and birth defects and possibly to long-term developmental difficulties. The children of alcoholics suffer from fetal alcohol syndrome, a condition of retardation and physical defects; even moderate drinking, though, may cause some fetal abnormality.

5. Various diseases, including rubella, herpes, and AIDS, cause fetal abnormalities or death.

6. The Rh factor is a particular red-blood-cell antigen. If the mother is Rh negative and the father is Rh positive, the offspring may be Rh positive and problems may arise. Antigens from mother may pass through the placenta and kill

red blood cells in the fetus. Today women with such problems receive a shot of RhoGAM, which blocks the creation of the antibodies.

7. Most birth defects are caused by prenatal insults, not genetic diseases. Women unwittingly expose their unborn children to such insults when they do not understand the danger, do not believe the warnings, do not realize they are pregnant at the time, or are not sufficiently motivated to stop a potentially dangerous activity.

8. A *critical period* is the time an event has its greatest impact. Some teratogens are more dangerous at some times than at others.

9. More women over thirty are having children. Although at this age the risk is greater for both mother and baby, good prenatal care can reduce the risk. Many pregnant teens do not receive the proper prenatal care, are exposed to many teratogens, and may suffer from malnutrition. The risk factor for this group is very high.

10. Serious malnutrition can lead to fewer fetal brain cells. Specific vitamin and mineral deficiencies may lead to fetal deformities. The effects of mild and moderate malnutrition are controversial, but malnutrition may serve to weaken the fetus.

11. Maternal stress has been liked to babies who are irritable as well as to obstetrical problems.

12. Paternal drug-taking prior to pregnancy may affect the father's genes. In addition, if the father continues to indulge in drinking and smoking, the pregnant woman may find it more difficult to refrain from such behavior herself.

13. New technologies now give the doctor and patient more information and choices. Sonography uses ultrasonic soundwaves to create a picture of the unborn child in the womb. Amniocentesis and chorionic villus sampling are used to discover genetic problems, and fetal monitoring during labor gives doctors early warnings that something is wrong.

14. During the first stage of birth, the uterus contracts and the cervix dilates. The infant is delivered in the second stage, the placenta during the third.

15. Cesarean births have increased greatly since the early sixties, due to improvements in safety, new technology making it possible for doctors to know sooner if something is wrong, and the tendency of doctors to practice defensive medicine.

16. Newborns whose mothers were given medication to control labor pains are sluggish and not very alert. The long-term effects of obstetrical medication are controversial at the present time.

17. The Lamaze method of prepared childbirth emphasizes the importance of both parents' participation in the birth process. Relaxation and breathing techniques are used to reduce discomfort, and less medication is required.

18. The Leboyer method emphasizes the importance of the infant's experience. It involves delivering the child with dimmed lights and whispers, placing the infant on the mother's abdomen, waiting minutes before cutting the umbilical cord, and bathing and massaging the infant.

19. Premature infants are at risk for a number of intellectual, neurological, physical, and developmental disabilities. These infants have special needs, and parents must learn to cope with these greater demands. Extra stimulation appears to reduce the possibility that the infant will develop a disability.

20. The average American male infant weighs about 7½ pounds and measures about 20 inches. Females weigh slightly less than males, but are more mature as measured by skeletal age and more neurologically advanced. After birth, the child may be rated on the Apgar Scoring System, which provides caregivers with an idea of the infant's physical condition and chances for survival.

Answers to True or False Statements

1. *False*   Correct statement: The heart is the first organ to function during the prenatal period.
2. *False*   Correct statement: Some substances do cross over to the infant's system through the placenta.
3. *False*   Correct statement: Smoking is linked to lower-birth-weight infants.
4. *False*   Correct statement: Heavy exposure to

caffeine may be injurious, but current research shows that very small amounts do not seem to be very dangerous.

5. *False* Correct statement: The AIDS virus can cross the placenta and be found in the unborn child's system.

6. *True* An infant is more likely to suffer a prenatal insult than to be the victim of a genetic disorder.

7. *True* The number of women bearing children in this age-group has increased.

8. *True* Severe malnutrition may lead to an abnormally low number of brain cells.

9. *False* Correct statement: The number of cesarean sections has increased markedly.

10. *False* Correct statement: Despite improvements in medical care, the premature infant is still at greater risk for developmental problems than the normal infant.

11. *False* Correct statement: Girls are more neurologically mature at birth than boys.

12. *False* Correct statement: The infant mortality rate in the United States is not even in the lowest ten.

PART TWO

Infancy and Toddlerhood

Physical and Cognitive Development in Infancy and Toddlerhood

CHAPTER CONTENTS

Are the Following Statements True or False?

*Try the True-False Quiz below. See if your answers correspond to the information in
this chapter. Each question is repeated after the paragraph in which the answer can be found.
The True-False Answer Box at the end of the chapter lists the complete answers.*

_____ 1. The newborn infant is very nearsighted at birth.

_____ 2. Infants are born deaf, but quickly develop their sense of hearing.

_____ 3. Newborns are relatively insensitive to pain.

_____ 4. Most of the infant's reflexes become stronger with time.

_____ 5. An infant can be adequately fed using prepared formula instead of breast milk.

_____ 6. The injurious effects of malnutrition can be reduced by a good environment.

_____ 7. At birth, females are more mature and continue to develop at a faster rate.

_____ 8. The one-month-old infant believes that mother no longer exists when she leaves
the room.

_____ 9. Three-month-old infants can recognize their mothers' faces.

_____10. Scales measuring infant intelligence can accurately predict later childhood
intelligence.

_____11. Parents of competent infants spend many hours of time teaching them concepts.

_____12. Interactions with infants and toddlers of less than one minute have no effect on
their cognitive development.

The Newborn at a Glance

The newborn infant does not resemble the pictures we see on baby food jars, in soap advertisements, or in the movies. The **neonate,** or newborn, is covered with fine hair called **lanugo,** which is discarded within a few days. In the womb the baby's sensitive skin is protected by a thick secretion called **vernix caseosa,** which dries and disappears. The head is elongated and is about one-quarter of the baby's total length. The thin skin appears pale and contains blotches caused by the trip through the birth canal. The head and nose may be out of shape because their soft, pliable nature allows an extra bit of "give" during birth. They will soon return to normal, but it will be about a year and a half before the bones in the skull will cover the soft spots, or **fontanels.** The legs are tucked under the baby in a fetal position and will remain that way for quite a while. The infant wheezes and sneezes. The infant appears anything but ready for an independent existence.

But appearances can be deceiving. The infant's appearance has survival value (Morris, 1977). Some ethologists, scientists who study organisms in their native habitat, argue that the appearance of newborns elicits strong protective emotions in adults. The very shape of the infant is viewed positively by adults (Alley, 1981). In addition, scientists now know that newborn infants are better prepared for survival than was first thought and that their abilities develop quickly. Researching the sensory abilities of neonates is very challenging since they cannot verbally tell us what they see or how they are experiencing their environment. Careful and sometimes ingenious studies show that infants' use of their senses is first governed by inborn, prewired programs, but these quickly give way to more voluntary programs that are based on the babies' physical maturation as well as their experience with the environment.

How the Infant Experiences the World

Vision

Adults rely on the sense of vision for much of their information about the world, and so do infants. At birth,

neonate   The scientific term for a newborn infant.

lanugo   The fine hair that covers a newborn infant.

vernix caseosa   A thick liquid that protects the skin of the fetus.

fontanels   The soft spots on top of a baby's head.

the visual apparatus of an infant is immature but functional (Aslin, 1987). What can an infant see?

Acuity and accommodation.   Infants are very nearsighted at birth (Dayton et al., 1964). Neonates have a visual acuity of 20/150, which means they can see at 20 feet what an older child with normal vision could see at 150 feet. Other estimates are a little worse, approaching between 20/200 and 20/300 (Dobson and Teller, 1978). The infant also has difficulty focusing. The best focal distance for the newborn is about 19 centimeters (7½ inches). This serves infants well, though. When a newborn is held by the mother, the baby's face is usually less than 6 inches away, so the infant is able to see her during feeding. Infants have difficulty focusing on distant or approaching objects (Wickelgren, 1967). Visual abilities improve quickly, and within six months the infant's visual acuity approaches that of an adult (Cohen et al., 1979); by about two months the ability to focus approaches adult proportions (Aslin and Dumais, 1980).

True or False   The newborn infant is very nearsighted at birth.

Form and preference.   Newborns have visual preferences. They prefer curved lines to straight lines (Fantz and Miranda, 1975), patterned surfaces over plain ones (see Figure 4.1) (Fantz, 1963), and high-contrast edges and angles (Cohen et al., 1979). The infant's scanning is not random. It is directed by rules (Haith, 1980) that cause the baby to concentrate on the outline of a feature rather than explore its details (Milewski, 1976). By eight weeks or so, infants develop more adult patterns of scanning and will investigate the interior of a figure as well as its contours (Maurer and Salapatek, 1976). New research shows that infants are sensitive to patterned properties of stimuli from birth (Antell et al., 1985). Neonates can even discriminate different facial expressions (Field et al., 1982).

A preference for faces? How can visual patterns and preferences help the newborn survive? The newborn depends on others for the necessities of life, so a visual preference for human faces would be adaptive. In fact,

FIGURE 4.1

Visual Preferences in Infancy

The importance of pattern, rather than color or brightness, was illustrated by the response of infants to a face, a piece of printed matter, a bulls-eye, and plain red, white, and yellow disks. Even the youngest infants preferred patterns. Color bars show the results for infants from two to three months old; gray bars, for infants more than three months old.

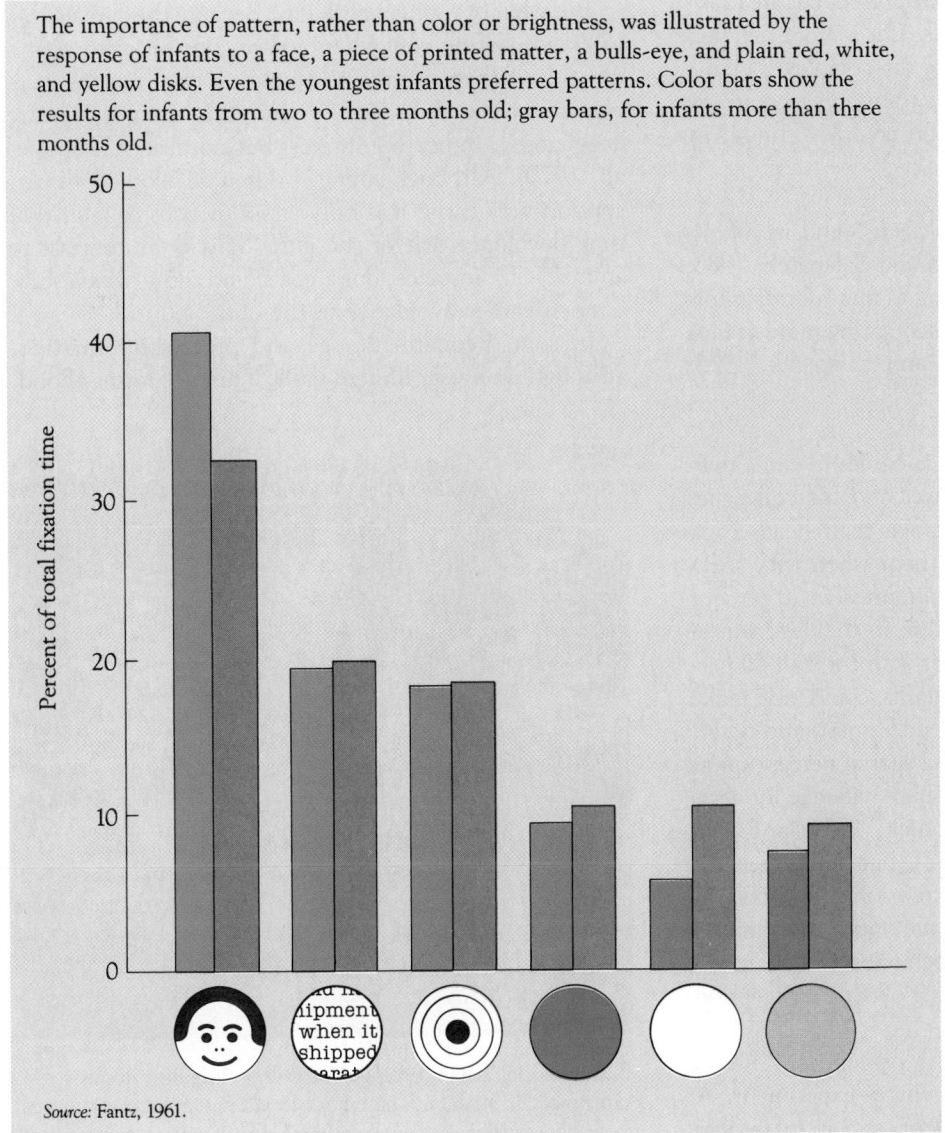

Source: Fantz, 1961.

the discovery by Fantz (1961) that this was true excited the scientific world. Fantz showed infants two pictures—one to the infant's right, the other to the left—and measured the time the infant's eyes spent fixated on either one. Fantz found that infants preferred patterned to nonpatterned surfaces and that a picture of a face attracted the most attention. Perhaps the infant comes into this world preprogrammed to recognize faces. But Fantz's argument that infants have a natural preference for faces may be premature. His conclusions have been reinterpreted in terms of the complexity of stimuli, and other research has not replicated his work (Cohen et al., 1979). At the present time, there is no final answer to this question. Perhaps both sides are correct but are looking at the issue at different levels. On a more detailed level, the infant has a preference for complex stimuli, while on the behavioral level this translates into an interest in faces, which are common complex stimuli in the infant's environment.

Color vision.   Color vision has been found in infants as young as three months (Banks and Salapatek, 1983; Bornstein, 1976). Infants as young as four months show the same color preferences as adults, gazing more at blue and red than at yellow (Banks and Salapatek, 1983; Banks, 1975).

Spatial and depth perception.   Do babies live in a two- or three-dimensional world? Bower and his colleagues (1970) found that infants will move their heads back and put their hands in front of them when they see a ball coming toward their face. An impressive 70 percent of the infant's hand extensions were in the direction of the ball, and infants made contact with the ball 40 percent of the time. When the infants could not make contact with the ball, they seemed surprised and upset. If this is true, it shows astonishing spatial perception at a very young age. Studies have found evidence for early spatial perception (Ball and Tronick, 1971) and eye-hand coordination (Hofsten, 1982), but some researchers do not believe these hand extensions are a coordinated defensive attempt to avoid the oncoming stimulus (DiFranco et al., 1978). Such behavior can be interpreted only as the earliest beginning of depth perception and eye-hand coordination.

In order to test an infant's depth perception, Gibson and Walk (1960) designed an ingenious experiment. A stand was constructed above the floor, and an infant was

placed on the stand, which had two glass surfaces. One half of this surface had a checkerboard pattern, the other half was clear glass. Underneath the clear glass was another checkerboard pattern, giving the impression of a cliff. This experiment, using what is called the **visual cliff,** showed that children six months or older would not crawl from the "safe" side over the cliff even if their mothers beckoned (see Figure 4.2).

But what of younger children? Because they are unable to crawl, testing very young infants on this apparatus is difficult. When infants as young as two months were placed on the deep side of the cliff, their heart rate decelerated, indicating interest but not fear (Campos et al., 1970). Although young children develop depth perception very early, it is only at six months or later that they develop a fear of the cliff. This is in contrast to animals—for instance, dogs, goats, and cats—which show a much earlier avoidance of the cliff.

In sum, neonates do see and process information, although on a very limited basis. They see forms (Bond,

Babies develop depth perception at a very early age; in this experiment, a six-month-old infant would not crawl across what looks like a cliff even though its mother beckoned.

FIGURE 4.2

The Visual Cliff Apparatus

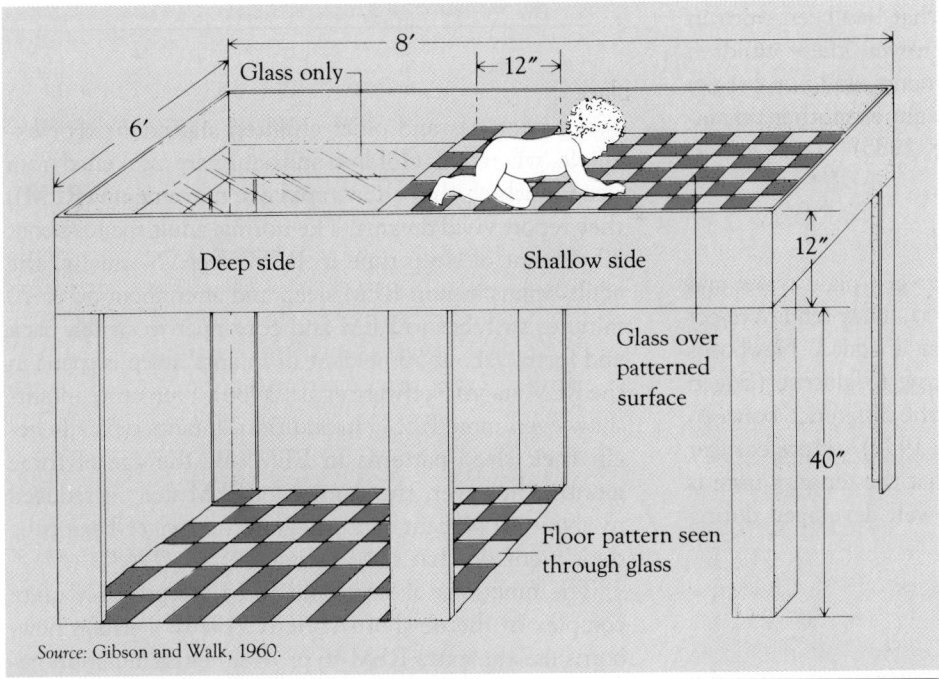

8'

Glass only

12"

6'

Deep side

Shallow side

12"

Glass over
patterned
surface

40"

Floor pattern seen
through glass

Source: Gibson and Walk, 1960.

1972) and can track slow moving targets (Kreminitzer et al., 1979), although their visual acuity and ability to focus are poor. Finally, they scan the field according to rules that may be innate, indicating that part of the visual processing is inborn. However, visual abilities develop quickly, and these primitive prewired programs give way to more adult scanning and visual processing.

Hearing

Infants can hear from the moment of their birth (Wertheimer, 1961; Muir and Field, 1979). In fact, the newborn's auditory abilities are better developed than the visual abilities. Newborns react to pitch, loudness, and even rhythm (Eisenberg, 1970). They coordinate their body movements to other people's speech rhythms (Condon and Sander, 1974).

True or False Infants are born deaf, but quickly develop their sense of hearing.

Just as the infant's visual abilities have survival value, so do the infant's auditory abilities. Human neonates respond to most sounds within the human voice range

(Webster et al., 1972) and are more responsive to sounds within that range than outside it (Kearsley, 1973). They are more sensitive to higher-pitched sounds (Aslin et al., 1983) and can discriminate one sound from another. DeCasper and Fifer (1980) reported that by three days of age neonates could discriminate between mother's voice and that of a stranger, as measured by differential sucking on a nipple. Infants will suck harder when they hear a familiar voice in a familiar intonation than when they hear the same voice with an altered intonation (Mehler et al., 1978). Infants are also tuned in to language from birth (Aslin et al., 1983). Infants as young as one month can tell the difference between the sound of a *P* and a *B* (Eimas, 1975). Infants are also partial to music (Walk, 1981), and rhythmic sounds tend to sooth them (Salk, 1960).

Smell

Newborns can also use their sense of smell. Neonates move away from unpleasant-smelling solutions (Lipsitt et al., 1963). Infants as young as seven days old turned differentially to their mother's breast pad even if offered another woman's breast pad, but two-day-old neonates did not do this (MacFarlane, 1975). Two-week-old breast-fed children could recognize the smell of their mother when presented with gauze pads that had been worn in the mother's underarm area. However, these children could not recognize their father's odors, and non-breast-fed children could not recognize either mother's or father's odors (Cernoch and Porter, 1985).

Taste

Infants can tell the difference between plain water and a sugar solution (Desor et al., 1973). They tend to reject plain water, but accept it if sugar is added. Newborns one to three days old prefer sucrose to glucose (Engen et al., 1973). They can even tell the difference between sour and bitter substances (Jensen, 1932) and prefer sugar to salt (Pratt, 1954). It is clear that the sense of taste is functioning in the neonate and well developed during infancy and toddlerhood.

Pressure and Pain

Neonates are responsive to tactile stimulation, especially around the mouth, but relatively insensitive to pain at birth. This reduces the infant's discomfort during the birth process. Within a few days, a dramatic increase in this sense occurs (Lipsitt and Levy, 1959), contributing to the baby's ability to respond to painful stimuli that might be injurious. The sense of pain reaches a plateau in later infancy and stays rather stable through childhood (Birren et al., 1981).

True or False   Newborns are relatively insensitive to pain.

Infants, then, are born with a number of sensory abilities that develop rapidly throughout infancy and toddlerhood. They actively seek out stimuli during their attempts to experience and understand the world. This process is facilitated by changes in the sleeping-waking cycle. As infants mature, they spend more time awake and alert, which allows for even more exploration of the environment.

The Sleeping-Waking Cycle

Neonates spend about sixteen or seventeen hours a day sleeping (Parmelee et al., 1964). The nature of these periods of sleep shows some interesting differences be-

---

Rapid Eye Movements (REM)   The movements of the eyes during sleep that are related to dreaming.

---

tween neonates and older children and adults. For example, when both children and adults are awakened from sleep in which they show **rapid eye movements (REM),** they report vivid dreams. The normal adult spends about 20 percent of sleep time in REM sleep. Normally, the adult begins in non-REM sleep and after about 50 to 70 minutes switches to REM and continues to switch back and forth. About 50 percent of infants' sleep is spent in the REM stage (Roffwarg et al., 1966). Premature infants show even more REM. In addition, infants typically begin their sleep patterns in REM. By the age of three months, however, the amount of REM sleep is reduced to about 40 percent, and they are no longer beginning their nights in that state (Minard et al., 1968).

The functions of sleep and REM are probably quite complex in the newborn (Brierly, 1976). Perhaps newborns use the extra REM to provide self-stimulation because they sleep so much of the day. The decrease in REM sleep as waking time increases provides some evidence in that direction (Roffwarg et al., 1966). Other psychologists argue that REM sleep fosters brain organization and development, which is particularly rapid at this stage of development (Berg and Berg, 1979).

It is relatively easy to describe waking and sleeping in adults, but not so easy with infants. Waking and sleeping do appear in the newborn, but a number of transitional states that fit into neither category are present too. As the infant grows, these decrease, and the infant's state can more easily be measured and classified. Wolff (1969) argues that infants show seven states:

Regular sleep. During this state, the infant lies quiet and subdued, with eyes closed and unmoving. The child looks pale, breathing is regular.
Irregular sleep. In this state the infant does not appear so still. There are sudden jerks, startles, and a number of facial expressions, including smiling, sneering, and frowning. The eyes, though closed, sometimes show bursts of movement, and breathing is irregular.
Periodic sleep. This is an intermediate stage between regular and irregular sleep. The infant shows some

periods of rapid breathing, and jerky movements followed by periods of perfect calm.

Drowsiness. In this state the infant shows bursts of "writhing" activity. The eyes open and close and have a dull appearance. Respiration is variable but regular.

Alert inactivity. The infant is now relaxed and inactive, but the eyes have a bright, shining appearance. Breathing is irregular, and the child searches the environment.

Waking activity. The infant in this state shows spurts of activity involving the entire body. Respiration is irregular. The intensity and duration of these movements vary with the individual.

Crying. In this familiar state the infant cries, and this is often accompanied by significant motor activity. The face may turn red.

It is estimated that infants spend 67 percent of the time in sleep, 7 percent in drowsiness, 10 percent in alert inactivity, 11 percent in waking activity, and 5 percent in crying (Berg et al., 1973).

The concept of infant state is important because the responses of infants to a stimulus are a function of the state in which they are tested (Parmelee and Sigman, 1983). Some reflexes are stronger and more reliable in one state than in the other. The infant's sensory thresholds are also mediated by the baby's state. In the alert inactive state, infants may turn away from strong auditory stimuli toward more gentle voices. Before comparing studies, the infant's state must be taken into consideration. The concept of state has practical implications for parents as well. During the transition states, the infant can go either way. If the stimuli awaiting the infant are pleasant, the baby is drawn out into an alert stage and is more responsive.

Infant Crying

Perhaps the most familiar infant state is crying. The cry of the infant has survival value. It not only informs others of the baby's condition but also encourages the parents to care for the infant. The cry of an infant can have a physical effect on parents. In one study, mothers' heart rates increased as they watched videotape recordings of infants, particularly their own, crying (Wiesenfeld and Klorman, 1978). Parents' sensitivity and responsiveness to infants' cries have a powerful effect on the infant. Infants whose mothers respond promptly to cries exhib-

ited less crying in later months (Bell and Ainsworth, 1972). Babies who are held may become more secure and require less contact later in the first year. Young parents are often concerned that they will not understand what the infant is communicating through the cry. However, there are qualitative differences in the cries (Wolff, 1965), and parents can usually understand what these cries mean from environmental cues as well.

The infant emits a number of different cries. The hunger cry is heard when the infant is hungry, but it is also heard if there is any environmental disturbance. It starts out arrhythmically and low in intensity, but gradually becomes louder and more rhythmic. The mad or angry cry follows the same general pattern as the hungry cry, except it is more forceful as more air is pushed past the vocal cords. The pain cry is different. The first cry is much longer, as is the first rest period. It lasts as long as seven seconds, during which time the infant lies still holding his or her breath. This is followed by the gasping intake of air and cries of shorter and varying duration. The pain cry begins suddenly, and there is no moaning preceding it. The initial segments of the pain cry are particularly potent stimuli for both adult males and females (Zeskind et al., 1985). Mothers can accurately discriminate between pain and anger cries, at least for their own infants (Wiesenfeld et al., 1981).

The Infant's Ability to Learn

If newborns are to survive, they must learn about their new world. Even neonates can learn through the three processes described in Chapter 1—classical conditioning, operant conditioning, and imitation.

Classical Conditioning

Researchers report some success using classical conditioning with infants (Blass et al., 1984). For example, Lipsitt and Kaye (1964) succeeded in classically conditioning the sucking reflex by sounding a tone that acts as the conditioned stimulus and following it by inserting in the mouth of the infant a nipple, which acts as the unconditioned stimulus. After pairing the tone and insertion of the nipple, the infants sucked to the tone (the conditioned response). Other studies also reported success in classically conditioning infants (Rovee-Collier, 1987), but it should be noted that only about half of all the studies report success (Fitzgerald and Brackbill, 1976).

Perhaps infants experience difficulty associating the conditioned and unconditioned stimuli (the tone and the insertion of the nipple, for example) because of lack of experience. While acknowledging that the research results are mixed, we can conclude that classical conditioning has been established in the neonate (Sameroff and Cavanaugh, 1979).

Operant Conditioning

No such problem exists with operant conditioning. In one study, Siqueland (1968) successfully trained newborns to turn their heads for a chance to suck on a nipple. The creativity of researchers working with young infants is shown by a Butterfield and Siperstein (1972) study on the musical preferences of young infants. Infants were allowed to suck on a nipple and were rewarded by being allowed to hear music. The longer they sucked, the more music they heard. Two-day-old infants sucked longer and longer to hear the music, but they would not do this if sucking led to the music's being turned off.

Imitation

Neonates also imitate. Meltzoff and Moore (1977) claim that twelve- to twenty-one-day-old infants imitate facial and manual gestures. Infants opened their mouths and stuck out their tongues when the same behaviors were modeled by an adult. Infants only 60 minutes old show imitative responses. In another study, newborn infants ages 0.7 to 71 hours imitated an adult's facial gestures of opening the mouth and sticking out the tongue (Meltzoff and Moore, 1983). Neonates are more likely to imitate movement than static conditions. In other words, they are more likely to imitate a hand opening and closing if they see the hand open and close, than if they see merely an open hand or a closed hand (Vinter, 1986).

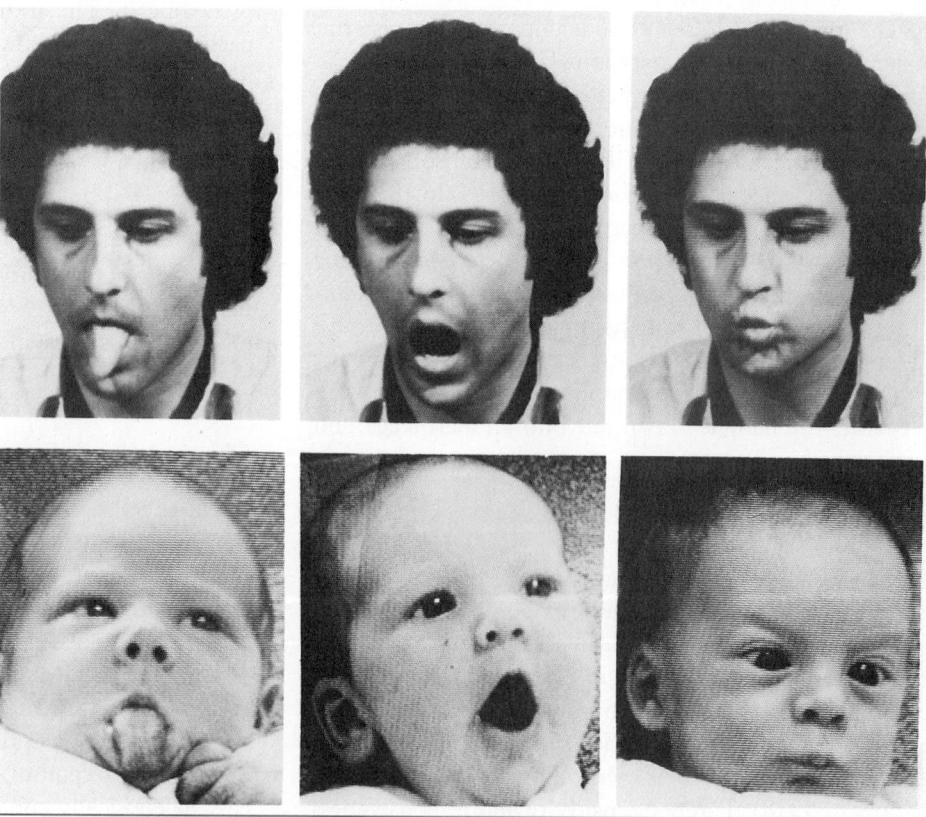

Infants show imitation at very early ages. In the top row, Andrew Meltzoff makes facial gestures at an infant. In the bottom row, you can see the infant's responses.

Habituation

Imagine looking at the same picture hanging over your desk day after day. Eventually you wouldn't even notice it. But what if someone changed the picture while you were out of the room? Would you notice the change? The process by which you spend less and less time attending to a familiar stimulus is known as **habituation** (Brierly, 1976). In order to respond to the new picture, you must notice that it is different.

Psychologists have used the process of habituation to test a number of infant perceptual abilities in the visual, auditory, and even tactual realms (Streri and Pecheux, 1986; Kisilevsky and Muir, 1984). An infant is presented with one stimulus, and the baby's behavior is observed closely. At first the infant shows some interest, but after a time the baby pays less attention to it, finally perhaps ignoring the stimulus altogether. Now you present the infant with another stimulus and observe the behavior. If an increase in attention occurs, the infant has noticed the difference between the pair of stimuli.

The habituation design has been used on infants as early as the first few days after birth. Infants one and a half days old to three days old habituate to a checkerboard pattern placed on the side of the crib (Friedman and Carpenter, 1971). The three-day-old infants habituated faster to the visual stimuli than younger infants did.

Reflexes in the Newborn

Infants also enter the world preprogrammed with a number of specific responses to stimuli in the form of reflexes (see Table 4.1). A **reflex** is a simple automatic reaction to a particular stimulus (Kalat, 1981). Reflexes connected with feeding are well established in the newborn; place something in an infant's mouth, and the baby will **suck** vigorously. The infant also shows the **rooting reflex**—if you stroke the neonate's cheek, the baby turns toward that side to find the breast. The swallowing reflex is also well developed in the newborn, as are a number of digestive reflexes, including hiccuping, burping, and regurgitation.

The functions of other reflexes are either unknown or can only be guessed at. For example, if you slide your finger along the palm of a neonate, the infant's fist will close. This **grasping reflex** is strongest at birth, weaker by two months of age, and usually disappears by about

habituation   The process by which organisms spend less and less time attending to familiar stimuli.

reflex   A relatively simple automatic reaction to a particular stimulus.

sucking reflex   A reflex found in young infants, in which they automatically suck when something is placed in their mouths.

rooting reflex   The reflex in young infants in which a stroke on a cheek causes them to turn in the direction of the stimulus.

grasping reflex   A reflex in which a stroke on the palm causes the infant to make a fist.

Babinski reflex   The reflex in which stroking the soles of the feet results in the toes fanning out.

Moro reflex   A reflex elicited by a sudden loud noise or momentary change in position, causing the back to arch, an extension of the arms and legs, and finally their contraction into a hugging position.

stepping reflex   A reflex in which if the baby is held upright and the soles of the feet are placed on a hard surface while the baby is tipped slightly forward the infant makes a stepping movement.

three months (Illingworth, 1974). In the evolutionary perspective, the grasping reflex might have some survival value. Most primates must hold on to their mothers for protection, and this reflex would facilitate that attachment. The reflex may have once had the same purpose for human infants. Persistence of this response well past the three- to four-month period may indicate brain damage.

If someone tickled you on the sole of your foot, your toes would curl in. When an infant's sole is stroked, the toes fan out. This reflex, known as the **Babinski reflex,** disappears by the end of the first year. The **Moro reflex** may be the strangest. A sudden loud noise or momentary change in position may cause infants to extend their arms and legs while arching their back, then contract them into a hugging position; the infant also cries (Brazelton, 1981). The presence of this reflex past six months or so is a sign that there may be some neurological dysfunction.

The **stepping or walking reflex** is exhibited by stepping motions elicited by holding infants upright and pitched a bit forward, making certain the soles of the

TABLE 4.1

Some Neonatal Reflexes

Reflex	Eliciting Stimulus	Response	Developmental Duration
Babinski	Gentle stroke along sole of foot from heel to toe	Toes fan out, big toe flexes	Disappears by end of first year
Babkin	Pressure applied to both palms while baby is lying on its back	Eyes close and mouth opens; head returns to center position	Disappears in 3–4 months
Blink	Flash of light, or puff of air delivered to eyes	Both eyelids close	Permanent
Diving reflex	Sudden splash of cold water in the face	Heart rate decelerates, blood shunted to brain and heart	Becomes progressively weaker with age
Knee jerk	Tap on patellar tendon	Knee kicks	Permanent
Moro reflex	Sudden loss of support	Arms extended, then brought toward each other; lower extremities are extended	Disappears in about 6 months
Palmar grasp	Rod or finger pressed against infant's palm	The object is grasped	Disappears in 3–4 months
Rage reflex	Place both hands on side of alert infant's head and restrain movement; block mouth with cheesecloth or covering for 10 seconds	Crying and struggling	Disappears in 2–4 months
Rooting reflex	Object lightly brushes infant's cheek	Baby turns toward object and attempts to suck	Disappears in 3–4 months
Sucking reflex	Finger or nipple inserted 2 inches into mouth	Rhythmic sucking	Disappears in 3–4 months
Walking reflex	Baby is held upright and soles of feet are placed on hard surface; baby is tipped slightly forward	Infant steps forward as if walking	Disappears in 3–4 months*

*Recently, the disappearance of the walking reflex has been questioned. Esther Thelen (Thelen, 1986; Thelen and Fisher, 1982) noted a similarity between the stepping reflex and infants' kicks when lying on their back. As infants mature, they show more kicking and Thelen argues that these kicks are a forerunner of stepping. The walking reflex disappears because, as the mass of their legs increases, it alters the way they can move. The infants' strength is sufficient when the body weight is supported as in the supine position (laying on the back) and the movement is aided by gravity. However, the strength is inadequate to lift the legs or support the weight when the infant is upright. The underlying mechanism, then, has not disappeared, but physical factors such as muscle strength make it impossible for the infant to show it.

Source: Dworetsky, 1984.

feet make contact with some hard surface (Cratty, 1979). Another interesting reflex is the swimming reflex. If infants are placed in water stomach down, they make swimming movements. These babies do not swallow water and can hold their breaths. Sometimes "instructors" capitalize on this swimming reflex during the first months of life to "teach" babies to swim. However, *extreme caution* must be taken, because these infants cannot hold their heads above the water and may drown easily. It is best to get both a physician's opinion concerning this activity and an expert's participation, because there is such a clear danger in this practice. The swimming reflex normally disappears by about the fourth month.

Brain Development and Behavior

The change from automatic, preprogrammed sensory, perceptual, and motor behavior to more voluntary activity is partly due to the development of the infant's central nervous system. At birth, the infant's brain weighs between 325 and 350 grams, while an adult male's brain weighs about 1,400 grams and a female's weighs 1,200

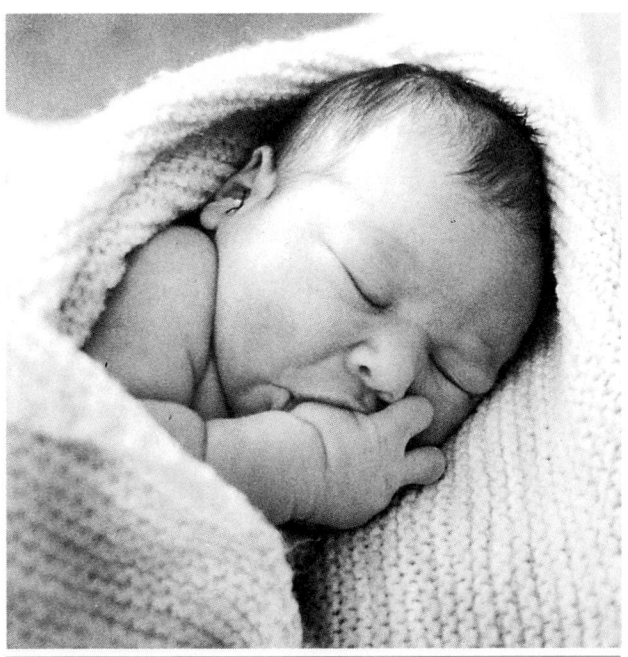

The sucking reflex is perhaps the most familiar reflex in young infants.

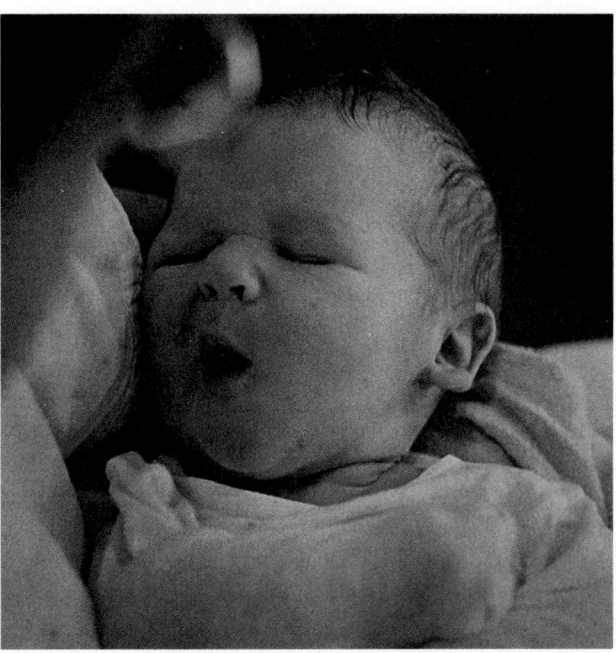

If an infant's cheek is stroked he turns his head in that direction.

grams. (There is no relationship between brain weight and intelligence, although an adult brain of less than 1,000 grams usually indicates intellectual retardation.) The newborn's brain weighs about 25 percent of a mature adult brain; by six months it weighs about 50 percent, and at two years of age it weighs about 75 percent (Brierly, 1976).

Most areas of the brain are not well developed at birth. The brain stem and spinal cord are the most advanced (Hutt and Hutt, 1973), because they are involved in critical psychological functions and behavioral responses. Most areas of the upper region of the brain, the cortex, are relatively undeveloped. The sensory and motor areas are functional, but at a primitive level. The neurons that carry instructions from the cortex to the motor nerves do not yet have the insulating cover called a myelin sheath, which is necessary for efficiently conducting impulses and increasing the speed of conduction (Strand, 1983). The process of myelinization is faster for the sensory tract than for the motor cortex. This has survival value, because the infant needs information from the senses in order to negotiate the environment safely.

Between three and six months a very important change occurs. The upper portion of the brain, the cortex, develops more rapidly. This switch from control by the lower, more automatic section of the brain to control by the upper, more voluntary centers affects behavior. For instance, many neonatal reflexes disappear within the first half-year of life because the upper centers of the brain are inhibiting these reflexes (Kalat, 1981).

True or False   Most of the infant's reflexes become stronger with time.

The Brain and Experience

The brain does not develop in a vacuum. Rosenzweig and his colleagues (1972), for instance, showed that the brains of rats who are raised in an enriched or impoverished environment differ. Experience makes an imprint on the brain, and lack of basic experience may hinder brain development. Although brain development is partly programmed by genes, experience is important. Visual experience speeds up myelinization of nerves in the visual cortex (Morrell and Norton, 1980). Wiesel and Hubel (1965) sewed one eye of a kitten closed for the first four to six weeks of life. After the sutures were cut and the kitten was allowed full use of its eyes, the cells that normally process visual information were unable to do so. There is a critical period of four to six weeks in which the cortical cells develop an ability to process informa-

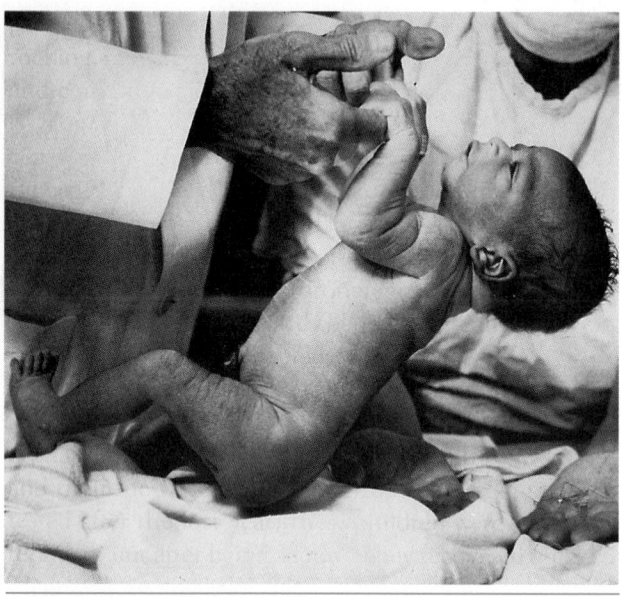

The grasping reflex is quite strong in infants.

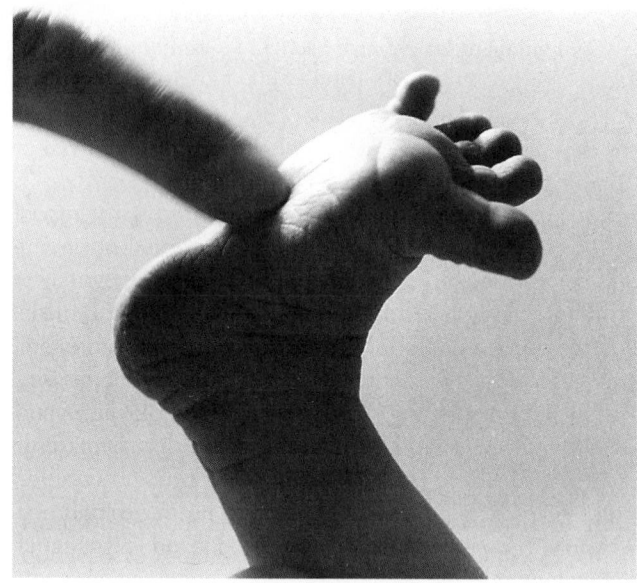

In the Babinski reflex, the toes fan out when the sole of the infant's foot is stroked.

tion from the eye. After that period, suturing the eye had little or no effect on the kitten.

Experiments like this cannot be performed on human beings, but there is evidence that there may be a similar critical period in the development of human sensory abilities. People who are cross-eyed have difficulty focusing both eyes and sometimes undergo operations to reverse the condition. If the operation is performed early in life—up to three years—the condition can be corrected and something like normal vision restored. But this is not true for adults who have the operation; they still show poor focusing even after the operation (Banks et al., 1975).

Sudden Infant Death Syndrome

A seemingly healthy baby goes to sleep. In the morning the baby is found dead. There is no sign of a struggle, no sign of any fight for life. An autopsy fails to discover any life-threatening condition. The cause of death is listed as Sudden Infant Death Syndrome (SIDS) commonly called crib death.

Perhaps as many as 10,000 infants in the United States die from this mysterious killer every year (DeFrain et al., 1982). Victims are usually between two and four months of age. Some 90 percent are younger than six months; 97 percent are younger than one year. SIDS is more common among the poor, but no family, regardless of income and social status, is immune. The child's mother is more likely to be a smoker, to have received less medical care, and to be either young or have had many children with short intervals between pregnancies (Guntheroth, 1982). However, many mothers of SIDS victims do not fit this pattern.

The cause of Sudden Infant Death Syndrome remains elusive. SIDS is indicated only where no other cause of death can be found. It is strange that a healthy infant would die in the night with no apparent cause. However, research has found that these infants may not be as healthy as they first seem. Between 40 and 50 percent of SIDS victims suffer from some respiratory infection right before their death. Some have a history of stress both before and after birth. The Apgar scores of these infants are significantly lower than those of babies who did not suffer SIDS (Guntheroth, 1982). These babies, then, appear to be members of an "at risk" population although they are essentially normal.

Because many victims of SIDS suffer from mild respiratory infections, research interest has centered on finding a relationship between SIDS and respiration. Many infants stop breathing for brief periods during sleep. These pauses are called apneic pauses. Perhaps the SIDS victim does not recover from these periods. But why? The SIDS victim may be weaker and possibly does not develop the

A sudden loud noise can cause the Moro reflex in which infants extend their arms and legs while arching their back, then contract them into a hugging position and cry.

The young infant shows swimming motions when placed in water.

ability to react to threats to survival. One theorist, Lewis Lipsitt (1978), argues this position. In the first month or so, the infant's defensive reactions to respiratory distress are reflexive. However, a learned reaction soon takes place. Perhaps the victim of SIDS fails to learn to defend against such dangers because of some subtle neurological problem. Other suggested causes of SIDS include botulism (poisoning due to a toxin transmitted by bacteria), heatstroke, and hormone imbalances (Fogel, 1984). Perhaps no single cause will explain every case of SIDS; a number of different agents are implicated in the disorder.

At times we can predict which infants will be at risk for SIDS, but not all victims fit any specific pattern. Among those who are most at risk are infants who have suffered an oxygen deficiency, have a high apnea rate, or have almost died from the disorder (near misses). These infants may be monitored in their own homes using an apnea monitor. The device rings an alarm if the infant stops breathing for a specific period of time, allowing parents to respond to the problem. But use of the monitor does not guarantee the infant's survival, and monitors may cause parents much distress. Parents may feel they cannot go outside or use a noisy appliance because they will not be able to hear the monitor ring.

Sudden Infant Death Syndrome is a family tragedy. Parents suffer self-doubt, guilt, and pain. There is a high rate of marital problems and divorce following the experience. When a child is born very prematurely or suffers some lingering disease, parents have time to prepare

for the possibility of an impending death, but SIDS does not afford parents that opportunity. The shock is great, the questions are many, and the answers are few.

Parents of SIDS victims can be helped in coping with their grief. Social support is available from groups of parents who have suffered similar tragedies, where parents of SIDS victims discuss their feelings and help one another. Professionals may also aid the family by offering parents the facts about SIDS as we know them today. Sometimes just the knowledge that an autopsy shows no cause of death alleviates some of the guilt.

Though Sudden Infant Death Syndrome is a mystery today, there is hope that research will reveal more about its causes so that we can prevent this silent killer from striking.

Growth and Motor Development

Nowhere are the changes in the infant more noticeable than in the areas of growth and motor development. Growth and weight gain during infancy and toddlerhood are shown in the Appendix. Heights and weights that fall between the 25th and 75th percentile are considered normal. For instance, a one-year-old male infant may weigh anywhere between 9.49 and 10.91 kilograms and still be within normal range. Those that fall outside these figures should be investigated by a doctor but may not indicate any problems.

Within six months the infant has grown more than 5 inches, and in the next three months 3 more inches will be added to the baby's length. In the entire second year the child grows approximately 4 inches. As impressive as the growth and weight gain in infancy may be, it represents a slowing down since the prenatal stage, in which sometimes weight doubles within a month.

A self-correcting process also takes place. If a baby's father is tall but the mother is short, the child's growth may be limited in the womb but the child may catch up during the first six months and return to normal growth rate (Tanner, 1970). Each child has a preordained path to travel in physical development (Waddington, 1957). Illnesses, stress, and nutritional inadequacy deflect the path for a time, but a self-righting tendency called **canalization** takes place. The child's natural growth trajectory may be permanently deflected from its course only if environmental deficiencies continue for a long period of time or are very severe.

Principles of Growth and Development

Infants do not develop haphazardly. Their development follows consistent patterns (Shirley, 1931) and is governed by principles that are now well understood. For instance, the head and brain of the infant are better developed at birth than the feet or hands. The **cephalocaudal principle** explains that development begins at the head and proceeds downward (cephalocaudal actually means from head to tail). Control of the arms develops ahead of control of the feet.

A second rule of development notes that organs nearest the middle of the organism develop before those farthest away. The **proximodistal principle** explains why the internal organs develop faster than the extremities. It also correctly predicts that control of the arms occurs before control of the hands, which predates finger control (Whitehurst and Vasta, 1977).

Muscular development follows a path from control of mass to specific muscles. First the individual develops control over the larger muscles, which are responsible for major movements. Then, slowly, control is extended to the fine muscles. This is why younger children use broad, sweeping strokes of the forearm or hand when coloring with a crayon. Only later does the child gain the dexterity to use finger muscles in a coordinated manner.

Development is also directional. It moves from a state of largely involuntary, incomplete control to one of voluntary control—from undifferentiation toward subtle

canalization The self-righting process in which the child catches up in growth despite a moderate amount of stress or illness.

cephalocaudal principle The growth principle stating that growth proceeds from the head downward to the trunk and feet.

proximodistal principle The growth principle stating that development occurs from the inside out, that the internal organs develop faster than the extremities.

differentiation. Under normal circumstances the movement is forward, with new abilities arising from older ones.

Motor Development

The first step a child takes is a milestone for the child and a joyous occasion for the parents. A new world of exploration is now open. Many parents may not be fully aware of the series of accomplishments that lead up to walking. Today we can predict what advancements in motor control will occur next, but not necessarily when they will happen. Shirley (1933) made exhaustive observations of a group of children beginning on the day of their birth. These infants all progressed through the same sequence, leading up to walking. Shirley was interested only in when infants would first perform any of the acts on her chart (see Figure 4.3), such as sitting with support or standing with help, not in how well they performed it. Each of these abilities is perfected with practice. Although the sequence of motor development stands, the ages noted are merely guidelines. Radical departures should be investigated, but each infant will negotiate each stage at his or her own rate. Some will stay longer at one stage than others. The age at which a child develops these abilities is a function of that child's maturation rate, as long as the child is well fed and healthy and has an opportunity to practice these skills.

The Question of Cultural Differences

Although individual differences in the rate of motor development are well accepted, the question of cultural differences is more difficult. For example, most researchers agree that African infants reach motor milestones like sitting and walking before European or American infants (see Super, 1981). How can we explain these differences?

The most obvious explanation involves a difference in the rate of maturation, which is largely influenced by genetics. This may be partly true, but there may be another explanation too. In many African societies, infants are reinforced for their motor behavior, even at very early ages. Parents play games with them using these emerging motor skills. In some tribes, mothers begin walking-training very early, and African children are placed in a sitting position and supported much more often than American babies. Differences in child-rearing procedures may thus partly explain the motor advancement. African infants are precocious with motor skills they have the most practice with (Super, 1981).

This raises two questions. What is the effect of lack of practice on the development of motor skills? Can motor skills be accelerated through a special training program?

The Effects of Practice and Stimulation

No one doubts that some opportunity to practice motor skills is necessary for development of these skills, but there are many roads to mastering them. Hopi children who were reared in the restrictive environment of the cradleboard still walked at about the same age as infants not reared on the cradleboard (Dennis and Dennis, 1940). These children received excellent stimulation and were allowed off the cradleboard more often as they matured. When Dennis and Najarian (1957) investigated the development of children growing up in a Lebanese orphanage, they found these children to be retarded in motor development in their first year. By the time they reached four to six years of age, however, they were normal. The greater opportunities these children experienced after the age of one was sufficient to counter their poor early environments. Although Dennis admitted that severe malnutrition results in motor retardation, he argued that it was due to environmental restriction and that this deficit could be remedied. If corrected, the effects of a deprived environment could be reduced and children can catch up on their motor skills. If nothing in the environment improves, these children would not develop normal motor abilities. Finally, Dennis argued that Shirley's mean ages for achievement of motor milestones are met only under favorable environmental conditions (Dennis, 1960). In other words, maturation alone

is not sufficient to explain motor development. The environment must be stimulating and provide opportunities for practice as well.

For most parents, however, the question is not one of overcoming stimulus deprivation but one of fostering motor development. To that purpose, a number of programs aimed at improving motor development have been advanced and have been shown to be somewhat effective. In one experiment, Zelazo and his colleagues (1972) found that a specific program of practice capitalizing on the stepping reflex enabled children to walk at an earlier age than expected. This is a controversial question, however, and evidence on both sides exists (Ridenour, 1978). Parents should be wary of stimulation programs that promise large gains in motor and cognitive development. Efforts would better be spent on optimizing the environment, allowing each child to take advantage of opportunities to explore and learn when the child is ready.

Choices

Most of the choices that affect the child in infancy are made by parents. These include feeding, toilet-training, and the extent to which children will be treated differently because of their gender.

Infant Nutrition

One of the first choices parents must make is whether to breast-feed or bottle-feed the baby. Infants' nutritional needs are different than those of adults (see Figure 4.4). Although bottle-feeding is popular in the United States, there has recently been a resurgence of breast-feeding. The overwhelming majority of women in third world countries breast feed their infants. However, there has been some decline in the practice (Lightbourne et al., 1982). This is unfortunate, because medical checkups to determine whether infants are getting the proper nutrition are not usually available. Misuse of prepared infant formulas has reportedly caused some infant deaths. In addition, the cost of prepared formula can be as much as half the family income in underdeveloped nations, which means families go without other necessities of life (Wade, 1974). The problem is not only one of encouraging breast feeding but promoting its continued use after the first few months. The experience of one country, the Philippines, is presented in the Cross-Cultural Current on page 108. In an attempt to encourage breast-feeding,

FIGURE 4.3

The Sequence of Motor Development Leading to Walking

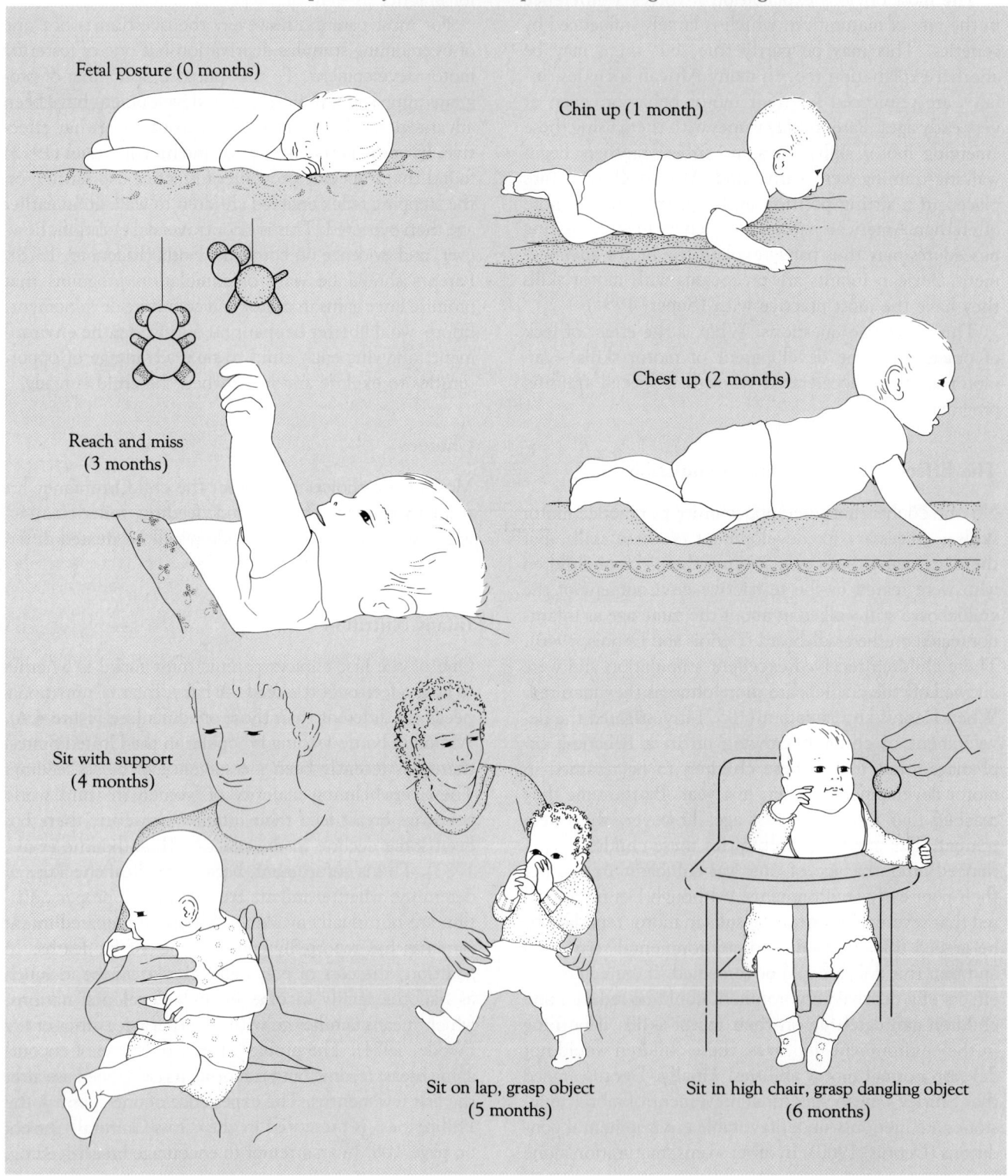

Fetal posture (0 months)

Chin up (1 month)

Chest up (2 months)

Reach and miss (3 months)

Sit with support (4 months)

Sit on lap, grasp object (5 months)

Sit in high chair, grasp dangling object (6 months)

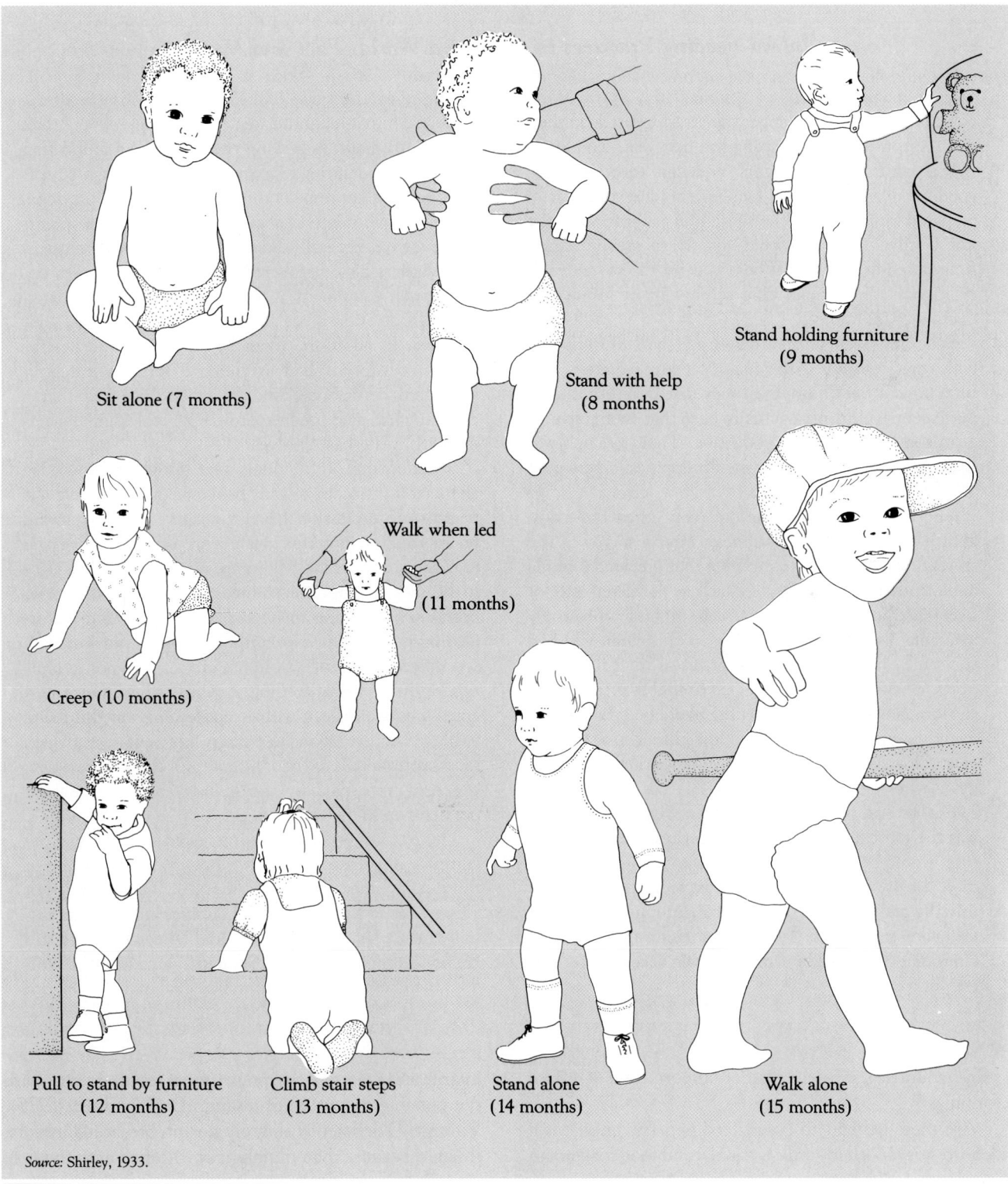

Sit alone (7 months)

Stand with help
(8 months)

Stand holding furniture
(9 months)

Creep (10 months)

Walk when led

(11 months)

Pull to stand by furniture
(12 months)

Climb stair steps
(13 months)

Stand alone
(14 months)

Walk alone
(15 months)

Source: Shirley, 1933.

Infant Feeding Practices in the Third World: Fact and Myth

Picture yourself as head of a project in a Third World country trying to encourage women to breast-feed their infants from birth and during the first year. You know this is better for the infants, and you know it makes good economic sense for families, because the cost of prepared formula would be so high in proportion to the low family incomes. Would you try to prevent stores from carrying formula? Would you try to prevent multinational corporations from selling infant formula to doctors or midwives?

Such steps seem logical, but when Charles Griffin and colleagues researched the infant-feeding situation in a rural area of the Philippines, they discovered that what may seem logical may actually be either ineffective or even sometimes counterproductive. Their research was done in the Bicol region of the Philippines, a very poor area about the size of the state of New Jersey.

The researchers' first question concerned the availability of breast-milk substitutes. After a survey of the stores in the area, they concluded that prepared formula and/or other milk substitutes, such as powdered milk or sweetened condensed milk, were almost universally available and that people living in this rural area had the same choices at the same prices as their urban cohorts. The investigators expected to find that the higher the formula prices, the greater the likelihood that infants would be breast-fed from birth and throughout the first year. However, this was not the case. The price and availability of formula did not affect the use of substitutes. Instead, proximity to a store carrying a substitute was the most important factor affecting whether substitutes would be used. The farther away the store was, the more likely women were to breast-feed their children initially and continue through the third month without using any substitutes. So the major factor in choice and continuation of feeding method was accessibility, not cost or availability.

The researchers also looked into the activities of the formula companies in the area. They surveyed more than 400 health facilities serving the region and found that most of the facilities received samples of prepared formula either all or some of the time. However, traditional midwives, who deliver about 65 percent of the infants in the region, generally did not receive such free samples. Interviewers also discovered that many companies donated such equipment as tape measures, growth charts, and identification bracelets and sponsored medical conferences. In addition, about 23 percent of the health-care professionals had attended a formula-industry-sponsored conference, and 5 percent reported that a company had paid their expenses for a professional meeting within the past two years.

When health professionals were tested for knowledge about and attitudes toward breast-feeding, the average health-care professional had a positive attitude toward breast-feeding, but the mean score on knowledge was only about 55 percent. Midwives, who are usually thought to be more supportive of breast-feeding, scored lower both on knowledge about and attitudes toward breast-feeding. We might expect that attending an industry-sponsored conference would lead to a less-positive attitude toward breast-feeding, but only when the conferences specifically dealt with infant-feeding was this found to be so. Neither talking to industry representatives (which most professionals did) nor attending a conference where expenses were paid by the industry was a significant predictor of knowledge.

The researchers were also interested in the actual occurrence of breast-feeding, not only at birth but also at three, six, nine, and twelve months. They found that 93 percent of a sample of 600 families with infants initially breast-fed their children, and 74 percent were still breast-feeding at one year. Some 62 percent of the children had also been fed formula, evaporated milk, or

some countries severely restrict importation of infant formulas.

Are there benefits to breast-feeding? The answer is a definite yes. Mother's milk is the natural food for human

infants and meets all their nutritional requirements, with the possible exception of vitamin D (Woodruff, 1978). Vitamin D deficiency is rarely seen in breast-fed infants, though, because that vitamin is synthesized with the help

other milk substitutes by the end of the first year. By the third month, 12 percent of the infants were being fed supplemental foods, and by the end of a year nearly all were getting solid foods.

What is the effect of receiving free samples of formula in the hospital? According to the researchers, this did not significantly affect whether a woman would initially breast-feed her infant, but it did lead to an increase in the probability that a woman would introduce breast-milk substitutes after three, six, or nine months.

If hospitals and local health professionals were given formula samples to distribute, women were less likely to breast-feed initially and more likely to use substitutes later, especially at nine and twelve months. Here the most important effect is the reduced probability of breast-feeding initially, at birth. But the decrease is quite small. If the average baby were taken from an area where health facilities did not distribute free samples to an area where samples were distributed, instead of having a 96 percent chance of being breast-fed at birth the chances would drop to 90 percent.

A debate is currently raging over the role multinational companies play in health care, especially in the Third World. But the debate often lacks hard facts, and studies, like this one offer some badly needed information. The researchers claim that their study provides important information that can be used to answer the following questions:

1. *What would be the effect of removing formula from stores?* Such a policy would not encourage initial breast-feeding behavior. In addition, in this study women were deterred from using substitutes not by the absence of formula or its price, but by the distance from the store.

Before removing the formula, the authors suggest that research determine whether the formula will be replaced by breast milk or by some other substitute.

2. *What would be the effect of restricting contacts between medical and formula company sectors?* This would reduce the amount of medical supplies and have a negative impact on the supply of medical information. However, it would have no effect on the traditional midwives, whose attitudes toward and knowledge about breast-feeding were generally poor. It does not seem the best way to proceed.

3. *What would happen if distribution of formula samples to mothers was curbed or eliminated?* This would result in a slight increase in breast-feeding at birth and reduce the probability that breast-milk substitutes would be introduced at three months. It would have its strongest effect on reducing the incidence of mixed feeding, which would indirectly increase long-term breast-feeding.

The real need is to get the information concerning breast-feeding to the midwives and other health professionals as well as to mothers. The promotion of prepared formula by formula companies appears to affect not so much the initial decision as to whether to breast-feed as an early switch to substitutes. In this regard, this study points out an area that has not been examined—how to encourage mothers to *continue* to breast-feed once the initial decision to do so is made. In the larger context, the study shows that the effects of formula promotion and availability on incidence of breast-feeding may not be as straightforward as first thought. Before jumping to what may seem like logical conclusions concerning the effects, we should first conduct painstaking research and consider the results carefully.

Source: Griffin, C. C., Popkin, B. M., and Spicer, D. S. Infant Formula Promotion and Infant-Feeding Practices, Bicol Region, Philippines. *American Journal of Public Health*, 1984, 74, 992–997.

of a normal amount of exposure to sunlight. Mother's milk also contains helpful substances not found in prepared formulas. Some antibodies protect the infant against intestinal disorders, and the mother's immunities are passed

on in breast milk. Mother's milk also contains chemicals that promote the absorption of iron. In addition, breast-feeding produces fewer fat infants, and the incidence of allergies is less than in infants raised on artificial for-

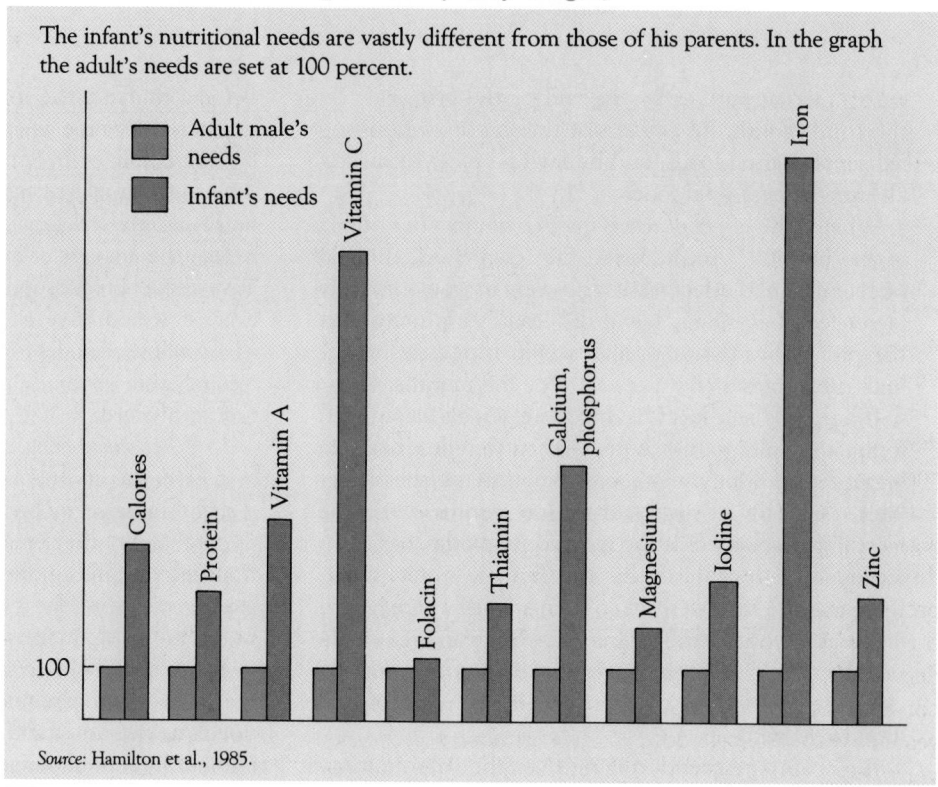

FIGURE 4.4

Nutrient Needs of Three-Month-Olds and Adult Males
(per unit of body weight)

The infant's nutritional needs are vastly different from those of his parents. In the graph the adult's needs are set at 100 percent.

- Adult male's needs
- Infant's needs

Calories · Protein · Vitamin A · Vitamin C · Folacin · Thiamin · Calcium, phosphorus · Magnesium · Iodine · Iron · Zinc

100

Source: Hamilton et al., 1985.

mulas. Breast-feeding also promotes better tooth and jaw alignment (Hamilton et al., 1985).

Breast feeding, then, is nutritionally sound. But what of bottle-feeding with prepared formulas? Some advocates of breast-feeding make outlandish unsubstantiated claims about the benefits of breast milk that causes guilt in mothers who want to bottle-feed, but there is no evidence of long-term differences between breast-fed and bottle-fed babies (Schmidt, 1979). However, bottle-feeding may require more thought and concern because the infant's nutritional and psychological needs are naturally satisfied during breast-feeding. The caregiver must be certain to hold the baby close to give the child the physical contact that is so important to infants.

Today, many infant formulas meet the nutritional standards set by the Committee on Nutrition of the American Academy of Pediatrics. Most formulas are based on fortified cow's milk, but the incidence of allergies to cow's milk is estimated to be less than 1 percent of the infants (Woodruff, 1978). Although breast-feeding may be preferable, there is no reason that a loving, caring parent should feel guilty about bottle-feeding an infant.

True or False An infant can be adequately fed using prepared formula instead of breast milk.

Infant Malnutrition

Severe malnutrition in infants has long-term consequences. Laboratory studies of inadequately fed animals indicate that malnutrition leads to deficits in the size and number of brain cells (Dobbing, 1975), and autopsies of severely malnourished infants show they have between 15 and 20 percent fewer brain cells than average healthy infants (Winick et al., 1970; Winick and Russo, 1969). Infants who are severely undernourished may develop marasmus A condition of severe underweight, heart irregularities, and weakened resistance caused by malnutrition.

kwashiorkor A nutritional problem often found in toddlers and preschoolers who are newly weaned and then subjected to a protein-deficient environment.

---

marasmus, a condition that involves severe weight problems. These children are literally all skin and bones. The heart is weakened, and resistance to disease is low. Between the ages of one and three, a common form of malnutrition in the Third World involves a protein deficiency called kwashiorkor, which occurs in newly weaned children when the child is subjected to a diet that is very deficient in protein. With this disorder, the child becomes apathetic and inactive, which is probably the body's defense against malnutrition. Fluid fills the abdomen and legs, and the child is quite weak. Normal childhood diseases can become life-threatening. Most of the time, protein and calorie deficiencies are found together. In the Third World this combination, called protein-calorie deficiency, is the most common nutritional problem, contributing to the death of millions of children each year. Malnourished children who survive may suffer severe growth problems, and malnutrition may permanently affect intellectual and emotional development (Eichenwald and Fry, 1969).

Although severe cases of malnutrition are relatively rare in Western, developed countries, they do sometimes occur in the poorest areas of those countries. However, a number of other deficiencies exist in developed nations. The most common is iron deficiency anemia. In addition, deficiencies in vitamin A, vitamin C, and riboflavin (a B vitamin) are not unusual (Eichorn, 1979).

Scientists have become more cautious in interpreting the data on the effects of malnutrition (Ricciuti, 1980a) because we now better understand the complex relationship between malnutrition and intellectual development. Malnutrition is found mostly among the poor, and it is difficult to evaluate the "independent" effects of malnutrition on the child (Ricciuti, 1980b). A malnourished child is probably experiencing poor housing, poor sanitation, little or no medical care, increased exposure to disease, poor feeding and child-care practices, and severely limited educational and vocational opportunities (Ricciuti, 1980b). Much of the early evidence linking malnutrition to intellectual and emotional deficits may have confused the injurious effect of malnutrition with the effects of poverty.

There is now evidence that the effects of malnutrition are mediated by a person's environment. Korean children suffering from various degrees of malnutrition and adopted before the age of two by middle-class families developed normal intelligence and did well in school (Winick et al., 1975). Jamaican children suffering from early severe malnutrition whose families scored fairly high on social-background measures had intelligence scores only slightly lower than average (Richardson, 1976). Intelligence test scores for malnourished children whose families scored low on social-background factors scored far below children whose families scored higher. Malnutrition may have a greater impact on children who come from poor environments, and the injurious effects of malnutrition can be moderated by improvements in the home environment. Malnutrition is likely to lead to permanent physical and intellectual damage if it is prolonged, if it occurs early in life, and if it is left untreated. Field work in Guatemala among children who suffer mild to moderate malnutrition demonstrates that dietary supplements can improve intellectual functioning somewhat (Townsend et al., 1982). If we are to help malnourished children develop normally, however, the entire environment must be substantially improved.

True or False The injurious effects of malnutrition can be reduced by a good environment.

Toilet-Training

An important event in toddlerhood is the beginning of toilet-training. One of the most common questions is how early to start. In one study, McGraw (1940) started to train one twin from each of two pairs as early as two months of age, while their siblings were allowed to wait. This early training did not help. The later-trained children trained much more quickly and were soon up to the others. Training started later is faster (Sears et al., 1957). It is best to train a child when the child is ready.

Some parents place a great deal of importance on early training. To expect a one- or two-year-old to be completely dry day and night is not only unreasonable but also possibly harmful, because it leads to criticism from parents when the child has an accident.

Once a child is maturationally ready, toilet-training should not take long. Azrin and Foxx (1976), authors of a book on the subject, do not recommend training a child much younger than two years old, and then they advocate using reinforcement and imitation. The toddler is carefully taught the mechanisms of going to the bathroom, including how to lower and raise his or her pants, being reinforced each step of the way. Then a doll that wets is used to illustrate the elimination process. The child sees the doll placed on a potty and wet. The child is then reinforced for doing the same. Sometimes candy is used to prompt the child to eliminate. Using this learning technique, the child who is ready can be trained quickly.

Sex Differences

The first announcement usually made to new parents is the baby's sex. In fact, the first question people ask when told a new baby has arrived concerns gender (Intons-Peterson and Reddel, 1984). How important is gender to the way infants are treated? Do any inborn physical differences exist at birth?

Sex differences at birth.   One of the most common sex differences at birth is that females are more physically mature and continue to develop at a faster rate. At birth, girls are four weeks more advanced in skeletal development (Tanner, 1970), and they reach later motor milestones faster than males. The average female child sits, walks, toilet-trains, and talks earlier than the average male child (Kalat, 1981). Another difference is that the average female infant performs more rhythmic behaviors, such as sucking and smiling, than the average male infant (Feldman et al., 1980). Still another is that males exceed females in large-muscle movements, such as kicking. Males also show greater muscular strength and can lift their heads higher at birth (Korner, 1973). However, when we take into account all the possible differences, the similarities between the sexes are more impressive than the differences.

True or False   At birth, females are more mature and continue to develop at a faster rate.

Interpreting early differences.   Early sex differences may affect parental behavior, magnifying the effects of the differences. The developmentally superior females may be more responsive and their ability to do things at an early age may be more reinforcing to parents. For these reasons, advanced development can be said to lead to more attention from and different types of interaction with the caregivers.

Some differences in parental treatment of sons and daughters are based not on any real differences but on the different expectations parents have of infant sons and daughters. For example, even when male and female infants are the same size, weight, and physical condition, parents see daughters as weaker and more sickly, and males as sturdier and more athletic (Rubin et al., 1974). When parents who had not even held their newborns, but merely seen them behind the nursery glass, were asked to describe their children, both fathers and mothers described the males as more alert and stronger and the girls as more delicate (Rubin et al., 1974). This labeling process continues throughout infancy and toddlerhood. College students were shown videotapes of nine-month-old infants demonstrating negative responses to a loud buzzer. When the subjects were told that the infants were male, they described the emotion as anger, but if the infants were described as female, the emotion was labeled fear (Condry and Condry, 1976). In another study, thirteen-month-old infants were observed in a play group. Although in one study no sex differences were found in assertive acts or attempts to communicate with adults, the adults attended more to boys' assertive behaviors and less to those of girls. However, adults attended more to girls when they used less-intense forms of communication. Eleven months later, sex differences were observed as boys were more assertive but girls talked to "teachers" more (Fagot et al., 1985).

As boys and girls develop, other differences become noticeable. Males are reinforced for attempts to develop gross motor skills involved in large-scale physical play more than females are (Smith and Lloyd, 1978). Boys are allowed to play alone more than girls (Fagot, 1978). Girls receive more praise and more criticism than boys. Fathers are more concerned with sex-appropriate behavior, giving more negative feedback to boys who play with dolls and other soft toys.

Three major conclusions stand out from the research on gender differences in treatment in infancy and toddlerhood. First, the initial differences between the sexes are quite limited at birth (Bee, 1978). Second, the treatment of males and females tends to be more similar than different, although the difference may in the end turn out to be important. Parents give both sons and daughters affection and do not usually tolerate aggression from either. Third, although parents often do not vocalize their sex-stereotyped opinions, they may show them in some of their behavior toward their children. Fathers are stricter in reinforcing these stereotyped "sex-appropriate" behaviors, especially in their sons, than mothers.

As children develop their physical skills, they travel from a state of reflexive, involuntary behavior to one of more voluntary control over the immediate environment. But the most important choices are made by others. The same pattern can be found in the cognitive development of the infant and toddler.

The Wonder of Cognitive Development

During the first two years of life, children develop a basic understanding of the world around them. They learn to recognize objects and people, to search for objects that are not in their field of vision, to understand cause and effect, and to appreciate the concept of space. The average adult takes this knowledge for granted, but a child's understanding of these concepts takes many months to develop.

Piaget's Theory of Sensorimotor Development

The manner in which infants develop an understanding of their world was described in detail by Jean Piaget. The infant is negotiating the first stage of cognitive development, the **sensorimotor stage** (Piaget, 1962). It is called "sensorimotor" because infants learn about their environment through their senses (hearing, vision, touching) and through their motor activity (reaching, grasping, kicking) (Piaget, 1967). How else does anyone get to know the world?

Much of our knowledge of the environment is symbolic. It is based on words and language and requires an ability to represent, or create, a mental picture of what is going on around us. For instance, when your friend tells you not to sit on the chair that has spilled coffee on it, you don't have to see the coffee or get your pants soggy. You understand the idea behind the statement and can create a mental picture of what has happened. All this is far beyond the abilities of the infant.

The Substages of Sensorimotor Development

It is easy to overlook the basic cognitive advances in infancy. The ideas that objects exist even if they are out

---

sensorimotor stage The first stage in Piaget's theory of cognitive development, in which the child discovers the world using the senses and motor activity.

---

of sight, or that by tugging at a string with a toy on the end, the toy will come toward you, must be learned. Piaget describes the development of elementary concepts in terms of six substages.

1. Reflexes (0–1 month). In substage one, infants are basically organisms reacting to changes in stimuli. The behavior of infants is rigid and reflexive. They are almost entirely dependent on these inborn patterns of behavior. Yet infants do learn and can be conditioned. During the first month, reflexes are often modified in an infant's everyday experience. For instance, an infant may suck harder if instead of a toy a bottle containing milk is placed in the mouth (Ault, 1977).

2. Primary circular reactions (1–4 months). The most prominent feature of substage two is the emergence of actions that are repeated again and again. These actions develop from modified reflexes and are called primary circular reactions. They are primary because they are focused on the infant's body instead of on any outside object (Phillips, 1975). They are circular because they are repeated. The infant tries to recreate some interesting happening. For example, the infant may have had a thumb drop into his or her mouth by accident. This is pleasurable, so after the thumb falls out, the infant attempts to find the mouth again (Ault, 1977).

3. Secondary circular reactions (4–8 months). An important change occurs in substage three. Secondary circular reactions are observed. Infants now focus their interest not only on their own bodies but also on the consequences of some action on the external environment. That is why they are secondary rather than primary reactions. The infant does something that is intended to create some environmental reaction. For instance, an infant shakes a rattle and is surprised to find that it produces a sound. The child may pause, then shake it again, hear the sound, and continue the activity (Flavell, 1985).

4. Coordination of secondary reactions (8–12 months).

In substage four, the child coordinates two or more secondary circular reactions to reach a goal. This shows intention. Means and ends are now separated. The child begins to show perseverance in spite of being blocked. For instance, if you place your hand in front of a toy, the child will brush it away. The change can also be seen in terms of play activities. Children will enjoy stacking items again and again, or banging a pot with a spoon over and over (Willemsen, 1979).

5. Tertiary circular reactions (12–18 months).

We now begin to see tertiary circular reactions—substage five. Although actions are still repeated and circular, they are no longer carbon copies of one another. Children now seek out novelty (Ault, 1977). They are little scientists, experimenting with their world in order to learn its characteristics and mysteries. The substage-five child picks up objects from the crib and throws them out, listening and watching intently to learn what they sound like and how they look on the floor (Willemsen, 1979). When you put them back in the crib, the child may do it again.

Ault (1977) describes the difference between the child's employing secondary circular reactions and using tertiary circular reactions. Suppose the child is placed in a playpen with lots of toys. The infant in the secondary circular reaction stage drops a block from a certain height again and again. He does not vary the action. The child in the stage of tertiary circular reactions may drop different items out of the playpen, and at different distances from the ground.

6. Invention of new means through mental combination (18–24 Months).

Substage six marks the beginning of representation, or the use of symbols (Flavell, 1977). The child can now think of an object independent of its physical experience. The character of play and imitation changes. Children are now capable of deferred imitation—that is, they can observe some act and later imitate it. Before going to bed, eighteen-month-olds may make pedaling motions with their feet, just as they saw older siblings do while riding bicycles hours before. Children also show some pretend play in this substage (Belsky and Most, 1982). Until now, spoons were something to suck on, to eat with, or to bang. Now a spoon may stand for another, unrelated object, such as a person or a piece of corn on the cob. The infant

> **object permanence** The understanding that an object exists even when it is out of one's visual field.

has moved from the realm of coordinated actions to that of symbolic representation.

Object Permanence

"Out of sight, out of mind" the saying goes. But to the young infant, objects that are out of sight quite literally cease to exist for him. Most students are surprised to discover that infants must torturously develop an understanding that objects exist outside their perception of them, an understanding known as **object permanence**.

The development of object permanence. Researchers study the development of object permanence by hiding objects in a variety of ways and observing children's search patterns. Infants develop their ability to understand object permanence in a series of substages identified by Piaget (1954). In substage one (0–1 month), infants look at whatever is in their visual field but will not search when the item or individual disappears. For instance, the infant looks at mother but doesn't search for her when she leaves the room (Ault, 1977). Instead, the infant looks at something else.

True or False The one-month-old infant believes that mother no longer exists when she leaves the room.

During substage two (1–4 months), the infant looking at some item will continue to look in the direction of the item after it disappears. However, Piaget does not see this as true object permanence because the search is basically passive (Piaget, 1954).

During substage three (4–8 months), we begin to see some active search for items. If an object is partially covered by a handkerchief, the infant tries to lift the cloth to discover the rest of the object (Diamond, 1982). Children who drop something from a high chair look to the ground for it. It is as if they can now anticipate the movement of an item. However, the child at this stage does not show complete object permanence; the search for the hidden object consists only of a continuation of eye movement—some expectation that something in motion may continue its trajectory. The child will not search for an object if it is completely hidden from view.

In substage four (8–12 months), the child will search for an item that is completely covered by a handkerchief.

In early infancy, babies do not show object permanence, the understanding that objects exist even though they are out of sight.

But if the child is allowed to find the item in one place, and the item is then hidden elsewhere while the child watches, the child will search in the first location. The child has simply identified the object with a particular location (Diamond, 1982).

In substage five (12–18 months), children can follow the object through the displacements. They no longer search for an item under the first pillow if it has been moved to a second pillow while they are watching. But the stage-five child's understanding of object permanence is far from perfect. Piaget designed a simple test to demonstrate the child's limitations. His daughter had been playing with a potato and placing it in a box that had no cover. Piaget (1954, p. 266) notes:

> I then take the potato and put it in the box while Jacqueline watches. Then I place the box under the rug and turn it upside down, thus leaving the object hidden by the rug without letting the child see my maneuver, and I bring out the empty box. I say to Jacqueline, who has not stopped looking at the rug and who has realized that I was doing something under it: "Give papa the potato." She searches for the object in the box, looks at me, again looks at the box minutely, looks at the rug, etc., but it does not occur to her to raise the rug in order to find the potato underneath.

Note that in this stage the movement from one hiding place to the other must be performed under the child's gaze. The child's search for a hidden object is still based on visual information. No logical inferences are formed, and there is no mental representation of the object.

During the last substage (18–24 months), children become free from the concrete information brought in through their senses. They can now construct a mental representation of the world and locate objects after a series of invisible displacements. They can imagine where an item might be (Diamond, 1982).

Object permanence and infant behavior. Piaget's description of the infant's cognitive development explains some common infant behaviors. For instance, children in substage five of the sensorimotor period who are dropping toys out of their playpens are not doing this out of any malicious intent—they are practicing tertiary circular reactions. And take the example of the old game of peekaboo, in which you cover your face with your hands, then take them away. As a child gains more knowledge of object permanence, the child will pull down your hands, exposing your face. The child is validating the expectation that you are still there. Or perhaps a four-month-old begins to cry hysterically after playing alone for a while, and you notice that the baby has dropped a toy out of sight. Because children younger than six months do not search for hidden objects, merely picking the toy up and putting it in the baby's field of vision may stop the crying.

Piaget's Theory Under Scrutiny

Piaget's description of infant and toddler cognitive development is accepted by many psychologists. Studies conducted all over the world have generally supported Piaget's view of the sequence in which children develop these skills (Nyiti, 1982; Kramer et al., 1975; Uzgiris, 1973). Piaget's descriptions hold under a variety of environmental conditions, although the development of object permanence and causality is delayed in some cultures and more advanced in others (Dasen and Heron, 1981).

Some problems remain, however. First, the way Piaget presented the tasks to infants may have affected their reactions. Second, a fundamental error in logic may have crept into these studies. Just because infants do not successfully complete a particular task does not mean they can't do it. Perhaps they have the ability to perform some task but either are not motivated to do so or cannot perform the motor activity required.

These arguments are too logical to dismiss without further consideration.

The competency-performance argument. The most intriguing argument is the contention that children may be capable of doing something but for some reason cannot or do not. Have you ever "known" something but been unable to put it into words? Perhaps you failed an essay test but felt that you knew the information—you just could not perform the required action of putting your knowledge on paper. Perhaps you didn't have the vocabulary or the time. Maybe the pressure was too great. Perhaps the questions were phrased in such a way that the correct response in your memory wasn't tripped.

Whenever an infant does not perform a particular task, Piaget interprets it in terms of competency: the child does not have the necessary cognitive sophistication. But some psychologists are not so sure about that. If we change the physical composition of the task, maybe the results would be different.

Characteristics of the task and the infant. There is some evidence that infants are more capable than Piaget believed. Individual and situational factors influence performance. When examining object permanence studies, such factors as familiarity with the object and motivation must be taken into account (Lingle and Lingle, 1981).

The testing procedures can lead investigators to make the logical but erroneous assumption that performance always reflects competency. Even the type of cover used when hiding an object seems to make a difference. Rader and his colleagues (1979) studied object permanence in infants whose median age was 160 days. They hid plastic keys in a well and covered the keys with either a 12-by-12-inch washcloth or a 7-by-7-inch piece of manila paper covered with blue felt. Infants differed in their success with the task. Some succeeded in uncovering the keys when the paper cover was used but not when the cloth cover was hiding their toys. The awkwardness of the covers used in an object permanence test may affect its outcome. The infant's physical abilities may be an important confounding factor in tests of object permanence.

The very nature of the three-dimensional task may also affect the infant's search pattern. Young infants have difficulty when an object is put inside another object. When a rattle is placed in a box, infants are confused, because they see the rattle not as being hidden but as having been replaced by the box (Bower, 1979). Bower and Wishart (1972) found that infants who could not find an object hidden under a cup could grasp an object dangling in front of them when the lights were turned out in the room. Infants can successfully retrieve objects from behind a two-dimensional barrier, such as a screen, before they can do so from a three-dimensional barrier,

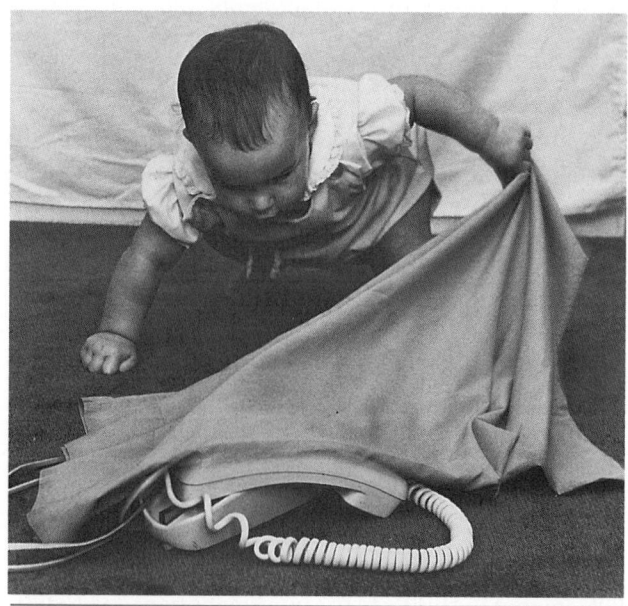

Later in infancy, children develop object permanence. This child isn't fooled by the presence of the blanket that conceals the telephone.

such as a box. The response demand of the search, such as whether a researcher demands successful retrieval or mere looking, is also a factor (Dunst et al., 1982). Bower (1971) argues that object permanence develops much sooner than Piaget believed, that infants do not show it because most studies force children to engage in an active search, which involves eye-hand coordination and motor skills. Another possible confounding variable is memory. Infants of about eight or nine months old were presented with the standard task of watching a researcher hide an object in Place A, then move it to Place B. The babies were forced to wait different amounts of time before being allowed to search for the item. If the infants were allowed to search immediately, they did not make the mistake of searching in Place A first, but if the babies were held back from searching for anywhere between three and fifteen seconds, some of them made the common error of searching in Place A (Gratch et al., 1974). Memory, then, is a factor as well. One reason older children perform better than younger children is that the former have better memories than the latter (Diamond, 1985).

Putting it all together.   We have two sets of findings. First, much evidence substantiates Piaget's contention that infants progress through a series of substages during the sensorimotor stage. Second, there is evidence that such factors as how the task is structured and the infant's memory, motivation, and physical skills affect performance on sensorimotor tasks. These findings do not disprove Piaget's theory, but rather extend it.

Piaget's description of infant cognitive growth is an excellent starting point. His descriptions of how a child progresses in infancy are well accepted and his descriptions have focused attention on this area and encouraged us to ask more detailed questions (Gratch, 1979). At the same time, however, the evidence showing that other factors may affect performance should make us wary of making generalizations about what an infant or toddler can or cannot do. The specific type of task presented to the infant, and its memory requirements, must always be noted. Infants follow Piaget's progression if tested in the standard Piagetian way. However, infants are very sensitive to the demands of the task. Analysis of what skills are necessary for success may yield information concerning why a child fails at a task. When a child must retrieve a hidden object, eye-hand coordination skills, motor skills, three-dimensional perception, and memory abilities are required. Piaget did not detail these skills. That task remained for others. Children who fail

recognition   A way of testing memory in which the subject is required to choose the correct answer from a group of choices.

recall   A way of testing memory in which the subject must produce the correct response given very limited cues.

a particular task may lack any one (or more) of these skills or abilities.

Memory in Infancy and Toddlerhood

The idea that infants remember things is easy to demonstrate experimentally but difficult to comprehend. We rarely retrieve memories from infancy or toddlerhood, yet memory is basic to the learning process.

Research on early memory focuses on recognition and recall. **Recognition** involves the ability to choose the correct response from a group of answers and is similar to the multiple-choice questions on a test. **Recall** involves producing the correct response on the basis of very limited cues and is similar to the task you face when taking an essay test. As a rule, our ability to recognize is far better than our ability to recall information (Wingfield and Byrnes, 1981).

Studies show that recognition is excellent even in very young infants. Three-month-old infants were presented with pictures of their mother. They were later able to tell the difference between their mother's face and that of a stranger (Barrera and Maurer, 1981). And infants show a surprising ability to retain information. Infants as young as two months were able to recognize a visual pattern and retain it for twenty-four hours (Martin, 1975). Fagan (1973) found that five- to six-month-old infants familiarized with a face for only two minutes were able to recognize it after a delay of two weeks. After performing a series of experiments, Fagan (1977) concluded that loss in recognition is the exception rather than the rule. Recognition does improve with age, with older infants showing superior retention on tests of recognition (Rose, 1981).

True or False   Three-month-old infants can recognize their mothers' faces.

Studies of recall are not as plentiful as research on recognition. Although Piaget (1968) argued that children do not show true recall before one-and-a-half to two years of age because of lack of representational skill, a memory process similar to recall has been found in eight-month-old infants (Brody, 1981). An increase in the ability to recall seems to take place between eight and twelve months. This period is one of rapid change in the infant's cognitive abilities. Neurological changes that improve memory occur (Kagan, 1979a; 1979b). The infant develops an ability to retrieve older information spontaneously and apply it to current circumstances. An improvement in recall is partly responsible for the child's increased ability to follow objects through displacement in object permanence studies in which toys are hidden in one place, a brief delay occurs, and then in sight of the child changed to place B (Diamond, 1985). As infants develop, they can tolerate longer and longer delays, making this mistake less and less unless the delay is fairly long. This improvement in memory can help us understand infant behavior. Suppose the father of a ten-month-old leaves the room. The child remembers his former presence and compares it with the current scene in which father is not here. If the child cannot resolve the difference, distress may occur. In addition, the ten-month-old may cry when mother walks toward the exit without leaving. Kagan believes that this child can now generate hypotheses about what might happen in the future and anticipates the mother's exit.

Cognitive Development in Infancy and Toddlerhood

Infants are hardly passive beings just waiting for the world to teach them something (Restak, 1982). They are quite active and develop their abilities quickly. During the first year, the infant becomes a goal-directed being and develops some idea of causality. By one year the child can search for completely covered objects and has developed some measure of object permanence. The child's memory is also developing, as is the ability to anticipate outcomes. At about one year, the child utters his or her first word(s). This is the culmination of a year of verbal and nonverbal communication with caregivers. The one-year-old knows the difference between a stranger and a loved one and may be walking or about to talk.

Cognitive development during the second year is impressive. The ability to walk allows children of this age to explore the environment more fully, and their vocabulary grows. They master the finer points of object permanence and in the last six months of their second year can no longer be confused by difficult hiding pro-

cedures. By the end of the second year, the child has developed representational thought—that is, can now think without acting (Ault, 1977). Children at this point are no longer sensorimotor in the truest sense of the term—relying solely on the information they have obtained through the senses and motor activity. They can now construct a mental image of the world, and they can defer imitation—seeing an event at one time and imitating it later.

Predicting Later Intelligence

Psychologists are always interested in predicting some future behavior on the basis of past behaviors or circumstances. For instance, what if we knew which behaviors or capabilities in early infancy are forerunners of intellectual achievement during the school years? We could then isolate these important abilities that predict later achievement and perhaps help children develop them. A number of such possible predictors already exist, including infant intelligence tests, socioeconomic status, information-processing abilities, and the characteristics of the home.

Predictions from Tests: The Bayley Scales

The most popular way to measure the intellectual abilities of the infant and toddler was devised by Nancy Bayley and her colleagues (Bayley, 1969; Bayley and Oden, 1955). The **Bayley Scales of Infant Development** can be used to assess the abilities of infants from two months through two and a half years. The Mental Scale measures such functions as perception, memory, learning, problem-solving, and vocalization (Anastasi, 1976). The Motor Scale measures such motor abilities as sitting, standing, stair-climbing, hand skills, and coordination. The Infant Behavior Record is designed to assess such qualities as attention span, persistence, and emotional and social behavior. The observer is asked to rate the infant on responsiveness, cooperativeness, fearfulness, and activity level. The Bayley Scales describe the infant at the time the assessment is done but do not seem to have much predictive validity with normal infants (McGowan et al., 1981; McCall, 1979). Only after eighteen months does the child's score on infant intelligence tests have any predictive abilities, and then only when added to some measure of socioeconomic status (McCall, 1979). However, the Bayley Scales are useful in predicting the intelligence of infants who are neurologically impaired or have some other defect (Rubin and Balow, 1979; McCall et al., 1972).

True or False Scales measuring infant intelligence can accurately predict later childhood intelligence.

Information-Processing Skills

Some researchers have recently tried to isolate certain infant behaviors or skills that may predict later development (see Bornstein and Benasich, 1986). One behavior showing promise in this regard is the speed of habituation during infancy which is related to measurements on such Piagetian tasks as object permanence during early toddlerhood (Miller et al., 1977) and speaking vocabularies at twelve months (Ruddy and Bornstein, 1982). Another study showed that visual recognition memory at six months predicted scores on tests of cognitive skills from two to six years in preterm infants (Rose and Wallace, 1985). Such information-processing abilities as the ability to encode visual stimuli efficiently and to remember visual or auditory stimuli are related to superior performance on traditional tests of verbal intelligence and language tests during childhood (Bornstein and Sigman, 1986). Although these developments are interesting, more research in this area is needed.

Socioeconomic Status and Cognitive Development

The socioeconomic status of the child in the first twelve to eighteen months appears to be a good predictor of later intellectual development (McCall et al., 1972). Socioeconomic status is usually analyzed in terms of income, parental educational level, and occupational rating (Rubin and Balow, 1979). Low-socioeconomic-status homes differ greatly from middle- and higher-socioeconomic homes, especially in the area of verbal behavior (Tulkin and Kagan, 1972). Low-socioeconomic-class mothers talk much less to their infants. Perhaps because of lack of education or the stresses of poverty,

Home Observation for Measurement of the Environment (HOME) A scale that provides a measure of the quality and quantity of the emotional and cognitive elements in the home.

they may not provide the verbal stimulation or the environment necessary for their children to develop adequate cognitive skills.

Yet there is something unsatisfactory about the entire concept of socioeconomic status. It is too broad and too general a consideration, and it ignores the wide variations in intelligence within socioeconomic levels. It would be better to focus on the differences among families (Ramey et al., 1979). General statements noting that the lower-socioeconomic-status parent does this or that ignore these differences and stigmatize an entire group of people. Finally, socioeconomic status is not an easy variable to change. Poverty, lack of education, and a low-status job cannot be altered overnight by a child development specialist. Because these factors are so important, professionals may have an obligation to help improve the lot of the poor. However, a specific approach stressing behaviors and specific environmental variables instead of social class may be more helpful in uncovering clues to intellectual development. These environmental factors may be more susceptible to change. For instance, if we find that children of parents who are responsive and who speak to them are intellectually advanced in middle childhood, we can help parents develop these skills and change the pattern of parent-child interactions. If we find that the absence of books in the house makes a difference, we can not only provide the books but also teach parents how to use them. There has already been a start in this direction. We have discovered that certain types of parent-child interactions and discrete elements of the physical environment facilitate cognitive growth.

Predictions from the Home Environment

One instrument frequently used to measure various aspects of the home environment is called the **Home Observation for Measurement of the Environment,** or **HOME** for short. This scale provides a measure of the quality and quantity of the emotional and cognitive elements in the home setting (Elardo et al., 1977). The inventory measures six factors, including the mother's emotional and verbal responsiveness, the avoidance of restriction and punishment, the organization of the environment, provision of appropriate play materials, maternal involvement with the child, and opportunities for variety in the daily routine (see Figure 4.5). Information is collected through an interview and observation.

Using the HOME instrument, Bradley and Caldwell (1980, p. 1145) discovered a "substantial relationship between home environment in the first year of life and IQ at age three." The HOME score is an effective predictor of IQ and language. Evaluations of specific elements of the home environment are more efficient in predicting future intellectual growth than either infant tests or parental education (Elardo et al., 1975). For example, the intensity and variety of stimuli are related to intellectual development (Wachs, 1971). Carew and his colleagues (1975) found that positive experiences in verbal and symbolic learning—such as labeling objects, perceptual, spatial, and fine motor experiences such as matching, color discrimination, and problem-solving activities—were related to IQ scores at three years.

At this point, some tentative conclusions can be drawn. Such factors as the responsiveness of the caregiver, parental involvement with the child, the variety of stimulation available, the organization of the environment, the caregiver's restrictiveness, and the play materials available at an early age predict later cognitive development. One point should be kept in mind, though. A healthy environment in infancy is usually carried over throughout childhood. An unhealthy environment in infancy rarely improves greatly in childhood. Some of the relationship between the environment during in-

---

FIGURE 4.5

The HOME Inventories: Assessing a Child's Home Environment

The importance of a child's home environment is a favorite theme of developmental psychologists. Bettye M. Caldwell formulated a tool which attempts to assess this crucial element in the child's development. An observer spends about an hour in the family's home watching the normal daily routine and occasionally asking a question. The observer checks off items on the inventory.

This instrument, called the HOME Inventory, exists in two forms. The first is meant to assess the home environments of children from birth to age three and consists of forty-five items; the second is used to assess the environments of preschoolers (three- to six-year-olds) and contains eighty items. Although the full inventories are too long to present here, the main categories are noted below.

Home Observation for Measurement of the Environment (Birth to Three Years)

Categories

1. Emotional and verbal responsivity of mother
2. Avoidance of restriction and punishment
3. Organization of physical and temporal environment
4. Provision of appropriate play materials
5. Maternal involvement with child
6. Opportunities for variety in daily stimulation

Home Observation for Measurement of the Environment (Three to Six Years)

1. Provision of stimulation through equipment, toys, and experiences
2. Stimulation of mature behavior
3. Provision of a stimulating physical and language environment
4. Avoidance of restriction and punishment
5. Pride, affection, and thoughtfulness
6. Masculine stimulation (involves time spent with father and the availability of toys such as jump ropes, swings, and balls which encourage large-muscle development)
7. Independence from parental control

fancy and later intellectual ability is a reflection of the cumulative effects of the environment throughout childhood and does not solely demonstrate the importance of the earliest environment.

Parents and Cognitive Development

Most factors that affect cognitive development are determined by the child's parents. White (1971) studied the differences between mothers of competent infants and mothers of less-competent infants and found three major differences. The mothers of competent children were designers—that is, they constructed an environment in which children were surrounded with interesting objects to see and explore. They were able to understand the meaning an activity or experience might have for a child and build on it. Second, parents of competent children interacted frequently with their children in interplays of twenty- to thirty-second duration. The children were not smothered with attention, but these parents were always available and ready to help their children experience events. They often labeled the environment for them and helped to share a child's excitement. Third, the parents of these children were not overly permissive or overly punishing. They had firm limits, but they were not unduly concerned about such minor problems as mess and bother.

True or False Parents of competent infants spend many hours of time teaching them concepts.

The research on cognitive development can be translated into a number of parental activities that encourage the cognitive growth of children. Some of these are as follows.

Provide opportunities for exploration. Children are active learners and need to have all their senses stimulated. Such environmental stimulants as a mobile above the crib and a few safe, brightly colored toys are important. A bit later, try to provide experiences for the infant that involve materials of different colors, textures, and shapes.

Label the environment. It is important to label the environment. When the child appears to be communicating in a prelinguistic mode, it is beneficial to say "So you want a cookie?" while holding the cookie up and emphasizing the word.

Encourage verbalizations. As children grow, the number of verbalizations they utter will increase. The child begins to use words usually in the second year of life. Encourage communication even in the prelinguistic stage. When children become older and begin using words, encourage them to expand their vocabulary. Children need a willing audience and encouragement to develop their linguistic skills.

Read to the child. Reading to the child can start early, and you can tailor your technique to the age and ability of the child. For instance, young children can point to various objects in a book, such as a ball. Later your questions can expand to questions of color, shape, and so on.

Ensure brief interactions between parents and child. Those twenty-to thirty-second encounters can be valuable. Some people believe that spending every minute of their time with their children is desirable, but this is not the case. As children mature, their attention span will increase, and interactions can become more involved and longer. However, sharing even a brief experience with a child is beneficial.

True or False Interactions with infants and toddlers of less than one minute have no effect on their cognitive development.

Tailor activities to the child's developmental level. Most child specialists who write books about parental activities that can optimize cognitive growth note that these activities should be low-key and fun. A problem arises when parents believe they are conducting an academic activity and put pressure on their children to achieve too early (Zinsser, 1981). Parental disappointment, anxieties, and expectations can be communicated to young children quite early and may hinder the very development that parents seek to improve. Infants and toddlers have limited attention spans and may go from activity to activity quickly. Equally important is understanding that enriched environments do not always lead to accelerated or enhanced cognitive or perceptual development. Enhanced environments help when there is a match between the encounter and the child's abilities (Hunt, 1961).

The Question of Acceleration: The "American Question"

American educators and parents often ask how fast or how early a child can accomplish a certain academic task. We are impressed by the child who is reading at the age of three or solving algebraic equations at age eight. Reflecting this fascination with speed, researchers have raised the question of whether infants can be accelerated through the various periods of sensorimotor experience. The entire idea actually runs counter to Piaget's ideas.

Piaget was reluctant to make any recommendations to teachers or parents concerning how to maximize a child's potential, let alone how to accelerate the child (Vernon, 1976). Remember that Piaget's theory emphasizes the importance of maturation and giving children an opportunity to interact with the environment—and deemphasizes formal instruction. Parents can help their children by designing an environment that is appropriate for the children at their particular point in development and elaborating on that environment, giving children plenty of opportunity to discover things on their own. For instance, when presenting children with objects of different textures, it is beneficial to have a variety of such objects in the environment and to allow the children to explore them at their own rate. This does not mean that the parents remain passive. Indeed, parents should be available to answer questions, interact with the child, and so on, but the emphasis is on discovery, not on formal teaching and programming.

Perhaps we should put the question a different way. The purpose of improving interaction with parents and designing a stimulating and appropriate atmosphere for infants is to provide the optimal atmosphere for children to develop their cognitive potential. At certain stages, certain experiences are beneficial, but the goal should not be to see how fast a child can get through Piaget's stages. Instead, the goal is to provide experiences that will help the child develop according to his or her own rate and abilities. Such an environment is child-centered and provides the child with the opportunities to interact and learn.

There are times when parents and professionals must become more active in designing a program of stimulation. Rose (1981) found significant differences in the recognition memories of full-term and preterm infants, but when preterm infants received extra stimulation during the early weeks of life, their performance on memory tasks was similar to that of full-term infants. Infants who are not at risk might also benefit from a more active program, but the power to accelerate development is not unbounded. If cognitive development can be accelerated, an upper limit to this acceleration probably exists.

And there are risks. Parents may put pressure on their infants and toddlers to perform and may have unreasonable expectations that can interfere with normal development.

The value of trying to accelerate infants through the sensorimotor period is doubtful, especially since correlations between sensorimotor intelligence and later cognitive achievement are so low (Lewis and McGurk, 1972). The best course is to design a stimulating environment for children and to have parents interact with their infants so that they can gain the appropriate skills. Rushing a child through this stage accomplishes little. Because development is faster does not necessarily make it better.

Conclusions

The infant begins life with certain preprogrammed physical and cognitive behaviors. As the child matures and interacts with the environment, he or she develops new physical and cognitive skills that allow the infant and toddler both to explore the environment and to develop an understanding of the world around them. Such activities as labeling the environment, interacting in a positive manner with children, and encouraging children

The intellectual level of the home and nature of the parent-child interaction may affect later cognitive abilities.

to investigate and explore their world are clearly helpful in promoting development. Parents can and should be active in these areas, but they must also beware of overdoing it, of pressuring their infants, of believing that faster is always better, or of becoming schoolteachers instead of being parents.

Finally, there is no magic age at which it is "all over." Infant development is important, but it is possible to improve the lot of a child who has not experienced an optimal early environment—if there is a significant change in the environment (Clarke and Clarke, 1976). Of course, the sooner such a positive change is made, the better it is for the child. Although we should not underestimate the importance of early development, neither should we overestimate it.

We have now seen how the child develops from a newborn infant with few skills to a two-year-old with an impressive repertoire of abilities. But the rash of interest in early cognitive development should not blind us to the importance of the child's personality and social development. After all, we want our children not only to be intellectually advanced but also to develop their personality and social abilities. It is to these qualities that we turn next.

Summary

1. The neonate is born with characteristics and abilities that make survival possible. Newborns can see, hear, smell, and taste. Although they are relatively insensitive to pain at birth, this sense increases dramatically during the next few days.

2. Neonates spend between sixteen and seventeen hours a day sleeping. The infant's state is related to behavior. A number of cries have been identified, including hunger, pain, and angry cries.

3. Classical and operant conditioning has been demonstrated in the infant. Infants can also imitate.

4. The neonate is born with a number of reflexes, such as the sucking, rooting (turning the head toward a source of stimulation when a cheek is stroked), grasping, stepping, and swimming reflexes. The functions of other reflexes, such as the Babinski reflex (fanning of the toes when soles of the feet are stroked) and the Moro reflex (extending arms and legs while arching the back, then contracting them in a hugging manner) are not known.

5. The brain grows rapidly in the months following birth, and such factors as nutrition and experience are important in optimizing growth.

6. There are nutritional and health advantages to breast-feeding, but there is no evidence of long-term differences between children who were breast-fed and those who were bottle-fed. In the Third World, malnutrition is a major problem that leads to many developmental problems, including a smaller number of brain cells. The effects of lesser degrees of malnutrition is more controversial. The effects of malnutrition are mediated by the environment.

7. Genetic considerations and nutrition both affect development. Acute illnesses and stress may deflect children from a normal growth trajectory, but a self-righting process enables them to return to normal when the stress is past. Development occurs in a consistent pattern from the head downward (cephalocaudal) and from the inside out (proximodistal), and muscular development progresses from mass to specific.

8. Sex differences in infancy are moderate and unstable, but parents tend to treat infant sons and daughters differently.

9. According to Jean Piaget, infants are negotiating the sensorimotor stage, during which they use their senses and motor skills to learn about the world. They do not have the ability to create mental images or to use language or symbols to represent anything.

10. The development of object permanence, the understanding that an object or person exists even if it is out of sight, is an important achievement in infancy.

11. One should not equate competency (knowledge and ability) with performance. Performance depends on motivation, the type of task presented to the infant, and other environmental factors.

12. Infants have the ability to recognize faces very early. Between eight and twelve months they show some recall abilities.

13. Scores on infant intelligence tests do not predict later intellectual ability well, but some information-processing abilities such as visual recognition hold some promise in this area. The responsiveness of the caregiver, parental involvement with the child, the variety of stimulation the child receives, the organization of the environment, and the play materials available relate to later cognitive development.

14. The so-called "American question" asks whether we can and should accelerate cognitive growth. Such acceleration was discouraged by Piaget, who believed that if children live in an appropriately designed environment and are given an opportunity to discover the mysteries of life, they can develop their cognitive abilities.

Answers to True or False Statements

1. *True*   The newborn is nearsighted at birth, but by six months visual acuity approaches that of a normal adult.

2. *False*   Correct statement: Newborns can hear at birth.

3. *True*   Newborns are relatively insensitive to pain, but sensitivity to pain develops quickly.

4. *False*   Correct statement: Many infant reflexes become weaker and finally terminate.

5. *True*   Many infant formulas meet nutritional standards for infants.

6. *True*   We now know that a good environment can reduce the injurious effects of malnutrition.

7. *True*   The average female infant is more mature at birth than the average male infant and develops at a faster rate.

8. *True*   At this age it is literally "out of sight, out of mind."

9. *True*   Research shows that three-month-old infants can recognize their mothers' faces.

10. *False*   Correct statement: For normal infants, scores on infant intelligence tests do not predict later intelligence.

11. *False*   Correct statement: Parents of competent infants do not smother their children with attention.

12. *False*   Correct statement: Interacting briefly with children to share experiences with them is one way to encourage cognitive development.

CHAPTER 5

Social and Personality Development in Infancy and Toddlerhood

Are the Following Statements True or False?

Try the True-False Quiz below. See if your answers correspond to the information in this chapter. Each question is repeated after the paragraph in which the answer can be found. The True-False Answer Box at the end of the chapter lists the complete answers.

_____ **1.** Fear of strangers is an abnormal response in infants and toddlers and indicates insecurity.

_____ **2.** Poor mothering in early infancy results in permanent retardation, even if the child's environment is later improved.

_____ **3.** The quality of a child's attachment to the primary caregiver cannot change after the age of six months.

_____ **4.** Older mothers have a more positive attitude toward motherhood than younger mothers do.

_____ **5.** Firstborn children receive more attention than later-born children.

_____ **6.** Early and extended contact immediately after birth is necessary if infants are to develop a healthy attachment to their mothers.

_____ **7.** Infants become attached to their fathers as well as to their mothers.

_____ **8.** Most children in need of day care attend licensed day-care centers.

_____ **9.** Children in day care do not form attachments to day care workers since they have already formed attachments to mother and father.

_____**10.** Fathers are generally more active in child care when mothers are employed.

_____**11.** Maternal employment has no effect on a child's social or cognitive development.

_____**12.** Toddlers interact more if many small toys, rather than a few larger toys, are available.

The Changing Patterns of Child Care

Like so many American families, Lisa and Tim Walters needed every penny to keep their heads above water. With two children (Beth, age two, and Jon, eight months), a modest home, and two cars, they were just breaking even. They had decided that Lisa would stay home and be a full-time homemaker until the youngest child entered elementary school. Then she would return to work. Both agreed that this was the best strategy. It combined their belief that the early relationship between mother and child was important and the reality of needing two incomes as the children grew.

But then Tim was laid off from his job. Unable to afford a long layoff, he took a lower-paying position and returned to school for retraining. Trapped by car payments and a hefty mortgage, Lisa and Tim fell into debt. They finally decided that Lisa should go back to work.

Lisa and Tim are concerned. The two-year-old will have to enter a day-care program, while the baby will either be in day care too or be taken daily to Lisa's mother. The parents have many questions. How will the experiences affect the children? How will these constant but temporary separations affect their relationship with their youngsters? How will Lisa's working affect the family? Is day care harmful to children?

Many American families are asking the same questions. Over the past thirty years, the number of women in the labor force and the proportion of working mothers has increased dramatically (see Table 5.1 and Figure 5.1). Some 18.6 percent of married mothers with preschoolers worked in 1960, while 54.4 percent did so in 1986. About two thirds of all divorced mothers with preschoolers work. Many people equate the working mother with the single parent, and indeed most single parents work—but more than half of all parents in two-parent families also work (U.S. Bureau of the Census, 1986).

So the Walters' dilemma is not unusual, and the questions they ask are vital. This chapter will investigate the social, emotional, and personality development of infants and toddlers and answer the Walters' questions.

Emotional Development in Infancy and Toddlerhood

How Emotions Develop

One of the Walters' concerns involves the emotional development of the children. Emotional development in infancy follows a distinct pattern. Early emotions re-

---

T A B L E   5.1

Women in the Labor Force with Young Children (in thousands)

Today, many women are entering the labor force when their children are small.

Presence and Age-Group of Children	Civilian Noninstitutional Population	Civilian Labor Force	Civilian Labor Force Participation Rate
Total women, 16 years and over	94,490	51,732	54.7
No own children under 18 years*	61,653	31,112	50.5
With own children under 18 years	32,837	20,620	62.8
Children 6 to 17 years	17,143	12,075	70.4
Children 6 to 13 years	11,315	7,866	69.5
Children under 6 years	15,694	8,545	54.4
Children under 3 years	9,421	4,786	50.8

*Children are defined as "own" children of the family. Included are never-married daughters, sons, stepchildren, and adopted children. Excluded are other related children, such as grandchildren, nieces, nephews, and cousins, and unrelated children.

Source: Bureau of Labor Statistics, 1986.

flected in the infant's cry and smile are reflexive. As children develop, these early emotional responses begin to be triggered by specific environmental stimuli. Mother's voice may bring forth a smile in the infant, and later in infancy seeing the doctor's office may lead to crying. As the child develops, emotions such as fear, anxiety, joy, pleasure and surprise become more differentiated from one another (Yarrow, 1979; Bridges, 1933). Emotional development occurs in a sequential pattern, as outlined in Table 5.2. Both experience and central nervous system development are implicated in the child's expanding repertoire of emotions.

A child's emotions affect the caregiver. When parents label emotions in the first few months, they rely on the context to appreciate what the child is experiencing. Although context remains important, children's emotions become more recognizable as children develop. Later,

parents learn to elicit positive emotions, such as smiling, in their infants, which in turn reinforce the parents' own behavior.

Fear and Anxiety

Two situations commonly produce fear or anxiety in infants and cause parents concern: fear of strangers and separation anxiety. Both Beth and Jon Walters show some fear of strangers, and their parents want to know if this is normal. In addition, Beth and Jon don't like being left with a baby-sitter, and the parents wonder how the children will react to being left in a day-care environment.

Fear of strangers. Sometime in the second half of the first year, parents are surprised by the way their infants react to kindly strangers. In the past the baby showed

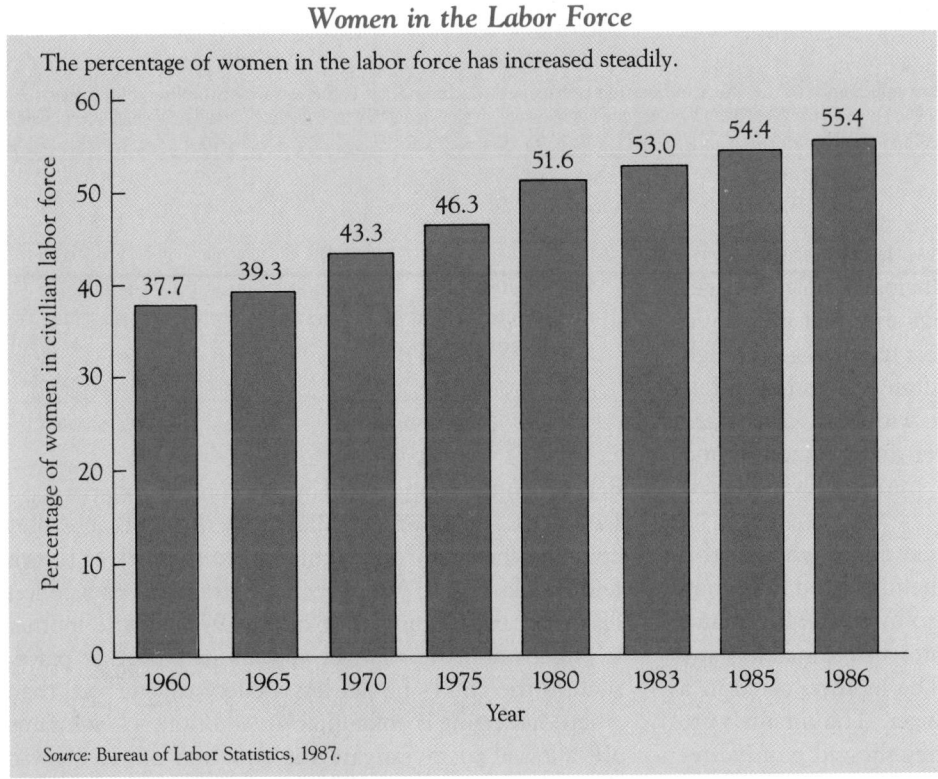

FIGURE 5.1

Women in the Labor Force

The percentage of women in the labor force has increased steadily.

Source: Bureau of Labor Statistics, 1987.

T A B L E   5.2

The Development of Some Basic Human Emotions

Emotions develop in a sequential pattern, becoming more complex as the child ages.

Age (months)	Pleasure-Joy	Wariness-Fear	Rage-Anger
0	Endogenous smile	Startle/pain	Distress due to: covering the face, physical restraint, extreme discomfort
		Obligatory attention	
1	Turning toward		
2			
3	Pleasure		Rage (disappointment)
4			
	Delight	Wariness	
	Active laughter		
5			
6			
7	Joy		Anger
8			
9		Fear (stranger aversion)	
10			
11			
12	Elation	Anxiety	Angry mood, petulance
		Immediate fear	
18	Positive valuation of self-affection	Shame	Defiance
24			Intentional hurting
36	Pride, love		Guilt

Note: The age specified is neither the first appearance of the affect in question nor its peak occurrence; it is the age when the literature suggests the reaction is common.

Source: Sroufe, 1979a.

curiosity, but now the child shows fear, manifested by crying and agitation. Until about four months of age, infants smile even at strangers, but after that they do so less and less (Bronson, 1968). Most children go through a period in which they react to strangers, and even relatives they do not see regularly, with fear. This stage usually comes between about seven and ten months and may last through a good portion of the second year (Lewis and Rosenblum, 1975).

Some studies, though, have questioned whether this **fear of strangers** is inevitable. Rheingold and Eckerman (1973) allowed an adult female to interact with infants and their mothers for ten minutes before making any attempt to pick up the babies. The mothers acted in a friendly manner toward the stranger. The infants were neither fearful nor upset, and they showed positive responses to the stranger. Infant responses to strangers

fear of strangers   A common phenomenon beginning in the second half of the first year, consisting of a fear response to new people.

depend on the stranger and on the context. Infants show less or no fear of other children, perhaps because they compare the size of these children to themselves (Lewis and Brooks-Gunn, 1972). Female strangers produce less fear than male strangers (Skarin, 1977). If the mother is present and the stranger appears in a familiar place, such as the child's home, less anxiety is generated than when the setting is unfamiliar. In addition, when infants are allowed to investigate the situation on their own, they do not always show stranger anxiety.

Stranger anxiety, then, is mediated by a number of factors, and Lisa and Tim Walters can be assured that a fear of strangers is normal at their children's ages. Because stranger anxiety can be reduced if the meeting takes place in a familiar setting in the presence of the mother (or perhaps the father), and if the child is allowed time to warm up to the stranger, unfamiliar Aunt Gertie would do better to get acquainted again with mother and dad before trying to interact with eight-month-old Jon.

True or False Fear of strangers is an abnormal response in infants and toddlers and indicates insecurity.

Separation anxiety. Parents are familiar with **separation anxiety.** As they are about to go out for the evening, young children begin to cry and protest loudly. The memory of that scene may haunt the parents throughout the evening.

Separation anxiety begins at about eight or nine months and peaks at between twelve and sixteen months (Metcalf, 1979). It may continue throughout the second year, but is not as intense, if found at all, in the third year. Some separations are predictable, as in the case of the mother who every weekday morning takes her child to the day-care center. The child can anticipate predictable separations and knows that mother will return. The environment is familiar, and the child is well acquainted with the substitute caregivers. After a while, children become used to an environment, such as a day-care center, and do not show much if any separation anxiety when mother leaves (Maccoby, 1980). Unpredictable separations, as when a child must enter the hospital, are different. The child is now presented with an unfamiliar environment, strange people who wear frightening uniforms, and a new situation.

How a child reacts to any separation depends on the child's age, how familiar the situation is, and previous experiences. In addition, if the child has familiar toys or a companion (such as a sibling), or is left with a substitute caregiver for whom she has an attachment, separation anxiety will be reduced. Kagan (1976) found that children who had a history of day care and home care still reacted with separation anxiety when tested in the laboratory. But children familiar with day care did not show protest in the day-care center when the caregiver departed (Maccoby, 1980). When children are left in their own homes with a grandmother, the separation anxiety is reduced (Bowlby, 1969). Even the possibility that mother might leave may be enough to provide some problems,

separation anxiety Fear of being separated from caregivers, peaking at between twelve and sixteen months.

protest stage The initial reaction to separation, in which the infant cries and refuses to be cared for by substitute caregivers.

despair stage The second stage in prolonged separation from the primary caregivers, in which the child becomes apathetic.

detachment stage The last stage in prolonged separation from the primary caregivers, in which the child cannot trust anyone else and becomes detached from other people.

especially in unpredictable situations. For example, when mother begins to pack for a trip, the child may start to cry and cling to her. The child is anticipating the loss. Any increase in the risk of separation may trigger some anxiety (Bowlby, 1982).

The psychological impact of separation depends partly on the length of the separation. Robertson and Bowlby (1952) argue that the child's reaction to *prolonged* separation goes through three stages—protest, despair, and detachment. In the **protest** stage, children cry and do not allow anyone else to care for them (Schaffer, 1977). The dominant emotion appears to be anger (Shiller et al., 1986). In the next stage, **despair,** the children become apathetic and may gaze at the ceiling from the crib for hours at a time. Then the final stage, **detachment,** is reached. Now the child "comes to terms with the situation but at a cost of his emotional tie with his mother and his ability to put his trust into any relationship" (Schaffer, 1977, pp. 96–97). If the separation is temporary, upon reunion the child may react to the parents with a detached attitude. A bit later the youngster may become clingy and refuse to be left alone.

What are the long-term effects of *prolonged* separation? The early work of Bowlby showed that these breaks could lead to emotional disturbances, but we now know that experience is cumulative and that an excellent later environment can mitigate the effects of a poor early environment. A study of children raised in institutions for the first few years and then adopted found no evidence of extensive emotional disturbance. These children also developed good relationships with their adoptive parents (Tizard, in Schaffer, 1977). In addition, many of the problems Bowlby attributed to separation may have been due to problems that existed before the breaks (Rutter,

Sometime in the second half of the child's first year, most infants develop a fear of strangers.

1979). Finally, the separations were frequently long and severe, not the type of predictable temporary separations so common when children are involved in a day-care situation.

Lisa and Tim Walters can now understand the difference between predictable and nonpredictable temporary separations. To reduce their children's anxiety, they should let them get acquainted with their new environments and try to maintain a routine so that the separations will be predictable. Allowing children to take a familiar toy with them at the beginning may be necessary, and allowing them time to get used to a new environment is important. Finally, individual differences abound in separation anxiety. Some children react better than others, and Lisa and Tim will have to be alert to individual patterns.

Attachment

When children show a fear of strangers or anticipate a separation, they often stay close to or seek contact with the caregiver. Children most often develop a relationship with the mother as the primary caregiver and cling to her for safety. Lisa and Tim are aware of the importance of the early mother-child bond and are concerned that the day-care experience will affect that relationship.

> **attachment** An emotional tie binding people together over space and time.

The Nature of Attachment

Study of the caregiver-infant relationship usually centers on the concept of **attachment.** According to Ainsworth (1974, p. 135), "An attachment is an affectional tie that one person forms to another specific person, binding them together in space and enduring over time." Attachment is specific, but an infant may be attached to more than one person. It implies an emotional bond that is a positive force in an individual's life. Infants become attached to the primary caregiver, in most instances the mother. How this occurs and the functions of this attachment are still a matter of controversy.

One theory of attachment emphasizes its biological roots. Attachment is necessary for the survival and normal development of the infant (Ainsworth, 1974; Bowlby, 1973). Attachment takes time to form, and it develops along with the child's cognitive abilities. The infant is not born with a natural affinity to the mother; this affinity is learned (Waters and Deane, 1982). So, although attachment has biological roots, learning and cognition also play a part.

Attachment Behavior

Infants begin to recognize the difference between strangers and familiar people in the first four months, but only at about six months do proximity-maintaining behaviors—such as seeking out the caregiver when afraid, crying when mother leaves the room, or following mother around—occur (Ainsworth, 1967).

The concept of attachment differs from "attachment behavior." **Attachment behavior** involves actions by a child that result in the child's obtaining proximity to another person whom the child views as better able to cope with the world (Bowlby, 1982). In other words, under certain circumstances, such as stress or anxiety, children are motivated to seek out the individual to whom they are attached.

We may think of attachment as a type of control system (Bretherton, 1985). The function of the behavioral control system is to "maintain a balance between attachment and exploratory behavior in a wide range of contexts" (Waters and Deane, 1985, p. 42). When the child perceives little danger, the balance favors exploration, although the child will check where the adult is. In other more risky environments, the balance favors physical contact over exploration. If the system works properly, it encourages both social and cognitive development.

As children age, these attachment behaviors change somewhat, and they can accept temporary separations from the mother. They may feel secure enough to be left with a warm substitute figure without creating so much fuss. Even here, though, acceptance of separation is conditional (Bowlby, 1982). The child must be familiar with the sitter, not be anxious or ill at the time, and be secure enough to be able to resume contact with the primary caregiver in a short period of time.

Although shown less frequently and less urgently after the third birthday, attachment behavior is not completely absent even then. During years four, five, and six, and even through early middle childhood, children may seek out their parents when they have been frightened or have a difficult day. If, as Bowlby believes, this attachment is necessary for the emotional growth and development of the infant, we would expect children who have not been able to develop such attachments to suffer greatly.

Maternal Deprivation

Many theorists argue that the early interactions between mother (usually the primary caregiver) and child are crucial to a child's later development. Freud (1935) believed that difficulties in this early relationship were the foundation for emotional disturbance. Children who do not receive adequate care become anxious and are unable to relate to others.

The Results of Poor Mothering

Many early studies found that the consequences of a breakdown in the early mother-child relationship were serious (Rutter, 1979). Spitz (1965, 1945) compared children who were raised in an orphanage, where they received impersonal care from the staff, and another group raised by their mothers in what amounted to a prison nursery. The children raised in the prison nursery thrived, while those raised in the orphanage without much attention suffered greatly. Emotional disturbances, failure to gain weight, and retardation were common. The orphanage-raised children also suffered many more physical illnesses. Spitz coined the term **hospitalism** to describe these symptoms.

Some studies of maternal deprivation have been performed on animals. The results offer more evidence about the tragic effects of maternal deprivation (Harlow, 1971, 1959; Harlow and Suomi, 1971). Harlow raised rhesus monkeys with either a terrycloth monkey or a wire monkey. When frightened, the infant monkeys clung to the terrycloth mothers even if they had received nourishment in the form of milk from a bottle placed in wire mother's "breast." They were greatly comforted by the softness of these dolls. But even though the monkeys raised on the terrycloth mother were more normal than those raised on the wire mother, abnormalities were still present. These monkeys did not play normally, showed rocking movements, bit themselves, were withdrawn, and could not function sexually.

Human infants may also have this need for **contact comfort.** In other studies, Harlow demonstrated that the injurious consequences of a lack of caregiving need not be permanent (Harlow and Harlow, 1962). If a monkey is placed with companions before six months of age, the effects of a motherless environment were not as severe and were gradually reversed, but if the situation was not reversed early, these problems remained.

Researchers have reported similar problems in human infants. Dennis (1973) followed children raised in an orphanage in Lebanon. They received little attention, and their life was one of uninterrupted boredom. When tested after the first year, these children were extremely retarded, but after being adopted they recovered quickly. Those adopted prior to the age of two recovered well. At about six years of age, those who were not adopted were transferred to other institutions—one for males, the other for females. The institution serving the females was just as bad as the one from which they had come. When tested during middle childhood, the girls were quite retarded, but the institution for males was run differently and provided a more stimulating environment, filled with toys, educational equipment, and films. The boys had an average IQ of 80—far above the intelligence scores for the girls. Dennis' observations led to two conclusions. First, these children had suffered from **stimulus deprivation**—that is, their environments were so unstimulating that it prevented them from developing normally. Second, the consequences of these unfavorable environments, although quite serious, could be remedied to some degree by placing them in a better, more stimulating environment, and the earlier this occurred, the better.

True or False Poor mothering in early infancy results in permanent retardation, even if the child's environment is later improved.

The Effects of Institutionalization

The work of Spitz, Bowlby, and Dennis led to great changes in institutional practices. Children's needs for attention, fondling, warmth, and care are now more fully appreciated. Ways to meet their need for a stimulating environment comprised of human beings as well as things to see, hear, and handle have been incorporated into

contact comfort The need for physical touching and fondling.

stimulus deprivation The absence of adequate environmental stimulation.

trust vs. mistrust Erikson's first psychosocial stage, in which the positive outcome is a sense of trust while the negative outcome is a sense of suspicion.

autonomy vs. doubt The second psychosocial stage, in which the positive outcome is a sense of independence, and the negative outcome is a sense of doubt about being a separate individual.

many institutional environments. We have learned at least some of our lessons. Institutionalization, then, need not lead to retardation (Saltz, 1973; Wolins, 1970). It is not the institutionalization itself, but rather the quality of the care provided, that determines the outcome.

The Caregiver-Child Relationship

All roads seem to lead back to the basic caregiver-child relationship. But what is it in this relationship that seems to affect infants so greatly? Let us focus on the elements of the relationship that may contribute to the development of a healthy personality.

Trust vs. Mistrust and Autonomy vs. Doubt

According to Erik Erikson (1963), our basic attitude toward people develops from the early relationship with our caregiver. If our early needs are met in a warm environment, we develop a sense of **trust,** a feeling that we live among friends and that we can trust others. If our needs are met with rejection or hostility, we develop a sense of **mistrust,** perceiving the world as a hostile, nonaccepting place and developing an inability to relate warmly to others.

Erikson argued that as children negotiate toddlerhood, it is important for them to gain a sense of **autonomy,** an understanding that they are someone on their own and have some control over their own behavior. However, if parents do not allow their children to do what they are able to do and are greatly overprotective, or if they rush their children into doing something for which they are not ready, the children may develop a sense of **shame** or **doubt** concerning their ability to deal with the world around them. Parents do not help children acquire a sense of autonomy by allowing them to do everything for themselves. Rather, encouraging children to do what they can do is the key to their developing a sense of autonomy. Children's relationships and early experiences form the basis of how the children will see the world later in life.

Classifying Attachment Behaviors

Attachment behaviors can be measured by means of a standardized procedure called the **strange situation** (Ainsworth and Wittig, 1969). The "strange situation" consists of eight standardized episodes in which children are brought to an unfamiliar room where a series of brief separations and reunions with their mothers are observed (Waters and Deane, 1982). Infants are classified as **secure** if they greet their mothers positively, actively attempt to reestablish proximity during reunions, and show few if any negative behaviors toward them. Secure infants explore the room just prior to the separation episodes and use their mothers as a base of operations to explore the environment when the mother is present (Sroufe, 1979a).

Two other classifications can be grouped under the heading of **anxious attachment.** Infants who are classified as being **anxious/avoidant** ignore their mother's entrance into the room in the reunion episodes and may actively

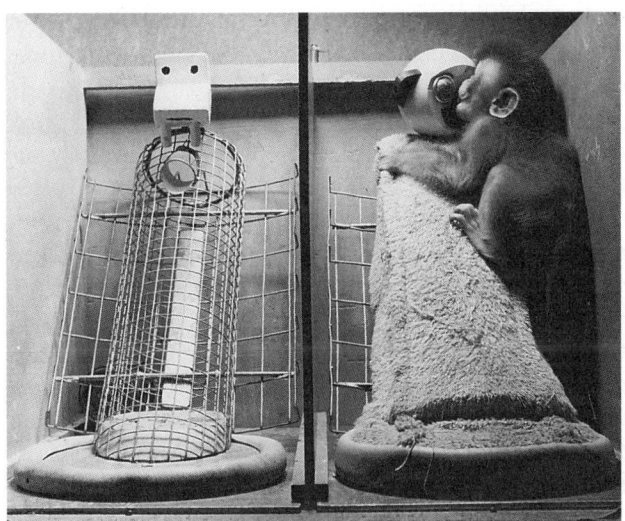

Harlow's experiments show the importance of contact comfort. When frightened, this infant monkey clung to its terrycloth substitute even if it was fed by the wire substitute mother.

strange situation   An experimental procedure used to measure attachment behaviors.

secure attachment   A type of attachment behavior in which the infant in the "strange situation" uses the mother as a secure base of operations.

anxious attachment   A general classification of insecure attachment shown in the "strange situation," consisting of either avoidant behavior or ambivalent attachment behavior.

anxious/avoidant attachment   A type of attachment behavior shown in the "strange situation," in which the child avoids reestablishing contact with the mother as she reenters the room after a brief separation.

anxious/ambivalent attachment   A type of attachment behavior shown during the "strange situation," in which the child both seeks close contact and yet resists it during the mother's reentrance after a brief separation.

avoid reestablishing contact. Infants classified as **anxious/ambivalent** show an angry resistance toward the mother upon reunion (Joffe and Vaughn, 1982). These babies show a great deal of anxiety about entering the room, even before the session begins, and are quite distressed by the separation. In the reunion they are ambivalent, seeking close contact and yet resisting it (Ainsworth, 1979). These patterns are relatively stable (Sroufe, 1985), but they can change if there is a major improvement or worsening in the child's environment.

True or False   The quality of a child's attachment to the primary caregiver cannot change after the age of six months.

How Attachment Relates to Later Behavior and Personality

Studies have found a relationship between the quality of an infant's attachment to the caregiver and later behavior and personality characteristics. Infants classified as securely attached at eighteen months were more enthusiastic, more persistent, and less easily frustrated than infants from the two other groups at two years of age (Matas et al., 1978). Securely attached infants are more socially and cognitively competent as toddlers (Waters, 1978). Securely attached toddlers are better at negotiating the environment, maneuver more successfully around toys and furniture, and reach more often for objects with-

Secure infants explore the environment more than insecurely attached infants. Behavioral differences are found even three years later. Here, a child heads for parts unknown.

out stumbling than anxiously attached infants (Cassidy, 1986). The ability of securely attached infants to explore their environment, and their superiority in other areas, carries over into early childhood (Arend et al., 1979). Infants who were securely attached at twelve months interact faster and more smoothly with a strange visitor at three years of age than children classified as avoidantly attached (Lutkenhaus et al., 1985). These children are also more likely to accept suggestions from mother (Matas et al., 1978), are more cooperative, and comply more readily with their mother's instructions (Londerville and Main, 1981). Toddlers who were securely attached at eighteen months received a greater number of positive responses from their peers at three years (Jacobson and Wille, 1986). When children were rated on classification of attachment at eighteen months, and when their behaviors were observed at four and a half and five years, the pattern of the superiority of securely attached children was evident on a number of social skills (Erickson et al., 1985). Secure infants also differ in their play, being more sociable toward both mothers and peers (Pastor, 1981). Attachment classifications, then, are related to competence in interpersonal situations (Waters et al., 1979).

The Effect of the Parent-Child Relationship on Attachment

Securely attached infants are superior to anxiously attached children on many measures of behavior and development, and this superiority continues at least through early childhood and perhaps beyond. But what is it in the early parent-child relationship that may lead to these differences?

The home environments of securely attached and anxiously attached infants differ. Mothers of securely attached infants pick them up and hug them more often than parents of anxiously attached infants do. Most research has focused on the parents of anxious/avoidant children, because their mothers appear to be more rejecting than mothers of securely attached and ambivalently attached infants (Ainsworth et al., 1971). Whereas parents of anxious/avoidant infants disdain physical contact with their infants (Ainsworth et al., 1978), they do show affectionate behavior. They tend to kiss their infants, but do not encourage physical contact (Tracy and Ainsworth, 1981). These children avoid contact in the "strange situation." Not all modes of showing affection are equal. When infants are upset, they require physical contact. Perhaps avoidant children desire the contact, but they realize they will not get it from their mothers. The avoidance may be a defensive reaction to past disappointments in this area.

Factors Determining the Patterns of Parent-Child Interaction

The importance of the child's relationship with the primary caregiver is confirmed by research. Some caregivers are more competent than others, and we have some idea of what characteristics comprise competent caregiving (see Table 5.3). If we could predict the nature of the parent-child relationship and target parents who are at risk for poor parent-child relationships, we could prevent some problems, but the situation is complicated because a number of factors affect the caregiver-child relationship and shape the interactions.

Attitudes and expectations are factors in this relationship. The ability of an individual to visualize oneself as a parent seems to be an important aspect of parenting (Heinicke et al., 1983). People who understand realistically how their lives will change now that they are parents find it easier to adopt to their new roles. Parents who have positive expectations about parenting adapt well to their new roles, while those who are overly anxious do not (Maccoby and Martin, 1983). Parents who know what to expect of a child at a particular age are less likely to lose their patience. For example, the parent who thinks that a newborn will sleep through the night, or that a baby will be quiet during his or her favorite television program, is likely to be disappointed. Attitudes and expectations are somewhat related to age. Many young parents have unrealistic expectations for their infants, thinking of them as toys or dolls (Wise and Grossman, 1980). Reality may come as a shock, and this may affect their relationship with the child. Older mothers are more likely to have a more positive attitude toward parenthood and to be more responsive to the needs of their children. They also report spending less time away from their children than younger mothers (Ragozin et al., 1982). Perhaps older mothers are more secure and more likely to have realistic expectations of parenthood.

True or False Older mothers have a more positive attitude toward motherhood than younger mothers do.

The parents' background is also important. Children who are abused or mistreated grow up to use similar, but not necessarily the same, behavior with their own children (Martin, 1975). People generally believe that what they have experienced is the normal way of interacting with others. If children are raised with kindness and love, they will find it easier to give such attention to their own children. Sensitivity is still another variable (Schaffer, 1977). Parents who form warm and loving relationships with their infants are sensitive to the baby's signs and can interpret baby's behavior. And social support is important as well. The social support received from both family and friends is related to maternal sensitivity (Crockenberg and McCluskey, 1986). This is most true for parents of irritable infants and shows that mothers require the support of other people, especially when dealing with more difficult children.

In the past it was popular to look only at the parents' contribution to the parent-child relationship, but we now realize that certain characteristics of the child can also help or hinder that relationship. For example, the responsive, capable infant is more likely to elicit favorable responses than an infant who is unresponsive (Brazelton et al., 1974). The appearance of the child also may affect how the child is treated. For instance, parents may not be able to cope adequately with their feelings toward children who suffer from some deformity. They know they should love their children, but their feelings may not be equal to that ideal. Even birth order may affect treatment. Firstborn children normally receive the most attention from parents, for everything the child does is new and exciting. Adults have different expectations for the oldest and youngest children in the family. The oldest child is expected to be more outgoing, dominant, obedient, and responsive as well as secure and self-confident. The youngest is expected to be likeable, sociable and not as obedient or secure (Baskett, 1985). These expectations affect how they are treated. Temperament also enters the picture; parents behave very differently with children of various temperaments (Dunn, 1981). The difficult child may elicit different reactions from caregivers. For example, parents who consider their children difficult are less responsive to their children than parents who do not consider their infants difficult (Donovan et al., 1978). Finally, as we saw in the last chapter, gender can affect how children are treated.

True or False Firstborn children receive more attention than later-born children.

Bi-directionality

Parent-child interactions are actually a chain of quick actions and reactions. An action on the part of the child

TABLE 5.3

Characteristics of Competent Infant Caregivers

On the left side of this table, the desirable characteristics of caregivers are shown; on the right side are some behaviors that reflect these characteristics. Research shows that the caregiver's ability to provide for the infant's physical, social, cognitive, and psychological needs is an important factor in the infant's development.

Desired Caregiver Characteristics	Cues to Desirable Caregiver Characteristics
Personality Factors	
Child-centered	Attentive and loving to infants
	Meets infants' needs before own
Self-confident	Relaxed and anxiety free
	Skilled in physical care of infants
	Individualistic caregiving style
Flexible	Uses different styles of caregiving to meet individual needs of infants
	Spontaneous and open behavior
	Permits increasing freedom of infant with development
Sensitive	Understands infants' cues readily
	Shows empathy for infants
	Acts purposefully in interactions with infants
Attitudes and Values	
Displays positive outlook on life	Expresses positive affect
	No evidence of anger, unhappiness, or depression
Enjoys infants	Affectionate to infants
	Shows obvious pleasure in involvement with infants
Values infants more than possessions or immaculate appearance	Dresses practically and appropriately
	Places items not for infants' use out of reach
	Reacts to infant destruction or messiness with equanimity
	Takes risks with property in order to enhance infant development
Behavior	
Interacts appropriately with infants	Frequent interactions with infants
	Balances interaction with leaving infants alone
	Optimum amounts of touching, holding, smiling, and looking
	Responds consistently and without delay to infants, is always accessible
	Speaks in positive tone of voice
	Shows clearly that infants are loved and accepted
Facilitates development	Does not punish infants
	Plays with infants
	Provides stimulation with toys and objects
	Permits freedom to explore, including floor freedom
	Cooperates with infant-initiated activities and explorations
	Provides activities which stimulate achievement or goal orientation
	Acts purposefully in an educational role to teach and facilitate learning and development

Source: Jacobson, 1978.

prompts an action on the part of the parent, which may then elicit another action on the part of the child, and so on. The beginning and the end are difficult to define. Infants are small but powerful. "Their power lies in the baby's ability to compel action by its eye-to-eye gaze, smiling, crying, appearing helpless, or thrashing" (Bell, 1979, p. 824). The child's behavior elicits behavior from the parents. For example, many abusing parents report that their children were annoying, showed persistent crying, and were generally "abrasive." These behaviors elicited abusive behavior from their parents.

The Synchrony Between Parent and Child

Any understanding of the parent-child relationship must look at the second-by-second interactions between the two. This is often summarized under the term **synchrony**—referring to the basic rhythms that underlie the interaction between parent and child (Schaffer, 1977). Watch a mother feeding her baby some mushy cereal, and the meaning of synchrony will become obvious. The infant's head turns, the baby looks here and there, spits out a little, blows a bubble, and kicks both feet. At just the right second, as the baby looks up at the mother, she has the spoon ready. The timing is amazing. The infant was an active participant too, looking at mother at just the right moment, knowing what was coming. The timing was based on an accurate reading of cues by both parent and child.

Caregiver and child must cooperate, and each must adapt to the other's behaviors (Osofsky and Connors, 1979). Development of a warm relationship hinges on the development of synchrony—this understanding of what will happen next—which in turn helps foster a sense of trust. The beginning of this mutual understanding, as well as the basic attachment sequence discussed earlier, starts at birth.

How Important Is Early Mother-Child Contact?

Yet in many cases mothers do not have contact with their infants for some time after birth. Is early contact vital to development of a healthy mother-child relationship? For many species, separation immediately after birth results in rejection. If a goat is separated from her kid right after delivery, she will reject it when reunited, but if the separation occurs ten minutes after delivery, no rejection occurs (Klaus and Kennell, 1976). In other species, there is also a critical period for attachment. Lorenz (1937) found that geese will follow and attach themselves to the first object they see. When the goslings opened their eyes and saw Lorenz, he became the object of attachment. They followed him everywhere. But the geese were capable of forming such a relationship only

synchrony The coordination between infant and caregiver in which each can respond to the subtle verbal and nonverbal cues of the other.

imprinting An irreversible, rigid behavior pattern of attachment.

in the first day and a half. This unlearned, rigid, irreversible behavior pattern is called **imprinting.** Could there be such a sensitive period in attachment for human beings? Could the first minutes, hours, or even days after birth be critical for the formation of a bond between mother and child?

Klaus and Kennell stirred up controversy by arguing that such a sensitive period in human beings did exist. The normal procedure in many hospitals was routine separation after birth, with the mother going to the recovery room and the infant to the nursery. Even days

When these goslings hatched, the first thing they saw was Konrad Lorenz. These goslings have imprinted on Lorenz and now will follow him everywhere.

later, contact was often limited. Klaus and Kennell suggested that this lack of early contact was responsible for some later problems in the parent-child relationship. In addition, some research showed that mothers who maintained early contact with their infants demonstrated more maternal behaviors (Kennell et al., 1974).

Most studies, though, have not found such a linkage, or they found that any differences disappear in a very short time (Grossman et al., 1981; Svejda et al., 1980). Even when separations are long, as in the case of premature babies, no significant differences in security of attachment were found between infants separated from their parents at birth and those who were not separated (Rode et al., 1981). The claims of Klaus and Kennell appear to be "exaggerated" (Belsky, 1982, p. 33). Attachment is based on the cumulative effects of mother-child interactions, not on any single brief encounter (Sroufe and Waters, 1977).

True or False Early and extended contact immediately after birth is necessary if infants are to develop a healthy attachment to their mothers.

The Father-Child Relationship

Up to this point, it must have seemed as if children only had one parent—the mother. Where is the father? Interest in the father's influence is quite recent (Hodapp and Mueller, 1982), and some of the latest findings in this area are surprising.

Where Is Father?

Child specialists are taking a long look at the father-child relationship. So are fathers, who are more interested and involved in their role than they were generations ago. This "paternal consciousness" (Lamb, 1979) may be a response to changes in society. The number of single male parents is increasing, and movies such as *Kramer v. Kramer* have dealt with the problems and possibilities of father involvement. Generally, fathers have less contact with their infants and toddlers than they do when the children are somewhat older. Although there is evidence of movement toward greater father involvement with young children, it would be wrong to be overenthusiastic or to begin speaking in terms of the egalitarian family where father and mothers are equally involved (Chibucos and Kail, 1981).

How Do Fathers Interact with Infants?

Mothers and fathers generally do not interact with their infants for the same reasons, nor do they share the caregiving duties equally. Fathers are much more likely to play with their infants than to care for them (Parke, 1981). The routine day-to-day child care is apt to fall squarely on the mother's shoulders (Kotelchuck, 1976).

The nature of father-child interactions differs from mother-child interactions. Both parents play with their children, but differently. Fathers play with their infants more physically than mothers do (Hodapp and Mueller, 1982). These differences remain fairly constant throughout infancy. Fathers are more likely to engage in physical-social games than mothers (Clarke-Stewart, 1978). Fathers also engage in more unconventional, unpredictable play (Lamb, 1976), but mothers are more responsive to infant cues of interest and attention (Power, 1985).

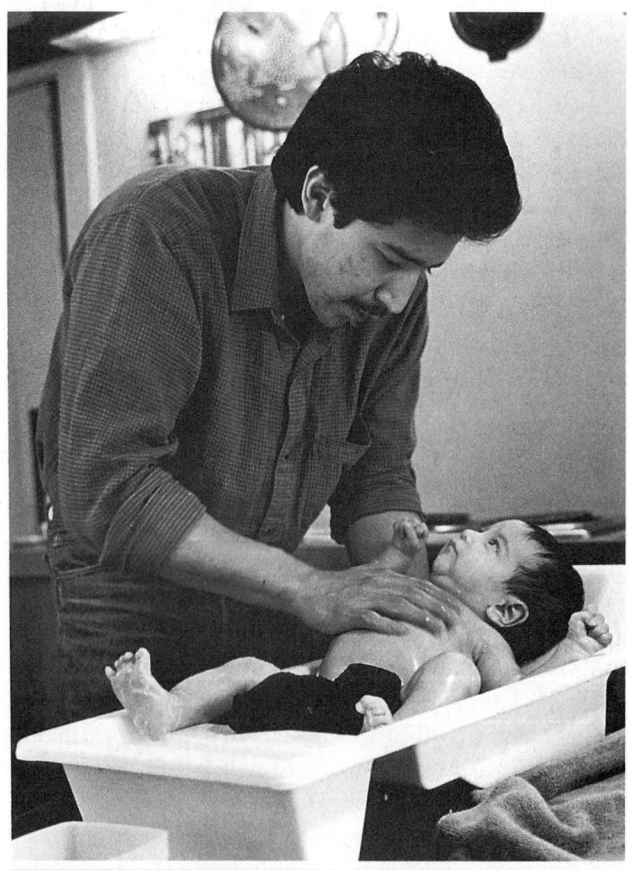

Mothers tend to perform many more of the day to day child care duties such as bathing the infant than most fathers do.

These differences in interaction explain why children seek out each parent for different reasons (Biller, 1982). This is not a function of gender, but the type of interaction that mothers and fathers engage in. The preference is based on the past experience of the child. The interactional difference is culturally determined. Swedish fathers and mothers do not play differently with their infants (Lamb et al., 1983), but American fathers interact with their infants differently from mothers, and spend much less time with their children.

Do Infants Become Attached to Their Fathers?

Infants do form an attachment to their fathers, even though their interaction with them is limited. In fact, they become attached to many people, not just the mother. The quality of this attachment depends on the history of the interactions the child has had with a person. Many people think of love as a type of pie in which a child can give only certain amount, that if love is portioned out to too many people, the amount available for mother is less. But this is not true. "Love in babies has no limits" (Schaffer, 1977, p. 104).

True or False Infants become attached to their fathers as well as to their mothers.

Infants who are attached to their fathers spend more time looking at them and react emotionally when their fathers enter or leave the room. In addition, "well-fathered" infants are more curious and more likely to explore the environment, more secure, and more advanced in motor development (Biller, 1982). Infants tend to choose mothers over fathers when they are hungry, wet, or under stress, but in a stress-free environment they show no preference and may even seek out fathers when they want to play. Fathers and mothers mean different things to children, based on the roles they choose to fulfill (Parke, 1981). The attachment to both can be quite strong, though. When mother, father, and stranger are present, the child will stay closer to the mother than to the father, and closer to the father than to the stranger (Cohen and Campos, 1974). In the "strange situation," children protest the departures of both mothers and fathers, and their play decreases (Kotelchuck, 1972). It is possible for a child to be securely attached to one parent and insecurely attached to another. In an interesting study, Main and Weston (1981) first classified infants according to their attachment behaviors with mothers and fathers. These infants were then exposed to a clown who sought to

establish a friendly relationship. Infants who were judged secure with both mother and father were more responsive to the clown than those who were securely attached to only one parent. Infants who were insecurely attached to both parents were least responsive to the clown. The study shows that the infant's relationship with both parents is important and can affect behavior in social situations.

The Cultural Context of Fathering

Given the opportunity and enough encouragement, fathers can do a fine job with their children and show many nurturant behaviors. Fathers are just as likely as mothers to hold newborn infants, to rock them, and to talk to them in the hospital (Parke and Sawin, 1976). Fathers are very interested in their children, and they act in a nurturant manner even though they do fewer caregiving chores (Parke, 1979). Fathers can accurately recognize the meaning of infant cries and are responsive to the infant's signals, sounds, and motor movements (Parke, 1981), although not as responsive as mother.

If fathers are capable of such behaviors, why aren't they more involved in the daily child-care activities when they are available? The answer is found in our American culture and its gender expectations, which are made clear very early in childhood. In our culture, little girls often run to a toddler and say "How cute!" while little boys try to look as bored as possible. Raising children is still considered woman's work. Throwing a baseball to a son or daughter is another story. In this area, fathers are supremely confident. Many fathers do not have the confidence, the experience, the encouragement, or the social supports necessary to take a more active role in the day-to-day care of their children. This situation is not unique to our culture (see the Cross-Cultural Current on page 142). Parenthood training may be helpful for both males and females (Parke, 1979). In one study, fathers who had the opportunity to learn and practice caregiving skills in the hospital were more involved in the care of their infants and in household tasks at three months (Parke, 1979).

Children attach themselves to many people, depending on the nature of the interactions. The quantity of the interactions is not as important as their quality. When one asks, then, just what the role of the father in the family should be, the answer given by Schaffer (1977, p. 104) is, "Just what he and his wife choose it to be."

Just How Involved Is Daddy?

It's no secret that mothers do most of the child-rearing duties in the average family. Fathers do not bathe, dress, or feed their children very much. Mother predominates, even in such activities as playing, reading stories, and helping children with schoolwork. This is disheartening, because studies show that paternal involvement in child-rearing is related to a child's academic competence as well as to a number of other desirable outcomes.

Just what keeps fathers from being more involved with their children? Could it be that fathers view diapering, feeding, and comforting as feminine activities that are not appropriate for a male?

This was the question Graeme Russell sought to answer. To understand his research the term androgyny must be introduced. **Androgyny** is the state of possessing the best characteristics of masculinity and femininity. For instance, many people think of being objective, competitive, aggressive, and not expressing one's feelings easily as masculine traits and being tactful, gentle, not being very aggressive and being sensitive to other people's feelings as feminine characteristics (Broverman et al., 1972). Whether these characteristics are adaptive or maladaptive depends on the situation. Emotionality and subjectivity may be adaptive in some situations but not in others. Both extremely high masculinity and very high femininity are associated with a narrowness of sex role. The individual who has the best of both worlds is in the most flexible position to react, being capable of both showing emotions and not showing them, being subjective or objective as the situation warrants. People who are androgynous have the flexibility to combine the best characteristics of both males and females. Russell reasoned that fathers who score high on a scale that measures androgyny would be more likely to perform such child-rearing tasks as diapering and feeding and

androgyny   The state of possessing the best characteristics of masculinity and femininity.

would interact more frequently with their children than men who score low on the androgyny dimension. Because the role of mother is so well stereotyped, whether or not a woman is androgynous probably would not matter as much.

To test this hypothesis, Russell interviewed forty-three couples living in the Sydney, Australia, area. He asked questions relating to the amount of time each parent spent at home or at work, the amount of time father and mother spent in child-rearing activities, and the kinds of activities that parents and children participated in together. Each parent was also given the Bem Sex Role Inventory, which measures androgyny.

Some of Russell's results are found in Table A. Notice that the father diapered the child only 19 percent of the time and fed the child only 14 percent of the time. One reason often advanced for this dismal record is lack of time. If father works all day and comes home late at night, he simply doesn't have the time to interact with his children. But this explanation does not fit the facts. Although all the fathers in Russell's sample had full-time positions, almost half the women were also employed either full- or part-time. In addition, duties performed mostly at night, such as helping children with schoolwork, playing with them, attending to their needs before bed, and reading them stories, are also heavily weighted toward the mother, even though most of the fathers were at home and available. These percentages are very close to those found in studies done in the United States (see Table B).

The Issue of Day Care

Lisa and Tim Walters' concerns center on the children's experience in day care. Many people today think of day care only in terms of large urban care centers, but most

day care does not take place in such centers. A government survey found that about 31 percent of the young children whose mothers' work were cared for in the child's home most likely by a relative, while about 40 percent were cared for in someone else's home where the child

TABLE A

Mean Parent-Child Interaction for Mothers and Fathers Expressed in Hours/Week (H) and Percentage of the Total Mother- and Father-Child Interaction (%)

	Feed	Dress	Change Diapers	Bathe	Attend at Night	Read Stories	Help School	Play
Mothers								
H	10.5	3.39	1.43	1.52	.38	1.37	.29	13.73
%	86	86	81	74	72	70	62	61
Fathers								
H	1.76	.5	.34	.52	.15	.59	.17	8.88
%	14	14	19	26	28	30	37	39

Russell also found a relationship between father-child interaction and androgyny. The degree to which fathers interacted with their children was related to their scores on the androgyny scale, while mother's interactions were not. Androgynous fathers interacted more with their children and performed more of the child-care responsibilities than nonandrogynous fathers. Perhaps androgynous fathers are more nurturant because they do not label child-care activities as strictly mother's work.

Russell also found that fathers low in androgyny married to women high in the characteristic participated more in child care than low-androgyny fathers married to low-androgynous women. High-androgynous mothers may insist that their husbands participate whether or not they think the duties are appropriate. Situational factors, such as employment status or physical health, may also be at work here.

To summarize, fathers do not perform many child-care duties, but androgynous fathers are more involved

TABLE B

Australian Data Compared with U.S. Data

	Mother		Father	
	Australia	United States	Australia	United States
Time present	9.0	10.0	3.2	5.4
Feeding	1.5	1.5	.25	.26
Cleaning	.91	1.1	.19	.3
Play	1.96	2.0	1.3	1.25

Note: Figures are in hours/day.

with their children than nonandrogynous fathers. Since paternal involvement is so important in child development, a redefinition of the father's role in child care is necessary. Fathers must be convinced that helping to care for children is not an exclusively female task.

Source: Russell, G., The Father's Role and Its Relation to Masculinity, Femininity, and Androgyny. *Child Development,* 1978, 49, 1174–1181.

was about as likely to be cared for by a non-relative as a relative. This is often called family day care. About 15 percent were cared for in group care centers and about 9 percent were cared for by mother while she worked. A very small number (about .2 percent) made other arrangements including allowing these children to care for themselves. About five percent of the people surveyed did not choose to provide this information (U.S. Bureau of the Census, 1986). The overwhelming majority of infants under one year of age whose mothers worked were cared for by relatives or the parents themselves (Klein, 1985). Thus, many forms of day care exist and the day-care center is the answer for the minority. Among those who do attend a day-care center, only 17 percent attend a center that is licensed (Zigler and Muenchow, 1983).

True or False Most children in need of day care attend licensed day-care centers.

Day Care and Attachment

Lisa Walters is concerned that the day-care professional will become a mother substitute and affect Lisa's relationship with her children. Some studies have shown differences between home-reared and day-care children on measures of attachment in the "strange situation" (Blehar, 1974). A recent study found some negative effects, mostly for children who received out-of-home care prior to their first birthday. Secure children who had entered out-of-home care after their first birthday did not show any problems (Vaughn et al., 1985).

In another study, infants whose mothers were employed and experienced day care in their own homes by an unrelated person were more likely to show insecure-avoidant attachment patterns in the "Strange Situation" than infants whose mothers had remained at home. However, 53 percent of those infants whose mothers worked showed secure attachment and some as yet unidentified factors must moderate the effects of these daily separations for these securely attached infants (Barglow et al., 1987). These studies have raised concerns about substitute care for infants and launched a great debate on infant day care (see Belsky, 1987; 1986).

While some studies may show the possibility that infant day care may heighten the risk of infants developing insecure-avoidant attachment patterns, these findings still seem like the exception to the rule (Phillips et al., 1987a). Controlled studies of infant day care are few, and there is no doubt that the quality of such care makes a great difference. It would be most unwise to come to any negative conclusion about the effect of infant day care on attachment patterns. Years ago many people believed that institutional rearing of children always led to negative outcomes, but after more research was performed it became clear that the key issue was one of the quality of the institutional care not institutional care itself (Chess, 1987). The same may be true for infant day care which is becoming more prevalent in our society. The overwhelming majority of these infants are cared for in private homes not day care centers (Kammerman, 1986). These homes vary widely in quality, making assessment very difficult. We will have to watch for more research on the issue of infant day care and attachment in the future. However, infant day care appears to be here to stay and hopefully future research will discover exactly what types of infant day care environments lead to positive or negative outcomes.

Lisa's children will form an attachment to their substitute caregivers (Lewis, 1987). Children show less distress when left with a familiar caregiver than when left with a stranger, and they even show some distress when separated from the caregiver (Ricciuti, 1974). Anderson and her colleagues (1981) found that the extent of this attachment depended on the quality of the day-care worker's interaction with the child. Children showed attachment behaviors to high-interaction competent caregivers, and low levels of attachment to low-interaction caregivers. In the presence of a high-interaction caregiver, the child feels secure enough to explore the environment. Again, the quality— not the quantity— of interaction is most important for the development of positive interpersonal relationships.

True or False Children in day care do not form attachments to day care workers since they have already formed attachments to mother and father.

Day Care and Intellectual Development

We might assume that if a child went from a stimulating environment to a good day-care center, little gain or loss should occur. But if a child came from a nonstimulating environment to a stimulating environment, some gain should result. If a child came from a stimulating environment to a poor day-care center, negative effects should be apparent. Indeed, the research supports these notions (Belsky and Steinberg, 1979).

Day care seems to have no injurious effects on the cognitive development of low-risk children (Belsky and Steinberg, 1978). For disadvantaged children, an enriched day-care program may encourage cognitive development. In some studies, disadvantaged children reared at home showed a decline over the first three years or so in intelligence scores, while those enrolled in day care did not.

Day Care and Social Development

The evidence on the effects of the day-care experience on social development is interesting. Studies show that generally the overall social and emotional adjustment of day-care children is good and compares well with that of home-raised children (Watkins and Bradbard, 1984; Etaugh, 1980). Some differences have been noted. Children who experience day care are more outgoing, but they are also more aggressive and boisterous (Clarke-Stewart, 1982). Children enrolled in day care are inclined to be more impulsive and egocentric as well (Belsky and Steinberg, 1978). The more time spent in day care, the more time children as young as two years of age spend associating with peers, and the less time they spend time just looking at others and playing alone (Schindler et al., 1987). Children in day care interact more with their peers. However, the type of program makes a difference. Children enrolled in a cognitively oriented day-care establishment were more aggressive in the early years of elementary school than children who had attended more typical programs that focus more on social skills. These children, though, were not considered difficult to manage, and the aggression decreased over time (Haskins, 1985). When more attention is given to prosocial behaviors in these programs, aggression is reduced and cognitive gains are not affected (Finkelstein, 1982). These results may also be affected by culture, for studies in other countries do not find these differences. In summary, there are differences in the social-emotional area, but there is no evidence that day care causes serious emotional or social problems for children.

The Quality of Day Care

Much depends on the quality of the day-care center (Phillips et al., 1987b). All the effects described above are mediated by the characteristics of the day-care center and the home. But how can we evaluate a day-care center? The Day-Care Checklist shown in Figure 5.2 may help. Certain factors are especially important. The caregiver-to-child ratio is one such factor. If attention and face-to-face interactions are vital to development in early childhood, the better the ratio of caregivers to children, the more likely it is that day care will be a positive experience. If the caregiver-to-infant ratio is too great, the children cry more and become withdrawn or apathetic (Ruopp et al., 1983). Another factor is the nature of the day-care program. Although day care should not be thought of in terms of school, such activities as reading to children and playing social games can contribute to social and intellectual growth. Such other factors as safety, ventilation, security, cleanliness, conven-

ience, staff turnover, and cost should also be taken into consideration.

Day care is neither a panacea nor a hell. Some facilities are excellent, others are poor. The nature of the interactions between day-care workers and the child will in part determine the quality of the experience. Research shows that children given high-quality day care do not suffer, and in some cases may even benefit from the experience.

The Working Mother

Most parents send their children to day-care centers because they both work. Slightly over half the mothers of preschool children are employed outside the home, and this figure is rising. What effect does a mother's working have on a child's development?

Right from the start, you may say that asking what affect a mother's working is a sexist question. What about father? This is a reasonable criticism, but because mothers usually act as the primary caregivers, the question is proper. Even in homes where both parents work, the mother usually has the responsibility for the bulk of the child-care and household chores. In a recent poll, 93 percent of the respondents said parents should share the chores equally when both work. Yet in 57 percent of the homes where both spouses work, women did most of the housework (*Newsday*, June 17, 1986). Studies show that when mothers work, fathers do take on more child-rearing responsibilities (Rutter, 1981). The qualitative differences between mother-child interactions and father-child interactions decline somewhat as well (Stuckey et al., 1982). However, fifty-fifty splits are unusual, and the mother remains the focal point of the home.

True or False Fathers are generally more active in child care when mothers are employed.

Mother-Child Interactions: Working vs. Nonworking Mothers

Opinions on whether working mothers interact differently with their children vary. Some studies show that employed and nonemployed mothers interact similarly with their children (Hock, 1980), that child-rearing practices do not vary according to whether the mother is employed or not (Yarrow, 1962). But other studies come up with different findings. One found that nonworking mothers give more positive attention, including affectionate touching, and vocalize more to their infants, than mothers who work (Cohen, 1978).

A Day-Care Checklist

It's not easy to choose a day-care facility. The following checklist can be used as a basis for comparing day-care centers.

Yes No Space and Equipment

— — 1. There is adequate space to play.
— — 2. Sufficient storage for materials is available.
— — 3. The furniture is child-size and in good condition.
— — 4. The temperature is comfortable (68 to 70 degrees).
— — 5. The lighting is adequate.
— — 6. Materials are available in sufficient numbers so children don't have to wait long to use them.
— — 7. There is enough space outside or inside (a playground or a gym) for children to run or engage in other physical activities.
— — 8. There is adequate space for resting.
— — 9. The eating area is clean and bright.
— — 10. Bathroom facilities are designed for small children.
— — 11. Bathroom facilities are convenient.
— — 12. Electrical outlets are covered when not in use.
— — 13. First-aid supplies are available.
— — 14. All equipment is in good repair (no broken toys or sharp edges).
— — 15. Material is available (e.g., pots or cages) for growing things or taking care of animals.
— — 16. Books are visible.
— — 17. Puzzles are available.
— — 18. Adequate space is available for dramatic play (raised platforms, rows of wooden crates, etc.)
— — 19. Emergency procedures are clear, and environment allows for safe exit in case of emergency.
— — 20. Smoke detectors and fire extinguishers are evident.

The Program

— — 1. There is an organized daily program.
— — 2. There is variety within the program.
— — 3. Students are encouraged to talk with each other.
— — 4. Children participate in projects.
— — 5. Activities are planned to encourage children to learn by using their senses.

Yes No

— — 6. Self-expressive activities such as painting and various forms of art are programmed.
— — 7. Children are generally busy, not just sitting around.
— — 8. Children show evidence of learning through discovery and asking questions of the staff.
— — 9. Small-group activities are encouraged.
— — 10. Reading and storytelling are part of the program.
— — 11. Activities that develop the large muscles are evident.
— — 12. Activities that develop fine-muscle control are evident.
— — 13. Boys and girls are encouraged to participate in all activities.

Teacher-Child/Teacher-Parent Relationships

— — 1. Sufficient staff is available so each child may receive individual attention at some point in the day.
— — 2. A warm relationship with the children is evident.
— — 3. Staff circulates among all children, does not spend an inordinate amount of time with only one child.
— — 4. Staff offers suggestions in a positive manner.
— — 5. Staff trusts and respects children.
— — 6. Staff encourages children to do things.
— — 7. Staff does not use threats or punishment.
— — 8. Staff does not smoke around the children.
— — 9. Children understand their responsibilities.
— — 10. Staff has sufficient training in the field.
— — 11. Children seem happy.
— — 12. Children seem to get along with one another.
— — 13. Staff appears vigilant, knows what is going on at all times.
— — 14. Staff and administrator encourage parents to visit and become involved.
— — 15. Communication with parents, such as written notices of special events or changes in program, is adequate.

Yes	No		Staff/Child Ratio		
—	—	16. Checks on who can take child home (dismissal procedures) are adequate.	Minimum staff-child ratio for day-care centers:		
—	—	17. Staff/teacher conferences are held regularly.	*Age*	*Maximum group size*	*Staff/child ratio*
			Birth to 2 years	6 children	1 adult: 3 children
			2 to 3 years	12 children	1 adult: 4 children
			3 to 6 years	16 children	1 adult: 8 children

Source: Adapted from Stines, 1983, and Clarke-Stewart, 1982.

The attitude of the parents toward the mother's working was found to be important. More problems arose in families where negative attitudes toward maternal employment existed. For example, if parents believed that it was harmful to the children to have the mother work, or that the children required full-time mothering, more rejection and criticism was directed toward the children. Whether the mother is employed outside the home or a full-time homemaker, how she feels about her role is as important as what that role is.

The stereotype of the unhappy homemaker has become common. Depression and boredom were supposedly related to full-time homemaker status. The happy, satisfied working woman was held in high esteem. There may well be some advantages in self-esteem for women who work (Rutter, 1981). However, the personal benefits are much more likely to be found in mothers who are working because they want to work than in mothers who are working because of financial necessity (Alvarez, 1985). The stereotype of the unhappy homemaker is only partly accurate. Most studies simply compare working mothers with nonworking mothers and report the differences. But if you split homemakers into those who want to work and those who don't, a different picture becomes apparent (Tavris, 1976). The stereotype is accurate only for the woman who finds herself trapped and wants out. The homemaker who is satisfied is just as happy as the working woman.

Effects of Maternal Employment on Children

Does the mother's working affect a child's development? Before answering this question, a few cautions are nec-

essary. Even if a mother is home, it does not mean that she is paying much attention to the children. A home-based mother does not necessarily mean a full-time mother (Hoffman, 1979). In addition, while some people may uncritically accept the belief that full-time mothering is best, this may not be the case. One study found that although boys who received full-time mothering during the preschool period are more intellectually advanced, they are also more fearful, more conforming, and more inhibited as adolescents (Moore, 1975). The full-time mother may be too involved with the children. In addition, the effect of employment is mediated by such factors as the type of day care provided, the attitude of the parents, and their behavior when they return home from work.

But some differences between children of working and nonworking mothers have surfaced. These depend on the child's gender and social class. Maternal employment does not have a negative effect on girls and may actually be a positive influence on their development. Daughters of working mothers tend to be higher achievers, and the mother may serve as an achieving role model (Hoffman, 1979). Sons of working mothers do not have the traditional sex stereotypes that children of nonworking mothers frequently have.

Social class is another variable. Males from low socioeconomic backgrounds may view the need for their mothers to work as a reflection on their father's failure to earn a living. This could lead to a strain in the father-son relationship. Generally, though, maternal employment does not adversely affect the cognitive development of lower-income children. Studies of middle-class youngsters, however, sometimes show differences in cognitive development. Middle-class toddlers of nonemployed mothers were more cognitively advanced than those of employed mothers. These differences are most likely to be found in males. Some studies of middle-class males show that they do not do as well on intelligence tests as children raised by nonworking mothers (Hoffman, 1979). Although the majority of studies have not shown this superiority in cognitive development, it has come up enough to indicate that there is room for additional research in this area. Why this may occur is open to question. Perhaps the care received by some middle-class children in day care does not match that provided by a nonemployed mother. Perhaps some working mothers are not as involved with their children when they get home.

Differences in social behavior between children of working and nonworking mothers do appear, but they are minor. Schachter (1981) found that preschool children of employed mothers are more peer-oriented and self-sufficient. Children of nonemployed mothers seek out more help and protection and show more jealousy. No differences in emotional adjustment were found.

In summary, the effects of maternal employment can be either negative or positive, depending on many factors. It does not lead to massive personal or emotional problems (Hoffman, 1979; 1974), although there is room for some concern about the cognitive development of middle-class males. The possible problem may be reduced by providing better substitute care and encouraging parents to become more involved in their children's cognitive development.

True or False Maternal employment has no effect on a child's social or cognitive development.

Relationships with Grandparents, Siblings, and Peers

So far we have looked at the nature of children's social relationships with their mothers, fathers, and day-care workers, but many children also form early relationships with grandparents, siblings, and peers.

Grandparents and Their Grandchildren

Grandparents often develop special relationships with their grandchildren. Some even help out with their care. The nature of the grandparent-child relationship depends on the quality of their interactions, and the nature

formal-style grandparents Grandparents who are not too involved in bringing up their grandchildren.

fun-seeking grandparents Grandparents who are indulgent to their grandchildren and enjoy doing things with them.

surrogate-parent grandparents Grandparents who take on a parenting role, usually so the mother can work.

reservoir-of-family-wisdom grandparents An older style of grandparenting in which the grandparents, most often the grandfather, is the authority figure for the family.

distant-figure grandparents Grandparents who are basically not involved with their grandchildren and have little contact with them.

of these interactions depends on the style of grandparenting undertaken by the child's grandparents.

Neugarten and Weinstein (1964) interviewed seventy pairs of middle-class grandparents and isolated five different grandparenting styles. The **formal style** is adopted by grandparents who are not really involved in the upbringing of the child other than an occasional babysitting chore but who are interested in the grandchildren. **Fun-seeking** grandparents are playmates for the grandchildren. They are indulgent and enjoy taking part in activities with them. The **surrogate parent** style, more common for grandmothers than for grandfathers, is especially important. This type of grandparent takes on a parenting role, often so the child's mother can work. The style known as the **reservoir of family wisdom** involves an older type of grandparenting in which the grandparent, usually the grandfather, is the titular head and the authority figure for the entire extended family. This grandparent's position is supreme. The **distant-figure style** involves a noninvolved grandparent who may have very little contact with grandchildren except for a birthday party.

Each style of grandparenting has a direct or indirect impact on the child. Grandparents may have an indirect impact on a child by providing a safety valve for new parents who need help adjusting to their role and who benefit from advice (Spock, 1974). Grandparents have a direct impact through their relationship with their grandchildren. If grandparents spend a considerable amount of time in active interaction with their grandchildren, an attachment will probably grow and develop.

Grandparents may indeed play a part in the development of their grandchildren.

Interactions with Siblings

From our earliest days, we have significant relationships with our siblings. Sibling relationships are variable and can result in help and protection or anger and despair. And the presence of other children may affect how much attention a child receives.

Most children have siblings. Older siblings may provide some small measure of caring for an infant by feeding, playing with, or in some way comforting the baby (Bank and Kahn, 1982), but this can be a mixed blessing.

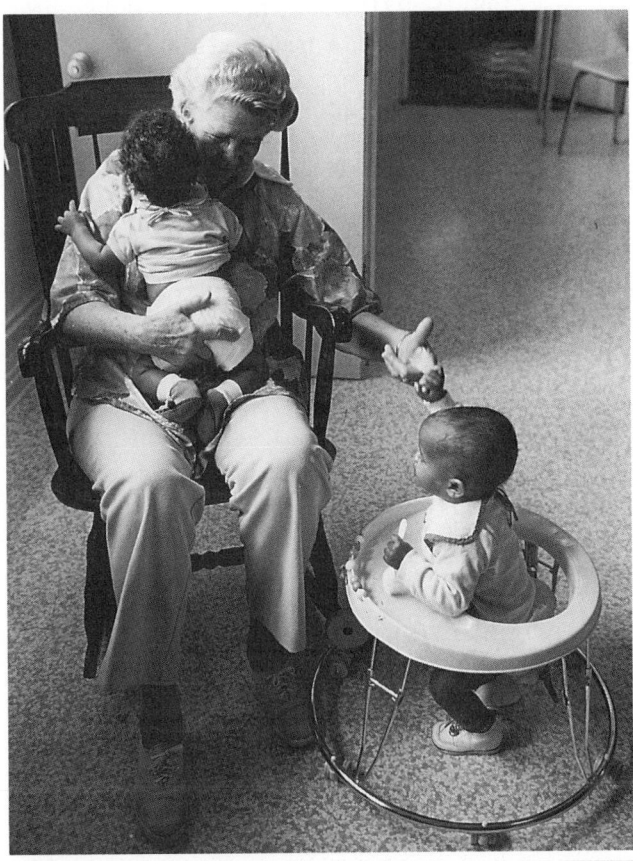

About 60 percent of women with children aged three to five work. Half the women with infants and toddlers are now in the work force and these percentages can be expected to increase in the coming years. Relatives will care for some of these children; others will be cared for in day care centers (New York Times, July 12, 1985).

The younger child may expect and desire a protective, warm relationship and receive anger and hostility instead, thus forming a lasting pattern of poor sibling interactions. On the other side, older siblings may have a sense of pride in their position as the oldest.

Infants can become attached to their siblings. Those who had a brother or sister with them in the nursery were much less distressed when separated from their parents (Dunn, 1977). The siblings were only two or three years older themselves, so the comfort was not the result of being mothered. This sibling bond does not compare with the child's primary attachments. Because of sibling immaturity, the bond is often inconsistent and anxiety-provoking. However, infants do form attachments to older children, imitate them, and follow them around. These interactions may influence social and emotional development.

Interactions with Peers

As infants develop into toddlers, their relationships with peers become a factor in development. Few parents introduce peer interactions into the daily schedules of infants, but infants react to the presence of other children, and during their first year they interact with them.

Social behavior progresses with age and experience (Mueller and Vandell, 1979). Visual recognition of peers begins at about two months. If placed near each other at three or four months, infants will touch. At six months or so, infants begin to direct their attention to other infants and to smile in response to the coos of their peers. By seven or eight months, they follow a peer. Between nine and twelve months, we begin to see exchanges involving social play. For example, children begin to play social games using rubber balls. By thirteen or fourteen months, they readily imitate their peers.

After the first year, peer interactions take on a more recognizable quality. The number of interactions increases, and some negative interactions, such as tugging with another child for a desired toy, are seen. Although even one-year-olds share (Hay, 1979; Rheingold et al., 1976), cooperative and sharing behaviors increase greatly during the second year. In this second year, children will turn less toward their mothers and more toward both toys and peers if placed in a novel play setting (Eckerman et al., 1975). As toddlers, their social games become more sophisticated (Ross, 1982). The amount of social interaction will depend on a number of factors. Children interact more with familiar peers—and when only one other toddler is present, rather than a group. A few large toys, or even no toys at all, encourage interactions, and more interaction takes place in familiar settings (Mueller and Vandell, 1979). In conclusion, infants and toddlers do interact with one another from early ages. They come to prefer peers in certain situations, perhaps because their behavior is more novel than that of their parents and because their actions are more easily imitated (Eckerman et al., 1975).

True or False Toddlers interact more if many small toys, rather than a few larger toys, are available.

Lisa and Tim Walters now have some of the answers to their questions about day care and maternal employment being harmful to their children. They must be certain that the day care provided is of excellent quality. Tim's attitude toward Lisa's working bears scrutiny, as does his ability and willingness to help with child-care and household chores. Finally, both parents must realize that their responsibilities do not end when they come home from work. They must build active involvement with their children into their schedules. If they choose to leave their children either at a day-care center or with the grandparents, the children will develop some attachment to others, but it will not be at the parents' expense.

Many Roads to Travel

We now have a general picture of how a child forms relationships and becomes a social being. The caregiver-child attachment is important. Securely attached children are superior to anxious/avoidant and anxious/ambivalently attached children on a variety of measures. The child forges bonds and close relationships with many people, including mother, father, grandparents, day-care workers, siblings, and peers. The quality of the interactions is more important than the quantity.

Much has been said about meeting the needs of the child, and warm, responsive, understanding adults are required if children are to develop socially and emotionally in a healthy manner. Yet the research shows there is no single way these needs must be met. As Chess and Thomas (1981, p. 221) note, "Just as the child's nutritional requirements can be met successfully with a wide range of individual variation, so can his psychological requirements." Many roads can lead to the same destination. Some are more difficult than others. Parents can provide for their children's needs in many ways, taking into account the personality of the child, the children's own needs and requirements, and the family's circumstances.

Summary

1. The infant's earliest emotions are reflexive. As the child develops, emotions become more differentiated and attached to particular social stimuli.

2. A child's fear of strangers begins sometime in the second half of the first year and lasts through most of the second year. The child will show less fear of strangers if the stranger is small or female, or if the child is allowed to get used to the stranger.

3. Beginning at about eight months, and peaking somewhere between twelve and sixteen months, children show separation anxiety. Long-term separations from the caregiver may lead to protest, despair, and finally a detachment that can end in death.

4. Infants must attach themselves to a caregiver if they are to develop normally. Children who have

not had the opportunity to form such an attachment often suffer retardation. The tragic consequences of maternal deprivation may be reduced if the child receives excellent care later on.

5. Erikson argues that the psychosocial crisis during infancy is trust versus mistrust. If the child's needs are met, the child develops a sense of trust. If not, a sense of mistrust may develop. The psychosocial crisis of the toddler stage is autonomy versus doubt. If children are allowed to do what they are able to do on their own, they develop a sense of autonomy. If children are thwarted in their attempt to do things on their own that they are capable of doing, they develop a sense of doubt or shame.

6. Attachment behaviors can be measured using a standardized procedure of brief separations and

reunions known as the "strange situation." Three classifications of attachment behavior have surfaced: secure attachment, anxious/avoidant attachment, and anxious/ambivalent attachment. Children classified as securely attached are superior to those in other classifications on a variety of measures.

7. Many factors affect the parent-child relationship, including the age of the parent, the parents' attitudes and expectations concerning their new role, and the parents' background and sensitivity to the infant's needs. The infant's abilities, appearance, birth order, temperament, and gender also affect the relationship. While the parent affects the child, the child also affects the parents.

8. Although early and extended contact between mother and infant may be desirable, it is not absolutely necessary for establishing a healthy mother-child relationship.

9. Infants form attachments to their fathers as well as to their mothers. Mothers and fathers interact differently with their infants—mothers often performing more of the daily caregiving chores, and fathers playing with them more physically. Infants often seek out father when they want to play, and mother when they are in distress. The involvement of fathers with their infants varies from culture to culture and from family to family.

10. The day-care experience may be a positive, neutral, or negative one, depending on the quality of the day care, the attitudes of parents, and the parent-child interactions after work. Studies show that, in general, day care does not injure the child and in some instances may actually promote development.

11. Maternal employment does not have a negative affect on daughters, and working mothers can serve as achieving role models. There is some evidence that middle-income males whose mothers are employed are not as cognitively advanced as sons of nonemployed mothers. This may be remedied by providing extra attention after work. The differences in social behavior between children of working and nonworking mothers are minor.

12. Children may become attached to their grandparents and siblings. Grandparents differ in their styles of grandparenting.

13. Interaction with peers begins very early in infancy. Peer interaction increases as the child matures.

Answers to True or False Statements

1. *False* Correct statement: A fear of strangers is common in older infants and toddlers.

2. *False* Correct statement: The effects of a poor early environment may be at least partly reduced by a significant improvement in the child's later environment.

3. *False* Correct statement: Although they are usually stable, attachment patterns can change.

4. *True* Older mothers have a more positive attitude toward parenthood than younger mothers do.

5. *True* Firstborn children receive more attention than their later-born siblings.

6. *False* Correct statement: Although such early contact may be desirable, it is not absolutely necessary for development of a healthy mother-child relationship.

7. *True* Infants become attached to their fathers as well as to their mothers.

8. *False* Correct statement: Only a very small percentage of the children in day-care situations are cared for in licensed centers.

9. *False* Correct statement: Children in day care form attachments to their day care workers.

10. *True* Although mothers continue to perform most of the child-care and household duties, fathers generally pitch in more when the mother is employed outside the home.

11. *False* Correct statement: The effects of maternal employment may be positive or negative, depending on a number of factors.

12. *False* Correct statement: Toddlers tend to interact more with their peers if there are only a few larger toys present.

The Development of Language and Communication Skills

Are the Following Statements True or False?

Try the True-False Quiz below. See if your answers correspond to the information in this chapter. Each question is repeated after the paragraph in which the answer can be found. The True-False Answer Box at the end of the chapter lists the complete answers.

_____ 1. The terms *language* and *communication* can be used interchangeably.

_____ 2. Infants as young as one month can understand the spoken word.

_____ 3. When infants babble, they utter every sound the human vocal apparatus is capable of producing.

_____ 4. Children who use incorrect forms of words, such as *goed* and *drinked* instead of *went* and *drank,* need formal language training.

_____ 5. Children produce many more words than they can understand.

_____ 6. Parents use well-formed sentences when speaking to toddlers.

_____ 7. Parents are just as likely to correct children's statements for grammatical errors as they are for truthfulness.

_____ 8. Middle-class children use more complex sentences and fewer commands than children of working-class parents.

_____ 9. Twins are generally not as advanced in linguistic development as their nontwin peers.

_____10. On the average, American girls acquire language faster than American boys.

_____11. Black English is a dialect of Standard English.

_____12. Bilingualism, itself, leads to cognitive difficulties and academic problems in school.

The Mysteries of Language

Most of you have taken a foreign language in high school or college. There you sat, struggling over a text, trying to learn a different grammar and vocabulary. The task is time-consuming and arduous. Has it ever occurred to you that infants who come into this world with no prior knowledge of any language learn their own language within a few years on the basis of very little formal teaching? Somehow infants master the basics of their native tongue, including the difficult sounds and pronunciations that wreak such havoc on students desperately trying to master a second language? How does the child accomplish this feat?

A related mystery involves children's ability to generate sentences they have never heard before. Spend an hour or so listening to preschoolers converse. The creativity involved in generating a new thought will amaze you. But the simplicity of a child's communication should not blind us to the wonder of how a child creatively uses language.

But why single out language development for special treatment and devote a special chapter to it? First, the acquisition of language is probably the greatest intellectual feat a person will ever perform. Children are born without knowing any language, and within five years or so they are communicating their thoughts, feelings, and ideas to those around them. Second, language defines humanity. No other species shows the depth and complexity that human beings show in language formation and use. Third, the way children acquire language is really quite complex. And finally, the issues involved in language, such as bilingualism, the importance of the environment, and language and subculture, transcend all ages and stages.

The Nature of Communication

Language and communication are not the same. Language is only one part of communication. **Communication** is the process of sharing information, including facts, desires, and feelings (Shatz, 1983). It entails a sender, a receiver, and a message. **Language** involves "strings of symbols that represent meaning in some per-

communication   The process of sharing information.

language   The use of symbols to represent meaning in some medium.

ceptible medium" (Shatz, 1983, p. 844). It involves arbitrary symbols with agreed-on meanings. While communication is a process, language is one means of conveying the meaning to someone else. The medium is usually speech, but it does not have to be.

True or False   The terms *language* and *communication* can be used interchangeably.

For instance, consider the plight of a two-and-a-half-year-old who wants a cookie but can't reach the jar. The child wants to send a message to mommy, who is reading a magazine. He can communicate with her in a number of ways. He can verbally interrupt her by saying, "Mommy, gimme cookie," but there are other avenues of communication. He can cry, make nonlanguage sounds to gain her attention, or physically lead her to the cookie jar and point.

As receiver of the communication, the mother must interpret the message—not always an easy task. Children mispronounce words or express their thoughts in individualistic ways. Parents and children often have special words or phrases that stand for particular things. If a child said, "My stomach hurts," it would normally indicate that the child was experiencing gastric distress. However, one of my daughters would use that phrase to mean that she was either hungry of very full. We understood the phrase, and it carried a specific meaning for us, but when the child visited her grandmother, this phrase was interpreted differently, leading to a nap and no more cookies—much to my daughter's distress.

Once mother has interpreted the message, she must communicate an answer. The roles are now reversed: the mother becomes the sender, the child becomes the receiver. Let's say that mother nods her approval. As long as the child understands that this means yes, it is as effective as verbal communication.

The Nature of Language

Just what do children learn when they acquire language? Language has a number of subsystems. These include phonology, morphology, syntax, and semantics, as well as the rules for social language use, sometimes called pragmatics. **Phonology** includes the sounds of a language, the rules for combining them to make words, and the stress and intonation patterns (Gleason, 1985). For example, the sound "cl" occurs in English, but not "kx." Children also must learn how these sounds combine to become words. The **morpheme** is the smallest unit of meaning in a language. Some morphemes such as "dog" and "little," can stand by themselves, while others, such as "ed" and "ing," must be added to another word. The rules of morphology make certain that some sequences (such as "walked") will occur, and that others (such as "walkness") will not. Every language also has its own

phonology The study of the sounds of language, the rules for combining them to make words, and the stress and intonation patterns.

morphology The study of the patterns of word formation in a particular language.

morpheme The smallest unit of meaning in a language.

syntax The rules for combining words to make sentences.

semantics The study of the meaning of words.

rules for how to combine words to make sentences, called its **syntax.** For instance, "Johnny hit Mary" conveys a meaning quite different from "Mary hit John." The child must also acquire a vocabulary and understand the meaning behind the words. This area is called **semantics.** The

Children use a number of mediums to communicate with their parents including gestures and facial expressions.

general term **grammar** is used to refer to our total linguistic knowledge of phonology, morphology, syntax, and semantics (Best, 1986). The child must also be able to use language appropriately, to express his or her ideas efficiently and to get things done. This ability is called **pragmatics.** For example, children must learn the proper way to ask for something and how to use language in social situations. Each language has its own rules, and each culture has its own idea of how language should be used.

The Development of Language

Few events bring parents as much joy as their child's first word. It is easy to forget that much has taken place before the child says "Dada" or "Car." Under normal circumstances, every human child in every culture proceeds through similar steps in reaching linguistic competence (see Table 6.1).

Prelanguage Communication

Communication between infants and their caregivers does not require language. Smiles, cries, gestures, and eye contact all form a basis for later communication. The nonlanguage interaction between parent and infant approximates a conversation. Although very young infants cannot understand words, they do respond to the caregiver's language, and some linguistic abilities are present almost from birth (Molfese et al., 1982). One-day-old infants respond to speech sounds by moving their bodies in rhythm to them (Condon and Sander, 1974). One-month-old infants are able to discriminate between certain vowels, such as "-u" from "i-a," and "pa" from "pi" (Trehub, 1973).

True or False Infants as young as one month can understand the spoken word.

The infant's ability to respond to language and to other nonverbal cues leads to a kind of turn-taking called **proto-conversations.** A parent speaks, and the baby responds by smiling or later cooing. The parent then says something else, and the pattern continues. The interactions are spontaneous. Let's say mother is feeding the baby. When the infant spits the nipple out, the mother says, "No, I don't want any more. I want to burp." These interactions are the beginning of a conversation mode and are the basis for later communication.

grammar A general term that refers to the total linguistic knowledge of phonology, morphology, syntax, and semantics.

pragmatics The study of how people use language in various contexts.

proto-conversations The infant's responses to verbal and nonverbal cues that resemble turn-taking, as in a conversation.

cooing Verbal production of single-syllable sounds, like "oo."

babbling Verbal production of vowel and consonant sounds strung together and often repeated.

Such "conversations" are not as random as they seem. Mothers use a rising pitch when their infants are not paying attention and mothers want eye contact (Stern et al., 1982). In addition, yes-no questions are spoken with a rising pitch, whereas questions having to do with what and where, and various commands, are accompanied by a falling pitch.

The infant is also the master of another ability, **cooing.** Cooing involves production of single-syllable sounds, such as "oo." Vowel sounds are often led by a consonant, resulting in a sound like "moo." Infants enjoy listening to themselves vocalize, but these early noncrying vocalizations are not meant to be formal communication.

The next step in language development is **babbling.** Babbling involves both vowel and consonant sounds strung together and often repeated. Babbling may begin as early as three months, and it gradually increases until about nine to twelve months of age. Then it decreases as the child begins to use words (deVilliers and deVilliers, 1978). Most infants are babbling by the age of six months (Dale, 1976). Some people believe that when children babble they vocalize every possible speech sound the human vocal apparatus is capable of producing. This is not the case. Although the variety and range of speech sounds produced is impressive, it does not approximate all the sounds that humans can produce (deVilliers and deVilliers, 1978).

True or False When infants babble, they utter every sound the human vocal apparatus is capable of producing.

No one really knows why infants begin to babble, but we do know that they do so both when they are alone and when they are in the presence of other people. Per-

T A B L E 6.1

Patterns of Normal Speech Development

Child's Chronological Age	Child's Normal Speech Development
6 months	Repeats self-produced sounds; imitates sounds; vocalizes to other people; uses about 12 different speech sounds (known as phonemes).
12 months	Commonly uses up to 3 words besides mama and dada; may vocalize such words as bye-bye, hi baby, kitty, and puppy; and uses up to 18 different phonemes.
18 months	Commonly uses up to 20 words and 21 different phonemes; jargon words or phrases are present and often automatically repeats words or phrases said by others (echolalia); uses names of objects that are familiar, one-word sentences such as go or eat, and uses gestures; uses words such as no, mine, good, bad, hot, cold, nice, here, where, more, and expressions such as oh-oh, what's that, and all gone; the use of words at this age may be quite inconsistent.
24 months	Commonly uses up to 270 words and 25 different phonemes; jargon and echolalia are infrequent; averages 75 words per hour during free play; speaks in words, phrases, and 2- to 3-word sentences; average 2 words per response; first pronouns appear such as I, me, mine, it, who, and that; adjectives and adverbs begin to appear; names common objects and pictures; enjoys Mother Goose; refers to self by name such as Bobby go bye-bye, uses phrases such as I want, go bye-bye, want cookie, up daddy, nice doll, ball all gone, and where kitty.
30 months	Commonly uses up to 425 words and 27 different phonemes; jargon and echolalia no longer exist; averages 140 spoken words per hour; says words that name or identify items such as chair, can, box, key, and door; repeats 2 digits from memory; average sentence length is about 2½ words; uses more adjectives and adverbs; demands repetition from others (such as do it again); almost always announces intentions before acting; begins to ask questions of adults.
36 months	Commonly uses up to 900 words in simple sentences averaging 3 to 4 words per sentence; averages 15,000 words per day and 170 words per hour; uses words such as when, time, today, not today and can repeat three digits, name one color, say name, give simple account of experiences, and tell stories that are understandable; begins to use plurals and some prepositions; uses commands such as you make it, I want, and you do it; verbalizes toilet needs.
42 months	Commonly uses up to 1,200 words in mostly complete sentences that average between 4 and 5 words in length; 7 percent of the sentences are compound or complex and average 203 words per hour; rate of speech is faster; relates experiences and tells about activities in sequential order; can say a nursery rhyme; asks permission (such as Can I? or Will I?).
48 months	Commonly uses up to 1,500 words in sentences averaging 5 to 5½ words in length; averages 400 words per hour; counts to 3, repeats 4 digits, names 3 objects, and repeats 9-word sentences from memory; names the primary colors, some coins, and relates fanciful tales, enjoys rhyming nonsense words and using exaggerations; demands reasons why and how; questioning is at a peak, up to 500 a day; passes judgment on own activities; can recite a poem from memory or sing a song and uses such words as even, almost, now, something, like, and but.
54 months	Commonly uses up to 1,800 words in sentences averaging 5½ to 6 words but now averages only 230 words per hour and is satisfied with less verbalization; does little commanding or demanding; about 1 in 10 sentences is compound or complex and only 8 percent of the sentences are incomplete; can define 10 common words and count to 20; asks questions for information and learns to control and manipulate persons and situations with language.
60 months	Commonly uses up to 2,200 words in sentences averaging 6 words; can define ball, hat, stove, policeman, wind, and can count five objects and repeat 4 or 5 digits; definitions are in terms of use—can single out a word and ask it meaning; makes serious inquiries (such as what is this for, how does this work, etc.); uses all types of sentences, clauses, and parts of speech, reads by way of pictures and prints simple words.
66 months	Commonly uses up to 2,300 words in sentences that average 6½ words in length; grammatical errors continue to decrease as sentences and vocabulary become more sophisticated.
72 months	Commonly uses up to 2,500 words in sentences averaging 7 words in length; relates fanciful tales, recites numbers up to 30; asks the meaning of words; repeats five digits from memory; can complete analogies such as: A table is made of wood, a window of _____. A bird flies, a fish _____.

Source: Adapted and abridged from Weiss and Lillywhite, 1976.

haps babbling serves some self-stimulatory function or is part of a drive to master an emerging ability. Whether it be sitting, standing, or vocalizing, infants have a drive to practice and gain control of their emerging abilities. Even though infants do not need social stimulation to begin to babble, babbling can be increased through social reinforcement (Dodd, 1972). Although babbling begins as a relatively uncoordinated activity, social stimulation does affect the amount of babbling children produce.

The First Word

What exactly constitutes a child's first word? Specialists in language development use two criteria (deVilliers and deVilliers, 1978). The word must approximate some adult word and must be used consistently in similar situations. If the baby says "ca" whenever she sees a car, it meets both criteria, but if the infant says it once, it may be pure coincidence. Trying to convince a proud parent of this is useless.

Children usually utter their first word any time between ten and fifteen months, but there is considerable individual variation. Children's first words are not usually those they hear most often. Nelson (1973) studied early word acquisition in a number of children and was able to divide the children into two categories. **Expressive children** used words that were involved primarily in social interactions, such as "bye-bye" and "stop it." The early language of **referential children** involved the naming of objects, such as "dog" and "penny." These differing styles followed the linguistic style used by the children's caregivers. The parents of referential children named objects very frequently, while those of expressive children directed their children's activities and emphasized social interactions. The early language of both groups differed. Referential children used many more different words. Expressive children began to use language in a social context, while referential children used it in a cognitive context, such as labeling items when looking at a book (Nelson, 1981).

Words are used at first in isolation and then gradually generalized to similar situations. Babbling continues during this one-word stage. For years psychologists have argued about the meaning of these one-word utterances. Francis (1975) asks what a child really means when uttering the single word "jam." Does it mean that some jam is on the table or that the child wants jam on a piece of bread? Psychologists call this one-word utterance a

expressive children   Children who use words involved in social interactions, such as "stop" and "bye."

referential children   Children whose early language is used to name objects, such as "dog" or "bed."

holophrase   One word used to stand for an entire thought.

telegraphic speech   Sentences in which only the basic words necessary to communicate meaning are used with helping words such as "a" or "to" left out.

holophrase, meaning a single word that stands for a complete thought. For instance, a child says "Up" and means "Pick me up," or the child says "Wet" and wants to be changed. Parents must go beyond the word and use the context in order to interpret the child's ideas. The child saying "Wet" may be labeling the condition and not want to be changed at all. This interpretation casts doubt on whether the child is really using one-word expressions to indicate entire thoughts. If a child wanders over to the refrigerator and says "Jam," mother may say, "So you want some bread and jam." When parents interpret one-word utterances so loosely, establishing what a child really means becomes difficult.

Telegraphic Speech

The child's early speech, whether it is constructed of two- or three-word sentences, leaves out small words like "a," "to," or "from" and concentrates on the more important words. This is called **telegraphic speech** because it is similar to the language found in telegrams where the sender includes only the words absolutely necessary for communication. For example, "Mommy go store" may mean "Mommy is going to the store" or may be thought of as a command: "Mommy, go to the store!" Parents must still interpret the child's meaning according to the context of the remark, but the thoughts are communicated more precisely at this stage. If the child has just discovered there are no more cornflakes in the house, the mother may interpret "Mommy go store" as a command. If mother has just taken her coat off the hanger and begun to put it on, the child's comment may simply indicate that mother intends to go to the store.

Whatever this utterance means, the child has used only the words that are absolutely necessary for conveying meaning. These important words are commonly stressed by other speakers in the environment, which makes them easier to imitate and learn (Brown, 1973).

Approaching Mastery

By about three and a half years of age, children begin to use sentences of approximately four or five words, and by five years their syntax is quite good. The three-year-old has a vocabulary of about 900 words and begins to use plural nouns and the past tense. By age four, conjunctions are being used and the sentence structure is more complex. By age five or six, syntax has improved and approaches that of an adult (Smith and Neisworth, 1975), although tense errors and other grammatical irregularities still occur in speech until eight to ten years of age.

How Words Are Used

If you listen even casually to the speech patterns of young children, you will find some striking differences between their use of language and that of adults. Young children overextend and underextend their use of words and follow grammatical rules with what seems to be blind devotion.

Overextensions and Underextensions

"Look! Daddy!" the child says when noticing a man's picture on the wanted poster in the post office—to the embarrassment of mother. As they learn language, children make certain kinds of mistakes (Griffiths, 1986). For instance, a young child looking at a magazine might label every picture of a man "Daddy" and every four legged animal "Dog," even though the child knows his or her father and is probably aware of the difference between a cat and a dog.

The type of error in which children apply a term more broadly than is correct, called an **overextension,** is probably a problem of production more than one of comprehension (Whitehurst, 1982). That is, children understand the difference, but they have difficulty producing the correct labels. This was demonstrated in a study by Nelson and her colleagues (1978), who found that a child would call a variety of vehicles—such as an airplane, a truck, or even a helicopter—a car, but could pick out the correct object when asked to do so. In another study, a child who overextended the word "apple" to include

overextensions A type of error in which children apply a term more broadly than it should be.

underextension A type of error in which children apply a term more narrowly than it should be.

overgeneralization A type of error in which children overuse the basic rules of the language. For instance, once they learn to use plural nouns they may say "mans" instead of "men."

a number of different foods was able to choose an apple from a group of foods when asked to do so (Thomson and Chapman, 1975).

Children also **underextend**—that is, they use a term to cover a smaller universe than it should (Anglin, 1977). Young children often use "animal" to define only mammals and may deny that people, insects, or birds are also animals.

Why do children make these errors? Perhaps they learn nouns in terms of features (Clark, 1978). For example, dogs have four legs and fur. If this were so, the child would call all four-legged animals with fur "dogs." Categorization problems may also arise from the speech that is directed at children by adults (Anglin, 1977). When a child is young, parents are apt to use such terms as "car" and "dog" instead of "Chevrolet" or "German shepherd." This is functional because children need to recognize the difference between a car and a truck but not between a Chevy and a Dodge, but it restricts the child's experience with labels and explains these phenomena. Overextensions and underextensions may also simply reflect the child's current mental abilities and difficulty in categorizing items.

Overgeneralization of Rules

Once children begin to acquire some of the basic rules of English, they overuse—or, as psychologists say, **overgeneralize**—them (Goodluck, 1986). For example, to pluralize a noun, we ordinarily add an "s" to its end, as in "dogs" or "pencils." However, exceptions abound, and the plural of "man" is not "mans" but "men." When creating a past tense, we normally add the suffix "ed," as in "walked" or "talked." But again exceptions are plentiful; the past tense of "go" is not "goed" but "went," and the past tense of "see" is not "seed" but "saw." Children will often overuse these rules and use words

"I drinked the waters!" Once children begin to master the rules of grammar, they often overgeneralize them.

like "seed" or "goed." They may have used the word correctly in the past, but now that they know the rule, they apply it to every case producing such gramatically incorrect forms. With experience, children correct themselves, and most gradually learn the exceptions with little or no formal training.

True or False Children who use incorrect forms of words, such as *goed* and *drinked* instead of *went* and *drank*, need formal language training.

Comprehension and Production

So far we have looked at the **production** of language, but there is another important area—**comprehension,** the understanding of language. As noted, infants can differentiate between sounds very early. Early in infancy they react to the tonal quality of a voice (Wolff, 1963). The baby shows pleasure and contentment when exposed to a pleasant, soothing voice. Later, children can understand words they cannot produce (Bloom, 1974). A fourteen-month-old child could point out his own shoe and his mother's shoe when asked to do so, even though he was unable to speak a word (Huttenlocher, 1974).

At every age, children understand more words than they can produce. As children grow into adulthood, they use a greater variety of words in their writing than in

| **production** | The ability to verbalize language. |
| **comprehension** | The understanding of language. |

their speech. We recognize many more words in print and in someone else's speech than we ourselves use, and this imbalance remains throughout life.

True or False Children produce many more words than they can understand.

How We Learn Language

The simplest questions are often the most difficult to answer. This is especially true in the area of language-learning. For years, psychologists have been struggling over the question of how a child develops from a being that understands and produces no language to one that can use language with great ease.

Reinforcement and Imitation

At first glance, it appears that children learn language through imitation. This is true of vocabulary. Words are symbols that stand for things or ideas. The vocabulary of each language differs. The Spanish word for chair is "silla," and in Hebrew it is "keesay." Children do learn vocabulary through imitation. Children learn the word "cookie" when they have need for the word. They master words in an attempt to communicate with others (Hoff-Ginsberg, 1986). When they finally say "chair," they have imitated what they have heard in their environment.

The vocabulary growth of children shown in Figure 6.1 is impressive. Between the ages of one and a half and six and a half, the child learns about ten new words each week, yielding a rate of one and a half new words a day (Smith, 1926, in Whitehurst and Vasta, 1977).

The effect of imitation on word acquisition is evident. A parent who labels common, everyday items is more likely to have a child who has a superior early vocabulary (Nelson, 1973). Children may also pick up unusual words that have shock value. My two-year-old daughter learned the words "horrible," "ridiculous," and "disgusting" very early—no doubt from her older sisters. She would try some new food, make a face, and say "disgusting," with all the intonation the word requires. She generalized the use of this word and, after receiving a big kiss from one of her great-aunts, wiped her face and said, "Disgusting." The power of the environment is shown by the way children learn words from older siblings and peers, often using them at the wrong time.

It is a mistake to think that because the child learns vocabulary through these processes, all language development can be explained by imitation and reinforcement. There is more to it. Children must acquire rules for changing tense, creating word order, and the like—called syntax—in order to use language correctly. Some of the rules are quite complicated. Try describing the rule by which you would use the phrase "a thing" or "the thing." Most of us use the rule perfectly, but we would be hard-pressed to formulate it. Can children learn the syntax of a language through the processes of reinforcement and imitation, or is language too complicated to be explained by these processes?

According to Skinner (1957), operant conditioning—including the processes of reinforcement, generalization, and discrimination—are responsible for language development. Children learn language the same way they learn everything else. They are reinforced for labeling the environment and for asking for things. Through the process of generalization and discrimination, children come to reduce their errors and use the appropriate forms. Of course, imitation also enters the picture, as the child imitates parental speech. Skinner looks at the acquisition of grammar as a matter of generalizing and making inferences. For example, a child may learn the meaning for the phrase "my teddybear" and then infer that it is also "my cookie," "my television"—"my" everything.

Although learning must be involved in language acquisition, the theory does not seem sufficient to explain totally how a child acquires language. Learning theory may explain acquisition of vocabulary, but how does a child learn to create an original sentence? It is difficult to explain the simple but brilliant creativity and originality of a child's sentences. All children create original sentences they have not heard before. In addition, how can a child of limited cognitive abilities master the complicated rules of grammar that even adults cannot ex-

plain—and do all this without formal training (Bloom, 1975)? Finally, if only the processes of learning are involved, why do children make the same mistakes as they develop their language abilities, and why do they produce such childish speech patterns as telegraphic speech, which they do not hear around them? These problems, among others, have led some authorities to argue that an innate biological mechanism must be responsible for language acquisition.

Is Language Acquisition Innate?

Noam Chomsky (1972, 1965, 1959), the leading advocate for the biological or **nativist explanation** argued

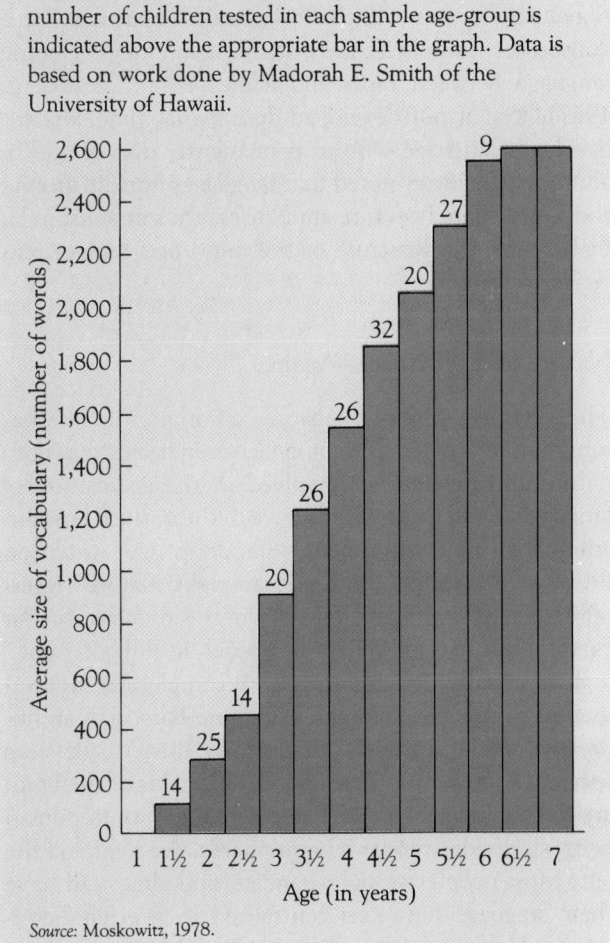

FIGURE 6.1

Children's Average Vocabulary Size

Children's average vocabulary size increases rapidly between the ages of one and a half and six and a half. The number of children tested in each sample age-group is indicated above the appropriate bar in the graph. Data is based on work done by Madorah E. Smith of the University of Hawaii.

Source: Moskowitz, 1978.

that human beings are preprogrammed to learn language. Children require only exposure to the language prevailing in their own culture. Human beings are born with an innate, biological ability to learn language—called a **language-acquisition device.** Children can acquire the grammar of the particular culture's language because their brain is biologically patterned to understand the structure of languages. Children acquire and use the basic rules of language and form hypotheses about them, which they then test out.

Chomsky's position excited many psychologists and **psycholinguists,** scientists who study the nature of languages. It explained the interesting similarities we find in language development around the world. Children proceed through the same steps when learning language in all cultures (Slobin, 1972) and make the same mistakes. These similarities could be explained if the acquisition of language rests on some shared neurological foundation. Language acquisition becomes a maturational activity coinciding with brain developments. Some authorities claim there is a critical period for developing language between birth and adolescence (Lenneberg, 1967), that if not developed during that time, the individual's language will be permanently disordered. In addition, Chomsky noted that languages from all around the world shared certain similarities, thus establishing a fit between the structure of the mind and human language in general.

Nature and Nurture—Again

The Chomsky-Skinner debate is a variation of the nature-nurture debate. Current evidence indicates that both nature and nurture are involved in the acquisition of language. Even those who believe in the nativist position admit that the environment is important. As Aitchison (1978, p. 89) states, "Both sides are right: Nature triggers off the behaviour, and lays down the framework, but careful nurture is needed for it to reach its full potential."

It is equally difficult to take a completely environmental perspective. Human beings are born with an impressive vocal apparatus that allows them to develop speech (Aichison, 1978), and specific areas of the brain are devoted to language. The cerebral cortex in human beings is divided into two hemispheres, the right and the left. Most people are right-handed, and almost all have their language functions centralized in the left hemisphere. Half the left-handed people also have their lan-

language-acquisition device An assumed biological device used in the acquisition of language.

psycholinguistics The study of the nature of language.

Broca's area An area in the brain responsible for producing speech.

Wernicke's area An area in the brain responsible for comprehension of language.

guage areas localized in the left hemispheres (Gleason, 1985). Scientists found that when specific areas of the brain are injured, certain language-related problems occur. For example, the area responsible for producing speech is called **Broca's area.** Damage here causes difficulties in producing language, but the person is still able to comprehend it. Damage to another area, called **Wernicke's area,** causes a person to have poor comprehension and speech filled with nonsense words, even though it is fluent. The brain also has areas associated with written language (Gleason, 1985).

A number of factors already noted indicate that some biological basis for language acquisition may exist too. Human infants can make impressive phonetic distinctions and are attentive to speech quite early in life. Some strategies for processing language may be innate (Slobin, 1973; McNeill, 1970). Finally, certain informational processes, such as memory and attention, may develop according to maturational rules that we are only just beginning to appreciate. Some biological or innate factors are at work in language acquisition, but a complete biological position does not match the facts.

The weaknesses in the nativist position are evident. For example, the existence of a language acquisition device has not yet been demonstrated. In addition, even if we agree that a neurological basis for language exists, it does not explain the processes involved in language-learning. Finally, although the similarities between how children learn language around the world are impressive, recent evidence shows that there are some differences that reflect the nature of the language being learned (Akiyama, 1985). In one study, children were tested on the order in which they acquired four types of statements: true affirmatives such as "You are a child," false affirmatives like "You are a baby," false negatives like "You aren't a child," and true negatives like "You aren't a baby." Three- and four-year-old Japanese-speaking and

English-speaking children were asked whether such statements were right or wrong. The English-speaking children found verifying true negatives most difficult, whereas the Japanese-speaking children had the greatest problem with false negatives. The difference in acquisition pattern is due to linguistic differences between English and Japanese (Akiyama, 1984). So, although some biological foundation for learning language is probable, the nativist position does not fully explain language acquisition either.

The strictly-learning theory and nativist positions thus fail as complete explanations for language acquisition. Two other approaches to language acquisition, which emphasize the importance of cognitive and social factors, are now popular and have begun to fill this void.

Cognitive Theory and Language Development

Language-learning involves such cognitive processes as attention, information-processing, and retention. For instance, paying attention to stimuli that are loud or attached to some vital activity (such as feeding), remembering them, and making discriminations and judgments about these stimuli (such as whether they are the same or different and classifying according to these judgments) are all cognitive processes related to language-learning (Peters, 1986). How could children create sentences if they did not have the cognitive ability to remember words? In addition, children must understand something about an object or an idea before using words in a meaningful manner. Linguistic growth necessarily parallels cognitive growth. Children may learn language by first understanding the meaning of words spoken in their environment and then coming to appreciate the relationship between what the words mean and the language used (MacNamara, 1972). The child first uses simple words for things, then proceeds to define classes in terms of their more abstract qualities, such as color. Language-learning follows cognitive advancements. As a child's cognitive development proceeds, expressions become more exact. Children may understand some concept and want to communicate it, yet not have the proper words in their vocabulary. In fact, if children cannot express a thought using a word they know, they will invent a word (Nelson, 1974). Scientists are now searching for specific identifiable relationships between cognitive advancements and linguistic expression. Although this approach is interesting, only further experimentation can determine how fruitful that search will be.

Social Interaction and Language Development

Children do not acquire language in a vacuum. They are affected by the total linguistic environment that surrounds them, including the home and the day-care center they may attend. (See Cross-Cultural Current on page 164.) Recent investigations of the nature of the child's early linguistic environment have uncovered information that runs counter to conventional wisdom.

The child's early language environment. Consider the situation in which infants find themselves. They can hear and discriminate certain sounds, but everyone is talking quickly in a complex and difficult-to-understand manner with little repetition. At first glance, the linguistic environment appears to be confusing, and its level seems to be much too high for infants. Yet children learn to communicate through language in a relatively short time. Such a scenario appealed to the psychologists who argued in favor of an innate language mechanism. After all, children acquire language on the basis of very fragmented and cognitively advanced input. It all seemed impossible.

But this particular argument in favor of the innate mechanism has been refuted. Communication aimed at children is neither fragmented nor confusing. Infants receive verbal stimulation from the first days of their lives. This verbal input is well structured and tuned to their level. It begins in the hospital nursery. Certainly new mothers and fathers speak to their newborn infants from birth. Even hospital workers not only use soothing sounds and baby talk but actually speak to newborns as if they expect them to understand speech (Rheingold and Adams, 1980). At times, they engage in a dialogue; the child's movements encourage the adult to say something. And at times the staff ask and answer their own questions as they think the baby would. In all, the earliest verbal communication is anything but impersonal and random. Infants elicit a great deal of stimulation, and from the first they are exposed to a rich linguistic environment.

The idea that early verbal interchanges are confusing and too difficult for infants is in error. When people talk to infants, they modify their speech. Parents talk to their older infants in shorter sentences, but these sentences are very well formed (Bowerman, 1981; Newport et al., 1977). The language that parents use for talking to toddlers is simple and repetitious. It contains many questions and commands, few hesitations, focuses on the present tense, is highly pitched, and is spoken with an exagger-

Day Care and Language Development

What happens to the language development of children when they attend a day-care center for long periods of time? That depends on the day-care center, according to Kathleen McCartney, who investigated the language development of 146 preschoolers attending nine day-care centers in Bermuda. Because language skills are so important to later success in school, the effect the day-care experience has on development of these skills is worth addressing.

The choice of Bermuda as the site for the study is interesting in itself. First, 84 percent of all Bermudan children spend the majority of the work week in some form of nonmaternal substitute care by age two. When studies of children in American day care are performed, the possibility that these children differ from the average child becomes a problem. In Bermuda, the child not in some day-care arrangement is unusual. Another frequent problem in day-care research is that programs differ so much that the results of research using one or two centers may be biased. This study used all nine day-care centers in Bermuda that accepted children from infancy through the preschool years and that had been in operation for five or more years. All children three years and older who attended any of these centers for six months or more, and their parents, were asked to participate.

The children ranged in age from thirty-six months to sixty-eight months. Previous research had demonstrated that the amount and nature of the verbal interchanges between parents and their children are major factors in determining language skill. McCartney hypothesized that the amount and nature of the verbal interchanges between children and caregivers at the day-care center would also predict language skill.

Many aspects of the day-care environment, and the children's intellectual and language development, as well as their homes and backgrounds, were carefully measured. Verbal interactions with caregivers and peers were divided into four categories. *Control statements* involved commands like "Stop talking." *Expressive comments* involved the expression of feelings and attitudes, such as "I like your shirt." *Representational statements* were defined as the giving and receiving of information, as in the statement "The toys are over there," and *social comments* were aimed at establishing and maintaining social relationships, as in the statement "Let's play with this."

McCartney found that the overall quality of the day-care center was a positive predictor of children's language development, as was the amount of verbal interaction between caregiver and child. The type of caregiver-child interchange was important too. The proportion of control statements was a negative predictor of language development—that is, children who received many commands were hampered in their development of important language skills. It is interesting to note that control and

---

ated intonation (Garnica, 1977). In short, parents' speech to their linguistically limited children is restricted; it uses common nouns and comments on what their children are doing (Molfese et al., 1982). The use of simplistic, redundant sentences is normally referred to as **motherese.** All adults, and many older children, tailor their language use to the age and comprehension level of younger children. Even young children use these strategies, but do not present their little siblings with much nonverbal information and are not as proficient in the use of these strategies (Tomasello and Mannle, 1985).

True or False Parents use well-formed sentences when speaking to toddlers.

motherese The use of simple repetitive sentences with young children.

The child's reaction to parental speech determines the speaker's choice of words (Bohannon and Marquis, 1977). If a two-year-old shows a lack of comprehension, an adult immediately reduces the number of words in the next sentence. Children are not merely passive receivers of information. Their show of comprehension or noncomprehension serves to control their linguistic environment.

Verbal exchanges between adults and young children

representational statements were inversely related to each other. The more control statements (as in commands) given by the caregivers, the fewer the representational statements (giving and receiving information) communicated to them. On the other hand, the proportion of representational statements was positively related to language skills. Children benefit when they are given and asked for information.

Another important predictor of linguistic ability was the child's willingness to initiate a conversation with a caregiver. This was related to the atmosphere created by the caregiver. Children's language skills are optimized when children are encouraged to initiate conversations.

Some specific aspects of the day-care center were particularly important in determining a child's language abilities. Children did better in more-structured centers with low noise levels and little time for free play. But this does not mean children should be regimented, and we should not conclude that any one educational theory is superior. It does demonstrate that children benefit when caregivers structure children's activities to some extent and create an organized environment.

But how about peer exchanges? After all, children do talk to one another in day-care centers. McCartney found that the greater the number of peer conversations, the lower the language scores of the children. Perhaps peer conversations of lesser quality replaced important caregiver talk.

This study demonstrates that a number of factors predict children's language abilities, including the amount and type of caregiver utterances, children's willingness to initiate interactions with caregivers, and the overall quality of the day-care center, as well as some specific aspects of the way the center is organized. Good things seem to occur together. It is likely that superior day-care centers are well organized with structured activities, create an atmosphere in which children talk more with their caregivers, and contain personnel who are more concerned with giving and receiving information than with giving commands.

Studies like this emphasize the importance of the environment in determining language skills. No matter which theory of language acquisition one subscribes to, the child's linguistic environment is a major predictor of language skills. The challenge is to create a linguistic environment that will help children develop language skills to the fullest. Day-care centers clearly have a role to play in this area.

Source: McCartney, K. Effect of Quality of Day-Care Environment on Children's Language Development. *Developmental Psychology,* 1984, 20, 244–260.

do not constitute formal language lessons. The idea that parents somehow sit down and teach their children how to talk is not supported by the facts. For example, parents usually do not correct their children for grammatical errors or reward them for using correct grammar. They are more interested in the correctness of their children's utterances (Brown et al., 1969). If little Sharon says, "Me girl," her mother is likely to say, "That's right, you are a girl." On the other hand, if Sharon says, "I am a boy," her mother is likely to straighten her out immediately. A recent study confirmed this finding that parental approval of what the child says follows both grammatically correct and incorrect utterances to the same degree. However, Penner (1987) also found that parents

were more likely to expand on their replies when their young children used grammatically incorrect statements than when they used grammatically correct ones. For example, if a child said, "Ball fall," parents said, "Yes, the ball fell down," rather than simply "Go get the ball." This did not occur all the time, but it still happened more than would be expected by chance. Notice that the parent first reinforced the child for the correctness of the statement and then expanded on the statement, changing the grammar of the sentence and expanding on its content.

True or False Parents are just as likely to correct children's statements for grammatical errors as they are for truthfulness.

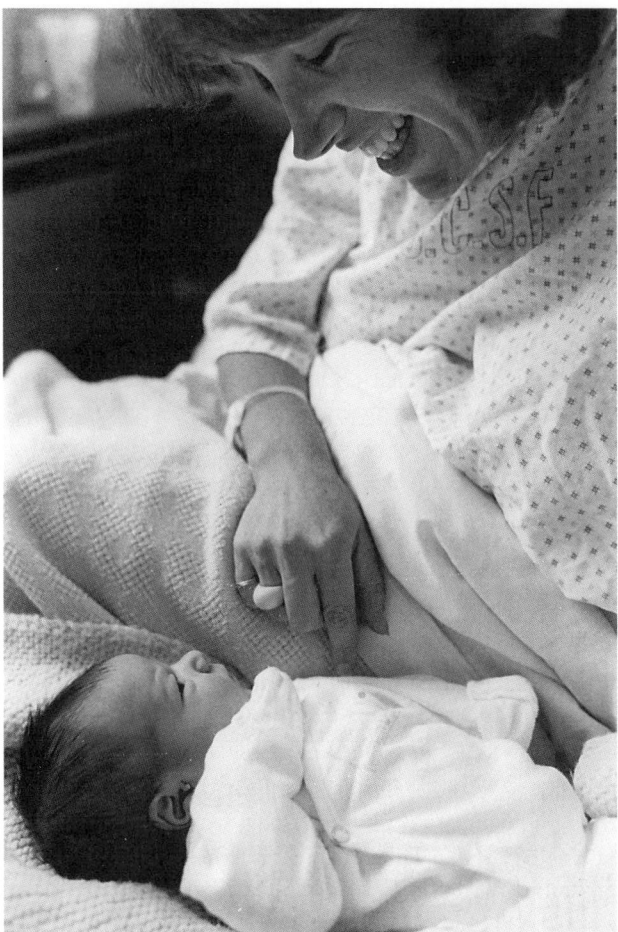

Children are spoken to from earliest infancy.

Language acquisition involves learning a social skill that is useful in the interpersonal context. Language is purely functional. The purpose of speech and language is to communicate thoughts, ideas, and desires to others. Psychologists have become more interested in the nature of this give-and-take on the part of parents and their children. Even before learning language, children begin actively communicating with their parents through gestures and vocalizations (Bruner, 1978a, 1978b). These prelinguistic modes are replaced by standard linguistic modes. Indeed, the child is an active and willing partner. The interactions between mother and child are very much structured in the form of a dialogue and show a progression from the simple to the complex. Even though parents may not be aware of their role as teachers, they do teach their children their native tongue. The infant

begins to communicate, and mother responds. The interaction between the two is intense and functional.

Language is used to direct the actions of others. The child learns that communication involves signaling meaning, sharing experiences, and taking turns. One eminent psychologist, Jerome Bruner (1978a) sees language development in terms of problem-solving. Children must solve the problem of how to communicate their wishes and thoughts to others. They learn language through this interaction with others and by actively using language. The opportunity to engage actively in communication is necessary. Children acquire grammar and vocabulary because they are useful to them in accomplishing their aim of getting across to others what they want and what they are thinking. Notice that, in this conception of language development, parents tune their linguistic input to the ability level of the child. This theory is sometimes called the **fine-tuning theory.** It explains the finding that children encounter language in a very structured and progressively more difficult and complex manner. Language is learned as an extension of nonlinguistic communication.

Bruner also believes that cognitive development precedes linguistic development. Children know what they want to communicate, and language becomes the necessary vehicle for doing so when they are mature enough to produce it. The view sees language acquisition as arising from need and based on carefully fine-tuned interactions between mother and child and as an outgrowth of solving the problems of communicating with another individual. When studying a child's linguistic progress, the transactions between mother and child should be investigated. Bruner (1978a, p. 38) notes that language-learning is not a "solo flight in search of rules, but a transaction involving an active language learner and an equally active language teacher."

Encouraging Linguistic Competence: What Parents Can Do

Children learn language through an active process that involves exposure to a particular linguistic environment.

The finding that the nature of this early linguistic interaction determines the child's later language abilities comes as no surprise. Children who are encouraged to verbalize and expand on their language skills develop superior language abilities (Hoff-Ginsberg, 1986). A number of studies have found that language usage among middle-class and working-class people differ. Middle-class youngsters use more expansive language and do better in language activities in school. Children of working-class parents use simpler sentences and more commands (Olim et al., 1967). But we must remember that language is functional and that these children are not deficient in their own native environment. What is somewhat lacking are the specific language abilities required in school. When we consider how well a child knows his or her own dialect, there is no deficiency in rate and amount of linguistic knowledge (Menyuk, 1977). The importance of the linguistic environment is also shown by a study that compared the language development of twins to nontwins. The twins were not as advanced as single children. The communication pattern between these twin pairs and their mothers was more directive and contained fewer questions or statements that required the children to answer (Tomasello et al., 1986). There is no doubt that the child's linguistic environment affects language development.

True or False Middle-class children use more complex sentences and fewer commands than children of working-class parents.

True or False Twins are generally not as advanced in linguistic development as their nontwin peers.

Most suggestions for improving linguistic competence are based on the premise that children learn language both by listening and by participating. Parents should not take an artificial attitude toward language development, for the natural flow of parent-child interactions is sufficient for the child to learn the appropriate language. Parents can do more harm than good by trying to force a child to say something the youngster is not ready to say, or by providing the child with a language environment that is too complex or inappropriate. Nevertheless, parents can help children in the development of their language.

Give the child an opportunity to talk. Acquisition of language is an active process. Children need an opportunity to talk and to communicate their thoughts (Cazden, 1981). When children are young,

ask "wh-" questions and encourage them to use more than just a yes or no answer.

Expand on the child's statements. Middle-class parents often expand on their children's statements. For example, if the child says "Throw ball," a parent might say "Throw the ball to daddy." Such expansions have a positive effect in broadening the child's language usage (Hovell et al., 1978).

Label things in the environment. Children benefit from listening to speech that labels the environment. When a baby points at the bottle, it is worthwhile to say, "You want your bottle."

Read to the child. Reading to a child is beneficial, but there are many ways to do this. When the child is old enough to give some response, try to ask questions that are age-appropriate and allow the child to participate in the story. When reading a story, you may ask the youngster to point to the cow or the dog. In time, when children can talk, they can label things themselves and answer such questions as what color it is. Even later, the story may lead to a discussion about farm life and the like.

Provide good language models. Because children tend to copy the way their parents express themselves, reasonably good linguistic models are important. Finishing sentences, answering questions in an expanded way, using adjectives, and so on, contribute to a rich linguistic environment.

Encourage verbal interaction. Instead of forcing a child to speak and verbalize, using praise and engaging the child in meaningful verbal interactions are worthwhile (Hess and Shipman, 1967).

Current Issues in Language and Communication

We have been looking at the general sequence of development and some theoretical viewpoints that explain how children develop language. The general process by which language unfolds is universal, although individual differences in the paths a child may follow do exist (Nelson, 1981). The theoretical attempts to answer the simple question of how children learn language seem confusing, but we can surmise that innate factors, cognitive growth, the principles of learning, and social interactions are involved in some complicated manner. With this basic knowledge in hand, let's look at some of the fascinating issues in the area of language development.

Even young children reduce the length of their sentences when faced with a younger sibling who does not understand.

Sex Differences in Language Acquisition

Do girls learn language faster than boys? The evidence on this question is mixed. Many early studies found that girls acquire language more quickly than boys do (McCarthy, 1954). Smith (1926) found that two- and three-year-old girls had larger vocabularies than boys of the same age, although the differences were negligible by age four. Some later studies confirmed this, but other studies did not. This led Maccoby and Jacklin (1974) to conclude from the literature that the only consistent female advantage is found in the area of verbal fluency. Females are more fluent in language than males. But additional recent evidence again supports the earliest evidence that girls speak earlier and make longer utterances than boys (Schachter et al., 1978). We may conclude that, although not all studies are in agreement, the evidence does generally favor females in this area.

True or False On the average, American girls acquire language faster than American boys.

The advantage would not be surprising, because girls are physically more advanced at birth and mature more quickly. If language acquisition partly involves the maturation of some complex neurological structures, we would expect girls as a group to develop language faster than boys. Perhaps the greater responsiveness of females encourages verbal communication from those around them. Some studies suggest that mothers talk more to daughters than to sons (Goldberg and Lewis, 1969).

The superiority of females in this respect may also be a function of culture. One study investigating sex differences in early vocal responsiveness discovered that Greek infant males raised at home were superior to infant females also raised at home on a measure of verbal responsiveness (Roe et al., 1985). In addition, Greek mothers spoke differently to infant sons than to daughters. Perhaps we should keep in mind that the studies showing female superiority in early language development were conducted in the United States, and consider the possibility that cultural forces are operating. The researchers who performed the study in Greece cite evidence that "male children in Greece are much more welcomed, valued and interacted with than female children" (Roe et al., 1985, p. 372). This pattern is more pronounced than in the United States. Therefore, when speaking of sex differences in language we must be careful to note the culture.

Does the linguistic superiority of American girls continue? Until about the age of three, girls seem to be superior, but boys do catch up. In middle childhood no differences are found except among very poor groups, in which girls remain superior to boys (Bee, 1978). In adolescence, females again begin to show greater verbal abilities than males (Maccoby and Jacklin, 1974). Of course, individual differences are plentiful, and it is easy to find a male who is superior in linguistic abilities.

Black vs. Standard English: Difference or Deficit?

"By the time I get there, he will have gone."
"Time I git dere, he be done gone."

If you were asked which of the above sentences would be best received by an English teacher, you would certainly choose the first. While the first sentence illustrates Standard English, the second is Black English. **Black English** is a dialect spoken throughout the United States by lower-income blacks and understood by almost all black people (Raspberry, 1970). It contains a consistent logical, and coherent grammar (Labov, 1970).

True or False   Black English is a dialect of Standard English.

At one time it was thought that Black English was simply mispronounced and poorly spoken Standard English, and it was accorded no respect. In fact, because children from ghetto areas have many language difficulties, it was thought that their problems were caused in part by their initial exposure to and learning of this dialect. This led to what has been called the **deficit hypothesis.** Basically, the dialect was considered to be a deficit—something wrong, not merely different. It was something that a child should give up somewhere along the educational ladder.

Beginning in the late 1960s, however, social scientists began to reconsider this position. After all, if Black English is understood in the child's environment and has a consistent set of rules, why treat it differently from Spanish or French? In some ways, it is even more precise

Black English   A dialect spoken throughout the United States by lower-income blacks but understood by the overwhelming majority of blacks.

linguistic deficit hypothesis   The belief that a dialect such as Black English is a hindrance to learning.

linguistic difference hypothesis   The belief that a dialect such as Black English is different from Standard English but not a deficit.

than Standard English. When a teacher asks a black child why her father couldn't make a meeting the night before, the child might answer, "He sick." But when asked why the father had not attended any of the meetings during the year, the child says, "He be sick" (Raspberry, 1970). Inclusion of the word "be" shows an ongoing chronic status. In Standard English, the answers to both questions might simply be that the father was ill.

Black English is closer to Standard English than French or Spanish, but the black child who has mastered Black English might best be considered bilingual for educational purposes. Standard English could be taught as a second language. This extreme position is not accepted by most authorities, who argue instead that Black English is a valid dialect. Black children do not suffer from linguistic deficits, but they do experience some academic difficulties due to **linguistic differences,** and differences are not necessarily deficits.

If teachers consider Black English to be inferior to Standard English, they may reject these children's ideas, essentially turning them off and reducing communication between teacher and child. Students may also develop feelings of inferiority. Teachers must understand that Black English is a dialect and should accept the child's ideas without reacting negatively to the dialect. When a teacher misunderstands Black English, it may also lead to frustrating situations for both teacher and pupil. Dale (1972) notes that black children read the words "I saw it" as "I see it," because both "see" and "saw" are pronounced "see" in this dialect. Correcting the error is difficult because black children do not understand that it is an error.

Whether it is called a deficit or a difference, Standard English presents difficulties for lower-income children from ghetto areas. Perhaps both the deficit hypothesis and the difference hypothesis miss the mark in one regard. Children must be able to deal with their environment, and Black English is useful for this. However, even though Black English may be accepted as a dialect, children must learn Standard English if they are to succeed in school and in the world of work. When six black college women were sent for interviews, those that spoke Black English were given shorter interviews and received fewer offers. The offers that were made were for lower-paying positions. Children who are encouraged to speak Black English in order to keep their heritage may risk being handicapped in the job market (Raloff, 1982).

Most people who want to accept Black English as a dialect agree that black children must still learn to speak and write Standard English. Perhaps there has been too much focus on the deficit and difference hypotheses, and not enough on how one teaches children a different dialect, one they will not hear around their homes or neighborhoods very much. Some suggest using techniques developed to teach children a foreign language. The most modern way of learning a foreign language is total immersion—living, breathing, and thinking that language for weeks until one is thoroughly familiar with it. This is not a practical strategy in this case. We certainly need more research into alternative methods of teaching Standard English to children who speak other dialects.

The Bilingual Puzzle

What of the thousands of children in the United States who come from homes in which a foreign language, commonly Spanish, is the primary language (see Table 6.2)? These children, who often come also from impoverished backgrounds, face many of the same problems blacks do, although their language itself is accepted as a true language. English is the second language for these children, and their success in the United States depends partly on learning Standard English.

What is the best way to educate these children? Some educators propose that a bilingual program be introduced in the school, that subjects such as math and social studies be taught to Spanish-speaking students in Spanish until the children gain sufficient ability in English to function effectively in that language. At the same time, these children would receive instruction in Standard English. Evaluations of these programs have been mixed. Some evidence shows that the programs have helped students achieve scholastically (Crawford, 1987; Willig, 1985). Other researchers disagree, noting that these pro-

TABLE 6.2

Languages Other Than English Spoken at Home

Many people are surprised by the number of children who come from homes in which a language other than English is spoken. As this table indicates, many of these children have difficulty with English.

Current Language Spoken	Total (1,000)	Difficulty with English (percent)
Total persons	47,494	—
Speaking a language other than English	4,568	14.0
Spanish	2,952	15.4
Italian	147	5.4
French	223	6.8
German	192	6.2
Polish	41	5.7
Chinese	114	20.9
Greek	66	5.2
Philippine languages	63	8.9
Portuguese	68	10.3
Japanese	34	18.7
Korean	60	17.0
Vietnamese	64	36.0
All other	544	12.3

Source: U.S. Bureau of the Census, 1980.

grams have not been as successful as hoped (Baker and de Kanter, 1981). Some note that there is a strong need to emphasize English, instead of the child's native language, through a process that is similar to immersion. In such programs, students are taught in English by teachers who know other languages but use it only to help students who do not understand the material. Students are encouraged to use English, but also to ask questions in their native language when necessary (*U.S. News & World Report*, 1986). Other detractors note how difficult it is to recruit effective bilingual teachers and that there are problems involved when more than one foreign language is used by various children in the class.

The debate over the best way to teach these children English is ongoing, and more research is needed (August, 1986). Congress has passed legislation encouraging bilingual education, and the courts have mandated it when appropriate. Bilingual education is a fact of life in the United States although it is increasingly under attack.

The psychological issues surrounding bilingualism are still with us, and debate over the consequences of bilingualism continues.

At first glance, people who can function in society using more than one language would seem to be at a great advantage. However, research in the 1950s indicated that bilingual children did poorly in school and suffered retarded language development in both languages (Segalowitz, 1981). These studies have been criticized for their poor methodology and questionable testing devices.

Recently, though, an about-face on the issue of bilingualism itself has occurred. McLaughlin (1978, 1977) found no clear evidence that bilingualism leads to intellectual or cognitive problems in school. Some of the difficulties encountered by bilingual students are due not to their bilingual nature but to poverty, poor housing, lack of intellectual stimulation, and other socioeconomic variables (Diaz, 1985). In fact, there is evidence that bilingual children are high in verbal and nonverbal intelligence scores and show more cognitive flexibility (Segalowitz, 1981).

True or False Bilingualism, itself, leads to cognitive difficulties and academic problems in school.

What can we conclude about the bilingual child? First, there is nothing inherently inferior about bilingualism, and there is evidence that bilingual children have certain advantages over monolingual peers. Second, poverty and bilingualism are often confused. Many minority groups in the United States that speak a language other than English suffer from the degradations of poverty, and all that entails—including poor self-concept, disillusionment, discrimination, poor opportunity, and so forth. It may be that the clash of cultures, rather than bilingualism, actually causes many of the problems experienced by teachers in the public schools. Finally, we still do not know the best way to teach children English, and there is probably room for many different approaches.

If bilingual programs in the schools are to work, they must ensure that *all* children learn English in a way that will allow them to function reasonably well, not only in the outside world but also in academic settings. If children leave school knowing math, science, and social studies, but function poorly in language-related areas, such as reading, writing, and speaking, their prospects for educational advancement will be poor and their vocational opportunities limited. To be certain that these

children are learning and using English, such programs must be continuously evaluated.

A Wonder Rediscovered

Language development is an area of developmental psychology that is filled with controversy. We have looked at many of the issues surrounding language acquisition, especially the question of how language is acquired. The certainty with which so many psychologists embraced Skinner's and Chomsky's work has long passed. Neither the radical innate posture of Chomsky nor the behavioral-learning ideas of Skinner seem sufficient to explain the development of language in children, although they both explain some aspects of language-learning. The more modern approach takes both the laws of learning and

Should bilingual children be taught subjects other than English in their native language or in English?

According to Professor Higgins in My Fair Lady *it is the way language is used that separates social classes from each other.*

the biological basis for language-learning into consideration, but it also looks at the nature of the interactions between the developing child and the child's parents. This position views language development as a carefully orchestrated progression of interchanges between an active learner and active teachers, who may not be aware of the role they are playing in the child's language development.

This chapter has focused on issues surrounding language-learning in childhood. However, the language learned in childhood is carried over into adulthood. Adults are frequently judged on their linguistic abilities, including their vocabulary and the ability to express themselves. Adults who have limited linguistic abilities may find themselves limited in the job market and in certain interpersonal interactions, such as dealing with supervisors or making a positive impression at job interviews. Thus, language abilities take on an importance for the entire life span.

As we begin to tear down the curtain of mystery that surrounds language development, we can appreciate the wonder of it all. The simple sentence of a child is not just an imitation of what the child has heard, nor is it something preprogrammed. It is a creative expression of an inherently human ability. Looking at it from this standpoint, we can see that learning our native tongue is perhaps the greatest intellectual feat any one of us ever performs.

Summary

1. Communication is the process of sharing information. It may be verbal or nonverbal. Language is a set of agreed-on, arbitrary symbols used in communication. Language consists of a number of subsystems, including phonology, morphology, syntax, semantics, and pragmatics.

2. Infants communicate with the people around them by smiling, crying, and gesturing. They are sensitive to speech sounds from the moment they are born.

3. Babbling, which involves verbalization of vowel and consonant sounds, begins as early as three months. Children utter their first word any time between ten and fifteen months of age. Some psychologists argue that children use one word, called a *holophrase,* to stand for an entire thought. The child's early sentences are called *telegraphic* because they contain only words absolutely necessary for communicating the meaning to other people.

4. The length of children's sentences gradually increases, and conjunctions begin to be used. By the age of five or six, a child's syntax approaches that of an adult.

5. Young children make predictable errors. They overextend, using words in a wider manner than is proper, and they underextend, using words in a more restrictive sense than is appropriate. Children also overgeneralize rules; when children begin to learn the rules of a language, they use them indiscriminately and have difficulty with exceptions.

6. Behaviorists, such as Skinner, use the processes of reinforcement and imitation to explain language

acquisition. Chomsky argues that a human being is preprogrammed to learn language and merely requires exposure to a language in order to master it. The nativist position sees language acquisition as having a biological basis and stresses the importance of maturation.

7. Cognitive psychologists argue that such factors as attention and memory are involved in language acquisition. In addition, a child must know something about an object in order to use a word correctly.

8. Adult speech to young children is well constructed and consists of short, simple sentences with many repetitions. Social interaction is important in language acquisition, because children learn language through interaction with caregivers, who fine-tune their language to the developmental level of the child.

9. The average girl is ahead of the average boy in language development.

10. Black English is a dialect spoken by lower-income blacks and understood by most black people in the United States. It has a consistent, logical, and coherent grammar. Many authorities believe that it should be accepted as a valid dialect and that teachers should not reject the ideas of students using this dialect. But children who use Black English sometimes have difficulty with Standard English, which is necessary for success in the academic and vocational world.

11. Early studies seemed to show that bilingualism was a deficit to learning, but more recent studies stress the advantages a bilingual child has. Much controversy surrounds bilingual programs, and much research concerning the best way to teach English remains to be performed. It is important that every child learn Standard English.

Answers to True or False Statements

1. *False* Correct statement: The terms *language* and *communication* are not synonymous.

2. *False* Correct statement: Although young infants can differentiate between sounds, they cannot understand language.

3. *False* Correct statement: Although the range of sounds babbled by infants is impressive, it does not approach every sound humans are capable of producing.

4. *False* Correct statement: Children often overgeneralize the rules of grammar, but they learn the correct irregular forms without formal training.

5. *False* Correct statement: Both children and adults understand many more words than they use in their own speech.

6. *True* Although the sentences are usually shorter, they are well formed.

7. *False* Correct statement: Parents are more likely to correct their children for the truthfulness of their statements than for their grammar.

8. *True* Children from middle-class families use a more expansive language than children from working-class families.

9. *True* When compared with children of the same age who are not twins, twins are generally not as advanced in linguistic development.

10. *True* Generally, American girls learn language faster than American boys.

11. *True* Today, Black English is generally accepted as a dialect of Standard English.

12. *False* Correct statement: Bilingualism itself does not lead to academic problems in school.

PART THREE

Early Childhood

Physical and Cognitive Development in Early Childhood

Are the Following Statements True or False?

Try the True-False Quiz below. See if your answers correspond to the information in this chapter. Each question is repeated after the paragraph in which the answer can be found. The True-False Answer Box at the end of the chapter lists the complete answers.

_____ 1. During early childhood, the rate of growth increases.

_____ 2. The leading cause of death among preschoolers is accidents.

_____ 3. During the preschool years, the child begins to reason in a manner that is very similar to that of an average adult.

_____ 4. Preschoolers are better able to take someone else's point of view than older children.

_____ 5. Young preschoolers believe that even inanimate objects are capable of being alive and conscious.

_____ 6. Surprisingly, preschoolers perform better on new, unfamiliar tasks than on familiar tasks.

_____ 7. Preschool children do not use memory strategies, like rehearsal, spontaneously.

_____ 8. Reading to young children is not an effective way to promote reading skills.

_____ 9. Preschoolers average almost four hours a day watching television.

_____10. Preschool children cannot tell the difference between commercials and the programs they accompany.

_____11. Fewer children are attending nursery schools in the 1980s than in 1970.

_____12. Children who attended Project Head Start classes were less likely to be found in special-education classes than their peers who did not participate in the program.

The Time-Life Remover

"She (turned) almost full blue. My mother was screaming at me to get away from her. I ignored her. I knew what to do. I said to my mother, "I saw this on 'Benson' [the television situation comedy]. I lifted her up and banged her on her feet. She bended over and she coughed and it plopped out." This is how five-year-old Brent Meldrum saved the life of six-year-old Tanya Branden who had something stuck in her throat. He is the youngest person ever known to have used the Heimlich maneuver, which he calls "the time-life remover" (*Los Angeles Times*, August 7, 1986).

This incident demonstrates how great the physical and cognitive advances of preschoolers are. Brent showed a surprising ability to learn from television and to translate that learning into action. For Brent to have performed this act, he had to size up the situation correctly, understand what to do, be physically able to perform the maneuver, and finally, ignore the pandemonium that surrounded him as he did so.

Anyone who works with preschoolers will be impressed by their newfound abilities. Yet we are often surprised when preschoolers treat inanimate objects as if they are real, have difficulty understanding that squat 8-ounce cups and tall 8-ounce glasses hold the same amount, and have problems solving what seem like simple problems.

Physical Development in the Preschool Years

In this chapter we'll look at the physical and cognitive development of preschool children. The expanding motor abilities of preschoolers allow them to attend to what is going on around them instead of having to concentrate just on how they walk and hold things. They can now easily take part in many physical activities, satisfying some of their curiosity about the world and learning from their experiences. Their physical skills give them more independence. They now interact more frequently with other children and learn from these social interactions. Eating is no longer a great physical challenge either, for they can handle eating implements with some skill. They can eat by themselves and are affected by the nutritional

information around them, especially on television. Finally, many children now attend a preschool in which their new physical and sensory abilities are used as a tool to encourage social and cognitive abilities.

Growth and Development

The rate of growth slows during the early childhood years. About twice as much growth occurs between the first and third years as between the third and fifth years (Cratty, 1970), but growth is still readily apparent during this period (see Appendix for growth charts). The average three-year-old girl stands about 37 inches (94.1 cm) tall and weighs about 29 pounds (13.11 kg). By the age of six, she stands just over 45 inches (114.6 cm) tall and weighs almost 40 pounds (17.8 kg). Boys are a bit taller and heavier throughout this stage, and remain so until

Five-year-old Brent Meldrum saved the life of six-year-old Tanya Branden by using the Heimlich maneuver. Brent had seen it on television.

about the age of eleven. The average three-year-old boy stands just over 37 inches (94.91 cm) tall and weighs about 32 pounds (14.62 kg). By the age of six, he stands almost 46 inches (116.1 cm) tall and weighs 45.5 pounds (20.69 kg) (Hamill, 1977). The preschool child grows approximately 3 inches a year.

True or False During early childhood, the rate of growth increases.

Of course, variation from the statistical average can be expected. As noted on page 103, scientists usually speak of a range of heights and weights (between the 25th and 75th percentiles) that are usual for a child of a certain age in a certain culture. Deviations from this range may not indicate a problem, but it may alert us to a possible problem and many doctors will look into the situation.

During the preschool period, body proportions change. At age two, the head is about one-fourth the total body size, by age five-and-a-half it is one-sixth the body size, and at adulthood it is about one-tenth (Cratty, 1970). The preschooler gradually loses that baby-like appearance. The amount of fat decreases during this period, the added weight resulting from growth and development of muscle tissue. Boys generally have more muscle tissue, while girls have a bit more fat, but many individual differences can be found. At the beginning of this preschool period, children usually have a full set of baby teeth, which at the end of the period they begin to shed.

Motor Skills

By the beginning of the early childhood period, children have mastered the basics of walking and no longer need to pay so much attention to standing steadily on two feet. Now they attempt to master the physical environment. They are as likely to run as to walk, their movements are smoother, and they turn corners better. The four-year-old can stand on one foot for two seconds and can negotiate a 6-centimeter walking board with a bit of stepping off (Heinicke, 1979). Large muscles are still much better developed than fine muscles, but by age four the child can hold a pencil in something that resembles

an adult's style and can fold a paper diagonally (Heinicke, 1979).

Children at this stage master many motor skills, including running, jumping, hopping, skipping, and climbing. (The motor development of children in the pre-school period is summarized in Table 7.1.) Children younger than about eighteen months do not usually have the power or balance to leave the ground with both feet in the air, making running and jumping difficult. By the age of three, however, 42 percent can jump, and by four and a half years, 72 percent can (Cratty, 1970). By about three and a half, most children can hop from one to three steps, but they cannot do it with much precision or control. By about five, most can hop for ten seconds or so. Girls are better than boys at this. Skipping is more difficult and is generally not well developed until about five years of age (Corbin, 1980). Catching a ball is a skill that develops in early childhood too. At about age four, the hands are at least open to receive the ball, although the elbows are fixed. By about five, the arms and elbows are held to the sides of the body, allowing them to give when the ball arrives. The development of such motor skills allows children to explore and physically master the world around them.

Fine Motor Control

The three-year-old riding a tricycle is the picture many people have when they think of a preschooler. Indeed, the development of gross motor skills—such as running, hopping, and climbing—is readily visible at this stage. But the advances in fine motor control are also impressive, although fine motor control lags behind gross muscle development and control. The more subtle development of fine motor control shows itself in the way a child controls a crayon or pencil.

If you give crayons to children of various ages and watch how they hold and use them, you might be surprised at the progress preschoolers show when compared with younger children. Babies use their entire fists. Toddlers progress to holding the crayon fairly well but use their wrist for drawing, while preschoolers by about age five have improved to the point where they are now holding the crayon better and using the small muscles

Development of Locomotor Skills in Early Childhood

This table outlines the development of locomotor skills in early childhood. Keep in mind that some children will develop these skills earlier than other children.

Locomotor Skill	Three-year-old	Four-year-old	Five-year-old
Running	Runs with lack of control in stops and starts	Runs with control over starts, stops, and turns	Running well established and used in play activities
	Overall pattern more fluid than 2-year-old	Speed is increasing	Control of running in distance; speed and direction improving
	Runs with flat foot action	Longer stride than 3-year-old	Speed increasing
	Inability to turn quickly	Nonsupport period lengthening	Stride width increasing
		Can run 35 yards in 20–29 seconds	Nonsupport period lengthening
Galloping	Most children cannot gallop	43 percent of children are attempting to learn to gallop	78 percent can gallop
	Early attempts are some variation of the run pattern	During this year most children learn to gallop	Can gallop with a right lead foot
		Early gallop pattern somewhat of a run-and-leap step	Can gallop with a left lead foot
			Can start and stop at will
Hopping	Can hop 10 times consecutively on both feet	33 percent are proficient at hopping	79 percent become proficient during this year
	Can hop 1–3 times on one foot	Can hop 7–9 hops on one foot	Can hop 10 or more hops on one foot
	Great difficulty experienced with hop pattern	Hop pattern somewhat stiff and not fluid	Hop characterized by more spring-like action in ankles, knees, and hips
	Attempts characterized by gross overall movements and a lot of arm movement		Can hop equally well on either leg
Climbing	Ascends stairs using mark-time foot pattern	Ascends stairs using alternate foot pattern	Climbing skill increasing
	During this year, ascending stairs is achieved with alternate foot pattern	Descends stairs with alternate foot pattern	70 percent can climb a rope ladder with bottom free
	Descending stairs mostly with mark-time foot pattern	Can climb a large ladder with alternate foot pattern	37 percent can climb a pole
	Climbing onto and off of low items continues to improve, with higher heights being conquered	Can descend large ladder slowly with alternate foot pattern	32 percent can climb a rope with bottom free
			14 percent can climb an overhead ladder with 15 degree incline
			Climbing includes more challenging objects such as trees, jungle gyms, large beams
Balance	Balance-beam walking pattern characterized by mark-time sequences	Balance-beam walking pattern characterized by alternate shuffle step	Balance-beam walking characterized by alternate step pattern
	Can traverse 25-foot walking path that is one inch wide in 31.5 seconds with 18 step-offs	Can traverse 25-foot walking path that is one inch wide in 27.7 seconds with 6 step-offs	Can traverse 25-foot walking path that is one inch wide in 24.1 seconds with 3 step-offs
	Can walk 3-inch-wide beam forward 7.4 feet, backward 3.9 feet	Can walk 3-inch-wide beam forward 8.8 feet, backward 5.8 feet	Can walk 3-inch-wide beam forward 11 feet, backward 8.1 feet
	44 percent can touch knee down and regain standing position on 3-inch-wide beam	68 percent can touch knee down and regain standing position on 3-inch-wide beam	84 percent can touch knee down and regain standing position on 3-inch-wide beam

Development of Locomotor Skills in Early Childhood (Continued)

Locomotor Skill	Three-year-old	Four-year-old	Five-year-old
Skipping	Skip is characterized by a shuffle step Can skip on one foot and walk on the other Actual true skip pattern seldom performed	14 percent can skip One-foot skip still prevalent Overall movement stiff and undifferentiated Excessive arm action frequent Skip mostly flatfooted	72 percent are proficient Can skip with alternate foot pattern Overall movements more smooth and fluid More efficient use of arms Skip mostly on balls of feet
Jumping	42 percent are proficient Jumping pattern lacks differentiation Lands without knee bend to absorb force Minimal crouch for take-off Arms used ineffectively Can jump down from 28-inch height Can hurdle jump 3½ inches (68 percent)	72 percent are proficient Jumping pattern characterized by more preliminary crouch Can do standing broad jump 8–10 inches Can do running broad jump 23–33 inches 90 percent can hurdle jump 5 inches 51 percent can hurdle jump 9½ inches	81 percent are skillful Overall jumping pattern more smooth and rhythmical Use of arm thrust at take-off evident More proficient landing Can do standing broad jump 15–18 inches Can do running broad jump 28–35 inches, vertical Can jump and reach 2½ inches 90 percent can hurdle jump 8 inches 68 percent can hurdle jump 21½ inches

Source: Corbin, 1980.

in the fingers for control. Still, they must concentrate, and the effort lacks the smoothness it will have later. Both maturation and practice are responsible for this improvement in control and coordination (Kellogg, 1970).

Growing Independence and the Need for Supervision

Children use these motor skills to explore the environment and do things on their own. They can dress themselves with some degree of care, eat by themselves, and play by themselves for significant periods of time. Their advances in both gross and fine motor control open new opportunities for private play. Preschoolers no longer need to be watched every second, and active, independent preschoolers are engaging beings. Yet their motor skills and desire for independence are greater than their mental ability to understand what is good for them. This can lead to problems in the areas of safety and nutrition.

Safety

Accidents are the leading cause of death during the preschool years, accounting for more than one-third of all deaths among children (Talbot and Guthrie, 1976). The danger from disease has decreased steadily over the past fifty years, but the same cannot be said of accidents. The most common causes of accidental death are motor vehicle accidents, drowning, fires, and poisoning. Although not all accidents can be avoided, precautions—such as using restraints in cars, fencing and locking pools, and placing poisons in locked storage cabinets where young children cannot enter—can prevent many of them.

True or False The leading cause of death among preschoolers is accidents.

Nutrition

Infants eat, or don't eat, what you give them. However, preschoolers know what foods are in the house and can tell you what they want. They may want a particular cereal and cry until they get it, refusing anything else. They are old enough to take certain foods, especially snacks, by themselves. Three- and four-year-old children can rank-order their food preferences, and these preferences are related to eating habits (Birch, 1979). For example, preschoolers prefer soup that contains more salt, and they prefer salted pretzels to unsalted pretzels (Cowart and Beauchamp, 1986).

It is not surprising that the diet of many preschoolers is filled with high-calorie, low-nutrition foods—especially snacks. Preschoolers receive much of their information about food from watching television. Spend a Saturday morning watching children's television, and you'll find that the commercials are often more colorful and impressive than the programs themselves. The cartoon characters selling sugar-coated cereals are appealing to the preschoolers who watch these commercials and then demand these foods. Most commercials glorify processed and sweet foods, encouraging poor eating habits. One study found that 22 percent of the calories ingested by preschoolers came from snacks (Beyer and Morris, 1974). Many parents also use sweets as rewards, which is another mistake. Learning to eat right is an important skill learned in childhood. An apple or a carrot can be a snack; it doesn't always have to be cookies or candy.

Children's appetites are variable. At about twelve months their appetites usually decrease, probably in accord with the decrease in the rate of growth (Hamilton and Whitney, 1982). It is not unusual for preschoolers to have periods in which they eat very little. Breakfast is often their best and most important meal, for they are usually hungry in the morning and therefore more likely to be cooperative. Unfortunately, many families place little emphasis on breakfast, so a plan to improve children's diets should begin with providing a nutritious breakfast.

The advances in motor control and coordination in early childhood enable preschoolers to master the physical environment and learn about their world. They actively encounter the physical world and, as we shall see, try to comprehend the phenomena they see around them. In Piagetian theory, children actively learn through their physical and social interactions. It is natural that their expanding physical abilities would allow them to experiment with all sorts of activities and bring them into contact with many new social situations. Their physical

development therefore has an impact on their cognitive development. As we turn to the cognitive domain, we should remain aware of how preschoolers' expanding physical abilities make experimentation and interaction possible, thus encouraging cognitive growth.

Cognitive Development in the Preschool Years

Where do babies come from? Most of us learned the facts of life long ago and understand the sophisticated physiological explanations. But preschoolers do not. Even if they parrot parents' explanations, it does not necessarily mean they understand them. For instance, Bernstein and Cowan (1975) asked preschoolers where babies came from. All the children had seen their mothers pregnant with younger siblings and had their questions answered factually by parents. Preschoolers could not understand the biological explanations involving sperm, egg, and prenatal development. Many preschoolers believed that babies are bought. They thought in terms of their own experiences, such as buying something new in a store. When faced with development within the womb, many believed the mother swallowed something that grew, or that after buying the bones and other organs from a store she assembled them in her tummy. Preschoolers take bits and pieces from what they are told, combine them with their own experiences, and come up with explanations that cause us to ask ourselves, "Where did they get that from?"

Preoperational Thought

The study of how preschoolers understand birth demonstrates the qualitative differences between preschool and adult thought patterns. These differences are found in preschoolers' understanding of many common situations including buying and selling as well as their appreciation of the value of money as shown in the Cross-Cultural Current on page 184. The distinct manner in which preschoolers think was described by Piaget who argued that the child from the age of two to seven progresses through the preoperational stage (Piaget, 1952; Piaget and Inhelder, 1956). It is a stage marked by many advances, but at the same time many limitations.

preoperational stage Piaget's second stage of cognitive development, marked by the appearance of language and symbolic function and the child's inability to understand logical concepts, such as conservation.

deferred imitation The ability to observe an act and imitate it later.

inductive reasoning Reasoning that proceeds from specific cases to the formation of a general rule.

deductive reasoning Reasoning that begins with a general rule and then is applied to specific cases.

transductive reasoning Preoperational reasoning in which young children reason from particular to particular.

seriation The process of placing objects in size order.

classification The process of placing objects in different groupings.

Symbolic function. The **preoperational stage** begins when the child is able to use one thing to represent or symbolize another (Mandler, 1983). One major illustration of this ability is the acquisition of language. Words represent particular concepts and objects. The ability to use symbolism also manifests itself in nonlinguistic areas. Children may use a spoon to represent a hammer, or a toy person to represent the mail carrier. Another manifestation of the ability to use symbolism is known as **deferred imitation.** The child can see something occur, store the information, and perform that action at a later date. To do this, the child must preserve a symbolic representation of the behavior during the intervening time. For example, hours after a child sees a brother or sister doing exercises, the child may be found doing a version of the same exercises.

How preschoolers reason. To understand preschoolers, one must realize that they often reason differently from adults. Adults reason either inductively or deductively. **Inductive reasoning** proceeds from the specific to the general. For instance, after examining a number of causes, we may say that children who do not do their homework do not receive good grades. Adults also use **deductive reasoning,** beginning with a general rule and proceeding to specifics. They may form a rule concerning homework and grades and then apply it to specific cases.

Transductive reasoning and causality. Preschool children, though, reason from particular to particular, in a **transductive** manner. The simplest example of such reasoning is that if A causes B then, according to the preschooler, B causes A. For example, Piaget found that his daughter believed that, because his shave required hot water, the appearance of hot water meant that daddy would shave (Phillips, 1975). The child's understanding of causality is based on how close one event is to another. As Pulaski notes, "The road makes the bicycle go; by creating a shadow one can cause the night to come. The thunder makes it rain, and honking the horn makes the car go" (1980, p. 49).

True or False During the preschool years, the child begins to reason in a manner that is very similar to that of an average adult.

Seriation and classification. Parents are often surprised when preschoolers show a different logic or have difficulty with a particular problem that seems so simple to adults. For instance, ask preschoolers to put a series of sticks in order from biggest to smallest, an operation called **seriation** (see Figure 7.1 on page 186). They simply cannot seem to do it. Nor can they **classify** items, at least at the beginning of the preoperational stage (see Figure 7.2 on page 186). When young children are given a number of plastic shapes—including squares, triangles, and rings of different colors—and asked to put things that are alike into a pile, most children younger than five do not organize their choices on any particular logical basis. They may put a red triangle and a blue triangle together, but then throw in a red square. No central organizing principle is evident. Some young children do not understand the task at all (Ault, 1977). Later in the preoperational stage, some progress in classification is made. They can sort items on the basis of one overriding principle—most often form—but they fail to see that multiple classifications are possible.

Preschool children also have difficulty understanding subordinate and superordinate classes (see Figure 7.3 on page 187). For example, a child may be shown seven green beads and three white beads, all made of wood, and asked whether there are more green beads or more wooden beads. The child will usually say more green beads. Show children a picture of a bouquet containing five roses and three tulips and ask them whether there

The Value of Money

You are in a store with your young daughter and she is looking longingly at every toy. She tells you she wants this one and that one and the other one. When you tell her you can't afford it, she acts shocked and states emphatically "You have money in your pocket." Later, she is thrilled when you hand a twenty-dollar bill to the cashier and receive "more" in change: a five, three singles, and five other coins. You gave one bill and received nine "pieces of money" in return.

The development of children's understanding of money has been studied in a number of societies. Most recently, Anna Berti and Anna Bombi used a Piagetian approach to study how children gain their understanding of money and exchange.

Eighty children between the ages of three and eight were selected from a middle-class area of a city in Italy. At first, a single 100 lira coin and three bills of different denominations (500 lira, or 60 cents; 10,000 lira, or 12 dollars; and 100,000 lira, or 120 dollars) were shown to children to determine whether they recognized money and knew what it was used for. Unlike U.S. currency, Italian currency varies in size; the larger the bill, the more it is worth. The children were then told that four items were to be purchased: chocolate candy, a comic

book, a doll, and a real automobile. The children were asked, "If I go to a store with just this money [one of the four types the experimenter had in her hand], can I buy a ———?"

The second part of the experiment involved a short game-playing sequence in which children were asked to play the role of the customer or the store owner. The experimenters could then ascertain whether children understood that they had to pay for their purchase, what change was, and the like. All the children were tested a second time one year later.

The experimenters were able to show that children develop their understanding of money and exchange in stages. In the first stage, children are only vaguely aware that money has anything to do with buying or selling. In the second stage, they understand that they must pay for candy and toys but they think all types of money are the same; to them, a quarter and a dime have the same value. In the third stage, they are aware that there is some difference in money, but they don't really understand the rules for buying and selling. In the fourth stage, they understand that different items cost different amounts and that they may not have enough money to buy what they want, but they really don't understand why. In the

---

are more roses or more flowers. They will often say more roses. Preschoolers cannot make comparisons across levels and usually get the problem wrong.

Transitive inferences. Preschoolers also cannot seem to understand **transitive inferences.** If Ed is taller than Sue, and Sue is taller than Tim, then Ed is taller than Tim is an example of such an inference (see Figure 7.4 on page 188). The preoperational child views comparisons as absolute (Piaget and Inhelder, 1974) and does not understand that an object can be larger than one thing and at the same time smaller than another.

Conservation problems. Nowhere are the preschooler's difficulties so obvious as in the child's inability to solve conservation problems (see Figure 7.5 on page

transitive inferences Statements of comparison, such as "If X is taller than Y, and Y is taller than Z, the X is taller than Z."

conservation The principle that quantities remain the same despite changes in their appearance.

189). **Conservation** involves the ability to comprehend that quantities remain the same regardless of changes in their appearance. You can test this out yourself in a number of ways. For example, show a preschooler displays of seven pennies in which the coins are either grouped close together or spread apart. The four-year-old is certain that the spread-out display has more pennies than the one that is packed closer together. Or take two

fifth stage, children understand the value of various denominations and the correspondence between money and the price of the toy. In the last stage, they understand that the storekeeper should give a certain amount of change back, along with the item.

Here we see the development of the concept of money. The changes are predictable in terms of the order in which they will appear. What is not predictable is the precise age at which the child will exhibit a particular stage of understanding. Berti and Bombi found that of sixteen four-year-olds tested, two were in stage one, seven were in stage two, five were in stage three, and two were in stage four. Each child's individuality entered into the equation. Developmental psychologists can demonstrate sequences and make some rough statements about age distributions surrounding some behavior. For example, the average three-year-old recognized that money was necessary to buy an item, but had no idea of anything else. Most children do not achieve the sixth, or last, stage until about the age of seven. However, we cannot say that a four-year-old is definitely in a certain stage, because children enter and leave these stages according to their own timetable. Within the year, about half the children in the study had progressed one level, while about one-quarter had advanced two levels. The experimenters note that the first four stages depend upon preoperational reasoning and that the last two stages require establishment of a one-to-one correspondence between money and the prices of the objects, which requires more sophisticated reasoning found at the beginning of the concrete operational period.

This sequence matches and extends the general outline found by experimenters working with children from other cultures. It also gives us some insight into why children act the way they do in toy stores and supermarkets. Some parents become annoyed when their young children show immature beliefs concerning money and economic exchange. This study, and others from cultures around the world, show that parents should expect such behavior from young children and, to understand their children's behavior better, should appreciate just what they do and do not understand about money and exchange.

Source: Berti, A. E., and Bombi, A. S. The Development of the Concept of Money and Its Value: A Longitudinal Study. *Child Development*, 1981, 52, 1179–1182.

equal lumps of clay and roll each one into a ball. Then, in the child's view, roll one ball into a worm and ask the child which clay form has more clay. The preschooler fails to understand that they are still equal and believes that one has more clay. Present a preschooler with two identical half-filled beakers of water. The child will tell you they are equal. Now transfer one to a squat cup and ask the child which has more. The answer will usually be that the taller beaker contains more liquid.

All these are examples of the preschooler's failure to understand and successfully perform conservation tasks. The fact that preschoolers cannot correctly judge that pouring a liquid from a tall beaker to a squat beaker does not change the amount of water has fascinated psychologists for years. But why can't preschoolers solve these simple tasks? The answer lies in certain characteristics of preschoolers' thinking.

centering The tendency to attend to only one dimension at a time.

Characteristics of preschoolers' thinking.

Centering. Most preschool children can concentrate on only one dimension at a time (Piaget and Inhelder, 1969). This is known as **centering.** For instance, try to explain to a preschooler that a particular cup and a tall glass hold the same amount of liquid. Because the containers are shaped differently, preschoolers believe that one is larger than the other. They rely on a visual comparison and believe that the taller glass contains more liquid than the fatter cup. Preschoolers can attend

FIGURE 7.1

Seriation

Young children have difficulty placing things in size order.

to only one measure at a time, and appearances confuse them. In the same way, they have no difficulty telling you that two balls of clay are the same. But if one is rolled into the shape of a worm, they compare the clay shapes on the dimension of length and cannot take both the length and the width into account.

Appearance vs. reality. Generally, preschoolers confuse how things look with what they really are. In other words, preschoolers are confused by the appearance of objects in their environment. For example, show a three-year-old a red toy car and cover it with a green filter that makes it look black. Now hand the car (without the filter) to the child and put it behind the filter again. When the child is asked what color it is, the child says "Black" (Flavell, 1986). Preschoolers are perception-bound, basing their judgments simply on how things look to them at the present time, and they have difficulty going beyond the visual information given.

reversibility Beginning at the end of an operation and working one's way back to the start.

Irreversibility. Most preschoolers cannot **reverse** operations. If a clay ball is rolled into a worm in front of them, they cannot mentally rearrange the clay back to its original form (Piaget, 1926). This inability to reverse an operation affects preschoolers' answers to what seem like simple questions. When a preschooler was asked whether he had a sister, he answered yes and gave her name. When asked whether his sister had a brother, he replied no.

Transformations. When preschoolers notice that change has occurred, they can point to the beginning

FIGURE 7.2

Classification

Young children have difficulty with tasks that require the ability to classify items into various groupings.

FIGURE 7.3

Subordinate and Superordinate Classification

Are there more green beads or wooden beads? Young children answer more green beads because they have difficulty making comparisons across levels.

"Are there more green beads or wooden beads?"

"Green beads."

egocentrism A thought process described by Piaget in which young children believe everyone is experiencing the environment in the same way they are. Children who are egocentric have difficulty understanding someone else's point of view.

animism The preschooler's belief that inanimate objects have a consciousness or are alive.

and the end but do not realize the sequence involved in the change. For example, when young subjects were asked to draw successive movements of a bar falling from a vertical position to an upright position, the children did not draw (nor did they later understand) that it went through a series of intermediate positions between the first and last position (Phillips, 1975). In the same way, children faced with a conservation task judge equality on the basis of the beginning and end states. They cannot take intervening states into consideration.

Egocentrism. Underlying all the child's reasoning is a basic **egocentrism**. The use of this term is unfortunate, because it connotes selfishness. Piaget (1954) argues that children see everything from their own point of view and are not capable of taking someone else's view into account. Young children believe that everything has a

purpose that is understandable in their own terms and relevant to their own needs. For instance, a boy once asked Piaget why there were two mountains above Geneva. The answer the boy wanted was that one was for adults to climb while the other little one was for children (Pulaski, 1980). Preschoolers see the entire world as revolving around them. The sun and moon exist to give them light; mothers and fathers exist to give them warmth and to take care of them.

True or False Preschoolers are better able to take someone else's point of view than older children.

This egocentrism is seen in children's interpretations of their physical world and their social world. Children who know their left hand from their right may not be able to identify correctly the left and right hands of a person standing opposite. Nursery school teachers are aware of this, and when facing preschoolers they raise the left hand when requesting that the children raise their right (Davis, 1983). Piaget showed a model of three mountains to young children and asked them to consider how the display might look to a doll sitting in different positions around the model (see Figure 7.6 on page 191). Preschool children could not do this accurately. They reason that everyone sees the world as they do.

Egocentrism is found in a number of different situations. I can remember coming home on a particularly hard day. It was 98 degrees and the humidity was horrendous. The car had broken down, and a number of other smaller catastrophes had occurred. Seeing me tired and upset, my four-year-old came over and asked if I wanted her to read a story to me. Since stories make her feel better, she supposed they would do the same for me.

Animism and artificialism. One of the charming aspects of early childhood is the child's belief that everything is capable of being conscious and alive, which is called **animism** (see Figure 7.7 on page 192). A paper turtle can be alive; a hammer has a life of its own. This

Transitive Inferences

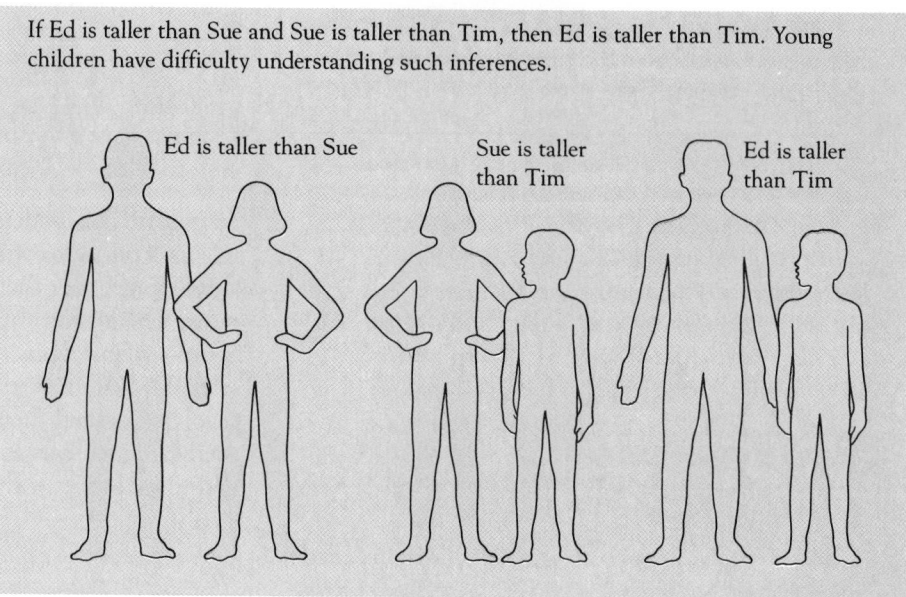

If Ed is taller than Sue and Sue is taller than Tim, then Ed is taller than Tim. Young children have difficulty understanding such inferences.

Ed is taller than Sue   Sue is taller than Tim   Ed is taller than Tim

results in unusual behavior. If you step on the turtle, you've just killed something, not just smashed a small toy. A preschooler may bump into a desk, smack it, and say, "Bad desk!" A book that falls from a shelf does not want to be with the other books. A balloon that has soared to the ceiling does not want to be held. Animism is most characteristic of the early part of this stage. It becomes less evident as children reach the age of four or five (Bullock, 1985).

True or False Young preschoolers believe that even inanimate objects are capable of being alive and conscious.

The child's reasoning also reflects **artificialism,** the belief that natural phenomena are caused by human beings. This is a natural outgrowth of what children see around them. Everything is viewed as intentional and organized for human use, so children explain the world in terms of human causation (Piaget, 1927). Thus, the lake near Geneva was created not by natural forces but by a group of men digging (Pulaski, 1980).

Recent challenges to Piaget's views. Preschool children have made great strides since infancy and toddlerhood. They can use language more efficiently and show deferred imitation. However, it is their limitations that

artificialism The belief that natural phenomena are caused by human beings.

are often emphasized. The child is described as lacking communication skills, number concepts, order concepts, and memory skills and having problems in causal relationships, as well as being egocentric, perception-bound, and unable to understand states and transformations (Gelman and Baillargeon, 1983; Gelman, 1979). Preschoolers are described more by what they cannot do (Flavell, 1985), and their charm is due to their ignorance. Of course, preschoolers' reasoning appears reasonable to them. It is only when we take an adult perspective that it seems unusual.

But many of Piaget's ideas concerning the limitations of preschool thought have recently been challenged. These challenges are not just based on the age at which these abilities appear. Psychologists are beginning to realize that preschoolers may not be as limited as we first thought. Perhaps they can classify, are not so egocentric, and can perform transitive inferences—if the situation is structured correctly.

FIGURE 7.5

Conservation

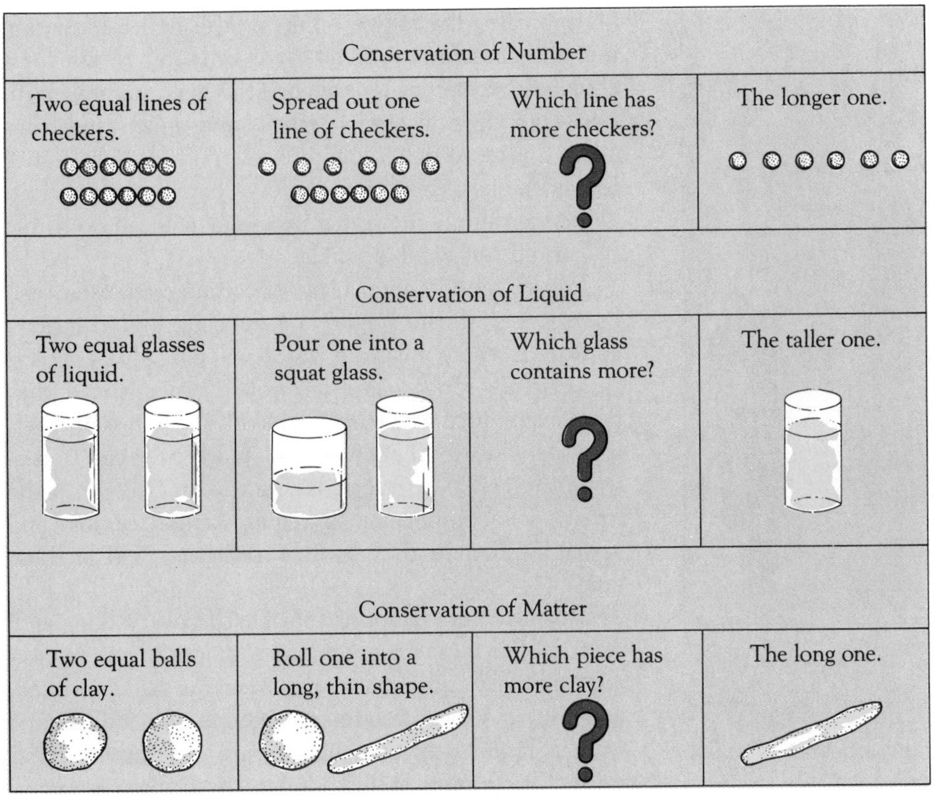

Conservation of Number			
Two equal lines of checkers.	Spread out one line of checkers.	Which line has more checkers?	The longer one.

Conservation of Liquid			
Two equal glasses of liquid.	Pour one into a squat glass.	Which glass contains more?	The taller one.

Conservation of Matter			
Two equal balls of clay.	Roll one into a long, thin shape.	Which piece has more clay?	The long one.

The observations Piaget made of preschoolers using his standard testing procedures are well founded, and no one seriously doubts their reliability (Gelman and Baillargeon, 1983). If you test a preschooler the same way Piaget did, you will get the same results. However, the assumption that because preschoolers fail these tests they cannot seriate, classify, or decenter is questionable. Perhaps if we tested the children differently, they might succeed. Indeed, this is exactly what researchers have found.

Preschoolers can arrange things in size order, classify items, and understand inferences if we design the tasks in a manner that is ideal for the preschooler's interests and abilities. First, we have to strip away anything that might distract the preschooler, leaving only the elements most essential to the task. Second, the task situation must be familiar (Brown et al., 1983). Preschoolers are easily sidetracked and do poorly in situations that are strange to them. Their abilities are also easily taxed, so

that memory and lack of comprehension can affect performance (Trabasso, 1975).

True or False Surprisingly, preschoolers perform better on new, unfamiliar tasks than on familiar tasks.

At times, simple modifications in Piaget's method change the results of the experiment. For example, Inhelder and Piaget (1964) argue that children can seriate if they can place the items in correct order, put additional items into the series, and correct any errors. So far this is reasonable. But Piaget used a total of ten sticks in his observations and concluded that true seriation did not occur at this stage. Koslowski (1980) used a similar approach, but instead of ten sticks she used four. Using the same criteria, she found that three-quarters of the three- and four-year-olds could put the sticks in size order, about four-fifths could insert new sticks into the order, and all the children could correct the incorrect insertions. The ability to seriate is present in these chil-

Preschoolers do not show the ability to conserve.

dren, but a set of ten sticks is simply too many for the preschooler to deal with at one time.

Piaget's conception of egocentrism has also been the focus of much criticism (Ford, 1979). Under specific circumstances, preschoolers are not egocentric—that is, they can understand the viewpoint of others. Flavell and his colleagues (1981) found that preschoolers understood that objects with different sides, like a house, look different from various perspectives, but that objects with identical sides, like a ball, look the same. In another experiment, one- to three-year-old children were given a hollow cube with a picture pasted to the bottom of the inside. The children were asked to show the picture to an observer sitting across from them. Almost all the children who were two years or older turned the cube away from them and toward the observer, demonstrating some understanding of the other person's perspective (Lempers et al., 1977). Other studies note that preschoolers can sequence events, especially in forward order. Piaget found that children were unable to recall the sequence of events in a story when asked to do so using pictures depicting story events, but recent studies found that if the pictures and stories are meaningful, pre-

schoolers can indeed sequence stories (Fivush and Mandler, 1985; Mandler and Johnson, 1977).

Harmonizing the views. Putting this new information into perspective is difficult. It is only fair to ask for a conclusion concerning the preschoolers' mental abilities—can they decenter, seriate, and understand causality in a more or less mature manner? At first glance the research seems contradictory, but it really is not. Under certain circumstances preschoolers can do things Piaget did not think possible.

The key phrase here is "under certain circumstances." Preschool skills are fragile and delicate, and children's abilities in these areas are just developing. Preschoolers can classify, seriate, and are not as egocentric if they have experience in a particular skill, if the task is clear, if it does not tax their memory, and if they can understand the verbal instructions. On the other hand, if the situation is complicated or requires more memory and verbal skills than they have, preschoolers fail at these tasks.

This new information is valuable. People working with preschoolers must design an environment in which tasks are simplified and memory requirements are minimized, and they must be certain that preschoolers understand what is required of them if they are to bring out these newly developing skills. Under these circumstances, preschoolers can do some surprising things. Situational and task factors are then of paramount importance. This is also shown in the preschool child's information-processing abilities.

Information-Processing in the Preschool Years

Attention

Adults working with preschoolers do not expect these young children to maintain their attention for long periods of time, and neither do the designers of television programs aimed at young children. Certain aspects of the programs—such as color, movement, surprise, and novelty—are likely to attract and hold attention. Much of the information on preschoolers' attention span comes from studies on how children view television. For instance, puppets and animation usually attract children, probably because of the unusual voices that accompany them (Anderson et al., 1979). A drum roll or loud crash of music signals an important event and gains attention

(Huston and Wright, 1983). However, it would be incorrect to view preschoolers merely as beings who are passively manipulated by the environment. Preschoolers attend to messages from television that they understand and that are focused on their interests (Anderson and Field, 1983).

This means that even young children can use some limited decision-making power in focusing their attention on television and are not simply manipulated by sights and sounds. This purposeful, planful aspect of attention is commonly accepted in older children and adults. People enter different situations with ideas about what they should watch for and may voluntarily focus on different aspects of the situation. If you attend a hockey game and are interested in how people play defense, you may follow a particular player for a few minutes without following the flight of the puck. Psychologists have found that as children mature their ability to focus their attention voluntarily in a planned, organized, systematic, goal-oriented manner increases (Daehler and Bukatko, 1985;

F I G U R E 7.6

Egocentrism

In Piaget's three-mountains experiment, preschool children had difficulty visualizing the doll's perspective of the three-mountain display.

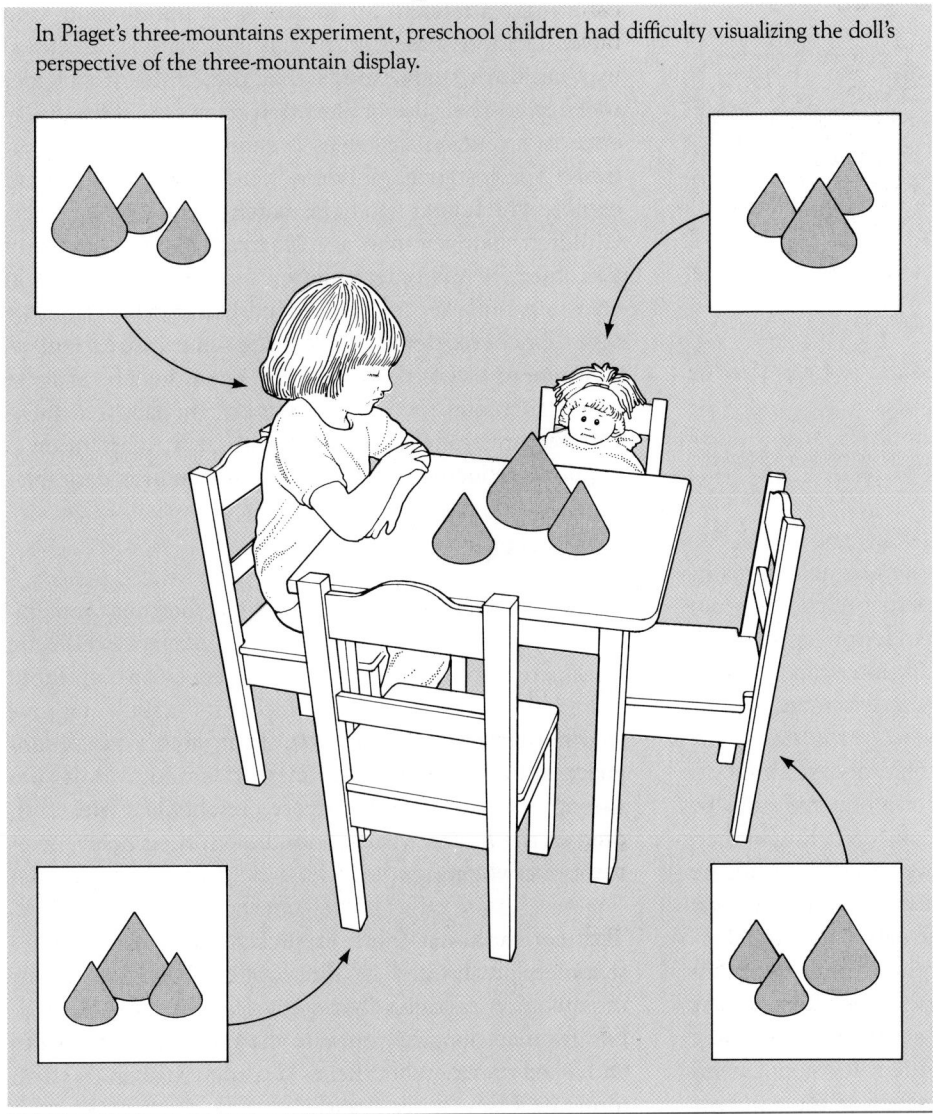

FIGURE 7.7

Animism

Young children often ascribe characteristics of living things to inanimate objects.

instead of the full twelve used by older children. The best way to accomplish this task is to focus attention on window one of house one and switch attention to window one of house two and so forth. This requires planning. Not one child in the preschool group did this, but almost all the eight- and nine-year-olds did.

These findings on the subject of attention have important implications for people who deal with preschoolers. The fact that their attention can be gained and to some degree held by using elements of sound, color, novelty, and movement is well known, but their ability to comprehend the material should not be forgotten. Their lack of sustained attention requires that material be presented in small segments. The fact that preschoolers do not attend to all the relevant information, and make decisions based on partial information, as shown in Vurpillot's study, shows that they differ from older children in their use of attention strategies. This difference in attention strategies is exhibited in many situations. For instance, children were given an object to explore which later had to be matched with a like object. Children younger than age six fixated at the center of the object, while older children focused their attention on the boundaries and performed better on a matching task (Zinchenko et al., 1977). Specific instructions as to where to place their attention, then, may be of some help (Hochman, 1987). In addition, the fact that these children are easily distracted implies that, if attention is required, reducing other competing stimuli is desirable.

Memory Skills

Even if children attend to something, they must remember it if is to be useful. Preschoolers' memory skills are far superior to those of toddlers. Between two and four years old, their already good recognition skills improve (Perlmutter and Myers, 1979). Their ability to use language allows them to store memories using words. On the other hand, if you compare preschoolers with children in the middle years of childhood, their deficiencies seem overwhelming.

The conventional view of preschool memory. Preschoolers are limited by their ability to spontaneously use memory strategies that many of us take for granted. For instance, suppose you were shown a group of pictures and asked to remember them. You might first group them into categories (foods, buildings, people), then rehearse

Wright and Vliestra, 1975). They are also able to maintain their attention for longer periods because they are becoming less easily distracted (Anderson and Lorch, 1983). A fourfold increase in attention span is found between the ages of one and four (Anderson and Levin, 1976).

The gradual development of voluntary, planned attentional behavior is shown in an often-quoted study by Vurpillot (1968; Vurpillot and Ball, 1979). Children between the ages of four and nine were asked to compare two pictures of houses, each of which contained at least six windows with objects such as flowerpots, hearts, curtains, socks, and other objects in their windows. Their task was to judge whether the houses were identical. As they inspected the houses, their eye movements were tracked. Preschoolers often made their decisions on incomplete information, using only seven of the windows

them. Preschoolers do not use these strategies on their own (Kail and Hagen, 1982). In order to remember successfully, you had to understand the task, have some idea of its difficulty, and then devise an appropriate strategy. You had some idea of what was involved in the memory task. This knowledge of memory processes, called **metamemory,** will be discussed more extensively in Chapter 9.

If you had been presented with only two items to remember, you probably would have used only a bit of rehearsal. When preschoolers were asked to remember a string of digits, they did not spontaneously use any rehearsal—the simplest strategy, but if they were instructed in the use of rehearsal, their ability to remember the list improved greatly (Flavell and Wellman, 1977). Children can be taught to use rehearsal, but at a later time children will not use this strategy spontaneously when confronted with the same task with no instructions as to the use of rehearsal (Keeney et al., 1967). In other words, young children apparently can use this strategy, but do not unless they are told to do so.

True or False Preschool children do not use memory strategies, like rehearsal, spontaneously.

Children's lack of understanding concerning the demands of the task was demonstrated by Appel and his colleagues (1972). They presented pictures to four-, seven-, and eleven-year-old children using two different instructions: "Look at the pictures" or "Remember the pictures." If you were told to remember the pictures, you might repeat to yourself what they are or write them down. If you were told to look at them, you wouldn't do anything special. However, you understand the problem, whereas preschool children do not. They don't seem to know that the problem requires some voluntary, purposely cognitive activity. Indeed, the four-year-olds did not act any differently when presented with either instruction, but the older children did. Perhaps preschoolers show such poor use of memory strategies because they do not understand what is involved in the memory tasks (Flavell and Wellman, 1977).

The memory of preschoolers has traditionally been viewed as rather passive, nonstrategic, and nonplanful (Brown et al., 1983), but if we look more deeply, we can see the beginning of strategy use, and at times children will surprise you with their memories. Again, the characteristics of the task and the test conditions are most important.

A more recent look at memory skills. Many studies have used artificial situations that require remembering new information for its own sake (Paris and Lindauer, 1982). When the information and situation are more familiar, and the goals of the remembering are clear, preschoolers show the beginnings of memory strategies, and their ability to recall improves markedly. For instance, children three to seven years of age were asked to remember a list of five words under two different conditions. Under one condition, the children played a game of grocery store and had to recall the items so they

Seriation involves the ability to place things in size order. Some studies show that if we reduce the difficulty of some tasks, such as seriation, some preschoolers can perform them.

could buy them. Under the second condition, children were simply told to remember the items. Children recalled significantly more items in condition one than in condition two (Istomina, 1975). When children were tested on the task of remembering a list, young children did quite well when the words were comprised of familiar categories, such as names of their teachers and television shows (Lindberg, 1980).

Even the idea that preschoolers are nonstrategic needs rethinking. Preschoolers do use some strategies for remembering such as pointing and looking (Kail and Hagen, 1982). They are competent when asked to use these motor and sensory strategies, but their ability to use verbal strategies, such as rehearsal, is greatly limited.

Memory reconsidered. The more recent look at the memory skills of young children matches the newer appreciation of what preschoolers can and cannot do in other cognitive areas. If we watch the children during their normal day, amid familiar situations and tasks whose goals are clear, we find they can remember more and do begin to use strategies. But the abilities of preschoolers are fragile. Young children are easily confounded, and artificial tasks are likely to show their limitations. Taken as a group, the studies in cognition and memory should keep us from generalizing about what abilities children do or do not have. Even though they may not show these abilities when tested in a certain way, it does not nec-

script A structure that describes an appropriate sequence of events in a particular context.

essarily mean they do not have them. Instead, it is important to note the situations in which children can and cannot successfully perform particular tasks.

The Importance of Prior Knowledge

Psychologists have recently been focusing on the importance of what people know—their knowledge base—to what people are trying to know or remember (Chi and Glaser, 1985). For instance, if you were asked what happens when you visit a restaurant or go to the doctor's office, you probably would have no difficulty constructing a sequential series of events. You enter the restaurant, sit down, order the food, eat it, pay the check, and leave. A **script** is a "structure that describes an appropriate sequence of events in a particular context" (Schank and Abelson, 1977, p. 41). There are numerous scripts, including birthday parties, job interviews, and a school day. Adults show a great deal of agreement on these scripts (Bower et al., 1979), and so do young children on familiar scripts. Nelson (1978) found that four-year-olds described daily events at home, in a day-care center,

Even young children know a great deal about certain scripts such as what is supposed to happen at a birthday party and the order of events.

or at a McDonald's restaurant in much the same way as adults. Preschoolers, though, are rather rigid in their ideas of what should take place and when (Wimmer, 1980). They will often rebel if people do things that are not in keeping with their idea of the script. Older children also produce more alternative paths in their scripts. For instance, when describing activities, such as making a campfire, they offer many more possible paths to accomplishing the task than younger children do. Scripts, then, become more flexible and more complex as children develop (see Mandler, 1983).

Scripts form the base for remembering stories and events that are familiar. If you are given information and are familiar with the script, you can fill in missing information (Chi and Glasser, 1985). Prior knowledge represented by the script makes the story easy to follow.

If preschoolers are presented with a script that is out of order and asked to recall it, they either omit the misordered event or put it in the place that is in keeping with their knowledge of how it usually is (Nelson and Gruendel, 1981). Children recognize deviations from the proper script and correct them (Wimmer, 1979). Preschoolers misremember stories if the stories differ from their familiar scripts. For instance, children invent and put appropriate material in stories when they cannot recall what they were told (Mandler and Johnson, 1977).

The knowledge of scripts also affects how children make inferences. Children need not be told that someone looked at a menu or had a glass to hold his milk in. They understand this is so, and they infer it because they are familiar with the script. Scripts show how prior knowledge affects the way new material is processed. One's prior knowledge makes new material meaningful, suggests how one can bridge gaps in what one knows, and helps organize material (Saloman, 1983). Some of the differences in memory between adults and children are caused by the more extensive knowledge base of adults (Chi, 1978). In summary, the child's knowledge base is an important variable in understanding how the child functions. Knowledge facilitates memory and affects performance on a variety of tasks.

The Environment and Cognitive Development in the Preschool Years

Jason lives in a home filled with books. His mother reads to him daily, and he watches "Sesame Street" at least once a day. He attends nursery school, where he plays with other children, takes short trips around the neighborhood, and learns about colors and shapes. Jason's parents encourage him to describe what he sees around him.

Craig's parents put him in front of a television set right after breakfast to watch cartoons for hours. They never read to him. Craig plays mostly by himself, and his parents speak to him only to demand something. They never have much time for Craig, and he is often cared for by his older brother, who would rather be doing something else.

It probably won't surprise you to find that Jason is doing well in elementary school and that Craig is having difficulty. Will Craig catch up? For most such children, the answer is no. In fact, just the opposite may occur: they may fall even further behind. But this does not mean the game is all over by age five. Early experience is important, but later experience can compensate for poor earlier experiences. If the environment is not improved, however, the child will not catch up. Only with a concerted and time-consuming effort on the part of his teachers will Craig close the gap between himself and Jason. It would have been easier to prevent this problem, to structure the environment so that Craig was as ready as Jason for elementary school. Before we can do this, we must understand the three most important environmental influences on the preschool child: the home, television, and the nursery school.

The Home

The atmosphere at home is a vital factor in the development of a child's cognitive abilities. Children who are more cognitively advanced come from homes in which language is used in an expansive manner. The children are encouraged to express themselves, to label the environment, and to describe their world (Chazan and Cox, 1976). Parents who give information, explain events, and encourage curiosity and exploration develop their children's minds so that when they enter elementary school they are ready for new challenges (Katz, 1980). In a study of sixteen five-year-old readers and nonreaders, Briggs and Elkind (1973) found that early readers came from homes in which the parents' occupational and educational levels were high and parents read to their children. Even when not directly involved in a parent-child interaction, children observe those around them. An environment filled with books is not stimulating unless the books are read. If preschoolers see their parents and older siblings enjoying reading, they are more likely to develop a positive attitude toward the activity.

True or False   Reading to young children is not an effective way to promote reading skills.

How can parents optimize a preschooler's cognitive development? There are two models here. The first views parents as environmental engineers who at the appropriate times provide materials and opportunities that help their children explore and learn about the world. These parents construct an environment rich in opportunities, allowing the children to discover the world at their own pace and stimulating them to think. Although Piaget never listed recommendations on child-rearing (Vernon, 1976), this type of strategy is in line with his thinking. The child learns through discovery, and readiness is taken into consideration. Formal instruction is deemphasized. The everyday experiences of the child are educational. A simple walk around the neighborhood becomes a learning experience. There are traffic signs, people working, and a hundred different things to discuss. The other approach emphasizes the importance of formal instruction. Parents are encouraged to teach their preschooler skills. There is less emphasis on self-discovery and more on planned activities that impart knowledge to the child.

Both extreme positions should be questioned. The parent who merely produces an environment suitable for a child but does not actively interact with the youngster is not maximizing the child's experiences. On the other side, too formal or unnatural a structure may cause a child to resent the parents and reject the instruction. It becomes a "grim business" (Zinsser, 1981). There is no joy, merely pressure. In addition, not all preschool children can be early readers. Many preschoolers do not have the physical abilities, such as the ability to focus on printed words, necessary for success in reading (Moore and Moore, 1973). In such cases, children may feel they cannot live up to their parents' expectations and tension could develop, which would interfere with normal development.

Television

Some 98 percent of all American households have television sets, and 52 percent have more than one—the extra set for the children (Parke and Slaby, 1983). On the average, preschoolers spend 27.8 hours a week watching television (Anderson et al., 1986). Many par-

ents use the television set as a baby-sitter. If children spend that much time in one activity, its effects may be substantial (Rubinstein, 1983).

True or False   Preschoolers average almost four hours a day watching television.

But exactly what do children learn from what they see and hear on television, and how do they process this information? For example, do children understand the differences between commercials and regular programs? Do they comprehend the purpose behind advertising?

Advertising aimed at children.   The average child is exposed to about 20,000 commercials a year. About 5,000 of these are for some type of food (Stoneman and Brody, 1981). By the time a child is twenty years old, he or she has watched one million commercials. Commercials are as carefully produced as the programs they accompany. Children's advertising has three goals: to increase a child's desire for a particular product, to influence the child to ask parents to purchase the item, and to change consumption patterns—that is, encourage a person to use more of the product (Atkin, 1980).

Advertising is effective in achieving each of these goals. Children do remember what they see on television and ask their parents to purchase the items. In one study, 75 percent of the mothers of preschoolers noted that their children sang commercial jingles by the age of three, and 91 percent reported that their children asked for the toys they saw advertised on television (Lyle and Hoffman, 1972). In another study, 90 percent of the children exposed to a particular cereal commercial wanted to eat that brand, compared with about 67 percent of a control group (Atkin and Gibson, 1978). Most advertising aimed at children involves toys, cereals, candy, and fast-food restaurants. As children got older, more personal products take center stage (Liebert et al., 1973).

And children do attempt to influence the purchasing patterns of their parents. Galst and White (1976) followed children ages three through eleven who had been exposed to commercials in a lab setting on a trip to the supermarket. On the average, children tried to influence the purchases of particular foods fifteen times. Children who paid more attention to the advertisements made more requests. The extent to which these attempts are successful will vary from parent to parent. Young children make more efforts to influence parental purchases, but older children are more successful. Mothers report yielding more often to older children than to younger children (Ward and Wackman, 1972, cited in Liebert et al., 1973).

Children exposed to a particular commercial are more likely to increase their use of the product too (Atkin, 1980). As children watch the programs, they are reminded of the product, and this alters their consumption patterns.

Television advertising aimed at children is controversial. It is too easy to condemn advertising in general. Advertising is a process that is useful for introducing people to a product, but adults have the ability to recognize and interpret the commercials for what they are—attempts to persuade one to buy. Until recently, it was thought that young children could not even make the distinction between commercials and the television programs they were watching, but we now know that children as young as three years old can tell the difference between commercials and regular programs, though the ability increases with age (Levin et al., 1982). This does not mean that children understand the intent and motives behind commercials. Such understanding is not expressed until age seven or eight (Levin et al., 1983). By the sixth grade (age eleven or so), children are downright cynical about commercials (Rubinstein, 1978).

True or False Preschool children cannot tell the difference between commercials and the programs they accompany.

The effectiveness of commercials is increased by the skillful manner in which they are produced. Advertisers know how to capture and hold the attention of children. About 80 percent of the cereal commercials use animation in conjunction with nonanimated scenes (Barcus, 1980). Advertisers frequently use unusual sound and visual effects, violent activity, magic, and fantasy to attract attention. Few rational arguments are presented. Cereal ads usually concentrate on taste and texture and give little information about the ingredients except to say that the product is "fortified with essential vitamins" (Barcus, 1980).

The combination of efficient and effective psychological techniques of persuasion and an audience incapable of understanding the motives behind these commercials may cause us to consider whether television commercials aimed at young children should be permitted at all. But cleaning up children's advertising is not a simple matter. There are strong political and economic forces at work (Adler, 1980). In addition, censorship and freedom-of-speech issues are often raised (Heinz,

1983), and these should not be taken lightly. Finally, many of the recommendations to improve the children's advertising are based on what seems appropriate rather than on solid evidence (Rossiter, 1980). Even so, children do not have the cognitive sophistication to understand the motives behind the commercials and to resist the messages that are presented so well. Children do need some additional protections.

Children's television. Prior to the late 1960s, children's programs had little focus. Although some were produced by concerned individuals, they were not based on the needs and abilities of young children as determined by psychological research. That all changed when public television began showing their blockbuster children's programs "Sesame Street" and "Mister Rogers' Neighborhood." Children's television will never be the same.

Sesame Street. Big Bird, Grover, Bert and Ernie, Oscar the Grouch. Most preschoolers know these characters well. Since 1969 the face of television has been irreversibly changed as bold new experiments in television programming demonstrate that children's programs can be both entertaining and educationally valuable. "Sesame Street" is directed toward teaching inner-city youngsters basic numerical, language, and problem-solving skills (Lesser, 1976). It emphasizes cognitive concerns, although over the years prosocial behavior, tolerance for others, and attitudinal issues have been covered. The producers of "Sesame Street" knew it had to compete with commercial television to be successful (O'Bryan, 1980), that it had to be entertaining as well as educational. The show was fitted to the needs and level of its intended audience. The pace is varied and quick, the now-famous Muppets are present, and animation, splashy color, repetition, and music are used. The show is fun to watch, and children do watch it.

Children who watch "Sesame Street" regularly learn the central concepts and have an advantage over those who do not watch. These advantages seem to hold regardless of socioeconomic level, sex, or ethnicity of the viewer (Ball and Bogatz, 1970; Bogatz and Ball, 1971). Children gain more from the program if they watch with a parent who can interpret the material and act as a guide (Peters, 1977). Children also imitate the cooperation they see if they are placed in a situation like the one on television, but no generalized effects have been found (Watkins et al., 1980).

The show is not without critics. The very fast, perhaps frenetic, pace does not leave room or time for rehearsal (Tower et al., 1979). "Sesame Street" also depicts such undesirable behavior as violence and trickery (Coates et al., 1976). And some claim the effects of the show are not as pronounced as some of the research leads us to believe (Cooke et al., 1975).

Mister Rogers' Neighborhood. A show with a completely different format is "Mister Rogers' Neighborhood." This is a slower-paced, adult-led show that emphasizes interpersonal skills, imagination, and understanding one's emotions (Tower et al., 1979). Research on "Mister Rogers' Neighborhood" shows that it is successful in promoting prosocial behavior, although the

The characters on "Sesame Street" are well known to most preschoolers. The program is both entertaining and educationally valuable.

effect is not lasting (Friedrich and Stein, 1973). In one study, preschool children were exposed to daily viewing of either "Mister Rogers' Neighborhood," aggressive cartoons, or neutral programs for nine weeks. Children who saw "Mister Rogers" improved in task persistence and prosocial behavior, such as cooperation. Watching that show also led to an increase in fantasy play and imagination (Singer and Singer, 1976). This increase is noteworthy, since fantasy and pretend play are considered important aspects of a child's development (Rubin et al., 1983). Children who show more imaginative play have better social skills, show greater concentration and more positive affect, are less impulsive, and exhibit more internal control (Tower et al., 1979). The success of "Mister Rogers' Neighborhood" demonstrates that a deliberately slow-paced program can be successful in aiding both cognitive and affective development (Singer and Singer, 1983).

"Mister Rogers' Neighborhood" has also been criticized. Its slow pace sometimes makes young children restless, and some parents have difficulty getting their children to watch the program. But there is a trade-off in pacing. In one study, kindergarten and first-grade children attended more to fast-paced programs but showed greater recall for the material in slow-paced shows (Wright et al., 1984).

Television has great potential for helping preschoolers develop cognitively and socially. Commercial television has learned something from the success of these shows, and its offerings have improved. But television has a long way to go to reach its potential.

Nursery School

The third environmental factor in cognitive development is nursery school. The growth in nursery school attendance has been impressive. Nursery school enrollment of three- and four-year-olds doubled between 1970 and 1983. In 1970, 15.3 percent of the three- and four-year-old population were attending nursery school while in 1983 the percentage stood at 33.6. This trend towards increased enrollment in nursery school is continuing through the middle 1980s. The percentage of children attending preschools increases with age. Ninety-three percent of the five-year-olds were enrolled in kindergarten in 1983 versus 80 percent in 1970 (Galinsky, 1986). The need for many women to work and the growth of one-parent families account for part of this increase (Busch-

Rossnagel and Vance, 1982). In other cases, parents worry that unless their children receive a preschool education they will enter elementary school at a disadvantage.

True or False   Fewer children are attending nursery schools in the 1980s than in 1970.

Many authorities no longer differentiate between nursery schools and day-care programs. Today, day-care programs, community preschools, and experimental early education programs are all included under the heading of early childhood education (Clarke-Stewart and Fein, 1983). One additional term should be introduced here. **Compensatory education** involves an attempt to compensate for some difference between one group and another. Many preschool programs, such as Project Head Start, try to help children from economically disadvantaged families develop the attitudes and skills necessary for later success in school.

There are many approaches to preschool education. Some emphasize the importance of social skills and emotional development, including in their programs stories, listening to music, art, and trips and encouraging cooperation and sharing (McClinton and Meier, 1978). Others are more cognitively oriented. Many are sponsored by religious groups and emphasize moral education and personal and family-related activities. Generally speaking, nursery schools accomplish their purposes. Children who attend nursery schools are generally more advanced than their nonattending peers. This is especially true for children in lower-income groups (Minuchin and Shapiro, 1983). Children who attend preschool programs are more socially competent, outgoing, self-assured, curious, independent, and persistent on a task than those who do not attend. In elementary school they are better adjusted and more task-oriented, goal-directed, persistent, cooperative, and friendly (Clarke-Stewart and Fein, 1983). In a review of 56 studies of children attending nursery school, only 3 studies showed no difference between those attending and those not attending (Sjolund, 1971). Some 53 showed advantages for those attending preschool. Of 36 studies on the cognitive development of children attending and not attending nursery school, 21 found higher intellectual performance for children who attended nursery school (Sjolund, 1971).

Project Head Start.   The finding that children, especially those from poor backgrounds, are likely to benefit from the preschool experience is important. If children from poverty backgrounds enter school behind their middle-class counterparts, these children are likely to fall further behind as they progress through school. Perhaps if these children could attend a preschool that would help compensate for their different experiences this cycle could be stopped and they would have a reasonable chance for academic success. This was partly the thinking behind one of the greatest educational social experiments of the past fifty years: Project Head Start (Cooke, 1979).

Since its inception in 1964, millions of American children have taken part in the great experiment called **Project Head Start** (Zigler and Valentine, 1979), and the program continues today. The hope was that a program instituted early enough could give children in poverty situations a head start in school and reduce or eliminate the social-class difference in education achievement (Zigler and Berman, 1983).

Project Head Start had both cognitive and noncognitive goals (Washington, 1985). Children were to learn to work and play independently, become able to accept help and direction from adults, learn competence and worth, sharpen and widen language skills, be curious, and grow in ability to channel inner, destructive impulses (Head Start Rainbow Book No. 4, 1965, cited in Miller, 1979). There were also health goals.

Hopes were high for Project Head Start, but soon controversy, disappointment, and disillusionment set in. The first evaluations were impressive, and studies showed sizable gains in cognitive abilities and self-esteem (Zigler and Berman, 1983). Soon, though, it was found that the intelligence gains noted did not continue as the child progressed through second and third grade (Weinberg, 1979; Westinghouse Learning Corp., 1969). This was often called the fade-out phenomenon. In other words, the gains in intelligence seemed temporary, and by the second grade or so, Head Start children did not differ from their classmates in intelligence. This led to a period of intense skepticism on the part of critics, and defensiveness on the part of the program's supporters.

However, recent research demonstrates the beneficial effects of the Head Start experience. They are obvious once you know where to look. The most recent studies looked at other measures besides intelligence and reported that, like other preschool programs, students who took part were significantly less likely to be retained in grade or to be found in special-education classes. The results of studies on reading and math achievement of children who attended a Head Start program are mixed, with some showing Head Start children achieving more in math and reading (Lazar et al., 1982; Darlington et al., 1980; Palmer and Andersen, 1979).

True or False Children who attended Project Head Start classes were less likely to be found in special-education classes than their peers who did not participate in the program.

Other advantages have been found, especially for Head Start programs in which parental participation is encouraged and high (Mann et al., 1978). The children of parents who were very active in Head Start as board members, volunteers, and so forth performed better on achievement tests (Washington, 1985). Involvement in the program is often the first community involvement for many parents, and most authorities believe even more emphasis should be placed on involving parents (Sprigle and Schaefer, 1985; Oyemade, 1985). In one Wisconsin community, not only did a majority of the parents become involved in the program but 44 percent continued to serve in other community organizations for years after (Zigler and Berman, 1983). Parental involvement helps parents deal with younger siblings as well. Gray and Klaus (1970) found that the younger siblings of children who had taken part in the Head Start program had significantly higher intelligence scores, perhaps because the improved parental interactions carried over to other children. On the whole, Head Start has been successful.

Two Dangers

Cognitive development during the preschool period is certainly impressive. Piaget described the preschooler's abilities and limitations, and new research shows just how sensitive young children are to the type of task and the environment surrounding the challenge. Psychologists have gained a genuine respect for the preschool child's abilities. We now also have a better understanding of how important it is for children to be ready for the formal school experience and of the part the home, television, and preschool programs can play in fostering cognitive development.

Yet in the midst of the tremendous interest in preschool education and cognitive development, two cautions are necessary. First, there is a real danger of overemphasizing early cognitive education, making parents quasi-teachers who grimly and joylessly drum facts and skills into children's heads (Zinsser, 1981). One parent I met truly believed that the right preschool education and home environment would guarantee her son an Ivy League education and eternal success. She was busy teaching him to read, even though he did not have the physical ability—in this case the ability to focus on the printed word—necessary for such success. Second, there is a danger that the child's social and personality development will be submerged in the rush to "school" our children. Social and personality development is just as important, and people sometimes forget that children learn much through interacting with other people and in play. It is to the preschoolers' development in these areas that we turn next.

--- Summary ---

1. During the preschool years, the rate of growth declines.
2. Preschoolers develop a number of motor skills, including jumping, running, and hopping. The development of the large muscles precedes that of the fine muscles.
3. The leading cause of death among preschoolers is accidents, including motor vehicle accidents, fires and burns, drowning, and poisoning. Many of these accidents can be prevented.
4. According to Piagetian theory, children between about two and seven are in the preoperational stage. These children can now use symbols and have the capacity to view an action, remember it, and repeat it later.
5. Children in the preoperational stage also tend to

be egocentric (see everything from their own point of view). They are also animistic, believing that everything is capable of being conscious and alive, and they reason transductively (from specific event to specific event).

6. Preschoolers have difficulty placing things in size order (seriation), and at least at the beginning of this stage they have problems sorting items into different classes (classification).

7. Preschoolers cannot solve conservation problems (challenges that involve the understanding that quantities remain the same even if their appearance changes). Their tendency to center on one dimension and to base their judgments on appearances, and their inability to reverse operations and to understand transformations, are responsible for the problems they have in this area.

8. New evidence shows that many of these abilities are present if preschoolers are tested on tasks that are meaningful to them, simple, and clearly defined. However, these abilities are fragile, and preschoolers will not show these skills all the time.

9. The attention span of preschoolers is superior to that of toddlers, but it is still not as long as it will be in middle childhood. Children are attracted by many aspects of the situation, such as movement, color, and loud noise. As children age, their ability to voluntarily focus their attention in a planned, organized manner increases. This ability is not well developed in the preschooler.

10. Preschoolers do not spontaneously use verbal strategies—such as rehearsal—as memory aids, but they do show such strategies as looking and pointing. Children do better in familiar situations and with tasks that are meaningful.

11. The child's knowledge base affects memory and performance on a number of tasks. Both children and adults possess a number of scripts or structures describing the sequence of events in a particular situation. These form the basis for understanding events.

12. Parents who label the environment, encourage their children's curiosity, and read to them tend to maximize their children's cognitive development.

13. Advertising aimed at children is very effective. Children often ask for the products they see on television. "Sesame Street" and "Mr. Rogers' Neighborhood" are two successful television shows combining entertainment with education.

14. More and more preschoolers are attending early childhood education programs. Children who attend preschool gain from their experience.

15. Project Head Start is an attempt to provide experiences to help close the gap between children from lower socioeconomic backgrounds and their peers from middle-class backgrounds. While the immediate gains in intelligence are not sustained throughout elementary school, children who attend Head Start classes are less likely to be left back or to be found in special-education classes. Some studies show that they do better in math and reading as well. Parental involvement in such programs is related to the best outcomes.

Answers to True or False Statements

1. *False* Correct statement: The rate of growth decreases markedly during early childhood.
2. *True* Accidents are the number-one cause of death during early childhood.
3. *False* Correct statement: Even though new research shows that preschoolers can do more than we originally thought, their logic does not approach that of the average adult.
4. *False* Correct statement: Generally, older children show a superior ability to take someone else's point of view.
5. *True* Young preschoolers believe that inanimate objects are capable of being alive and conscious.
6. *False* Correct statement: Preschoolers perform better on familiar tasks than on tasks that are new to them.
7. *True* Preschoolers may use rehearsal if they are directed to do so on a particular task, but they do

not use it on their own.

8. *False* Correct statement: Reading to children is an effective way to promote reading skills.

9. *True* Preschoolers spend about four hours every day watching television.

10. *False* Correct statement: Recent evidence shows that preschoolers can tell the difference between the commercials and the programs, but do not understand the motives behind the advertising.

11. *False* Correct statement: The popularity of nursery schools has increased greatly since 1970.

12. *True* Children who took part in the Head Start Program were less likely to be placed in special-education classes than their peers who did not attend the program.

Social and Personality Development in Early Childhood

Are the Following Statements True or False?

Try the True-False Quiz below. See if your answers correspond to the information in this chapter. Each question is repeated after the paragraph in which the answer can be found. The True-False Answer Box at the end of the chapter lists the complete answers.

____ 1. An activity is considered play only if it is enjoyable.

____ 2. Role reversal—acting the part of a doctor or parent instead of a child or patient—during play is a sign of behavioral disturbance.

____ 3. Two-year-olds are known for cooperative play, in which they take specific roles in an organized game and interact extensively with others.

____ 4. Boys show significantly more rough-and-tumble play than girls.

____ 5. Children actually spend less time with peers during early childhood than during the toddler stage.

____ 6. Siblings are more likely to fight than to play with each other.

____ 7. Children of parents who allow the child maximum freedom with few if any restrictions are usually self-reliant and show excellent self-control.

____ 8. Unusual as it may seem, parents who abuse their children often believe that physical punishment is wrong.

____ 9. Research has failed to establish any consistent differences between the sexes in personality or behavior.

____10. Girls generally receive more punishment than boys, while boys receive more praise.

____11. Fathers are more likely than mothers to treat their sons and daughters equally.

____12. Preschoolers are more likely to accept female sex-role violations than male sex-role violations.

You Stay Home, I'm Going Fishing

"You stay home with the mommies and the babies. I'm going fishing," said a four-year-old boy to the little girl he was playing with.

"But I want to come too," she protested.

"No, you can't, but I'll take you to a Chinese restaurant when I get home."

The little girl was quieted by that promise. (After Carper, 1978)

When the nursery school teacher reported this conversation to the boy's mother, the mother told her that when her husband did go fishing the whole family always went along. Children's play does not always accurately reflect their home surroundings. Play can be very imaginative. In fact, the ability to use imagination is a major difference between toddlers and preschoolers. We have already looked at some of the other differences—their physical and cognitive skills have improved, and their language and speech abilities are far superior to what they were in the toddler stage.

During early childhood, preschoolers are able to plan, and they enjoy being on the move and taking the initiative (Erikson, 1963). Erikson considers **initiative** the positive outcome of this preschool stage, while the negative outcome is **guilt.** If parents appreciate the importance of encouraging a preschooler's self-guided initiatives and curiosity, the child will leave the stage with a sense of initiative. If a child's curiosity and activities become a bother to parents and they react with verbal scorn and restrictions, the child is likely to become timid and fearful.

In this chapter we will look at the preschooler's expanding social world and consider some areas in which the changes are quite dramatic—play, relationships with parents and siblings, and children's understanding of sex roles.

The Mysteries of Play

Play is so much a part of childhood that you might think we would know a lot about it. Although most people can accurately judge when children are playing, actually defining play is difficult (Smith and Vollstedt, 1985).

> **initiative vs. guilt** The third psychosocial stage, in which the positive outcome is a favorable view of one's own desires and actions and the negative outcome is a sense of guilt over one's actions.
>
> **play** An activity dominated by the child and performed with a positive feeling.

Stop and think about it. Just what is play? Do adults play too? Is a child who is painstakingly assembling a model of the starship *Enterprise* with a determined look playing? There is no single accepted definition of play today, but this does not mean we cannot study it, for play has some unique characteristics (Vandenberg, 1978).

What Is Play and Why Do Children Play?

An activity that is performed for sheer enjoyment with no ulterior motive is **play.** In play, the focus is on the child instead of on what the child is holding, bouncing, or coloring. Play activities are activities performed for their own sake (Vandenberg, 1978); there is no payoff in candy, attention, or money. Finally, play is enjoyable.

True or False An activity is considered play only if it is enjoyable.

Two young boys were asked why they continued to throw a rubber ball to each other for hours at a time. The boys answered, "We like it." When asked what they liked about the activity, they just shrugged their shoulders. To the casual observer, the activity seems to have little value or purpose.

Isolating the functions of play is difficult. For some activity to be considered play, it must be voluntary, enjoyable, and basically purposeless. The fact that the activity is enjoyable masks the fact that play is essential to a child's development. Since we often think that only work is valuable, we tend to overlook all the possible values in play. For instance, the children playing ball are exercising their muscles and improving their eye-hand coordination. Play often involves muscular activity that is vital for optimal physical development. It also helps develop a child's mental abilities. Preschoolers often

In play, children often exchange roles enabling them to understand other people's roles.

use their imagination during play (Howes, 1985). They may imagine themselves flying, or take on the role of some fictional character. Often this play is social, and the combination of social and pretend play appears during the third year of life (Howes, 1985). Such play helps children develop their problem-solving abilities too.

The social functions of play are obvious. Children who play with others soon learn the need for cooperation and sharing. They learn that they will not always win, that compromises are sometimes necessary. Their interactions with other children teach them the social skills necessary to live in society. In addition, children often exchange roles during play, pretending that they are doctors, nurses, fathers, and so on. This helps them understand other people's roles. In the children's museum in Seattle, Washington, child-sized grocery stores, post offices, doctors offices, and the like are available for children to use. There young children can easily take on the role of a checker in a grocery store or a doctor, for instance.

Children experiment with new roles, and they often reverse them from roles of submission to roles of dominance (Sutton-Smith and Roberts, 1981). The five-year-old acting the part of a doctor has experienced being a patient quite often. In play, children try out other roles. They can actually control the behavior of the people in these roles in a way that is not possible in the real world. They can create a world in which they can control and dominate situations. They use play to cope with their sense of powerlessness.

True or False Role reversal—acting the part of a doctor or parent instead of a child or patient—during play is a sign of behavioral disturbance.

Play may also function as an outlet for pent-up frustration and anger. It makes it possible for children to express some of their anger in a safe way. This is essentially the Freudian or psychoanalytical viewpoint—children act out their problems and thereby reduce their anxieties (Erikson, 1959). One four-year-old played house with small, doll-like figures. At home, she had to share the attention of her parents with a baby sister, who required much care. In her play, daddy would come home and, instead of kissing her and going to see the baby, he would say "I want to play only with you, not that silly baby. I don't care about her." In her play she was expressing her true feelings. Observing a child at play often allows professionals to gain deeper insights into a child's problems (Axline, 1969).

Finally, play is a vehicle for exploring new ways of acting. Once children realize they will not be ridiculed or made to suffer because they make a mistake, they will try out new ways of behaving and relating to other people.

The Development of Play

Try this experiment. Visit a playground and watch the children play. Try to estimate their ages, and then note *how* they are playing. You will probably notice a definite progression (Rubin et al., 1983).

A baby will be relatively uninvolved with other children. Anything that occurs may be of interest to the infant for only a few seconds. Such unoccupied behavior is the first stage of play, since these children may stroke their bodies, play with their hands, or hug a stuffed animal. Later in the first year, children play with simple toys, banging them against something or dropping them. They are basically exploring the properties of the toy and are uninvolved with any other children around them. They may play simple peek-a-boo games with a parent, but the other individual is essentially a toy, and no mutuality is evidenced.

Independent or **solitary play** can be seen in young children and remains important in the second and third years of life. However, the transition to a more social type of play can be seen in what Parten (1932) called **onlooker play.** During this stage, children watch others with considerable interest and frequently ask questions about what they are doing, yet they are not able to join in and therefore remain on the outside. This leads to a type of play in which children may seek out the company of others but still not interact extensively with them.

During the second year, children are often brought together with their peers. These two-year-olds engage in **parallel play.** They play in the presence of other children, but not with them. They do not really interact or cooperate with one another. An observer gets the feeling

solitary play Independent play in which the child shows no interest in the activities of others.

onlooker play A classification of play in which the child watches others play and shows some interest, but is unable to join in.

parallel play A type of play common in two-year-olds in which they play in the presence of other children but not with them.

associative play A type of play seen in preschoolers who are actively involved with one another but cannot sustain these interactions.

cooperative play A type of play seen in the later part of the preschool period and continuing into middle childhood, marked by group play, playing specific roles, and active cooperation for sustained periods of time.

that if one child left, the other could go on without any problem. The quality of the sand castles built by either child does not depend on the participation of the other. Parallel play is found throughout the preschool period, but it decreases with age. It is the primary play behavior in two-year-olds and in some three-year-olds (Smith, 1978).

True or False Two-year-olds are known for cooperative play, in which they take specific roles in an organized game and interact extensively with others.

During early childhood, true interaction with others emerges. Preschoolers actively **associate** with other children and may share, cooperate, have verbal arguments, and play together, but these periods are not sustained. There is a flightiness to the play and to their interactions with others. Much of the play of preschoolers involves practice of physical skills that have been, or are being, mastered. As the preschool stage continues, social interaction, cooperation, and sharing increase (Howes, 1985).

Beginning in the later part of the preschool period and continuing into middle childhood, children actively **cooperate** with one another. This involves a more-or-less unified group playing a particular game, in which one or two children often take the lead. Children are able to take specific parts in a game, and they have a more mature understanding of what their role in the group is. If you watch a group of five-, six-, or seven-year-olds at the park, you may see this type of behavior.

dramatic play A type of play in which children take on the roles of others.

Some children are leaders and allot roles to the others. Sometimes rebellions break out in the ranks, but their need for one another is obvious.

During the preschool stage, **dramatic play,** which involves taking the roles of others, increases. This requires the ability to imitate and put oneself in another person's place. This ability is primitive in preschoolers, but it develops as children find themselves in different social situations. Preschoolers are essentially egocentric, but you can see some attempts at role-taking in their dramatic play. Usually this play takes a standard form. Garvey (1977) observed a number of preschool children at play. Each child was paired with another and allowed to play undisturbed in a room that contained a number of play materials. Children as young as two and three years of age engaged in some dramatic play, often involving mothers and infants. Most of the dramatic play centered on common home situations and everyday challenges. Some involved participation in fantasies, including protecting others from monsters and putting themselves in fairy tales as characters. The dramatic play was spontaneous and flexible. The sophistication of such play increases with age.

Sex Differences in Play

As you watch the children play, you may notice some sex differences. Many studies indicate that boys and girls play in characteristic fashions. Simply stated, boys play much more roughly than girls. DiPietro (1981) brought same-sex groups of four-and-a-half-year-old children three at a time into a mobile home from which the furnishings had been removed. A few toys were present, including a beach ball, a small trampoline, and a Bobo doll. DiPietro noted that the girls organized themselves and made rules. The girls argued, but they did not resort to physical means of persuasion. The boys played in a rougher fashion, often wrestling. They did not seem angry, nor did they attempt to injure one another. They simply played differently. The difference is also seen in animal studies performed on chimpanzees. When chimps were allowed contact only with their peers, characteristic play patterns could be seen. The males were more aggressive. Because

these chimps had been separated from their parents at birth, they could not have learned the patterns from them, and some biological factor—perhaps hormones—must be responsible (Harlow and Harlow, 1966).

True or False Boys show significantly more rough-and-tumble play than girls.

It is difficult to do the kinds of controlled studies necessary to understand the cause of sex differences. As we shall see, this is a field of great interest and controversy at the present time. Although Harlow's experiments with chimps are interesting and suggestive, they are not conclusive. Such research may suggest models and hypotheses, but we must be careful when we try to generalize from animal research to human beings. Any cross-species generalizations are dangerous. Research on cats may not generalize to dogs or horses, let alone to human beings. We may question whether the same cognitive processes involved in thinking, planning, and interpreting, which are so obvious in human beings, should be automatically ascribed to other species. Although animal research is interesting, generalizations should be made with care.

While some may argue that males are biologically predisposed to aggressive patterns, other explanations are possible. For example, various societies may expect males to act more aggressively, so males may simply be complying with society's expectations. The presence of some biological predisposition does not negate the importance of learned behavior.

The Rise of the Peer Group

Preschoolers are more socially oriented in their play than toddlers and prefer to play with familiar peers (Rubin et al., 1983). The amount of social play increases as children become familiar with each other (Harper and Huei, 1985). As the child's interpersonal world expands in early childhood, peers begin to have more influence.

With increasing age, children spend more time with peers and less with their parents. While the peer group does not have the power it will have during middle childhood and adolescence, it does have an influence on the preschooler. The growth of early childhood programs has exposed many children to the social demands of other children at a very early age. In addition, the structure of the child-rearing environment may affect one's relationships with peers. (See the Cross-Cultural Current on page 211.) While toddlers show some ability to participate in social activities, it is in early childhood that such activities come closer to what we might call friendship. A considerable degree of sharing and cooperation begins to manifest itself, and the play of the child becomes more social, more dramatic, and more sophisticated. As preschoolers mature, the number of children they play with at one time increases. Preschoolers are no longer merely limited to one-on-one situations. Groups of three and four children are not uncommon.

True or False Children actually spend less time with peers during early childhood than during the toddler stage.

Most of the preschooler's interactions with others, especially their peers, are positive (Hartup, 1970). Preschoolers are more prosocial and playful with peers than with their older or younger siblings (Abramovitch et al., 1986). There are fewer arguments than one might think. Children are accepted on the basis of how friendly and outgoing they are. Preschoolers are not very sympathetic to others, probably because of their egocentric mentality. However, cooperation as well as competition increases with age.

The peer experience sometimes modifies parental authority, but the preschooler's family remains the primary influence on the child's activities. Parents and siblings are still the most significant people in the interpersonal environment of a child.

The Sibling Experience

"My children fight like cats and dogs," a mother of two active boys told me one night. She had come for counseling because she could no longer take the noise, the bickering, and the constant fighting. She and her husband had just broken up some "vicious" verbal exchanges, and peace seemed unobtainable.

The very presence of siblings affects a child's development. Unlike friends, siblings do not leave the home. You can limit your contact with them, but you cannot totally avoid them. They compete for parental attention, and their joys and pains affect everyone in the household.

Discussions about siblings usually revolve around sibling rivalry, but psychologists have noted that siblings encourage prosocial actions and fill definite psychological

As children negotiate the preschool stage, they begin to play in groups.

Child-Rearing Environments: Do They Make a Difference?

Most of you were raised in a fairly standard American home. You slept under your parents' roof each night. Your contact with peers was limited—at least in the early years. Your primary associations were with parents and siblings. All your friends were brought up the same way. But what if you were raised in a completely different environment, perhaps a communal home? Would your personality and social relationships be much different?

This was one question that Rachel Levy-Shiff and Michael Hoffman tried to answer in their study of urban and kibbutz-raised children. In Israel, some children are raised on communal agricultural establishments called kibbutzim. These children sleep in a children's house with other preschoolers, instead of in their parents' quarters. *

The kibbutz-raised children were compared with preschoolers raised in the modern city of Tel Aviv. The parents of all the children in the study were born in Israel, were middle class, had similar educational backgrounds, and enjoyed similar standards of living. The fathers of the kibbutz-raised children were involved primarily in agricultural work or worked in light industry, while the mothers held jobs in social services or education. The parents of the urban preschoolers held white-collar jobs in business and social services. Previous research had reported that older children raised in the communal environment showed better group-oriented skills but less warmth and personal intimacy in interpersonal contact. Perhaps these behaviors have their roots in this early arrangement, where children are likely to have to depend on one another and do not develop the same intense relationship with parents.

Both groups of children were observed in free-play situations, either at the urban nursery school or in the

kibbutz children's house. An assortment of play materials was provided, and observers used a checklist to indicate the type of interpersonal behavior shown by the subjects, such as responding positively to a playmate's initiatives, showing cooperative and coordinated play, competitive behaviors, and the like.

The results showed that even at the early preschool stage the differences were apparent. Among the most important findings were that the kibbutz preschoolers—compared with the urban children—were less competitive, engaged more frequently in coordinated play, displayed less warmth toward their peers, and were more verbally aggressive. They also showed more solitary play. Urban preschoolers spent more time exchanging toys and objects and struggling over who would get the toys.

The researchers conclude that the larger amount of coordinated play, reduced competition, and avoidance of physical conflict shows greater group-oriented skills and enhanced group cohesion. The increased amounts of verbal aggression, reduced warmth in interpersonal relations, and more solitary play demonstrate greater emotional distancing in kibbutz-raised children, compared with their urban peers.

These findings parallel those found for older children in kibbutzim, showing that the roots of these behaviors can be found even in very young preschoolers. In the United States, the typical upbringing is quite different from kibbutz upbringing. In other areas of the world, especially in Africa and Asia, children are raised in environments that are very different from the standard American nuclear family. The results of this study, as well as other similar studies, suggest that the child-rearing arrangement itself may help shape the child's behavior and orientation toward others. The roots of the person's personality may be found in the child-rearing environment of the society or subculture that structures the child's early peer and parental interactions.

*Not all kibbutzim are structured this way. In some communal establishments, children sleep in the same house as their parents.

Source: Levy-Shiff, R., and Hoffman, M. A. Social Behavior of Urban and Preschool Children in Israel. *Developmental Psychology*, 1985, *21*, 1204–1205.

needs. Not only do siblings play together and experience each other's joys and pains firsthand, but they often help one another (Brody et al., 1985). Sometimes they provide support and affection that may not be forthcoming from the parents (Dunn and Kendrick, 1982). In one study, preschool children acted as substitute attachment figures for their younger siblings in the presence of a stranger (Stewart, 1983). In a series of studies, Abramovitch and colleagues (1986, 1980, 1979) followed siblings as they matured, starting when the younger siblings were one and a half years old and when the older siblings were preschoolers, to a time when the younger ones were five years old and the older ones were in middle childhood. As these children matured, a common pattern became apparent. The older children initiated more prosocial and combative behaviors, and young children imitated more. The older sibling clearly dominated the younger one. Although the distinctions lessened over time, birth order rather than age seemed to be the cause of the domination. Although there was antagonism, prosocial and play-oriented behaviors constituted a majority of the interactions. Abramovitch asserts that it is incorrect to think of sibling relationships as primarily combative or negative. Sibling relations often grow warmer with time, and in adulthood siblings give each other great support in family crises.

True or False Siblings are more likely to fight than to play with each other.

In terms of influence, siblings have one advantage over parents. They are of the same generation, which gives them a special social status, especially during adolescence. Siblings have an effect on each other, and any understanding of a child's environment must take the sibling experience into account.

When people discuss sibling relations they often emphasize fighting and bickering. However, siblings also provide a great deal of support for each other.

Parents and Preschoolers

Throughout the preschool period, parents have the greatest influence on the child's social and personality development, but the preschooler's relationship with his or her parents is very different from what it was in toddlerhood. As preschoolers achieve more independence, their relationship with their parents changes, and parents face many questions concerning discipline and punishment.

Parenting Styles

Parents differ in the ways they control their children's behavior. Some exercise a great deal of direct control, others believe that having fewer rules is better. The effects of differing parenting styles were investigated by Baumrind (1980, 1978, 1971, 1967), who isolated three different styles.

Authoritarian parents try to control their children's conduct by establishing rules and regulations. Obedience is greatly valued, and the threat of force is used to correct behavior. A parent's decisions cannot be questioned. The authoritarian parent's word is law.

Permissive parents make few demands on their children. They are nonpunishing, open to communication, and do not attempt to shape the children's behavior. The children regulate their own activities. When necessary, permissive parents use reason rather than power to control their children.

Authoritative parents encourage verbal give-and-take and explain the reasons behind family policies. Both autonomy and discipline are valued. Limits are set, but the child's individuality is taken into consideration. The parents are warm, and do not see themselves as infallible (Baumrind, 1971).

As a group, the children of authoritative parents are the most self-reliant, self-controlled, explorative, and contented. The children of permissive parents are least self-reliant, explorative, and self-controlled. The children of authoritarian parents are the most discontented, withdrawn, and distrustful.

True or False Children of parents who allow the child maximum freedom with few if any restrictions are usually self-reliant and show excellent self-control.

Authoritative parents combine firm control, encouragement of individuality, and open communication—

authoritarian parenting style A style of parenting in which parents rigidly control their children's behavior by establishing rules and value obedience while discouraging questioning.

permissive parenting style A style of parenting marked by open communication and a lack of parental demand for good behavior.

authoritative parenting style A style of parenting in which parents establish limits but allow open communication and some freedom for children to make their own decisions in certain areas.

discipline An attempt to control others in order to hold undesirable impulses in check and to encourage self-control.

punishment The process by which some physical or emotional pain is inflicted in order to reduce the probability that misbehavior will reoccur.

producing children who are independent and competent. They are also warmer and more nurturant than authoritarian parents. Some permissive parents are warm, others show a coolness and detachment toward their children.

Parental control does not interfere with independence as long as children have opportunities to develop their own abilities and make their own decisions, within limits. Yet the total parental control that authoritarian parents use leads to children who are less competent, less contented, and suspicious. Warmth and discipline are the keys to producing independent, competent children.

Discipline and Punishment

For many families, punishment is synonymous with discipline, but there are important differences. **Discipline** involves control of others for the purpose of holding undesirable impulses or habits in check and encouraging self-control. It may include reasoning and positive reinforcement for the correct behavior. Discipline also occurs before the infringement. **Punishment** is a process by which an undesirable behavior is followed by a negative consequence. It is administered after the damage is done and is always negative. Its purpose is to decrease or completely eliminate a behavior in a particular circumstance. Most behaviors are correct in one instance but not in another. While hitting another child to get a toy is unacceptable, defending oneself when being hit by another child is acceptable. Punishment may teach a child what not to do, but it does not provide any instruction in what the child *should* do under the circumstances.

Discipline style. Parents' attempts to control their children's behavior can be put under two headings. **Power-assertive discipline** involves physical punishment, yelling, shouting, and forceful commands, while **love-oriented discipline** involves praise, affection, reasoning, showing disappointment, and the withdrawal of love (Maccoby and Martin, 1983). Authoritarian parents use power-assertive discipline; authoritative parents use both power-assertive and love-oriented discipline. Permissive parents use very little discipline, but when discipline is necessary they use reasoning, a love-oriented approach.

power-assertive discipline   A type of discipline relying on the use of power, such as physical punishment or forceful commands.

love-oriented discipline   A type of discipline relying on the use of reasoning or love.

These discipline styles interact with the emotional tone of the parent-child relationship. When restrictiveness occurs within a context of warmth and acceptance, it can lead to obedience, nonaggressiveness, and other positive outcomes. When it occurs in the presence of hostility, it leads to withdrawal and anxiety (Becker, 1964). In investigating techniques of discipline, both the type of approach (power-assertive or love-oriented) and the emotional tone of the relationship (warm or hostile) must be considered.

It is not easy to find the most effective way of disciplining a child.

time out A punishment procedure in which a person is denied access to positive reinforcement for a certain period of time. A child who misbehaves may be isolated from the group for a brief period.

Discipline and verbal abilities. Preschoolers can get into more trouble than infants or toddlers because their physical abilities are greater. However, their ability to use language gives parents more options in dealing with misbehavior. As children mature, they respond to a more rational approach. In a study of one-and-a-half-year-olds, two-and-a-half-year-olds, and three-and-a-half-year-olds, toddlers responded better to simple commands than to suggestions or questions, and preschoolers responded more to suggestions (McLaughlin, 1983). Parents who realize that preschoolers' verbal abilities give them more options are likely to change their discipline strategy and use more complicated verbal techniques instead of mere commands.

Each of the three parenting styles uses discipline in a different way, resulting in different outcomes. Authoritarian parents rely on punishment, which gets them obedience in the short term and rebellion in the long term. Permissive parents rarely use any type of discipline, and this can result in a child who lacks direction and self-control. Authoritative parents use both approaches, depending on the situation, but they encourage independence by allowing children freedom within limits. Perhaps authoritative parents notice the change in a child's verbal and physical abilities and tailor the discipline to the emerging abilities of the child.

Punishment: Uses and abuses. Psychologists recognize that punishment may be necessary under certain circumstances, but they are concerned about the type of punishment used and the way it is administered. Punishment can be administered in two ways (Karen, 1974). First, a positive reinforcer may be removed. A parent may remove a toy or turn off the television set to punish a misbehaving child. In the technique called **time out,** children are removed from the reinforcing circumstances for a brief period of time (Kazdin, 1984). For example, the child who is misbehaving while the family is watching a television program may be sent out of the room for ten minutes. The second procedure involves following the

undesirable action with an unpleasant action—a child who whines may be yelled at or spanked.

While punishment can decrease the frequency of an undesirable behavior, it often fails in its purpose because it is administered incorrectly. It may be overused by some parents, who never compliment their children but are always ready with a criticism, and even the strap. In order to be effective, punishment should be moderate, swift, certain, and combined with rewards for the correct behavior (Altrocchi, 1980). Unfortunately, parents often delay punishment, are inconsistent, use overly severe punishments, and constantly threaten their children—practices that are ineffective over the longer term.

Effective punishment. Punishment has a place in child-rearing, but using punishment correctly is more difficult that most parents realize. The effects of a poorly administered punishment may linger for some time. In addition, parents often forget to include reinforcement for good behavior along with punishment for inconsiderate actions. A punishment is likely to be more effective if children know they are capable of meeting the standards of conduct and that the parent will notice when they do and praise them for it.

The aim of punishment is to decrease or eliminate a behavior, so if a parental action, no matter how severe, fails to do that, it has been a failure. Here are some guidelines for effective punishment:

1. Be as consistent as possible about which behaviors are acceptable and which are not.
2. Although a warning may be in order, continually threatening a child without carrying through a reasonable disciplinary action decreases the adult's influence over the child.
3. Never threaten to give a child a punishment that either cannot be carried out ethically or that you would not be willing to administer.
4. Especially when dealing with younger children, punishment should be as immediate as possible. However, if you know yourself to be emotional, be careful not to administer punishments that are too severe for the misbehavior. You may regret the overreaction later.
5. Moderate punishments are usually more effective than severe ones. After you have used your harshest punishment on a child, you have nowhere to go from there. In addition, if the punishment is

too severe for the "crime," the child tends to reflect on the punishment instead of on what was done to deserve it.

6. Do not use the "wait until father (or mother) comes home" approach.
7. Give your child a chance to answer any accusations.
8. Punishment is most effective when it is combined with reinforcement for the correct response. Using positive reinforcement along with disciplinary action increases the effectiveness of both.
9. Overreliance on punishment decreases communication, as children become afraid to confide in adults. Keep the lines of communication open.
10. Use the minimum amount of punishment that will successfully accomplish your goal.
11. Punish only the child's action. Some parents make statements concerning how "bad" the child is, which focuses on the *child* rather than on the child's inappropriate *behavior*. Punishment should be aimed at reducing or eliminating the troublesome behavior, not at injuring the child's self-concept.

The effects of harsh punishment.   Some parents are proud that they are severe disciplinarians and do not spare the rod. They claim their method is successful and find it difficult to understand why other parents do not use as much punishment. To the casual observer, the harshly disciplined child may seem well behaved, but a deeper look reveals a different picture. Harsh punishment is effective in temporarily decreasing the undesirable behavior, but over the long term it is less successful and can even be damaging (Martin, 1975). Children may correct their behavior temporarily, especially in the presence of the feared parent, but their frustration and anger builds up and eventually explodes. These children may become sullen and suspicious of authority. According to Martin (1975), many children who are problems in school are disciplined harshly at home. Thus, the stereotype that the problem child in school is rarely disciplined at home may not be accurate.

Child Abuse

Sometimes punishment goes beyond the point of reason and leads to abuse. **Child abuse** occurs when parents

> **child abuse**   A general term used to denote an injury that is intentionally perpetrated on a child.
>
> **child neglect**   A term used to describe a situation in which the care and supervision of a child is insufficient or improper.

intentionally injure their children. **Neglect** refers to a situation in which the physical care and supervision of the child is inadequate or inappropriate. States vary in their definitions of abuse and neglect, and many states now require such professionals as doctors, nurses, and teachers to report suspected cases of child abuse or neglect. There were 1.7 million cases of child abuse and neglect reported in 1984 (American Humane Association, 1986). Most people would like to think that child abusers are mentally ill, but although parents who abuse their children suffer from a number of psychological problems (Lystad, 1975), only 10 percent can be confidently classified as mentally ill (Kempe and Kempe, 1978). Sometimes it is easier to see abusing parents as something less than human, but in the vast majority of cases this is not true. Child-abusing parents cannot be detected just by looking at them, nor is it always easy to identify them.

Sexual Abuse

One type of child abuse—sexual abuse—has been the subject of much discussion in the media. Beginning in the mid-1970s and continuing in the 1980s, the public has been swamped with well-publicized cases of sexual abuse (Finkelhor, 1984a). Sexual abuse may involve forcible rape, statutory rape, sodomy, incest, or "indecent liberties," such as genital exhibition and physical advances (Sarafino, 1979). About 23,000 cases of sexual abuse were reported in 1982 (Finkelhor, 1984a), but the incidence of such abuse is grossly underreported, and it is the least-reported type of child abuse (Schultz and Jones, 1983). In a recent study of 521 families in the Boston area, 9 percent of the parents said one of their children had been a victim of an attempted or actual incident of sexual abuse (Finkelhor, 1984b).

Sexual abusers are mostly men, and girls constitute the majority of victims (Canavan, 1981). Sexual abuse is most likely to occur between people who are related, but a child may also be victimized by a stranger. The consequences of sexual abuse may be both physical—such as venereal disease and pregnancy—and emotional. Long-term effects include depression, self-destructive behavior, anxiety, feelings of isolation and stigma, poor self-esteem, difficulty trusting others, substance abuse, and sexual maladjustment (Browne and Finkelhor, 1986; Adams-Tucker, 1982).

Parents often ask what they can do to prevent sexual abuse. Knowing where their children are, what they are doing, and who they are with are obvious precautions, but parents cannot foresee every circumstance. For instance, one six-year-old boy was abused by an older boy when he went to the bathroom of a supermarket while his mother waited in the checkout line (De Vine, 1980). Parents should remind their children not to accept money or favors from strangers, and not to accept a ride or go anywhere with someone they do not know. If they think they are in danger, they should be told that making a scene by running away and screaming for help is acceptable. Because the sexual abuser may be someone they know and trust, children should be told that they do not have to agree to demands for physical closeness even from relatives. Finally, children should be encouraged to report any instances of people touching them in intimate places or asking them to do the same (Queens Bench Foundation, 1977). The increase in publicity surrounding sexual abuse has led to frank public discussion of the problem. This offers some hope that we can reduce its incidence through prevention and its consequences through early discovery and treatment.

Emotional Abuse

Does child abuse have to be physical? What of parents who constantly yell at and berate their children? Imagine a four-year-old who has just spilled some juice hearing a parent shout, "You're a stupid, rotten kid. If I had any sense I'd give you away!" Such statements can actually influence children to believe they are "stupid" or "rotten" and as a result begin to act that way—the way they think people expect them to. This is an example of the **self-fulfilling prophecy,** the phenomenon in which a person's expectations concerning some event affects the probability that it will occur.

It is difficult to define **emotional abuse,** sometimes

self-fulfilling prophecy   The concept that a person's expectations concerning some event affect the probability that it will occur.

emotional abuse (psychological maltreatment)   Psychological damage perpetrated on the child by parental actions, which often involves rejection, isolation, terrorizing, ignoring, and/or corrupting.

called **psychological maltreatment** (Rosenberg, 1987). Certain parental actions can lead to a loss of self-esteem in the child and interfere with emotional development, but defining these actions and describing remedial steps are difficult. Conceptually, such parental behaviors as rejecting, isolating, terrorizing, ignoring, and corrupting constitute psychological maltreatment (Garbarino et al., 1986). These forms of abuse frequently produce emotional and behavioral problems in children (Hart and Brassard, 1987). However, it is not easy to define the behaviors constituting such abuse objectively enough to allow for mandatory intervention (Melton and Davidson, 1987). In the absence of such specific guidelines, the courts have taken a hands-off attitude toward everything but the most extreme forms. Perhaps in the future the more obvious cases will be identified and some help for parents will be forthcoming. At this point, however, emotional abuse is a concept in search of a solid definition and some guidelines for action.

Causes of Child Abuse

In order to understand the causes of child abuse, we must take into account the characteristics of a parent, the child, and the situation.

The abusive parent.   What kind of parent abuses a child? As a group, parents who abuse their children are impulsive, have unmet dependency needs, have a poor self-concept and a poor sense of identity, are defensive, and project their problems onto their children (Green et al., 1974). They are immature, socially isolated, believe in the value of physical punishment, afraid of spoiling their children, and have difficulty empathizing with their offspring (Martin, 1978). Although child abuse can be found in every age-group and economic level, it is most common among young parents. Young parenthood, though, is related to poverty, poor health care, poor housing, poor family background, and other social factors, so it may be the socioeconomic situation and impoverished background, not necessarily the age itself, that contributes to the abuse (Kinard and Klerman, 1980).

But many parents who are impulsive and isolated, for example, do not abuse their children, and this fact has led many professionals to deny that there is any definite "abusive" personality (Green et al., 1974). Although abusive parents have different reactions to stressful family situations (Frodi and Lamb, 1980), it is difficult to predict abuse from a personality profile of a parent.

Many—between 25–35 percent—of the parents who were abused as children abuse their own children (Kaufman and Zigler, 1987). In a study of 436 families with 73 abused children, Galdston (1975) found that two factors kept appearing in abusive parents. One was sexual frustration within the marriage, the other was the lack of a healthy relationship with their own parents. Abusive parents who experienced neglect or abuse in childhood do not think what they are doing is wrong. They know no other way to relate to their children. Violent individuals were often the victims of physical brutality or rejection in their own childhood. Thus, abusive parents are apt to create hostile, disturbed, unhappy children who grow up and perpetuate the cycle.

True or False Unusual as it may seem, parents who abuse their children often believe that physical punishment is wrong.

The abused child. Certain characteristics of a child may predispose that child to being a victim of abuse. This statement causes some people to feel uneasy. Any suggestion that the child contributes to the problem is usually met with hostility. The reaction is understandable. It is easier to see a child as a helpless victim of a vicious adult than to look at characteristics of a child that may bring out the worst in a parent. No one is excusing such behavior or blaming an innocent victim. However, a child's personality or physical and intellectual characteristics, in combination with an inadequate parent, may cause problems (Parke and Collmer, 1975).

For instance, children who are premature, who have physical handicaps, or who are mentally retarded are abused more often than children who do not suffer from these conditions (Friedrich and Boriskin, 1976). In addition, children who have difficult temperaments—that is, whose emotional reactions are intense and demanding—are also prone to being abused. The common char-

displacement The process by which an emotion is transferred from one object or person to another, more acceptable substitute.

acteristic in all these groups is the need for special care. The child whose needs are greater is at risk for abuse.

Abusing parents often hold unreasonable expectations for their children and distorted perceptions of what their children can do (Martin, 1978). Children with physical, emotional, or mental handicaps who cannot meet their parents' expectations are more likely to be abused. Consider the premature baby, who requires a great deal of care. The demand may be more than an impulsive, unrealistic parent can take, and the parent may resort to violence to quiet the child. As the child grows, the pattern is reinforced; physical violence keeps the child in line until it is well established and continues throughout childhood. These abused children often justify the parent's actions on the basis of their own behavior, believing themselves to be generally bad (Dean et al., 1986). The child whose needs are greater, who engenders anger in a parent, or who is difficult to care for is more likely to set in motion abusive parental responses that may become the standard parent-child interaction.

The situation. Any situation that raises the level of tension and stress can promote abuse. For instance, neglect and abuse increase when economic problems within the community increase (Steinberg et al., 1981). Unemployment and underemployment cause stress. Parents may **displace**—that is, transfer their feelings from one person or object to another. Thus, the child may become the object of a parent's anger toward the boss or the life situation in general.

Preventing Child Abuse

It is important to take all three elements—the parent, the child, and the situation—into account when seeking to understand child abuse. We have learned much about the causes of child abuse, and we have also made some progress in preventing and treating abusers and victims. Some prevention programs involve enrolling parents in educational programs, having professionals visit the homes of parents who have the potential to become abusers, and offering courses in child development in high school.

In such courses, teens are taught child-care techniques, given information concerning the nutritional and emotional needs of children, and told where parents can turn for help. The results of such programs are encouraging (Starr, 1979).

Many approaches treat child abusers after the fact. Individual and family therapy, self-help groups such as Parents Anonymous (which provide emotional support), and group treatment all claim some success. About half the parents involved in abusive situations can be helped at least to stop physically abusing their children. The victims also need help. Many improve even when there is only a mild to moderate improvement in the home situation (Jones, 1977).

During the course of this chapter we have looked at a number of influences on the preschooler, including peers, parents, and siblings. There are many other influences—for example, nursery school, books, and the television set. The greater the number of influences on the child, the more difficult it is to focus on the exact cause of a behavioral pattern. Nowhere is this more obvious than in the case of how the child acquires his or her sex role.

Sex-Role Acquisition

What sex differences have been substantiated by research? How do children form their conceptions of sex roles? These two questions have been researched extensively, and we have quite a bit of data. Unfortunately, there is little agreement about how to interpret the data.

Sex Differences

The term **sex differences** describes differences between the sexes that have been established by scientific research. For example, the average female matures more rapidly than the average male. Maccoby and Jacklin (1974) reviewed more than 1,600 studies concerning sex differences and concluded that only four differences appeared consistently. Most studies indicate (1) that males are generally more aggressive than females, (2) that girls have greater verbal ability, (3) that boys excel in visual-spatial ability, and (4) that boys excel in mathematical ability. A number of supposed differences were not supported by scientific studies. The hypotheses that girls were more suggestible, had lower self-esteem, were less motivated, were more social, were better at rote learning,

sex differences   The differences between males and females established through scientific investigation.

were less analytical, were affected more by heredity, and learned better using their auditory sense than boys were dismissed as not supported by the research. A number of other hypotheses were still in question. These include the questions of male dominance, female compliance, female nurturance, male activity level, female passivity, and male competitiveness.

True or False   Research has failed to establish any consistent differences between the sexes in personality or behavior.

As valuable as it is, the work of Maccoby and Jacklin is not the last word on the subject. There have been a number of criticisms. For example, Block (1976) noted a number of technical objections to the way the review of the literature had been performed. Others reviewed much the same literature and came to different conclusions. Bardwick (1971) argued that females show more dependent behavior than males. Eagly (1978) suggested that women are more suggestible and more fearful than men. Minton and Schneider (1980) suggest that while males and females do not differ in general ability, they differ in specific abilities: "Females generally surpass males in verbal fluency, reading comprehension, finger dexterity, and clerical skills, whereas males are superior on mathematical reasoning, visual-spatial ability, and speed and coordination of large bodily movements" (p. 319). These authors also argue that "females are better at rote memory, especially of verbal and social material" (p. 319).

Three Considerations

The study of sex differences has become frenetic. Some consider any positive finding on sex differences sexist, others seem anxious to demonstrate the superiority of one gender over the other in some area. Three considerations should be kept in mind whenever anyone announces a positive finding on sex differences.

First, even though a difference between the genders on some characteristic—such as verbal ability—is found, that tells us nothing about its cause. Are males generally more aggressive than females because of some environmental factor, such as reinforcement, because of some genetic or hormonal factor, or because of some interaction between the two? Even the finding that some genetic or hormonal element may underlie the behavior does not mean the behavior itself cannot be modified. Genetic contribution does not imply immutability. Rather, the individual's genotype may influence the range of possible behaviors, but it remains the environment that determines the behavior itself.

Second, most sex differences should not be seen as absolute. The overlap between the sexes is tremendous. The average difference between the sexes on any particular trait is normally very small, even if it does exist. The differences between individuals within the same gender are far greater than the average differences between males and females. Thus, although males generally seem to perform better at math, you will find excellent female math students and males who receive terrible math grades. Stating that males are better in one trait or that females are superior in another should not blind us to the overlap that exists in these skills or characteristics. The sexes are more similar than they are different.

This leads to the third consideration. Just how much of any particular trait can you predict on the basis of an individual's sex alone? As Plomin and Foch (1981, p. 383) ask, "How much do we know about an individual's verbal ability if all we know is the individual's sex?" These researchers note that sex differences provide only about 1 percent of the variation on verbal ability and only about 4 percent of the differences in math ability. Hyde (1984) suggests that only about 5 percent of the difference in aggression between males and females is due to gender. Although these differences exist, they explain little about the variation between individuals on any of these traits.

Sex Typing and Sex Roles

The research on sex-role acquisition is also difficult to interpret. For instance, consider the following statement: "Women cook, take care of the children, ask for help, are rescued from trying circumstances (by men), and play with dolls. Men work full-time jobs, don't ask for help, are action-oriented, and are strong." Such generalizations still exist in our society. **Sex typing** is the process by which an individual acquires values and behaves in a manner appropriate to one sex more than the other sex (Mischel, 1976). Sex-typed behavior can be seen in many

sex typing The process by which people acquire, value, and behave in a manner appropriate to one sex more than the other.

sex roles Behaviors expected of people in a given society on the basis of whether they are male or female.

areas of development—for example, boys play with trucks, girls play with dolls. Such behavior patterns as methods of aggression, behavior while dissecting a frog, and emotional expressiveness are examples of sex-typed behavior. Girls learn that crying is acceptable when they are sad, boys learn to hold it in. Boys avoid showing an interest in babies, females pay more attention to infants (Blakemore, 1981).

When we add up all the behavior patterns and psychological characteristics that seem appropriate for each sex, we are describing the concept of **sex roles.** Sex roles permeate many other roles. Not only are they involved in the choice of occupation (truck drivers are men, nurses are women), but they also are related to a number of social expectations. For example, consider some social conventions in the areas of dating and family life—the male picks up the female at her house for the date and drives the car, and the male is the primary breadwinner. Some of these conceptions are changing, but many are still with us today.

In order to understand just how children acquire the behaviors that are considered "appropriate" for their gender, we must examine a number of different approaches. No single approach adequately explains it, but each has something to offer.

The Biological Approach

There is no biological explanation that successfully explains why males may act one way and females another. Instead, a number of biological factors to take into account when studying sex roles are suggested.

Hormones. Males produce more testosterone, females produce more estrogen. In laboratory studies, the hormone testosterone is linked to aggressive behavior (Rogers, 1976). However, variations in human behavior cannot be explained merely by citing hormonal factors. Learned behavior is important too. Money and Ehrhardt (1972) studied children who were born with ambiguous genitals. Some were surgically altered very early in childhood, and these children made successful adjustments to their gender if the surgery took place before the age of two. Those who became female did, however, show a tomboyish nature, showing more rough-and-tumble play. This tendency might be caused by the greater concentrations of testosterone in their systems. Perhaps males are more inclined to be aggressive than females, but despite this inclination both males and females can be taught to settle disagreements by nonaggressive means.

Differences in maturation. The average female is born more ready for life than the average male is. Females are more advanced in central nervous system development and bone formation. Some sex differences may be caused by the interaction of rates of maturation and the environment surrounding the child. For example, while gross muscle development in males is superior, females develop fine muscle control more quickly (McGuinness, 1977; 1976). Because children are apt to do both what is easiest and what yields the most positive reinforcement, males may turn their attention to activities in which gross muscle ability and reaction time are vital. Females, on the other hand, having better fine motor control, are more apt to concentrate on tasks involving such control.

McGuinness, then, is arguing that society merely reinforces a difference in abilities that is already present. Boys find baseball easier, succeed at it, and then are reinforced for their efforts. Girls find activities that require fine motor control easier, succeed at them, and are reinforced. The interaction of maturation and the environment may also help explain why boys have so many more reading problems than girls. Females also have a greater attention span, and their eyes are better developed by the time they enter school. Female superiority in language development and reading does not excuse males from learning to read. It only suggests that the average male may find language skills more difficult and may require additional instruction.

Genetic differences. We have already discussed the possibility that genetic differences may affect behavior. The male Y chromosome contains many fewer genes than the female X chromosome, and some characteristics—such as color blindness—are sex-linked. There is evidence that this may also be true of spatial ability, although some studies cast some doubt on this (Vandenberg and Kuse, 1979).

Even if you are impressed by the biological approach, assignment of unequal roles on the basis of biological argument cannot be either condoned or justified by the evidence (Archer, 1976). In the case of sex roles and behavior, biology is not destiny. At this point in time, the biological contribution to our understanding of how a child acquires a sex role is a large question mark.

Behavior Theories

The most obvious reason that males and females act differently is that they learn different behaviors. These learning experiences can be roughly divided into two categories. First, boys and girls are treated differently and reinforced for different actions. Second, the role models that surround boys and girls differ, and children learn at least some of their sex role by observing others.

Different treatment for sons and daughters. Are boys and girls reinforced for different behaviors? Do parents treat boys and girls differently? Parents do expect different behaviors from sons and daughters, expecting sons to be stronger and tougher (Richmond-Abbott, 1983). Parents provide sons with different toys and decorate their rooms in a "sex appropriate manner" (Rheingold and Cook, 1975). One recent study found that although parents may not consciously reinforce young children for playing with sex-stereotyped toys (boys with trucks, girls with dolls), they actively channel their children into such standard play (Eisenberg et al., 1985). The same parents who may say it would not bother them if their son played with dolls are apt to provide only balls, gloves, and trucks for him to play with and to encourage him to play with such toys.

Differences in treatment are not difficult to find. Parents encourage sons to be independent, competitive, and achieving (Block, 1979). They encourage daughters to be more passive and seek protection (Chafetz, 1974). Girls are viewed as more fragile, and parents play with sons more roughly than they do with daughters (Bee, 1978). Parents also supervise daughters more, allowing sons more freedom (Block, 1979). Males are punished more, and parents are more likely to be physical with sons than with daughters. Girls tend to receive more praise than boys, but also more criticism (Fagot, 1974). Mothers talk differently to toddler and preschool sons and daughters. Males receive more verbal stimulation, which is thought to encourage cognitive development

(Weitzman et al., 1985). Boys are also more likely to be discouraged by adults and peers for engaging in sex-inappropriate behavior (Langlois and Downs, 1980). Fathers are more likely than mothers to treat sons and daughters differently (Bee, 1978). A father is more likely to criticize his son when he sees him playing with dolls than he is to criticize a daughter who is observed beating up a Bobo doll. Mothers, generally, are more likely to treat sons and daughters equally.

True or False Girls generally receive more punishment than boys, while boys receive more praise.

True or False Fathers are more likely than mothers to treat their sons and daughters equally.

Boys are more likely to hold rigidly to sex-typed behaviors than females. Even though preschool boys and girls both prefer sex-stereotyped toys, boys avoid cross-

It is easier to get girls to play with male-stereotyped toys than to get boys to play with female-stereotyped toys.

sex toys more often than girls do (Williams et al., 1975). Indeed, preschool boys choose sex-typed toys and cling to their choices even if told that toys not chosen were appropriate for both boys and girls (Frasher and Walker, 1972). It is also easier to get girls to switch toy preferences than boys. Females have more flexibility in behavior than males. In one study, preschoolers judged female sex-role violations more permissible than male sex-role violations. They were also much less committed to maintaining the female sex-typed behaviors than the male sex-typed behaviors (Smetana, 1986).

True or False Preschoolers are more likely to accept female sex-role violations than male sex-role violations.

As impressive as they are, though, these differences do not tell the entire story. Some authorities are more impressed by the similarities in the way males and females are treated by their parents than by the differences (Maccoby and Jacklin, 1974). The evidence does not indicate that a simple, straightforward reinforcement approach can answer the question of sex typing. For example, Maccoby and Jacklin (1974) did not find that boys were necessarily reinforced for aggressiveness more than girls. The question is not whether boys and girls are treated differently. They are. The question is whether these differences are enough to explain later sex-typed behavior patterns. Although some differences in treatment do exist, it is difficult to see how these could be the *sole* determiners of later personality and behavioral differences between the sexes. They are, then, only one part of the puzzle. Another part may be found in the understanding of the role models that surround a child.

Role models and imitation. The use of modeling and imitation to explain the acquisition of sex role is appealing. If a boy sees his father cooking dinner and enjoying it, he gets the idea that it is manly to cook dinner for the family. The strength of the imitative response is especially noticeable in young children, who may act like their mothers or fathers or imitate older brothers or sisters—to the delight or despair of the parents. Because parents are the most important people in the life of preschoolers, the children may model themselves after them (Mischel, 1970). For example, daughters of working mothers hold less-traditional role concepts and have higher aspirations than girls whose mothers do not work (Hoffman, 1974). They benefit from observing that mother as well as father is valued in the labor market and performing useful functions outside the home.

Peers, teachers, and heroes. We must remember that parents are not the only models in their children's lives. Children are also exposed to models in the outside world—for example, peers, teachers, and characters in children's books and television. While it is difficult to analyze the effect these other models have on a child's understanding of sex roles, their role should not be minimized.

Psychoanalytic Theory

No theory is more controversial than Freud's ideas about the development of sex-typed behavior. According to Freud (1924), the development of sex roles arises from events that occur during the **phallic stage.** Until early childhood, both boys and girls have similar psychosexual experiences, but in the phallic stage the **Oedipal** situation occurs. The little boy experiences sexual feelings toward his mother, views his father as a rival for his mother's affection, and resents his father. The child fears that his father will find out how he feels and retaliate by castrating him. At the same time, the father is respected as a model of masculinity who is superior to the child. As he matures, the little boy represses his feelings toward his mother and identifies with the father. In this way he becomes like his father and takes on the appropriate sex role.

The process with females is more convoluted. It is sometimes called the **Electra complex.** The little girl is also originally sexually attached to the mother, but slowly turns her attention to her father when she realizes she does not have a penis (Mullahy, 1948). Blaming her mother for her lack of a penis, she competes with her mother for the father's attention. She does not have to resolve this situation fully, since she doesn't have to worry about castration. She may never fully accept the "appropriate" sex role. Because of this, Freud believed that women were more likely to have personality difficulties than men (Freud, 1933; Schaffer, 1981).

An important idea underlying the psychoanalytic concept of sex roles is **identification.** Children identify with the parents of the same sex and thereby acquire the appropriate sex role. Perhaps the most controversial portion of this theory involves Freud's argument that the girl's discovery that she lacks the male organ is a turning point in her life, which is now dominated by the desire to attain one through her father and later through her husband by having a baby. Freud sees every imaginable character trait of females beginning with this "penis envy,"

phallic stage Freud's third psychosexual stage, occurring during early childhood, in which the sexual energy is located in the genital area and the Oedipal or Electra conflicts take place.

Oedipus complex The conflict during the phallic stage in which a boy experiences sexual feelings toward his mother and wishes to do away with his father.

Electra complex In Freudian theory, the female equivalent to the Oedipus complex, in which the female experiences sexual feelings toward her father and wishes to do away with her mother.

identification The process by which children take on the characteristics of another person, often a parent.

including inferiority, physical modesty, envy, and psychosexual difficulties. In the end, however, Freud's ideas in this realm have been largely rejected by developmental psychologists because evidence is lacking (Sears et al., 1965). The clinical problems Freud noted can be interpreted in terms of the social roles traditionally thrust on women by society (Horney, 1967; 1939). In addition, even though the Oedipal situation has been found in a number of societies (Kline, 1972), it is not universal (Mead, 1974).

Sex-Role Theories Reconsidered

No single theory can adequately explain how a child acquires a sex role, but each can add greatly to our knowledge. Behavior theory makes us aware of how important differential treatment of boys and girls by parents and teachers can be. Social-learning theory stresses the importance of imitation and the models that surround the child. While few scientists today believe that biological explanations are by themselves sufficient to explain sex roles, maturational, hormonal, and genetic differences add pieces to the puzzle. Finally, despite the problems inherent in the Freudian approach, the importance of identification must be remembered.

Sex-Role Stereotypes and Androgyny

Does it really matter whether a child has a narrow or a broad definition of what is appropriate as a sex role? The answer is a definite yes. Let's say that little Joey feels like crying but refuses to do so because he thinks it is not manly. He decides that it's best not to express his emotions. Emotional expression remains inconsistent with his definition of gender role. Later in life, Joey may have difficulty expressing his feelings. His definition of being male limits his flexibility. Little Kate, who believes that girls don't get dirty or take leadership positions, has also limited her future activities unnecessarily.

Because the traditional, rigid sex roles seem to be so limiting, Bem (1975, 1974) claims that people are better off if they are flexible enough to combine the best characteristics of males and females. Such people are called **androgynous.** Both extremely high masculinity and extremely high feminity are associated with very poor adjustment. These people are limited by the narrowness of their conception of sex role. Androgynous college students have higher self-esteem (Spence et al., 1975). Fathers who score high in androgyny tend to spend more time with their children (Russell, 1978). The more flex-

androgyny   The state of possessing the best characteristics of masculinity and femininity.

ible androgynous individuals also have a wider number of behavioral choices available to them and are capable of adapting to new situations more easily. An androgynous individual is no less a man or a woman. When a woman feels secure enough to act assertively and a man is secure enough to show emotion without being afraid it is not masculine, both have gained.

Socializing children into androgynous roles is not easy. My daughters have often been examined by female pediatricians, yet one surprised me by stating that boys can be doctors while girls are nurses. She certainly didn't get that limitation from us, or from her medical experiences

This young girl may believe that men can also cook and, if her mother works, that a woman's role is not restricted to the home.

or her parents. However, her peers and the media often stereotype these roles, and she picked them up. Trying to broaden children's conceptions of sex roles is sometimes an uphill battle, but it is worth the effort.

Ready for New Challenges

Early childhood is a time of great change. The preschooler's social world is expanding rapidly. Parents, peers, nursery school teachers, and siblings all have an effect on the child. Preschoolers are active, curious, and playful. If parents and teachers encourage healthful activities, the children gain the sense of initiative that Erikson believes is so important. If parents set limits in a loving atmosphere and allow preschoolers some freedom to choose, the children become competent and independent and develop a positive view of themselves. Such children are ready for the challenges of middle childhood and school that come next.

Summary

1. Play is an activity performed for sheer enjoyment with no ulterior motive. It helps develop a child's mental, physical, and social abilities. It serves as an outlet for the child's frustrations and allows the child to experiment with new roles. The complexity of play increases with age. Boys play more roughly than girls.

2. Preschoolers have more contact with peers than when they were toddlers. They show more prosocial behavior with peers than with siblings.

3. Siblings may offer support and help, as well as serve as sources of discord. Although antagonistic behavior among siblings is not uncommon, most interactions are positive and play-oriented.

4. Baumrind identified three types of parenting styles. *Authoritarian parents* seek to control a child's every action, causing the child to become suspicious and withdrawn. *Permissive parents* allow almost total freedom and rarely use discipline. These children do not show much self-control or self-reliance. *Authoritative parents* give their children freedom within limits. These children are competent and self-controlled.

5. Discipline involves training in self-control; punishment involves inflicting physical and/or psychological pain for violating a rule. Punishment is most effective when it is moderate, swift, certain, and combined with positive reinforcement for the correct behavior.

6. Child abuse is a major societal problem. In order to understand abuse, the characteristics of the parents, child, and situation must be taken into account. Sexual abuse is the least-reported type of abuse. Many parents who physically abuse their children can be helped to stop abusing them.

7. Research has generally found that males are more aggressive than females, that girls have greater verbal abilities, and that boys excel in visual-spatial tasks and ability in math. Sex differences tell us nothing about the cause of the differences and account for very little of the behavioral differences between individuals. In addition, a great deal of overlap exists between the sexes.

8. Sex roles involve the behavioral patterns and psychological characteristics that are appropriate for each sex. Biological factors—including hormonal, genetic, and maturational differences—have been advanced as explanations for these differences, but a completely biological explanation is untenable. Children learn their sex roles through operant conditioning and imitation of role models in the environment. Freud saw sex roles in terms of the resolution of the Oedipal situation in the phallic stage, when children identify with the parent of the same sex.

9. People who have the best of both stereotyped male and female characteristics are said to be *androgynous* and are more flexible in their behavior.

1. _True_ The activity must be enjoyable to be considered play.

2. _False_ Correct statement: Role reversal is a normal and healthy aspect of play.

3. _False_ Correct statement: Such cooperative play does not take place during toddlerhood.

4. _True_ Boys play much more roughly than girls.

5. _False_ Correct statement: Children spend much more time with their peers during early childhood than they did in the toddler stage.

6. _False_ Correct statement: Although antagonistic behavior between siblings is not unusual, the majority of the interactions are positive and play-oriented.

7. _False_ Correct statement: Children of permissive parents do not show much self-reliance or self-control.

8. _False_ Correct statement: Parents who abuse their children believe in physical punishment.

9. _False_ Correct statement: Some consistent sex differences have been found.

10. _False_ Correct statement: Boys are punished more, and girls generally receive more praise.

11. _False_ Correct statement: The opposite is true. Mothers are more likely than fathers to treat their sons and daughters equally.

12. _True_ Preschoolers are more likely to judge female sex-role violations more permissible than male sex-role violations.

PART FOUR

Middle Childhood

CHAPTER 9

Physical and Cognitive Development in Middle Childhood

Are the Following Statements True or False?

Try the True-False Quiz below. See if your answers correspond to the information in this chapter. Each question is repeated after the paragraph in which the answer can be found. The True-False Answer Box at the end of the chapter lists the complete answers.

____ 1. During the elementary school years, the child's growth rate increases.

____ 2. On the average, girls weigh more than boys at age ten.

____ 3. During middle childhood, boys are superior in running speed, and girls are better in tasks that require agility.

____ 4. School-age children can solve abstract, hypothetical problems.

____ 5. When elementary school children claim they understand something, a parent or teacher can be reasonably certain that they do.

____ 6. Reading achievement has declined among elementary school children in the past ten years or so.

____ 7. American children are superior to Japanese children in achievement in mathematics.

____ 8. By the end of elementary school, girls are doing better in reading, while boys excel in math.

____ 9. Intelligence is highly related to school achievement.

____10. By law, every exceptional child must be mainstreamed—that is, placed in a class with "normal" students.

____11. Hyperactivity can be cured through correct use of medication.

____12. Children who are intellectually gifted tend to be socially backward.

The Photo Exercise

Collect a group of your childhood photographs. Then guess what age you were when they were taken. Baby pictures are easy. The infant's distinctive look is a give-away. The changes between ages one and two, two and three, and perhaps three and four are so distinctive that you probably have little difficulty guessing your age. But look at your school photographs. It is difficult to tell whether you were seven or eight, nine or ten. You may make the decision by looking at other cues, such as your hairstyle or clothing. As children develop during the school years, physical changes occur at a slower rate. Children appear to be marking time, filling in.

Physical Development in Middle Childhood

Middle childhood is indeed a time of horizontal growth. The gradual changes in height, weight, and appearance can lead us to conclude that little of interest is going on. But this is a mistake. Though the changes may be less spectacular than those that occur in earlier years, they are no less important.

Growth

The rate of growth continues to decline during middle childhood until about age ten, eleven, or twelve. Girls are a bit shorter than boys until adolescence, but because girls experience their adolescent growth spurt about two years earlier than boys, girls are actually taller for a couple of years (see Appendix). By age fourteen or so, boys regain their height advantage (Tanner, 1978). Normal height and weight are best viewed in terms of a range of values—between the 25th and 75th percentile.

True or False During the elementary school years, the child's growth rate increases.

Chronological and maturational age.
People often pay lip service to the fact that children mature at their own pace. One child may lose baby teeth at an earlier age or grow faster during childhood than another child. Still, this mental acceptance of individuality often does not coincide with our feelings. Parents are concerned if their

chronological age A person's age according to birthdays.

maturational age A person's level of maturation relative to his or her peers.

child's development is slower than they expected—even though it may still be within normal range. We tend to use chronological age as the marker, and therein lies a problem.

Imagine that you have three well-nourished, healthy ten-year-old boys standing next to each other. By coincidence, all were born on the same day in the same year. Would they be the same height? Probably not, you might answer, because their genetic endowment differs. This is true, but there is another possibility. What if I tell you that Boy 1 is only 8.5 years old in biological or maturational terms, that Boy 2 is exactly 10 years old in those terms, and that Boy 3 is 11.5 years old. Boy 3 is far older than Boy 1 biologically, even though their **chronological ages** as measured in birthdays are the same (Krogman, 1980). This concept of **maturational age** can help us better understand the timing and rate of children's growth. Perhaps we should think of growth from the prenatal period to adulthood as a race that some of us run faster and some run slower. At any point in the twenty years, some of us may be ahead, some just on schedule, and some behind. Those who are ahead are maturationally more advanced than those who are behind (Krogman, 1980).

If we think in terms of maturational age, we are forced to consider development as an individual process. In addition, maturational age is a better measure of what can be expected of a child than chronological age. Consider the six-year-old who is maturationally behind but who may be the same height as another child who is "right on schedule." The child "on schedule" will be more advanced and more ready for school. In fact, studies have shown that many children entering school are not physically mature enough to handle the work expected of them and consequently are likely to experience failure in school (Ames, 1986). Some states are now considering using maturation level rather than chronological age as the criterion for entrance into public school.

Weight

Although boys are heavier at birth, both sexes are about equal in weight at eight and a half years of age. Then girls become heavier at about nine or ten, and this remains true until they are about fourteen and a half, when boys equal or surpass girls (Tanner, 1978). Again, we should be wary of averages and speak in terms of percentiles. For example, a ten-year-old girl may weigh anywhere between 63 pounds (28.71 kg) and 82.6 pounds (37.53 kg) and still be considered "normal." Substantial deviations from these marks should be investigated. Many deviations reflect differences in physique or developmental age, but some may indicate physical problems. Substantial deviations in weight may contribute to psychological problems, as in the case of the overweight or obese child.

True or False On the average, girls weigh more than boys at age ten.

Childhood obesity. More than 20 percent of school-age children are considered obese (Hamilton and Whitney, 1982). These children are more likely to be shunned (Richardson et al., 1961), to have fewer friends (Staffieri, 1967), and to have a poor body image (Mendelson and White, 1985).

Parents often fall victim to the "baby fat" theory, in the belief that a fat child is a healthy child. Other parents argue that children who are obese will simply grow out of it on their own. Both points of view are wrong. Obese children are not especially healthy, and juvenile obesity is related to adult obesity (Corbin, 1980a). The longer a child is obese, the more difficult it is to modify the condition. Obesity seems to run in families. A child has only a 7 percent chance of becoming obese if neither parent is overweight, a 40 percent chance if one parent is overweight, and an 80 percent chance if both are overweight (Winick, 1975). But this does not prove that obesity is inherited, because it is during childhood that people learn how and what to eat. Perhaps they are urged to eat everything set before them and to take second helpings. Perhaps they see their parents overeating or consider the evening gluttony the highlight of the day. Some children learn to eat the wrong foods and consume thousands of empty calories from junk food each day. Lack of exercise may also be an important consideration. Obese children are less active than their nonobese peers, although they may not always be aware of it (Bullen et al., 1964). Genetic endowment may play some part in obesity as discussed in the cross-cultural current in chapter two, but the child's environment and activity level must also be taken into account.

Childhood obesity is difficult to correct (Becker and Drash, 1979), and very heavy dieting may injure children as they develop. One promising approach is to feed children in a nutritious way that will help them maintain a constant weight while they grow. This promotes normal development while restricting the accumulation of body fat (Cataldo and Whitney, 1986). Other approaches involve providing psychological support and increasing the amount of exercise the child gets. Any dietary plan should be executed under a doctor's care.

Nutrition. No one doubts the importance of good nutrition during childhood, but children seem to have little chance to develop good eating habits. All around them they see commercials for sugar-coated foods, overindulgence, and an emphasis on tastiness, and they are forced into poor eating habits, such as having to finish everything on their plates.

During the middle childhood years, children accumulate a store of nutrients—especially calcium—that will be drawn on by the body during the upcoming growth spurt. The more dense their bones are before the growth spurt, the better prepared they are for it (Whitney and Hamilton, 1987). Children cannot be counted on to choose a balanced, nutritious diet in a society in which most of the dietary influences are against them. It is the responsibility of parents and schools to educate children and to counter the prevailing influences. As early as possible, children should be taught to eat correctly and slowly, to eat moderate amounts, and to make mealtimes relaxing occasions during which they can enjoy the company of the others who are eating.

Besides height and weight gains, a number of other physical changes occur during middle childhood. The forehead becomes flatter, the arms and legs get more slender, the nose grows larger, the shoulders squarer, the abdomen flatter, and the waistline more pronounced. These changes occur gradually. The more noticeable changes are the shedding of baby teeth and the eruption of permanent teeth.

Dentition

The shedding of **deciduous teeth** is perhaps the most obvious physical occurrence during early middle childhood. For children, losing their teeth is a sign that they are growing up. But the gaps left in the mouth can cause temporary cosmetic problems as well as difficulty in pronunciation.

Human beings have a complement of twenty baby teeth and thirty-two permanent teeth (see Figure 9.1). The first permanent tooth is usually the "six-year molar," which does not replace any baby tooth (Smart and Smart, 1978). This tooth may erupt at any time between four and a half and eight years of age (Krogman, 1980). It is not easily recognizable, and it may become decayed and lost if not properly cared for. Many parents do not put much effort into dental care for their young children, thinking they have "only baby teeth" anyway. This is unfortunate, however, because premature loss can lead to dental problems, including difficulties with the bite. As a rule, girls lose their baby teeth before boys do.

Again, the importance of nutrition should be noted. First, adequate nutrition—such as ample supplies of calcium, phosphorus, vitamins A, C, and D, and protein—is required for healthy formation of the mouth and teeth. Second, restricting the supply of fermentable carbohydrates is important, as are avoiding sticky sweets and brushing after meals, in order to help prevent tooth decay.

Motor Skill Development

The pattern of gradual growth and development that we saw with height, weight, and changes in proportion is also shown in the areas of motor and skill development. If you watch elementary school children during recess and compare them with preschool children, the differences are obvious but hard to describe. The elementary school children run, hop, jump, and throw more easily

deciduous teeth The scientific term for "baby teeth."

than the nursery school children. By the time children enter elementary school, they have developed many motor skills. They can run, climb, gallop, and hop. Skipping is just being mastered, as are throwing, catching, and kicking, and balancing is reasonably good. During the next six years, skills are refined and modified (DeOreo and Keogh, 1980).

During middle childhood, running speed and the ability to jump for distance increases. The ability to throw both for accuracy and for distance also improves (Cratty, 1978), as does balance. These improvements are due both to maturation and to practice. Are boys better than girls at these skills? Boys are superior in running speed and throwing, while girls excel in tasks that require agility, rhythm, and hopping (Cratty, 1978). Boys are also stronger than girls during this period, but girls show more muscular flexibility. Although balance is good in both sexes, girls between the ages of seven and nine tend to be superior (Cratty, 1978). Boys jump higher and longer, girls tend to hop better. Girls also learn to skip sooner (DeOreo and Keogh, 1980).

True or False During middle childhood, boys are superior in running speed, and girls are better in tasks that require agility.

As with almost all sex differences, the overlap between the sexes is great (Lockhart, 1980), and training and motivation are important factors. Frequently boys are more motivated to perform on tests of physical ability and are more likely to practice certain skills, such as throwing, that involve the large muscles. In addition, the differences between the average boy and girl on many of these tasks are not very great. If girls are encouraged to develop their skills, they can improve them greatly.

As boys and girls get older, however, differences in their physical abilities become more noticeable. Differences in performance before the age of about eleven or twelve are small (Corbin, 1980b), but during adolescence males continue to improve, while females tend to level off or may even decrease in physical ability (Espenschade, 1960). The decreased performance may be due to lack of motivation, fear of physical injury to female internal organs, or fear of appearing too masculine (Corbin, 1980b). It may also be due to society's expectations.

FIGURE 9.1

Average Ages for (a) Eruption and Shedding of Baby Teeth and (b) Eruption of Permanent Teeth

Both the eruption and shedding of baby teeth and the replacement of baby teeth by permanent teeth are maturational changes.

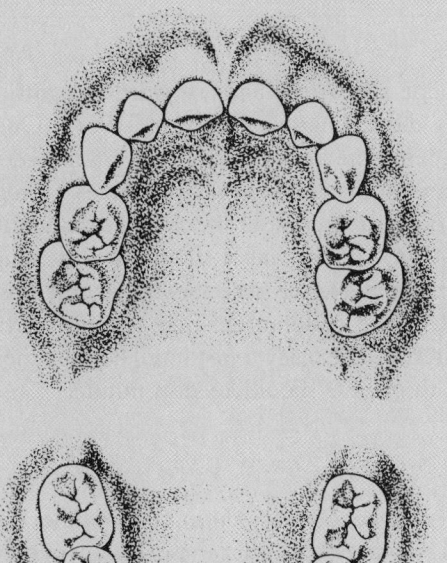

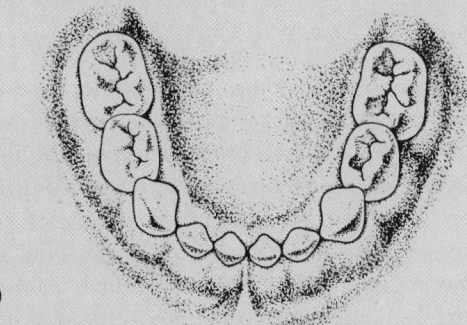

(a)

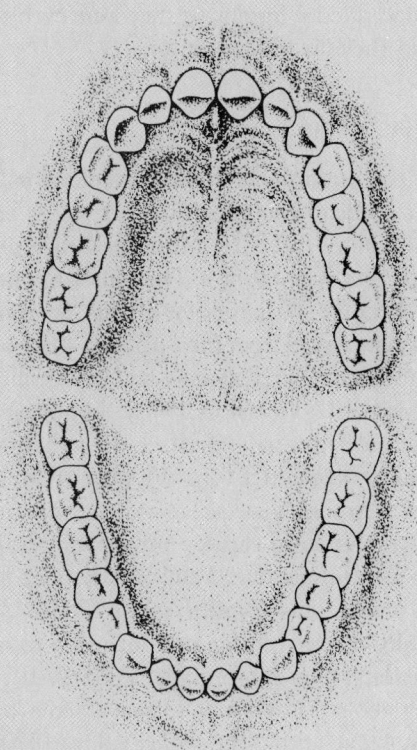

(b)

Upper Teeth	Eruption Date	Shedding Date
Central incisor	8–12 months	6–7 years
Lateral incisor	9–13 months	7–8 years
Canine (cuspid)	16–22 months	10–12 years
First molar	13–19 months	9–11 years
Second molar	25–33 months	10–12 years

Lower Teeth	Eruption Date	Shedding Date
Second molar	23–31 months	10–12 years
First molar	14–18 months	9–11 years
Canine (cuspid)	17–23 months	9–12 years
Lateral incisor	10–16 months	7–8 years
Central incisor	6–10 months	6–7 years

Upper Teeth	Eruption Date
Central incisor	7–8 years
Lateral incisor	8–9 years
Canine (cuspid)	11–12 years
First premolar (first bicuspid)	10–11 years
Second premolar (second bicuspid)	10–12 years
First molar	6–7 years
Second molar	12–13 years
Third molar	17–21 years

Lower Teeth	Eruption Date
Third molar	17–21 years
Second molar	11–13 years
First molar	6–7 years
Second premolar (second bicuspid)	11–12 years
First premolar (first bicuspid)	10–12 years
Canine (cuspid)	9–10 years
Lateral incisor	7–8 years
Central incisor	6–7 years

Source: American Dental Association

For example, males are expected to participate in rugged sports that require strength, and females are more likely to be encouraged to engage in physical activity involving agility. Females may not be taught the same physical skills as males. Society's different expectations for the physical abilities and training of males and females are somewhat reduced today from what they were even twenty years ago, but they are still present.

Readiness for School

Think of all the physical, mental, and behavioral skills necessary for academic success. Children must be able to sit in one place, listen to an adult, and attend to lessons (Blank and Klig, 1982). They must be intellectually mature enough to understand what is going on, emotionally emancipated from their parents—so that they can form relationships with others—and have some measure of self-control (Kohen-Raz, 1977). In almost every culture, children begin to attend school sometime between the ages of five and seven. We have traditionally used the child's chronological age to indicate school readiness but, as we discussed earlier, only a very weak case can be made for this practice. Many children are simply not ready to master schoolwork (Ames, 1986).

For example, many children are not ready to master reading in kindergarten or first grade (Perkins, 1975). A mental age of about six and a half years is often considered necessary for acquiring the skill (Durkin, 1970), but this presents a problem. Some children may not be mentally, physically, or emotionally mature enough to tackle the challenge. Some children may not have the ability to focus on the reading matter (Moore and Moore, 1976) or may lack a left-right sequence. They may be too immature to sit in a chair, listen to the teacher, and follow instructions. If children cannot recognize shapes, they cannot begin to learn their letters (Blank and Klig, 1982). Parents may read to their children, provide a home where reading is considered an enjoyable activity, and generally instill in their children a positive attitude toward learning, but even with this excellent background some children, especially boys, will not be ready for reading instruction (Ilg and Ames, 1972).

Many schools now give reading readiness tests to determine whether a child is ready to learn to read. Reading readiness tests measure a number of skills and abilities, including associating pictures with the spoken word, visual discrimination, sentence comprehension, the ability

concrete operational stage Piaget's third state of cognitive development—lasting from about seven through eleven years of age—in which children develop the ability to perform logical operations, such as conservation.

to count and write numbers, word recognition, and auditory discrimination (Heilman, 1967). Once a child's weaknesses are discovered, a decision is made about how to remedy the deficiency. Sometimes a program of instruction is required, at other times maturation must be allowed to take its course. If children are taught reading before they have the necessary skills, only frustration can result. Since children develop at their own rate, some children will be ready to read well before others—a point anxious parents should keep in mind.

The Stage of Concrete Operations

The school experience during the middle years of childhood is so important that these years are often called the school years. As children enter first grade, at about the age of six, the long preoperational stage is drawing to a close and children are entering the stage of concrete operations. The shift from the preoperational stage to the **concrete operational stage** is gradual. A child does not go to sleep one night in the preoperational stage and wake up the next morning in the concrete stage. The child does not go to sleep egocentric and unable to fully understand classification and conservation, and wake up with fully developed abilities in these areas. These skills develop gradually over the years. During the concrete operational stage, children can deal with concrete objects rather than with abstractions when they consider change (Forman and Kuschner, 1977). They must either see or be able to imagine objects. If children in this stage are presented with a purely verbal problem that involves hypotheses, they cannot solve it, but if you explain it in real, concrete terms, they have no difficulty with the challenge (Wadsworth, 1971).

The Decline in Egocentrism

Children in the stage of concrete operations become less egocentric. They understand that other people see the world differently, and they seek to validate their own view of the world. This is accomplished through social interaction during which they can share their thoughts and verify their view of the world (Piaget, 1928). In addition, they can now take the perspective of the other person and can imagine what others are thinking of them in a relatively simply way (Harter, 1983). They are capable of being more sensitive to the feelings of others and imagining how others would feel in various situations. Language becomes less egocentric. Preschoolers often use such pronouns as "he" or "she" without offering enough information for the listener to know to whom they are referring. They figure that since *they* know who they are talking about, so do you (Pulaski, 1980). As the child matures, this tendency is greatly reduced.

Reversibility, the Ability to Decenter, and Transformations

During middle childhood, the limitations of preoperational thought begin to fade slowly. Children develop the ability to reverse operations—to realize that if you roll a clay ball into a long worm you can reverse your operation and recreate the ball of clay. They develop the ability to decenter, to take into consideration more than one dimension. Children now realize that the increase in the length of the clay worm compensates for the decrease in its width. They also begin to understand transformations—to understand that as objects change positions or shape they progress through a series of intermediate points. Piaget did not find these abilities in preschoolers.

Conservation

The crowning achievement of the concrete operational stage is the ability to conserve. The simplest example is the famous beaker experiment mentioned in Chapter 7, in which a researcher takes two identical beakers that are long and thin and pours equal amounts of liquid in each. Then, in front of the child, the contents of one tall beaker is poured into a squat beaker. The preschool child cannot take both height and width into consideration—cannot reverse the operation of pouring—and attends to the end state rather than to transformations, making conservation impossible (Piaget and Inhelder, 1969). But school-age children find such problems rel-

In some school districts, young children are screened to be certain they have the abilities necessary to succeed in school.

atively easy. They may even show surprise when younger children don't get them right.

Conservation of number, substance, weight, and volume occur at different ages but in a specific order. Piaget (1952) noted this uneven performance within a developmental stage and used the term **horizontal decalage** to describe the phenomenon whereby the child has acquired the underlying principle for solving a problem such as conservation but is not able to apply it across contexts.

Conservation in number. Show children displays of seven pennies in which the coins are either grouped in very close density or spread out. The four-year-old is certain that the spread-out display has more coins than the other one. The six- or seven-year-old develops a sense of conservation of number and knows that the spacing does not matter.

Conservation of weight. The seven-year-old may understand that no clay was lost during the transformation,

> **horizontal decalage**   A term used to describe the unevenness of development in which a child may be able to solve one type of problem but not another, even though a common principle underlies them all. A child may be able to solve one problem concerning conservation of length, but not a problem involving conservation of volume.

but this child probably will not understand that they both still weigh the same. Conservation of weight comes later, at about age nine or ten (Piaget and Inhelder, 1969).

Conservation of volume. Make two balls of clay and put them in two identical beakers containing equal amounts of water. The child should understand that the clay balls are equally large and equally weighted. Then put the clay balls in the containers and show that they displace the same volume of liquid because they cause

School age children show their ability to classify when they start collections of various items such as rocks or sea shells.

Learning and Cognition

When you think of the term learning, *what comes to mind? The most common picture seems to be a child sitting in a classroom reciting the alphabet or memorizing the sixteen exports of a certain country. But learning involves much more than the acquisition of academic skills. We must also learn the physical and social skills that are necessary for us to meet everyday challenges.*

Cognitive or intellectual development has been the focus of much research in recent years. We now have some understanding of how a person develops from a newborn unable to understand simple concepts of space and causality to an adolescent who has the ability to use abstract thought to unravel complex scientific mysteries. Psychologists have also examined the nature of cognitive development in adulthood, being especially interested in how people use their experience and learning abilities throughout life to solve the problems that arise every day.

The life-span perspective views learning and such cognitive skills as memory and problem solving as developing throughout the entire life span.

(Above left) Learning and cognitive development are active processes often involving discovery and investigation.

(Above right) Physical skills are learned and become more refined through practice.

People can continue to learn new physical skills throughout adulthood. Some technical work such as assembling computers requires extensive use of small muscles and sometimes sophisticated troubleshooting skills as well.

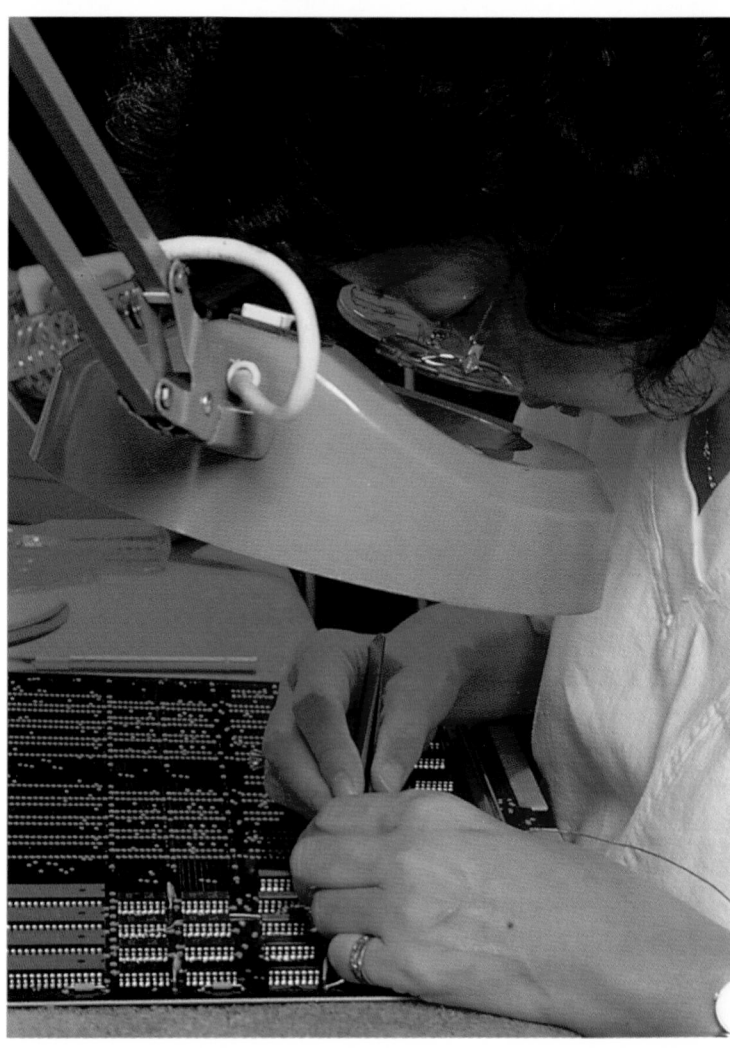

(At left) Do you relate differently to people now than you did five or ten years ago? The social skills needed to converse and develop a personal relationship are learned and refined as we negotiate adulthood.

(Above) Altruism—doing things for others without regard to tangible personal reward— is a desirable behavior.

These people interacting at an employee production meeting must learn group interaction skills that are different from those necessary to relate to others on a one-to-one basis.

(Above) The ability to use abstract symbolic thought to solve difficult problems is an important cognitive ability not found in young children.

(At right) Learning academic skills such as reading and writing is a vital part of a child's education. In today's society we cannot underestimate the importance of basic skills.

Learning new skills can be a lifelong activity, as shown by these adults trying to master some aspect of computer use.

the level of water to rise the same amount. Now change the shape of one of the balls and ask whether it would still make the water level rise to the previous height (Diamond, 1982). Typically, conservation problems concerning volume are the last to be solved. The ability to solve them appears at about age eleven or twelve (Piaget and Inhelder, 1969).

Seriation and classification.   School-age children also further develop the ability to seriate and to classify. They can easily arrange a series of sticks in terms of length, and later weight and finally volume (Wadsworth, 1971). Their ability to classify improves greatly too. In fact, school-age children are known for their propensity to collect things (Kegan, 1982). They will collect anything, and thereby practice their skills of classification. They begin to realize that an item can be classified in many ways and can belong to a great many classes at one time.

How the School-Age Child Thinks

The school-age child's thought processes are a great improvement over those of the preschoolers. The logic of preschoolers often defies analysis for the parent who is unfamiliar with Piaget's theories. Irreversibility, egocentrism, and the rest are very different from what we encounter in adult life. The more logical, less egocentric ways of elementary school children are more recognizable. The children go beyond what the situation looks like and infer from it what reality is. In the conservation situation, they are not taken in by the fact that the amount of liquid in one beaker looks greater. They can now decenter and take many more elements of the problem into consideration.

Cultural and Individual Differences

Piaget was well aware that children in other cultures show variability in the age at which they develop concrete operational skills (see Bringuier, 1980). Children in the rural areas of Iran showed two-, three-, and even four-year delays in passing through the same stages, compared with their urbanized peers. The environment becomes more important as a child becomes older. Many studies show that children with no schooling who have little contact with Westerners and who live in poor rural environments do poorer on Piagetian tasks than urbanized schooled children (Laboratory of Comparative Hu-

man Cognition, 1983). Such factors as schooling, urbanization, and the relevance of a particular skill for a particular society affect the onset of concrete operational abilities (Dasen and Herron, 1981).

The Limitations of Concrete Operational Thought

While they are impressive, the cognitive abilities of school-age children show a number of limitations. For instance, ask a seven-year-old to interpret a proverb like "You can lead a horse to water, but you can't make him drink," and you will be very surprised at the answer. The child may say something about not being able to force an animal to drink, or show a puzzled expression or attempt a literal interpretation of the saying. These children do not understand the more general, abstract meaning of the saying. Political cartoons also require the ability to think in the abstract, and children do not understand them very well. Teachers who are aware of this may attempt to explain difficult concepts, such as democracy, in more concrete terms that children can understand, perhaps through elections in class, instead of trying to define concepts in abstract, dictionary terms.

Children also have difficulty with hypothetical situations. Ask a child, "If all dogs were pink and I had a dog, would it be pink too?" Children often rebel at such statements (Ault, 1977). They insist that dogs are not pink and that's that. Children in the concrete state of operations have difficulty accepting hypothetical situations.

True or False   School-age children can solve abstract, hypothetical problems.

Memory in Middle Childhood

Any attempt to understand cognitive functioning during the school years must look at information-processing abilities, most notably memory. Think back at all the tests you took in your early school years. You had to memorize poems, lyrics to songs, lists of presidents, state capitals, and the twenty-eight exports of whatever country. Success in elementary school requires a good memory, and school-age children make impressive gains in this important area.

Recall, Recognition, and Memory Strategies

No matter how it is measured, memory improves as children negotiate middle childhood. Short-term memory improves with age from five to ten years. The typical five-year-old can recall four or five numbers after a single presentation, a ten-year-old can recall six or seven (Williams and Stith, 1980). Recognition memory is generally good at all ages, but it too shows improvement with age (Dirks and Niesser, 1977). Retention is also superior in both recall and recognition.

Children in middle childhood also begin to use verbal memory strategies on their own. Flavell and colleagues (1966) showed pictures to five-, seven-, and ten-year-olds. The researchers pointed to certain pictures that were to be remembered, and measured the rehearsal strategies used by the children. Only 10 percent of the five-year-olds showed any rehearsal, while 60 percent of the seven-year-olds did once, but only 25 percent used the strategy regularly. Some 85 percent of the ten-year-olds verbalized, and 65 percent did consistently. As one might expect, recall improved with age. Preschoolers can be trained to use verbal strategies, and these do improve their performance, but when faced with similar problems preschoolers do not use these strategies spontaneously. Perhaps they do not understand the memory process well enough to know they should. Children in the school years begin to use the strategies more consistently. As children progress through middle childhood, they also become aware that some strategies are superior to others. In one study, second-graders showed no preference for categorization over rehearsal, while sixth-graders demonstrated a clear preference for categorization, a more sophisticated strategy (Justice, 1985). Progress in understanding the relative effectiveness of different strategies continues throughout the elementary school years.

The developmental progression in the use of strategies is quite clear. Preschoolers may occasionally name an item to be remembered, point, or pay greater attention to it, but they do not yet use any verbal strategy spontaneously. Children in the middle years of childhood rehearse, use repetition, and later demonstrate planning and flexibility in their use of strategies (Brown et al., 1983).

Metamemory

"After you study the names of the presidents and know them well, come downstairs and I'll test you," said Rachel's mother. With that, nine-year-old Rachel ran upstairs and studied. A little while later, she was ready. Asked whether she knew the presidents, she confidently answered yes.

metamemory People's knowledge of their own memory processes.

metacognition People's awareness of their own cognitive processes.

However, it soon became apparent that she knew very few. Rachel's mother got angry, and Rachel ran upstairs in tears.

This scene is repeated in many homes each night. Actually, Rachel and her parents would have an easier time if they understood the concept of **metamemory,** which is defined as knowledge of one's own memory processes. Another term, **metacognition,** refers to knowledge of one's own thought processes. Children's knowledge of these processes increases with age. Rachel probably did not know that she didn't understand the work.

A pioneer in metamemory research, John Flavell (1985), suggests that metamemory should be understood in terms of two major categories. The first is sensitivity. Children must understand—that is, be sensitive to—the meaning of instructions, which often involve words like "remember." Although this may be a problem with very young children, most school-age children have little problem with such instructions. The second category involves three types of variables or factors that interact to determine how well an individual performs on a memory problem (Flavell, 1985). The first is knowledge of one's own memory abilities. Young children tend to overestimate the number of items they can remember (Flavell et al., 1970). In one study, Markman (1973) found that second-graders and fourth-graders were better than kindergartners and first-graders in understanding whether they knew items after studying them.

The second involves the nature of the task. Young children often have difficulty separating the important material from the not-so-important material (Brown and Smiley, 1977). In addition, children must learn what is required of them. Rogoff and colleagues (1974) told six-, eight-, and ten-year-olds that they would be tested on their recognition of forty pictures after a few minutes, a day, or a week. Only the older children studied longer when told they would have to remember the material for a longer period of time.

The third variable is knowledge of strategies. As children mature, they gain the ability not only to use more strategies but also to understand the situations in which one strategy is more useful than another.

Metamemory is a promising area of research. Academic progress may be related to children's ability to comprehend their own level of understanding. John Holt, in his influential book *How Children Fail* (1964), noted that part of being a good student is understanding one's level of comprehension. Good students may be those who often say they do not understand because they are aware of their level of knowledge. Poor students may not really know whether they understand the material. Holt (1964, p. 29) notes, "The problem is not to get students to ask us what they don't know; the problem is to make them aware of the difference between what they know and what they don't." Some evidence indicates that children can be taught to improve their understanding of memory and their use of strategies (Leal et al., 1985; Masters, 1981). We may be able to train children to monitor whether they are truly understanding the material. This is important, because children who are superior on measures of metacognition are better readers (Stewart and Tei, 1983).

True or False When elementary school children claim they understand something, a parent or teacher can be reasonably certain that they do.

Mastering The Basic Skills

Children in elementary school are expected to master the basics of reading, writing, and arithmetic. This mastery is crucial in two ways. First, these skills form the bases for later success in school. They affect how a child sees himself or herself. Erik Erikson viewed the psychosocial crisis of this stage in terms of **industry vs. inferiority.** Children who do not measure up to other children in these skills may feel inferior, while children who do well develop a positive sense of achievement. Interest in how children acquire these basic skills has increased since we have begun to look critically at our educational system.

Reading and Writing

Reading is fundamental to school achievement, and learning to read at the appropriate time is crucial to academic success. Failure to learn to read by the end of first grade is associated with later academic failure. The level of reading achievement by the end of sixth

> **industry vs. inferiority** The fourth psychosocial stage, in which the positive outcome is a sense of confidence concerning one's accomplishments and the negative outcome is a sense of inadequacy.

grade can predict academic achievement in high school (Bloom, 1976). This does not mean that a poor reader in the second grade cannot be helped but, without special help, children who are behind tend to stay behind. In fact, studies have found that ratings of the child's general cognitive abilities, classroom skills, and personal social characteristics made by kindergarten teachers, as well as measures of the child's early cognitive abilities—includ-

The ability to read is a crucial skill in elementary school that affects not only success in one's school work, but also one's self concept.

ing naming letters, memory, perception, and word-matching skills—predicted later achievement (Stevenson et al., 1976). A later study found that the prekindergarten measures of the ability to name letters and common categories of objects, the ability to associate visual and verbal stimuli, and some other early skills predicted measures of academic performance in high school (Stevenson et al., 1986). Without any special help, children who are ahead stay ahead, and those who are behind stay behind.

How has reading ability fared in the last decade? The most recent surveys show that basic reading skills continue to gain slightly and that the largest gains are found in minority group children. Advanced reading skills showed small but steady declines from the early 1960s to the late 1970s, after which they leveled off and started to climb slightly (The Report of Commission on Reading, 1986).

True or False Reading achievement has declined among elementary school children in the past ten years or so.

The ability to write is another important skill that is essential for academic achievement. The results of studies on achievement in writing are similar to those for reading. Basic writing skills have shown some improvement in the lower grades, but writing in junior and senior high schools remains a serious problem (Wheeler, 1979).

Arithmetic

The third basic skill is arithmetic. Studies show that American students spend less time on math and do more poorly in that subject than children in many other societies. In one study, first-grade and fifth-grade students in Japan, Taiwan, and the United States were tested. Students in Japan and Taiwan were superior to elementary school students in the United States on basic mathematical skills (Stigler et al., 1987; 1982). The differences can be explained by the time devoted to these skills as well as by the practice demanded of students. Other differences in achievement between American students and other students around the world have been studied. (See the Cross-Cultural Current on page 242.)

True or False American children are superior to Japanese children in achievement in mathematics.

Factors in Academic Achievement in Middle Childhood

Reading, writing, and math skills do not develop in a vacuum. The general achievement of a child in school depends on a number of factors, including the nature of the school experience, the child's home, and the student's personal characteristics.

The School Experience

Each school has its own atmosphere, its own "feeling." Some are orderly, others have a carnival atmosphere. Some schools are doing a better job than others. Such factors as a safe and orderly environment, an understanding of the goals of the school, administrative leadership, a climate of high expectations, allocation of time to instruction in the basic skills, and frequent monitoring of student progress have been suggested as factors that differentiate schools that are more successful from those that are less successful (Lezotte, 1982; Cohen, 1982). A good relationship between home and school is also important. Especially in the early grades, and in schools where students require remedial work, smaller classes are an advantage (Rutter, 1983).

Everyone knows that some teachers do a better job than others, but it is difficult to discover just what qualities are common to superior teachers. In fact, no single pattern predominates (Centra and Potter, 1980; Hamachek, 1969). One aspect of teaching that is well related to effective learning is the amount of time spent in direct instruction (Davis, 1983; Brophy, 1982).

The Home

Do children who come from poor socioeconomic backgrounds do as well as their middle-class peers? The answer is a clear no (Anderson and Faust, 1973; Coleman, 1966). Children from poor families live in crowded conditions, have poorer health care, are not exposed to such middle-class experiences as trips and books, have lower career aspirations, and may not know how to succeed in public school (Biehler, 1982; Mandell and Fiscus, 1981). These conditions may lead to failure, and a vicious cycle can ensue. Failure leads to lack of interest and motivation, which leads to more failure. The children's expectations for success are lower as well, although they increase with age (Fulkerson et al., 1983).

Some of these generalizations are now being challenged. The correlations between socioeconomic status and academic achievement are indeed positive, but they range anywhere from a low of +.1 to a high of +.8 (White, 1982). (Remember, a correlation of +1.00 is perfect.) Although socioeconomic status is correlated with achievement it can explain only about 5 percent of the final results in academic achievement. The traditional indicators of socioeconomic status are occupational level, education, and income, but many studies add to these such factors as family size, educational aspirations, ethnicity, and the presence of reading material in the home. Measures of home atmosphere such as the availability of books in the home, educational aspirations, and the like correlate more highly with academic achievement than any single or combined group of the traditional indicators of socioeconomic status.

Because this is true, we would do better to concentrate on what home factors affect academic achievement. Many poor families do promote academic achievement in their children. For example, the parents read to their children, help them with homework, take them to the library, and expand on their language. If we know that these home variables are more predictive of academic achievement, we can then educate parents to change the ways they interact with their children. In addition, by concentrating on home environment instead of socioeconomic status, we turn our attention away from a particular group and toward particular parent-child relationships, home variables, and child-rearing strategies. Socioeconomic status may mask truly important home variables that are good predictors of academic achievement.

Parents both create an atmosphere in the home and also teach children through their interactions with them. Parents must understand what their children can and cannot do. Unfortunately, many parents tend to overestimate their children's abilities and what children can do in general (Miller, 1986). The more accurate a parent's judgment of the child's developmental level, the better the child's academic performance, probably because parents who understand their children's abilities are able to structure the environment in ways that can promote cognitive growth. Perhaps parents need to be educated so that they can understand what their children

can and cannot do and helped to structure better learning environments for them.

Some children from the same families attending the same schools do very well in school, while others do not. The reasons involve such individual variables as gender, attitudes, cognitive styles, and intelligence.

Gender

Do girls or boys do better in elementary school? Even though no sex differences exist in intelligence, girls perform better than boys on measures of reading, spelling, and verbal abilities, while boys, at least in the later elementary school years, do better in math and problems involving spatial analysis (Busch-Rossnagel and Vance, 1982; Burstein et al., 1980). A great deal of overlap occurs, with some girls performing better than boys in math, and some boys reading better than girls. In addition, many of these gender differences, such as those found in verbal ability, are relatively small (Hyde, 1981), and the differences in math achievement normally show themselves only in the later years of elementary school (Dembo, 1981) or at the onset of puberty (Paulsen and Johnson, 1983).

True or False By the end of elementary school, girls are doing better in reading, while boys excel in math.

Why should these sex differences exist? Perhaps girls are more physiologically ready for school and this readiness gives them an edge toward academic achievement (McGuinness, 1979). Perhaps the atmosphere of the school is considered feminine, with its great percentage of female teachers and its emphasis on obedience and sitting still. Boys and girls experience school in very different ways, and both male and female teachers value the stereotyped feminine traits of obedience and passivity rather than aggressiveness and independence (Etaugh and Hughes, 1975). At least in the early grades, boys may find school achievement more difficult and not in keeping with their view of the masculine role model.

Attitudes, Motivation, and Work Habits

Students with positive attitudes toward school and with high motivation do better than children who dislike learning and school and don't care how they do. One

Achievement Differences Among American, Japanese, and Chinese Students: Answering the Question of Why

Time after time, studies have shown that Japanese children perform better than their American peers on a wide range of academic tests. In fact, Asian-American children in American schools generally achieve well above average. The question is, Why? Some authorities claim that the cognitive abilities of the Japanese and maybe also the Chinese children simply exceed those of American children. Perhaps the superior cognitive skills of Japanese and Chinese children in the areas of spatial relationships, various types of memory, and vocabulary explain the differences in achievement, especially in the area of reading.

Harold Stevenson and his colleagues decided to test whether this superiority in reading was really due to superior cognitive skills. Specifically, they wanted to know whether children in Japan, Taiwan, and the United States had different scores on particular cognitive tasks. Their second purpose was to discover whether scores on different cognitive tasks could predict reading achievement in the three different cultures.

Some 240 first-graders and 240 fifth-graders were selected in each of the three cultures. The American children were from Minneapolis, Minnesota; the Japanese children were from the city of Sendai; and the Chinese children came from the city of Taipei on the island of Taiwan. Great care was taken to ensure that these children were representative of all the elementary school children in those cities.

A variety of cognitive tasks were designed for use in all three cultures. Again, care was taken to create tasks that were relevant, interesting, comparable in terms of

language, and appropriate for all the children. The cognitive tasks measured a wide range of abilities, including spatial relationships, perceptual speed, auditory memory, serial memory for words, serial memory for numbers, verbal memory for brief stories, and vocabulary. Children were also given tests of reading skills that measured comprehension, vocabulary, and the percentage of the text read correctly, and tests of math skills.

The researchers reasoned that if the children's scores on the various cognitive measures and reading differed significantly, the superiority of achievement might be attributed to differences in cognitive abilities. However, if the scores of the children in the three cultures on measures of reading achievement differed, but no differences in cognitive abilities were evident, then differences in reading achievement are probably due to other factors found in the home and school.

The researchers did find differences in achievement among students in the three cultures. The Chinese children generally scored the highest, followed by Japanese children. In math, the Japanese children performed better than the Chinese children, but both were superior to the American children. There were some exceptions—for example, first-grade American children scored higher on vocabulary than Japanese children. But generally the achievement results indicated that the Japanese and Chinese children had performed better than the American children on tests of these basic skills.

So far, this is in keeping with previous findings. However, what about the children's performance on the cognitive tasks? On a number of cognitive tasks, the Amer-

reason put forward for male superiority in math in the later grades is that males expect to do better. These higher expectations are found as early as the first grade, even though the grades and abilities of boys are not superior to those of girls (Entwisle and Baker, 1983). Differences in performance are not inevitable, especially when females have positive attitudes toward math (Paulsen and Johnson, 1983). Work habits are another variable. Children who know how to study and how to take tests are likely to do better than those who don't. Work habits and study skills can be taught.

Cognitive Style

Some children are quick to answer but make many mistakes, while others take a while to answer but make fewer

ican first-graders exceeded the scores of both the Chinese and the Japanese children. Generally, the scores of the first-grade Japanese children exceeded those of the Chinese first-graders. Although some differences among children in the three cultures did exist in fifth grade, for the most part any differences evident in first grade had disappeared by the fifth grade. Children from all three cultures scored similarly on a variety of cognitive measures by the fifth grade.

The results of this study, then, do not support the hypothesis that differences in cognitive abilities are responsible for the superiority of the Japanese and Chinese children in reading and math. Although children in each of these cultures have their own strengths and weaknesses, by the fifth grade they are very similar in level and scores on a variety of cognitive tasks. The same two factors—general cognitive ability and serial memory ability—predicted reading achievement for children in all three cultures.

The importance of environmental differences was evident. For example, the Chinese first-graders scored rather low on a number of verbal tasks. In China, a young child is taught to be thoughtful but not talkative. By fifth grade, these children had experienced numerous verbal interactions in school and had caught up. The initial superiority of American first-graders on some tasks was explained by their more frequent early exposure to events outside the home—for example, outings to museums, movies, sporting events, and the zoo. The Chinese and Japanese children experienced many fewer such outings.

Although the differences in reading achievement are definite, the investigators were impressed by the similarities rather than the differences that characterized cognitive functioning among the Japanese, Chinese, and American youngsters. Based on the results of this study, we might conclude that the answer to the question of why Japanese and Chinese children read better does not lie in the area of differential cognitive abilities. It suggests that we should turn our attention toward a search for more subtle factors in the school and home that may lead to superior achievement. Perhaps such factors as motivation, work habits, parental expectations, or the amount of time spent on developing reading skills in the classroom are the important factors differentiating children in one culture from children in another. Only more research will indicate elements of the environment that are responsible for the differences.

Source: Stevenson, H. W., Stigler, J. W., Lee, S., Lucker, G. W., Kitamura, S., and Hsu, C. Cognitive Performance and Academic Achievement of Japanese, Chinese, and American Children. *Child Development*, 1985, 56, 718–734.

errors (Yap and DeV. Peters, 1985). The first cognitive style is labeled **impulsive,** the second is **reflective.** Children who have a reflective cognitive style generally make fewer errors on a variety of different tests, including those involving recognition, memory, and inductive reasoning (Borkowski et al., 1983). Impulsive children make more errors in reading (Kagan, 1965) and are more likely to fail in the early grades (Messer, 1970). Reflective chil-

impulsive style A cognitive style marked by cursory examination of a problem and answering questions very quickly.

reflective style A cognitive style marked by thorough exploration of a problem, consideration of various alternatives, and finally, answering the question or performing the tasks.

dren also use different problem-solving skills. They gather more information and analyze the problem and their answers more thoroughly. Reflective children also have higher metamemory scores—that is, they are more aware of how they solve problems (Borkowski et al., 1983). Reflective children can adapt to a faster pace if necessary, whereas impulsive children are locked into a less-adaptive style (Kogan, 1983). Although reflectivity seems better than impulsivity, both extremes can cause problems. Most people fall somewhere in between.

Although these styles are rather stable, they can be altered. For example, children with impulsive styles can be taught to be more reflective (Kogan, 1983). One way is to teach them to utter certain self-statements in which children monitor their own progress and remind themselves to "go slow" (Meichenbaum and Goodman, 1971).

Intelligence

Of all the factors that contribute to academic achievement, none is more controversial than intelligence. Just what does it mean when we say someone is intelligent?

Approaches to intelligence. The ability to profit from one's experiences, a cluster of cognitive abilities, the ability to well in school, and whatever an intelligence test measures—all these have been used as definitions of **intelligence.** Intelligence has also been considered a measure of one's rate of development relative to the rate of development of one's peers (Blank, 1982). Piaget did not view intelligence as a "thing," but rather as an ongoing process by which children use qualitatively different ways to adapt to their environment.

An important question to ask about intelligence is whether it is one quality or composed of a number of separate and distinct components (Kail and Pelligrino, 1985). If it is one quality, then you would expect people who are "intelligent" to show this quality across a wide variety of tasks. On the other hand, some psychologists argue that some people perform much better on some tasks than on others, and that in addition to this general factor there are specific abilities (the s factor) (Spearman, 1904). Still others deny that any general factor for intelligence exists, insisting that a number of primary abilities are present. For example, Thurstone (1938) argued that there are seven primary abilities: verbal comprehension, word fluency, number, spatial abilities, associative memory, perceptual speed, and general reasoning.

intelligence A measure of one's rate of development relative to one's peers. The ability to profit from experience. A cluster of abilities, such as reasoning and memory. In the Piagetian view, any behavior that allows the individual to adapt to the environment.

triarchic theory of human intelligence A theory of intelligence based on information-processing considerations advanced by Robert Sternberg, who postulates the following mechanisms of intelligent functioning: *metacomponents*, which involve the individual's skills used in planning and decision-making; *performance components*, which relate to the basic operations involved in actually solving the task; and *knowledge acquisition components*, which involve processes that are used in acquiring new knowledge.

Today this viewpoint is expanded in a new approach by Howard Gardner (1983), who advanced the theory of multiple intelligences—that is, that a number of different types of intelligence exist, including musical, linguistic, logical and mathematical, visual and spatial conceptualization, bodily-kinesthetic, and interpersonal (social and interpersonal skills). Another new approach is based on an information-processing model. Here investigators try to understand intelligence in terms of the mental processes that relate to performance on a task. For example, Robert Sternberg (1985, 1984) advanced the **triarchic theory of human intelligence.** Sternberg argues that intelligence involves purposeful adaptation to the real-world environment. What is adaptive in one culture may not be in another. An intelligent person in the United States might be quite unable to cope with the requirements of living in a mountainous Asian country. Sternberg also argues that intelligence is shown both with tasks and situations that are either novel or so "customary" that performance on them is automatic.

According to Sternberg, intelligence is composed of three components. First, there are *metacomponents*, or executive skills, used in planning and decision-making, including recognition of what the problem is, the various processes involved in selecting a strategy, the allocation of time, and the monitoring of the solution, among others. Second, there are the *performance components*, which are the basic operations involved in actually solving a problem, such as encoding information, inferring relationships between different aspects of the problem, and comparing and contrasting different answers. The third component of intelligence is *knowledge acquisition*. This involves processes useful in acquiring new knowledge, including selective encoding (sifting the relevant from the irrelevant), selective combination (integrating the knowledge in a meaningful way), and selective comparison (rendering the information meaningful by appreciating its relationship to other information).

Sternberg uses his theory to explain both giftedness and mental retardation. He defines *giftedness* as the ability to think in new and insightful ways. He notes that the differences between the gifted and those that are not gifted can be found in the knowledge-acquisition component. He describes the case of Alexander Fleming, discoverer of penicillin, who showed selective encoding when while gazing at a petri dish containing a moldy culture he noticed that the bacteria in the area of the mold had been destroyed, presumably by the mold. Fleming encoded the information in a highly selective way, focusing on the part of the field that was relevant to discovery of the drug. On the other hand, Sternberg suggests, the mentally retarded show difficulties mostly in the metacomponents area and differ in the way they

The skills and abilities one society considers "intelligence" may seem unimportant to another society. No one really knows what intelligence means in cultures whose problems and challenges are different from one's own.

mental age The age at which an individual is functioning.

intelligence quotient (IQ) A method of computing intelligence by dividing the mental age by the chronological age and multiplying by 100.

use these executive skills. For example, even when mentally retarded people have the knowledge, they don't seem to be able to use it to solve the problem.

Clearly, the definition one uses affects the way intelligence tests will be constructed. Most intelligence tests are targeted at school-age populations. Intelligence tests are often given for screening purposes—for example, they are often used to determine which students are intellectually gifted. At other times they are used for diagnostic purposes. Since there is a high correlation between school achievement and performance on intelligence tests, about .6 or so (Zigler and Berman, 1983), children who score very low may have difficulty in school. Because the correlation is not perfect, however, other factors—such those discussed previously—are also important.

True or False Intelligence is highly related to school achievement.

The Stanford-Binet and Wechsler tests. In the early 1900s, Alfred Binet created a test to identify students who could not benefit from traditional education. Binet used a series of tests that measured a sample of children's abilities at different age levels. At each level some children performed better than others. Binet simply compared children's performances on these tests to that of others in the age-group. If a child had less knowledge than the average child of the same age, that child was said to be less intelligent; if the child knew more, the child's intelligence was said to be higher. Binet used the term **mental age** to describe the age at which the child was functioning. Later, another psychologist, William Stern, proposed the term **intelligence quotient** or **IQ,** which is arrived at by taking the mental age of the child and dividing it by the child's chronological age (age since birth) and then multiplying by 100 to remove the decimal. The problem with the IQ is that it assumed a straight-line (linear) relationship between age and intelligence. This is not the case, especially after age sixteen. The problems of defining, measuring, and comparing intelligence levels of adults are discussed in the sections of the text devoted to cognitive development in adulthood. Today a more statistically sophisticated way of calculating the intelligence score, called a *deviation IQ,* is used. The original Binet test has gone through a number of revisions and today is called the Stanford-Binet Intelligence Test.

Beginning in the 1930s, David Wechsler began to develop another set of individualized intelligence tests. The Wechsler Intelligence Scale for Children (revised edition) contains a number of subtests that can be divided into two categories: verbal and performance. The five verbal subtests are information, similarities, arithmetic, vocabulary, and comprehension. The five performance subtests include picture completion (pointing out what is missing in a picture), picture arrangement (arranging a group of pictures in sequential order), block design (copying a pattern with blocks), object assembly (putting together puzzle pieces) and coding (a test in which people are asked to translate one set of symbols into another). Two additional subtests, one verbal and one performance, are sometimes used: digit span (a test of immediate recall in which the test taker is asked to repeat random series of digits sometimes in forward order and sometimes in reverse order) and mazes. A composite, or total, intelligence score may also be obtained.

The correlation between the Stanford-Binet and Wechsler varies, but for the full scale it is +.73 (Brown, 1983). There is also a good relationship between Piagetian tests and scores on the Wechsler Intelligence Scale for Children (Humphreys et al., 1985). This indicates that different tests of intelligence do not tap identical skills, but are related.

How intelligence tests can be misused. In recent years, much controversy has arisen over the use of intelligence tests. Some criticism has been directed at the possible cultural bias against minority groups. In 1971 a group of parents of black children who were placed in classes for the retarded sued in federal court, claiming that the placements were discriminatory because they were based on intelligence tests that were culturally biased. Eight years later the court ruled that IQ tests were culturally biased. This famous case, *Larry P. v. Riles,* is well known. However, about nine months later, in the case of *PASE v. Hannon,* after hearing similar testimony and looking over the test one question at a time, a judge decided that these intelligence tests, when used with other cri-

teria for determining educational placement, were not discriminatory (Bersoff, 1981a; 1981b). Some psychologists argue that these tests do not show consistent bias against minority groups (Cole, 1981). Lack of bias does not make the test socially beneficial, though, and even the appearance of bias—as when more minority group students are placed in classes for the retarded—is undesirable. In addition, because these tests are highly verbal they may be inappropriate for children for whom English is not the primary language (Heward and Orlansky, 1984). Problems with how the tests are used, rather than with their technical fairness, may be at the center of the controversy (Reschly, 1981). In an attempt to free standardized tests of any bias, culture-fair tests have been formulated. These depend less on language abilities and speed of responding, and they eliminate items that reflect differential cultural or social experiences. Such tests use matching, picture completion, copying block designs, analogies, spatial relations, and the ability to see relations between patterns (Brown, 1983). But a perfect culture-free test has yet to be invented. Even if one is formulated, it is questionable whether it will predict school performance as well as our present standardized tests.

Another problem is the interpretation of intelligence as if it were a fixed quality etched in stone. As we have noted many times, it is not. Intelligence can change with one's experience. Finally, although scores on an intelligence test correlate with academic achievement, there is a tendency to overrate the test's predictive abilities and to categorize children rigidly (Kaplan, 1977). For example, one of my acquaintances was shocked when her child's fifth-grade teacher told her that her son was doing fine, considering he had an IQ of "only" 105. If intelligence test scores are used in such a manner, the child can truly suffer. Even though these problems exist, intelligence tests will continue to be used, especially in the diagnosis and placement of exceptional children. However, they must be used with care and interpreted correctly if they are to be an aid in the educational process.

Exceptional Children

Intelligence tests are often administered to children thought to be in need of special services. In the last decade or so, the schools have become involved in the challenge of educating exceptional children. An **excep-**

tional child is a child whose intellectual, emotional, or physical performance falls either above or below that of his or her normal peers (Haring, 1986). These children require special services to maximize their functioning in certain areas, such as academic achievement and/or personal-social functioning. Everyone deviates from the mythical average, but there is a range of normal performance expected from children at particular stages in their lives. Children who deviate appreciably from this norm in both directions are considered exceptional.

The Law

Just how many children are exceptional is difficult to say. One estimate is shown in Table 9.1. Today, exceptional children and their parents have rights and opportunities that are new and challenging, mostly as a result of the sweeping changes brought about by Public Law 94-142, the Education for All Handicapped Children Act (see Table 9.2).

This law guarantees every child a free and appropriate education, and no school district can claim that a child cannot be educated. It is the district's responsibility to educate the child. In addition, the guarantees that due process be used in placing a child in some educational program mean not only that certain procedures must be followed, but also that all testing must be performed in a nondiscriminatory manner. A Spanish-speaking child

> **exceptional child** A child whose intellectual, emotional, or physical performance falls substantially above or below that of "normal" peers.
>
> **Individualized Education Program (IEP)** An individual plan outlining educational goals for an individual and methods for attaining them.

can no longer be given an intelligence test written in English, nor can only one test be relied on for any decision. The law also encourages educational accountability, because teachers must develop an **Individualized Education Program,** or **IEP,** which states the goals of each exceptional child's schooling and the methods for attaining them. Parents have the right to participate in all phases of the child's placement and education. Finally, the law mandates that each child be placed in the *"least restrictive environment."* Figure 9.2 shows the placement alternatives. The most restrictive are at the top, while integration into the normal classroom is the least restrictive possible. When disabled children are placed in a regular classroom, they are said to be mainstreamed.

Mainstreaming: Problems and Potential

The most controversial part of Public Law 94-142 has to do with the practice of mainstreaming. Actually,

---

TABLE 9.1

Prevalence of Exceptional Children in the United States

The number of exceptional children in the population is significant, usually more than most people would think.

Exceptionality	Percent of Population	No. of Children Ages 5–18*
Visually impaired (includes blind)	0.1	55,000
Hearing impaired (includes deaf)	0.5 to 0.7	275,000 to 385,000
Speech handicapped	3.0 to 4.0	1,650,000 to 2,200,000
Orthopedically and health impaired	0.5	275,000
Emotionally disturbed	2.0 to 3.0	1,100,000 to 1,650,000
Mentally retarded (both educable and trainable)	2.0 to 3.0	1,100,000 to 1,650,000
Learning disabilities	2.0 to 3.0	1,100,000 to 1,650,000
Multihandicapped	0.5 to 0.7	275,000 to 385,000
Gifted and talented	2.0 to 3.0	1,100,000 to 1,650,000
Totals	12.6 to 18.0	6,930,000 to 9,900,000

*Number of children based on 1985 population estimates

Source: Gearheart and Weishahn, 1984.

TABLE 9.2

Major Provisions of PL94-142 (Education for All Handicapped Children Act)

Public Law 94-142 ensured that all handicapped children would receive a free and appropriate education.

Each State and Locality Must Have a Plan to Ensure:

Child identification	Extensive efforts must be made to screen and identify all handicapped children.
Full service at no cost	Every handicapped child must be assured an appropriate public education at no cost to the parents or guardians.
Due process	The child's and parents' rights to information and informed consent must be assured before the child is evaluated, labeled, or placed, and they have a right to an impartial due process hearing if they disagree with the school's decisions.
Parent consultation, parent surrogate	Parents or guardian must be consulted about the child's evaluation and placement and the educational plan; if parents or guardian are unknown or unavailable, a surrogate parent to act for the child must be found.
Least restrictive environment (LRE)	The child must be educated in the least restrictive environment that is consistent with his educational needs and, insofar as possible, with nonhandicapped children.
Individualized education program (IEP)	A written individualized education program must be prepared for each handicapped child. The plan must state present levels of functioning, long-term and short-term goals, services to be provided, and plans for initiating and evaluating the services.
Nondiscriminatory evaluation	The child must be evaluated in all areas of suspected disability and in a way that is not biased by his language or cultural characteristics or his handicaps. Evaluation must be by a multidisciplinary team, and no single evaluation procedure may be used as the sole criterion for placement or planning.
Confidentiality	Results of evaluation and placement must be kept confidential, and parents or guardian may have access to records regarding their child.
Personnel development, in-service	Training must be provided for teachers and other professional personnel, including in-service training for regular teachers in meeting the needs of the handicapped.

There are detailed rules and regulations of the federal government regarding implementation of each of these major provisions. The definitions of some of these provisions—LRE and nondiscriminatory evaluation, for example—are still being clarified by federal officials and court decisions.

Source: Adapted from Hallahan and Kauffman, 1986.

mainstreaming is not really part of the law at all. The law mandates that a child be placed in the "least restrictive environment," but it does not require that all children be mainstreamed. Still, for many children the law has meant integration into regular classrooms.

True or False By law, every exceptional child must be mainstreamed—that is, placed in a class with "normal" students.

The thinking behind such integration is obvious. Both the disabled child and the nondisabled benefit from being exposed to and interacting with each other. The disabled child learns to live in the nondisabled world and gains the social skills necessary for independent living. The nondisabled child becomes more accepting of the disabled and less prejudiced. But mainstreaming has brought

mainstreaming A term used to describe the process by which exceptional children are integrated into classes with "normal" peers.

problems. Teachers walked into classrooms to find they had disabled children to teach but little or no training in how to meet the special needs of these children. There was little, if any, time included in the day to work with experts in special education. And the exceptional child was not given much preparation for entering the mainstream either (Tolkoff, 1981).

It is difficult to evaluate mainstreaming. The practice has apparently not led to a reduction in prejudice or to increased acceptance on the part of the nondisabled (Gresham, 1982). In other words, despite being placed in regular classrooms, exceptional children have not been integrated into the social framework of the classroom. This does not mean, however, that mainstreaming or the concept of the least restrictive environment is a failure. All it means is that we cannot merely place disabled students into regular classrooms and expect events to take their course. Proximity gives us only an opportunity to help; it does not ensure better acceptance. Strategies aimed at enhancing cooperation between the disabled and the nondisabled are required (Johnson, 1983). In addition, exceptional children must be taught appropriate social skills, including conversation and listening skills, so that they can handle social situations (Wanat, 1983). Perhaps all children could use a dose of such

training, but it is vital to the success of the exceptional child, who may be negotiating a new situation at an initial disadvantage. The most successful mainstreaming programs have (1) developed specific criteria indicating who should and should not be mainstreamed, and to what extent, (2) prepared disabled students and their nondisabled peers, (3) promoted communication among educators, and (4) continually evaluated the progress of exceptional children and provided teacher in-service training to enable teachers to deal better with the challenge of serving students with exceptional needs (Salend, 1984).

It is impossible to cover even briefly all the problems and potentials of all categories of exceptional children. However, we can focus on children from four classifications of exceptionality: students with learning disabil-

FIGURE 9.2

A Continuum of Educational Services for Exceptional Children

This figure shows the many alternatives available for placing handicapped children. Notice the continuum of services ranging from placing the child in a regular classroom with few or no supportive services (1) to placement in a hospital or institution (10). Children are placed in the least restrictive environment in which they can effectively function.

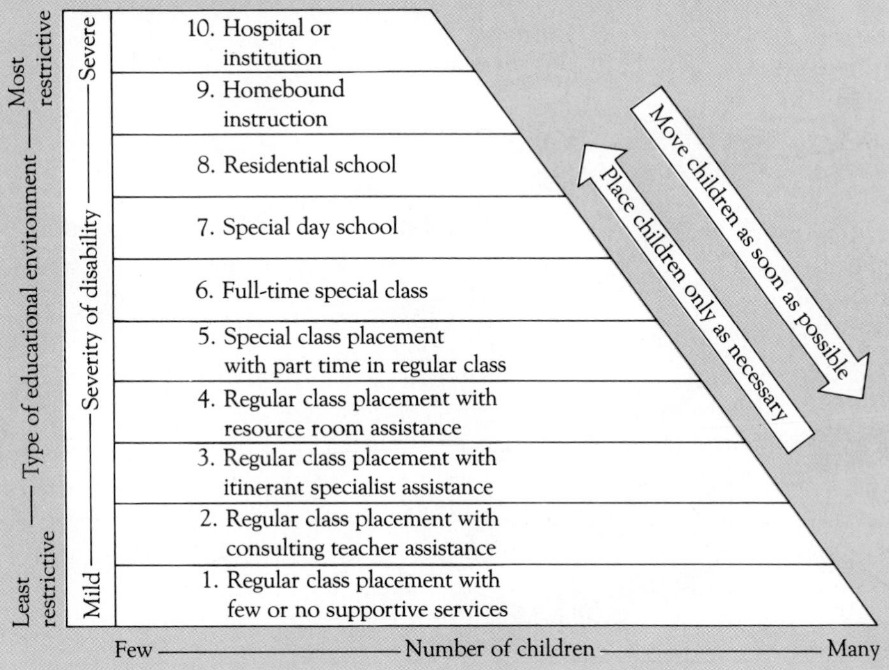

Source: Deno, 1973.

ities, students who are hyperactive, students who have been diagnosed as mentally retarded, and students who are gifted.

Learning Disabilities

Richard has had little success in learning to read. Now, at the end of second grade, he has been sent for testing by the school psychologist. She noted that there is a great discrepancy between what Richard's intelligence says he should be doing and his actual achievement.

Richard is suffering from a **learning disability.** The term "learning disabilities" refers to a group of disorders marked by significant difficulties in acquiring and using listening, speaking, reading, writing, reasoning skills, or math. These disorders are intrinsic to the child (within the child) and are presumed to be due to central nervous system dysfunction (Hammill et al., 1981). In other words, children with learning disabilities do not achieve up to their age and ability in some basic skill. This problem is not the result of sensory handicaps—such as blindness, mental retardation, or emotional disturbances, or to environmental, cultural, or economic disabilities (*Federal*

> **learning disabilities**   A group of disorders marked by significant difficulties in acquiring and using listening, speaking, reading, writing, reasoning, or math.

Register, 1977, *42*, 65082–65085). When diagnosing learning disabilities, three factors stand out: (1) there are academic problems; (2) there is a discrepancy between ability and performance; (3) these problems are not due to the exclusions noted previously (Mercer et al., 1985).

The learning-disabled child experiences great difficulty in learning to read and developing other academic skills. When the child grows up, such problems as low motivation, distractibility, low self-concept, and organizational problems remain (Buchanan and Wolf, 1986). The child needs and deserves special help.

There are two major approaches to helping such children learn. The *underlying-abilities approach* focuses on improving the psychological processes in which the child shows some deficiency by teaching the child to compensate for the deficiencies. This approach claims that cen-

Due to changes in the law, many disabled students are now "mainstreamed" into regular classrooms. The challenge is to integrate them into the social fabric of the classroom.

tral nervous system problems can affect one or more of the basic abilities involved in perception, psycholinguistic abilities, and cognition. Exercises that help the child's perceptual and motor functions involved in balance, developing a left-right sequence, gross and fine motor coordination, rhythm, eye control, training in auditory discrimination, and the like are used. The second approach, called the *observable skills approach*, assumes that the only way to help the child with a learning disability is to teach the child the skills he or she must learn. To do this, each skill is analyzed and broken into small parts, and direct instruction in these skills is given. Besides concentrating on cognitive weaknesses, this approach uses behavior modification and other techniques to help the child achieve better impulse control and perseverance (Adelman and Taylor, 1986).

Children with learning disabilities often experience social as well as academic problems. They may be rejected because of the way they interact with others (Vaughn, 1985). Learning-disabled children often do not interpret verbal communications properly and respond in ways that may not be appropriate or sensitive. The parents of learning-disabled children rate their children significantly lower in social competence and social involvement, and claim that they display more behavior problems, than did parents of non-learning-disabled children (McConaughty and Ritter, 1985). In addition, these children are keenly aware of their deficits (Cohen, 1983). Children who are learning disabled require training in both academic and social skills.

Hyperactivity

Timothy does not pay attention in class. He walks around the room, touches everything, seems out of control, and is easily distractible. He is impulsive and always in motion.

If you spend a few minutes with a hyperactive child, you begin to appreciate the patience and skill required for dealing with these children. **Hyperactive** children are impulsive, highly distractible, inattentive, and show a great deal of inappropriate behavior (Ross and Ross, 1976). They have difficulty in school, and their relationships with teachers are often strained. They are often considered aggressive and annoying and are not accepted by their peers. Their parents find them less compliant and less responsive to their questions, and parents report many more conduct problems than they do for their nonhyperactive children (Tarver-Behring et al., 1985).

hyperactivity A term used to describe the behavior of children who are impulsive, overly active, highly distractible, and inattentive.

Most hyperactive children are male, the ratio being about 3:1 to 9:1 (Gelfand et al., 1982). As these children mature, about 80 percent carry some of the symptoms of hyperactivity into adulthood. They do not fidget as much, but they are likely to be impulsive and to have difficulty forming relationships. They also suffer from more car and motorcycle accidents and move frequently. On the other hand, their impulsivity is not necessarily a problem in the workplace; employers do not see them as very different from nonhyperactive workers (Sobel, 1979).

Three basic approaches are being used to treat hyperactivity. Hyperactive children are often treated with stimulant medications to reduce the symptoms of the disorder. Under such medications, these children become calmer and more attentive (Clampit and Pirkle, 1983). Some people have criticized the use of these drugs because they treat only the symptoms, not the underlying cause, and may produce unpleasant side effects. Finding the correct dosage for a particular child is often a problem too (Varley and Trupin, 1983). Others question the effectiveness of these drugs (Gadow, 1983). No one claims that drug therapy will improve intelligence or even schoolwork, but medication may reduce the symptoms so that the children can learn. An analysis of 135 studies of stimulant use with hyperactive youngsters concluded that stimulants are effective (Kavale, 1982). This does not mean that drug therapy is always the treatment of choice. The very idea of a child taking medication over a period of years should make us cautious. Some authorities claim that such treatment should be used only as a last resort, and then always in combination with another type of treatment. In any event, because medication only reduces the symptoms of hyperactivity, other techniques must be used to compensate for the child's academic and social problems.

True or False Hyperactivity can be cured through correct use of medication.

One popular nondrug treatment is the *Feingold diet*, named after the physician who developed it, Dr. Norman Feingold. Feingold noted that hyperactivity was related to the consumption of food additives, such as preservatives and artificial flavorings. Even some natural chemicals, such as salicylates, might be implicated, and he suggested that children may be genetically predisposed to react to these additives. He claimed that if hyperactive children were put on a diet free of these compounds, a significant number would improve (Johnson, 1981; Feingold, 1975).

Some clinical support for the Feingold diet has been found (Holborow et al., 1981), but controlled studies have been difficult to conduct, and each has been criticized on methodological grounds. Johnson (1981) suggests that a scarcely significant relationship exists between diet and hyperactivity, especially among young children, and that the success rate with the diet is lower than claimed. Others either argue that the diet is generally ineffective or note that it is successful in only a small number of cases (Kavale and Forness, 1983; Mattes, 1983), but some authorities argue that this negative assessment is premature and may be inaccurate (Rimland, 1983). More research is needed in this area. At this point, it is reasonable to conclude that the diet may be effective for some children, but not for as many as first thought.

The third approach to treating hyperactivity (which may be used in combination with either of the first two) involves manipulating the environment and its reinforcements. For example, providing structure and solid routines and using positive reinforcements are helpful (Walden and Thompson, 1981). Some claim that behavioral intervention is superior to medication (Gadow, 1983). Perhaps in the future we will discover new techniques to give hyperactive children the opportunity to learn and succeed in school.

The Mentally Retarded

You are told that a group home for mentally retarded people will be established in your neighborhood. One of your neighbors asks you to sign a petition opposing it. The neighbor tells you that "these people" will bring an "undesirable element" into the community and will depress home values. Would you sign the petition?

Such scenes are repeated in hundreds of communities around the nation. Community opposition appears even after data showing that property values do not suffer and that neighborhoods will not be adversely affected is pre-

sented (Landesman-Dwyer, 1981). Why is there so much prejudice against the mentally retarded?

To understand this, we must look at just who is considered mentally retarded. In order to be considered mentally retarded, three criteria must be met. First the individual must show an intelligence score of below 70 on an individualized intelligence test given in the child's primary language. Second, the retardation must occur before the age of eighteen. Third, a substantial failure in adjustment must be present (President's Commission on Mental Retardation, 1977). Some explanation here is necessary. As we've seen, intelligence testing is not an exact science, and a child's intelligence score may change over time. Significant gains have been noted after periods of intensive instruction (Heward and Orlansky, 1984), so borderline children should be labeled with care. In addition, as noted earlier, some authorities argue that even our best intelligence tests are culturally biased against children from minority groups. Thus, defining anyone as mentally retarded simply on the basis of intelligence is dangerous. The requirement that there be some adjustment problem is based on more subjective data. Although some objective tests measure adjustment problems, they are of questionable validity (Brown, 1983). Even so, this criterion is important, because adjustment problems relate to the individual's performance in the areas of social responsibility and self-sufficiency (Grossman, 1973). A child who shows a lack of reasoning or an inability to communicate with others certainly has an adjustment problem.

Years ago, the mentally retarded were classified into the categories of idiot, imbecile, and moron, which have negative connotations. Then, the terms *educable*, *trainable*, and *custodial* were introduced, and these are still in use. The problem here is the connotation that children who are trainable cannot be educated. Today many authorities use the terms *mild*, *moderate*, *severe*, and *profound* to indicate levels of retardation. Even so, you may find the older titles—educable, trainable, and custodial—being used. About 85 percent of the mentally retarded are in what was called the educable category, about 12 percent are deemed trainable, and 3 percent are categorized as custodial. The great majority of those diagnosed as mentally retarded are found in the upper levels, near normal intelligence levels.

Our knowledge of the causes of mental retardation, especially of mild and higher-level moderate retardation

TABLE 9.3

Educational Achievement Among the Mentally Retarded

The mentally retarded are frequently able to surprise people with what they can achieve if given the best educational and familial environments possible.

Degree of Mental Retardation	Potential for Educational Achievement	Potential for Adult Functioning
Mildly retarded: IQ approximately 51–65	"Educable"; capable of third- to sixth-grade educational achievement; able to read and write and use basic mathematics.	Able to be independent personally and socially; able to be self-supporting; frequently lose identification as retarded and blend into "normal" population.
Moderately retarded: IQ approximately 36–50	"Trainable"; capable of kindergarten through third-grade achievement; typically not able to read and write.	Able to be employed in unskilled occupations if supervision available; typically incapable of independent living or marriage.
Severely retarded: IQ approximately 21–35	Able to acquire some self-care skills; able to talk and express self; unable to acquire any academic skills.	Need permanent care from family or society; some are capable of performing simple chores under total supervision.
Profoundly retarded IQ approximately 20 or lower	Unable to speak; some are capable of self-ambulation, but many remain bedridden throughout their lives.	Incapable of any self-maintenance; require permanent nursing care.

Source: Suran and Rizzo, 1983.

(educable), is limited. Identifiable causative agents have been discovered in fewer than 10 percent of the cases (Polloway and Patton, 1982). As intelligence scores decrease, however, the number of cases caused by known organic and genetic factors increases. Some of these factors include infections, trauma, metabolic problems, prenatal problems, genetic and chromosomal abnormalities, and brain damage (Grossman, 1977).

Most mildly retarded individuals do not look any different from the general population. The cause of their retardation is generally unknown, but it may be linked to environmental factors. For that reason, the cause is often listed as cultural familial. These mentally retarded individuals have difficulty with abstractions and show slower cognitive development (Kirk and Gallagher, 1986). Despite these problems, if they receive good care and a proper education many mildly retarded people can learn to lead independent, productive lives (see Table 9.3). For many mildly retarded students, vocational training is important. Vocational training includes behavioral and social training as well as learning occupational skills. These people can successfully work in unskilled or semiskilled jobs, and research shows them to be effective workers (Brickley and Campbell, 1981).

The moderately retarded will probably not be able to lead an independent existence. About one-third of the children in this category have a known brain dysfunction, and another third suffer from Down's Syndrome. In the past these children were immediately institutionalized, but today many are raised at home. The moderately retarded are very slow, especially in language development. Their educational program stresses self-help skills, proper behavior, and limited simple verbal communication (Telford and Sawrey, 1981). The vast majority of the moderately retarded need care throughout their lives, and special instruction in self-contained classrooms is the rule. Moderately retarded individuals are often employed in sheltered workshops (Rusalem and Malikin, 1976). The workshop environment is noncompetitive and friendly. The jobs may include sorting and packaging. For example, one workshop might require workers to take one item from three or four piles and place them in a bag, which is brought to another worker who seals it. Such labor gives workers a sense of satisfaction, a feeling of productivity, along with a few extra dollars for their enjoyment, although some parents report that their mentally retarded adolescents are bored on such jobs (Hirst, 1983). Most of the severely and pro-

This gifted fourth grader is solving a difficult problem in a special workshop setting for gifted students. Gifted children also need special educational services.

foundly retarded are found in institutions and suffer from multiple disabilities, including sensory or motor problems.

Attempts to help the mentally retarded center on educational experiences. Today the emphasis is on developing the social and personal skills necessary for success in the outside world. Because many mildly retarded individuals are capable of living productive, independent lives, this emphasis is well placed. There is also a movement toward community-based group homes, where the retarded can live in dignity and with a degree of independence. In this area, the watchword is normalization—that is, the trend is to try to integrate the individual into normal society as much as possible. The degree to which this can be accomplished depends on the severity of the retardation, the education and social training the person receives, and public acceptance of the retarded as individuals with full rights in the community.

The Gifted and Talented

Pretend you are an expectant parent who has learned that a certain treatment will ensure that your child will have an IQ of 160 safely and without any danger. Would you seek out this treatment?

I often ask my students this question, and after assuring them that safety is no problem, the stereotypes begin to unfold. "He would be a misfit," one told me. "She would be socially backward," another noted. Stereotypes about the gifted are probably as great as for any other exceptionality, and most are false.

The federal government defines a gifted child as any child who either has demonstrated or seems to have the potential for high capabilities in intellectual, creative, specific academic, or leadership areas or in the performing or visual arts (Gifted and Talented Children's Act of 1978). Thus, not only general intellectual abilities, but also aptitude, creative thinking, leadership ability, and talent, are considered in this definition (Torrance, 1980). Although creativity is difficult to define, it is usually looked at in terms of types of thinking. Guilford (1967) differentiated between two kinds of thinking—convergent and divergent. *Convergent thinking* involves arriving at an answer when given a particular set of facts and is the type of thinking measured by intelligence tests. *Divergent thinking* involves the ability to see new relationships between things that are still appropriate to the situation. It is measured in many ways, but the most common is ideational fluency—the ability to come up with a large quantity of ideas (Kogan, 1983). Intelligence and creativity are positively related, but there are many exceptions, and intelligence tests do not always identify all creative students (Goetzels and Jackson, 1962). And identification is not always easy, especially when dealing with minority group children. Some gifted minority students may not do as well on regular intelligence tests (McCallum et al., 1984). Others may have difficulty with language. Identification of the gifted handicapped is also a problem (Wolf and Stephens, 1986).

Stereotypes of the gifted sometimes prevent society from meeting the special needs of such children (Treffinger, 1982). For example, many people believe that the gifted are socially backward, have little or no common sense, and look down on people (Rickert, 1981). These stereotypes should be laid to rest. In a longitudinal study of about 1,000 children, Terman and his colleagues (Terman and Oden, 1959; Terman, 1925) found that gifted children who had an IQ of 130 or more were fast learners and interested in school. They also tended to be the oldest child in the family, well adjusted, energetic, and physically healthy. They are also more curious. In another study the gifted were found to be intuitive, perceptive, a bit rebellious, and original (MacKinnon, 1978).

acceleration An educational program in which a gifted child skips a grade or a particular unit, or in which material is presented much more quickly than it would be for an average student.

enrichment An educational program in which a gifted child is given special, challenging work that goes beyond the usual.

The gifted child usually has a positive self-concept (Maddux et al., 1982), and most have good interpersonal relationships (Austin and Draper, 1981).

True or False Children who are intellectually gifted tend to be socially backward.

Any pictures of the gifted must be drawn with care. The gifted are not a homogeneous population (Juntune, 1982), and even though most seem well adjusted, others are not. Overgeneralizations can be dangerous. For example, although most gifted children are quick learners, we should not equate being smart with being fast (Sternberg, 1982). Very intelligent people may spend more time planning how they are going to solve a problem instead of merely jumping into a solution.

Two approaches—acceleration and enrichment—are widely used to help the gifted. **Acceleration** involves skipping a grade or a particular unit and placing the child in a more challenging situation. **Enrichment** involves staying on grade level but assigning work that goes beyond the usual. In addition, children may either be kept in their normal classroom, be placed in a special room for a few hours a day, or even be placed in separate classes. In any case, gifted children require a program that is qualitatively different from the normal school environment if they are to fulfill their potential (Wolf and Stephens, 1982).

The Total Child in School

The middle years of childhood are dominated by school experiences. School-age children are expected to learn to read, write, and be proficient at math. When children succeed in school, they develop a positive sense of achievement about their work that Erik Erikson calls industry. As we have seen, the nature of the school experience depends on many factors.

However, it is wrong to emphasize school as merely a place of academic learning. It is also a place to meet friends, to learn to deal with hundreds of social situations, and to begin to develop more personal autonomy and move away from parents. Of course, the family remains the most important influence on the child, but children during the middle years of childhood are deeply affected by an ever widening variety of social experiences and it is to these experiences that we turn next.

—————————————— *Summary* ——————————————

1. The rate of growth slows during middle childhood. At about age nine, girls become heavier and remain so until about age fourteen. Obesity is a major problem for about 20 percent of all schoolchildren. These children usually do not grow out of the problem unless they receive a nutritious diet that maintains a constant weight while they grow. Children's motor skills improve and are refined with maturation and experience. Physical changes during middle childhood are gradual.

2. In almost every society, children begin their education or training at about age six. Still, some children may not be ready to learn to read or to perform school tasks successfully because of physical, cognitive, or behavioral immaturity.

3. According to Piaget, the school-age child is negotiating the stage of concrete operations. Egocentrism declines, and the child improves in the ability to solve problems that entail reversibility and in the ability to decenter, and do transformations, seriation, and classification. The crowning achievement is development of the ability to conserve. The child develops the ability to conserve number, substance, weight, and finally volume.

4. Children in the stage of concrete operations are limited by their inability to understand abstractions and hypothetical problems.

5. During middle childhood, memory abilities

increase. In addition, children begin to use verbal memory strategies, such as rehearsal and classification, spontaneously.

6. Elementary school children are expected to learn to read, write, and solve math problems. Recent studies show that reading and writing achievement in elementary school students has increased slightly in the past decade. American children spend less time learning math and do not do as well as Japanese students on math achievement tests.

7. A child's academic achievement is affected by the nature of the school and the teachers and the pupil's socioeconomic status, home environment, gender, attitudes, work habits, motivation, cognitive style, and intelligence.

8. There are many different approaches to defining intelligence. Performance on intelligence tests is related to school achievement, but other factors—such as motivation and adjustment—are important.

9. An exceptional child is one whose intellectual, physical, or emotional performance falls either much above or much below that of peers. Public Law 94-142 requires educational districts to provide an appropriate free education for every child. It also mandates nondiscriminatory testing and educational accountability through an Individualized Education Plan. Finally, it requires that children be placed in the least restrictive educational environment. Mainstreaming is the process by which disabled children are placed in regular classrooms.

10. Children who achieve much below what their intelligence and educational experiences indicate they should be achieving are considered learning disabled. The cause of this discrepancy may not be cultural differences, socioeconomic level, or sensory disability. Today, some educational techniques promise help for these children.

11. Hyperactive children are impulsive and distractible. They are treated with medication, changes in diet, and behavior modification.

12. Most mentally retarded individuals are mildly retarded, and the cause of their retardation is unknown. Many can be educated to lead productive, independent lives. The moderately retarded can be taught self-care and some skills, but only rarely can they live independent lives. The severely and profoundly retarded require institutional care.

13. Gifted children are children who have superior intellectual, creative, or academic capabilities, or manifest talent in leadership or in the performing or visual arts. The gifted are generally well adjusted.

Answers to True or False Statements

1. *False*   Correct statement: During these years the child's growth rate actually decreases.
2. *True*   Generally, ten-year-old girls both weigh more and are slightly taller than ten-year-old boys.
3. *True*   During middle childhood, boys are superior in running speed, while girls are better in tasks that require agility.
4. *False*   Correct statement: School-age children have tremendous difficulties with abstract, hypothetical problems and cannot solve them.
5. *False*   Correct statement: The research on metamemory shows that many children do not understand their own level of comprehension.

6. *False*   Correct statement: Reading achievement among elementary school students has shown modest improvement over the past decade.
7. *False*   Correct statement: Japanese children tend to score higher on tests of mathematical knowledge.
8. *True*   In general, girls do better in reading, and boys (at least in the later elementary school grades) perform better in math.
9. *True*   Intelligence is positively related to school achievement, but other factors—such as motivation and adjustment—can also influence learning.
10. *False*   Correct statement: The law requires that

the child be placed in the "least restrictive environment." This may or may not mean the regular classroom setting.

11. *False*   Correct statement: Medication may reduce the symptoms, but it does not cure the disorder.

12. *False*   Correct statement: Most intellectually gifted children are socially well adjusted.

Social and Personality Development in Middle Childhood

Are the Following Statements True or False?

Try the True-False Quiz below. See if your answers correspond to the information in this chapter. Each question is repeated after the paragraph in which the answer can be found. The True-False Answer Box at the end of the chapter lists the complete answers.

——— **1.** Friendly contacts between boys and girls increase during middle childhood.

——— **2.** Parents show less physical affection for their school-age children but spend more time with them.

——— **3.** After a divorce, the custodial parent becomes stricter while the other parent becomes more permissive.

——— **4.** Children from one-parent families have less academic ability than children from two-parent families.

——— **5.** There is little or no difference in the adjustment and cognitive functioning between children in stepfamilies and children in nuclear families.

——— **6.** Children who are popular with their peers one year tend to be popular throughout the elementary school years as well.

——— **7.** Girls have stricter ideas about sex roles than boys do.

——— **8.** Girls' friendships are more likely to be characterized by conflict than boys' friendships.

——— **9.** As children mature, they tend to share with other children more often.

———**10.** Aggressive behavior is one of the most common types of interaction between children.

———**11.** Most aggressive children grow out of this troublesome behavioral pattern.

———**12.** There is a scientifically recognized relationship between watching violence on television and aggressive behavior.

Through a Child's Eyes

Karen quickly looked around and put the wallet in her pocket. No one had noticed. The wallet had a lot of money in it and she had so many things she wanted to buy. She could return it, since she knew the man who had lost it—a wealthy business executive. Karen's parents would want her to return the wallet, but they were so busy with their own problems, and Karen was considered the "bad one" anyway. Her parents were always saying how dumb she was, and her father usually lost his patience when trying to explain something to her.

Then Karen saw her best and almost only friend, Linda, and got an idea. Linda was very poor and Karen would enjoy sharing the money with her. She could buy Linda some nice slacks and they could go to the movies. To Karen's surprise, however, Linda didn't think they should keep the wallet. "Maybe the man needs it badly and won't be able to buy food for the family," she told Karen. Karen replied that the man who lost it was rich, but Linda just said, "It isn't right to keep it." Karen valued Linda's opinion and realized that if she returned it there might be a nice reward. Yet she still couldn't decide what to do. Now that Linda knew about the wallet, Karen had to make up her mind quickly.

Looking at Middle Childhood

During the school years, the social world of children expands rapidly. They begin to attend school, and the number and importance of their friendships increase. The relationship with their parents undergoes a subtle but definite shift toward greater independence. Children also now receive feedback from many more sources and must develop a sense of their own abilities, strengths, and weaknesses. They are also considered more responsible for their own actions and develop a sense of right and wrong. They are likely to be faced with moral and ethical dilemmas concerning cheating, lying, and stealing, as well as more positive prosocial qualities, including helping and cooperating with others. Even though these changes take place slowly over a number of years, they are real and important.

Industry and Inferiority

School-age children become more project-oriented and are faced with many academic challenges. If they succeed, they gain a sense of **industry,** the sense that their work and efforts are valued. If not, they develop a sense of **inferiority,** a belief that they are incompetent and do not measure up to their peers (Erikson, 1963). During this stage, children take comparisons seriously. If parents compare their work unfavorably with that of their siblings, they may stop trying. One difficult parenting task is valuing the competencies of each child in the family, especially when one child may be superior to the others in a number of areas. Even if parents avoid direct comparisons, implicit comparisons are still present.

These comparisons can cause a special problem for minority group children. Children are aware of their racial and religious identifications before middle childhood, but now they become aware of how their group's standing compares with that of the majority. These children often learn that their group is not as valued (Spurlock and Lawrence, 1979) and develop a sense of inferiority.

The Misunderstood Latency Phase

In Freudian theory, the child has now negotiated the Oedipal situation and enters the **latency stage.** This phase is often misunderstood. A boy resolves his Oedipal problem by identifying with his father ("me and you, dad") and repressing his feelings toward his mother, and indeed

> **industry**   The positive outcome of the psychosocial crisis in the middle years of childhood, involving a feeling of self-confidence and pride concerning one's achievements.
>
> **inferiority**   The negative outcome of the psychosocial crisis in the middle years of childhood, involving the child's belief that his or her work and achievements are below par.
>
> **latency stage**   The psychosexual phase, occurring during middle childhood, in which sexuality is hidden.

all females. Girls experience less pressure to resolve their conflicts in this stage, and many do not fully do so. Sexuality in this phase is hidden or latent, and a segregation of children by gender appears. Boys play with boys, and girls play with girls.

True or False Friendly contacts between boys and girls increase during middle childhood.

Why does this segregation occur? A Freudian might explain that these children have repressed their feelings toward the opposite sex in order to resolve their Oedipal conflicts and that contact may reawaken these disturbing

Many young children become project-oriented in middle childhood.

| self-concept | The picture people have of themselves. |
| self-esteem | The value people place on various aspects of their self. |

emotions. In addition, because girls are ahead of boys developmentally, this grouping allows each sex to explore issues in sexual curiosity and fantasies at its own rate in a more comfortable and less stimulating manner (Solnit et al., 1979). Sexuality, however, is not absent in this stage, as has often been asserted, but rather hidden from view.

The Developing Self-Concept

In the opening vignette, Karen saw herself as the "bad" child in the family. Psychologists call the picture a person has of himself or herself the **self-concept.** Another term, **self-esteem** refers to the value a person may place on various aspects of his or her self (Kaplan and Stein, 1984). For instance, she may think of herself as being a good friend to Linda but as poor in other areas.

How the Self-Concept Affects Behavior

A child's self-concept colors how the child interprets certain situations, as well as his or her behaviors and attitudes. Consider Karen's problems in school. If she is faced with a difficult arithmetic problem and believes she is a poor student, she will probably give up easily. If she has a positive view of herself as a mathematician she would approach the problem with the attitude that she *can* do it. Children with a positive view of their physical self will join in and play baseball with the other children, but those who don't think they are good enough will refuse to join in. A vicious circle ensues, for children who do not practice their motor skills will not develop them to their fullest. They fall further behind their peers until they do not measure up to them at all. This causes them to refuse to play, leading to a further lack of development.

Early Development of the Self-Concept

We can trace the development of the self-concept back to infancy, when children begin to differentiate themselves from the outside world. In early childhood, the self-concept is based on external factors like physical characteristics (Burns, 1979), possessions (Damon and Hart, 1982), and such activities as playing a sport well. In middle childhood, though, especially after age eight, a shift from physical to psychological conceptions of the self takes place (Damon and Hart, 1982). Now personality characteristics take center stage. Children between seven and fourteen years old often make statements referring to personal attributes, interests, beliefs, attitudes, values, and relationships with the opposite sex. Social conceptions of belonging—such as being a member of a family—are also common. There is a decrease in statements concerning possessions and appearance (Livesley and Bromley, 1973). As the self-concept develops, there is a change from an external frame of reference to a more internal frame of reference.

Focus on Process

The self-concept evolves from a combination of the feedback a child receives from others and the child's evaluation of his or her own subjective experiences. The child receives feedback from peers, parents, and teachers. If a parent continually tells a daughter she has "no brains" and is "stupid," as Karen's father had done, she may believe it.

But children are not just passive recipients of feedback. They also evaluate their own experiences. They experience themselves as being good, bad, aggressive, calm, or honest, and they compare their experience against a standard set by society, parents, peers, and finally themselves. Even in the absence of direct feedback, they evaluate these experiences. If a child's experience is not in keeping with the youngster's sense of self, the child may reject the subjective experience. For instance, children may believe they are honest and have difficulty coming to grips with the fact that they copied from a friend during an exam—or, in Karen's case, kept the wallet when she could have returned it. The experience of dishonesty may not match their conception of themselves as honest.

In middle childhood, the situation becomes complicated. First, children receive feedback from many more sources. They encounter more children and adults, not all of whom will like them. Some of this feedback is likely to be negative, or at least conflicting. The child who has been the center of attention at home may find that this is not the case in school. Second, children's newly developing cognitive skills affect the self-concept. Children in the concrete operational stage can reason more logically, which makes it possible for them to verify the attributes of their self. Children are especially good at developing a self-theory from inductive (specific) experience. They may conclude that they are smart because they are good at reading and math (Harter, 1983), or honest because they gave something back. Children now develop the ability to take another person's point of view, as Linda did when she reasoned that the person who lost the wallet might be sad and just as in need of the money (Froming et al., 1985). They test their self-concepts by comparing themselves with others, and because they are no longer as egocentric, they develop the ability to imagine what others are thinking of them. This allows them to anticipate evaluations and to correct their behavior, or to evaluate an action and react to it emotionally with pride or disappointment. In order to understand better the nature of the events that affect a child's self-concept in middle childhood, we must look at the changes in the child's interactions with family and peers.

The Family Today

The family remains the most powerful influence on the child's development and mental health (Bower, 1979). On paper, the family may appear to be a relatively simple institution—a mother, a father, child one, child two. But many variables influence the nature and quality of family interactions—including stress, economic problems, the physical environment, and illness. In addition, the family is not a static institution. Parents may change over time, and relationships in the family are reciprocal—the child affects the parents just as the parents affect the child (Hartup, 1979). The newest model posits a control system in which people have upper and lower limits of tolerance for a particular behavior. When the upper limit is approached, the person reacts in a way that reduces the behavior. If the lower limit of a parent's tolerance is approached, perhaps because the child is not doing something he ought to, such behaviors as prompting and urging may take place (Bell and Chapman, 1986). In Karen's case, her slowness at catching on to her schoolwork caused her father to lose patience and react to her negatively, calling her "dumb." Such interactions can be quite complex (Mink and Nihira, 1986).

Parent-child relationships are also influenced by other relationships within the family structure. The family is composed of many small interpersonal systems, each affecting the other. For example, when there are marital problems, fathers tend to give their children less positive reinforcement and are more likely to interrupt them at work and complete a task for them even before their children ask for help (Brody et al., 1986). Perhaps some of the difficulties Karen experienced with her father actually come from the problems he has within the marriage. These new conceptions of family life show how difficult it is to study family interactions. Despite these difficulties, however, psychologists have learned much about the nature of family interactions during middle childhood.

The Changing Relationship Between Parent and Child

The relationship between parent and child changes in middle childhood. Parents show less physical affection for their children, are not as protective, and generally spend less time with them (Maccoby, 1980). Children are quite verbal, and parents reason with them more. Children also perceive their parents differently. During the early years of middle childhood, children strive to please parents and teachers. They derive great pleasure from reaching the goals these adults set for them and from acting in a way that meets their standards.

True or False Parents show less physical affection for their school-age children but spend more time with them.

Later in this stage, the child's peers become more important, and fitting in and being accepted in the group take center stage. Children begin to identify less with adults and more with peers. They become more argumentative, discourteous, and rebellious and complain about what they perceive as unfairness. These children now see their parents' authority as having limits. Ten-year-olds believe that decisions about who their friends are, and other decisions that affect only them, are outside parents' authority (Tisak, 1986). Parents are now seen as fallible human beings who can be, and often are, arbitrary and wrong. Children ask more questions, and parents may get tired of explaining the reasons for certain rules.

Child-Rearing Strategies Reconsidered

In Chapter 8, the studies conducted by Baumrind (1971, 1967) were discussed. Baumrind identified three different child-rearing strategies, or parenting styles. The *authoritarian* strategy involves the use of demands, power, placing strict limits on children's behavior, and no discussion of rules. *Permissive* parents make few demands on their children and are willing to discuss issues. They let their children regulate their own behavior and adopt a very tolerant attitude toward aggressiveness. *Authoritative* parents expect mature behavior, enforce firm rules, encourage independence and communication between parents and children, and recognize the rights of both parents and children. A factor that complicates any analysis of child-rearing strategies is nurturance. Parental warmth is related to positive outcomes, while coldness and hostility are related to negative outcomes.

Baumrind's (1979) original studies were based on observations of children in nursery school. She continued her studies, examining the behavior of these children when they were eight or nine years old, and found that the problems of authoritarian-raised children continued at those ages, especially for boys. Boys showed less interest in achievement and withdrew from social contact. Children who were raised permissively lacked self-confidence and were not achievement-oriented. The authoritative-raised children were again superior. The combination of firm rule enforcement, demands for more mature behavior, better communication, and warmth led to a desirable outcome.

This combination also leads to greater self-esteem. Fifth- and sixth-grade boys who have high self-esteem have parents who set and enforce high standards of competence, do not often use coercion, practice a more democratic style of decision-making in which children can question parental judgments, and use punishment that children deem fair. A warm relationship exists between these parents and children (Coopersmith, 1967). The child-rearing style in which parents use power and are not open to rational argument is associated with low self-esteem in boys. Loeb and his colleagues (1980) found that high self-esteem was associated with parents who offered suggestions but left the child some freedom of choice, rather than with a directive style in which parents told the child what to do.

Neither the unbridled use of power, then, nor the permissive style, benefits most children. Children of authoritarian parents lack social competence with peers,

The "traditional" family consisting of parents with two children is less common today than it was years ago.

do not take the initiative, lack spontaneity, and have external rather than internal moral orientations to right and wrong. Karen's parents use this style. Children from permissive families are impulsive, aggressive, and lack independence and a sense of responsibility. Children of authoritative parents are independent, take the initiative in the cognitive and social areas of life, are responsible, control their aggressive urges, have self-confidence, and have high self-esteem (Maccoby and Martin, 1983).

The Changing Family

These prescriptions seem viable in every family context, but the family of the 1980s is a far cry from what families were even thirty years ago. Today the structure of the family is more variable. The traditional family—consisting of a mother who is a homemaker, a father who works, two children, and a dog—is less common today. Many women with young children work full-time or part-time. The number of single-parent families increased more than 75 percent in the 1970s (Skolnick and Skol-

nick, 1983) and more than a million divorces take place each year (see Figure 10.1). About half of all first marriages now end in divorce, and 59 percent of these now involve children under eighteen (Glick, 1984).

By 1990, one-third of the nation's children will have parents who have been divorced (Kurdek, 1981). As many as three-quarters of all divorced people will remarry, and these children will spend an average of six years in a family headed by a single parent—usually the mother (Hetherington, 1979).

The reasons for this increase are many and varied, including the lessening of sanctions for divorce, the growing realization that it may be better for a child to grow up in a happy one-parent family than in an unhappy two-parent family, and a liberalization of the divorce laws. Whatever the reasons, the problems of the one-parent family are of great concern to psychologists.

The Experience of Divorce

Divorce is not only an event; it is an experience that affects the entire family forever. Five and ten years after a divorce, it remains the central event in childhood years and casts a "long shadow" over those years (Wallerstein, 1983, p. 233).

Divorce itself brings many changes. Not only is the child's world torn asunder, but the entire lifestyle may be disrupted. Financial problems may force the family to move to a new neighborhood, and the daily routine will be altered. Most children do not see these changes in a positive light even years after the divorce.

Immediate reactions to divorce.   Almost all children find divorce a painful experience. The early symptoms may differ, but they include anger, depression, and guilt (Hetherington, 1979). Children often show such behavioral changes as regression, sleep disturbances, and fear (Wallerstein, 1983). Parent-child relationships also change. The custodial parent, usually the mother, becomes stricter and more controlling, while the other parent becomes permissive and understanding, though less accessible. Both parents make fewer demands on children to mature, become less consistent in their discipline, and have more difficulty communicating with the children (Hetherington et al., 1978).

True or False   After a divorce, the custodial parent becomes stricter while the other parent becomes more permissive.

How quickly children recover from the initial shock depends on whether a stable environment is created after the divorce and on the social supports available to the child (Kurdek, 1981). Often these supports are unavailable. Parents are confused and must rearrange their own lives. Grandparents, aunts, and uncles are often judgmental, and their relationships with both parents and children may change. Peer relationships may suffer, as some children feel guilty about what is happening. Family friends may be forced to take sides and maintain contact with only one parent. The main social supports are weakened at a time when increased support is required.

FIGURE 10.1

Divorce in the United States, 1960–1986

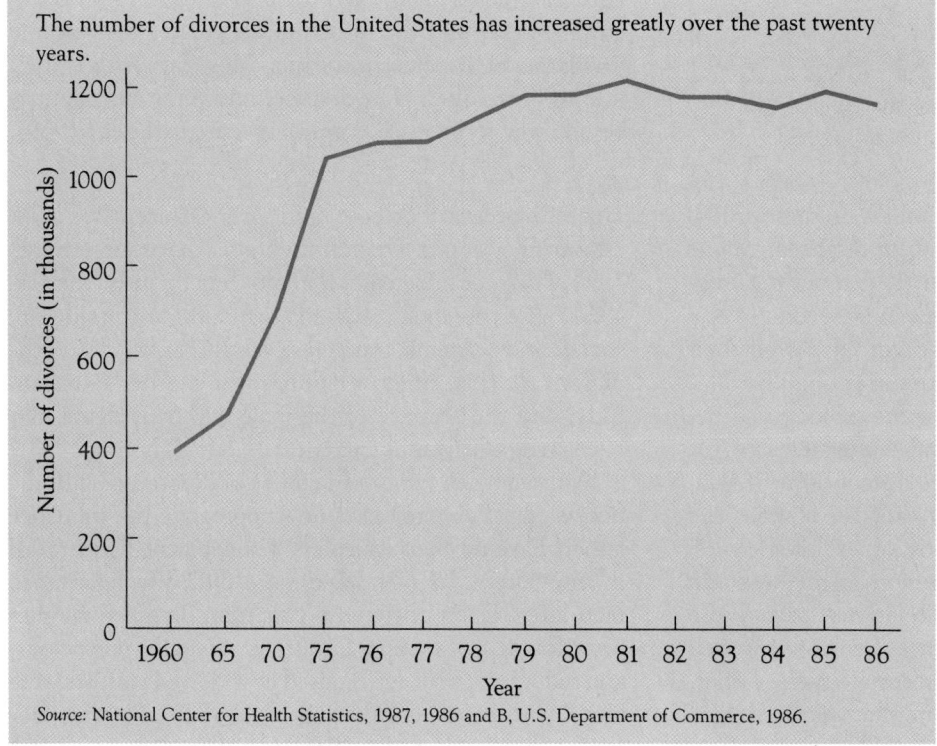

The number of divorces in the United States has increased greatly over the past twenty years.

Source: National Center for Health Statistics, 1987, 1986 and B, U.S. Department of Commerce, 1986.

There has been a dramatic increase in the number of single-parent families.

True or False   Children from one-parent families have less academic ability than children from two-parent families.

The long-term effects, though, are dependent on a number of factors. For example, if parents continue to quarrel whenever they meet after the divorce, children will suffer (Wallerstein, 1983). On the other hand, the child benefits if both parents remain concerned and active in the child's life. Adjustment problems will be less severe if financial problems and parental conflict are minimized and if social supports exist (Kurdek, 1981).

The quality of the parent-child relationship also contributes to reduction in long-term problems. Children do better when parents form and maintain a warm relationship with their children (Hess and Camara, 1979). The child's general adjustment before the divorce is still another factor (Fine et al., 1983). Unfortunately, parents' difficulties involving finances, loneliness, fear, anxiety about the future, and the loss of social supports reduce their ability to give the children what they need in order to soften the blow.

Children do best, then, when both parents are involved and there is a minimum of conflict (Abarbanel, 1979). Based on these findings, new custody arrangements, such as shared custody, are now being tried. When both parents have custody, the child is not a stranger in either house, and the father shows greater interest and involvement in the child's life. Most fathers see their role as diminished after divorce, and joint custody may be one way to increase their involvement (Greif, 1979).

Long-term effects of divorce. Many of these initial reactions either become less severe or disappear by the end of the first year (Hetherington, 1979), but the long-term effects of divorce on children can be severe. In one study of children whose parents divorced during their middle childhood years, the functioning of half had improved while about one-quarter of the subjects had become significantly worse (Kelly and Wallerstein, 1976). Children from one-parent families do not differ in academic ability or intelligence, but they are absent from school more often, are more disruptive, have lower grades, and are viewed by teachers as less motivated (Minuchin and Shapiro, 1983). Parent-child relationships may also worsen. Children in divorced families often perceive their relationships with their parents, most often the father, more negatively than children from intact families (Fine et al., 1983).

Does divorce affect boys and girls differently? One almost unanimous research finding is that long-term effects of divorce are greater for boys than for girls (Kurdek, 1981). Boys are much more likely to suffer psychological, social, and academic problems. We can only guess at the reasons for this. In most families, the mother gains custody, and the absence of the male authority figure may have an especially injurious effect on boys (Huston, 1983).

Although the long-term effects of divorce on girls are not as great, psychologists now appreciate the influence fathers have on their daughters' development. Girls raised in one-parent families have more difficulty relating to men later on. In one study, girls from divorced families were found to be more flirtatious, sexually precocious, and seductive, while girls raised in widowed families were more withdrawn (Hetherington, 1972). Paternal absence, then, affects daughters as well as sons.

peer Any person of a similar age.

The problems may begin before the divorce. Sometimes the divorce itself is blamed for the children's problems, but family turmoil—whether it ends in divorce or not—creates problems for children (Emery, 1982). The more open and intense the hostility, the more serious the children's difficulties. Marital turmoil is also related to underachievement in school. In one interesting longitudinal study, the personalities of children from intact families were assessed. A number of these families later experienced divorce. The behavior of the boys prior to divorce was affected negatively by the stress in the family. Such problems as uncontrolled impulsiveness and aggressiveness were common. Again, the behavior of girls was found to be less affected than that of boys. The researchers conclude that some of the problems considered to be consequences of divorce may be present prior to divorce (Block et al., 1986).

Stepchildren

Most parents who divorce will remarry. In fact, five out of six men and three in four women eventually remarry, with half of all remarriages taking place within three years of the divorce (Cherlin, 1981). About one in six children under eighteen is now a stepchild, and about 35 percent of all children born in the United States in the early 1980s will spend a portion of their childhood in a stepfamily (Glick, 1984; Visher and Visher, 1979).

The experience of parents who remarry will be discussed in Chapter 15. Here we are interested in how the step-experience affects children. When positive relationships exist between stepparents and stepchildren, children are less aggressive and females especially, show higher levels of self-esteem (Clingempeel and Segal, 1986). In addition, it is commonly believed that children do not thrive in stepfamilies because the adjustments are so difficult. However, the most common finding of studies comparing stepfamilies with nuclear families on adjustment or cognitive functioning is that there is little or no difference (Clingempeel and Segal, 1986). In fact, when you compare stepfamilies and single-parent families, the presence of a stepfather reduces some of the negative effects of divorce for boys and males score higher both on measures of cognitive development and on measures

of adjustment (Oshman and Manosevitz, 1976; Santrock, 1972).

True or False There is little or no difference in the adjustment and cognitive functioning between children in stepfamilies and children in nuclear families.

There is no doubt that stepchildren are faced with many adjustments. However, research in this area shows that living in a stepfamily can be a positive experience, depending upon the quality of the relationship between parents and children.

Peer Relations in Middle Childhood

During middle childhood the influence of peers and friends grows substantially. Elementary school children form their own groups and now interact extensively with them. Friends take more of a central position, and being popular is more important.

Spending More Time with Other Children

At age two, about 10 percent of a child's social interactions involve other children, while by age eleven the percentage increases to 50 percent (Barker and Wright, 1955). Peer interactions are very different from adult-child interactions. Child-child interactions involve companionship and amusement, adult-child interactions involve protection, care, and instruction (Damon, 1983). Children turn to parents for affection and reliable aid, but they turn to their friends when they want companionship (Furman and Buhrmester, 1985). They have more power with friends as well. Children understand this difference. They see adults and older children as more helpful, but they look to age-mates for play. Their behavior reflects these perceptions. They show more submission and appeal when interacting with adults, and more social behavior and domination when interacting with peers (Edwards and Lewis, 1979).

Children learn a great deal from their peers. They learn social skills and obtain information by comparing themselves with others. Such interactions foster a sense of group belonging (Rubin, 1980). Peer interaction allows children to gain a better sense of social events (Hartup, 1979) and to learn self-control.

But a peer and a friend are not the same. Although **peer** once meant someone of equal status, the word is now used to indicate anyone of similar age (Hartup,

1983). **Friendship** connotes a positive, reciprocal relationship (Shantz, 1983). Children in the same class are peers, yet a particular child may have few, if any, friends. In fact, 5 to 10 percent of all elementary school children are named as a friend by no one in their class (Asher and Renshaw, 1981), and about 12 percent are named by only one person (Gronlund, 1959). Such a lack of popularity may have many undesirable consequences for the child.

What Makes a Child Popular?

Children who are not popular are more likely to be low achievers and dropouts (Putallaz and Gottman, 1981) and to suffer from emotional difficulties (Newman, 1982). Teachers are able to identify the children who are popular, as well as those who are having difficulty relating to other children (Vosk et al., 1982). Popularity and rejection are also fairly stable patterns across time (Bukowski and Newcomb, 1984).

> *True or False* Children who are popular with their peers one year tend to be popular throughout the elementary school years as well.

Children who are popular are physically attractive, share interests with other children, are friendly, outgoing, and enthusiastic, know how to give positive reinforcement, and have interpersonal skills (Hartup, 1970; Dion, 1973). Late in middle childhood, such traits as loyalty and empathy become important. Deviant and negative reactions to others are related to rejection (Hartup, 1983). Children who are unpopular are likely to have deficits in social skills (Asher and Renshaw, 1981). They do not interact well with other children, criticize others, and are aggressive. One way to help unpopular children is to teach them the social skills they lack. Such a program can work if it is combined with structured peer involvement. In other words, children who learn social skills need to be included in programs that allow them to show and practice their new skills (Bierman and Furman, 1984).

Friendship

Although children interact with other children from infancy, they first begin to form friendships in early childhood. Like all preschool interpersonal relationships, these friendships are fragile (Corsaro, 1981) and fleeting. When four-year-olds were asked why they like their friend, 47

friendship   A positive reciprocal interpersonal relationship.

percent mentioned common activities, 34 percent mentioned play, and 28 percent mentioned possessions (Hayes, 1978). When asked why they did not like some children, 46 percent mentioned aggressive behavior, 32 percent mentioned deviant behavior, and 28 percent mentioned violation of certain rules. Preschoolers see friends in terms of playmates, and friendship is defined by momentary interactions. The main factors in preschool friendships are physical characteristics and transitory play (Selman, 1981). The qualification for friendship is simply being physically present and willing to play (Rubin, 1980). Friendships form and disintegrate very quickly, and relationships are not based on any real intimacy.

In the early school years, a gradual change takes place. Furman and Bierman (1983) investigated the change in children's perceptions of friendship between age four and age seven. Common activities, affection, support, and being near were all found to be important, but expectations concerning affection and support increased with age, while references to physical characteristics decreased. Older children saw support, helping, sharing, and affection as more important than common activities. Children in the early grades of elementary school are likely to form friendships on the basis of sharing and helping (Bigelow, 1977). By the second grade, they are aware of the differences between friends and mere acquaintances (Furman and Bierman, 1984). They expect to receive more support from friends than acquaintances and may be surprised when they receive less support than expected from friends and more support than they expected from acquaintances (Berndt and Perry, 1986). Friendships become more stable as children progress from grade one to grade four (Berndt and Hoyle, 1985). As children mature, they begin to look at psychological compatibility (Rubin, 1980) and see friends as people with whom they can share both good times and problems. Friendships become based on deeper values, such as intimacy, trust, loyalty, and faithfulness (Berndt, 1981).

Selman's developmental model.   A useful model describing the development of friendship devised by Robert Selman (1981) is summarized in Table 10.1. Selman sees

How Children Perceive Friendship: Selman's Model

Children's understanding of friendship changes as they mature and affects how they will behave towards their companions.

Stages of Reflective Understanding of Close Dyadic Friendships

Stage 0: Momentary physicalistic playmates. Conceptions of friendship relations are based on thinking which focuses upon propinquity and proximity (i.e., physicalistic parameters) to the exclusion of others. A close friend is someone who lives close by and with whom the self happens to be playing with at the moment. Friendship is more accurately playmateship. Issues such as jealousy or the intrusion of a third party into a play situation are constructed by the child at Stage 0 as specific fights over specific toys or space rather than as conflicts which involve personal feelings or interpersonal affection.

Stage 1: One-way assistance. Friendship conceptions are one-way in the sense that a friend is seen as important because he or she performs specific activities that the self wants accomplished. In other words, one person's attitude is unreflectively set up as a standard, and the "friend's" actions must match the standard thus formulated. A close friend is someone with more than Stage 0 demographic credentials; a close friend is someone who is known better than other persons. "Knowing" means accurate knowledge of other's likes and dislikes.

Stage 2: Fair-weather cooperation. The advance of Stage 2 friendships over the previous stages is based on the new awareness of interpersonal perspectives as reciprocal. The two-way nature of friendships is exemplified by concerns for coordinating and approximating, through adjustment by both self and other, the specific likes and dislikes of self and other, rather than matching one person's actions to the other's fixed standard of expectation. The limitation of this stage is the discontinuity of these reciprocal expectations. Friendship at Stage 2 is fair-weather—specific arguments are seen as severing the relationship, although both parties may still have affection for one another inside. The coordination of attitudes at the moment defines the relation. No underlying continuity is seen to exist that can maintain the relation during the period of conflict or adjustment.

Stage 3: Intimate and mutually shared relationships. At Stage 3 there is the awareness of both a continuity of relation and affective bonding between close friends. The importance of friendship does not rest only upon the fact that the self is bored or lonely; at Stage 3, friendships are seen as a basic means of developing mutual intimacy and mutual support; friends share personal problems. The occurrence of conflicts between friends does not mean the suspension of the relationship, because the underlying continuity between partners is seen as a means of transcending foul-weather incidents. The limitations of Stage 3 conceptions derive from the overemphasis of the two-person clique and the possessiveness that arises out of the realization that close relations are difficult to form and to maintain.

Stage 4: Autonomous interdependent friendships. The interdependence that characterizes Stage 4 is the sense that a friendship can continue to grow and be transformed through each partner's ability to synthesize feelings of independence and dependence. Independence means that each person accepts the other's need to establish relations with others and to grow through such experiences. Dependence reflects the awareness that friends must rely on each other for psychological support, to draw strength from each other, and to gain a sense of self-identification through identification with the other as a significant person whose relation to the self is distinct from those with whom one has less meaningful relations.

Source: Asher and Gottesman, 1981.

children as developing their conceptions of friendships in stages. In stage 0, friendship is based on proximity. Stage 1 (called one-way assistance) involves a rather selfish view in which friends are seen as important if they satisfy the child's own needs—our friend knows what we like and what we don't like. When children enter stage two—fair-weather cooperation—they see friendship as a two-way street. However, these reciprocal relationships are tenuous, and simple arguments often wreck the friendship. In stage 3—intimate and mutually shared relationships—some understanding of continuity, affection, mutual support, and the sharing of personal problems exists. On the negative side, possessiveness is apparent in this type of close relationship. Finally, stage 4—autonomous interdependent friendships—involves both independence and dependence, accepting each other's needs to have separate friendships outside the relationship.

As children develop, their definition of friendship changes from one involving concrete behaviors to more abstract terms. It changes from the self-centered orientation of perceiving friends as satisfying one's own needs to perceiving friendship as mutually satisfying, and from an emphasis on the momentary or transient positive interactions between individuals to a relationship that endures over time and conflict. In order for these changes to occur, advances in cognitive functioning are necessary. Children cannot develop mutuality unless they can take a friend's point of view into consideration, an ability that develops in middle childhood.

Why Boys Stay with Boys, and Girls Stay with Girls

Same-sex friendships are the rule during middle childhood. Boys and girls do speak to each other, but their relationships lack intimacy and involvement. Active rejection of the opposite sex is rare; avoidance is the usual course of action (Hartup, 1983). Whatever cross-sex friendships do develop are less stable than same-sex relationships (Tuma and Hallinan, 1979). This segregation reaches its peak during the late elementary school or early junior high school years (Schofield, 1981). Of course, individual differences do exist, and some fast-developing seventh-graders may be ready to develop cross-sex friendships.

Why do boys stay with boys, and girls with girls, during this period? Freud explained it in terms of the resolution of the Oedipal situation, as mentioned earlier in this chapter. Other interpretations for gender segregation have been advanced. These include lack of compatibility in play, encouragement from parents to form friendships with children of the same sex, and the formation of sex-role stereotypes (Hartup, 1983). Boys simply do not expect girls to want to join in their games (Schofield, 1981). They perceive girls as having different interests and participating in different activities. They may also be aware of the relationships between the genders that await them in adolescence—including dating, romance, and sex. Peer pressure may also be a factor. A sixth-grade boy interested in forming a relationship with a girl may find himself under peer pressure not to do so. The young girl may also be the butt of rumors and jokes and find it easier to avoid a boy than risk her friends' criticism. Whatever the reasons, the growth of same-sex friendships during this period helps the child develop the ideals of friendship and intimacy that prove so important when

the child begins to form cross-sex relationships in adolescence.

Sex Stereotypes: Alive and Well in the 1980s

A few years ago there was a commercial in which a mother stated her approval of her daughter's attempt to emulate her older brother. The picture showed the girl in pigtails sliding safely into third base. Because the purpose of a commercial is to sell a product, this must mean that being a tomboy—having what we might call male-stereotyped interests—is acceptable for elementary school children. The opposite would probably never be shown. Can you imagine a commercial showing a boy playing with dolls with a girl and mother saying, "When my little boy wants to keep up with his sister, I let him"? Girls are allowed to take on some of the characteristics usually assigned to males during the elementary school years, but boys are not encouraged to take on the stereotyped competencies of females.

It is acceptable for girls to take on some of the "stereotyped competencies" of males. Do you think boys are as free to adopt such "females stereotyped competencies" as being gentle or playing with dolls?

Young elementary school children know what activities are associated with males and females and are rather inflexible in their assignment of "sex appropriate" activities (Williams and Stith, 1980). They have acquired their initial sex stereotypes. As children mature, they become somewhat less rigid in their stereotypes (Huston, 1983). After about age seven, children no longer accept such stereotypes as absolute and are willing to make exceptions (Carter and Patterson, 1982). This tendency should not be overemphasized, for children have limits to what they will accept, and the resistance of boys to change is likely to be greater than that of girls. Whereas boys show an increased preference for male-stereotyped activities, girls do not show the same growing preference for stereotyped female activities (Carter and Patterson, 1982). Boys have much stricter ideas about sex-role preferences than girls do (Nadelman, 1974), and boys value their own stereotyped competencies greatly.

True or False   Girls have stricter ideas about sex roles than boys do.

Parents continue to treat their sons and daughters differently. Parents allow sons more freedom than daughters (Newson and Newson, 1976). Differential treatment is also found in schools. Although elementary school teachers interact more with boys than with girls, much of this interaction is critical. Teachers are more likely to reprimand boys (Serbin et al., 1973). Boys are more likely to be seen as causing trouble, and girls do not receive as much harsh discipline in school as boys. Role models in schools are quite stereotyped. Teachers are likely to be female, reinforcing the male view that school is a female-oriented experience (Busch-Rossnagel and Vance, 1982).

The Development of Morality in Middle Childhood

Whether children are male or female, though, we are interested in their moral development—their sense of right and wrong. The second Karen picked up the wallet, she was faced with a moral question. Moral questions arise anytime a person is in a position to do something that helps or injures someone else (Carroll and Rest, 1982). Three distinct approaches to the study of morality have been advanced. The first studies the child's **moral reasoning**—ideas about justice and about right and wrong—and is typified by the theories of Jean Piaget and

moral reasoning   An approach to the study of moral development, stressing the importance of the child's ideas and reasoning about justice and right and wrong.

moral realism   The Piagetian stage of moral reasoning, during which rules are viewed as sacred and justice is whatever the authority figure says.

moral relativism   The Piagetian stage of moral reasoning, in which children weigh the intentions of others before judging their actions right or wrong.

Lawrence Kohlberg. The second is the psychoanalytic viewpoint, which stresses the development of a child's conscience. The third is in the diverse social-learning and behavioral tradition, which emphasizes how such behaviors as honesty and altruism are learned. Each approach looks at moral development in a different way and taps different elements of morality.

Piaget's Theory of Morality

Piaget looked at morality in terms of how a child develops a sense of justice and a respect for the social order. He argued that children's understanding of rules follows a general sequence. Preschoolers and children in the early school years consider rules sacred and untouchable and created by an all-powerful authority figure. In this stage, called **moral realism,** rules are viewed as inflexible, and justice is whatever the authority or law commands. At about age seven or eight the intermediate stage is reached. Children now interact with peers and develop some type of reciprocal give-and-take understanding. What is fair is more important than the position of authority. Punishments may or may not be fair, depending on the crime committed. In the stage called **moral relativism,** emerging at about age eleven or twelve, children take extenuating circumstances into account and weigh them in their moral judgments. Children become more flexible, and rules are changeable. In the same way, children in the stage of moral realism do not take intent into account when assessing moral questions. For instance, ask a young child, "Who was 'naughtier'—the child who broke one dish trying to sneak into the refrigerator to get some jam, or another child who broke five dishes trying to help her mother?" Children in the stage of moral realism claim that the second child was naughtier, but children in the stage of moral relativism argue that the first child committed the worst act. Children younger than seven years old, then, rely primarily on consequences when evaluating another person's actions. Children older than age ten or so rely on intentions. Between about age seven and age ten, children rely on either one of these (Ferguson and Rule, 1982).

Piaget's ideas in this area have been criticized. First, making judgments about who is naughtier is a very special type of moral judgment. Piaget does not deal with questions about what a child *should* do (Rest, 1983). Second, a number of studies have varied such factors as the amount of damage and the degree of intentionality and found that under certain circumstances even small children understand that deliberate damage is naughtier. Piaget's findings are valuable, even though the area of moral development he covers is narrow. The most complete theory of moral reasoning was developed by Lawrence Kohlberg.

Kohlberg's Theory of Moral Reasoning

Heinz's wife has cancer. There is a drug that might cure her, but the only dose is owned by a pharmacist who wants a great deal of money for it. Heinz doesn't have the money. Should he steal the drug? Lawrence Kohlberg (1976, 1969) presented dilemmas like this to many subjects, and after careful study he proposed a model that describes the development of moral reasoning. Kohlberg sees moral reasoning as developing in a three-level, six-stage sequence, which is summarized in Table 10.2. These stages are sequential and universal—that is, they are applicable to every culture, and no stage is ever skipped. Each stage requires more sophisticated skills than the one that preceded it.

How would you have answered the dilemma of Heinz described above? Most students state immediately that Heinz should steal the medication. But Kohlberg is not interested in the answer itself. It is the reasoning behind the choice that is of interest and that determines what stage of moral reasoning a person is in. Karen's dilemma is perhaps more personally relevant, but any moral question—for example, cheating on a test—could be analyzed the same way. As Kohlberg's three levels and six stages are reviewed below, keep in mind that it is the moral reasoning, not the answer itself, that determines one's stage of moral development.

preconventional level Kohlberg's first level of moral reasoning, in which satisfaction of one's own needs, and rewards and punishment, serve as the bases for moral decision-making.

conventional level Kohlberg's second level of moral reasoning, in which conformity to the expectations of others and society in general serves as the basis for moral decision-making.

Level one: Preconventional level. At the **preconventional level,** people make decisions on the basis of reward and punishment and the satisfaction of their own needs. If Karen reasoned at this level, she might keep the wallet because it satisfies her immediate desires. On the other hand, she might not, because she is afraid of getting caught and being punished. Morality is defined strictly by the physical consequences of the act.

Stage 1: Punishment and obedience orientation. An individual in Stage 1 avoids breaking rules because it might lead to punishment. This person shows complete deference to rules. The interests of others are not considered.

Stage 2: Instrumental-relativist orientation. In Stage 2, the right actions are those that satisfy one's own needs and only sometimes the needs of others. However, the only reason for helping others is that they will then owe you something, to be collected at a later time. There is a sense of fairness in this stage, and a deal is acceptable.

Level two: Conventional morality. At the **conventional level,** conformity is the most important factor. The individual conforms to the expectations of others, including the general social order. Karen might keep the wallet if she reasons that anyone would keep it—and it's just too bad for the owner. On the other hand, she might not keep it if she reasons that it is against the rules and she would not be doing the "right" thing or being a good girl.

Stage 3: Interpersonal concordance, or "good-boy/ nice-girl" orientation. Living up to the expectations of others and being good are the important considerations for a person in Stage 3. The emphasis is on gaining approval from others by being nice.

Stage 4: "Law-and-order" orientation. A person in Stage 4 is oriented toward authority and maintaining the social order. The emphasis is on doing one's duty and showing respect for authority. Sometimes people in this stage reason, "If everyone did it, then . . ."

Level three: Postconventional morality. People in the **postconventional level** have evolved moral values that have been internalized. These values are individualized and do not depend on membership in any particular group. Usually such moral reasoning does not occur until

---

T A B L E 10.2

Kohlberg's Stages of Moral Reasoning

Lawrence Kohlberg views the development of morality in terms of moral reasoning. The stage of moral reasoning at which people can be placed depends upon the reasoning behind their decisions, not the decisions themselves.

I. Preconventional Level

The child is responsive to cultural rules and labels of good and bad, right or wrong, but interprets these either in terms of the physical or hedonistic consequences of action (punishment, reward, exchange of favors) or in terms of the physical power of those who enunciate the rules. The level is divided into two stages:

Stage 1: Punishment and obedience orientation. The physical consequences of action determine its goodness or badness regardless of the meaning or value of these consequences. Avoidance of punishment and unquestioning deference to power are valued in their own right, not in terms of respect for an underlying moral order (the latter being Stage 4).

Stage 2: Instrumental relativist orientation. Right action is that which instrumentally satisfies one's own needs and occasionally the needs of others. Human relations are viewed in terms of the marketplace. Fairness, reciprocity, and equal sharing are present, but are always interpreted in a physical, pragmatic way. Reciprocity is a matter of "you scratch my back and I'll scratch yours," not of loyalty, gratitude, or justice.

II. Conventional Level

Maintaining the expectations of the individual's family, group, or nation is perceived as valuable in its own right, regardless of consequences. The attitude is not only one of *conformity* to personal expectations and social order but also of loyalty to it, of actively *maintaining,* supporting, and justifying it, of identifying with the persons or group involved in it. This level has two stages:

Stage 3: Interpersonal concordance or "good boy/nice girl" orientation. Good behavior is that which pleases or helps others and is approved by them. There is much conformity to stereotypical images of what is majority or "natural" behavior. Behavior is frequently judged by intention—"he means well" becomes important for the first time. One earns approval by being "nice."

Stage 4: "Law and order" orientation. Orientation is toward authority, fixed rules, and the maintenance of the social order. Right behavior consists of doing one's duty, showing respect for authority, maintaining the social order for its own sake.

III. Postconventional, Autonomous, or Principled Level

The person makes a clear effort to define moral values and principles that have validity and application apart from the authority of the groups or persons holding these principles, and apart from the individual's own identification with these groups. This level has two stages:

Stage 5: Social-contract, legalistic orientation. Generally with utilitarian overtones. Right action is defined in terms of general individual rights and standards that have been critically examined and agreed upon by society. The person is clearly aware of the relativism of values and opinions and so emphasizes procedural rules for reaching consensus. Aside from what is constitutionally and democratically agreed upon, right is a matter of personal "values" and "opinion"; emphasis is thus on the "legal point of view," but with the possibility of changing law in terms of rational considerations of social utility rather than freezing in terms of Stage 4. Outside the legal realm, free agreement and contract is the binding element. This is the "official" morality of the American government and Constitution.

Stage 6: Universal ethical principle orientation. Right is defined by the decision of conscience in accord with self-chosen *ethical principles* appealing to logical comprehensiveness, universality, and consistency. These principles are abstract and ethical (the Golden Rule, the categorical imperative); they are not concrete moral rules like the Ten Commandments. At heart, these are universal principles of *justice of the reciprocity and equality of human rights* and of respect for the dignity of human beings as individual persons.

Source: Jensen, 1985.

adolescence, at the earliest, so we would not expect Karen to show such reasoning. However, if this dilemma occurred at a later age, she might return the wallet because she herself values honesty and integrity, even if it means she has to do without something. In Karen's case, the reasoning for keeping the wallet is admittedly strained. However, she might reason that the wealthy person who lost it does not need the money as much as she and Linda need it, and that even if she were caught she would be helping another human being in need—her friend. Karen's values of friendship, loyalty, and giving to others would become most important here.

Stage 5: Social contract, legalistic orientation.
In Stage 5, correct behavior is defined in terms of individual rights and the consensus of society. Right is a matter of personal values and opinions, but the emphasis is on the legal point of view.

Stage 6: Universal ethical principle orientation.
In this highest stage, Stage 6, the correct behavior is defined as a decision of conscience in accordance with self-chosen ethical principles that are logical, universal, and consistent. These are very abstract guidelines (Kohlberg and Kramer, 1969).

People rarely reason solely in one stage. More often, they are predominantly in one stage but also partly in the stages before and after. A person may be 40 percent in Stage 3, 30 percent in Stage 2, and 30 percent in Stage 4. Change involves a gradual shift in the percentage of reasoning from one stage to the next, rather than a wholesale switch from one stage to the next higher stage (Carroll and Rest, 1982).

Kohlberg's theory has been applied successfully to many cultures (Snarey et al., 1985). In one study, Nisan and Kohlberg (1982) studied rural and city subjects ages ten through twenty-eight in Turkey and found evidence for the universality of the stage sequence. City subjects were well ahead of the villagers in development. People's experiences influence their level of moral reasoning. Perhaps the constant interpersonal contacts and possibility for experiencing more sophisticated moral dilemmas lead to higher moral reasoning in urban-dwellers.

There is also evidence that the stages are indeed sequential (Walker, 1982; Kohlberg et al., 1978). People do not skip stages, although they enter and leave them at varying times. Sequential development in non-West-

postconventional level Kohlberg's third level of moral reasoning, in which moral decisions are made on the basis of individual values that have been internalized.

ern cultures has been shown at least through Stage 4 (Carroll and Rest, 1982). Cross-cultural studies have not been clear, though, in finding level-three (postconventional) moral reasoning in all non-Western cultures.

Moral reasoning and gender. If you look at the descriptions of Kohlberg's stages, it is clear that the emphasis in the higher stages of moral reasoning is on justice and on individual rights and the rights of others. Higher moral reasoning seems to have little to do with interpersonal relationships. According to Gilligan (1982, 1977), women have a different orientation to moral questions. They see moral questions more in terms of how these issues affect interpersonal relationships, rather than in strictly individualistic terms.

Females learn this different orientation toward moral issues. For example, boys learn to be independent, assertive, achievement-oriented, and individualistic and to attach great importance to the rule of law. This is similar to the Stage 4 perspective. On the other hand, women are raised to be more concerned with the rights and needs of others and to be interested in interpersonal relationships. They tend to see moral difficulties as conflicts between what they themselves want and the needs and wants of others, and they may base their decisions on how relationships with others will be affected. Harmony, rather than justice, may be the guiding principle. Sensitivity to the needs of others, instead of strict individual rights, becomes the criterion to apply in such dilemmas. This seems more like the Stage 3 perspective. However, Gilligan notes that neither reasoning is superior—they are just different, and these differences should be understood and respected.

Kohlberg's theory fails to take these differences into account. Karen may look at how her actions might affect her relationships with others, rather than simply looking at some abstract rules of justice. Some interesting evidence in favor of this point of view comes from studies showing that five- and seven-year-old boys and girls settle their disputes differently. Boys are more likely to use threats and physical force and to pursue their own goals, while girls try to reduce conflict and their goal is to improve harmony (Miller et al., 1986). Boys also experience more conflict with peers than girls do.

True or False Girls' friendships are more likely to be characterized by conflict than boys' friendships.

Gilligan's ideas have become popular, but they are not completely accepted. For instance, Walker (1984) reviewed the literature in the field and failed to find evidence of consistent sex differences in moral development. But others have criticized Walker's research (see Baumrind, 1986), while Walker (1986) has steadfastly defended it. So the argument continues with no end in sight. All we can say at the present time is that sex differences in moral reasoning may exist and that we should be careful in stating that a particular type of reasoning is higher or lower—it may simply be different.

Kohlberg's theory stresses the importance of the reasoning behind an act—why this boy sneaked these cookies—rather than the act of "stealing" itself.

Is moral reasoning related to moral behavior? Would a person reasoning at a Stage 5 level act differently from a person reasoning at a Stage 1 level? As the individual progresses toward Stage 6, we would think that moral behavior such as honesty and resisting temptation, would increase. Indeed, most studies do find a relationship between moral reasoning and moral action (Blasi, 1980; Kohlberg, 1987), but the strength of the relationship varies from area to area. Some support is found for the idea that people at higher moral stages are more honest, but there is little support for the idea that people at the postconventional level resist social pressure to conform in their actual moral actions. Only relatively weak associations are found between progressing to higher levels of moral reasoning and whether a child will cheat, yield to temptation, or behave altruistically if there is a personal cost attached to it (Maccoby, 1980). In one study, college students were found to cheat less as their level of their moral reasoning increased. However, although subjects low in moral judgment cheated more, those high in moral judgment also cheated when the temptation became strong (Malinowski and Smith, 1985). Therefore, although a relationship between moral reasoning and moral behavior exists, other factors help determine whether a person will perform a particular act.

Evaluating Kohlberg's theory. Although Kohlberg's theory gives us a valuable framework for understanding moral development, it has been criticized. One problem is the discrepancy between reasoning and action. For whatever reason, people sometimes proceed in ways they think are theoretically best, and sometimes they do not (Chandler and Boyes, 1982). In addition, it is possible to reason at any level and still find a reason to cheat, lie, or steal. More predictability is needed. Perhaps the greatest problem with Kohlberg's theory is that moral reasoning may be only a part of the overall process people use to convert environmental information into an action sequence. According to Rest (1983), there are four stages to this sequence. First, a person must be sensitive enough to notice and evaluate a situation in terms of moral questions. Then the person attempts to reason the problem out. (This is where Kohlberg's moral-reasoning theory fits in.) In the third stage, environmental influences are taken into consideration. How much will the decision personally cost the person? How important is getting a good grade when cheating may be easy? Finally, there may be practical difficulties in implementing the plan of action. You may want to help someone who has just suffered a heart attack but not know how to do cardiopulmonary resuscitation.

Can We Teach Moral Values?

How can we encourage moral values in children? We can preach to them and demand that they parrot our speeches, but because the sentiments will not be internalized, this is ineffective. Kohlberg's theory leads to another approach—challenging children by bringing up various moral dilemmas and encouraging them to discuss the cases from a variety of viewpoints. The idea is that the children will be challenged by the reasoning of the other children, impelling them toward higher stages of reasoning. The teacher's job is to present the moral dilemmas, to facilitate the discussions and role-playing, and to see that each side is fairly presented. Evaluations of such programs, often called **values clarification courses,** are mixed. Some show moderate success (Blatt and Kohlberg, 1975). However, it is difficult to raise the average level of moral judgment of any group, and thus a number of studies show no changes (Rest, 1983). When change does occur, it is relatively slight but always in the upward direction. A reasonably long term is required to produce any changes—usually at least three months.

It may be necessary to change the school experience itself if we want to improve moral reasoning (Kohlberg and Lickona, 1987). The school climate and child's experiences in society exert a stronger influence than any classroom learning. It is impossible to divorce the moral context of the home and the school from the development of morality. If the school environment fosters undemocratic values, it will affect the child. This is, in part, the thinking behind the "just community" programs that attempt to impart a different attitude in the classroom and the school. Teachers are encouraged to be more open and democratic, to discuss moral issues with students, to hold class meetings, and to encourage an atmosphere that facilitates individual responsibility and moral development. The change in atmosphere is successful, especially in small schools that stress participation in school affairs, but more research is needed before this method can be applied successfully in larger schools.

The Psychoanalytic Conception of Morality

When children are considering an action, do they hear a "small, critical voice" exhorting them to improve their

values clarification courses   Approaches to improving moral decision-making skills based on presenting students with problems and helping them to perceive issues from many different viewpoints and to consider many different solutions.

superego   In Freudian theory, the part of the mind that includes a set of principles, violation of which leads to feelings of guilt.

ego ideal   The individual's positive and desirable standards of behavior.

conscience   Part of the superego which causes the individual to experience guilt when transgressing.

behavior? Do they experience guilt if they do something forbidden? Psychologists who follow Freud believe so. They view morality as involving the development of the **superego.** Children between the ages of about four to six resolve their sexual fantasies toward their parents—called the Oedipal situation—by identifying with the parent of the same sex. The superego arises out of this identification. The superego consists of two parts: the **ego ideal** and the **conscience.** The ego ideal consists of the individual's standards of perfect conduct, which are formed when the child identifies and internalizes the ideals and values of the adults around him. The second part of the superego is the child's conscience, which causes the child to experience guilt when misbehaving (Eidelberg, 1968; Freud, 1933). Before the superego is formed, all resistance to temptation exists outside the individual (Solnit et al., 1979). The child is afraid that he or she will lose the parents' love or that they will punish the child. After the formation of the superego, the regulation is internalized. Even if the parents are not present, the child acts in ways that would make the parents proud and experiences guilt when acting badly.

Research on the psychoanalytic conception of morality is mixed. Children do identify with older people, including their parents (Kline, 1972), but their moral values are hardly carbon copies of their parents' values. Although some similarity exists, the idea that children totally copy their parents is unacceptable (Damon, 1983).

The Learning-Theory Approach to Morality: Study the Behavior Itself

Some psychologists approach moral development by studying the behavior itself—including sharing, helping, and giving, as well as lying, stealing, and being aggressive—instead of looking at the moral reasoning of the individual. They explain moral behavior in terms of the situation, the child's background, the models available to the child, and the reinforcements that are present in the environment.

Learning theorists argue that moral behavior is learned like any other behavior. Operant conditioning explains some of it. Children who are reinforced for giving and sharing are more likely to give and share. Social-learning theorists add imitation to the picture. Much of behavior is influenced by watching how others—both adults and peers—deal with life's challenges (Bandura, 1986). If we observe people we respect helping others or giving to charity, we are more likely to do so ourselves. Of course, this may not always be the case. We do not imitate everything we see. Such factors as the character of the model, the consequences of the behavior, and our own characteristics affect imitation (Bandura, 1977). Cognitive factors, such as how we perceive the situation and process the information, are important. For instance, aggressive children are more likely to believe that aggression will get them what they want and find it easier to be aggressive than nonaggressive children (Perry et al., 1986). Another factor is competence to deal with a particular situation (Mussen and Eisenberg-Berg, 1977). If you feel you are competent, you may act one way; if you are bewildered, you may act in a totally different manner.

Prosocial and Antisocial Behavior in Middle Childhood

It is tempting to divide the world into those who are honest and helpful and those who are not, those who give and share and those who are selfish. In our everyday conversations, we are likely to do this—for example, labeling one child as honest, another as selfish. This trait-like approach has not worked well. In their landmark studies, Hartshorne and May (1928) tested thousands of children on a number of different tasks. They concluded that children's behavior varied with the situation. A child could be honest in one situation and not in another. One who cheated on an athletics test might or might not cheat on an arithmetic test (Cairns, 1979). This situational view of honesty prevailed for some time, but further research using statistical techniques not available to Hartshorne and May discovered a carryover of honesty from one situation to the next, although it was not very strong (Burton, 1963). It seems

that although some people are more honest than others, we cannot say that a person will be honest in every situation.

Prosocial Behavior

A number of factors influence prosocial behavior (see Yarrow et al., 1983). For example, one's culture is important. We pride ourselves on being a prosocial society, and indeed Americans donate a good deal of money to charity. Yet American children are not as willing to share or to give as children in other societies. In one study, children from six different cultures—India, Kenya, Okinawa, Mexico, the Philippine Islands, and the United States—were observed (Whiting and Whiting, 1975). Every one of the Kenyans and 73 percent of the Mexican children showed prosocial behavior in amounts that exceeded the median of all children in the study, while only 8 percent of the American children exceeded this median. Differences were found among the three societies that showed the most prosocial behavior—Kenya, Mexico, and the Philippines—and the other three. Such behaviors were encouraged in cultures where children lived in extended families and had greater responsibilities, and where the social structure was simpler.

Certain child-rearing practices also lead to internalization of values and prosocial behavior. Parents who use reasoning techniques combined with affection outside the discipline situation raise children who practice prosocial behavior (Hoffman, 1979). This is especially true if parents make the effort to point out to children the effect of this behavior on the other person. Parents also serve as models for their children. If children observe their parents helping and sharing, they are more likely to do the same.

Other factors enter into the equation. Older children are more likely to show altruism than younger children (Peterson, 1983), probably because they are able to understand what other children are feeling. In addition, children are more likely to show prosocial behavior when happy than when sad (Mussen and Eisenberg-Berg, 1977). Finally, the situation is important. A child will be more likely to help another if the personal cost is low than if it is high. Asking a five-year-old to share green beans is likely to be greeted with joy, but ask the same child to share a piece of cake and you get a different reaction. The reinforcement properties of the situation are factors too. Children will help and share more if they are rewarded for that behavior.

Soviet and American Children's Conceptions of Nuclear War

Nuclear war is unthinkable, but it is clear that people of all ages are thinking about it. In 1977 about 1,000 American elementary and high school students polled believed that nuclear war was possible, and many believed their city or country would be obliterated. Many admitted that the threat of nuclear war affected their future plans for marriage and children. During interviews, these children showed uncertainty, anxiety, hopelessness, sadness, cynicism, and bitterness. Concern about nuclear war seems to be increasing. About ten years ago, around 7 percent of 19,000 seventeen- to eighteen-year-olds polled said they worried frequently about nuclear war. In 1982 that percentage had jumped to 31 percent. Studies from all around the Western world show this concern among children for their future. Although older children articulate their concerns better, younger children also show awareness of this threat.

But how do Soviet children feel about nuclear war, and how do their attitudes compare with those of American children? In the summer of 1983, Dr. Eric Chivian and three associates traveled to the Soviet Union to conduct research on just this subject. They visited two children's summer camps, one near Moscow and the other near the Black Sea. The children were all between the ages of ten and fifteen, and the researchers took pains to be certain the children were not primed for the occasion. The interviewees were selected by the children's governing council and were often council members themselves, but the American interviewers chose other subjects as well and were allowed to interview anyone they wanted. Some 293 children completed questionnaires, and 50 Soviet children were interviewed. A similar questionnaire had been given to 900 American students in 1983. The questions concerned many aspects of their knowledge about nuclear war, including how old they were when they learned about the problem, their sources of information, their understanding of the consequences of nuclear war, and their beliefs about the possibility of war in their lifetime and whether they would survive it. The investigators compared the Soviet children's responses with the responses of the sample of children from Los Angeles and San Jose, California.

Some of the findings are found in Table A. Notice that the Soviet children were more hopeful that war would not occur during their lifetime. Over half believed that a nuclear war would either "definitely not" or "probably not" occur, while only about 17 percent of the American children answered that way. The Soviet children were far more pessimistic about their chances of survival in a nuclear holocaust. More than 80 percent believed their families would "definitely not" or "probably not" survive a nuclear war, while about 41 percent of the American children answered in this manner. About 37 percent of the American children thought the United States would not survive a nuclear war, while about 75 percent of the Soviet children believed their nation would not survive. In addition, more Soviet than American youngsters believed nuclear war was preventable. About 92 percent of the Soviet children, compared with about 65 percent of the American children, believed nuclear war could be prevented.

So the Soviet children were more hopeful that nuclear war can be averted and more likely to believe that no one would survive such a conflict. The researchers found that the Soviet children learned about nuclear war a bit

---

True or False   As children mature, they tend to share with other children more often.

Helping to Develop Prosocial Behavior

Prosocial behavior can be encouraged. Rational methods of discipline and pointing out how a child's prosocial behavior helps others encourages such behavior. Because models are important, demonstrating prosocial behaviors and rewarding their behavior through nodding, affection, and the like may be helpful. In some areas of prosocial behavior, such as aiding others in distress, a feeling of competence is helpful. In addition, as children mature

TABLE A

Responses of American and Soviet Samples to Questions* on Prospects for Nuclear War
(in Percents)

Response	Question A		Question B		Question C		Question D	
	USA	USSR	USA	USSR	USA	USSR	USA	USSR
Definitely not	2.5	24.9	11.9	45.1	11.9	54.3	4.5	2.0
Probably not	14.4	28.3	29.4	35.5	25.9	22.5	10.0	0.7
Uncertain	44.8	33.8	40.8	16.4	39.8	15.4	19.9	4.8
Probably yes	28.9	9.2	11.4	2.4	16.9	3.1	39.3	16.7
Definitely yes	9.5	3.4	5.0	0.3	5.0	3.8	25.9	75.1

*A - Do you think that nuclear war between the USSR and the USA will occur within your lifetime?
B Do you think that you and your family could survive a nuclear war?
C Do you think the Soviet Union and the United States could survive a nuclear war? (American sample asked only about U.S. survival.)
D Do you think it is possible to prevent a nuclear war between the USSR and USA?

earlier than the American children (between the ages of six and eight), probably because units on nuclear war are taught in all Soviet elementary schools. Like the American children, the Soviet children learn about nuclear war principally through television programs and school. Soviet children are also exposed to more detailed information about nuclear weapons and the effects of these weapons on society, while the education of American children in these areas is more variable.

Therefore, Soviet children are apparently quite concerned about the prospect of nuclear war and, although they are hopeful about averting it, are realistic about its consequences. American children seem more pessimistic about averting war and more optimistic about surviving the conflict, but they are concerned too.

Dr. Chivian and his colleagues note that in 1983 a major American correspondent told the American public that Soviet children were not realistically taught about the threat or consequences of nuclear war because the Soviet authorities believed it was better for their children not to fear the possible use of nuclear weapons in "defense" of their country. This study shows that this is not true. Children in both the East and West are concerned and frightened about the specter of nuclear war, and many have a realistic view of its consequences.

Source: Chivian, E., Mack, J., Waletzky, J. P., Lazaroff, C., Doctor, R., and Goldenring, J. M. Soviet Children and the Threat of Nuclear War: A Preliminary Study. *American Journal of Orthopsychiatry,* 1985, *55,* 484–501.

they are better able to read subtle cues and react in ways that take the other person's perspective into consideration. Such taking of another's perspective can be encouraged, as long as one realizes that the younger the child the clearer and less complicated the signals must be.

Aggressive Behavior

A casual look at the newspapers may lead you to believe that aggressive behavior in childhood is common, but it is not. A study of highly aggressive boys found that only two to three aggressive actions occur per 1,000 inter-

Children learn how to solve their disputes partly by observing how their parents deal with interpersonal problems.

actions (Patterson and Cobb, 1971). The behavior is common enough, though, and almost all parents have had to deal with aggressiveness in their young children (Sears et al., 1957). Aggressive behavior in the classroom is a serious problem, and the aggressive-disruptive behavior pattern is one of the most common problems in mental health facilities (Cullinan and Epstein, 1982).

True or False   Aggressive behavior is one of the most common types of interaction between children.

The social consequences of aggressive behavior are great. Aggressive children are generally unpopular (Clarizio and McCoy, 1983) and likely to be targets of aggressive behavior themselves (Dodge and Frame, 1982; Cairns, 1979). Aggressive children are more likely to be male. Between three and six times as many boys than girls are referred to mental health agencies for aggressive behavior (Cullinan and Epstein, 1982). The sex differences are rather constant across age and culture (Maccoby and Jacklin, 1980; 1974). Some argue that hormones predispose males to be aggressive (Maccoby and Jacklin, 1980), and the evidence for the hormonal theory in animals is strong. The question is whether it holds

instrumental aggression   Aggression that involves struggles over possessions.

for human beings. Some argue that the evidence does not indicate such a link (Tieger, 1980), while others note that the research, although inconclusive, does lean toward such a conclusion (Maccoby and Jacklin, 1980). This argument will continue for many years, but both sides readily acknowledge that social factors are involved in aggressive behavior.

Some people believe that an aggressive child will grow out of the tendency to aggressive behavior, but this is just wishful thinking (Cullinan and Epstein, 1982); aggressiveness tends to be stable over long periods of time for both boys and girls (Olweus, 1982; 1979; 1977). Highly aggressive children tend to show such patterns year after year. However, the nature of the aggressiveness is likely to change. Hartup (1974) divided aggressive behavior into two categories. **Instrumental aggression** involves struggles over possessions. It is not personal, and its aim is to secure an item. **Hostile aggression** is person-oriented. This type of aggressive behavior is aimed at injuring the other party. Most preschool children use instrumental aggression when they wrench a toy from someone else or try to gain space (Hay and Ross, 1982). The general finding that aggression gradually decreases with age is probably explained by the striking decrease in instrumental aggressive behavior as the child matures. With maturity, verbal alternatives replace physical means (Parke and Slaby, 1983).

True or False Most aggressive children grow out of this troublesome behavioral pattern.

Factors Affecting Aggressive Behavior

The most important factor affecting aggressive behavior is the family situation. Consider children who watch their parents argue violently, who are hit hard and often, and who discover that they get what they want by being aggressive toward others. We could predict that these children would become aggressive, and research confirms our hypothesis (Sears et al., 1957; Parke and Slaby, 1983).

Aggressive behavior can also be learned through modeling. A child who sees authority figures being aggressive may act aggressively too. In a series of studies, children were exposed to live or filmed models acting aggressively against a Bobo doll. They were then given the opportunity to play with the doll too. Usually the children imitated whatever they saw. If exposed to aggressive actions, they acted aggressively; if shown constructive actions, they imitated those actions (Bandura, 1986; Bandura et al., 1961). Children who witness aggressive behavior in the homes or feel that such behavior is condoned are more likely to be aggressive. Some peer groups also influence aggressive behavior. Children may model themselves after an aggressive individual who gains something of value through violence. In addition, the peer group may reinforce violent deeds.

Television and Aggressive Behavior

Another influence on aggressive behavior is television. By the time a child graduates from high school, he or she has seen 13,000 violent deaths on television (Gerbner and Gross, 1980). Children spend more time watching television than engaging in any other single activity.

hostile aggression Aggression aimed at injuring another person.

More than 70 percent of prime time television contains violence (Parke and Slaby, 1983), and two-thirds of all television programming aimed at children is violent (Gerbner and Gross, 1980). Since children may learn to be aggressive by viewing violent behavior, the possible link between watching violent television programs and aggressive behavior is a crucial issue.

If every child exposed to violence on television imitated it, there would be no question that watching aggressive acts on television affects children. But this is not the case. The decision to be aggressive is not a simple one, and it is difficult to determine exactly what causes a violent action. However, there is evidence that viewing television increases the likelihood of violent action (Liebert, 1986; Parke and Slaby, 1983; Singer and Singer, 1983), and most experts agree that there is at least a positive relationship between aggressive behavior and viewing violence on television (Pearl, 1984; Rubinstein, 1980).

However, a relationship does not demonstrate cause and effect. Perhaps aggressive children simply watch more violent television. There is some truth to this. In an analysis of two very long-term studies, Eron (1982) concluded that television violence is indeed one cause of aggressive behavior. But he also found that aggressive children prefer to watch more and more violent programs, establishing a circular pattern. Eron also reasoned that aggressive children are unpopular and spend more time watching television. The violence they see reassures them that their behavior is appropriate and teaches them new ways to act aggressively. This make them even more unpopular and sends them back to the television for another dose of violence. Whatever the reasons, the link between aggressiveness and viewing violence on television is fairly well established.

True or False There is a scientifically recognized relationship between watching violence on television and aggressive behavior.

But television violence has another, more subtle effect. We get used to violence on television and come to accept it as a normal part of life (Drabman and Thomas,

1975). We become desensitized to violence and no longer take it that seriously (Thomas et al., 1977; Cline et al., 1973). We begin to think that violence is a natural and "normal" part of life and accept it as such.

Although some people seem to be more susceptible to violent suggestion than others, children of all ages, social classes, ethnic groups, and personality characteristics may be affected (Huesmann et al., 1984). Both males and females may be equally influenced, with people who are more aggressive within each sex being more affected than others. Although children at every age are susceptible, a particularly sensitive period during late middle childhood—around eight or nine years old—has been found (Eron et al., 1983). Exposure to violence peaks at about the third grade, but the correlation between aggressiveness and viewing violence increases until age ten to eleven, suggesting that there is a cumulative effect beyond this sensitive period.

Help for the Aggressive Child

There are no magic solutions to reducing aggressiveness in children. At times, a behavioral approach reinforcing prosocial behavior—such as sharing—and ignoring aggressive behavior may be successful (Clarizio and McCoy, 1983). But the second part of the prescription is often impractical, so when ignoring the behavior is impossible or undesirable, the child must know what behaviors will not be tolerated and the consequences of misbehavior.

Punitiveness and firmness are not the same, and it is best to avoid generating additional frustration and anger through physical punishment. Social isolation for aggressive behavior, and explaining the reasons for punishment, are better. For instance, in the technique called time out described in Chapter 8, children who show aggressive behavior are removed from the reinforcing circumstances for a brief period of time (Kazdin, 1984). Because aggressive behavior is learned through operant conditioning and imitation, children must be provided with rewards for prosocial behavior and receive no rewards for antisocial acts. Finally, aggressive children should be exposed to models who are constructive, competent, and rewarded for nonaggressive but assertive actions.

The Calm Before the Storm

The school-age period is often considered a time of horizontal growth. Middle childhood is often seen as the calm before the storm of change that occurs in adolescence. Unfortunately, this has led to the mistaken notion that middle childhood is a stagnant period, which is untrue. Unlike the earlier years of childhood and the coming years of adolescence—when cognitive, physical, and social growth are more obvious—changes during the middle years are more gradual. We must look harder to find them. However, as we have seen, significant changes *are* taking place. The child's social world is expanding as friends and teachers become more important and children are given more freedom and responsibility at home. Because parents will not be with them all the time, children must develop their own sense of right and wrong and decide how they will handle their interpersonal relationships.

These trends are seen in Karen's dilemma. There are no parents or even adult figures present to tell her what to do. She must reason and act on her own, and decide whether to give the wallet back or keep it. Her background, her relationship with her parents, her self-concept, and numerous other factors will influence her reasoning and final behavior.

It comes as no surprise, then, that psychologists have found that children who emerge from middle childhood with a positive self-concept, good working relationships with their parents, a healthy relationship with friends, and a good feeling about their own academic and social capabilities are ready to tackle the challenges that await them during adolescence.

--- Summary ---

1. According to Erikson, the positive outcome of middle childhood is the development of a sense of industry, while the negative outcome is a feeling of inferiority.

2. Freud noted that children resolving the Oedipal situation next enter a latency phase, when sexuality is hidden. Boys' and girls' groups are segregated.

3. During middle childhood, children get feedback from many different people. Their self-concept develops from a combination of this feedback and their own evaluation of their subjective experiences.

4. Children's relationships to their parents change during middle childhood. Children become more independent and, later in the stage, are greatly influenced by peers. They also become more argumentative and question parental judgment more often.

5. Children's immediate reaction to divorce involves anger, depression, and guilt. Normally children recover from the initial shock after a year or so, but the long-term effects of divorce can be serious if parents continue to argue, if serious financial problems exist, and if social supports are unavailable. Generally, boys are affected more adversely than girls.

6. Children's conceptions of friendship changes over time as they become more cognitively sophisticated.

7. In middle childhood, boys show an increased preference for male-stereotyped activities, while girls do not show such a preference for stereotyped female activities. Parents continue to treat sons and daughters differently.

8. Piaget and Kohlberg both advanced theories of moral reasoning. Piaget noted that young children do not take intention into consideration when judging actions and that they see rules as unchangeable. Older children are more flexible and consider intent when judging actions. Kohlberg explained the development of moral reasoning in terms of three levels, each of which contains two stages. It is the reasoning behind the moral decision, not the decision itself, that determines the level of moral reasoning.

9. Gilligan argues that males and females reason differently on moral issues. While males are oriented toward individual rights and legal issues, women are more concerned with how their decision will affect their social and interpersonal relationships.

10. Freud viewed morality in terms of the development of the superego. The child identifies with the parent of the same sex and internalizes ideals and values.

11. Behaviorists are more interested in studying moral behaviors—such as cheating and altruism—than in the reasoning behind the behavior. The environment as well as the situation itself affects moral behavior.

12. Prosocial behavior is encouraged when parents use rational methods of discipline and point out how the child's behavior helps others. The models children observe around them, as well as the reinforcements they experience or witness, are also important.

13. Instrumental aggression involves struggles over possessions; hostile aggression is more person-oriented. Instrumental aggression decreases significantly with age.

14. Children who observe a great deal of aggressive behavior at home, who are harshly disciplined, or who are taught that aggressiveness is an acceptable method of getting what they want tend to be aggressive. Aggressive behavior can also be imitated.

15. Most studies indicate that observing violent behavior on television makes it more likely that a child will act aggressively. It also desensitizes children to violence.

Answers to True or False Statements

1. *False*   Correct statement: Boys and girls tend to avoid each other during middle childhood.

2. *False*   Correct statement: Parents show less physical affection for their school-age children and spend less time with them.

3. *True*   A common complaint of the custodial parent is that the other parent plays the part of candy man or woman and is constantly taking the child's side in disputes.

4. *False*   Correct statement: Although children from

one-parent families do not do as well in school as children from two-parent families, they do not differ in academic ability.

5. *True*   Most studies find little or no differences between children from nuclear families and children from stepfamilies in adjustment and cognitive functioning.

6. *True*   Popularity tends to be rather stable from year to year.

7. *False*   Correct statement: Boys have much more rigid conceptions about what is appropriate for each sex than girls do.

8. *False*   Correct statement: Just the opposite is true. Boys' friendships are characterized by more conflict than girls' friendships are.

9. *True*   Generally speaking, children show more prosocial behavior as they mature.

10. *False*   Correct statement: Aggressive behavior is fairly uncommon in child-child interactions.

11. *False*   Correct statement: Aggressive children tend to remain aggressive.

12. *True*   Most studies find that there is a positive relationship between watching violence on television and aggressive behavior.

PART FIVE

Adolescence

CHAPTER 11

Physical and Cognitive Development
in Adolescence

Are the Following Statements True or False?

Try the True-False Quiz below. See if your answers correspond to the information in this chapter. Each question is repeated after the paragraph in which the answer can be found. The True-False Answer Box at the end of the chapter lists the complete answers.

_____ 1. The sequence of developmental changes in adolescence is still largely a mystery.

_____ 2. Menstruation is one of the earliest signs of puberty in females.

_____ 3. Twelve- or thirteen-year-old girls are generally taller and heavier than the average boy of that age.

_____ 4. Early maturing boys have a social advantage in adolescence.

_____ 5. Most sufferers of anorexia nervosa, a condition marked by self-starvation, come from poor, uneducated, lower-income families.

_____ 6. The ability to interpret proverbs and political cartoons develops during adolescence.

_____ 7. Most early adolescents believe that everyone will be looking at them when they walk into a restaurant, store, or classroom.

_____ 8. Most college freshman still believe that the activities of married women are best confined to their homes and families.

_____ 9. The number of adolescents who consider themselves politically conservative has increased about 20 percent in the last fifteen years, while the number of those who see themselves as politically middle-of-the-road has decreased about 5 percent.

_____10. During the past twenty years, the sexual attitudes of females have changed much more than those of males.

_____11. Most adolescents do not seek out contraceptive assistance until they have been sexually active for about a year.

_____12. About 20 percent of all parents refuse to let their children participate in sex education programs in school.

Physical Change in Adolescence

Ask anyone to state the ways adolescents differ from elementary school children and you will probably get a long list of the physical differences. These changes are well known and quite obvious. Much less obvious and rarely listed are the cognitive changes that take place during this period. In this chapter we will look at the meaning of these physical and cognitive changes for adolescents as well as for those around them.

Most adolescents are acutely aware of their physical selves. Early adolescence is a time of tremendous physical change that affects the adolescent's self-concept and behavior. Although the sequence of this physical change is predictable, the timing of the changes varies considerably from person to person. For example, the average age of the first menstrual flow among American teens is approximately 12.8 years (Tanner, 1970), but a girl may begin menstruating any time between age ten and sixteen and a half and still be within the normal range.

True or False   The sequence of developmental changes in adolescence is still largely a mystery.

Puberty and Adolescence

Some people use the terms *puberty* and *adolescence* synonymously. Actually, **puberty** refers to the physiological changes involved in the sexual maturation of the individual, as well as to other body changes that occur during this period (Sommer, 1978). Body changes directly related to sexual reproduction are called **primary sex characteristics.** These include maturation of the testes in males and of the ovaries in females. Changes that are not directly related to reproduction but that distinguish boys from girls are called **secondary sex characteristics** (Forisha-Kovach, 1983). Secondary sex characteristics include beard growth in males and breast development in females. When the term *puberty* is used to mark an event in someone's life, it refers to the time at which the reproductive system becomes mature and sexual reproduction is possible (Chumlea, 1982). In females, puberty is marked by the onset of menstruation. In males it is not as easily determined and relates to the ability to ejaculate mobile sperm. Puberty, then, is a biological

puberty   Physiological changes involved in sexual maturation, as well as other body changes that occur during the teen years.

primary sex characteristics   Body changes directly associated with sexual reproduction.

secondary sex characteristics   Physical changes that distinguish males from females but are not associated with sexual reproduction.

adolescence   The psychological experience of the child from puberty to adulthood.

ripening, while adolescence is a behavioral and cultural ripening (Krogman, 1980). **Adolescence** refers to the stage from puberty to adulthood and covers all the psychological experiences of the person during that period.

The Female Adolescent Develops

Many people believe that menstruation is the first sign of puberty. Menarche—the first menstrual flow—actually occurs late, after a number of other changes have taken place (see Table 11.1). Shortly after the growth spurt begins, girls develop breast buds and the breadth of their hips increases. Then, when the growth spurt is at its maximum, changes in the genital organs take place. These include maturation of the uterus, vagina, labia, and clitoris as well as the breasts. When growth slows considerably, menarche takes place. At this point, a number of other changes in fat and muscle composition are also occurring. Following menarche, most of the changes are nonsexual, including further changes in body shape and voice (Krogman, 1980). Each pubescent female develops within her own environment, specific culture, and subculture and is exposed to a different set of peers and parents. The importance of her subjective experience should not be lost in any biological discussion of general physical development or norms.

True or False   Menstruation is one of the earliest signs of puberty in females.

TABLE 11.1

Maturation in Girls

Although there may be normal variations in the sequence of physical and sexual maturation in girls, a typical sequence of events is:

1. Adolescent growth spurt begins.
2. Downy (nonpigmented) pubic hair makes its initial appearance.
3. Elevation of the breast (the so-called bud stage of development) and rounding of the hips begin, accompanied by the beginning of downy axillary (body) hair.
4. The uterus and vagina, as well as labia and clitoris, increase in size.
5. Pubic hair is growing rapidly and becoming slightly pigmented.
6. Breasts develop further; nipple pigmentation begins; areola increases in size. Axillary hair is becoming slightly pigmented.
7. Growth spurt reaches peak rate and then declines.
8. Menarche, or onset of menstruation, occurs (almost always *after* the peak rate of growth in height has occurred).
9. Pubic hair development is completed, followed by mature breast development and completion of axillary hair development.
10. Period of "adolescent sterility" ends, and girl becomes capable of conception (up to a year or so after menarche).

Source: Conger and Petersen, 1984.

The Growth Spurt

The growth spurt is one of the earliest and most recognizable body changes. Because this spurt begins about two years earlier in girls than in boys, twelve-year-old girls are generally taller and heavier and have larger muscles than twelve-year-old boys (Tanner, 1970). Although all structures grow at this time, they do not enlarge at the same rate. Hands and feet reach adult size first, causing many adolescents to complain about having hands or feet that are too big. Parents can alleviate some of this distress by simply telling their children that when they are fully grown their proportions will be correct.

True or False Twelve- or thirteen-year-old girls are generally taller and heavier than the average boy of that age.

If girls of twelve or thirteen are physically more advanced than boys the same age, why do early adolescent boys outshine girls in sports? The answer may involve differences in physiology, but different interests and training—both environmental factors—are probably the keys. In our society, males are encouraged to develop their bodies through athletic competition, while females are not. With the growth in popularity of such sports as tennis and jogging, some changes are taking place. We might also expect that, because of different rates of maturation, female athletes may be capable of developing their potential at an earlier age than men. Indeed, female champions in gymnastics are often much younger than their male counterparts. The earlier growth spurt and maturation, combined with excellent training, allow females to develop their full potential at an earlier age than males.

Menstruation. Of all the body changes that occur in adolescence, menstruation is the most dramatic (Logan, 1980). It is also the most ritualized. Various societal laws and customs prescribe what may and may not be done during the time of the menstrual flow. For example, one tribe in Borneo confines girls going through menarche in dark cells suspended by poles for long periods of time. When they conclude menarche, they are again introduced to the sun, flowers, earth, and so forth. One South African cattle-rearing tribe believes that the cattle would die instantly if they walked on ground on which even a drop of menstrual blood had fallen. To prevent this, special paths are available for women so they will not have contact with the ground cattle may frequent (Williams, 1977).

Even in our own society, taboos are plentiful. In some homes, women are considered too unclean to touch food or utensils during their period, and daughters are often taught to be ashamed of menstruation. This contrasts with the experience of male adolescents, who are taught to focus on their body changes as symbols of sexual strength (Breit and Ferrandino, 1979). The reproductive function of the menstrual cycle is underscored, while female sexuality is denied. A number of cultural "don'ts"—such as swimming, going barefoot, and participating in sports during the menstrual period—appear, and girls are told that no one should know they are having their period.

Some teens know little about this important change, but some educational progress has been made in this area. Today, most female adolescents have at least been given some biological information about what is happening (or about to happen) to them. They are subjected to fewer restrictions, and discussion today is likely to be more honest.

How do teenage girls evaluate the experience? Most American women consider it a negative or, at best, a neutral experience. Many feel insufficiently prepared and experience surprise, embarrassment, or fear (Logan, 1980). At the same time, they often feel pride (Whisnant and Zegans, 1975). When girls in late elementary school, junior high, and high school were asked for their reactions to their first menstrual period, the reactions were decidedly mixed. Most reported some physical distress and an immediate desire for secrecy. Girls who were less prepared to who began menstruating very early were most likely to evaluate the experience negatively. The researchers conclude that although the experience produces some confusion and ambivalence, especially in those who are very young or who are not well prepared, it is not as traumatic as once thought (Ruble and Brooks-Gunn, 1982; Brooks-Gun and Ruble, 1982). The initial reaction to the first menstrual period may be anxiety, but this decreases rapidly as the months pass (Rierdan and Koff, 1980). In summary, if young girls are prepared for menstruation, they will probably experience some ambivalence and anxiety, but these feelings will dissipate with time.

The Male Adolescent Develops

The first signs of puberty in males are the growth of the testes and scrotum along with the appearance of pubic hair. This is followed about a year later by a spurt in

Girls experience their growth spurt about a year and a half to two years before boys.

TABLE 11.2

Maturation in Boys

Although there may be some individual—and perfectly normal—variations in the sequence of events leading to physical and sexual maturity in boys, the following sequence is typical:

1. Testes and scrotum begin to increase in size.
2. Pubic hair begins to appear.
3. Adolescent growth spurt starts; the penis begins to enlarge.
4. Voice deepens as the larynx grows.
5. Hair begins to appear under the arms and on the upper lip.
6. Sperm production increases, and nocturnal emission (ejaculation of semen during sleep) may occur.
7. Growth spurt reaches peak rate; pubic hair becomes pigmented.
8. Prostate gland enlarges.
9. Sperm production becomes sufficient for fertility; growth rate decreases.
10. Physical strength reaches a peak.

Source: Conger and Petersen, 1984.

height and the growth of the penis (see Table 11.2). The prepubertal growth spurt in males occurs approximately two years after the average female has experienced her growth spurt and takes the boy well beyond the height of the average female. Often a male who has not started his growth spurt will see friends pulling away and yearn to recover his status in the group. Generally, if he was tall compared with his peers before puberty, he will return to this relative position after puberty (Tanner, 1970).

As is often the case, we can predict the sequence of events, but the time at which they occur varies from person to person. The trunk and legs elongate. Leg length reaches its adult proportions before body breadth. Growthwise, the last change to occur is a widening of the shoulders (Stolz and Stolz, 1951). This progression demonstrates why a young adolescent boy grows out of his trousers a year before growing out of his jackets (Tanner, 1970). His voice deepens and facial hair appears. Muscles develop, in part because of the secretion of testosterone, and the heart and lungs increase dramatically, as does the number of red blood cells.

The Secular Trend: Taller, Earlier, and Heavier

In the past 100 years or so, each new generation has been taller and heavier than the preceding one. In addition, each new generation has entered puberty at a slightly earlier age. These developmental tendencies, as

secular trend The trend toward earlier maturation today, compared with past generations.

well as others, known collectively as the **secular trend,** have been the focus of much research. The trend is unmistakable. Since 1900, children have been growing taller at the rate of approximately one centimeter and heavier by half a kilogram (1.1 pounds) each decade (Katchadourian, 1977).

Menstruation is also occurring at an earlier age. In Norway in the 1840s, the average age was 17; in 1950 it was 13 years, 4 months. In Germany in 1860 it was 16 years, 6 months; in 1955 it was 13 years, 5 months. Generally, among European populations the age of menarche has decreased over the past century from a range of 15 to 17 years to 12 to 14 years today (Roche, 1979). Not everyone agrees with the conclusion that women are menstruating at a much earlier age than previous generations. After a review of very early records, Bullough (1981) concluded that adolescent women from ancient times through the Middle Ages experienced their first period between the ages of 12 and 15. The situation is also complicated by the fact that even within the same country there may be substantial differences in the age at which people reach their adult height or girls menstruate. For example, in Romania the average age of menarche is 13.5 years in larger towns and cities, and 14.6 years in smaller villages (Tanner, 1970). The secular trend is thought to be due to improvements in health and nutrition, to a decline in growth-retarding illnesses during the first five years of life, and better medical care (Krogman, 1980). Whether the decrease has been substantial or minimal, the secular trend is definitely leveling off in the United States and Western Europe (Steinberg, 1985). This leveling off may indicate that there are limits to how much these factors can affect the onset of puberty and influence the course of the physical changes that occur during this stage of life.

What Causes Puberty?

Three structures are thought to be primarily responsible for puberty. These are the hypothalamus (a part of the brain), the pituitary gland, and the gonads, or sex organs—the testes in males and the ovaries in females (Sommer, 1978). The hypothalamus produces chemicals known as "releasing factors" which are carried in the bloodstream to the pituitary gland, stimulating it to pro-

duce substances called gonadotropins, which stimulate the gonads. The gonads then produce the sex hormones that cause changes in the body (see Figure 11.1) (Sommer, 1978).

The level of hormones in the body is kept in balance. During childhood the level of gonadotropins is quite low, but for some reason in later childhood secretion of these hormones increases. The gonads grow and produce more sex hormones. The hypothalamus is sensitive to sex hormones circulating in the body. As the amount of sex hormones increases, the output of the releasing factors from the hypothalamus decreases, thereby reducing the pituitary's output of gonadotropins and regulating the amount of sex hormones in the body.

Just why these changes are triggered by the hypothalamus remains a question. Scientists now believe that during childhood the hypothalamus is extremely sensitive to the amount of sex hormones secreted. As puberty approaches, however, the central nervous system matures and becomes less sensitive to the hormone levels, causing the hormones to appear in greater concentrations (Chumlea, 1982).

The changes that take place during adolescence, then, are largely determined by hormones. One group of such hormones are the sex hormones. Scientists use the term

Women champions in gymnastics are usually much younger than their male counterparts, partly because of their earlier maturation.

FIGURE 11.1

Observable Effects of Sex Hormones

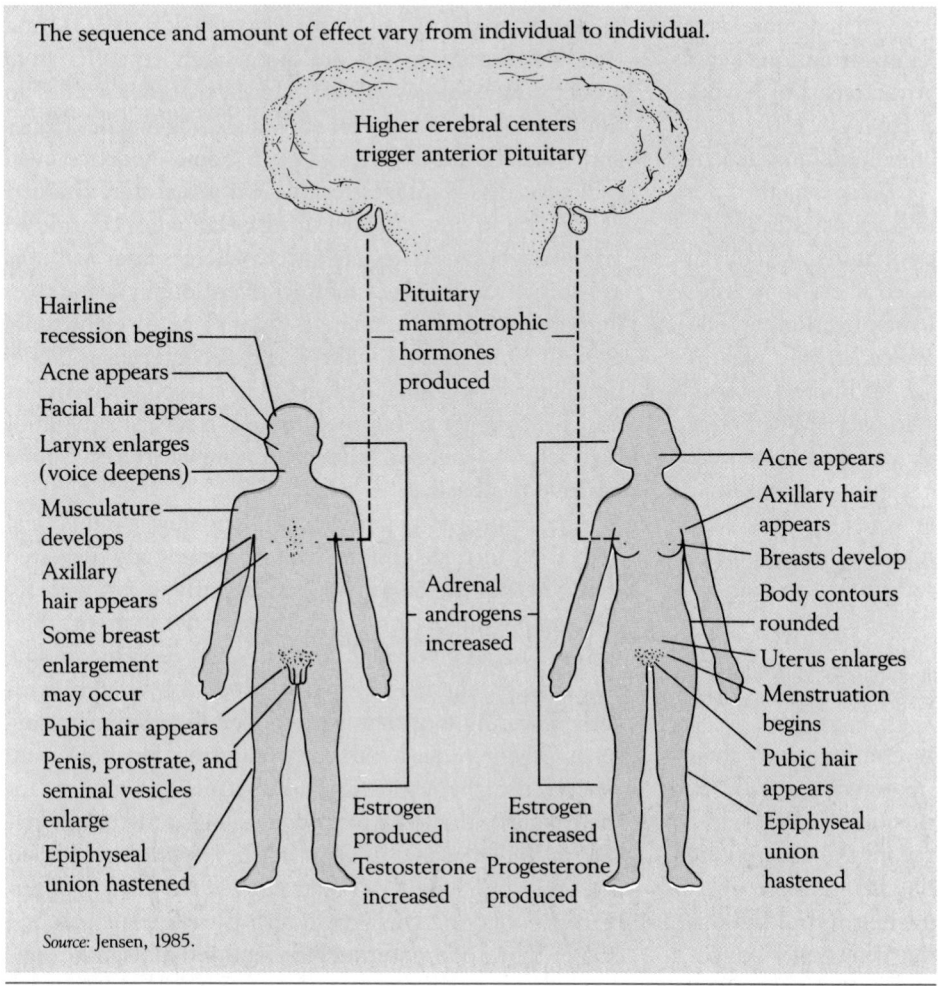

The sequence and amount of effect vary from individual to individual.

Higher cerebral centers trigger anterior pituitary

Pituitary mammotrophic hormones produced

Hairline recession begins

Acne appears

Facial hair appears

Larynx enlarges (voice deepens)

Musculature develops

Axillary hair appears

Some breast enlargement may occur

Pubic hair appears

Penis, prostrate, and seminal vesicles enlarge

Epiphyseal union hastened

Adrenal androgens increased

Estrogen produced

Testosterone increased

Estrogen increased

Progesterone produced

Acne appears

Axillary hair appears

Breasts develop

Body contours rounded

Uterus enlarges

Menstruation begins

Pubic hair appears

Epiphyseal union hastened

Source: Jensen, 1985.

---

androgens A group of male hormones, including testosterone.

estrogens A group of female hormones, including estradiol.

---

androgens to refer to the group of male hormones, including testosterone, and the term **estrogens** to denote a group of female hormones, including estradiol (Kalat, 1981). Although both males and females produce both sets of hormones, females produce more estrogens and males produce more androgens. During adolescence, the

sex hormones are secreted into the bloodstream in great quantities. The androgens cause secondary sex characteristics—such as lower voice, beard growth, the growth of hair on the chest and in the underarm and pubic areas. Estrogens encourage breast development and broadening of the hips (Kalat, 1981).

Early and Later Maturation

Most people are neither very early in maturing or very late. They fall somewhere in between. There is some evidence, however, that teens who mature either very early or very late may be affected by this experience. Early maturing males seem to have a substantial social advantage over late maturers. Adults rate early maturers more positively than late maturers. Early maturing boys are considered more masculine, more attractive, and better groomed. Late maturers are considered tense and childish and are seen as always seeking attention. Peers see them as bossy, restless, less attractive, and having less leadership ability (Jones and Bayley, 1950). Late maturers are also viewed as more rebellious and dependent (Mussen and Jones, 1957). The fact that they are both more rebellious and dependent demonstrates a basic conflict in their personalities. Late maturers of college age have not yet resolved their basic conflicts from childhood, tend to seek both attention and affection, and do not gain positions of dominance or leadership (Weatherley, 1964). The late maturer separates himself psychologically from both his parents and his peers. Weatherley also found that early and average maturing boys were very similar in personality structure, meaning that early maturation itself may not be the benefit it has been thought to be. It may be that what has actually been measured in previous studies is the lack of late maturation.

True or False   Early maturing boys have a social advantage in adolescence.

The problems of later maturers continue into their thirties (Jones, 1957). The late maturers are still less settled, less self-controlled, and still more rebellious, and they have a lower self-concept. Not all the findings are negative, however, as late maturers also are more assertive and insightful. In addition, in their forties the differences diminish greatly and some personality advantages in favor of later maturers are found. The early maturers become more conforming and rigid, whereas the late maturers become more flexible and, again, more insightful (Jones, 1965).

Other studies have hinted at advantages for the late maturer. Peskin (1973, 1967) found that early maturing boys became less active, more submissive, and less curious as they matured. Whereas the early maturing boy may have a social advantage, the later maturer was superior in some intellectual areas. Ames (1957) found that early maturers had more personal and social success but were not as happy in their marriages as later maturers. The problems that seem to arise in early maturers in middle age—namely, inflexibility and being very conforming—were present even in adolescence (Peskin, 1973).

In adolescent girls, the effects of early and later maturation are less clear. Some studies find that early maturing girls are better adjusted in young adulthood, as measured at the age of thirty years (Peskin, 1973), and that late maturing girls are more likely to suffer from anxiety (Weatherley, 1964). However, other studies do not find any advantages for early maturing females (Jones and Mussen, 1958; Jones, 1949). Some evidence even indicates disadvantages for the early maturer. Staffieri (1972) found that early maturing girls are not considered attractive because they are fatter, whereas later maturers are thinner and judged more conventionally attractive. Perhaps whether the changes take place in elementary or junior high school makes a difference (Faust, 1960). Early developing girls in elementary school receive fewer positive comments, but the situation is reversed in junior high school, where early developing females receive more positive feedback.

The timing of puberty may affect how parents deal with their teenage children. One recent study suggested that whether the child experiences early or late puberty seems more important to the perceptions of parents than to how the adolescents look at themselves. One finding was that parents perceive they have *less* conflict with early maturing sons than with moderate or late maturing sons. On the other hand, early maturing daughters were perceived to be a source of *more* stress and anxiety for their parents than late and on time maturing daughters. (Savin-Williams and Small, 1986). The adolescents, on the other hand, generally did not see the timing of puberty as affecting their relationship with their parents, except that early maturing girls reported a bit more conflict with their parents.

In summary, then, early maturation in males is a definite social advantage during adolescence, but the advantage diminishes in middle age, where there is perhaps some reversal. In females, the situation is less definite and no one single pattern has been found. Last, the timing of puberty may affect how parents see their children and relate to them.

Body Image and the Self-Concept

Just about every television situation comedy has a scene in which the entire family is waiting for the teenager to leave the bathroom after having just broken the "total time spent in the bathroom" record. Yet behind this comedy lies something deeper. Teenagers' bodies are changing quickly. Although some teens cope very well with these changes, many are not always comfortable with their new bodies. Many want to change aspects of their physical selves—mostly their height, weight, and complexion (Burns, 1979). For example, in one sample of teenage girls, although 81 percent of the subjects were assessed to be within the ideal weight range or even underweight, 78 percent wanted to weigh less and only 14 percent were satisfied with their current weight (Eisele et al., 1986). In adolescence, a good part of one's self-esteem is determined by body image. There is a link between physical attractiveness and self-esteem, and between dissatisfaction with one's body and low self-esteem (Grant and Fodor, 1986; Garner and Garfinkel, 1981).

The combination of peer pressure and media advertising encourages teens to try to meet a stereotyped socially approved body image. It takes time for them to become comfortable with their bodies and accept the elements, such as height, that cannot be changed. As the adolescent matures, a compromise in physical appearance is often struck between the stereotype and the reality, and a positive body image is attained.

Nutrition and Eating Problems in Adolescence

Since many teens are concerned with body image, it stands to reason that eating and weight would be a major concern. Eating disorders are not rare in adolescence. Although obesity is the most talked about problem, other eating disorders, including anorexia nervosa and bulimia, are also serious concerns.

Obesity

Between 10 and 25 percent of all teenagers are obese (Whitney and Hamilton, 1984). The estimate depends upon the standard used for determining obesity. Some authorities define it as 20 percent over chart weight, others as low as 15 percent over normal weight while others opt for 25 percent over chart weight (Hamilton et al., 1985). Obesity is not solely dependent on weight, however, as body build and age should also be taken into account. Obesity increases risks for hypertension and coronary disease, and it leads to negative body images and poor self-concepts. Obese teenagers also have more difficulty developing a coherent identity (Shestowsky, 1983). Obesity creates a social problem for the teen.

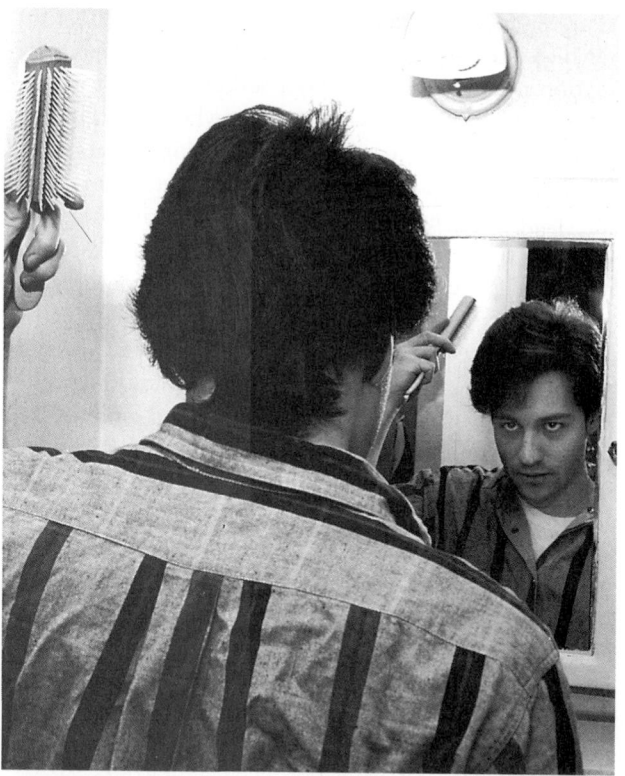

In adolescence a part of one's self-esteem is determined by body image.

Because our society's view of beauty and attractiveness is equated with being thin, the obese person is out of step with current fashion.

Obese children become obese teens, and obese teens become obese adults. Obese teens with a history of overweight have a 28 to 1 chance of becoming obese adults (Zakus et al., 1979). But people may become obese at any age. Parental supervision of eating habits during the teen years usually wanes as the adolescent gains personal freedom. Social and academic pressure may lead to increased caloric intake (Hubble et al., 1969). Many students use food to quiet their anxiety, and the less physically active life many older teens lead runs counter to the active life some led in childhood.

There is no easy cure for obesity. Certainly nutritional information is needed, because teens eat an enormous amount of junk food and their diet is often rich in starch but deficient in basic nutrients (Miller, 1980). However, not everyone appreciates or accepts such information. Schafer (1979) found a relationship between self-concept, choice of diet, and acceptance of nutritional information. Women with positive self-concepts both chose better diets and were more influenced by nutritional information than women with poor self-concepts. It is often difficult to motivate obese people, who generally have poor self-concepts, to accept nutritional information and to change their eating habits. In addition, many teens use crash diets, semi-starvation, or fad diets in a desperate attempt to lose or maintain weight. This can cause physical damage, especially to the kidneys, and these approaches are not effective in the long run.

Perhaps a combination of increased physical activity under a doctor's supervision, nutritional information, a reduction in the consumption of junk food, and psychological support provided by peer group and family members can help the obese teen lose weight and keep it off. It is often easier to prevent obesity than to cure it. But some modest success in weight reduction has been reported for a program that included nutritional information, identification of behaviors contributing to obesity, and alteration of these behaviors, as well as an increase in physical activity (Brandt et al., 1980). However, long-term weight loss is difficult, and the battle against fat is a lifelong process.

Anorexia Nervosa

When Karen Carpenter, a well-known singer, lost her twelve-year battle to anorexia nervosa in 1983, many people had never heard of this unusual and sometimes fatal disorder. Today most people know about it because the media have given it so much attention, but few truly understand it.

Although **anorexia nervosa** literally means loss of appetite (Wenar, 1982), the name is misleading. It is a disorder marked by self-imposed starvation and involves an abnormal fear of becoming obese, a disturbance of body image, significant weight loss, and a refusal to maintain even a minimal normal body weight (American Psychiatric Association, 1980). Anorexics have an appetite, but they are proud of being able to control their hunger. Anorexia nervosa is one of the few psychological problems that can be fatal, claiming between 15 and 21 percent of those afflicted (Halmi, 1978). The overwhelming number of anorexia sufferers are female—about 96 percent (Halmi, 1978)—and the onset of the condition is typically between the ages of twelve and eighteen. No one knows for sure why so many sufferers are female. It may have to do with the difference between

anorexia nervosa A condition of self-imposed starvation found most often among adolescent females.

how females and males perceive their bodies. Females tend to see their bodies as effective only if they are attractive, which means thin, while males prize dominance, which translates into large proportions and physical strength (Grant and Fodor, 1986).

Anorexics usually show little overt rebellion toward their parents, but they suffer deep conflict on the dependent-independent dimension. They are often raised in educated, success-oriented, middle-class families that are quite weight conscious. They are also perfectionistic and are described by their parents as model children (Smart et al., 1976). The disorder is not rare. About one in 250 female adolescents suffers from this condition.

True or False Most sufferers of anorexia nervosa, a condition marked by self-starvation, come from poor, uneducated, lower-income families.

Anorexics are obsessed with food, weight loss, and compulsive dieting and are quite active physically (Grant and Fodor, 1986). Once they achieve significant weight loss, anorexics do not stop, but continue until they are too slim to be physically healthy. Losing weight becomes an obsession, and they fear they will lose control if they eat a normal diet. Controlling their weight becomes the passion of life. Changes in their physiology, thinking, and personality occur. They misperceive their weight, believing they are fat or about to become so. Their condition becomes serious as their body begins to waste away. Menstruation ceases, they become ill and anemic, they cannot sleep, they suffer from low blood pressure, and their metabolism rate decreases (Bruch, 1978).

The cause of anorexia is still a mystery. One theory emphasizes the effects our society's view of the glamorous female as very thin, and the popularity of books on dieting, have on teens. Yet females receive double messages because the same women's magazines are likely to give advice on how to make rich desserts, and at social functions women find themselves surrounded by calorie-rich foods. Unable to integrate these messages, the anorexic develops a fear of losing control, of eating too much and gaining weight. Freudian theory asserts that anorexia is a defense against sexuality and an attempt to regress back to a preteen stage, especially since the anorexic stops menstruating. Those emphasizing a family approach note that anorexics come from rigid, overprotective families where conflicts are avoided and people are overinvolved with each other. This interferes with formation of a personal identity. Still others believe that there is some basis in biology or that a neurological dysfunction exists (Muuss, 1985).

The treatment for anorexia is varied. In severe cases, intravenous feeding is necessary. Family therapy that focuses on the relationships among family members and behavior modification to reinforce the anorexic to eat properly may be required (Muuss, 1985). This combination of therapies is often successful.

Anorexia nervosa is a serious disorder in which people sometimes literally starve themselves to death. This young lady has been working to overcome this problem.

bulimia An eating disorder marked by episodic binging and purging.

Bulimia

Imagine someone eating a gallon of ice cream and tens of brownies and doughnuts, and then purging the system of the food by forcing herself to vomit. Such a dangerous pattern of behavior is characteristic of another eating disorder, known as bulimia. **Bulimia** involves episodic binging often followed by induced vomiting (Voget, 1985). The sufferer is aware that the behavior is abnormal, but is afraid of losing control over her eating. Depression and extreme self-criticism are common after the binging period. Often the food is sweet and easy to chew, high in calories, and eaten very quickly. The binging may be brought on by some emotional difficulty, such as stress, loneliness, depression, rejection, or rage (Muuss, 1986). It may also be preceded by a diet (Whitney and Hamilton, 1984).

Bulimics binge secretly. They stop eating when they experience stomach pain, require sleep, are interrupted by someone, or induce their own vomiting. Just as in the case of anorexia, bulimic teens are obsessed with their body image. However, the fluctuations in body weight are rarely extreme enough to be as life-threatening as they are in anorexia, and these teens often appear physically normal—unlike the anorexic.

Estimates of the prevalence of bulimia differ widely. About 5 percent of college students show occasional bulimic eating patterns, but other estimates run as high as 15 or 20 percent (Muuss, 1986). Only 5 or 10 percent of all bulimics are males. Bulimics are perfectionistic, high achievers, and fear losing control. They often believe that others are watching them, and they are constantly worried about how others are perceiving them. Bulimics are very concerned about pleasing men and being attractive. They often jump from one eating fad to another. They make lists of forbidden foods and begin by denying themselves these foods. Later they break down and binge. They have unreasonably high goals and may believe that if they gain any weight at all they will be fat, or that if they can't stick to a diet they are failures (Muuss, 1986).

The treatment for bulimia involves group therapy in which bulimics have the support of others to help them overcome their problems. They often need to be taught how to handle stress and to define femininity in a broader context (Rosenhan and Seligman, 1984).

Cognitive Advances in Adolescence

During our discussion of the physical changes that occur in adolescence, as well as the eating disorders, some patterns appear repeatedly. Adolescents are capable of perceiving the world as other people do and evaluating themselves as they think others will. Their self-consciousness seems to stem from their ability to consider how other people might be evaluating them and then to act to influence this assessment. This attitude that "people will think I am . . ." is especially powerful in early and middle adolescence.

At the same time, other cognitive changes that relate directly to behavior are taking place, although these are less obvious. These changes allow teens to think differently from elementary school children and to begin to develop their own values.

The Stage of Formal Operations

Between the ages of about eleven or twelve and fifteen, many adolescents enter the **formal operations stage** and develop some interesting capabilities (Piaget, 1972; Inhelder and Piaget, 1958). As with all the other abilities described by Piaget, these develop over time, and an adolescent may show one skill but not another at a particular point in development.

Combinational Logic

Give elementary school children a problem in which they must find all the possible alternatives. You may be surprised to find that they do not approach the task in a scientific manner. For example, Inhelder and Piaget (1958) presented subjects of varying ages with five jars of a colorless liquid and told them that some combination of two of these chemicals would yield a yellow liquid. Preschoolers, who are in the preoperational stage, simply poured one into another, making a mess. Children in the concrete state of operations combined the liquids, but did not approach the task with a systematic strategy. Adolescents formed a strategy for making all possible combinations of liquids and finally solved the problem.

This finding can be extended to other situations. Adolescents can give all the possible solutions to a particular problem. If asked why something might happen, they understand that there are many different motives behind behavior. If you ask adolescents to answer the question "Why didn't Justin do his homework?" you'll get a number of answers—some possible and many improbable. This demonstrates another similar skill—being able to divorce oneself from what is real.

Separating the Real from the Possible

"What if human beings were green?" Ask a child this question, and the youngster may insist that human beings are not green. But adolescents can accept a proposition and separate themselves from the real world (Ault, 1977). They can form hypotheses and test them, which entails separating oneself from the real and considering what might be possible (McKinney et al., 1982). Adolescents can reflect on a verbal hypothesis even though its elements do not exist in real life.

Some parents may have difficulty with adolescents who can and do suggest alternatives that may not be feasible or that parents simply do not like. The separation of what *is* from what *can* or *could be* allows the adolescent to begin to think about a better world. Their "why" questions are based on possibilities divorced from reality, and they are capable of suggesting other alternatives. But their lack of experience in the real world limits their ability to consider these possibilities in practical terms.

Using Abstractions

The ability adolescents have to separate themselves from the trappings of what is real stems partly from their new-found ability to create and use abstractions. Children in the stage of concrete operations have difficulty understanding political cartoons and such sayings as "You can lead a horse to water, but you can't make him drink." They are still reality-bound and therefore have difficulty with abstract thought. They may actually picture a horse being led to water. But adolescents develop an ability to interpret abstractions, which allows them to develop internal systems of overriding principles. They can now talk in terms of ideals and values. Freedom, liberty, justice, and other such concepts take on added significance when they are separated from their specific situational meaning. Adolescents are now able to form their own values based on these overriding principles.

True or False   The ability to interpret proverbs and political cartoon develops during adolescence.

Hypothetical-Deductive Reasoning and Thinking

These emerging abilities allow the adolescent to engage in hypothetical-deductive reasoning. Basically, this is the ability to form a hypothesis, which then leads to certain logical deductions. Some of the hypotheses may be untestable, such as "What if all humans were green?" while others may be capable of being investigated scientifically. This type of reasoning is necessary for scientific progress. No one has ever seen an atom, but the developments in atomic theory have greatly affected our lives (Pulaski, 1980).

The abilities to use combinational logic, separate the real from the possible, interpret abstractions, and engage in hypothetical-deductive logic combine to allow adolescents to reason about problems on a higher level than they could during childhood. Adolescents are capable of accepting assumptions in the absence of physical evidence, developing hypotheses involving if-then thinking, testing out these hypotheses, and reevaluating them (Salkind, 1981). The thinking of adolescents is also more flexible, because they can consider a number of alternatives, weigh them, and then discard those that do not fit the situation. This ability to attack problems logically has great value in math and science and in life generally.

Adolescents also develop the ability to think about thinking (Ault, 1977). Teens can look back on their own thought processes and see one thought as the object of another. This ability allows them to consider the development of their own concepts and ideas.

Evaluating Piaget's Ideas

These abilities sound quite impressive, and they are. But not all adolescents—or, for that matter, even all adults—reason on this level (Neimark, 1982; 1975). Although older adolescents tend to be further along in using formal operational thinking, they do not use it on every problem where it would be appropriate (Roberge and Flexer, 1979; Martorano, 1977). It is estimated that only about half the adult population attains the final stage of formal operations (see Muuss, 1982).

Why doesn't everyone show formula operational reasoning? Some claim that people may be competent enough to succeed at a task, but for one reason or another do not perform it successfully (Flavell and Wohlwill, 1969). They fail because of fatigue, the way the problem is structured, or lack of experience with problems requiring such abilities. There is some evidence that people can be taught to use formal operational reasoning when appropriate (Kuhn et al., 1979; Danner and Day, 1977).

Others suggest that not all people require the use of formal operations in their daily life. Consider the cross-cultural differences that have been discovered. Studies of formal operations in non-Western cultures show that people in these cultures generally perform more poorly when presented with Piagetian tasks that require formal operational reasoning (Dasen and Heron, 1981). It may be that Piaget's stage of formal operations is basically applicable only to adolescents in Western technological societies who are exposed to a great deal of formal education. Indeed, schooling does seem to be an important variable in determining whether people reach the formal operational stage. Schooled non-Western adolescents do better on these tests than unschooled non-Western adolescents (Rogoff, 1981).

Such evidence led Piaget (1972) to reevaluate this area of his theory. He recognized that education, vocational interests, and the society and culture determine performance on tests of formal operations. Perhaps the environments necessary to progress to concrete operational thinking are basic and exist in the overwhelming majority of societies, but formal operational reasoning may require a more technological, structured environment. It requires a particular type of stimulation found most often at the upper levels of schooling. At this level, the nature of the environment may have more of an effect on performance than at earlier levels. In addition, this type of abstract reasoning may not be necessary for effective functioning in many societies. Piaget viewed it as the ultimate achievement, but that may be so only in Western cultures. We have little idea what may constitute the ideal last stage of cognitive growth in some other societies.

Finally, even within the same age-groups in Western societies, some people perform better than others on tasks requiring formal operations. People mature at different rates and are exposed to different challenges. Individual differences in attaining formal operations skills should be expected, and indeed are found.

Cognitive Growth and Behavior in Adolescence

The formal operational abilities just described can help us understand how teenagers come to be concerned with societal problems and develop their own morals and values. It also helps us understand much of the social behavior that is common in teenagers.

Adolescent Egocentrism

The self-consciousness of adolescents (especially early adolescents) is legendary. In fact, early adolescent eighth-graders in one study were found to be significantly more self-conscious than both younger children and older adolescents (Elkind and Bowen, 1979). Adolescents often look at themselves in the mirror and imagine what others will think about them. Adolescents can now think about thoughts—both their own and those of others. However, a logical error occurs. Teenagers can understand the thoughts of others, but they fail to differentiate between the objects toward which the thoughts of others are directed and those that are the focus of their own thoughts (Peel, 1969). Because teens are concerned primarily with themselves, they believe everyone else is focusing on them too and is as obsessed with their behavior and appearance as they are. The inability to differentiate between what one is thinking and what others are thinking constitutes what David Elkind (1967) called **adolescent egocentrism.** This leads to two interesting phenomena: the imaginary audience and the personal fable.

The imaginary audience. Adolescents often believe that when they walk into a room everyone focuses their attention on them. Then they anticipate the reactions. Teenagers create an **imaginary audience,** believing that everyone is looking at and evaluating them. The people in this "audience" are real, but it is imaginary because most of the time the adolescent is not the focus of attention. The imaginary audience phenomenon leads to self-consciousness and the adolescent's mania for privacy.

adolescent egocentrism The adolescent failure to differentiate between what one is thinking and what others are considering.

imaginary audience A term used to describe adolescents' belief that they are the focus of attention and being evaluated by everyone.

personal fable The adolescents' belief that their experiences are unique and original.

The self-consciousness stems from the conviction that others are seeing and evaluating them in the same way that they see themselves. The mania for privacy may come either from what Elkind calls a "reluctance to reveal oneself" or from a reaction to being constantly scrutinized by others. Privacy becomes a vacation from evaluation.

True or False Most early adolescents believe that everyone will be looking at them when they walk into a restaurant, store, or classroom.

Adolescents, then, are deeply involved with how others will evaluate them. As they dress, act, and groom, they imagine how others will see them. Elkind notes that when the boy who combed his hair for hours and the girl who carefully applied makeup meet, both are more concerned with being observed than with being the observer.

During later adolescence, the imaginary audience disappears considerably. Teens begin to realize that people may not react to them the way they think they do. They also realize that people are not as interested in them as they thought. However, another phenomenon caused by adolescent egocentrism lasts much longer—the personal fable.

The personal fable. "You can't know how it feels to be in love with someone who doesn't know you exist," said one adolescent to his parents. He was convinced that only he could suffer such feelings of unrequited love, of loneliness, of despair. As adolescents reflect on their own thoughts and experiences, they come to believe that what they are thinking and experiencing is absolutely unique in the annals of human history. The belief that what they are experiencing and thinking is original, new, and special is known as the **personal fable.** Evidence of the personal fable is found in the diaries of adolescents.

Young people are often involved in political demonstrations as their values and ideals become more definite. Here Amy Carter celebrates on being found not guilty of charges of trespassing and disorderly conduct during a 1986 demonstration on a college campus.

The personal fable declines somewhat as the adolescent enters young adulthood, but it may never be completely extinguished.

Morals and Values in Adolescence

Look at any mass demonstration for a cause and you will usually see young people in the thick of it. Whether the cause be nuclear disarmament, free speech, or a cleaner environment, the idealism and values of adolescents often show themselves in a visible activism. Adolescents who do not join groups and demonstrate also develop their own values and personal philosophy of life. Their new-found abilities to understand abstract and overriding principles and values—such as freedom, liberty, and justice—and to separate the real from what is possible allow them to formulate their own personal principles and ideas about right and wrong.

Cognitive Development and Moral Reasoning

Lawrence Kohlberg, whose theory of moral reasoning was outlined and discussed in Chapter 10, argues that moral reasoning is related to cognitive growth. The higher stages of moral reasoning require more-sophisticated cognitive abilities. If this is true, adolescents progressing from concrete to formal operations should show an increased ability to reason at higher levels. Indeed, research has demonstrated a correlation between the cognitive level and moral reasoning (Kohlberg, 1987). Adolescents operating at the formal operations stage have the ability to reason at Kohlberg's higher stages, but as we shall see, still may not do so (Weiss, 1982).

The higher stages of moral reasoning. Just what is the nature of these higher stages of moral reasoning? Stage 4 involves reasoning that is oriented toward doing one's duty and maintaining the social order for its own sake. Stage 5 involves a contractual legalistic orientation that emphasizes not violating the rights of others and a respect for the welfare and majority will of others. Stage 6 is a more individualistic orientation, in which decisions are made involving one's own conscience and principles. Adolescents who are developing formal operational skills are better able to reason at these higher levels of moral reasoning. But even if they have this ability, many adolescents do not function at this level. In fact, most people do not develop beyond Stage 4 (Shaver and Strong, 1976).

Why doesn't everyone reason at stage 6? Why do some people use Stage 6 reasoning, based on individual principles and values, while others do not? Perhaps the best way to understand this is to invoke the competency-performance argument. Cognitive advancement makes more sophisticated moral reasoning a possibility but does not assure it. Other factors may enter the picture. One variable is the *content* of the problem (Fischer, 1980), another is *consequences* of the moral decision. When people are faced with a dilemma in which the personal consequences are great, they are likely to demonstrate lower-level moral thinking (Sobesky, 1983). Generally, when people are confronted with a problem, their cognitive skills form the upper limits of their abilities to reason, but the situation itself will affect the actual behavior.

The adolescent's moral reasoning cannot be neatly placed in a single stage (Kohlberg, 1969). At times, adolescents operate on a higher level, but at other times they operate on a lower one (Holstein, 1976). Thus, moral reasoning may be inconsistently applied to various problems. Indeed, we see this inconsistency often, and parents may have difficulty understanding their child's highly moral stand on one issue and lower-level reasoning on another.

Moral Reasoning and Prosocial Behavior

Are high levels of moral reasoning related to more prosocial behavior? Kohlberg says yes (Kohlberg and Turiel, 1971), others are skeptical (Wonderly and Kupfersmid, 1980). You may remember Milgram's (1968) famous study, in which he asked students to obey a researcher and deliver what they thought were painful shocks to an innocent subject whose only crime was answering a question incorrectly on a learning-memory test. No shocks were really delivered, but the "teachers" did not know this. The study was really one of obedience. Kohlberg and Turiel (1971) reported that 75 percent of the Stage 6 subjects tested on Milgram's obedience tests did not comply, while only 13 percent of the subjects reasoning at the other moral stages refused to deliver the shocks. This sounds impressive, but notice that 25 percent of

values Constructs that serve as internal guides for behavior.

the Stage 6 sample did deliver the shocks. In addition, some studies have failed to find differences between the behavior of people reasoning in the upper stages and those in the lower stages (Wonderly and Kupfersmid, 1980). All we can say at this point is that there is a positive relationship between level of moral reasoning and behavior, but it has not been found in all studies, and even where it has been found it is far from perfect.

Values, Attitudes, and Political Beliefs

We noted that the development of formal operations is related to certain cognitive abilities that allow adolescents to develop their own values. But what values do most adolescents hold, and have these changed over the years?

Values. Constructs that serve as internal guides for behavior are called **values** (McKinney and Moore, 1982). Values are beliefs that certain patterns of conduct or certain goals are better than others (Rokeach, 1973). To some extent, values are culturally determined (see the Cross-Cultural Current on page 303). For example, many hunting-gathering societies require teamwork to survive, so the values of cooperation and sharing are crucial. Obedience was a value that the Pilgrims and the Puritans greatly admired.

A poll of 17,000 high school students found that more than 75 percent of the students stated that their goal was a good marriage and a happy family life. Over two-thirds thought that having strong friendships was important, and only 4 percent of noncollege youths and 10 percent of the college freshmen thought that being a community leader was important (Bachman and Johnston, 1979). This generation adheres to conventional values of marriage and parenthood, friendships, and meaningful work. Their lack of community involvement is somewhat of a disappointment, but their parents probably approve of these values.

Some values and attitudes have changed significantly over the past twenty years. Each year since 1966, the attitudes and values of 280,000 college freshman have been surveyed at about 550 two- and four-year colleges

Dividing the Rewards in Two Cultures

Consider the following problem. You've asked three people to help you move a piano and some furniture. You would like to give them some monetary reward after the job is done. Worker 1 did the hardest work, with Worker 2 a bit behind. Worker 3 carried the piano bench and didn't work up a sweat. You want to give them fifteen dollars, but how would you divide it up?

As most psychologists see it, you have two main choices. You can use an *equality norm,* in which all people receive the same amount of money no matter how much effort they put in or how much they need the money. In this equality model, each worker would get five dollars. This norm promotes harmony and solidarity among the members and avoids conflicts. On the other hand, you could use the *equity norm* and divide the reward up depending on some other criterion—in this case the amount of effort. You might give Worker 1 seven dollars, Worker 2 five dollars, and Worker 3 three dollars. This would lead to higher levels of motivation and task performance the next time these people worked, and it reinforces hard work. Which norm would you use?

This is essentially what Gerardo Marin wanted to find out when he compared college students in Chicago with college students attending a university in Bogotá, Colombia. Each subject was given a booklet in which a mythical psychological experiment was described. In this imaginary study, people were asked to perform some task, and the allocator had to reward them. Some of the students were told that the allocator used the equality principle, while other students were told that the equity principle was used. The subjects were then asked to rate how fair they thought the division of money was and to tell how they would have divided the reward. Finally, they were asked to describe why the allocator had chosen

a particular method to reward the subjects.

The results showed that most students—both in the United States and in Colombia—preferred the equitable distribution of reward and perceived it as fairer. The preference for the equity norm was more marked among Colombian subjects. When asked how they would have divided the rewards, again there was preference for the equitable distribution, and again the preference was more marked among Colombians than among Americans. No sex differences were found.

The subjects also understood the reasons behind the allocators' division of the rewards. They noted that the equal allocator was more concerned with avoiding conflict, maintaining good interpersonal relations, and promoting friendliness, and that the equitable allocator wanted to be as fair as possible.

So college students in each culture seem to prefer the equity norm over the equality norm, at least in the situation described. The fact that the subjects in both countries saw the motives of the equal allocator in terms of promoting friendliness, and saw the equity norm as fairer, shows a similarity between the two cultures.

The lack of sex differences was a bit surprising. Early studies showed that males prefer the equity norm and that females prefer the equality norm. Perhaps this study, and other recent research efforts that have not found sex differences, reflect the changes in society that accompanied the women's movement. It would be interesting to see whether the pattern would hold if different segments of each society—perhaps rural, agricultural subjects rather than college students—were used or if people from more tribal cultures were tested in the same way.

Source: Marin, G. Perceiving Justice Across Culture: Equity vs. Equality in Colombia and in the United States. *International Journal of Psychology,* 1981, *16,* 153–159.

and universities nationwide. Astin and colleagues (1986) took data from nearly 6 million students and analyzed it for trends. In the United States, the 1960s were a time of social upheaval, involving civil rights and great changes in sexual attitudes. When adolescent values in the 1960s,

1970s, and 1980s were compared, some interesting trends appear. In the late 1960s, students were more interested in social interpersonal morality. Values relating to one's relationship with society were most important. By 1975, however, the climate had changed, and students were more interested in personal achievement and less involved with society. For example, while only 44 percent of the 1967 sample believed it was essential to be well-off financially, 71 percent of the freshmen believed so in 1985. While 14 percent of the 1966 freshmen planned to major in business, 25 percent of the 1985 group did (Astin, 1986; Greene, 1986). The changes in freshmen's views of social roles are startling. In 1967, some 57 percent of freshmen believed that activities of married women are best confined to the home and family, while only 22 percent of the 1985 group believed the same. Figure 11.2 depicts some of these changes.

True or False Most college freshmen still believe that the activities of married women are best confined to their homes and families.

Political philosophy. Values and attitudes affect one's view of politics. Adolescents see law and politics differently from the way younger children see them. When adolescents and younger children were asked "What is the purpose of laws?" Adelson (1972) found striking differences between the answers of adolescents and preadolescents. Younger children answered that laws were necessary so people didn't get hurt or so people wouldn't kill or steal. Adolescents of about fifteen or sixteen years old viewed law in more abstract and principled terms—laws ensure safety, enforce government policy, and act as guidelines for determining right and wrong. Subjects younger than age eleven focus on the consequences of law and order for themselves, while older adolescents go beyond this and see the legal system from the point of view of the community as a whole (Adelson and O'Neil, 1966). Preadolescents look at law and government in terms that are concrete, absolute, and authoritarian and evaluate them on the basis of how they affect particular individuals—for example, seatbelts are necessary to protect the driver and passengers. Older subjects are less authoritarian and more sensitive to individual rights and personal freedom. Adolescents may see the conflict between requiring seatbelts for the good of everyone and the loss of personal freedom that comes with regulation—a conflict that younger children do not see. When Gallatin and Adelson (1971) asked what these younger children thought of a law requiring men to have a yearly medical checkup, they noted the good the law might do and frequently were willing to accept the idea. Older subjects saw that the good must be weighed against individual freedom. Preadolescents see government in per-

genital stage The final psychosexual stage, occurring during adolescence, in which adult heterosexual behavior develops.

sonal terms, personifying it in terms of the president, mayor, or police officer, while older adolescents see it in terms of abstract properties (Sprintall and Collins, 1984). Children see government as powerful and good, but by about the eighth grade they are more skeptical (Merelman, 1971).

The political attitudes of today's freshmen are different from what they were just two decades ago. In 1970, some 34 percent thought of themselves as liberal, while in 1985 only 21 percent did. However, whereas 45 percent saw themselves as middle-of-the-road in 1970, some 57 percent now do. The percentage of freshmen considering themselves politically conservative increased from 17 percent in 1970 to 20 percent in 1985. College freshmen are less liberal today, and more describe themselves as middle-of-the-road.

True or False The number of adolescents who consider themselves politically conservative has increased about 20 percent in the last fifteen years, while the number of those who see themselves as politically middle-of-the-road has decreased about 5 percent.

Adolescent Sexuality

The physical and cognitive changes that we have been looking at thus far affect many areas of functioning, but one area that is currently the center of attention is sexuality. Sexuality is a basic concern of adolescence. According to Freud, the teen enters the **genital stage,** during which the libido—hidden during the latency phase—reappears. Physical drives are strong and cannot easily be repressed, and as a result adolescents turn their attention to heterosexual relationships (Freud, 1925/1953).

The Revolution in Attitudes

The traditional attitude concerning sexuality reflects the double standard. Males were permitted sexual freedom, females were denied it. Males were encouraged to experiment, yet sanctions against female sexuality were great. The sexual needs of males were recognized, but females' desires were denied, even during marriage. At least to some degree, however, the double standard has been reduced (Shope, 1975). Attitudinal differences between males and females have narrowed, as the results of a questionnaire given over the years to groups of college students show (see Figure 11.3).

The attitude change is in the direction of greater acceptance and a live-and-let-live orientation to sex. Sorenson (1973) found that adolescents did not believe that premarital sex, in and of itself, was either right or wrong. As long as both partners were willing (force was

---

FIGURE 11.2

Changes in Freshman's Attitudes

Alexander Astin, Kenneth Green, and William Korn surveyed nearly six million first year college students. Some of their results are graphically represented in the following frames.

Identify themselves as politically liberal.

| 1970 | 1985 |
| 34% | 21% |

Identify themselves as middle of the road politically.

| 1970 | 1985 |
| 45% | 57% |

Identify themselves as politically conservative.

| 1970 | 1985 |
| 17% | 20% |

Plan to major in business

| 1966 | 1985 |
| 14% | 25% |

Plan to pursue elementary or secondary teaching careers.

| 1968 | 1985 |
| 24% | 6% |

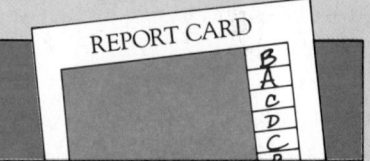

Believe college grades should be abolished.

| 1970 | 1984 |
| 44% | 14% |

Believe it is essential or very important to be very well-off financially.

| 1967 | 1985 |
| 44% | 71% |

Believe the activities of married women are best confined to the home and family.

| 1967 | 1985 |
| 57% | 22% |

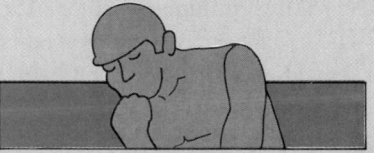

Believe it is essential or very important to develop meaningful philosophy of life.

| 1967 | 1985 |
| 83% | 43% |

Source: Green, 1986.

FIGURE 11.3

The Drift Toward More Liberal Attitudes

Depicted below are the percentages of college students in 1965, 1970, 1975, and 1980 strongly agreeing with certain statements regarding the morality of premarital sexual relationships.

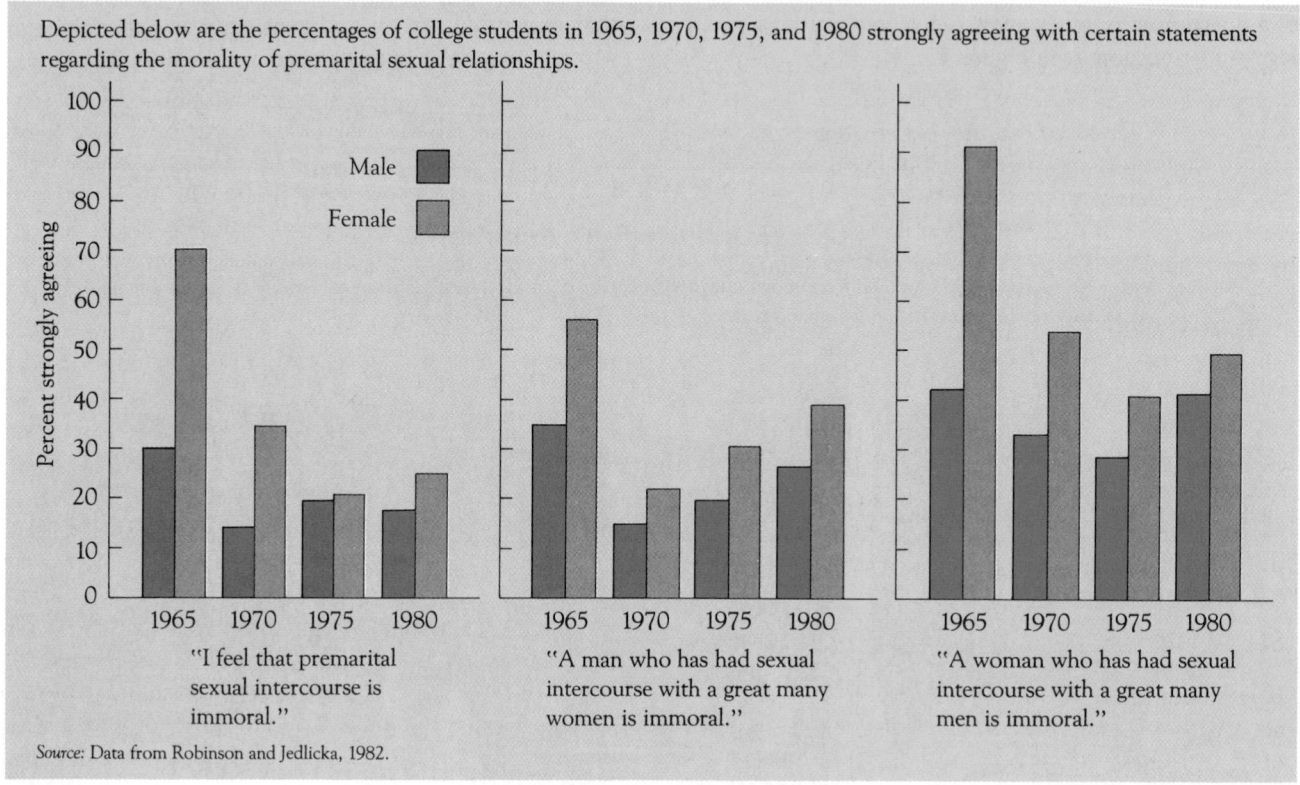

Source: Data from Robinson and Jedlicka, 1982.

unacceptable) and it occurred within an affectionate relationship, no negative sanctions were attached to it. Sexual behavior is considered more a matter of personal choice than the business of society (Chilman, 1983). The attitudes of adolescents are likely to be much more permissive than those of their parents. Most adolescents understand this, and while they disagree, they respect their parents' different opinions (Sorenson, 1973).

The revolution in attitudes appears to have been greater for females than for males, probably because women had more conservative attitudes to start with. Yet the idea that sex itself is looked on casually or that the attitudes of males and females are identical is false. Females are still more conservative than males and more likely to view sex as part of a loving relationship. Adolescents' attitudes toward what is proper depend on how serious they think the relationship is. Both males and females become more permissive as the relationship gets more serious. And both believe that more sexual intimacy is proper when one is in love or engaged than when one

is dating without affection or even with affection but without love (Roche, 1986). However, males and females show differences in what they believe is appropriate at the beginning stages of dating, with males being more permissive than females. In the later stages, which include dating only one person, being in love, and engagement—the differences for the most part disappear. Males, then, expect sexual intimacy earlier in the relationship, while females tie sexual intimacy to love and commitment (Roche, 1986). Adolescents today show less fearful and more matter-of-fact attitudes than teens in the previous generation, and less moral conflict or guilt about sex. However, sexual affairs are still not viewed by the majority as casual encounters.

True or False During the past twenty years, the sexual attitudes of females have changed much more than those of males.

Adolescents' attitudes are generally more liberal than their actual behavior. While they are tolerant of other people's sexuality, their personal standards are somewhat stricter. Females are more likely to live up to their standards than males (Chilman, 1983). Hass (1979) found that in a study of fifteen- to nineteen-year-old males and females, 95 percent of the males and 83 percent of the females approved of heavy petting, such as genital touching, but only 55 percent of the males and 43 percent of the females had participated in such activities. As for sexual intercourse, 83 percent of the males and 64 percent of the females approved of it, while only 56 percent of the males and 44 percent of the females had participated in sexual intercourse.

Four conclusions are indicated by the data. First, adolescent sexual attitudes are quite tolerant and more liberal than in the past. Second, the attitudes of male adolescents are still more liberal than female attitudes, especially concerning sex in the early part of a relationship. Third, sex is not seen as a casual act. And fourth, adolescents seem to be somewhat more conservative in their behavior than in their attitudes.

Sexual Behavior

If attitudes have changed quite a bit, what about the actual rate of sexual behavior? The most common type of sexual experience for adolescence is masturbation, but when people speak of the sexual revolution they are usually referring to what they see as the tremendous increase in the rate of sexual intercourse. Has there been a revolution in sexual behavior?

After reviewing a number of studies on the subject, Dreyer (1982) notes that between 1925 and 1973 the percentage of high school girls reporting premarital sex tripled from 10 percent to 35 percent, and that the rate for college females rose from 25 percent to 65 percent. Recent studies show that approximately 44 percent of high school females and 74 percent of college females reported engaging in premarital sex. For males the rates have risen, but because the initial rates were higher the rise is not as dramatic. In 1925 about 25 percent of high school males and 55 percent of college men reported having premarital sex. Today, about 56 percent of high school males and 74 percent of college men report experiencing sex. The most recent studies indicate that high school males are more likely to be sexually active than high school females but that the virginity rates among college men and women are almost the same (Dreyer, 1982). Zelnik and Kantner (1980: 1978, 1977,

1971) studied teenage sexual behavior in the 1970s and noted an increase in the percentage of females between the ages of fifteen and nineteen experiencing sexual intercourse—from 27.6 percent in 1971, to 39.2 percent in 1976, to 46 percent in 1979.

The increase in premarital sexuality is now accepted by most researchers. However, whether one wants to call this a revolution or an evolution depends on one's personal point of view. Certainly the change in attitudes has been more radical than the change in behavior (Lerner and Spanier, 1980).

Yet the picture of adolescent sexuality is not one of rampant promiscuity. In Hass' (1979) study, one-fifth of the sexually active boys and almost half the girls age fifteen to nineteen reported having sex with only one partner. In Zelnik and Kantner's 1977 study, only about 10 percent of the subjects reported having sex with more than one partner, and only about half had had intercourse within a month of being interviewed. Less than 30 percent had engaged in sex as often as three times a month, and 15 percent had experienced it only once.

The explanations for the increase are many and varied. Some explain it in terms of the more open sexuality shown in the media, the reduction of sanctions against premarital sex, the movement toward women's equality, the increased availability of contraceptives and abortion, earlier maturation, and the faster pace of our society.

Contraceptive Use

If rates of premarital sex have increased substantially and attitudes have become more liberal, what about contraceptive use? The statistics are astounding. Zelnik and Kantner (1977) report that only 30 percent of their sample always used contraception; 45 percent sometimes did, and 25 percent never did. Younger teens are less likely to use contraception than older teens, and it is usually left up to the male. Many teens run the risk of becoming pregnant either because they use no contraception or because they use an ineffective method. Between one-third and two-thirds use no contraception during first intercourse (Morrison, 1985). In one startling study, Zabin and colleagues (1979) found that the majority of teens do not look for any contraceptive assistance until they have been sexually active for about a year. This is distressing because so many pregnancies occur during the first six months after teens begin engaging in intercourse. Most sexually active teens have had intercourse at least once without using any form of birth control (Dreyer, 1982). Contraceptive use increases with age, and the use of an oral contraceptive increases in steady relationships and in marriage (Luker, 1975). Although some increases in contraceptive use during the late 1970s and the early 1980s may have occurred (scientifically valid studies are absent), these increases are not significant. Many teens are experimenting with sex and not protecting themselves against pregnancy. Why?

True or False Most adolescents do not seek out contraceptive assistance until they have been sexually active for about a year.

Cognition and contraception. Many teens simply do not consider the possibility that they will get pregnant, and if they do think about it, it is only a passing thought. As many as 40 percent of the females in Sorenson's (1973) study stated that sometimes they do not really care whether they get pregnant or not. Asked "Do you ever worry about the possibility that you might become pregnant?" 16 percent of the nonvirgin girls said "Never," 14 percent said "Hardly ever," 41 percent said "Sometimes," and 29 percent said "Often." When Sorenson asked nonvirgin males whether they ever worry about getting a girl pregnant, 18 percent said "Never," 6 percent said "Hardly ever," 48 percent said "Sometimes," and 28 percent said "Often." Some 25 percent of the males also stated that they always trusted to luck that the girl would not become pregnant.

We often think that the sexually active teen is a well-informed person and knowledgeable about the facts of conception, but that is not what the research shows (Morrison, 1985). Between 10 and 25 percent of teens questioned did not believe they could become pregnant the first time they had intercourse. When adolescents were asked to identify the time during the menstrual cycle when the greatest risk of pregnancy existed, fewer than half answered correctly. Fewer than half the teens sampled knew that sperm could live for three days, with one-third believing they live less than one day. About one-third of Sorenson's respondents believed they couldn't get pregnant if they didn't want to, even if they had sex without using some contraceptive method, while one-quarter of another sample believed that a woman must have an orgasm to become pregnant.

Adolescents know something about the different methods of contraception, with older teens knowing more than younger teens. However, their attitudes toward contraception are negative or neutral at best. Many do not believe that even reliable forms of contraception really work.

Adolescents do not use contraception regularly because of erroneous beliefs about fertility, indifference to becoming pregnant, not knowing where to get contraceptives, and negative attitudes toward contraceptive devices themselves (Morrison, 1985). Some teens are afraid of using an oral contraceptive or note that they are not in a continuous sexual relationship. The fact that contraception must be planned and that planned sex seems to lose its romantic quality and spontaneity may also be another reason for the sporadic use of contraceptives (Reichelt, 1976). Many teens also deny that they are sexually active and may not be mature enough to accept the fact that they are engaging in intercourse (Dreyer, 1982). The first encounter is rationalized as an accident—a moment of passion or a chance event. Most methods of birth control demand that the person acknowledge that he or she is sexually active and view sexual encounters realistically (Pestrak and Martin, 1985). Many adolescents do not have the cognitive ability to cope with these facts. For example, the "personal fable" enables adolescents to believe they are immune to danger and cannot get pregnant. Some are restricted to here-and-now thinking, and younger teens find the entire subject of conception difficult to understand.

Teenage Pregnancy

One in five fourteen-year-old girls today will become pregnant before reaching the age of eighteen, and more than one million teenagers become pregnant each year (Allgeier and Allgeier, 1984). Of these, 600,000 give birth (Perlez, 1986). Some 95 percent of these young mothers keep their infants (Connolly, 1978). The odds are quite high that a second pregnancy will occur within the next three years. In fact, over half the pregnant teens in one study became pregnant again within three years (Furstenberg, 1979). Women who are poor or very young are most likely to become pregnant again.

Consequences of teenage pregnancies. The consequences of adolescent pregnancies are serious for the entire family. If the pregnant teen decides to get married, the odds against a successful marriage are great. The rates of separation and divorce are much greater among couples where the woman was pregnant at the time of marriage than among couples where she was not pregnant (Kelly, 1982). Teenage marriages are generally less stable, and if the extra stress of pregnancy is added, the potential for discord increases.

The infant. The consequences for the baby born to a teenage mother can be serious. These infants have more health problems than the average infant. They have a 30 percent greater risk of dying before their first birthday, compared with babies born to mothers between the ages of twenty and twenty-four (Foster and Miller, 1980). Babies born to teenagers have lower birth weights, are more often premature, and have a greater chance of having a birth defect. These problems are caused by poor nutrition, drugs, and a lack of prenatal care. Although some problems may stem simply from the immaturity of the childbearing system in some very young females, many of these problems are not inevitable. But igno-

Teenage pregnancy is a national problem with more than one million teenagers becoming pregnant each year.

rance, denial, and other psychological factors combine to prevent the pregnant adolescent from seeking out the best care for herself and her infant during the crucial prenatal period. The rate of child abuse is also higher in young families, as is the chance that they will be living in poverty.

The mother. Pregnancy is the most common reason that female students drop out of school. Somewhere between 50 percent and 66 percent of female dropouts claim that pregnancy was the reason for their failure to finish school. Some 70 percent of all pregnant teenagers do not finish high school (Gordon and Dickman, 1980). The younger a woman is when she bears her first child, the fewer the years of education she will receive (Moore and Waite, 1977). Mothers who have babies in their teens have lower incomes and hold lower-prestige jobs than their classmates. They also express less satisfaction with their jobs in their twenties. They often suffer from depression and experience a conflict between independence and submission to their parents, who helped them through the trying time (Zougher, 1977). In fact, family support is of vital importance to these young mothers and their babies. Those who receive family support adapt better to these challenges than those who do not receive such social, psychological, and financial help (Furstenberg, 1981).

It would be wrong to believe that all teenage pregnancies are the result of accidents and ignorance. One pregnant sixteen-year-old told a reporter, "I figured this would be something that could be mine—nobody could take it, and I would have a little piece of me left that would give me a reason for living." Some girls become pregnant as a way to get attention or to get a boy to marry them (Perlez, 1986). It is only after they give birth that the financial problems, the rigors of parenthood—with its loss of freedom—and either a poor marriage or lack of any support from the father forces these young women to regret the decision.

The father. Little information about adolescent fathers is available. We are usually most interested in identifying the father and forcing him to accept his legal responsibilities, not in finding out more about him. The stereotype of the adolescent father as uncaring, uninterested, and immature may not always be accurate. As a group, these fathers are more similar to adolescents who have not fathered a child than they are different from them (Earls and Siegel, 1980). However, the profiles of the unwed father that do exist show that he is frightened, withdrawn, confused, and often feels guilty about his girlfriend (Barret and Robinson, 1981). He may not come forward out of fear, and many cannot deal with the pregnancy at all (Freedman, 1986).

The consequences of early parenthood can be severe for the father too. Teenage mothers and fathers are both educationally retarded, and it is an uphill climb to succeed in the world of work (Card and Wise, 1978). They often have dead-end jobs and, faced with the difficulty of supporting a family, many "slide into unemployment" (Freedman, 1986, p. 5). They may also not have the maturity necessary to handle the situation, whether they get married or not.

The extended family. Most parents are shocked to learn that their unwed daughter is pregnant (Furstenberg, 1976). Teens who seek abortions do not usually consult their parents, but teens who carry their pregnancies to term almost always do. When the decision is made to bear the child, a definite progression is seen. First, there is anger and disappointment, followed by a stage of gradual acceptance and a growing closeness between mother and daughter. The quality of the relationship between the pregnant teen and her parents during the pregnancy determines what will happen after the birth. If the bond is close, marriage is much less likely to occur, and young mothers are apt to stay with their parents (Furstenberg, 1981). Most young mothers will stay at home if their mother signals a desire to help them. In fact, young mothers who are helped by their parents, especially until the child is attending school, are in a better economic position than others who leave to be on their own. Grandmothers provide much of the child care in these situations (Forbush, 1981). Many young mothers who return to school are better off years later, although problems do exist and the benefits should not be overstated. As the child matures, sometimes there is a deterioration in family relationships. The child's mother remains in a subordinate position because she is dependent on her family. Even considering these problems, though, it is clear that young parents need help. Whether they live at home or marry, or whether the new mother tries to make it on her own, the young parents(s) need counseling and support from the time the pregnancy begins

through the prenatal period and delivery and into the early years of parenthood. Because subsequent pregnancies are common, sex education is also required.

Sex Education

The majority of people have had no formal sex education, either from teachers or from parents; they learned about sex from their peers (DeLora et al., 1981). However, most parents do favor sex education in the schools (Shope, 1975), but the controversial question is what to teach. Most parents want their own values taught. Even so, when sex education is offered in school, less than 3 percent of parents refuse to let their children participate (Scales, 1978). After the biological aspects of sexuality have been covered, the questions of contraception and values arise. Some parents do not want contraception taught or birth control devices made available to students, although most do (Rinck et al., 1983). Other parents are afraid that the teacher will encourage sexuality or teach values that are different from those "taught" at home. The main problem is that parents do not often talk with their children about contraception, morals, or ethics or help them learn decision-making skills. Instead, the information is often in the form of an explicit warning: "Don't do it."

True or False About 20 percent of all parents refuse to let their children participate in sex education programs in school.

What can a sex education program accomplish? Any program based on the idea that it relieves parents and the religious establishment of the responsibility to educate children about values, or that it will lead to less promiscuity or stimulate sexual play, or that it will automatically reduce venereal disease and pregnancy rates, or that it will prevent ill-advised marriages, is unrealistic (Dale and Chamis, 1981). The purpose should be to "equip young people with the skills, knowledge, and attitudes that will enable them to make intelligent choices and decisions" (Scales, 1981, p. 220). The decision about whether to have sex does not appear to be influenced by sex education. However, there is evidence that sexually active young women who have been exposed to sex education courses are less likely to become pregnant (Zelnik and Kim, 1982). In summary, sex education is likely to continue to be a controversial topic, but the need for it remains great.

Adapting to Change

It is easy to recite the list of physical changes that occur in adolescence, but more important than any list is an understanding of the subjective experience of each adolescent in coping with these changes. Although it is more difficult to cite the cognitive changes that take place during adolescence, they are just as important, and their contribution to adolescent behavior should be appreciated.

When these changes are applied to an issue such as sexuality, adolescent behavior becomes more understandable. But how can parents and teachers help adolescents deal with the issues surrounding sexuality? The answer seems to lie in helping them use their developing cognitive abilities to make sound personal decisions. Adolescents need information, but they also need help in developing their decision-making skills (Scales, 1983). These skills require the ability to communicate, the development of personal and religious values, and the ability to see the problems and consequences of any decision. These abilities can be taught and developed, but they come through dialogue, not lectures (Tangri and Moles, 1987).

Adolescents must make decisions in other areas besides sexuality, decisions about identity and vocational choice, as well as whether to engage in such activities as using drugs. They must also make decisions about interpersonal relationships. It is to these areas of social and personality development that we turn next.

Summary

1. *Puberty* refers to the physiological changes leading to sexual maturity, while *adolescence* refers to the individual's psychological experiences during this period of life. The sequence of physical development during adolescence is predictable, although the age at which each change occurs varies from person to person.

2. Females normally experience their growth spurt before males do. After the growth spurt, the genital organs and breasts develop. Then menstruation occurs.

3. In males, pubic, body, and facial hair appear after the growth spurt. At about the same time, the sexual organs mature. Deepening of the voice and enlargement of the shoulders occur later.

4. The fact that each new generation for the past hundred years or so has been taller and heavier and menstruated earlier than the previous one is known as the *secular trend*. It is leveling off or even stopping in the United States.

5. Early maturation in males is a social advantage during adolescence and early adulthood. In middle adulthood, however, early maturers tend to be less flexible and less insightful. The effects of early and late maturation in females is unclear.

6. Nutrition and eating disorders are not uncommon in adolescents. Obesity is a major medical and social problem. Anorexia nervosa, a disorder involving self-imposed starvation, can be fatal. Bulimia involves binging and purging of the system.

7. During the stage of formal operations, adolescents develop the ability to find possible alternatives to problems, to separate the real from the possible, to form hypotheses and test them out, to understand propositions, to interpret abstractions, and to think about their own thoughts.

8. Adolescents often have difficulty differentiating between their own thoughts and those of others, leading to egocentric thinking. Out of this egocentrism comes the *imaginary audience*, in which adolescents often believe everyone else is looking at them, and the *personal fable*, in which they believe their experiences and thoughts are absolutely unique in the annals of human history.

9. According to Kohlberg, adolescents' more sophisticated cognitive abilities allow them to function at higher levels of moral reasoning. However, most people do not develop past Kohlberg's Stage 4. In adolescents, there is a positive relationship between the level of moral reasoning and prosocial behavior.

10. Adolescents value marriage, family life, and friendships, and their values are apt to be similar

to those of their parents. During the past twenty years, values relating to personal achievement have become more prominent than those having to do with one's relationship with society.

11. School-age children tend to see law and government in terms that are concrete, absolute, and authoritarian. Adolescents view these areas on a more abstract basis, are less authoritarian, and are more sensitive to individual rights. Adolescents understand the conflict between society's and individual's rights. Today, as opposed to fifteen years ago, many more college freshmen see themselves as middle-of-the-road politically.

12. Adolescent attitudes toward sexuality are more liberal than in the past. Females are still more conservative than males, although the gap is narrowing. Males expect intimacy sooner in a relationship than females do.

13. There has been an increase in premarital sex over the past fifty years, but adolescent sexual behavior tends to be more conservative than adolescents' attitudes would indicate.

14. Many sexually active teens do not use contraception regularly. Use does tend to increase with age. Many teens do not use any contraceptive device because they deny their sexuality, do not believe they can become pregnant, believe that contraception diminishes the romantic nature of the experience, or are ignorant of the biological facts of life.

15. Teen pregnancy is a widespread problem for everyone concerned, including the infant, mother, father, and the extended family. Infants born to teenage mothers have more health problems, and teen mothers are more likely to drop out of school. Teenage fathers are often found in dead-end jobs.

16. Most parents favor sex education in school but want their own values taught. Sexually active young women who are exposed to sex education are less likely to become pregnant. Sex education should aim at giving young people the skills, knowledge, and attitudes that will allow them to make intelligent choices. Sex education courses do not relieve the home of its responsibility in this area.

Answers to True or False Statements

1. *False*   Correct statement: The general sequence is quite predictable, although the age at which any particular change occurs varies from person to person.

2. *False*   Correct statement: Menstruation is actually one of the later changes in puberty.

3. *True*   Girls experience their growth spurt before boys, which makes them taller and heavier at this age.

4. *True*   Although research shows early maturation to be a mixed blessing, there is a social advantage to early maturation for males during adolescence.

5. *False*   Correct statement: Most sufferers of anorexia nervosa come from well-educated, affluent, middle-class families.

6. *True*   The ability to interpret proverbs and political cartoons develops during adolescence.

7. *True*   Early adolescents believe that when they walk through the door they will be noticed and evaluated by everyone in the room.

8. *False*   Correct statement: Most college freshmen do not believe that a woman's activities should be confined to home and family.

9. *False*   Correct statement: The number of college freshmen who call themselves conservative has increased about 3 percent, while the number who consider themselves middle-of-the-road has increased 12 percent.

10. *True*   Female sexual attitudes have changed more than those of males, probably because they were more conservative to begin with.

11. *True*   Most adolescents do not seek out advice on contraception until about a year after they have become sexually active.

12. *False*   Correct statement: Only about 3 percent of all parents refuse to allow their children to participate in sex education courses.

CHAPTER 12

Social and Personality Development in Adolescence

No Easy Task
In Search of an Identity
Relationships with Parents and Peers in Adolescence
CROSS-CULTURAL CURRENT   Peers, Parents, and Religion
Career Choice
Four Problems Common in Adolescence
Exploding the Myths

Are the Following Statements True or False?

Try the True-False Quiz below. See if your answers correspond to the information in this chapter. Each question is repeated after the paragraph in which the answer can be found. The True-False Answer Box at the end of the chapter lists the complete answers.

_____ 1. It is more difficult for a person to achieve an identity today than it was a century ago.

_____ 2. Males can achieve intimacy before they find their identity, whereas females must find their identity before they can achieve true intimacy.

_____ 3. Peer influence usually peaks during the late junior high school and early high school years.

_____ 4. Most parents think the generation gap is greater than it actually is.

_____ 5. When parents communicate with their adolescent children, they tend to explain their views rather than trying to understand their teens' opinions and attitudes.

_____ 6. Friends try to control the adolescent's behavior more than parents do.

_____ 7. Daughters who choose to enter male-dominated vocations tend to have distant relationships with their fathers but very close relationships with their working mothers.

_____ 8. The average high school dropout has an average intelligence score.

_____ 9. Alcohol is the most popular drug used by adolescents.

_____ 10. Antismoking advertisements have been more successful at preventing teens from beginning to smoke than at motivating older people to stop smoking.

_____ 11. Cocaine, like alcohol, is a central nervous system depressant that slows down body functioning.

_____ 12. People who talk about committing suicide rarely make a suicide attempt.

No Easy Task

Many people see adolescence as a period of perpetual storm and stress during which teens trade in their dependence on parents for dependence on their peers. They are sometimes viewed as physically mature children who are not quite normal and are negotiating a period in which they show some deviant, confused, but understandable behavior that will disappear by the end of adolescence. With the possible exception of old age, no stage of life is subjected to more stereotyping than adolescence. The stereotypes and misconceptions are responsible for the dislike and distrust that many people hold for adolescents (Varenhorst, 1984).

It is true, however, that adolescents have difficult tasks. They must develop their own sense of individuality, evaluate their unique abilities, make tentative decisions concerning vocational choice and personal definitions, and renegotiate their interpersonal relationships with parents and friends. To do this, they must somehow integrate the lessons of the past with the realities of the present and the possibilities of the future. None of these tasks is easy. In this chapter we look at adolescent social and personality development and examine some of the major challenges confronting adolescents today.

In Search of an Identity

Who am I?
Where do I belong?
Where am I going?

These three questions typify the adolescents' search for a personal identity (Ruittenbeck, 1964). Erik Erikson (1959) saw the positive outcome of adolescence as the formation of a solid, personal **identity,** while the negative outcome of adolescence is an aimlessness known as **role confusion** or **role diffusion**—the state of not knowing who one really is. Adolescents are walking a tightrope. Their task is to surrender the old, dependent ties and childhood identifications with their parents and to develop a separate identity, while continuing a healthy relationship with their elders (Siegel, 1982). If they are to function as adults, they must be able to make their own decisions. They cannot simply be carbon copies of their parents. On the other hand, the attitudes and val-

> **identity** The sense of knowing who you are.
>
> **role confusion (role diffusion)** In psychosocial theory, the negative outcome of adolescence, which involves a failure to develop a personal identity and feelings of aimlessness.

ues gained from parents during childhood serve as anchors, providing security in a sea of change. If they totally abandon these values, they may become bewildered and utterly confused. In addition, surrendering older ideals assumes them all to be dysfunctional—a conclusion that is difficult to support. Adolescents, then, have a difficult course to chart. But is it more difficult today than it was years ago?

Is Finding an Identity More Difficult Today?

Developing an identity involves choosing from various alternatives. Knowing what alternatives are available, as well as having some freedom to choose, are important factors. Imagine yourself a farmer in the plains of the old American West in the early 1800s. Your life is mapped out for you. You will marry the boy or girl a few farms down the road, buy a farm in the same area, and have as many children as possible so the land can be worked efficiently. Because news and information travels slowly, your knowledge of the alternatives available is minimal, and your freedom to act is even less.

Now let's look at the situation in that same area of the West today. Television, the print media, and the movies bring instant information to the community from all over the world. Schooling is universal, and farming has become so technological that it sometimes requires higher education. Along with this information explosion, different values and many new choices surround teenagers. No longer is the teenage girl expected to bear as many children as possible. No longer is farming the only vocation available. No longer are people so isolated that they do not know about other possibilities. You now have many more choices, and a greater degree of freedom to choose your own course. And with choice comes doubt and anxiety.

These factors—more choices and a greater degree of freedom to choose—combine to make forming an identity more difficult today than it was years ago. One other factor is important. Many contemporary observers believe that society is changing at a faster rate than ever before (Toffler, 1970). The skills needed for you to prosper in the years ahead are likely to change along with the rest of our society. Not long ago, a high school education was considered relatively unnecessary, computers were the toys of science fiction writers, and manufacturing jobs were considered secure. The lack of stability in society means that teens must predict what vocations and skills will be needed in a changing world if they are to prepare adequately for it.

True or False   It is more difficult for a person to achieve an identity today than it was a century ago.

The Four Identity Statuses

Achieving an identity depends on two variables—**crisis and commitment** (Marcia, 1967). In a **crisis,** one actively faces and questions aspects of one's personal identity. For instance, a college student may have to choose a major and be faced with this decision when approaching the junior year. In the personal sphere, the student may be dating someone for a while and may have to

Finding an identity one hundred years ago was easier than it is today, simply because there were fewer alternatives available.

identity diffusion An identity status resulting in confusion, aimlessness, and a sense of emptiness.

identity foreclosure An identity status marked by a premature identity decision.

identity moratorium An identity status in which a person is actively searching for an identity.

identity achievement An identity status in which a person has developed a solid, personal identity.

---

decide whether to get more deeply involved. The second aspect, **commitment,** involves making a firm decision concerning some question and following a plan of action that reflects the decision. A person who investigates many vocational choices and decides on a business career will follow the appropriate course of study. The decision to end a relationship or to become engaged leads to different behavioral paths.

Adolescents differ in the extent to which they have experienced crises or made commitments. A prominent researcher in this field, James Marcia (1980, 1967), grouped adolescents into four categories, according to their experiences with crises and commitments (see Table 12.1). One group of adolescents, termed **identity diffused,** consisted of adolescents who may or may not

have experienced a crisis but have not made any commitments. The **identity foreclosed** group consisted of teens who had not experienced a crisis but had made commitments anyway. The **identity moratorium** group contained adolescents who were presently experiencing a crisis but had not yet made any commitments. The **identity achievers** group consisted of adolescents who had already experienced crises and made their commitments. It is worth taking a more detailed look at each status.

Identity diffusion. An individual with identity diffusion has not made any commitments and is not presently in the process of forming any. The adolescent may or may not have experienced a crisis. Even if there has been a crisis, it has not resulted in any decision (Waterman, 1982). Identity-diffused people may actively seek noncommitment, actually avoiding demanding situations. They may also appear aimless, aloof, drifting, and empty (Orlofsky et al, 1973). But people in this status are not mentally ill. Their psychological profiles appear normal (Oshman and Manosevitz, 1974), although their self-esteem is not very high. Some students become alarmed at this description, because they have experienced periods in which the description fits them or someone they are close to very well. But identity diffusion is negative

---

T A B L E 12.1

James Marcia's Four Identity Statuses

Identity Status	Definition
Identity Achievement	An Identity Achiever has experienced doubt (crisis) in personal goals and values, has considered alternatives, and is committed at least tentatively to some expressed value positions and career plans.
Identity Foreclosure	A Forecloser displays a commitment similar to that of the Identity Achiever but has not appraised alternatives to personal goals and values; choices often express parental preferences.
Identity Moratorium	A Moratorium has questioned goals and values and considered alternatives but is still doubtful and uncommitted; predominating is an active effort to become informed and to make suitable choices.
Identity Diffusion	An Identity Diffuser might or might not have experienced doubt over goals and values; he or she does not evidence a serious or realistic inclination to examine concerns about goals and values; he or she expresses no commitments to an ideology or to career plans.

Source: Hummel and Roselli, 1983.

only when a person leaves adolescence without making commitments. A period of confusion often precedes establishment of a firm identity (Erikson, 1959).

Identity foreclosure. Do you know people who always seem to have it "all together," who knew what they wanted at a very early age and appear confident and secure? These seemingly lucky people have formed a commitment, but it may not be their own. It may be one handed down to them by their parents. They identify very well—perhaps too well—with their parents. For example, some people may go into their parents' business because it was always expected of them. They were not permitted, or did not permit themselves, to search for other alternatives. In another situation, a young woman may have chosen a mate very early in life and not explored other possible choices or alternatives to early marriage.

Identity foreclosure can be a secure status. These people appear to function well and do not suffer periods of crisis. They show little anxiety (Marcia and Friedman, 1970). Identity-foreclosed people are often envied by their peers. After all, they have a direction in life and are following a definite path. But this security is purchased at a price. The path is not one they might have chosen, and foreclosed individuals sometimes find themselves mired in an unhappy lifestyle later in life (Petitpas, 1978).

There is another side to identity foreclosure. Some adolescents may be foreclosed because they do not have the opportunity to search or to know what is available. Many poor and minority group youths do not believe they have many choices. Some must enter the labor force as soon as possible to support themselves and their families. Others may not have the basic academic skills necessary for more advanced study, which would allow them to explore alternative vocational opportunities. For these teens, foreclosure is forced on them by circumstances, by lack of knowledge about their choices, or by their belief that they do not have any control over their own destinies.

Identity moratorium. Adolescents who are presently experiencing a crisis but whose commitments are vague are considered to be in the moratorium status. This is a period of delay in which a person is not yet ready to make definite commitments (Erikson, 1968). Many possibilities are being explored, some of them radical, but

There is nothing wrong with people entering the "family business" as long as it is their own choice and not forced upon them.

final commitments tend to be more conservative. Many who were radicals during the 1960s are now living conservative lives and are members of the political establishment. They often made professional commitments that involve human services (Nassi, 1981).

The moratorium state is not a happy one. The adolescent may be dissatisfied with everything and everyone. The campus reformer may indeed be searching for something. He or she sees everything that is wrong but is less successful when it comes to suggesting what realistic steps can be taken to alleviate the problems. People in this status are active and troubled. Quick to debate and frequently in opposition to their parents, they are often hostile toward peers as well. They are engaged in seemingly perpetual struggles with authority figures (Donovan, 1975).

Identity moratorium is the least stable of all the statuses (Waterman, 1982). However, it may be necessary for a person to experience, for then when a person does make a commitment it is his or her own, made after a period of searching for answers. Studies show that about 75 percent of all college students who were in the moratorium state when they began college could later be said to have achieved an independent identity by graduation (Waterman and Waterman, 1971).

Identity achievement. Identity achievers have made it. They have experienced their crises, solved them, and made their commitments. Their goals are realistic, and they can cope with shifts in the environment (Orlofsky et al., 1973). These independent personal identities are not carbon copies of their parents' identities, nor are they totally the opposite (Donovan, 1975). Their identity includes some of the parents' values and attitudes, while omitting others. They are well adjusted (Bernard, 1981) and have good relationships both with peers and with authority figures (Donovan, 1975).

Predictions from Identity Status

If you know someone's identity status, can you predict anything about that person's behavior or standing in the community? The answer is yes, but we must keep in mind that people can move from one group to another as they experience a crisis or make a new commitment. Although the identity-achiever status is relatively stable, it can change (Douvan and Adelson, 1966). An unusual experience might lead one back to a moratorium—for example, after spending a number of years preparing to become a newspaper reporter, one young woman found she could not find a job and had to search for an occupational identity all over again. Or the divorced person may have to search anew for a personal or social identity because the original one is no longer viable.

Research shows that there is a relationship between one's present status and specific behaviors. For example, identity achievers have the highest grade-point averages of any of the other statuses (Cross and Allen, 1970) and have better study habits (Waterman and Waterman, 1971). Identity achievers also perform better under stress (Muuss, 1982). If we compare people in all four statuses, identity achievers show the least self-consciousness, while identity-diffused individuals exhibit the most self-consciousness—perhaps because identity achievers have

intimacy vs. isolation   The sixth psychosocial stage, occurring during young adulthood, in which the positive outcome is a development of deep interpersonal relationships and the negative outcome is a flight from close relationships.

a higher acceptance of self and a more stable self-definition (Adams et al., 1987). Identity-foreclosed people score much higher on measures of authoritarianism and are more conservative, obedient, and loyal to conventional values than people in the other statuses (Muuss, 1982). Moratorium subjects are the most anxious.

Probably the most important finding is that identity achievement has been linked to the depth of intimacy developed in early adulthood. The ego crisis of young adulthood can be expressed as **intimacy vs. isolation** (Erikson, 1968). Intimacy involves the development of very close personal relationships, while isolation involves a lack of commitment. Intimacy requires that two people share their identities, not that there be a complete merging of selves. Problems may occur for people who choose marriage or parenthood as a way out of an identity dilemma. These people really have not resolved the identity issue—it is still on the back burner, waiting for an opportunity to show itself. Resolution of identity issues can be delayed, but not always shelved forever.

People in the moratorium and achievement statuses experience deeper levels of intimacy than people in the other two statuses (Fitch and Adams, 1983). In a landmark study, Orlofsky and colleagues (1973) determined the identity status of fifty-three male juniors and seniors at a university in New York. The researchers also rated the subjects on the presence or absence of close interpersonal relationships and the degree of openness, closeness, and commitment in these relationships. Data on personality and social relationships was also collected. Identity achievers scored very high on measures of intimacy, while the identity-diffused and foreclosed subjects scored poorly. The foreclosed and diffused subjects were the most isolated. The moratorium subjects were somewhere in the middle. Identity-foreclosed subjects had the greatest need for social approval, were least autonomous, and had not modified their family ties. Autonomy and intimacy were related, and identity achievers were found to have successful, mature, intimate relationships; moratorium subjects were similar to achievement subjects, but a bit behind. Most moratorium subjects had intimate relationships with close friends but had not formed enduring heterosexual relationships. Foreclosed and diffused subjects were involved in some relationships, but these lacked the depth and genuine closeness of the achievement group. The results of this study confirm that progress toward achieving a mature identity is related to the ability to achieve intimacy.

Although the basic relationship between identity and intimacy is correct, some authorities now claim that the relationship may be slightly different for males and females. In one study, a number of women but only one man was found to be high in intimacy but low in identity. It may be that some women deal successfully with intimacy issues prior to identity issues (Schiedel and Marcia, 1985), while most men do not. This surprising finding may have to do with the difference between the search for identity that males and females conduct.

> *True or False*   Males can achieve intimacy before they find their identity, whereas females must find their identity before they can achieve true intimacy.

Do Males and Females Take Different Paths to Identity?

The key to identity formation is searching and exploring. The process of identity formation requires that a person combine considerations from the past, the present, and the future. The years between eighteen and twenty-one seem especially crucial to development of an identity. Before this time, the overwhelming number of young adults are either foreclosed or diffused (Archer, 1982; Meilman, 1979), and only very limited changes occur prior to or during the high school years (Waterman, 1982). The experience of schooling, especially college, seems to encourage young people to question. Because such searching is not easy, it is not unusual for adolescents to take shortcuts by joining cults or blindly adopting and espousing a cause that becomes the consuming passion in their life.

Males and females may approach identity formation from different perspectives. Their searches and their abilities to explore alternatives may differ. For one thing, their parents' attitudes toward lifestyles, and the models available to males and females, are not the same. In addition, males tend to focus on intrapersonal factors, such as vocational identity and personal identity, while

women are more likely to tie their identities to interpersonal relationships (Schiedel and Marcia, 1985).

I sometimes ask students in my classes whether they think about the impact their future vocation will have on their family life. The responses of males and females differ. Males are more likely to focus solely on economic issues, while females, who are interested in economic issues too, also focus on how their vocational pursuits will combine with future family and caregiving responsibilities. Jobs and vocational identities, which are now considered by females to be part of their lives, are not necessarily seen as vital factors in self-actualization, but rather viewed as something they can fall back on, allowing some measure of independence (Hyde, 1985). The future family remains the focus of their quest (Greenglass and Devins, 1982). Like any generalization, this is not true in every case. Some men do consider their family roles, and some women do not define achievement in interpersonal terms. However, the differences do seem to exist. The extent to which this may change in the future is open to question. Neither males nor females now see women's place as exclusively in the home (Astin, 1986). This may mean that women are accurately perceiving their new role as both worker and primary family caregiver. Men may not yet see their dual responsibility in these balanced terms.

Relationships with Parents and Peers in Adolescence

> "I wish my parents would get off my back. They're always criticizing everything I do. They must have been saints when they were in their teens. If they would just leave me alone, I'd be okay."
>
> "My parents and I get along pretty well. They listen to me and I listen to them—although we don't agree on everything. I have a good set of friends, and my parents like them."
>
> "The one problem I have with my parents is that they don't seem to trust me. They think I'm still eleven years old. They don't want to discuss rules, they just want to lay down the law. They repeat everything four hundred times, especially the warnings."

These are some of the responses from fourteen- and fifteen-year-olds when I asked about their relationships with parents. During adolescence, the relationship between parents and children changes. One task of adolescence is to establish a personal identity, and this requires that there be some separation between parent and child and attainment of some degree of independence and autonomy.

Parental and Peer Influence

It is no secret that peer influences increase during middle childhood and into adolescence. The amount of time spent with parents declines, and the sheer quantity of time spent with friends increases. The peer group serves a number of functions in adolescence. It often provides support for adolescents who are striving for independence, because peers are facing the same challenges. Peers help adolescents develop social skills and an identity (Coleman, 1981). The peer group serves as a reference group and gives teens another evaluation of their actions. In early adolescence, dependence on parents decreases and dependence on peers increases. Adolescents become more emotionally autonomous from their parents; they idealize them less and relinquish some of their childhood dependence on them. This is accompanied by increased susceptibility to peer influences (Steinberg and Silverberg, 1986).

Adolescents in late junior high and early high school (eighth- and ninth-graders) seem to be most influenced by peers. One study (Berndt, 1979) presented children from the third, sixth, ninth, and eleventh or twelfth grades with hypothetical situations in which a child was encouraged by peers to perform antisocial acts (such as stealing or cheating), neutral acts (such as choosing hobbies or entertainment and eating places), or prosocial acts (such as performing charitable deeds). The children's responses to these situations showed that conformity to peers for antisocial acts peaked at the ninth-grade level and declined thereafter (Berndt, 1979). Males are generally more willing than females to follow their peers in antisocial behavior, but in other facets of conformity this is not the case (Brown et al., 1986). Traditionally, females have been considered less autonomous and more conforming. However, any gender gap that may have existed in autonomy and conformity is narrowing and even disappearing (Steinberg and Silverberg, 1986; Eagly, 1978).

True or False Peer influence usually peaks during the late junior high school and early high school years.

Peer pressure can be great even in the younger grades. Third-graders often experience conflicts between parents and peers, but usually decide in the direction of their parents' wishes. Peer influences become more evident between the third and sixth grades, but there is little evidence of increased conflict (Berndt, 1979). In this period, children can isolate the peer world from the familial environment. Many early adolescents use language with their peers that they do not use at home. Early adolescents seem to be able to separate their worlds— not discussing with their parents what they do with their peers, and vice versa. By ninth grade, peer conformity is at its peak and conflict between parents and adolescents is common.

Berndt believes that two factors are involved in this increasing conflict. First, antisocial conformity is at its peak here, and parents—who may be able to look the other way when it comes to hairstyles and taste in music—cannot disguise their concern about antisocial behavior. Second, the push toward independence is particularly strong at this age. At this point, adolescents often report the greatest number of disagreements with their parents. By the junior and senior years of high school, some conflict remains, but peer influence seems to decline somewhat and conventional behavior increases. This pattern continues into young adulthood.

Areas of Influence

We can better understand the influence of parents and peers by looking at specific situations. If teenagers have questions about the newest styles or musical trends, whom would they consult—parents or peers? If they had questions concerning their future occupation, would they ask peers or seek out some older person? The influence of either generation depends on the situation (Brittain, 1969; 1963). Adolescents perceive peers and parents as competent guides in different areas. The peer group is viewed as more knowledgeable in surface and social areas—such as styles and feelings about school—but in deeper values adolescents report being closer to their parents. (The Cross-Cultural Current on page 323 examines peer and parental influence on religious beliefs and behavior during adolescence.)

This division of influence meshes well with common experience. Adolescents are influenced by people who they believe have superior knowledge in a particular area. For instance, students eager for vocational information consult sources of expertise—often older adults. They

Peers, Parents, and Religion

When asked in what areas peers or parents are more influential, the common response of most social scientists is that peers are more influential in "surface areas," such as styles and language, and that parents are more influential in the "deeper areas," such as values. On the other hand, some authorities claim that the youth subculture has distinctive values of its own. One of these areas of "deeper values" is certainly religion. Do parents' religious values have more influence on older adolescents, or do the values of the peer group influence the religious orientation of the adolescent more?

Up to this point, there has been little research on the influence of parents and peers on religious orientation, and the studies we do have are inconclusive. Some research in the United States showed that peers are more important in the area of religion, while other studies showed the opposite. One problem may be the very definition of what should be studied under the heading of "religion." There is a difference between religious values and religious behavior. For example, believing in a particular religious philosophy is different from attending church every Sunday. In addition, when we talk of peer or parental influence, we should be more specific. Are we talking about mothers or fathers, close friends, or "the crowd"?

David de Vaus looked at the importance of peer influence and parental influence in relation to religious values and behavior in Australian teenagers. Some 375 sixteen-to eighteen-year-olds from the state of Victoria were randomly chosen for the study. Subjects were asked about their religious activities—such behaviors as church attendance and prayer—and their perceptions of parents' and peers' religious beliefs. Then they were asked to rank-order the people who had influenced their religious beliefs and behaviors.

De Vaus wanted answers to three questions. First, was the religious orientation of adolescents most similar to that of parents or that of peers? Second, when parents and peers hold different religious beliefs, to whom is the adolescent most similar? Third, are parents or peers most likely to be considered referents for adolescents?

The results show that, at least for religious activity (behavior), both parents and peers were about equal in importance. Adolescents were more similar to their close friends than to "the crowd," and closer in religious activity to their mothers than to their fathers. When parents and peers held different orientations (values and attitudes), parents were relatively more important than peers.

The results also show that peers are more likely to have influence over overt behavior than values, ideals, and beliefs. When asked who had been most influential in development of their religious feelings, the most common answer was the mother (51 percent), followed by the father, at 42 percent. Close friends were ranked third, at 15 percent, and the crowd was ranked last. It is interesting to note that, when asked whose opinions mattered most, close friends were most important, but parents—especially the mother—were considered important too. Because the assessments of others have a great deal of influence on self-concept, the peer group seems greatly but not solely influential here. However, the peer group does not seem to influence religious values very much.

Why the peer group does not have much effect on religious values is not clear. Perhaps religious orientation is simply not an important factor in how teens are evaluated by their friends. On the other hand, in Australia religion is viewed as a private matter, and attempts to influence the religious views of others are not acceptable.

This study demonstrates that it is important to separate the influence of mother and father, close friends, and "the crowd." In addition, separation of religious values from religious behavior is important. There is evidence that mother and close friends were generally more important than father and the crowd.

It would be fascinating to repeat this study in countries where religious orientation is less of a private matter. The results might be different and might help us better understand the effect culture could have on parental and peer influence on adolescents.

Source: De Vaus, D. A. The Relative Importance of Parents and Peers for Adolescent Religious Orientation: An Australian Study. *Adolescence,* 1983, *18,* 147–158.

may discuss career options with their friends, but they know that in this area some older people know more.

The Generation Gap Revisited

In order for adolescents and adults to interact effectively, they must have some idea of how each views the other, as well as some ability to communicate. Just how accurately do adolescents and their parents see each other and understand each other's point of view? Lerner and his colleagues (1975) asked undergraduate students and their parents to note their feelings on a number of issues—such as racism, war, sex, and drug use. Subjects checked the alternatives from number 1, meaning "strongly agree," to 7, indicating "strongly disagree." They were asked to rate not only statements that reflected their own attitudes, but also statements mirroring the beliefs of their parents and peers. Parents were asked to rate their own stands on issues, as well as to predict where their children and other teens stood on those issues.

generation gap   The differences in attitudes among various generations.

The results? Most actual differences were in the direction of intensity. In other words, the differences between the generations are a matter of degree, with one generation agreeing or disagreeing more strongly with a position than the other. The popular term **generation gap** is often used to denote what is seen as the ever-widening gap between the standards, values, and opinions of generations. Most studies find that the generation gap is more apparent than real (Lerner et al., 1975), and the differences are more a matter of degree or intensity than anything else. Only on the subjects of sex and drugs do qualitative differences exist (Chand et al., 1975).

Although the generation gap may not be as great on most issues as first thought, the perceptions each group has of the attitudes of the other group are mistaken.

When it comes to styles in clothing or music, young people are likely to value each other's opinions greatly.

Adolescents overestimate the gap between their parents and themselves, while parents consistently underestimate it. Each group views the other as more conservative than it actually is (Lerner et al., 1976).

True or False Most parents think the generation gap is greater than it actually is.

Why should this perceived gap be so much greater than the actual gap? Perhaps parents want to see themselves as closer to their children, while adolescents are motivated to separate themselves more from their parents. But this could also reflect poor communication between the generations.

Communication with Parents and Peers

Communication with peers differs greatly from communication with parents during adolescence. Parents are more directive, sharing their wisdom, whereas communication with peers often shows greater mutuality and sharing of similar experiences (Hunter, 1984). Parents may not like to listen to their adolescents who are in the process of formulating their own values and opinions, especially if their children are taking positions that are different. On the other hand, parents may counter these unwanted views with a long lecture, which is usually an ineffective method of communication. Parents tend to concentrate more on explaining their own viewpoints than on trying to understand their child's views (Hunter, 1985). In short, parents are more directive with their adolescents, while peers tend to share more and appear to be more open with their peers. In addition, much parental communication comes as criticism. This is unfortunate because positive and supportive communication enables children to explore their identity in greater depth. Generally, parents who support their children by creating an atmosphere that fosters respect for the opinions of others, mutuality, and tolerance make it possible for their children to explore identity alternatives (Grotevant and Cooper, 1986a). And adolescents who have the support of their families actually feel freer to explore identity issues (Cooper et al., 1982).

True or False When parents communicate with their adolescent children, they tend to explain their views rather than trying to understand their teens' opinions and attitudes.

Adolescents perceive this difference more clearly than parents do. Adolescents see significantly less openness

and more problems in intergenerational communication (Barnes and Olson, 1985). However, there are communication problems on both sides.

Renegotiating Relationships with Parents

Now that some groundwork has been laid, we can look at the nature of the relationship between parents and their children during adolescence. There are two popular models (Grotevant and Cooper, 1986b). The first sees the adolescent severing his or her ties with parents, often leading to a new dependency on peers. The other sees parent-child relationships basically as stable throughout adolescence and downplays the idea that meaningful conflict arises. If we look at early adolescence, we see some evidence for the first theory, and if one looks at late adolescence, some evidence for the second can be deduced. However, the newer perspective of adolescence as a whole sees the relationship between adolescents and their parents as moving toward a new symmetry and equality as the years of adolescence roll by. This view sees autonomy and remaining connected with one's family as complementary, not opposite, processes. In one study, adolescents who considered themselves most autonomous rated their relationships with their parents as close, perceived them as role models, and often turned to their parents for advice (Kandel and Lesser, 1969). Adolescence is not a time of complete break or total stability. Instead, a gradual renegotiation between parents and adolescents takes place as the relationship changes from the authoritarian, superior-subordinate relationship to one that involves greater mutuality (Grotevant and Cooper, 1986b).

Just how does this renegotiation take place? Hunter and Younis (1982) looked at changes in three functions of interpersonal relationships in students in the fourth, seventh, and tenth grades and in college. The *control function* involved being told what to do and disagreeing. The *intimacy function* described self-disclosure and empathy, among other aspects of the relationships. The *nurture function* referred to giving and helping acts.

The control function was found to be greater in the parent-adolescent relationship across all age-groups. In other words, at every age parents try to control the behavior of adolescents much more than friends do. The attempts at control, though, lessen as the adolescent enters college. The intimacy function showed a change as the adolescent matures. It was greater for parents at fourth grade, but was surpassed by peers in tenth grade. By mid-adolescence to late adolescence (seventh to tenth grade), friendship patterns become more intimate, and there was a decrease in this function for parents, after which there was a characteristic increase.

True or False Friends try to control the adolescents' behavior more than parents do.

Again we see the pattern in which mid-adolescence seems to be the most trying period for parent-child relationships, with improvement occurring later on. Even though friendships continue to become more intimate in later adolescence, the increase in parental intimacy demonstrates that the growing intimacy with age-mates need not interfere with that portion of the relationship with parents. The nurturance factor remains very high throughout adolescence for the parent-child relationship. Although there is an increase in this helping function for friends, it never surpasses the level of helpfulness in parent-child interactions.

The most interesting change is in intimacy. Sharabany and her colleagues (1981) investigated changes in this area in fifth-, seventh-, ninth-, and eleventh-graders. Intimacy involves frankness and spontaneity, sensitivity and knowing, attachment, exclusiveness, imposing and taking, trust and loyalty. Male relationships generally show a lower degree of intimacy than those formed by females. Females are more expressive and report more giving and sharing than males. Females also develop intimacy with the opposite sex faster than males do. In the fifth grade, boys and girls relate to the opposite sex with little intimacy. By the seventh grade, girls report far more intimacy toward boys than boys report toward girls. This discrepancy is maintained through the eleventh grade. Intimacy with same-sex friends remains strong, but with maturity a reduction in attachment and exclusiveness takes place. By the eleventh grade, the differences in intimacy between same-sex and opposite-sex friends is reduced. It appears that girls in mid-adolescence are more ready to commit themselves to intimate friendships than boys are. The socialization of males away from expressiveness may partly explain this finding. Because boys are not as ready to form relationships at this age, it may be wise for a girl to understand that she may be more ready to share than the average male of her age-group.

These studies show that the adolescent's relationships with parents and with peers are dynamic, changing with maturity and experience. Peers and parents provide dif-

ferent social worlds for adolescents (Montemayor, 1982). Adolescents interact with their parents in such activities as shopping, eating, and doing chores, but spend more time with peers, playing games and talking. Most of the free time spent with parents involves watching television, for which many adolescents do not show much enthusiasm. Perhaps parents would do better if they reduced the amount of time they spent watching television with their adolescents and directed their efforts to more active social activities.

Still, there is some good news in this for parents. The restructuring of relationships during early and middle adolescence may be difficult, but it does not put parents out in the cold. In addition, by late adolescence an improvement in the parent-child relationship occurs, and there is less conflict.

Career Choice

"If I only knew what I wanted to be, I'd be able to do better in school." This is one of the more common complaints of adolescents. Erik Erikson acknowledged the importance of a vocational identity (Erikson, 1968). The interrelationship is nicely shown by the fact that college students who chose occupations that mirrored their measured abilities and interests showed more successful resolutions of Erikson's first six stages, including identity formation in adolescence (Munley, 1977; 1975). Students begin thinking about their vocational futures long before high school begins. The process of vocational development starts in childhood, as children observe the occupations around them and imagine themselves working in them (Super, 1953). But it is in high school and later in college that students begin to realize that a career decision is facing them.

Is Career Choice Different Today?

The labor market changes quickly. Career choice today differs from what it was even twenty years ago and a number of emerging trends are worth noting. The 1970s saw for the first time in history the mean educational attainment level in the United States surpass the average education level required for jobs (Scott, 1983). This has resulted in artificially high educational requirements for some jobs. Some of these job requirements are greater than the skills really necessary to perform them.

In addition, the population of the United States is becoming older. Fewer teenagers are around to take up the many lower-paying jobs that exist, and studies show that this change toward an older population will continue (Supple, 1986). The median age of all American workers in 1970 was twenty-eight, but it will be age thirty-five by the year 2000. Fewer workers mean that there will be supply shortages, but determining in precisely what fields these will occur is difficult. Technological advances are also important, and economic changes are coming faster than they did twenty-five years ago. Finally, many of the better-paying jobs are rather invisible—that is, unlike doctors and lawyers they are not in the public eye—making vocational information more important.

Gender and Socioeconomic Status

Ideally, people take their abilities, interests, and future goals into consideration when they choose a vocation. Chance factors enter into the equation too. But vocation is a conscious choice only when people consider what they want to do and then follow some program of study or training to achieve it. Not everyone makes such a conscious decision. Conscious career choice is viable only for people who believe they have the opportunity and the resources to succeed and who live in an environment that makes it possible for them to carry out their plans (Harmon and Farmer, 1983). For some women and members of many ethnic and racial minority groups, this is not always the case.

Women and careers. Years ago, one could say that a girl would grow up, get married, and lead a rather conventional existence. Few women who worked could be found in professional jobs. This is not so today. Studies predict that, by the year 1990, nine of every ten women can expect to work outside the home sometime in their lives (Clarey and Sanford, 1982). In fact, most women today state that they prefer to combine marriage and career pursuits (Fitzgerald and Betz, 1983). In addition, although women are still over represented in certain fields, such as clerical and service positions, more women than ever before are entering what might be called non-traditional fields. A nontraditional field is one in which the overwhelming majority of workers are men, such as engineering.

Nontraditional careers for women: Two views. The trend for women to enter nontraditional fields can be analyzed in two ways. The first is pessimistic. For example, 74 percent of all schoolteachers are female, as

are 69 percent of retail sales workers. Women comprise 87 percent of librarians, 96 percent of nurses, and 99 percent of secretaries. They comprise only 1 percent of firefighters, 2 percent of construction workers, 3 percent of mechanics, 6 percent of police officers, and just 6 percent of engineers. Although 45 percent of all workers are women, only 36 percent of the executives or managers are women. In the largest 500 companies, only one chief executive is a woman (Bloom, 1986). Most women are still opting to enter traditional fields, even if these fields are professional, such as teaching (Lueptow, 1981). There is some change in the number of women who want to enter nontraditional fields, such as the sciences, but it has been a relatively small change overall.

The other evaluation is more optimistic. It sees women as making substantial if uneven progress. For example, in 1970 only 5 percent of lawyers were female, while it is 20 percent today. Some 18 percent of all physicians are female today, up from 10 percent in 1970. Women comprise 28 percent of computer scientists today, com-

There are now more career opportunities open to women than ever before.

pared with 14 percent in 1970. Today, 8 percent of architects are women, double the percentage in 1970, and the percentage of college and university professors has increased from 29 percent in 1970 to 37 percent today. In the area of business executives, the rise is also significant. In 1972, women comprised only 27 percent of the managers, but in 1986 that percentage stood at 36 percent (Bloom, 1986). One-third of all students in law school, and one-quarter of students in medicine, veterinary medicine, and business administration, are women (Wilson et al., 1982).

These figures show that women are entering these male-dominated fields in greater numbers. But cultural attitudes and beliefs concerning women's roles and capabilities, including occupational stereotyping, act to restrict women's career goals. Some young women learn that their adult roles should include being a wife and mother and that if they must work they should choose a stereotyped female-dominated occupation. This limits their choice of occupation (Fitzgerald and Betz, 1983). The same argument can be made for men, who usually do not consider female-dominated occupations.

Both men and women who enter nontraditional career areas must deal with special difficulties.

Women who enter nontraditional careers differ from those who do not (Auster and Auster, 1981). Women who achieve in male-dominated professions often have mothers who worked and acted as role models for them. The higher the social status of the position held by the mother, the less traditional the choice made by the daughter (Treiman and Terrell, 1975). The father influences this decision too. Daughters choosing nontraditional careers also have close relationships with their fathers and model themselves after the male parent as well. Both parents also support the daughter's decision to enter a nontraditional field. Socioeconomic status enters the picture too, as there is a positive relationship between higher socioeconomic status and a nontraditional career choice. Women choosing nontraditional careers also tend to be oldest or only children and come from relatively small families. Peers may exert a positive or negative influence on the choice of a nontraditional career.

True or False Daughters who choose to enter male-dominated vocations tend to have distant relationships with their fathers but very close relationships with their working mothers.

Other studies found a positive correlation between androgyny in women (females whose personalities comprise both masculine and feminine traits) and choice of nontraditional careers (Clarey and Sanford, 1982). Mentors and husbands may also be important sources of encouragement (Wilson et al., 1982). Women choosing nontraditional careers also believe in a more equitable division of labor in marriage and generally have attitudes that are less conventional (O'Donnell and Andersen, 1978), including less-traditional beliefs about "appropriate" sex roles (Keith, 1981).

Socioeconomic status. Career choice is also a misnomer for the poor, many of whom belong to minority groups. Many poor do not have any choices, or at least do not see any, and adolescents from poverty backgrounds are less likely than middle-class teens to have high vocational aspirations (Bachman, 1978). For many poor, black males, there is no real career exploration period. They may take a job in their teens, but after that job there may be a succession of unrelated jobs for fifty years. No career ladder is present.

Occupational choice may also be limited by lack of economic resources and racial discrimination, and the lack of high-achieving role models complicates the situation. Adolescents from middle-class families believe they can influence their own futures—that is, they have an **internal locus of control.** But this is not the case with poorer youngsters, who often have an **external locus of control** and see themselves as at the mercy of the system, the outside world, or luck. They are more fatalistic in their outlook (Farmer, 1978). If they don't have the power to change things, why plan?

All in all, the poor face barriers of discrimination and a history of lack of success with the system. This does not mean they lack motivation to succeed, though, only that in order to succeed there must be some belief in the effectiveness of one's own efforts. For example, say you want to become a chemist but don't believe that you can make it even if you study hard. You might not even know what is necessary. The first problem is one of changing a view toward life, the second requires adequate vocational information and counseling. The disadvantaged are also hindered by their poorer educational background and academic skills.

As in the case of women, there is both good and bad news concerning career choices for minorities. For example, in 1970 about half a million black men and women were attending college, while in 1985 that figure stood at about 755,000. The proportion of blacks in white collar jobs has increased greatly over the past 25 years and the percentage of blacks in professional and technical areas has increased somewhat. In 1970 blacks constituted 2 percent of the doctors, 1 percent of the lawyers and judges, and 2.9 percent of the teachers. In 1985, 3.7 percent of the doctors, 3.3 percent of the lawyers, and 9 percent of all teachers were black (U.S. Department of Commerce, 1987). While this shows some progress, the progress has been slow. In addition, the unemployment rate is greater for minority group youths than for whites. The unemployment rate for black youths is 28 percent, 14 percent for Hispanics, and 11 percent for Caucasian youths not in school (U.S. Department of Labor, 1986b). This higher unemployment rate probably reflects both the lack of skills and the high percentage of high school dropouts found among minority group youths.

Four Problems Common in Adolescence

Adolescence is often linked to specific problems, such as dropping out of high school, delinquency and crime, drug abuse, and suicide. Although the last three are not the sole province of adolescents, they are serious problems during this stage.

Dropping Out of School

High school dropouts are more likely to live on or near the poverty level, to experience unemployment, and to depend on government for support (Steinberg, 1985). Although the majority of students finish high school, a large minority do not. About one in four students who enroll in high school drop out before graduation (Boyer, 1983). Students from minority groups, who are usually poor, have a higher dropout rate than middle-class youths. The dropout rate is distressing because it represents a waste of human resources. Although some studies have found that the average dropout has a lower intelligence score, most more recent studies show that this is true only for those who drop out before high school. The average high school dropout has an average intelligence score (Sprintall and Collins, 1984; Voss et al., 1966). Many students who do not finish high school have not developed their potential. In addition, the financial differences between graduates and nongraduates is great, especially as they move through adulthood. Dropouts do not usually find jobs that have solid futures because their skills are poor. Third, many dropouts will face unemployment or underemployment throughout life, which will affect their self-concepts and family relationships.

True or False The average high school dropout has an average intelligence score.

School holds little promise for dropouts. As a group, they are poor readers. In one study, 80 percent of the dropouts were one year behind peers in reading, and 50 percent were at least two years behind (Grinder, 1973). Dropouts have poor grades, experience failure, and show little or no interest in school. Many of these students have been left back a grade. They often come from backgrounds of poverty, large families, or families in which discord and divorce are common (Bachman et al., 1972).

These homes generally do not offer much intellectual stimulation. Dropouts also show a history of school-related problems, including high rates of delinquency and school suspension (Sprintall and Collins, 1984). Their personality profiles show that they are hostile and resentful, have low self-esteem, and are less likely to have definite values and goals than high school graduates (Conger and Petersen, 1984).

Most factors that differentiate graduates from dropouts are present before these teens dropped out (Bachman et al., 1978). The low self-esteem, higher rates of delinquency, and higher rates of drug abuse are found before the students stop attending school, so they are not the consequences of dropping out. Dropping out is not an event as much as it is the result of a long process of failure, poor adjustment, low aspirations, low intellectual stimulation, and poverty. It can be predicted.

Many school districts recognize that the dropout problem is a serious one that requires bold new approaches. Some have instituted programs in which potential dropouts attend alternative schools or work-study programs and receive more attention and tutoring in basic academic skills. All these show promise, and because the problem is such a complicated one, the solution may require a variety of programs and approaches.

Delinquency

Adolescents who have difficulty in school and are potential dropouts are frequently involved in delinquent activities. Concern about youth crime or delinquency is certainly not new, and statistics show that it is a serious, ongoing problem. In 1985, some 31 percent of the arrests for the crime index offenses of murder, forcible rape, robbery, assault, burglary, larceny-theft, motor vehicle theft, and arson were under the age of eighteen and 47 percent were under the age of 21 (FBI, 1986). Males comprise 80 percent of all arrests and 89 percent of the arrests for violent crimes. Of course, most delinquent actions are not as serious as murder and rape. The most frequent complaints against boys involve joyriding, drunk driving, burglary, malicious mischief, auto theft, and illegal drug use. Girls are most likely to be reported for running away and for illicit sexual behavior (U.S. Department of Commerce, 1986). More than 1,400,000 people under the age of eighteen were arrested in 1985 (FBI, 1986).

Most people think of delinquents as coming from broken homes and poverty-stricken backgrounds. Indeed, delinquency flourishes where family discord and abuse are prevalent, where gangs reinforce criminal acts, and where discipline is either very severe and punitive or very lax (Fox, 1985; Hardert et al., 1984). Delinquency has been thought of as a problem emanating from lower-income youths, and there is some evidence for this, but the relationship between delinquency and socioeconomic status is found only in large cities and not in smaller cities and towns (Clarizio and McCoy, 1983). In addition, studies of undetected delinquency—that is, self-reported delinquent acts, many of which are never reported to the police—show no significant differences in delinquent behavior across socioeconomic groups (Clarizio and McCoy, 1983). Some 80 percent of all young people admit doing something delinquent at one time or another, and the fastest rate of increase in delinquent behavior is among suburban teens (Steinberg, 1985). This might be expected, since abuse, family discord, antisocial peer groups, and inconsistent discipline exist in the suburbs as well. Perhaps the statistics that show greater prevalence of delinquent acts in poor areas are skewed because the justice system is more likely to try and imprison the poor than the more affluent (Jensen, 1985).

Delinquents are impulsive, resentful, socially assertive, defiant, suspicious, and lack self-control. They often feel inadequate and see themselves as lazy or bad (Conger and Petersen, 1984). Relationships with parents are usually poor. In many of the homes that yield delinquents, there is a lack of family routine, inconsistent discipline in which parents yell, threaten, and nag but do not follow through, and an inability to deal with family problems (Wilson and Herrnstein, 1985). Parent-child interactions lack warmth and intimacy and are characterized instead by rejection or indifference. Lack of supervision is also a problem, especially in single-parent families. In one study, single-parent families headed by mothers were found to have more difficulty controlling their teenagers. Adolescents in these mother-only households were more likely to make decisions without direct parental input, lacked parental supervision, and were more likely to exhibit deviant behavior when compared with two-parent or extended families controlled for socioeconomic status (Dornbusch et al., 1985). The importance of peer influence, especially during the early and middle years of adolescence, when peer pressure is at its strongest, should also be considered.

There are no simple answers to delinquency. Some programs have attempted to prevent delinquency, but many have not been effective. In one well-publicized program, budding delinquents were taken to Rahway State Prison in New Jersey, where they got a glimpse of their future. Inmates spent hours talking to the young people about prison life. Unfortunately, however, follow-up studies showed that this program was not effective in preventing delinquency (Finckenauer, 1979). Some community-based programs have been successful, especially those that provide recreational activities, work directly with both gangs and individuals, and include campaigns for community improvement (Clarizio and McCoy, 1983). Community involvement seems to be the key. In the educational realm, alternative schools offer some hope. Finally, some have advocated family interventions. For instance, delinquents usually have negative interpersonal relationships with others, including family members, often because of their social behavior and the reactions others have to it. Some programs hope to reduce these negative interactions by teaching the parties better ways to interact (Henggeler et al., 1986).

Drug Use

Adolescents are likely to come in contact with the police for drug-related incidents. In some cases, this involves drunk driving, while in other cases possession or sale of a narcotic substance may be the charge. While many adolescents who take drugs may not get into trouble with the police, there is a positive relationship between drug use and criminal behavior. For example, alcohol consumption is related to both major and minor juvenile crimes (Dawkins and Dawkins, 1983).

Adolescent drug use is common. According to a survey conducted by the National Institute on Drug Abuse, 93 percent of high school seniors sampled had used alcohol, 57 percent had used marijuana, 16 percent had

---

FIGURE 12.1

Drug Use Among High School Students, 1975–1986

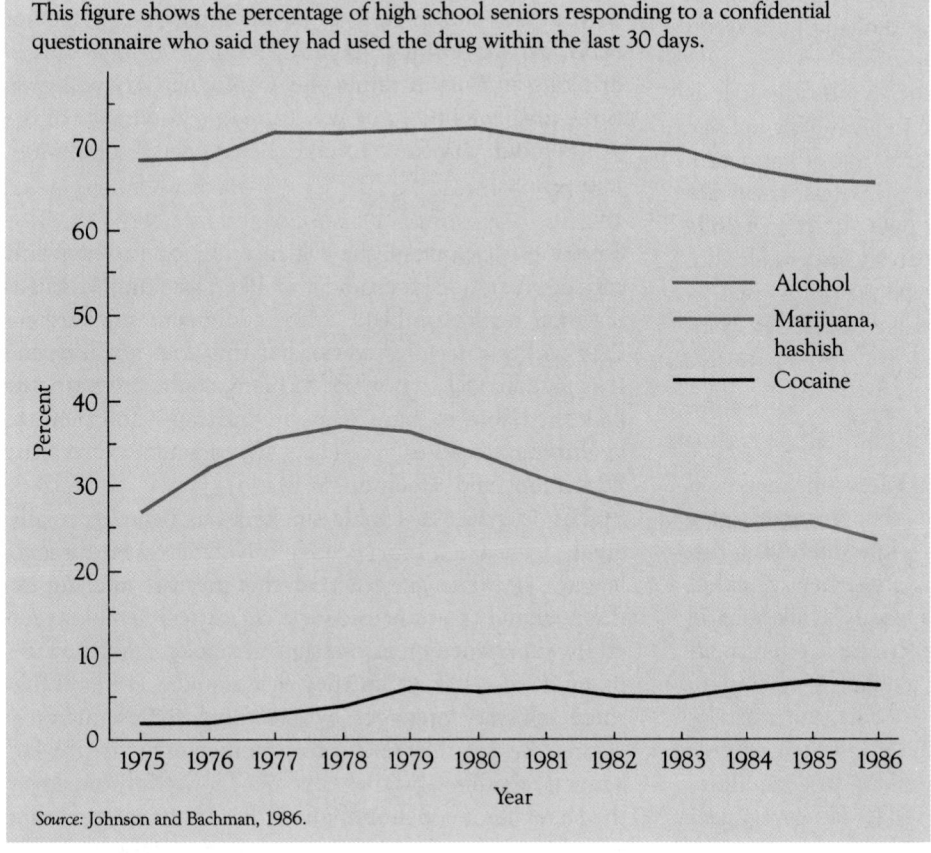

This figure shows the percentage of high school seniors responding to a confidential questionnaire who said they had used the drug within the last 30 days.

Alcohol

Marijuana, hashish

Cocaine

Source: Johnson and Bachman, 1986.

used cocaine, 14 percent had used sedatives, and 35 percent had used stimulants. Various studies yield different percentages, but the pattern of significant drug use is apparent (see Figure 12.1). In one survey, 92 percent of the undergraduates at a midwestern university had had a drink in the past month, and 21 percent were classified as heavy drinkers (fifty-six drinks or more during the past month) (Conye, 1984). A recent government survey showed that 37 million Americans, about one in five people twelve years of age or older, used one or more illicit drugs in the last year (Brinkley, 1986). Although there has been a small decline in the use of drugs in high school, the use of cocaine has increased significantly (Snider, 1987; Brinkley, 1985). Drug use is affected by the models and reinforcements in the home as well as by the peer environment. In every drug-related category, dropouts have higher rates of drug use than students who graduate (Rosenberg and Berberian, 1975).

Alcohol. When I served as a counselor in a junior high school, one teacher reported a student who constantly reeked of alcohol. His mother was called to school. When I told her that her son had a drinking problem, she sighed with relief and said, "Gee, and I thought he was on drugs."

Just like this parent, many other adults think it is natural for teens to get drunk once in a while or to have a drink or two. Males look at it as a rite of passage, a sign of maturity. Although females drink less, their rate of alcohol consumption has risen over the past decade (Lowney et al., 1981). The figures on adolescent alcohol use show that it is by far the most popular drug used by youths between the ages of twelve and seventeen (Nathan, 1983).

True or False Alcohol is the most popular drug used by adolescents.

The overwhelming majority of adolescents have used alcohol at some time in their lives, but frequently this is in the presence of their parents—one interesting difference between the use of this drug and others. Alcohol is the drug of choice because it is readily available and in many circles socially acceptable. Its use is often modeled by parents. Parental use of alcohol is related to adolescent use (Blum et al., 1970). Parental attitudes are also important. Adolescents who think their parents have permissive views about drug-taking in general are more likely to drink (McDermitt, 1984). However, peer pressure is also a factor, as peer attitudes and use are important influences on the adolescent.

Many adolescents drink only occasionally, but the figures on daily use of alcohol show that it is a significant problem. Between 2 and 6 percent of adolescents are classified as problem drinkers (Braucht et al., 1973). About 5.5 percent of all high school seniors use alcohol on a daily basis (U.S. Office of Drug Abuse, 1978). Although people tend not to take it as seriously, the facts prove otherwise. Some 54 percent of the jailed inmates convicted of violent crimes were drinking before they committed the offense, and in 1984 more than half the highway deaths were alcohol-related (New York State Council on Alcoholism, 1986). A disproportionate percentage of the dead and injured were adolescents (Hardert, 1984). The carnage on our highways has caused an outcry. People are demanding action.

How do we combat the problem of teenage alcohol and drunk driving? A number of programs have been offered. Some states have raised the legal age for drinking. Education programs, both those that are preventive in nature and those aimed at people arrested for various alcohol-related crimes, have become more common in high school and in college, but such programs have not been too successful (Nathan, 1983). The high cost of drinking in human terms and in productivity will continue until we find some way to redraw the image of the drinker and get people to take the teenage alcohol problem seriously.

Smoking. Despite all the evidence linking smoking with cancer, heart disease, and the like, smoking is still a national health problem. Most adolescent smokers say they will quit in a few years, but this does not happen. It is paradoxical that while so many adults are trying to kick the habit, so many teens are starting—and they are beginning at earlier ages (U.S. Department of Health, Education, and Welfare, 1978).

The increase in female smokers has been especially great. In a fascinating study, Silverstein and his colleagues (1980) suggested that this increase was due to the availability of low-nicotine cigarettes. Females generally experience great pressure to smoke, and they are likely to feel sick when they first smoke. They resolve these contrary pressures by switching to low-nicotine cigarettes. Another reason for the increase may involve general rebellion and the movement toward throwing off the shackles of conventionalism. For instance, girls who smoke are more socially outgoing but much more rebellious. They report getting drunk more often, have lower grades, dislike school more, and are more likely to have sexual relations and use marijuana than nonsmoking peers (Jarvik et al., 1977).

Smokers generally score higher on extroversion but lower on other personality measures, such as agreeableness and strength of character (Smith, 1969). Cigarette ads for men show the macho image; the ads directed toward females show the independent, sexy, outgoing, having-fun, rebellious attitude that often is attractive to females seeking an identity in a world that now gives them more choices. Smoking follows the same peer-parent use pattern as alcohol consumption. Both peer and parental factors predict future smoking. Those who have friends and parents who smoke, experience lower levels of parental support, and those whose friends have lower expectations for general and academic success are more likely to smoke (Chassin et al., 1986).

Antismoking campaigns have been directed at various segments of the population—pregnant women, fathers who have young children who may imitate, teenage girls who are trying to maintain an image, and so on. These campaigns have been more successful in motivating adults to quit smoking than in encouraging teens not to start.

Studies suggest that adolescents perceive smoking as having social benefits (Leventhal and Cleary, 1980). Whether or not an adolescent smokes may depend on that teen's view of the social image of the smoker. If it is close to a teenager's view of the ideal person, he or she is likely to smoke.

True or False Antismoking advertisements have been more successful at preventing teens from beginning to smoke than at motivating older people to stop smoking.

One study found that sixth-graders and eighth-graders had mixed views of smokers (Barton et al., 1982). Smokers were rated as less healthy, less wise, less obedient, and less likely to act their age. The sixth-graders also perceived smokers as less likely to achieve in school and less desirable as friends. However, smokers were also rated as tougher, more interested in the opposite sex, and wanting to be with "the group" more than nonsmokers. These are powerful positive attributes in early and mid-adolescence. Students in both grades believed that smokers were more likely to drink—a negative for sixth-graders, but not for eighth-graders. Findings for males and females were similar. According to Barton and

his colleagues, children in the younger grades are most affected by the negative image of the smoker. The more negative the image, the less likely the sixth-graders were to smoke. But in the eighth grade, smoking is related to the positive qualities of the smoker—especially interest in the opposite sex, wanting to be with the group, and the idea of being relaxed. Perhaps antismoking campaigns directed at younger children should stress the negative view of the smoker, while those directed at the mid-adolescent must improve the image of the nonsmoker. Only time will tell whether this strategy will be effective.

Illicit drugs. Marijuana is used much more frequently by adolescents than by adults (Archer and Lopata, 1979). Perhaps more than any other drug, marijuana symbolizes adolescent rebellion. In fact, its use is correlated with feelings of rebellion against parental rules and tolerance

In the eyes of adolescents, the image of the smoker and nonsmoker differ greatly. Despite the health warnings about smoking many adolescents still choose to smoke.

for deviant behavior (Brook et al., 1978). Whereas marijuana use tends to decline as people age, alcohol and cigarette use continues to expand. According to a National Institute on Drug Abuse study (1983), 57 percent of their sample of high school seniors had used marijuana once, and 5.5 percent were daily users. About the same percentage of adolescents use marijuana on a daily basis as drink alcohol. A recent survey found a decrease in marijuana use among high school students (*New York Times*, February 24, 1987).

Most marijuana use takes place only occasionally and for recreational purposes and users are not much different from nonusers. Differences have been noted though—for example, nonusers have more affectionate relationships with their fathers (Brook et al., 1981)—but many differences are found at the extreme (Archer and Lopata, 1979). Regular heavy users are much more rebellious and angry, show a lack of responsibility, and score high on measures of sensation-seeking (Brook et al., 1981). They see themselves as inadequate, have friends who smoke marijuana heavily, often come from turbulent homes filled with discord, and show an inability to conform to rules. For these heavy users, marijuana use is an act of defiance against parents and authority figures. It modifies such disturbing emotions as anger, reinforces fantasies of effortless and grandiose success, and enables the adolescent to withdraw from conflicts, especially those having to do with competition and achievement (Hendin et al., 1981).

An adolescent's first drink is usually in the family setting, but peer pressure is more important in determining the initial use of marijuana (Sorosiak et al., 1976). However, peer pressure is not necessarily the only or most critical factor in initiation of drug use, although it may contribute to it (Norem-Hebeisen and Hendin, 1984). In one challenging study, most adolescents surveyed said that, although they had been offered marijuana at parties, they had never felt pressured to use it. Those who had experienced peer pressure in this area stated they had felt the pressure only once or twice. Sheppard and colleagues (1985) argue that although some young people are exposed to peer pressure, it is not the predominant reason for drug use. They suggest that one reason users spend time with other users is that drug-taking is often a group activity. In addition, drug users may actively seek out others who use the drug, who are likely to share similarities in personality and social desires.

Of all the illicit drugs, cocaine has recently been the subject of more media attention than any other sub-

stance. Cocaine is a stimulant, affecting the central nervous system and producing feelings of euphoria. Physiological changes include extreme changes in blood pressure, increase in heart and respiration rates, insomnia, nausea, tremors, and convulsions. Cocaine use can lead to paranoid behavior, and potent forms like crack are highly addictive (New York State Division of Substance Abuse Services, 1986).

Use of cocaine has increased markedly in only the past few years. Nearly 5.8 million people use cocaine at least monthly, a 38 percent increase in three years. The number of people using cocaine less often but at least once a year showed a modest increase between 1982 and 1985. Because the levels were already quite high in 1982, this is especially significant. Much of the increase is due to the popularity of a very dangerous and highly potent form of cocaine called crack. The number of emergency room visits for cocaine-related problems has increased dramatically over the past five years (Kerr, 1986). Although the recent cocaine-related fatalities of athletes such as Len Bias and Don Rogers have focused more public attention on the dangers of the drug, the need for continuing education in this area is clear.

True or False   Cocaine, like alcohol, is a central nervous system depressant that slows down body functioning.

Adolescent Suicide

The attention drug abuse gets from the media is constant. However, the attention given to another problem—adolescent suicide—is much more sporadic. Consider these facts:

- Suicide is the second leading cause of death among people between the ages of fifteen and twenty-one (accidents are first). Nationally, suicide increased by more than 200 percent between 1960 and 1980. (Frederick, 1985)
- It is estimated that 11 percent of youths in the fifteen- to nineteen-year-old age-group have attempted suicide, with more than 5,000 succeeding in taking their own lives during 1985. (Hobart, 1986; Frederick, 1985)
- The death rate for suicide is two to three times higher for males than for females, and for each death there may be fifty to sixty attempts. Most people who commit suicide had a history of self-destructive behavior and previous attempts. (Gispert et al., 1985)

Adolescent suicide is a major problem. The most common cause of suicide, according to most experts, is depression (Gispert et al., 1985). A sense of hopelessness seems to pervade suicide victims (Farberow, 1985; Schneidman, 1970). Those who attempt suicide often have a family history of breakdown, divorce, and suicide in the family, and they have few friends and suffer from rejection (Wenar, 1982). Most experienced a large number of stressful events in childhood, with a marked increase in stress in the year preceding the suicide attempt (Gispert et al., 1985). Other predisposing factors include early death of a parent, rejection in love, academic pressure to achieve, and failure (Hendin, 1985).

Whenever a suicide occurs in a community, people start looking for answers and clues. Indeed, research has provided us with some clues to predict the possibility of suicide, but unfortunately we do not always pay attention to them. For instance, many people believe that people who talk about suicide never actually do it. But this is not so. People who talk about suicide are actually more likely to attempt it. Other warning signs include giving things away and talk about "ending it." A previous attempt at suicide is also a warning that a future attempt might be made if the predisposing factors are not controlled or adequately dealt with (Colt, 1983). Situations that cause extreme anxiety, depression, and hopelessness should put a person on guard that suicide may be contemplated (Schneidman, 1970). In many communities, suicide prevention centers have hotlines for emergency help. Although these are quite effective (Farberow, 1985), long-term help is usually necessary.

True or False People who talk about committing suicide rarely make a suicide attempt.

Exploding the Myths

With the possible exception of old age, adolescence is the most stereotyped period of life. But the caricature of the adolescent as giving up dependence on parents and forming a total dependence on peers is incorrect. The commonly held belief that parents' relationships with their adolescents are uniformly poor must also be reevaluated in view of recent research. This chapter has exposed, and hopefully exploded, a number of myths.

The period of adolescence is one in which people are faced with important decisions in every area of life. A great deal has recently been written about moral education and the nature of these personal choices. As we have seen, parents need not abdicate their special relationship with their children during this stage. Supervision and guidance are part of a parent's responsibilities, but so is preparation for independent adulthood. Constant criticism, harsh punishment, and strict warnings are often ineffective, especially if they occur in a cold, hostile environment. Adolescents will be affected most by what they see and experience—and communication is most important.

Haim Ginott (1969, p. 243) said, "Character traits cannot be taught directly: no one can teach loyalty by lectures, courage by correspondence, or manhood by mail. Character education requires presence that demonstrates and contact that communicates. A teenager learns what he lives, and becomes what he experiences. To him, our mood is the message, the style is the substance, the process is the product."

Summary

1. Erikson viewed the formation of a personal identity as the positive outcome of adolescence. Identity diffusion—failure to answer the fundamental questions of identity—is the negative outcome of the stage.

2. Marcia extended Erikson's conception of identity to include four identity statuses. *Identity diffusion* is a status in which a person has not begun to make any commitments. This status is considered negative only when an individual leaves adolescence without making reasonable progress toward finding an identity. *Identity foreclosure* is a

status in which a person has made commitments prematurely. *Identity moratorium* is a temporary status in which an individual is not ready to make commitments but may be exploring possibilities. *Identity achievers* have gone through their crises and made their commitments. People who are identity achievers are generally more ready to form intimate relationships.

3. Males and females may take different paths to identity formation. Males focus on intrapersonal factors, while women tend to tie their identities to interpersonal relationships. Some changes are

taking place in this area, however, as many women now seek to balance a career with family responsibilities.

4. Peer influence peaks in the late junior high or early high school years. Traditionally, females have been considered less autonomous and more conforming, but these differences are narrowing and even disappearing. Peer influence is greater in the areas of social interaction, styles, and attitudes toward school than in the realm of deeper values.

5. The generation gap in attitudes is not as wide as first thought. Differences in the way the generations see the world are often a matter of degree, but each generation usually misperceives the opinions of the other.

6. Parents are more likely to be directive, to want to share their wisdom, and to explain their views than to listen to the opinions of their teens. Peer communication shows more give-and-take.

7. The popular picture of adolescence as a period of continuous conflict between parents and children is not substantiated by research. During adolescence, the parent-child relationship moves toward greater symmetry and equality. Most adolescents have good relationships with their parents.

8. The choice of a vocation affects one's entire lifestyle. For many women and minority group youths, vocational choice is limited. However, women have made progress entering male-dominated occupations. The choice of a nontraditional career requires family support and adequate models. There has been some progress for minority group youths entering the professions, but many minority adolescents do not have high vocational aspirations, lack adequate role models, and find that their choices are limited by lack of academic skills, economic resources, or racial discrimination. In addition, these youths are less likely to believe that they have the power to influence their own futures.

9. Most high school dropouts have average intelligence scores but lack academic skills, have little interest in school, and show a history of school-related problems. They are more likely to come from poor, large families or families where there is discord and divorce. Dropouts are more likely than graduates to find themselves in dead-end jobs.

10. Almost one-third of all arrests for serious crimes in 1985 were of adolescents under the age of eighteen. Delinquents are more likely to come from homes filled with discord, where there is no supervision and where discipline is inconsistent and either very lax or very stringent.

11. Adolescent drug use is common, with alcohol, tobacco, and marijuana leading the list. The recent increase in cocaine use is significant. Alcohol is the most abused drug, and its social acceptability makes combating excessive use difficult. Cigarette-smoking has increased greatly among females. Despite the health hazards, to many teens the social image of the smoker is a positive one. More than any other drug, marijuana use symbolizes adolescent rebellion. Although some differences between users and nonusers have been found, they are for the most part more similar than different. Heavy users, however, are quite different. They are more angry, show a lack of responsibility, have difficulty conforming to rules, and are defiant. They use marijuana to reinforce fantasies of effortless success and to withdraw from conflicts.

12. Suicide is the second leading cause of death among people between the ages of fifteen and twenty-one, with accidents leading the list. Most suicide victims are depressed and have a pervading sense of hopelessness. Many give clues, such as talking about suicide or giving treasured items away, or have a history of a previous suicide attempt or a suicide in their family. Suicide prevention centers are effective in giving help in emergency situations.

───────── *Answers to True or False Statements* ─────────

1. *True* There are more alternatives open to adolescents today, making identity formation

more difficult.

2. *False* Correct statement: For both males and

females, identity achievers are generally better able to form intimate relationships. When a sex difference is found, females can sometimes achieve intimacy before identity, but very few men can.

3. *True*   Peer influence usually peaks during the late junior high school and early high school years.

4. *False*   Correct statement: Most parents minimize the differences in attitudes between them and their children.

5. *True*   Parents tend to explain their own views rather than listen to those of their adolescent children.

6. *False*   Correct statement: Parents usually try to control the adolescent's behavior more than friends do.

7. *False*   Correct statement: Women who choose to enter male-dominated vocations tend to have close, supporting relationships with their fathers as well as with their mothers.

8. *True*   The average high school dropout has an average intelligence score, but dropouts prior to high school tend to have scores that are below average.

9. *True*   Alcohol is the most commonly used drug among adolescents.

10. *False*   Correct statement: Antismoking campaigns are more successful in motivating people to stop smoking than in preventing adolescents from starting to smoke.

11. *False*   Correct statement: Cocaine is a stimulant that leads to increases in blood pressure, heart and respiration rates.

12. *False*   Correct statement: People who talk about committing suicide are more likely to attempt it.

PART SIX

Early Adulthood

New Perspectives on Adulthood

Are the Following Statements True or False?

Try the True-False Quiz below. See if your answers correspond to the information in this chapter. Each question is repeated after the paragraph in which the answer can be found. The True-False Answer Box at the end of the chapter lists the complete answers.

____ 1. Historically, interest in adult development is at least as great as it has been in child development.

____ 2. Freud was one of the first theorists to emphasize the importance of adulthood as a developmental period.

____ 3. Very few theories can be considered true life-span theories.

____ 4. One challenge of middle age is to remain mentally flexible and open to new ideas.

____ 5. During the decade from age thirty to age forty, most men concentrate on vocational pursuits.

____ 6. People often find older employees at the workplace who serve as guides or confidants, and these relationships usually last for two decades or more.

____ 7. The status of older people in our society is quite high.

____ 8. People from higher socioeconomic groups can delay movement from one stage of adulthood to the next more easily than people from lower socioeconomic groups.

____ 9. The mid-life crisis that occurs around age forty is a time of reevaluation and questioning, but for most people not a time of dramatic change.

____10. Generally speaking, males and females have different attitudes toward social relationships and experiences, with women seeing relationships and attachment as central, and men seeing autonomy and personal identity as most important.

The New Fascination with Adulthood

The terms "mid-life crisis," "age-thirty transition," "career consolidation," "mentor," and "the dream" have become part of our language. For many years, psychologists were oblivious to the possibility of adult development (see Honzik, 1984; Rubin, 1981). A few psychologists, such as G. Stanley Hall (1922), looked at adulthood, but little developmental research was conducted, and no one seemed interested in creating a theoretical framework from which to understand adulthood. After all, Freud emphasized the importance of early experience, and his psychosexual stages ended at adolescence. Piaget did not believe that any qualitative changes occurred during adulthood (Piaget, 1972). This began to change with Erik Erikson's work, but only within the past decade or so have sweeping changes taken place. We are now inundated with interest in adulthood, and aging is no longer thought of only as an inevitable process ending in death. New theorists who focus solely on adulthood have appeared, and a number of best-sellers, led by Gail Sheehy's *Passages* and *Pathfinders,* have popularized these new theories.

True or False Historically, interest in adult development is at least as great as it has been in child development.

True or False Freud was one of the first theorists to emphasize the importance of adulthood as a developmental period.

One reason for this interest in adulthood is increased longevity. There is now a longer period of time between physical maturity and decline, and this period may continue to increase (Vaupel and Gowan, 1986). In addition, we are a better-educated society, aware that there is life after adolescence.

Developmental theories have already been discussed in Chapter 1, so why this special introduction to adulthood? With the exception of Erikson's psychosocial theory, none of the other theories discussed is truly a lifespan theory—that is, they do not continue their analysis throughout adulthood. The newer theorists of adulthood—for instance, Vaillant, Levinson, and Gould, whose theories will be described in this chapter—begin their analyses either in late adolescence or in early adulthood. They seek commonalities in adult life and are less concerned with childhood. Therefore, the newer theories of

These days interest in adult development is high and books on the subject are very popular.

adulthood are not really life-span theories either. As we look at these theories, remember that they are the first attempts to put together some coherent framework from which to understand adulthood. There will be unanswered questions and gaps in the theories. With time, these questions will be answered and the gaps will be reduced.

True or False Very few theories can be considered true life-span theories.

Erikson's Later Psychosocial Stages

Most of the credit for our new appreciation of adulthood must go to Erik Erikson (Cohler, 1982). Erikson's emphasis on the life cycle affected psychologists greatly. We discussed the basics of his theory in Chapter 1. Here we look at how he views adulthood.

Intimacy vs. Isolation

The young adult has already acquired an identity and is now ready to share that identity with others. In other words, young adults are ready for **intimacy,** which is the capacity to commit oneself to others, to make commitments, and to keep those commitments, despite the sacrifices and compromises that may be necessary (Erikson, 1963). This describes marriage, but intimacy may include deep friendships as well. It involves a commitment to meaningful and satisfying relationships. When ones makes a commitment to another person, it is deep and abiding and can endure despite adversity.

The negative outcome of the psychosocial stage of young adulthood is **isolation**—the unwillingness or inability to commit oneself to others. An inability to share one's innermost feelings and thoughts may cause isolation, and isolation leads to loneliness and despair (Salkind, 1981). Such a person may opt for isolation, perhaps because it does not require the risk of being hurt in a relationship.

Generativity vs. Stagnation

The next stage has the positive outcome that Erikson calls generativity. **Generativity** is primarily concerned

intimacy According to Erikson, the positive outcome of the psychosocial crisis of young adulthood, involving development of close interpersonal relations, most often typified by marriage.

isolation The negative outcome of Erikson's psychosocial crisis of young adulthood, resulting in a lack of commitment to others.

generativity The positive outcome of Erikson's psychosocial crisis of middle age, which involves giving of oneself and one's talents to others.

stagnation The negative outcome of Erikson's psychosocial crisis of middle age, in which one becomes completely absorbed in one's self.

ego integrity The positive outcome of Erikson's last psychosocial stage, in which an older person experiences a sense of satisfaction with life.

despair The negative outcome of Erikson's last psychosocial stage, in which an older person experiences a sense of bitterness about lost opportunities.

with establishing and guiding the next generation. Erikson notes that although it is common for people to say that children need adults, the opposite may also be true—that mature adults need the younger generation. Generativity involves investing something of oneself in the future (Giele, 1980) and may easily extend beyond one's children to grandchildren (Pearlin, 1980). People may develop generativity through other means besides rearing children, such as through community involvement and helping others or through creative acts (Katchadourian, 1978). **Stagnation,** the negative outcome of this stage, involves absorption in one's own personal needs and an inability or unwillingness to give to others (Salkind, 1981).

Integrity vs. Despair

Erikson's final stage of life can be described in terms of **ego integrity** versus **despair.** People who have developed ego integrity realize that their life has been worthwhile. After an entire lifetime of facing challenges and problems, they can look back on a productive life. Mature adults have a different perspective on life and see their lives as having a purpose. People who see only missed opportunities may become bitter and depressed and develop a sense of despair.

Peck's Elaboration of Erikson's Theory

Robert Peck (1968) accepted much of Erikson's theory but argued that Erikson's stages of middle and late adulthood were just too vague.

Challenges and Tasks in Middle Age

Peck notes that people in middle age face the following four challenges or tasks:

Socializing vs. sexualizing in human relationships. The capacity to find deep and meaningful interpersonal relationships is in part determined by a change from looking at people in terms of sexuality to appreciating their companionship. As children grow up and leave home, it is possible to find deeper meaning in interpersonal relationships. As we shall see in Chapters 15, 17, and 20, marital relationships change as people negotiate adulthood. Although sexuality remains important, other interpersonal factors involving companionship come to the forefront.

Valuing wisdom vs. valuing physical powers. In the forties there is some physical decline. People who consider this a catastrophe may become depressed, but people who can learn to appreciate their cognitive abilities are more successful in negotiating middle age. If people define their value in terms of physical attractiveness or strength, they may have difficulty with their definition of themselves as these fade somewhat.

According to Erikson, the positive outcome of middle age is generativity which involves giving to the younger generation.

Mental flexibility vs. mental rigidity. It is easy for people in middle age to become rigid in their thinking and closed to new ideas. Dwelling on the past is likely to be stifling, and allowing past rules and attitudes to determine the present and the future may lead to dissatisfaction. Many middle-aged people live rather stable lives and may not try anything new and open their minds to fresh ideas and possibilities. Peck believes that middle-aged people must become more open to new experiences and challenges.

True or False One challenge of middle age is to remain mentally flexible and open to new ideas.

Cathectic flexibility vs. cathectic impoverishment. Consider the emotional attachments of middle-aged people. Their children are leaving home, and their parents are negotiating old age—or perhaps no longer living. In addition, groups of friends may break up as premature death, early retirement, or other events separate people from their natural groups. The task here is to enlarge one's social world so that one is not lonely and can find new meaningful relationships.

Challenges and Tasks in Old Age

Peck also formulated three challenges or tasks of old age.

Ego differentiation vs. work-role preoccupation. The issue of one's role being almost exclusively defined by one's work is likely to arise at retirement. Peck argues that retirees must realize that their value lies beyond work and parenting. They must place value on their leisure time and their relationships with others. They need to become involved in other activities and to make meaningful use of their increased free time.

Body transcendence vs. body preoccupation. Old age brings with it an assortment of physical ailments. Those who can transcend these physical problems and enjoy activities and social interactions in later life are happier.

Ego transcendence vs. ego preoccupation. The final task is to come to terms with one's own mortality. People are more likely to accept their mortality if they feel they have made a contribution to the future through their children or their own creative accomplishments. This involves transcending the fear of death. A person who fails to do this is likely to suffer from depression.

The Importance of Peck's and Erikson's Work

Peck and Erikson have presented us with an interesting overview of adult development. They have established three periods of adulthood—young adulthood, middle age, and later maturity—and given us our first psychological maps of the tasks faced at each age. Their work is important in that it demonstrates the changing nature of the challenges in adulthood. Certain challenges occur during certain periods of adulthood, and Peck and Erikson offer a framework for understanding these challenges. Unfortunately, these challenges are described in very broad and global terms (Thomas, 1979) and make their work difficult to test experimentally.

George Vaillant and the Grant Study

Another theorist who expanded Erikson's theory is George Vaillant. Vaillant analyzed the results from a longitudinal study, called the Grant Study, which followed Harvard University students throughout their adult years. Only students who showed no sign of physical or mental disturbance were used in the study. Much of this study's fame comes from the description of ninety-five men who had graduated between 1942 and 1944, which can be found in Vaillant's popular book *Adaptation to Life*. Although these men did not differ physically from other college men, they belonged to a privileged socioeconomic group. Extensive interviews, physical exams, and psychological testing were performed during their college years, and information concerning family, employment, health habits, and political attitudes was obtained in adulthood through questionnaires and interviews. The findings involve not only a look at common points of crisis in adulthood, but also an analysis of various methods of coping with stress as people age.

Career Consolidation and Keeping the Meaning

Vaillant found support for Erikson's basic stages in adulthood—intimacy, generativity, and integrity. However, he found an uncharted period for development for men in their thirties and another in the fifties. Between the development of intimacy in one's twenties and the generativity of middle age comes the stage of **career consolidation,** when men are busy concentrating on their careers and ascending the career ladder. At this point, their focus is likely to become quite narrow and they tend to be conforming and materialistic.

True or False During the decade from age thirty to age forty, most men concentrate on vocational pursuits.

Most people eventually grow out of the crassness of this stage. At thirty-one years of age one of Vaillant's subjects wrote, "I've reached the point where I would appreciate material gain and improvement in status. I'm striving towards that goal, and this makes me enthusiastic about my work and career" (Vaillant, 1977, p. 219). The same man at forty noted that he enjoyed watching others become successful and trying to win the affection of the shop steward. He had moved on to generativity

Vaillant argued that men in their thirties direct most of their energy to climbing the career ladder.

career consolidation A period suggested by Vaillant that occurs in the thirties and is marked by concentration on careers and ascending the career ladder.

keeping the meaning and rigidity A period suggested by Vaillant, occurring in the fifties, in which a person needs to find new meaning in life and to avoid falling into rigid patterns.

too. Vaillant noted that at age forty, men become less compulsive about their vocational pursuits and become "explorers of the world within." This change arises chiefly from a reexamination of one's talents and values. It is a transitional period to middle age, which brings with it conflict—often called the mid-life crisis.

This period called the mid-life crisis is controversial. Some argue that it is a period of dramatic change, similar to a second adolescence, and filled with turmoil. Vaillant says, "The term mid-life crisis brings to mind some variation of the renegade minister who leaves behind four children and the congregation that loved him in order to drive off in a magenta Porsche with a twenty-five-year-old striptease artist" (1977, p. 222). Instead, Vaillant found little evidence of any dramatic change, but he did see the period as one of continuous rediscovery. He also found that men who did not leave the career consolidation stage did not achieve generativity.

Vaillant tentatively posits another period in addition to Erikson's stages—beginning after the attainment of generativity and before integrity. He summarizes the period in terms of **keeping the meaning and rigidity.** The fifties are a quieter, more relaxed time of life. It is a time of accepting both successes and failures, and people must find new meaning for their lives. There is danger of falling into a rigid pattern that does not allow for the meaningful enjoyment of life.

The Importance of Vaillant's Work

Vaillant's work extends Erikson's theory by adding the two intermediate stages: career consolidation in the thirties and keeping the meaning and rigidity in the fifties. His findings also support some of Erikson's ideas. Finally, Vaillant does see the forties as a time of change and reawakening, but not as a time of high drama and radical changes. Unfortunately, Vaillant's work leaves open the question of how these stages apply to women, to people of other social classes, or even to people in different historical times.

Daniel Levinson's "Seasons of a Man's Life"

The most famous theorist of modern adulthood is Daniel Levinson (1980, 1978), whose book *The Seasons of a Man's Life* had a tremendous impact on our thinking about adulthood. Beginning in 1969, Levinson conducted a longitudinal study of a group of forty men age thirty-five to forty-five. Ten were executives, ten were factory workers, ten were biologists, and ten were novelists. Levinson conducted five to ten detailed biographical interviews for a total of ten to twenty hours. The subjects were asked to tell the stories of their lives, and then Levinson analyzed the hundreds of pages of transcripts looking for differences and commonalities in their experiences.

The Four Eras of Life

Levinson found his commonalities. He divided life into four eras. (Remember that Levinson's subjects were men, so we summarize his findings in this section as he reported them, from the man's point of view. How these findings relate to women is yet to be established.) The preadulthood era extends from birth to age 22 and is the time of rapid growth in every area of life. The second era, called early adulthood, lasts from age 22 to age 45. In this era a person establishes himself and raises a family. It ends with his reaching a senior position in his occupation. It is a period of rich satisfaction in terms of love, sexuality, family, and occupational advancement. However, it is also marked by marital, parenting, and vocational problems, as well as by many personal choices. Middle adulthood, from about age 45 to age 60 or so, is a time of great transition, reappraisal, and coping with diminished physical abilities. It is also a time of achieving a dominant position and seeking more meaning in our own lives, as well as of giving to others. In late adulthood, about age 60 to age 85, the individual must confront the problems of aging. In addition, he may no longer dominate and must cope with the changing relationship between the society and himself, finding a new balance and becoming more interested in realizing and using his inner resources. Levinson suggests that

another era, late-late adulthood, exists beyond, but he did not describe it in detail.

Levinson's Periods of Adult Life

Within these eras, Levinson identified a number of periods. One period does not flow right into the other—there are transitional periods that connect them. Each transition involves termination of an existing life structure and initiation of a new one. During these transitions, a person must reappraise and modify. Each period also contains its own developmental tasks. Levinson notes that each period begins and ends at a particular age, with a range of about two years above or below the average. Levinson describes the seasons of a man's life as follows.

The early adult transition (ages 17–22). The early adult transition forms the bridge between adolescence and adulthood. One task of this transition is to change one's life structure by altering one's relationship with parents and institutions. This involves separating oneself from one's family. Externally a person may leave his home and parents and become more self-sufficient. Internally, he must explore new possibilities of the adult world and make tentative choices. Levinson notes that people can live with their parents and still become more self-sufficient.

Entering the adult world (ages 22–28). The transition is followed by a rather stable period in which a new life structure is created. The key elements of this period are exploration and creating a new and stable structure so that "the dream" can be fulfilled. This involves exploring the self and the world of work, making choices, and searching for alternatives. It also means making a new home and family life and increasing commitments. Decisions about occupation, love relationships, lifestyle, and values, which are not always lasting, are made.

The age thirty transition (ages 28–33). Now that the exploratory period is over, the person has established a more-or-less stable lifestyle. The questioning becomes overwhelming: What have I done with my life? What new directions shall I choose? Questions about the nature of the vocational and familial choices abound. Did I make the right choices? Although I really care about my spouse, do I really love her? There is a sense of urgency to these questions, and a reexamination of what one has built. This is a time of great introspection. Levinson sees this period as an opportunity to work out flaws in the twenties' lifestyle and create the basis for a more satisfactory life structure later. On the other hand, people who have not made commitments during their twenties may be bothered by a lack of roots and feel it is time to make a change. This transitional stage ends either with major changes or with a recommitment to family and occupation.

Levinson sees the major tasks of early adulthood in terms of making family and occupational commitments. In addition, however, there are two other tasks that are especially interesting. First, during this phase a dream is forged. **The dream** consists of some understanding of the life a person wants to live. It becomes more definite as people develop. In addition, many men find a mentor during this stage. A **mentor** is a person, usually at the workplace, who is older and serves as a guide, confidant, counselor, or teacher helping you grow. The mentor supports and helps you realize your dream. Mentor relationships need not last long—two or three years on the average to ten years at the most.

True or False People often find older employees at the workplace who serve as guides or confidants, and these relationships usually last for two decades or more.

Settling down and becoming one's own man (ages 33–40). The next major task is to build a second life structure and within this framework to work toward the dream. This consists of two subtasks. The first is to establish one's own place in society, to anchor oneself to career and family, and to deepen one's roots. The second is to work toward advancement. Stability and progression are the key words here. During this period, family and vocational demands are especially high. Between the ages of 36 and 40 a distinct phase occurs that Levinson calls **becoming one's own man.** This is where ambition peaks and a person is blessed with more authority. The person is eager to accomplish goals, becomes more independent, and is more likely to speak with confidence and authority. An interesting change occurs when the person is no longer considered "promising" but must now achieve personal goals and move up.

Mid-life transition (ages 40–45). This bridge between early and middle adulthood brings with it great struggle and turmoil. Three major tasks have been identified. As in all transitions, the first task in **mid-life transition** is

the dream What a person wants in life, according to Levinson.

mentor An older person, usually at the workplace, who serves as a guide and confidant to a younger worker.

becoming one's own man Levinson's stage between the ages of about thirty-six and forty marked by ambition, authority, independence, and confidence.

mid-life-transition A period of reassessment, suggested by Levinson and others, occurring in early middle age and causing turmoil. ("Transition" and "crisis" are sometimes used synonymously, but whether the period of questioning is a crisis is a matter of controversy.)

a reappraisal of lifestyle and goals and a critical examination of one's life structure. For the first time a person may become personally aware of his own mortality and recognize that time is now limited and must be used wisely. Again, questions are raised. What have I done with my life? What do I really get from and give to my family? What do I truly want? How am I using my talents? How satisfactory is my present life?

The second task in mid-life transition is to integrate what Levinson calls the great polarities. These involve four conflicts that arise during this transition. The first polarity is young/old. The person entering middle age is neither young nor old, but actually feels both ways. If one clings to youth, however, he does not adjust to the challenges of middle age. But if being young is surrendered completely, the risk of rigidity increases. The second polarity is the destructive/constructive problem. Middle-aged people are aware of the transient nature of many achievements, their own mortality and the extent to which others have hurt them and they have acted destructively towards others. The desire to be more creative and to leave some sort of positive legacy arises. The masculine/feminine issue is a third polarity. The gender lines become less important and men (remember again, Levinson's subjects were men) must come to terms with the feminine side as well as the masculine side of their nature. Finally, the fourth polarity, the attachment/separation polarity, must be resolved. One must integrate the need for attachment to others with the need for separateness.

The third task in mid-life transition is to build a new structure for successful negotiation of middle adulthood.

Some men make significant changes in external commitments, such as changing careers or getting a divorce. For others, recommitment is in order. However, even if there is a recommitment, marital relationships do change. Levinson found that 80 percent of his subjects found this period a time of great struggle. They described crises that were either moderate or severe, and they questioned every aspect of their selves and their lives. During this period the dream is also modified, and people sometimes become mentors to others. At times it is the wife who reassesses the marriage. She may want changes, and the husband may be the one who opposes them.

Entering middle adulthood (ages 45–50). During this period people build a new life structure for middle age. They must cope with aging or dying parents and the knowledge that they are also growing old. This is also a time of deeper commitments to the younger generation.

The later stages. Levinson actually says very little about the stages of later middle adulthood and old age. He tentatively maps out a stage called the "Age-Fifty Transition," which is a smoother transitional stage than the earlier ones and in which only modest changes are made. People who had easy mid-life transitions may find this transition more difficult than those who settled the mid-life issues. In the next stage, called "Culmination of Middle Adulthood," another structure is built. This is followed by a "Late-Adult Transition," from age 60 to 65 in which the individual must psychologically consider the questions that come with entering old age. Finally, Levinson posits the stage of late adulthood.

The Importance of Levinson's Work

Levinson's theory offers us a more concrete framework within which to consider the challenges and opportunities of adulthood. It is a dynamic theory because it sees adults as faced with a series of crises and challenges and having to make decisions and suffer the consequences for them. Levinson identifies the transitional stages during which particular questions arise. He also raises a number of interesting theoretical points, such as the true meaning of mid-life crisis, that are the subject of much research which will be presented later in this book. The criticisms revolve around the question of whether the theory can be applied to women and to the poor, as well as to people of other generations and cultures.

Roger Gould's Transformations

One researcher whose sample included both males and females was Roger Gould (1980, 1978, 1975). Gould's theory arises from a cross-sectional study of 524 middle-class men and women between the ages of sixteen and sixty. Gould, a psychoanalyst, noted that his outpatients at a university clinic suffered from similar problems at similar ages. From their answers on questionnaires, he found that adulthood was marked by a pattern of predictable transitions. Of course, the use of a clinical sample like this raises the question whether these people are generally representative of adults. Gould found adulthood to be a time of change, rather than stability, that is made up of seven phases.

Levinson found that many people find a mentor who is an older person who acts as a confidant and helps the younger person grow.

In midlife transition, a great deal of reevaluation takes place as questions concerning one's accomplishments and goals are raised.

Gould's Seven Phases

According to Gould, the first phase of adulthood (ages 16–18) is the time when an identity is formed and there is an increasing desire to escape from parental control and achieve independence.

In the second phase (about ages 18–22), young adults are in the process of leaving home and believe that true adulthood and independence await them. At this point, there is flexibility and an openness to new ideas.

The third phase (ages 22–28) is a time when young adults are devoted to attaining their goals and are autonomous. There is increasing commitment to family and a growing confidence.

In the fourth phase (ages 29–34), goals and marriages are questioned and reevaluated. Economic problems become more important, and there is increasing dissatisfaction with one's lifestyle. Self-reflection is a key, and confusion arises.

During the fifth phase (ages 35–43), people continue to question their values, but now they begin to feel the pressure of time. They must act now or never if they are to make any new moves. This is also marks the beginning of an awareness of one's own mortality. This unstable and uncomfortable time is marked by increasing concerns about one's own health and that of one's parents. There is also an urgency to obtain life goals.

The sixth phase (ages 44–53) is one of relative stability. Marital satisfaction increases and friends become more important. Life is accepted for whatever it is, but there arises a feeling that there is not enough time left to do what you want. Concerns about personal health become more common.

The last phase described by Gould covers age 54 through the early sixties, in which people mellow and accept themselves. They are more relaxed and begin to reflect on the meaning and purpose of their life.

The Importance of Gould's Work

Gould's discussion sounds a great deal like the stages described by Levinson, but he believes that in order to negotiate these stages successfully one must take on a new consciousness and view the world differently. His inclusion of women is also valuable, since he found these trends in their lives as well.

Social Norms, Culture, and History: Bernice Neugarten

Any consideration of adulthood would be incomplete without looking at the historical and societal aspects of life. This perspective is taken by Bernice Neugarten, whose varied research will be described throughout the chapters that follow.

Culture, History, and Social Clocks

Each culture has its own **norms,** rules that regulate behavior in certain situations. For instance, parenthood brings with it new social roles and obligations. Some norms are based on a person's age. These **age norms** legislate the types of behaviors appropriate for people of that age-group. For instance, if we see a young person looking outrageously punk, we shrug it off. But if grandma tries to achieve the same look, we consider it an oddity. Table 13.1 shows age norms of twenty years ago—the results of a study by Neugarten and colleagues (1965). Such age norms add constraints to behavior as people internalize them and realize how someone else may react to any given violation. Many societies also have **age-status systems,** in which people are given power and status based on their age. Our society gives the elderly a fairly low status.

True or False   The status of older people in our society is quite high.

Each society also has its own **social clock,** which is an internalized sense of timing that tells us whether we are progressing too fast or too slowly in terms of social events in our lives (Neugarten, 1968). A forty-year-old who has not married, or someone who has not made an occupational commitment in his or her twenties, may experience internal as well as external pressure to do so.

age-status systems   The status accorded different age-groups in various societies.

social clock   The internalized sense of timing that tells people whether they are progressing too fast or too slow in terms of social events.

Social clocks depend partly on social class. People from lower-income groups proceed through adult stages at a faster pace. They marry at a younger age and tend to have their children earlier in adulthood. People from higher socioeconomic groups are able to delay movement from one stage of adulthood to the next (Neugarten and Moore, 1968). Consider the plight of a rich person and

T A B L E   13.1

How a Middle-Class Sample Viewed Age-Related Characteristics

This table shows how a middle-class, middle-age sample viewed age-related characteristics in 1965. Do you think today's middle-aged people would also agree with these views?

	Age Range Designated as Appropriate or Expected	Percent Who Concur	
		Men	Women
Best age for a man to marry	20–25	80	90
Best age for a woman to marry	19–24	85	90
When most people should become grandparents	45–50	84	79
Best age for most people to finish school and go to work	20–22	86	82
When most men should be settled on a career	24–26	74	64
When most men hold their top jobs	45–50	71	58
When most people should be ready to retire	60–65	83	86
A young man	18–22	84	83
A middle-aged man	40–50	86	75
An old man	65–75	75	57
A young woman	18–24	89	88
A middle-aged woman	40–50	87	77
An old woman	60–75	83	87
When a man has the most responsibilities	35–50	79	75
When a man accomplishes most	40–50	82	71
The prime of life for a man	35–50	86	80
When a woman has the most responsibilities	25–40	93	91
When a woman accomplishes most	30–45	94	92
A good-looking woman	20–35	92	82

Source: B. L. Neugarten et al., 1965.

a poor person in early adulthood. The rich person can afford to lose a term in school or to delay getting started in a career, but someone from a poverty-stricken background cannot. He or she must make occupational commitments earlier and has less freedom to delay choices.

True or False People from higher socioeconomic groups can delay movement from one stage of adulthood to the next more easily than people from lower socioeconomic groups.

Social clocks and age norms are affected by the historical period in which people live. In the late twentieth century, retirement is not just a dream for many, it is a reality for millions. Years ago, retirement simply meant illness and the inability to work. Couples used to have as many children as possible and spent most of adulthood raising them. But today a good portion of adulthood is spent without children to raise. Social clocks change with historical periods. We are now more flexible in determining when people "ought" to take jobs, marry, or retire (Schlossberg, 1984).

The Importance of Neugarten's Work

Neugarten's emphasis on culture, the social clock, and historical time puts our look at adulthood in broader perspective and allows for cross-cultural appreciations of adulthood. It also focuses attention on changes within our own culture and forces us to reevaluate older ideas of what is and is not appropriate adult behavior in the light of such cultural changes.

What Can We Learn from These Theories?

Many people feel uneasy after looking at these theories. After all, the theories are a bit vague and not based upon hard, statistical evidence, and none of the research seems to have utilized control groups. In addition, most of the subjects are white upper-middle-class males. Still, these theories can form a useful framework for analyzing adulthood. Certain similarities in these theories allow us to come up with a tentative structure for understanding adulthood.

The age-groups. Most psychologists today accept early and middle adulthood as distinct stages. No one seriously questions whether later adulthood is a stage. Neugarten

young–old Younger elderly people who are fully functioning and independent.

old–old Elderly people who have a number of deficits and infirmities that decrease their ability to function on their own.

(1975) suggests that because of our increased longevity we divide later maturity into two different stages: the young–old stage and the old–old stage. The **young–old** are fully functioning, independent people, while the **old–old** suffer from a number of infirmities and deficits that decrease their ability to enjoy life and function autonomously.

Developmental tasks throughout adulthood. The theorists all concluded that adults face challenges throughout the life span and that these tasks are identifiable and predictable. For many years, we have understood the tasks associated with marriage, career advancement, and raising children, but these theorists have pointed out periods in which the individual considers the *value* of these pursuits in his or her quest for fulfillment in life.

The concept of transitions. Most of these theories predict a period of intense questioning followed by periods of relative stability (Thomas and Kuhn, 1982). The transition leading to the thirties and the mid-life transition are especially important. There is the possibility of another transition into late maturity as well. The most controversial is certainly the mid-life transition. Theorists agree that this is a time of questioning and searching, but they disagree on just how dramatic it is. At present, most research does not show it to be very dramatic, and the questioning may take place at an earlier or later time (Perlmutter and Hall, 1985).

True or False The mid-life crisis that occurs around age forty is a time of reevaluation and questioning, but for most people not a time of dramatic change.

The importance of love and work. All these theories emphasize the relationship of people to their families and to their careers. At different times, one seems to eclipse the other, but the basic importance of both remains throughout the adult life cycle. The transitions are often based on reevaluations of these two basic areas of human endeavor.

Looking for both stability and change. Continuous growth and change occur throughout adulthood, and many of these changes are predictable. Yet none of these theorists sees any one stage as totally separate from the one that came before it. There is stability as well. One period builds on the next, and any decisions to change are based both on past experiences and on hopes for the future.

Aging and physiological changes are important. Beginning in middle adulthood, physiological changes, aging, and the recognition of one's own mortality are potent forces that drive a person to a reconsideration of life. Though these concerns may be more serious for some people than others, the awareness of aging touches all adults.

The Need to Look at the Female Perspective

The definite male orientation of these theories needs to be corrected. One problem with Levinson's and Vaillant's work is the lack of females in their samples. Levinson (1980) believes that in early adulthood women proceed through the same periods as men, but that there are important differences in the way men and women negotiate the periods. However, little research on the life paths of women has been conducted. The extent to which the theories of Levinson and Vaillant generalize to women is at present questionable.

Perhaps males and females have a different orientation toward life. Gilligan (1982) notes that whereas separation and autonomy are basic to the male, attachment and empathy are of central importance to females. By the time children reach adolescence, each sex has a different orientation toward social experiences and social relationships. For women, relationships are most important, and the key to understanding female development is to understand how important attachment is to them. To men, the keys involve autonomy and personal identity. Women and men define themselves and their experiences in different ways.

True or False Generally speaking, males and females have different attitudes toward social relationships and experiences, with women seeing relationships and attachment as central, and men seeing autonomy and personal identity as most important.

The Importance of Life Events and Culture

Certain events in the lives of men and women are important to keep in mind. Marriage, parenthood, divorce, unemployment, illness, the death of one's parents, and so many other identifiable life events cause us to rethink paths and values, and we must cope with them. Although most of the theories described in this chapter are grounded in late-twentieth-century middle-class experiences, it is important to understand that different cultures have different values, support different social clocks, and have different norms and role expectations. In some Eastern societies, such as Japan, the elderly are expected to live with their children, but in the United States independent existence as long as possible is considered desirable. Developmental psychologists are aware of the importance of culture, and attempts are being made to discover whether people from other cultural backgrounds share similar developmental tasks and periods (see the Cross-Cultural Current on page 354). In addition, we should always be aware of the historical period with which we are dealing. People who went through early adulthood during the depression of the 1930s had an experience that is very different from that of today's young adults.

The Theme of Adulthood: Paths and Choices

Each of us is faced with many choices and alternatives. We can choose a number of life paths. For instance, consider the person who wants to become a doctor but also an engineer. Most of us would think that this goal is impossible and that a choice must be made—doctors and engineers have different paths. A decision here has definite consequences and opens up different opportunities. Now let us say that this person is dating steadily and considering marriage. Three paths are open: the person can do nothing and continue to date, the couple can get married, or the relationship can be terminated. Again, each choice leads to another path. The same analysis can be made when the couple decides whether to have children. What causes us to choose one decision over another and to follow one life path instead of another? Personal background, learning, and socialization are factors, but so are one's subjective experience and personal dream.

As we investigate young adulthood, middle adulthood, and later maturity, the theme of choice will be

Adult Development Among Immigrants

A major question that people explaining the new theories of adulthood face is the extent to which these theories reflect the experience of members of the diverse cultural groups that live in the United States. Many of the new theories of adulthood were formulated on the basis of relatively small samples or special groups. Are these theories useful for looking at the adult development of people from different cultures who have immigrated to the United States? Can the life histories of these immigrants fit into the general framework of Levinson's theory? Are the developmental tasks of these people similar to those found in the majority group? Do they negotiate the same transitions? David Ross addressed some of these questions when he compared the life histories of Mexican-Americans to those of Americans born and raised in the United States.

To answer these questions, fifteen Mexican-Americans referred through social service professionals and community contacts were compared with a group of fifteen nonimmigrants randomly selected from a pool of men enrolled at a community college. The immigrants had all come to the United States in their young adult years and were now middle-aged. All subjects were interviewed, and translators were used when necessary. The tape-recorded information from these interviews was used to create a biography of these men from the time they were seventeen years old to the present. The information was subdivided into time periods corresponding to those advanced by Levinson (17–22 years of age, early adult transition; 22–28 years, entering the adult world; 28–33 years, age thirty transition; 33–40 years, settling down; and 40–45 years, mid-life transition).

The researcher then asked judges to listen to each interview and look for the presence or absence of important elements of Levinson's theory, such as "the dream," a mentor, the formation and development of marital relationships, vocational experiences, the existence of the "age-thirty transition," the mid-life transition, and the like. In addition, the judges were asked to identify important life events in a more qualitative manner, listing the most important personal, vocational, and familial events and placing them into various age periods.

When the data were analyzed, there were interesting similarities and differences between the two groups. The two groups were similar in many ways. In early adulthood, "dreams" were developed, and the men worked in their twenties to entrench themselves in their personal and occupational worlds. Around age thirty, some adjustments were made. Between age thirty and age forty, they were deeply involved with work and family, trying to improve the lot of their families as much as possible. Some reevaluation and questioning was present at age forty for both groups. In addition, both groups showed a desire to have a family and a home, and within both groups the questioning surrounding the transition periods was caused by some external event.

emphasized. This new look at adulthood, as exemplified by the theories covered in this introduction, does not view adulthood as a passive stage of life in which the aging process takes its toll, cognition steadily declines, and social interaction becomes limited. Rather, adulthood is a period of life that brings with it the need to adapt to new circumstances and to make various choices. It is a time of both challenge and choice, and it provides us with opportunities for growth and personal fulfillment.

Summary

1. According to Erikson, the positive outcome of the psychosocial crisis of the young adulthood is a sense of intimacy that involves forming deep and satisfying relationships, usually through marriage. The negative outcome is a sense of isolation. The positive outcome for the psychosocial crisis of middle adulthood is the development of a sense of generativity, which involves giving to the younger

Differences between the groups were also evident. Comparatively few people in either group reported having a mentor, but when they did an interesting group difference arose. According to Levinson's theory, a mentor is someone outside the family who helps give support and helps one begin the quest for the dream. Although this was so for the nonimmigrant group, the immigrant group was more likely to cite a family member, perhaps an uncle or cousin, who helped. Education was by far the greatest difference between the two groups. The Mexican-American group of immigrants averaged 7.3 years of education, while the nonimmigrant group averaged 13.8 years. This lack of education and training limited career options and carried over into life goals. To the immigrants, work did not mean status or achievement, but a way to earn a living and support one's family. The nuclear family was very important to both groups, but the immigrants maintained stronger relationships with parents, siblings, aunts, and uncles, whom they often consulted about major decisions in their lives. Both groups experienced the transitions described in Levinson's theory, although individual differences were great. However, the immigrants' experiences during these transitions were generally less intense and less difficult. This may be because immigration itself acted as an important transition in their lives. All but one of the immigrant

men had originally come to the United States on a temporary basis, but later all decided to stay. This necessitated a restructuring of their lives. Ross suggests that this need to cope with the major transition of immigration made the later transitions, such as those of mid-life, seem not as difficult.

In general, the findings support the proposition that the framework of Levinson's theory can be used to investigate the adult development of this group of immigrants as well as that of the native group. Both groups seem to encounter similar developmental tasks and transition periods. The greatest differences were in the areas of education, which led to differences in occupational experience, and relationships with extended family members. Although Levinson's theory demonstrated its usefulness with this subcultural group, it remains to be seen whether the theory can be used to investigate the adult development of people from other subcultural groups residing within the United States. It would also be interesting to discover whether the basic framework is useful for analyzing adult development in other societies around the world. Such research is difficult and time-consuming, but it remains the only way we can discover the extent to which our new theories of adulthood can be used.

Source: Ross, D. B. Cross-Cultural Comparison of Adult Development. *Personnel and Guidance Journal,* 1984, 62, 418–421.

generation. The negative outcome is stagnation or self-absorption. The positive outcome of the psychosocial crisis of old age is a sense of ego integrity. This involves being able to evaluate one's life positively. The negative outcome is a sense of despair, which is shown through bitterness.

2. Peck elaborated on Erikson's theories, enumerating four challenges in middle adulthood and three in old age. The middle adulthood challenges involve socializing versus sexualizing in human relationships, valuing wisdom versus valuing physical powers, maintaining mental flexibility

versus becoming mentally rigid, and cathectic flexibility (forming new relationships) versus cathectic impoverishment (the failure to form new relationships). The challenges of old age include ego differentiation versus work-role preoccupation, in which the person must realize there is value in activities beyond work and parenting; body transcendence versus ego preoccupation, in which people must overcome physical ailments to enjoy life; and ego transcendence versus ego preoccupation, which involves coming to terms with one's own mortality.

3. Vaillant found an uncharted period for men in

their thirties and fifties. The thirties is a time of career consolidation, in which people concentrate on their careers, while the fifties is a quieter time marked by the danger of falling into rigid patterns.

4. Levinson's theory of adult male development divides adulthood into four eras—preadulthood, early adulthood, middle adulthood, and late adulthood—and into a number of periods, each with its own problems and challenges. Levinson sees periods of transition and periods of stability. The most prominent and controversial transition is the transition to middle age, which Levinson, unlike most other theorists, sees as a crisis.

5. Gould divides adulthood into seven phases. He believes that to negotiate adulthood successfully, people must view the world differently. His research included women as well as men.

6. Culture, history, and social clocks are also important for understanding adult development. One's culture determines the rights and responsibilities of adulthood. The historical period in which a person lives has a profound effect on his or her outlook. A social clock is an internalized sense of timing, telling us whether we are progressing too fast or too slowly in terms of social events.

7. Most theorists agree that early, middle, and old age are reasonable divisions, although dividing older adulthood in terms of the young-old and old-old is becoming more popular. There is also agreement that developmental tasks continue throughout adulthood, that transitions do occur, that love and work are the key elements in adult life, and that aging and physiological changes are important.

―――――――――――――― *Answers to True or False Statements* ――――――――――――――

1. *False*   Correct statement: Developmental interest in adulthood has not been great until recently.
2. *False*   Correct statement: Freud emphasized the importance of early childhood and sees the final psychosexual stage as occurring in adolescence.
3. *True*   Very few theories begin their analysis in childhood and continue throughout the life span.
4. *True*   One challenge of middle age is to remain mentally active and receptive to new ideas.
5. *True*   Generally, the thirties are a time when men dedicate themselves to vocational pursuits.
6. *False*   Correct statement: Although people often find mentors at work, the relationships usually do not last more than two years or so.

7. *False*   Correct statement: The status of older people in our society is fairly low.
8. *True*   People in the higher socioeconomic groups can delay passage from one stage to the other more easily.
9. *True*   Although a period of questioning and reevaluation is common, most studies fail to find it a period of dramatic change and crisis for most people.
10. *True*   Males and females have different attitudes toward social relationships and experiences.

Physical and Cognitive Development in Early Adulthood

CHAPTER CONTENTS

The Bet
Research on Young Adulthood
Health and Physical Functioning in Young Adulthood
CROSS-CULTURAL CURRENT   An Unexpected Consequence of Moving
Cognitive Processes and the Body in Young Adulthood
Cognitive Functioning in Young Adulthood
Morals and Ethics in Young Adulthood
Reconsidering the Bet

❖

Are the Following Statements True or False?

Try the True-False Quiz below. See if your answers correspond to the information in this chapter. Each question is repeated after the paragraph in which the answer can be found. The True-False Answer Box at the end of the chapter lists the complete answers.

_____ **1.** Chronic diseases are more common in young adulthood than in any other adult age-group.

_____ **2.** Females reach their average final adult height before males do.

_____ **3.** Adults gain weight through age forty, after which they begin to lose weight.

_____ **4.** Most authorities believe that regular exercise does help prevent cardiovascular disease.

_____ **5.** Exercise increases appetite.

_____ **6.** About one-third of all smokers try to quit each year, and more than half are successful.

_____ **7.** There is a major decline in visual acuity after age thirty.

_____ **8.** Young adulthood is the least stressful stage of life.

_____ **9.** The age at which the average person's intelligence is thought to peak has decreased over the past fifty years.

_____**10.** Young adults tend to have more abstract values than adolescents.

_____**11.** Vocational interests become less rigid with age.

_____**12.** More than 95 percent of American adults believe in God.

The Bet

"Even though you're in good physical shape, your body's not what it was when you were in your teens," the commercial on the radio stated. As Trudy, age twenty-five, nodded agreement, her twenty-seven-year-old husband, Marc, was incredulous. "I'm in better shape now than I was ten years ago, especially since we started that exercise program. What's more, I'm sharper mentally," he said. Trudy ignored the comment, but Marc pressed her. Finally she said, "Well, we're both healthy. But face it— right after your teens you decline sharply." They continued the discussion, expanding into other areas. For example, Trudy said she and Marc were more rigid than they had been in college, while Marc said they were much more flexible. Marc offered to bet Trudy twenty dollars that he was right. Trudy smiled, but raised the stakes. "I'll take that bet, but I don't want *our* money. If I'm right, you get up and feed Kathy every night for two weeks." "Done," said Marc, "but you better get ready to wake up night after night for a while."

The contrasting positions of Marc and Trudy hint at two conflicting views of young adulthood. The first, represented by Marc, looks at this stage of life as a period of peak functioning. The second reflects Trudy's opinion that young adulthood is the beginning of decline. Which viewpoint matches the facts?

Research on Young Adulthood

Marc and Trudy will not find it easy to locate research to back up their positions. Any changes that Trudy thinks take place are likely to be gradual and not easy to spot. Compared with the research on physical and cognitive changes in middle and late adulthood, changes that take place in young adulthood have not been researched very thoroughly. It is far more common to find young adults used as a control group and compared with people in later life, than to find studies that investigate the changes in physical or cognitive functioning during the young adult years (Tyler, 1986; Honzik, 1984).

When Does Adulthood Begin?

Right from the start, our bettors will have difficulty defining their area of interest. There is no objective, agreed-upon age at which everyone enters adulthood. Certainly, there are religious and cultural rites of passage in which people symbolically assume the responsibilities of adulthood, but many of these date back to a simpler era and today hold largely symbolic meaning. In fact, there is no single event in our society negotiated by everyone that can represent the passage to adulthood. For example, if we choose marriage as that point, what do we say about people who either do not marry or who marry later in life? If supporting oneself is used as a measure of entry into adulthood, what do we do with medical students who may not leave school and earn their own living well into their twenties? Each state has legally decreed that a person is an adult at a certain age, usually eighteen or twenty-one, but only a weak case can be made for any particular age.

The only tenable conclusion is that in our society no single event signifies passage into adulthood for every person. For some, a significant event—such as a death in the family or an unplanned pregnancy—may catapult a person into adulthood. For most of us, though, the passage into young adulthood is slow and gradual.

In this chapter, we look at the physical and cognitive changes that take place during young adulthood—roughly corresponding to the years between age twenty and age forty—and in doing so, we'll try to settle Trudy and Marc's bet.

Health and Physical Functioning in Young Adulthood

Marc and Trudy believe they are healthy, and according to a government survey more than nine out of ten young adults rate their health as excellent or good (U.S. Department of Health, Education, and Welfare, 1976). Young adults don't get sick very often, and when they do they bounce back quickly. They are not hospitalized much either. Hospitalization occurs chiefly for childbirth, accidents, and digestive and genital-urinary problems (U.S. Department of HEW, 1976). Chronic diseases—such as high blood pressure, arthritis, and diabetes—are relatively rare in young adulthood (Troll, 1985). After about age thirty the death rate increases dramatically and the male death rate throughout young adulthood is higher than that for females.

True or False Chronic diseases are more common in young adulthood than in any other adult age-group.

Height and Weight

The age at which people reach their final adult height is controversial. Roche and Davila (1972) note that the average male reaches his adult height at 21.2 years, while the average female reaches her adult height earlier, at 17.3 years. Other researchers say that people reach their full height in their mid-twenties as 1 to 2 centimeters of additional height may be added each year between the ages of nineteen and twenty-eight (Hammar and Owens cited in Stevens-Long, 1984). Although these increases in height are trivial, the average person's increase in weight in young adulthood may become a problem.

True or False Females reach their average final adult height before males do.

Adults gain weight through about age fifty-five, after which progressive weight loss seems to be the rule (Troll, 1985). Between the ages of eighteen and twenty-four, the average man gains about 13 pounds. Weight gain during the rest of young adulthood is more gradual, and the average male gains another 5 pounds or so. The average female's weight gain in young adulthood does not show this precipitous increase during its early stage and is more uniform throughout early adulthood. She gains about 17 pounds during young adulthood (Abraham, 1979). Many adults have sedentary jobs, which contributes to a reduction in physical activity. Unless there is a reduction in caloric intake, a gain in weight may occur (Newman, 1982). In addition, if an individual eats as much or even increases caloric intake during this time of inactivity, weight gain will be the result. For specific populations that have migrated from rural areas and have changed their eating habits and lifestyle, obesity can be a major problem (see the Cross-Cultural Current on page 362).

True or False Adults gain weight through age forty, after which they begin to lose weight.

Few among us have never seen "ideal weight" tables and not felt a twinge of emotion—be it anger, disappointment, or depression. Such tables are often used by insurance companies, and they are sometimes changed in the upward direction (Metropolitan Life Insurance Co., 1983). The ideal weights as well as the actual average weights for young adults can be found in the appendix. A few points concerning ideal weights should be noted. First, one's ideal weight changes with age. As people age and become less active, the amount of muscle tissue decreases and bone tissue becomes less dense. People who were lean and muscular during their twenties may weigh the same forty years later and yet appear much fatter (Whitney and Hamilton, 1984). In addition, fat may be distributed differently as people age, giving people a weightier appearance. For some, this process of weight gain becomes especially dangerous because it may be related to heart disease in later life (Botwinick, 1984). People who were overweight as children tend to be overweight adults (Starfield and Pless, 1980), partly because of the excessive number of fat cells created during childhood that stay with the individual throughout life and partly because of poor eating habits established earlier in life.

Many previously active young adults have sedentary jobs; if they do not watch their caloric intake, they may gain weight.

An Unexpected Consequence of Moving

When people move from a rural area to the city, or from one country to another, we might expect that they would experience some problems. They might have to change occupations, learn a new language, and adjust to a different culture. But we might not realize that the migration can lead to physical changes that can have a negative impact on health. As groups migrate to new geographical locations and into a larger and different culture, changes in diet and exercise patterns could affect their physical health. To see whether this might be the case, a researcher must first choose a sample from a minority group that has migrated and compare it with a group that has not left their native land. This is just what Ivan Pawson and Craig Janes did when they compared a group of Samoans living just south of San Francisco to groups of Samoans who live in American Samoa, Western Samoa, and Hawaii.

An estimated 60,000 to 80,000 Samoans live in California. Because most Samoans are involved in church activities, Pawson and Janes considered the church a logical place to obtain a sample, which consisted of eighty-eight males and ninety-one females.

Various physical measurements were taken and medical tests were performed on the subjects. Height and weight were taken, as well as a measure of fatness (triceps skin-fold). Blood pressure and fasting blood-glucose levels were also determined. The findings were then compared with those for Samoans living in American Samoa, Western Samoa, and Hawaii.

The results were startling. Although the height of the Samoans living in California generally fell between the 25th and 50th percentile of the U.S. population, about half the sample exceeded the 95th percentile for weight. In the California sample, 55 percent of all males and 46 percent of females exceeded the age-specific 95th percentile for weight in the U.S. population. Samoans living in California were significantly heavier than those living in Samoa or Hawaii. For some unknown reason, however, this extra weight was not reflected in the measure of skinfold thickness, which did not differ significantly across samples.

The incidence of hypertension (high blood pressure) was also higher in the California sample. Unfortunately, only a little more than 40 percent of the California

Exercise and Health

Trudy and Marc do not really think they are out of shape, although Trudy believes they are past their peak. Marc is a stockbroker and Trudy works part-time as an accountant and cares for their two children, age three and age four months. Even though they both watch their weight, they are gaining a little. When they were younger they were fairly active. Trudy enjoyed swimming and racquetball, Marc used to play full-court basketball and tennis. Now they don't get much exercise. Marc commutes every day to the city and sits in an office, and Trudy's exercise consists of running after the preschooler and shopping. But they both felt exhausted at the end of a day, and this concerned them.

While there is no single accepted definition of physical fitness, it can be considered the ability to complete one's daily tasks without fatigue and exhaustion and with en-

ergy left over for leisure or evening activities (Diekelmann, 1977). Faced with the feeling of being out of shape and a tendency to put on weight, Marc and Trudy began an exercise program. Exercise is important in early adulthood, because the lives of many once-active adolescents become sedentary in this period when career and family become the focus. Really for the first time, people must make an effort to set aside time for a regularly scheduled exercise program.

Is exercise really good for you? Exercise seems to have become a national obsession. Health clubs are flourishing, and the neighborhood jogger is a common sight. Exercise and aerobics classes are being advertised, and miracle fitness machines are offered to an exercise-conscious public in all the media. What kind of exercise program is best, and what are the benefits of physical exercise?

sample followed the fasting procedure necessary to get accurate readings of fasting blood glucose, but analysis of this partial sample showed that females who were overweight also had elevated blood-glucose levels. Elevated blood-glucose level is an indicator of possible metabolic problems.

Definite conclusions are difficult to draw from this data because of a lack of information concerning the backgrounds of subjects within these samples. In addition, we really do not know whether these people became obese after they reached California or before. However, even taking these problems into consideration, the study raises many important issues and questions. If the obesity and hypertension problem is so serious in the Samoan community, then it could lead to long-term and widespread health problems. In addition, we need answers to questions concerning cultural beliefs that de-termine attitudes toward food and obesity. Cultural beliefs or eating habits may become counterproductive when transferred to different environments, or perhaps they change after migration and exposure to other environments. In addition, exercise patterns and other lifestyle changes need to be investigated.

Understanding this phenomenon can help us see how the changing lifestyles of immigrants and migrants can affect their physical stature and health. American society has experienced and still is experiencing extensive im-migration. In addition, migration from rural to urban environments and from older industrial states to those in the Sunbelt are just two of the patterns we've seen in the past fifty years. Understanding the possible effects of such migration may be vitally important to safeguard-ing the health and well-being of various populations throughout the nation.

Source: Pawson, I. G., and Janes, C. Massive Obesity in a Migrant Samoan Population. *American Journal of Public Health.* May 1981, 71, 508–513.

As long as young adults are in good health, most au-thorities agree that they can participate in vigorous exercise programs (Rosentsweig, 1980). Exercises that require in-creased oxygen consumption, called **aerobic exercises**— including brisk walking, jogging, bicycling, and swim-ming—are best. For maximum advantage, however, ex-ercise should be performed regularly (at least four times a week), sustained, and exercise the heart (Diekelmann, 1977). The Sunday-morning jogger or Wednesday-evening bowler will not receive the greatest benefits.

Although there are many claims that have no basis in fact, research generally shows exercise to be quite beneficial. Regular exercise leads to greater vigor (de Vries, 1975) and improved cardiovascular functioning. The regular exerciser can achieve the same cardiac out-put with a lower heart rate (Strand, 1983), and the heart and circulatory system do not have to work as hard during

aerobic exercise Exercise that requires increased rates of oxygen consumption, such as brisk walking or bicycling.

more vigorous activity. Although the studies are not unanimous, excellent research shows that regular exer-cise plays a part in preventing cardiovascular disease (Curfman, 1985). Exercise also burns up calories and can convert fat to muscle, which while it does not lead to a reduction in weight, can improve one's appearance. Reg-ular exercise can also lead to a better self-concept (Hilyer and Mitchell, 1979) and an increase in feelings of well-being. Regular exercise may lead to a reduction in stress and anxiety and to improvements in mood and work performance, although many studies in these areas are poorly designed and in need of better controls (Folkins and Sime, 1981). Indeed, an increasing number of adults are now exercising. It is estimated that 54 percent of adults between the ages of twenty and forty-four exercise regularly (U.S. Department of Commerce, 1979).

True or False   Most authorities believe that regular exercise does help prevent cardiovascular disease.

There are a number of erroneous ideas about exercise. Some people believe that if they exercise their appetite will increase, but the opposite actually occurs—exercise actually reduces appetite (Diekelmann, 1977). And some people equate being in shape with thinness. This is incorrect too. A thin person may be lean but out of shape and weak (Whitney and Hamilton, 1984). People also sometimes rely on physical exercise as their only weight-loss program. If your caloric intake stays the same but your activity level increases, your weight will decrease somewhat; in addition, regular exercise increases the heat output of the body, burning up more calories even when you are not exercising. But the amount of exercise necessary to burn a pound of weight is relatively great, so even though exercise is a useful adjunct to a weight-reduction program, it should not be thought of as the total program. Physically inactive young adults must look to their diets as well.

True or False   Exercise increases appetite.

Exercise in aulthood.   Okay, so we should exercise—but how much is necessary, and are there any dangers? Too often the general recommendation to get more exercise is made without a discussion of such matters. According to medical evidence, if the goal is to prevent heart problems later in life, most people need to incorporate exercise into leisure activities. In one study of college alumni, Paffenbarger and colleagues (1978) found that leisure-time activities that burn up at least 2,000 calories a week were effective in reducing one's chances of having a heart attack. This is equal to 1 hour of fast walking at 4 miles an hour each day, or 30 minutes of jogging a day. However, other combinations—which include stair-climbing, cycling, and swimming—are also effective. After looking at the evidence, Curfman and colleagues (1985) suggest that even low-level activities, such as walking and gardening, offer some protection, but only if they are done regularly. More vigorous activities probably confer additional protection, and one study

The keen interest of contemporary young adults in exercise has played a large part in making it a major industry in the United States today.

suggests that activities using up 7.5 calories a minute—such as cycling, swimming, and running—are ideal (Morris et al., 1980).

Can exercise be dangerous? The new convert to vigorous exercise may not be concerned about possible dangers of exercise, but they do exist. The increased interest in physical exercise has brought with it a great deal of research on muscle and skeletal injuries and a spate of unusual warnings, including warnings about joggers being attacked by predatory birds. Knee, leg, and foot injuries to runners are common (Soloman, 1984). Novice exercisers sometimes begin strenuous exercise without an adequate stretching or warmup period and injure a muscle.

The most serious concern, however, is sudden cardiac death. The newspapers often carry articles about an adult in seemingly excellent physical condition who exercised regularly and suffered a sudden heart attack. But this worry needs to be put in perspective. A study of men who had suffered their first coronary found that in habitually active men the overall risk of sudden cardiac death was only 40 percent of that for habitually inactive men (Siscovick et al., 1984). Although the risk of sudden death increases during strenuous physical exercise for both inactive men and active men, regular physical activity seems to protect against sudden cardiac death. In addition, most sudden cardiac deaths occur in individuals with preexisting coronary disease (Curfman et al., 1985). Individuals over forty should undergo intensive exercise stress-testing before initiating a physical activity program. But how about people under forty? Any such program should be phased in gradually, and the intensity of the exercise should be increased slowly over a period of weeks or months. In addition, whenever symptoms remotely suggest a cardiac problem, testing should be performed. Finally, people with high cholesterol levels should consult a doctor before beginning an exercise program. Even young adults who are out of shape should first consult a physician.

The evidence showing that increased activity equaling 2,000 calories a week can help prevent later heart attacks is important. Simple changes in lifestyle can be a start. For instance, walking uses about 3 to 7 calories a minute, so a person walking briskly might consume 5 calories a minute for 30 minutes, expending 150 calories, compared with only 45 calories used up sitting in an auto. Climbing stairs consumes about 11 calories a minute, and if a person climbs twenty flights of stairs a day, about 50 calories are utilized. This may contribute to the amount needed to reduce heart problems.

Drug Use

Another area of concern in the health area is drug abuse. Most articles on drug use focus on the adolescent, but what happens when drug-taking adolescents graduate from high school and enter the job market? Table 14.1 shows trends in drug use over the past decade among young adults. If we compare the age-groups—ages 12–17, 18–25, and 26 and older—we see some interesting trends. Although marijuana use decreases sharply after age twenty-six, alcohol and cigarette-smoking do not show the same major reductions after that age (U.S. Department of Commerce, 1986).

But this is not the whole story. Over the past decade some major attitudinal and behavioral changes have taken place. According to a Louis Harris poll, adults now claim that alcohol plays less of a role in their lives than it did in their younger years, and almost half those surveyed believed they drank less than they did five years ago (*Business Week,* 1983). These changes may be due to an increased awareness of the dangers of drinking and driving, or to the trend toward a healthier lifestyle, but drug and alcohol abuse remains a serious problem in adulthood. Some 3 to 7 percent of the employed population use some form of illicit drug on a daily basis (Quayle, 1983), and between 5 and 10 percent of the work force suffers from alcoholism. Alcohol abuse is associated with a number of physical problems later in life, including liver problems.

The statistics on tobacco use in adulthood over the past four decades tell an interesting story too. Between 1950 and 1979, the percentage of adult men who smoke declined from 53 percent to 37 percent. The percentage of adult women who smoke was close to 33 percent through 1976, but by 1979 it had decreased to 28 percent (U.S. Department of Health and Human Services, 1980). Among people who smoke, however, the number of cigarettes smoked per day has increased. About one-third of adult smokers try to quit each year, but only about one-fifth of those are successful (Oskamp, 1984). In 1982, some 39.5 percent of people within the age-group between eighteen and twenty years old, and about 34.6 percent of all adults over age twenty-six, were smoking (U.S. Department of Commerce, 1986). The decrease over the decades is probably due to the public's increasing

Drug Use in Youth and Adulthood

Note the decrease in the use of marijuana and some other drugs and the sustained use of other drugs like tobacco and alcohol.

	Percent of Youths (age 12–17)				Percent of Young Adults (age 18–25)				Percent of Adults (age 26+)			
	Ever Used		Current User		Ever Used		Current User		Ever Used		Current User	
	1974	1982	1974	1982	1974	1982	1974	1982	1974	1982	1974	1982
Marijuana	23.0	26.7	12.0	11.5	52.7	64.1	25.2	27.4	9.9	23.0	2.0	6.6
Inhalants	8.5	(NA)	.7	(NA)	9.2	(NA)	(Z)	(NA)	1.2	(NA)	(Z)	(NA)
Hallucinogens	6.0	5.2	1.3	1.4	16.6	21.1	2.5	1.7	1.3	6.4	(Z)	(Z)
Cocaine	3.6	6.5	1.0	1.6	12.7	28.3	3.1	6.8	.9	8.5	(Z)	1.2
Heroin	1.0	(Z)	(Z)	(Z)	4.5	1.2	(Z)	(Z)	.5	1.1	(Z)	(Z)
Stimulants*	5.0	6.7	1.0	2.6	17.0	18.0	3.7	4.7	3.0	6.2	(Z)	.6
Sedatives*	5.0	5.8	1.0	1.3	15.0	18.7	1.6	2.6	2.0	4.8	(Z)	(Z)
Tranquilizers*	3.0	4.9	1.0	.9	10.0	15.1	1.2	1.6	2.0	3.6	(Z)	(Z)
Alcohol	54.0	65.2	34.0	26.9	81.6	94.6	69.3	67.9	73.2	88.2	54.5	56.7
Cigarettes	52.0	49.5	25.0	14.7	68.8	76.9	48.8	39.5	65.4	78.7	39.1	34.6

NA = Not available.   Z = Less than .5 percent.   *Prescription drugs.

Source: Statistical Abstracts, 1986.

belief that cigarettes represent a significant health risk, to the modern emphasis on a healthier lifestyle, and even perhaps to the increasing militancy of the nonsmoking population, which discourages smoking in their presence.

True or False About one-third of all smokers try to quit each year, and more than half are successful.

Another area of concern is cocaine use, which in the 1980s increased substantially among both teens and adults. Unfortunately, it is regarded by some as a "glamorous substance" because its use has been linked to some famous people and cuts across socioeconomic social and economic classes (Wynder et al., 1981). In a study of cocaine-using adults, Spotts and Shontz (1980) found that most users had tried an average of five drugs prior to their first use of cocaine and that most had been introduced to the drug by friends. These users all admitted a strong craving for the high the drug induced. Cocaine users often find the drug irresistible, and it may come to dominate a person's whole life.

Can drug use in young adulthood be viewed simply in terms of a continuation of drug-taking habits from adolescence? Jerald Bachman and his colleagues (1984) looked at the pattern of drug use right after high school and found they could predict drug use in young adulthood from patterns of drug use in the senior year of high school. Except for smoking, however, the rate of drug use de-

> **Acquired Immune Deficiency Syndrome (AIDS)** A fatal disease causing a breakdown of the body's natural defenses, leaving the body vulnerable to diseases that the body cannot then fight.

pended on living arrangements. Those who continued to live with their parents showed no significant change, but those who married decreased their drug use. Those who left their parents' home to live with someone else or who lived in dormitories actually showed an increase. These associations were unaffected by student status, employment, or other personal factors.

So drug-taking in young adulthood remains a serious concern, although with age it generally becomes less of a problem. Alcohol and tobacco use, however, remains high throughout adulthood. People who settle down and get married, especially to a non-drug taking spouse, tend to reduce drug use. They may see drug-taking merely as a stage they went through or perhaps the act of taking on the responsibility of a family causes them to rethink their behavior.

AIDS

No disease in the past 100 years has had the shocking effect that **AIDS,** or **Acquired Immune Deficiency Syn-**

drome, has had on the American public in the past several years. Many people who have AIDS are young adults. The median age is thirty-four years, and 92 percent are under the age of fifty (Foege, 1983). By the end of 1986, more than 29,000 Americans had contracted AIDS, and it is projected that by 1991 the figure will be close to 270,000 (*U.S. News & World Report*, 1987). At the present time, there is no cure for AIDS, although some new medications—such as azidothymidine, or AZT—which stops the virus from reproducing, show promise for treatment of the disease. AIDS cripples the body's natural defenses, leaving it vulnerable to opportunistic diseases that healthy bodies fight easily (Schram, 1986). Symptoms of AIDS include unexplained weight loss, oral thrush (an infection of the tongue and mouth), persistent diarrhea, coughing or shortness of breath, skin rashes and spots, bruising and bleeding, and severe fatigue (Gong, 1985a). The disease is caused by a virus called by some the lymphadenopathy virus (LAV) and by others the HTLV-111 virus (the human T-cell lymphotrophic virus) (Gong, 1985b). But not everyone who comes in contact with the virus will get AIDS. An estimated 1.5 million Americans now carry the virus but display no symptoms (*U.S. News & World Report*, 1987). No one knows for certain what percentage of these people will eventually display symptoms of AIDS. Some estimate that only a minority, between 20 and 30 percent, will actually suffer the ravages of the disease (Koop, 1987) but estimates on the percentage vary, and no one knows for sure.

Certain groups are more likely to contract AIDS than others. Some 73 percent of AIDS victims in the United States are homosexual or bisexual men, 17 percent are intravenous drug users, 2 percent are blood transfusion recipients, and 1 percent are hemophiliacs (Schram, 1986). The sexual partners of anyone in each of these groups are also at risk.

Fear of contracting AIDS has led to a massive interest in how the virus is transmitted. A number of people—including health-care workers, funeral directors, and law enforcement personnel—have shown reluctance or sometimes outright refused to deal with AIDS patients (Sensakovic and Greer, 1985). AIDS is transmitted through contact with infected body fluids. It is a sexually transmitted disease, but it can be spread through blood transfusions with infected blood. In addition, intravenous drug users often share needles, making it possible for infected blood to pass from one person to another (Hirsch, 1985). The disease can also be spread from an infected mother to her unborn infant during the prenatal stage (Sande, 1986). And there is no longer any doubt that it can be contracted through heterosexual sex, although the number of such cases, at least in the United States, remains low at this time (Sande, 1986). By 1991, however, it is expected to increase tenfold to an estimated 23,000 heterosexuals (*U.S. News & World Report*, 1987). Even though the AIDS virus has been isolated in tears and saliva, a discovery that concerned many more people, there is no evidence at the present time that the AIDS virus can be spread through these media (Schram, 1986). In fact, there is no evidence that casual contact spreads the disease. Studies of health-care professionals or families living with AIDS victims find that they do not catch the virus from casual contact (Friedland et al., 1986). Still, the general public is frightened of even casual contact with an AIDS victim and have stigmatized people belonging to groups at risk (Altman, 1986).

People can reduce their chances of contracting AIDS by taking some simple precautions. Among other things, people providing health care for AIDS patients should wear gloves and clean spills with chlorine bleach. Intravenous drug users are urged not to share needles. Since AIDS is spread most often through sexual contact, it is recommended that people refrain from engaging in sexual practices that might cut or tear the skin, avoid sex with people who engage in activities that place them at greater risk for contracting the virus (such as intravenous drug use), use condoms, and take whatever other precautions are necessary to avoid transmission of the virus.

Unfortunately, the sufferings of AIDS victims are often forgotten in the public's extreme fear of the disease. Since many victims are young adults, their care is often left to aging parents, forcing a new and unwanted dependency on both patient and family (Lehman and Russell, 1985). The AIDS sufferer must not only come to accept the diagnosis, but also deal with the rejection and stigma attached to the disease.

AIDS must be fought on three levels. First, new treatments and ways to combat the disease must be found through research. Second, people must be educated about how to reduce the risk of contracting the disease. Third, there must be an educational program aimed at separating myth from fact.

The Physical Abilities of Young Adults

One tragedy of AIDS is that it strikes mostly young adults in the prime of life and at the height of their physical abilities. Indeed, physically speaking, young adulthood marks the peak of physical prowess. The picture of the professional athlete most of us hold is a person in the early to middle twenties, and indeed this is accurate. Most Olympic athletes in rigorous competition such as running and jumping tend to be in this age-group (Tanner, 1964). We hit our peak in physical strength, speed, and agility during the mid-twenties (Newman, 1982; Hershey, 1974). Yet by the end of the twenties and the beginning of the thirties, certain changes take place. The capacity to perform physical labor at extreme temperatures begins to decline before the age of thirty (Stevens-Long, 1984). The heart and circulatory system begin to lose their elasticity. Cardiac output—the volume of blood pumped by the heart each minute—decreases about 1 percent a year beginning at age twenty (Kohn, 1977). There is a slow decline in strength after age thirty, and a gradual decrease in muscular endurance after age twenty-five (Rosentsweig, 1980). The decrease in strength is usually in the legs, and indeed aging professional athletes often complain that this loss is the first physical problem they sense. Between the ages of thirty and forty, there is some loss of speed and agility (Newman, 1982)

and a gradual decrease in the secretion of gastric juices after age thirty, which may explain the increase in digestive problems later in young adulthood (Timiras, 1972). Reaction time increases too—it takes longer to respond to a stimulus. Bromley (1974) suggests that there is a 17 percent increase in reaction time between the ages of twenty and forty.

Two points are crucial for understanding these trends. First, physical decline is probably due as much to disuse of muscles as to degeneration of muscles. Individuals who exercise can remain in excellent physical shape. Indeed, cross-cultural research demonstrates that older people in other cultures in which activity is the rule do not show some of the signs we attribute to aging, including reduction in strength and agility (Rosentsweig, 1980). Second, the decline of these abilities is quite gradual. Strength declines only about 10 percent between age thirty and age sixty (Troll, 1985). These slight declines in strength, agility, and speed probably go unnoticed by most of us during our late twenties and thirties, and it is understandable that Marc thinks he is still in the same shape he was in during his teenage years. For the vast majority of us, these decreases are of little consequence, but

Most Olympic athletes who compete in active sports requiring running or jumping are young adults.

professional athletes may find this loss a problem and attempt to compensate by using their experience. Most athletes, as they progress through their thirties, know that their athletic careers are winding down are are keenly aware of any decrease in physical abilities or increase in time necessary to prepare for a season.

Sensory Functioning

If the physical declines in young adulthood do not seem to be very important, what of sensory functioning? During young adulthood, sensory functioning remains excellent, although some gradual changes do occur. Visual acuity is perhaps best at the age of twenty and remains relatively constant until age forty (Timiras, 1972). The changes that do occur are minor and inconsequential (Botwinick, 1984). There is a small decline in the ability to see details after age twenty-five or thirty (Stevens-Long, 1984; Newman, 1982). It also takes longer for the eyes to adapt to the dark (Corso, 1981). Hearing declines a bit from about age twenty, especially for high-pitch sounds (Birren, 1964). There is little indication that smell, touch, or taste decline at all during the young adult years.

True or False There is a major decline in visual acuity after age thirty.

Physical Changes in Young Adulthood: A Summary

At this point, neither Trudy nor Marc can claim victory (and two weeks of blissfully undisturbed sleep). Evidence indicates that during the young adult years physical functioning is excellent. Many systems are functioning at or around their peak. Any declines are very minor and hardly noticeable. At the same time, health habits established at this stage in life may affect physical functioning later on. Lack of physical exercise and failure to change eating habits can lead to heart problems in middle and late adulthood.

Cognitive Processes and the Body in Young Adulthood

To this point, we have focused exclusively on physical functioning in early adulthood. Trudy and Marc's bet treated physical and cognitive functioning as separate entities. They did not even take into account how physical functioning might affect mental abilities and how cognitive processes might affect physical abilities. But some appreciation of this interaction is important. On the surface, it is obvious that one must affect the other. People who are overweight often have a poor view of themselves, and people who are in good physical shape are apt to have a more positive self-concept (Burns, 1979). Yet some areas are not as obvious. To demonstrate this interaction, we'll look at two important areas—stress, and the effects of hormones on mood and behavior.

Stress in Young Adulthood

Although stress is present in the childhood and adolescent years, negotiating the stage of young adulthood is particularly stressful. Any changes in one's life are inherently stressful (Milsum, 1984), and the average young adult must negotiate many major and minor life changes. Holmes and Rahe (1967) formulated a life-events scale that rated forty-three life events according to the amount of stress imposed upon a person (see Table 14.2). The more changes in life events, the greater the chance of mental or physical illness. If you look at Table 14.2, you will see how many of the events are tied to young adulthood—including marriage, pregnancy, gaining new family members, and work-related events. Of course, older adults are subjected to stress too. The greatest stressor—loss of a spouse—is most likely to occur in old age. However, the number of life changes in young adulthood that take place in a relatively short amount of time is impressive. Even positive changes—such as marriage, the birth of a child, or buying a house with a substantial mortgage—are stressful. And young adults seem to take stressful events harder than middle-aged adults. When asked to describe how disruptive certain life events were, older people consistently produced lower ratings. They worry less than younger people and report less job stress (Chiriboga and Cutler, 1980). While Holmes and Rahe concentrated on specific stressful events, others emphasized the importance of daily problems and stressors (DeLongis et al., 1982). We all are exposed to daily hassles, those little stressors that mount up. The traffic jam that causes us to be late for a meeting, a cranky child, the television that breaks two days after the warranty runs out, and the inability to lose that extra five pounds—all contribute to the stress in our lives. Envi-

TABLE 14.2

The Social Readjustment Rating Scale

Life changes bring about stress and too many changes within a relatively short amount of time increase the chances that a person may suffer mental and/or physical illness.

Rank	Life Event	Mean Value	Rank	Life Event	Mean Value
1	Death of spouse	100	25	Outstanding personal achievement	28
2	Divorce	73	26	Wife beginning or ceasing work outside the home	26
3	Marital separation from mate	65	27	Beginning or ceasing formal schooling	26
4	Detention in jail or other institution	63	28	Major change in living conditions (e.g., building a new home, remodeling, deterioration of home or neighborhood)	25
5	Death of a close family member	63	29	Revision of personal habits (dress, manners, associations, etc.)	24
6	Major personal injury or illness	53	30	Trouble with the boss	23
7	Marriage	50	31	Major change in working hours or conditions	20
8	Being fired at work	47	32	Change in residence	20
9	Marital reconciliation with mate	45	33	Changing to a new school	20
10	Retirement from work	45	34	Major change in usual type and/or amount of recreation	19
11	Major change in the health or behavior of a family member	44	35	Major change in church activities (e.g., a lot more or a lot less than usual)	19
12	Pregnancy	40	36	Major change in social activities (e.g., clubs, dancing, movies, visiting, etc.)	18
13	Sexual difficulties	39	37	Taking out a mortgage or loan for a lesser purchase (e.g., for a car, TV, freezer, etc.)	17
14	Gaining a new family member (e.g., through birth, adoption, oldster moving in, etc.)	39	38	Major change in sleeping habits (a lot more or a lot less sleep, or change in part of day when asleep)	16
15	Major business readjustment (e.g., merger, reorganization, bankruptcy, etc.)	39	39	Major change in number of family get-togethers (e.g., a lot more or a lot less than usual)	15
16	Major change in financial state (e.g., a lot worse off or a lot better off than usual)	38	40	Major change in eating habits (a lot more or a lot less food intake, or very different meal hours or surroundings)	15
17	Death of a close friend	37	41	Vacation	13
18	Changing to a different line of work	36	42	Christmas	12
19	Major change in the number of arguments with spouse (e.g., either a lot more or a lot less than usual regarding child-rearing, personal habits, etc.)	35	43	Minor violations of the law (e.g., traffic tickets, jay-walking, disturbing the peace, etc.)	11
20	Taking out a mortgage or loan for a major purchase (e.g., for a home, business, etc.)	31			
21	Foreclosure on a mortgage or loan	30			
22	Major change in responsibilities at work (e.g., promotion, demotion, lateral transfer)	29			
23	Son or daughter leaving home (e.g., marriage, attending college, etc.)	29			
24	Trouble with in-laws	29			

Source: Holmes and Rahe, 1967.

psychosomatic or **psychophysiological disorders**
Physical disorders, such as ulcers and colitis, that are contributed to or caused by emotional factors, including reactions to stress.

ronmental insults—such as crowding, noise, and pollution—are stressful too (Oskamp, 1984).

True or False Young adulthood is the least stressful stage of life.

People react to stress in different ways. How a perceives the stressor is an important factor. One person's tragedy is another person's challenge. Past experiences, physical and emotional stamina, and basic outlook all affect how we perceive the stressful situation, which in turn may affect how we are affected by it (Kaplan and Stein, 1984).

Stress is an important concern partly because it is linked to a number of illnesses (Krantz et al., 1985). It is estimated that between 50 and 80 percent of all illnesses have emotional components and are stress-related

(Pelletier, 1977). Stress can lead to such physiological responses as increased heart rate and blood pressure (Krantz et al., 1985). If prolonged, these changes can be dangerous, sometimes leading to **psychosomatic** or **psychophysiological** disturbances that are real physical disorders in which stress and emotional reactions play a part. Such disorders as ulcers, colitis, and high blood pressure are related to the body's reaction to stress.

Type A and Type B Personalities

Are certain people more likely than others to suffer from these disorders? The search for personality types and specific behavioral reactions that predict later physical problems is ongoing. One interesting finding is that a particular type of personality, labeled Type A, is related to coronary disease, while people of another personality type, labeled Type B, are more resistant to such disease (Friedman and Rosenman, 1975). Type A people are overly competitive, do everything in a hurry, are quite time-conscious, feel guilty when they relax, and take life very seriously. Type B people are more easygoing and do the things they have to do in a less-hurried fashion.

Even positive experiences such as buying a new home can be a source of stress.

There is a correlation between Type A behavior and coronary disease later in adulthood (Rosenman et al., 1970; Rosenman et al., 1964).

Even if such factors as smoking, diet, and lack of physical exercise are controlled, the Type A personality pattern remains an important factor in predicting later heart trouble (Brand et al., 1978). Perhaps the problem stems from the greater reaction that Type A people have to threatening situations, compared with the reactions of the Type B person. Type A people appear to be more sensitive to negative sources of stress in their lives, especially those that threaten their control over the environment. Their physiological reactions to these circumstances weaken the body and increase the chances of heart disease (Glass, 1977). They are always shifting into emergency reactions, increasing their heart rate and blood pressure and producing high amounts of adrenalin and noradrenalin (Rosenman et al., 1975). These patterns are found in women as well as in men (Matthews, 1982). Type A behavior also affects other areas of life. One study found that Type A behavior adversely affects marital satisfaction. Wives of Type A husbands reported more conflict in their marriages (Burke et al., 1979).

The majority of heart attacks do not occur in young adults, so why cover this material here? One challenge of the life-span developmental perspective is to identify early patterns that affect later behavior and experience. Type A behavior begins very early in life and continues throughout adulthood, if no intervention occurs. A mere two years of Type A behavior in middle adulthood would probably not be responsible for a coronary. It is lifelong health habits and behaviors that are responsible. The discussion here does not mean that other factors—such as genetic considerations—cannot also contribute to heart attacks. However, young adulthood is a time of change. Exercise should be built into the daily schedule, and watching one's diet becomes more important, Establishing such good health practices at this stage in life can affect physical health later. Exercise, making time for relaxation, and taking a broader look at life's challenges can help reduce stress and even the Type A behavior that is related to later coronary artery disease (Suinn, 1982).

Hormones and Behavior

Hormones are defined as "chemical substances that deliver a message from one part of the organism to another" (Doering, 1980, p. 230). They are produced in the en-

premenstrual syndrome (PMS) An assortment of symptoms—including tension, depression, irritability, and fatigue—that occur in many women just prior to and at the start of their period.

docrine glands and circulated throughout the body by the blood. Hormonal increases and decreases during the life span can have physical and behavioral effects. The inability to manufacture insulin leads to diabetes, and thyroid secretions affect metabolism.

But most of the controversy and interest today has to do with hormones that affect the menstrual cycle and the possibility that they also affect mood and behavior. The traditional interpretation of the psychological implications of hormonal fluctuations in women is rather sexist. Some have used the research to support the incredible supposition that raging hormones cause wild mood swings and make women incapable of handling certain situations and holding some types of jobs (Paige, 1973). Any research purporting to show psychological and behavioral changes during the monthly cycle can be misused to rationalize such sexism if one is not careful. We must also note here that hormonal shifts have been found in men too (Hyde, 1985). Ramey (1972) reported the results of a sixteen-year study of Danish males that showed rhythmic changes in hormone levels on a monthly cycle and corresponding changes in irritability and efficiency with the hormonal fluctuation. However, the males in the study did not perceive their behavior as subject to cyclical hormonal influences, although their responses to psychological tests did reflect mood shifts. The possibility that men experience these cycles has not received nearly as much attention as the hormonal cycles in women.

Part of the controversy over such hormonal fluctuations has to do with the symptoms reported by many women immediately prior to and during the first day or so of the menstrual period. These symptoms include tension, depression, anxiety attacks, irritability, headaches, backaches, fatigue, water retention, and lower self-esteem, among others (Doyle, 1985). The symptoms are referred to collectively as the **premenstrual syndrome,** or **PMS.** Actually, more than 150 symptoms have been associated with PMS (Knox, 1984). Symptoms vary from woman to woman, with some women reporting some symptoms but not others, and some women reporting none. Although the various symptoms reported are real, there is some difference of opinion about whether PMS is a distinct entity because the symptoms vary so much (Hongladarom et al., 1982). It has been suggested that labeling be avoided while the specific symptoms are studied.

The percentage of women who suffer from PMS is also a matter of controversy. Some studies claim that almost 70 percent of the women surveyed suffered from these symptoms, while others claim only 30 percent (Hyde, 1985). This discrepancy is partly due to the vague definition of PMS and the great variation in the nature and severity of the symptoms.

The cause of PMS is controversial too. Some emphasize the overwhelming importance of hormonal fluctuations as the cause (Bardwick, 1971), and one important study gives validity to this notion. Women who used oral contraceptives reported less variation in mood during the menstrual cycle than those not taking the pill. Since the pill reduces hormonal fluctuation, this might be some support for hormonal involvement in PMS (Paige, 1971). The steadier and higher levels of female hormones produced by the pill may have reduced the symptoms associated with PMS.

Other researchers believe that PMS cannot be understood without looking at culture, learning, and expectations. Although hormones play some part, social and cultural influences are also important (Paige, 1973). Attitudes toward menstruation have traditionally been negative, and women are often taught to perceive it as a time when their abilities are reduced. When people expect to feel a particular way, they usually do, and women who see menstruation in terms of weakness expect to experience more symptoms than women who perceive it in a more positive way (Brooks et al., 1977).

The importance of expectation in premenstrual symptoms was shown by a study conducted by Ruble (1977). College students were tested about a week before the onset of their menses and told that they were participating in a study validating a new technique for predicting the expected date of menstruation using an electroencephalograph, a machine for measuring brain waves. Although the women did not differ significantly in the actual time at which their period would start, one group was told that they were premenstrual and their period was due in one or two days, another group was told that they had at least a week to ten days before their period arrived, and the control group was not given any information about when their period would begin. Women then completed self-reports on their feelings about men-

struation. Those who believed they were in the premenstrual phase reported more water retention, pain, and changes in eating habits although no significant differences between the groups were found on measures of emotionality. This study demonstrates the importance of expectations in understanding PMS.

Another consideration is the learning factor as women learn how to cope with physical symptoms by observing their mother or older sisters. The influence of environmental factors, such as stress, may be important too. Events that produce stress—for example, divorce or getting fired—can play a role in increasing PMS symptoms (Parlee, 1973). These possible nonhormonal factors do not mean that PMS is not real. They simply indicate that we must look at how hormonal factors and individual psychological factors interact.

What effect do hormonal variations have on women's performance? Studies find no fluctuations in intellectual performance that can be attributed to hormonal variations over the menstrual cycle (Golub, 1976). This may be because most women cope very well with their symptoms (Kerr and Scully, 1982). In addition, for most women, the symptoms are moderate and their coping mechanisms are more than sufficient to deal with any unpleasant symptoms they do experience.

In sum, despite the controversies that surround PMS, it is a real phenomenon but the type and severity of symptoms vary widely. Hormones do play a role, but so do learning and cultural expectations. Most women cope very well with these symptoms, and trying to use PMS as an excuse for discrimination against women is indefensible.

Cognitive Functioning in Young Adulthood

What about the second part of Trudy and Marc's bet? What happens to cognitive functioning during young adulthood? Young adults must learn skills necessary to obtain and keep a job. They face a host of moral and ethical questions concerning marriage, family life, and job behavior—and these questions are real, not just hypothetical, as they often are in adolescence. The young adulthood period is certainly a change from college, when facing these questions lay in the future and opinions were not encumbered by the limitations of the real world. Again, there are two ways to look at young adulthood, reflecting Marc's and Trudy's viewpoints. According to Marc, young adults are at the zenith of their cognitive powers and have ideals, morals, and ethics that compare favorably to those of younger as well as older people. But Trudy believes that their cognitive powers are waning and that young adults are less idealistic and more conservative than adolescents. Which view is correct?

Piaget and Adult Cognition

Piaget had little to say about adult cognitive development. He considered the stage of formal operations to be the final qualitative change in cognitive functioning (Piaget, 1970). Piaget believed that any changes after adolescence were quantitative and based on experience rather than on maturation. He differentiated formal operational behavior from the other stages, though, by admitting that a person's interests and vocational specialization were factors in determining the areas in which this advanced reasoning would be shown.

Not all adolescents or adults function at the stage of formal operations (Kuhn et al., 1977), and among those who do it will be used only under certain circumstances (Piaget, 1972). For instance, Marc and Trudy might show formal operational reasoning in their areas of specialization and not in other areas. In addition, because the development of formal operational thought is closely related to education, you would expect well-educated people in every culture to perform better on tests of formal operations, and indeed this is so (Keating and Clark, 1980).

Because Piaget had so little to say about adult cognitive development, a number of theorists looked for ways to extend Piaget's ideas. A number of suggestions for a fifth stage have been made. For example, Arlin (1977, 1975) argues that after the formal operations stage a person may enter the problem-finding stage, in which a person develops the ability to generate new problems or to raise questions about problems that are not well defined. Other theorists have also attempted to demonstrate different modes of cognition beyond formal operations (Commons et al., 1982). Although these attempts hold promise for going beyond the stage of formal operations, they are still tentative and await further development.

Intelligence Testing

How do young adults do on standardized tests of intelligence? Most do very well. Studies indicate that scores on intelligence tests, such as the Wechsler Adult Intelligence Scale, peak in the twenties and show a small decline in the thirties (Botwinick, 1977; Wechsler, 1958). Other studies show no decline until much later in adulthood (Bayley, 1968; 1966). One factor important in determining when and if there will be a decline is how the study is performed. Cross-sectional studies are more likely than longitudinal studies to show a decrease in intelligence with age (Whitbourne and Weinstock, 1979). Some reasons for this will be described later. However, the entire idea of measuring intelligence in adulthood is questionable. Intelligence is correlated with academic achievement (Horn and Donaldson, 1980), and this may have some meaning for children, but what meaning does it have for a thirty-year-old adult who is out of school? Because intelligence tests are geared toward younger people, testing adults on such youth-oriented tests is a questionable practice (Willis and Baltes, 1980). Although the problem is not acute when testing twenty-year-olds, by the end of young adulthood it can become a significant question.

Another problem involves individual differences. Children's experiences are individualistic and vary from child to child, but some researchers argue that individual differences become even more important in adulthood (Fischer and Silvern, 1985). This makes generalizing from studies of groups of adults to individuals difficult. Although schools differ in their academic standing, al-

Some authorities claim that there are many types of intelligence. This artist may or may not have a high verbal intelligence.

most every child in the Western world will be exposed to prolonged schooling. But adults differ even more widely in their academic experiences after graduation. Some never read a book and do not use advanced logic in their jobs, others are constantly learning and using complex problem-solving skills.

If you define intelligence in terms of adaptability, it is very difficult to measure adult intelligence. We have not had much success in determining what cognitive abilities are part of an adult's everyday experience (Kuhn et al., 1983). We still do not understand what role formal logic or deductive reasoning plays in an adult's everyday world (Labouvie-Vief, 1982; 1980). In addition, because there are many different kinds of intelligence (Gardner, 1983), emphasizing verbal intelligence may be unfair to artists, musicians, mechanics, or other specialists whose ability to cope with problems within their own discipline is excellent. Although no one is saying that musicians, artists, or mechanics cannot or do not have superior verbal intelligence, measuring only verbal intelligence may be unfair to them.

Despite these problems, we can tentatively conclude that intelligence measured by scores on standardized intelligence tests remains relatively stable throughout young adulthood. Although the question of decreases of intelligence with age remains controversial, we can safely say that any decreases that do take place are minor. In addition, individual differences are especially important, because experiences after high school seem to affect later intellectual functioning greatly.

Cross-Sectional and Longitudinal Studies of Intelligence

Whether one sees a decline in intelligence in young adulthood depends somewhat on what type of study is done. If you used a cross-sectional study, comparing groups of people in their twenties, thirties, forties, and fifties, you might find decreases in intelligence. If you use a longitudinal format, comparing the same people over a long period of time, you will not see this decline (Whitbourne and Weinstock, 1979). Why does this occur?

The cohort effect. Suppose you perform a cross-sectional study. You compare people in their twenties, thirties, forties, and fifties on some intelligence test. You find that there are reductions in scores over the years. How do you interpret your results? They may be real, or

cohort effect The effect of living in a particular generation or historical period, particularly important to consider when comparing generations.

they may be due to the generational differences between the groups—which would be called the **cohort effect,** the effect of living in a particular historical period. The cohort effect is considered a major issue when comparing sixty-year-olds with twenty-year-olds, but society is changing so fast that comparing a person entering middle age with one entering young adulthood may not be fair today. Perhaps the most important cohort effect regarding intelligence is due to differential levels of schooling between the generations. It is difficult to compare groups of people from different generations on intelligence tests, because educational background is so important to performance on these largely verbal tests. The improvement in education with each generation is reflected in the point at which intelligence supposedly peaks. In 1916, intelligence was considered to peak at age sixteen; by 1930, the peak age was twenty; by 1939, it had been raised to between twenty and twenty-four; and in the 1950s researchers argued that the peak could be found somewhere between age twenty-five and age thirty-five (Schaie, 1983). This probably reflects the increase in education over the years, since education is well correlated with intelligence.

True or False The age at which the average person's intelligence is thought to peak has decreased over the past fifty years.

The problem with averaging intelligence scores. In order to solve this problem, you decide to perform a longitudinal study. You test the same group of twenty-year-olds every five years for thirty years and find no significant reductions in intelligence. But there are problems with this approach too. First, a number of people will probably drop out as your study continues. These people tend to be the least educated and the physically ill. So your study may be comparing an ordinary group of twenty-year-olds with a superior group of forty-year-olds. In addition, the stability of intelligence noted in longitudinal studies may reflect the averaging of different abilities measured under the heading "intelligence." In other words, some aspects of intelligence may increase while others may decrease. In that case, they would average out. For example, suppose an intelligence test was made up to measure two abilities, A and B. As people age, Ability A increases but Ability B decreases. If you test your subjects every five years, their intelligence scores may stay the same, because for every increase in A there is a corresponding decrease in B. There is evidence that this might be the case.

Fluid and crystallized intelligence.   Cattell (1963) argued that although intelligence may consist of a number of abilities, two factors are most important—fluid intelligence and crystallized intelligence. **Fluid intelligence** is essentially the basic capacity for learning and problem-solving and is independent of education and experience (Sattler, 1974). It refers to such abilities as memory, reasoning, and the speed at which the mind works (Brim

> **fluid intelligence**   The basic capacity for learning and problem-solving, independent of education and experience.
>
> **crystallized intelligence**   Learned knowledge and skills.

and Kagan, 1980). **Crystallized intelligence** is basically learned knowledge, such as information and skills, and what we might call wisdom. The abilities that comprise crystallized intelligence increase over most of the life span, and certainly throughout early and middle adulthood (see Figure 14.1). However, the curves look very different for fluid abilities (Figure 14.2), which show a decline beginning in young adulthood. Notice that although each ability has a different curve, the general

FIGURE 14.1

Changes in Crystallized Intelligence Over the Life Span

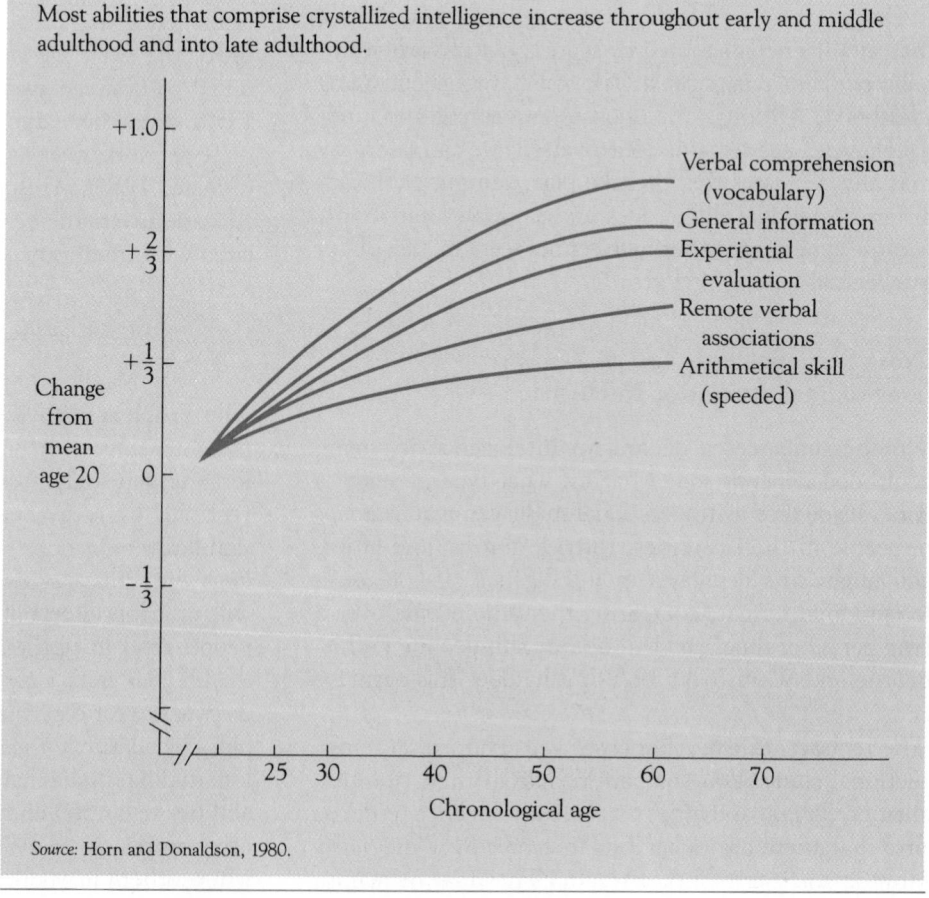

Most abilities that comprise crystallized intelligence increase throughout early and middle adulthood and into late adulthood.

Source: Horn and Donaldson, 1980.

FIGURE 14.2

Changes in Fluid Intelligence Over the Life Span

The curves for the abilities that comprise fluid intelligence show a decline beginning in young adulthood and continuing throughout middle and late adulthood.

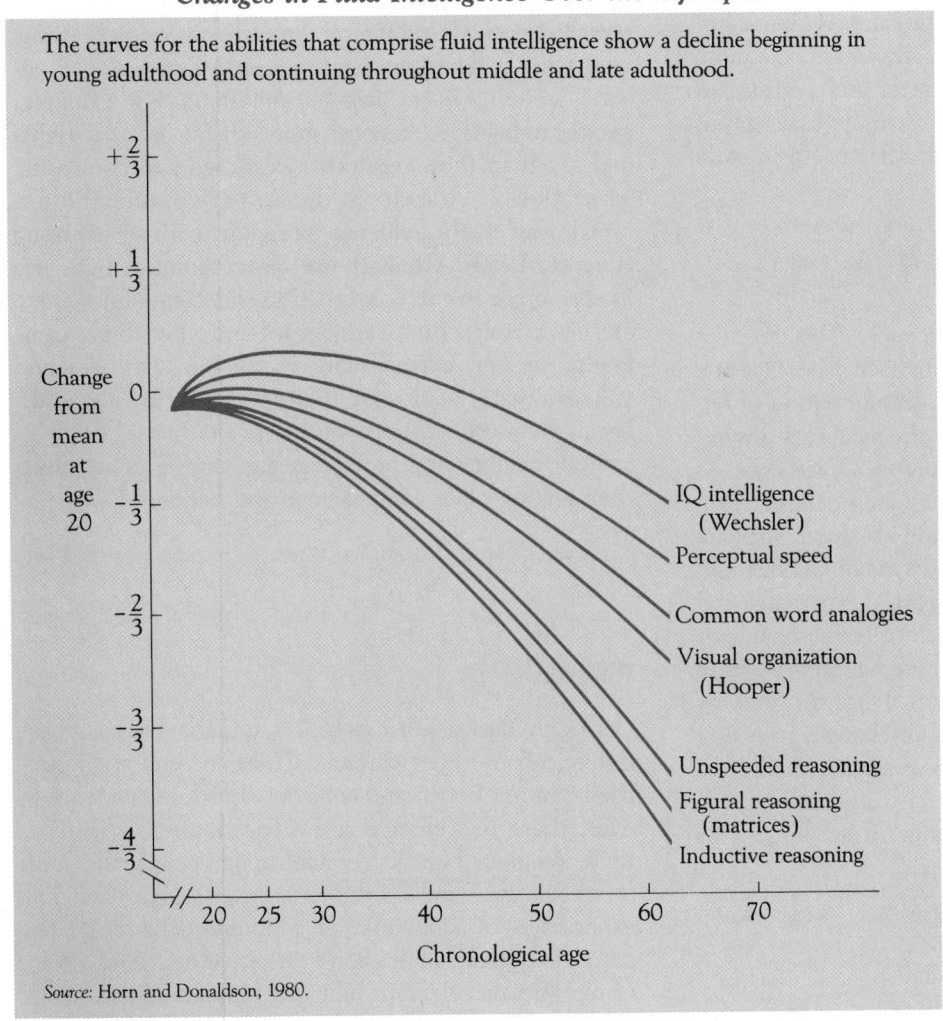

Source: Horn and Donaldson, 1980.

pattern is obvious. The reason for this decline is thought to be small changes in the central nervous system (Horn, 1980).

This analysis is not accepted by everyone. Some scientists criticize the evidence that purports to show this decline (Schaie and Hertzog, 1982), noting, among other technical objections, that Horn's data is based largely on cross-sectional studies. However, others defend the evidence (Horn and Donaldson, 1980). We cannot come to any definite summary about whether this theory is correct. However, despite the controversies in the field of intelligence some tentative conclusions are possible.

First, any decreases in fluid intelligence in young adulthood are quite minor and again are hardly noticeable in daily life. Second, crystallized intelligence increases throughout this period. Third, although scientists argue over whether groups of people show predictable changes in intelligence, they agree that individual differences are important to any understanding of intelligence. Fourth, the entire concept of intelligence may require some revision. The usefulness of this concept for describing adult intellectual functioning is questionable, since adults are already doing or have already done the things the tests were designed to predict.

Morals and Ethics in Young Adulthood

It is conventional wisdom that, during adulthood, ideals decrease, attitudes become more rigid, and religious commitment increases with age. After all, we become more fixed in our ways and more practical and realistic in outlook. This raises two questions. Are the basic trends cited above correct? If they are, do they begin in early adulthood?

Ideals

Idealism is identified with adolescence. The development of formal operational reasoning (see page 298) and college experiences often result in the formation of fervent beliefs. Increasing exposure to the media also invites adolescents to question. The ideals of adolescence do change in early adulthood, but they are not lost. Adolescent values tend to be abstract and absolute. They are polar and largely philosophical and symbolic (Bocknek, 1980), and they are based on very partial experience and an impatience for change that may not be reasonable or practical. Things are either right or wrong, but the desire to end the wrongs is not based on a realistic look at possibilities or practicalities. This all changes in young adulthood. Now ideals become more pragmatic, and there is more emphasis on putting them into effect in the real world. The focus of idealism changes from abstract to functional (White, 1952).

True or False Young adults tend to have more abstract values than adolescents.

Attitudes

Do people become more conservative and less likely to change with age? Consider the person who has a home, a family, and a job. That person wants to keep what he or she has and sees no need to risk everything on new ideas. Because things are still somewhat fluid in early adulthood, some consider young adulthood the last chance to change. The rapid changes that occur in young adulthood involving marriage, children, and career require a certain amount of flexibility. When these choices are made, an increasingly conservative stance can be seen, and there is less flexibility in attitude. One study found a steady decline in changes in voting behavior after ages twenty to twenty-four; with the decline continuing throughout the twenties and early thirties.

Much of the evidence that people become more conservative with age right after the earliest portion of young adulthood is based on cross-sectional data—and, as always, cohort effects may be important. For example, people today have become more liberal on civil rights and sex than they were thirty years ago and comparing generations is difficult. In the area of vocational interests, however, the evidence for rigidity with age is strong (Glenn, 1980). Changes are quite common from age fifteen to age twenty, and then they decrease until there are few changes in vocational interest after forty. Generally, we can expect more changes in attitudes and values in early adulthood than in middle or late adulthood, but some change occurs even then. However, attitude changes appear to be greater among young adults than among older adults (Hoge and Bender, 1974).

True or False Vocational interests become less rigid with age.

Religion

During childhood, religious beliefs and behaviors are greatly influenced by one's parents. Children tend to imitate their parents' beliefs and behavior. In adolescence, however, there is a change and a questioning of many of these religious beliefs. At adulthood, people are more on their own, and questions concerning the religious experiences of adults take on a different shade. At this point, the young adult chooses whether to attend a place of worship or celebrate religious holidays. In addition, many of the important decisions faced by young adults—including marriage, children, abortion, divorce, and personal ethics—have to do directly with religious beliefs and teachings. The answers your religion gives in these and other adult situations may be taught in childhood, but children are never faced with having to make these important decisions.

Between 96 and 98 percent of the American public believe in God (Princeton Religion Research Center, 1980). When asked whether their religion was important to them, 72 percent of the young adults eighteen to twenty-four years old said it was either very important or fairly important, while 91 percent of those over the age of fifty said the same. This indicates a reduction of

17 percent in the responses of young adults over the past twenty years. Church attendance also increases with age, as does confidence in organized religion (Princeton Religion Research Center, 1980). However, a sizable minority of young adults attend church or synagogues and adhere to the beliefs of an organized religion. Beginning with the age twenty-five to twenty-nine group, more than half said their religious beliefs were very important to them.

True or False More than 95 percent of American adults believe in God.

What of religion's effect on behavior? There is evidence that it has a restraining effect on divorce, perhaps because religious people often agree on such areas as sex roles and life goals (Spilka, 1985). Spilka concludes that having firm religious beliefs is associated with marital happiness and being able to maintain loving relationships. Religious people are less likely to engage in non-marital sexual activity, more likely to avoid illicit drugs, and less likely to abuse alcohol. In short, religious beliefs have a great effect on certain areas of decision-making.

Moral Development

Ideals, attitudes, and religious values influence an individual's beliefs about right and wrong. Lawrence Kohlberg's theory of moral reasoning, as described in Chapters 10 and 12, is important here. What happens to moral reasoning during the years of young adulthood? In a longitudinal study of Harvard students, not one student younger than twenty-three demonstrated postconventional reasoning (reasoning in which moral decisions are made on the basis of individual values that have been internalized). Most did not reach it even after age thirty. The majority were reasoning at the conventional level, in which conformity to the expectations of others and society in general serves as the basis for moral decision-making. Most adults reason at the conventional level (Kohlberg's Stages 3 and 4) and believe in upholding laws and conventions because they are there. In one study, Kohlberg and associates (Colby et al., 1980) followed Kohlberg's original 1956 sample for twenty years and found that reasoning at Stages 1 and 2 (the preconventional level, at which moral reasoning is based on

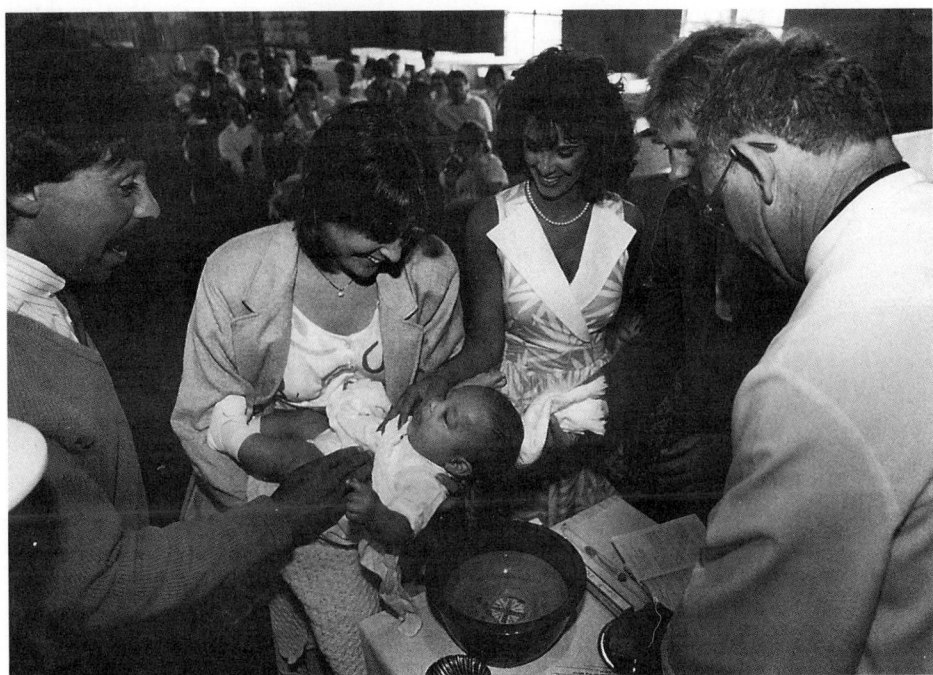

Young adults are free to make their own decisions concerning their religious convictions and practices.

satisfaction of one's own needs as well as on the desire to obtain rewards and avoid punishments) decreased and that reasoning at Stage 4 (the stage evidenced by an orientation toward authority and doing one's duty), which did not appear in ten-year-olds, existed in 62 percent of the thirty-six-year-olds. Moral reasoning at Stage 5 (post-conventional reasoning) did not appear until the age of twenty to twenty-two and never rose above 10 percent of the subjects.

There is evidence that even some regression may take place between late adolescence and early adulthood. However, when moral reasoning was measured differently, using a standard of commitment in relativism (believing other views besides one's own are possible) and of tolerance, rather than in terms of absolute hypothetical principles of justice, subjects actually showed progress in moral reasoning. Such progress is related to having personal experiences of moral conflict where behavioral choices are present (Murphy and Gilligan, 1980). The idea that qualitative differences in moral reasoning show themselves when we change our perspective was shown in Chapter 12, when we noted that gender differences in moral reasoning might exist. Women may see moral questions more in terms of how they affect interpersonal relationships and the rights and needs of others, than in strictly individualistic, legalistic terms (Gilligan, 1982). Perhaps our approach to understanding moral reasoning must be broadened if we are truly to understand the phenomenon.

What conclusions can we make about the values, moral reasoning, attitudes, and religious beliefs of young adults? First, their ideals change because they become more pragmatic and the emphasis is placed on doing something that can realistically succeed. Second, although there is more change in young adulthood than in other later stages, there is a reduction in flexibility in some areas, especially in occupational interests. Third, religion remains an important influence in some areas of life, and it increases in importance throughout adulthood. Fourth, moral development continues in a positive direction throughout early adulthood.

Reconsidering the Bet

So who collects on the bet? Both viewpoints match the facts. During young adulthood, strength, coordination, health, efficiency, and general functioning are at their highest. It almost seems as if we have hit a plateau during this period (Troll, 1985). If one looks carefully, however, significant but gradual physical and cognitive changes are taking place. But the importance of individual differences should always be kept in mind. People who take good physical care of themselves and are mentally active may show little, if any, decline. Neither the extreme view of precipitous change nor the view that nothing changes during young adulthood is consistent with the facts. So Trudy and Marc will have to continue sharing the feeding duties for Kathy and wake up for the two o'clock feeding.

─────────────────────── *Summary* ───────────────────────

1. Most young adults are in excellent or good health. Both men and women gain weight throughout the early adulthood stage, probably because with age they become less active but have not yet begun to restrict their intake of calories.

2. Vigorous exercise is beneficial to health. It improves cardiovascular functioning, burns up calories, and increases feelings of well-being. People should see a doctor before beginning an exercise program.

3. Most drug use declines in young adulthood. Alcohol consumption and cigarette-smoking remain problems throughout the young adult years.

4. Although early adulthood represents the peak of physical conditioning, some abilities begin to decline during the late twenties and throughout the thirties. These reductions are hardly noticeable. The same pattern of slight decline is found in sensory functioning as well.

5. Young adulthood is a very stressful period. Stress may be due to life events, such as getting married, as well as to the hassles of everyday life. Because stress has been related to illness, it is important that young adults learn to deal with

these new stresses. Two personality types, the aggressive, hurrying Type A and the more relaxed Type B have been identified. Type A behavior is related to heart attacks in later life.

6. Premenstrual syndrome, or PMS, is a collection of symptoms that include irritability and depression. PMS is caused by hormonal fluctuations but the effects of culture, learning and expectations are factors as well. Its severity varies widely and it does not appear to affect a woman's intellectual performance.

7. Well-educated early adults perform well on tests of formal operational reasoning. Researchers are now looking at the possibility that there might be stages beyond Piaget's formal operational stage. Although some have been suggested, none have been widely accepted.

8. Most young adults perform well on intelligence tests. Cross-sectional research studies tend to show some declines with age, but interpretation of these studies is difficult because of the cohort effect. Longitudinal studies show fewer or no declines. Whatever declines take place in young adulthood are very minor.

9. Fluid intelligence is the basic capacity for learning and problem-solving, including memory, reasoning, and speed of mental work. Crystallized intelligence is learned knowledge, such as information and skills. Fluid intelligence begins to decline in young adulthood, while crystallized intelligence continues to increase during early and middle adulthood and into old age.

10. Ideals are not lost in early adulthood, but they do become more practical. Emphasis is put on what can be realistically accomplished. Although young adults change their attitudes less than they did in adolescence, their attitudes are more flexible than they will be in middle and old age. Most young adults believe in God. Religious beliefs have an effect on certain interpersonal realms, such as divorce, nonmarital sexual activity, and drug-taking.

11. The majority of early adults reason at Kohlberg's conventional level of moral reasoning. Young adults are more likely to believe that other views besides their own are possible and to be more tolerant than adolescents.

Answers to True or False Statements

1. *False* Correct statement: Chronic diseases such as arthritis are less common in young adults.

2. *True* The average female reaches peak height before the average male does.

3. *False* Correct statement: The average adult gains weight through about age fifty-five, then shows a weight loss.

4. *True* Most authorities believe regular physical exercise can help reduce chances of cardiovascular disease.

5. *False* Correct statement: Evidence indicates that exercise reduces appetite.

6. *False* Correct statement: Although about one-third try to quit, only about one-fifth are successful.

7. *False* Correct statement: There is no major decline in visual acuity during the young adult years.

8. *False* Correct statement: Many experts believe that young adulthood is a very stressful time of life.

9. *False* Correct statement: The age at which the average person's intelligence is thought to peak has increased consistently over the past fifty years.

10. *False* Correct statement: The values of young adults are more realistic and less abstract.

11. *False* Correct statement: Vocational interests become more rigid with age.

12. *True* More than 95 percent of all American adults believe in God.

CHAPTER 15

Social and Personality Development in Early Adulthood

Lifestyle Choices
Marriage
Cohabitation
The Singles Alternative
Friendships in Young Adulthood
Parenting
CROSS-CULTURAL CURRENT   East Meets West:
Child-Rearing in Hong Kong
Divorce
After the Divorce
Vocational Development
Choices and Paths

Are the Following Statements True or False?

Try the True-False Quiz below. See if your answers correspond to the information in this chapter. Each question is repeated after the paragraph in which the answer can be found. The True-False Answer Box at the end of the chapter lists the complete answers.

_____ 1. The median age at which females choose to marry is declining.

_____ 2. Almost two-thirds of all women with children under six are in the work force.

_____ 3. Generally, wives have fewer complaints about their marriages than their husbands do.

_____ 4. Most cohabiting couples live together for at least one year before breaking up or marrying.

_____ 5. More than in any other period in our nation's history, couples are choosing not to have any children.

_____ 6. Career-oriented women are more likely to get divorced than women who are full-time homemakers.

_____ 7. Women are more likely to ask for a divorce than men are.

_____ 8. Divorced people considering remarriage look for the same qualities in the second spouse that they sought in their first.

_____ 9. Most people say they would work even if they did not have to.

_____10. Today's employees are more loyal to their companies than workers in the past.

_____11. Most women work because they are bored at home.

_____12. People who are fired or laid off tend to blame the employer rather than themselves.

Lifestyle Choices

It is 1888 and James Cole and Kaye Butler are pondering their future. They will get married and have a large family. James will work while Kaye stays at home with the children. If the marriage is unhappy, they will probably not get a divorce, because that would be socially unacceptable and a very difficult process.

Consider the alternatives available to James and Kaye if they were living in today's world. They may choose not to marry but to cohabit—that is, live together. If they marry, they may decide either not to have any children or to limit their family. Kaye may continue to work throughout the marriage, or take some time off during the children's early years and then return to work. In some countries, the same option is available to James. If the marriage does not work out, divorce is an option, followed perhaps by remarriage for both or either partner.

Young adults today have many more alternatives than they had years ago. Their life revolves around love and work, and the principal choices they must make are in these two areas. The importance of these areas did not escape modern theorists of adult development. Erikson saw the major psychosocial crisis of young adulthood in terms of intimacy versus isolation. The young adult makes commitments to another person, which is most often reflected in marriage. The negative outcome of the young adult years is isolation—the unwillingness or inability to commit oneself to others. Levinson sees the ages from about seventeen to twenty-two in terms of an "Early-Adult Transition," in which a person separates from his or her original family and becomes more self-sufficient. This is followed by a stage during which a new life structure is formed as choices concerning love and work commitments are made. During the late twenties and early thirties, the "Age-Thirty Transition," a time of questioning and perhaps change, takes place. During the thirties, people deepen their roots and become more committed to career and family. This is a time of stability and progression. In the late thirties, ambition peaks along with confidence and authority.

Vaillant basically agrees with Erikson's emphasis on intimacy, but he argues for the importance of vocational pursuits during this period. He posits that, especially during the thirties, there is a stage of "Career Consoli-

dation" in which people are busy concentrating on their careers and become more materialistic. Gould too emphasizes the importance of achieving independence in early adulthood and attaining goals in the areas of love and work in one's twenties, and posits a period of questioning beginning in the late twenties and lasting through early thirties. The theorists all agree that the concerns of young adulthood revolve around intimate interpersonal relationships and work. In this chapter, we examine some of the choices and opportunities available to young adults today and the nature and consequences of their decisions in these two areas.

Marriage

The overwhelming majority of young adults choose the alternative of marriage (Brehm, 1985). The percentage of both males and females who marry increases throughout young adulthood (see Figure 15.1). Although most young adults marry, they do so slightly later than twenty years ago. The median age at which males marry rose from 22.8 years to 24.4 between 1960 and 1983 and the age of the first marriage for women increased from 20.3 years to 22.5 (National Center for Health Statistics, 1986). Young people today are under less pressure to marry at an early age. The need for education beyond the high school level means that many people are not financially able to marry at young ages. Because couples no longer try to have as many children as biologically possible, as was common years ago, they no longer worry about being twenty and unmarried. Although the present increase in the average age at which young adults marry is modest, it is a trend that will probably continue.

True or False   The median age at which females choose to marry is declining.

Choosing a Spouse

Although most people marry, and many marry more than once, we really do not know much about what determines people's choice of a spouse—that is, how they select a mate (Murstein, 1982). Few decisions in life are as important as the choice of a spouse, and yet most theories about why people choose one person over another have not successfully explained the dynamics of the choice. Certainly, people get married because they love each other, but they could also marry for other reasons—for example, companionship, a desire for children, or financial security. Most people have been taught that love is the foundation of marriage (Golanty and Harris, 1982), but this tells us nothing about why people fall in love with some people and not others, and why some people who fall in love get married and others do not.

Similarity. According to the research, if James marries Kaye we can expect them to be similar in many ways. People who marry usually share similar backgrounds, re-

ligious beliefs, educational level, race, interests, and personality characteristics (Brehm, 1985; Schulz and Rodgers, 1975). However, there are at least two different ways this can be interpreted. First, we can say that people are attracted to people who are similar to them, perhaps because communication is easier and people with similar interests enjoy doing the same things together. Two people who like camping will have something to talk about and a hobby to share. Or consider two people who love popular music. They both attend concerts and take music courses. They have a greater opportunity to meet than two people who do not share this similar interest. People who are wealthy usually meet others who are well-to-do because they congregate in the same places and are in-

FIGURE 15.1

Marital Status of the Population

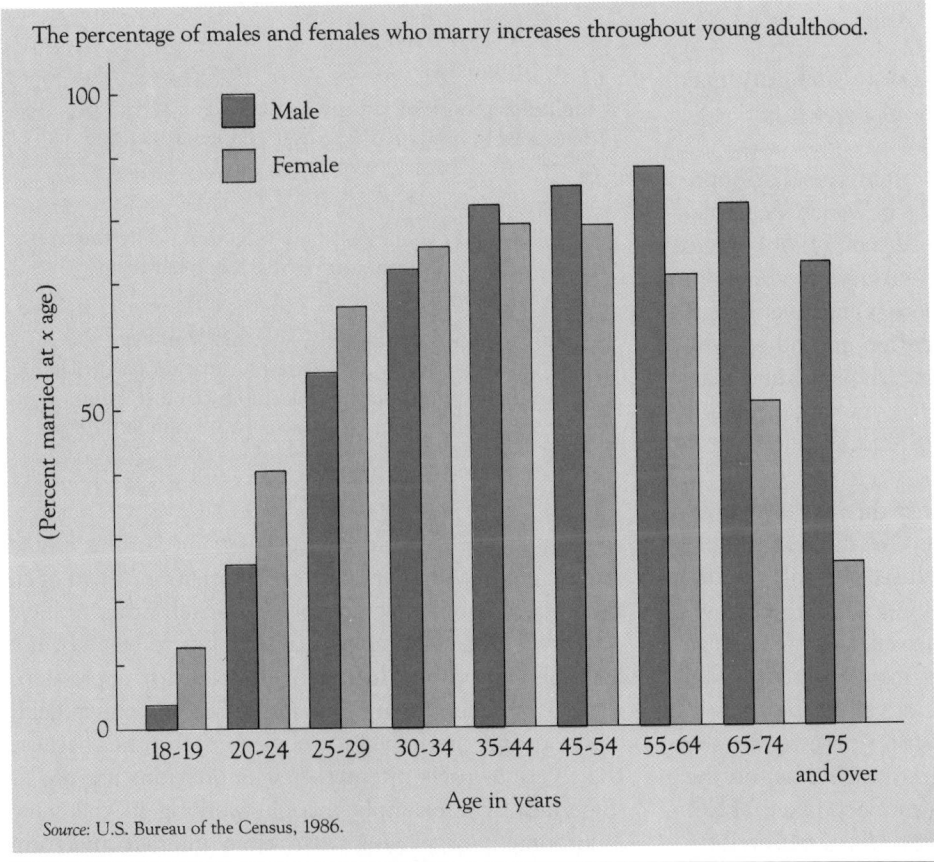

The percentage of males and females who marry increases throughout young adulthood.

Source: U.S. Bureau of the Census, 1986.

Most young adults marry although they do so at slightly older ages than they did a decade ago.

vited to the same parties. In this way, **similarity** may help determine the people you are likely to meet.

Complementary opposites.   It is often said that opposites attract, and this is the basis for Winch's **complementary theory of mate selection.** Winch (1958) argues that complementary opposites do attract. A dominant person seeks out a spouse who is more submissive. People who want to be the center of attention find others who will not compete with them. But although some marriages may work this way, evidence has not generally supported this thesis (Murstein, 1982).

Stimulus-value-role theory.   Other theories have been advanced, but all have weaknesses. One theory that does hold some promise is the **stimulus-value-role theory** (Murstein, 1982; 1976). According to this theory, selection of a marital partner is viewed as a three-stage progression, each stage involving more intimacy. The theory emphasizes the importance of values and roles in the later stages of the mate-selection process. In the stimulus stage, people are attracted to each other on the basis of physical and social attributes. Such external features as physical attractiveness, poise, dress, personality,

similarity theory of mate selection   The theory of mate selection emphasizing that people attract and marry on the basis of underlying similarities in a variety of areas.

complementary theory of mate selection   The theory of mate selection emphasizing that complementary opposites attract.

stimulus-value-role theory   The theory of mate selection that sees the selection of a marital partner as a three-stage progression involving initial attraction, value comparisons, and analyses of role compatibility.

and reputation are important. First impressions would seem vital, but this depends on the situation. In an open field where two people do not know each other or have only a slight acquaintance, both are free to begin or not begin a relationship. In this open field, first impressions and surface qualities are important, but in a closed field, where people are forced to relate to each other because their various roles interact, first impressions are not as important. For example, people working in the same environment or playing on a team interact and form relationships. In a closed system, the first stage, or stimulus stage, is not as important because people have an opportunity to go beyond their first impressions and relate to each other.

In the second stage, the value stage, values are compared. Communication proceeds to a deeper, more personal level. They begin to talk about their dreams, fears, hopes, and concerns. They explore their political and religious attitudes. They reflect on how comfortable they are with each other, and self-disclosure increases. Sometimes marriage occurs after this stage, but couples must often go beyond to the third stage.

In the third stage, or role stage, people ask themselves whether the roles they see themselves playing in the future are compatible with those of their partner. People consider how they and the other person function together and compare their relationship with their concept of the ideal relationship.

Expectations for Marriage

If James and Kaye have already progressed in their relationship to the point where they are considering marriage, they must deal with what each expects of the relationship. Their expectations for marriage are likely to be different from the expectations their parents had when they were young. For example, it is likely that James and Kaye will plan to have fewer children than previous generations (Doherty and Jacobson, 1982). More than 90 percent of all young women express a desire to have children (Rossi, 1984), but most are planning to have fewer. In addition, Kaye is more likely to continue to work even after the children arrive. Women now comprise more than 45 percent of the work force, and 55.4 percent of all women age sixteen and older are employed outside the home (U.S. Bureau of Labor Statistics, 1987). The increase continues unabated. In addition, the number of mothers with young children who work outside the home has grown steadily and continues to do so. About 54 percent of all women with children under six are in the labor force, and 70 percent of all women with children between six and seventeen are employed outside the home (U.S. Department of Labor, 1987). Half of all mothers of children under three are in the labor force—up from only one-third in 1975 (U.S. Department of Labor, 1985). Black mothers are more likely to be in the labor force, but the gap is narrowing. Most employed mothers work full-time.

romantic love Love that is basically erotic in nature and involves a strong need for the physical presence of the other and for contact.

realistic or **companionate love** Love that is characteristic of people in a long-term relationship involving steady concern and caring.

True or False Almost two-thirds of all women with children under six are in the work force.

Love and Marriage

Modern psychologists look at the development of love within a relationship in terms of a romantic love and companionate love, also called realistic love. **Romantic love** is basically erotic in nature. There is a strong need for the presence of the loved one and for physical contact. It is characterized by a belief that love conquers all and that a person has only one true love, and by idealization of the other person. Although some people believe that romantic love and infatuation are the same, others claim that infatuation is only the first step in a love relationship. In addition, infatuation is often used to describe romantic love that is of fairly short duration and has failed to develop into a meaningful relationship.

Realistic love, sometimes called **companionate love,** is more characteristic of people who have been involved in a relationship for an extended period of time. It is less intense, but it involves steady concern and caring. People in a realistic love relationship do not expect their partners to be perfect and do not believe that love will solve all their problems. This is not to say that romance is no longer a factor as the years of marriage roll by. Indeed, romantic and passionate moments do occur, but they are not of the same intensity (Schultz, 1984). In addition, when high school seniors, people married about five years, and people married for twenty years were compared on love attitudes, both the high school seniors and the older group were quite romantic—much more so than those who had been married five years. The older group tended to believe that the person they married was the only one for them. Others believed they had grown to love the other person. Of course, when so much time has been invested in a relationship, people are likely to feel this way. The lack of romantic feeling in the group married for five years is understandable, because some of the initial fantasy had turned to realism. These couples were still very much in love, but their love had probably changed to a more realistic type with the need to make a living, care for children, and the like (Knox, 1985).

Sex and Marriage

The importance of sex in marriage varies from couple to couple. For some, sexual satisfaction is vital and the need for sex is great. For others, it takes on lesser importance, and tenderness and loving concern may be more important. Some studies have found a relationship between satisfactory sexual relationships within marriage and general marital satisfaction (Hunt, 1974). Indeed, there is evidence that sexual problems within marriage are sometimes a reason for divorce (Levinger, 1966). Others argue that sexual problems may be the result—not the cause—of marital dissatisfaction. It is difficult to maintain a loving sexual relationship if you are continually angry at your spouse. In addition, happy marriages exist even when sexual relations are neither frequent nor very exciting to the partners (Frank et al., 1979).

With time, the frequency of sexual relations in marriage decreases. Greenblatt (1983) found that the average couple in his study had sex fifteen times a month during the first year of marriage, while those who had been married for six years averaged six times a month. Other studies may come up with different figures, but the trend is unmistakable (James, 1981; Trussell and Westoff, 1980). The reasons are many, ranging from various daily worries about vocational or financial problems to simply boredom. Children are also partly responsible. Their presence may inhibit parents, and child-rearing responsibilities may cause parents to be too tired at night to consider their own intimate relationship. The focus of sexuality changes with age too, from an emphasis on passion and sexual intimacy to one in which tender feelings of affection and loyalty are more important (Reedy et al., 1982).

Types of Marriage

Because marital relationships differ in many ways, trying to categorize them is difficult. However, a well-known study by Cuber and Harroff (1965), who interviewed hundreds of people, came up with five specific types of marriage.

Conflict-habituated. The conflict-habituated marriage is typified by constant arguing and conflict. The spouses are basically incompatible, but they consider arguing acceptable and do not see this as a reason for divorce.

Devitalized. The devitalized marriage is typified by a lifeless and apathetic relationship. There is little arguing, just a great deal of boredom. Once the couple shared good times, but the marriage has lost any vitality it might have had.

Passive-congenial. The passive-congenial marriage is a polite and stale relationship. All the couple's interests and energy are directed toward careers and children. There is little or no conflict.

Vital. The vital marriage is one in which the marital relationship is central to the couple's satisfaction in life. They share both emotional closeness and the desire to do things together. They are highly involved with each other in every aspect of life.

Total. The total marriage is similar to a vital marriage, except that each spouse actually schedules his or her day around the other, and the couple try to spend a great deal of time together. The sharing is more complete.

Some movement between categories is possible as when a marriage starts with a total relationship and proceeds to a devitalized or conflict-habituated one, but stability is most common. Couples in all five types of marriage stated that they were content if not happy, and about four-fifths of the marriages fell into the first three categories.

Marital Satisfaction

If this is the case, just how satisfied will James and Kaye be in their marriage? Marital satisfaction is almost always very high at the beginning of marriage, but the honeymoon ends quickly, and a decrease in satisfaction becomes evident. There are many reasons for this. The presence of children is one. Studies show a decline in marital satisfaction, more evident in the wife than the husband, with the transition to parenting (Belsky et al., 1985). Caregiving duties may take up time once used for interactions between husband and wife. Young children especially require a great deal of time and may affect the course of the relationship negatively (Anderson et al., 1983). However, one study found that this reduction in satisfaction might be more likely to occur in low-income mothers who were employed full-time and had too little time to discuss daily matters with their husbands (Schumm and Bugaighis, 1986). Although the presence of children generally may bring on additional stresses, dissatisfaction may be most severe among poor families. Whatever the factors involved, the decline in marital satisfaction after the initial phase is real.

Will Kaye be more satisfied with the marriage, or will it be James? If they are like most couples, James will be more satisfied than Kaye. Generally, men have fewer complaints about their marriages and are more satisfied than their wives (Rhyne, 1981). Wives are often asked to make more sacrifices in marriage and parenting. In addition, women are socialized to consider love, marriage, and parenthood the prime sources of satisfaction, and actual experience may not meet these expectations.

True or False Generally, wives have fewer complaints about their marriages than their husbands do.

Keys to Marital Satisfaction and Adjustment

Although a number of factors affecting adjustment to and satisfaction in marriage have been suggested, including maturity and willingness to compromise, the keys appear to be sensitivity and the ability to communicate. Satisfaction is higher when people can discuss their experiences and solve problems without completely sacrificing their own interests (Golanty and Harris, 1982). When people feel that their partner understands their needs, they express greater satisfaction with the marriage (Tiggle et al., 1982). Measures of communication predict marital adjustment and satisfaction, especially after the first year. In addition, couples who indicated that their communication was good before marriage tended to have happier marriages (Markman, 1981).

Studies of communication note the importance of giving support, sharing emotions, and being sensitive to and showing an understanding of the spouse's needs and feelings. In fact, communication patterns often differentiate happy couples from unhappy couples. Happily married spouses are better able than strangers to understand exactly what their spouses mean, but in troubled marriages this is not so (Goleman, 1985). Happy couples show a high degree of responsiveness and share everyday events with each other. Without such sharing, tension can result, and perhaps even estrangement. Some specific examples of positive and negative communication are found in Table 15.1. A person who is unable to communicate

cohabitation   The state of living together without being married.

is likely to find that adjustment is more difficult and that the satisfaction of at least one of the parties is reduced.

Cohabitation

Instead of marrying, Kaye and James may decide to **cohabit,** or live together. This choice is becoming more popular. About 1,983,000 couples are cohabiting today, up from approximately 500,000 in 1970 (U.S. Department of Commerce, 1987). Although this represents only 3 percent of all the households in the United States, the increase is significant. About 25 percent of people in college surveys report that they have cohabited (Macklin, 1978), and many older couples cohabit (Cox, 1984). In fact, cohabitation may not always signify and intimate relationship, because some people cohabit in order to reduce expenses somewhat like the "Three's Company" situation comedy on television a few years ago. This arrangement may have a special advantage for women in that they may feel a bit safer, especially in apartments, not having to live alone.

James and Kaye might decide to cohabit for a variety of reasons. It may be a temporary convenience, or it may simply be a continuation of an affectionate relationship where two people enjoy each other but do not want to consider marriage. They may also view it as a trial marriage, or a temporary alternative to marriage until they feel ready for the commitments of marriage. They may also consider it a permanent relationship without the legal sanction (Macklin, 1978).

Most cohabiting relationships, however, are anything but permanent. In one survey, 82 percent of young men under twenty, and 63 percent of older men, claimed their longest cohabitation was three months. For females under twenty, 67 percent reported that their longest cohibation was three months or less, and 40 percent of women above that age reported the same (Peterman et al., 1974). Other studies show that cohabitation is far from a permanent lifestyle choice for the vast majority of young adults (Glick and Spanier, 1980). Men are much less committed to a cohabitation relationship than women are (Macklin, 1983), and most couples break up

TABLE 15.1

Characteristics of Productive and Nonproductive Communication

Some patterns of communication add to understanding while others are potentially harmful to a relationship.

Productive Communication	Nonproductive Communication
1. Avoidance of behaviors in column 2.	1. Blaming—"You're lying around the house while I do the work."
2. Neutral statement rather than accusation—"I thought we agreed . . ."	2. Name calling—"lousy lover," "tramp."
3. Acknowledgment of responsibility for partner's discomfort—"Well, I guess we did discuss my sharing the work."	3. Threatening—"I'm going to leave."
4. Expression of willingness to alleviate problem—"What do you want me to do?"	4. Using sarcasm—"What would you know about sensitivity?" "Right again, Sherlock."
5. Positive labeling of suggestion—"It would be nice if . . ."	5. Being judgmental—"You're being hateful and mean."
6. Reciprocity—"I'll handle it MWF."	6. Changing issues—"No sex again tonight."
7. Positive expression at end of conflict—"Okay. I guess I'm on for Thursday night, eh?"	7. No attempt to stop escalation of conflict.
8. Brief—Each person takes two turns speaking.	8. Lengthy—Each person takes six turns speaking.

Source: Knox, 1985.

quickly. Of course, some will marry (Watson, 1983). While some people argue that cohabitation will become a recognized step before marriage for the majority of people in the future, this does not seem likely. Although for some it is a time to find out more about themselves and their partners (Murstein, 1971), it is a step toward marriage only for a minority of young adults (Macklin, 1983).

True or False   Most cohabiting couples live together for at least one year before breaking up or marrying.

Married couples who lived together before marrying each other regard that experience as positive. However, there is more physical violence in cohabiting relationships than in married relationships (Yilo and Straus, 1981). In addition, studies have not found that marriages preceded by cohabitation are any better, more satisfying, or more egalitarian than marriages of couples who did not cohabit (Macklin, 1983; Risman, 1981). The finding that they are not any more egalitarian may be surprising, because many consider this lifestyle somewhat radical or

rebellious. This could have been predicted, however, because the division of labor in most cohabiting relationships is actually very traditional (Macklin, 1983). In addition, the divorce rate for couples who live together before marriage is similar, when compared with couples who married without cohabiting. One study of couples married from between one and two years found cohabitation before marriage was associated with a lower perceived quality of communication for wives and lower marital satisfaction for both spouses (DeMaris and Leslie, 1984). All things considered, cohabitation does not seem to contribute to later marital satisfaction or to a lower rate of divorce.

The Singles Alternative

Another choice is to remain single. In 1985, some 25.2 percent of all men and 18.2 percent of all women over the age of eighteen in the United States were single (U.S. Department of Commerce, 1987), and this does not include the percentage of widowed or divorced people. If you include all single people in the count, about 40 percent of the American population is single. Approximately 8 or 9 percent of all people who are now twenty years old will never marry (Van Hoose and Worth, 1982). In the past, people who remained single were scorned or pitied. It was believed that there was something wrong with them or that they were unfortunate enough never to have the opportunity to marry. Single people have been described by others as selfish, irresponsible, impotent, frigid, hedonistic, or immature (Edwards, 1977). Some people have images of the "swinging single," others see the single person as lonely and depressed or a misfit (Stein, 1976). Actually, none of these descriptions is correct, for singles have a variety of lifestyles. People today appear less likely to stereotype singles, and the decision to remain single is apt to be greeted with more respect and tolerance (Thornton and Freedman, 1978). Because singles are not a homogeneous group, we should distinguish between the experience of the single divorced person and that of the never-married single.

Remaining single has some advantages. Singles have more time for personal development, and then have more control over their own lives and destiny (Gigy, 1980; Stein, 1976). However, the key word is *choice*. Those who choose the single life and have plenty of opportunity for meaningful relationships are apt to experience more satisfaction than those who would like to get married but cannot find a suitable mate.

Friendships in Young Adulthood

It is wrong to treat Kaye and James as existing in a vacuum. Even if they do get married, they will probably develop close relationships with others. Friends form the basis for social life, and their support and help can be vital in times of crisis. Most friendships in young adulthood are based on similarity and proximity. We tend to become friendly with people who live close to us (Kahn, 1984). We see these people more often, and first impressions are not so important. One study of women's friendships in early adulthood showed that women were likely to be friendly with neighbors, and that often their children were friends too (Athanasiou and Yushioka, 1973). The women were close in age and income level too. Shared interests and attitudes are also important. All these factors work together, since people who live near

---

motherhood mandate Term used to describe society's expectations that women should desire to be mothers.

---

each other are likely to be similar in income, social status, and attitudes.

The same-sex friendships formed by men and women differ. Women's friendships are likely to be deeper and more intimate than friendships formed by men (Caldwell and Peplau, 1982). Friendships formed in early adulthood tend to endure, probably because families follow the same developmental course and share the same problems (Lowenthal et al., 1975). Young adults tend to have more friendships than they did in late adolescence or will in middle or late adulthood (Weiss and Lowenthal, 1975). As young couples form relationships with other couples who live near them or whom they meet at work, some of their previous friendships dissipate. Friendships fade for many reasons, whether it be disagreements or simply moving away (Parlee, 1979).

Parenting

Few decisions in life are more important and have more lasting consequences than the decision to become pregnant and raise a child. Attitudes toward parenting differ, depending upon the culture. (See Cross-Cultural Current on page 392.) The nature and development of the parent-infant relationship was discussed in Chapters 4 and 5, so here we focus on its effect on the parents and the marriage. If James and Kaye decide to have children, their whole lives, as well as their relationship, will be affected.

To Have or Have Not

Despite increasing tolerance of different lifestyles in American society, a kind of **motherhood mandate**—in which society expects and encourages a woman to want to be a mother and considers it strange if she does not choose this course—exists (Russo, 1979). Still, a growing segment of the population is deciding not to have children. While in 1965 some 2 percent of the married couples under age forty said they did not want any children, 6 percent of the couples surveyed in 1975 did not want any children (Hoffman, 1982). Some of these cou-

East Meets West: Child-Rearing in Hong Kong

Consider the traditional Chinese family with its great respect for age and authority. Now consider the Western family, where there is much less filial devotion. Consider the traditional Chinese child-rearing belief that young children cannot understand much, and the indulgence of young children that goes along with it. Now consider the modern Western view that emphasizes the early learning potential of children. The Chinese and Western views clash. What happens when Chinese are exposed to Western ideas about parenting and child-rearing?

Traditional child-rearing attitudes and behaviors in China can be summarized as follows. The Chinese believe that a child's social environment is more important than any genetic factor. Chinese parents do not believe young children are capable of learning very much and young children are not disciplined severely. Strict discipline is applied to older children when they have reached the age of understanding, which is believed to be around age six. Fathers have little to do with their infants, but they assume the role of disciplinarian as the child matures.

David Ho and T. K. Kang reasoned that changes in parenting attitudes and practices due to Western influences could be investigated by comparing current parental attitudes and behaviors with those of grandparents. Seventeen pairs of grandmothers and mothers were interviewed, and information on major areas of child-rearing practices was obtained. Most of the grandmothers had spent at least half their lives in Mainland China, while the mothers had been raised in Hong Kong. Although there was little difference in social status, the mothers were better educated than the grandmothers.

In a related study, twenty pairs of fathers and grandfathers (unrelated to the mothers and grandmothers used in the first study) were also interviewed concerning their attitudes toward child-rearing, filial devotion, and their general beliefs about parenting and children. All the grandfathers were over sixty years old and had spent at least fifteen years in Mainland China. Again, fathers were better educated and spent the greater part of their lives in Hong Kong.

The differences between the mothers and the grandmothers were small. The mothers reported more paternal interest in infants than the grandmothers did. In addition, the mothers followed a less rigid schedule for feeding. But that was about the extent of the intergenerational differences. Both the mothers and the grandmothers emphasized sexual modesty and control of aggressiveness. The intergenerational comparisons were marked more by stability than by change.

ples will change their minds, others will not be able to have children for physical reasons. While this increase may seem considerable, it does not nearly reach percentages of couples not having children in other historical periods. An estimated 8.2 percent of married women born between 1846 and 1855 did not have children, and more than 20 percent of the married women born between 1901 and 1910 did not have any children. Notice that women born in the latter time period were of childbearing age during the Great Depression of the early 1930s. Of women born between 1931 and 1935, some 7.3 percent did not have any children (Bane, 1976). While the increase is not of historic proportions, it is a trend to watch.

True or False More than in any other period in our nation's history, couples are choosing not to have any children.

The stigma of not having children has led some professionals to decry the very word "childless" because it implies that something is missing in a marriage, that somehow childless unions are less than perfect. The new term sometimes used is "child-free," which has a different connotation (Hyde, 1985). The evidence is that the wife is the decision-maker in this area (Richmond-Abbott, 1983). Two types of child-free marriages have been identified. First, some women declare their desire not to have children early in life, well before they get married, and they seek out a mate who agrees with that plan. Second, there are couples who delay having children, often for career reasons, until they make the decision not to have children at all (Houseknecht, 1979).

Are couples who prefer not to have children more selfish than those who decide to have children? When

Intergenerational differences between the fathers and the grandfathers were more pronounced. The fathers showed much less filial devotion than the grandfathers did, which the researchers believe translates into less emphasis on strictness, obedience, and following the principles and attitudes of one's father. In addition, significant differences were found in the age at which children are thought to understand things. Grandfathers estimated the age of understanding at 6.5 years, while fathers considered it to be much earlier—at 3.5 years. Grandfathers estimated the age at which children know what is right or wrong at 7 years while fathers thought it was 5 years. Fathers were also much more likely than grandfathers to report having performed certain child-care duties, including soothing the crying baby and helping to feed and change the infant. It is surprising that there were no significant intergenerational differences in attitudes concerning the desirability of fathers participating in early child care since obviously fathers were participating more than the grandfathers in such early child care.

Fathers and grandfathers agreed on many issues. Both believed that the child's environment was more important than genetic factors and that children are basically good. In addition, both generations agreed on the desirable characteristics of children when they grow up, especially moral character and competence needed to achieve.

Chinese attitudes toward child-rearing, then, do show some changes. Younger fathers are more interested in their infants and are more aware of the young child's ability to learn. Mothers are more traditional, showing less change and more continuity with past generations. The finding of both change and stability should be expected. The idea that the influence of Western ideas overwhelms traditional patterns of child-rearing does not hold up. At the same time, the idea that child-rearing is so insulated that it does not change is also not supported by the evidence. Perhaps the best conclusion is that links with the past are modified but certainly not severed.

Source: Ho, D. Y. F., and Kang, T. K. Intergenerational Comparisons of Child-Rearing Attitudes and Practices in Hong Kong. *Developmental Psychology,* 1984, 20, 1004–1016.

couples are asked why they want to remain child-free, they often cite a desire not to interfere with the marital relationship or the freedom to work or enjoy traveling (Richmond-Abbott, 1983). On the other hand, the reasons for having children also revolve around personal fulfillment. Children are seen as satisfying basic psychological needs—for instance, the need to be loved or the need for stimulation—or as a vehicle for finding special meaning and fulfillment in life (Hoffman and Manis, 1979). Although the reasons for having or not having children differ, it is difficult to label one choice more selfish than the other. Child-free marriages are apt to be found among the better educated and tend to be happy (Hoffman, 1982; Campbell et al., 1975; Ryder, 1973). Couples who decide on child-free marriages must be stronger because they are going against the current of

societal expectations. The most important conclusion we can make regarding voluntary child-free marriages is that they are happy and both husband and wife are satisfied. It is an option, but one that is taken by a comparatively small minority of couples.

Motherhood

Although women may be raised from childhood with the goal of becoming mothers (Chodorow, 1978), evidence for the instinctual basis of motherhood is weak (Field and Widmayer, 1982). Child-care and child-rearing practices are the product of lifelong learning. In our culture, we tend to believe that parents are the most important determinants of children's attitudes, behaviors, and development, and this can produce great stress in parents who are contemplating their new roles (Cohler, 1982).

When a pregnancy is welcomed, it is easy to see how the initial reaction may be one of both joy and doubt on the part of the mother. The doubt may come from some concern about her ability to parent. She may also feel more vulnerable, distress about the physical changes in her body, and anxiety concerning the infant's physical condition (Field, 1980). At the same time, positive feelings about the pregnancy are not uncommon. Bearing a child changes a woman's status and life. It entails a redefinition of her identity and sometimes, abandonment or suspension of her own interests. She may see herself as more responsible and mature, but also as more restricted. Some women expect to be tied down by the demands of young children, but feel that there will be time for personal freedom later, when the children grow up.

After the birth, postpartum depression is not uncommon (Hopkins et al., 1984). Hormonal and psychological factors are considered probable causes, and stress has been implicated as well. The presence of a child in the family brings about drastic changes in routine. Because the mother is likely to take on the greater share of the child-rearing responsibility, this places additional stress on her. She is expected to know how to do everything, even though child care is not instinctual. Although there is stress, parents also report feelings of creativity, accomplishment, and competence from having and rearing children (Williams, 1977). When asked how much satisfaction they obtained from each of several areas of life—including jobs, marriage, leisure activities, housework, and being parents—parents reported that all areas provided some satisfaction, but none as much as parenthood. Among employed mothers, 94 percent said that being a parent provided great satisfaction, while only a little more than half that many indicated such satisfaction from their jobs (Hoffman and Manis, 1978). When parents were asked how having a child changes a person's life, the answers were primarily positive. So despite the many problems and self-doubts, parenting is a significant source of satisfaction in adulthood (Hoffman, 1982).

How does parenthood affect the marriage? The birth of the child creates additional stresses and is seen as a crisis by some because it means so many changes in lifestyle (Hobbs and Cole, 1976). It disrupts marital roles, and women may experience some loss of power because their roles change so much more than those of the hus-

Despite the trials and tribulations of being a parent, most mothers, including those employed, consider parenting a source of great satisfaction.

band (Richmond-Abbott, 1983). As the child grows, another infant may be added, increasing the mother's responsibilities as well as the pressure and stress. When children start school, it may or may not be a painful experience for the parents. For some it means greater freedom, for others it is a reminder of aging and a time for questioning of purpose.

Fatherhood

The changes in a new father's lifestyle are apt to be less than the changes in the new mother's life, and fathers are usually not so ambivalent about a pregnancy. For one thing, they do not anticipate as many changes in their lives (Yarrow et al., 1971). However, fathers may find themselves under a good deal of pressure when it comes to financial considerations, which they often see as their primary concern.

Society's views of fathering have changed, and with them so have fathers' attitudes. Fein (1978) posits three views of fatherhood. In the traditional view, the father is aloof and distant. He may provide some emotional support for the mother, but his primary job is to support the family. He has little or no involvement with the children. In the 1960s this began to change. Fein notes that fathers had come to be regarded as important to the successful development of the children and vital in certain areas—including the proper development of masculinity and femininity, academic performance, and moral development. A great deal of this concern came from studies of father-absent homes in which there were deficits in these areas (Biller, 1982; 1974). Unfortunately, many of these studies on father absence did not control for stress and socioeconomic status. The more modern perspective is one in which fathers have some duties. The fathers' guidance and presence are deemed important, which is a significant change from the traditional view.

The emergent perspective on fathering is that men are psychologically able to participate in all parenting behaviors and that children's lives are improved by the opportunity to develop personal relationships with both parents. Fathers are no longer seen as deficient in child-rearing skills just because they are males. This new view is reflected in the sections on fathering throughout this text. But fathers still do much less of the housework, and mothers have the primary responsibility for child-rearing. The situation is changing, but slowly. Fathering too is a skill that must be learned. Fathers who remember their fathers as nurturant and actively involved tend to act the same way with their children (Manion, 1977). The slow changes in the attitudes of males toward fathering is an ongoing process. Fathers can play a greater role in the lives of their children, and they probably will in the future.

Divorce

Whether James and Kaye have children or not, if their marriage is unhappy they may decide to get a divorce. For more than one million couples a year, marital breakdown and divorce are facts of life (U.S. Department of Commerce, 1987). Half of all divorces occur within the first seven years of marriage, and more than one million children each year are affected by divorce. If the current rate of divorce continues, about half of all new marriages will end in divorce (Skolnick and Skolnick, 1983; Weed, 1980). Most people are aware that the divorce rate has increased substantially, actually increasing seventeen-fold from 1867 to 1979. But most people are unaware that a gradual decline began to take place in the early 1980s, from a peak of 5.3 per 1,000 population in 1979 to 4.8 per 1,000 population at the end of 1986 (U.S. Department of Health and Human Services, 1987).

But divorce cannot be understood only in terms of statistics. If Kaye and James get a divorce, they will go through a period of crisis and pain. In one survey of 500 divorced males and females, one-quarter of the people involved said the divorce was very traumatic and described their experience as a nightmare, while 40 percent reported that it was stressful but bearable. Only one in five reported little difficulty with the experience (' brecht, 1980).

Predictors of Divorce

Some people are more likely to get divorced than others. Men who marry before the age of twenty and women who marry before they are eighteen are twice as likely to get divorced (Glenn and Supancic, 1984). If the pregnancy begins before the marriage, divorce is also more likely (Coombs and Zumeta, 1970). Traditionally, the poor and the undereducated have had much higher divorce rates than the middle class and the educated, but the gap has been closing rapidly and is now small (Norton and Glick, 1979). Some groups of middle-class and educated people are now statistically at risk for divorce. For example, career-oriented women with graduate educations are more likely to get a divorce than other groups of women (Glick, 1984a). Perhaps these women are financially secure and do not have to depend on their husbands for support, so they need not stay in an unpleasant situation for financial reasons.

True or False Career-oriented women are more likely to get divorced than women who are full-time homemakers.

Kaye is more likely than James to make the move to divorce. It is estimated that in three-quarters of the cases the woman takes the initiative (Wallerstein and Kelly, 1980). It is not uncommon for the other spouse to claim surprise at the decision, although he or she will readily admit that there were problems in the marriage. Mutual agreement on divorce is relatively rare. It is not a decision that is made on the spur of the moment either, although frequently one incident, such as physical abuse, an extramarital encounter, or a big argument, is the last straw (Kelly, 1982). The person who is most surprised is likely to experience the greatest stress, but both will probably suffer.

True or False Women are more likely to ask for a divorce than men are.

The Causes of Divorce

People seeking divorce give many reasons for their decision. Communication problems, simple unhappiness, incompatibility, emotional abuse, financial problems, sexual problems, and alcohol problems are among the most prominent. But societal changes are important factors too. Divorce laws have been liberalized to make divorce easier. In addition, the stigma attached to being divorced is not nearly so great. Historically, many women had to stay with their husbands because they had no other means of supporting themselves. Today, however, they are less likely to feel they have to stay married, because there are more women in the work force. Finally, people today expect to get more out of marriage. They expect to actualize themselves and grow within the marriage. In fact, older studies of reasons for divorce usually note that drinking or nonsupport are important factors. Newer studies emphasize breakdowns in affection and communication. In these studies, women almost always voice more complaints than men do but both emphasize the lack of communication (Kelly, 1982). Spouse violence or involvement in an extramarital relationship is often a precipitating or last-straw factor.

The Consequences of Divorce

The divorce experience is a trauma for everyone involved. Social supports are reduced as friendships cool (Hetherington et al., 1977). Divorced people are likely to find it more difficult to continue their friendships with couples they knew before the divorce. Sometimes remaining friends with both parties after a divorce is difficult, while at other times the single person may not fit in with an evening of couples getting together.

After the divorce, both males and females are more disorganized, and it takes some time for them to put their new lives in order. Divorce may even lead to physical problems. Studies show that divorcees have poorer health, a higher mortality rate, and more accidents than married people. They are also more likely to have emotional problems (Goetting, 1983). It may be that the stress more than the divorce itself causes these difficulties. The financial problems are significant. Many men do not pay child support, or when they do it is sporadic. Even wives who do receive support regularly are likely to find that two households cannot be maintained on the same paycheck that was barely enough before the divorce. Women with young children must often return to work, but find that reasonable alternative child care is not available. More than two-thirds of the women in one study reported their income had dropped significantly after the divorce (Albrecht, 1980). After a divorce, women are likely to suffer a significant drop in living standard, while some men actually experience an increase.

How do people see divorce years later? One study found that while half the men opposed separation and divorce at the beginning, five years later two-thirds expressed a positive view of divorce. Only 30 percent of all males responding in the study were content though. On the female side, the opposite occurred. The number of women viewing divorce as positive decreased, although still more than half considered it a positive step (Kelly, 1982). Despite the tremendous stress involved, most people eventually do start a new life and build new relationships. The healthier and better adjusted a person is before the divorce, the more quickly that person is likely to adjust to the problems of divorce (Wallerstein and Kelly, 1980). It often happens that only one of the spouses involved in divorce shows an improvement, as indicated in a ten-year follow-up study of divorced couples (Wallerstein, 1986). In almost two-thirds of the families studied, only one spouse had substantially improved his or her overall quality of life, which was measured by such factors as the nature and quality of their interpersonal relationships, general contentment with life, and freedom from loneliness. In fact, in one-fifth of these divorces both partners were worse off. Even ten years after the divorce, feelings of anger were common. Some 40 percent of the women and almost 30 percent of the men still felt hurt and angry. However, the majority do recover and rebuild their lives, and we find increases in general happiness and self-esteem two years following the divorce (Hetherington et al., 1976). Many divorcees overcome the economic and social problems,

Interpersonal Relationships

*O*ur greatest source of joy comes from our relationships with other people. They celebrate our good fortune and serve as playmates and companions. In times of trouble we receive support and help from others, and people often give us encouragement to persevere and succeed. We are deeply affected by other people's behavior. Along with the joy and benefits of interpersonal relationships comes the possibility of pain and trouble as when we are hurt by something someone else did. But relationships are reciprocal, and we both affect and are affected by many others in our environment.

Our relationships with others start from birth and develop rapidly. Our early relationships with others have a considerable affect upon our development, although we now know that experience is cumulative and later positive experiences can compensate at least to some degree for poor early experience. With increasing age, the number of our interpersonal relationships increases as we go beyond the family and develop relationships with friends and teachers. Later, we form our own families and develop relationships with people at work. Relationships differ from each other in a qualitative manner, and our relationships with spouse, partners, parents, children, supervisors, co-workers, and friends differ substantially. Psychologists have traced the development of these relationships from infancy through later adulthood, allowing us to better understand how they affect us throughout life.

(At right) The earliest relationship is with our parents. This relationship is crucial to the future development of the child.

(Above) From a life-span perspective, our longest relationships are often with our siblings. Although sibling rivalry is a reality, siblings also serve as playmates and confidants.

Friendship in middle childhood differs greatly from the fleeting peer relationships of earlier years and is based upon mutual interest and personal qualities.

As we develop we must relate to other authority figures besides our parents, such as teachers. The quality of these relationships differs greatly from those we have with our parents.

(Above) Social interactions in adolescence take on a different quality as friendships deepen and relationships with the opposite sex become more important.

The most important relationships in adulthood for most people are formed with spouses and children. These intimate relationships require playing new roles and developing new interpersonal skills.

In adulthood, relationships are often formed on the job. Some of our co-workers become friends while others remain only acquaintances. Still other relationships are formed with supervisors.

It is most common for people of the same age to be friends since they share so much as they negotiate a particular developmental stage of life. Friendships are very important to the well-being of older people.

One aspect of interpersonal relationships rarely considered is the need to form social relationships with people from other cultures. The Olympic games is one place where people from many nations meet and hopefully achieve better understanding.

including loneliness and the need to make new friends, although it takes a significant amount of time and effort to do so.

Two factors mentioned as the "last straw" are often spouse abuse or an extramarital relationship. Although neither is new to our society, both appear to be on the increase.

Spouse Abuse

One wife signed a nominating petition for a candidate her husband didn't like, so he beat her badly, as was his habit. Then he went to sleep, and while he was sleeping his wife clubbed him to death with a baseball bat (Meyers, 1978). About 4.1 percent of all the homicides in the United States involve wives killing husbands, and 4.9 percent involve husbands killing wives (Brehm, 1985). Most physical abuse, of course, falls short of murder.

It is difficult to obtain reliable figures on the extent of the problem, but it is estimated that 3.3 million wives are severely beaten and that 250,000 husbands share the same fate (Steinmetz, 1978). A government survey estimates that 40 percent of all marriages are marred by at least one incident of violence. In 15 to 20 percent of all marriages, abuse is periodic, and in 5 percent it is chronic (U.S. Department of Labor, 1978). It is not surprising that there has been much more research on husbands abusing wives than on wives abusing husbands, since the physical advantage men have usually makes their abuse more serious.

While there are many theories why such abuse takes place, certain factors predispose marriages to abuse (Ponzettie et al., 1982). First, many men who abuse their wives either had witnessed their mothers being abused or were victims of abuse as children (Kalmuus, 1984). Early in life they learn that physical force is a way to settle conflicts. The second factor in spouse abuse is alcohol and drug dependencies, and a third involves the inability to express oneself. When abusive males cannot explain their point of view they often become frustrated and resort to violence. The fourth factor is emotional dependence. Abusive males are emotionally dependent on their partners and feel very jealous and possessive. They often use violence as a way to keep a spouse from leaving. Finally, abusive males are less assertive than nonabusive males and may use violence to "prove" they are men. Abusive husbands are not usually psychotic and do not require institutionalization (Steinmetz and Straus, 1973). External factors may interact with these individualistic factors—for example, economic stress, isolation, and a cultural belief that violence is legitimate. About 20 percent of all Americans approve of physical force in marriage (Meyers, 1978). Abuse is a learned behavior that has deep psychological and sociological roots.

It may be easier to understand the sad pattern of violence on the part of the husband than to understand why the wife does not leave. We hear of cases of wife-beating and child abuse that go on for years. Sometimes the wife leaves for a short period of time and then returns, only to be abused again. Many women do not leave at all, or return after a brief time because they hope their husband will change, have nowhere to go, fear that their husbands will find them and punish them for leaving, are concerned about their children's need for a father, or cannot support themselves financially (Hyde, 1985). The longer someone has been married, the more they have committed themselves to the marriage and the less willing they will be to leave (Strube and Barbour, 1983). On the other hand, women who have a job are less likely to stay (Gelles, 1980), probably because they are not so dependent on their husbands for financial support.

Abuse often begins even before the marriage. In one study, more than 20 percent of all respondents had been involved in one or more violent premarital relationships (Cate et al., 1982). Some people raised on violence believe it is a normal part of the relationship. Women who consider violence improper and demeaning are less likely to be abused, simply because they will not accept such treatment.

Victims of abuse need shelters, hotlines to call for immediate help, and police protection, as well as counseling. The abuser needs to be restrained, but also requires counseling in the hope that he or she will reform.

Extramarital Relationships

If you watch some soap operas you might begin to think that everyone is having an extramarital affair. Actually, we have no authoritative estimates of such practices. Our figures come from surveys by popular magazines, which are hardly representative or accurate. These reports lead some to estimate that 50 percent of husbands and 20 to 40 percent of all wives have such encounters (Knox, 1985). In one study, 28 percent of the men and 5 percent of the women who had extramarital relationships said they lasted only one night (Spanier and Margolis, 1983). Despite these figures, the overwhelming majority of Americans are opposed to extramarital sex (Reiss, 1980; Golanty and Harris, 1982).

Researchers have been able to gather some information about extramarital relationships. Men are more likely than women to engage in extramarital sex, and many such relationships have some connection with work. They are more likely to take place when the marriage is poor, and having a close friend who is involved in such a relationship increases the chances. The reasons for affairs vary, and there may be general gender differences in motivation. Men may be motivated by a desire for variety. In fact, twice as many men say they have extramarital encounters for sex only (Thompson, 1983). Wives are more likely to have extramarital sex when they find some deficit in their marriage, be it sexual or emotional (Knox, 1985).

After the Divorce

What happens after the divorce? For many, they are faced with the challenges of single parenting and then remarriage and stepparenting.

Single Parenting

Imagine you are divorced with two small children. Your parents live far away, and you do not have many friends. You must go to work to support your family, but good alternative child care is expensive. In addition, your former spouse complains about everything you do and you think he (or she) may be trying to undercut your authority with the children.

We looked at the experiences of the children raised in single-parent families, most often because of divorce (see Chapter 10), but what of the parents' experience? Most parents are single because of divorce, although some are widowed parents or single mothers who never married. About 12.8 million families contain a single parent living without a spouse. Some 10.5 million families are headed by single women and 2.3 million by single men (U.S. Department of Labor, 1985). The problem of single parents include loneliness, lack of social support, financial difficulties, and a lack of day-care availability (Wallerstein and Kelly, 1979).

The experiences of single divorced parents with and without children differ. The divorced parent without children need not have any contact with the former spouse, and studious avoidance is quite common. Each is free to establish a completely independent life. This is not so when children are involved. In this case, financial support is always an issue, as are child-rearing practices. One woman who had just gone through an ugly divorce told me her husband was "always looking over her shoulder ready to pounce on everything and anything." Her former husband blamed all the child's problems on her, threatening to take her to court and gain custody of the child.

Financial pressure is great too. One-parent families are likely to be living in poverty (Reiss, 1980). Payment of child support and alimony is variable, and many men simply do not send the money (Wallerstein and Kelly, 1979). When small children are involved, the practical problems mount up. One woman had to give up a good job because she could find no one to look after her child before and after school. Another found that it was difficult or impossible to find people to get her child to and from extra tutoring help after school, and the child could not join the soccer club because there was no one to drive him to practice.

Sometimes the child will say or do something that causes the parent with physical custody to almost give

The single parent has more stress and responsibilities than parents in a two-parent family.

up. Often the noncustodial parent, especially right after the divorce, will act very sweet and give the child everything possible, as well as agree with the child's complaints about the custodial parent. This may undercut the custodial parent's authority, making discipline difficult. Because the majority of children live with their mothers, it is easy to find such examples, but fathers and noncustodial mothers have complaints as well. Sometimes the custodial parent continually tells the child how terrible the other parent is, trying to turn the child against that parent. At other times, the child may play one parent against another. Still others have valid complaints about the custodial parent's child-rearing strategies but because of the strained relationship with the ex-spouse they have little influence. Fathers who have physical custody have their own problems. Many must learn a child-rearing routine that is foreign to them. They also have the same problems as mothers who have physical custody.

Although the problems described above are real, single-parenting does have rewards. If the home was filled with violence, it is less violent now. If it was fraught with emotional conflict, the conflict is reduced. On the other hand, many single parents find that they have turned in one set of problems for another.

Remarriage

Remarriage is common in the United States today. In 1980, of all the people between the ages of sixty-five and seventy-four who had been divorced, 84 percent of the men and 77 percent of the women had remarried (Glick, 1984b). The remarriage rate has shown a decrease since the 1960s, although it is still high (Glick and Ling-Lin, 1986). The decrease may be partly due to increases in cohabitation (Glick, 1980). In any event, the large number of people who remarry demonstrates that people who get a divorce have not soured on marriage, only on their particular marriage. In order to remarry, a person must have some belief that things will be different another time around. The second marriage differs greatly from the first. The first experience will never be forgotten.

In what is perhaps the most important study of its kind, divorced residents of a Pennsylvania community in 1977 were followed and interviewed. A number of differences between first and second marriages were noted (Furstenberg, 1982). Most blamed their divorces on marrying the wrong person, and they looked for different things in their second spouse than they did in the first. They were more pragmatic than romantic. The first time they emphasized appearance, ambition, and occupational status; the second time they placed importance on stability and respect. There was less fantasy, and the attachment was more qualified. Their expectations for the marriage were reduced. In addition, there was more informality in their dating, and rather than project an ideal image, they presented themselves honestly. The unhappy experience of the first marriage makes an indelible impression on the choice for the second.

True or False Divorced people considering remarriage look for the same qualities in the second spouse that they sought in their first.

Stepparenting

About half a million people annually become stepparents (Prosen and Farmer, 1982). People often see stepfamilies as identical to nuclear families, but they are very different. Not only are children living with a new parent, but most people come to the new family after having experienced a loss. Stepparents must learn to share the child with the biological parent, who lives in another home, and the child must relate to a new parent. The problems of readjustment can be difficult. In addition, each parent may have his or her own children as well, so two or more children may be living with one biological parent and one stepparent.

In such fairy tales as "Cinderella" and "Sleeping Beauty," the stepmother is wicked and the father is good but weak. This stereotype has been passed down to us, and many people regard the state of being a stepmother as the epitome of wickedness. In one study, college students from single-parent families, stepfamilies, and intact families all rated stepparents, particularly stepmothers, less positively than natural parents. However, students from stepfamilies and single-parent families were significantly less stereotyped in their perception of stepmothers than those from intact families (Fine, 1986). In reality, stepparents are neither as bad as Cinderella's nor as good as what was portrayed on the television show "The Brady Bunch."

Another myth is the myth of instant love—that the nuclear family once torn asunder by divorce is now back together and living happily ever after. This conflicts with the wicked stepparent myth, but it is just as false. Stepparents may not instantly fall in love with their step-

In many fairy tales, the stepmother is considered wicked.

children, and children may resent or merely tolerate the presence of stepparents. Stepparenting presents definite problems, especially in the area of discipline and adjustment. Imagine marrying into a family with a parent and two children. They have been a one-parent family for some time and have established certain patterns. You as the new parent must learn how to discipline the children, what changes are feasible, and what areas must be left alone. It is a difficult job, and one for which little training is available.

The clinical literature concerning stepparenting stresses its problems—which include acceptance of the new spouse by family members, difficulties with discipline, problems coping with new relationships and with the impact of an absent biological parent who probably has some say in the child-rearing practices—mainly because clinicians are likely to work with families that are troubled (Ganong and Coleman, 1986; Kosinski, 1983). In many states, the stepparent is not considered a parent and does not have any legal rights (Rallings, 1976). However, they are expected to take on financial, educational, and so-

cialization responsibilities. Stepmothers are expected to perform a nurturant role in the family, but at the same time some of the power rests with the biological parent, who is likely to be overcritical of her efforts.

Stepparents do have an effect on their children, but that effect can be positive or negative (Parish, 1982; Duberman, 1973; Bernard, 1956). In some studies, no significant adjustment differences between biological children and stepchildren were found (Wilson et al., 1975). There is even evidence that the presence of a stepfather can reduce the problems of father absence (Oshman and Manosevitz, 1976) and has positive effects on the cognitive development of boys (Santrock, 1972).

As the experience of the child in a stepparenting situation may be positive or negative, so it is with the stepparent. For some, stepchildren are a source of pride, but other stepparents consider them a bother and constant conflict typifies the relationship. Still others do not have much involvement with their stepchildren. There are so many variables involved in stepparenting that it is impossible to make any generalization about its effect on everyone in the family. One thing is clear, though. Stepparenting is a difficult role that offers significant challenges to everyone in the family.

Many Roads to Travel

Times have changed. While 100 years ago few people made a conscious choice to remain single, today some people do. While single parenthood resulted mostly from death of the spouse, today it is mostly due to divorce. There are even a number of people who elect to adopt or have children without marriage, although studies of them are rare. Others divorce and elect to remarry. The choices are many, and people have greater freedom to choose a lifestyle than any generation has ever had.

Vocational Development

The second area of life that is so important to young adults is their vocation or career. When people mention the words "career" or "job," most people think of money. But pay is just one aspect of the world of work, Think of all the functions of work. First, it keeps you busy. About 80,000 hours, or 30 percent of your lifetime, is taken up by work (Miller, 1964). It also provides an outlet for personal satisfaction and is a significant source of social interaction. We often form friendships at work. Work also affects one's self-concept (Kennedy, 1978), because working is connected with feelings of self-worth. When people are unemployed, it affects more than their pocketbooks—it affects every aspect of their life. Satisfaction with one's job is related to general happiness (Freedman, 1978), and vocational success to self-esteem (Marshall, 1983). Work is a central part of our lives. When people were asked whether they would continue to work even if they inherited enough money and did not need to work anymore, 84 percent of the males and 77 percent of the females said they would continue to work, although not necessarily at the same job (Yankelovich, 1981).

True or False Most people say they would work even if they did not have to.

There are developmental changes in what people see as most important in work. Young adults typically are interested in advancement, but in middle adulthood job security becomes more important (Krausz, 1982). This is mirrored in job mobility statistics, which show that workers in their twenties tend to change jobs more often than workers in their thirties. Middle-age workers change jobs even less often.

Are Today's Workers Different?

Many people complain that today's workers are not at all like the hardworking employees they remember from years ago. This sounds a bit like the older generation sounding off against the younger, but there is some truth to it. The modern worker is different, but different does not have to mean better or worse.

The modern worker is better educated than ever before. Most manual workers have completed high school, and one-fourth have had some college experience. The number of college-educated workers doubled between 1960 and 1980, and many are overqualified for the work they perform. It is estimated that one in four take a position that does not require a college education (Kossen, 1983). On the other side, many more jobs require basic academic skills, such as reading, or more advanced skills, such as computer literacy, than ever before. And educated workers are more likely to want to exercise some control over decision making on the job and show their competence (Rubin, 1976). Perhaps the supervisor-worker relationship needs reevaluation.

Another major change is in the area of the work ethic—the idea that work is valuable for its own sake. In one survey, 85 percent of workers rejected work as an end in itself (Fein, 1976). In addition, workers appear to be valuing work less and their leisure time more (Quinn and Staines, 1979). For many, such matters as working conditions and time off have become more important than other more traditional factors (Featherman, 1980).

Other attitudes have changed too. The ideas that money and status are measures of achievement, that employees owe their loyalty to the employer, and that as long as a job is decent and provides a living it is sufficient are no longer accepted (Albanese and Van Fleet, 1983). People who are unhappy at work are more likely to leave for a job that is more interesting (Renwick and Lawler, 1978), and workers today are less likely to feel they owe the company anything even if they were trained at company expense. Such lack of company loyalty may simply reflect the lack of job security and feelings of dissatisfaction some people experience in their jobs.

True or False Today's employees are more loyal to their companies than workers in the past.

Faced with these changing attitudes, many companies find it less expensive to satisfy their present employees than to continue to train new people. They provide a better work environment and look at the totality of the workers' experience. Many companies now provide health and fitness facilities so workers can exercise during the workday to reduce stress. Studies show that such fitness programs also reduce turnover and absenteeism (Brody, 1985). Other companies allow workers to participate in management decisions and give employees more autonomy.

These new attitudes are reflected in the career desires of many young adults. When asked what they want from their jobs, many young adults cite not only money and advancement but also interest and a feeling of accomplishment. People expect more from their careers today. It remains to be seen whether the world of work can satisfy these demands.

Job Satisfaction

Job satisfaction was certainly not a major issue for our grandparents. They were lucky even to have a job and to make a living for the family. But times have changed, and both workers and companies are concerned about job satisfaction. It is reasonable to assume that satisfied employees are more productive, but that relationship is complex, and when it does exist the correlation tends to be positive but low (Iaffaldino and Muchinsky, 1985). However, job dissatisfaction is related to absenteeism and especially high turnover (Young, 1983), and to the physical and mental health problems of workers.

Studies show that people are generally satisfied with their jobs. The data pooled from nine surveys of job satisfaction shows that slightly more than 85 percent of the males and females said they were satisfied. About half of those surveyed considered themselves very satisfied and less than 4 percent were very dissatisfied (Glenn and Weaver, 1985). Most but not all authorities agree that there has been a recent drop in job satisfaction, especially among young workers (Thayer, 1983; Havighurst, 1982; Quinn and Staines, 1979). But what makes someone satisfied? So many variables are involved that it is impossible to list them all. Money, job security, and the relationship with one's immediate superior are important (Nord, 1977), as are whether the work is challenging and whether the worker gets enough recognition for his or her contributions (Renwick and Lawler, 1978).

> **hygiene factors** Such factors as adequate salary, good working conditions, and job security—whose absence causes workers to be dissatisfied with their jobs.
>
> **motivational factors** or **satisfiers** Such factors as a sense of achievement, recognition, and esteem, the presence of which leads to job satisfaction.

Herzberg and colleagues (1959) argued that the factors that led to worker satisfaction were not the same as those that led to dissatisfaction. Salary, working conditions, and one's relationship with the boss are considered physical needs, or **hygiene factors.** Their absence causes dissatisfaction, but just because they are present does not indicate that the worker will be satisfied. **Motivational factors** or **satisfiers**—including personal growth, achievement, creativity, and autonomy—are important factors in job satisfaction, although their absence does not necessarily lead to job dissatisfaction. When people cite what they do not like about their jobs, pay is often given as a reason (Lawler, 1971). When workers are asked to cite their greatest satisfactions at work, they are most likely to mention the recognition they get, self esteem, and the sense that they are doing something valuable.

When people begin their first real job, satisfaction is high. After all, they are now self-sufficient and the whole world of work is new. Then there is a steep decline in worker satisfaction, followed later by an increase (Rhodes, 1983). Perhaps when the first flush of excitement about working ends, reality—for instance, the disappointments and the need to make compromises—sets in. Part of the dissatisfaction younger workers feel may arise because they tend to be given the least-creative and fulfilling work, whereas older, more experienced workers with more seniority may be able to choose the most interesting jobs.

Just as age seems to predict changes in job satisfaction, so does race. Nonwhite workers are twice as likely as white workers to be dissatisfied with their jobs. One-third of all nonwhites have jobs that are at the very lowest vocational level and offer minimal pay and little chance for advancement. Even in higher-level jobs, however, the rate of dissatisfaction is higher for nonwhite workers than for white workers, and this is especially evident in white-collar jobs (Schultz, 1978). This holds true up to age forty, after which the dissatisfaction rate for both whites and nonwhites becomes equal.

If age and race make a difference, what about gender? The situation with women is not so clear. Some studies show that women are as satisfied as men, others show that women are less satisfied (Schultz, 1978).

Women and Work

In 1893 only 5 percent of all women worked outside the home (Troll, 1985). By 1980 there were more women working outside the home that there were full-time homemakers (Maymi, 1982). The trend is unmistakable. About 55 percent of all women are in the labor force up from 41 percent in 1970 (U.S. Bureau of Labor Statistics, 1987). And that percentage continues to rise. Two-thirds are employed full-time (U.S. Department of Labor, 1985b). The increase, especially in young women entering the labor force, is remarkable. In 1966, some 44 percent of twenty to twenty-four-year-old women worked, and by 1986 it had risen to 72 percent. Between 1973 and 1986 the number of working mothers with children under six rose from 33 percent to 54.4 percent. About 70 percent of all women with children from age six to age seventeen are in the labor force, and 50.8 percent of all women with children under three are employed outside the home (U.S. Bureau of Labor Statistics, 1986). By 1990, some 85 percent of women between the ages of twenty and twenty-four will be in the work force (Maymi, 1982). Indeed, a survey of female high school seniors showed that almost 88 percent believed that work was either important or very important to their future (Wagenaar, 1981). The attitudes of the population are generally positive toward women working, with more than three quarters of the public approving of women working, even if the husband's job was sufficient to care for the family (Cherlin and Walters, 1981).

Most women work because they have to. Two-thirds of all women in the labor force are single, widowed, divorced, separated, or married to husbands who earn less than $10,000 a year (Maymi, 1982). In other words, most women work out of economic necessity. This does not mean that women get no sense of accomplishment or personal satisfaction; studies show that they do (American Council of Life Insurance, 1983). And women are committed to their jobs. This commitment depends on how long they have been employed, how satisfying it is and how much training they have had (Haller and Rosenmayr, 1971). A woman who has gone through six years of higher education to get a good job is less likely to give it up for a career as a full-time homemaker.

True or False Most women work because they are bored at home.

Women's lifestyle patterns follow one of six paths (Mueller in Havighurst, 1982). First, there is the *stable homemaking career pattern*. In this pattern, women marry shortly after leaving school and devote themselves to homemaking and family life. Women in the *conventional career pattern* work before marriage and then take up full-time homemaking. The *stable working career pattern* involves training for a position and a continuing devotion to employment as the most important area of the woman's life. The *double-track career pattern* involves women going to work after completing their education, marrying, and continuing with the double career of working outside the home and homemaking. The *interrupted career pattern* involves periods of working, homemaking, and then working again while homemaking or instead of it. Resumption of employment depends on the age of the children and financial needs. The *unstable career pattern* involves alternating working and homemaking, with the amount of employment dependent on economic needs or health. This is most common for low-income women. It is clear that the first two patterns are declining while the next three are increasing. It is difficult to make any statement concerning the sixth pattern.

Women employed outside the home face a number of challenges both in the workplace and at home. In the workplace, discrimination, sexual harassment, and being given low-paying, low-prestige jobs are important concerns. However, some progress has been made, even in the last decade or so. For example, the percentage of women in managerial and professional specialties rose from 17.3 percent to 23.6 percent between 1973 and 1986 (Bureau of Labor Statistics, 1987; see Figure 15.2).

Female workers do not make as much as male workers (see Table 15.2). They make approximately 68.8 percent of what men make (U.S. Department of Labor, 1987), but this means very little when one can say that women are clustered in lower-paying occupations. Because of laws that make sex discrimination in the workplace illegal, it is rare to find women performing the exact same job and being paid less—almost everyone is opposed to this type of discrimination.

Recently, however, there has been a clamor for elimination of a different type of bias. Although women are

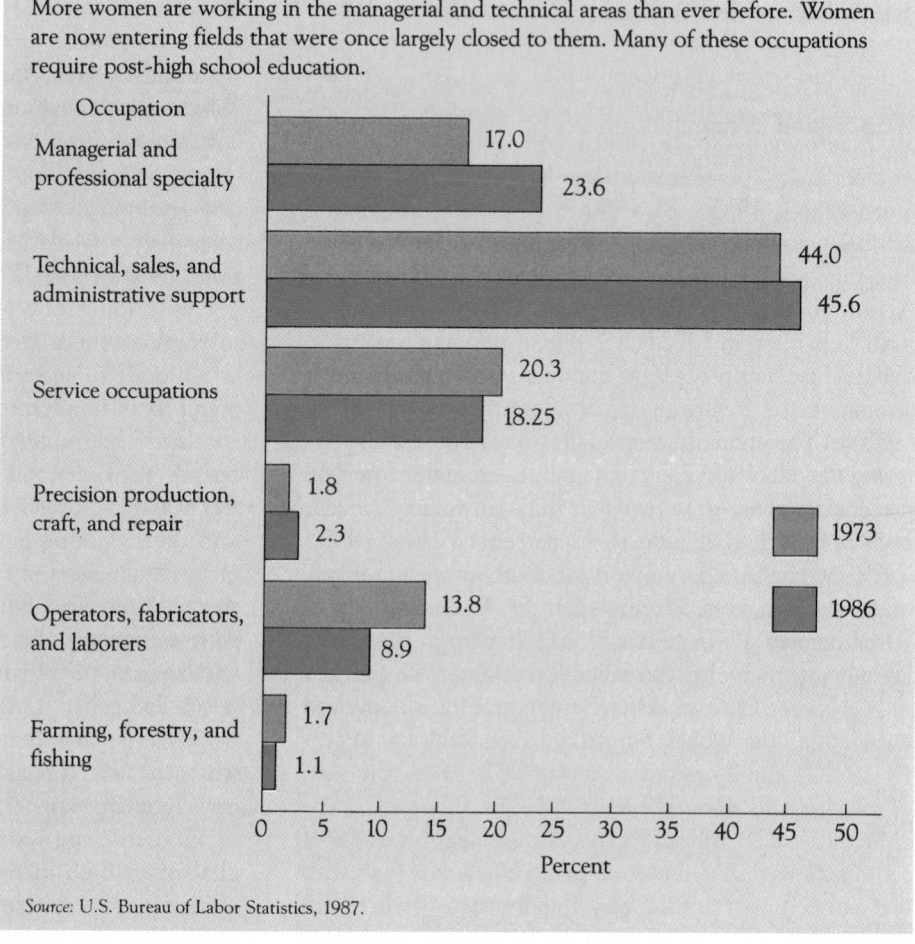

FIGURE 15.2

Employed Women by Occupation, 1973 and 1986, Annual Averages

More women are working in the managerial and technical areas than ever before. Women are now entering fields that were once largely closed to them. Many of these occupations require post-high school education.

Source: U.S. Bureau of Labor Statistics, 1987.

clustered in low-paying jobs, these positions often entail as much training and are as valuable to the company as positions usually occupied by men. This, some argue, can be corrected only by paying people according to their **comparable worth.** This would entail an analysis of the skills and values of various jobs and paying according to those criteria. In other words, if two jobs require the same amount of knowledge or skill and are of the same value, they would be paid the same. Proponents of a comparable worth program believe it is really the only way to address the problem. Opponents argue that it is impossible to determine whether—for example—a nurse is equivalent to a carpenter.

Women may find that their job does not end when they come home. Studies show that a woman must put

comparable worth   The principle by which jobs that require the same amount of knowledge or skill, or whose value to the employer are equal, are paid equally. Thus, a nurse and a carpenter might be paid the same.

in not only the same hours at work as her husband, but also be responsible for most of the household and child-rearing duties. A mother with a full-time job puts in about eighty hours a week working, while the father puts in sixty-two hours (Vanek, 1980). In addition, she must deal with the everyday stresses and illnesses that come

TABLE 15.2

Median Weekly Earnings of Full-Time Men and Women

The earnings gap is closing, but very slowly.

Year	Usual Weekly Earnings (Current Dollars)		Women's Earnings as Percent of Men's
	Women	Men	
1979	$176	$286	61.5
1980	199	306	65.0
1981	212	337	62.9
1982	235	358	65.6
1983	251	376	66.8
1984	258	400	64.5
1985	277	406	68.2
1986	287	419	68.4
1987*	299	434	68.8

*First quarter results.

Source: Bureau of Labor Statistics, 1987, 1986, 1985.

with leading two lives. Usually it is the mother who takes off from work when the children are sick and who is responsible for child care. Yet there are benefits to holding a job outside the home. Many women are afraid of being out of touch with the world, and they want the stimulation and companionship available in the workplace. There is some evidence for an increase in self-esteem among women who work (Rutter, 1981), but the personal benefits depend on whether she really wants to work or would rather be a full-time homemaker (Alvarez, 1985). The simple fact is that people are happier when they are living the lifestyle they want to live.

The Dual-Career Marriage

There is a good chance that James and Kaye will fit into the category of the dual-career marriage. The fact that both husband and wife work does not make it a dual-career marriage though. In a dual-career marriage, two people are engaged in a lifestyle in which each pursues an independent career yet is committed to the intimate relationship (Parker et al., 1981). The key term is "career" rather than "job." A career involves a sequence of steps leading to greater responsibility. It entails a greater degree of commitment than a job.

The advantages of this lifestyle include the possibility of greater financial independence, intellectual growth,

and a more equal distribution of power in the marriage. The problems involve a possible decline in interaction between husband and wife and sometimes too much competition between the two. Success in dual-career marriages is possible when there is flexibility, mobility, a balance of independence and interdependence, and communication (Maples, 1981). The mobility question is interesting. What if Kaye has an excellent job opportunity in Kansas City and must move there from Savannah, where they now live? Can James find a position equivalent to the one he now has? This depends on the skills each has and on the job market.

Many dual-career couples delay having children until they are older, and this is so common that the phrase "thirty-year baby panic" is now found in the literature (Parker et al., 1981). Even though Kaye's ability to have children does not end at thirty, this age milestone seems to trigger a social clock. It is common for dual-career couples to begin having children at this age, although Kaye will probably return to work soon after the child is born.

Unemployment

Name any negative event or experience, and you will find that unemployment is related to it. Unemployment is related to low self-esteem (Perfetti and Bingham, 1983), to suicide rates (Vigderhous and Fishman, 1978), to divorce, alcoholism, and drug abuse, to abuse of spouse and children, and to juvenile delinquency (Riegle, 1982). As noted earlier, people's self-respect and self-esteem are usually rooted in their work, and these often decline when a person becomes unemployed. In a study comparing unemployed men with employed men, the unemployed men showed more symptoms of depression, anxiety, and ill health than the employed group (Linn et al., 1985). People who are unemployed, even through no fault of their own, tend to blame themselves.

True or False People who are fired or laid off tend to blame the employer rather than themselves.

Unemployment brings financial pressures that can become intolerable. Men and women both are affected by unemployment, but because men tend to define success and failure more in terms of vocational achievement, they are apt to be more psychologically devastated. Women with children may define their self-esteem in terms of both employment and family, so success in the family

Unemployment affects a person's self-esteem and causes a number of physical and emotional disturbances.

sphere may balance out occupational problems. A study of unemployed Israelis by Shamir (1985) showed that the financial state of the men in his sample was more strongly affected by unemployment than the financial state of the women. But Shamir points out that recent studies of American blue-collar workers show that the financial impact of a plant closing is similar or greater for women. Therefore, the effects of unemployment on women will vary with a women's family status, the husband's employment status, and family earnings. Poor women who are supporting families are more vulnerable to the negative effects of unemployment than women who are married to a husband with a good income (Shamir, 1985).

The young are more likely to be unemployed than older people (Kossen, 1983). Because they are the last

to be hired and therefore have less seniority, they are the first to be fired. However, they are also likely to be out of work for less time than older people.

Choices and Paths

In this chapter we've seen just how many different paths are open to James and Kaye. No doubt, some are more socially acceptable today than others, but attitudes are changing. With greater tolerance of alternative lifestyles comes the need to assess one's own personal needs and to understand what one wants from a relationship and a career. This takes maturity and a great deal of self-knowledge. If James and Kaye know what they want, they will find that the late 1980s and 1990s will offer many paths they can choose from to reach their goals.

1. The major theorists of adulthood—Erikson, Levinson, Gould, and Vaillant—agree that the basic concerns of early adulthood lie in the areas of love and work.

2. Early adulthood offers many different lifestyle choices. Most young adults marry, but we do not have a clear idea why someone chooses one person over another. Some authorities believe that similarity is the key to understanding mate selection, others argue that complementary opposites attracts. The stimulus-value-role theory suggests that the decision to marry entails a three-stage progression toward a deeper sense of intimacy. Young adults' expectations for marriage today are somewhat greater than years ago. They expect marriage to help them actualize their own abilities and potentials.

3. Marital satisfaction is high at the beginning of the marriage, then it declines somewhat. Communication is a key to marital satisfaction and adjustment.

4. The importance of sexual relations in marriage varies from couple to couple. The frequency of sexual relations decreases with time.

5. Cohabitation, or living together, has increased in popularity. Most cohabiting couples break up before a year has passed. Remaining single is a viable lifestyle today.

6. Most couples want to have children, but an increasing percentage of couples are deciding not to. Motherhood brings with it joys, strains, and self-doubt. Fatherhood affects the lifestyle of men less than motherhood affects women's lives. Our conception of fathering has changed, and the emergent viewpoint is that fathers are able to participate in all facets of parenting.

7. Divorce is a serious problem in our society. The divorce rate has increased because divorce is now easier to obtain, there is less stigma attached to being divorced, women are increasingly able to support themselves, and people expect more out of their marriages. Breakdowns in affection and communication are commonly cited as reasons for divorce too. Divorce is a wrenching experience, but most divorced people do rebuild their lives. Women with young children often have serious economic difficulties.

8. Spouse abuse is a serious problem. Abusive males often have a history of using physical force to settle disputes, may be drug-dependent, and may have difficulty expressing their emotions.

9. Single-parent families are becoming more common today, primarily because of the increased divorce rate. Remarriage is also common. Stepparenting is a challenging role that may be a satisfying experience or fraught with anxiety and conflict.

10. Today's workers are different from those of previous generations in that they are better educated, value their leisure time more, have less company loyalty, and want more autonomy and input in the decision-making process. Most young adults are generally satisfied with their jobs, but there has recently been a drop in job satisfaction among young workers.

11. Most women work outside the home today because they need the money to maintain a reasonable standard of living. Women may follow a number of different vocational life paths. Women are concentrated in lower-status positions, although they have made some progress entering the professions.

12. Dual-career marriages are also becoming more common as both marital partners establish and maintain their careers. These couples usually delay having children. Unemployment is related to low self-esteem, suicide, and divorce, among other problems. Younger adults are more likely to be unemployed than older people, but they will be out of work for less time.

Answers to True or False Statements

1. *False* Correct statement: The age at which females choose to marry is increasing.

2. *False* Correct statement: A bit more than half the women with children under six are in the work force.

3. *False* Correct statement: Wives have more

complaints about their marriage than their husbands do.

4. *False*   Correct statement: The majority of cohabiting couples live together for less than a year before breaking up.

5. *False*   Correct statement: Although the percentage of couples choosing not to have children has increased, there are other historical periods in which the percentage of such couples has been higher.

6. *True*   Working women, especially career-oriented women, are more likely to get a divorce than full-time homemakers, probably because they are not financially dependent on their husbands.

7. *True*   Women are more likely to ask for a divorce than men are.

8. *False*   Correct statement: Divorced people who are considering remarriage look for different qualities in their next spouse.

9. *True*   Most people say they would work even if they didn't have to.

10. *False*   Correct statement: Company loyalty is on the decline.

11. *False*   Correct statement: Most women work because financial pressures force them to.

12. *False*   Correct statement: Even if they were fired or laid off through no fault of their own, people tend to blame themselves.

Middle Adulthood

Physical and Cognitive Development
in Middle Adulthood

Are the Following Statements True or False?

Try the True-False Quiz below. See if your answers correspond to the information in this chapter. Each question is repeated after the paragraph in which the answer can be found. The True-False Answer Box at the end of the chapter lists the complete answers.

____ 1. In middle adulthood, coordination decreases and flexibility increases.

____ 2. Most college students underestimate their parents' sexual activity.

____ 3. Middle-aged men take less time to achieve orgasm than young adult men.

____ 4. A dramatic increase in estrogen production causes women to experience uncomfortable physical symptoms in menopause, such as hot flashes.

____ 5. Cardiovascular disease is the most common cause of death among middle-aged men and women.

____ 6. Most people are not aware of the link between heart disease and diet.

____ 7. As people age, their health habits improve.

____ 8. As people age, they often become more farsighted.

____ 9. Middle-aged people often have difficulty hearing high-frequency tones.

____10. Reaction time generally slows with increasing age.

____11. In middle age there is a decline in ability to solve practical problems.

____12. Abilities that are exercised show no decline until old age.

A Positive Look at Middle Adulthood

Everyone knows that the best part of life is when you belong to the Pepsi generation. When you're a footloose teenager with a transistor plugged into your ear and have time to sit home and style your hair all day. When you're so cool you can stop in the middle of the ski slope and light up a Salem for your new bride. When you're home with a teething baby watching television, commercials idolize you as the couple just meant for that special low-low-fare of sizzling and snorkeling in Jamaica. What comes later is better left unsaid. After all, middle age is when everything turns gray, leaves home, is harder to see, or you've already seen it. Right?

Wrong. If people in the Comeback Decade (Americans between the ages of 45 and 54) got into a game of Monopoly with people of the Entry Decade (those between 25 and 34), it would be the oldies who got Boardwalk and Park Place and all the other valuable holdings—to reflect the share of property they actually own in this country—while the young ones would be lucky to get Marvin Gardens. And every time the gray-haired ones passed "Go," they would collect an extra $5,000 to reflect the elevation of their annual income over that of the young competitors. (Sheehy, 1981, p. 218)

This passage from one of Gail Sheehy's popular books on adulthood aptly demonstrates the "new look" at middle age. The graying hair, wrinkles, bulge around the middle, and all the other outward signs of aging that were once the themes of chapters such as this one have given way to a more optimistic, or perhaps realistic, look at middle age. As we shall see in this chapter and the next, no one denies the basic facts of aging, just the results of it. The new look at middle age fits in perfectly with the theme of adulthood—choice. With its improved economic situation, the status of middle adulthood gives us personal choices that were not available to us in early adulthood. However, the extent to which these opportunities are appreciated depend on how we deal with the aging process.

Physical Changes in Middle Adulthood

Some of the physical changes that occur in middle adulthood have major implications for our health and physical functioning. Others are purely cosmetic, but they may still be of great social and personal importance.

Commercials often lead us to believe that the late teen-early adulthood years are the "best of our lives." However, middle-aged people are quite active and have far greater incomes.

Changes in Appearance and Physical Functioning

The physical changes in middle adulthood are quite visible. They include graying hair, wrinkles, and a bulge around the middle (Lidz, 1976). At the same time, the legs become thinner and the amount of muscle tissue decreases as fat and connective tissue replace it. The decline in physical fitness is marked, it takes longer to get in shape, and it is harder to maintain that shape (Newman, 1982). The lungs work less efficiently. There is a decrease in the density of bone and muscle, and soreness in the joints is not unusual (Diekelmann, 1977). This may be the result of obesity, or simply a case of the joints wearing thin after years of use. The metabolic rate declines during middle age, and if people do not reduce their caloric intake, a slow but steady weight gain is the result (Diekelmann, 1977). The skin lines and begins to sag, stamina decreases, reflexes slow down, hair thins, muscle strength decreases, and the amount of blood pumped by the heart decreases (Tierney, 1982). Coordination and flexibility decrease as well (Shock and Norris, 1970). Despite this impressive list, these changes themselves are not the cause of much immediate discomfort. Yes, there is an increase in fatigue, minor backache, and other somatic complaints, but these are relatively minor (Barrow and Smith, 1983) and usually take place so gradually that most people hardly notice them in their daily life. In addition, conditioning and health habits can decrease their effect. A person who is overweight, smokes, and gets little exercise is likely to show the effects of these physical changes more than people who exercise, watch their diet, and refrain from smoking.

True or False In middle adulthood, coordination decreases and flexibility increases.

Even people in good physical shape may be bothered by the physical changes in appearance. This is especially true for those who define themselves in terms of their youthful appearance. You may remember that many of the theorists of adulthood stressed the importance of turning from defining oneself physically to valuing wisdom and experience (Peck, 1968), as well as coping with the diminished physical abilities of middle age (Levin-son, 1978). People who define themselves in terms of physical abilities or beauty may find middle age a wrenching experience. In middle age, people may have to redefine the self, putting less emphasis on youthful appearance and physical performance and more emphasis on wisdom and experience (Shanan, 1983). The athlete who is annoyed that he or she can no longer beat a youngster at tennis may find solace in knowing that well-conditioned middle-aged athletes can easily beat their nonexercising cohorts, as well as some younger nonexpert adults, in any sport they want to pursue. Some governing bodies in professional sports recognize the folly of allowing well-conditioned middle-aged athletes to retire simply because they cannot compete successfully with the twenty-two-year-old professional. This has led to senior leagues, in which such athletes can compete against their cohorts.

Sex differences in aging. Next time you watch television, make note the commercials aimed at middle-aged men and women. The differences are significant. Those aimed at females tell women that they need not show their age. They can use a skin cream to keep age wrinkles from appearing, dye their hair so no one will know they are graying, and use a certain detergent for washing dishes so that when she and her daughter compare hands an observer won't be able to tell which hand belongs to mother and which to daughter. Hanging onto youth is the key.

Now consider the commercials aimed at men. They have a different emphasis. The only area of a man's appearance that might be hinted at is increasing baldness or graying. But even when it comes to graying, men are told simply to moderate it, that they need not hide all of it. A little gray makes a man look distinguished (Schaffer, 1981).

The double standard of aging. Society does not see middle-aged men and women as aging in the same way, and men and women do experience the physical aging process differently. We have a double standard of aging in our society (Sontag, 1977; 1972). Although both men and women negotiate the inevitable aging process—for example, loss of skin elasticity, increasing fat, graying

The signs of aging in middle age are visible and include graying hair and wrinkles.

hair—aging affects women more than men. A man may find that he has to give up football and basketball and go on to other sports, or that he can no longer beat his eighteen-year-old son at tennis, but his aging is seen as graceful. His graying is said to show maturity, and his features are now considered handsome in a mature way (Schaffer, 1981). He is now on the top of his occupational ladder. If successful aging involves switching from a body orientation to an intellectual orientation, men can and often do succeed (Shanan, 1983).

A woman is faced with a different prospect. As she ages, she loses her girlish figure and look and is no longer admired for her sexuality. She must fight against the aging process. While men grow from boy to young man to middle-aged maturity, and with it to a new vision of excellence, women do not (Schaffer, 1981; Sontag, 1977). There is no counterpart to the distinguished middle-aged gentleman. He accepts aging and makes only limited accommodation to it, while women desperately fight it.

He develops toward a new prospect of physical handsomeness, women do not.

It is therefore not surprising to find that cosmetic surgery and the use of cosmetics among middle-aged women are aimed not so much at making women look like more attractive middle-aged women but at reducing and hiding the effects of aging. When middle-aged women between the ages of forty-five and fifty-five are shown pictures of other middle-aged women, they rate them very negatively. In fact, they rate them more critically than men and women of all other ages who are shown the same pictures (Nowak, 1977). This emphasis on physical aging may explain why older women argue that middle age begins at thirty-five while older men believe it begins much later, at age fifty (Jackson, 1974).

Thus, women are faced with two problems of aging. First, people do not seem to have the very positive physical image of the older woman that they have of the middle-aged man. Women do not have any model to grow into. Second, if a woman defines herself in terms of her body image and attractiveness, as stereotyped by society, she is likely to find that she is fighting a losing battle and may experience a crisis of confidence in herself. On the other hand, her husband is less likely to define himself in these physical terms, and aging is psychologically a more gentle process for him.

Sexuality

When we think about sexuality, we get a picture of teenagers or young adults in the throes of passion. The idea that our parents, and especially our grandparents, are sexually active is rejected, if it even occurs to us at all. When I was once lecturing on the increase in interest in sexuality shown by this generation's middle-age and older people, one eighteen-year-old blurted out, "My father maybe, but my mother never." When 646 college students were asked to estimate the extent of their parents' sexual activity, half these students believed that their parents had sexual intercourse about once a month or less (Pocs and Godow, 1976). The researchers had no real data on how often these students' parents engaged in intercourse, but comparing the results with Kinsey's data of about seven times a month for people in their forties, these students drastically underestimated their parents' sexual activity. Younger people refuse to see older people as having any interest in sex.

True or False   Most college students underestimate their parents' sexual activity.

Shortly after getting married, there is a considerable decline in sexual activity, but this does not mean that middle-aged adults lose interest in sex. Just the opposite is true. There is evidence that middle-aged people are having more sex and using a greater variety of techniques than people in the middle years did a generation or two ago (Hunt, 1974). Some physical changes in middle age can affect sexual interest and activity but do not really interfere with the enjoyment of sex in middle age. Some changes may even enhance it.

The well-known research team, Masters and Johnson (1966), studied 270 married couples and 142 unmarried males and females ranging in age from eighteen to eighty-nine and found that sexual response could be conceptualized as occurring in four stages. In the *arousal stage*, the penis becomes erect and the woman's vaginal secretions increase. Muscle tension increases, the body be-

comes flushed, and the heart rate increases. During the *plateau stage*, the penis is fully erect and the vagina is well lubricated. The uterus becomes elevated and the testicles become enlarged and also somewhat elevated. In the *orgasm stage*, a pulsating release of sexual tension occurs, which is followed by the *resolution stage*, in which the body returns to its normal state. In males, the resolution stage is followed by a period of inactivity, called the refractory period, in which genital activity is not possible. The most common effect of aging on male sexuality is that each stage of the cycle lasts longer. Thus, the older male takes more time to obtain an erection and is capable of keeping one for a longer period of time before ejaculating. This can actually lead to an improvement in a couple's sex life, because the man can prolong the experience, allowing his partner more time to reach a climax. Other physical changes in males include a reduction in testosterone levels between the ages of forty and sixty, after which it levels off, an increase in the refractory period, and a qualitative change from an intense genital focus to a more diffused generalized pleasure (Knox, 1985).

True or False   Middle-aged men take less time to achieve orgasm than young adult men.

Some of the changes in middle-aged women that relate to sex have a similar effect. It now takes longer for women to become aroused. Lower levels of sex hormones cause the vagina to become shorter and narrower, and the vaginal walls become thinner and less expansive. Vaginal lubrication becomes slower and less intense. Middle-aged women also have fewer contractions during the orgasm stage (Rosen and Rosen, 1981). Sexual interest remains high, and there is evidence that postmenopausal women have an increased interest in sex (Knox, 1985). When sexual problems in aging couples do occur, it is much more likely that they are due to situational or psychological problems than to physical difficulties.

How sexually active middle-aged adults are depends on their sexual practices in early adulthood (Pfeiffer and Davis, 1972). People who have a high interest in sex and were sexually active in their younger days continue to remain interested as they advance through life. Between the ages of forty-five and sixty-nine, health status and life satisfaction correlate positively with sexual functioning for men, while certain medications and an in-

In some sports, older champions such as Arnold Palmer continue to play on a tour in which they compete with other middle-aged champions.

creased concern for physical well-being seem to decrease sexual interest. For women, the overwhelming determinant of sexual expression in middle age is marital status: married women engage in a much greater amount of sexual activity than women who are not married.

In sum, biological changes do not limit sexual activity in middle age. The most important physiological change affecting sexual activity is that each stage is reached more slowly (Pfeiffer, 1983), which does not reduce pleasure but may actually enhance it. In addition, the greatest predictor of sexuality in aging is past sexuality. If a couple has a satisfying sex life in young adulthood, chances are it will continue to be satisfying in middle age.

Menopause

Few events in an individual's life have been as misunderstood as menopause. **Menopause** is the cessation of a woman's menstrual cycle. Another term often confused with menopause is **climacteric,** which encompasses all the physical changes that bring someone from a state of fertility to a state of infertility. The climacteric is the counterpart to puberty, whereas menopause is the counterpart to menstruation (Timiras and Meisami, 1972).

Most women experience menopause somewhere between the ages of forty-two and fifty-two. Menopause is caused by a reduction in estrogen secretions. Estrogen and progesterone secretion declines as the functioning of the ovaries decreases. The pituitary still tries to stimulate the ovaries to produce sex hormones, but the ovaries do not respond. Ovulation ceases, the menstrual cycle disappears, and the woman becomes infertile (Strand, 1983; Williams, 1977). Estrogen found in postmenopausal women is derived from the conversion of a hormone produced in the adrenal glands.

Other biological changes associated with a woman's climacteric include shrinking of the external genitalia, a decrease in pubic hair, thinning of the vaginal canal and reduction in vaginal secretions, and a decrease in size of the ovaries and uterus. The ligaments supporting these structures lose their elasticity, as do muscles and skin (Saxon and Etten, 1978).

The drastic decline of estrogen precipitates the physiological symptoms associated with menopause (Doering, 1980). The physical symptoms include hot flashes, depression, irritability, dizziness, heart palpitations, and headaches (Smallwood and Van Dyck, 1979). In a much-quoted British study of 638 women, 30 to 50 percent reported experiencing some of these symptoms, with about half experiencing hot flashes. About half of those experiencing hot flashes reported that the hot flashes made them uncomfortable (McKinlay and Jeffreys, 1974). When a symptoms checklist was given to 460 women in six age-groups, the groups with the highest symptoms were adolescents and menopausal women. Nonmenopausal women in the group of women age forty-five to fifty-four reported fewer symptoms than menopausal women. Postmenopausal women reported the fewest number of physical complaints (Neugarten and Kraines, 1965). Although many women surveyed experience some discomfort, most do not seek medical treatment for it (Neugarten,

menopause The cessation of a woman's menstrual cycle.

climacteric A term used to describe all the physical changes bringing someone from a state of fertility to one of infertility.

> **heart attack** (also **myocardial infarction**)   The death of a part of the heart muscle due to interruption of the blood supply.

1970). Many studies concentrating on menopausal women receiving medical treatment for their symptoms do not reflect the experience of most women during this stage.

> *True or False*   A dramatic increase in estrogen production causes women to experience uncomfortable symptoms in menopause, such as hot flashes.

Although the majority of women report some symptoms, most are not unduly affected by them. Yet menopausal women are stereotyped as unreliable and emotional. In 1976 a Canadian judge ruled against a forty-eight-year-old woman on the grounds that "women at that age may be menopausal and it is known that the testimony of that age group is unreliable" (Palmore, 1983, p. 55). The evidence does not support this judge's conclusions at all. When 100 women were asked to select causes of stress that bothered them, only 4 cited menopause as a major source of worry. When asked what they disliked about middle age, only one mentioned menopause. Only 12 women could not mention anything good about menopause, while 30 could not think of anything bad about it (Neugarten, 1970).

Women may be negatively affected by their attitudes toward menopause. The degree of anxiety depends on how they feel about no longer being able to have children, what they know about the symptoms of menopause, and their anxiety about growing old (Newman, 1982). Young women often fear menopause, perhaps because they confuse the physiological changes with the negative connotation of growing older. Neugarten and her colleagues (1963) found that among their sample of women over age forty-five who had already negotiated menopause, attitudes toward menopause were positive. They were aware that it brought freedom from the worry of pregnancy and an upsurge in sexual interest and activity. Culture too affects psychological reactions to menopause. In a survey of various cultures around the world, Griffen (1977) found a number of different reactions to menopause. In eight cultures there were no behavior changes for postmenopausal women. Women in India greeted menopause with relief. In a small minority of cultures menopause is considered a disorder. In other cultures, taboos present during the childbearing years, such as eating certain meats, are erased at menopause. Cultural beliefs, then, are likely to affect one's view of menopause as well as one's behavior.

The Male Climacteric

We are slowly accumulating research data showing that males also proceed through a climacteric, although it is slower and more gradual (Bischof, 1976). Between the ages of about forty and sixty, testosterone levels decline, causing a decrease in the size of the testes. Fewer sperm are produced, ejaculatory force is diminished, and the size of the prostate gland increases. In addition, sexual excitement develops more slowly (Saxon and Etten, 1978). Enlargement of the prostate may lead to urinary-tract problems, and cancer of the prostate during middle age is not uncommon. Mood swings and changes in self-concept also occur, but these problems are more likely to stem from difficulties in coping with aging than from the biological changes themselves (Williams, 1977). Men have the ability to impregnate females their whole lives.

Health Factors in Middle Adulthood

We are shocked to hear that a young adult has died of cancer or heart disease. We are more likely to shake our heads and accept the death of a middle-aged person who succumbs to one of these killers. In fact, after the age of thirty the number of deaths from accidents declines and deaths from disease increase. Among males age forty-five to sixty-four, the most common cause of death is related to cardiovascular problems, while among women of the same age, cancer is the most common cause of death (Pacovsky and Hermanova, 1983). The incidence of cancer and heart disease, as well as the death rate from these diseases, increases steadily in middle age (see Figures 16.1 and 16.2).

> *True or False*   Cardiovascular disease is the most common cause of death among middle-aged men and women.

Heart Attack and Hypertension

A **heart attack** involves the death of a part of the heart muscle caused by an interruption of the blood supply. A heart attack is also called a **myocardial infarction** (Gasner and McCleary, 1982). This is caused by a clot in a branch of a coronary artery. The problem is in the arterial walls. As people age, their arteries lose their elasticity and begin to thicken. This hardening of the arteries is called **arteriosclerosis.** Although we do not know the exact cause of this phenomenon, we do know that it is associated with genetic factors, hormones, diet, and certain diseases, such as diabetes (Napoli, 1982). Although most people have some form of the condition, they experience no bothersome symptoms. It may start very early. Autopsies on American soldiers killed in action during the Korean War showed that more than 75 percent had some form of arteriosclerosis, and 15 percent had severe cases. This was not the case for Koreans killed in action (Napoli, 1981; Chew, 1976).

One form of arteriosclerosis is called **atherosclerosis,** in which the inner walls of the artery are made thick and irregular by a fatty substance called *plaque.* This plaque consists of a fat called cholesterol, as well as other materials. The blood clots on top of this plaque. Due to elevated levels of cholesterol, however, the blood clot does not disintegrate, but actually grows. When these

arteriosclerosis A condition in which the arteries lose their elasticity as they harden.

atherosclerosis A condition in which the inner walls of the artery become thick and irregular due to a buildup of plaque.

hypertension High blood pressure.

plaques block the blood flow or break off and lodge somewhere else in the coronary artery, a portion of the heart is starved from lack of oxygen and nutrients and dies. The person has now suffered a heart attack (Gasner and McCleary, 1982). If an artery that serves the brain is obstructed, brain cells will be starved and some loss of function may occur. We call this a *stroke.* Although a stroke or heart attack may occur suddenly, it is actually the result of many years of arterial narrowing (Simons, 1972).

Hypertension, or high blood pressure, contributes to many heart problems. High blood pressure damages and weakens the lining of the coronary and cerebral (brain) arteries and causes vascular problems in the brain. It may also damage the eyes and kidneys and injure the heart muscle (Gasner and McCleary, 1981). It also contributes to arteriosclerosis. About 60 million Americans suffer from hypertension, but only in about 5 percent of the cases is the actual cause known.

There are many suspected causes of hypertension and heart disease, including obesity, excessive intake of salt, stress, smoking, personality factors such as the Type A personality (see Chapter 14), and genetic predisposition. These factors have a cumulative effect: the more factors present in a person's life, the greater the likelihood of developing heart disease. The frightening thing about hypertension is that about half the people who have it are not aware that they do (Diekelmann, 1977). In fact, hypertension is called the silent killer because in the early stages it does not have any noticeable symptoms. Only by having their blood pressure checked can people be certain that their blood pressure is within normal limits (Weaver, 1980). People who have high blood pressure can be treated with medication and/or changes in diet and lifestyle.

Although it is still the number-one killer in the United States, the death rate from heart disease has decreased over the past thirty years. One reason for the decrease is medical breakthroughs, including better medication

---

FIGURE 16.1

Deaths from Heart Disease

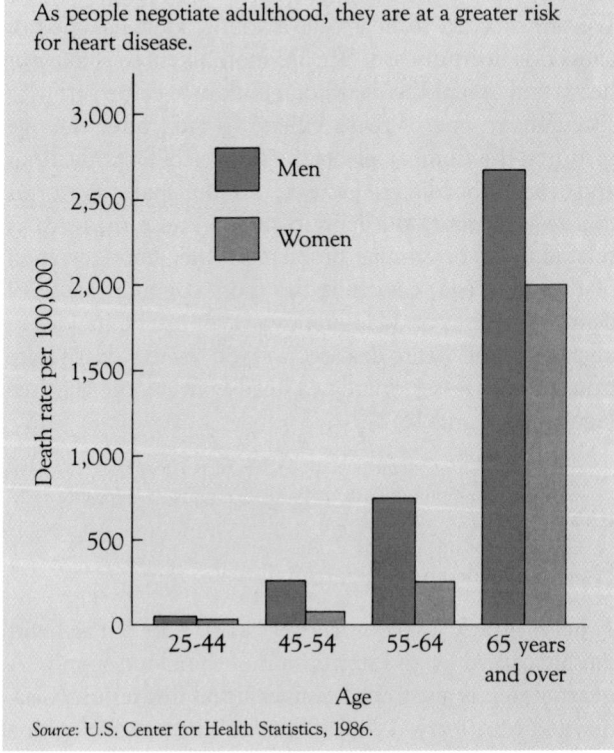

As people negotiate adulthood, they are at a greater risk for heart disease.

Source: U.S. Center for Health Statistics, 1986.

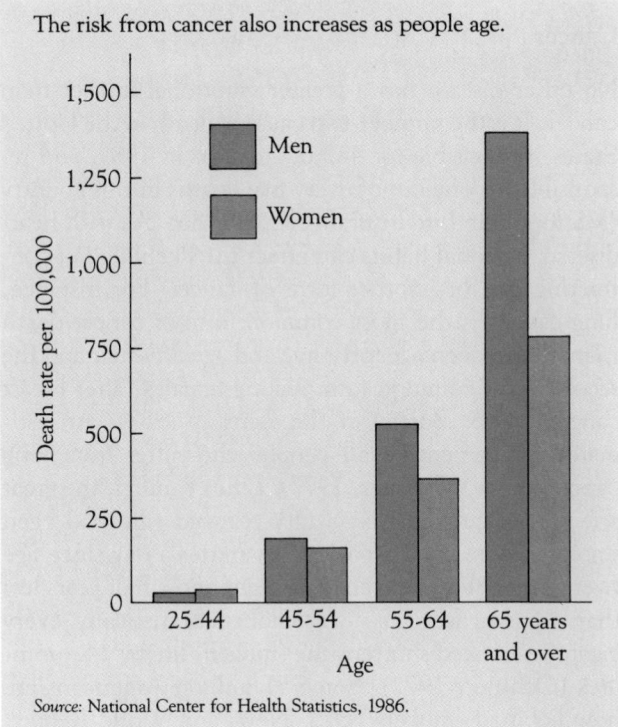

FIGURE 16.2

Deaths from Cancer

The risk from cancer also increases as people age.

Source: National Center for Health Statistics, 1986.

to control hypertension and improved surgical procedures, but credit must also go to preventive steps taken by people who are now better educated concerning the risks of heart disease. People are much more aware of how lifestyle affects health. More than three-fourths of the public understand that hypertension is related to diet, and over half know that salt or sodium and consumption of cholesterol and fats are related to heart disease. Even since 1979 there has been an increase in understanding (Heimbach, 1985).

True or False Most people are not aware of the link between heart disease and diet.

And people are putting what they know into practice. In one study, young, middle-aged, and older adults were asked about sleep habits, avoidance of salt, diet, how they coped with stress, and other factors. The results showed that as people aged they began living healthier lives. The middle-aged group was more likely than younger adults to eat a balanced diet, obtain good medical information, avoid smoking, use salt sparingly, and eat

high-fiber foods. The elderly were even more likely than the middle-aged subjects to take these steps. The same pattern held for stress reduction, with middle-aged people reporting avoidance of stress, having a good family life, avoiding anger, and thinking more positively than younger adults, but less than the elderly. The only health practice that declined with age was exercise (Prohaska et al., 1985). However, this may change somewhat in the future, as young adults—who are exercising at a higher rate than young adults did a generation ago—become middle-aged and, it is hoped, continue the practice.

True or False As people age, their health habits improve.

Stress

In Chapter 14 we saw that both everyday stresses and changes in life events, as well as certain aspects of the personality, were important in understanding stress. People with the Type A personality pattern are hostile, aggressive, impatient, ambitious, and do everything in a hurry, while Type B people take life easier and are not as rushed. Although we do not know for sure why this is related to coronary artery disease, hormonal changes and increased heart rate may be factors. A number of studies show that Type A people show greater cardiovascular and neuroendocrine responses to life events. Although both men and women are thought to be at risk, not all the evidence has found greater cardiovascular responsivity in Type A women as compared with Type B women (Harbin and Blumenthal, 1985). How people cope with stress may also be a factor in the effect stress has on the body. Our own inner resources—plus support from family and friends, professional help, and our attitudes toward life events—are important factors (Ebersole and Hess, 1981).

These basic elements in stress are the same at any age, but stress in middle age is different from stress during the young adult period in two ways. First, it takes longer for middle-aged people to cope with and bounce back from stress (Chew, 1976). Second, the effects of stress are cumulative and take time to show up; in middle age, they may finally show through in heart attacks and other illnesses.

Many major companies, recognizing the relationship between stress and illness and other work-related problems such as absenteeism, have established programs to help employees deal with stress. Such programs may involve physical activity, relaxation-training, and alcoholism and drug-counseling. About 20 percent of the largest firms in the United States have some sort of stress-management program. For example, the Equitable Life Assurance Society in New York gave employees who frequently reported stress-related health complaints an opportunity to participate in a stress-reduction program. It reduced the number of visits to the medical office from an average of twenty-four to about six. The company saved $5.52 in medical costs for every dollar it invested in the program. At New York Telephone, periodic health exams and meditation lessons for those with stress-related symptoms cut the hypertension rate among workers from 18 percent to about 9 percent, and saved an estimated

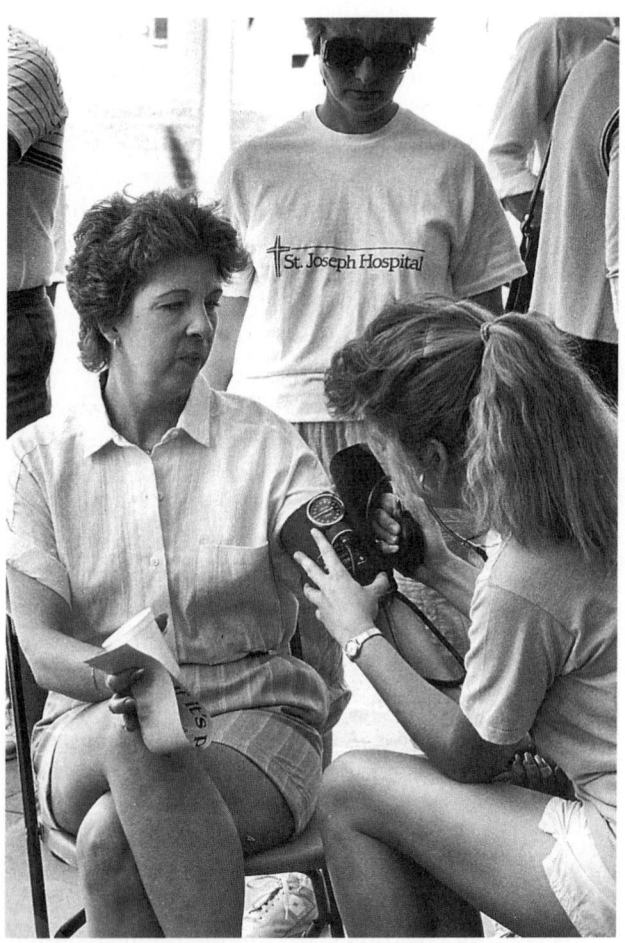

About 60 million Americans suffer from hypertension, also known as high blood pressure.

$130,000 a year from reduced absenteeism alone (*Time*, 1983).

Cancer

No other disease has a greater emotional impact than cancer. It is the number-two cause of death in the United States, responsible for 462,000 deaths in 1985, and responsible for one out of every five deaths in this country (Metropolitan Life Insurance Co., 1986). As with heart disease, personal habits can affect the likelihood of contracting one or another form of cancer. For instance, lung cancer is the most common form of cancer death in males between age forty-five and age fifty-four and the second most common form among females (after breast cancer) (U.S. Bureau of the Census, 1985). An estimated 90 percent of all people who suffer from lung cancer smoke (Ochsner, 1972). Linus Pauling, the great scientist calculated that a fifty-year-old who had been smoking more than a pack of cigarettes a day since age twenty-one lives an average of eight and a half years less than someone who has never smoked. Statistically, every cigarette smoked shortens the smoker's life by 14.4 minutes (Ochsner, 1972). Some 51 million Americans are now habitual smokers (U.S. News and World Report, August 17, 1987). Smoking is the most preventable cause of major health problems, including heart disease and cancer, in the United States today (Krantz et al., 1985).

Breast cancer is the leading cause of death among women between the ages of thirty and fifty-five. One in thirteen women will develop it (Hellman, 1982). Self-examination and periodic gynecological procedures can help detect such cancer early and lead to more successful treatment.

Diet

The nutritional problems that were evident during the early adulthood stage—namely, ingestion of too many calories for the amount of physical activity engaged in—become even more pronounced during the middle adult years. People are likely to be even less active, and basal metabolism (the rate at which food is burned) decreases. This means that even if caloric intake remains the same, a person will gain weight (Long and Shannon, 1983), perhaps a couple of pounds a year. During this stage of life, fat intake—which increases risk of heart disease and cancer—should be reduced as well as calorie intake. In addition, certain minerals are especially important. Women's need for iron remains high at least until menopause. In addition, the need for calcium to maintain healthy bones and teeth is great, and for postmenopausal women the daily calcium requirement actually increases (Notelovitz and Ware, 1982). Long-standing inadequate calcium intake is one factor implicated in osteoporosis, a disorder in which the bones become brittle and lose their mass (Hongladarom et al., 1982). Osteoporosis (see Chapter 18) is much more frequent in females than in males.

The relationship of diet to disease is not a simple one. The public has accepted this relationship with respect to heart disease, and as a result people are watching their salt and fat intake more. But the question of how diet and cancer may be related has recently taken a controversial turn. Certain types of cancer, such as colon and rectal cancer, appear to be related to an excessive amount of fat and a low amount of fiber in the diet. A number of new "anti-cancer" diets have been formulated. They include greater amounts of fiber, based on evidence that fiber shortens the amount of time cancer-causing agents are in the colon and rectum (Burkitt, 1978). They also involve reducing ingestion of fat, which has been linked to the incidence of cancer as well (Hamilton and Whitney, 1982), and eating more fruits and vegetables, especially those in the cabbage family. However, it is important to note that other factors, such as environmental exposure to cancer-causing substances and genetic factors, may be involved and that no one knows the extent to which such dietary corrections will help reduce the risk of cancer.

Sensory Changes in Middle Adulthood

Any sensory decline during early adulthood is minor, but in middle age the declines become more noticeable. Yet some important factors should be kept in mind. First, a person's general physical health should be taken into consideration. In healthy middle-aged people who take care of themselves by exercising and practicing good health habits, the declines are not nearly so great as in adults who do not follow these health practices. Second, the decline that does take place may not have any effect at all on a person's day-to-day life. For instance, the increase in reaction time of a fraction of a second makes no difference in our daily life. Whether one responds to a telephone signal a tenth of a second more or less makes

presbyopia A form of farsightedness occurring in late middle age and beyond.

little difference. Many of the studies performed on sensory functioning take place in the laboratory under artificial circumstances. Middle-aged people may not be as motivated on such artificial tasks, which have little or nothing to do with real-life problems. Third, middle-aged people can compensate for some of the decline. Eyeglasses, hearing aids, and, above all, experience are helpful. Finally, most of the changes reflect more the need of each sense for a higher level of stimulation in order to function, rather than any traumatic reduction in the sensory functioning itself (Newman, 1982). For example, middle-aged people may find they need more light to read or may need to turn up the volume slightly to hear the whispers of people on the television set.

Vision

Until middle adulthood there is little change in visual acuity. Thereafter, a decline becomes apparent (Botwinick, 1984; Chown, 1983). Middle-aged people may have difficulty seeing things very far away. At the same time, reading may become a problem since the aging eye may also have more difficulty focusing on objects that are very close. The middle-aged person holding a newspaper at arm's length is a common sight. With age, people also become more farsighted, or **presbyopic.** Farsightedness is caused by a decrease in the elasticity of the lens. Bifocals are often used to compensate for these visual problems. Other effects of middle age include a thickening of the lens of the eye and a decline in the ability of the lens to focus (Fozard et al., 1977); increased sensitivity to glare, probably due to the increasing cloudiness of the lens (Walk, 1981); more difficulty with driving at night and less-efficient dark adaptation, making it harder to see in a darkened room (Newman, 1982); decreased depth perception; and smaller pupil size, meaning that more light is needed to see (Saxon and Etten, 1978).

True or False As people age, they often become more farsighted.

Hearing

The ability to hear generally declines in middle adulthood (Schaie and Geiwitz, 1982), specifically the ability to hear high-pitched sounds. This condition, called **presbycusis,** is probably caused by a general degeneration of the auditory system. Men show this decrease before women, possibly because more men than women are exposed to noise pollution in their occupations, such as assembly line work (Marsh and Thompson, 1977). They do not lose their ability to hear these frequencies, but they find it difficult to hear them unless the volume is increased (Corso, 1971). In addition, middle-aged people may find it more difficult to discriminate certain sounds from others and to separate out the sounds they want to hear from background noise. For most people, the practical significance of these hearing losses is not great. For middle-aged people, a bit more volume and concentration may be all that is necessary, and they may not even be aware of the decline in their ability to hear.

True or False Middle-aged people often have difficulty hearing high-frequency tones.

Other Senses

Less research has been performed on the senses of taste, smell, and touch, but it appears that these senses decline slightly throughout middle adulthood. A gradual loss of sensitivity to sweetness and saltiness takes place (Moore et al., 1982; Grzegorczyk et al., 1979), and there is some evidence for a slight decline in general taste sensitivity (Engen, 1977). The decrease in the number of taste buds and the higher threshold of sensitivity needed to activate them begins to show itself in the forties but is of little importance in middle adulthood (Saxon and Etten, 1978). The changes in the ability to smell are more controversial, and although some decrements may take place, they do not appear to be important either (Walk, 1981).

Reaction Time

Perhaps the most common finding is that there is some slowing of most processes in middle adulthood. For example, the time it takes to respond to a stimulus, called reaction time, increases with age (Newman, 1982). Reaction time is measured in two different ways. *Simple reaction time* involves pressing some key or making some response after detecting a stimulus—for example, when

presbycusis The decline in the ability to hear high-pitched sounds.

a buzzer rings, the subject must push a button as soon as possible. *Choice reaction time* involves making one of a number of choices, depending on the stimulus presented (Coren et al., 1979)—for instance, subjects may be asked to push one button when a red light comes on and another when a blue light is flashed. No matter what sense organ is stimulated, an increase in reaction time is found. The slowdown is not from lack of motivation in a laboratory setting, because this has been taken into account in a number of studies (Welford, 1977). Both simple reaction time and choice reaction time are adversely affected by age. In order to succeed on a test of choice reaction time, a subject must first identify which signal has been presented, then make the choice, then initiate the action. All of these processes slow to some extent, causing an increase in reaction time.

True or False Reaction time generally slows with increasing age.

Why the increase in reaction time? If every older person performed worse than every younger person in every study of reaction time and mental processing, it would be easy to explain the slowdown. But this is not the case. In one experiment, Botwinick and Thompson (1968) tested the reaction time of older men averaging above age seventy and young men about twenty years old. Younger subjects were divided into two groups—athletes and nonathletes. The elderly subjects as a group showed slower reaction times than the young athletes did, but they were not much slower than the nonathletes. In fact, 30 percent of the younger subjects were slower in reaction time than the fastest 30 percent of the older sample. The speed of the young nonathletes varied considerably, with some performing better than the older people and some doing not as well. This appears to be true when comparing middle-aged adults with younger adults as well. Age is one factor explaining the slowdown, but other individual factors are important too. When age is correlated with speed on a number of different behaviors, the time it takes to react to stimuli generally increases with age. Yet the relationship is relatively low, showing that more is involved than simple age (Salthouse, 1984). Other variables include the subjects' health, motivation, and training.

A number of theories attempt to explain this increase in the time necessary to respond to a stimulus with age. Some argue that there is a general slowing in the central nervous system—in other words, one consequence of aging is a reduction in the speed at which impulses are conducted in the central nervous system (Botwinick, 1984). Another theory argues that atherosclerosis reduces psychomotor speed. A third theory argues that neural noise is responsible. As people age, cells begin to fire more at random, creating neural noise and making it difficult for older people to differentiate one stimulus from the other. Still others argue that it may result partly from a change in strategy, as older people show more cautious behavior (Welford, 1977). It is possible that some combination of these is correct. The same theories are often used to explain some changes that occur in cognitive functioning in middle adulthood.

Cognition in Middle Adulthood

Suppose you were hiring a group of one hundred people to do a certain job. They must be able to learn a new task, remember how to do it, and do it accurately. Al-though it is illegal to discriminate on the basis of age, let's say you were allowed to hire either a group of young adults or a group of middle-aged people. Which group would you hire?

When I've asked my students this question, they usually choose the young adults—because they believe this group would be more efficient at both learning and performance. But is this really the case? To determine whether the age discrimination that is found so frequently is based on fact or fantasy, we turn to the cognitive development of middle-aged adults—first their intellectual ability, then their memory, then their learning and problem-solving abilities.

Intellectual Abilities

Which of the following statements is correct?

Intellectual abilities increase in mid-life.
Intellectual abilities decrease in mid-life.
Intellectual abilities remain stable throughout middle age.

Research supports all three statements. One reason for this is that individual differences—for example, health, education, and mental and physical fitness—are factors

If you had to hire someone to learn a new task, would you look for a young adult or one who was middle-aged?

Job Structure and Intellectual Functioning

We know that job structure affects the intellectual processes of workers. An exciting, creative job filled with challenges is likely to demand that people exercise their minds to the fullest, while a dull, boring job is likely to demand next to no intellectual skills. However, a finding that people who have intellectually demanding work actually use these processes not only at work but also in other areas of life, such as leisure activities, is more interesting. Simply stated, work is so important that it affects workers' intellectual processes and generalizes to other areas of life. People with challenging jobs exercise their intellectual powers and show more logic and reasoning power, not only at work but also at home.

Does this transfer continue across the life span, or is it specific to one adult period of life—young adulthood, middle age, or later maturity? In addition, exactly what is the relationship between the structure of a person's job and various intellectual processes? These are the basic questions that Joanne Miller, Kazimierz Slomczynski and Melvin Kohn sought to answer using a sample of workers from the United States and Poland. This cross-cultural analysis is especially interesting because it compares workers in a capitalistic state with those in a socialistic or communistic state.

Miller and her colleagues measured the structure of the job by looking at the amount of self-direction it offered. *Self-direction* involves use of "initiative, thought, and independent judgment in work" (p. 595). It was measured in terms of three variables—the complexity of the work, the closeness of supervision, and just how routine the work was. The researchers focused on two aspects of intellectual processes. The first was *ideational flexibility*, which involves the use of logical reasoning, the ability to see both sides of an issue, and independent judgment. The second was *authoritarian conservatism*, which is a measure of obedience to authority and intolerance of nonconformity. It is the opposite of open-mindedness.

More than 3,000 male workers in the United States and more than 1,500 workers in Poland were interviewed and tested. Both samples were stratified by age into three groups: workers younger than thirty, workers between thirty-one and forty-five, and workers older than forty-six. A subgroup of these men was followed for ten years.

The results showed that occupational self-direction affects intellectual process in workers from both countries, and to an almost identical degree. The relationship between the variables involved in self-direction (job complexity, closeness of supervision, and routinization of work) and the two intellectual processes (ideational flexibility and conservative authoritarianism) in Poland and the United States is interesting. In both countries,

that are especially important in mid-life and beyond. People who are healthy and do not abuse drugs score higher on intelligence tests than those who are not well or use drugs. Educated people tend to have an edge in intelligence testing because they are apt to remain intellectually active throughout life. Even the type of job and the way it is structured can affect intellectual functioning. (See the Cross-Cultural Current on this page.)

When people are followed throughout late adolescence and middle adulthood, we find that the intelligence of some people increases while that of others decreases. Still others stay relatively stable in intelligence. One study found that people whose intelligence increased had traveled extensively overseas, had spouses whose adult intelligence was high, and had enjoyed stimulating experiences all through adulthood. People whose intelligence had decreased had drinking problems and experienced little mental stimulation (Honzik, 1985). In fact, until about age seventy, the differences between people of the same chronological age are larger than the differences between age-groups (Schaie and Parham, 1977). As we negotiate middle age, individual differences become more important, but something more than individual differences is involved here.

The relationship of age to different abilities varies, depending on what is being tested and how it is measured

work complexity had the greatest effect on ideational flexibility. The closeness of supervision was more important in the Polish sample than in the American sample, with the routineness of the job being more important in the American sample. As for authoritarian conservatism, job complexity was most important to the American sample, routinization was moderately important, and closeness of supervision was not very important. For the Polish sample, closeness of supervision was the most important factor. The authors believe that in Poland, the authority of basic institutions is more important and obedience is stressed. This generalizes to worker-supervisor relationships. In the United States this is not the case.

These results held for each group. In other words, in the older group the structure of the occupation was just as important to the worker's intellectual functioning as it was to the younger group. The researchers also found interesting reciprocal effects between occupational self-direction and ideational flexibility—that is, the occupational self-direction affects ideational flexibility, and ideational flexibility affects occupational self-direction. In other words, workers both are affected by their job and help create the atmosphere and structure that sur-

round the job. This effect was even stronger for the older group than for the younger group, possibly because those in the older group have advanced to jobs that allow for more self-direction and flexibility.

The researchers conclude that job conditions affect intellectual processes in older men just as much as in younger men. Job conditions can encourage workers to use their intellectual powers, and this was true of workers across the adult life span and in both countries, even though they work under very different economic systems. If workers generalize from work to their outside lives, as prior research shows, the importance of the structure of work takes on new importance. Dull, routine, repetitive jobs stultify intellectual processes both on the job and after work in every age-group. In addition, the finding that people in some ways affect their own jobs shows that people are not entirely at the mercy of others. They can help create the job structure and atmosphere at work. The relationship between job structure and intellectual processes shows how important it is to design jobs so that people are challenged and kept stimulated.

Source: Miller, J., Slomczynski, K. M., and Kohn, M. L. Continuity of Learning-Generalization: The Effect of Job on Men's Intellective Process in the United States and Poland. *American Journal of Sociology,* 1985, 92, 593–615.

(Denney, 1982). For instance, **fluid intelligence,** which is the basic capacity for learning and problem solving including such abilities as memory and the speed of mental work tends to decrease beginning in early adulthood (Botwinick, 1977; Horn and Cattell, 1966). In a similar vein, nonverbal and abstract abilities also decline with age (Bayley, 1970). Studies on the nonverbal performance subtests of the Wechsler Adult Intelligence Scale, such as making a design out of blocks and completing a picture in which something is left out, show a decline in these nonverbal abilities with age (Honzik, 1985). On the other hand, **crystallized intelligence** which involves learned knowledge and skills tends to increase

fluid intelligence The basic capacity for learning and problem solving. It is independent of education and experience.

crystallized intelligence Learned knowledge and skills.

throughout middle adulthood (Horn and Donaldson, 1980; McCarthy et al., 1982).

But are we really measuring familiarity of task on these tests? After all, many people use their verbal skills throughout life but allow nonverbal skills, which may not be as useful in middle age, to decline. When abilities are exercised, they remain relatively constant throughout most of adulthood, but abilities that are not used decline (Denney, 1982). In other words, adults might find nonverbal tasks more difficult merely because they have not used the skills involved for years. Indeed, studies have found that as people age they find tests of fluid ability more difficult and less familiar than verbal tests (Cornelius, 1984).

The old problem of how these skills are measured arises too. Longitudinal studies tend to show less of a decline throughout adulthood than cross-sectional studies. However, even those who argue that there is a decline throughout adulthood find that the decline in fluid intelligence is moderate until after age fifty, while crystallized intelligence tends to improve through middle age and into later adulthood (Horn and Donaldson, 1980). Others deny that much of a decline in intelligence occurs during middle age, and in one fourteen-year study of people age twenty-two to sixty-seven, the decline in adult intelligence became evident between age fifty-three and age sixty-seven but was most definite after age sixty (Schaie and Hertzog, 1983). What made this study special was the combination longitudinal and cross-sectional design. As you would expect, the effects of aging differed, depending on the way the material was measured as well as on the task itself. For example, in the longitudinal study, inductive reasoning was found to improve from age twenty-five through age thirty-nine, but in the cross-sectional study there was a decline between age thirty-two and forty-six. However, there was no further decrease throughout the rest of middle age. The researchers note that although a decline may begin during late middle age, it does not become clearly evident until age sixty. They deny that any major decline in intelligence occurs during the period of middle age.

There is little disagreement that intellectual abilities decline sometime in adulthood—the question is when and why. Some say the decline begins early, others say not until old age. What causes the decline is of vital importance and remains controversial. No one really knows why fluid intelligence decreases, and the theories attempting to explain this phenomenon are mainly repetitions of theories seeking to explain the increase in reaction time with age. If the decrease is due to central nervous system decline resulting from the normal aging process (see Horn and Donaldson, 1980), then we will all be affected to some extent as we age. On the other hand, the evidence that people who are mentally active, physically fit, and watch their eating and health habits show few if any of these declines indicates that experience is probably as or more important than physiological factors.

Memory

People are always complaining about their memories, and they tend to blame their age when they can't remember something. To what extent do various memory functions decline with age?

Visual memory declines only minimally until age sixty, after which a significant decline occurs (Riebe and Inman, 1981). Auditory memory shows a drop between the ages of twenty and forty, and no decline after. Tactual memory shows a gradual decline with age. There is no evidence that sensory memory—memory that lasts for only a second before it must be attended to—changes much over the life span (Baltes et al., 1980). The number of items held in short-term memory—memory that lasts for about thirty seconds—increases during childhood, peaks in early adulthood, and declines thereafter (Baltes, 1980). The differences in short-term memory ability throughout adulthood are relatively small (Wingfield and Byrnes, 1981). The time it takes to scan information increases with age (Anders and Fozard, 1973). These changes, though, are also minor.

Long-term memory declines somewhat during middle adulthood, but again the changes are not great. There is an age-related decline in recall, with young adults performing better than middle-aged adults, who in turn do better than the elderly (Smith, 1977). However, recognition remains excellent (Schonfield and Robertson, 1966). In one study, young adults right out of high school and older adults of about fifty years of age were tested on both recall and recognition of high school acquaintances. In recognition, the older adults did just about as well as the eighteen-year-olds, even though they had been out of high school for so long (Bahrick et al., 1975). Other studies measuring memory for news items found a decline in recall with increasing age, but not much change in recognition ability (Warrington and Silberstein, 1970). Whatever reductions in memory abilities do occur are probably the result of an increase in the time people take to process information with increasing age (Salthouse and Kail, 1983).

Middle-aged people can easily improve their memory by using better organization and imagery. Mason and Smith (1977) tested young, middle-aged, and late adults on free recall of words from a list. Middle-aged people benefited from instructions that told them to use visual imagery, while the others did not. Hultsch (1975) found that when middle-aged people age forty-five to fifty-four were told how best to organize material, they improved their memory ability greatly. Finally, people who use their memory do well on tests of memory. In one study, ten young adults, ten middle-aged students in a university, ten middle-aged people not attending school, and ten elderly people were compared on memory ability and the strategies they used. On all measures of memories and strategies used, the two groups attending school were more alike and the two out-of-school groups were more similar to each other than the two middle-aged groups (Zivian and Darjes, 1983). Perhaps the educational experience requires people to practice their memory skills. Declines in memory and memory strategies may not be due to age alone. The researchers note that "adults of the same age may differ in memory performance, and adults differing in age may perform similarly" (Zivian and Darjes, 1983, p. 519).

The results of these studies are heartening. Some deficits may occur in recall, but not in recognition memory (Botwinick, 1973). As people age, it may take them longer to recall certain events, but these changes are not serious and do not appear to affect daily functioning. Again, activity and practice appear to be important. In addition, the slight loss in recall can be compensated for by better organization and the use of imagery.

Learning and Problem-Solving in Adulthood

One controversy surrounding hiring middle-aged people is how well they can learn new skills and information. Some people are surprised to discover that most studies find little or no differences in adult learning until about age sixty (Botwinick, 1977). This is especially true if the material is meaningful for the adult. When Denney and Palmer (1980) tested adults across the age span on both abstract and realistic problems, a performance decline on abstract problems was found beginning in early adulthood, but performance on realistic and practical problems peaked in the forties or fifties and showed some decline thereafter. In an extensive study, known as the Baltimore Longitudinal Study, learning and memory tasks

were analyzed cross-sectionally across the age span. Very small age differences were found prior to age sixty (Arenberg and Robertson-Tchabo, 1977).

True or False In middle age there is a decline in ability to solve practical problems.

This does not necessarily mean that there are no differences between middle-aged and younger learners in the learning process. The retrieval and response time of older learners tends to be greater (Monge and Hultsch, 1971). Allowing additional time for study and learning will lead to better performance. Actually, everyone performs better under these conditions, but the middle-aged and the elderly are likely to benefit even more from these changes. Sometimes middle-aged people need help in organizing new material, especially if it is unfamiliar. Again, all people improve when they are taught how to organize material for efficient learning, but older people benefit even more. When Rowe and Schnore (1971) investigated the use of such strategies as repetition and visual imagery, young adults performed better than the middle-aged, whose performance was in turn superior to that of the elderly. Younger adults use mnemonic devices and other strategies that organize the material more often than older adults. Education may be as or more important than age in determining the use of these strategies (Zivian and Darjes, 1983). However, studies with middle-aged and older workers show that they need help learning to attend to relevant cues and must be taught to use control strategies (Arenberg and Robertson-Tchabo, 1977). When this is done, middle-aged people do well with learning and problem-solving tasks.

In summary, while the learning and problem-solving abilities of middle-aged people are truly excellent and show little or no decline, there are some qualitative differences in learning. Their response time is slower, and they are helped significantly by superior organization and by instruction in strategies that are useful in discriminating between what is relevant and what is not and if the problems are realistic.

What can we conclude concerning hiring middle-aged or young adults as workers and trainees? Judith Stevens-Long (1984, p. 287) answers this question. "It would seem wise to enlist the services of the young if one needed to receive and decode fast-paced messages transmitted at high frequencies by the light of the waning moon, especially if the messages were constantly interrupted by CB radio transmission and masked by static noise. Still, it might be useful to have a middle-aged person on hand to decide how the information should be used." The evidence indicates that middle-aged people are very capable learners and trainees and that age is no impediment to learning.

Formal Education

Even a casual look around a college campus will tell us that more middle-aged adults are taking courses and graduating from colleges and universities than ever before. In 1970, males over age thirty-five accounted for 2.4 percent of the college population, while in 1982 they accounted for 4 percent. In 1970, females over the age of thirty-five accounted for 2.5 percent of the college enrollment, while in 1982 they accounted for 7.3 percent. Projections of college populations through 1990 show that this trend will probably continue.

Why are middle-aged people returning to school in such numbers? For some, a career change necessitates further training. A man who found he could not get anywhere in the mailroom returns to school for accounting courses. A homemaker returns to school to prepare

Studies show that this mentally active middle-aged person should have no difficulty remembering the important material being taught here.

for a job selling insurance. Others return to school in order to broaden their horizons. A middle-aged man once told me he was taking psychology, philosophy, and mythology and loving it. It was a way to use his mind—something he couldn't do on his boring job. Others have no specific goals in mind but return to school because they crave more stimulation in life. Some might return to school to achieve the dream of receiving the college education they either could not or did not pursue in their earlier years.

Middle-aged learners have a number of assets when it comes to learning, as well as some special problems. Haponski and McCabe (1982) list the following assets for adults returning to college: The life experiences of adults often help them contribute more to the class. They show a greater eagerness to learn, and more commitment, because attending school often requires some personal sacrifice. They spend more time studying and show a willingness to ask questions. They often have a better idea of why they are there. The liabilities of being an older student include greater susceptibility to fear of failure and greater external pressures, which make it difficult to study.

Learning Throughout Adulthood: A Model

No one knows the extent to which the relatively small age-related changes in learning and memory affect middle-aged people trying to learn something new. As we have seen, the changes do not seem very great. Some difficulties probably arise because the abilities required in academic areas have not been used extensively for years. Studies have shown that abilities that are not used tend to decay more rapidly than those that are used. Nancy Denney (1982) argues that the decline after early adulthood is definite in abilities that are not exercised but that practice and experience clearly have an influence on cognitive abilities. Figure 16.3 demonstrates this concept. Unexercised abilities are a function of both biological potential and normal environmental experience. Optimally exercised abilities reflect the maximum ability attained by a normal, healthy person under optimal training and exercise. The space between the curves is the amount that both practice and training affect performance. Denney uses the example of running to illustrate how this model operates. The curve for unexercised ability indicates how well an individual could run at any age if he or she did not have any practice. The optimal

Developmental Functions of Unexercised and Optimally Exercised Cognitive Abilities

The curve for unexercised abilities reflects biological potential and normal experience. The curve for optimally exercised ability reflects the ability attained through optimal training and exercise while the space between the curves shows how practice and training affects performance. Notice how much better people do when their abilities are exercised.

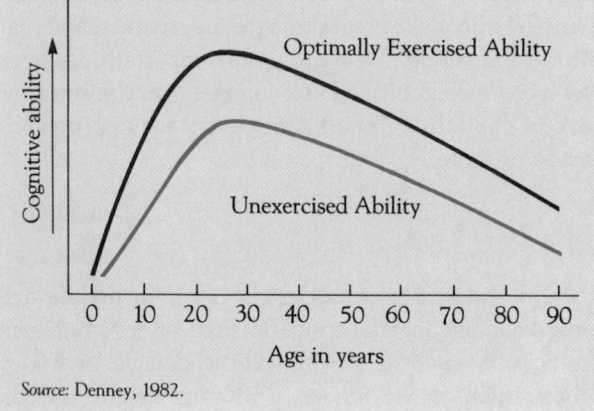

Source: Denney, 1982.

exercise curve shows how well that person could perform if given the best training. Notice that if given enough training an individual could run better at age fifty than he would at age twenty with no practice. However, a seventy-year-old with training would not do so well as a twenty-year-old without training.

True or False Abilities that are exercised show no decline until old age.

The analysis is the same for cognitive abilities. For example, if this curve was used to analyze cognitive abilities it would show a decline starting in early adulthood for unexercised abilities—for instance, abstract problem-solving. However, people can improve their abilities throughout life with training and practice, and the decrease in exercised abilities is not as much as for unexercised abilities. The curve for optimally exercised abilities also is shown to decline, although the decline may not take place until later in life. Keep in mind that there is much individual variation, depending on native ability, training, and experience. Different abilities follow different curves over the life span. For instance, the curve for nonverbal abilities such as picture completion and

block design show a curve similar to that for non-exercised abilities because these abilities are not used very much in adulthood. Verbal abilities are exercised and remain stable throughout middle adulthood. The same analysis is useful when looking at problem solving abilities. Traditional laboratory tests often use problems that are abstract and so one would expect a decline and indeed one is found. However, when middle aged people are asked to solve practical problems they show an improvement through the forties and fifties and some decline after.

This model is important because it explains the decline or lack of decline in specific abilities across the life span. Abilities that are exercised decline less than those that are not exercised, and different abilities follow different paths.

Creativity in Adulthood

Creativity is not an easy term to define or study (see Chapter 9). Evaluating one adult achievement as creative and another as not is very difficult. Although everyone agrees that creativity is possible at every age, psychologists have long been interested in when people are most creative.

The most famous studies on adult creativity were performed by Harvey Lehman (1963; 1953), who spent twenty years looking at the quantity and quality of the work of scientists and philosophers, among other professionals. Lehman argued that the thirties were the most productive years from the point of view of quality work. This fits well with Vaillant's (1977) belief that the thirties were the more career-conscious decade for workers. In terms of quality, creative work then peaks before middle age or during the very beginning of the period, although some creative work of lesser value continues throughout life (see Figure 16.4). People in certain fields produced their most important work earlier than people in other fields. For example, astronomers produced their best work in their mid-forties, psychologists in their late thirties, and musicians at an even younger age (Lehman, 1965). For philosophers with long lives, the peak was much later, actually in the sixties. Throughout his work, Lehman stressed that quality of work was not bounded by age, that he was dealing only with the most important discoveries and the average age at which they were made.

Lehman has been criticized severely for his conclusion that creativity peaks early in life. One major argument is that he did not take into consideration the fact that

FIGURE 16.4

Creative Output in Relation to Age

Lehman argues that the quality of creative work peaks relatively early in adulthood.

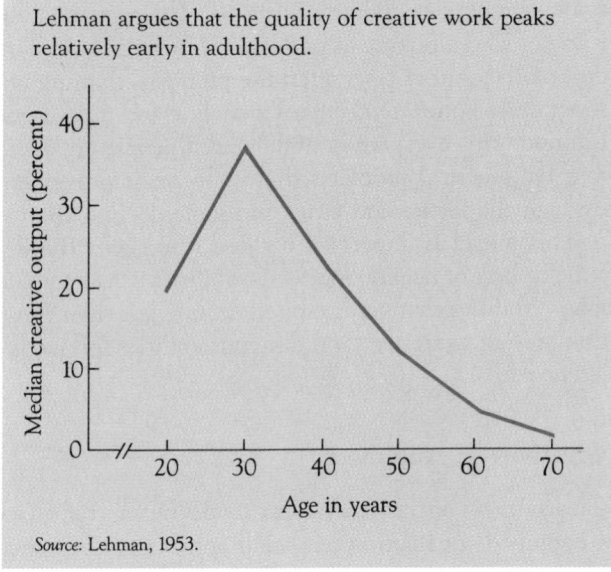

Source: Lehman, 1953.

years ago people did not live as long. In other words, a person who lived only to age forty did not have a chance to produce quality work past that age. Dennis (1966) believes that this invalidates Lehman's conclusions. Dennis analyzed the work of people who lived long lives and found that peak performances occur throughout the entire age range. There are differences in peak performance for the humanities, sciences, and arts (Figure 16.5), but creative acts continued at a high rate throughout life. Dennis found that creativity began to decline during the decade before death and that some decline may occur in late middle age in the fields of music and literature. One problem with Dennis' work is that it may reflect *quantity* of output, while Lehman looked at *quality*. Of course, quality is a difficult element to measure. In another study, Simonton (1977) found that while total production of music from great composers peaked between the ages of forty-five and forty-nine, their most original contributions peaked between thirty and thirty-four years of age and then declined. Other studies suggest that the peak age for producing creative work is in early middle age, between forty and forty-four, and suggest a slower decline that Lehman does (see Cole, 1979). In almost all these studies, early middle age seems to be a very productive time in life.

What can we conclude about creativity across the life span? Some argue that creativity does show some decline after the forties (Chown, 1977), but everyone agrees that high-quality creative work can be produced throughout adulthood. If creative work does decline after early middle age, the vital question becomes why. One possibility is that creative middle-aged people are often placed in charge of others and become more involved in administration and management (Diamond, 1986). In other words, they switch career paths and do not have as much opportunity in their own field to be creative. In addition, scientists who make breakthroughs may spend many years following them up. While the most important discovery may have been published at a younger age, the intensive work of capitalizing on this discovery may go on for a decade or more.

A Positive Look at the Present

Physical and sensory changes do occur in middle age. Some that are merely cosmetic take on psychological significance, such as graying hair and facial wrinkles. Others, such as the tendency to gain weight and the reduction in heart and lung capacity, may affect general

FIGURE 16.5

Performance in the Humanities, Sciences, and Arts in Relation to Age

The percentage of total output for people in the humanities, sciences, and arts differs throughout adulthood.

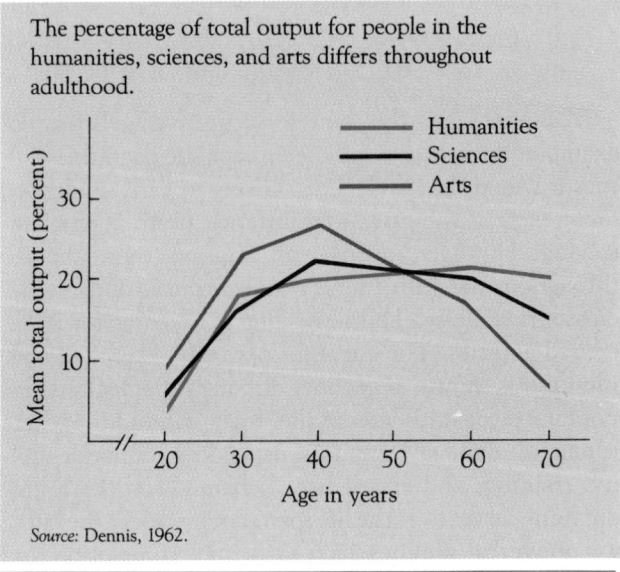

Source: Dennis, 1962.

health as well as the ability to perform certain tasks. Changes in the sex organs and declines in the sensitivity of sensory receptors also take place. Cognitive changes occur too, although they are more controversial. A person may find that it takes more time to learn something and that the ability to solve nonverbal abstract problems declines. Some decline in memory abilities may show itself as well.

What do these changes mean? For most middle-aged people, they mean very little. People can compensate for many sensory deficits, and while a middle-aged person may no longer be able to beat a well-trained younger person in a strenuous game of tennis or in a laboratory reaction time exercise, does it really matter? The important factor is one's attitudes and the recognition that these changes do not restrict enjoyment of life or participation in most activities.

In addition, the finding that trained people in middle age actually perform better than untrained early adults (Denney, 1982) shows that practice and activity can change the curve of decline greatly. Finally, the findings that individual differences in health, interest, motivation, experience, and training are more important than any biological factors in solving real problems demonstrate that how one lives makes all the difference.

However, if a person's attitude toward no longer being able to have children, no longer being able to beat youngsters in tennis, or no longer being able to read a newspaper without some aid is that these are catastrophic occurrences, that person is likely to go through a crisis of personal confidence. If, on the other hand, a more realistic and optimistic attitude is taken, middle-aged people can adjust to these changes and enjoy the financial and experiential rewards of middle adulthood.

Summary

1. Physical changes—for example, gray hair, wrinkles, and a redistribution of weight—are quite visible in middle adulthood. The lungs work less efficiently, and there is a decrease in the density of bone and muscle. Metabolic rate also declines.

2. Heart attacks become more frequent in middle age, and hypertension is a major problem. However, over the past thirty years better medical care and changes in lifestyle have reduced the death rate from heart disease. Older people tend to be more careful about their health habits than young adults, with the exception that they get less exercise. Stress is a factor in heart disease, and many companies are instituting stress-reduction programs. Cancer is the second most common cause of death. Although the cause of cancer is unknown, cigarette-smoking and diet have been linked to it.

3. There is a double standard of aging for men and women. Men age to a new concept of being handsome, while females are encouraged to continue to look like they did as young adults.

4. Evidence indicates that middle-aged people are engaging more frequently in sexual intercourse than middle-aged people did a generation ago. Physical changes in the sexual organs during middle age lead to an increase in response time required in all phases of sexual response.

5. Menopause involves cessation of a woman's menstrual cycle, while the term climacteric refers to all physical changes that bring someone from fertility to infertility. During menopause, women are likely to have physical symptoms, especially hot flashes, but most cope well with the discomfort. In addition, postmenopausal women have positive attitudes toward menopause because it brings freedom from pregnancy. Males may also proceed through a climacteric, although it is much more gradual than that experienced by women.

6. During middle age, sensory declines occur, although they do not affect daily life much. Visual acuity worsens, and glare becomes a problem. Hearing also declines somewhat. There is some loss of taste, smell, and touch sensitivity. Reaction time increases, probably because the speed of impulse conduction in the nervous system is slower.

7. In middle adulthood fluid intelligence continues to decline, but crystallized intelligence may increase. Individual differences in cognitive functioning are great and increase in importance with age. Middle-aged people who are mentally

active, physically fit, and healthy do very well on intelligence tests.

8. Memory declines little if at all in middle adulthood. There is some decline in recall, but recognition remains excellent.

9. Middle-aged people benefit when they are given additional time to study and learn, and receive help in organizing new material. Abilities that are exercised show less decline than those that are not exercised, and different abilities show different curves of decline throughout middle adulthood.

10. In most fields, creative work peaks in late early adulthood or early middle age, perhaps because middle-aged people are often placed in management positions or spend many years following up their discoveries. However, creativity can be found in people of every age.

--- Answers to True or False Statements ---

1. *False*   Correct statement: Both coordination and flexibility decrease in middle age.

2. *True*   Most young people underestimate their parents' sexual activity.

3. *False*   Correct statement: Middle-aged people take longer to achieve orgasm.

4. *False*   Correct statement: It is the dramatic decrease in estrogen that leads to the uncomfortable physical symptoms.

5. *False*   Correct statement: Cardiovascular disease is the most common cause of death for middle-aged men, but cancer is the primary cause of death among women of that age-group.

6. *False*   Correct statement: Most people are aware of the link between heart disease and diet.

7. *True*   People tend to eat better and become more concerned about their health habits as they age.

8. *True*   People usually become more farsighted as they age.

9. *True*   Middle-aged people often have difficulty hearing high-frequency tones.

10. *True*   Reaction time does slow with increasing age.

11. *False*   Correct statement: There is no decline in the middle-aged person's ability to solve practical, realistic problems.

12. *False*   Correct statement: Abilities that are exercised may still show some decline during adulthood, but the decline is less than for unexercised abilities.

CHAPTER 17

Social and Personality Development in Middle Adulthood

Are the Following Statements True or False?

Try the True-False Quiz below. See if your answers correspond to the information in this chapter. Each question is repeated after the paragraph in which the answer can be found. The True-False Answer Box at the end of the chapter lists the complete answers.

_____ 1. Women entering middle adulthood today are taller and heavier than their mothers.

_____ 2. According to Erikson, one positive outcome of middle adulthood is a commitment to helping the younger generation.

_____ 3. During early middle age, most couples report being more satisfied with their marriage than at any other time in the life cycle.

_____ 4. The relationship between middle-aged people and their parents is marked by strain and obligations.

_____ 5. Most middle-aged children see their elderly parents infrequently.

_____ 6. Most middle-aged people look forward to the empty-nest stage and report greater marital satisfaction during that time in life.

_____ 7. Salary is the most important element for job satisfaction among poor people who work.

_____ 8. Age-related decreases in job performance with age are a fact of life.

_____ 9. Middle-aged people are more likely to be unemployed than younger colleagues, but they are not likely to be out of work as long.

_____10. Job burnout is a real phenomenon.

_____11. Personality generally changes substantially throughout middle age.

_____12. Most people experience a substantial mid-life crisis, during which they make radical changes in their lives.

Passage to Middle Adulthood

What is the difference between thirty-nine years and forty years? Usually the answer "one year" is correct, but not when we are talking about age. Forty seems to have a special status attached to it, because it represents the passage into middle age. At numerous fortieth-birthday parties, birthday cards joking about the loss of youth are read out loud as everyone roars with laughter. It is as if a door has closed on one part of life—the part called youth.

Middle adulthood brings special challenges. When a friend dies of a heart attack, we are forced to face our own mortality. We begin to recognize the limits of our own physical and psychological abilities and to understand that we may not achieve all we had hoped to. We assess our careers and the meaning of our successes or failures (McIlroy, 1984). If we have children, we are likely to be dealing with adolescents and being constantly reminded that a newer, fresher generation is coming into maturity.

Many middle-aged people are at the top of their power and can influence the decisions of others. This is the generation that is very much in command. Maturity and experience become more useful, and middle-aged people are in a position to help both the older and the younger generation with social support, the benefit of their experience, and sometimes with their financial resources.

Middle adulthood is a time of mystery and controversy for modern psychologists. Some see it as a time of stability, when people use all their resources to cope with the normal developmental challenges of the age. Some reevaluation is required, but stability is the rule. Others disagree, seeing middle age as a period of crisis, of turbulent change in all areas of life. In this chapter, we look at the social and personal challenges facing middle-aged people and try to discover which is closer to the truth.

The Baby-Boom Generation Hits Middle Age

The population now entering middle adulthood today is the largest in the history of the United States and is different from past generations in some ways. When World War II ended, millions of men who had been in the armed forces were discharged. Many had waited to have families. The peak years of the "baby boom" were from the late 1940s through the early 1960s (see Figure 17.1). The boom continued for a number of years while these couples completed their families. This generation is now reaching middle age.

The very size of this generation caused problems as they matured. When the baby-boomers entered school, many districts were forced to build new facilities. Child-related industries, such as those producing toys and baby food, boomed along with them. So many applied to colleges and universities that those educational institutions had to expand to accommodate them. Now they are entering middle adulthood. In the early twenty-first century, when they begin to retire and reach later maturity, they will demand the social security and social services they deserve and place a tremendous burden on the delivery of such services.

One's fortieth birthday usually represents entrance into middle age.

FIGURE 17.1

Fertility Rates for Women, 1917–1979

The phrase "baby boom" accurately reflects the bulge in the U.S. population. Some of these boomers are now entering middle age.

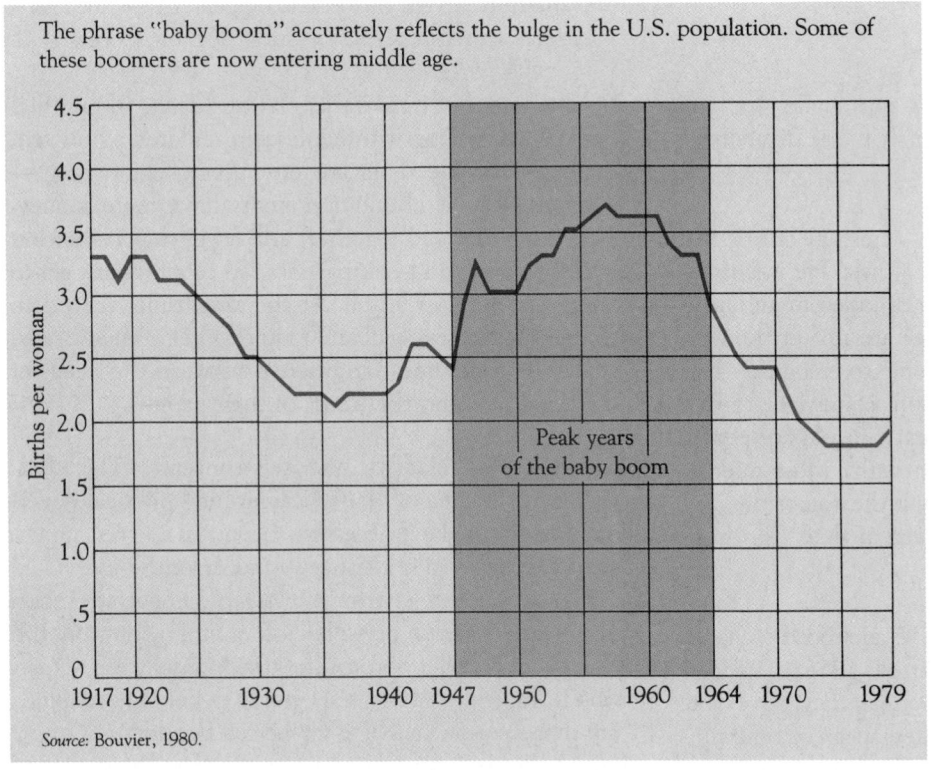

Peak years
of the baby boom

Source: Bouvier, 1980.

The baby-boom generation differs greatly from the generation of their parents. Physically they a bit taller, but forty-year-old women are a bit lighter than their mothers, while men weigh about the same as their fathers. They eat differently, consuming more chicken, fish, and low-fat milk and less beef. This generation smokes a bit less as well, and exercises more. They are by far the best-educated generation, with an average of 12.9 years of schooling. More than 84 percent have completed high school, 44.5 percent have finished one year of college, and 25.1 percent have had four years or more of higher education. They've experienced the sexual openness of the sexual revolution of the late 1960s and early 1970s. They are much more likely to be divorced than their parents at the same age and to be remarried. A forty-year-old woman today is more likely to be working outside the home than her mother. Postwar baby-boomers tend to own their own homes. They save only about 3 percent after taxes and have substantial debts (*U.S. News & World Report,* March 10, 1986).

True or False Women entering middle adulthood today are taller and heavier than their mothers.

What implications for society and for the social sciences does the arrival of the baby-boomers at middle age have? Because this generation is more affluent and entering the period in life when they will reach the top of their earning power, their preferences for food, leisure activities, and material comforts may dominate the marketplace. And because they are better educated, they may expect more self-direction and autonomy in their jobs. The fact that they are so numerous means that as they move through middle age into later maturity and begin to suffer from long-term debilitating illnesses, they will tax our existing health-care resources and require an increasing amount of social services. This new generation is now ready to tackle the developmental tasks and concerns of middle age.

The Tasks of Middle Adulthood

Every age brings with it problems and challenges, and middle adulthood is no exception. It is the diversity of these challenges that is impressive.

Dealing with one's own mortality. Imagine one of your friends dying suddenly of a heart attack. He was not a member of the "older" generation or killed in an unfortunate accident. Such occurrences are not uncommon in middle age, and they cause people to recognize their own mortality. Young adults rarely come face-to-face with catastrophic disease, and in extreme old age people may consider the threat of death daily. Most middle-aged people do not think they will die tomorrow, but they do begin to cope with the idea of their own mortality.

A new time perspective. At middle adulthood a change in time perspective occurs (Neugarten, 1968a). Middle-aged people tend to look at the time they have left, rather than at the past. People often speak of time running out, and there is an increased emphasis on using time wisely.

Recognizing biological limitations and health risks. Although today's middle-aged people are more likely to be in better shape, they are scarcely able to compete with well-conditioned young adults. Middle-agers must come to grips with the cumulative effects of their diet, smoking, drinking, and lifestyle in general. Young adults often believe they will live healthier lives when they get older, but middle-aged people do not have that luxury and may find it difficult to change health habits that are so deeply ingrained.

Reorientation to work and achievement. In the American dream, the worker who was shining door handles works himself up to be president of the company. In another dream, the medical researcher becomes famous for her breakthrough in medicine, and the police officer

successfully solves the big crime and gains detective rank. Some people make it, but many do not. There is simply less room at the top today. The realization that a doctor will continue to treat acne, that the police officer will not become a detective, and that the keys to the executive washroom are not within one's reach forces some reevaluation. Even those who appear to be successful may have to reassess the meaning of their success.

Reassessment of important relationships. In mid-life, parents are dealing with adolescent children who eventually leave home. They are left with an "empty nest"— a home without children. Parents have more money, more time to spend together, and fewer responsibilities. After years of child-rearing, married couples must get to know one another again. At the same time, their own parents are becoming ill and requiring help. Middle-aged adults are sometimes sandwiched between the needs of their children and the needs of their parents.

Restructuring identity and self-concept. The challenges in the area of family, career, and physical development may make it necessary to reassess and restructure one's identity and self-concept. Consider the individual for whom success on the job is most important, then imagine that person being laid off or finding out that the big promotion will not come through. Consider the woman who has spent so many years giving to her children finding that she now has time for herself but does not know what to do with it. Her role as mother has been diminished. Questioning values, achievements, and the meaning of life is also a part of middle adulthood (McIlroy, 1984). Sometimes people find areas of their selves that have been neglected—for example, the wife may rediscover her ambition, or her husband may take up a new interest, such as music or art.

Do all these tasks reflect only the experience of the white middle class? While there is evidence that white middle-class people are more likely to face these problems and challenges, interviews of blue-collar workers showed similar themes (Danielson and Cytrynbaum, 1979).

Theories About Middle Adulthood

Midlife is a fertile area for theorizing, but the basic tenets of reevaluation, change, and recommitment are common themes in most theories of middle adulthood. Keep in mind that the theories outlined here are based primarily on observations of the experiences of males (see page 351). Erik Erikson (1963) sees the psychosocial crisis of middle age as the attainment of **generativity,** or a sense of giving to others, versus **stagnation** and self-absorption. Generativity means giving not only to one's own children but also to grandchildren and the community. It may involve creative work and the ability to open oneself up to new experiences. Stagnation involves self-centeredness. In his elaboration on Erikson's theory, Robert Peck (1968) notes the importance of changing one's social emphasis from emphasizing sexuality to dealing with people on a more social level, as companions. As physical powers wane, middle-aged people must come to value wisdom over physical powers and maintain their mental flexibility.

True or False According to Erikson, one positive outcome of middle adulthood is a commitment to helping the younger generation.

Perhaps the most controversial theory of middle age was advanced by Daniel Levinson, who sees entrance into middle adulthood as a great struggle, and the mid-life years as a time for reevaluating one's entire life structure. Levinson (1978) believes that in middle age a number of conflicts, called polarities (see pages 348–349), must be faced and that a new life structure must be built. Another theorist, Roger Gould (1975), also sees the need for a basic reevaluation of life during these years.

Changes in Family Life

Throughout adulthood, the most important areas of concern are love and work. These areas give us our greatest satisfactions in life, but they are also the cause of our greatest trials.

Middle-aged parents are likely to have teenage children. If parents married in their early twenties, had their first child a few years later and their last child at about age twenty-nine, then by the time parents are forty their children are well into adolescence (Spanier et al., 1985). Within the next ten years, while the couple are in their fifties, their children are being launched to be on their own. After the last child leaves home, the empty-nest period begins. By the time middle age rolls around, marriages that have survived are about twenty years old. As noted, the poor tend to enter and leave these stages before their middle-class cohorts.

Marriage in Middle Adulthood

Marriage in middle adulthood has stood the test of time so far, but still faces many challenges. First, raising teen-agers is stressful. Second, the period of middle age is one of reevaluation and the marriage is one of the areas that is reevaluated. Third, our spouses are likely to remind us that we are aging, and this itself can be a source of stress. Fourth, both spouses are likely to be working and to some extent leading their own lives. They may have to infuse new energy into the marriage in order to revitalize it. Finally, the empty nest can bring many surprises as children no longer dominate their parents' every motivation and action.

The elements that comprise a happy and successful marriage come as no surprise. When seventy-two middle-aged middle-class spouses who had indicated they were very happy were interviewed, they reported similar sexual needs and viewed sex as a way of expressing deep emotional commitment. There was evidence of mutual support, and the couples made it clear that they cared very much for each other. Each was very committed to the marriage and expressed a deep desire to work things through. And each person was a fully functioning, mature and independent individual with a solid ego (Fincham and O'Leary, 1983). In successful marriages, positive actions are the rule and are not related to any specific situation, while in unhappy marriages negative behaviors were extensive and considered to be deliberate. In a study of 438 spouses, age twenty through seventy-eight, four areas—communication, love, respect, and religion—were found to be most important (Stinnett et al., 1982). Of these, the last requires some explanation. Among middle-aged couples, high degrees of religious practice, religious experience and feeling, and religious beliefs are related to superior marital adjustment—defined in terms of agreement on issues of basic importance to the relationship, satisfaction with and commitment to the relationship, and tendency to engage in activities together, among other things (Wilson and Filsinger, 1986).

The position of the couple in the family life cycle is also a factor in marital satisfaction (Spanier et al., 1979). Marital satisfaction is very high right after marriage and then declines afterward. It increases during the later stages of marriage. There is evidence that marital satisfaction, particularly for women, is low at the beginning of middle age (Pineo, 1961) and rises in later middle age, but the timing of the rise may depend upon gender. Because children can have a negative effect on marital satisfaction, this effect may be greater for women than for men (Rollins and Galligan, 1982), which is interesting, because many women cite their children as a prime source of satisfaction. Middle-aged people are much more likely to be living with teenage children or alone than with preschoolers. If the children were planned and wanted, they do not seem to be as great a factor in reducing marital satisfaction. Rollins and Feldman (1970) found a steady decline from the beginning of marriage to the school-age stage for women. The decline then levels off and begins a rapid rise from the empty-nest stage to the retirement stage. For husbands, a slight decline is found from the beginning of the marriage to the school-age stage, then there is an increase to the empty-nest stage and all through the retirement stage. The rate of increase during the later years of marriage is more dramatic for wives than for husbands.

We can conclude that the earliest and later stages of marriage are the most satisfying (Benin and Nienstedt, 1985). Other studies also found this relationship between marital satisfaction and the life cycle, but doubts have been raised about the strength of that relationship. Other factors, such as the number of children, are involved (Anderson et al., 1983). Still, generally, the connection is there.

True or False During early middle age, most couples report being more satisfied with their marriage than at any other time in the life cycle.

Parents and Adolescents

"Mental illness is catching—you get it from your teenagers." We've all heard some variation of this saying. As we've seen in Chapters 11 and 12, conflict between parents and teens tends to be overemphasized (Thurnher et al., 1974). Some conflict does take place. Both middle-aged people and teenagers are going through a period of evaluation or reevaluation. The middle-aged couple is concerned about aging, about the disparity between their dreams and reality, about keeping meaning in life, and about how to deal with aging parents. Their children are dealing with their identities, hopes for the future, concerns about adulthood, and trying to get along with their parents. Parents may be overburdened by the problems of both generations—their adolescent children, on one side, and their elderly parents, on the other. Little research has been done on the effects adolescents have on their parents (Alpert and Richardson, 1980). Some believe that adolescence is the most stressful period in a mother's life (Field and Widmayer, 1982). The rapidly changing relationships affect the mother, as she finds it difficult to allow her children more freedom. The relationship between parents and adolescents remains important and is the best predictor of adolescent adjustment (Bachman, 1970).

The father finds himself no longer as powerful, and his control wanes. He may be in need of some recognition and overt signals that he is making the right decisions, while his teenagers may be rejecting or modifying those decisions in order to be independent (Bozett, 1985). Consider the father who is proud of his achievements in business and in providing a good home being told by his son that materialism is "the pits." Consider the father who is proud of his involvement in community activities, only to be told by his daughter that politics is dirty. Conflict reaches its height during early to middle adolescence and then declines. Fathers often have different relationships with their sons and their daughters, being more concerned with a son's success than a daughter's (Bozett, 1985).

The main complaints most teens have concerning their parents have to do with overprotectiveness and interference (Field and Widmayer, 1982). Of course, what a teen may see as overprotection and interference may not coincide with the parents' view. On the other hand, parents are generally not eager to admit that their children are ready for more independence, and they may be overprotective and interfering. Two-way communication is important, but unfortunately parents spend more time explaining their own viewpoints than trying to understand their teenager's views (Hunter, 1985).

Parents of adolescents have special concerns. One parent once told me, "When you have small children you have small worries, but when you have big children you have big worries." Parents of teens worry about their companions, their future, their sexual activities, their choice of vocation and school, and their values. Parents are concerned that their children not get trapped into an unwanted pregnancy, make a poor choice of spouse, or get involved in a dead-end job. During this period of life, conflict has a different quality to it. Younger children may argue about bedtime, but such arguments pale next to disagreements about curfews, dating, and other adolescent concerns. Parents hope their children will make reasonable career decisions, and would like to help, but they must be careful not to be overinvolved or underinvolved. During these years, parenting requires delicacy, a sense of balance and skill.

Relationships with the Older Generation

When you are forty years old, your parents are sixty, sixty-five, or even seventy. They are entering late adulthood. The relationship between grown children and their parents is often looked at in terms of formal obligations and financial help. The picture is one of the dutiful child, usually a daughter, taking care of elderly parents—a role reversal. Instead of parents taking care of children, the children now take care of their parents. The older person is seen as taking and dependent (Shanas, 1973). The truth is quite different.

The relationship between parents and children in middle age is actually quite good and characterized by mutual support and voluntary activity. Baruch and Barnett (1983) found that women between the ages of thirty-five and fifty-five saw their relationships with their parents as rewarding. One married woman of thirty-five was asked whom she like to be with when she felt down, and she said, "It's really embarrassing to say, but it's my mother" (p. 605). Contrary to the popular stereotype, little conflict with mothers was found. The relationship is instead marked by concern and close emotional attachment (Shanas, 1979a). Most parents live close to their children and see them often (Shanas, 1979b). The middle generation's relationships with their parents are quite good, and middle-aged parents often show a greater degree of obligation than their parents expect. Older people prefer adult children to be providers of emotional support and financial management, but not of income. They expect their middle-aged children to modify family schedules for the sake of their elderly parents, but the majority of each generation believes that adult children should not share households with elderly parents (Brody et al., 1984).

About one in six middle-aged couples will have an aged parent living with them at one time or another.

True or False The relationship between middle-aged people and their parents is marked by strain and obligations.

True or False Most middle-aged children see their elderly parents infrequently.

Most do not share their homes with their parents, but a significant minority do. An estimated one in nine middle-aged couples will have an elderly parent in their home while one or more of their own children is still at home, and one in six middle-aged couples will have an aged parent in the household at some time or another (Beck and Beck, 1984). Sharing one's home with an elderly parent is often a last resort and frequently occurs when the parent cannot live independently because of financial or medical reasons. But sharing a home has a positive side that is often left unmentioned. The older person has much to give—for example, household and babysitting help, sometimes a financial contribution, and other services.

Concern for the family's elderly is the rule, not the exception (Botwinick, 1984). But as parents age, chronic illness sets in, and they require more care, the situation becomes increasingly difficult. Both generations want their independence, and as long as this is possible, relationships stay quite good. The role reversal and major problems arise when additional daily help is required and when medical needs become more serious. This usually happens late in the middle-adulthood period, during the empty-nest stage.

The Empty Nest

After spending much of the adult years involved with the children, the children leave home to make their own way in the world. How does this affect middle-aged parents? Two different scenarios can be anticipated.

First, consider the woman who has invested a tremendous amount of energy in raising children. They are her career. But when they leave home her role expires, and with it her self-esteem decreases, resulting in depression (Bart, 1971). Some evidence for this view is found in a study showing that women who work exhibit less depression during the empty-nest period than women who were full-time homemakers confirms this (Powell, 1977). Presumably, working mothers have followed a dual-career life path and do not find their role reduced as much during the empty-nest stage.

In the other scenario, the empty-nest period is a time of renewal, of improved financial status, of spouses becoming reacquainted, and of relief that the task of raising children is over. The overwhelming majority of studies show that most women find increased satisfaction during this stage (Neugarten, 1977) and that the most common reaction is relief (Neugarten, 1974). In one of the most-quoted studies, Rubin (1979) studied 160 middle-aged women who had given up work to assume a traditional housewife role for ten years or more. These women had invested a great amount of time and effort in their children and had sacrificed to stay at home with them. If any group should show symptoms of empty-nest problems, this group should. But they did not. Some experienced moments of sadness and loneliness after the children had gone, but they were definitely not depressed, and again the most common feeling was relief. Now they could spend time on other pursuits. Renewal of interest in oneself, and a feeling of being released, are also reported quite often (Harkins, 1978; Glenn, 1975). The sense of increased freedom and opportunity far outweighs the supposed loss of role (Neugarten and Datan, 1973). Most studies find no negative effects of children leaving home, and significant positive effects (Palmore et al., 1979).

The effect of the empty nest on men is not as clear, because theoretically men do not invest as much time in their families. The evidence that is available shows the empty-nest stage to be a happy time in their life (Fiske and Weiss, 1977). In late middle age, men become less work-oriented and concentrate more on the family, and this may contribute to the reported increase in marital satisfaction (Lowenthal and Chiriboga, 1972).

For most, then, the empty-nest stage is a positive one. With both people often working, the financial picture improves. Fewer family responsibilities make it possible to take vacations and extra evenings out. Both spouses may be at the top of their earning power. Time is plentiful, they are mature enough to appreciate it, and most are in good health. They can live life to its fullest.

True or False Most middle-aged people look forward to the empty-nest stage and report greater marital satisfaction during that time in life.

Vocational Development

One reward of middle adulthood is financial. Middle-aged people are earning more and are often in management positions. Because men rarely interrupt their vocational life voluntarily—for example, to stay home with the children, as many women do—they are likely to be at the top of their earning power. Most middle-aged women work. In fact, almost 65 percent of women between the ages of forty-five and fifty-four, and 42 percent of the women in the fifty-five to sixty-four age group, are now employed (U.S. Department of Labor, 1985), and that percentage will increase as the present group of early adults age. The middle-aged woman who has been working throughout her adult years is also probably at the top of her earning power. Even if she delayed entering the work force or interrupted her career to raise the children, she will probably reach her earnings peak sometime in late middle adulthood.

Job Satisfaction

Let's say you found your dream job at age twenty-two. Now you are forty-five years old and you've spent more than twenty years in the field—and probably a good part of that where you are presently employed. How do you think you would rate your job now?

Middle-aged people usually express satisfaction with their work (Havighurst, 1982; Weaver, 1980). When asked to rate their job satisfaction, older people reported that it increased up to late middle age, ages fifty to fifty-nine, then decreased thereafter, often during the last five years of their working life (Saleh and Otis, 1964). Some argue that job satisfaction increases to about age forty-five and then declines somewhat (Meltzer, 1965).

The research on job satisfaction can be interpreted in many ways. People become used to their jobs in middle adulthood and, faced with less opportunity to change jobs, simply adapt to them. In a more positive vein, middle-aged workers are more likely than their younger cohorts to have attained a favorable position, received promotions, and make good salaries. They may have a position that allows for more self-direction and choice. So the high level of job satisfaction reflects the increased individual freedom available in higher-level positions. Job satisfaction is related to how challenging the position is, as well as to the financial security it offers, and higher-level positions are more likely to be challenging. Salary is the most important factor affecting job satisfaction among low-income workers, but this is not true among middle-class blue- or white-collar workers who already earn good salaries. If people have certain abilities and skills, they want to use them. The decline in satisfaction during the later years of middle adulthood may stem from

The decline in work satisfaction in late middle age is probably due to the realization that one will not attain one's dream.

an awareness that promotion is no longer likely and that one's dream will not be realized. It may also reflect the vision of retirement. But age-related changes in satisfaction should not be overemphasized. Chronological age is probably less important than other factors, such as the type of job, the company one works for, the challenges the job offers, and a number of other job-related variables (Chown, 1977).

True or False Salary is the most important element for job satisfaction among poor people who work.

Age and Job Performance

Everyone is interested in the bottom line. When middle-aged workers seek employment, the question of how they compare with younger workers is raised. The conventional wisdom is that job performance declines with age

(Stagner, 1985; Rhodes, 1983). After all, middle-aged people are slower than younger workers so one would expect some decline in performance. On the other hand, it is said that middle-aged people are better and more efficient workers because they have more experience. For instance, an experienced salesperson may know which leads are best to follow up, while a younger worker may waste time trying to follow all the leads. Others argue that it is a standoff, that the middle-aged worker's experience compensates for any loss of speed. Which of these three hypotheses is supported by research?

Actually, all of them are. Studies concerning the relationship of age to job performance have found that job performance sometimes increases with age and sometimes decreases. At times, no relationship between aging and job performance was found (Rhodes, 1983). The available evidence does not reveal any large age differences

in performance at work (Salthouse, 1982). It may be unfair to make any generalization in this area because there are so many individual differences. Older workers with direct experience may show equal or even higher performance, compared with younger workers. Older, inexperienced workers in technically complex and rapidly changing work environments may not compare as well (Waldman and Avolio, 1986). Individual differences should be taken into account, and two workers of the same age may be performing quite differently.

True or False Age-related decreases in job performance with age are a fact of life.

Functional Age

Because individual differences are so important, many psychologists argue that chronological age is a poor measure to use in making social policy, such as when a worker should retire or be shifted to a less-demanding job. The fact that some older workers outperform younger workers should make us wary of such generalizations. Instead, the concept of functional age should be used instead of chronological age. **Functional age** is an individual's level of capacity relative to others of his age for functioning in a given environment (Birren and Renner, 1977). The basic idea is to substitute some measure of a person's functioning for chronological age (Salthouse, 1982). Unfortunately, we do not yet have an acceptable way of measuring functional age. Although functional age is an interesting concept, scientifically valid measuring instruments must be formulated before it can be used (Schaie and Parr, 1983).

Job Discrimination

People often base job discrimination against workers over the age of forty on the argument that job performance declines with age. But as we have just seen, there is no basis for that position. Still, job discrimination because of age is a fact of life (Gannon, 1982). According to federal law, it is illegal to discriminate on the basis of

This middle-aged salesperson probably knows from experience which leads are best to follow up and which will probably be dead ends.

burnout A state of physical, emotional, and mental exhaustion, found mostly in people whose jobs require working in emotionally demanding circumstances.

age with respect to terms and conditions of employment for people between the ages of forty and seventy, but a variety of discriminatory practices still exist. Older workers may be laid off, fired, involuntarily retired, not given the promotions they deserve, or even denied a job on the basis of age alone (Pritchard et al., 1984).

Often the older worker has nowhere to go after being laid off. The chances of landing a new job are slim. In a Ford Foundation study of formerly unemployed people who were able to get new jobs, workers under the age of thirty-five received far more increases in pay than decreases, but after age forty there were more decreases than increases. At age fifty-five and older, the chances of finding a higher-paying job were slight (Kossen, 1983). Many adults find that they are trapped. They cannot reach their goals in the job they have, but there is nowhere else to go. This may be one cause of the depression and other psychological problems that occur in middle age.

When middle-aged people do lose their jobs, chances are that they will be unemployed for a longer time than their younger colleagues. Statistics show that they are less likely to be laid off because of seniority provisions but that once they are out of work they are more likely to stay unemployed (Kossen, 1983). The effects of this long-term unemployment are serious. In one study, a group of subjects age thirty-five through sixty who were unemployed was compared with a similar group who held jobs. The unemployed group showed many more symptoms of depression and anxiety. The changes in self-concept depended on the social support received from family and friends. Those with family support did better, but in general the self-esteem of the unemployed group was lower (Linn et al., 1985).

True or False Middle-aged people are more likely to be unemployed than younger colleagues, but they are not likely to be out of work as long.

Some employers believe that older workers are more costly. They think that older workers will use health benefits more frequently, have fewer years to offer the company, are absent from work more often, or are phys-

ically unable to do the job. But in fact, older workers are not absent more and do not change jobs as often as younger workers. The increased use of health benefits can be offset by savings in turnover and training, and whether older workers can meet the physical demands of the job depends on the job and the functional age of the person (Kossen, 1983).

Older workers have a number of advantages over their younger colleagues. Their attitudes toward work tend to be stable (Staw and Ross, 1985), and an older worker who has a history of positive work attitudes is less likely to be affected by situational and external influences. A survey of attitudes and values of more than 3,000 workers ranging in age from seventeen to sixty-five showed that older workers placed greater emphasis on the moral importance of work and took greater pride in craftsmanship, while younger workers placed greater emphasis on money and the importance of friends (Cherrington et al., 1975).

Burnout

Consider the middle-aged social worker who after years of work can no longer face his job. He feels irritable, restless, and tense. He is very passive, seems almost apathetic, and experiences intense frustration that carries over to his family life. These are the symptoms of **burnout,** which can be defined as a state of physical, emotional, and mental exhaustion in workers whose jobs thrust them into emotionally demanding situations (Etzion, 1984). The symptoms of burnout include exhaustion, fatigue, psychosomatic illness, insomnia, negative attitudes toward others, negative attitudes toward work, poor work performance, absenteeism, increased use of drugs, loss of appetite or overeating, negative self-concept, aggressive feelings, irritability, restlessness, tension, anger, hopelessness, apathy, depression, or boredom (Maher, 1983). Of course, no one person will suffer all these symptoms.

Since it was defined in descriptive terms more than a decade ago (Freudenberger, 1974), burnout has become a popular diagnosis, and everyone with a problem is said to be "burned out." This is unfortunate, because when a term is overused it can become meaningless. But burnout is real (Maher, 1983). It is related to stress on the job, lack of positive feedback, and lack of appreciation. Workers in service occupations are especially prone to burnout. The exact causes of burnout are unknown, but it does not result from a single event. It is probably tied

Middle-aged workers often show greater pride in craftsmanship than younger workers.

to daily hassles, disappointments, and frustrations, caused by such things as an excessively large and difficult client load, long hours, too many secondary duties such as paperwork, poor relationships with or isolation from colleagues, lack of control over outcomes, lack of preparation for dealing with job stress, unrealistic expectations, and guilt (Maher, 1983). Imagine the front-line social worker dealing with clients. He has responsibility, but little or no input into administrative decisions (Ellenbury, 1981). He is given more and more work, and difficult cases, but gets little appreciation and no positive feedback for what he is doing. As the work piles up, he feels as if he is not accomplishing anything. And whether he does his job well seems to make no difference.

True or False Job burnout is a real phenomenon.

The concept of burnout has been ridiculed as merely an excuse for poor work. Why has it only just appeared? One answer is that burnout may have gone unrecognized until recently. But it is more probable that burnout is a result of an increasing emphasis on human services. Many new jobs are being created in the area of human services, and it is workers on these jobs who are most likely to become burned out. One high school science teacher admitted that he found no satisfaction teaching students who read so poorly that the same materials had to be gone over again and again. Teaching in a difficult situation, receiving no positive feedback, and finding that his students showed no interest in the lesson he had tried so hard to present made him apathetic. He could hardly wait for the end of the period, day, week, and term. In a recent study of why teachers leave teaching for other careers, the most frequently cited cause was low salary, but 36 percent cited working conditions, 17 percent said lack of respect, 13 percent listed boredom, 10 percent were dissatisfied with the administration, and 5 percent said they lacked fulfillment. Eight percent mentioned burnout itself (Newsday, March 14, 1986). One wonders whether these teachers would have stayed if the other aspects of teaching were more satisfying even at a low salary.

For some, the term *burnout* itself is a problem, because it implies that people have only so much to give before they, like a lightbulb, burn out. In reality, energy is expandable, but whatever we label the problem, the problem is there. The principal question is how to avoid burnout and help people maintain their performance and commitment to the field. This is especially relevant for middle-aged people who have spent fifteen or more years in a career and find it difficult to recapture the excitement and optimism of their first years of work. A recommitment to the field is fostered when the activities are enjoyable, there is loyalty to others, extrinsic rewards are expected, or there is a desire to avoid repercussions from shoddy performance (Marks, 1977). Unfortunately, many human services jobs can become boring and repetitive and are low-paying. In addition, relationships with students or clients and administrators are sometimes poor. Finally, in such jobs it is also difficult to evaluate workers, and positive feedback and reinforcements are rare.

The first step in reducing burnout—or avoiding it—is to recognize the potential for it. Social support seems to be very important (see the Cross-Cultural Current on page 448). In addition, a good relationship with the boss, positive reinforcements for good work, and good communication with one's supervisors can help. In some areas, more participation by workers in policy-making is necessary too. Whatever burnout is, it does prevent people from working up to their potential, and it may require some restructuring of the job itself.

Changing Jobs in Midstream

Between the ages of forty and sixty, about 10 percent of all workers change the type of work they do (Havighurst, 1982). People voluntarily change their careers in middle age for many reasons. First, some careers end after twenty years or so. Police and firefighters are sometimes encouraged to retire after twenty years, and athletes retire before middle age. Most people in these situations enter new fields. Second, many women find that they are free at middle age to make some kind of career commitment. Some of these women have worked in the past, but in jobs that allowed them to spend more time with their family. During the empty-nest stage, they may make a career change. Third, some people find themselves in dead-end jobs, unable to go any further. They may return to school and prepare for a career change. Fourth, some people find that their jobs do not satisfy their personal needs—for example, the successful business leader who finds that she would rather work with delinquent adolescents, or the social worker who believes she would be happier in business.

Many theorists believe that career reevaluation takes place during middle age. Levinson (1978) believes that middle-aged people are apt to be concerned about the difference between the dream and the reality and seek out a change. In a similar manner, Neugarten (1976) believes that during middle age people see time beginning to run out and are forced to evaluate their career accomplishments and potential in their quest for success. Men especially identify with their role as provider, and their definition of themselves often depends on how they evaluate their achievement and power at work (Skovholt and Morgan, 1981). Success and failure may depend upon how they see themselves at work. With time running out, they may opt for a change in career.

It is difficult to evaluate the success of these changes, especially for those who leave what they see as dead-end jobs or for those who leave jobs because they have reevaluated what they want to do with their lives. In one study of white-collar career changes, Thomas (1980) found that 62 percent described the change as very rewarding, while only 4 percent expressed general unhappiness with their new careers. However, these people were executives—they knew how to make decisions and how to prepare for change. This may not always be the case.

Some people seeking to change careers do not investigate choices thoroughly or seriously consider more than one option (Armstrong, 1981). For instance, a person who was musically inclined in youth but chose a more secure career may decide to return to music during middle age, but unless he has kept up with his music on the side he may find the field has passed him by. Although a number of excellent counseling centers run by universities are available for helping the mid-career-changer, many do not seek counseling (Gannon, 1982). The tendency to make a career change without proper preparation is a significant problem. For example, some people return to school only to find that their money runs out after a year. Many people changing careers experience time pressures, know little about career-planning, and do not have adequate information (Frederickson et al., 1978). Some may be moving from a career whose weaknesses they know to one about which they hold some idealistic notion. Not all changes in career are radical. For example, a broker with a relatively secure job may choose to open his own firm, or a top-level banker with computer experience may go into management in a computer company. These are changes too, but in each the person has a better knowledge of the area he or she is moving into.

Any mid-career change is a gamble, and many more workers express a desire to change careers than actually do (Isaacson, 1981). Career change will probably continue to be an important part of mid-career evaluation for some, but not for the majority.

Personality in Middle Adulthood

Think of all the changes that occur during middle adulthood. Physical changes require scrutiny and adjustment. People are confronted with their own mortality as people close to them pass away. A shift of time perspective occurs as people look at the time they have left rather than to the past (Neugarten, 1976). Dealing with aging parents requires some change in attitude, and being the middle generation presents unique challenges. It is a time for recognizing talents that have been neglected and have to be fulfilled either now or never. It is a time for reassessing careers. It is a time for recognizing one's power in earnings and decision-making, as well as perhaps a

Coping with Burnout

We've come to think of burnout as an American problem, but it really isn't. It is a problem in many industrialized societies. Burnout is a state of physical, emotional, and mental exhaustion found mostly in people whose jobs require working with others in emotionally demanding circumstances. Burnout is related to stress, and stress on the job may be caused by work overload, bureaucratic pressures, lack of feedback, too little autonomy, and insufficient appreciation.

According to some authorities, these stresses can be reduced by what social scientists call *social support*. Social support involves interactions through which people show concern for the worker's welfare, give positive reinforcement, or communicate understanding. It can reduce stress, and consequently burnout, in two ways. First, social support can directly reduce the stress in the environment. A boss who lets workers know he or she understands their problems and gives them positive reinforcement creates an atmosphere in which stress is reduced. Second, social support can moderate the impact of stress and burnout by modifying the relationship between stress and burnout. In other words, the amount of stress on the job may remain the same, but social support may help workers under stress cope better with the situation. This moderating effect is especially important when it

is not possible to reshape the job or the manager-worker relationship directly.

Dalia Etzion first investigated the general relationship between stress, burnout, and social support. Then she turned her attention to the question of whether social support could moderate the relationship between stress and burnout. More than 600 Israeli managers and social workers were given questionnaires measuring burnout, stress in work and in life outside work, and the amount of social support in and outside of the work situation. Data was analyzed separately for males and females.

Etzion found that burnout was positively related to stress in life and at work for both men and women. Burnout was negatively related to social support in life and in work. In other words, as social support increased, burnout tended to decrease. Some interesting gender differences were discovered. Women reported significantly more burnout and more life stress (outside work) than men. No significant differences were found between males and females for stress on the job or for social support at work. Women reported higher social support outside work.

As expected, then, there is a relationship between stress and burnout. Would this relationship be moderated by social support? The answer is yes, but Etzion

second adolescence—in which people must ask questions of identity all over again (McIlroy, 1984). Faced with these issues, it is fair to ask what happens to a person's personality throughout adulthood. Do the same traits shown in adolescence continue throughout adulthood, or does some radical restructuring or change occur?

Does Personality Change in Middle Adulthood?

A famous study that investigated personality from birth through adulthood was conducted at the Fels Research Institute (Kagan and Moss, 1962). Eighty-nine children were studied as they matured. Correlations for various traits were found for the first fourteen years of life and then throughout early adulthood. Here we are interested

only in stability or change from childhood through adulthood. In certain areas, considerable stability was found. Girls who were passive and dependent during childhood established similar relationships with males in adulthood and remained dependent on their families as well. These girls also withdrew from stress in adulthood. This was not true for males, but aggressive behavior in males during childhood was well related to such behavior in males in adulthood. Achievement orientation was also relatively stable, and adult achievement was related to achievement by the age of ten for both males and females. Intellectual competence in adolescence was a predictor of intellectual ability in adulthood as well. Some traits, such as compulsivity, were not stable. The overt behaviors indicating passivity, dependence, aggressive-

found that this moderation followed different paths for men and women. The relationship between *work stress* and burnout was moderated by support outside the work situation for women and by support in the work situation for men. The relationship of *life stress* to burnout was not moderated by any source of social support for men or women. In other words, men used relationships with co-workers to moderate the relationship between stress and burnout, while women more often used sources outside work, including family and friends. Perhaps women are more willing than men to talk, or actually do talk, more to family and friends about the stress they experience.

Why does social support moderate work stress but not stress outside the job? Complaints about the boss, working conditions, and the like are easily discussed with others, while the more intimate and unique life stresses are more difficult to share. But social support cannot be elicited without some degree of self-disclosure and communication.

The conclusion that social support at work for men, and at home with friends for women, seems to moderate the relationship between stress and burnout should not be quickly generalized to other cultures. The cultural background of the subjects should be kept in mind. Previous research by Etzion showed that Israeli men and women did not use the coping strategy of talking as much as American men and women in the same professions did. And other cultural factors, including the availability of social support, the extent of such support, and the cohesiveness of the community, may differ among cultural groups and influence the relationship between stress and burnout. Sex roles differ across cultural groups, and that must be taken into consideration too.

Any research on the effectiveness of social support in reducing stress should take cultural factors into consideration. Even so, the possible effectiveness of social support in moderating the relationship between stress and burnout is worth investigating in different situations and in different cultures. As human services vocations expand, we will need as much information about reducing burnout as possible. We may find that certain programs are more effective in one culture than in another, but the possibility that social support groups at work or in the community can help reduce burnout is an important first step toward this goal.

Source: Etzion, D. Moderating Effect of Social Support on the Stress-Burnout Relationship. *Journal of Applied Psychology,* 1984, 69, 615–622.

---

ness, and achievement changed from childhood to adulthood, but childhood behaviors were predictive of analogous socially acceptable behaviors indicative of these underlying traits in adulthood.

In another major study conducted at the Institute of Human Development of the University of California at Berkeley, a tremendous amount of data was gathered on subjects from early adolescence to middle adulthood (Block, 1971). Consistency was found for males in such traits as dependability, responsibility, impulsiveness, and inability to delay gratification. Stability for females was found in submissiveness, sociability, rebelliousness, and nonconformity. Some developmental changes were gender-related. Between adolescence and middle adulthood, both males and females changed in ways that showed acceptance of the stereotyped male and female in our society. Males became more self-assured, exhibited greater self-control and self-confidence, and became more serious. Females showed increases in sympathy, protectiveness, warmth, ease in social situations, security, and dependability. For most people, Block found considerable evidence for stability across ages.

In another longitudinal study, Neugarten (1964) tested people age forty through eighty for a decade and found that personality was basically stable but that some age-related changes took place. Styles of coping and strength of goal-directed behavior remained stable. However, the sample of forty-year-olds believed they had more control over their environment and life and took more risks than sixty-year-olds, who were more likely to view the en-

Extraversion is one characteristic that is stable throughout middle age.

vironment as dangerous and to take a more passive stance. Neugarten argued that people proceed from an active to a passive mastery over their environment. She also found that men became more nurturant and females became more understanding of their aggressive tendencies in later adulthood. In other words, personality remains relatively stable across middle adulthood, but some age-related changes occur late in mid-life and continue into later adulthood.

Bronson (1967; 1966) followed eighty-five boys and girls from the Berkeley Guidance Study until they were about thirty years old, and he found stability for males in the dimension of warmth, self-acceptance, and productivity, and for females in expressiveness. Males who were controlled in childhood were rigid in adulthood, and females who were placid in childhood were calm in adulthood. In a study of middle-class adults ages forty-five to seventy, Conley (1984) found long-term stability for social extroversion and agreeableness. Steinberg (1985) found that behavior and temperament in early childhood were predictors of Type A behavior in adults. Veroff and colleagues (1984) found achievement and affiliation motives in men, and power motives in women, remaining stable. They also found that achievement and affiliation motives decline in older ages and that men's hope for power is very high at middle age.

Although the evidence for consistency in personality is plentiful, a number of cautions must be applied to these findings. In most of these studies, the correlations between early and later measures of personality are positive—but sometimes low. Therefore, although there is good evidence for stability even over a decade or more (Conley, 1985), some changes do occur. These changes may reflect age. For instance, toward the end of middle age, people may become more cautious and passive. In addition, some changes are gender-related. As people negotiate middle adulthood, men become more nurturant and women become more assertive. Because the relationship between early and later personality dimensions is far from perfect, some evidence for individual change can be gleaned from the data. Perhaps the best way of looking at personality is that it remains generally stable but some changes may occur.

True or False Personality generally changes substantially throughout middle age.

Mid-life Crisis: Fact or Fiction?

The idea that middle adulthood is a period of crisis has recently become popular. Magazine articles announce that people in middle age face a crisis of reevaluation and of confidence. The term *mid-life crisis* has actually become part of our language. We read in the print media about people married twenty years who suddenly have affairs and split up, of men suddenly changing careers, of women discovering that what they have is not what they want and making some radical shift. But is the reevaluation that occurs in middle age truly a crisis?

To understand this, we must first define the term. A **mid-life crisis** is a perceived state of physical and psychological distress that results when a person's internal resources and external social support systems threaten to be overwhelmed by developmental tasks that require new adaptive resources (Cytrynbaum et al., 1980). In other words, people at mid-life are faced with tremendous tasks—for example, dealing with their own mortality, recognizing their biological limitations, and reorientating themselves to work—which cause distress that threatens to overwhelm their ability to cope.

The most important advocate of the crisis viewpoint is Daniel Levinson (1978), whose theory was discussed on pages 345–349. Levinson argued that people in middle age negotiate a period of self-recrimination, asking such questions as "Where did I fail?" Questions like "Who am I?" and "What do I want to do with the rest of my life?" become important too, just as they were in adolescence. About 80 percent of Levinson's sample went through a period of substantial instability and change. Levinson noted five possible outcomes for mid-life crisis:

1. *Advancement within a stable life structure.* The men in this group, which comprised a majority of Levinson's sample, had achieved a moderate degree of success and stability. However, they wanted more. For example, some novelists were not interested only in writing another successful novel; they wanted to win the Pulitzer prize and be acclaimed. They now wanted to leave something for posterity. There is a recommitment in this group—one last push to make it.

2. *Serious failure or decline within a stable life structure.* The men in this group were unable to advance in their occupations, and their marriages were lifeless and failing. They had to face their failures. "What do I do now that I can't make foreman or president of the board of directors?" is a key type of question for this group. Some never recover from recognition of failure. Others may begin to define success more broadly and may recover.

3. *Breaking out: Trying for a new life structure.* Some men broke out of their stable patterns. The breaking out included some significant change, such as quitting a job

> **mid-life crisis** A perceived state of physical and psychological distress that results when a person's internal resources and external social support systems are overwhelmed by developmental tasks that require new adaptive resources. (*Note:* Both *mid-life crisis* and *mid-life transition* are used interchangeably to refer to a period of questioning at the beginning of middle age. There is general agreement that questioning does occur, but whether the term *crisis* should be applied is controversial.)

or moving to another region or leaving a wife. The next years were spent building a new structure, but at this age it is difficult and the new life is often a compromise. The outcome for the men who broke out was quite variable. Some were disappointed with the results, others were pleased.

4. *Advancement that itself produces a change in life structure.* A few men received promotions that produced qualitative changes in their lifestyles. For example, one worker received an extraordinary promotion, becoming a full manager of the purchasing department at age thirty-seven and at age forty becoming head of manufacturing. These promotions allowed him to move to a different neighborhood and adopt a different lifestyle, but these leaps did not always yield positive results.

5. *Unstable life structure.* Men in this group were not able to stabilize their lives and were unfulfilled. They changed jobs, lovers, and spouses frequently and were unable to cope with life's tasks. One man was not able to hold a stable job, even though he was thirty-seven years old. Another changed jobs frequently, was involved with drugs, did not marry, and formed no stable interpersonal relationships.

The mid-life crisis can provide opportunities for growth. Gould (1978) also found a mid-life crisis between the ages of thirty-five and forty-three, which he called the crisis of urgency. He saw mid-life as a kind of second adolescence and every bit as turbulent. People become aware that they are mortal, that time is running out, and make one last attempt to achieve their goals. Life becomes unstable and uncomfortable. Gould believed that the age at which the conflict comes depends on the person's personality, lifestyle, and subculture. Further evidence for a crisis at mid-life comes from figures showing that at mid-life the rates for first admission for alcohol abuse are high and suicide rates increase. Also, infidelity and desertion are significant problems, and physical problems related to stress—such as ulcers, hypertension, and heart disease—increase significantly (Rosenberg and Farrell, 1976).

Others do not agree that the mid-life transition is a crisis. They see a crisis as an exception rather than the rule. George Vaillant (1977) was especially interested in how people coped with conflict and stress. In his study he classified certain coping mechanisms, used in childhood and early adolescence, as immature. For example, Vaillant labeled such behavior as expressing anger and hostility indirectly and ineffectively as passive-aggressive. Such behavior is exhibited when, for example, a person is always late and procrastinates when faced with decisions. Mature coping mechanisms are the healthy ways adults deal with stress—for instance, suppression involves a conscious effort to postpone dealing with a source of conflict. Someone angry at the boss might realize she should mull over her alternatives before quitting the job.

Vaillant classified six coping mechanisms as "mature" and six as "immature." He compared twenty-five men who used mostly mature defense mechanisms with thirty-one men who used mostly immature mechanisms. Members of the first group were more successful, had satisfying friendships and marriages, and were sick less often than members of the second group. According to Vaillant, successful adjustment involves changing from immature to mature defense mechanisms. Vaillant also found that the use of mature coping mechanisms increased to mid-life and then remained constant throughout adulthood. Although he was not so interested in the mid-life crisis as such, his research suggests that its occurrence reflects a failure in the ability to cope and is not an inevitable part of the aging process (Botwinick, 1984).

Costa and McCrae (1980) administered a scale that measured distress in men between the ages of thirty-three and seventy and found no age differences in the amount of turmoil reported. No one age stood out as most stressful. People who did experience a crisis during middle age were prone to having crises at other points in their lives and had long-standing adjustment problems. Most middle-aged people report that early adulthood was a period of greater strain (Gurin et al., 1960). In one study, men between the ages of 35 and 39, 41 and 46, and 48 and 53 were interviewed about mid-life, including the meaning and usefulness of their lives, their fulfillment of "the dream," and their productivity. No age differences were

found in these areas, leading the investigators to argue that reevaluation may be a continual process rather than belonging only to the mid-life period (Hedlund and Ebersole, 1983).

Most psychologists today do not consider the mid-life period to be a time of crisis or tumult. Yet no one doubts that reevaluations do occur and that increased reflection is common. Life events probably trigger bouts of reevaluation. For example, when a parent dies we become more aware of our own mortality and must deal with questions concerning time and death. Still, this reevaluation is rarely a crisis, and most people handle it well.

True or False Most people experience a substantial mid-life crisis, during which they make radical changes in their lives.

A Model for Reevaluation in Middle Adulthood

In the last two chapters we outlined a number of issues that middle-aged people must face and master. Figure 17.2 shows a model for how this occurs, suggested by Solomon Cytrynbaum and colleagues (1980). The person enters mid-life with a unique personality, with coping strategies, and with different internal and external resources—for instance, some people have families who care and can help, others do not. In the second column, factors that may precipitate the destructuring process or attack equilibrium are noted. These are usually some incident, such as an encounter with death, illness, or a reduction in parenting duties. The task is to deal with each problem as shown in the third column—"developmental tasks." The person proceeds through a process of destructuring, reassessment, and reintegration and restructuring, leading finally to behavior and role change (column four). These changes can be adaptive or maladaptive (column five). For example, take the case of a person who finds that he will not get the promotion he dreamed of. At forty-seven he now finds himself in a dead-end job. Remember, there are also other problems at this time, including changes in family life. This causes him to reassess his life and dream, and we can imagine how he feels about having given so much at work for many years and not receiving a just reward. The reassessment may involve emotional trauma, but it can lead to a reintegration or restructuring. Perhaps he decides that his long-neglected hobbies or talents should be explored and decides to invest more time in his marriage. Perhaps he decides to change jobs. Whatever his decision, it leads to behavioral and role changes as he puts more emphasis on different areas of life.

This model makes it clear that middle adulthood is a time of facing specific questions and answering them. Most people deal quite well with these challenges. This period is both a time of stability and a time of change. Middle-aged people have the experience, financial resources, and maturity to deal with the basic questions of life, enjoy their new-found freedom, and recommit themselves to each other, family, and community. This recommitment satisfies Erikson's concept of generativity, of growing through experiencing and giving to others. Instead of seeing middle age as a time of stress and struggle, perhaps we should regard it as a time of growth, choice, and opportunity. It may be true after all that life begins at forty!

FIGURE 17.2

How People Deal With Issues in Middle Adulthood—A Model

Predispositions	Developmental Processes			Outcomes
Personality	Precipitating Events	Developmental Tasks	Developmental Processes	Adaptive
Differences in personality (ego strength, narcissism, coping strategies, defenses, etc.) that predispose individuals to respond differently to the mid-life transition. ⇑ Interacts with ⇒ ⇓	Individual: Encounter death anxiety; shift in time orientation. Stressful or Unanticipated Life Events: Biological changes; illness or death of parents, spouse, friends; life-threatening illness.	Accept death and mortality. Accept biological limitations and risks. Restructure self-concept and sexual identity. Reorientation to work, creativity, and achievement. Reassess primary relationships.	Destructuring ⇓ Reassessment ⇓ Reintegration and restructuring ⇓ Behavioral and role change ⌐⇒	Acceptance of mortality; achieve a sense of individuation and coherent identity; integration of creative and destructive forces; attain a sense of community; integrate masculine, feminine, and related emergent components of personality; reinvest narcissism in self. ⌐⇒ Able to cope with developmental tasks of the second half of life. *Maladaptive* Failure to establish sexual bimodality which integrates male and female components of personality; failure to transfer narcissism; inability to accept mortality and associated losses.
Support Systems Extent to which primary systems (couples, family, work organization) can adapt and support individual member's engagement with mid-life tasks as assessed by system's flexibility, communication, boundary management, leadership, role differentiation, culture, and myths; varies by social class, racial, ethnic background, etc.	Social System: Reduction in parental imperative; work organization or professional culture signals limitations on mobility and rewards or pressures to retire.			⌐⇒ Casualties of one's own developmental potential expressed in mid-life-related symptoms (depression, anxiety, decreased appetite for food and sex, poor concentration, fear of homosexuality, alcoholism, psychosomatic disorders) or in vulnerabilities and predispositions to distress and maladaptive symptoms as older adults.

Source: Slightly adapted from Cytrynbaum et al., 1980.

Summary

1. Middle age is commonly said to begin at forty. The present generation entering middle age, called the baby-boom generation, differs greatly from their parents in eating habits, attitudes, and education.

2. Middle-aged people must learn to deal with their own mortality, use their time wisely, recognize physical limitations, deal with long-standing health habits, reassess the value of their careers and family relationships, and identify which parts of the self remain unfulfilled.

3. Theorists generally see middle age as a time of reevaluation, reassessment, and commitment. The positive outcome of the psychosocial crisis of middle age, according to Erikson, is attaining a sense of generativity that involves helping the younger generation. The negative outcome is stagnation. Peck notes the importance of changing from viewing people sexually to seeing them as companions, of valuing wisdom, and of maintaining mental flexibility. Levinson views middle age as a turbulent time of reassessment and of solving the great dilemmas of middle-age existence.

4. Marital satisfaction, especially for women, is low at the beginning of middle age, but increases later for both men and women. Dealing with teenage children can create tension, but this aspect is often overemphasized. Adolescents complain that parents are overprotective and interfere.

5. The relationship of middle-aged people to their aging parents is generally good and characterized by mutual support. They visit their parents often, and both generations desire independence.

6. The empty-nest stage is a time of considerable opportunity, and most people look forward to it. The most common reaction is relief, and negative reactions are few.

7. Middle-aged people usually express satisfaction with their jobs. Many have attained positions that are challenging and allow for self-direction and expression as well as financial rewards.

8. Some studies find increases in job performance with age, some show decreases, and some find no relationship. In understanding job performance, individual differences are far more important than chronological age. Some psychologists argue that *functional age*, the age at which the person is actually performing, be substituted for *chronological age.*

9. Job discrimination on the basis of age is a fact of life. It is often based upon such arguments as poorer performance, greater absenteeism, physical limitations, and fewer years of employment remaining to older workers. Each can be effectively refuted, and it has been shown that older workers take more pride in craftsmanship.

10. Burnout is a real phenomenon. It is a state of mental exhaustion that leads to a number of troublesome symptoms. It is most common in human services occupations, where the pay is low, client work load is high, there is little input into decision-making, and little positive feedback or reinforcement.

11. Of people who opt for a career change at mid-life, some later express satisfaction with the change, others do not. However, some career-changers may not be planning for such moves as effectively as they should.

12. The evidence for stability in personality throughout adulthood is strong. However, some age-related and gender-related changes do occur, often in late middle age, and continue through later maturity.

13. Although middle age is a time for reevaluation, most psychologists today believe it need not be a time of crisis.

Answers to True or False Statements

1. *False* Correct statement: Women entering middle age today are a bit taller but a few pounds lighter than their parents were at the same age.

2. *True* Erikson argues that one positive outcome of the psychosocial crisis of middle age is a commitment to help the younger generation.

3. *False*   Correct statement: Couples express more marital satisfaction right after marriage and during late middle age and beyond.

4. *False*   Correct statement: The relationship between middle-aged children and their parents is marked by mutual support and satisfaction.

5. *False*   Correct statement: Most middle-aged children see their elderly parents fairly often.

6. *True*   Most middle-aged people look forward to the empty-nest stage and report greater marital satisfaction during this period.

7. *True*   Among the poor, salary is the most important determinant of job satisfaction.

8. *False*   Correct statement: Research fails to find any major decreases in job performance with age, and some studies show increases.

9. *False*   Correct statement: Middle-aged people are less likely to be unemployed, but once they are out of work it takes them longer to find another job.

10. *True*   Although the term is overused, job burnout is a real phenomenon.

11. *False*   Correct statement: Most studies find more stability than change in personality over middle age.

12. *False*   Correct statement: Most studies find that a reevaluation takes place but that it is not necessarily a crisis.

Later Adulthood

Physical Development in Later Adulthood

Are the Following Statements True or False?

Try the True-False Quiz below. See if your answers correspond to the information in this chapter. Each question is repeated after the paragraph in which the answer can be found. The True-False Answer Box at the end of the chapter lists the complete answers.

_____ 1. There are societies in which almost everyone lives to a very old age.

_____ 2. After a number of gains, the last few years have brought decreases in the average life expectancy of Americans.

_____ 3. Life expectancy for infant females is greater than for infant males in the United States.

_____ 4. The gap between the life expectancies of blacks and whites has been narrowing since the turn of the century.

_____ 5. Cancer is the most common cause of death in the elderly.

_____ 6. The elderly have the highest accident rate of any age-group.

_____ 7. People in their sixties and seventies describe their health status in positive terms.

_____ 8. Mental illness occurs more often in young adults than in the elderly.

_____ 9. Alzheimer's disease is a communicable disease.

_____10. Most elderly people are out of shape and do not exercise regularly.

_____11. Elderly men have more difficulty hearing and discriminating speech than elderly women.

_____12. The elderly experience pain more intensely than younger people do.

The Search for Methuselah

On February 22, 1986, the oldest known man in the world, Shigechio Izumi, died peacefully in his home on the Japanese island of Tokuno Shima. At 120 years of age, Izumi took daily walks. At age 116 he stopped smoking at his doctor's suggestion, but he refused to stop drinking his daily glass of shochu, a liquor made from unrefined sugarcane. He began this moderate drinking when he was seventy. When his doctor suggested that he give this up too, Izumi said he would rather die than stop. His diet consisted mainly of the vegetables he grew in his garden—potatoes, tomatoes, beans, spinach, and cabbage. His secret for long life was not to worry (*Newsday*, February 22, 1986).

Shangri-las

People who live extremely long lives are always of interest both to researchers and to the general public. Newspapers publish their secrets of longevity, and people rush to buy these words of wisdom hoping to discover something of personal use. The search for societies where people live very long lives continues, and some researchers claim to have found places where people well over one hundred years old are common. Three such places head the list: Abkhazia, in the Caucasus Mountains of the Soviet Union; Hunzakut, in the Karakoram Mountains of Pakistan; and Vilcabamba, in the Andes mountains of Ecuador. These societies share some interesting similarities (Leaf, 1973). They are all rural and situated at high altitudes, the people are poor, diets are low in calories and animal fat, and the people show a high level of physical activity and fitness. Many farm until they are very old. There is no obesity, and alcohol and tobacco use is very moderate. The elderly people lead active social lives—retirement does not exist. A sense of purpose pervades their lives. We may be able to learn something from these people. However, new research has cast doubts on these Shangri-las, because many of the people are not as old as they claim to be (Medvedev, 1974) and scientific research has failed to substantiate the claims (see the Cross-Cultural Current on page 462).

life span The biological limit to the length of life of a particular species.

life expectancy The average remaining lifetime for a particular population of a given age.

True or False There are societies in which almost everyone lives to a very old age.

Life Span and Life Expectancy

In order to understand the whole picture of longevity, two terms that are often used incorrectly must be defined. **Life span** is the biological limit to length of life (Fries and Crapo, 1981, p. xii). **Life expectancy** is the average remaining lifetime for a population at any given age (Jackson, 1980). A person's life expectancy from birth cannot exceed the life span, but it can approximate it.

If we conquered all disease, would human beings live forever? Most scientists say no. Our bodies seem programmed to "wear out," and death would come anyway. In fact, our life span has probably not increased for 100,000 years (Fry, 1985). The maximum number of years that humans live is somewhat over 100, perhaps up to 120 or so. Each species has its own characteristic life span. The Norway rat lives four years, the gray squirrel can live fifteen, the kangaroo twenty years, the capuchin monkey forty, the coyote sixteen, the Asiatic elephant seventy, the hippopotamus fifty-one (Sacher, 1977). These are, of course, approximations. Like any other species, our human species is also bounded. We live a finite number of years. The intriguing question is, What causes us to age and then die?

Theories of Aging

No one really dies from old age. When we say that, we mean the normal aging process has reduced the person's ability to fight disease and that the person finally succumbed to a disease. The official cause of death for Shigechio Izumi, our 120-year-old man, was actually pneumonia. As we negotiate later maturity, we are statistically more likely to suffer from heart disease, cancer, diabetes, and cerebrovascular diseases, as well as die from pneumonia. Why is this so, and why do we show the changes in physical appearance and functioning that accompany old age? Scientists have been looking for answers to these questions for years, and some interesting theories have been advanced. None is fully accepted today as an explanation for aging and there is probably some truth in all of them.

An Evolutionary Viewpoint

When Darwin noted that the fittest survive, he was really talking about procreation. The fittest live long enough to bear and protect their offspring. Many animals do not survive much past the time they stop being able to produce offspring. But human beings do. Why does nature allow human beings to enjoy old age?

A partial answer lies in an analogy presented by Fries and Crapo (1981). When you manufacture a car, you build it just well enough to last as long as it has to. It must last through the warranty period and remain in good running condition for a while so that the owner will return to buy another car from you at a later date. But because you cannot be certain about the conditions in which the car will be used, you add a reserve factor to it. You design and build it well enough to last 80,000 or 90,000 miles.

This theory can be applied to human beings. We are built well enough to live through the reproductive years, and then nature throws in a reserve period. Longevity has an evolutionary advantage, since it allows parents and grandparents to protect the young for a longer period of time. This is especially important in a species like ours in which the young take a very long time to mature. Thus, our bodies are designed to last through the parenting period with some reserve. We are not built to last much longer. After the reserve period, human beings—like their automobiles at 90,000 miles—are on a straight line to complete breakdown.

The evolutionary theory is interesting, but it cannot explain why we live to an age at which our parenting duties are far behind us. However, it does lead us to search for biological factors behind the aging process and decline in old age.

The Elusive Search for the Aging Gene

The search for genes involved in the aging process is ongoing. Scientists are not really looking for a single gene, but rather for some genetic control over the biological process of aging. For example, chemical processes within the cell might be controlled by genetic endowment. Changes in these processes, including a loss of

There are specific areas of the world where people supposedly live very long lives.

Living to a Ripe Old Age in Ecuador: Fact or Fiction?

Think of what it would be like to live in a place where one-hundred-year-old people were not unusual. Our quest for answers to the riddle of longevity has brought scientists to many isolated communities around the world. One of the most prominent of these communities is Vilcabamba, in southern Ecuador. Claims of extreme longevity in this area of the world have met with either uncritical acceptance or harsh rejection, often without sufficient study. Richard Mazess and Sylvia Forman decided to look carefully into the phenomenon.

First the researchers had to find out how old the people in this community claimed to be. To accomplish this, Forman conducted a household census in the village, which included about 80 percent of the actual population living there. The results, combined with a few other surveys, provided this vital piece of information.

The second step, trying to find proof of the ages reported, was more difficult. Mazess examined any available birth and baptismal records from 1860 to 1940, as well as death and marriage records from this century. These frequently referred to older Vilcabamba residents, giving their ages while they were still young adults. For example, if a few records referred to a certain villager in 1940 as thirty-five years of age, he would be seventy-five years old in 1980. If he claimed to be eighty-six, the discrepancy would be obvious. The researchers were looking for significant differences between the actual ages and stated ages.

But they ran across a problem few would have considered before the study began. Positive identification of particular individuals was a nightmare, mainly because many people had the same names as their fathers and uncles and few familial names are used. For example, the last names of Carpio and Toledo are very common. Because the village is so insulated and the intermarriage

rate is great, it is possible for someone to have the same patronym (father's last name) and matronym (mother's maiden name). The same given names were used over many generations in some families, which explains why a cursory review of some records can support claims of extreme longevity—these reviews often mistook father and uncle for son or nephew. No one took the time and effort to reconstruct genealogies.

After painstakingly ascertaining the identities of their subjects, Mazess and Forman concluded that the older people in the community greatly exaggerated their ages. Up to about the age of 60 or 70 there was little systematic age exaggeration, but after that the exaggeration became clear. Generally, people claiming to be 80 were more likely to be about 77 and those claiming to be between 100 and 130 were more likely to be between 84 and 95.

Why do people exaggerate their ages when they get old? There seem to be no economic benefits, but the great respect and prestige accorded the very old may explain the phenomenon. Some have claimed that the increased attention and tourism causes the exaggeration, but this tendency existed long before the village became famous.

This does not mean that there are not very old people in the region. There is indeed a greater percentage of older people in this area than in other parts of Ecuador, but this can be explained by the migration of younger people to other areas that offer more economic opportunity, leaving a greater proportion of elderly behind. Still, many of the older people in Vilcabamba remain physically active and seem to maintain excellent cardiovascular health. Whether the person is really one hundred as claimed, or eighty, may not be as important as looking into how and why these older people seem to remain active. Future research can look into this.

Source: Mazess, R. B., and Forman, S. H. Longevity and Age Exaggeration in Vilcabamba, Ecuador. *Journal of Gerontology,* 1979, 34, 94–98.

efficiency in the cell's operation, might be built in (Watkin, 1983). Some evidence for genetic control comes from studies that show rats can be bred for longevity. In addition, a group of diseases causing very early and very fast aging, called **progeria,** appear to be genetically in-

progeria Disorders characterized by premature aging, ending in death. Children with the disease take on the appearance of the aged.

duced. In one of these disorders, called the Hutchinson-Gilford Syndrome, one-year-old children begin to show signs of rapid aging, including baldness, prominent bulging eyes, diminished fat, and large head size. After a few years their appearance is unmistakably like that of an elderly person, and victims usually die in their teens or before (McClearn and Foch, 1985). Other progerian disorders are found in early adults. These disorders are fascinating, but it is doubtful that a rare disorder can serve as a model for normal aging.

Other evidence for genetic participation in aging comes from twin studies. When 1,000 pairs of twins were followed for years to study their aging processes, monozygotic (identical) twins were consistently more similar than dizygotic (fraternal) twins. For example, identical twins were more likely to contract certain diseases, like cancer, and died closer together than fraternal twins did (Jarvik and Falek, 1962; Kallman and Jarvik, 1959). In addition, a relationship exists between parental longevity and the longevity of the offspring, although the relationship is less than earlier studies indicated (Palmore, 1983). However, interpreting such relationships is difficult, because environmental factors must be taken into account. Parents who live a long time may provide better nutrition or education, or simply be able to protect their children more than parents who do not live as long.

The most important evidence in favor of the genetic theory of aging comes from some unique studies performed by Leonard Hayflick (1977, 1976, 1974). Hayflick grew embryonic tissue in the laboratory in a disease-free environment and found that these cells grew and divided perfectly for months. Then they began to slow down, stopped dividing, and died. These cells underwent fifty cell divisions and then died. Cells obtained from young adults multiplied only about thirty times. Some cultures were allowed to divide thirty times and then were frozen. When thawed, these cultures divided only another twenty times or so and then died. As these cells aged, it took more time for them to double. In addition, a definite reduction in metabolic rate was evident. An accumulation of cellular debris and a total degeneration of the cell tissue took place (Hayflick, 1977). People do not die because their cells stop regenerating (Hayflick, 1976). We all die well before this. What is most important is the potential limit on life and the possibility that the changes in cell biochemistry associated with the aging cell may tell us something about why we age.

The evidence for some genetic participation in aging is strong. Although we have not yet found the gene or genes that control the aging process, it does not mean they do not exist (McClearn and Foch, 1985).

The Immunological Theory

When a germ invades the body, the immune system recognizes that the germ is a foreign body and fights the germ while leaving our own cells, which it can recognize, alone. As we age, our immune system breaks down (Walford, 1983). It loses its ability to protect us and no longer recognizes the difference between foreign bodies and our tissue. We begin to destroy our own cells. Evidence for this theory is fairly strong. Fighting disease depends on two cells. B cells are formed in the bone marrow, and T cells are produced in the thymus. T cells are responsible for the rejection of foreign cell tissue, including organ grafts and cancer cells. The thymus begins to degenerate shortly after sexual maturity. Studies show that people who are taking drugs to suppress the rejection of organ transplants are more susceptible to cancer. We may find an answer to the reduced immunity of the elderly by looking at the causes for the decline of the thymus (Makinodan, 1977). Immunological theory may well explain why the elderly are more vulnerable to disease, but whether it can explain the aging process itself is still controversial.

The Cellular Error Theory

For the body to survive, cells must reproduce, and the result must be a perfect copy of the parent cell. According

There is a relationship between parental longevity and the longevity of their offspring, but the question is whether the relationship is due to environmental or genetic factors or both?

to the cellular error theory of aging, as we age more mistakes in the copying process occur, allowing inaccurate genetic information to be delivered to the next generation of cells. This impairs the functioning of these cells, and aging—perhaps even death—results when the errors are great (Saxon and Etten, 1978).

The Cross-Linking and Free Radical Theories

Two biochemical theories show some promise in explaining aging. The cross-linking theory notes that elastin and collagen are proteins that form connective tissue. Collagen itself comprises about one-third of all the protein in the body. With age, these proteins form cross links or bonds with other molecules, resulting in more rigidity and less elasticity and leading to physical aging (Balasz, 1977; Bjorksten, 1968).

"Free radicals" are very reactive chemicals that are the by-product of normal cell metabolism. These chemicals are capable of damaging tissue and cell membranes. As they react with cell material, more free radicals are released, increasing the damage (Rockstein and Sussman, 1979). According to this "free radical theory," then, cell changes are responsible for aging. Some evidence for this theory comes from laboratory studies showing that certain enzymes counter these free radicals and reduce the amount of cell damage (Harman, 1981).

The Accumulation Theory

According to the accumulation theory, as cells age they become cluttered with waste products and partly completed proteins. This material interferes with the cell function, causing death. The most commonly researched waste product is lipofuscin, which does interfere with cell function. Shock (1977) found that lipofuscin comprises about one-third of the total heart muscle volume in the very elderly. It is still not clear, however, whether this is the cause or the effect of aging, and the actual effects of these materials are not clearly understood.

The Homeostasis Theory

The body is a system that can make adjustments to changing environments and keep a balance. Homeostasis is the process of keeping this balance. For example, body chemicals are regulated closely, and body temperature is constantly monitored. After a change, the body restores equilibrium (Fries and Crapo, 1981). As we age, our body's ability to maintain this balance declines. If homeostasis is not maintained, life cannot continue. The young person can respond better to major injury, whereas an older person dies from the flu. When organs cannot adapt to changes in the environment and their functioning sinks below what is necessary for life, we die.

The Wear-and-Tear Theory

The most common-sense theory is that as we age we simply wear out. Think of our bodies as machines. No matter what we do, the engine parts become less efficient and eventually wear out. Of course, if we take better care of the machine it lasts longer, and this applies to human beings as well as to machines. However, this theory is quite simplistic and ignores the fact that the body can repair itself and is not a helpless machine.

Lengthening the Life Span?

If we found out why we age, could we change our life span? Could we live 150 or even 200 years? It's only fair to admit that all these theories are really in their infancy. But a number hold promise for the future. For example, if there are specific genes that control the aging process, it may be possible in the far future to alter these genes so that we age more slowly. In addition, we may discover certain regimens that increase life span. Perhaps the most startling discovery in this area was made fifty years ago, when McCay and colleagues (1935) found that if they fed rats a very restricted caloric diet, but one with the correct nutrition, these animals lived longer than theoretically predicted by their life span. This has also been found in mice and fish (Barrows and Roeder, 1977). When the caloric intake of animals is restricted, immunological responses characteristic of young animals are greatly prolonged (Watkin, 1983). Before you start restricting your caloric intake to increase your life span, consider that half of McCay's rats died very early and that the restriction was very severe. The restricted animals were also retarded, and many were malformed as well (Whitney and Hamilton, 1984). In addition, making generalizations across the species is dangerous, and the meaning of these experiments is not yet apparent. Others deny that the life span of the rats was increased, arguing that some rats merely approximated their life span (Fries and Crapo, 1981). It is doubtful that the life span will be lengthened in the near future.

Life Expectancy

But perhaps we've been asking the wrong question. Perhaps we should forget about living 200 years and concentrate on living our full 100 or so years that we appear to be programmed to live. Progress in this area has been nothing short of spectacular.

The Increase in Life Expectancy

Someone born in 1900 could expect to live a little past age 49. By 1951, life expectancy had leaped to more than 68 years and as of 1984 it had increased to 74.6 (Metropolitan Life Insurance Co., 1985) (see Figure 18.1). Gains are still being made, although they are not continuous. The 1970s saw significant increases when compared with the relative stagnation of the 1960s (Metropolitan Life Insurance Co., 1986). The life expectancy for people in a number of developed nations is shown in Table 18.1. Although there are gaps between these countries, they have narrowed substantially.

True or False After a number of gains, the last few years have brought decreases in the average life expectancy of Americans.

F I G U R E   18.1

Gains in Life Expectancy Since 1900

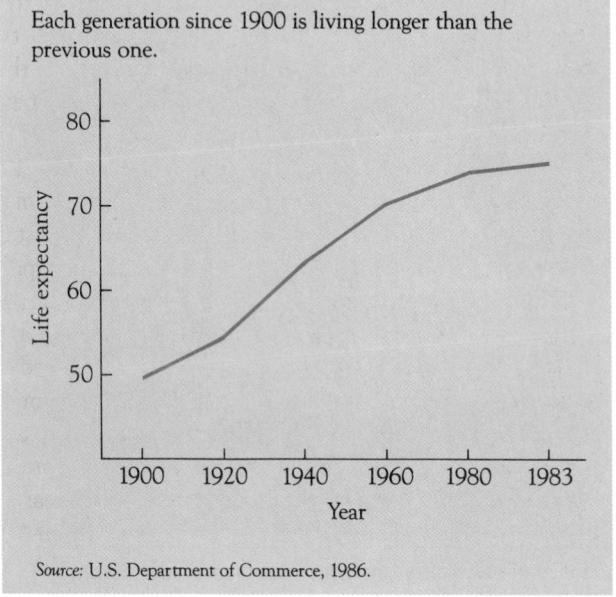

Each generation since 1900 is living longer than the previous one.

Source: U.S. Department of Commerce, 1986.

T A B L E   18.1

Life Expectancy by Sex and Age in Selected Countries (in Years)

The gap between life expectancy among developed nations is fairly narrow.

Country/Year(s)	Males	Females
Canada (1980–82)	71.9	78.9
United States (1979–81)	70.1	77.6
Denmark (1980–81)	71.1	77.2
France (1981)	70.4	78.5
Germany, F.R. (1979–81)	69.9	76.7
Netherlands (1981)	72.7	79.3
United Kingdom		
England and Wales (1980–82)	71.1	77.1
Northern Ireland (1979–81)	69.5	75.1
Scotland (1980–82)	69.0	75.2
Australia (1981)	71.4	78.4
Israel (1981)	72.7	75.9
Japan (1981)	73.8	79.1

Source: Metropolitan Life Insurance Company.

A word about life expectancy tables such as the one found in the Appendix is in order. They show how long a group of people of a particular age are expected to live. Of course, everyone is interested in the number of years a person can expect to live from birth. However, you will notice that some tables give the figures for other ages as well. For example, a person born in 1982 could expect to live 74.6 years, but if you were sixty years of age you could expect to live another 20.4 years. It seems that the older you are, the longer you are expected to live! Indeed, this is true. By the time you have reached sixty, you have escaped death at earlier ages and statistics tell us that you have a better chance of living even past the average life expectancy. If you are eighty-five your life expectancy is still another 6.3 years, but relatively few people reach that age.

Do Women Live Longer?

Do women outlive men? The clear answer is yes. At every age the life expectancy of women is significantly higher than that of men. For example, life expectancy for a boy born in the United States was 66.8 years in 1982, but 75 years for a baby girl. In developed countries throughout the world, the pattern is the same (Metropolitan Life Insurance Co., 1986). This does not hold in some underdeveloped countries, where males are valued more and given better nutrition during childhood. At age sixty, the average male could expect 16.8 more years of life, while the average female could expect 21.5 more years. This differential for people over sixty-five has actually widened since the turn of the century. In 1900 the differential mortality rate for men and women over sixty-five was only 6 percent, while today it hovers at about 40 percent (Turner, 1982). By the year 2000, the ratio of women to men will be 154 to 100 for those over age sixty-five, and 191 women per 100 men for those over age seventy-five (Ebersole and Hess, 1981).

Why do women outlive men at every age? Some argue that genetic differences can explain some of the pattern. Infant mortality is considerably higher for males than for females. Females have more resistance than males to infectious diseases, presumably because the X chromosomes carry genes for producing disease-fighting immun-ities (Goble and Konopka, 1973). Researchers point out that more males than females die before birth—a difference that cannot be attributed to socialization differences. Genetic differences may be one key.

True or False Life expectancy for infant females is greater than for infant males in the United States.

Lifestyle differences may be another possibility. The most common causes of male death at older ages are heart disease, cancer, stroke, and cirrhosis of the liver. Although genetic factors may be involved in these diseases, lifestyle differences between the sexes are significant. Between one-third and two-thirds of the difference have been attributed to smoking, which is related both to heart disease and to cancer (Botwinick, 1984; Waldron, 1976). Although the trend toward women smoking more has been noted, women usually smoke low-nicotine cigarettes and do not inhale as deeply. However, it would not be surprising to see health problems relating to smok-

Since women live to older ages than men in our society, there are many more older women available than men.

ing become more common among women. Cirrhosis of the liver is related to excessive alcohol consumption, another category in which men surpass women. Men are also more likely to die from traffic and hunting accidents. Diet may be still another factor, because until recently women were much more likely than men to watch their diets.

Some have pointed to the stress-filled life of males who are career-oriented, aggressive, and obsessed with achievement. The Type A behavior pattern appears more frequently in males than in females (Friedman and Rosenman, 1974), and this pattern is more related to life-threatening diseases. As more women enter the career world, they will be subject to the same stress-related illnesses that men are. However, work itself does not seem to be the problem. One study showed that Type A women between the ages of forty-five and seventy-four who have been in the labor force for more than half their lives have similar rates of heart disease when compared with Type A homemakers (Haynes et al., 1978). In addition, although women have been entering the labor force in unprecedented numbers since the end of World War II, heart disease in women has also declined as it has in men. In the Soviet Union, where the overwhelming majority of women work, women still outlive men by ten years (Botwinick, 1984). At the present time, we do not know exactly why women outlive men, but both genetics and lifestyle probably contribute to this phenomenon.

Racial Differences in Life Expectancy

Tables of live expectancy are also stratified by race. Throughout life, white males have higher expectancies than nonwhite males, and the same relationship holds for females. Nonwhite females, though, live longer than white males. The gaps are narrowing considerably. In 1900–1902, white females could expect to live 51.1 years, and white males 48.2 years, while nonwhite females had a life span of 35 years and nonwhite males 32.5 years. White females could expect to live about sixteen years longer, and white males about the same (Jackson, 1980). This has changed considerably. A white male infant born in 1981 could expect to live 71.1 years, while a black male infant could expect to live 64.4—a differential of about seven years. A white female infant born in 1981 could expect to live 78.5 years, while a black female infant could expect to live 73 years—a difference of

about four and a half years (U.S. Bureau of the Census, 1985). At age sixty the difference in life expectancy between white and nonwhite males is 17.7 versus 15.8 years, or about two years, and for females it is 22.7 versus 20.3 years, or about two and a half years. At age seventy-five and after, though, nonwhites die at later ages than whites (Botwinick, 1984). The difference in race and survival is probably due mostly to social factors, such as medical care and nutrition. Also, minority groups in the United States tend to live in environments where violent crime is more common. In the future, the gap will probably narrow even more, but it will take some time until the statistics will show no difference between whites and blacks.

True or False The gap between the life expectancies of blacks and whites has been narrowing since the turn of the century.

Physical Aging and Health in Later Adulthood

"Every man desires to live long, but no man would be old." This statement made more than 250 years ago, by Jonathan Swift in *Gulliver's Travels*, is as true today as it was then. For most of us, physical aging is linked with decline. In fact, psychologists use the term *senescence* to describe the period of life during which losses in physical capacity are most common (Levin and Levin, 1980). For too many people, however, aging is synonymous with senility. As we shall see, the changes that accompany aging need not be incapacitating, or even very disturbing, and individual differences become more pronounced with age.

Physical Signs of Aging

The most obvious changes are in skin and general appearance. Skin loses its elasticity, and there is a decrease in skin secretions. Fatty tissue underlying skin is lost, allowing veins to show (Ebersole and Hess, 1981). The skin becomes wrinkled and develops areas of darker pigment. Because blood vessels become more fragile, older people are more sensitive to bruises (Levin and Levin, 1980). When skin does bruise, it takes longer to heal. The body's ability to regulate temperature decreases, which partly explains why older people are likely to feel the cold more. The nose becomes elongated and the abdomen may bulge. The nails become tougher, grow more slowly, and become yellowed or weathered. Hair loses its pigment and thins.

Other noticeable changes are seen in teeth and height. Most elderly people do not have all thirty-two teeth, and gum and bone diseases are not uncommon (Rossman, 1981)—leading to problems in eating. When they were children, the current generation of elderly did not have the quality dental care available today to the upcoming generation, so perhaps the coming generation can avoid or at least reduce these dental problems. People also shrink with age. By age fifty to fifty-five there is a decrease of about one-half to three-quarters of an inch. This is attributable to a number of factors, including a flattening of the disks between vertebrae, making them smaller. In later life, changes in bone and other tissues, especially in the spine, lead to an increase in the curve of the spine that gives the elderly a more stooped appearance (Rossman, 1981).

Bones and muscles show signs of aging too. In later adulthood, muscles become weaker, and older people have less strength and move more slowly. Flexibility also declines with aging (Saxon and Etten, 1978). However, the effect of the aging process on muscles seems less than

Older people are more sensitive to the cold than younger people.

the effect of disuse. Regular physical exercise can maintain muscle strength and flexibility. As we age, bones lose mass and become less dense (Saxon and Etten, 1978). Older people, especially women, are prone to a disorder called **osteoporosis,** in which the bone tissue becomes absorbed and the bones become porous, causing them to fracture easily.

Changes occur in all body organs and systems. Blood pressure increases with age. Cardiac output is also reduced. Usually, this does not cause much of a problem, since demands are minimal and basal metabolism declines. However, when stressed the heart has less reserve capacity. Lungs become more rigid, perhaps because of cross linkage (see page 464) (Ebersole and Hess, 1981). Changes in the skeleton limit rib-cage expansion, and the muscles responsible for inhalation and exhalation become weaker. Changes in the digestive system include a decrease in digestive juices, making indigestion even more common among the elderly. Some foods are not as easily absorbed, and because of this some elderly are deficient in vitamins, such as B_1 and B_{12}, and minerals, such as iron and calcium (Ebersole and Hess, 1981).

The brain also changes with age (Bondareff, 1985). The speed at which nerve impulses are transmitted declines, which may explain their slower reaction times. This reduction affects all sensory, perception, and cognitive processes. Studies by means of electroencephalographs show that brain-wave patterns slow with age too (Saxon and Etten, 1978). Blood circulation and the utilization of oxygen by brain cells are reduced somewhat. Loss of cells with age has also been found, but the effects of this loss in normal aging is unknown. Sleep patterns also change. One-third of the elderly complain of sleep problems (Woodruff, 1985). Rapid-eye-movement sleep, associated with dreaming, also declines somewhat. Older people are less likely to sleep through the night and also spend less time in deep sleep (Saxon and Etten, 1978).

If these changes sound a bit depressing, consider these points. First, they occur gradually over a number of years. Second, there are many individual differences in aging—a sixty-year-old man may have a full head of hair, while a thirty-year-old may find his hair thinning and falling out. Third, aging is affected by individual health habits. For instance, people who drink and smoke immoderately are more likely to show age-related deficits than people who watch their health habits. Fourth, the extent to which these changes affect the lives of the elderly is a matter of controversy. If older people walk a bit slower, does it really matter? If older people feel the cold more, they can compensate by dressing properly. Finally, many of the physical problems we see in the elderly are really the result of disease, not aging.

Threats to Health

Too often, aging and disease are linked. Some physical age changes may bring about health problems. Increases in blood pressure and reduced elasticity of the arteries may lead to heart and circulatory problems. However, most physical aging can be summed up as a general slowing and is not in itself related to illness. But there is no denying that the elderly are more vulnerable to disease. As we age, chronic diseases become more frequent, while acute diseases become less so. **Chronic diseases,** such as diabetes, heart disease, and arthritis, are long, lingering affairs. They are usually progressive and irreversible. About 85 percent of all people over age sixty-five suffer from at least one chronic disease (Kalish, 1977). **Acute diseases** make sudden appearances, run their course, and disappear. The elderly are more likely to suffer from chronic health problems, tend to suffer more complications from all illnesses, and require longer periods of hospitalization when they become ill, whether the condition is acute or chronic (Metropolitan Life Insurance Co., 1984).

Heart Disease and Cancer

Heart disease is the most common cause of death in the elderly (Wolanin, 1981). It is estimated that 72 percent of all adults over age sixty-five have some cardiac disease

(Ebersole and Hess, 1981). Hypertension, or high blood pressure, affects a slightly greater percentage of those over sixty-five than those under that age, but it is a major health problem for both (Barrow and Smith, 1983). It is controllable, but half of all elderly sufferers do not take the medication needed to control the condition (Baltes, 1983).

The second most common cause of death among the elderly is cancer. It also shows an increase in incidence as we age (Upton, 1977). The most common fatal cancers among elderly males include cancers of the respiratory, digestive, and genital organs, while cancer of the digestive organs, breast, and respiratory system cause the most fatalities among females (U.S. Bureau of the Census, 1985). The cause of cancer is still unknown at the present time, as is the reason for the elderly's special vulnerability to the disorder.

True or False Cancer is the most common cause of death in the elderly.

Cerebrovascular Disease

Cerebrovascular disease, most commonly called *stroke*, is the third leading cause of death among elderly adults. Strokes are related to hypertension and arteriosclerosis. A stroke may result either from a substantial reduction in blood flow to the brain or from bleeding in the brain. The reduced blood flow is sometimes caused by a blood clot in the lining of the cerebral artery. Bleeding may be caused by a rupture of blood vessels in the brain, causing brain damage. Strokes are characterized by periods of unconsciousness and some degree of paralysis. How severe a stroke is depends on where the blockage in the brain is located as well as the amount of brain tissue involved. Although all strokes cause some permanent damage, their effects vary greatly. Some stroke victims die, others suffer from some loss of muscular function that responds successfully to rehabilitation, while others become greatly impaired and difficult to care for (Barrow and Smith, 1983). The long-term nature of the disease has led many researchers to look for ways to prevent strokes by identifying people who are at risk. There is hope that certain drugs and vascular surgery may help prevent them in the future (Steffl, 1981).

Osteoporosis

A condition that people have become very aware of because of recent widespread publicity is osteoporosis, which involves a gradual decrease in bone mass (see Figure 18.2). Osteoporosis is most commonly found in postmenopausal women. By about sixty years of age, 20 to 25 percent of women and 5 percent of men have osteoporosis (Hongladarom et al., 1982). Everyone loses bone mass with age, but the process can be dangerous if it is accelerated. As bones become more brittle and weak, falls are more likely to cause fractures. One of the most dangerous fractures is the hip fracture. Some 160,000 elderly Americans suffer broken hips each year, and one-sixth die from complications following them (Sterns et al.,

1985). Osteoporosis can also lead to physical deformities, including a stooping posture (Notelovitz and Ware, 1982). The cause of osteoporosis is thought to be a long-standing calcium deficiency, along with the decrease in the ability to absorb the mineral (Hamilton and Whitney, 1982). The calcium need of late middle-aged and elderly people is actually greater than that of younger people, but older people may not consume enough food containing calcium. The sex hormones—estrogen and androgen—both work against the process by which bone is broken down (Hongladarom et al., 1982). The reduced estrogen pro-

FIGURE 18.2

Osteoporosis

Spinal vertebrae weakened by osteoporosis collapse causing loss of height (all from the upper part of the body), inward curvature of the lower spine, outward curvature of the upper spine, and protruding of the abdomen.

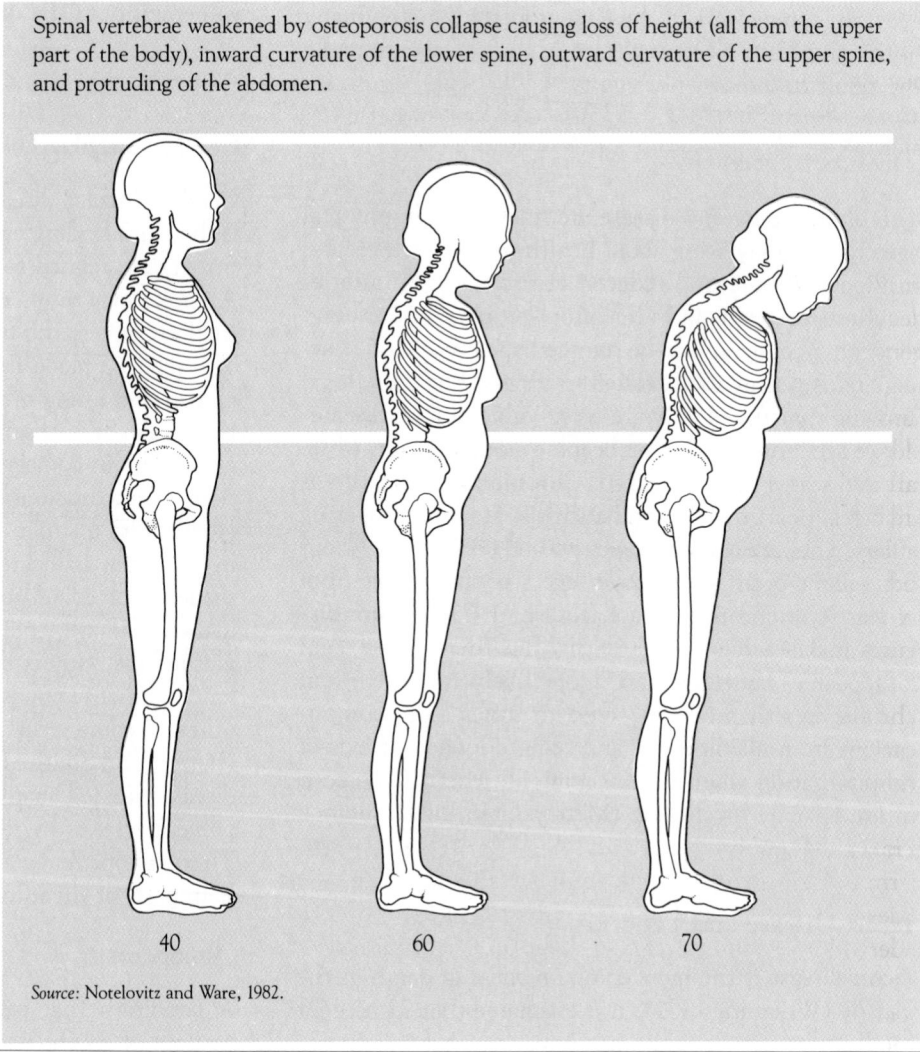

Source: Notelovitz and Ware, 1982.

duction in menopause increases the rate of bone loss. There is no way to restore bone that has been lost, but the rate of loss can be reduced and perhaps prevented through diet, adequate exercise, and sometimes hormone treatment (Notelovitz and Ware, 1982). The use of hormone therapy, consisting of estrogen, has been known to be successful for years, but with it came an increased risk of cancer. Now, however, estrogen is given with progesterone, another hormone, and this reduces the risk of cancer (Notelovitz and Ware, 1982).

Accidents

Children have the highest accident rate in the United States, but older adults have the highest disability and death rate from accidents. The accident rate among older adults is relatively low, compared with other age-groups, but when the elderly have an accident it tends to be more serious (Sterns et al., 1985). Falls and motor vehicle accidents are the most common.

True or False The elderly have the highest accident rate of any age-group.

Falls. "She fell and broke her hip. That's when the decline started." This is not an unusual statement. Degeneration and brittleness of bones, often caused by osteoporosis, frequently result in fractures from falls. Fractures in the elderly take a long time to heal, and the elderly are more likely to suffer from complications. Most falls occur in the home, but outside environmental hazards, such as ice and stairs, also take their toll.

Physical changes in the body contribute to falls. The reduction in visual and auditory abilities, the decrease in muscle strength, endurance, and coordination, impairments in balance, and the slowing of reaction time contribute to falls (Ochs et al., 1985; Bernard, 1969). The chances of an accident occurring can be reduced somewhat by examining the house or apartment for possible dangers, including mats and carpets that slide.

Traffic accidents. There is some disagreement concerning the frequency of highway accidents among the elderly. If we look at the number of accidents in which elderly drivers are involved, it does not appear that they are poorer drivers. For example, in 1985 only 6.6 percent of all accidents involved drivers over age sixty-five, while 9.8 percent of all the drivers in the United States are

over sixty-five (National Safety Council, 1986). Elderly drivers were involved in 8.3 percent of the fatal accidents, which is not out of line with their numbers, but the older driver does not drive as many miles as the younger adult. When statistics are adjusted for this fact, drivers over the age of sixty and below the age of twenty-five are involved in more accidents than other age-group. In terms of the number of miles driven, an increase in accidents begins between the ages of forty-five and sixty and continues throughout the rest of the life span.

The accident record of older drivers is nearly as bad as the record of young drivers (Salthouse, 1982). Older drivers are more likely to be involved in accidents involving improper lane changes, improper turning, failing to yield right of way, and ignoring traffic signals. Drivers under the age of twenty-five are involved in far more accidents involving excessive speed, fatigue, or driving on the wrong side of the road. Many accidents involving the elderly are the result of an inability to process information quickly or to notice signs while traveling at speed, a problem that will be described in detail later (Salthouse, 1982). Older drivers are not oblivious to their physical changes. They compensate by driving more cautiously and more slowly, driving fewer miles, using less-demanding roads, and not driving at night (Sterns et al., 1985). Most studies show that older drivers can do well on tasks relating to driving when the pace of making decisions on the road is similar to their speed of information-processing. It is when faster-paced decision-making is required that they do not do as well (Sterns et al., 1985).

It would be wrong to conclude that most elderly drivers constitute a safety hazard on the road, just as it is incorrect to argue that all young drivers are safety hazards. I have heard calls for the elderly to give up their licenses after age seventy, but this ignores the wide range of individual differences among the elderly. If we are interested in reducing traffic accidents, the number-one offenders are younger, inexperienced drivers. The answer lies in more stringent tests and physical examinations for drivers over the entire life span. In addition, driver education programs could stress special safety and driving tips for the elderly.

Stress

"Enjoy your golden years," the ads say, "those wonderful years when stress is minimal and you can live the good life." It is as if the older person suddenly becomes immune to the stresses of everyday life. Are the elderly less likely to experience stress?

The life stresses the elderly are most likely to experience, as detailed by the life-events scale (page 370), include the death of a spouse (the greatest stress on the scale), death of close family members, injury and illness, retirement, change in a family member's health, change in residence, and change in financial status. However, stress also arises from everyday hassles. The elderly do appear to suffer from less of these daily hassles—for example, they don't have to cope with daily commuting or office politics. Even if they do work, they are not likely to be trying to claw their way up through the ranks. They are also finished raising their children. The daily lives of the elderly can be organized around what they want to do; the daily rushing around of younger years is over. When older people were given questionnaires concerning sources of stress, they reported fewer than younger individuals (Chiriboga and Cutler, 1980). They also seem to be less preoccupied with these stresses. In fact, not only are these stresses less frequent, but the elderly appeared better able to distance themselves from them (Chiriboga and Dean, 1978).

Perhaps the best conclusion is that some types of stress are reduced in old age, while other types are not. For example, the elderly report more stress relating to health and less relating to family and work (McCrae, 1982). Many of the stresses in old age entail "exit events" like death and leaving work, while the stresses of the young involve "entrance events," such as starting a family (McCrae, 1982). However, socioeconomic status enters the picture. For the elderly who are poor or trying to live on a moderate fixed income, financial stresses can be significant and daily life a series of stresses as they try to pay their bills.

Stress is related to physical and psychological problems at every age. Stress may accelerate the aging process, or lead to physical disease by reducing the organism's capacity to respond to the stress (Eisdorfer and Wilkie, 1977). On the other hand, it may be considered a challenge by some people. As shown in earlier chapters, the cognitive interpretation of the stress is a vital factor.

Some authorities claim that the elderly are more likely to use more primitive defense mechanisms to cope with stress (Pfeiffer, 1977). Vaillant (1977) found a decrease in the use of immature defense mechanisms through middle age, but no evidence was presented for the elderly. Perhaps some slippage occurred? In two important studies, though, McCrae (1982) found that older people cope very much the same way younger people do; they do not show more rigidity. He found only one difference in coping style related to age. His middle-aged and older subjects did not use immature mechanisms, including escapist fantasy and hostile reactions, as much as younger subjects did. One caution should be noted. McCrae's study included older individuals who were in good mental and physical health and had ample financial resources. Different results might be obtained for elderly people who are infirm or poor.

Other evidence shows that certain changes in reaction to stress do occur with age. The elderly have less reserve capacity (ability to handle sudden stresses), and it takes longer for them to regain their equilibrium after they have experienced stress (Saxon and Etten, 1978). Others believe that a change from active to passive mastery of stress occurs. Increased dependence on passive strategies may be health-promoting (Chiriboga, 1980). Cohen (1980) found that elderly surgical patients who used denial were better off than those who used a more active, confrontational approach. Perhaps when there is nothing to be done, denial is a reasonable way of coping.

In conclusion, then, the elderly experience stress just as people of all ages do. However, the real difference may be in the type of stress-related events they experi-

Are elderly drivers involved in more than their share of auto accidents? It depends upon what figures one looks at.

ence. They are less likely to have day-to-day family and work stressors, but more likely to be dealing with "exit events" and chronic health stresses. They are also likely to need more time to recover from the stress. The inconsistent data on how the elderly cope may be explained by these differences in types of stress. When faced with the same daily problems, the coping styles of the elderly do not seem very different from younger people's. However, when faced with stressors for which little or nothing can be done, a more passive type of strategy, such as denial or acceptance, may be more suitable than a strategy of challenge and confrontation.

The Health Status of the Elderly

After looking at all these health risks, it is easy to think of the health status of the elderly as uniformly poor, but the majority are in fairly good health (Barrow and Smith, 1983) and rate their own health positively (see Table 18.2). Even people over seventy-five view their health optimistically (Ferraro, 1980). Most elderly people are active, and although they suffer from chronic conditions, they deal with them well (Botwinick, 1984). Robert Peck (1968) noted that a central issue in later adulthood was body transcendence versus body preoccupation. In order to enjoy life, the older person must learn to deal with chronic health problems and transcend them. Most elderly people do this successfully.

True or False People in their sixties and seventies describe their health status in positive terms.

The health status of the elderly affects every area of functioning. The healthier the person, the better his or her outlook on the world, and the worse a person's health, the less satisfied that person is (Schmitz-Scherzer, 1983). Health affects life satisfaction, morale, and cognitive functioning (Birren and Renner, 1983; Coleman, 1983). Subjective experience is also very important, and how the elderly view their health may be the most important factor in life satisfaction (Larson, 1978).

How can we explain the fact that despite objective declines in health status even very elderly people see their health as positive? The elderly compare their health status with others of the same age instead of with younger people. In addition, people rate their health as negative when it requires some limitation of activity. Since the elderly are usually less active, their symptoms do not limit their activity as much as we would think. This

---

T A B L E   18.2

How the Elderly Rate Their Own Health

Most elderly perceive their health as good, very good, or excellent.

Perceived Health Status	65–74 Years	75 Years and Over
Excellent	15.5	15.8
Very good	19.6	18.6
Good	32.5	30.8
Fair	21.4	21.3
Poor	10.6	13.0

Source: National Center for Health Statistics, 1986.

---

explains why people entering their sixties begin to define their health as better than the health of people in the younger years of adulthood (Cockerham et al., 1983).

Mental Health

Mental illness occurs more often in older adults than in younger people. Between 18 percent and 25 percent of the elderly suffer from mental health problems (Burnside, 1984). Some of these problems involve chronic organic mental disorders, such as Alzheimer's disease, but depression and alcoholism are common among the elderly too.

True or False Mental illness occurs more often in young adults than in the elderly.

Depression

The most common emotional problem found in the elderly is depression (LaRue et al., 1985). In fact, depression is found more frequently in the elderly than in any other age-group (Altrocchi, 1980). About 10 to 15 percent of the elderly require treatment for depression. The symptoms of depression are the same as for depression in other age-groups. Sadness, lethargy, and low self-concept are prominent (Wigdor, 1983). The causes of depression in the elderly include isolation and loneliness, bereavement, loss of role, poor health, and changes in brain chemistry—for example, some researchers link depression to changes in neurotransmitters (LaRue et al., 1985). It is possible that such neurological changes make the elderly more vulnerable to depression. However, environmental causes are also important. In a survey conducted for the National Council on Aging, 12 percent of the sample of people over age sixty-five reported being lonely (Burnside, 1984). Some 50 percent of the women and 13.6 percent of the men over age sixty-five were widowed and suffered from depression during bereavement. In addition, loss of role is a factor. Unlike other societies, where the role of the elderly is spelled out clearly and older adults are rewarded for their status and wisdom, the elderly population in the United States is not given a socially important role. In societies where the elderly do have such a role, they suffer less depression (Altrocchi, 1980).

Depression in the elderly is often treated successfully if the cause is environmental and not due to deterioration of the brain (Van de Plaats, 1983). The treatment for depression is varied and may include social support, improved nutrition, and medication.

Suicide Among the Elderly

Suicide among the elderly is anything but rare. The rate for suicide among women increases until the mid-forties, then declines through the eighties. No figures beyond age eighty are available. The suicide rate for men rises and falls between age twenty-five and age forty, but then continues to rise through the eighties. Although together the overall statistic for the suicide rate is 21.2 per 100,000 people, the rate for men is 42.5 and for women 7.5 (Kastenbaum, 1985). Although the suicide rate among the elderly is still the highest among all age-groups, there has been a slight but steady decline in the rate over the last twenty-five years (Kastenbaum, 1985). Almost three-quarters of all elderly suicide victims visit a doctor in the month before committing suicide. The doctor probably does not recognize the suicide potential (Levy et al., 1980). Among the potential warning signs of suicide are depression, withdrawal, bereavement, expectation of death, less organization and complexity of behavior, helplessness, institutionalization, physical illness and pain, alcoholism, reaching a decision that one's life has no purpose, and organic deterioration (Pelizza, 1979). However, these are symptoms that are found in many people who will not attempt suicide. Although predicting suicide is difficult in many cases, being aware that there is a potential for it is a place to start.

Organic Syndromes

The most serious threats to the mental health of the elderly are chronic brain dysfunctions. About 5 percent of the population over age sixty-five suffer from some chronic brain dysfunction that interferes with functioning, and another 10 percent suffer mild to moderate cognitive impairment (Coyle et al., 1983). There are many such disorders.

Senile dementia. Although depression may be the most common mental health problem, senile dementia is the most feared (Gatz et al., 1980). Actually, senile dementia is better thought of as a syndrome—a collection of symptoms—than as one disease. This term is used to encompass a number of organic disorders that involve loss of intellectual abilities, such as memory, judgment, abstract thought, and changes in personality and behavior (American Psychiatric Association, 1980). However, many people show signs of these disorders, especially if they are depressed, and some have argued that dementia is mistaken for depression in between 8 percent and 15 percent of all cases (Ron et al., 1979).

The differences between depression and dementia are important. Depressed elderly people often show cognitive problems, such as failing memory and the like, but when motivated to perform they can succeed. Depression is primarily a disturbance of mood; the cognitive deficits are secondary. In dementia, disordered intellectual functioning is primary and the mood abnormalities are less pervasive. In depression, we can often point to an event or a date as its start, whereas this is not the case with dementia. The symptoms of depression progress more rapidly (American Psychiatric Association, 1980). In addition, when elderly people are treated for depression, their cognitive functioning improves significantly, but this is not the case for people suffering from dementia (LaRue et al., 1985).

There are many types of senile dementia, which is also called primary degenerative dementia. In *multi-infarct dementia*, there is a patchy intellectual deterioration. Some functions are left intact, while others wither. This type of dementia is caused by multiple blood clots in parts of the brain, which kill cells and reduce functioning. Of the elderly who have serious cognitive impairment, between 15 percent and 40 percent suffer from this multi-infarct type, while 60 percent suffer from one of the most mysterious diseases of our time—Alzheimer's disease (Burnside, 1984).

Alzheimer's disease.   A leading cause of death among the elderly is **Alzheimer's disease,** but that fact is not shown clearly by the statistics. Patients with Alzheimer's often linger in a very weakened state for fifteen or more years and finally die from another disorder because of their weakened condition (Heckler, 1985). Alzheimer's disease is a progressive and irreversible deterioration of brain tissue that is marked by mental disorientation, social withdrawal, and loss of memory (Heckler, 1985). Alzheimer's patients have difficulty naming objects and show other semantic problems, such as not being able to describe how a table and a chair are alike (Nebes et al., 1986). It is the most common cause of severe intellectual impairment in older people (Rickards et al., 1985). The symptoms of memory loss, bizarre behavior, and intellectual deficits result from changes that take place within the brain. Estimates of its prevalence vary, but among people age sixty-five to seventy-five about 6 percent have the disorder, about 10 percent of the population between seventy-five and eighty-five have it, and 20 percent of those over eighty-five suffer from Alzheimer's (Heckler, 1985).

Since Alzheimer's disease was first identified in 1906, we have learned much about it, but its cause remains unknown. Diagnosis is difficult because the symptoms are common to other disorders found in the elderly (Khachaturian, 1985). The only way to diagnose Alzheimer's disease positively is through examination of brain tissue (Heckler, 1985), but of course this is not a practical method, and the most common method of diagnosis is to rule out all other possible reasons for the behavior. The search is on for new ways to diagnose the disease through both brain scans and behavioral and psychological measures. Incorrect diagnosis occurs in between 10 percent and 30 percent of all cases (Khachaturian, 1985), which is a problem both for researchers, who must be certain of the disorder they are studying, and for clinicians, who must treat the illness.

What causes the disease? Some researchers believe that neurotransmitter and neurochemical deficits are the culprit, others argue that it is a slow virus, and still others point to an excessive accumulation of toxins in the brain, one being aluminum. Abnormally high levels of aluminum have been found in many (but not all) people suf-

> **Alzheimer's disease**   An organic disorder of the elderly involving progressive and irreversible deterioration of brain tissue, causing cognitive and behavioral deficits.

fering from the disease. Although we are all exposed to large amounts of aluminum, most healthy people show very little of it in their systems. Why and how people with Alzheimer's retain such quantities of the substance is not known yet. Research on how this toxin is implicated in the disease is ongoing (Turkington, 1987). Still others believe Alzheimer's disease is an autoimmune disorder (Heckler, 1985).

The course of the disease is variable, but it can be described in terms of four phases. In the first phase, the person has less energy and drive and reacts slowly. Throughout the course of the disease, memory impairment becomes progressively more serious (Vitaliano et al., 1986). In the second phase, the patient's speech slows and he or she has difficulty planning ahead, becomes mentally confused, cannot follow a story, and becomes self-absorbed and insensitive to the needs of others. In the third phase, the patient loses orientation to time and place and may not be able to identify familiar people. In the fourth and last phase, the patient is apathetic and completely unable to function, even in familiar surroundings, requiring help with everyday living. Sometimes depression, delusions, and delirium occur (Powell and Courtice, 1983). The disease may develop either slowly or rapidly.

When autopsies are performed on victims of Alzheimer's disease, certain irregularities of the brain can be observed. One of these irregularities is the accumulation of abnormal fibers in the neuron, called neurofibrillary tangles. They occur mostly in a part of the brain called the hippocampus, which controls memory and emotion, so this might explain the memory and emotional problems. Other observable irregularities in the brain are neuritic plaques, or collections of degenerated cell material, and granulovacuolar degeneration, which occurs when the cell becomes filled with cavities, called vacuoles, and fluid and other material—the greater the degeneration, the greater the loss of mental functions (Powell and Courtice, 1983). Treatment involves administration of drugs to limit symptoms. Research into

Alzheimer's disease is expanding rapidly, but it will be some time before we have all the answers.

True or False Alzheimer's disease is a communicable disease.

Factors Related to Longevity

Harping on these physical and mental problems leaves the wrong impression. Most elderly people are optimistic about life, and despite these problems, most people want to live long lives. Shigechio Izumi had his own secret of life and every one-hundred-year-old person has his or her own secrets. Science has also found some interesting predictors of long life. Although these are based on correlational studies that do not indicate cause and effect (see pages 27–28) and the correlations are not perfect, they do present us with some interesting data.

Predictors of Longevity

Fries and Crapo (1981) list nine factors that slow the rate of aging, delay the development of disease, and correlate with longevity: exercise, not smoking, moderation in alcohol consumption, not being obese, proper diet, avoidance of environmental toxins, use of mature defense mechanisms (such as humor, altruism, mild denial, or suppression), a belief in one's own worth, and avoidance of injury by taking such precautions as wearing seat belts. Studies consistently show that proper diet, not smoking cigarettes, and exercise and activity are factors important to health and long life (Botwinick, 1984). Another factor is genetics. People whose parents live a long time are more likely to have long lives too, so heredity may be important (Palmore, 1983). However, it does not appear to be a factor after age sixty, although people surviving beyond sixty probably have sound genetic constitutions. Of these factors, two require further explanation—exercise and diet.

Exercise

The elderly are woefully out of shape. Between 60 percent and 70 percent are physically unfit, according to the President's Council on Physical Fitness (Clarke, 1977). Exercise is a low priority on their list of preferred leisure activities. The elderly hold a more negative view of physical exercise than any other group (Burrus-Bammel and

Bammel, 1985). This is especially unfortunate because the benefits of physical fitness are great—for instance, leg strength, flexibility, endurance, cardiac output, and respiration are all affected in a positive way by exercise (Clark, 1977). It helps develop and maintain an efficient cardiovascular system, lowers blood pressure, relieves stress, controls body fat, decelerates the deterioration of bone tissue, and leads to an increase in feelings of well-being (Shock, 1983; Steffl, 1981). The lack of physical exercise is not just a problem of Americans. A study of pensioners in the Soviet Union found that even though people had more free time, there was no increase in physical exercise (Sachuk and Moskalets, 1983).

True or False Most elderly people are out of shape and do not exercise regularly.

Although some reduction in activity with age may be expected, it does not have to be as great as indicated. Of course, any physical activity program for the aged must take into consideration the person's health and physical condition (Kalish, 1975). We may see some

The beneficial effects of exercise are not restricted to any age group.

changes in this area, though, and cohort effects may be strong. Many young and middle-aged adults are products of generations that are more concerned about physical fitness. As they progress through the life cycle, perhaps they will continue to exercise. The elderly of the future may be more physically fit.

Nutrition

Some authorities estimate that one-third to one-half of health problems experienced by the elderly are related to nutrition (Long and Shannon, 1983). Disorders such as iron deficiency anemia, deficiency in vitamins, and obesity are directly related to malnutrition, while diabetes, hypertension, cardiovascular diseases, and osteoporosis are influenced by nutrition (Long and Shannon, 1983). Some argue that cancer should be included on this list. Some emotional and behavioral problems, such as listlessness and confusion, may be caused by nutritional deficiencies as well, and dehydration among the elderly is a significant health concern too (Steffl, 1981). In addition, obesity is common. One survey found that 84 percent of the men and 71 percent of women over the age of fifty are overweight (Saxon and Etten, 1978).

Nutritional requirements of the elderly are similar to those of other groups, although less-active older people require fewer calories (Saxon and Etten, 1978). Caloric requirements decrease with age because metabolism rate declines with age. The rule of thumb is that there is a reduction in caloric need of about 7.5 percent for each decade past twenty-five years (Diekelmann, 1977). Although caloric intake should decrease somewhat, there is no decline in the need for essential vitamins. The answer is to eat less fat and less fried food and to substitute fruit for sweets. Increasing fiber intake, decreasing salt, and sufficient fluid intake are also important dietary considerations (Diekelmann, 1977). According to the ten-state nutrition survey, undernutrition in the elderly was not limited to the very poor or to any one ethnic group. It was mostly due to poor food choices. Some nutritional deficiencies are seen in the elderly, including deficiencies in vitamins D, C, and A. Both vitamin A and vitamin C help fight infection, and because the elderly absorb iron poorly, they are more likely to become anemic. Calcium intake is also important because it is needed for bone strength (Long and Shannon, 1983).

Many elderly adults lose interest in food when their spouses and friends die. Eating is a social activity and many people are not used to eating alone. For some, poverty does not allow them to eat balanced meals, and older people with time on their hands are apt to snack on high-sugar foods. Another important element is loss of teeth and problems with dentures that make it uncomfortable to eat.

Drug-Nutrient Interactions

The elderly take many medications, and new research shows that these sometimes interact with food, causing unusual problems. Some cancer drugs decrease appetite and alter tastes. Antacids, laxatives, and antibiotics decrease nutrient absorption, and some hypertension drugs inhibit the production of enzymes necessary for the body to use vitamin B_6. Some drugs, such as some anticonvulsive drugs used to treat epilepsy, increase the body's use of vitamins. Food may also affect the effectiveness of drugs. One well-known example involves the antibiotic tetracycline, which loses its effectiveness if dairy products are consumed with it. The most hazardous interaction between medication and food involves monoamine oxidase, which is sometimes prescribed for depression and high blood pressure.* When this medication reacts with a substance in foods called tyramine, the result can be dangerously high blood pressure, hemorrhage, and sometimes death. Such foods as pickled herring, sharp or aged cheese, bananas, and a variety of other foods can contain tyramine (Long and Shannon, 1983).

Sensory Changes in Later Adulthood

The quality of daily life for older people depends on their health and the way they can cope with chronic illness, but it also depends on how well their senses—their windows on the world—function.

Vision

Vision worsens with age, and many of the changes can be thought of as progressive deterioration continuing from middle age. Pupil size decreases, and the lens loses its elasticity, thickens, and yellows. The elderly often

---

*There are now new medications for high blood pressure which may not involve such risks, but patients taking any medication should consult their doctor concerning drug-nutrient reactions.

complain of difficulty seeing in conditions of glare. Depth perception begins to decline in the fifties, and this decline is significant by the seventies (Walk, 1981). There is less sensitivity to low-level illumination, and dark adaptation worsens. In fact, by the age of eighty, dark adaptation levels off to be one hundred times worse than in the thirties (Walk, 1981). Older people also have more difficulty discriminating colors, especially blue, blue-green, and violet (Schaie, 1981). The ability to discriminate objects at a distance also decreases. The visual field shrinks by about two degrees per decade beginning at age forty-five (Salthouse, 1982).

Static visual acuity is usually measured in a stationary manner by reading letters off a chart. **Dynamic visual acuity** involves the visual processing of information while in motion. Studies have found that people over age seventy-five have worse dynamic visual acuity than younger people, even when they have the same static visual acuity. This decrement is even more evident when dynamic acuity is measured under conditions of poor illumination. Driving at night, then, becomes a significant problem. Studies comparing older and younger adults show that elderly people do not process the information on highway signs until they are much closer to them, giving them less time to react. The combination of motion and low illumination causes problems for the elderly driver (Salthouse, 1982).

The meaning of these deficits is clear. Visual abilities are reduced in the elderly, especially under conditions of low illumination, glare, and motion. Even surfaces like shiny floors are likely to cause problems for the elderly, and rapid changes in lighting conditions that require quick readjustment of the lens are especially troublesome. The finding that dynamic visual acuity is poor in the elderly explains some of the driving problems they have. When an elderly driver going sixty miles an hour says he did not see the sign until the last minute, it is probably true. Combined with problems of glare and dark adaptation, many elderly drivers would be wise to curtail their night driving, and many do.

The effects of aging on vision described above are gradual and can be compensated for by using glasses and care. However, the elderly are also more likely to suffer from eye disease than younger adults, although most elderly will not experience serious visual impairment. Of the 1.4 million people suffering from severe visual impairment, such as inability to read newspaper print even with glasses, 990,000 are over the age of sixty-five. Of

dynamic visual acuity   The ability to process visual information while in motion.

550,000 people who are legally blind, about half are over sixty-five (Kline and Schieber, 1985).

The most common visual problems are cataracts and glaucoma. A cataract is a pathological increase in the opacity of the lens. Between 20 percent and 25 percent of the elderly in their seventies have cataracts (Botwinick, 1984). Cataracts diminish visual acuity and can cause blindness, but the condition can be surgically corrected, and the procedure is now the fifth most frequent major surgery performed in the United States. Glaucoma, which occurs in about one out of 200 people past the age of forty and is most common in people in their sixties (Rockstein and Sussman, 1979), is really a group of disorders characterized by an increase in pressure in the eyeball and a degeneration of the optic nerve. Unfortunately, the most prevalent type of glaucoma among the elderly does not produce symptoms until damage to the retina has already occurred. It can be detected by a simple test in the doctor's office and treated through medication (Kline and Schieber, 1985).

Hearing

From a behavioral viewpoint, the decline in the auditory sense may be more important than the decline in the visual sense. Hearing loss begins early in the thirties for both males and females, but the degeneration in the auditory system, called presbycusis, increases as we age, and these physiological changes are the cause of the reduction in auditory ability (Olsho et al., 1985). The incidence of hearing impairments rises sharply after age sixty. By the seventies, as many as 75 percent have some problem, and 15 percent of the population over sixty-five are deaf (Botwinick, 1984).

Hearing loss shows itself in the increase in thresholds for pure tones. The elderly have difficulty hearing faint noises. Loss of hearing among high-pitch sounds causes difficulty in speech and pitch discrimination. Any competing noise in the environment adds to their auditory problems (Schaie, 1981). Men suffer greater hearing loss at high frequencies (Schaie, 1981). Some authorities claim that women suffer greater hearing loss at low frequencies, while others say that it is about equal (Schaie, 1981; Corso, 1977). Because of their greater hearing loss at high frequencies, men are likely to show more problems in speech discrimination than women, especially when the environment is noisy.

True or False Elderly men have more difficulty hearing and discriminating speech than elderly women.

Progressive hearing loss often leads to interpersonal problems. For example, older people may not realize that they do not hear as well and accuse someone of talking too softly or talking behind their back. They may also misunderstand verbal communication. When someone talks very loudly in response to their lack of comprehension, they may ask the communicator to quiet down because they are not deaf. The elderly may sometimes be helped by hearing aids that amplify sound, but these hearing aids do not make it clearer. Some changes in the environment are helpful as well, such as rearranging furniture to provide more face-to-face contact and reducing background noise generated by household appliances (Olsho et al., 1985). Finally, speaking slightly louder, at a normal rate but not rapidly, keeping lip movements visible, making certain you have the attention of the elderly person before speaking, and rephrasing rather than merely repeating the message can also help (Hull, 1984).

Taste and Smell

Some evidence indicates a change in taste preferences with age. There is an increase in sensitivity to bitter tastes and a decrease in sensitivity to saltiness (Engen, 1977). Older people gradually lose sensitivity to sweet tastes with age, but the recent studies report this loss as much smaller than was found in earlier studies, and large individual differences are found (Moore et al., 1982). One study found that the elderly rated high concentrations of salt and sugar as more pleasant than younger subjects (Murphy and Withee, 1986). Some decline in the sense of smell occurs too (Botwinick, 1984). In one experiment, Schiffman and Pasternak (1979) found that older people age seventy-two to seventy-eight were not as good at discriminating food odors as young adults.

Some of the decline in these senses may be more the result of disease, smoking, and gender than aging itself (Engen, 1977). Women show less of a decline than men, and people who smoke show a greater decline in taste than people who do not.

Touch and Pain

Sensitivity to touch and pain decreases with age (Walk, 1981; Kenshalo, 1977). When people between the ages of nineteen and eighty-eight were tested, a reduced sensitivity to touch was found across the life span (Thornbury and Mistretta, 1981). However, significant individual differences were found, and the decreasing sensitivity did not interfere with normal functioning. The changes are relatively minor.

There is evidence that older people do not feel pain as intensely as younger people (Botwinick, 1984). The time it takes to become aware of pain increases slightly up to age sixty, after which the increase is even more noticeable (Botwinick, 1984). If this is so, why would the elderly feel it less but seem to complain about it more? Two reasons are given. First, this reduction in pain sensitivity does not mean that the elderly do not experience pain, only that the pain is relatively less intense than when they were younger. Anyone who has seen the elderly in pain knows that they feel pain readily. Second, the elderly suffer from chronic pain, such as from arthritis, much more than the young.

True or False The elderly experience pain more intensely than younger people do.

Reaction Time

Perhaps the most common finding in the aging research concerns the general slowing with age. Activities that are a part of daily living—such as dialing a telephone, zipping up a jacket, or cutting with a knife—are all slowed with age (Salthouse, 1985). Older adults both make their decisions more slowly and execute them more slowly. This slowing may be the result of physiological changes in the sense organs and the decrease in the speed of neural transmission. All processes slow in the aged, including those involved in sensation, perception, and cognitive abilities (Botwinick, 1984). The extent to which each of these contributes to the slowness in behavior is debatable. Another cause is the tendency of older adults to react with more caution than younger adults, as well as their desire to be accurate rather than simply fast (Botwinick, 1984).

But predicting a person's speed of performance on the basis of age alone is hazardous, because individual differences are plentiful. Healthy individuals of all ages react faster than those in poorer health, and physically healthy older adults who are physically active have faster reaction times than sedentary middle-aged adults (Salthouse, 1985). It is then possible to find a physically healthy active group of older adults who may be equal or superior to physically inactive unhealthy younger adults in reaction time (Salthouse, 1985). One interesting finding is that when older people are given practice, they respond well, improving significantly on speed-related tasks (Welford, 1977).

The Senses and the Real World

Few would disagree that generally the senses show some slowing and decline with age, although individual differences are great. However, most elderly adults compensate for these changes. Almost all the decrements noted here can be compensated for through medical intervention, environmental manipulation, and careful individual planning. For instance, visual and auditory problems may be reduced with eyeglasses and hearing aids. The environment can also be manipulated so that the elderly can pay greater attention to what is being said and taking place and thereby become more a part of the action. Or older people who understand that they react more slowly or do not see well can plan vacations so that they do not have to drive at night and reduce speed on the road to one that is safe yet does not hinder traffic. For most elderly, the decreases in sensory acuity need not unduly affect their enjoyment of life.

The Rectangular Curve of the Future

It will be some time before the human life span is increased, but good health practices, good medical care, and good nutrition affect how long we live within this life span. What will the future bring? Many scientists believe that eventually more and more people will reach older and older ages. This is graphed on the rectangular survival curve (see Figure 18.3). The initial dip represents infant mortality, a statistic that will probably always be with us. The slow decline in mortality from age one through age seventy shows the relatively small percentage of deaths occurring during these ages. After age sev-

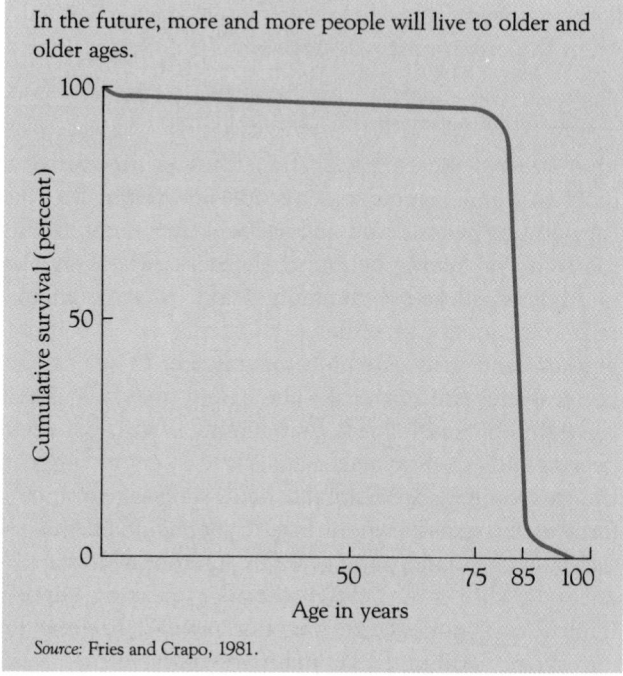

FIGURE 18.3

The Rectangular Survival Curve

In the future, more and more people will live to older and older ages.

Cumulative survival (percent)

Age in years

Source: Fries and Crapo, 1981.

enty-five, the curve drops sharply and within a few years most have died. Finally, the curve slackens to represent those few who survive to very old age. In the future, the curve will shift so that the sharp drop occurs at older ages. We have seen this trend develop and accelerate as more people than ever before live to a ripe old age.

The question is no longer so much one of survival but one of quality of life. Most of the normal physiological and sensory changes that occur with aging need not greatly impair the ability of elderly people to enjoy their lives. In addition, good health habits can increase their vitality and their resistance to disease and injury. Social and medical personnel interested in the physical and psychological health of the elderly must now be concerned not only with prolonging survival but also with providing the necessary preventive and remedial care so the elderly can remain fully functioning members of the community for their entire life.

Summary

1. Although claims of extreme longevity in some rural societies have been made, scientists have proven them incorrect.

2. *Life span* is the maximum life expected of a species, while *life expectancy* is the number of years remaining to a group of a particular age

within a society. The human life span has not changed for thousands of years, but within the past century life expectancy has increased greatly.

3. There are many theories of aging in human beings. The evolutionary view argues that an evolutionary advantage to longevity allows us to protect the young for a longer period of time. The genetic view argues that we are genetically programmed to age. Some theorists believe that aging is due to a breakdown of the immune system, leaving the elderly more vulnerable to disease, others believe that errors in cell reproduction lead to aging and death. The "cross-linking theory" argues that, with age, the elastin and collagen in the body link to other substances and cause rigidity and aging, while the "free radical theory" notes that certain very reactive by-products of cellular metabolism may cause cell damage. The accumulation theory assumes that aging is caused by a buildup of waste products within the cell. The homeostasis theory argues that, with age we lose the ability to cope with changes in the internal and external environment. The wear-and-tear theory argues that bodies simply wear out. No single theory of aging is fully accepted.

4. The average life expectancy of people born in Western societies has increased dramatically since the turn of the century. The life expectancy for females is greater than that for males. The reasons may be genetic and/or environmental. Although whites have a longer life expectancy than blacks, the gap is narrowing.

5. The most obvious changes due to aging are seen in physical appearance, as the skin wrinkles and loses elasticity, the nose elongates, the person shrinks slightly, and teeth are lost. In addition, muscles decrease in strength, bones become more rigid and fracture more easily, blood pressure increases, cardiac output decreases, and changes in the digestive system make the system less efficient, transmission of brain impulses slows and sleep patterns change.

6. Aging and illness are not the same. In general, with aging comes a slowing of body processes. The elderly are more likely to suffer from chronic diseases than younger people, and heart disease, cancer, and cerebrovascular disease (stroke) are

the three most common causes of death for the elderly.

7. Although the accident rate is lower among the elderly than among some younger groups, the elderly are more likely to suffer death or disability from accidents. Falls are relatively common and often result in fractures. One reason for these fractures is the condition of bone loss in the elderly known as osteoporosis. Traffic accidents are also a concern. Although the gross number of traffic accidents in which the elderly are involved is not out of line with their numbers, it is when this figure is corrected for number of miles driven that it is clear that the elderly are involved in more accidents than we would expect from their numbers.

8. The causes of stress in the lives of the elderly are different. The elderly are less likely to experience daily hassles or stress due to entrance events, such as starting something new, but they are more likely to suffer from health-related stresses and stresses arising from exit events, such as loss of a loved one. The elderly take a longer time to return to equilibrium after experiencing stress.

9. Despite suffering from chronic diseases, most elderly people evaluate their health in positive terms.

10. Mental illness is more prevalent among the aged than among younger groups. Depression is the most common problem, and the suicide rates among the elderly are quite high. A number of organic disorders are major causes of mental illness, the most prominent being Alzheimer's disease.

11. Alzheimer's disease involves a progressive deterioration of brain tissue resulting in cognitive impairments in memory and judgment and disorganized behavior. The cause of this disease is not known.

12. Vision worsens in old age. The elderly have more difficulty seeing under conditions of low illumination, glare, or when in motion. Visual problems are commonly caused by cataracts and glaucoma. Hearing loss in old age may affect the ability to understand spoken language. The evidence on smell and taste is inconsistent, but some relatively minor decrements occur here as well. The sense of touch also decreases slightly

with age, and the elderly feel pain less intensely and take longer to react to it. The elderly react more slowly, perhaps due to decreases in the speed of neural transmissions.

Answers to True or False Statements

1. *False* Correct statement: Under closer scrutiny, these claims have been disproved.
2. *False* Correct statement: The life expectancy of Americans continues to increase, although it does not show an increase each year.
3. *True* As a group, females can expect to live longer than males in the United States.
4. *True* The life expectancy gap between blacks and whites has narrowed considerably.
5. *False* Correct statement: Heart disease is the most common cause of death in the elderly.
6. *False* Correct statement: Children have more accidents, but those suffered by the elderly are more likely to be life-threatening or to lead to disabilities.
7. *True* People in their sixties and seventies describe their health in positive terms.

8. *False* Correct statement: Mental illness occurs more often in the elderly than in younger people.
9. *False* Correct statement: Although the exact cause of Alzheimer's disease is presently unknown, it is not communicable.
10. *True* Most elderly people are not physically fit and do not exercise regularly.
11. *True* Elderly men lose more of their ability to hear high-frequency sounds, and this causes them to have difficulty discriminating speech sounds.
12. *False* Correct statement: The elderly experience pain less intensely than younger people do, but because of chronic conditions they must live with it daily.

Cognitive Development in Later Adulthood

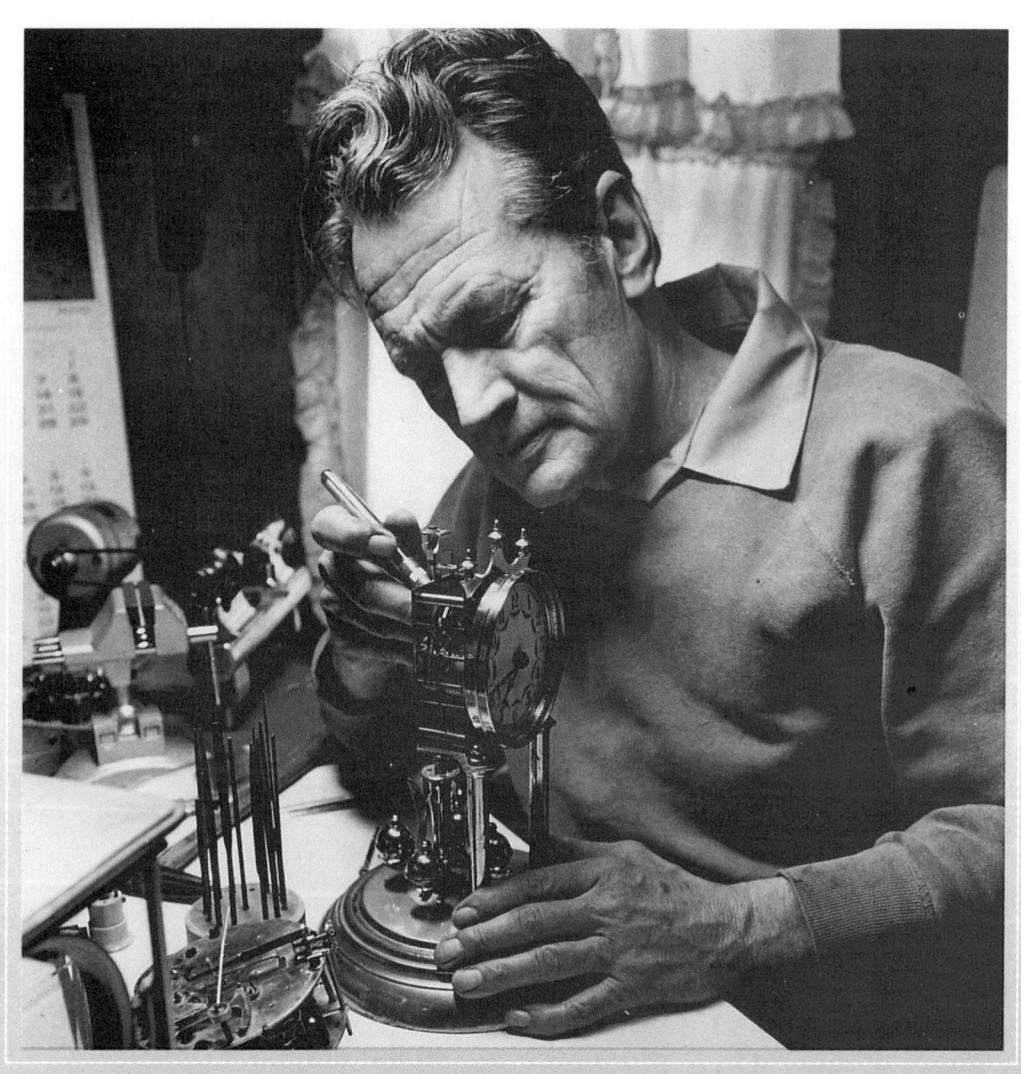

The Graduate
Interpreting Research with the Elderly
Intelligence in Later Adulthood
Factors Affecting Aging and Intelligence
CROSS-CULTURAL CURRENT   Improving the Performance of Elderly People
Information-Processing in Later Adulthood
Learning in Later Adulthood
Where Do We Go from Here?

Are the Following Statements True or False?

Try the True-False Quiz below. See if your answers correspond to the information in this chapter. Each question is repeated after the paragraph in which the answer can be found. The True-False Answer Box at the end of the chapter lists the complete answers.

_____ 1. When playing "Twenty Questions," the elderly get the answers by using more efficient strategies than young adults use.

_____ 2. Most verbal skills decline significantly after age sixty-five.

_____ 3. Nonverbal skills, such as solving puzzles, improve between the ages of sixty and seventy, after which they decline sharply.

_____ 4. Most cognitive deficits before age sixty are due to illness.

_____ 5. When time limits on intelligence tests are removed, the elderly do as well as young adults.

_____ 6. People show a significant drop in cognitive functioning prior to death.

_____ 7. The elderly commonly complain about their inability to remember things.

_____ 8. The changes that take place in sensory and short-term memory with age are quite minimal.

_____ 9. The saying "He who hesitates is lost" aptly describes problem-solving strategies in the elderly.

_____10. The elderly always choose the course of action that involves the least degree of risk.

_____11. Most elderly people believe their ability to solve problems has increased with age.

_____12. The elderly learn better when material is presented using both visual and auditory means.

The Graduate

When Mary Robbins' name was announced at graduation, she walked to the rostrum, received her diploma, then triumphantly held it over her head, just like so many other graduates do. The difference is that Mary Robbins is seventy-three years old. Her husband, children, grandchildren, and even one great-grandchild, three months old, were in attendance. The entire graduating class stood and cheered. It brought tears of joy to her eyes.

Mary was married at the age of sixteen and immediately settled down to have a family. She had not even finished high school. Years later, she passed the test for a high school equivalency diploma. At the age of sixty-

Many elderly people attend college today.

eight, she announced to her family that she intended to enroll in college. Mary told me that the whole family was supportive, with her daughters and retired husband rooting for her. Her friends were not as certain, and even Mary doubted her decision at times. "I was not convinced that my memory or my ability to learn were good enough at my age," she told me. "And I wasn't sure how the younger students would accept me." Yet Mary persevered and graduated.

Mary is one of about 340,000 adults over the age of sixty-five who are enrolled in postsecondary education (U.S. Bureau of the Census, 1986), but she is unusual in that most of these older adults are not working toward an academic degree, but are enrolled in vocational programs or taking college-level courses for personal development, social or recreational purposes, or job improvement. The newspapers occasionally remind us that older people can achieve, and some of these older people are famous. Golda Meir was seventy-one when she became prime minister of Israel. George Bernard Shaw was ninety-four when one of his plays was first produced. Benjamin Franklin signed the Constitution of the United States when he was eighty-one. Yet these people are thought of as great intellects and exceptions to the rule. We do not seem to have much faith in the intellectual achievements of older adults. Most people still believe the saying "You can't teach an old dog new tricks."

Conventional wisdom holds that in old age cognitive abilities decline and that these declines are both general and deep. But other societies do not view the elderly this way. Many non-Western societies revere the elderly for their wisdom and look to them for guidance. Whatever is lost in quickness is more than compensated for by their life experience.

Interpreting Research with the Elderly

Before we take a look at cognitive development in later maturity by investigating the changes in intelligence, Piagetian skills, memory, problem-solving, and learning that occur with age, it is important to note that while the research results are consistent, interpretation of the data is difficult and controversial.

ecological validity The question of whether the tasks tested in a special environment, such as the laboratory, are relevant to those in real life.

The Competency-Performance Argument

If you show a group of pictures to subjects ranging in age from twenty to ninety and tell them their task is to ask questions until they can guess the picture you are thinking of, a task similar to the game of twenty questions, you'll find that the elderly subjects need to ask more questions than young or middle-aged adults. In addition, young adults are more likely to ask more general questions, like "Is it made of wood?" or "Is it bigger than a breadbox," while older adults use more specific questions that do not eliminate as many items (Denney and Denney, 1982). How would you interpret this finding? We might say that older adults do not play the game as well and are not as competent as younger adults. But research has found that after simple training elderly adults can ask the same types of questions younger people do—that is, that elderly people have the ability to use more efficient methods but, for whatever reason, simply do not (Denney et al., 1979). So it is difficult to come to any definite conclusions about competence based merely on performance.

True or False When playing "Twenty Questions," the elderly get the answers by using more efficient strategies than young adults use.

Differences Versus Deficits

Let's look at another problem. If you present groups of subjects with fifty pictures of everyday objects for sorting, you'll find differences between how your elderly subjects and younger subjects classify the items. The older subjects place a frying pan with the stove because that is where a frying pan is used, while younger subjects are more likely to create categories, such as "utensils" and "appliances" (Cicirelli, 1976). As people age, abstract grouping becomes less common, although most elderly people still use it. Is this a deficit? If we consider abstract grouping to be superior, it is a deficit, but it is not a deficit if we believe this type of sorting is reasonable for elderly people. Some researchers believe that we have been too quick to label differences as deficits just because we think the way young adults reason is optimal (Labouvie-Vief, 1982).

Ecological Validity

What if you find that the elderly do not perform as well on skills that relate to success in school? Such measurements may have great meaning for younger people, but much less for older people (Schaie, 1978). This presents us with a problem of **ecological validity**—whether the tasks being tested are those that the normal elderly person is usually faced with in the environment. It is not easy to find problems that both the elderly and the young must solve in their daily lives. Even when such problems are found, differences may reflect varying experience, not ability level. The fact that most elderly people function well in their daily lives and cope well with familiar challenges makes interpreting deficits found in artificial tasks performed in a laboratory difficult.

The Five Possible Patterns of Change in Cognitive Functioning

When examining cognitive change in later adulthood five possible patterns emerge (Willis, 1985). The first involves *irreversible decrement,* a pattern that would show an age-related decrease in an ability that is caused by some physiological change, such as slowing of brain waves with age. The second pattern is *decrement with compensation,* in which a decline occurs but the person can compensate for it—for example, a person whose eyes have worsened may need new glasses. The third pattern is *decrement due to disuse,* a decline in the ability to think at abstract levels, which may partly reflect lack of use. The fourth pattern is *continued increment,* which is demonstrated when some skills improve with practice. The fifth pattern is *stability,* where some abilities remain stable well into late adulthood.

Occasionally, the public has to be reminded that people can achieve all through life. Golda Meir became Prime Minister of Israel when she was 71 years of age.

Intelligence in Later Adulthood

What happens to intelligence in old age? Despite much data from excellent and thorough studies, we have only a partial answer to this question.

Change and Stability

We tend to assume that intelligence is a single construct that can decline or remain stable or even increase. Yet there may be many types of intelligence, such as musical, linguistic, numerical intelligence and the intelligence that is reflected in skilled movement or perception (Gardner, 1983). Some types may increase over time, others may decrease. In addition, there are several components to each of these types of intelligence. For instance, in verbal intelligence such abilities as information, vocabulary, and comprehension are important. Any one of these components may increase, decrease, or remain stable over time. In recognition of this fact, many researchers have divided intelligence into component

skills instead of looking at intelligence as a unified construct.

The Wechsler Adult Intelligence Scale (WAIS) allows a researcher to do just that. The 1981 version of the WAIS contains eleven subtests (see Table 19.1) that can be grouped into two categories—verbal and performance—just as in the case of its cousin, the Wechsler Intelligence Scale for Children (Wechsler, 1981). Verbal intelligence involves such subtests as information, comprehension, arithmetic, similarities, digit span (a test of memory), and vocabulary. Performance subtests include digit symbol, picture completion, block design, picture arrangement, and object assembly. The verbal subtests involve abilities that are academically oriented, the performance tests examine nonverbal skills (see Newmark, 1985).

When older people are tested, common developmental patterns are found. Vocabulary either remains stable or increases during the life span up to about age seventy. Information shows no age-related pattern at all in adulthood. Comprehension shows no difference until age fifty or sixty, after which it may decline somewhat. Similarities show a slight reduction with increased age (Salthouse, 1982). In all, the phrase that would describe older people's performance in these tests is *relative stability*. The data on the arithmetic test shows relative stability with age through age fifty, after which some decrease is found. However, studies with other arithmetic tests yield mixed results, apparently depending greatly on the type of arithmetic problem presented. The evidence for digit span shows that poorer performance accompanies age.

True or False Most verbal skills decline significantly after age sixty-five.

The pattern of achievement on the performance subtests is quite different. Scores on tests of spatial abilities, block design, and picture arrangement show decreases starting early in adulthood and continuing throughout later maturity (Salthouse, 1982). This pattern of relative stability in verbal performance, and continuous decline in performance of nonverbal tests, is known as the **classic pattern of aging** (Botwinick, 1984).

True or False Nonverbal skills, such as solving puzzles, improve between the ages of sixty and seventy, after which they decline sharply.

Fluid and Crystallized Intelligence

The division in the WAIS between verbal intelligence and performance intelligence corresponds roughly to the categories of fluid intelligence and crystallized intelligence. You will remember from Chapter 14 that *fluid intelligence* refers to basic processes, such as memory and reasoning, that allow people to understand relationships and draw inferences from their understanding, while *crystallized intelligence* involves basic knowledge and skills. Many of the verbal tests in the WAIS represent crystallized intelligence, and the performance tests measure fluid intelligence. Generally, fluid intelligence decreases with age, showing a steeper decline after age fifty, while crystallized intelligence improves even into old age up

to around age seventy (Horn and Donaldson, 1980). What happens after seventy? In a twenty-one-year longitudinal study, Schaie (1982) found no reliable age-related changes in ability before about age sixty, but he did find a decline in all abilities by age seventy-four.

Cross-Sectional and Longitudinal Studies

Both cross-sectional studies, in which people of various ages are tested at about the same time, and longitudinal studies, in which the same people are tested periodically over a period of years, show declines in general intelligence, but they differ as to when the decline begins. Cross-sectional studies also show a greater decline than longitudinal studies. Of course, the cohort effect reduces the usefulness of cross-sectional studies, and some experts do not believe that this type of study should be used to understand what happens with the elderly (Willis and

---

TABLE 19.1

Subtests on Wechsler Adult Intelligence Scale, 1981 Revision

These six verbal subtests and five performance subtests comprise the Wechsler Adult Intelligence Scale.

Verbal Scale	Performance Scale
Information: 29 items that measure the range of the examinee's knowledge and retention of learned materials, and assess the examinee's cultural background. Items are of the form "Where does wool come from?" and "Who wrote Paradise Lost?"	*Digit Symbol:* Measures flexibility and ability for new learning through a task requiring the substitution of symbols for numbers. Speeded.
Comprehension: 16 items measuring judgment and "common sense." Includes translation of proverbs and items of form "Why should children be warned against playing with matches?"	*Picture Completion:* 20 items that require examinee to tell what is missing in a picture of a common object. Measures perceptual ability, particularly ability to differentiate essential from unessential details.
Arithmetic: 14 items testing concentration, arithmetic ability, and problem-solving skill. All items have time limits and are simple word problems; for example, "If I have $15 and earn $8 more, how much money do I now have?"	*Block Design:* Examinee reproduces designs with colored blocks. Measures ability to analyze and organize. Good test for observing problem-solving strategy as well as distorted perception and visual-motor coordination. Generally considered best single performance test. Time limits. 9 items.
Similarities: 14 items measuring logical thinking and conceptual ability; a good measure of general intelligence. Items are of the form "In what way are a car and a boat alike?"	*Picture Arrangement:* Requires examinee to arrange a group of pictures (similar to comic strip panels) to tell a coherent story. Measures ability to comprehend a total situation. Bonus points for rapid solutions. 10 items.
Digit Span: Tests attention and immediate memory by items requiring examinee to repeat series of digits either forward or backwards.	*Object Assembly:* Task is to assemble pieces of a puzzle to form a common object. Speeded. Tests perceptual ability and persistence. 4 items.
Vocabulary: 35 words of varying difficulty. Is the best single index of Full-Scale IQ; indicates range of knowledge and cultural background.	

Source: Brown, 1983.

Baltes, 1980). Cross-sectional studies generally show that older people do poorer than younger people on almost any cognitive ability, and that the older the group of people the worse they compare with a group of young adults (Botwinick, 1977). Longitudinal studies find some loss in old age, but exactly when it begins is subject to question. In a major longitudinal study, Schaie and Herzog (1983) found such a decline in intelligence, but only a very small decrement was noted between the ages of fifty-three and sixty-seven. There were larger decrements thereafter. Schaie used a test called the Primary Mental Abilities Test, not the WAIS. When the Primary Mental Abilities Test, which also contains subtests, is divided roughly into verbal and performance categories, a pattern similar to the WAIS for verbal and performance abilities is noted (Botwinick, 1984). In another longitudinal study, there was some general decline in some cognitive abilities after age sixty, but many more after seventy (Schaie and Labouvie-Vief, 1974).

The difference between cross-sectional and longitudinal studies may not be as important for our purposes, since both show deficits occurring in later life (Salthouse, 1982). An important researcher in this field, K. Werner Schaie (1981), concludes that any intellectual decrement (except in speed of response) that occurs before the late fifties is probably due to illness. From the early sixties to the mid-seventies, there is some decline, but not with all abilities and with wide individual differences. Beyond age eighty, decrement is the rule for most.

True or False Most cognitive deficits before age sixty are due to illness.

So it seems that intelligence does decline in old age. However, unless one specifies the skill or ability measured, it is difficult to make any truly global statements about intelligence of people in their sixties and perhaps in their early seventies. The older the person is, the more likely it is that cognitive deficits will be found. At the same time, individual differences are plentiful. It is doubtful that our seventy-three-year-old Mary will show much of a deficit in verbal abilities, and she may even show gains in some skills.

Factors Affecting Aging and Intelligence

The factors that affect the relationship between aging and intelligence can be categorized into age-graded in-

age-graded influences Biological and environmental factors that are related to chronological age and may affect intelligence. For example, the increase in reaction time is generally age-related.

history-graded influences Events such as wars, depressions, revolutions, and social movements that are related to historical change and may affect the measurement of intelligence. For instance, the educational experiences of different generations differ.

fluences, history-graded influences, and non-normative influences (Willis and Baltes, 1980.)

Age-Graded Influences

Biological and environmental factors that are highly correlated with chronological age are referred to as **age-graded influences.** For example, the slowing of behavior with age is one of the most common findings. Mary Robbins recognized that she had slowed down and found certain aspects of her work, including tests that required rapid answers, quite difficult. Many intelligence tests contain timed subtests. If all processes slow down in the elderly (see Salthouse, 1985), wouldn't this adversely affect the scores that the elderly get on intelligence tests? The answer appears to be yes. When time limits are removed the elderly do better, but still not as well as younger people (Storandt, 1977). Still, such timed tests may accentuate the differences between older and younger samples, making the deficit seem greater than it really is.

True or False When time limits on intelligence tests are removed, the elderly do as well as young adults.

History-Graded Influences

Events that are correlated with historical change are referred to as **history-graded influences.** For example, wars, revolutions, depressions, epidemics, social movements, and technological changes affect each generation differently. If you were a teenager during the depression of the 1930s or the Vietnam War of the late 1960s, your experiences will affect your values and outlook on life. A recent study shows that military service during the late forties and Korean War affected the course of people's lives because it tended to delay marriage, parenthood, and stability in occupational achievement (Elder, 1986). Whenever one is comparing the elderly with young adults, historical periods must be taken into account. History-graded influences affect intelligence largely through generational differences in education.

Education and intelligence. One reason older people do not do as well as younger people on intelligence tests is that they lack education. Because, generally speaking, each generation is better educated than the previous one, comparing people born in 1900, who are now in their eighties, with those born in 1960, who are in their twenties, puts the older generation at a disadvantage (Labouvie-Vief, 1985). Future generations of elderly will be better educated than today's elderly. When educational differences are minimized, so are performance differences on intelligence tests (Salthouse, 1982; Green, 1969). If education is so important, why not simply test a group of young adults and elderly subjects who are similar in educational achievement? There are two problems here. First, many of the elderly today do not have a great deal of education, so the sample may not be representative of the elderly population generally. Second, and more important, merely matching for years spent in school does not mean equal schooling. At different historical periods, schools focused on different areas of study. For example, prior to World War II, memorization of facts was emphasized, while after that date schools focused on recognizing relationships between events (Schaie, 1981). In the late 1960s and early 1970s, the importance of emotions and interpersonal skills was stressed too. The educational scene is changing more and more quickly. Students educated during the present "back to basics" movement are likely to be different from those educated at a different time.

Non-Normative Influences

Events that relate to our individual life pattern are known as **non-normative influences.** Travel, medical problems, divorce, or periods of unemployment are examples of such influences. These can affect intelligence by narrowing or broadening one's experiences.

Individual differences. Each person's unique life experiences affect cognitive functioning. For example, Mary

non-normative influences Events such as medical problems or divorce that affect a particular individual's life and may affect intelligence too.

terminal drop A phenomenon in which there is a decline in intelligence scores, and personality changes, that is associated with death.

Robbins found her English courses fairly easy because she had been reading at least a book a week for many years while she was a homemaker. The more a skill is used, the less it declines over the life span (Denney, 1982). While psychologists perform most studies on groups, individual differences among the elderly must be appreciated. It is generally inaccurate to predict an individual's cognitive functioning solely on the basis of age.

Terminal drop. Important discoveries are sometimes made almost by accident. So it was in the case of a phenomenon called terminal drop. Over a dozen years, Kleemeier (1961) tested the intelligence of elderly men on four separate occasions. As expected, each subject showed some decrease. Right after the last test, four of the men died, and Kleemeier noted that the intelligence of these subjects had declined more sharply than that of the survivors. He analyzed additional data and found evidence that preceding the death of many elderly people, a significant drop in intelligence occurred. **Terminal drop** is the phenomenon in which there is a decline in intelligence scores (as well as personality changes) associated with death (Lieberman, 1983). Most psychologists believe it is the drop, not the score itself, that predicts death. Terminal drop is seen in both verbal scores and nonverbal scores. Lieberman (1965) gave twenty-five residents of a nursing home two psychological tests. Six of the eight who died within three months had performed much less well on the last test than on the first. Botwinick et al. (1978) studied 380 men and women, assessing a wide variety of functions that included cognitive and perceptual abilities as well as personality characteristics. During the five years following the testing, 83 subjects had died. Two-thirds of those who died could be predicted by their previous test scores. There were significant differences between survivors and nonsurvivors on speed of performance on psychomotor tasks, learning and memory skills, self-ratings of health, and personality characteristics, including depression and feelings of being in control.

True or False People show a significant drop in cognitive functioning prior to death.

The cause of this drop, which is not clear, may involve complex physiological and psychological factors. However, in evaluating cross-sectional studies of intelligence, one must take terminal drop into consideration. For example, if a sample of elderly people perform more poorly on an intelligence test, compared with young adults, how much of the collective decline can be attributed to terminal drop? The average intelligence score of the group may be held down by the few who are actually suffering from terminal drop. Of even more concrete importance for the elderly is the possibility that we may be able to predict death or significant deterioration from a precip-

itous drop in cognitive or psychological functions and provide some intervention at the appropriate time.

Training Studies

Can older people improve their scores on intelligence tests? We tend to think of younger people as being able to improve and to become smarter, and sometimes we equate maturation with development. But we are likely to equate old age with withering away. Yet new studies show that the cognitive behavior of older adults can be altered substantially.

Psychologists have used many methods to improve the performance of elderly adults on intelligence tests. Powell (1974) found that physical exercise itself could produce improvements. Birkhill and Schaie (1975) found that teaching the elderly alternative strategies and overcoming their reluctance to guess improved performance.

Older people who travel and remain active are less likely to show cognitive declines.

Willis and colleagues (1981) analyzed the skills necessary to perform well on problems measuring two aspects of fluid intelligence. After they taught an elderly sample rules for solving these problems, there was significant improvement on these measures. These findings have been replicated and expanded (see Cross-Cultural Current on page 494). The importance of practicing these skills should not be minimized (Denney, 1982). Hofland and colleagues (1981) argued that some of the supposed loss of intelligence was due to lack of test sophistication, slow response times, lack of motivation, and too much test anxiety. By giving the elderly practice in the skills required and by relaxing time restrictions, the performance of elderly subjects improved. In an important study, Schaie and Willis (1986) divided a sample of 229 people between the ages of sixty-four and ninety-five into those who had declined on inductive reasoning and spatial orientation and those who had showed stability on these two abilities. The sample was then assigned to a five-hour training program on either ability. In a substantial number of adults, the cognitive training techniques reversed the decline in both abilities and enhanced the performance of the older adults who had remained stable.

From these and many other studies, we can conclude that remarkable performance gains are possible with minor interventions (Labouvie-Vief, 1977). We cannot expect a short-term training course to alter the cognitive functioning of the elderly forever, but the positive findings of training studies demonstrate that age-related deficits in intelligence may not all be the result of irreversible biological processes. Environmental stimulation and continued use of skills are important too. The factor of age itself accounts for relatively little of the decline seen between sixty and seventy years of age, but it becomes a more important factor as elderly people negotiate the seventies (Willis and Baltes, 1980). Even in the seventies, however, nonbiological factors must be taken into consideration if we are to understand cognitive functioning. Finally, any decline found in the elderly should not be viewed as absolute and irreversible.

Piagetian Abilities in the Elderly

Standardized intelligence tests do not measure Piagetian skills, and some researchers have studied how the elderly do on tests of these abilities. However, such studies have been plagued by both practical and theoretical problems.

It is difficult to use the same procedures that Piaget used when testing classification, seriation, or conservation in children (Reese and Rodeheaver, 1985). Changing Piaget's procedures can alter performance on Piagetian tasks (see Chapter 7). In addition, many studies have shown that Piaget's last stage, the stage of formal operations, is not reached by everyone. In people who do develop this type of reasoning, its continuance depends on occupational and personal attributes (Piaget, 1972). If you were to test a group of elderly adults and young adults and found that the elderly people did not do as well as the young adults, how would you interpret the results? Because this data is cross-sectional, cohort problems arise. In addition, you cannot be certain that your elderly ever had the abilities that you now think are in decline. Only a long-term longitudinal study could show the development of these abilities. Finally, you could argue that the abilities that define formal operations—such as hypothetical-deductive reasoning, combinational logic, and the ability to deal with abstractions—are not relevant to the elderly and that therefore any decline shows nothing more than disuse (Reese and Rodeheaver, 1985).

Notwithstanding all these problems, some researchers have looked at the performance of elderly adults on Piagetian tests. When Denney and Cornelius (1975) studied Piagetian skills, such as classification, in middle-aged and elderly subjects, the former performed much better than the latter. When different types of conservation were tested in subjects from childhood through old age, older people showed a decline in their ability to handle tasks involving conservation of substance, weight, and volume (Papalia, 1972). Other researchers, though, have not found such a decline in conservation abilities (Reese and Rodeheaver, 1985). Generally, however, the research shows that the elderly do not do as well as younger people on Piagetian tests.

Some interesting relationships between performance on Piagetian tasks and other variables have been found. For instance, Hooper and colleagues (1971) found that performance on Piagetian tasks was related to fluid intelligence. Perhaps the decline in fluid intelligence explains the older person's poor showing on Piagetian tests (Storck et al., 1972). A relationship between health and Piagetian performance is also found in studies where cardiovascular problems have been related to poorer functioning (LaRue and Jarvik, 1982). To summarize, then, some but not all studies show a decline in Piagetian abilities in old age, and the studies that do are difficult

Improving the Performance of Elderly People

Most people today recognize that there is a decline in fluid intelligence in old age, although the extent of that decline is still controversial. Fluid intelligence refers to the basic cognitive processes that allow a person to perceive and understand relationships and to draw inferences from this understanding (Horn, 1982). However, be that decline great or relatively small, the question of whether fluid abilities can be improved in the elderly in an interesting one. Can social scientists improve an elderly person's fluid intellectual abilities through training, or is the loss irreversible? Recent studies noted in this chapter indicate that some fluid intellectual abilities, such as figural relations and induction, can be improved through training. Those studies were done in the United States, so Paul Baltes and his colleagues decided to replicate and extend the findings in another culture, in this case West Germany.

The researchers employed the same training program used in the United States in attempts to improve the performance of elderly people on figural relations and induction. *Figural relations* is the ability to see relationships within figural patterns. It can be measured in a number of ways, including presenting a subject with two groups of geometric patterns that are related to each other in some way, then presenting the subject with a third group and asking him or her to identify the group in which each figure in the third group belongs. For instance, group one might consist of shaded triangles, and group two of white triangles. Group three would consists of some shaded and some white triangles, and the subject would have to recognize the relationship between group one and group two and correctly place the triangles that are in group three into the appropriate

group. *Induction* involves identifying a general concept that applies to some display—be it letters, shapes, or hypotheses—and then choosing which element does not fit. One way to measure induction involves presenting subjects with a display consisting of five groups of letters and asking them to identify which group does not belong. Perhaps four of the groups contain letters in alphabetical order, while the other does not. A subject must recognize this rule and use it. These abilities are shown in Table A.

Some 204 healthy West German elderly adults living in Berlin were randomly divided into two groups. The experimental group received a pretest on these skills, cognitive training, and then three posttests administered one week, one month, and six months after training. The control-group subjects received none of the training, but were tested at the same intervals. The training program consisted of ten sessions conducted within one month. Five sessions dealt with figural relations, the other five dealt with induction. These training programs focused on helping subjects identify rules and concepts and teaching them how to use them to solve induction and figural-relations problems.

After the training, the researchers found significant differences between the experimental and control groups on tests of these abilities. The differences were maintained through the second and third posttest, although performance on the third posttest was not as good as on the second. Still, the performance of the experimental group was significantly better than the control group on all posttests. One particularly interesting feature of this study was an attempt to discover the nature of the experimental group's improved performance. For instance,

to interpret. Although some decline probably occurs, the reasons for it are unknown at the present time.

Information-Processing in Later Adulthood

When Mary Robbins started college, she was expected to learn, remember material for later testing, and solve

problems. These information-processing abilities are vitally important in daily life as well as in school.

Memory

How people function depends partly on their memory. Remembering where a store is, what to buy, whose birth-

T A B L E   A

Measuring Figural Relations and Induction

This figure shows a way to test figural relations and induction, two abilities that are often used to measure aspects of fluid intelligence.

Primary Ability Being Tested	Description of Tests	Sample Items
Figural Relations—being able to find rules or concepts relating figures, shapes, designs	Figure Classification—2 or 3 groups, each containing 3 geometric figures that are alike according to some rule. Choose figures out of 8 which fit each of the groups	Write the number under each figure that corresponds to its group
Induction—finding general concepts that will apply to various materials (letters, shapes, designs), testing hypotheses	Letter Grouping—Find the rule which relates sets of letters; choose the set which does not fit the rule	Which letter group does not belong? NOPQ DEFL ABCD HIJK UVWX

Source: Adapted from Whitbourne and Weinstock, 1979.

were experimental subjects answering more of the easy questions correctly? Were they simply answering more questions and getting more correct because they were guessing? Neither of these turned out to be the case. The experimental subjects answered more questions correctly at every level of difficulty than the control group. Subjects in the experimental and control groups did not significantly differ in the number of items attempted in the posttests. The improved performance was attributed to increased accuracy in solving easy, moderate, and difficult problems.

This study replicates others that found improvement in some elements of fluid intelligence with training. It does this by using the same experimental procedures in a different culture and coming up with similar results. Such replications are important if we are to understand the nature of cognitive functioning in elderly adults. The findings now both in the United States and in West Germany show that healthy elderly people have the capacity to improve their performance in areas of fluid intelligence that often show a decline. To further extend the universality of these results, it would be interesting to perform the same studies in Eastern societies as well.

Source: Baltes, P. B., Dittmann-Kohli, F., and Kleigl, R. Reserve Capacity of the Elderly in Aging-Sensitive Tests of Fluid Intelligence: Replication and Extension. *Psychology and Aging,* 1986, *1,* 172–177.

day is approaching, and when to make dinner are simple tasks, but Mary had to remember complicated academic information and retrieve it quickly under the stress of a test. Memory problems are one of the most common complaints of older people (Lowenthal et al., 1967). What happens to memory as we age?

True or False The elderly commonly complain about their inability to remember things.

Sensory memory. When a stimulus is first presented, it is registered initially in sensory memory. Age differences in sensory memory are small. Sometimes a small deficit is found (Cerella et al., 1982), sometimes none at all (Birren et al., 1983). Small changes are not necessarily unimportant, but at this point no one really understands how such losses contribute to any deficits in memory (Poon, 1985).

Short-term or primary memory. The information is transferred from sensory memory to short-term or primary memory. The time period for short-term memory is described variously as anywhere between fifteen seconds (Bransford, 1979) and thirty seconds (Best, 1986). Short-term memory has a limited capacity. Again, some change is found here, but actually very little (Craik, 1977). The most common test of this memory is the forward span task in which subjects are presented with a list of digits and asked to repeat them back immediately in order (Labouvie-Vief and Schell, 1982). The memory span, or the average number of digits that can be reproduced without error after one presentation, declines from seven to six some time in the late fifties and then remains at that level (Wingfield and Byrnes, 1981). The speed at which items are recalled is slightly slower for the elderly (Waugh et al., 1978). This optimistic finding is common when elderly adults can concentrate completely on the task (Hartley et al., 1980), but when their attention is divided they do not do as well (Birren et al., 1983). When some process must be performed on the memory trace, age-related differences arise—for instance, if we demand that subjects recall the digits in reverse order, the elderly perform much more poorly than younger subjects (Botwinick and Storandt, 1974). Under simple conditions, then, short-term memory deficits are minimal, but they become more prominent if the elderly must reorganize the material.

True or False The changes that take place in sensory and short-term memory with age are quite minimal.

Long-term or secondary memory. It is in long-term memory that we find the age-related deficits that elderly adults complain about so much (Labouvie-Vief and Schell, 1982). If we compare the performance of elderly people and younger subjects a few days after learning a list, we will find that the younger people remember more of the list. In a study of eyewitness testimony to a videotaped crime, elderly people were just as accurate as younger adults, but not as complete in their stories (List, 1986). When presented with a story and asked to remember it, they again do not remember as much as younger adults

(Petros et al., 1983). Such findings are common for verbal material (Zelinski et al., 1984). When older people are asked to repeat something verbatim, they are not as good as younger adults, but there is no age difference with reporting the gist of meaningful material (Hultsch et al., 1984). Memory problems are more likely to be seen when elderly adults are asked to recall information rather than recognize it. Recognition either does not decline, or it does slightly and certainly less than the ability to recall information (Craik, 1977).

Imagine Mary Robbins taking a human development course and facing an assignment of reading and understanding a text. As she reads, she must encode, or establish a memory. Then she must store the material. Finally, she must retrieve the material at the proper time. We can better understand the memory problems of the elderly by looking at these three processes.

Encoding, storage, and retrieval. Long-term memory deficits are found either at the encoding stage or the retrieval stage, or perhaps both, but not in storage (Birren et al., 1983; Labouvie-Vief and Schell, 1982). Some studies try to separate encoding and retrieval, but it is becoming more obvious that they interact—that encoding affects retrieval. Older people show a decreased ability to organize incoming material into meaningful clusters and process it. Studies show that when older people are shown how to organize material so it can be encoded more easily, they improve their performance on memory tests significantly (Hultsch, 1969). Older people also take longer to encode information. If older people are allowed sufficient time to respond to a test but are rushed in their initial acquisition of the material, they still perform more poorly than younger people (Botwinick, 1973). Older people benefit much more than younger people when the rate of presentation is slowed down (Craik, 1977) or when they are allowed to go at their own pace (Poon, 1985). When the elderly have time to encode and are taught how to use efficient strategies, the differences between older and younger adults are minimized (Smith, 1980). In addition, the more familiar the items, the better the performance of elderly people (Botwinick, 1973).

Encoding, then, is one source of the problem. Retrieval is another. The elderly have problems retrieving information, even if it is effectively learned. Recall is a more active and more difficult retrieval process than recognition. The elderly show more problems in recall, indicating that they are apt to have problems in the retrieval process. Other studies show that the elderly do not do as well with retrieving information even if it is familiar, although the deficits are not as pronounced as they are with unfamiliar material (Craik, 1977). Still further evidence for retrieval deficits comes from studies showing that if the elderly are given longer to respond they perform better on memory tests. In this case, the material is encoded and stored, but there is some delay in retrieval (Labouvie-Vief and Schell, 1982). Perhaps the best conclusion is that the memory problems of the elderly are probably caused by problems in both the encoding area and the retrieval area (Duchek, 1984).

Memory in everyday life. Age-related deficits in long-term memory are well documented. However, some psychologists are concerned that the artificial nature of these laboratory studies may exaggerate these deficits. Many studies involve learning words, phrases or stories under stringent conditions. While such studies help us understand the possible age-related deficits, the question of how they generalize to the real world is controversial. We are back to the ecological validity argument. Are

we testing adults on skills that are no longer needed? For instance, when older and younger adults were tested on their ability to remember information that was required for later action, called *goal-related memories,* as well as memory of incidental details not needed for future action, the young adults performed better than the older adults only on the incidental memories, not on the more functional, goal-related memories (Sinnott, 1986). Testing elderly people on memories needed to accomplish a preplanned activity leads to better performance than testing them on incidental details. To examine adequately the nature of memory in the elderly, we must look at what types of memory tasks are necessary in the life of the elderly and how elderly adults perform on these (Hartley et al., 1980). This is difficult to do, but there has been some research in this area.

Most elderly complain that they seem to be forgetting more and more. Elderly people often show deficits when it comes to estimating the amount of time it took to perform a task or the order in which tasks had been performed (Kausler et al., 1985). In an interesting study, Cavanaugh and colleagues (1983) asked young and elderly adults to keep diaries of their memory failures and

The elderly show fewer memory failures when they are assessed on familiar tasks within a meaningful context.

their use of memory aids. As expected, elderly people reported more memory failures than younger adults. However, generally, when the elderly are assessed on familiar tasks within a meaningful context, performance differences between them and young adults are reduced somewhat (Birren et al., 1983).

What happened when you were twenty? "It's been weeks since I've seen you," said the eighty-four-year-old woman to her fifty-five-year-old daughter. "Did you give the bracelet to Judy?"

"Mom, I saw you last Thursday and told you that I gave the bracelet to Judy two weeks ago."

With that, the elderly woman remained still, a bit embarrassed, and then went on to another subject. Later in the same visit, she was reminiscing about her days fifty years ago, when she lived with eight brothers and sisters in a three-room apartment. She seemed to remember everything in great detail.

This is a common phenomenon. In the late nineteenth century, Ribot (1882) attempted to explain it by noting that in old age newer and more complex abilities decline before older and simpler abilities. In other words, newer memories and more complex processes should show deficits before older, more established memories or simpler processes do. Although everyday experience seems to point to the validity of this phenomenon, the research evidence is decidedly mixed (Botwinick, 1984). Some studies even find that, contrary to popular belief, memory for recent events is retained better than for older events (Warrington and Silberstein, 1970).

If the phenomenon is real, how can we explain it? If there is no loss during storage, as seems to be the case (Walsh, 1983), older people may have the information stored from years ago and simply be awaiting the right cue to unlock the door. When speaking to elderly people, you may find that the longer you talk about a particular event that occurred years ago, the more they remember, as one memory leads to another. Of course, these memories are subject to distortions and interference with time. However, if older people encode material more poorly this can lead to difficulty remembering things. Also, these older memories are retrieved under different conditions. Forgetting something that happened forty years ago is not likely to cause as much anxiety as forgetting whether you paid the telephone bill this month. So, although the evidence is still mixed on this subject, it seems that encoding newer memories is a significant source of problems for many elderly people.

Memory in elderly adults: A reconsideration. How can we put all these findings in perspective? Sensory and short-term memory (primary memory) do not decline much in old age, but numerous long-term memory deficits have been found. Under some circumstances, however, these deficits are less-pronounced than others. For example, older adults do better when tested in supportive environments and when they are praised for their work (Lair and Moon, 1972). This also reduces anxiety. They benefit more from information if it is personally relevant or familiar. They do better if they are shown how to organize material. Older people also improve their performance if the material is presented using both the auditory and the visual modalities (Schaie, 1981) and if they are asked to recognize rather than recall the information. If they are given more time to encode and retrieve, they also perform better. Age-related deficits are more likely to be observed when attention is divided or when the person must reorganize information (Schaie, 1981). Memory is also related to intelligence, with people who are more intelligent showing comparatively less decline with age (Horn and Donaldson, 1980). The list of findings could go on and on.

The practical importance of these discoveries is that if you want older people to remember something, they must be given more time to encode and retrieve, the material must be carefully organized, their attention must be undivided, and their anxiety level must be lowered. People who work with the elderly can be more effective if they are aware of the circumstances under which the elderly are less likely to show these deficits.

The elderly are clearly bothered by their memory losses. In everyday life, though, familiar material is so overlearned that any pronounced deficit here is viewed by many as a sign of depression or organic damage (Schaie, 1981). The evidence on ecologically valid tasks shows that the deficits are less as the familiarity of material is increased (Labouvie-Vief and Schell, 1982). In addition, intervention studies show that the elderly can be helped to improve their memories somewhat. The elderly can learn to use various memory strategies, such as visual imagery or verbal association, although they seem to use these only when instructed to do so, not spontaneously (Botwinick, 1984).

The causes of this long-term loss are controversial at the present time. Some researchers believe that physiological changes in the nervous system, damage to brain structures, or the increased random firing of nerves that accompanies aging are responsible (Labouvie-Vief and Schell, 1982). Others point to the slowing of processing speed (Salthouse and Kail, 1983).

Problem-Solving

We are faced with hundreds of problems each day. These problems may be practical, such as how to challenge a bureaucratic snafu in the social security agency, or more academic, such as how to solve some math problem. Information from our senses, as well as our memory, serves to help us in this regard. Let's say Mary is driving to school and comes up on a traffic jam. She considers her past experience and decides that if she stays in bumper-to-bumper traffic she will miss class. She then uses one of three alternative routes she knows. Mary has just solved a problem. Notice that her sensory information, her judgment of how bad the traffic jam was, and her memory of other routes were involved. Researchers have been interested in just what happens to problem-solving with age, and the data show some interesting differences in how younger adults and the elderly approach and solve problems.

Cautiousness. "Look before you leap." This saying best describes what might go through the minds of older people confronted with a task. Young adults make more errors of commission, older adults are more likely to make errors of omission (Botwinick, 1967). In other words, the elderly are not likely to guess, and they tend to leave questions unanswered when they are not certain of the correct answers. Younger people are more likely to venture a guess even if it is wrong (Heyn et al., 1978). Older people value accuracy over speed and want to be confident in their judgments before answering a question (Botwinick, 1984). Simply stated, older people do not like to take risks (Labouvie-Vief, 1985). This is carried over into daily life, as the elderly are less likely to drive in poor weather, to invest their money in something new, or to experiment with a new food. This may be functional. They may recognize that their sensory and motor mechanisms are not as efficient, that their money cannot easily be replaced, and that the consequences of

mistakes in life are greater for them. Cautiousness, then, can be a rational response to the aging process (Okun, 1976). In one study, Wallach and Kogan (1961) presented a questionnaire containing twelve life situations to young and elderly adults. The subjects were asked to choose among courses of action that were evaluated for riskiness. Elderly people were more cautious, especially in financial decisions, than younger people. But this is only half the story. Older people try to minimize risks and avoid them if possible. But what happens when they cannot avoid them? Botwinick found that, when confronted with the Wallach and Kogan questionnaire, many elderly people choose the least risky alternative, even when the likelihood of success with just a little risk was high. Botwinick (1969) forced elderly subjects to encounter some risk by eliminating the alternative in the questionnaires that allowed the elderly to avoid risk. We might think that the elderly would simply choose the next conservative choice, but that is wrong. When risk was unavoidable, no significant differences between the elderly and younger adults were found. The elderly, then, avoid risks whenever they can. When faced with unavoidable risk, however, they are no more conservative than younger adults (Botwinick, 1984).

True or False The saying "He who hesitates is lost" aptly describes problem-solving strategies in the elderly.

True or False The elderly always choose the course of action that involves the least degree of risk.

Flexibility and rigidity. Older adults are also less flexible and show more rigidity in solving problems. In a variety of studies, older adults show a reluctance to change from one strategy to another when the task calls for it (Salthouse, 1982; Heglin, 1956). Older adults appear to be less flexible, but this may be because doing things in the accustomed ways may be safer.

Abstract and concrete problems. Everyone does better when problems are meaningful and concrete than when they are irrelevant and abstract. This is partly explained by differences in interest and in motivation. When tasks are meaningful and concrete, motivation is likely to be higher. When older adults are tested on concrete problems, they perform significantly better than they do on abstract problems, although they still do not do as well as younger adults (Labouvie-Vief, 1985; Arenberg, 1968).

Forming hypotheses and concepts. Older people also take longer to form concepts and hypotheses (West et al., 1978). In the game of "Twenty Questions" described earlier, the most efficient strategy is to ask questions that eliminate the largest number of possible answers. Older adults ask many more questions, their questions are more specific, and many of their questions are redundant (Denney and Denney, 1973). You may see some relationship between concept-attainment and fluid intelligence here, and so have some researchers. When matched on fluid intelligence, older adults can compete with younger adults on tests of concept-attainment (Wetherick, 1964). However, the average elderly person does not have as much fluid intelligence as the average younger adult, and this should be taken into consideration. Elderly people also show deficits in using the best strategy, defined as the most appropriate and efficient, to solve a problem (Salthouse, 1982). Finally, in many situations people must sort out the important details from the extraneous details. For example, what if I asked you how much fence is needed to surround a yard but instead of giving you just the dimensions of the yard I also added information about how long the grass is, how many trees there are, how big the house is, and the direction the wind blows. In order to solve this problem, you must ignore the irrelevant information and concentrate on what is important. Some research shows that the elderly are not as good as younger adults in doing this (Hoyer et al., 1979).

Teaching new problem-solving methods. Can elderly people be taught new ways to approach and solve problems? The research in this area is consistent. When older people receive training in these areas they improve, and that improvement lasts for a longer period of time than one would think (Giambra and Arenberg, 1980). In many cases, practice itself allows adults to develop their own effective strategies. Sanders and colleagues (1975) taught elderly subjects how to solve simple problems, then gradually introduced them to more difficult ones. Not only could these elderly solve problems that their cohorts could not, but this superiority was present one year later (Sanders and Sanders, 1978). The fact that such training was brief—only about three half-hour sessions—shows that it affected performance, not competence (Labouvie-Vief, 1985). Denney (1974) found that showing the elderly how to form better questions in the

"Twenty Questions" game significantly improved their performance in the game. It is clear that with minimal training elderly adults can greatly improve their abilities to solve problems.

Wisdom in everyday life. What do the elderly themselves think of their problem-solving skills? In one study, 76 percent believed their problem-solving skills had increased with age, about 20 percent reported no change, and only 4 percent reported some decline. When they were presented with facts from laboratory experiments showing the opposite, the majority simply stated that they were referring to different problems. Everyday challenges were different (Denney and Palmer, 1981). Most elderly people have a positive view of how they solve their everyday problems.

True or False Most elderly people believe their ability to solve problems has increased with age.

Problem-solving reconsidered. The evidence that the elderly solve problems differently from the way younger adults do is strong. Older adults take more time to form new concepts, are less likely to use efficient strategies,

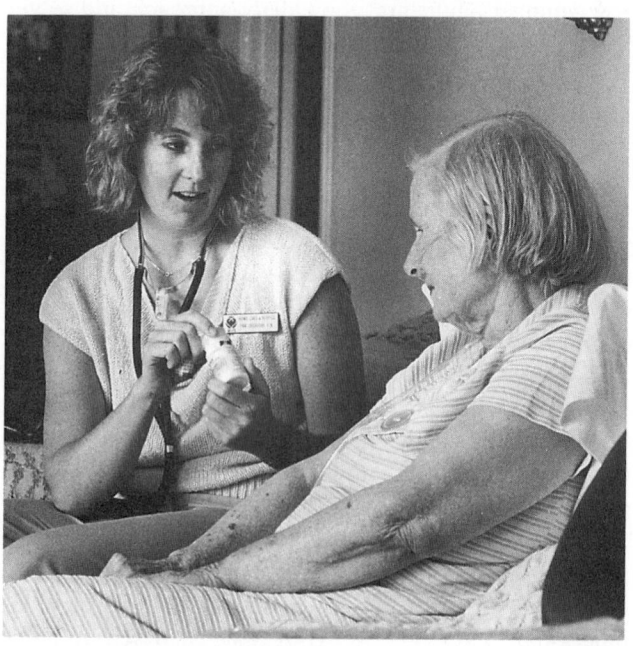

What is the best way to explain to this person that she must take medication three times a day right before meals?

are more likely to use a strategy rigidly even if a better strategy is available, and use more concrete concepts than abstract concepts. Whether these differences can be considered deficits probably depends on the particular situation. If elderly people are suddenly forced to deal with abstractions or to form new concepts after years of not using these skills, they are likely to find themselves at a disadvantage. However, most elderly solve everyday problems well, and their cautiousness may reflect rational changes in outlook. In addition, studies showing that performance can be significantly improved through training leads to the conclusion that the less-efficient problem-solving strategies demonstrated in laboratory studies, are performance deficits not competency deficits. Finally, experience is a great equalizer and should be considered a factor in evaluating problem-solving ability in real life.

Learning in Later Adulthood

Older people certainly can and do learn. Mary Robbins negotiated the same college program that many younger people did. Anyone who has ever visited retirement communities knows that people who are new to the community must learn many new rules and regulations, find out how to get to restaurants and movie theaters, and manage their resources differently. Older people read newspapers and magazines and are capable of discussing and integrating new material with their past experiences. The question surrounding adult learning is not whether it occurs but the conditions under which it can be facilitated.

The older learner faces some unique challenges, as do people who must teach them. Teachers may find elderly people in their classrooms. Nurses, health-care workers and even family members often need to teach the elderly new facts about biology, aging, and disease. What if you were faced with this situation? A seventy-five-year-old man with a heart condition must take medication three times a day, follow a specific diet, and exercise regularly. Although he is motivated to do these things, you find that he has difficulty planning menus and taking the correct medication, and sometimes cannot even remember whether he has taken his medication. Because he lives independently his children are concerned about this problem. In a case like this, we must find ways to help him learn his new regimen effectively.

Prescriptions for Older Learners

The information we have about intelligence, memory, and problem-solving, as well as the sensory changes described in Chapter 18, can help us formulate ways to help the elderly learn whether it be in a group situation or a one on one situation. We can manipulate certain factors to make learning more efficient for the elderly.

Altering the environment. The elderly are especially sensitive to environmental factors. Print should be large, the room comfortable, and the level of sound reasonable for their needs. For reading, even the type of paper can be a problem. Some glossy paper may look very nice but be troublesome to the elderly because of glare. In addition, minimizing extraneous noise that can interfere with concentration helps. Because the elderly do poorly if their attention is divided or if they have to attend to two tasks simultaneously, focusing their attention on a single item at a time improves their performance (Craik, 1977).

Changing the pace. Older adults need more time to learn material and more time to respond. Giving older people this additional time improves their performance. A nurse must understand that the elderly patient will learn better if the pace is slowed down. In a classroom situation, the fast pace is likely to reduce the amount of material the elderly learn, so slowing down the pace of instruction or providing extra help is beneficial. If assignments can be given far ahead of time, older adults can plan their readings more effectively. Any new procedures should be explained more slowly, and the elderly should be given more practice in performing the new skill.

Reducing anxiety. Everyone does better when anxiety is reduced and praise is plentiful, but the elderly seem especially sensitive to these conditions. The elderly need more social support and encouragement as well.

Using two-sense modalities. When at all possible, older people learn better when they can both see and hear the information. This can be accomplished through audio-visual presentations and a combination of reading, lecture, and recitation. The communication problems of the elderly can be acute. Speech discrimination declines, and older people may take longer to label objects and concepts (Obler and Alpert, 1985). The hearing loss is one culprit, and the suggestions on page 479 for communicating with the elderly should be noted.

True or False The elderly learn better when material is presented using both visual and auditory means.

Making the material relevant. The more meaningful the material, the better the learning and memory. Using examples that are relevant to the elderly, and showing how the information fits into their daily lives and goals, helps older people encode the information more efficiently.

Teaching memory and learning strategies. Because encoding can be a problem, the elderly sometimes need help in organizing information. Older people may not have had much experience with actual studying and may need help developing study habits. The use of mnemonic devices and other memory-training techniques can be helpful. For example, the "loci method" is an effective aid to learning items on a list. With this method a person can learn a list by mentally walking through a house and visualizing an item at each predetermined stopping place. When asked to recall the information, the trip can be repeated in the older person's mind, and the stopping

places can serve as effective cues for retrieving the words. The loci method works because the elderly do not have to learn a new memory scheme and because it uses familiar cues, such as the couch or dining room table (Arenberg, 1983). As we have seen, memory, reasoning, and problem-solving can be improved through practice and education (Willis, 1985; Denney, 1982). Some people may need such training. The elderly man may require some mnemonic device and record-keeping procedure tied to some visual cue to help him take his medication at the right time.

Compensating for problems. Many elderly people realize their memory may not be as good as it once was, so they compensate by using other devices more frequently. None other than the great behaviorist B. F. Skinner (1983) noted this strategy. At the age of seventy-nine, he realized that he was having age-related memory problems and discovered that his problems mostly involved retrieval. For example, he would listen to a weather report calling for rain and decide to take an umbrella the next day, only to forget it. He began to forget people's names and would forget to do things like making changes in articles. He solved these problems in simple ways. Now when he hears a weather report he immediately

Some environmental changes, such as large print, can help the elderly learn.

places an umbrella where he will be sure to see it when he leaves the next morning. Skinner tries to remember names by going through the alphabet, testing each letter to see if the person's name begins with that letter. He also uses lists more often, writing notes immediately or taping his ideas. Skinner believes the problem in old age is not generating ideas but retrieving them.

Assessing personal learning characteristics. Not all elderly people require extraordinary changes in the learning environment. Some have considerable experience in particular areas and may learn new ideas quickly, but others need help. In order to serve the elderly better, making some assessment of what they do know, their problems, the types of learning strategies they use, and their skills can be helpful.

Singling out the important points. The elderly learner often has difficulty singling out the important details from the less-crucial details. When faced with information overload, mistakes are common. This can be reduced through training in such skills as understanding the main points and through very specific instructions about what is and is not vital to learn.

Practice effects. Many adults are unfamiliar with the process of testing or, in the case of our elderly gentleman, planning and executing a strategy such as menu-planning. This can be overcome through practice. Studies show that the elderly improve greatly when they have time to practice, so rehearsal should be built into the learning process.

Where Do We Go from Here?

The evidence for some cognitive decline in memory, problem-solving, intelligence, and Piagetian skills is clear (Eisdorfer, 1983). However, these deficits are likely to show up under particular conditions, such as when the speed required for learning is great, when there is little time to respond, when the anxiety level is high, when the testing situation is uncomfortable, when the material is abstract or not very meaningful, when motivation is low, when there are many distractions, or when there are health problems (Barrow, 1986). Although everyone's performance improves when these conditions are reversed, the elderly improve much more.

When interpreting cognitive decline, however, three points should be kept in mind. First, studies show that we can minimize these declines through various intervention strategies. Some strategies—such as teaching memory strategies and problem-solving strategies—are cognitive, while others may involve nutrition and medical care, because the relationship between health and cognitive functioning is strong (Coleman, 1983). Second, individual differences are very important. In one study of memory and learning in later life, Arenberg (1983) found that 28 percent of the men over age seventy showed no decline and that their performance on a memory task was as good as the average younger adult. Age alone is not a particularly good predictor of intelligence. Statistical averages are not especially useful in predicting individual performance, and intelligent people tend to show fewer deficits (Salthouse, 1982). Third, experience compensates for some losses and is a factor that should not be taken lightly.

Where should we go from here? Arenberg (1983) suggests that we try to find new and effective training procedures that can be used outside the laboratory to reduce some of the deficits in cognitive functioning in the elderly. And we can learn much by following people like Mary Robbins, who show no decline or very little in old age, to gain more insight into why they continue to function at such a high level (Arenberg, 1983). Perhaps researchers have spent too much time concentrating on people who show a significant decline and not enough on those who do not or who do so in very minor areas. If we find answers to these questions, we may be able to forestall or at least reduce whatever declines in cognitive functioning are seen.

--- *Summary* ---

1. Verbal intelligence remains rather stable well into old age before it declines somewhat. Nonverbal skills show a decline in young adulthood that continues throughout life. When intelligence is examined in terms of crystallized and fluid intelligence, the same pattern is shown. Crystallized intelligence is much more stable than fluid intelligence.

2. Research from both cross-sectional and longitudinal studies shows a decrease in intelligence in old age. Usually cross-sectional studies show these deficits occurring earlier and being more severe than longitudinal studies.

3. Influences on intelligence can be grouped into three categories. Age-graded influences are biological and environmental factors that correlate with age, such as a decline in speed. History-graded influences are events that correlate with historical change, such as a revolution or educational practices. Non-normative influences are events that relate to our own unique life pattern, including divorce, travel, or unemployment. The phenomenon, called terminal drop, describes the severe drop in intelligence prior to death. Studies show that through a variety of training procedures the elderly can improve their performance on intelligence tests.

4. Most studies show that Piagetian skills decline in old age, but it is difficult to interpret the meaning of this decline.

5. Complaints about memory are common in the elderly. Studies show that sensory memory and short-term memory show little or no decline in old age. However, a variety of studies show declines in long-term memory. These declines may be due to problems in encoding and/or retrieval, but not in storage.

6. The elderly are more cautious and rigid in confronting and solving problems. They perform better on realistic, concrete problems than on abstract ones. They take longer to form concepts and hypotheses and use less-efficient problem-solving strategies. The elderly can be taught to solve problems more efficiently.

7. The elderly believe they are better at solving daily, practical problems now than they were in the past. The importance of experience in solving such problems should not be minimized.

8. Learning continues throughout life. Studies show that the elderly learn best in surroundings that meet their sensory needs, when the pace of instruction is slower, when anxiety is reduced, and when the material is meaningful. The elderly frequently require help in organizing the material, and they benefit when the important points are emphasized. Although these practices may help people of all age-groups, they benefit the elderly even more.

9. Studies show that we can minimize declines in cognitive skills through a variety of intervention strategies.

10. There are important individual differences in the cognitive functioning of the elderly, and age itself is not a particularly good predictor of functioning in later life.

Answers to True or False Statements

1. *False* Correct statement: The elderly often use strategies that are less efficient.

2. *False* Correct statement: Most verbal skills remain rather stable until after age seventy.

3. *False* Correct statement: Nonverbal skills show declines beginning in young adulthood and continuing throughout later maturity.

4. *True* Except for those involving speed of response, cognitive deficits before age sixty are mostly due to illness.

5. *False* Correct statement: The elderly do much better when time limits are suspended on intelligence tests, but they do not do as well as younger adults.

6. *True* The decline in intelligence prior to death, called terminal drop, is a real phenomenon.

7. *True* Memory problems are one of the most common complaints of older people.

8. *True* The changes in sensory and short-term memory are very small.

9. *False* Correct statement: The elderly tend to be very cautious in their approach to problem-solving.

10. *False* Correct statement: The elderly avoid risk whenever possible, but when risk is unavoidable they are no more conservative than younger adults.

11. *True* Most elderly believe that their ability to solve problems has increased with age.

12. *True* Using both sense modalities improves learning in the elderly.

Social and Personality Development in Later Adulthood

The New Breed
CROSS-CULTURAL CURRENT   These Days, Money Is Love:
The Elderly in Nepal
Interpersonal Relations in Later Adulthood
Retirement
Work and Leisure in Later Adulthood
Personality in Later Life
Religion in Later Life
Successful Aging
A New Look at Aging

Are the Following Statements True or False?

Try the True-False Quiz below. See if your answers correspond to the information in this chapter. Each question is repeated after the paragraph in which the answer can be found. The True-False Answer Box at the end of the chapter lists the complete answers.

_____ 1. The elderly comprise just over 5 percent of the population today.

_____ 2. The ratio of elderly females to elderly males has increased significantly since 1900.

_____ 3. The elderly are twice as likely to live in poverty as children are.

_____ 4. Only 5 percent of the elderly live in nursing homes and other residential facilities.

_____ 5. The elderly accept the negative stereotypes concerning aging, but see themselves as exceptions.

_____ 6. Elderly Japanese people are less likely to live with their children than elderly Americans are.

_____ 7. One hundred years ago, the extended family was the most common family structure in America.

_____ 8. The grandparent role has tremendous personal significance for the elderly.

_____ 9. Eighteen months after retirement, most people are happier and more satisfied with their lives than they were a month after retirement.

_____10. Retirement leads to a decline in health.

_____11. Elderly workers express more satisfaction with their jobs than younger workers.

_____12. Personality traits remain basically stable throughout adulthood and old age.

The New Breed

Rebecca and Bill Stone live in a retirement community in Boca Raton, Florida. Every day Bill works out in the gym and swims in the pool, while Rebecca attends aerobics class and does household chores. Their afternoons are spent visiting with others, participating in one of many planned daily activities, or going to town. Their evenings are spent at special shows, socializing, or just watching television.

Rebecca had looked forward to retiring from her job as a cashier for the New York State Motor Vehicle Bureau, while Bill, who owned a fashionable ladies' clothing store, was not so sure about retirement. He had always spent long hours at work and considered business a challenge. How would he do without it? Twice a year or so, they fly north to see their family, spending a few months at a time in a small apartment. They have a positive view of themselves and their lifestyle.

The media tend to concentrate on the plight of the poor elderly. We read almost daily about those who live from hand to mouth or who cannot afford to live in dignity and comfort. We read about depression, isolation, and negativism. The stories about the elderly who become impoverished providing nursing care for their beloved spouses move us emotionally, and the newspapers are filled with reports of the elderly living afraid in squalid surroundings with no one to care for them. We are constantly bombarded with the economic and social problems of the elderly. To what extent is this the real picture of the social and personal functioning of the elderly? Are Rebecca and Bill Stone simply an exception to the depressing picture of the elderly, or are they a new and growing breed?

Portrait of a Population

In 1900 people over sixty-five years of age comprised only 4 percent of the population. Today they comprise somewhat over 10 percent. By the year 2000 the elderly will comprise a full 12 percent of the population, by the year 2020 their proportion will jump to ·15.5 percent, and by the year 2040 it may stand as high as 18 percent (Morrison, 1982). The fact that people are living longer,

combined with the decline in the fertility rate, will translate into an increased proportion of elderly in the population. Those over sixty-five will comprise the fastest growing segment of the population in the next seventy years (Flynn et al., 1985). The population over eighty will increase four times more than any other age-group (Metropolitan Life Insurance Company, 1984).

True or False   The elderly comprise just over 5 percent of the population today.

The elderly population is predominately female. In 1900 the ratio of elderly males to females was 102 : 100, probably because many women died in childbirth. By 1960 it was 83 : 100, and by 1975 it was 60 : 100 (National Council on the Aging, 1978). In 1983 the ratio was 67.1 : 100 (U.S. Bureau of the Census, 1985).

True or False   The ratio of elderly females to elderly males has increased significantly since 1900.

This increase in the numbers of elderly in the population has implications for social and medical services. For example, in 1940 less than 100,000 people were

A growing number of the elderly live in retirement communities where the emphasis is on enjoying leisure-time activities.

receiving social security. Today the figure stands at 21 million (Morrison, 1982), and that figure will rise. As the baby-boom generation born after World War II enters old age, social and medical services will be strained. Because the elderly suffer from more chronic disorders, more long-term health-care facilities and specialized housing will be needed in the future.

The late-middle-aged people and the elderly represent a potent economic force in the country. Those over the age of fifty comprise a $800 billion market of buying power today—far greater than that of the younger generation (Kahn, 1986). Those over age sixty-five now have about 30 percent of the discretionary spending power in the United States (Eisdorfer, 1983). Companies will be scrambling for a larger share of this consumer market.

The economic status of the elderly. Is the average elderly person poor, trying desperately to manage on an insufficient income, or comfortably middle class? Income figures are readily available, but they can be interpreted in many ways. Traditionally, the elderly have been poor, and economic trends, such as inflation, were thought to reduce their buying power. Indeed, heads of households over sixty-five years of age earn little more than half what younger families earn (Botwinick, 1984). The elderly are overrepresented among the poor and the near poor (Clark and Spengler, 1980). Older adults comprised nearly 30 percent of those with an annual income below $3,200 in 1980 (Poon, 1980).

However, another view has been argued recently. The poverty rate for people age sixty and older declined from 21 percent to 14 percent between 1970 and 1982, while the poverty rate for people under sixty rose from 11 percent to 15 percent (Barrow, 1986). Figures for after-tax income from the 1980 census showed that people over age sixty-five averaged $6,299 annual income per family member, $335 more than the national average, and this was greater than any other age-group except for the age fifty to fifty-nine group (Barrow, 1986). The number of individuals over sixty-five with incomes below the social security administration's poverty level declined from 5.5 million in 1959 to 3 million in 1976, from 35.2 percent to 15 percent (Clark and Spengler, 1980).

Why this seeming improvement? The elderly pay very little income tax and have fewer members in their households. Their expenses may not be as great in some areas, such as food. In addition, the social security that now covers most elderly is linked to inflation, and as inflation increases, so do social security payments. Most of the sources of income for the elderly rise with increasing prices, and inflation may not have the crippling effect on the elderly that has been traditionally assumed (Clark and Sumner, 1985).

Perhaps the best conclusion is that, as a group, the elderly are better off today than they were years ago. However, many still live at or near the poverty level. Age itself, though, is not a particularly good predictor of need. As a group, children are more likely to live in poverty than older people (Kutza, 1981).

True or False The elderly are twice as likely to live in poverty as children are.

Housing. The overwhelming majority of older people, about 70 percent, own their own homes (Ebersole and Hess, 1981). About 25 percent live in hotels, rent apartments, or live in public housing projects, and 5 percent are institutionalized most often in nursing homes. There is a shortage of appropriate housing for the elderly, and many elderly do not live in housing that fits their physical or social needs. Those who own their own homes face a number of decisions. They may not have the financial resources or physical ability to maintain their homes. It is expensive to run a large home, to pay high utility bills, and to keep the grounds presentable. The value of the home has probably increased, and the house may be the largest asset. They may elect to move to a retirement community, often made up of condominiums, or a smaller home of their own. The elderly seem happiest in small clusters, where they can be together with others their age but are close to areas where different age-groups exist (Regnier and Gelwicks, 1981). Yet, moving means making new friends and breaking old neighborhood ties. In the case of the Stones, they were able to maintain a small apartment in their old community. Most elderly cannot.

True or False Only 5 percent of the elderly live in nursing homes and other residential facilities.

Most older adults are proud of their independent existence and their ability to care for themselves and their homes. When they need help, they prefer to have a relative or a paid helper come to the home. They fear and do not want to enter nursing homes, but generally prefer this alternative to living with their children (McAuley and Blieszner, 1985).

Nursing homes. Even though only 5 percent of the elderly live in nursing homes, the percentage of elderly who can expect to live in one sometime in their life is estimated at between 25 percent and 40 percent. The percentage of the elderly living in nursing homes increases with age. About 22 percent of those age eighty-five and over live in such arrangements (Ward, 1984). The elderly view nursing homes in terms of a loss of independence, rejection, and as a prelude to death (Shanas, 1961).

The public's conception of nursing homes is generally poor, mainly because of the negative publicity the industry has had over the recent past. Horror stories concerning mistreatment and bad conditions capture the public's attention. It is often with a great deal of guilt and anguish that both the elderly and their children find themselves in a position where there is no other alternative.

The portrait of the elderly person in a nursing home shows this quite well. The typical patient is female, white, widowed, and age seventy-nine, and most come from another institution, such as a hospital, rather than from their own homes. The typical patient has multiple physical problems and is confused, angry, and depressed. Some 77.7 percent need help dressing, 40.4 percent require assistance in eating, 63.3 percent with elimination, and 91.2 percent with bathing (National Center for Health Statistics, 1987) (see Table 20.1). With these types of needs and problems, professional full-time care is often unavoidable, but there are negative consequences to institutionalization—for example, low morale, negative self-image, feelings of personal insignificance, anxiety, depression, and premature death (Tobin and Lieberman, 1976). Many nursing homes do not offer much. When Gottesman and Bourestom (1974) observed more than 1,000 residents in nursing homes, they found that over half the residents' time was spent doing nothing and only a small percentage of the day was spent in contact with any other person.

But the picture may not be as bad as that, and some argue that nursing homes are frequently blamed for conditions they did not cause. Many of the problems associated with nursing homes, such as isolation and depression, existed prior to institutionalization but increase in severity when the older person is placed in the home (Tobin and Lieberman, 1976). Institutionalization may not cause these problems but may make them worse.

These symptoms, though, need not be inevitable (Moos and Lemke, 1985). The quality of the institution is crucial. Homes with better staff-to-patient ratios, better

---

TABLE 20.1

The Status of the Elderly in Nursing Homes

More than half the elderly in nursing homes require assistance in bathing, dressing, and performing other normal daily chores. They require full-time professional help.

Dependency Status	Total	Age			Sex	
		65–74 Years	75–84 Years	85 years and over	Male	Female
Type of Dependency				Percent		
Requires assistance in bathing	91.2	84.8	90.3	94.1	86.9	92.6
Requires assistance in dressing	77.7	70.2	75.9	81.9	71.5	79.7
Requires assistance in using toilet room	63.3	56.6	60.3	68.2	56.2	65.7
Requires assistance in transferring	62.7	52.1	59.7	69.0	55.3	65.2
Continence—difficulty with bowel and/or bladder control	54.5	42.9	55.0	58.1	51.9	55.3
Requires assistance in eating	40.4	33.4	39.1	44.0	34.8	42.3

Source: National Center for Health Statistics, 1987.

medical record-keeping procedures, and superior nutrition programs are associated with improvement in functioning (Linn et al., 1977). If an institution provides a more stimulating environment, encourages interpersonal relationships, provides a healthy nutritional program, and has a good staff, the results can be beneficial (Lieberman, 1974). In one study, Myles (1978) compared a group of institutionalized elderly and community residents who had the same level of illness and disability and found the nursing home residents had a higher subjective rating of health, which is an important determinant of morale. Another positive finding is that family interaction improves after admission to an institution as intergenerational stress is reduced (Montgomery, 1982; Smith and Bengtson, 1979). Family visits are important because they reduce elderly person's feeling of being alone and are related to better integration into the nursing home environment (Shuttlesworth et al., 1982). Institutions frequently rob the elderly of any sense of responsibility and control. In a series of studies, people in nursing homes were divided into two groups, each of which received potted plants. Subjects in the experimental group were given responsibility for the day-to-day care of the plant, while subjects in the control group had someone else taking care of it for them. Experimental-group subjects participated in many more daily social activities and nursing home projects and demonstrated better health over the next year and a half. In fact, many more of the control group died than the experimental group (Rodin and Langer, 1977; Langer and Rodin, 1976). It is important for the institutionalized elderly to have some degree of responsibility and autonomy.

How Society Views the Elderly

Next time you watch television in the evening, keep track of the total number of characters in the show and the number of elderly people. Then make note of how the elderly are portrayed. In a well-known study, Gerbner and colleagues (1980) found that heavy television viewers believed that the number, health, and survival of older people was declining and that the elderly were not open-minded, adaptable, or alert and did not accomplish anything. They saw the elderly as stubborn, eccentric, and foolish. The elderly are underrepresented on television shows. Even though the elderly comprise over 10 percent of the population, only about 2 percent of all characters in dramatic programming are elderly (Passuth

and Cook, 1985). The portrayal of the elderly on television is not entirely negative, because elderly women are sometimes given strong roles in soap operas (Passeth and Cook, 1985), but the elderly, most frequently elderly males, are often shown as ineffectual (Schlossberg, 1982).

Older people, though, are certainly not portrayed as active, engaging people in children's books. When they do work, older people are often seen in unskilled jobs and portrayed as lacking in intellectual ability (Barnum, 1977). In a survey of more than 700 books, Ansello (1977) found that the aged were portrayed as unimportant, unimaginative, unintelligent, dependent, and boring. The older king in fairy tales is often portrayed as good but very foolish. Older people are also the butt of jokes, and many of these have negative sexual connotations (Richman, 1977).

What do people think of the elderly? Although the evidence is not entirely consistent, they are generally seen as ill, tired, not interested in sex, isolated, depressed, slow, and not intellectually alert (Runback and Carr, 1984; McTavish, 1971). Children see the aged as having some positive personality traits but as being physically incapable of doing many things (Mitchell et al., 1985). In one study, Kahana (1970) looked at how people of different ages view one another. Elementary school children, adolescents, young adults, middle adults, and the elderly were asked to rate all ages as to hopefulness, activity, independence, involvement, heartiness, stability, and wisdom. Young adulthood was seen as the most desirable age, followed by middle adulthood and adolescence. Old age was the most undesirable period, an opinion shared by many elderly people. The elderly were seen as more hopeless, helpless, passive, uninvolved, wise, stable, and fragile. Fortunately, some recent studies find a reduction in the stereotypes of the elderly (Barrow, 1986; Kahana, 1982). It is sometimes easier to emphasize the negative than to see any positive side. The elderly are frequently seen as having good interpersonal relationships with others (when they are not seen as isolated), and some of their personality characteristics are positive.

How the Elderly See Themselves

When elderly people are asked about their lives and the lives of their cohorts, three points stand out clearly. First, they share many of the stereotypes that the younger people do; second, they are much less extreme in these beliefs; and third, they usually see themselves as exceptions to the rule (see Table 20.2). Notice that only 35 percent of the young adults believe the elderly are very good at getting things done, while 38 percent of the people over sixty-five believe that their cohorts (others over sixty-five) can accomplish tasks well. However, 55 percent believe they themselves are good at getting things done. Elderly people who are either educated or affluent are not as likely to hold stereotypes of their cohorts as those who are uneducated or poor (Hellebrandt, 1980). Older people in a Florida retirement community saw the elderly as active, competent, and optimistic (Kahana et al., 1980).

True or False The elderly accept the negative stereotypes concerning aging, but see themselves as exceptions.

How do these stereotypes affect the elderly? Comedian George Burns, now over 90 years old, noted that older people can convince themselves to act according to the stereotype and think of themselves as passive and unproductive. People practice getting old. "They start to walk slower and they hold on to things. They start practicing when they're seventy, and when they're seventy-five they're hit. They've made it. They are now old" (Burns in Butler, 1980, p. 72).

The self-concept of elderly people is determined partly by their acceptance of or rejection of the stereotype as well as by their attitude toward aging. People below the age of thirty or above sixty mention age as a defining characteristic more often than people of any other age-group (Burns, 1979). It is also affected by their ability to adapt to changes in their lives and how they experience themselves in relation to others.

Cross-Cultural Studies in Aging

Most Americans believe that the position of elderly people in Eastern societies is much better than it is in Western societies. But the situation is more complicated than that, and any generalization is misleading (see the Cross-Cultural Current on page 514). A number of researchers have recently taken an interest in Japanese society because it combines an Eastern heritage with a Western technological base. Some interesting facts emerge. For example, most large firms retire their workers at the young age of fifty-five or fifty-seven, even though traditional Japanese society defined old age as over sixty years (Maeda, 1978). Traditionally, a ceremony took place at the person's sixty-first birthday in which a red vest was presented to the elderly person, signifying the beginning of a second childhood. The person was now permitted to become dependent again, usually on their adult sons, and were no longer obligated to work in order to earn a living. Most elderly people continued to work for money or satisfaction anyway. Early retirement causes a number of problems, for often the last child may still be attending college, with all the costs this entails. In addition, pension benefits are rather low, and retired people are forced to take jobs with much lower pay and prestige than the one from which they were forced to retire. Most Japanese would rather stay on the job.

T A B L E 20.2

How the Elderly are Viewed by Others and by Themselves

	Percent Saying That Most People Age 65+ Are:		Percent of Those 65+ Saying They Are:
	Age 18–24	Age 65+	
Very friendly and warm	82	25	72
Very wise from experience	66	56	69
Very bright and alert	29	33	68
Very open-minded and adaptable	19	34	63
Very good at getting things done	35	38	55
Very physically active	41	43	48

Source: Harris and Associates, 1975, pp. 48, 53.

The comedian George Burns argues that people can convince themselves to act according to the negative stereotype of the elderly.

As the last child leaves home, it is not unusual for the older couple to move in with their children, with the eldest son taking responsibility for them. Older people are expected to be dependent on their children. A popular Japanese proverb is "When old, obey your children." Most elderly and middle-aged people believe it is natural for the generations to live together. This is in sharp contrast to feelings of the elderly in Western cultures, where independent living is a badge of honor (Havighurst, 1978).

True or False Elderly Japanese people are less likely to live with their children than elderly Americans are.

What of the position of the aged in less-technological societies? Most studies confirm that by and large the elderly are more respected and better treated in less-industrialized societies than in industrialized countries (Lehr, 1983). It must be remembered, however, that the percentage of elderly in these societies is very small and that prestige may come with low numbers (Cowgill and Holmes, 1972). As the percentage of elderly people increases, it is possible that their prestige will decrease. In addition, if the elderly can perform some valuable function, their status is high (Lehr, 1983). The elderly are appreciated most when they control something valuable. In a rural African culture called the Gesuii, elderly people often become healers or spiritual leaders who can perform certain ceremonies which increase their power (LeVine, 1978). In some societies, the elderly control valuable information and are respected for this (Maxwell and Silverman, 1970). For example, in the Bakongo culture in Zaire, the elderly have technical information about fishing that is not available to others (Missinne, 1980). In other cultures, they control land or cattle or political power (Fry, 1985).

What happens when industrialization occurs? The status of elderly people decreases and quickly (Rosenmayr, 1985). They no longer have the necessary skills, and as their children leave the traditional village or lifestyle for industry, the elderly lose their control and power. Industrialization has come to be linked with loss of the extended family and an increase in the nuclear family and with a subsequent decrease in power and status. There is some indication that in the later stages of industrialization the status of the old improves again (Palmore and Manton, 1974), though not everyone believes this increase exists.

Generally, then, we can say that the status and power of the elderly in less-technological, more traditional societies is superior to what it is in industrialized societies. However, individual differences in the treatment of elderly are found in every society—just as some elderly are treated better than others in the United States, this is true for other societies as well. In addition, we should be wary of taking attitude surveys and thinking that behavior always follows from these. Studies in a number of cultures—including the Ibo in Nigeria and various areas of Taiwan—show that behavior does not always match attitudes (Fry, 1985). Sometimes the attitude toward the aged is very positive while their actual treatment is less so. The ideal in China is reverence for the elderly, but research in both Hong Kong and rural Taiwan shows that the ideal is not often matched by practice (Fry, 1985). So we should not worship an idealized view of the status and role of the aged in other societies. Industrialization often brings with it increases in survival rate and superior material benefits for the elderly as well as for everyone else.

These Days, Money Is Love: The Elderly in Nepal

When an elderly Hindu woman living with her son in Kathmandu, Nepal, was asked whether elderly people need their own money and income, she replied, "These days, money is love." This certainly does not fit the stereotype of the elderly in non-Western societies. We generally think of them as living in the extended family, honored and cared for by family members who feel both an obligation to the elderly family member and a genuine respect for his or her age and life experience. It is unfortunate that little research has been done with the elderly non-Western population, especially because the majority of the elderly population in the world live in non-Western countries. Two questions seem most pertinent. First, is the extended family breaking down? and second, if it is not, does its presence imply that the status, life satisfaction, and security of the elderly is high?

These are two questions that researchers Melvyn Goldstein, Sidney Schuler, and James Ross sought to answer. The first is relatively easy, as data from the non-Western world clearly indicates that the extended family continues to exist. They quote data from a survey of eight rural and urban studies in India showing that between 50 percent and 75 percent of all elderly people live with a married son and that well over 90 percent live with some relative. In Japan, three-quarters of Japanese elderly live with their children. So the extended family is still popular in non-Western cultures.

But does this translate into high status and caring? To answer this question, a series of interviews were held with 87 percent of the high-caste elderly adults over sixty years of age in a neighborhood of Kathmandu, Nepal. The interviews were conducted at the end of another extensive study, when the residents were acquainted with the researchers and a good rapport had been established. Each interview lasted between one and a half and three hours and covered health, economics, values, and attitudes. While Western values emphasize independence in aging, the traditional Hindu ideal is dependence. Indeed, 61 percent lived with at least one married son, and 96 percent lived with other relatives, including spouses. Many of those living with spouses or others had sons who were married. Therefore the mere existence of the married son did not result in automatic shared residence status. Most elderly were not supported by their married sons and were economically independent and surviving on their own resources. In half the households where the elderly did reside with a married son, all or most of the expenses were paid for by the elderly themselves. Asked whether it was necessary or important for elderly people to have their own private income, every one of the respondents—100 percent—said yes.

When elderly people lived with their sons but had no income, they received next to nothing for their own needs. One respondent told of an old man with four sons and four daughters who received little care or love. He went to his friend and told him everything. His friend brought him a big box and locked it with seven locks. The friend told the old man to inform his sons that all his gold and jewelry had been kept at his friend's house but that since he was old he had decided to bring it back to his own home. After this, he was loved, well respected, and well cared for. The respondent then pointed to a red box in the corner of his room. Most of these people, the researchers remind us, were not forgotten and lived with their families. They just did not believe they could depend on their children anymore.

One major reason for this attitude is the reduced importance of the extended family as a unit of production. Father's authority was very strong in Hindu life, not only because of traditional values but also because he owned land. Elderly parents depended on their sons to work the land, and the relationship was not one of giving charity to one's poor elderly parents but rather one of a superior-subordinate. With increasing urbanization and more independent employment, this changed. When sons get jobs outside the traditional family, they become independent both economically and socially.

In the traditional Nepalese family, the more sons you had, the more security for old age you possessed, since some sons were likely to survive. Taking from one's married sons was acceptable, but not taking from one's married daughters. Today, however, in order to make a living and obtain some creature comforts, education is necessary and parents must make substantial investments in their children's education. The number of children must be limited. When older people were asked about the ideal family size, 81 percent stated that it was two or three children—not a large family by Nepalese standards. Older people are placed in a paradoxical situation. If sons are not successful, they cannot support their parents. If these sons are successful, they are not only independent economically but also find themselves exposed to such values as individualism and independence, instead of obedience and deference to the elderly. The son's primary responsibility is now to his nuclear family, and he tries to provide support for them, leaving little for his parents. The inflation, poverty, and generally low salaries in Nepal make it difficult to provide modern comforts for one's family and a good education for one's children while supporting one's parents at the same time. Interviews with grown sons showed that they do respect their obligation to their parents but cannot satisfy their families' higher expectations as well as their parents. In this tug of war, parents are the losers—and they know it.

The elderly in Nepal are adapting to the situation in two ways. First, they are keeping control of their property and renting it whenever possible. In addition, elderly men sometimes transfer their property to the wife so that after their death the surviving spouse can remain independent and not have to depend on their sons. Most elderly women who were interviewed and owned property thought it was this wealth that was responsible for the honor and deference they received from their sons, not their position in the family hierarchy. These elderly are helping out their children, sometimes paying for household expenses to allow their sons to send their children to better schools and acquire material goods. At the same time, they are moderating their expectations somewhat. Many no longer expect to be consulted by their sons about family decisions and do not expect daughters-in-law to provide such services as massaging their feet at night.

But what of the poor elderly who have no property? The wealthy have adapted to the changing social system, but unfortunately the poor suffer. Many of the poor elderly interviewed expressed a desire to die, either now or soon. Many had asked their children for support, which is a culturally proper request, and grudgingly received only a minimum. For many, it placed them at a survival level but left nothing for any personal needs. When asking for more, many received a lecture on the difficulty of living in the modern world. This ruined their self-esteem, and the shame of becoming a beggar in their own family was great. These elderly stop asking for anything, and their sons do not give. Even if they live in the same home, these elderly become socially and psychologically isolated.

So although the extended family still exists, it is being radically changed. This demonstrates the importance of seeing the family as a dynamic, changing institution. For those who control property and wealth, the adaptation has been relatively easy; but the lot of the poor has worsened, even if they live in an extended-family situation. Older people in Nepal are not passively accepting the changes. They are keeping their land, transferring their assets to their wives, and trying to cope with modernization. Most of the elderly who were interviewed understood the importance of family planning and limiting the size of families.

The fact that the wealthy are adapting faster and better than the poor is something we see in our own society as well. The wealthy have alternatives not open to the poor. The authors suggest that perhaps it is not Westernization that is the problem as much as poverty. And poverty in the Third World is a problem that is increasing. Any solution to the problems of the Third World elderly poor must include better social services and national economic growth. With the results of this study in mind, we can understand one statement by an elderly Hindu woman: "These days, money is love."

Source: Goldstein, M. C., Schuler, S., and Ross, J. L. Social and Economic Forces Affecting Intergenerational Relations in Extended Families in a Third World Country: A Cautionary Tale from South Asia. *Journal of Gerontology,* 1983, *38,* 716–724.

Three important points stand out. First, each society gives the elderly certain duties and rights. Second, while looking at aging, we must consider the attitudes and practices of the society. Third, where the elderly are seen as serving a useful purpose, they tend to have a higher status. This purpose may involve transmission of culture, special knowledge, control of production, or wisdom. As we look at such areas as changes in personality, family and work relationships, and the entire area of retirement, the cultural context of these changes should be kept in mind.

Developmental Tasks of the Elderly

People negotiating old age must cope with diminished physical skills, chronic illness, loss of friends and family members, and recognition of their own mortality. According to Erikson (1963), the psychosocial crisis of old age is **ego integrity** versus **despair.** The older person reviews his or her life and accomplishments. If the sum total of life's achievements in all spheres is positive, a sense of satisfaction emerges and ego integrity is achieved. But if the life of the elderly person is strewn with failures and missed opportunities, a sense of despair emerges, which exhibits itself in bitterness and frustration.

Peck (1968) noted that the elderly had to meet three challenges. The first consists of ego differentiation versus work-role preoccupation—older people must value leisure time and make meaningful use of it. The second challenge is ego transcendence versus ego preoccupation. The elderly must come to terms with their own mortality and transcend their fear of death. Third, they must meet the challenge of body transcendence versus body preoccupation. The elderly must live a satisfying life, including having good interpersonal relations, despite chronic illness.

Interpersonal Relations in Later Adulthood

Good interpersonal relations are important to the maintenance of high morale (Mancini, 1979). Other people give us support in time of crisis, serve as confidants, and help us spend our leisure time. It is difficult to exaggerate the importance of interpersonal relationships in old age.

Marriage in the Golden Years

Marital satisfaction increases and reaches its peak in old age (Foner and Schwab, 1981; Gilford and Bengtson,

ego integrity   The positive outcome of Erikson's last psychosocial stage, in which an older person experiences a sense of satisfaction with life.

despair   The negative outcome of Erikson's last psychosocial stage, in which an older person experiences a sense of bitterness concerning lost opportunities.

1979). The increase begins in the empty-nest stage and continues into later maturity. Most elderly adults are satisfied with their marital relationships, which do show some change in old age. More sharing occurs, and more activities are performed together (Keating and Cole, 1980). There is more emphasis on relating to each other in an honest, expressive manner.

The blurring of sex roles is one reason for the change (Ward, 1984). Older males do not need to live up to a male stereotype that no longer has much meaning to them. Older females may still be working when their husbands retire, or may be taking care of older, physically ill husbands. For whatever reason, older women find themselves with more power. These changes should not be interpreted to mean that the truly egalitarian marriage emerges and that housework and other responsibilities are shared equally. Immediately after retirement, more sharing of the household duties is evident, but gradually it reverts back to a more stereotyped pattern (Keating-Groen, 1977). In fact, the wives of retired men have more tasks to perform than they did when the husband was working (Turner, 1982).

There is an old saying that when a man retires the wife receives half the income and twice the husband. After retirement, husbands are around the house more and see their wives doing their chores. Husbands may become more critical. When housewives were asked their reactions to the early years of retirement, they were happy that the time available to do things together had increased substantially and that companionship was more plentiful. Some 28 percent noted that husbands helped with more of the housework, many stated that their husbands were happier. The most negative aspects were financial problems, husbands not having enough to do, and too much togetherness (Hill and Dorfman, 1982). When asked to give their advice to other wives, most argued that wives must try to keep their husbands busy, continue their own preretirement activities and do more together and that the wives should maintain their privacy. The marital relationship, then, does change after retirement. The possibilities for sharing and traveling are great, but so is the need for privacy and continuation of personal interests.

Sex and the elderly.   If people have difficulty seeing their parents in sexual terms, imagine how difficult it is to view their grandparents as sexual beings. Older people are "desexed," and many believe that sex is the province of the young (Ludeman, 1981). This is unfortunate, since sexual activity can remain a satisfying part of life throughout old age. Other cultures do not shackle their elderly with such stereotypes. In one survey, Winn and Newton (1982) found that 70 percent of the societies they researched expected continued sexual activity, especially for males.

Evidence concerning sexuality among the elderly is not very extensive. The frequency of intercourse decreases every year, beginning in middle age (Pfeiffer et al., 1972). Yet frequency and quality are not the same, and in one study of 800 elderly people, 75 percent of those who were still sexually active believed that their lovemaking had improved with age (Starr and Weiner, 1982). For older men, quality of performance was more impor-

tant to self-esteem than frequency (Stimson et al., 1981). In a long-term study of aging, Pfeiffer (1969) found that 80 percent of elderly men continued to be interested in sex, and he found only a small decline in sexual activity in the decade between age sixty and age seventy. Some 70 percent of the men were still active at age sixty-eight, but there was a marked decline at age seventy-eight, when only one-quarter of the sample of males was sexually active. Between 20 percent and 25 percent of the men report an increase in sexual expression over the ten years between age sixty-eight and age seventy-eight, and sexual activity for some continued up to one hundred years old.

A significant number of elderly people, then, do not continue to engage in sex. The two most important reasons are lack of opportunity and lack of activity. For women, lack of a partner is the most significant problem. Women are much more likely to live a portion of old age without a spouse than men are. Men die at an earlier age, leaving their wives without sexual partners. Some 51 percent of the women over the age of sixty-five, but only 13.6 percent of the men over that age, have been widowed at least once (LaRue, 1985). Because women outnumber men in this age-group by a substantial margin,

More sharing occurs in marriage as couples negotiate later maturity.

fewer older men are available. Marital status is not an important factor in the frequency of intercourse for males, but it is significant for females (Pfeiffer, 1983). For women living with a spouse, continued sexual activity depends on the male (Ward, 1984). Continued sexual activity in the elderly male is related to their sexual practices at the earlier stages of life. Those who were high in sexual interest and activity in early adulthood continue to be active later in life (Pfeiffer and Davis, 1972).

Many reasons are cited to explain the cessation of sexual behavior in elderly males, including poor health and loss of interest. Many men are afraid they will not be able to perform. Some physical changes in the elderly do affect sexual activity, including the need for much more time to achieve erection and ejaculation, but these need not lead to a cessation of sexual activity (Masters and Johnson, 1966). Sexuality is found even in nursing homes, a setting that is less than ideal. Some 40 percent of the females in nursing homes said that they would be sexually active if they had a partner available, and 30 percent of the males said the same (Loeb and Wason, 1985).

Although, sexuality continues to be a source of satisfaction for some older adults, many discontinue their sexual expression. Perhaps the sexual revolution has come too late for this older generation, but the next generation may be less affected by the cruel stereotype of the sexless older person.

Widowhood. Imagine being married to someone for fifty years. You've raised your children together, retired, and lived your later years depending on each other. Then your spouse dies. On the Life Events Stress Scale devised by Holmes and Rahe (Table 14.3, page 370), death of a spouse is the most stressful situation, achieving a 100-point score. When one becomes a widow or widower, life changes considerably. Years ago, widows were incorporated into the extended family and considered a family responsibility, but times have changed. Today women are more independent, have full inheritance rights, and are more likely to have outside social activities than in the past. On the other hand, widows are also more isolated from family and often suffer financial problems (Lopata, 1979).

Much more is written about widows than about widowers. There are over 10 million widows in the United States, but fewer than 2 million widowers (Lopata, 1983). Three out of four women can expect to be a widow,

while only if a man lives to be eighty-five years old does he have an even chance of becoming widowed (Barrow, 1986). The disparity in the amount of research probably reflects this difference in numbers.

The sense of personal loss is extreme, and the memories constantly surround the surviving spouse. In a study of widows in the Chicago area, widowhood was related to weight loss, irritability, depression, and insomnia (LaRue et al., 1985; Lopata, 1973). Widows have a higher rate of mortality and suicide and report poorer health (Fenwick and Baresi, 1981). Widows often must deal with situations that are new and strange. For instance, the husband may have always taken care of the cars or the finances, and suddenly the widow must learn about investments. Stories of widows being taken by irresponsible and even criminal "advisers" are frequently true. Some widows are left in poverty, but for many others unwise investments strip them of their financial resources. The more the widow has identified with the wifely homemaker role, the more she will be affected by the loss of the spouse. Most widows continue to live alone, and half find loneliness to be a great problem (Lopata, 1973). Many widows have difficulty recognizing their rights and taking advantage of whatever community resources are available (Lopata, 1983). Widows are also apt to curtail their social activities, often because they do not feel accepted and are uncomfortable in couple-oriented situations or when they are alone. Children and other family members help the widow adjust to life during the first months, but nonfamily contacts become more important as time passes (Pihlblad and Adams, 1972).

Most widows eventually regain their equilibrium and create a new life, yet one in five claim never to have recovered from the grief (Lopata, 1973). The process of coping with widowhood involves, first, initial recognition of the event, followed by a temporary disengagement and a period of limbo. Finally, a new life structure is built (Barrow, 1986; Lopata, 1973).

What about the widower? Some believe that he has an even more difficult job adjusting to the loss (Berardo, 1968). The incidence of low morale, mental disorders, and suicide and death are higher for widowers than for widows (Stroebe and Stroebe, 1983). The widower must learn to deal with many new elements of life. He may never have had to prepare meals or do the laundry. On the other hand, the widower is more likely to find a mate than the widow, simply because there are more older women than older men.

Relations with Children

Most elderly people have children, and most are pleased with their relationship with their middle-aged children. Before taking a look at these relationships, we must first explode a myth.

It is popular to mourn the death of the extended family and extol its virtues. The argument goes something like this: In the past, three-generation families living together and constantly helping one another were common, but with the advent of industrialization and urbanization the extended family became almost extinct and this special closeness was lost. This is generally untrue. The extended family was never common in the United States. Even in our earliest days of colonization, in the seventeenth century, the extended family was rare, if for no other reason than that grandparents were not as likely to be alive (Ward, 1984). In fact, at no point in American history did the percentage of extended families living in the same house exceed 10 percent (Aizenberg and Treas, 1985). In addition, the overwhelming majority of older people do not and did not want to live with their children (Bengtson and DeTerre, 1980; Shanas et al., 1968). Our society values independence, and older people show a great desire to be independent and live their own lives without interfering much with those of their children, but this does not mean that parents don't care about their children or that children don't care about their aged parents.

True or False One hundred years ago, the extended family was the most common family structure in America.

Older people expect and receive a great deal of help from their children during crisis situations (Shanas, 1979), but the help is reciprocal, and older people emphasize their contributions to the welfare of their adult children. According to a national survey of the National Council on the Aging (1975), 68 percent of the respondents helped their adult children in time of illness, 42 percent helped with financial assistance, 34 percent shop or run errands for them, and 26 percent reported helping their children fix things.

Relationships between parents and their children are marked by warmth, but the best relationships occur when neither interferes with the other. This sort of distant intimacy is the cultural norm respecting the independence of each (Stevens-Long, 1984). However, when elderly parents become depressed and very sick, the relationship becomes strained (Johnson and Bursk, 1977).

Relationships with the frail elderly change, because they cannot visit their children and often cannot see their grandchildren. Illness demoralizes older people and alienates family members as responsibilities grow (Aizenberg and Treas, 1985). As the elderly progress from the ranks of the young-old to those of the old-old, their need for care increases. Children provide much of the care, but the situation is complicated because one in ten elderly people have a child who is at least sixty-five, and these children may not be in good health (Aizenberg and Treas, 1985).

Grandparenting. This may be the wrong place to discuss grandparenting. If you are married and have your first child at age twenty-five, you could easily be a grandparent by fifty. Still, grandparenting is associated with older adulthood and is a role that continues to develop into one's sixties and beyond.

Some 70 percent of the elderly are grandparents (Barrow, 1986). A grandparent today is also much more likely to be in good physical health than fifty years ago (Aizenberg and Treas, 1985).

We have already described the five styles of grandparents set out by Neugarten and Weinstein (1964) (see Chapter 5). Most young grandparents fit into the fun-seeking or distant-figure styles—that is, they are either playmates or uninvolved except for an appearance at a birthday party or other family gathering (Troll and Bengtson, 1982). When a daughter becomes divorced and temporarily moves in with a grandchild, or if they are called upon to take care of their grandchildren so their children can work some grandparents are asked to play the part of a surrogate parent. Older grandparents are much more likely to take the formal role.

Grandparents are apt to have considerable contact with their grandchildren if they live close by. In one study, about three in four grandparents saw their grandchildren at least twice a month, and almost one in two had even more frequent contact with them (Harris et al., 1975). The overwhelming majority of grandparents see their new role as grandparents positively, but one-third do not feel quite comfortable with it (Neugarten and Weinstein, 1964). Some feel they are too young to be grandparents or find it difficult to play the role of grandparent. However, more than one-third of the grandparents polled in another study said they preferred the grandparenting role to the parental role, one-quarter liked both equally, while another third preferred the parenting

Most grandparents enjoy their role but do not define themselves in terms of the grandparent role.

role (Robertson, 1977). Grandparents like younger grandchildren better (Clark, 1969). Young grandchildren look foward to their grandparents' indulgence. As grandchildren age and create lives of their own, the relationship becomes less satisfying. Parents influence how involved their children will be with their grandparents (Gilford and Black, 1972). If the children's parents are not close to their own parents, it is unlikely that the children will be close to the grandparents (Matthews and Sprey, 1985).

Despite the positive nature of the grandparenting role, it has only limited personal significance for most elderly people (Troll, 1980). Being a grandparent does not play a central role in grandparents' self-definition (Wood and Robertson, 1976). In a survey of more than one hundred grandmothers, Robertson (1976) found that more than half had either remote or symbolic relationships with grandchildren, and less than one-third attached much personal significance to this role. Grandchildren have significance as a source of biological renewal and a symbol of the continuation of the family line (Neugarten and Weinstein, 1964). Although most grandparents are thrilled to watch their grandchildren develop, they do not define

themselves in terms of their relationships with grandchildren and are not likely to find a great deal of personal significance in the role.

True or False The grandparent role has tremendous personal significance for the elderly.

Great-grandparenting. A relatively new status is great-grandparenthood, as four-generation families become more common. It is estimated that half of all people over age sixty-five with children are great-grandparents (Shanas, 1978). Great-grandparenting differs from grandparenting in at least two ways. First, great-grandparents are much older. Using the model of having your first child at age twenty-five and becoming a grandparent at fifty, you could be a great-grandparent at age seventy-five. Second, instead of there being only one generation between grandparent and child, there are now two. The relationship is mediated by both parents and grandparents (Robertson, 1975). Grandparents visit their grandchildren, but because of their age and lack of transportation, they must wait for visits from great-grandchildren, who have grandparents to visit as well.

Little research exists on the subject of great-grandparenting. Wentowski (1985) interviewed nineteen great-grandmothers, and their comments are interesting. Again, as in the case of grandparents, great-grandparents prefer younger children. One great-grandmother said, "Young children don't think about age the same way grownups do. They love you anyway. Even if you are old, they don't notice. If they did notice, they would say so" (Wentowski, 1985, p. 593). In addition, while younger grandparents have energy to play and deal with grandchildren, great-grandparents often say that their very young great-grandchildren cannot stay long. They also felt that these youngsters were more wearing now that they are older. Great-grandparents realize they cannot do as much for great-grandchildren, and they recognize their limitations. They do not tend to be as involved as they were with grandchildren. Great-grandparents experience pleasure and a degree of ambivalence. The positive symbolic meaning of great-grandchildren is also an undeniable sign of aging. They are emotionally remote from the generation, admitting to being closer with grandchildren. Relationships with children were most important, then grandchildren, then finally great-grandchildren.

Siblings

A person's longest-lasting relationship is most likely to be with his or her siblings. An estimated 80 percent of the elderly have siblings (Atchley, 1977). Contact is fairly frequent, although the figures differ widely (Bild and Havighurst, 1976). About 17 percent of the elderly report seeing a sibling once a week, and about one-third claim to see them monthly (Cicirelli, 1979). About two-thirds of all elderly report feeling close or very close to siblings, and only 5 percent claim not to be close (Cicirelli, 1979). Even though they may drift apart in the middle years of adulthood, contacts remain strong, and closeness is emphasized (Scott, 1983). When siblings live far from each other, it is more difficult to be close. Visits and other contacts may then decrease somewhat with age (Rosenberg and Anspach, 1973), but feelings of closeness do not. In some cases, the relationship between siblings in old age becomes closer, since other family responsibilities decrease (Manney, 1975). Both men and women tend to name sisters and middle-born siblings as the closest sibling (Cicirelli, 1980). Gender also affects sibling closeness. Sister-sister relationships are the closest, followed by sister-brother, and then finally brother-brother relationships (Barrow, 1986). Siblings share a number of commonalities. Their memories may be similar, they are of the same generation, and as they age they can form part of a social network that will support one another in time of grief and crisis. Sibling relationships are especially important to the married elderly who have no children and to the widowed, the divorced, and the never married (Watson, 1982). The death of a sibling is a tremendous shock and one that deeply affects the elderly. The youngest member of the family is especially hard hit, as he or she may experience the loss of a number of older siblings with age.

Friendships

Although the actual number of friends people have usually decreases in old age, the importance of friends increases (Ebersole and Hess, 1981). Friends provide a buffer against stress (Lowenthal and Haven, 1968) and help maintain good morale in old age (Burrus-Bammel and Bammel, 1985). Many leisure-time activities, such as card-playing, require social intersection. According to the National Council on the Aging (1975), 60 percent of the elderly surveyed had seen a close friend within a day or so, and another one-third within the last week. Proximity to friends becomes very important in old age, as poor health and transportation difficulties make it difficult to travel long distances. We have all heard stories of elderly people refusing to leave changing neighborhoods where they have lived for so long. Part of this reluctance is leaving longtime friends. Most elderly people say that they feel no need to make new friends but would like more interaction with those they have (Atchley, 1977).

Friends often act as confidants, and most elderly have at least one intimate friend with whom they can discuss problems (Powers et al., 1975). Women are more likely to have more intimate friends with whom they can share personal secrets and problems, while men are more likely to have friends who share recreational pursuits. Older men usually stress the importance of similarities in interest, while understanding and support are more important for women (Lowenthal et al., 1975).

Retirement

Retirement is a relatively new concept. In the early years of this century, no one planned to retire. You worked until you were too ill to continue or you died. However, now that people live longer, a new viewpoint has emerged—voluntary retirement. In fact, early retirement, retirement before age sixty-five, has become relatively popular. Many firms and some government agencies give bonuses to people who retire early so they can replace these workers with younger, less-expensive employees. Poor health and dissatisfaction with one's job are the most potent predictors of early retirement (Palmore et al., 1982). Today retirement is a fact of life for most elderly, and people are constantly warned to save and prepare for their retirement.

Attitudes Toward Retirement

How do people feel about retirement? A study of fifty-five to sixty-four-year-old men varying in occupation, education, and a number of other factors showed that many look forward to retirement (McPherson and Guppy, 1979). About one-third of all people close to retirement look forward to it, another third view it with misgivings, and another third view it with uncertainty or fatalism or never even think about it (Belbin, 1983). Very few actually dread retirement. Attitude differences seem to depend on the person's job, health, financial prospects, and chances of finding meaningful activities in retirement. For example, people who believe that their income will be sufficient have more positive attitudes toward retirement than people who do not (McPherson and

Guppy, 1979). People who find their jobs either unsuitable or very boring also look forward to retirement (Barfield and Morgan, 1978). Positive attitudes toward retirement are also related to number of friends, preparation for retirement, and having outside interests (Ward, 1984).

The relationship between work commitment, job status, and retirement attitudes is complex. Generally, people who are highly committed to their work are less likely to retire, but this does not mean their attitudes toward retirement are negative (George, 1980). Very committed workers do not see retirement in negative terms, but they do see work more positively. The professional enjoying his or her work is less likely to retire (Riley and Foner, 1968). The white-collar worker with little commitment is most likely to retire. Blue-collar or poor workers hold positive attitudes toward retirement, especially if they do not like their work, but they fear the loss of income that accompanies retirement.

Phases of Retirement

Retirement is an exciting time. No longer do you have to get up at six in the morning or fight traffic on the way to work. Everything seems perfect—there is no other way to live. Does this honeymoon continue?

One prominent researcher, Robert Atchley (1977, 1976) suggests that preretirement and retirement occur in a series of definite phases (see Figure 20.1). The first

FIGURE 20.1

Atchley's Phases of Preretirement and Retirement

Robert Atchley suggests that people negotiate preretirement and retirement itself in a series of phases.

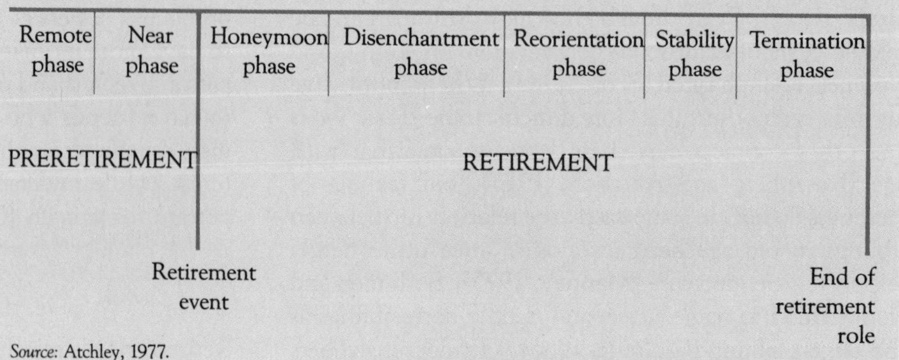

Remote phase	Near phase	Honeymoon phase	Disenchantment phase	Reorientation phase	Stability phase	Termination phase
PRERETIREMENT		RETIREMENT				

Retirement event

End of retirement role

Source: Atchley, 1977.

postretirement phase, called the **honeymoon phase** is a time of joy and excitement. People are very busy doing all those things they could not do when working full-time. Not everyone goes through a honeymoon period, though, for attitudes and financial resources may prevent some people from enjoying their immediate postretirement activities. This phase may last for months or years.

After the honeymoon phase is over, many people experience a letdown or even become depressed. Poor planning may show itself in this **disenchantment phase,** as the original choices may have been unrealistic. One retired man told me he intended to spend six hours a day at the beach and would make other plans only after he was "thoroughly rested." Another was certain that fishing and camping would suffice. For a time both did, but after a year or so disenchantment arose. David Ekerdt and his colleagues (1985) compared men who had retired thirteen to eighteen months before with new retirees. The former group was less satisfied and optimistic about the future than the latter group. They argue that the immediate postretirement period is marked by more enthusiasm and that some temporary letdown is normal during the second postretirement year.

True or False Eighteen months after retirement, most people are happier and more satisfied with their lives than they were a month after retirement.

The letdown often requires a reevaluation, and the **reorientation phase** begins as people begin to take stock of their lives and develop realistic alternatives. They may become involved in senior-citizen clubs (which they might have shunned earlier) and begin to make realistic choices. This leads directly into the **stability phase,** in which these realistic plans come to fruition. Now life is pleasant, satisfying, and predictable. Atchley notes that although many people pass directly into this phase from the honeymoon phase, some must negotiate disenchantment and some unfortunately never reach it. Finally, there is the **termination phase,** in which people either return to work or have their more active retirement role disrupted by illness or disability.

The Consequences of Retirement

What are the consequences of retirement? In a major study of retired people, Streib and Schneider (1971) studied 4,000 people who held many different types of jobs and varied greatly. No sharp decline in health was

honeymoon phase The first phase after retirement, a time of joy and excitement.

disenchantment phase The letdown and sometimes depression that follow the honeymoon phase, often experienced by people whose retirement planning may have been unrealistic.

reorientation phase The retirement phase following the disenchantment phase, during which people develop realistic alternatives.

stability phase The retirement phase following the reorientation phase, during which realistic plans are put into effect.

termination phase The final phase of retirement, during which people either return to work or find their stable lifestyle, disrupted and sometimes ended by illness or disability

found, and there was even some improvement. In a recent study, retired workers perceived their health as improved, probably because of reduced stress. This was especially true for people who had health problems before retirement (Ekerdt et al., 1983). Of course, perception of health is not the most objective measure of physical condition, but it is important. In Streib and Schneider's sample, one-third reported that retirement was better than they expected, while only 4 to 5 percent thought it was worse. Most were satisfied with their lives, and again good health and adequate income were related to satisfaction. There was some increase in the number of people who felt useless some of the time, but about seven in ten retirees never felt useless. Self-esteem in retirement appears to be high as well (Cottrell and Atchley, 1969).

True or False Retirement leads to a decline in health.

Most people cope well with retirement. Satisfaction with retirement is related to good health, adequate income, and substituting new satisfactions for old ones (Botwinick, 1984). If this is the case, we could predict that those with marginal incomes or poor health would have more difficult adjusting to retirement. In fact, this is true. Poorly adapted people have inadequate financial resources, poor health, and few friends or family. They also lack clear-cut goals and often feel they were forced to retire (Fillenbaum et al., 1985; Barfield and Morgan, 1978). People who find all their satisfaction in work are likely to find adjusting to retirement difficult (Atchley, 1980). They must develop new interests or rediscover old talents in order to adjust successfully.

Women and Retirement

Most studies of retirees involve only men. When studying retiring women, we must realize that most of today's elderly female retirees entered the work force late, that they interrupted their careers for their family for long periods of time, and that their working years spanned a time when women were most likely to have less-skilled jobs. Studies on women and retirement show mixed results. Some studies show that women generally have a more difficult time in retirement than men (Szinovacz, 1982; Atchley, 1976). Women have fewer financial resources (Rogers, 1985). They are more likely than men to miss the people at work and the positive feeling of achievement that sometimes comes with employment (Streib and Schneider, 1971). However, certain groups of women adjust better than others. Never-married women adjust better to retirement than widowed, divorced, or separated women (Keith, 1985). Never-married women are more likely to have participated longer in the labor market, and this difference may simply mirror a better financial position. Other studies find that retirement has less effect on the self-esteem and satisfaction of women than on that of men (Palmore et al., 1979) and that retired women were more likely than men to be happy if money was adequate (Jaslow, 1976).

It is too soon to come to any conclusion concerning the consequences of retirement for women. Gender itself may be too large a variable, and although certain groups of women may look forward to retirement, others do not. A woman who finds fulfillment on the job will have difficulty returning to housework if she has not developed outside interests.

Work and Leisure in Later Adulthood

The Stones have no thought of returning to work. They are leisure-oriented. But not all elderly people want to retire, and others, who do retire, sometimes return to work, taking another full-time job or part-time employment.

Working Through Old Age

The percentage of elderly men working has declined sharply since 1900. In 1900 about 70 percent of American men over the age of sixty-five were employed, but by 1975 it stood at 22 percent and by 1983 at 17 percent (Donovan, 1984). A decline is found in most countries around the world, but it has been very sharp in the developed countries (Pampel, 1985). The major reason for this drop is the development of retirement as an acceptable and expected alternative. About 10 percent of the elderly females continue to work (Ward, 1984). In addition, about 20 percent of all retirees work part-time, about half of these in the same industries they worked in previously (Parnes, 1981). People may choose not to retire for many reasons, including lack of financial resources, fear of retirement, or extreme commitment to work. Some may fear the loss of status that may come with retirement (Pampel, 1985).

Among those who work into late adulthood, job satisfaction is rather high, and there is a trend toward increased satisfaction with age (Glenn and Weaver, 1985). More than 80 percent of the working elderly age seventy and older said they were very satisfied with work. The cohort effect should be taken into consideration, because each generation has recently been less satisfied with work than its predecessor. In other words, the elderly may differ from the young adults in these studies not only in age but also in attitudes and feelings toward work. This cohort of elderly may have more positive feelings toward work than the next generation of elderly.

True or False Elderly workers express more satisfaction with their jobs than younger workers.

The elderly seeking work or trying to stay at their present positions face serious barriers of discrimination. Discrimination against the elderly in hiring, training, and even in keeping their jobs is extensive (Stagner, 1985). Some 61 percent of the chief executives of major corporations surveyed agreed that there was discrimination against the elderly in industry (Mercer, 1981). When prospective employees were given descriptions of various potential employees differing only in age, discrimination became evident. The elderly were simply not wanted as new employees (Craft et al., 1979). When readers of a prestigious business magazine were polled to make personnel decisions in fictitious cases, discrimination was rampant (Rosen, 1978). Older workers are very likely to be laid off (especially since seniority provisions are being scrapped), and when they find a job it is less prestigious and pays less than the one they had previously (Warner and McDonald, 1983).

This discrimination against the aged, referred to as

ageism   Discrimination on the basis of age.

ageism, is based on faulty premises. Some believe that the elderly are absent more often, are less productive, and do not have the new skills required for the job. Each of these is either untrue or a half-truth. Absenteeism actually declines with age (Spencer and Steers, 1980). In 1981, workers age sixty-five and over were absent for 4.2 days per year, compared with 4.1 days for workers age seventeen to twenty-four and 5.7 for workers age forty-five through sixty-four (Coberly and Newquist, 1984). The elderly also have a better safety record than younger workers. The lowest accident rates are found in the seventy to seventy-four age-group (Barrow, 1986). The elderly are very reliable and punctual. In addition, their performance on the job tends to be quite good (Foner and Schwab, 1981). Many elderly do have the necessary skills for the jobs they apply for, but discrimination in training often does not allow the older worker a chance to learn new skills (Spencer and Steers, 1980).

Again, because trained younger workers tend to leave jobs quickly while older workers tend to stay, this is a shortsighted policy.

Mandatory Retirement

Pilot Jack Young's Lockheed 1011 took off from Kennedy Airport in New York one snowy night in 1977 en route to Montreal. The plane was barely off the ground when one of its three engines failed. His wide-body jet was packed with passengers and fully fueled, heavier than usual for landing, and Young had to think quickly. He decided to turn the plane around and go back to Kennedy, rather than take the time to lighten the load by dumping fuel. He alerted the traffic controllers to make room, and with emergency crews waiting, he brought his plane down safely.

Young had dealt with failed engines before. And he dealt with many life-threatening situations as a pilot in the U.S. Army Air Corps during World War II. He knew how to handle the routine and the unexpected. But nothing in all his training and years of experience prepared him for the personal crisis he would face just two years after the incident at Kennedy.

On December 5, 1979, his career was over—not because he wanted it to be over, not because he failed a medical

About 17 percent of all elderly men and 10 percent of the elderly women continue to work full time in later maturity.

examination, and not because he flunked a proficiency test that airline pilots must pass. He was grounded that day because of his age. He had turned sixty, and no pilot can fly a plane for a U.S. airline at that age. The federal government says so. (Gilgoff, 1986, p. 9)

Mandatory retirement rules are controversial. Recent laws in the United States and other countries have raised the mandatory retirement ages (Belbin, 1983). Indeed, federal law now covers age discrimination until age seventy, and court decisions have mandated that municipalities must show why mandatory retirement policies are necessary and appropriate prior to that age (Levin and Levin, 1980; Gilgoff, 1986). Federal law-enforcement agents must retire at age fifty-five unless they were hired after the age of thirty-five, a rare occurrence. On the surface, mandatory retirement laws for public servants involved in safety-related jobs may make sense. How could a sixty-year-old police officer hope to match physically a twenty-year-old burglar running from the scene of a crime? However, not all jobs require these types of skills, and some elderly people function better than younger people on the job. It seems reasonably simply to mandate testing of all people over a particular age and retire or reassign them only if they cannot do the job any longer. The problem is that experts disagree on how accurate and relevant such testing would be, especially in predicting behavior in emergency situations. In addition, it is argued that older people are more prone to disabling illness that may occur at any time.

Some reasons for mandatory retirement are social and economic. Mandatory retirement encourages more upward mobility for the young worker, and it reduces costs because younger workers are paid less (Levin and Levin, 1980). On the other hand, being forced to retire even if one can and still wants to perform is degrading and causes undue financial hardship. It completely ignores the productive talents of older people and individual differences (Barrow, 1986). Mandatory retirement obviously does not affect the majority of workers who retire at sixty-five, but it is a challenging issue.

Leisure Time

When older people are asked what the best thing about being over sixty-five is, they often say having more leisure time (National Council on the Aging, 1975). A number of factors influence participation in leisure-time activities. First, some people are so work-oriented they find it almost impossible to deal with their increased leisure time. Second, people in poor health cannot always participate in their desired leisure activities. A person may love to read but not be able to see the print. Of course, some books can be found in large print, but perhaps not the ones a person is interested in reading. Mobility is also a prime concern. Many older adults depend on others for transportation, and 22 percent of the elderly surveyed have difficulty walking and climbing stairs (National Council on the Aging, 1975). If an elderly person likes to bowl but cannot get to the bowling alley, that person can't participate in this activity. In addition, lack of companionship is often a major problem (Burrus-Bammel and Bammel, 1985). If you enjoy playing poker, bridge, or gin rummy, you need a group. Finally, there is the income barrier. You may have always wanted to travel but find you cannot afford it.

How do the elderly spend their leisure time? The most common leisure-time activity is watching television, followed by visiting, reading, gardening, going for walks, and handiwork (Atchley, 1977). Travel is also an important leisure activity for the young-old, and many elderly belong to travel clubs. Fewer than 5 percent of the elderly are involved in volunteer work.

The elderly devote a greater amount of time to leisure pursuits, but the scope of their activities is frequently narrow. In addition, activities tend to become more sedentary with age (Burrus-Bammel and Bammel, 1985; Gordon and Gaitz, 1983). In other words, as people age they devote more time to less-active pursuits, such as television-viewing, and less time to more socially active participation. Perhaps declining health, the loss of friends, and mobility are the culprits. This is unfortunate, because people who are more involved with other people through such pursuits as bridge, photography competitions, civic projects, and square-dancing are more satisfied with life (Gordon and Gaitz, 1983). For those who move to retirement communities, high degrees of participation are related to increased life satisfaction (Gordon and Gaitz, 1983).

Leisure activities do not change much in old age. Few older adults take up totally new interests. The amount of time devoted to these interests increases with retirement though. There is a strong relationship between the number of hours spent on leisure-time activities and degree of life satisfaction (Parnes and Less, 1985).

Unfortunately, only 5 percent of the elderly do volunteer work, something which could prove to be a major source of satisfaction in their lives.

Life Satisfaction

The Stones are basically satisfied with their lives, as are most elderly people. Older people rate their present lives positively, and better than the average person's life (Borges and Dutton, 1976). Does satisfaction change with age? The answer is generally no. Most studies find little or no relationship between age itself and happiness (Kozma and Stones, 1983; Larson, 1978). Satisfaction with health declines, but satisfaction with home, government, religion, and involvement with organizations increases somewhat (Cutler, 1979).

Certain factors are related to life satisfaction. Among the most important are good health, socioeconomic status, and participation in social activities (Palmore and Kivett, 1977; Bengtson et al., 1977). However, it may not be the amount of activity that is related to well-being as much as the quality of the activity (Hoyt et al., 1980). The availability of a confidant is another major factor (Botwinick, 1984). Retirement and loss of work role is not related to lack of satisfaction, as long as the individual retired close to or at the age he or she chose (Beck, 1982). Despite some contradictory evidence, there appear to be no sex differences in life satisfaction among the elderly (Liang, 1982). In addition, the ability to cope well with problems in everyday life and to use the opportunities available is another factor (Thomae, 1983).

Two points stand out. First, health, financial status, and a fair level of interpersonal relationships are important in determining life satisfaction. Second, the continued happiness in old age shows that continuity rather than discontinuity is the key to understanding satisfaction in the elderly. Factors that are apparent in young adulthood or even earlier may be predictive of happiness in old age. In an involved study, Caspi and Elder (1986) found that personal resources and social involvement were important bridges to life satisfaction in old age and that those who coped well with problems in the past coped well presently. In conclusion, we would expect that if health, income, and social contacts are available, a happy, mature, satisfied person in early adulthood and middle adulthood would continue to be so into later adulthood.

Personality in Later Life

Are continuity and stability the keys to understanding personality as well? As we age, do our personalities change? Numerous studies have looked into this question. The overwhelming majority of modern studies have found that personality characteristics such as openness and extroversion remain rather stable in old age (Costa et al., 1986; Moss and Susman, 1980). When personality tests were given to a group of adults over a twenty-five-year period, no significant changes were discovered (Woodruff and Birren, 1972). In a study that combined both longitudinal and cross-sectional analyses no significant personality changes were found as well (Siegler et al., 1979).

True or False Personality traits remain basically stable throughout adulthood and old age.

Although stability in personality traits is common, some changes in personality with aging have been suggested. The aged are more likely to show an increase in **interiority**, a preoccupation with the inner life (Neugarten, 1968). Older people are likely to be more introspective (Schulz, 1985) and to participate in **life review** (Butler, 1963), a process of looking back and evaluating life which will be described in chapter 21. Such a process may be important in putting one's life in perspective.

Other changes have been noted in other chapters. Older people tend to be more cautious, slower, and more practical, and there are some sex differences. "Older men are more willing to accept their impulses to like and be with other people, to help others, and to gratify their senses than are younger men. Older women are more willing to accept their aggressive and egocentric impulses than are younger women" (Atchley, 1977, p. 77). Self-acceptance, then, increases in old age.

How can we explain these findings? If we look at people as they negotiate adulthood and old age, stability in personality traits is the most common pattern. A friendly person at age thirty-five is likely to be friendly at age fifty and age seventy-eight. Age-related changes, such as the increase in interiority and practicality, are adaptations to old age. However, this does not mean that the individual's personality must be absolutely stable. Some-

interiority The introspection and preoccupation with one's inner life that occur during later life.

life review The process of reviewing and evaluating one's past, usually found in older people.

times changes occur as people negotiate personal crises (Schaie, 1981). In addition, certain personality traits may be shown in a different way at different ages. If people were active in their younger years, they are likely to remain active in older adulthood if their health is good, but they do not show it in the same way. We might expect a young adult to play basketball, while an older adult might walk. We can conclude, then, that stability in personality traits should be expected. However, some changes do occur and are adaptive. The slowness, practicality, and cautiousness are reasonable adaptations to the challenges of aging.

Religion in Later Life

The increase in introspection, the life-review process, and the increase in interiority are attempts to place one's life into perspective and come to grips with one's own mortality. Older people are faced with many terminal events, such as the death of loved ones and incapacity. Religion may have much value for people in understanding these events. In addition, religious involvement may be a source of social contact with the community and the church or synagogue a place to interact with other people.

A serious problem in measuring religiosity through such variables as church attendance and observance of ritual is that these activities are greatly affected by health and, for church attendance, the ability to travel. As far as attitudes are concerned, older people are more likely than younger people to believe that religion is very important in their lives (Ward, 1984). In addition, certain personal activities such as reading the Bible, listening to religious programs on radio and television, and personal prayer increases in old age (Clark and Anderson, 1967). Religious attitudes tend to be rather stable in late adulthood (Blazer and Palmore, 1976), although there may be an increase in self-reported religiosity with age, especially for those who are somewhat religious as they enter old age. When Markides (1983) interviewed elderly Mexican-Americans and Anglo-Americans in 1976 and then again in 1980, he found that self-rated religiosity increased somewhat over the four years. While there is little evidence that older people turn radically to religion as they age, there is little doubt that it plays a part in the lives of many elderly people. Not only are beliefs a source of comfort, but the religious institution may help the elderly integrate into the community.

Successful Aging

After looking at so many aspects of the elderly person's life is it fair to ask the question, "What is successful aging?" Two theories of aging—the disengagement theory and the activity theory, have been advanced to explain successful aging. Each looks at aging from a very different perspective.

The Disengagement Theory

According to the **disengagement theory,** it is both normal and inevitable that people and society "disengage" from each other (Cumming and Henry, 1961). As the individual negotiates old age, he reduces the ties that bind him to others, becoming more isolated, less socially active, more introspective, and more passive. At the same time, society disengages from the individual as retirement is expected and society's push toward efficiency leaves the older person at a disadvantage. The aged escape the stress that would come with the inability to function at previous levels. After an initial period of depression and anxiety, disengagement is accepted and tranquillity is established. Some of the changes we have seen in old age—including the change from active to passive mastery, the increase in introspection, the reduction of activity, and narrowing of interests—fit this model. Successful aging in the context of this theory would be the progressive disengagement and acceptance of one's position, which should eventually lead to higher morale.

Criticisms of this approach are many, and most research is either mixed or runs contrary to its predictions. For many, what may seem like disengagement—the decrease in community involvement, reduction in interpersonal contacts, and the like—may actually be caused by poor health and travel difficulties (Kleiber and Kelly, 1980). Lack of opportunity may also lead to an unwilling disengagement, as when older people do not live near other elderly people (Carp, 1968). In addition, many

disengagement theory The theory relating successful aging to the reduction in the bonds that tie the elderly person to society.

activity theory The theory relating successful aging to the maintenance of activity throughout later maturity.

lives simply do not fit this pattern. One study of eighty-year-olds did not find a general trend toward disengagement (Granick and Patterson, 1971). In addition, morale does not seem to increase with disengagement (Tallmer and Kutner, 1970). Last, many studies find some positive relationship between activity, social involvement, and life satisfaction (Markides and Martin, 1979). Havighurst and colleagues (1968) found that there was a decline in social interaction, but as level of activity declined, so did feelings of contentment. The relationship between life satisfaction and activity was positive but moderate. Many elderly were not satisfied with their "disengagement" and placed great importance on social interaction.

The disengagement theory may be helpful in understanding some individuals but not all. Disengagement is most likely seen among the very old, whose health does not permit them to maintain their more active, engaged lifestyles. It is also seen in people for whom disengagement was a lifestyle before old age (Maddox, 1966). Some elderly disengage from some ties that are less satisfying in order to strengthen others that are more satisfying (Brown, 1974). A study of people in a retirement community showed that some were pleased to get away from children and neighbors in their older community and enjoy their relatively new relationships in the retirement community, which were more satisfying (Kahana and Kahana, 1980).

The Activity Theory

The **activity theory** emphasizes the importance of social activity in promoting life satisfaction and sees the maintenance of activities and attitudes of middle age to be most important in successful adjustment to aging (Havighurst, 1961; Havighurst and Albrecht, 1953). If a role is lost, such as losing a spouse or the work role because of retirement, some substitute must be found. But this approach is too simplistic. The link between social activity and life satisfaction is moderately positive, but not as strong as would be required to base a case for successful aging on this variable. In addition, activity can decline without affecting morale (Maddox, 1970). Some research also shows that loss of role, as in retirement, is not related to less life satisfaction (Lemon et al., 1972). Although many older people remain active, activity may not be the key to everyone's happiness.

Two Keys: Choice and Personality

Neither the disengagement theory or the activity theory is entirely successful in predicting successful aging. It may be that both theories are correct and that to understand aging we must look at two key factors that influence one's adaptation to life.

The first factor is choice. People who voluntarily decide to reduce some of their bonds, for whatever reason, are likely to show high morale with disengagement (Neugarten et al., 1968). People who retire because they want to, and not because they are forced, are happier. Choice is, of course, related to control. People who maintain some degree of personal control over their own life decisions are more likely to be happy in old age.

Personality is the second factor. Neugarten and her colleagues (1968; 1961) identified four personality types and discovered their relationship to life satisfaction and activity. Those with an **integrated personality** are flexible, open to new stimuli, mature, and basically function well in the cognitive domain. They have a high level of life satisfaction, but differed greatly from each other regarding their activity level. Some were highly active substituting new activities for older ones, some showed moderate levels of activity, being more selective in their choice of activities, while others were disengaged and showed low levels of activity.

The second personality type was the **armored-defended** personality. These people were striving, ambitious, and achievement oriented, with high defenses against anxiety and the need to control impulses. Some showed medium or high levels of activity and life satisfaction trying to hold on to middle age as long as possible. Others were preoccupied with losses and deficits and voluntarily reduced their social interactions and closed themselves off showing a medium level of satisfaction.

The third personality type was labeled **passive-dependent.** Some of these people showed a strong need to depend on others and required others to be very responsive to their needs. They showed a medium level of

> **integrated personality** A personality pattern marked by an openness to new stimuli.
>
> **armored-defended personality** A personality type marked by high defenses against anxiety and the need to control impulses, as well as striving, ambition, and continued achievement-orientation.
>
> **passive-dependent personality** A personality type marked by passivity and dependence on others.
>
> **unintegrated personality** A personality type marked by disorganized patterns and defects in both thought and psychological functioning.

activity and medium satisfaction. Others were basically passive and apathetic, showing low levels of activity and either low or medium life satisfaction.

The last personality type was the **unintegrated personality.** These people showed a disorganized pattern of aging, including defects in psychological functioning and deteriorating thought processes. They showed low activity levels and reported poor life satisfaction.

The researchers argue that neither the activity theory nor the disengagement theory accounts for their findings. The relationship between social activity and life satisfaction is mediated by personality type and pattern, which show consistency over the life span. People are not merely at the mercy of the social environment but rather make choices and select their degree of involvement in accordance with their own needs.

A New Look at Aging

It is common to dwell on the problems of old age— inadequate income and housing, poor health, and general decline. These problems are real. Providing adequate care for the old-old who may need constant monitoring is a challenge that must be faced. On the other hand, if we merely focus on the problems of aging, we overlook the possibilities for great satisfaction in later life. It is clear that our present psychological theories of aging are inadequate. Neither the disengagement theory nor the activity theory alone explains aging. Because of increases in longevity and better health, many of today's elderly are not only evaluating their past but also living active, involved satisfying lives in the present.

We tend to think of choice as being central to the lives of young and middle-aged adults, and to see older adults as having most decisions forced on them or made by someone else. This is not true. Most elderly are independent and have a number of choices concerning their engagement or disengagement, activity or lack of activity. As is true of young and middle-aged adults, they make their choices on the basis of their needs and circumstances. By emphasizing the possibilities for personal choice and satisfaction, we are not neglecting the real problems of aging. We are merely realistically echoing sentiments that are present in the elderly community today.

Summary

1. The proportion of elderly people in the United States stands at more than 10 percent today and will increase substantially during the first half of the next century. The elderly population is predominately female. Although the elderly are better off financially today than years ago, many still live below or near the poverty level.

2. Only 5 percent of the elderly live in institutions, such as nursing homes. Institutionalization takes place when no other alternatives are open. Many elderly nursing home patients have serious chronic disorders and need help eating and dressing. Depression and other psychological symptoms are common, but if the nursing home is excellent, these symptoms may not appear.

3. The image the general population holds of the aged is complex, showing both positive and negative features. The elderly too have stereotypes about the aging population, but not to the same extent. They also see themselves as exceptions to the rule.

4. Each culture has its own roles and responsibilities for older people. In tribal or preindustrial societies, the status of the elderly is somewhat higher than in industrialized societies.

5. Marital satisfaction among the elderly is quite high. More sharing takes place in old age, and more activities are performed together. Sex-role distinctions blur somewhat. Sexuality can be a source of satisfaction, but many elderly have ceased to function sexually. Lack of a partner is the most frequent reason for women's lack of sexual activity, while fear of failure, poor health, and lack of interest are cited as common reasons for males to cease sexual activity.

6. Women are much more likely to become widows than men are to become widowers. Most widows and widowers eventually build a new life.

7. The extended family—where three generations live together—was never very popular in America. Most elderly people want to live independent lives. Older people are frequently visited by and visit their children. They receive help from them in times of crisis. However, older people also point to the help they give their children. Their relationship with their children is good, although it may become more strained when the elderly become very ill and require more attention and care.

8. Most grandparents have frequent contact with grandchildren and enjoy their role. However, grandparenting does not rate very highly in their self-definition. Great-grandparents are less involved with their great-grandchildren than they were with their grandchildren.

9. Siblings are also important to older people, and closeness may increase with age. Most elderly adults have at least one very close friend who acts as a confidant. Women are more likely to have close friends than men.

10. Most people hold a positive view of retirement, although not everyone wants to retire. The retired individual may pass from the satisfaction of the initial honeymoon stage to disenchantment. This is frequently followed by a reorientation phase, when a more realistic lifestyle is built. In the stability phase, life becomes satisfying and predictable. The last phase, called termination, occurs either when the retiree returns to work or when he or she cannot continue normal activities because of illness or disability. Most people adjust well to retirement.

11. Most elderly who continue to work show high job satisfaction. Discrimination due to age, called ageism, seriously hampers older workers. Older workers are more safety conscious than younger

workers and are absent fewer days. Their performance on the job is good.

12. Mandatory retirement is a very controversial question. Most elderly adults are pleased that they have more leisure time. In old age, leisure pursuits tend to narrow and become more sedentary.

13. Life satisfaction is determined by health, economic circumstances, and social activities. It is predicted by emotional stability, personality characteristics, and a history of coping with past problems.

14. Most personality characteristics are rather stable throughout adulthood. Older people, though, do

tend to be more cautious, slow, introspective, and accepting of their own desires.

15. The disengagement theory states that successful aging involves progressively loosening the bonds that bind the individual to society. The activity theory states that people who stay active and maintain middle-aged attitudes are more likely to be satisfied in old age. Neither theory, by itself, is totally accepted. Two important variables involved in successful aging are (1) choice and personal control and (2) personality type and pattern.

Answers to True or False Statements

1. *False*   Correct statement: People over age sixty-five comprise more than 10 percent of the population.

2. *True*   The ratio of elderly females to elderly males has increased significantly since 1900.

3. *False*   Correct statement: Children are slightly more likely than older adults to live in poverty.

4. *True*   Only 5 percent of the elderly live in nursing homes and other residential facilities.

5. *True*   The elderly accept a number of negative stereotypes, but seem themselves individually as exceptions to the rule.

6. *False*   Correct statement: Elderly Japanese are more likely to live with their children.

7. *False*   Correct statement: The extended family never comprised more than 10 percent of all the households in America.

8. *False*   Correct statement: Studies show that the role of grandparent does not have much personal significance for the elderly.

9. *False*   Correct statement: Most people are not as happy or optimistic about their lives eighteen months after retirement, but then they reorganize their activities and build a new and more satisfying life structure.

10. *False*   Correct statement: There is evidence that health may even improve somewhat following retirement.

11. *True*   Elderly workers express considerable satisfaction with their jobs.

12. *True*   Most studies find that personality traits remain stable throughout adulthood and old age.

Dying, Death, and Coping with Loss

The New Interest in Death and Dying
Death: A Developmental Perspective
On Dying
Appropriate Death
Bereavement, Grief, and Mourning
Personal Choices
CROSS-CULTURAL CURRENT   Culture and Death

Are the Following Statements True or False?

Try the True-False Quiz below. See if your answers correspond to the information in this chapter. Each question is repeated after the paragraph in which the answer can be found. The True-False Answer Box at the end of the chapter lists the complete answers.

_____ 1. About 70 percent of all people who die today are over sixty-five compared with about 80 percent in the year 1900.

_____ 2. Most children understand that death is irrevocable, universal, and irreversible by the age of seven.

_____ 3. Adolescents tend to romanticize death.

_____ 4. As a group, older people fear death less than middle-aged people or young adults.

_____ 5. The tendency of older people to dwell on the past is a definite sign of organic deterioration.

_____ 6. When dying patients finally accept their fate, their communication with others increases and they become more lively and animated.

_____ 7. Most elderly people want to die at home.

_____ 8. Most elderly people die in their own home or in that of one of their children.

_____ 9. A hospice is a place where dying people get the most advanced experimental treatments for their diseases.

_____10. As a group, the elderly are less likely than younger people to favor euthanasia.

_____11. The initial reactions to the death of a close relative differ so greatly among people that no accepted description of them exists.

_____12. Recovery from the grief following the death of a loved one is more rapid if the death was expected.

The New Interest in Death and Dying

A pregnant California woman, declared legally dead from a severe brain seizure in January, was put on life support systems to allow the fetus to mature. After a healthy baby was delivered on March 24, the woman was taken off the machines and immediately stopped breathing.

A Los Angeles judge dismissed charges that two physicians had violated their legal responsibilities by ordering that a comatose patient be taken off the respirator and intravenous feedings.

A federal judge struck down the Reagan administration's "Baby Doe" rule that urged hospital employees to tell federal officials if defective infants were being denied food or medical treatment. (*U.S. News & World Report,* July 11, 1983, p. 62)

After years of ignoring issues involving death, we are now in the midst of a tremendous rebirth of interest in the subject. Colleges and universities all across the nation are offering courses on death, and books about death and dying are well received by the general public. The interest in death pervades every age-group, even though death is more and more a phenomenon of old age. In 1900 only 25 percent of those who died were over age 65 (Albert and Steffl, 1984). Today the figure stands at about 70 percent (Barrow, 1986).

True or False About 70 percent of all people who die today are over sixty-five, compared with about 80 percent in the year 1900.

The increase in interest may be partly due to the technological revolution in medicine. Medical science has found ways to prolong survival. People are now more likely to linger for months, perhaps years, in terrible pain. This raises questions concerning the right of patients and their families to refuse treatment. On the other hand, the resurgence of interest in the area may be a reaction to our society's long denial of death. For many years, dying was simply not discussed. The depressing subject was avoided at all costs by almost everyone, including health professionals. Many physicians are uncomfortable with dying patients, often avoiding them whenever possible (Schulz and Aderman, 1976). This uneasiness with death reflects the denial often seen in society. The word

"death" is rarely used, even when it appears to be unavoidable. For example, condolence cards use the terms "gone," "departed," and "no longer with us" and rarely is there a direct reference to death. However, we are now beginning to face issues involved with death that were once taboo.

Death: A Developmental Perspective

Do you remember your first experience with death? Was it the death of a favorite pet or of some neighbor or friend? Was it casual, as in the withering of a flower, or more dramatic, such as seeing someone die of a heart attack on the street? As we age, our experiences with death are likely to change, and death has a different meaning to people of different ages.

Children's Understanding of Death

Most people would like to believe that children are sheltered from the death and destruction of life, that they can go about their daily lives without thinking of the end. According to this thinking, death is and should be a stranger to the child (Ward, 1984). In one way, this is true. Unlike years ago, children today are not likely to experience the death of parents and siblings. Still, children are exposed to death early and often (Hardt, 1979). Every child sees death on television, much of it violent. Every child has heard fairy tales tell about the death of a parent. Every child has experienced the death of a plant or other living thing. Although they may not be able to put in into words or understand its full significance, death is real to young children.

Perhaps the most widely quoted study on children's understanding of death was conducted by Maria Nagy (1948) in Budapest, Hungary. She interviewed 378 children ranging from age 3 to age 10. A clear developmental progression was found.

Stage one: about age 3–5. Children about the ages of three to five do not view death as universal, irrevocable, or irreversible. Rather, the dead are just a little less alive. They believe that the dead can return. Even after seeming to accept the fact that grandma has died,

Children's first real brush with death often occurs when a family pet has died.

they may ask when grandma is coming for a visit. To these young children, death may be akin to a separation or a trip; it is transitory and reversible. When the child finally acknowledges that grandma is not going to visit any more, he or she may ask such questions as "Who is going to bring me candy?" This may infuriate the grieving parent, who would like grandma remembered for other reasons. Yet at this age, children often think instrumentally; no disrespect is meant. Young children often equate sleep with death, which can cause some problems at bedtime (Kastenbaum, 1977). Preschoolers are also very curious about death. They are interested in details and may search for the reasons behind it. Preschoolers often believe that death is caused by some misbehavior on the part of the deceased, such as "eating a dirty bug" (Koocher, 1973).

Stage two: about 5 or 6 to age 9. Children slowly learn that death is indeed final, although it may not be completely accepted until the end of this stage. Nagy found that children personify death, seeing it as an ugly old person, a bogeyman-type of conception; the skeleton was very commonly cited by children. Most recent studies, however, have failed to find this personification, and it may represent a cultural rather than universal phenomenon (Koocher, 1973). Despite the advancement in understanding, children still think that death can be avoided by being clever. This reflects the child's real experiences. Children understand that people can be killed crossing the street, but they know that if you are careful this will not happen (Kastenbaum, 1977). Kastenbaum describes the child's understanding of death at this stage as "finality with an escape hatch" (1977, p. 119).

Stage three: about age 9 or 10 and beyond. Children now understand that death is universal and inevitable. Death is understood as the termination of life and every living thing is acknowledged as having an end point in time.

Nagy's conclusions that children proceed through an orderly, sequential stage-related progression in understanding death has been generally supported by other research. Childers and Wimmer (1971) found that by the age of ten, 90 percent of all children recognize the universality of death, but that children had more difficulty understanding death as final and irrevocable. Even at age ten, about one-third did not fully understand that death was final. By age ten or so, though, most children understand that death is irrevocable, universal, and inevitable. Of course, as with any other stage-like progression, age is no more than a guideline. A child's understanding of death is related to cognitive level as measured by Piagetian tests (Koocher, 1973). In addition, research with terminally ill children shows that they seem to understand death's finality, inevitability, and completeness at earlier ages than the developmental progression described above would indicate (Bluebond-Langner, 1977). Terminally ill children understand the changes in their own condition from how their parents, doctors, and nurses respond. Their time perspective changes, and they talk very little about the future and much more about the present.

True or False Most children understand that death is irrevocable, universal, and irreversible by the age of seven.

Three important points stand out in the developmental progression in children's understanding of death. First, it progresses in an orderly manner. Second, personal experience with death seems to hasten the process of understanding. We might expect that children exposed to war, as in Lebanon, Israel, and Vietnam, would develop a more sophisticated understanding of death at an earlier age. In fact, lower-income children, who frequently come in contact with personal death at an earlier age because of violence and accidents, are more advanced in their understanding of death (Kastenbaum and Costa, 1977). Third, from a very early age, children are exposed to death and are curious about it, even if they cannot understand the entire concept or put their thoughts into words.

Helping Children Deal with Death

When Will Lee, who played Mr. Hooper the shopkeeper on the children's television show "Sesame Street," died in December 1982, the program's writers were in a quandry. How should they explain his absence to the millions of preschoolers who watch the program every day? It wouldn't be honest to tell viewers that he had moved to Florida, so the writers decided to deal with the difficult concept of death.

But they did not do this by explaining the causes of death or the process of aging. Instead, the resident five-year-old on the show, Big Bird, was forthrightly told that Mr. Hooper had died. Like most preschoolers, Big Bird didn't understand the irreversibility of death and asked when his friend Mr. Hooper was coming back. Later, as the reality sunk in, Big Bird's attention centered on his own loss. "Who will make me birdseed milkshakes and tell me stories?" he asked. Told that his friend David would do that, Big Bird remained unhappy, knowing it would never be the same. He drew a picture of Mr. Hooper and hung it over his nest. But Big Bird's mood brightened as a new baby was presented on the show, demonstrating the continuity of life (*New York Times*, August 13, 1983).

Eventually, all parents must explain death to their children and decide whether the child should attend the

funeral. Although death is a difficult subject to discuss with one's children, the following guidelines may help.

1. *Be honest.* Hardt (1979) notes that parents can use either a religious or a secular approach with children. Telling the child that the person is now with God, or simply informing the child that when death occurs life stops and the dead cannot return, are both reasonable approaches. Combinations are possible as well. The important thing is that the communication be honest.

2. *Do not confuse death with any other state.* Have you ever heard parents tell their children that the dead are only sleeping or on a long trip? Not only is this dishonest, but it may cause major problems at bedtime.

3. *Be a good listener and observer.* Parents are sometimes more interested in explaining death to the child than in observing and listening to the child. By observing and listening, you can gain a better understanding of what the child does and does not understand.

4. *Do not explain everything at one sitting.* Some parents try to explain everything to the child when grandma dies. However, the death of pets or the death of

When Will Lee who played the shopkeeper on "Sesame Street" died, the writers had to decide how to explain his death to the many young children who watched the program daily.

a character on television can lead into a discussion of death with a child without the stress and intense grief that accompanies the death of a close relative.

5. *Explain death in simple terms and do not sermonize.* Sometimes parents get so involved in the subject that they drone on and on. Instead, ask the child to show his understanding by telling you in his own words what you just explained to him.

6. *Remember the developmental progression.* Many parents expect a child to grieve the same way they do, but because young children do not understand death the way adults do, this is impossible.

7. *Talk about fear.* Children are both very curious about death and fearful of it. Children may need to express their feelings and talk about experiences with the deceased.

8. *Prepare the child for funerals.* How early should children be allowed to attend funerals? We cannot simply posit an age. Some children are more mature than others. Hardt (1979) suggests that children age seven and above may go, but should never be forced to. Other people may argue for different ages. The child should always be told what will happen at the funeral.

Adolescents, Young Adults, and Death

Adolescents are likely to experience the death of distant elderly relatives like great-aunts and grandparents, again reinforcing the relationship between aging and death. However, adolescents will also probably come in contact with sudden death, most commonly death from motor vehicle accidents, suicide, and homicide. The unfairness of death—its randomness—is what may impress them. Adolescents do romanticize death somewhat. In one study, high school students were given a group of metaphors that describe death and asked to rank-order the metaphors in terms of how appropriate they were for describing death. Overall, high school students saw death as the "last adventure," "the end of a song," and a "misty abyss." Males were a bit less romantic than females (Farley, 1979).

True or False Adolescents tend to romanticize death.

The extent to which young adults think about or express anxiety about their own death is a matter of controversy at the present time. In one *Psychology Today*

study, most readers claimed to be unafraid, while a little more than one-third felt either fearful, discouraged, or depressed at the thought of death. Most did think occasionally about their own death, but about one-fourth said they never or rarely thought about it; only one-fifth thought about it frequently.

Middle Age and Death

Most theorists of adulthood see middle age as the first time many people are forced to come to grips with death. Younger people see death in terms of a specific occurrence, such as an accident or something that happens to much older people. The middle-aged person does not have that luxury. Experiences with the death of one's parents, or the heart attack that takes the life of a friend, force thoughts concerning one's own mortality into consciousness. Although death may not be coming tomorrow, time is running out. The physical decline that takes place becomes noticeable, and personal confrontations with death are inevitable (Cytrynbaum et al., 1980). It is not difficult to understand why an increase in belief about the afterlife and heaven occurs, especially after age fifty-five (Spilka et al., 1985).

How the Elderly View Death

The elderly are more likely to think about death and more likely to talk about it, but less likely to show a fear of death (Wass and Myers, 1982; Marshall, 1980). It is not difficult to encourage the elderly to talk about death, and they often talk to one another about it. Generally, the elderly show less fear of death than younger groups (Kalish and Reynolds, 1976). Perhaps older people recognize the limits of life, and those who are beset by health problems and economic problems see their more active roles as behind them. When older people were asked whether they wanted to live to be one hundred, many answered no and none said yes without qualifying the answer (Marshall, 1980). Older people anticipated a life span of sixty-five to seventy-five years, and many seemed to have outlived their own expectations. Finally, people are socialized to understand that death and aging are related. By the time people reach old age, they have suffered through the deaths of many other people (Kalish, 1976). They have been forced by circumstances to admit their own mortality.

True or False As a group, older people fear death less than middle-aged people or young adults.

Although the elderly show less death anxiety, this does not mean they welcome death or do not fear it at all. Many fear the loss of control, the unknown, and losing those who are close to them and still alive. The relationship between age and fear of death is not a simple matter. When McCrae and colleagues (1976) interviewed about 1,000 people ranging in age from twenty-five through ninety, they found that some people in each age-group showed high, moderate, or low fear of death. In addition, in one study of the young-old (ages sixty-five to seventy-five) and the old-old (age seventy-five and beyond), the latter group had a greater fear of death than the former group (Mullins and Lopez, 1982). Perhaps an increase in death anxiety occurs when death is very close at hand. The aged are a heterogeneous group. Elderly people who are in poor physical and emotional health, elderly people in institutions, and those who have unrealized dreams or who have not been satisfied with their lives report a greater fear of death (Ross et al., 1975). So, although as a group the aged fear death less, to say that the elderly do not fear death is patently false.

The Life Review

The finding that people's evaluation of their past affects their attitude toward death fits well with Erikson's concept of integrity, as well as with some of the changes in attitude and outlook discussed in Chapter 20. The increase in interiority and evaluation of one's past life, called **life review** (Butler, 1975; 1974) is part of the process of accepting death.

The elderly frequently talk about and dwell on the past. They are deeply involved with their past opportunities, relationships, and mistakes. Too often these reminiscences have been undervalued or even regarded as symptoms of senility. But such a life review fills a need because it permits the elderly to make their peace with life and to accept death. During these reviews, the elderly put their life decisions in perspective and work out conflicts and mistakes. The preoccupation may be mild and show itself as nostalgia or regret, or in its most severe form it may show itself in terms of anxiety and depression (Botwinick, 1984; Diekelmann, 1977).

Such reviews may take place anytime in life. In some African tribes, young adults make their own funeral arrangements, including some statement of their accomplishments and social value (Fry, 1985). They are en-

life review The process, usually found in older people, of reviewing and evaluating one's past.

couraged to do this at other times in their lives as well. In the United States, such a life review often occurs during late middle age, as men begin to think about retirement and as women evaluate their lives after the children leave home. However, the nature of the review in old age is more global. The reminiscences that make up the life review represent living history, and it is unfortunate that we have not taken more of an interest in them. Such reflections can serve as a valuable source of family history. Some families have taped stories about life years ago and preserved them for generations to come. The life review is a natural and functional attempt to place one's life in order and work through conflicts. Its value to the older person and to the family itself is now just beginning to be appreciated.

True or False The tendency of older people to dwell on the past is a definite sign of organic deterioration.

On Dying

Imagine you have just been told that Uncle Edward has advanced lung cancer and only three months to live. Uncle Edward has just been told of his impending death. You go to visit him. You walk into his room. What would you expect? What would you say? Until recently, there has been little research on how people come to deal with the knowledge of their own impending death. In this area, the great pioneering studies were performed by Elisabeth Kübler-Ross.

From Denial to Acceptance

After interviewing more than 200 dying patients, Elisabeth Kübler-Ross (1972, 1969) suggested that people come to accept their own death by going through five specific stages.

Stage one: Denial. "No, not me. It can't be true." The first reaction to being told one is dying is denial. Some use denial for a long time, but less than 1 percent continue to deny the truth until death. For others, a type of isolation takes place in which people talk about their own death in a very objective manner, as if it was happening to someone else. This is the time families come to visit but do not know what to say. They are uncomfortable and become distant. They may avoid the subject or simply engage in hours of small talk.

Stage two: Anger. "Why me?" Denial often gives way to anger. "Why am I dying while others live without pain?" One patient expressed his feelings this way. "An old man whom I have known ever since I was a little kid came down the street. He was eighty-two years old, and he is of no earthly use as far as we mortals can tell. He's rheumatic, he's a cripple, he's dirty, just not the type of a person you would like to be. And the thought hit me strongly, now why couldn't it have been old George instead of me?" (Kübler-Ross, 1969, p. 52). This is a very difficult stage for the dying patient, the family, and health-care professionals who must deal with the patients who displace their anger onto everyone and everything. Such patients may criticize the nurses for coming into the room and shaking the pillow when they wanted to nap, or criticize them for not doing so, or the family is always too early or too late. Such anger is understandable, for family members and nurses can come and go as they want, while the patient is left with pain and a death sentence. Patients need to express this anger (Kübler-Ross, 1972).

Stage three: Bargaining. "Yes me, but, please let me live long enough to attend my son's wedding." After the anger has abated, the dying patient may begin to bargain with God or the doctors. Some of the bargains with God are kept secret. Most are meant to postpone the inevitable, but Kübler-Ross found that few are kept. One patient in extreme pain who was taught self-hypnosis to allow her to attend her son's wedding for a few hours returned from the wedding and told Kübler-Ross, "Now don't forget I have another son." Kübler-Ross suggests that the clergy may play a significant role here, for some bargaining with God may reflect guilt, as when a person would like to live long enough to make amends for a past misdeed. The dying patient may need to work these feelings through.

Stage four: Depression. "Yes, me." Depression is the most common response to dying (Hinton, 1972). Patients at this stage may be grieving for loss of independence, loss of a part of what was once a functioning body, loss of relationships with others, or loss of the ability to do things for themselves. On the other hand, the depression may be one way of withdrawing into themselves to prepare for the loss of everything they have loved.

Stage five: Acceptance. In this last stage, the patient has accepted his or her fate. Feelings of envy for the healthy living and feelings of anger have been expressed. Losses have been mourned. Acceptance is not a happy stage. By this time the patient may be very weak and have little emotion left. One patient described it as "the final rest before the long journey." The patient has now found peace and acceptance, and interest in the outside world is reduced. He or she is not talkative and prefers short visits. The television is no longer left on. Being able to sit in silence with another person is greatly appreciated.

True or False When dying patients finally accept their fate, their communication with others increases and they become more lively and animated.

Evaluations of Stage Theory

Although Elisabeth Kübler-Ross' description of the process of dying has been enthusiastically accepted by the public and many professionals, there is little evidence that this sequence is either universal or invariable (Schulz and Aderman, 1974). Patients can and do switch back and forth—for example, from bargaining to denial and back again. Many do not go through these stages in any particular order, and others never enter some of them (Shneidman, 1973). Other studies show that contrary to Kübler-Ross' findings many dying people use denial until the last moment (Hinton, 1976). In addition, although acceptance is a frequent response, so are apathy and apprehension (Weisman and Kastenbaum, 1968). Stage theories usually describe development in terms of invariable, sequential steps with no regression to previous stages. This is clearly not the case here.

Other criticisms have focused on the methodology of Kübler-Ross or argued that other factors, such as the nature of the illness, may affect the patient's emotional response to it. Kübler-Ross' theory gives little attention to the particular illness, mode of treatment, ethnicity, or lifestyle. Still others point to the danger in wholesale acceptance of this progression. The dying patient may be pressured to leave one stage and graduate to the next, and acceptance may be demanded before the patient is ready (Kastenbaum, 1978). Kübler-Ross did recognize that individual differences occurred, but this caution was lost in the excitement of finally having some guidelines that were useful in understanding the dying patient. Despite the many criticisms of her work, no one doubts the exceptional contribution Kübler-Ross has made to the field or the need for people to understand the emotional experience of the dying patient.

Phases of Dying

Another way to look at the process of dying is to deny that any optimal progression of stages exists and to divide the process into three phases. In the first or *acute phase*, the patient is told about the impending death. A personal crisis ensues, and he or she experiences a great deal of anxiety and anger. Bargaining may occur here. When the person adjusts to being terminally ill, the second phase, or *chronic living-dying phase*, begins. Here fear of the unknown, loneliness, anticipatory grief, and depression are common. Anxiety and sorrow can coexist with hope and acceptance. In the last, or *terminal phase*, withdrawal from the outside world is common, and the patient may experience many different emotions (Pattison, 1977).

These phases of dying are affected by what are called *dying trajectories*, which describe the time and form of the dying process (Glaser and Strauss, 1968). Four basic trajectories have been outlined. Two deal with expected death and two deal with unexpected death.

Trajectory one: Certain death with an anticipated time limit. In this trajectory, certain death is anticipated and the person is told the approximate time he or she can expect to live—for example, three months.

Trajectory two: Certain death without a definite time limit. In this trajectory, the individual is told that he or she has a terminal disease but that the amount of time remaining is unknown. It can be months or years.

Trajectory three: Uncertain death, but the question will be resolved at a future time. Sometimes the patient does not know whether the illness is terminal but will know within a stated period of time. For example, exploratory surgery may be performed in a few days, and

then after receiving the pathologist's report the question of survivability can be assessed.

Trajectory four: Uncertain death at an uncertain time. In this trajectory, it is uncertain whether the patient will die, and there is no time that we will know definitely one way or another. Certain chronic diseases, such as serious heart disease, are typical of this pattern.

Both during the acute phase and when death is uncertain, as in trajectories three and four, anxiety is heightened. The uncertainty may cause behavioral changes, especially on trajectory four.

Two important points about this phase model stand out. First, we need not view the process in terms of an invariably sequential stage-like theory, where certain emotions are found at particular times. In the phase approach, emotions are variable, even at the very end. Second, the course of the disease and its trajectory may affect the person's reaction to it. The dying process probably cannot be described in universal terms, since the person's philosophy, the amount of pain and discomfort he or she is experiencing, the nature of the disease itself, how the patient copes with crises, religious orientation, family support, and many other variables enter the picture. For instance, the greater the level of discomfort or pain, the less able people are to make a successful emotional adjustment in the last stages of life. Having been close with a person who accepted death calmly is a positive factor relating to adjustment, while witnessing a person being angry until the end is negatively related to adjustment (Carey, 1975). The phase approach allows us to incorporate these variables into our analysis of the dying process. Perhaps the dying process is too complicated to describe in simple, straightforward terms.

Dealing with Dying People

When you walk into Uncle Edward's room and say, "Hello, Uncle Edward," he turns to you and says, "I think I'm going to die soon. I wish I could just end it all." What would you say?

When 200 attendants and nurses were asked to respond to this situation, more than 80 percent avoided the statement by telling the patient that he doesn't really mean that, by changing the subject, or by telling him that we are all going to die sometime. Some told the dying patient he was doing well now and not to worry. Others asked the patient what made him feel that way and suggested that he talk about it (Kastenbaum and Aisenberg, 1976).

Most people, even trained health professionals, are uncomfortable around dying people. Kübler-Ross (1974) found that nurses in a California hospital took much longer to respond to the call buzzer of dying patients than to buzzers of those who were not dying. This was not an indictment of the nurses, but rather an understanding of their inability to deal with the patient's anger and special needs. The dying patient requires open and honest communication. At times, the mere presence of someone who cares is important (Albert and Steffl, 1984). The dying patient deserves to be treated as a responsible human being with choices and alternatives, even though they may be limited. The patient should continue to participate in treatment decisions, as well as in everyday choices such as what to eat or wear.

Family members must understand that the dying person is working through conflicts and complex emotions and may feel the need to talk about the meaning of life and death. Some people believe that such talk will depress the terminally ill, but if it is initiated by them this is not true. In addition, one should never deemphasize the importance of hope and optimism. Hope is a part of the dying process. The person may hope for a miracle cure or remission, a painless day or painless death, that he will not be alone at the end, or a number of other things. Hope does not mean the patient is denying the seriousness of the condition. Finally, studies show that many elderly dying patients fear the ravages of prolonged illness, dependency, and pain more than death itself (Saxon and Etten, 1978). They are often afraid of being a burden to others or of leaving loved family members who will not be given adequate care. In one study, half of all terminally ill patients were very concerned about how those they will be leaving will be able to care for themselves (Carey, 1975). It is important to deal with these practical issues because this allows the patient time to deal with his own, inner feelings about death.

Appropriate Death

Medical care has advanced to the point that the final drama of life takes longer and longer to be played out. Life can now be prolonged through the use of technology, and new medicines hold out hope for extending life for an additional period of time. Today, many people who would not have survived just twenty years ago are alive.

appropriate death   A death that fulfills the needs and expectations of the patient and gives the individual some control over his or her destiny.

This tendency to prolong life is seen as a blessing by some, but others have pointed out that the patient often lives with extreme pain and that the burdens on the dying person and his or her family are tremendous. At this point a role reversal may occur, and children may have to provide the care necessary for the dying patient's daily existence. Bitterness may mix with pain, creating stress in relationships with loved ones. Some have focused on what Weisman (1972) called an **appropriate death,** which is a death that fulfills the needs and expectations of the individual, showing adequate concern for the needs and desires of the patient and giving the patient some control over his or her destiny. In this regard, we will look at two issues typifying this approach—the right to choose the place of death and issues relating to euthanasia.

The Place of Death

Although two-thirds of all dying people want to die at home, only 20 percent, one in five, will do so (Ryder and Ross, 1977). For the vast majority of elderly people, death will come in a hospital or nursing home. It is estimated that an average of two people die each month in a nursing home (Ingram and Barry, 1977). This mortality figure contributes to the depressing atmosphere of some nursing homes, as well as to the difficulty nursing homes have keeping adequate staff. If some elderly see nursing homes merely as places where they stay while waiting to die, their view is reinforced by these mortality figures. Although only 5 percent of the elderly are presently in nursing homes, about 25 percent of all elderly deaths occur in such homes (Kastenbaum, 1978).

But perhaps we should not look at death in the patient's own home as the ideal for everyone. There may be no one living at home who can take care of the patient. Living with children during these times is difficult, for the symptoms and suffering of the terminally ill can be severe. Yet the hospital does not seem especially capable of caring for terminally ill people either.

True or False   Most elderly people want to die at home.

Dying in a hospital.   Hospitals are not prepared to serve the needs of the dying, which include the need to feel valued, to talk and be listened to with understanding, to preserve personal identity, to maintain self-respect, to come to terms with the inevitability of death, to give love and be loved, and to be free from pain (Ebersole and Hess, 1981). The average general hospital does not, and perhaps cannot, meet these needs. For example, visiting rules make no sense for the dying patient, who may want to see family at different times. The terminally ill person may need to have a loved one nearby to hold hands or cry with at a time other than visiting hours. The family may find visiting hours inconvenient too. The patient may need more time and understanding than busy doctors and nurses can provide.

Hospitals are also poor when it comes to reducing or eliminating pain for the terminally ill patient. The basic rule of many hospitals is to wait until the patient complains or needs a painkiller, not to prevent the onset of pain. The basic worry is that the patient will become habituated to the painkiller, but such a worry is not reasonable when working with the terminally ill. Furthermore, the hospital philosophy is strongly weighted toward getting better, and this is as it should be. But the disease is treated, rather than the person. All medical procedures are directed toward the ultimate aim of defeating the disease. Such an orientation is incorrect for the terminally ill patient who requires services directed at him or her as a person and to the family, instead of the disease (Cassell, 1974). Finally, death in medicine is often seen as a failure of medical technology. Extensive and heroic efforts are used to keep patients alive using all types of medical machinery, but this may not be the desire of the patient or the family. The conclusion that many general hospitals cannot offer the dying the services they need is inescapable.

The hospice movement.   The **hospice** is a home specifically designed for the care of the terminally ill (Holden, 1976). Hospices do not offer high-tech medical services or advanced medication for the treatment of such diseases as cancer. Rather, the hospice offers a concern for the patient and his or her family, and expansive pain control. Death is not considered failure, and the nursing staff and volunteers who work there are sensitive to the

hospice   A center specifically designed for short-term care of the terminally ill. Hospices offer pain control and an atmosphere of understanding and concern, but no high-tech medical services.

needs of the patients and their families. Time is willingly spent with these people, the atmosphere is brighter, the staff is not running around as much, and families may visit at any time. Birthday celebrations are not uncommon, but death is expected. Hospices are not extended-care facilities, but rather short-term facilities catering to the special needs of the terminally ill.

True or False   A hospice is a place where dying people get the most advanced experimental treatments for their diseases.

The model for most hospices today is St. Christopher's in London, England. In this fifty-four-bed inpatient facility, relief of symptoms and pain is combined with an emphasis on meeting the emotional needs of patients and their families. Rather than waiting for a patient to request a painkiller, doses of special painkillers, which often contain heroin or cocaine, are used to prevent the onset of pain. Sometimes the patients are given steroids to improve their appetite, increase their sense of well-being, and reduce inflammation (Ryder and Ross, 1977). The staff is encouraged to form relationships with the patients, and the clergy play a significant role in helping patients come to grips with their fate. Between 8 percent and 10 percent of the patients go into remission (Saunders, 1977), but the focus is on living the last weeks of life as fully as possible, not on lengthening life through artificial means. Studies show that, compared with terminal patients in a general hospital, hospice patients are more likely to view the institution as comfortable and less likely to view the staff as busy (Saunders, 1977). Children are around, and there is a nursery for them as well (Holden, 1976). The first hospice in the United States was opened in New Haven, Connecticut, in 1974, and today many have been established in communities throughout the United States. Although some hospices are institutions like St. Christopher's, many are not. The hospice movement is also a philosophy. Some hospices provide home-care service for dying patients and their families, others function as houses where the terminally ill and their loved ones can go for counseling (Barrow, 1986).

Hospices provide an alternative to death in the hospital, but they do not solve the problem of long-term care for the terminally ill who cannot live at home. They remain an option, though, for those who want to live their lives out without machines or experimental drugs in an atmosphere of acceptance and caring.

Is There a Right to Die?

Should an elderly woman with failing mental powers have the right to refuse an operation for cancer that might cure her?

Should a hospital allow a severely burned patient to leave, even though he would probably die from infection within forty-eight hours?

Should a hospital refuse to disconnect life-support systems from a drug-overdose victim who suffers from ir-

The hospice is a short term facility where the terminally ill live out their final time in a brighter atmosphere, where pain is controlled but no high-tech medical services are offered.

> **euthanasia** A general term defining an act of putting a person to death painlessly. Euthanasia may involve passive acts, such as not giving exceptional treatment, or may be active, as when a terminally ill person in great pain is given something that causes death.

reversible and extensive brain damage, when taking her off the respirator would mean immediate death?

These are just a few of the dilemmas institutions and families face in the area of euthanasia. **Euthanasia** is defined by the dictionary as the act of putting a person to death painlessly. This may involve acts of commission or omission. For instance, a doctor may not make the maximum effort to revive a patient who is terminal and comatose—an act of omission. An act of commission would involve taking someone on a respirator off, even though it will probably speed the person's death. Because the gap between commission and omission is tenuous at best, euthanasia has been conceptualized in terms of four categories (Koza, 1977).

Voluntary and direct euthanasia. The death is voluntary and carried out by the patient. Suicide falls into this category, as would refusal to take medication.

Voluntary but indirect euthanasia. The patient gives to the doctor, family, or any other person the right to end medical treatment or life-prolonging medical treatment if he or she becomes comatose or dysfunctional. Many people have signed "living wills," documents in which they state that they do not want certain heroic attempts to save them if they should suffer from such conditions as irreversible brain damage. The legal status of such wills varies from state to state.

Involuntary and direct euthanasia. This is an active form of euthanasia in which something is done to hasten death such as giving a person a lethal injection to end life. It is involuntary because the person is not able to give consent and is close to what most people mean by mercy killing.

Involuntary and indirect euthanasia. In this case, treatment is stopped and the patient is allowed to die a natural death. In some circumstances, a doctor may not do everything possible to save a terminally ill person. This is sometimes called passive euthanasia.

The practice of euthanasia raises serious ethical questions. For example, under what circumstances can we allow others to make conscious decisions to end their lives? Consider the case of a severely burned person whose chances for survival are slim. Some physicians will tell the victim, "We cannot predict the future. We can only say that, to our knowledge, no one in the past of your age and with your size burn has ever survived this injury either with or without maximum treatment." The burn victim, who at this early point may not be in great pain, is then allowed to make his or her own decision. If the patient wants to receive maximum care, everything possible is done. If not, the patient is allowed visitors while only ordinary medical care is given. In this case, the individual makes the decision. But what if the patient is in extreme pain or not mentally healthy? Should such a person be allowed to choose?

Proponents of euthanasia note that medical science has developed to the point where people can be kept alive artificially to suffer lingering deaths, but that such medical treatment is not effective if its aim is to cure. Euthanasia is a compassionate answer for some, recognizing the importance of suffering and the right of the individual to make a choice based on the best information we can provide. It is part of the patient's right to make such decisions. These advocates argue that doctors should not be obligated to continue heroic medical measures to keep someone alive. Of course, these arguments are much easier to make if the dying patient is conscious, rational, and capable of making his or her own decision. When this is not the case and other people must decide, the moral and ethical problems multiply. For example, how do we know that a family is acting in the dying patient's best interests?

Opponents of euthanasia note that medicine is not an exact science and that people who have been diagnosed as hopeless have gone into remission. In addition, most advocates of euthanasia differentiate between heroic extraordinary measures and normal regular care. However, what was heroic years ago might be considered normal today. They also argue that last-minute medical developments might save some patients, although the odds are against this. Opponents fear that any reduction in the prohibition against taking life or not doing everything possible to prolong life may lead to serious social collapse. For example, what would stop people from terminating the life of deformed people or people who are senile? What would stop someone from shortening the life of a terminally ill person because one or more functioning organs is needed for a transplant? Finally, most dying patients are depressed and in pain. Under those conditions, can we really consider any decision truly voluntary? Some people simply take the view that the distinction between omission and commission makes all the difference. Physicians cannot actively engage in behavior that kills, but failure to use extraordinary measures permitting death is acceptable because this does not interfere with the *natural* process of dying (Kieffer, 1977). The problem here is that the distinction between omission and commission is not always so simple and that under our legal system a person may be prosecuted for not doing something that could have been done.

How does the public feel about euthanasia? Many health professionals agree with the practice of passive euthanasia (see Table 21.1). Some studies have found greater acceptance of euthanasia today than ever before in our history. When samples of the population in 1950, 1973, and 1977 were asked "When a person has a disease that cannot be cured, do you think doctors should be allowed by law to end the patient's life by some painless means if the patient and his family request it?" 36 percent agreed in 1950, some 53 percent agreed in 1973, and 63 percent agreed in 1977 (Ward, 1984; 1980). The clergy also favor the practice. In one study, 96 percent of the clergy favored passive euthanasia (cases in which pain is severe, quality of life is low, death is imminent, and the question is whether heroic measures should be withheld), while 21 percent agreed with it in active form (actively terminating life when the case is hopeless, pain is great, and the quality of life is poor) (Carey and Posavac, 1978). Support for passive euthanasia is always greater than that for active euthanasia. However, one important segment of the population opposes euthanasia strongly. The aged themselves are strongly opposed to even the practice of passive euthanasia (Kieffer, 1977). Agreement with euthanasia declines with advancing age.

True or False As a group, the elderly are less likely than younger people to favor euthanasia.

There are no simple answers to the questions surrounding euthanasia. Catchy phrases such as "death with dignity," "the right to die," and "heroic efforts" do not solve problems because they are so difficult to define. Perhaps what we need are accepted guidelines for deciding cases. However, such guidelines will always be controversial, and though they may be of some help, each case will eventually have to be decided on its own merits.

Bereavement, Grief, and Mourning

Thus far our focus has been on the dying person, but those who survive have suffered a loss and must cope with it. The death of a spouse, a parent, a sibling, a friend, and a child can leave a void, a feeling of emptiness in our lives. The task of recovery is difficult and fraught with mental and sometimes physical pain. The terms bereavement, grief, and mourning are often used incorrectly. **Bereavement** involves the status of having lost someone. **Grief** is the state of distress that occurs after the death. **Mourning** includes the cultural behaviors that follow such a loss (Kastenbaum and Costa, 1977).

How do people deal with the knowledge that someone they love has just died? The most important work in this area was performed by Erich Lindemann (1944), who observed and interviewed 101 people, some of whom were related to members of the armed forces who had been killed in action or whose relatives were victims of the Coconut Grove Fire in Boston, in which many people were killed. Lindemann found that the reaction to the losses followed a common progression. At first, somatic distress occurred in waves, lasting from twenty minutes to an hour and including a tightness in the throat, choking or shortness of breath, need for sighing, an empty feeling in the abdomen, muscular weakness,

bereavement The status of having lost someone.

grief The state of distress occurring after death.

mourning The cultural and societal behaviors that follow someone's death.

and tension and mental anguish. Just the mention of the deceased's name can bring on these symptoms. The grieving relative is preoccupied with the deceased relative and shows some desire for emotional distance from others. Sometimes feelings of guilt were present, as those who survive blame themselves for supposed negligence and exaggerated minor injustices to the deceased. For example, after her husband was killed in a fire, one young woman felt guilty because they had quarreled the day before. Some grieving people show hostility to others. Some are restless, cannot attend to anything, and appear aimless and disorganized. The most common symptoms following the death, then, are somatic distress, preoccupation with the deceased, guilt and hostility, and disorganized, restless patterns of conduct.

These reactions lessen with time. A number of models have been advanced to understand the process of grief. Although the phases used to describe them differ some-

T A B L E   21.1

How People Feel About Euthanasia

No. in Group*	Strongly Agree (%)	Agree (%)	Undecided (%)	Disagree (%)	Strongly Disagree (%)
Question 1: Regardless of his or her age, disabilities, and personal preference, a person should be kept alive as long as possible.					
75 College students	8	19	19	37	17
108 First-year nursing students	4	13	30	41	12
75 Registered nurses	4	11	23	34	28
110 First-year medical students	2	6	21	36	35
30 Physicians	10	7	10	33	40
Question 2: Some patients should be allowed to die without making heroic efforts to prolong their lives.					
75 College students	20	41	16	13	9
108 First-year nursing students	19	47	19	11	5
75 Registered nurses	50	44	5	1	0
110 First-year medical students	27	50	19	3	1
30 Physicians	40	53	0	7	0

*Nonmedical personnel answering this question were asked to respond as they might *if* they were a doctor or a nurse.

Source: Winget et al., 1977.

The immediate physical and psychological reactions following a death in the family include tightness in the throat, weakness, and mental anguish.

anticipatory grief   The grieving that occurs prior to the expected death of a loved one.

what, the progression is uniform. The model proposed by Schulz (1978) typifies many of them.

Phase One (death to funeral). Shock or numbness, difficulty accepting the death.

Phase Two (shortly after the funeral). Episodes of pangs of grief and yearning. Symptoms of somatic distress, preoccupation with the deceased, guilt and hostility, disorganized and restless conduct, periods of silence and intense misery.

Phase Three (after family members have gone). Depression, apathy, loss of energy; life seems to have lost its meaning; pangs of grief less frequent and less intense as time passes, but they still occur; memories of the deceased are still painful.

Phase Four (resolution stage). Loss is accepted and a new life is built.

True or False   The initial reactions to the death of a close relative differ so greatly among people that no accepted description of them exists.

Most models posit an initial phase of shock and denial, followed by a stage of awareness in which the emotional and behavioral reactions defined by Lindemann occur. Then comes a prolonged intermediate phase, in which the individual resumes daily activities, slowly reduces obsession with the deceased, but still experiences feelings

of sadness. Then a recovery phase occurs, when there is a more positive attitude toward life and some pride in recovering from the loss (Parkes, 1972).

What determines the length and intensity of the grieving process? Bugen (1977) suggests that two principal factors are the centrality of one's relationship with the deceased and the extent to which the grieving person believes the death was preventable. Certainly we grieve more for a parent than for a great-uncle whom we rarely saw. We also grieve more when we think the death could have been prevented. For example, the parents of a young girl killed in a tragic automobile accident by a drunk driver had been a few minutes late getting out of the house that day. Her mother believed that if she had been on time the accident would never have happened. It is the person's belief about preventability that matters, not the facts themselves. Table 21.2 shows how the two factors of centrality and preventability interact to affect the grief process. The effectiveness with which the person is able to work through the complex emotions that accompany the death of a loved one is another factor that affects the duration and intensity of grieving (Burnside, 1981). The suddenness of the death is still another factor. If the family knew that the end was coming, they can prepare for it. **Anticipatory grief** involves doing some of the grief work before the death of the loved one (Schoenberg et al., 1974). The person anticipating the death of a relative has time to adjust to it and to visit the dying person and share some last moments with him or her. The family can also make their peace with the dying individual and know they are forgiven for past indiscretions. Recovery from grief is more rapid when the death is anticipated, and less successful when the death is sudden or unexpected (Wass and Myers, 1982; Kalish, 1981).

True or False   Recovery from the grief following the death of a loved one is more rapid if the death was expected.

The process of grieving is a trying one. A casual look at the symptoms most frequently reported by 109 widows during their first month after bereavement (see Figure 21.1) is sufficient to show why the grieving process often weakens the person who has just suffered a loss. The incidence

T A B L E 21.2

The Interaction of Preventability and the Centrality of the Relationship to the Experience of Grief

	Death Perceived as Preventable	**Death Perceived as Unpreventable**
Central relationship	Intense and prolonged	Intense and brief
Peripheral relationship	Mild and prolonged	Mild and brief

Source: Bugen, 1977.

of physical and mental disorders, as well as death itself, increases for those most affected by the loss (LaRue et al., 1985; Marshall, 1980). For these reasons, then, working through one's grief is important.

The grieving process is affected by the age of the person who has died. For example, parents who lose infants or young children often grieve not only for the infant or child but also for the person that child might have been (Callahan et al., 1983). These parents often experience considerable rage (Kübler-Ross and Goleman, 1976). Grieving for the elderly is a bit different. People tend to grieve for the person that was, and there is a great deal of nostalgia. People may take comfort in the belief that the person had lived a full life (Epstein et al., 1975).

Other important factors in the grieving and mourning process are one's culture and religious beliefs. Funerals and formal mourning rituals often help survivors accept the death of the loved one and show their grief in an acceptable manner. Customs and traditions differ (see The Cross-Cultural Current on page 550).

Some people require bereavement counseling—professional help in order to recover from their loss. The clergy may be helpful in this regard (Kastenbaum and Aisenberg, 1976). However, grieving people often suffer from a lack of energy and depression that inhibits them from seeking out this aid. Other people and responsible groups may have to reach out to the bereaved.

Death Education

Some refer to the new interest in death and dying as the "gloom boom" (*U.S. News & World Report*, 1983), but the popularity of books and educational programs on death and dying does not reflect a morbid fascination with death. It mirrors both society's new understanding of the role death, dying, and bereavement play in the life cycle and the many modern bioethical questions that have come up. The complex issues surrounding death and dying are the concern not only of health professionals but also of the public. Although courses in death and dying have a number of specific goals, one that is very important is what Bugen (1979) calls "humanization of dying." This involves helping students confront their own fears and concerns about death and dying, identification and creation of community resources for the terminally ill and their families, and the realization that patients' families and staff all have legitimate needs and responsibilities in the general area of death and dying. On a more personal basis, death education can help make the final phase of life more predictable and controllable, finally allowing people to express their emotions and to deal with death and dying (Schulz, 1978).

People of all ages need death education. The child asking questions about death or who has just suffered the loss of a beloved pet needs to confront his or her own fears and emotions and have questions answered honestly. The middle-aged person may experience elevated fears of dying and may have to work through feelings concerning losing parents and coping with aging. The elderly, who would seem to be the group most concerned, have been almost completely neglected as far as death education goes.

Personal Choices

This book emphasizes the concept of personal choice. As we mature, the number of choices we make increase, and the nature of these choices changes. Although we cannot control everything in our lives, we do have some control over the paths our lives take and the way we cope with life's challenges. Although death is inevitable,

Culture and Death

"When the time came to die, the Maya did not fight it. Old ones might at any time announce that their time had come and retreat to their mat or hammock, where they would lie quietly, awaiting death" (Steele, 1977, p. 1063). The dying person was required to perform duties and rituals to fend off evil spirits prior to death. After he died, the family must be concerned with outward appearances. The burial must meet the expectations of both the community and the entire family exactly. The person's former status in the community determined how elaborate the funeral should be. Elaborate rituals served the purpose of providing a separation for the spirit from the earth and speeding it on its journey to the next world, where the spirit could not endanger the living. Only the correct behavior and chants, and scrupulous attention to ritualistic detail, could help the soul or spirit through successive stages to its destination. The mourning period was measured in days and involved the public showing of intense feelings of loss and overt displays of despair. Death among the Mayan Indians involved elaborate rituals and responsibilities.

A very different type of ritual surrounding death is found among the Amish of Pennsylvania (Bryer, 1979). The funeral is not for the dead but for the living. The bereaved family appoints only two or three families to take full charge of all burial arrangements and draws up a list of those to be invited. Everything else is the responsibility of the community and neighbors. When the body is embalmed and returned home, family members dress the body in white garments. This is a labor of love—the last one to be performed. The body is then rested in a plain wooden coffin and placed in a room for friends and relatives to view. The funeral service is held in the barn in summer and in the house in winter and is conducted in German. The same service is used for every funeral. The coffin is again viewed at the cemetery entrance, and guests gather next to a grave dug by neighbors. A short service is held, and the family and neighbors return home for a meal. Communal ties are emphasized, as is the belief that those who are loyal to their way of life will go to their eternal reward.

Death rituals vary greatly from culture to culture. Each society's mourning rituals serve to channel and legitimate the normal expression of grief, defining the appropriate time frame for showing grief, and providing support for the bereaved family. When people talk about an American way of death, they often forget the many subcultures and religious groups that comprise our own unique society. Christians and Jews differ substantially in their mourning and burial customs. So do people from different ethnic groups. In a study by Kalish and Reynolds (1976) some 434 persons in Los Angeles were asked a number of questions regarding the length of time following the death of a spouse before it would be appropriate for a person to remarry, stop wearing black, return to work, and go out with other people. Black Americans, Anglo-Americans, Mexican-Americans, and Japanese-Americans were questioned, and these groups differed substantially in their opinions (see Table A).

Two points are clear. First, each culture handles death and dying in its own way. Second, it is important to take the individual's cultural background into account if we are to understand that person's attitudes and behaviors with regard to death and dying.

Source: Bryer, K. B. The Amish Way of Death. *American Psychologist,* 1979, 34, 255–261. Kalish, R., and Reynolds, D. *Death and Ethnicity: A Psychocultural Study.* Los Angeles: University of Southern California Press, 1976. Steele, R. L. Dying, Death, and Bereavement Among the Maya Indians of Mesoamerica. *American Psychologist,* 1977, 32, 1060–1068.

TABLE A

Black Americans, "Anglo" Americans, Mexican Americans, and Japanese Americans Answer Questions About Death and Dying

People from different ethnic groups answer questions about death and dying differently.

	Black Americans	Japanese Americans	Mexican Americans	"Anglo" Americans
Sudden death or slow death, which seems more tragic?				
Sudden	39%	43%	41%	20%
Slow	58%	50%	50%	68%
Equal	3%	7%	9%	12%
How long should a person wait before remarriage?				
Unimportant to wait	34%	14%	22%	26%
1 week–6 months	15%	3%	1%	23%
1 year	25%	30%	38%	34%
2 years +	11%	26%	20%	11%
Other	16%	28%	19%	7%
Do you believe you will live on in some form after death?				
Yes	59%	47%	40%	66%
If yes, in what form will you live on after death?				
Through children/works/ memory	20%	33%	27%	30%
Return to earth in spirit form	9%	43%	7%	7%
In heaven, paradise	70%	24%	67%	63%
At what age do you expect to die?				
Mean age	79.0	74.3	71.9	73.9
Now, if you could choose, to what age would you choose to live?				
Mean age	88.6	80.1	75.8	79.7
Where would you like to die?				
At home	44%	72%	54%	61%
In hospital	21%	16%	34%	14%
Others	35%	12%	11%	25%

Source: Kalish and Reynolds, 1976.

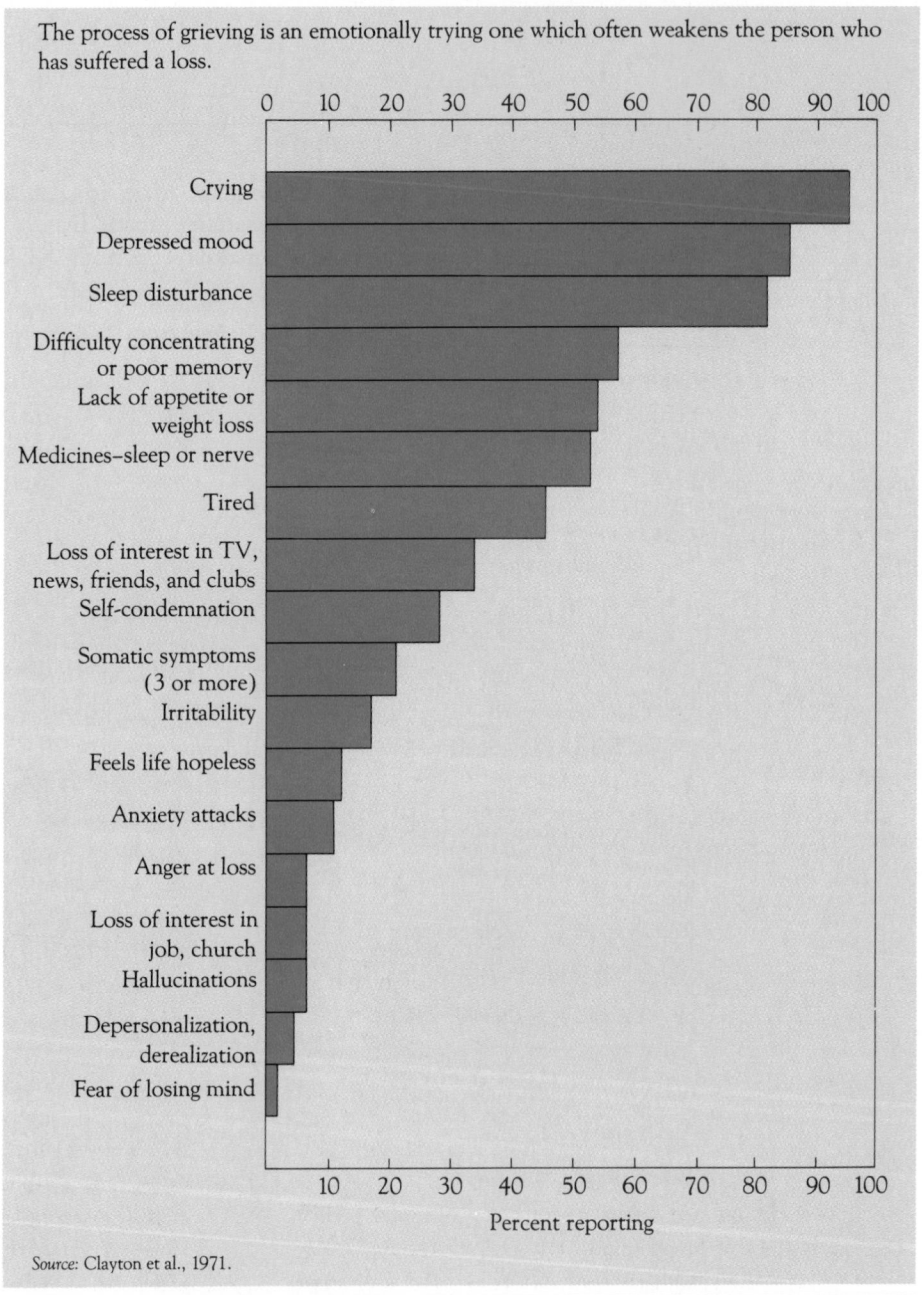

FIGURE 21.1

Symptoms of Bereavement as Reported by New Widows

The process of grieving is an emotionally trying one which often weakens the person who has suffered a loss.

Crying
Depressed mood
Sleep disturbance
Difficulty concentrating or poor memory
Lack of appetite or weight loss
Medicines–sleep or nerve
Tired
Loss of interest in TV, news, friends, and clubs
Self-condemnation
Somatic symptoms (3 or more)
Irritability
Feels life hopeless
Anxiety attacks
Anger at loss
Loss of interest in job, church
Hallucinations
Depersonalization, derealization
Fear of losing mind

Percent reporting

Source: Clayton et al., 1971.

people have many choices about how, when, and in what manner they will die. These choices represent the last choices in a long list of choices and alternatives available to people at different times in their lives. The choices we make concerning our own death, and how we handle the loss of loved ones, express our personal needs and values as much as any other choices made at any other time in life.

1. There is currently more interest in the areas of death and dying than at any time in the recent past. The resurgence of interest is partly due to the moral issues surrounding death raised by improvements in medical technology as well as by society's increased awareness of the importance of the dying experience.

2. Children understand death through a progression of three stages. In the first stage (three to five years), death is seen as reversible and transitory and the dead are merely less alive. From ages five to nine, death is irreversible but can be avoided. By about the age of nine or ten, children understand that it is universal, irrevocable, and irreversible, although some children that age still have not developed a completely adult-like understanding of death. Personal experience with death may influence the child's understanding of the concept.

3. Adolescents are more likely than children to come into contact with death. It is well established that the elderly do not experience as much death anxiety as younger groups. However, the elderly think and talk about death more often than younger people do.

4. The elderly negotiate a life-review process that allows them to put their lives in perspective. Their stories and reminiscences can be a source of living history.

5. After conducting many interviews, Elisabeth Kübler-Ross described the process by which dying people come to accept their fate. The first stage, of denial, gives way to the anger stage. In the next stage the patient may bargain with God or the doctors. The fourth stage involves depression, while the fifth stage is one of acceptance. Although it is a valuable starting point, this stage approach has been criticized. The stages are neither universal nor invariable. Dying people can go through stages more than once and sometimes do not negotiate all the stages. In addition, the nature of the disease and the dying patient's beliefs and background may affect how he or she copes with death.

6. The dying process can also be understood in terms of three phases—the acute phase, the living-dying phase, and the terminal phase. Each of these phases is affected by its trajectory—the form and progression of each disease. Because this approach does not posit any optimal progression of stages, there is allowance for variables—such as the nature of the disease, the individual's background—to be incorporated into the understanding of the dying patient.

7. The family and medical staff should understand the needs of the dying patient. The patient should be treated as a distinct individual and allowed to participate as much as possible in choices concerning treatment and daily activities.

8. Although most elderly people would prefer to die at home, most will die in hospitals or nursing homes. The average hospital is not well equipped to serve the emotional needs of the dying patient. Another alternative is the hospice, a short-term facility specializing in pain avoidance and pain reduction as well as serving the emotional needs of the patient. It does not offer highly technical medical care for treating the disease.

9. Euthanasia is the process of putting a person to death painlessly. It may be passive or indirect, in which an individual is allowed to die, or active and direct, in which something is done to hasten death. It may be voluntary, in that the patient either performs the act or asks someone to do something that hastens the death, or involuntary, in which the family or doctor makes the decision. Many important ethical questions surround the entire practice of euthanasia.

10. The most common symptoms in a bereaved person following a death are somatic distress, preoccupation with the deceased, guilt and hostility, and disorganized, restless behavior. Most models posit an initial phase of shock and denial, followed by a stage of awareness, in which many emotional and behavioral reactions occur. This is followed by a prolonged intermediate phase, in which the individual resumes activities and slowly reduces obsession with the deceased, but still has feelings of great sadness. Then a recovery phase occurs, when a more positive attitude toward life develops and some pride in recovering from the loss may be shown. The intensity and duration of

mourning depends on the centrality of the bereaved person's relationship with the deceased, whether the bereaved believes the death was preventable, and the ability of the grieving person to work through the grief, as well as whether the death was expected.

11. Death education aims at humanizing the process of death. It involves coming to grips with one's feelings about the subject, providing the necessary resources for the dying and their family, and recognizing the interests of everyone involved in the death and dying process.

Answers to True or False Statements

1. *False*   Correct statement: Only about 25 percent of those who died in 1900 were over sixty-five.
2. *False*   Correct statement: Most children do not understand that death is irrevocable, universal, and irreversible until the age of nine or ten.
3. *True*   Adolescents tend to romanticize death.
4. *True*   Older people show less death anxiety than either young adults or middle-aged people.
5. *False*   Correct statement: The elderly person's focus on the past is functional and does not indicate organic dysfunction.
6. *False*   Correct statement: In the stage of acceptance, communication is not great, and this is not a particularly happy or animated stage.
7. *True*   The overwhelming majority of elderly people want to die at home.

8. *False*   Correct statement: Most elderly people die in hospitals or nursing homes.
9. *False*   Correct statement: A hospice does not offer advanced medical care that holds out the promise or possibility of a cure.
10. *True*   The elderly are opposed to euthanasia, while younger groups tend to favor it.
11. *False*   Correct statement: The initial reactions to the death of a loved one are well researched and described.
12. *True*   If the death was expected, people have some time to deal with it before it occurs, and recovery tends to be more rapid.

acceleration An educational program in which a gifted child skips a grade or a particular unit, or in which material is presented much more quickly than it would be for an average student.

accommodation The process by which one's existing structures are altered to fit new information.

Acquired Immune Deficiency Syndrome (AIDS) A fatal disease causing a breakdown of the body's natural defenses, leaving the body vulnerable to diseases that the body cannot then fight.

activity theory The theory relating successful aging to the maintenance of activity throughout later maturity.

acute diseases Diseases with a sharp onset and rapid development.

adolescence The psychological experience of the child from puberty to adulthood.

adolescent egocentrism The adolescent failure to differentiate between what one is thinking and what others are considering.

aerobic exercise Exercise that requires increased rates of oxygen consumption, such as brisk walking or bicycling.

age-graded influences Biological and environmental factors that are related to chronological age and may affect intelligence. For example, the increase in reaction time is generally age-related.

age norms Rules that legislate types of behaviors appropriate for people in specific age-groups.

age-status systems The status accorded different age-groups in various societies.

ageism Discrimination on the basis of age.

Alzheimer's disease An organic disorder of the elderly involving progressive and irreversible deterioration of brain tissue, causing cognitive and behavioral deficits.

amniocentesis A procedure in which fluid is taken from a pregnant woman's uterus to check fetal cells for genetic and chromosomal abnormalities.

androgens A group of male hormones, including testosterone.

androgyny The state of possessing the best characteristics of masculinity and femininity.

animism The preschooler's belief that inanimate objects have a consciousness or are alive.

anorexia nervosa A condition of self-imposed starvation found most often among adolescent females.

anoxia A condition in which the infant does not receive a sufficient supply of oxygen.

anticipatory grief The grieving that occurs prior to the expected death of a loved one.

anxious attachment A general classification of insecure attachment shown in the "strange situation," consisting of either avoidant behavior or ambivalent attachment behavior.

anxious/ambivalent attachment A type of attachment behavior shown during the "strange situation," in which the child both seeks close contact and yet resists it during the mother's reentrance after a brief separation.

anxious/avoidant attachment A type of attachment behavior shown in the "strange situation," in which the child avoids reestablishing contact with the mother as she reenters the room after a brief separation.

Apgar Scoring System A relatively simple system that gives a gross measure of infant survivability.

appropriate death A death that fulfills the needs and expectations of the patient and gives the individual some control over his or her destiny.

armored/defended personality A personality type marked by high defenses against anxiety and the need to control impulses, as well as striving, ambition, and continued achievement-orientation.

arteriosclerosis A condition in which the arteries lose their elasticity as they harden.

artificialism The belief that natural phenomena are caused by human beings.

associative play A type of play seen in preschoolers who are actively involved with one another but cannot sustain these interactions.

attachment An emotional tie binding people together over space and time.

artherosclerosis A condition in which the inner walls of the artery become thick and irregular due to a buildup of plaque.

attachment behavior Actions by a child that result in the child's gaining proximity to caregivers.

authoritarian parenting style A style of parenting in which parents rigidly control their children's behavior by establishing rules and value obedience while discouraging questioning.

authoritative parenting style A style of parenting in which parents establish limits but allow open communication and some freedom for children to make their own decisions in certain areas.

autonomy vs. doubt The second psychosocial stage, in which the positive outcome is a sense of independence, and the negative outcome is a sense of doubt about being a separate individual.

babbling Verbal production of vowel and consonant sounds strung together and often repeated.

Babinski reflex The reflex in which stroking the soles of the feet result in the toes fanning out.

Bayley Scales of Infant Development A test of intelligence administered to infants between two months and two and a half years of age.

becoming one's own man Levinson's stage between the ages of about thirty-six and forty marked by ambition, authority, independence, and confidence.

bereavement The status of having lost someone.

Black English A dialect spoken throughout the United States by lower-income blacks but understood by the overwhelming majority of blacks.

blastocyst The stage of development in which the organism consists of layers of cells around a central cavity forming a hollow sphere.

Brazelton Neonatal Behavior Scale An involved system for evaluating an infant's reflexes and sensory and behavioral abilities.

Broca's area An area in the brain responsible for producing speech.

bulimia An eating disorder marked by episodic binging and purging.

burnout A state of physical, emotional, and mental exhaustion, found mostly in people whose jobs require working in emotionally demanding circumstances.

canalization The self-righting process in which the child catches up in growth despite a moderate amount of stress or illness.

career consolidation A period suggested by Vaillant that occurs in the thirties and is marked by concentration on careers and ascending the career ladder.

carrier A person who possesses a particular gene or group of genes for a trait, does not show the trait but can pass it on to his or her offspring.

cesarean section The birth procedure by which the fetus is surgically delivered through the abdominal wall and uterus.

case study A method of research in which one person's progress is followed for an extended period of time.

centering The tendency to attend to only one dimension at a time.

cephalocaudal principle The growth principle stating that growth proceeds from the head downward to the trunk and feet.

child abuse A general term used to denote an injury that is intentionally perpetrated on a child.

child neglect A term used to describe a situation in which the care and supervision of a child is insufficient or improper.

chromosomes Rod-shaped structures that carry genes.

chronic diseases Diseases, such as arthritis, that linger on for an extended period of time.

chronionic villus sampling A diagnostic procedure in which cells are obtained from the chorion (an early structure that later becomes the lining of the placenta) during the eighth to twelfth weeks of pregnancy and checked for genetic abnormalities.

chronological age A person's age according to birthdays.

classic pattern of aging The pattern of relative stability on verbal measures and decline in performance on nonverbal tests, commonly found when testing elderly people.

classical conditioning A learning process in which a neutral stimulus is paired with a stimulus that elicits a response until the originally neutral stimulus elicits that response.

classification The process of placing objects in different groupings.

climacteric A term used to describe all the physical changes bringing someone from a state of fertility to one of infertility.

clinical method A method of studying children that relies on both observation and individual questioning.

cohabitation The state of living together without being married.

cohort effect The effect of living in a particular generation or historical period, particularly important to consider when comparing generations.

commitment In psychosocial theory, making a decision concerning some question involved in identity formation and following a plan of action reflecting this decision.

communication The process of sharing information.

comparable worth The principle by which jobs that require the same amount of knowledge or skill, or whose value to the employer are equal, are paid equally. Thus, a nurse and a carpenter might be paid the same.

compensatory education The use of educational strategies in an attempt to reduce or eliminate some perceived difference between groups.

complementary theory of mate selection The theory of mate selection emphasizing that complementary opposites attract.

comprehension The understanding of language.

concordance rate The degree of similarity between twins on any particular trait.

conditioned response The learned response to the conditioned stimulus.

conditioned stimulus The stimulus that is neutral before conditioning and after being paired with the unconditioned stimulus will elicit the desired response by itself.

concrete operational stage Piaget's third stage of cognitive development—lasting from about seven through eleven years of age—in which children develop the ability to perform logical operations, such as conservation.

conscience Part of the superego which causes the individual to experience guilt when transgressing.

conscious Freudian term for thoughts or memories of which a person is immediately aware.

conservation The principle that quantities remain the same despite changes in their appearance.

contact comfort The need for physical touching and fondling.

control group The group in an experiment that does not receive any treatment.

conventional level Kohlberg's second level of moral reasoning, in which conformity to the expectations of others and society in general serves as the basis for moral decision-making.

cooing Verbal production of single-syllable sounds, like "oo."

cooperative play A type of play seen in the later part of the preschool period and continuing into middle childhood, marked by group, play, playing specific roles, and active cooperation for sustained periods of time.

correlation A term denoting a relationship between two variables.

crisis In psychosocial theory, a time in which a person actively faces and questions aspects of his or her own identity.

critical period The period during which a particular event has its greatest impact.

crossing over The process occurring during meiosis in which genetic material on one chromosome is exchanged with material from the other.

cross-sectional study A research design in which people of different ages are studied to obtain information about changes in some variable.

crowning The point in labor at which the baby's head appears.

crystallized intelligence Learned knowledge and skills.

cystic fibrosis A severe genetic disease marked by digestive and respiratory problems.

deciduous teeth The scientific term for "baby teeth."

deductive reasoning Reasoning that begins with a general rule and then is applied to specific cases.

deferred imitation The ability to observe an act and imitate it later.

delivery of the placenta The third and last stage of birth, in which the placenta is delivered.

defense mechanism A behavior that serves to relieve or reduce feelings of anxiety or emotional conflict.

dependent variables The factors in a study that will be measured by the researcher.

despair The negative outcome of Erikson's last psychosocial stage, in which an older person experiences a sense of bitterness concerning lost opportunities.

despair stage The second state in prolonged separation from the primary caregivers, in which the child becomes apathetic.

detachment stage The last state in prolonged separation from the primary caregivers, in which the child cannot trust anyone else and becomes detached from other people.

dilation The first stage of labor, in which the uterus contracts and the cervix flattens and dilates to allow the fetus to pass.

discipline An attempt to control others in order to hold undesirable impulses in check and to encourage self-control.

disengagement theory The theory relating successful aging to the reduction in the bonds that tie the elderly person to society.

discrimination The process by which a person learns to differentiate among stimuli.

disenchantment phase The letdown and sometimes depression that follow the honeymoon phase, often experienced by people whose retirement planning may have been unrealistic.

displacement The process by which an emotion is transferred from one object or person to another more acceptable substitute.

distant-figure grandparents Grandparents who are basically not involved with their grandchildren and have little contact with them.

dizygotic (fraternal) twins Twins who develop from two fertilized eggs and are no more genetically similar than any other sibling pair.

dominant traits Traits that require the presence of only one gene.

Down's Syndrome (mongolism) A disorder caused by the presence of an extra chromosome, leading to a distinct physical appearance and mental retardation.

dramatic play A type of play in which children take on the roles of others.

dream (the) A term used by Daniel Levinson describing what a person wants in life.

dynamic visual acuity The ability to process visual information while in motion.

ecological validity The question of whether the tasks tested in a special environment, such as the laboratory, are relevant to those in real life.

ego In Freudian theory, the part of the mind that mediates between the real world and the desires of the id.

egocentrism A thought process described by Piaget in which young children believe everyone is experiencing the environment in the same way they are. Children who are egocentric have difficulty understanding someone else's point of view.

ego ideal The individual's positive and desirable standards of behavior.

ego integrity The positive outcome of Erickson's last psychosocial stage, in which an older person experiences a sense of satisfaction with life.

Electra complex In Freudian theory, the female equivalent to the Oedipus complex, in which the female experiences sexual feelings toward her father and wishes to do away with her mother.

embryonic stage The stage of prenatal development, from about two weeks and to about eight weeks, when bone cells begin to replace cartilage.

emotional abuse (psychological maltreatment) Psychological damage perpetrated on the child by parental actions, which often involves rejection, isolation, terrorizing, ignoring, and/or corrupting.

enrichment An educational program in which a gifted child is given special, challenging work that goes beyond the usual.

epigenetic principle The preset developmental plan in Erikson's theory consisting of two elements: that personality develops according to maturationally determined steps and that each society is structured to encourage challenges that arise during these times.

eros In Freudian theory, the positive, constructive sex instinct.

estrogens A group of female hormones, including estradiol.

euthanasia A general term defining an act of putting a person to death painlessly. Euthanasia may involve passive acts, such as not giving exceptional treatment, or may be active, as when a terminally ill person in great pain is given something that causes death.

exceptional child A child whose intellectual, emotional, or physical performance falls substantially above or below that of "normal" peers.

experimental method A research strategy using controls that allows the researcher to discover cause-and-effect relationships.

expressive children Children who use words involved in social interactions, such as "stop" and "bye."

expulsion The second stage of birth, involving the actual delivery of the fetus.

external locus of control The belief that one is at the mercy of other people or fate.

extinction The weakening and disappearance of a learned response.

fear of strangers A common phenomenon beginning in the second half of the first year, consisting of a fear response to new people.

fetal alcohol syndrome A number of characteristics—including retardation, facial abnormalities, growth defects and poor coordination—caused by maternal alcohol consumption.

fetal stage The stage of prenatal development beginning at about eight weeks until birth.

fine-tuning theory A theory noting that parents tune their language to a child's linguistic ability.

fluid intelligence The basic capacity for learning and problem-solving, independent of education and experience.

fontanels The soft spots on top of a baby's head.

formal operations stage The last Piagetian stage of cognitive development, in which a person develops the ability to deal with abstractions and reasons in a scientific manner.

formal-style grandparents Grandparents who, although interested, are uninvolved in the raising of their grandchildren.

friendship A positive reciprocal interpersonal relationship.

fun-seeking grandparents Grandparents who are indulgent to their grandchildren and enjoy doing things with them.

functional age An individual's level of capacity relative to other people of the same age for functioning in a given environment.

gametes The scientific term for the sex cells.

gene The basic unit of heredity.

generation gap The differences in attitudes among various generations.

generativity The positive outcome of Erikson's psychosocial crisis of middle age, which involves giving of oneself and one's talents to others.

genital stage The final psychosexual stage, occurring during adolescence, in which adult heterosexual behavior develops.

genotype The genetic configuration of the individual.

germinal stage The earliest stage of prenatal development, lasting from conception to about two weeks.

grammar A general term that refers to the total linguistic knowledge of phonology, morphology, syntax, and semantics.

grasping reflex A reflex in which a stroke on the palm causes the infant to make a fist.

grief The state of distress occurring after death.

habituation The process by which organisms spend less and less time attending to familiar stimuli.

heart attack (also myocardial infarction) The death of a part of the heart muscle due to interruption of the blood supply.

heritability A term used to describe how much of the variation seen in any particular trait within a population is due to genetic endowment.

history-graded influences Events such as wars, depressions, revolutions, and social movements that are related to historical change and may affect some aspect of development.

holophrase One word used to stand for an entire thought.

Home Observation for Measurement of the Environment (HOME) A scale that provides a measure of the quality and quantity of the emotional and cognitive elements in the home.

honeymoon phase The first phase after retirement, a time of joy and excitement.

horizontal decalage A term used to describe the unevenness of development in which a child may be able to solve one type of problem but not another, even though a common principle underlies them all. A child may be able to solve one problem concerning conservation of length, but not a problem involving conservation of volume.

hospice A center specifically designed for short-term care of the terminally ill. Hospices offer pain control and an atmosphere of understanding and concern, but no high-tech medical services.

hospitalism A condition in children found in substandard institutions marked by emotional disturbances, failure to gain weight, and retardation.

hostile aggression Aggression aimed at injuring another person.

Huntington's Chorea A dominant and fatal genetic disorder affecting the central nervous system.

hygiene factors Factors such as adequate salary, good working conditions, and job security—whose absence causes workers to be dissatisfied with their jobs.

hyperactivity A term used to describe the behavior of children who are impulsive, overly active, highly distractible, and inattentive.

hypertension High blood pressure.

id In Freudian theory, the portion of the mind that serves as the depository for wishes and desires.

identification The process by which children take on the characteristics of another person, often a parent.

identity The sense of knowing who you are.

identity achievement An identity status in which a person has developed a solid, personal identity.

identity diffusion An identity status resulting in confusion, aimlessness, and a sense of emptiness.

identity foreclosure An identity status marked by a premature identity decision.

identity moratorium An identity status in which a person is actively searching for an identity.

imaginary audience A term used to describe adolescents' belief that they are the focus of attention and being evaluated by everyone.

imprinting An irreversible, rigid behavior pattern of attachment.

impulsive style A cognitive style marked by cursory examination of a problem and answering questions very quickly.

independent variables The factors in a study that will be manipulated by the researcher.

Individualized Education Program (IEP) An individual plan outlining educational goals for an individual and methods for attaining them.

inductive reasoning Reasoning that proceeds from specific cases to the formation of a general rule.

industry The positive outcome of the psychosocial crisis in the middle years of childhood, involving a feeling of self-confidence and pride concerning one's achievements.

industry vs. inferiority The fourth psychosocial stage, in which the positive outcome is a sense of confidence concerning one's accomplishments and the negative outcome is a sense of inadequacy.

inferiority The negative outcome of the psychosocial crisis in the middle years of childhood, involving the child's belief that his or her work and achievements are below par.

initiative vs. guilt The third psychosocial stage, in which the positive outcome is a favorable view of one's own desires and actions and the negative outcome is a sense of guilt over one's actions.

instrumental aggression Aggression that involves struggles over possessions.

integrated personality A personality pattern marked by an openness to new stimuli.

intelligence A measure of one's rate of development relative to one's peers. The ability to profit from experience. A cluster of abilities, such as reasoning and memory. In the Piagetian view, any behavior that allows the individual to adapt to the environment.

intelligence quotient (IQ) A method of computing intelligence by dividing the mental age by the chronological age and multiplying by 100.

interiority The introspection and preoccupation with one's inner life that occur during later life.

Internal Locus of Control The belief that one is in control of one's own fate.

intimacy According to Erikson, the positive outcome of the psychosocial crisis of young adulthood, involving development of close interpersonal relations, most often typified by marriage.

intimacy vs. isolation The sixth psychosocial stage, occurring during young adulthood, in which the positive outcome is a development

of deep interpersonal relationships and the negative outcome is a flight from close relationships.

isolation The negative outcome of Erikson's psychosocial crisis of young adulthood, resulting in a lack of commitment to others.

keeping the meaning and rigidity A period suggested by Vaillant, occurring in the fifties, in which a person needs to find new meaning in life and to avoid falling into rigid patterns.

kwashiorkor A nutritional problem often found in toddlers and preschoolers who are newly weaned and then subjected to a protein-deficient environment.

labor A term used to describe the general process of expelling the fetus from the mother's womb.

language The use of symbols to represent meaning in some medium.

language-acquisition device An assumed biological device used in the acquisition of language.

lanugo The fine hair that covers a newborn infant.

Lamaze method A method of prepared childbirth that requires active participation by both parents.

latency stage The psychosexual phase, occurring during middle childhood, in which sexuality is hidden.

learning Relatively permanent changes in behavior due to interaction with the environment.

learning disabilities A group of disorders marked by significant difficulties in acquiring and using listening, speaking, reading, writing, reasoning, or math skills.

Leboyer method A method of childbirth emphasizing the importance of the birth experience for the child and encouraging such practices as dim light, low voices, delay in cutting the umbilical cord, a bath, and a massage.

libido In Freudian theory, the energy emanating from the sex instinct.

life expectancy The average remaining lifetime for a particular population of a given age.

life review The process of reviewing and evaluating one's past, usually found in older people.

life span The biological limit to the length of life of a particular species.

life-span developmental psychology The study of human development that is concerned with describing, explaining, and at times modifying the changes that occur over the entire life span.

linguistic deficit hypothesis The belief that a dialect such as Black English is a hindrance to learning.

linguistic difference hypothesis The belief that a dialect such as Black English is different from Standard English but not a deficit.

longitudinal study A research design in which subjects are followed over an extended period of time to note developmental changes in some variable.

love-oriented discipline A type of discipline relying on the use of reasoning or love.

mainstreaming A term used to describe the process by which exceptional children are integrated into classes with "normal" peers.

marasmus A condition of severe underweight, heart irregularities, and weakened resistance caused by malnutrition.

maturation A term used to describe changes that are due to the unfolding of an individual's genetic plan. These changes are relatively immune to environmental influence.

maturational age A person's level of maturation relative to his or her peers.

meiosis The process by which sex cells divide to form two cells, each containing twenty-three chromosomes.

menopause The cessation of a woman's menstrual cycle.

mental age The age at which an individual is functioning.

mentor An older person, usually at the workplace, who serves as a guide and confidant to a younger worker.

metacognition People's awareness of their own cognitive processes.

metamemory People's knowledge of their own memory processes.

mid-life crisis A perceived state of physical and psychological distress that results when a person's internal resources and external social support systems are overwhelmed by developmental tasks that require new adaptive resources. (*Note*: Both *mid-life crisis* and *mid-life transition* are sometimes used interchangeably to refer to a period of questioning at the beginning of middle age. There is general agreement that questioning does occur, but whether the term *crisis* should be applied is controversial. For clarity, the definition for mid-life crisis differs from that for transition.)

mid-life-transition A period of reassessment, occurring in early middle age and causing turmoil. ("Transition" and "crisis" are sometimes uses synonymously, but whether the period of questioning is a crisis is a matter of controversy.)

monozygotic (identical) twins Twins who develop from one fertilized egg and have an identical genetic structure.

moral realism The Piagetian stage of moral reasoning, during which rules are viewed as sacred and justice is whatever the authority figure says.

moral relativism The Piagetian stage of moral reasoning, in which children weigh the intentions of others before judging their actions right or wrong.

moral reasoning An approach to the study of moral development, stressing the importance of the child's ideas and reasoning about justice and right and wrong.

Moro reflex A reflex elicited by a sudden loud noise or momentary change in position, causing the back to arch, an extension of the arms and legs, and finally their contraction into a hugging position.

morpheme The smallest unit of meaning in a language.

morphology The study of the patterns of word formation in a particular language.

motherese The use of simple repetitive sentences with young children.

motherhood mandate Term used to describe society's expectations that women should desire to be mothers.

motivational factors or **satisfiers** Such factors as a sense of achievement, recognition, and esteem, the presence of which lead to job satisfaction.

mourning The cultural and societal behaviors that follow someone's death.

multifactorial inheritance Traits influenced both by genes and by the environment.

nativist explanation An explanation of language development based on biological or innate factors.

naturalistic observation A method of research in which the researcher observes organisms in their natural habitat.

neonate The scientific term for a newborn infant.

non-normative influences Events such as medical problems or divorce that affect a particular individual's life and affect development.

norms Rules that regulate behavior in particular situations.

object permanence The understanding that an object exists even when it is out of one's visual field.

Oedipus complex The conflict during the phallic stage in which a boy experiences sexual feelings toward his mother and wishes to do away with his father.

old—old Elderly people who have a number of deficits and infirmities that decrease their ability to function on their own.

onlooker play A classification of play in which the child watches others play and shows some interest, but is unable to join in.

operant conditioning The learning process in which behavior is governed by its consequences.

osteoporosis A disorder, most or of postmenopausal women, characterized by a loss of bone tissue that causes the bones to become porous and fracture easily.

overextensions A type of error in which children apply a term more broadly than it should be.

overgeneralization A type of error in which children overuse the basic rules of the language. For instance, once they learn to use plural nouns they may say "mans" instead of "men."

parallel play A type of play common in two-year-olds in which they play in the presence of other children but not with them.

passive-dependent personality A personality type marked by passivity and dependence on others.

peer Any person of a similar age.

permissive parenting style A style of parenting marked by open communication and a lack of parental demand for good behavior.

personal fable The adolescents' belief that their experiences are unique and original.

phallic stage Freud's third psychosexual stage, occurring during early childhood, in which the sexual energy is located in the genital area and the Oedipal or Electra conflicts take place.

phenotype The observable characteristics of the organism.

phenylketonuria (PKU) A recessive genetic disorder marked by inability to digest a particular protein. If the disorder is not treated, it leads to mental retardation.

phonology The study of the sounds of language, the rules for combining them to make words, and the stress and intonation patterns.

play An activity dominated by the child and performed with a positive feeling.

polygenic (multigenic) inheritance Characteristics influenced by more than one pair of genes.

power-assertive discipline A type of discipline relying on the use of power, such as physical punishment or forceful commands.

postconventional level Kohlberg's third level of moral reasoning, in which moral decisions are made on the basis of individual values that have been internalized.

pragmatics The study of how people use language in various contexts.

preconscious Freudian term for thoughts or memories that, although not immediately conscious, can easily become conscious.

preconventional level Kohlberg's first level of moral reasoning, in which satisfaction of one's own needs, and rewards and punishment, serve as the bases for moral decision-making.

premature infants Infants weighing less than 5½ pounds or born less than thirty-seven weeks after conception.

premenstrual syndrome (PMS) An assortment of symptoms—including tension, depression, irritability, and fatigue—that occur in many women just prior to and at the start of their period.

preoperational stage Piaget's second stage of cognitive development, marked by the appearance of language and symbolic function and the child's inability to understand logical concepts, such as conservation.

presbycusis The decline in the ability to hear high-pitched sounds.

presbyopia A form of farsightedness occurring in late middle age and beyond.

preterm infants Infants born before thirty-seven weeks of gestation.

primary process The process by which the id seeks to gratify its desires.

primary sex characteristics Body changes directly associated with sexual reproduction.

production The ability to verbalize language.

progeria Disorders characterized by premature aging, ending in death. Children with the disease take on the appearance of the aged.

Project Head Start A federal funded compensatory education program aimed at reducing or eliminating the differences in educational achievement between poor and middle-class youngsters.

protest stage The initial reaction to separation, in which the infant cries and refuses to be cared for by substitute caregivers.

proto-conversations The infant's responses to verbal and nonverbal cues that resemble turn-taking, as in a conversation.

proximodistal principle The growth principle stating that development occurs from the inside out, that the internal organs develop faster than the extremities.

psycholinguistics The study of the nature of language.

psychosexual stages Stages in Freud's developmental theory.

psychosocial dwarfism A condition in which a child's small stature and lack of growth is due to psychological or emotional causes.

psychosomatic or **psychophysiological disorders** Physical disorders, such as ulcers and colitis, that are contributed to or caused by emotional factors, including reactions to stress.

puberty Physiological changes involved in sexual maturation, as well as other body changes that occur during the teen years.

punishment The process by which some physical or emotional pain is inflicted in order to reduce the probability that misbehavior will reoccur.

qualitative changes Changes in process or function.

quantitative changes Changes that can be considered solely in terms of increases or decreases, such as changes in height or weight.

Rapid Eye Movement (REM) The movements of the eyes during sleep that are related to dreams.

readiness The point in development at which a child has the necessary skills to master a new challenge.

realistic or **companionate love** Love that is characteristic of people in a long-term relationship involving steady concern and caring.

recall A way of testing memory in which the subject must produce the correct response given very limited cues.

recessive traits Traits that require the presence of two genes.

reciprocal interactions The process by which an organism constantly affects and is affected by the environment.

recognition A way of testing memory in which the subject is required to choose the correct answer from a group of choices.

referential children Children whose early language is used to name objects, such as "dog" or "bed."

reflective style A cognitive style marked by thorough exploration of a problem, consideration of various alternatives, and finally, answering the question or performing the tasks.

reflex A relatively simple automatic reaction to a particular stimulus.

reinforcement An event that increases the likelihood that the behavior that preceded it will reoccur.

reorientation phase The retirement phase following the disenchantment phase, during which people develop realistic alternatives.

reversibility Beginning at the end of an operation and working one's way back to the start.

reservoir-of-family-wisdom grandparents An older style of grandparenting in which the grandparents, most often the grandfather, is the authority figure for the family.

retrolental fibroplasia A disorder involving blindness caused by an oversupply of oxygen administered usually to premature infants.

Rh factor An antibody often, but not always, found in human beings.

role confusion (role diffusion) In psychosocial theory, the negative outcome of adolescence, which involves a failure to develop a personal identity and feelings of aimlessness.

romantic love Love that is basically erotic in nature and involves a strong need for the physical presence of the other and for contact.

rooting reflex The reflex in young infants in which a stroke on a cheek causes them to turn in the direction of the stimulus.

schizophrenia A severe mental disorder characterized by one or more of the following symptoms: delusions, hallucinations, disordered and illogical thinking, social withdrawal, inappropriate emotional responses, and bizarre behavior.

script A structure that describes an appropriate sequence of events in a particular context.

secondary sex characteristics Physical changes that distinguish males from females but are not associated with sexual reproduction.

secondary or **reality process** The process by which the ego satisfies the organism's needs in a socially appropriate manner.

secular trend The trend toward earlier maturation today, compared with past generations.

secure attachment A type of attachment behavior in which the infant in the "strange situation" uses the mother as a secure base of operations.

self-concept The picture people have of themselves.

self-esteem The value people place on various aspects of their self.

self-fulfilling prophecy The concept that a person's expectations concerning some event affect the probability that it will occur.

semantics The study of the meaning of words.

sensorimotor stage The first stage in Piaget's theory of cognitive development, in which the child discovers the world using the senses and motor activity.

separation anxiety Fear of being separated from caregivers, peaking at between twelve and sixteen months.

seriation The process of placing objects in size order.

sex chromosomes The twenty-third pair of chromosomes, which determines the gender of the organism.

sex differences The differences between males and females established through scientific investigation.

sex-limited trait A trait—for example, pattern baldness—that manifests itself in certain hormonal climates but not in others.

sex-linked traits Traits inherited through genes found on the sex chromosomes.

sex roles Behaviors expected of people in a given society on the basis of whether they are male or female.

sex typing The process by which people acquire, value, and behave in a manner appropriate to one sex more than the other.

sickle cell anemia An inherited defect in the structure of red blood cells found mostly in blacks and Latins.

similarity theory of mate selection The theory of mate selection emphasizing that people attract and marry on the basis of underlying similarities in a variety of areas.

small-for-date infants Infants born below the weight expected for their gestational age.

social clock The internalized sense of timing that tells people whether they are progressing too fast or too slow in terms of social events.

solitary play Independent play in which the child shows no interest in the activities of others.

sonogram A "picture" taken of the fetus through the use of ultrasonic soundwaves.

stability phase The retirement phase following the reorientation phase, during which realistic plans are put into effect.

stagnation The negative outcome of Erikson's psychosocial crisis of middle age, in which one becomes completely absorbed in one's self.

stepping reflex A reflex in which if the baby is held upright and the soles of the feet are placed on a hard surface while the baby is tipped slightly forward the infant makes a stepping movement.

stimulus deprivation The absence of adequate environmental stimulation.

stimulus generalization The tendency of an organism that has learned to associate a certain behavior with a particular stimulus to show this behavior when confronted with similar stimuli.

stimulus-value-role theory The theory of mate selection that sees the selection of a marital partner as a three-stage progression involving initial attraction, value comparisons, and analyses of role compatibility.

strange situation An experimental procedure used to measure attachment behaviors.

sucking reflex A reflex found in young infants, in which they automatically suck when something is placed in their mouths.

superego In Freudian theory, the part of the mind that includes a set of principles, violation of which leads to feelings of guilt.

surrogate-parent grandparents Grandparents who take on a parenting role, usually so the mother can work.

survey A method of study in which data is collected though written questionnaires or oral interviews from a number of people.

synchrony The coordination between infant and caregiver in which each can respond to the subtle verbal and nonverbal cues of the other.

syntax The rules for combining words to make sentences.

Tay-Sachs disease A fatal genetic disease found most often in Jews who can trace their ancestry back to Eastern Europe.

telegraphic speech Sentences in which only the basic words necessary to communicate meaning are used with helping words such as "a" or "to" left out.

temperament A group of characteristics reflecting an individual's way of responding to the environment and thought to be genetic.

teratogen Any agent that causes birth defects.

terminal drop A phenomenon in which there is a decline in intelligence scores and personality changes that is associated with death.

termination phase The final phase of retirement, during which people either return to work or find their stable lifestyle, disrupted and sometimes ended by illness or disability.

time out A punishment procedure in which a person is denied access to positive reinforcement for a certain period of time. A child who misbehaves may be isolated from the group for a brief period.

transductive reasoning Preoperational reasoning in which young children reason from particular to particular.

transitive inferences Statements of comparison, such as "If X is taller than Y, and Y is taller than Z, the X is taller than Z."

transition A period late in labor in which the contractions become more difficult.

triarchic theory of human intelligence A theory of intelligence based on information-processing considerations advanced by Robert Sternberg which postulates the following mechanisms of intellectual functioning: *metacomponents*, which involve the individual's skills used in planning and decision-making; *performance components*, which relate to the basic operations involved in actually solving the task; and *knowledge acquisition components*, which involve processes that are used in acquiring new knowledge.

trust vs. mistrust Erikson's first psychosocial stage, in which the positive outcome is a sense of trust while the negative outcome is a sense of suspicion.

unconditioned response The response to the unconditioned stimulus.

unconditioned stimulus The stimulus that originally elicits the response.

unconscious Freudian term for memories that lie beyond normal awareness.

underextension A type of error in which children apply a term more narrowly than it should be.

unintegrated personality A personality type marked by disorganized patterns and defects in both thought and psychological functioning.

values Constructs that serve as internal guides for behavior.

values clarification courses Approaches to improving moral decision-making skills based on presenting students with problems and helping them to perceive issues from many different viewpoints and to consider many different solutions.

vernix caseosa A thick liquid that protects the skin of the fetus.

visual cliff A device used to measure depth perception in infants.

Wernicke's area An area in the brain responsible for comprehension of language.

young—old Younger elderly people who are fully functioning and independent.

zygote A fertilized egg.

REFERENCES

Chapter 1

Adler, L. L. Cross-Cultural Research and Theory. In B. B. Wolman (ed.), *Handbook of Developmental Psychology*, 76–88. Englewood Cliffs, N.J.: Prentice-Hall, 1982.

Appelbaum, M. I., and McCall, R. B. Design and Analysis in Developmental Psychology. In P. H. Mussen (ed.), *Handbook of Child Psychology* (4th ed.), vol. 1, 415–477. New York: Wiley, 1983.

Baldwin, A. L. *Theories of Child Development.* New York: Wiley, 1967.

Baltes, P. B., Reese, H. W., and Lipsitt, L. P. Life-Span Developmental Psychology. In M. R. Rosenzweig and L. W. Porter (Eds.), *Annual Review of Psychology*, 1980, *31*, 65–111.

Bandura, A. *Social Foundations of Thought and Action: A Social Cognitive Theory.* Englewood Cliffs, N.J.: Prentice-Hall, 1986.

Bandura, A. *Principles of Behavior Modification.* New York: Holt, Rinehart, and Winston, 1969.

Bandura, A., Ross, D., and Ross, S. Transmission of Aggression Through Imitation of Aggressive Models. *Journal of Abnormal and Social Psychology*, 1961, *63*, 575–582.

Bandura, A., and Walters, R. H. *Social Learning and Personality Development.* New York: Holt, Rinehart, and Winston, 1963.

Barrera, M. E., Rosenbaum, P. L., and Cunningham, C. E. Early Home Intervention with Low-Birth-Weight Infants and Their Parents. *Child Development*, 1986, *57*, 20–34.

Baumrind, D. Research Using Intentional Deception: Ethical Issues Revisited. *American Psychologist*, 1985, *40*, 165–175.

Bell, R. Q. Parent, Child, and Reciprocal Influences. *American Psychologist*, 1979, *34*, 821–827.

———. A Reinterpretation of the Direction of Effects in Socialization. *Psychological Review*, 1968, *75*, 81–95.

Birren, J. E., Kinney, D. K., Schaie, K. W., and Woodruff, D. S. *Developmental Psychology: A Life-Span Approach.* Boston: Houghton Mifflin, 1981.

Blanck, I. D., Rosenthal, R., Snodgrass, S. E., DePaulo, B. M., and Zuckerman, M. Longitudinal and Cross-Sectional Age Effects in Nonverbal Decoding Skill and Style. *Developmental Psychology*, 1982, *18*, 491–498.

Botwinick, J. *Aging and Behavior* (3rd ed.). New York: Springer, 1984.

Bower, T. G. R. *A Primer of Infant Development.* San Francisco: Freeman, 1977.

Brainerd, C. J. *Piaget's Theory of Intelligence.* Englewood Cliffs, N.J.: Prentice-Hall, 1978.

Bronfenbrenner, U., and Crouter, A. C. The Evolution of Environmental Models in Developmental Research. In P. H. Mussen (ed.), *Handbook of Child Psychology* (4th ed.), vol 1, 357–415. New York: Wiley, 1983.

Bronstein, P. Differences in Mothers' and Fathers' Behaviors Toward Children: A Cross-Cultural Comparison. *Developmental Psychology*, 1984, *20*, 995–1004.

Brown, A. L., Bransford, J. D., Ferrara, R. A., and Campione, J. C. Learning, Remembering, and Understanding. In P. H. Mussen (ed.), *Handbook of Child Psychology* (4th ed.), vol. 3, 77–167. New York: Wiley, 1983.

Cairns, R. B. The Emergence of Developmental Psychology. In P. H. Mussen (ed.), *Handbook of Child Development* (4th ed.), vol. 1, 41–103. New York: Wiley, 1983.

———. *Social Development: The Origins and Plasticity of Interchanges.* San Francisco: Freeman, 1979.

Caspi, A., Elder, G. H., and Bem, D. J. Moving Against the World: Life-Course Patterns of Explosive Children. *Developmental Psychology*, 1987, *23*, 308–313.

Chodorow, N. Oedipal Asymmetries and Heterosexual Knots. In S. Cox (ed.), *Female Psychology: The Emerging Self*, 228–248. New York: St. Martin's Press, 1981.

Clarke, A. M., and Clarke, A. D. S. (eds.). *Early Experience: Myth and Evidence.* New York: Free Press, 1976.

Cooke, R. A. The Ethics and Regulation of Research Involving Children. In B. B. Wolman (ed.), *Handbook of Developmental Psychology*, 149–175. Englewood Cliffs, N.J.: Prentice-Hall, 1982.

Costa, P. T., and McCrae, R. R. Cross-Sectional Studies of Personality in a National Sample I: Development and Validation of Survey Measures. *Psychology and Aging*, 1986, *1*, 140–143.

Costa, P. T., McCrae, R. R., Zonderman, A. B., Barbano, H. E., Lebowitz, B., and Larson, D. M. Cross-Sectional Studies of Personality in a National Sample, II: Stability in Neuroticism, Extroversion, and Openness. *Psychology and Aging*, 1986, *1*, 144–149.

Dasen, P., and Heron, A. Cross-Cultural Test of Piaget's Theory. In H. C. Triandis and A. Heron (eds.), *Handbook of Cross-Cultural Psychology*, vol. 4, 295–343. Boston: Allyn and Bacon, 1981.

Dawkins, R. L., and Dawkins, M. P. Alcohol Use and Delinquency Among Black, White, and Hispanic Adolescent Offenders. *Adolescence*, 1983, *18*, 799–809.

Denney, N. W. Aging and Cognitive Changes. In B. B. Wolman (ed.), *Handbook of Developmental Psychology*, 807–828. Englewood Cliffs, N.J.: Prentice-Hall, 1982.

DiCaprio, N. S. *Personality Theories: A Guide to Human Nature* (2nd ed.). New York: Holt, Rinehart, and Winston, 1983.

Eidelberg, L. *Encyclopedia of Psychoanalysis.* New York: Free Press, 1968.

Erikson, E. *Childhood and Society.* New York: Norton, 1963.

Featherman, D. L. Life-Span Perspectives in Social Science Research. In P. B. Baltes and O. G. Brim (eds.), *Life-Span Development and Behavior*, vol. 5, 1–49. New York: Academic Press, 1983.

Felice, M. Reflections on Caring for Indochinese Children and Youth. *Journal of Developmental and Behavioral Pediatrics*, 1986, *7*, 124–128.

Flavell, J. H. On Cognitive Development. *Child Development*, 1982, *53*, 1–10.

———. *Cognitive Development.* Englewood Cliffs, N.J.: Prentice-Hall, 1977.

———. *Development of Role-Taking and Communication Skills in Children.* Huntington, N.Y.: Krieger, 1975.

Freud, S. *The Ego and the Id.* New York: Norton, 1962 (originally published 1923).

———. *New Introductory Lectures on Psychoanalysis.* New York: Norton, 1961 (originally published 1933).

———. *The Interpretation of Dreams.* In J. Strachey (ed.), *The Standard Edition of the Complete Psychological Works of Sigmund Freud,* vol. 4. London: Hogarth, 1957 (originally published 1900).

———. *An Outline of Psychoanalysis.* New York: Norton, 1949 (originally published 1940).

Frueh, T., and McGhee, P. E. Traditional Sex-Role Development and Amount of Time Spent Watching Television. *Developmental Psychology,* 1975, *11,* 109.

Furth, H. G., and Milgram, N. A. Labeling and Grouping Effects in the Recall of Pictures by Children. *Child Development,* 1973, *44,* 511–518.

Gallimore, R., Weiss, L., and Finney, R. Cultural Differences in Delay of Gratification: A Problem of Behavior Classification. *Journal of Personality and Social Psychology,* 1974, *30,* 72–80.

Galdston, R. Preventing the Abuse of Little Children: The Parents' Center Project for the Study and Prevention of Child Abuse. *American Journal of Orthopsychiatry,* 1975, *45,* 372–382.

Gergen, D. R. Childhood Lost. *U.S. News & World Report,* October 28, 1985, p. 78.

Giancotti, A., and Vinci, G. A. Major Depression of Psychogenic Origin in a Five-Year-Old. *American Journal of Orthopsychiatry,* 1986, *56,* 617–621.

Goertzel, V., and Goertzel, M. G. *Cradles of Eminence.* Boston: Little, Brown, 1962.

Goldfarb, W. The Effects of Early Institutional Care on Adolescent Personality. *Journal of Experimental Education,* 1943, *12,* 106–129.

Goleman, D. G. The Roots of Terrorism Are Found in Brutality of Shattered Childhood. *New York Times,* September 2, 1986(b), C1 and C8.

———. Child Development Theory Stresses Small Moments. *New York Times,* October 21, 1986a, C1 and C3.

Hall, C. S., and Lindzey, G. *Theories of Personality.* New York: Wiley, 1957.

Harrison, N. S. *Understanding Behavioral Research.* Belmont, Calif.: Wadsworth, 1979.

Hayes, D. S., and Birnbaum, D. W. Preschoolers' Retention of Televised Events: Is a Picture Worth a Thousand Words? *Developmental Psychology,* 1980, *16,* 410–416.

Heron, A., and Kroeger, E. Introduction to Developmental Psychology. In H. C. Triandis and A. Heron (eds.), *Handbook of Cross-Cultural Psychology,* vol. 4, 1–17. Boston: Allyn and Bacon, 1981.

Hess, R. D., Hiroshi, A., and Kashiwagi, K., et al. Family Influences on School Readiness and Achievement in Japan and the United States: An Overview of a Longitudinal Study. In H. Stevenson, H. Azuma, and K. Makuta (eds.), *Child Development and Education in Japan,* 147–166. New York: Freeman, 1986.

Hjelle, L. A., and Zeigler, D. J. *Personality.* New York: McGraw-Hill, 1976.

Holmes, D. S. Debriefing After Psychological Experiments, I: Effectiveness of Post-Deception Dehoaxing. *American Psychologist,* 1976a, *31,* 858–868.

———. Debriefing After Psychological Experiments, II: Effectiveness of Post-Experimental Desensitization. *American Psychologist,* 1976b, *31,* 868–876.

Hornstein, H. A. *Cruelty and Kindness: A New Look at Aggression and Altruism.* Englewood Cliffs, New Jersey: Prentice-Hall, 1976.

Hottinger, W. Early Motor Development: Discussion and Summary. In C. B. Corbin (ed.), *A Textbook of Motor Development* (2nd ed.), 31–41. Dubuque, Iowa: Brown, 1980.

Kadushin, A. Adopting Older Children: Summary and Implications. In A. M. Clarke and A. D. B. Clarke (eds.), *Early Experience: Myth and Evidence,* 187–213. New York: Free Press, 1976.

Kagan, J. Resilience and Continuity in Psychological Development. In A. M. Clarke and A. D. B. Clarke (eds.), *Early Experience: Myth and Evidence,* 97–122. New York: Free Press, 1976.

Kagan, J. and Klein, R. E. Cross-Cultural Perspectives on Early Development. *American Psychologist,* 1973, *28,* 947–961.

Kail, R., and Hagen, J. W. Memory in Childhood. In B. B. Wolman (ed.), *Handbook of Developmental Psychology,* 350–367. Englewood Cliffs, N.J.: Prentice-Hall, 1982.

Kline, P. *Fact and Fancy in Freudian Theory.* London: Methuen, 1972.

Laughlin, H. P. *The Ego and Its Defenses.* New York: Appleton-Century-Crofts, 1970.

Lazar, I., Darlington, R., Murray, H., Royce, J., and Snipper, A. Lasting Effects of Early Education: A Report from the Consortium for Longitudinal Studies. *Monographs of the Society for Research in Child Development,* 1982, *47,* (2–3, serial no. 195).

Milgram, S. Behavioral Study of Obedience. *Journal of Abnormal and Social Psychology,* 1963, *67,* 371–378.

Mullahy, P. *Oedipus: Myth and Complex.* New York: Grove, 1948.

Mussen, P. H., and Eisenberg-Berg, N. *Roots of Caring, Sharing, and Helping.* San Francisco: Freeman, 1977.

Navarick, D. J. *Principles of Learning: From Laboratory to Field.* Reading, Mass.: Addison-Wesley, 1979.

Noam, G. G., Higgins, R. O., and Goethals, G. W. Psychoanalytic Approaches to Developmental Psychology. In B. B. Wolman (ed.), *Handbook of Developmental Psychology,* 23–40. Englewood Cliffs, N.J.: Prentice-Hall, 1982.

Nunnally, J. C. The Study of Change: Measurement, Research Strategies, and Methods of Analysis. In B. B. Wolman (ed.), *Handbook of Developmental Psychology,* 133–149. Englewood Cliffs, N.J.: Prentice-Hall, 1982.

Nye, R. D. *Three Views of Man.* Monterey, Calif.: Brooks/Cole, 1975.

Olness, K. N. On "Reflections on Caring for Indochinese Children and Youth." *Journal of Developmental and Behavioral Pediatrics,* 1986, *7,* 129–130.

Olweus, D. Development of Stable Aggressive Reaction Patterns in Males. In R. Blanchard and C. Blanchard (eds.), *Advances in the Study of Aggression,* vol. 1. New York: Academic Press, 1982.

Orlofsky, J. L., Marcia, J. E., and Lesser, J. M. Ego Identity Status and Intimacy vs. Isolation Crisis of Young Adulthood. *Journal of Personality and Social Psychology,* 1973, *27,* 211–219.

Patterson, G. R., Littman, R. A., and Bricker, W. Assertive Behavior in Children: A Step Toward a Theory of Aggression. *Monographs of the Society for Research in Child Development,* 1967, *32,* no. 113.

Piaget, J. Piaget's Theory. In P. H. Mussen (ed.), *Handbook of Child Psychology,* vol. 1, 103–129. New York: Wiley, 1983 (originally published in *Carmichael's Manual of Child Psychology* [2nd ed.], 1970.

———. Intellectual Evolution from Adolescence to Adulthood. *Human Development,* 1972, *15,* 1–12.

———. *Genetic Epistemology.* New York: Columbia University Press, 1970.

———. *Six Psychological Studies.* New York: Vintage Books, 1967.

———. *The Construction of Reality in the Child.* New York: Basic Books, 1954.

———. *The Child's Conception of Number.* New York: Humanities Press, 1952.

Piaget, J., and Inhelder, B. *The Psychology of the Child.* New York: Basic Books, 1969.

Rachlin, H. *Introduction to Modern Behaviorism.* San Francisco: Freeman, 1976.

Ransom, J. W., Schlesinger, S., and Derdeyn, A. P. A Stepfamily in Formation. *American Journal of Orthopsychiatry,* 1979, *49,* 36–43.

Reese, H. W., and Lipsitt, L. *Experimental Child Psychology.* New York: Academic Press, 1970.

Rice, R. D. Neurophysiological Development in Premature Infants Following Stimulation. *Developmental Psychology*, 1977, *13*, 69–76.

Roche, J. P. Premarital Sex: Attitudes and Behavior by Dating Stage. *Adolescence*, 1986, *81*, 107–121.

Rogers, C. R. *A Way of Being*. Boston: Houghton Mifflin, 1980.

Ruittenbeck, H. M. *The Individual and the Crowd: A Study of Identity in America*. New York: New American Library, 1964.

Rutter, M. Maternal Deprivation, 1972–1978: New Findings, New Concepts, New Approaches. *Child Development*, 1979, *50*, 283–305.

Salkind, N. J. *Theories of Human Development*. New York: Van Nostrand, 1981.

Salthouse, T. A. *Adult Cognition: An Experimental Psychology of Human Aging*. New York: Springer-Verlag, 1982.

Sameroff, A. J. Developmental Systems: Contexts and Evolution. In P. H. Mussen (ed.), *Handbook of Child Psychology* (4th ed.), vol. 1, 237–295. New York: Wiley, 1983.

Schaie, K. W., and Hertzog, C. Longitudinal Methods. In B. B. Wolman (ed.), *Handbook of Developmental Psychology*, 91–116. Englewood Cliffs, N.J.: Prentice-Hall, 1982.

Schneider, E. L. *The Genetics of Aging*. New York: Plenum, 1978.

Selman, R. L. The Child as a Friendship Philosopher. In S. R. Asher and J. M. Gottman (eds.), *The Development of Children's Friendships*, 242–273. Cambridge: Cambridge University Press, 1981.

Spivack, G., Marcus, J., and Swift, M. Early Classroom Behaviors and Later Misconduct. *Developmental Psychology*, 1986, *22*, 124–131.

Sternberg, R. J. What Is an Information-Processing Approach to Human Abilities? In R. J. Sternberg (ed.), *Human Abilities: An Information-Processing Approach*, 1–5. New York: Freeman, 1985.

Stewart, M. J. Fundamental Locomotor Skills. In C. J. Corbin (ed.), *A Textbook of Motor Development*, 44–52. Dubuque, Iowa: Brown, 1980.

Stine, E. L., Wingfield, A., and Poon, L. W. How Much and How Fast: Rapid Processing of Spoken Language in Later Adulthood. *Psychology and Aging*, 1986, *1*, 303–311.

Thibault, J. P., and McKee, J. S. Practical Parenting with Piaget. *Young Children*. November 1982, *38*, 18–27.

Thomas, A., Chess, S., and Birch, H. G. The Origins of Personality. *Scientific American*, August 1970, *223*, 102–109.

Thomas, J. L. Gender Differences in Satisfaction with Grandparenting. *Psychology and Aging*, 1986, *1*, 215–219.

Thomas, R. M. *Comparing Theories of Child Development*. Belmont, Calif.: Wadsworth, 1979.

Triandis, H. C., and Brislin, R. W. Cross-Cultural Psychology. *American Psychologist*, 1984, *39*, 1006–1017.

Watson, J. B. *Behaviorism* (rev. ed.). Chicago: University of Chicago Press, 1930.

Wood, G. *Fundamentals of Psychological Research*. Boston: Little, Brown, 1974.

Wright, L. E. *Erikson: Identity and Religion*. New York: Seabury, 1982.

Wright, R. L. D. *Understanding Statistics*. New York: Harcourt Brace Jovanovich, 1976.

Chapter 2

Abroms, K., and Bennett, J. Current Genetic and Demographic Findings in Down's Syndrome: How Are They Presented in College Textbooks on Exceptionality? *Mental Retardation*, 1980, *18*, 101–107.

Ainslie, R. C. *The Psychology of Twinship*. Lincoln: University of Nebraska Press, 1985.

Altrocchi, J. *Abnormal Psychology*. New York: Harcourt Brace Jovanovich, 1980.

Apgar, V., and Beck, J. *Is My Baby All Right?* New York: Pocket Books, 1974.

Arehart-Treichel, J. Down's Syndrome: The Father's Role. *Science News*, December 1, 1979, pp. 381–382.

Berdine, W. H., and Blackhurst, A. E. *An Introduction to Special Education* (2nd ed.). Boston: Little, Brown, 1985.

Bouchard, T. J., and McGue, M. Familial Studies of Intelligence: A Review. *Science*, May 29, 1981, pp. 1055–1059.

Bridges, F. A., and Cicchetti, D. Mothers' Ratings of the Temperament Characteristics of Down's Syndrome Infants. *Developmental Psychology*, 1982, *18*, 238–244.

Cahill, G. G, Genetics and Inborn Errors of Metabolism. *Scientific American Medicine*, 1987, *9*, 1–17.

Carter, C. O. *Human Heredity*. Baltimore: Penguin, 1970.

Crandall, B. F., and Tarjan, G. Genetics of Mental Retardation. In M. A. Sperber and L. S. Jarvik (eds.), *Psychiatry and Genetics*. New York: Basic Books, 1976, 95–119.

Curtis, H. *Biology* (2nd ed.). New York: Worth, 1975.

Daniels, D., and Plomin, R. Origins of Individual Differences in Infant Shyness. *Developmental Psychology*, 1985, *21*, 118–122.

deVries, M. W., and Sameroff, A. J. Culture and Temperament: Influences on Infant Temperament in Three East African Societies. *American Journal of Orthopsychiatry*, 1984, *54*, 83–96.

Erlenmeyer-Kimling, L., and Jarvik, L. F. Genetics and Intelligence: A Review. *Science*, 1963, *142*, 1477–1479.

Feldman, M. W., and Lewontin, R. C. The Heritability Hang-up. *Science*, 1975, *190*, 1163–1168.

Fischman, S. E. Psychological Issues in the Genetic Counseling of Cystic Fibrosis. In S. Kessler (ed.), *Genetic Counseling: Psychological Dimensions*, 153–165. New York: Academic Press, 1979.

Fogel, A. *Infancy*. St. Paul: West, 1984.

Fuller, J. L., and Thompson, W. R. *Foundations of Behavior Genetics*. St. Louis: Mosby, 1978.

Gardner, H. *Frames of Mind*. New York: Basic Books, 1983.

Gardner, L. I. Deprivation Dwarfism. *Scientific American*, July 1972, *227*, 76–82.

Goldsmith, H. H. Genetic Influences on Personality from Infancy to Adulthood. *Child Development*, 1983, *54*, 331–355.

Goldsmith, H. H., and Gottesman, I. I. Origins of Variation in Behavioral Style: A Longitudinal Study of Temperament in Young Twins. *Child Development*, 1981, *52*, 91–103.

Goldsmith, H. H. et al. What Is Temperament? Four Approaches. *Child Development*, 1987, *58*, 505–530.

Gottesman, I. I. Genetics and Personality (1966). In J. J. Hutt and C. Hutt (eds.), *Early Human Development*, 17–25. London: Oxford University Press, 1973.

———. Schizophrenia and Genetics: Where Are We? Are You Sure? In L. C. Wynne (ed.), *The Nature of Schizophrenia*. New York: Wiley, 1978.

Gottesman, I. I., and Shields, J. *Schizophrenia and Genetics: A Twin Study Vantage Point*. New York: Academic Press, 1972.

Grossman, L. K., Holtzman, N. A., Charney, E., and Schwartz, A. D. Neonatal Screening and Genetic Counseling for Sickle Cell Trait. *American Journal of Disabled Children*, 1985, *139*, 241.

Hirsch, J. G. Helping the Family Whose Child Has a Birth Defect. In J. D. Noshpitz (ed.), *Basic Handbook of Child Psychiatry*, vol. 4, 121–128. New York: Basic Books, 1979.

Hodgkinson, S., Sherrington, R., Gurling, H., Marchbanks, R., Reeders, S., Mallet, J., McInnis, M., Petursson, H., and Brynjolfsson, J. Molecular Genetic Evidence for Heterogeneity in Manic Depression. *Nature*, 1987, *325*, 805–806.

Holden, C. Twins Reunited: More Than the Faces Are Familiar. *Science*, November 1980, *197*, 55–59.

Holtzman, N. A., Kronmal, R. A., Van Doorninck, W., Azen, C., and Koch, R. Effect of Age at Loss of Dietary Control on Intellectual Performance and Behavior of Children with Phenylketonuria. *New England Journal of Medicine*, 1986, *314*, 593–597.

Horn, J. M. Bias? Indeed! *Child Development*, 1985, *56*, 779–781.

Hyde, J. S. *Half the Human Experience: The Psychology of Women* (3rd ed.). Lexington, Mass.: D. C. Heath, 1985.

Jencks, C. *Inequality: A Reassessment of the Effects of Family and Schooling in America.* New York: Basic Books, 1972.

Jensen, A. R. How Much Can We Boost I.Q. and Scholastic Achievement? *Harvard Educational Review*, 1969, *39*, 1–123.

Kalat, J. W. *Biological Psychology.* Belmont, Calif.: Wadsworth, 1980.

Kamin, L. J. *The Science and Politics of I.Q.* Hillsdale, N.J.: Erlbaum, 1974.

Kermis, M. D. *The Psychology of Human Aging.* Boston: Allyn and Bacon, 1984.

Kirk, S. A., and Gallagher, J. G. *Educating Exceptional Children* (2nd ed.). Boston: Houghton Mifflin, 1979.

Kowles, R. V. *Genetics, Society, and Decisions.* Columbus, Ohio: Merrill, 1985.

Lappe, M., and Brody, J. A. Genetic Counseling: A Psychotherapeutic Approach to Autonomy in Decision Making. In M. A. Sperber and L. F. Jarvik (eds.), *Psychiatry and Genetics: Psychosocial, Ethical, and Legal Considerations*, 129–146. New York: Basic Books, 1976.

Lazar, I., and Darlington, R. Lasting Effects of Early Education: A Report from the Consortium for Longitudinal Studies. *Monographs of the Society for Research in Child Development*, serial number 195, *47*, nos. 2–3, 1982.

Linn, M. C., and Petersen, A. C. Emergence and Characterization of Sex Differences in Spatial Ability: A Meta-Analysis. *Child Development*, 1985, *56*, 1479–1498.

Loehlin, J. C., Lindzey, G., and Spuhler, J. N. *Race Differences in Intelligence.* San Francisco: Freeman, 1975.

Longstreth, L. E. Revisiting Skeel's Final Study: A Critique. *Developmental Psychology*, 1981, *17*, 620–625.

Mange, A. P., and Mange, E. J. *Genetics: Human Aspects.* Philadelphia: Saunders, 1980.

March of Dimes Foundation. *Tay Sachs, Public Health Education Information Sheet.* White Plains, N.Y.: March of Dimes Birth Defects Foundation, 1984.

———. *Genetic Counseling.* New York: March of Dimes Birth Defects Foundation, 1980.

Matheny, A. P. A. Longitudinal Twin Study of Stability of Components from Bayley's Infant Behavior Record. *Child Development*, 1983, *54*, 356–360.

Matheny, A. P., Riese, M. L., and Wilson, R. S. Rudiments of Infant Temperament: Newborn to Nine Months. *Developmental Psychology*, 1985, *21*, 486–495.

McBroom, P. *Behavioral Genetics.* National Institute of Mental Health Science Monograph. Washington, D.C.: Department of Health, Education, and Welfare, 1980.

McCall, R. B. Nature-Nurture and the Two Realms of Development: A Proposed Integration with Respect to Mental Development. *Child Development*, 1981, *52*, 1–12.

McCauley, E., Kay, T., Ito, J., and Treder, R. The Turner Syndrome: Cognitive Deficits, Affective Discrimination, and Behavior Problems. *Child Development*, 1987, *58*, 464–474.

Mirsky, A. F., and Duncan, C. C. Etiology and Expression of Schizophrenia: Neurobiological and Psychosocial Factors. *Annual Review of Psychology*, 1986, *37*, 291–321.

Mischel, W. *Introduction to Personality* (2nd ed.). New York: Holt, Rinehart, and Winston, 1976.

Nyhan, W. L. Neonatal Screening for Inherited Disease. *New England Journal of Medicine.* 1986, *313*, 43–44.

Pai, A. C. *Foundations of Genetics.* New York: McGraw-Hill, 1974.

Plomin, R., and DeFries, J. C. Genetics and Intelligence: Recent Data. *Intelligence*, 1980, *4*, 15–24.

Pogue-Geile, M. F., and Rose, R. J. Developmental Genetic Studies of Adult Personality. *Developmental Psychology*, 1985, *21*, 547–557.

Rainer, J. D. Genetics and Psychiatry. In A. M. Friedman and H. I. Kaplan (eds.), *Human Behavior: Biological, Psychological, and Sociological Perspectives*, 1–29. New York: Atheneum, 1972.

Reed, E. Genetic Anomolies in Development. In E. M. Hetherington, S. Scarr-Salapatek, and G. M. Siegel (eds.), *Review of Child Development Research*, vol. 4, 59–100. Chicago: University of Chicago Press, 1975.

Richmond-Abbott, M. *Masculine and Feminine.* Reading, Mass.: Addison-Wesley, 1983.

Rose, R. J., and Ditto, W. B. A Developmental-Genetic Analysis of Common Fears from Early Adolescence to Early Adulthood. *Child Development*, 1983, *54*, 361–368.

Rosen, R., and Rosen, L. R. *Human Sexuality.* New York: Knopf, 1981.

Rosenthal, D. *Genetic Theory and Abnormal Behavior.* New York: McGraw-Hill, 1970.

Scarr, S., and Kidd, K. K. Developmental Behavior Genetics. In P. H. Mussen (ed.), *Handbook of Child Psychology* (4th ed.), vol 2, 345–433. New York: Wiley, 1983.

Scarr, S., and McCartney, K. How People Make Their Own Environments: A Theory of Genotype-Environment Effects. *Child Development*, 1983, *54*, 424–435.

Scarr, S., and Weinberg, R. A. Gifted and Talented Children: State of Knowledge and Directions for Research. *American Psychologist*, 1986, *41*, 1147–1153.

———. The Minnesota Adoption Studies: Genetic Differences and Malleability. *Child Development*, 1983, *54*, 260–267.

Scarr-Salapatek, S. Genetics and the Development of Intelligence. In E. M. Hetherington, S. Scarr-Salapatek, and G. M. Siegel (eds.), *Review of Child Development Research*, vol. 4, 1–58. Chicago: University of Chicago Press, 1975.

Scarr-Salapatek, S., and Weinberg, R. A. IQ Test Performance of Black Children Adopted by White Females. *American Psychologist*, 1976, *31*, 727–739.

St. George-Hyslip, P. H. et al. The Genetic Defect Causing Familial Alzheimer's Disease Maps on Chromosome 21. *Science*, 1987, *235*, 885–886.

Schild, S. Psychological Issues in Genetic Counseling of Phenylketonuria. In S. Kessler (ed.), *Genetic Counseling: Psychological Dimensions*, 135–151. New York: Academic Press, 1979.

Schneider, E. L. *The Genetics of Aging.* New York: Plenum, 1978.

Segal, N. L. Monozygotyic and Dizygotic Twins: A Comparative Analysis of Mental Ability Profiles. *Child Development*, 1985, *56*, 1051–1058.

Shaw, M. W. Legal Issues in Medical Genetics. In M. A. Sperber and L. F. Jarvik (eds.), *Psychiatry and Genetics.* New York: Basic Books, 1976.

Sibinga, M. S., and Friedman, C. J. Complexities of Parental Understanding of Phenylketonuria. *Pediatrics*, 1971, *48*, 216–224.

Sirignano, S. W., and Lachman, M. E. Personality Change During the Transition to Parenthood: The Role of Perceived Infant Temperament. *Developmental Psychology*, 1985, *21*, 558–567.

Skeels, H. M. Adult Status of Children with Contrasting Early Life Experiences: A Follow-up Study: *Monographs of the Society for Research in Child Development*, 1966, *31*, no. 3.

Smith, R. M., and Neisworth, J. T. *The Exceptional Child: A Functional Approach*. New York: McGraw-Hill, 1975.

Sperber, M. A. Psychiatry and Metacommunication in Genetic Counseling. In M. A. Sperber and L. F. Jarvik (eds.), *Psychiatry and Genetics: Psychosocial Ethical and Legal Considerations*, 119–128. New York: Basic Books, 1976.

Steinberg, L. Early Temperament Antecedents of Adult Type-A Behavior. *Developmental Psychology*, 1985, *21*, 1171–1180.

Stunkard, A. J., et al. An Adoption Study of Human Obesity. *New England Journal of Medicine*, 1986, *314*, 193–197.

Sue, D., Sue, D. W., and Sue, S. *Understanding Abnormal Behavior*. Boston: Houghton Mifflin, 1981.

Sutton, H. E. *An Introduction to Human Genetics* (3rd ed.). Philadelphia: Saunders, 1980.

Tanzi, R. E., et al. Amyloid Beta Protein Gene: cDNA, mRNA Distribution and Genetic Linkage Near the Alzheimer Locus. *Science*, 1987, *235*, 880–884.

Thomas, A., Chess, S., and Birch, H. G. The Origins of Personality. *Scientific American*, August 1970, *223*, 102–109.

Thompson, R. A., Cicchetti, D., Lamb, M. E., and Malkin, C. Emotional Responses of Down's Syndrome and Normal Infants in the Strange Situation: The Organization of Affective Behavior in Infants. *Developmental Psychology*, 1985, *21*, 828–842.

Vandenberg, S. Hereditary Factors in Normal Personality Traits. In J. Wortis (ed.), *Recent Advances in Biological Psychiatry*, 1967, *9*, 65–105.

Walker, E., and Emory, E. Commentary: Interpretive Bias and Behavioral Genetic Research. *Child Development*, 1985, *56*, 775–779.

Walzer, S., Richmond, J. B., and Gerald, P. S. The Implications of Sharing Genetic Information. In M. A. Sperber and L. F. Jarvik (eds.), *Psychiatry and Genetics: Psychosocial, Ethical, and Legal Considerations*, 147–162. New York: Basic Books, 1976.

Weisfeld, G. E. The Nature-Nurture Issue and the Integrating Concept of Function. In B. B. Wolman (ed.), *Handbook of Developmental Psychology*, 208–230. Englewood Cliffs, N.J.: Prentice-Hall, 1982.

Wells, B. W. P. *Personality and Heredity: An Introduction to Psychogenetics*. London: Longman, 1980.

Whitten, P., and Kagan, J. Jensen's Dangerous Half-Truth. *Psychology Today*, August 1969, *3*, 18.

Willerman, L. *The Psychology of Individual and Group Differences*. San Francisco: Freeman, 1979.

Wilson, R. S. The Louisville Twin Study: Developmental Synchronies in Behavior. *Child Development*, 1983, *54*, 298–316.

Chapter 3

Abel, M., and Clark, A. L. Nutrition. In A. L. Clark and D. D. Affonso with T. R. Harris (eds.). *Childbearing: A Nursing Perspective* (2nd ed.), 175–215. Philadelphia: Davis, 1979.

Affonso, D. D. Psychological Concepts. In A. L. Clark and D. D. Affonso with T. R. Harris (eds.), *Childbearing: A Nursing Perspective* (2nd ed.), 609–630. Philadelphia: Davis, 1979.

Annis, L. F. *The Child Before Birth*. Ithaca, N.Y.: Cornell University Press, 1978.

Apgar, V. A Proposal for a New Method of Evaluation of the Newborn Infant. *Current Researches in Anesthesia and Analgesia*, 1953, *32*, 260–267.

Apgar, V., and Beck, J. *Is My Baby All Right?* New York: Pocket Books, 1974.

Apgar, V., Holaday, D. A., James, L. S., Weisbrot, I. M., and Berien, C. Evaluation of the Newborn Infant: Second Report. *Journal of the American Psychological Association*, 1958, *168*, 1985–1988.

Balinsky, B. I. *An Introduction to Embryology* (3rd ed.). Philadelphia: Saunders, 1970.

Berezin, N. *The Gentle Birth Book*. New York: Simon and Schuster, 1980.

Birch, H. G. Functional Effects of Fetal Malnutrition. *Hospital Practice*, March 1971, 134–148.

———. Health and the Education of Socially Disadvantaged Children (1968). In H. Bee (ed.), *Social Issues in Developmental Psychology*, 269–291. New York: Harper and Row, 1976.

Birch, H. G., and Gussow, J. D. *Disadvantaged Children*. New York: Harcourt, Brace, and World, 1970.

Blackeslee, S. Fetus Returned to Womb Following Surgery. *New York Times*, October 7, 1986, C1.

Bottoms, S. F. Rosen, M. G., and Sokol, R. J. The Increase in Cesarean Birth Rate. *New England Journal of Medicine*, March 6, 1980, pp. 559–563.

Brackbill, Y. Lasting Effects of Obstetrical Medication on Children. In J. Belsky (ed.), *In the Beginning*, 50–55. New York: Columbia University Press, 1982.

———. Obstetrical Medication and Infant Behavior. In J. D. Osofsky (ed.), *Handbook of Infant Development*, 76–125. New York: Wiley, 1979.

Brazelton, T. B. *On Becoming a Family: The Growth of Attachment*. New York: Delacorte, 1981.

———. Effects of Prenatal Drugs on the Behavior of the Neonate. *American Journal of Psychiatry*, 1970, *126*, 95–100.

Butler, N., Goldstein, H., Ross, K. Smoking in Pregnancy and Subsequent Child Development. *British Journal of Medicine*, 1972, *4*, 573–575.

Caputo, D. V., and Mandell, W. Consequences of Low Birth Weight. *Developmental Psychology*, 1970, *3*, 363–383.

Cave, V. G. The Role of Immunoglobulins in the Early Diagnosis of Congenital Syphilis. In L. Nicholas (ed.), *Sexually Transmitted Diseases*. Springfield, Ill.: Thomas, 1973.

Charles, A. G., Norr, K. L., Block, C. R., et al. Obstetric and Psychological Effects of Psychoprophylactic Preparation for Childbirth. *American Journal of Obstetrics and Gynecology*, 1978, *44*, 131.

Chasnoff, I. J., Burns, W. J., Schnoll, S. H., and Burns, K. Cocaine Use in Pregnancy. *New England Journal of Medicine*, September 12, 1985, *313*, 666–669.

Chervenak, F. A., Isaacson, G., and Mahoney, M. J. Advances in the Diagnosis of Fetal Defects. *New England Journal of Medicine*, July 31, 1986, *315*, 305–307.

Clark, A. L. Applications of Physiological Perspectives. In A. L. Clark and D. D. Affonso with T. R. Harris (eds.), *Childbearing: A Nursing Perspective* (2nd ed.), 277–322. Philadelphia: Davis, 1979.

Clarren, S. K., and Smith, D. W. The Fetal Alcohol Syndrome, *New England Journal of Medicine*, 1978, *298*, 1063–1067.

Cogan, R. Effects of Childbirth Preparation. *Clinical Obstetrics and Gynecology*, 1980, *23*, 1–14.

Copans, S. A. Human Prenatal Effects: Methodological Problems and Some Suggested Solutions. *Merrill-Palmer Quarterly*, 1974, *20*, 43–52.

Corey, L., and Spear, P. G. Infections with Herpes Simplex Viruses. *New England Journal of Medicine*, January 23, 1986, *314*, 749–754.

Counseling and Personnel Services Clearinghouse. *Teenage Pregnancy Factsheet*, Winter 1982, Eric/Caps.

Cox, F. D. *Human Intimacy: Marriage, the Family, and Its Meaning* (3rd ed.). St. Paul: West, 1984.

Curtis, H. *Biology* (2nd ed.). New York: Worth, 1975.

Dakshinamurti, K., and Stephens, M. Pyridoxine Deficit in Neonatal Rats. *Journal of Clinical Neurology*, 1969, *16*, 1515–1522.

Davies, R., Butler, N., and Goldstein, H. *From Birth to Seven*. London: Clowes, 1972.

DeHirsch, K., Langford, J., and Jansky, W. S. Comparison Between Premature and Maturely Born Children at Three Age Levels. *American Journal of Orthopsychiatry*, 1966, *36*, 61–78.

Drillien, C. M. *The Growth and Development of the Prematurely Born Infant*. Edinburgh: Livingstone, 1964.

Drugs and Pregnancy. Washington, D.C.: U.S. Department of Health, Education, and Welfare, October 1978, HEW pub. no. (FDA) 79–3083.

Eichorn, D. H. Physical Development: Current Foci of Research. In J. Osofsky (ed.), *Handbook of Infant Development*, 253–283. New York: Wiley, 1979.

Fielding, J. E. Smoking: Health Effects and Control. *New England Journal of Medicine*, August 22, 1985, *313*, 491–498.

Fitzgerald, H. E., Strommen, E. A., and McKinney, J. P. *Developmental Psychology: The Infant and Young Child* (rev. ed.). Homewood, Ill.: Dorsey, 1982.

Fogel, A. *Infancy: Infant, Family, and Society*. St. Paul: West, 1984.

Furey, E. M. The Effects of Alcohol on the Fetus. *Exceptional Children*, September 1982, *49*, 30–34.

Gleicher, N. Cesarean Section Rates in the United States. *Journal of the American Medical Association*, December 21, 1984, *252*, 3273–3277.

Goldstein, M. Parenthood After 30. *Long Island*, November 1980, 20–24, 64.

Gorsuch, R. L., and Key, M. A. Abnormalities of Pregnancy as a Function of Anxiety and Life Stress. *Psychosomatic Medicine*, 1974, *36*, 352–362.

Greenlund, S., Olsen, J., Rachootin, P., and Pedersen, G. T. Effects of Electronic Monitoring on Rates of Early Neonatal Death, Low Apgar Score, and Cesarean Section. *ACTA OBSTET. GYNCOL SCAND.*, 1985, *64*, 75.

Hanson, J. W. Unpublished manuscript, cited in *The Child Before Birth* by L. F. Annis. Ithaca, N.Y.: Cornell University Press, 1978.

Hanson, J. W., Jones, K. L., and Smith, D. W. Fetal Alcohol Syndrome: Experience with 41 Patients. *Journal of the American Medical Association*, 1976, *235*, 1458–1466.

Harlap, S., and Shiono, P. Alcohol and Incidence of Spontaneous Abortions in the First and Second Trimester. *The Lancet*, July 26, 1980, pp. 173–176.

Herbst, A. L. Diethylstilbestrol Exposure: 1984. *New England Journal of Medicine*, November 29, 1984, *311*, 1433–1435.

Hooker, D. *The Prenatal Origin of Behavior*. Lawrence: University of Kansas Press, 1952.

Householder, J., Hatcher, R., Burns, W., and Chanoff, I. Infants Born to Narcotic-Addicted Mothers. *Psychological Bulletin*, 1982, *2*, 453–468.

Hutchins, F. L., Kendall, N., and Rubino, J. Experience with Teenage Pregnancy. *Obstetrics and Gynecology*, July 1979, *54*, 1–6.

Jacobson, J. L., Jacobson, S. W., Fein, G., Schwartz, P. M., and Dowler, J. K. Prenatal Exposure to an Environmental Toxin: A Test of the Multiple Effects Model. *Developmental Psychology*, 1984, *20*, 523–533.

Jones, K. L., Smith, D. W., Streissguth, A. P., and Myrianthopoulus, N. Outcomes in Offspring of Chronic Alcoholic Women. *The Lancet*, 1974, *1*, 1076–1078.

Kline, J., Shrout, P., Stern, Z., Susser, and Warburton, D. Drinking During Pregnancy and Spontaneous Abortion. *The Lancet*, July 26, 1980, pp. 176–180.

Knothe, H., and Dette, G. A. Antibiotics and Pregnancy: Toxicity and Teratogenicity. *Infection*, 1985, *49*, 13.

Knox, D. *Human Sexuality: The Search for Understanding*. St. Paul: West, 1984.

Kopp, C. B. Risk Factors in Development in P. H. Mussen (ed.). *Handbook of Child Psychology* (4th ed.). New York: John Wiley, 1983, 1081–1188.

Kopp, C. B., and Parmelee, A. H. Prenatal and Perinatal Influences on Infant Behavior. In J. D. Osofsky (ed.), *Handbook of Infant Development*, 29–75. New York: Wiley, 1979.

Lamaze, F. *Painless Childbirth*. Chicago: Regnery, 1970.

Landesman-Dwyer, S., and Emanuel, I. (1979). Smoking During Pregnancy. In J. Belsky (ed.), *In the Beginning*, 37–45. New York: Columbia University Press, 1982.

Lawson, K. R. Auditory Responsiveness in Full-Term and Preterm Infants. *Developmental Psychology*, 1984, *20*, 120–127.

Leavitt, F. *Drugs and Behavior*. Philadelphia: Saunders, 1974.

Leboyer, F. *Birth Without Violence*. New York: Knopf, 1975.

Leifer, M. Psychological Changes Accompanying Pregnancy and Motherhood. *Genetic Psychology Monographs*, 1977, *95*, 55–96.

Lenz, W. Malformations Caused by Drugs in Pregnancy. *American Journal of Diseases of Children*, 1966, *112*, 99–106.

Lester, B. M., Heidelise, A., and Brazelton, T. B. Regional Obstetric Anesthesia and Newborn Behavior: A Reanalysis Toward Synergistic Effects. *Child Development*, 1982, *53*, 687–692.

Lewis, M., Bartels, B., Campbell, H., and Goldberg, S. Individual Differences in Attention. *American Journal of the Diseases of Children*, 1967, *113*, 461–465.

March of Dimes (Robert Matousek, Statistician). Personal correspondence concerning estimates of number of pregnant women who smoke, 1985.

March of Dimes. *Drug, Alcohol, Tobacco Abuse During Pregnancy*. White Plains, N.Y.: March of Dimes, 1983a.

———. *Be Good to Your Baby Before It Is Born*. White Plains, N.Y.: March of Dimes, 1983b.

Martin, J. C. Drugs of Abuse During Pregnancy: Effects upon Offspring Structure and Function. *Journal of Women in Culture and Society (Signs)*. Winter 1976, *2*, 357–368.

Mascola, L., Pelosi, R., Blount, J. H., Binkin, N. J., Harris, C. M., Jarman, B., Landon, G. P., and McNeil, B. J. Congenital Syphilis. *Journal of the American Medical Association*, October 5, 1984, *252*, 1719–1723.

McIntosh, I. D. Smoking and Pregnancy: Attributable Risks and Public Health Implications. *Canadian Journal of Public Health*, March–April, 1984, *75*, 141–148.

Melzack, R. The Myth of Painless Childbirth. *Pain*, 1984, *19*, 321.

Miller, R. W. Susceptibility of the Fetus and Child to Chemical Pollutants. *Science*, 1974, *184*, 812–813.

Mills, J. L., Braubard, B. I., Harley, E. E., Rhoads, G. G., and Berendes, H. W. Maternal Alcohol Consumption and Birth Weight: How Much Drinking During Pregnancy Is Safe? *Journal of the American Medical Association*, October 12, 1984, *252*, 1875–1879.

Murray, S. F., Dolby, R. M., Nation, R. L., and Thomas, D. B. Effects of Epidural Anesthesia on Newborns and Their Mothers. *Child Development*, 1981, *52*, 71–82.

National Center for Clinical Infant Programs. *Infants Can't Wait: The Numbers*. Washington, D.C.: National Center for Clinical Infant Programs, 1986.

National Center for Health Statistics. *Births and Deaths, 1984*. Washington, D.C.: U.S. Department of Health and Human Services, 1984.

National Center for Health Statistics. *Advance Report of Final Natality Statistics, 1985*. Vol. 36, number 4. Washington, D.C.: U.S. Department of Health and Human Services, 1987.

Nelson, N. M., Murray, W. E., Saroj, S., Bennett, K. J., Milner, R., and Sackett, D. L. A

Randomized Clinical Trial of the Leboyer Approach to Childbirth. *New England Journal of Medicine*, March 20, 1980, *302*, 655–660.

New York State Department of Health. *DES: The Wonder Drug Women Should Wonder About.* New York: New York State Department of Health, 1979.

Nielsen, T. F. Cesarean Section: A Controversial Feature of Modern Obstetric Practice. *Gynecological Obstetrical Investigations*, 1986, *57*, 21.

Obstetrical and Gynecological Survey. Comment on T. F. Nielsen's Cesarean Section: A Controversial Feature of Modern Obstetric Practice, 1986, *17*, 633–634.

Orenberg, C. L. *DES: The Complete Story.* New York: St. Martin's Press, 1981.

Ortho Diagnostic Systems. *What Every Rh Negative Woman Should Know About RhoGAM.* Raritan, N.J.: Ortho Diagnostic Systems, 1981.

Ounsted, M., Moar, V. A., and Scott, A. A. Risk Factors Associated with Small-for-Dates and Large-for-Dates Infants. *British Journal of Obstetrics and Gynecology*, 1985, *92*, 226.

Peterson, G. H., Mehl, L. E., and Leiderman, P. T. The Role of Some Birth-Related Variables in Father Attachment. *American Journal of Orthopsychiatry*, 1979, *49*, 330–339.

Pinching, A. J., and Jeffries, D. AIDS and HTLV-III/LAV Infection: Consequences for Obstetrics and Perinatal Medicine. *British Journal of Obstetrics and Gynecology*, 1985, *92*, 1211.

Planned Parenthood. *Daughters of DES Mothers.* New York: Planned Parenthood Federation of America, 1979.

Rhodes, A. J. Virus Infections and Congenital Malformations. *Papers Delivered at the First Conference on Congenital Malformations*, 106–116. Philadelphia: Lippincott, 1961.

Ricciuti, H. N. Adverse Environmental and Nutritional Influences on Mental Development: A Perspective. Paper delivered at the American Dietetic Association, Atlanta, 1980.

Rice, R. D. Neurophysiological Development in Premature Infants Following Stimulation. *Developmental Psychology*, 1977, *13*, 69–76.

Rosenberg, L., Mitchell, A. A., Parsells, J., Pashayan, H., Lovik, C., and Shapiro, S. Lack of Relation of Oral Clefts to Diazepan Use During Pregnancy. *New England Journal of Medicine*, November 24, 1983, *309*, 1185–1188.

Rugh, R., and Shettles, L. B. *From Contraception to Birth: The Drama of Life's Beginnings.* New York: Harper and Row, 1971.

Saco-Pollitt, C. Birth in the Peruvian-Andes: Physical and Behavioral Consequences in the Neonate. *Child Development*, 1981, *52*, 839–846.

Sameroff, A. J., and Chandler, M. J. Reproductive Risk and the Continuum of Caretaker Causality. In F. D. Horowitz (ed.), *Review of Child Development Research*, vol. 4. Chicago: University of Chicago Press, 1975.

Sande, M. A. Transmission of AIDS: The Case Against Casual Contagion. *New England Journal of Medicine*, February 6, 1986, *314*, 380–382.

Scarr-Salapatek, S., and Williams, M. L. The Effects of Early Stimulation on Low Birth Weight Infants. *Child Development*, 1973, *44*, 94–101.

Science News. Alcohol and Pregnancy. *Science News*, March 26, 1977, p. 12.

Self, P. A., and Horowitz, F. D. The Behavioral Assessment of the Neonate: An Overview. In J. Osofsky (ed.). *Handbook of Infant Development*, 126–165. New York: Wiley, 1979.

Simkin, P., Whalley, J., and Keppler, A. *Pregnancy, Childbirth, and the Newborn.* Deephaven, Minn.: Meadowbrook Books, 1984.

Singer, S., and Hilgard, H. R. *The Biology of People.* San Francisco: Freeman, 1978.

Solkoff, N., Jaffe, S., Weintraub, D., and Blase, B. Effects of Handling on the Subsequent Development of Premature Babies. *Developmental Psychology*, 1969, *1*, 765–768.

Sontag, L. W. War and the Fetal-Maternal Relationship. *Marriage and Family Living*, 1944, *6*, 3–4.

———. The Significance of Fetal Environmental Differences. *American Journal of Obstetrics and Gynecology*, 1941, *42*, 996–1003.

Stagno, S., and Whitley, R. J. Herpes Simplex Virus and Varicella-Zoster Virus Infections. *New England Journal of Medicine*, November 21, 1985, *313*, 1327–1329.

Stechler, G., and Halton, A. Prenatal Influences on Human Development. In B. B. Wolman (ed.), *Handbook of Developmental Psychology*, 175–189. Englewood Cliffs, N.J.: Prentice-Hall, 1982.

Stevenson, R. E. *The Fetus and Newly Born Infant: Influences of the Prenatal Environment.* St. Louis: Mosby, 1973.

Streissguth, A. P. Maternal Alcoholism and the Outcome of Pregnancy (1977). In J. Belsky (ed.), *In the Beginning*, 45–50. New York: Columbia University Press, 1982.

Streissguth, A. P., Martin, D. C., Barr, H. M., Sandman, B. M., Kirchner, G. L., and Darby, B. L. Intrauterine Alcohol and Nicotine Exposure: Attention and Reaction Time in Four-Year-Old Children. *Developmental Psychology*, 1984, *20*, 533–542.

Taina, E., Hanninen, P., and Gronroos, M. Viral Infections in Pregnancy. *ACTA OBSTET. SCAND.*, 1985, *64*, 167.

Thompson, M. Estimate of Opiate-Addicted Births. National Institute on Drug Abuse: Services Research Branch Notes, March 2–3, 1979, cited in F. Suffet, C. Bryce-Buchanon, and R. Brotman, Pregnant Addicts in a Comprehensive Care Program: Results of a Follow-up Survey. *American Journal of Orthopsychiatry*, 1981, *51*, 297–307.

Thompson, W. R., and Grusek, J. A. Studies of Early Experience. In P. H. Mussen (ed.), *Carmichael's Manual of Child Development.* New York: Wiley, 1970.

Trevarthen, C. Descriptive Analysis of Infant Communicative Behavior. In H. R. Schaffer (ed.), *Studies of Mother-Infant Interaction.* London: Academic Press, 1977.

Trotter, R. J. Born Too Soon. *Science News*, October 11, 1980, *118*, 234–235.

———. The New Face of Birth. *Science News.* September 15, 1975, *113*, 106–108.

Trulson, M. E. LSD: Visions or Nightmares. New York: Chelsea House, 1985.

Tucker, T., and Bing, E. *Prepared Childbirth.* New Canaan, Conn.: Tobey, 1975.

U.S. Department of Health and Human Services. *Prenatal Care.* Rockville, Md.: U.S. Department of Health and Human Services, Public Health Services, 1983, DHHS pub. no. 83–5070.

———. *Child Health and Human Development: An Evaluation and Assessment of the State of the Science.* Washington, D.C.: National Institute of Health, NIH pub. no. 82–2304, 1981a.

———. *The Health Consequences of Smoking for Women: A Report to the Surgeon General.* Washington, D.C.: U.S. Department of Health and Human Services, 1981b.

U.S. Department of Health, Education, and Welfare (HEW). *Smoking and Health: A Report of the Surgeon General.* Washington, D.C.: DHEW, no. 79–50066, 1979.

University of California. *Berkeley Wellness Letter*, vol. 1, no. 5, Caffeine, 1985.

Volpe, E. P. *Patient in the Womb.* Macon, Ga.: Mercer University Press, 1984.

Vorhees, C. V. and Mullnow, E. Behavioral Teratogenesis: Long-Term Influences on Behavior from Early Exposure to Environmental Agents in J. Osofsky (ed.) *Handbook of Infant Development* (2nd ed.). New York: John Wiley, 1987, 913–971.

Wenar, C. *Psychopathology from Infancy Through Adolescence.* New York: Random House, 1982.

Whitney, E. N., and Hamilton, E. M. N. *Understanding Nutrition* (3rd ed.). St. Paul: West, 1984.

Williams, J. H. *Psychology of Women: Behavior in a Biosocial Context.* New York: Norton, 1977.

Wilson, J. G. *Environment and Birth Defects.* New York: Academic Press, 1973.

Wilson, L. M. K., and Waterhouse, J. A. H. Obstetric Ultrasound and Childhood Malignancies. *The Lancet,* 1984, 997, 2.

Winick, M. *Malnutrition and Brain Damage.* New York: Oxford University Press, 1976.

Young, D. *Changing Childbirth: Family Birth in the Hospital.* Rochester, N.Y.: Childbirth Graphics, 1982.

Chapter 4

Alley, T. R. Headshape and the Perception of Cuteness. *Developmental Psychology,* 1981, *17,* 650–655.

Anastasi, A. *Psychological Testing* (4th ed.). New York: Macmillan, 1976.

Antell, S. E., Caron, A. J., and Myers, R. S. Perception of Relational Invariants by Newborns. *Developmental Psychology,* 1985, *21,* 942–948.

Aslin, R. N. Visual and Auditory Development in Infancy in J. Osofsky (ed.). *Handbook of Infant Development* (2nd ed.). New York: John Wiley, 1987, 5–98.

Aslin, R. N., and Dumais, S. T. Binocular Vision in Infants: A Review and a Theoretical Framework. In L. Lipsitt and H. Reese (eds.), *Advances in Child Development and Behavior.* New York: Academic Press, 1980.

Aslin, R. N., Pisoni, D. B., and Jusczyk, P. W. Auditory Development and Speech Perception in Infancy. In P. H. Mussen (ed.), *Handbook of Child Development* (4th ed.), vol. 2, 573–689. New York: Wiley, 1983.

Ault, R. *Children's Cognitive Development.* New York: Oxford University Press, 1977.

Azrin, N. H., and Foxx, R. *Toilet Training in Less Than a Day.* New York: Pocket Books, 1976.

Ball, W., and Tronick, E. Infant Responses to Impending Collision: Optical and Real. *Science,* 1971, *171,* 818–820.

Banks, M. S., Aslin, R. N., and Letson, R. D. Sensitive Period for the Development of Human Binocular Vision. *Science,* 1975, *190,* 675–677.

Banks, M. S., and Salapatek, P. Infant Visual Perception. In P. H. Mussen (ed.), *Handbook of Child Development* (4th ed.), vol. 2, 435–573. New York: Wiley, 1983.

Barrera, M. E., and Maurer, D. Recognition of Mother's Photographed Face by the Three-Month-Old Infant. *Child Development,* 1981, *52,* 714–716.

Bayley, N. Development of Mental Abilities. In P. H. Mussen (ed.), *Carmichael's Manual of Child Psychology.* New York: Wiley, 1970.

———. *The Bayley Scales of Infant Development.* New York: Psychological Corp., 1969.

Bayley, N., and Oden, M. H. The Maintenance of Intellectual Ability in Gifted Adults. *Journal of Gerontology,* 1955, *10,* 91–107.

Bee, H. *Social Issues in Developmental Psychology* (2nd ed.). New York: Harper and Row, 1978.

Bell, S. M., and Ainsworth, M. D. Infant Crying and Maternal Responsiveness. *Child Development,* 1972, *43,* 1171–1190.

Belsky, J., and Most, R. K. Infant Exploration and Play. In J. Belsky (ed.), *In the Beginning: Readings on Infancy,* 109–121. New York: Columbia University Press, 1982.

Berg, W. K. Adkinson, C. D., and Strock, B. D. Duration and Frequency of Periods of Alertness in the Newborn. *Developmental Psychology,* 1973, *9,* 434.

Berg, W. K., and Berg, K. M. Psychophysiological Development in Infancy: State, Sensory Functioning, and Attention. In J. Osofsky (ed.), *Handbook of Infant Development,* 283–344. New York: Wiley, 1979.

Birren, J. E., Kinney, D. K., Schaie, K. W., and Woodruff, D. S. *Developmental Psychology: A Life-Span Approach.* Boston: Houghton Mifflin, 1981.

Blass, E. M., Ganchrow, J. R., and Steiner, J. E. Classical Conditioning in Newborn Humans 2–48 Hours of Age. *Infant Behavior and Development,* 1984, *7,* 223–235.

Block, J. H. Assessing Sex Differences: Issues, Problems, and Pitfalls. *Merrill-Palmer Quarterly,* 1976, *22,* 283–308.

Bond, E. Form Perception in the Infant. *Psychological Bulletin,* 1972, *77,* 225–245.

Bornstein, M. H. Infants Are Trichromats. *Journal of Experimental Child Psychology,* 1976, *21,* 425–445.

———. Qualities of Color Vision in Infancy. *Journal of Experimental Child Psychology,* 1975, *19,* 401–419.

Bornstein, M. H., and Benasich, A. A. Infant Habituation: Assessments of Individual Differences and Short-Term Reliability at Five Months. *Child Development,* 1986, *57,* 87–99.

Bornstein, M. H., and Sigman, M. D. Continuity in Mental Development from Infancy. *Child Development,* 1986, *57,* 251–274.

Bower, T. G. R. *A Primer of Infant Development.* San Francisco: Freeman, 1977.

———. *Principles of Infant Development.* San Francisco: Freeman, 1977.

———. The Object in the World of the Infant. *Scientific American,* 1971, *225,* 30–38, offprint no. 539.

———. The Visual World of Infants. *Scientific American,* 1966, *215,* 80–92.

Bower, T. G. R., Broughton, J. M., and Moore, M. K. Infant Response to Approaching Objects: An Indication of Response to Distal Variation. *Perception and Psychophysics,* 1970, *9,* 193–196.

Bower, T. G. R., and Wishart, J. G. The Effects of Motor Skill on Object Permanence. *Cognition,* 1972, *1,* 165–172.

Bradley, R. H., and Caldwell, B. The HOME Inventory and Family Demographics. *Developmental Psychology,* 1984, *20,* 315–321.

Brazelton, T. B. *On Becoming a Family: The Growth of Attachment.* New York: Delacorte, 1981.

Brierly, J. *The Growing Brain.* Windsor, Eng.: NFER, 1976.

Brody, L. R. Visual Short-Term Recall Memory in Infancy. *Child Development,* 1981, *52,* 242–250.

Butterfield, E. C., and Siperstein, G. N. Influence of Contingent Auditory Stimulation upon Non-Nutritional Suckle. In J. F. Bosma (ed.), *Third Symposium on Oral Sensation and Perception: The Mouth of the Infant.* Springfield, Ill.: Thomas, 1972.

Campos, J., Langer, A., and Krowtiz, A. Cardiac Responses on the Visual Cliff in Prelocomotor Human Infants. *Science,* 1970, *170,* 196–197.

Carew, J. V., Chan, I., and Halfar, C. Observed Intellectual Competence and Tested Intelligence: Their Roots in the Young Child's Transactions and His Environment (1975). In S. Cohen and T. J. Comiskey (ed.), *Child Development: Contemporary Perspectives,* 29–44. Itasca, Ill.: Peacock, 1977.

Cernoch, J. M., and Porter, R. H. Recognition of Axillary Odors by Infants. *Child Development,* 1985, *56,* 1593–1598.

Cherry, L. and Lewis, M. The Pre-School Teacher-Child Dyad: Sex Differences in Verbal Interaction. *Child Development,* 1976, *46,* 532–535.

Clarke, A. M., and Clarke, A D. B. *Early Experience: Myth and Evidence.* New York: Free Press, 1976.

Cohen, L. B. Our Developing Knowledge of Infant Perception and Cognition. *American Psychologist,* 1979, *34,* 894–899.

Cohen, L. B., Deloache, J. S., and Strauss, M. S. Infant Visual Perception. In J. Osofsky (ed.), *Handbook of Infant Development,* 393–439. New York: Wiley, 1979.

Condon, W. S., and Sander, L. W. Neonate Movement Is Synchronized with Adult Speech: Interactional Participation and Language Acquisition. *SCIENCE*, 1974, *183*, 99–101.

Condry, J. G., and Condry, S. Sex Differences: A Study of the Eye of the Beholder. *Child Development*, 1976, *47*, 812–819.

Connolly, K., and Stratton, P. An Exploration of Some Parameters Affecting Classical Conditioning in the Neonate. *Child Development*, 1969, *40*, 431–441.

Cratty, B. *Perceptual and Motor Development in Infancy and Childhood.* New York: Macmillan, 1970. (2nd ed.) 1979.

Dasen, P., and Heron A. Cross-Cultural Tests of Piaget's Theory. In H. C. Triandis and A. Heron (eds.), *Handbook of Cross-Cultural Psychology*, vol. 4, 295–343. Boston: Allyn and Bacon, 1981.

Dayton, G., Jones, M., Aiu, P., Rawson, R., Steele, B., and Rose, M. Developmental Study of Coordinated Eye Movements in the Human Infant, I: Visual Acuity in the Newborn Human. Study Based on Induced Optokinetic Nystagmus Recorded by Electro-Oculography. *Archives of Ophthalmology*, 1964, *71*, 865–870.

DeCasper, A. J., and Fifer, W. P. Of Human Bonding: Newborns Prefer Their Mothers' Voices. *Science*, 1980, *208*, 1174–1176.

DeFrain, J., Taylor, J., and Ernst, L. *Coping with Sudden Infant Death.* Lexington, Mass.: D. C. Heath, 1982.

Dennis, W. Causes of Retardation Among Institutional Children: Iran. *Journal of Genetic Psychology*, 1960, *96*, 47–59.

Dennis, W., and Dennis, M. G. Cradles and Cradling Customs of the Pueblo Indians. *American Anthrolopogist*, 1940, *42*, 107–115.

Dennis, W., and Najarian, P. How Reversible Are the Effects? In S. J. Hutt and C. Hull (eds.), *Early Human Development*, 274–288. London: Oxford University Press, 1973.

———. Infant Development Under Environmental Handicap. *Psychological Monographs*, 1957, *71*, 1–13.

Desor, J. A., Maller, O., and Turner, R. E. Taste in Acceptance of Sugars by Human Infants. *Journal of Comparative and Physiological Psychology*, 1973, *84*, 496–501.

Diamond, A. Development of the Ability to Use Recall to Guide Action, as Indicated by Infants' Performance on AB. *Child Development*, 1985, *56*, 868–883.

Diamond, N. Cognitive Theory. In B. B. Wolman (ed.), *Handbook of Developmental Psychology*, 3–23. Englewood Cliffs, N.J.: Prentice-Hall, 1982.

DiFranco, D., Muir, D., and Dodwell, P. Reaching in Very Young Infants. *Perception*, 1978, *7*, 385–392.

Dobbing, J. Human Brain Development and Its Vulnerability (1975). In R. L. Smart and M. S. Smart (eds.), *Readings in Child Development and Relationships* (2nd ed.), 49–61. New York: Macmillan, 1977.

Dobson, V., and Teller, D. Y. Visual Acuity in Human Infants: A Review and Comparison of Behavioral and Electrophysiological Stimulation. *Vision Research*, 1978, *18*, 1469–1484.

Dunst, C. J., Brooks, P. H., and Doxsey, P. A. Characteristics of Hiding Places and the Transition to Stage 4 Performance in Object Permanence Tests. *Developmental Psychology*, 1982, *18*, 671–681.

Dworetzsky, J. P. *Introduction to Child Development* (2nd ed.). St. Paul: West, 1984.

Eichenwald, H. F., and Fry, P. G. Nutrition and Learning. *Science*, 1969, *163*, 644–648.

Eichorn, D. H. Physical Development: Current Foci of Research. In J. Osofsky (ed.), *Handbook of Infant Development*, 253–283. New York: Wiley, 1979.

Eimas, P. D. Speech Perception in Infancy. In L. B. Cohen and P. Salapatek (eds.), *Infant Perception*, vol. 2. New York: Academic Press, 1975.

Eisenberg, R. B. The Organization of Auditory Behavior. *Journal of Speech and Hearing Research*, 1970, *13*, 461–464.

Elardo, R., Bradley, R., and Caldwell, B. M. A Longitudinal Study of the Relation of Infants' Home Environments to Language Development at Age Three. *Child Development*, 1977, *48*, 595–603.

———. The Relation of Infants' Home Environments to Mental Test Performance from Six to Thirty-Six Months: A Longitudinal Analysis. *Child Development*, 1975, *46*, 71–76.

Engen, T., Lipsitt, L. P., and Peck, M. B. Ability of Newborn Infants to Discriminate Sapid Substances. *Developmental Psychology*, 1973, *10*, 741–744.

Fagen, J. F. Infants' Long Term Memory for Stimulus Color. *Developmental Psychology*, 1984, *20*, 435–441.

———. Infant Recognition Memory: Studies in Forgetting. *Child Development*, 1977, *48*, 68–78.

———. Infants' Delayed Recognition Memory and Forgetting. *Journal of Experimental Child Psychology*, 1973, *16*, 424–450.

Fagot, B. I. The Influence of Sex of Child on Parental Reactions to Toddler Children. *Child Development*, 1978, *49*, 459–465.

Fagot, B. I., Hagan, R., Leinbach, M. D., and Kronsberg, S. Differential Reactions to Assertive and Communicative Acts of Toddler Boys and Girls. *Child Development*, 1985, *56*, 1499–1505.

Fantz, R. L. Pattern Vision in Newborn Infants. *Science*, 1963, *140*, 296–297.

———. The Origin of Form Perception. *Scientific American*, May 1961, 16–21.

Fantz, R. L., and Miranda, S. B. Newborn Infant's Attention to Form of Contour. *Child Development*, 1975, *46*, 224–228.

Feldman, J. F., Brody, N., and Miller, S. A. Sex Differences in Non-Elicited Neonatal Behaviors. *Merrill-Palmer Quarterly*, 1980, *26*, 63–73.

Field, T., Woodson, R., Greenberg, R., and Cohen, D. Discrimination and Imitation of Facial Expressions by Neonates. *Science*, 1982, *218*, 179–181.

Fitzgerald, H. E., and Brackbill, Y. Classical Conditioning in Infancy: Development and Constraints. *Psychological Bulletin*, 1976, *83*, 353–376.

Flavell, J. H. *Cognitive Development.* Englewood Cliffs, N.J.: Prentice-Hall, 1977. Second edition 1985.

Fogel, A. *Infancy: Infant, Family, and Society.* St. Paul: West, 1984.

Friedman, S., and Carpenter, G. C. Visual Response Decrement as a Function of Age of Human Newborn. *Child Development*, 1971, *42*, 1967–1973.

Gibson, E. J., and Walk, R. D. The "Visual Cliff." *Scientific American*, April 1960, *202*, 64–71.

Gratch, G. The Development of Thought and Language in Infancy. In J. Osofsky (ed.), *Handbook of Infant Development*, 439–461. New York: Wiley, 1979.

Gratch, G., Appel, K. J., Evans, W. F., LeCompte, G. K., and Wright, N. K. Piaget's Stage 4 Object Concept Error: Evidence of Forgetting or Object Conception? *Child Development*, 1974, *45*, 71–77.

Griffin, C. C., Popkin, B. M., and Spicer, D. S. Infant Formula Promotion and Infant-Feeding Practices, Bicol Region, Philippines. *American Journal of Public Health*, 1984, *74*, 992–997.

Guntheroth, W. G. *Crib Death: Sudden Infant Death Syndrome.* Mount Kisco, N.Y.: Futura.

Haith, M. M. *Rules Babies Look By.: The Organization of Newborn Visual Activity.* Hillsdale, N.J.: Erlbaum, 1980.

———. The Response of the Human Newborn to Visual Movement. *Journal of Experimental Child Psychology*, 1966, *3*, 235–243.

Hamill, P. V. V. *NCHS Growth Curves for Children*. Vital and Health Statistics, Series 11, Data from the National Health Survey, no. 165. Washington, D.C.: U.S. Government Printing Office (DWEH no. 78–1650), 1977.

Hamilton, E. M. N., Whitney, E. N. *Nutrition: Concepts and Controversies* (2nd ed.). St. Paul: West, 1982.

Hamilton, E. M. N., Whitney, E. N., and Sizer, F. S. *Nutrition: Concepts and Controversies* (3rd ed.). St. Paul: West, 1985.

Hofsten, C. von. Eye-Hand Coordination in the Newborn. *Developmental Psychology*, 1982, *18*, 450–462.

Hunt, J. McV. *Intelligence and Experience*. New York: Ronald, 1961.

Hutt, S. J., and Hutt, C. R. *Early Human Development*. London: Oxford University Press, 1973.

Illingworth, R. S. *The Development of the Infant and Young Child: Normal and Abnormal*. Edinburgh: Livingstone, 1974.

Intons-Peterson, M. J., and Reddel, M. What Do People Ask About a Neonate? *Developmental Psychology*, 1984, *20*, 358–360.

Jensen, K. Differential Reaction to Taste and Temperature Stimuli in Newborn Infants. *Genetic Psychology Monographs*, 1932, *12*, 363–479.

Kagan, J. Overview: Perspectives on Human Infancy. In J. Osofsky (ed.), *Handbook of Infant Development*, 1–29. New York: Wiley, 1979a.

———. The Form of Early Development (1979b). In P. H. Mussen, J. J. Conger, and J. Kagan, *Readings in Child and Adolescent Psychology: Contemporary Perspectives*, 18–22. New York: Harper and Row, 1980b.

Kalat, J. W. *Biological Psychology*. Belmont, Calif.: Wadsworth, 1981.

Kaye, H. The Conditioned Babkin Reflex in Human Newborns. *Psychonomic Science*, 1965, *2*, 287–288.

Kearsley, R. B. The Newborn's Response to Auditory Stimuli: A Demonstration of Orientation and Defensive Behavior. *Child Development*, 1973, *44*, 582–590.

Kisilevsky, B. S., and Muir, D. W. Neonatal Habituation and Dishabituation to Tactile Stimulation During Sleep. *Developmental Psychology*, 1984, *20*, 367–374.

Korner, A. F. Sex Differences in Newborns with Special Reference to Differences in the Organization of Oral Behavior. *Journal of Child Psychology and Psychiatry*, 1973, *14*, 17–29.

Korner, A., and Thoman, E. The Relative Efficacy of Contact and Vestibular Proprioceptive Stimuli in Soothing Neonates. *Child Development*, 1972, *43*, 443–454.

Kramer, J., Hill, K., and Cohen, L. Infants' Development of Object Permanence: A Refined Methodology and New Evidence for Piaget's Hypothesized Ordinality. *Child Development*, 1975, *46*, 149–155.

Kreminitzer, J. P., Vaughn, H. G., Kurtzberg, D., and Dowling, K. Smooth-Pursuit Eye Movements in the Newborn Infant. *Child Development*, 1979, *50*, 442–448.

Kuczynski, L., Zahn-Waxler, C., and Radke-Yarrow, M. Development and Content of Imitation in the Second and Third Years of Life: A Socialization Perspective. *Developmental Psychology*, 1987, *23*, 276–283.

Lewis, M., and McGurk H. Evaluation of Infant Intelligence. *Science*, 1972, *178*, 1174–1177.

Lightborne, R. Jr., Singh, S. and Green, C. P. The World Fertility Survey: Charting Global Childbearing. *Population Bulletin*. Washington, D.C.: Population Reference Bureau, Inc., March 1982.

Lingle, K. M., and Lingle, J. H. Effects of Selected Object Characteristics on Object-Performance Test Performance. *Child Development*, 1981, *52*, 367–369.

Lipsitt, L. Perinatal Indicators and Psychophysiological Precursors of Crib Death (1978). In J. Belsky (ed.), *In the Beginning: Readings on Infancy*, 74–83. New York: Columbia University Press, 1982.

Lipsitt, L. P., Engen, T., and Kaye, H. Developmental Changes in the Olfactory Threshold of the Neonate. *Child Development*, 1963, *34*, 37–46.

Lipsitt, L. P., and Kaye, H. Conditioned Sucking in the Newborn. *Psychonomic Science*, 1964, *1*, 29–30.

Lipsitt, L. P., and Levy, N. Electrotactual Threshold in the Neonate. *Child Development*, 1959, *30*, 547–554.

Lunde, D. T., and Lunde, M. K. *The Next Generation: A Book on Parenting*. New York: Holt, Rinehart, and Winston, 1980.

MacFarlane, A. Olfaction in the Development of Social Preferences in the Human Neonate (1975), cited in T. B. Brazelton, *On Becoming a Family: The Growth of Attachment*. New York: Delacorte, 1981.

Martin, B. Parent-Child Relations. In F. D. Horowitz (ed.), *Review of Child Development Research*, vol. 4, 320–339. Chicago: University of Chicago Press, 1975.

Maurer, D., and Salapatek, P. Developmental Changes in the Scanning of Faces by Young Infants. *Child Development*, 1976, *47*, 523–527.

McCall, R. B. The Development of Intellectual Functioning in Infancy and the Prediction of Later I.Q. In J. Osofsky, *Handbook of Infant Development*, 707–742. New York: Wiley, 1979.

McCall, R. B., Hogarty, P. S., and Hurlburt, N. Transitions in Infant Sensorimotor Development and the Prediction of Childhood I.Q. *American Psychologist*, 1972, *27*, 728–748.

McGowan, R. J., Johnson, D. L., and S. E. Maxwell. Relations Between Infant Behavior Ratings and Concurrent and Subsequent Mental Test Scores. *Developmental Psychology*, 1981, *17*, 542–553.

McGraw, M. B. Neural Maturation as Exemplified in Achievement of Bladder Control. *Journal of Pediatrics*, 1940, *16*, 580–589.

Mehler, J., Bertoncini, J, Barriere, M., and Jassik-Gerschenfeld, D. Infant Recognition of Mother's Voice. *Perception*, 1978, *7*, 491–497.

Meltzoff, A. N., and Moore, M. K. Newborn Infants Imitate Adult Facial Gestures. *Child Development*, 1983, *54*, 702–709.

———. Imitation of Facial and Manual Gestures by Human Neonates. *Science*, 1977, *198*, 75–78.

Milewski, A. E. Infants' Discrimination of Internal and External Pattern Elements. *Journal of Experimental Child Psychology*, 1976, *22*, 229–246.

Miller, D. J., Ryan, E. B., Short, E. J., Ries, P. G., McGuire, M. D., and Culler, M. P. Relationships Between Early Habituation and Later Cognitive Performance in Infancy. *Child Development*, 1977, *48*, 658–661.

Minard, J., Coleman, D., Williams, G., and Ingledyne, E. Cumulative REM of Three to Five Day Olds: Effect of Normal External Noise and Maturation. *Psychophysiology*, 1968, *5*, 232.

Morrell, P., and Norton, W. T. Myelin. *Scientific American*, 1980, *242*, 88–119.

Morris, D. *Manwatching: A Field Guide to Human Behavior*. New York: Abrams, 1977.

Muir, D., and Field, J. Newborn Infants Orient to Sounds. *Child Development*, 1979, *50*, 431–436.

Nyiti, R. M. The Validity of "Cultural Differences Explanations" for Cross-Cultural Variation in the Rate of Piagetian Cognitive Development. In D. A. Wagner and H. W. Stevenson (eds.), *Cultural Perspectives on Child Development*, 146–166. San Francisco: Freeman, 1982.

Parmelee, A., and Stern, E. Development of States in Infants. In C. B. Clemente, D. P. Purpura, and F. E. Mayer (eds.), *Sleep and the Maturing Nervous System*. New York: Academic Press, 1972.

Parmelee, A. H., and Sigman, M. D. Perinatal Brain Development and Behavior. In P. H.

Mussen (ed.), *Handbook of Child Development* (3rd ed.), vol. 2, 95–157. New York: Wiley, 1983.

Parmelee, A. H., Wenne, W. H., and Schulz, H. R. Infant Sleep Patterns from Birth to Sixteen Weeks of Age. *Journal of Pediatrics*, 1964, *65*, 576–582.

Phillips, J. L. *The Origins of Intellect: Piaget's Theory* (2nd ed.). San Francisco: Freeman, 1975.

Piaget, J. *On the Development of Memory and Identity*. Worcester, Mass: Clark University Press, 1968.

———. *Six Psychological Studies*. New York: Random House, 1967.

———. The Stages of Intellectual Development of the Child, *Bulletin of the Menninger Clinic*, 1962, *26*, 120–128.

———. *The Construction of Reality in the Child*. New York: Basic Books, 1954 (originally published 1937).

———. *The Origins of Intelligence in Children*. New York: International Universities Press, 1952 (originally published 1936).

Pratt, K. C. The Neonate. In L. Carmichael (ed.), *Manual of Child Psychology* (2nd ed.). New York: Wiley, 1954.

Rader, N., Spiro, D. J., and Firestone, P. B. Performance on a Stage 4 Object-Permanence Task with Standard and Nonstandard Covers, *Child Development*, 1979, *50*, 905–910.

Ramey, C. T., Farran, D. C., and Campbell, F. A. Predicting I.Q. from Mother-Infant Interaction. *Child Development*, 1979, *50*, 804–814.

Restak, R. M. Newborn Knowledge. *Science*, January–February 1982, 58–65.

Ricciuti, H. N. Adverse Environmental and Nutritional Influences on Mental Development: A Perspective. Paper presented at American Dietetic Association Meeting, Atlanta, 1980a.

———. Developmental Consequences of Malnutrition in Early Childhood (1980b). In E. M. Hetherington and R. D. Parke (eds.), *Contemporary Readings in Child Psychology* (2nd ed.), 21–25. New York: McGraw-Hill, 1981.

Richardson, S. A. The Relation of Severe Malnutrition in Infancy of School Children with Differing Life Histories (1976), cited in S. A. Ricciuti, Developmental Consequences of Malnutrition (1980b). In E. M. Hetherington and R. D. Parke (eds.), *Contemporary Readings in Child Psychology* (2nd ed.). New York: McGraw-Hill, 1981.

Ridenour, M. V. Contemporary Issues in Motor Development. In *Motor Development: Issues and Applications*, 39–63. Princeton: Princeton Book Co., 1978.

Roffwarg, H. P., Muzio, J. N., and Dement, W. C. Ontogenic Development of the Human Sleep-Dream Cycle. *Science*, 1966, *152*, 604–619.

Rose, S. A. Developmental Changes in Infants' Retention of Visual Stimuli. *Child Development*, 1981, *52*, 227–233.

Rose, S. A., and Wallace, I. F. Visual Recognition Memory: A Predictor of Later Cognitive Functioning. *Child Development*, 1985a, *56*, 853–861.

Rose, S. A., and Wallace, I. F. Cross-Modal and Intramodal Transfer as Predictors of Mental Development in Full-Term and Preterm Infants. *Developmental Psychology*, 1985b, *21*, 949–963.

Rosenzweig, M. R., Bennett, E. L., and Diamond, M. C. Brain Changes in Response to Experience. *Scientific American*, February 1972, *226*, 22–29.

Rovee-Collier, C. Learning and Memory in Infancy in J. Osofsky (ed.). *Handbook of Infant Development* (2nd ed.). New York: John Wiley, 1987, 98–149.

Rubin, J., Provenzano, F., and Luria, Z. The Eye of the Beholder: Parents' Views of Sex of Newborns. *American Journal of Orthopsychiatry*, 1974, *43*, 720–731.

Rubin, R. A., and Balow, B. Measures of Infant Development and Socioeconomic Status as Predictors of Later Intelligence and School Achievement. *Developmental Psychology*, 1979, *15*, 225–227.

Ruddy, M. G., and Bornstein, M. H. Cognitive Correlates of Infant Attention and Maternal Stimulation over the First Year of Life. *Child Development*, 1982, *53*, 183–188.

Salk, L. The Effects of the Normal Heartbeat Sound on the Behavior of Newborn Infants: Implications for Mental Health. *World Mental Health*, 1960, *12*, 168–175.

Sameroff, A. J., and Cavanaugh, P. J. Learning in Infancy: A Developmental Perspective. In J. Osofsky (ed.), *Handbook of Infant Development*, 344–393; New York: Wiley, 1979.

Schmitt, M. H. Superiority of Breast-Feeding: Fact or Fancy. *American Journal of Nursing*, July 1979, 1488–1493.

Sears, R. R., Maccoby, E. E., and Levin, H. *Patterns of Child Rearing*. New York: Harper and Row, 1957.

Shirley, M. M. *The First Two Years: A Study of Twenty-Five Babies*, vol. 2: *Intellectual Development*. Minneapolis: University of Minnesota Press, 1933.

———. *The First Two Years: A Study of Twenty-Five Babies*, vol. 1: *Postural and Locomotor Development*. Minneapolis: University of Minnesota Press, 1931.

Siqueland, E. R. Response Patterns and Extinction in Human Newborns. *Journal of Experimental Child Psychology*, 1968, *6*, 431–442.

Smith, C., and Lloyd, B. Maternal Behavior and Perceived Sex of Infant: Revisited. *Child Development*, 1978, *49*, 1263–1265.

Strand, F. L. *Physiology* (2nd ed.). New York: Macmillan, 1983.

Streri, A., and Pecheux, M. G. Tactual Habituation and Discrimination of Form in Infancy: A Comparison with Vision. *Child Development*, 1986, *57*, 100–104.

Super, C. M. Cross-Cultural Research on Infancy. In H. C. Triandis and A. Heron (eds.), *Handbook of Cross-Cultural Psychology*, vol. 4: *Developmental Psychology*, 17–55. Boston: Allyn and Bacon, 1981.

Tanner, J. Physical Growth. In P. H. Mussen (ed.), *Carmichael's Manual of Child Psychology* (3rd ed.). New York: Wiley, 1970.

Thelen, E. Treadmill-Elicited Stepping in Seven-Month-Old Infants. *Child Development*, 1986, *57*, 1498–1506.

Thelen, E., and Fisher, D. M. Newborn Stepping: An Explanation for a "Disappearing" Reflex. *Developmental Psychology*, 1982, *18*, 760–775.

Thibault, J. P., and McKee, J. S. Practical Parenting with Piaget. *Young Children*, November 1982, *38*, 18–27.

Townsend, J. W., Klein, R. E., Irwin, M. H., Owens, W., Yarbrough, C., and Engle, P. L. Nutrition and Preschool Mental Development. In D. A. Wagner and H. W. Stevenson (eds.), *Cultural Perspectives on Child Development*, 124–146. San Francisco: Freeman, 1982.

Tulkin, S., and Kagan, J. Mother-Child Interaction in the First Year of Life. *Child Development*, 1972, *43*, 31–41.

Uzgiris, I. C. Patterns of Cognitive Development in Infancy. *Merrill-Palmer Quarterly*, 1973, *19*, 181–204.

Vernon, P. E. Environment and Intelligence. In V. P. Varma and P. Williams (eds.), *Piaget, Psychology, and Education*, 31–42. Itasca, Ill: Peacock, 1976.

Vinter, A. The Role of Movement in Eliciting Early Imitations. *Child Development*, 1986, *57*, 66–71.

Wachs, T. D., Uzgiris, I. C., and Hunt, J. M. Cognitive Development in Infants of Different Age Levels and from Different Environmental Backgrounds: An Explanatory Investigation. *Merrill-Palmer Quarterly*, 1971, *17*, 283–317.

Waddington, C. H. *The Strategy of the Genes.* London: Allen and Unwin, 1957.

Wade, N. Bottle-Feeding: Adverse Effects of a Western Technology. *Science,* 1974, *184,* 45–48.

Walk, R. D. *Perceptual Development,* Monterey, Calif.: Brooks/Cole, 1981.

Webster, R. L. Steinhardt, M. H., and Senter, M. G. Changes in Infants' Vocalizations as a Function of Differential Acoustic Stimulation. *Developmental Psychology,* 1972, *7,* 39–43.

Weisenfeld, A. R., and Klorman, R. C. The Mother's Psychological Reactions to Contrasting Affective Expressions by Her Own and Unfamiliar Infants. *Developmental Psychology,* 1978, *14,* 294–204.

Weisenfeld, A. R., Malatesta, C., and De-Loach, L. Differential Parental Response to Familiar and Unfamiliar Infant Distress Signals. *Infant Behavior and Development,* 1981, *4,* 281–295.

Weitz, S. *Sex Roles: Biological, Psychological, and Social Foundations.* New York: Oxford University Press, 1977.

Wertheimer, M. Psycho-Motor Coordination of Auditory-Visual Space at Birth. *Science,* 1961, *134,* 1962.

White, B. L. *The First Three Years of Life.* Englewood Cliffs, N.J.: Prentice-Hall, 1975.

———. *Human Infants: Experience and Psychological Development.* Englewood Cliffs, N.J.: Prentice-Hall, 1971.

Whitehurst, G. J., and Vasta, R. *Child Behavior.* Boston: Houghton Mifflin, 1977.

Whitney, E. N., and Hamilton, E. M. N. *Understanding Nutrition* (3rd ed.). St. Paul: West, 1984.

Wickelgren, L. W. Convergence in the Human Newborn. *Journal of Experimental Child Psychology,* 1967, *5,* 69–72.

Wiesel, T. N., and Hubel, D. H. Extent of Recovery from the Effects of Visual Deprivation in Kittens. *Journal of Neurophysiology,* 1965, *28,* 1060–1072.

Willemsen, E. *Understanding Infancy.* San Francisco: Freeman, 1979.

Wingfield, A., and Byrnes, D. L. *The Psychology of Human Memory.* New York: Academic Press, 1981.

Winick, M., Meyer, K. K., and Harris, R. C. Malnutrition and Environmental Enrichment by Early Adoption: Development of Adopted Korean Children Differing Greatly in Nutritional Status Is Examined. *Science,* 1975, *190,* 1173–1175.

Winick, M., and Russo, P. Head Circumference and Cellular Growth of the Brain in Normal and Marasmic Children. *Journal of Pediatrics,* 1969, *74,* 774–778.

Winick, M., Russo, P., and Waterloo, J. Cellular Growth of Cerebrum, Cerebellum, and Brain Stem in Normal and Marasmic Children. *Experimental Neurology,* 1970, *21,* 393–410.

Wolff, P. H. The Natural History of Crying and Other Vocalization in Early Infancy. In B. M. Foss (ed.) *Determinants of Infant Behavior,* vol. 4, 81–111. London: Methuen, 1969.

———. The Development of Attention in Young Infants (1965). In L. J. Stone, H. T. Smith, and L. B. Murphy (eds.), *The Competent Infant: Research and Commentary,* 307–314. New York: Basic Books, 1973.

Woodruff, C. W. The Science of Infant Nutrition and the Art of Infant Feeding. *Journal of the American Medical Association,* 1978, *240,* 657–661.

Zelazo, P. R., Zelazo, N. A., and Kolb, S. "Walking" in the Newborn. *Science,* 1972, *176,* 314–315.

Zeskind, P. S., Sale, J., Maio, L. W., and Weiseman, J. R. Adult Perceptions of Pain and Hunger Cries: A Synchrony of Arousal. *Child Development,* 1985, *56,* 549–554.

Zinsser, C. The Preschool Pressure Cooker. *Working Mother,* October 1981, 61–64.

Chapter 5

Ainsworth, M. D. S. Infant-Mother Attachment. *American Psychologist,* 1979, *34,* 932–938.

Ainsworth, M. D. S. The Development of Infant-Mother Attachment. In B. Caldwell and H. Riciutti (eds.), *Review of Child Development,* vol. 3. Chicago: University of Chicago Press, 1974.

———. *Infancy in Uganda: Infant Care and Growth of Attachment.* Baltimore: Johns Hopkins University Press, 1967.

Ainsworth, M. D. S., Bell, S. M., and Slayton, D. J. Individual Differences in the Strange Situation Behavior of One-Year-Olds. In H. R. Schaffer (ed.). *The Origins of Human Social Relations.* London: Academic Press, 1971.

Ainsworth, M. D. S., Blehar, M. C., Waters, E., and Wall, S. *Patterns of Attachment.* Hillsdale, N.J.: Erlbaum, 1978.

Ainsworth, M. D. S., and Wittig, B. A. Attachment and the Exploratory Behavior of One-Year-Olds in a Strange Situation. In B. M. Foss (ed.), *Determinants of Infant Behavior,* vol. 4, 113–136. London: Methuen, 1969.

Alvarez, W. F. The Meaning of Maternal Employment for Mothers and Their Perceptions of Their Three-Year-Old Children. *Child Development,* 1985, *56,* 350–361.

American Council of Life Insurance. *Factsheet on Women.* Washington, D. C.: American Council of Life Insurance, 1982.

Anderson, C. W., Nagle, R. J., Roberts, W. A., and Smith, J. W. Attachment to Substitute Caregivers as a Function of Center Quality and Caregiver Involvement. *Child Development,* 1981, *52,* 53–61.

Arend, R. A., Gove, F. L., and Sroufe, L. A. Continuity of Early Adaptation: From Attachment in Infancy to Ego-Resiliency and Curiosity at Age 5. *Child Development,* 1979, *50,* 950–959.

Bank, S. P., and Kahn, M. D. *The Sibling Bond.* New York: Basic Books, 1982.

Barglow, P., Vaughn, B. E., and Molitor, N. Effects of Maternal Absence Due to Employment on the Quality of Infant-Mother Attachment in Low-risk Sample. *Child Development,* 1987, *58,* 945–955.

Baskett, L. M. Sibling Status Effects: Adult Expectations. *Developmental Psychology,* 1985, *21,* 441–445.

Bell, R. Q. Parent, Child, and Reciprocal Influences. *American Psychologist,* 1979, *34,* 821–827.

Belsky, J. Risks Remain. *Zero to Three,* 1987, *7,* 22–24.

Belsky, J. Infant Day Care: A Cause for Concern. *Zero to Three,* 1986, *7,* 1–7.

Belsky, J. *In the Beginning.* New York: Columbia University Press, 1982.

Belsky, J., and Steinberg, L. D. What Does Research Teach Us About Day Care? *Children Today,* July–August 1979, *8,* 21–26.

———. The Effects of Daycare: A Critical Review. *Child Development,* 1978, *49,* 929–949.

Biller, H. B. Fatherhood: Implications for Child and Adult Development. In B. B. Wolman (ed.), *Handbook of Developmental Psychology,* 702–720. Englewood Cliffs, N.J.: Prentice-Hall, 1982.

Blehar, M. C. Anxious Attachment and Defensive Reactions Associated with Day Care. *Child Development,* vol. 45, 1974, 683–692.

Bowlby, J. Attachment and Loss: Retrospect and Prospect. *American Journal of Orthopsychiatry,* 1982, *52,* 664–678.

———. *Attachment and Loss.* New York: Basic Books, 1969.

———. *Maternal Care and Mental Health.* New York: Columbia University Press, 1951.

Brazelton, T. B., Koslowski, B., and Main, H. The Origins of Reciprocity: The Early Infant-Mother Interaction. In M. Lewis and L. A.

Rosenblum (eds.), *The Effect of the Infant on Its Caretaker*, 49–76. New York: Wiley, 1974.

Bretherton, I. Attachment Theory: Retrospect and Prospect. In I. Bretherton and E. Waters (eds.), *Growing Points of Attachment Theory and Research*, Monographs of the Society for Research in Child Development, 1985, *50*, nos. 1–2, serial no. 209, 3–39.

Bridges, K. M. B. A Study of Social Development in Early Infancy. *Child Development*, 1933, *4*, 36–49.

Bronson, G. The Development of Fear. *Child Development*, 1968, *39*, 409–432.

Broverman, I. K., Vogel, S. R., Broverman, D. M., et al. Sex-Role Stereotypes: A Current Reappraisal. *Journal of Social Issues*, 1972, *28*, 59–78.

Caldwell, B. M., Wright, C. M., Honig, A. S., and Tannenbaum, J. Infant Day Care and Attachment. *American Journal of Orthopsychiatry*, 1970, *40*, 397–412.

Cassidy, J. The Ability to Negotiate the Environment: An Aspect of Infant Competence as Related to Quality of Attachment. *Child Development*, 1986, *57*, 331–337.

Chess, S. Comments: "Infant Day Care: A Cause For Concern." *Zero to Three!* 1987, *7*, 24–25.

Chess, S., and Thomas, A. Infant Bonding: Mystique and Reality. *American Journal of Orthopsychiatry*, 1981, *52*, 213–222.

Chibucos, T. R., and Kail, P. R. Longitudinal Examination of Father-Infant Interaction and Infant-Father Attachment. *Merrill-Palmer Quarterly*, Winter 1981, *27*, 81–97.

Clarke-Stewart, A. The Day-Care Child. *Parents*, September 1982.

Clarke-Stewart, K. A. And Daddy Makes Three: The Father's Impact on Mother and Young Child. *Child Development*, 1978, *49*, 466–478.

Cohen, L., and Campos, J. Father, Mother, and Stranger as Elicitors of Attachment Behavior in Infancy. *Developmental Psychology*, 1974, *10*, 146–154.

Cohen, S. E. Maternal Employment and Mother-Child Interaction. *Merrill-Palmer Quarterly*, 1978, *24*, 189–197.

Crockenberg, S., and McCluskey, K. Change in Maternal Behavior During the Baby's First Year of Life. *Child Development*, 1986, *57*, 746–754.

Dennis, W. *Children of the Creche*. New York: Appleton-Century-Crofts, 1973.

Donovan, W. L., Leavitt, L. A., and Balling, J. D. Maternal Physiological Response to Infant Signals. *Psychophysiology*, 1978, *15*, 68–74.

Dunn, J. Studying Temperament and Parent-Child Interaction: Comparison of Interview and Direct Observation. In S. Chess and A. Thomas (eds.), *Annual Progress in Child Psychiatry and Child Development*, 415–430. New York: Brunner/Mazel, 1981.

———. *Distress and Comfort*. Cambridge: Cambridge University Press, 1977.

Eckerman, C. O., Whatley, J. L., and Kutz, S. L. Growth of Social Play with Peers During the Second Year of Life. *Developmental Psychology*, 1975, *11*, 42–49.

Erickson, M. F., Sroufe, L. A., and Egeland, B. The Relationship Between Quality of Attachment and Behavior Problems in Preschool in a High-Risk Sample. In I. Bretherton and E. Waters (eds.), *Growing Points of Attachment Theory and Research*, Monographs of the Society for Research in Child Development, 1985, *50*, nos. 1–2, serial no. 209, 147–167.

Erikson, E. *Childhood and Society*. New York: Norton, 1963.

Etaugh, C. Effects of Nonmaternal Care on Children: Research Evidence and Popular Views. *American Psychologist*, 1980, *35*, 309–319.

Finkelstein, N. W. Aggression: Is It Stimulated by Day Care? *Young Children*, 1982, *37*, 3–9.

Freud, S. A. *General Introduction to Psychoanalysis*. New York: Doubleday, 1953 (oroginally published in 1935).

Gerson, M. J., Alpert, J. L., and Richardson, M. S. Mothering: The View from Psychological Research. *Signs*, 1984, *9*, 434–453.

Grossman, K., Thane, E., and Grossman, K. E. Maternal Tactual Contact of the Newborn After Postpartum Conditions of Mother-Infant Contact. *Developmental Psychology*, 1981, *17*, 158–169.

Harlow, H. F. *Learning to Love*. San Francisco: Albion, 1971.

———. Love in Infant Monkeys. *Scientific American*, July 1959, *200*, 68–74.

Harlow, H. F., and Harlow, M. K. Social Deprivation in Monkeys. *Scientific American*, 1962, *207*, 136–146.

Harlow, H. F., and Suomi, S. J. Social Recovery by Isolation-Reared Monkeys. *Proceedings of the National Academy of Science*, 1971, *68*, 1534–1538.

Haskins, R. Public School Aggression Among Children with Varying Day-Care Experience. *Child Development*, 1985, *56*, 689–703.

Hay, D. F. Cooperative Interactions and Sharing Between Very Young Children and Their Parents. *Developmental Psychology*, 1979, *15*, 647–653.

Heinicke, C. M., Diskin, S. D., Ramsey-Klee, D. M., and Given, K. Pre-Birth Parent Characteristics and Family Development in the First Year of Life. *Child Development*, 1983, *54*, 194–208.

Hock, E. Working and Nonworking Mothers and Their Infants: A Comparative Study of Maternal Caregiving Characteristics and Infant Social Behavior. *Merrill-Palmer Quarterly*, 1980, *26*, 79–101.

Hodapp, R. M., and Mueller, E. Early Social Development. In B. B. Wolman (ed.), *Handbook of Developmental Psychology*, 284–298. Englewood Cliffs, N.J.: Prentice-Hall, 1982.

Hoffman, L. W. Maternal Employment. *American Psychologist*, 1979, *34*, 859–865.

———. Effects of Maternal Employment on the Child: A Review of the Research. *Developmental Psychology*, 1974, *10*, 204–228.

Jacobson, J. L., and Wille, D. E. The Influence of Attachment Pattern on Developmental Changes in Peer Interaction from the Toddler to the Preschool Period. *Child Development*, 1986, *57*, 338–347.

Joffe, L. S., and Vaughn, B. E. Infant-Mother Attachment: Theory, Assessment, and Implications for Development. In B. B. Wolman (ed.), *Handbook of Developmental Psychology*, 190–204. Englewood Cliffs, N.J.: Prentice-Hall, 1982.

Kagan, J. Emergent Themes in Human Development. *American Scientist*, 1976, *64*, 186–196.

Kammerman, S. Infant Care Usage in the United States (1986) cited in Belsky, J. Infant Day Care: A Cause for Concern. *Zero to Three*, 1986, *7*, 1–7.

Kennel, J. H., Voos, D. K., and Klaus, M. H. Parent-Infant Bonding. In J. Osofsky (ed.), *Handbook of Infant Development*, 786–799. New York: Wiley, 1979.

Klaus, M. H., and Kennel, J. H. *Maternal-Infant Bonding*. St. Louis: Mosby, 1976.

Klein, R. P. Caregiving Arrangements by Employed Women with Children Under 1 Year of Age. *Developmental Psychology*, 1985, *21*, 403–406.

Kotelchuck, M. The Infant's Relationship to the Father: Experimental Evidence. In M. Lamb (ed.), *The Role of the Father in Child Development*, 329–344. New York: Wiley, 1976.

———. The Nature of the Child's Tie to His Father (1972), cited in M. Kotelchuck. The Infant's Relationship to the Father: Experimental Evidence. In M. Lamb (ed.), *The Role of the Father in Child Development*, 329–344. New York: Wiley, 1976.

Lamb, M. Paternal Influences and the Father's Role: A Personal Perspective. *American Psychologist*, 1979, *34*, 938–944.

———. Interactions Between Eight-Month-Old Children and Their Fathers and Mothers. In

M. E. Lamb (ed.), *The Role of the Father in Child Development*, 307–329. New York: Wiley, 1976.

Lamb, M. E., Frodi, M., Hwang, C. P., and Frodi, A. M. Effects of Paternal Involvement on Infant Preferences for Mothers and Fathers. *Child Development*, 1983, *54*, 450–458.

Lamb, M. E., Frodi, A. M., Hwang, C. P., Frodi, M., and Steinberg, J. Mother- and Father-Infant Interaction Involving Play and Holding in Traditional and Non-Traditional Swedish Families. *Developmental Psychology*, 1982, *18*, 215–221.

Lewis, M. Social Development in Infancy and Early Childhood in J. Osofsky (ed.), *Handbook of Infant Development* (2nd ed.), 1987, 419–493.

Lewis, M., and Brooks-Gunn, J. The Reactions of Infants to People (1972). In J. Belsky (ed.), *In the Beginning*, 167–177. New York: Columbia University Press, 1982.

Lewis, M., and Rosenblum, L. A. (eds.), *Friendship and Peer Relations*. New York: Wiley, 1975.

Londerville, S., and Main, M. Security, Compliance, and Maternal Training Methods in the Second Year of Life. *Developmental Psychology*, 1981, *17*, 289–299.

Lorenz, K. The Companion in the Bird's World. *AUK*, 1937, *54*, 245–273.

Lutkenhaus, P., Grossmann, K. E., and Grossman, K. Infant-Mother Attachment at Twelve Months and Style of Interaction with a Stranger at the Age of Three Years. *Child Development*, 1985, *56*, 1538–1542.

Maccoby, E. E. *Social Development: Psychological Growth and the Parent-Child Relationship*. New York: Harcourt Brace Jovanovich, 1980.

Maccoby, E. E., and Martin, J. A. Socialization in the Context of the Family: Parent-Child Interaction. In P. H. Mussen (ed.), *Handbook of Child Development* (4th ed.), vol. 4, 1–103. New York: Wiley, 1983.

Main, M., and Weston, D. The Quality of the Toddler's Relationship to Mother and Father: Related to Conflict Behavior and Readiness to Establish New Relationships. *Child Development*, 1981, *52*, 932–940.

Martin, B. Parent-Child Relations. In F. D. Horowitz (ed.), *Review of Child Development Research*, vol. 4, 320–329. Chicago: University of Chicago Press, 1975.

Matas, L., Arend, R., and Sroufe, L. A. Continuity of Adaptation in the Second Year: The Relationship Between Quality of Attachment and Later Competence. *Child Development*, 1978, *49*, 547–556.

Metcalf, D. R. Organizers of the Psyche and EEG Development: Birth Through Adoles-

cence. In R. L. Noshpitz (ed.), *Basic Handbook of Child Psychiatry*, vol. 1, 63–72. New York: Basic Books, 1979.

Moore, T. Exclusive Early Mothering and Its Alternatives (1975), *Scandinavian Journal of Psychology*, 1975, *16*, 255–272, cited in L. W. Hoffman, Maternal Employment. *American Psychologist*, 1979, *34*, 859–865.

Mueller, E. C., and Vandell, D. Infant-Infant Interaction. In J. Osofsky (ed.), *Handbook of Infant Development*, 591–603. New York: Wiley, 1979.

Neugarten, B. L., and Weinstein, K. K. The Changing American Grandparent. *Journal of Marriage and the Family*, 1964, *26*, 19–206.

New York Times. Day Care Linked to Ills of Children. *New York Times*, June 27, 1984, C7.

Newsday. Polls Apart on Doing Chores. *Newsday*, June 17, 1986, p. 4.

Osofsky, J. D., and Connors, K. Mother-Infant Interaction: An Integrative View of a Complex System. In J. Osofsky (ed.), *Handbook of Infant Development*, 519–549. New York: Wiley, 1979.

Parke, R. D. *Fathers*. Cambridge, Mass.: Harvard University Press, 1981.

———. Perspectives on Father-Infant Interaction. In J. Osofsky (ed.), *Handbook of Infant Development*, 549–591. New York: Wiley, 1979.

———. Father's Role in Infancy: A Reevaluation. *The Family Coordinator*, 1976, *25*, 365–371.

Parke, R. D., and Sawin, D. B. The Father's Role in Infancy: A Reevaluation. *The Family Coordinator*, 1976, *25*, 365–371.

Pastor, D. L. The Quality of Mother-Infant Attachment and Its Relationship to Toddler's Initial Sociability with Peers. *Developmental Psychology*, 1981, *17*, 326–335.

Phillips, D., McCartney, K., and Scarr. S. Child-Care Quality and Children's Social Development. *Developmental Psychology*, 1987b, *23*, 537–543.

Phillips, D., McCartney, K., Scarr, S., and Howes, C. Selective Review of Infant Day Care Research: A Cause for Concern! *Zero to Three*, 1987a, *7*, 18–21.

Power, T. Mother- and Father-Infant Play: A Developmental Analysis. *Child Development*, 1985, *56*, 1514–1525.

Ragozin, A. S., Basham, R. B., Crnic, K. A., Greenberg, M. T., and Robinson, N. M. Effects of Maternal Age on Parenting Role. *Developmental Psychology*, 1982, *18*, 627–635.

Rheingold, H. L., and Eckerman, C. O. Fear of the Stranger: A Critical Examination. In

H. W. Reese (ed.), *Advances in Child Development and Behavior*, vol. 8. New York: Academic Press, 1973.

Rheingold, H. L., Hay, D. F., and West, M. J. Sharing in the Second Year of Life. *Child Development*, 1976, *47*, 1148–1158.

Ricciuti, H. Fear and Development of Social Attachments in the First Year of Life. In M. Lewis and L. A. Rosenblum (eds.), *The Origins of Human Behavior: Fear*. New York: Wiley, 1974.

Robertson, J., and Bowlby, J. Responses of Young Children to Separation from Their Mothers. *Courrier Centre Internationale Enfance*, 1952, *2*, 131–142.

Rode, S. S., Chang, P. N., Fisch, R. O., and Sroufe, L. A. Attachment Patterns of Infants Separated at Birth. *Developmental Psychology*, 1981, *17*, 188–191.

Ross, H. S. Establishment of Social Games Among Toddlers. *Developmental Psychology*, 1982, *18*, 509–518.

Ruopp, R., Travers, J., Glantz, F., and Coelen, C. *Children at the Center* (Final report of the National Day Care Study), cited in E. Zigler and S. Muenchow. Infant Day Care and Infant-Care Leaves: A Policy Vacuum. *American Psychologist*, 1983, *38*, 91–95.

Russell, G. The Father's Role and Its Relation to Masculinity, Femininity, and Androgyny. *Child Development*, 1978, *49*, 1174–1181.

Rutter, M. Social-Emotional Consequences of Day Care for Preschool Children. *American Journal of Orthopsychiatry*, 1981, *51*, 4–29.

———. Maternal Deprivation, 1972–1978: New Findings, New Concepts, New Approaches. *Child Development*, 1979, *50*, 283–305.

Saltz, R. Effects of Part-Time "Mothering" on IQ and SQ of Young Institutionalized Children. *Child Development*, 1973, *44*, 166–170.

Schachter, F. F. Toddlers with Employed Mothers. *Child Development*, 1981, *52*, 958–964.

Schaffer, R. *Mothering*. Cambridge, Mass.: Harvard University Press, 1977.

Schindler, P. J., Moely, B. E., and Frank, A. L. Time in Day Care and Social Participation of Young Children. *Developmental Psychology*, 1987, *23*, 255–262.

Shiller, V. M., Izard, C. E., and Hembree, E. A. Patterns of Emotion Expression During Separation in the Strange-Situation Procedure. *Developmental Psychology*, 1986, *22*, 378–382.

Skarin, K. Cognitive and Contextual Determinants of Stranger Fear in Six- and Eleven-Month-Old Infants. *Child Development*, 1977, *48*, 537–544.

Spitz, R. *The First Year of Life: A Psychoanalytic Study of Normal and Deviant Development of*

Object Relations. New York: International Universities Press, 1965.

———. Hospitalism: An Enquiry into the Genesis of Psychiatric Conditions in Early Childhood. *Psychoanalytic Study of the Child,* 1945, *1,* 53.

Spock, B. *Raising Children in a Difficult Time.* New York: Norton, 1974.

Sroufe, L. A. Attachment Classification from the Perspective of Infant-Caregiver Relationships and Infant Temperament. *Child Development,* 1985, *56,* 1–14.

———. Socioemotional Development. In J. D. Osofsky (ed.), *Handbook of Infant Development,* 462–519. New York: Wiley, 1979a.

———. The Coherence of Individual Development: Early Care: Attachment, and Subsequent Developmental Issues. *American Psychologist,* 1979b, *34,* 834–842.

Sroufe, L. A., and Waters, E. Attachment as an Organizational Construct. *Child Development,* 1977, *48,* 1184–1189.

Stines, J. *A Daycare Checklist* (1983) and personal communication, 1985.

Stuckey, M. F., McGhee, P. E., and Bell, N. J. Parent-Child Interaction: The Influence of Maternal Employment. *Developmental Psychology,* 1982, *18,* 635–644.

Svejda, M. J., Campos, J. J., and Emde, R. N. Mother-Infant "Bonding": Failure to Generalize. *Child Development,* 1980, *51,* 775–779.

Tavris, C. Women: Work Isn't Always the Answer. *Psychology Today,* September 1976, 78.

Tracy, R. L., and Ainsworth, M. D. S. Maternal Affectionate Behavior and Infant-Mother Attachment Patterns. *Child Development,* 1981, *52,* 1341–1343.

U.S. Bureau of the Census. *Statistical Abstracts of the United States,* 1986. Washington, D.C., 1986.

U.S. Department of Labor, Bureau of Labor Statistics. *Handbook of Labor Statistics.* Washington, D.C., 1983.

Vaughn, B. E., Deane, K. E., and Waters, E. The Impact of Out-of-Home Care on Child-Mother Attachment Quality: Another Look at Some Enduring Questions. In I. Bretherton and E. Waters (eds.), *Growing Points of Attachment Theory and Research,* Monographs of the Society for Research in Child Development, 1985, *50,* nos. 1–2, serial no. 209, 110–136.

Waters, E. The Stability of Individual Differences in Infant Attachment: Comments on the Thompson, Lamb, and Estes Contribution. *Child Development,* 1983, *54,* 516–520.

———. The Reliability and Stability of Individual Differences in Infant-Mother Attachment. *Child Development,* 1978, *49,* 483–494.

Waters, E., and Deane, K. E. Defining and Assessing Individual Differences in Attachment Relationships: Q-Methodology and the Organization of Behavior in Infancy and Early Childhood. In I. Bretherton and E. Waters (eds.), *Growing Points of Attachment Theory and Research,* Monographs of the Society for Research in Child Development, 1985, *50,* nos. 1–2, serial no. 209, 41–66.

———. Theories, Models, Recent Data, and Some Tasks for Comparative Developmental Analysis. In L. Hoffman, R. Gandelman, and R. Schiffman (eds.), *Parenting: Its Causes and Consequences,* 19–54. Hillsdale, N.J.: Erlbaum, 1982.

Waters, E., Wippman, J., and Sroufe, L. A. Attachment, Positive Affect, and Competence in the Peer Group: Two Studies in Construct Validation. *Child Development,* 1979, *50,* 821–829.

Watkins, H. D., and Bradbard, M. R. The Social Development of Young Children in Day Care: What Practitioners Should Know. *Child Care Quarterly,* Fall 1984, *11,* 169–187.

Whitney, E. N. W., and Hamilton, E. M. N. *Understanding Nutrition* (3rd ed.). St. Paul: West, 1984.

Wise, S., and Grossman, F. K. Adolescent Mothers and Their Infants: Psychological Factors in Early Attachment and Interaction. *American Journal of Orthopsychiatry,* 1980, *50,* 454–468.

Wolins, M. Young Children in Institutions. *Developmental Psychology,* 1970, *2,* 99–109.

Yarrow, L. J. Emotional Development. *American Psychologist,* 1979, *34,* 951–957.

Yarrow, M. R., Scott, P., de Leeuw, L. D., and Heinig, C. Child Rearing in Families of Working and Non-Working Mothers (1962). In H. Bee (ed.), *Social Issues in Developmental Psychology* (2nd ed.), 112–129. New York: Harper and Row, 1978.

Zigler, E., and Muenchow, S. Infant Day Care and Infant-Care Leaves: A Policy Vacuum. *American Psychologist,* 1983, *38,* 91–95.

Chapter 6

Aitchison, J. *The Articulate Mammal: An Introduction to Psycholinguistics.* New York: Universe Books, 1978.

Akiyama, M. M. Denials in Young Children from a Cross-Linguistic Perspective. *Child Development,* 1985, *56,* 95–102.

———. Are Language-Acquisition Strategies Universal? *Developmental Psychology,* 1984, *20,* 219–229.

Anglin, J. M. *Word, Object, and Conceptual Development.* New York: Norton, 1977.

August, D. L. Bilingual Education Act, Title 2 of the Education Amendments of 1984. *Washington Report,* Washington Liaison Office of the Society for Research in Child Development, May 1986.

Baker, K. A., and de Kanter, A. A. *Effectiveness of Bilingual Education: A Review of the Literature.* Washington, D.C.: U.S. Department of Education, Office of Planning, Budget, and Evaluation, 1981.

Bee, H. *Social Issues in Developmental Psychology* (2nd ed.). New York: Harper and Row, 1978.

Best, J. B. *Cognitive Psychology,* St. Paul: West, 1986.

Bloom, L. M., Language Development. In F. D. Horowitz (ed.), *Review of Child Development Research,* vol. 4. Chicago: University of Chicago Press, 1975.

———. Talking, Understanding, and Thinking. In *Language Perspectives: Acquisition, Retardation, and Intervention,* ed. R. L. Schiefelbusch and L. L. Lloyd. Baltimore: University Park Press, 1974.

Bohannon, J. N., and Marquis, A. L. Children's Control of Adult Speech. *Child Development,* 1977, *48,* 1002–1008.

Bowerman, M. Language Development. In H. C. Triandis and A. Heron (eds.), *Handbook of Cross-Cultural Psychology,* vol. 4, 93–187. Boston: Allyn and Bacon, 1981.

Brown, R. Development of the First Language in the Human Species. *American Psychologist,* 1973, *28,* 97–106.

Brown, R., Cazden, C., and Bellugi-Klima, U. The Child's Grammar from 1 to 11. In J. P. Hill (ed.), *Minnesota Symposia on Child Psychology,* vol. 2. Minneapolis: University of Minnesota Press, 1969.

Bruner, J. Learning the Mother Tongue. *Human Nature,* September 1978a, 11–19.

———. Learning How to Do Things with Words. In J. S. Bruner and A. Garton (eds.), *Human Growth and Development: Wolfson College Lectures,* 62–85. Oxford: Clarendon Press, 1978b.

Cazden, C. B. Language Development and the Preschool Environment. In C. B. Cazden (ed.), *Language in Early Childhood Education.* Washington, D.C.: National Association for the Education of Young Children, 1981.

Chomsky, N. *Language and Mind* (enl. ed.). New York: Harcourt Brace Jovanovich, 1972.

———. *Aspects of the Theory of Syntax.* Cambridge, Mass.: M.I.T. Press, 1965.

———. A Review of B. F. Skinner's *Verbal Behavior* in *Language,* 1959, *35,* 26–58.

Clark, E. V. Strategies for Communicating. *Child Development,* 1978, *49,* 953–959.

Condon, W. S., and Sander, L. W. Synchrony Demonstrated Between Movements of the Neonate and Adult Speech. *Child Development,* 1974, *65,* 456–462.

Crawford, J. Bilingual Education Works, Study Finds. *Education Week,* March 25, 1987, p. 16.

Dale, P. S. *Language Development: Structure and Function.* Hinsdale, Ill.: Dryden 1972. Second edition 1976.

deVilliers, J. G., and deVilliers, P. A. *Language Acquisition.* Cambridge, Mass.: Harvard University Press, 1978.

Diaz, R. M. Bilingual Cognitive Development: Addressing Three Gaps in Current Research. *Child Development,* 1985, *56,* 1376–1388.

Dodd, B. J. Effects of Social and Vocal Stimulation on Infant Babbling. *Developmental Psychology,* 1972, *7,* 80–83.

Francis, H. *Language in Childhood: Form and Function in Language Development.* New York: St. Martin's Press, 1975.

Garnica, O. K. Some Prosodic and Paralinguistic Features of Speech Directed to Young Children. In C. E. Snow and C. A. Ferguson (eds.), *Talking to Children: Language Input and Acquisition.* Cambridge: Cambridge University Press, 1977.

Gleason, J. B. *The Development of Language.* Columbus, Ohio: Merrill, 1985.

Goldberg, S., and Lewis, M. Play Behavior in the Year-Old Infant: Early Sex Differences. *Child Development,* 1969, *40,* 21–30.

Goodluck, H. Language Acquisition and Linguistic Theory. In P. Fletcher and M. Garman (eds.), *Language Acquisition* (2nd ed.), 49–69. London: Cambridge University Press, 1986.

Griffiths, P. Early Vocabulary. In P. Fletcher and M. Garman (eds.), 279–307. *Language Acquisition* (2nd ed.). London: Cambridge University Press, 1986.

Hess, R., and Shipman, V. Parents as Teachers: How Lower and Middle Class Mothers Teach (1967). In C. S. Lavatelli and F. Stendler (eds.), *Readings in Child Behavior and Development* (3rd ed.), 436–446. New York: Harcourt Brace Jovanovich, 1972.

Hoff-Ginsberg, E. Function and Structure in Maternal Speech: Their Relation to the Child's Development of Syntax. *Developmental Psychology,* 1986, *22,* 155–163.

Hovell, M. F., Schumaker, J. B., and Sherman, J. A. A Comparison of Parents' Models and Expansions in Promoting Children's Acquisition of Adjectives. *Journal of Experimental Child Psychology,* 1978, *25,* 41–57.

Huttenlocher, J. The Origins of Language Comprehension. In R. L. Solso (ed.), *Theories of Cognitive Psychology.* Potomac, Md.: Erlbaum, 1974.

Labov, W. *The Study of Nonstandard English* (1970). In V. P. Clark, P. A. Eshholz, and A. F. Rosa (ed.), *Language* (2nd ed.), 439–450. New York: St. Martin's Press, 1977.

Lenneberg, E. H. *Biological Foundations of Language.* New York: Wiley, 1967.

Lenneberg, E. H., Rebelsky, F. G., and Nichols, I. A. The Vocalizations of Infants Born to Deaf and Hearing Parents. *Human Development,* 1965, *8,* 23–37.

Maccoby, E. E., and Jacklin, C. N. *The Psychology of Sex Differences.* Stanford, Calif.: Stanford University Press, 1974.

MacNamara, J. Cognitive Basis of Language Learning in Infants. *Psychological Review,* 1972, *79,* 1–14.

McCarthy, D. A. Language Development in Children. In L. Carmichael (ed.), *Manual of Child Psychology.* New York: Wiley, 1954.

McCartney, K. Effect of Quality of Day Care Environment on Children's Language Development. *Developmental Psychology,* 1984, *20,* 244–261.

McLaughlin, B. *Second-Language Acquisition in Childhood.* Hillsdale, N.J.: Erlbaum, 1978.

———. Second-Language Learning in Children. *Psychological Bulletin,* 1977, *84,* 438–459.

McNeill, D. The Development of Language. In P. H. Mussen (ed.), *Carmichael's Manual of Child Psychology* (3rd ed.). New York: Wiley, 1970.

Menyuk, P. *Language and Maturation.* Cambridge, Mass.: M.I.T. Press, 1977.

Molfese, D. L., Molfese, V. J., and Carroll, P. L. Early Language Development. In B. B. Wolman (ed.), *Handbook of Developmental Psychology,* 301–323. Englewood Cliffs, N.J.: Prentice-Hall, 1982.

Moskowitz, B. A. The Acquisition of Language. *Scientific American,* 1978, *239,* 92–108.

Nelson, K. Individual Differences in Language Development: Implications for Development and Language. *Developmental Psychology,* 1981, *17,* 170–188.

———. Concept, Word, and Sentence. *Psychological Review,* 1974, *81,* 267–285.

———. *Structure and Strategy in Learning to Talk.* Monograph of the Society for Research in Child Development, 1973, *38,* nos. 1–2, serial no. 149.

Nelson, K., Rescorla, L., Gruendel, J., and Benedict, H. Early Lexicons: What Do They Mean? *Child Development,* 1978, *49,* 960–968.

Newport, E. L., Gleitman, H., and Gleitman, L. R. Mother, I'd Rather Do It Myself: Some Effects and Non-Effects of Maternal Speech Style. In C. E. Snow and C. A. Ferguson (eds.), *Talking to Children: Language Input and Acquisition.* Cambridge: Cambridge University Press, 1977.

Olim, E. G., Hess, R. D., and Shipman, V. C. Role of Mothers' Language Styles in Mediating Their Preschool Children's Development. *School Review,* 1967, *75,* 414–424.

Penner, S. G. Parental Responses to Grammatical and Ungrammatical Child Utterances. *Child Development,* 1987, *58,* 376–384.

Peters, A. M. Early Syntax. In P. Fletcher and M. Garman (eds.), *Language Acquisition* (2nd ed.), 307–326. London: Cambridge University Press, 1986.

Power, T. Mother- and Father-Infant Play: A Developmental Analysis. *Child Development,* 1985, *56,* 1514–1525.

Raloff, J. Reports from the 1982 Meeting of the American Speech Language Hearing Association's Meeting in Toronto, Canada. *Science News,* 1982, *122,* 360.

Raspberry, W. Should Ghettoese Be Accepted? *Today's Education,* April 1970, 59, 30–31, 34–41.

Roe, K. V., Drivas, A., Karagellis, A., and Roe, S. Sex Differences in Vocal Interactions with Mother and Stranger in Greek Infants: Some Cognitive Implications. *Developmental Psychology,* 1985, *21,* 372–378.

Schachter, E. F., Shore, E., Hodapp, R., Chalfin, S., and Bundy, C. Do Girls Talk Earlier? Mean Length of Utterance in Toddlers. *Developmental Psychology,* 1978, *14,* 388–392.

Segalowitz, N. S. Issues in the Cross-Cultural Study of Bilingual Development. In H. C. Triandis and A. Heron (eds.), *Handbook of Cross-Cultural Psychology,* vol. 4, 55–93. Boston: Allyn and Bacon, 1981.

Shatz, M. Communication. In P. H. Mussen (ed.), *Handbook of Child Psychology* (4th ed.), 841–891. New York: Wiley, 1983.

Shiller, V. M., Izard, C. E., and Hembree, E. A. Patterns of Emotion Expression During Separation in the Strange-Situation Procedure. *Developmental Psychology,* 1986, *22,* 378–382.

Skinner, B. F. *Verbal Behavior.* New York: Appleton-Century-Croft, 1957.

Slobin, D. I. Cognitive Prerequisites for the Development of Grammar. In C. A. Ferguson and D. I. Slovin (eds.), *Studies of Child Language Development.* New York: Holt, Rinehart, and Winston, 1973.

———. Children and Language: They Learn the Same Way All Around the World. *Psychology Today,* July 1972, 18.

Smith, M. E. An Investigation of the Development of the Sentence and the Extent of

Vocabulary in Young Children. *University of Iowa Studies in Child Welfare*, 1926, *3*, no. 5.

Smith, R. M., and Neisworth, J. T. *The Exceptional Child: A Functional Approach.* New York: McGraw-Hill, 1975. Second edition 1983.

Snow, C. E. The Development of Conversation Between Mothers and Babies. *Journal of Child Language*, 1977, *4*, 1–22.

Stern, D. N., Spieker, S., and MacKain, K. Intonation Contours as Signals in Maternal Speech to Prelinguistic Infants. *Developmental Psychology*, 1982, *18*, 727–736.

Thomson, J. R., and Chapman, R. S. Who Is "Daddy?" The Status of Two-Year-Olds Overextended Words in Use and Comprehension (1975), cited in J. G. deVilliers and P. A. deVilliers, *Language Acquisition.* Cambridge, Mass.: Harvard University Press, 1978.

Tomasello, M., and Mannle, S. Pragmatics of Sibling Speech to One-Year-Olds. *Child Development*, 1985, *56*, 911–917.

Tomasello, M., Mannle, S., and Kruger, A. The Linguistic Environment of One to Two Year Old Twins. *Developmental Psychology*, 1986, *22*, 169–176.

Trehub, S. Infants' Sensitivity to Vowel and Tonal Contrasts. *Developmental Psychology*, 1973, *9*, 81–96.

U.S. News & World Report. Educating the Melting Pot. *U.S. News & World Report*, March 31, 1986, pp. 20–21.

Weiss, C. D., and Lillywhite, H. S. *Communication Disorders: A Handbook for Prevention and Early Intervention.* St. Louis: Mosby, 1976.

Whitehurst, G. J. Language Development. In B. B. Wolman (ed.), *Handbook of Developmental Psychology*, 367–384. Englewood Cliffs, N.J.: Prentice-Hall, 1982.

Whitehurst, G. J., and Vasta, R. *Child Behavior.* Boston: Houghton Mifflin, 1977.

Wiig, E. H. Communication Disorders. In N. G. Haring (ed.), *Exceptional Children and Youth* (3rd ed.), 81–111. Columbus, Ohio: Merrill, 1982.

Willig, A. E. A Meta-Analysis of Selected Studies on the Effectiveness of Bilingual Education. *Review of Educational Research*, 1985, *55*, 269–317.

Wolff, P. H. Observations on the Early Development of Smiling. In B. M. Foss (ed.), *Determinants of Infant Behavior*, vol. 2. London: Methuen, 1963.

Chapter 7

Adler, R. P. Children's Television Advertising: History of the Issue. In *Children and the Faces of Television: Teaching, Violence, Selling*, 237–251. New York: Academic Press, 1980.

Alwitt, L. F., Anderson, D. R., Lorch, E. P., and Levin, S. R. Preschool Children's Visual Attention to Attributes of Television. *Human Communication Research*, 1980, *7*, 52–67.

Anderson, D. R., Alwitt, L. J., Lorch, E. P., and Levin, S. R. Watching Children Watch Television. In G. Hale and M. Lewis (eds.), *Attention and Cognitive Development.* New York: Plenum, 1979.

Anderson, D. R., and Field, D. E. Children's Attention to Television: Implications for Production. In M. Meyer (ed.), *Children and the Formal Features of Television.* New York: Sauer, 1983.

Anderson, D. R., and Levin, S. R. Young Children's Attention to Sesame Street. *Child Development*, 1976, *47*, 806–811.

Anderson, D. R., and Lorch, E. P. Looking at Television: Action or Reaction? In J. Bryant and D. R. Anderson (eds.), *Children's Understanding of Television*, 1–30. New York: Academic Press, 1983.

Anderson, D. R., Lorch, E. P., Field, D. E., Collins, P. A., and Nathan, J. G. Television Viewing at Home: Age Trends in Visual Attention and Time with TV. *Child Development*, 1986, *57*, 1024–1033.

Appel, L. F., Cooper, R. G., McCarrell, N., et al. The Development of the Distinction Between Perceiving and Memorizing. *Child Development*, 1972, *43*, 1365–1381.

Atkin, C. K. Effects of Television Advertising on Children. In E. L. Palmer and A. Dorr (eds.), *Children and the Faces of Television: Teaching, Violence, Selling*, 287–307. New York: Academic Press, 1980.

Atkin, C. K., and Gibson, W. Children's Nutrition Learning from Television Advertising (1978), cited in C. K. Atkin, Effects of Television Advertising on Children. In E. L. Palmer and A. Dorr (eds.), *Children and the Faces of Television: Teaching, Violence, Selling*, 287–307. New York: Academic Press, 1980.

Ault, R. *Children's Cognitive Development.* New York: Oxford University Press, 1977.

Ball, S., and Bogatz, G. *The First Year of "Sesame Street:" An Evaluation.* Princeton: Educational Testing Service, 1970.

Barcus, F. E. The Nature of Television Advertising to Children. In E. L. Palmer and A. Dorr (eds.), *Children and the Faces of Television: Teaching, Violence, Selling*, 273–284. New York: Academic Press, 1980.

Bernstein, A. C., and Cowan, P. A. Children's Conception of How People Get Babies. *Child Development*, 1975, *46*, 77–91.

Berti, A. E., and Bombi, A. S. The Development of the Concept of Money and Its Value: A Longitudinal Study. *Child Development*, 1981, *52*, 1179–1182.

Beyer, N. R., and Morris, P. M. Food Attitudes and Snacking Patterns of Young Children. *Journal of Nutrition Education*, 1974, *6*, 131–134.

Birch, L. L. Preschool Children's Food Preferences and Consumption Patterns. *Journal of Nutrition Education*, 1979, *11*, 189–192.

Bogatz, G., and Ball, S. *The Second Year of "Sesame Street:" A Continuing Evaluation.* Princeton: Educational Testing Service, 1971.

Bower, G. H., Black, J. B., and Turner, T. J. Scripts in Memory for Text. *Cognitive Psychology*, 1979, *11*, 177–220.

Brainerd, C. J. *Piaget's Theory of Intelligence.* Englewood Cliffs, N.J.: Prentice-Hall, 1978.

Briggs, C., and Elkind, D. Cognitive Development and Early Reading. *Developmental Psychology*, 1973, *9*, 279–280.

Brown, A. L., Bransford, J. D., Ferrara, R. A., and Campione, J. C. Learning, Remembering, and Understanding. In *Handbook of Child Psychology* (4th ed.), ed. J. H. Flavell and E. M. Markman, 77–167. New York: Wiley, 1983.

Brown, F. G. *Principles of Educational and Psychological Testing.* New York: Holt, Rinehart, and Winston, 1983.

Bullock, M. Animism in Childhood Thinking: A New Look at an Old Question. *Developmental Psychology*, 1985, *21*, 217–226.

Busch-Rossnagel, N. A., and Vance, A. K. The Impact of the Schools on Social and Emotional Development. In B. B. Wolman (ed.), *Handbook of Developmental Psychology*, 452–471. Englewood Cliffs, N.J.: Prentice-Hall, 1982.

Chazan, M., and Cox, T. Language Programmes for Disadvantaged Children. In V. P. Varma and P. Williams (eds.), *Piaget: Psychology and Education*, 182–299. Itasca, Ill.: Peacock, 1976.

Chi, M. T. H. Knowledge Structures and Memory Development. In R. R. Siegler (ed.), *Children's Thinking: What Develops?* Hillsdale, N.J.: Erlbaum, 1978.

Chi, M. T. H., and Glaser, R. Problem Solving Ability. In R. J. Sternberg (ed.), *Human Abilities: An Information Processing Approach*, 227–251. New York: Freeman, 1985.

Clarke-Stewart, K. A., and Fein, G. G. Early Childhood Programs. In M. M. Haith and J. J. Campos (eds.), *Handbook of Child Psychology*, vol. 2, 917–1001. New York: Wiley, 1983.

Coates, B., Pusser, H., and Goodman, I. The Influence of "Sesame Street" and "Mister Rogers' Neighborhood" on Children's Social

Behavior in the Preschool. *Child Development,* 1976, *47,* 138–144.

Cook, T. D., Appleton, H., Conner, R. F., Shaffer, A., Tomkin, G., and Weber, S. J. *"Sesame Street" Revisited.* New York: Russell Sage Foundation, 1975.

Cooke, R. E. Introduction. In E. Zigler and J. Valentine (eds.), *Project Head Start: A Legacy of the War on Poverty.* New York: Free Press, 1979.

Corbin, C. B. *A Textbook of Motor Development* (2nd ed.). Dubuque, Iowa: Brown, 1980.

Cowart, B. J., and Beauchamp, G. K. The Importance of Sensory Context in Young Children's Acceptance of Salty Tastes. *Child Development,* 1986, *57,* 1034–1039.

Cratty, B. J. *Perceptual and Motor Development in Infants and Children.* New York: Macmillan, 1970.

Daehler, M. W., and Bukatko, D. *Cognitive Development.* New York: Knopf, 1985.

Darlington, R. B., Royce, J. M., Snipper, A. S., Murray, H. W., and Lazar, I. Preschool Programs and the Later School Competence of Children from Low-Income Families. *Science,* 1980, *208,* 202–204.

Davis, G. A. *Educational Psychology: Theory and Practice.* Reading, Mass.: Addison-Wesley, 1983.

Fivush, R., and Mandler, J. M. Developmental Changes in the Understanding of Temporal Sequence. *Child Development,* 1985, *56,* 1437–1446.

Flavell, J. H. The Development of Children's Knowledge About the Appearance-Reality Distinction. *American Psychologist,* 1986, *41,* 418–426.

———. *Cognitive Development* (2nd ed.). Englewood Cliffs, N.J.: Prentice-Hall, 1985.

Flavell, J. H., Flavell, E. R., Green, F. L., and Wilcox, S. A. The Development of Three Spatial Perspective-Taking Rules. *Child Development,* 1981, *52,* 356–358.

Flavell, J. H., and Wellman, H. M. Metamemory. In R. V. Kail and J. W. Hagen (eds.), *Perspectives on the Development of Memory and Cognition.* Hillsdale, N.J.: Erlbaum, 1977.

Ford, M. E. The Construct Validity of Egocentrism. *Psychological Bulletin,* 1979, *86,* 1169–1188.

Friedrich, L., and Stein, A. *Aggressive and Prosocial Television Programs and the Natural Behavior of Preschool Children.* Monographs of the Society for Research in Child Development, 1973, no. 4, serial no. 151.

Galinsky, E. Investing in Quality Child Care: A Report for A.T.&T. New York: Bank Street College, 1986.

Galst, J., and White, M. A. The Unhealthy Persuader: The Reinforcing Value of Television and Children's Purchase-Influencing Attempts at the Supermarket. *Child Development,* 1976, *47,* 1089–1096.

Gelman, R. Recent Trends in Cognitive Development. In C. J. Scheirer and A. M. Rogers (eds.), *The G. Stanley Hall Lecture Series,* vol. 3, 141–176. Washington, D.C.: American Psychological Association, 1982.

———. Preschool Thought. *American Psychologist,* 1979, *34,* 900–905.

Gelman, R., and Baillargeon, R. A. A Review of Some Piagetian Concepts. In P. H. Mussen (ed.), *Handbook of Child Psychology* (4th ed.), vol. 3, 167–231. New York: Wiley, 1983.

Gelman, R., Bullock, M., and Meck, E. Preschoolers' Understanding of Simple Object Transformations. *Child Development,* 1980, *51,* 691–699.

Gray, S. W., and Klaus, R. A. The Early Training Project—A Seventh Year Report. *Child Development,* 1970, *51,* 908–924.

Gruendel, J. Scripts and Stories: A Study of Children's Event Narratives (1980), cited in J. M. Mandler, Representation. In P. H. Mussen (ed.), *Handbook of Child Psychology* (4th ed.), vol. 3, 420–495. New York: Wiley, 1983.

Hamill, P. V. V. *NCHS Growth Curves for Children.* Vital and Health Statistics,, Series 11, Data from the National Health Survey, no. 165. Washington, D.C.: U.S. Government Printing Office (DHEW no. 78–1650), 1977.

Hamilton, E. M. N., and Whitney, E. N. *Nutrition: Concepts and Controversies* (2nd ed.). St. Paul: West, 1982.

Heinicke, C. M. Development from Two and One-Half to Four Years. In J. D. Noshpitz (ed.), *Basic Handbook of Child Psychiatry,* vol. 1, 167–178. New York: Basic Books, 1979.

Heinz, J. National Leadership for Children's Television. *American Psychologist,* 1983, *38,* 817–820.

Hochman, D. (Chairperson, Early Childhood Education Program, Suffolk County Community College, Selden, N.Y.). Personal communication, 1987.

Huston, A. C., and Wright, J. C. Children's Processing of Television: The Informative Functions of Formal Features. In J. Bryant and D. R. Anderson (eds.), *Children's Understanding of Television,* 35–65. New York: Academic Press, 1983.

Inhelder, B., and Piaget, J. *The Early Growth of Logic in the Child.* New York: Harper and Row, 1964.

Istomina, Z. M. The Development of Voluntary Memory in Preschool-Age Children (1975), cited in S. G. Paris and B. K. Lindauer, The Development of Cognitive Skills During Childhood. In B. B. Wolman (ed.), *Handbook of Developmental Psychology,* 333–349. Englewood Cliffs, N.J.: Prentice-Hall, 1982.

Kail, R., and Hagen, J. W. Memory in Childhood. In B. B. Wolman (ed.), *Handbook of Developmental Psychology,* 350–367. Englewood Cliffs, N.J.: Prentice-Hall, 1982.

Katz, L. G. Should You Be Your Child's Parents? *Parents,* August 1980, 88–90.

Keeney, T. J., Cannizzo, S. R., and Flavell, J. H. Spontaneous and Induced Verbal Rehearsal in a Recall Task. *Child Development,* 1967, *38,* 953–966.

Kellogg, R. *Analyzing Children's Art.* Palo Alto, Calif.: Mayfield, 1970.

Koslowski, B. Quantitative and Qualitative Changes in the Development of Seriation. *Merrill-Palmer Quarterly,* 1980, *26,* 391–405.

Lamb, M. Interactions Between Eight-Month-Old Children and Their Fathers and Mothers. In M. Lamb (ed.), *The Role of the Father in Child Development,* 307–329. New York: Wiley, 1976.

Lazar, I., Darlington, R., Murray, H., Royce, J., and Snipper, A. *Lasting Effects of Early Education: A Report from the Consortium for Longitudinal Studies.* Monographs of the Society for Research in Child Development, 1982, *47,* nos. 2–3, serial no. 195.

Lempers, J. D., Flavell, E. R., and Flavell, J. H. The Development in Very Young Children of Tacit Knowledge Concerning Visual Perceptions. *Genetic Psychology Monographs,* 1977, *95,* 3–53.

Lesser, G. S. Applications of Psychology to Television Programming: Formulation of Program Objectives. *American Psychologist,* 1976, *31,* 135–137.

Levin, S. R., Petros, T. V., and Petrella, F. W. Preschoolers' Awareness of Television Advertising. *Child Development,* 1983, *53,* 933–937.

Liebert, R. M., Neale, J. M., and Davison, E. S. *The Early Window: Effects of Television on Children and Youth.* New York: Pergamon, 1973.

Lindberg, M. The Role of Knowledge Structures in the Ontogeny of Learning. *Journal of Experimental Child Psychology,* 1980, *30,* 401–410.

Los Angeles Times. Hero, 5, Can Do It but Can't Say It. *Los Angeles Times,* August 7, 1986, p. 2.

Lyle, J., and Hoffman, H. R. Explorations in Patterns of Television Viewing by Preschool-

Age Children. In E. A. Rubenstein, G. A. Comstock, and J. P. Murray (eds.), *Television and Social Behavior 4: Television in Day to Day Life, Patterns of Use.* Washington, D.C.: U.S. Government Printing Office, 1972.

Mandler, J. M. Representation. In P. H. Mussen (ed.), *Handbook of Child Psychology* (4th ed.), vol. 3, 420–495. New York: Wiley, 1983.

Mandler, J., and Johnson, N. Remembrance of Things Passed: Story Structure and Recall. *Cognitive Development,* 1977, 9, 111–151.

Mann, M. J., Harrell, A., and Hurt, M. A. *A Review of Head Start Research Since 1969 and an Annotated Bibliography.* Washington, D.C.: U.S. Government Printing Office, 1978, no. 017–092–00037–5.

McClinton, B. S., and Meier, B. G. *Beginnings: The Psychology of Early Childhood.* St. Louis: Mosby, 1978.

Miller, L. B. Development of Curriculum Models in Head Start. In E. Zigler and J. Valentine (eds.), *Project Head Start: A Legacy on the War on Poverty,* 195–221. New York: Free Press, 1979.

Minuchin, P. P., and Shapiro, E. K. The School as a Context for Social Development. In E. M. Hetherington (ed.), *Handbook of Child Psychology* (4th ed.), 197–275. New York: Wiley, 1983.

Moore, R. S., and Moore, D. R. How Early Should They Go to School? *Childhood Education,* October 1973.

Nelson, K. How Children Represent Knowledge of Their World In and Out of Language: A Preliminary Report in R. S. Siegler (ed.), *Children's Thinking: What Develops.* Hillsdale, N.J.: Erlbaum, 1978.

Nelson, K., and Gruendel, J. Generalized Event Representations: Basic Building Blocks of Cognitive Development in M. E. Lamb and A. L. Brown (eds.), *Advances in Developmental Psychology,* vol. 1. Hillsdale, N.J.: Erlbaum, 1981.

O'Bryan, K. G. The Teaching Face: A Historical Perspective. In E. L. Palmer and A. Dorr (eds.), *Children and the Faces of Television: Teaching, Violence, Selling,* 5–16. New York: Academic Press, 1980.

Oyemade, U. J. The Rationale for Head Start as a Vehicle for the Upward Mobility of Minority Families: A Minority Perspective. *American Journal of Orthopsychiatry,* 1985, 55, 591–602.

Palmer, F. H., and Andersen, L. W. Long-Term Gains from Early Intervention: Findings from Longitudinal Studies. In *Project Head Start: A Legacy of the War on Poverty,* ed. E. Zigler and J. Valentine, 495–509. New York: Free Press, 1979.

Paris, S. G., and Lindauer, B. K. The Development of Cognitive Skills During Childhood. In B. B. Wolman (ed.), *Handbook of Developmental Psychology,* 333–350. Englewood Cliffs, N.J.: Prentice-Hall, 1982.

Parke, R. D., and Slaby, R. G. The Development of Aggression. In E. M. Hetherington (ed.), *Handbook of Child Psychology* (4th ed.), 547–643. New York: Wiley, 1983.

Perlnutter, M., and Myers, N. A. Recognition Memory Development in Two-to-Four-Year-Olds. *Developmental Psychology,* 1979, 15, 73–83.

Peters, D. L. Early Childhood Education: An Overview and Evaluation. In H. L. Hom and P. A. Robinson (eds.), *Psychological Processes in Early Education,* 1–23. New York: Academic Press, 1977.

Phillips, J. L. *The Origins of Intellect: Piaget's Theory* (2nd ed.). San Francisco: Freeman, 1975.

Piaget, J. Piaget's Theory. In P. H. Mussen (ed.), *Handbook of Child Psychology* (4th ed.), vol. 1, 103–129. New York: Wiley, 1983 (originally published 1970).

———. *Understanding Causality.* New York: Norton, 1974.

———. *The Child's Conception of Time.* London: Routledge and Kegan Paul, 1970, (originally published 1926).

———. *The Construction of Reality in the Child.* New York: Basic Books, 1954.

———. *The Child's Conception of Number.* New York: Humanities Press, 1982.

———. *The Child's Conception of Space.* New York: Norton, 1956.

———. *Six Psychological Studies.* New York: Vintage Books, 1967.

———. *The Moral Judgment of the Child.* New York: Free Press, 1965 (originally published 1932).

———. *The Child's Conception of Physical Causality.* Totowa, N.J.: Littlefield, 1960 (originally published 1927).

Piaget, J., and Inhelder, B. *The Child's Construction of Quantities: Conservation and Atomism.* London: Routledge and Kegan Paul, 1974 (originally published 1942).

Pulaski, M. A. S. *Understanding Piaget: An Introduction to Children's Cognitive Development* (rev. ed.). New York: Harper and Row, 1980.

Rossiter, J. R. Children and Television Advertising: Policy Issues, Perspectives, and the Status of Research. In E. L. Palmer and A. Dorr (eds.), *Children and the Faces of Television:*

Teaching, Violence, Selling, 251–271. New York: Academic Press, 1980.

Rubin, K. H., Fein, G. G., and Vandenberg, B. Play. In E. Hetherington (ed.), *Handbook of Child Development* (4th ed.), 693–775. New York: Wiley, 1983.

Rubinstein, E. A. Television and Behavior: Research Conclusions of the 1982 NIMH Report and Their Policy Implications. *American Psychologist,* 1983, 38, 820–826.

———. Television and the Young Viewer. *American Scientist,* November–December 1978.

Salomon, G. Television Watching and Mental Effort: A Social-Psychological View. In J. Bryant and D. R. Anderson (eds.), *Children's Understanding of Television,* 181–196. New York: Academic Press, 1983.

Schank, R. C., and Abelson, R. P. *Scripts, Plans, Goals, and Understanding.* Hillsdale, N.J.: Erlbaum, 1977.

Singer, D. G., and Singer, J. L. Family Television Viewing Habits and the Spontaneous Play of Preschool Children. *American Journal of Orthopsychiatry,* 1976, 46, 496–502.

Singer, J. L., and Singer, D. G. Psychologists Look at Television: Cognitive, Developmental, Personality, and Social Policy Implications. *American Psychologist,* 1983, 38, 826–835.

Sjolund, A. The Effect of Day Care Institutions on Children's Development: An Analysis of International Research (1971), cited in K. Clarke-Stewart and G. G. Fein. Early Child Programs. In P. H. Mussen (ed.), *The Handbook of Child Psychology* (3rd ed.), vol. 2, 917–1001. New York: Wiley, 1983.

Sprigle, J. E. and Schaefer, L. Longitudinal Evaluation of the Effects of Two Compensatory Preschool Programs on Fourth- Through Sixth-Grade Students. *Developmental Psychology,* 1985, 21, 702–709.

Stoneman, Z., and G. H. Brody. Peers as Mediators of Television Food Advertisements Aimed at Children. *Developmental Psychology,* 1981, 17, 853–858.

Talbot, N. B., and Guthrie, A. Health Care Needs of American Children. In N. B. Talbot (ed.), *Raising Children in Modern America: Problems and Prospective Solutions.* Boston: Little, Brown, 1976.

Tanner, J. M. *Foetus into Man: Physical Growth from Conception to Maturity.* Cambridge, Mass.: Harvard University Press, 1978.

Tower, R. B., Singer, D. G., Singer, J. J., and Biggs, A. Differential Effects of Television Programming on Preschoolers' Cognition, Imagination, and Social Play. *American Journal of Orthopsychiatry,* 1979, 49, 265–281.

Trabasso, T. Representation, Memory, and Reasoning: How Do We Make Transitive Inferences? In A. D. Pick (ed.), *Minnesota Symposia on Child Psychology*, vol. 9 Minneapolis: University of Minnesota Press, 1975.

U.S. Bureau of the Census. *Statistical Abstract of the United States, 1986*. Washington, D.C., 1986.

Vernon, P. E. Environment and Intelligenc. In V. P. Varma and P. Williams (eds.), *Piaget, Psychology, and Education*, 31–43. Itasca, Ill.: Peacock, 1976.

Vurpillot, E. The Development of Scanning Strategies and Their Relation to Visual Differentiation. *Journal of Experimental Child Psychology*, 1968, 6, 632–650.

Vurpillot, E., and Ball, W. A. The Concept of Identity and Children's Selective Attention. In G. Hale and M. Lewis (eds.), *Attention and Cognitive Development*. New York: Plenum, 1979.

Ward, S., and Wackman, D. Television Advertising and Intrafamily Influence: Children's Purchase Influence Attempts and Parental Yielding. In E. A. Rubenstein, G. A. Comstock, and J. P. Murray (eds.), *Television and Social Behavior 4: Television in Day-to-Day Life: Patterns of Use*, 516–525. Washington, D.C.: U.S. Government Printing Office, 1972.

Washington, V. Head Start: How Appropriate for Minority Families in the 1980s. *American Journal of Orthopsychiatry*, 1985, 55, 577–590.

Watkins, B. A., Huston-Stein, A., and Wright, J. C. Effects of Planned Television Programming. In E. L. Palmer and A. Dorr (eds.), *Children and the Faces of Television: Teaching, Violence, Selling*, 49–71. New York: Academic Press, 1980.

Weinberg, R. A. Early Childhood Education and Intervention: Establishing an American Tradition. *American Psychologist*, 1979, 34, 912–916.

Westinghouse Learning Corporation. *The Impact of Head Start: An Evaluation of Effects of Head Start on Children's Cognitive and Affective Development*. Executive Summary. Ohio University, Report to the Office of Economic Opportunity. Washington, D.C.: Clearinghouse for Federal Scientific and Technical Information, June 1969 (EDO93497).

Wimmer, H. Children's Understanding of Stories: Assimilation by a General Schema for Actions or Coordination of Temporal Relations? In F. Wilkening, J. Becker, and T. Trabasso (eds.), *Information Integration by Children*. Hillsdale, N.J.: Erlbaum, 1980.

———. Processing of Script Deviations by Young Children. *Discourse Processes*, 1979, 2, 301–310.

Wright, J. C., Huston, A. C., Ross, R. P., Calvert, S. L., Rolandelli, D., Weeks, L. A., Raeisse, P., and Potts, R. Pace and Continuity of Television Programs: Effects on Children's Attention and Comprehension. *Developmental Psychology*, 1984, 20, 653–667.

Wright, J. C., and Vliestra, A. G. The Development of Selective Attention. In H. W. Reese (ed.), *Advances in Child Development and Behavior*, vol. 10. New York: Academic Press, 1977.

Zigler, E. Assessing Head Start at 20: An Invited Commentary. *American Journal of Orthopsychiatry*, 1985, 55, 603–609.

Zigler, E., and Berman, W. Discerning the Future of Early Childhood Intervention. *American Psychologist*, 1983, 38, 894–907.

Zigler, E., and Valentine, J. *Project Head Start—A Legacy of the War on Poverty*. New York: Free Press, 1979.

Zinchenko, V. P., Chzhi-Tsin, V., and Tarakanov, V. V. The Formation and Development of Perceptual Activity (1977), cited in E. J. Gibson and E. S. Spelke. The Development of Perception. In P. H. Mussen (ed.), *Handbook of Child Psychology* (4th ed.), vol. 3, 1–77. New York: Wiley, 1983.

Zinsser, C. The Preschool Pressure Cooker. *Working Mother*, October 1981.

Chapter 8

Abramovitch, R., Corter, C., and Lando, B. Sibling Interaction in the Home. *Child Development*, 1979, 50, 997–1003.

Abramovitch, R., Corter, C., and Pepler, D. Observations of Mixed-Sex Sibling Dyads. *Child Development*, 1980, 51, 1268–1271.

Abramovitch, R., Corter, C., Pepler, D. J., and Stanhope, L. Sibling and Peer Interaction: A Final Follow-up and a Comparison. *Child Development*, 1986, 57, 217–229.

Adams-Tucker, C. Proximate Effects of Sexual Abuse in Childhood: A Report on 28 Children. *American Journal of Psychiatry*, 1982, 139, 1252–1256.

Altrocchi, J. *Abnormal Psychology*. New York: Harcourt Brace Jovanovich, 1980.

American Humane Association, *Highlights of Official Child Neglect and Abuse Reporting, 1984*. Denver, Colo.: American Humane Association, 1986.

Archer, J. Biological Explanations of Psychological Sex Differences. In B. B. Lloyd and J. Archer (eds.), *Exploring Sex Differences*. London: Academic Press, 1976.

Axline, V. M. *Play Therapy*. New York: Houghton, 1947. Rev. ed., Ballantine Books, 1969.

Bardwick, J. *The Psychology of Women*. New York: Harper and Row, 1971.

Baumrind, D. New Directions in Socialization Research. *American Psychologist*, 1980, 35, 639–652.

———. Parental Disciplinary Patterns and Social Competence in Children. *Youth and Society*, March 1978, 9, 239–276.

———. Current Patterns of Parental Authority. *Developmental Psychology Monograph*, 1971, 4, no. 1, pt. 2.

———. Child Care Practices Anteceding 3 Patterns of Preschool Behavior. *Genetic Psychology Monographs*, 1967, 75, 43–88.

Becker, W. C. Consequences of Different Kinds of Parental Discipline. In M. L. Hoffman and H. W. Hoffman (eds.), *Review of Child Development Research*, vol. 1. New York: Russell Sage Foundation, 1964.

Bee, H. *Social Issues in Developmental Psychology* (2nd ed.). New York: Harper and Row, 1978.

Bem, S. Sex-Role Adaptability: One Consequence of Psychological Androgyny. *Journal of Personality and Social Psychology*, 1975, 31, 634–643.

———. The Measurement of Psychological Androgyny. *Journal of Consulting and Clinical Psychology*, 1974, 42, 155–162.

Berdine, W. H., and Blackhurst, A. E. *An Introduction to Special Education* (2nd ed.). Boston: Little, Brown, 1985.

Blakemore, J. E. O. Age and Sex Differences in Interaction with a Human Infant. *Child Development*, 1981, 52, 386–388.

Block, J. H. Socialization Influences on Personality Development in Males and Females. *American Psychological Association's Master Lecture Series*. Washington, D.C.: American Psychological Association, 1979.

———. Issues, Problems, and Pitfalls in Assessing Sex Differences: A Critique of the Psychology of Sex Differences. *Merrill-Palmer Quarterly*, 1976, 22, 283–308.

Brody, G. H., Zolinda, S., MacKinnon, C. E., and MacKinnon, R. Role Relationships and Behavior Between Preschool-Aged and School-Aged Siblings. *Developmental Psychology*, 1985, 21, 124–129.

Browne, A., and Finkelhor, D. Impact of Child Sexual Abuse: A Review of the Research. *Psychological Bulletin*, 1986, 99, 66–77.

Canavan, J. W. Sexual Child Abuse. In N. S. Ellerstein (ed.), *Child Abuse and Neglect: A Medical Reference*, 233–253. New York: Wiley, 1981.

Carper, L. Sex Roles in the Nursery. *Harper's*, April 1978, 35–42.

Chafetz, J. S. The Bringing-up of Dick and Jane (1974). In S. Cohen and T. J. Comisky (eds.), *Child Development: Contemporary Perspectives* 196–201. Itasca, Ill.: Peacock, 1977.

Dean, A. L., Malik, M. M., Richards, W., and Stringer, S. A. Effects of Parental Maltreatment on Children's Conceptions of Interpersonal Relationships. *Developmental Psychology*, 1986, *22*, 617–626.

DeVine, R. A. Sexual Abuse of Children: An Overview of the Problem. In *Sexual Abuse of Children: Selected Readings*. Washington, D.C.: Department of Health and Human Services, publ. no. 78–30161, November 1980, 3–7.

DiPietro, J. Rough and Tumble Play: A Function of Gender. *Developmental Psychology*, 1981, *17*, 50–58.

Dunn, J., and Kendrick, C. *Siblings: Love, Envy, and Understanding.* Cambridge, Mass.: Harvard University Press, 1982.

Eagly, A. H. Sex Differences in Influenceability. *Psychological Bulletin*, 1978, *85*, 86–116.

Eisenberg, N., Wolchik, S. A., Hernandez, R., and Pasternack, J. F. Parental Socialization of Young Children's Play: A Short-Term Longitudinal Study. *Child Development*, 1985, *56*, 1506–1513.

Erikson, E. H. The Problem of Ego Identity (1959). In L. D. Steinberg (ed.), *The Life Cycle: Readings in Human Development*, 189–198. New York: Columbia University Press, 1981.

———. *Youth and Crisis.* New York: Norton, 1968.

———. *Childhood and Society* (2nd ed.). New York: Norton, 1963.

Fagot, B. Sex Differences in Toddler's Behavior and Parental Reactions. *Developmental Psychology*, 1974, *10*, 554–558.

Finkelhor, D. How Widespread Is Child Sexual Abuse? *Children Today*, July–August 1984a, 18–20.

———. The Prevention of Child Sexual Abuse: An Overview of Needs and Problems. *SIE-CUS Report.* September 1984b, *13*, 1–5.

Frasher, R., and Walker, A. Sex Roles in Early Reading Textbooks. *The Reading Teacher*, 1972, *25*, 741–749.

Freud, S. *New Introductory Lectures on Psychoanalysis.* New York: Norton, 1965 (originally published 1933).

———. The Dissolution of the Oedipus Complex (1924). In J. Strachey (ed.), *The Standard Edition of the Complete Works of Sigmund Freud.* London: Hogarth, 1957.

Friedrich, W. N., and Boriskin, J. A. The Role of the Child in Abuse: A Review of the Literature. *American Journal of Orthopsychiatry*, 1976, *46*, 580–591.

Frodi, A. M., and Lamb, M. E. Child Abusers' Responses to Infant Smiles and Cries. *Child Development*, 1980, *51*, 238–241.

Galdston, R. Preventing the Abuse of Little Children: The Parents' Center Project for the Study and Prevention of Child Abuse. *American Journal of Orthopsychiatry*, 1975, *45*, 372–382.

Garbarino, J., Guttman, E., and Seeley, J. *The Psychologically Battered Child: Strategies for Identification, Assessment, and Intervention.* San Francisco: Jossey-Bass, 1986.

Garvey, C. *Play,* Cambridge, Mass.: Harvard University Press, 1977.

Gelles, R. J. Violence Towards Children in the United States. *American Journal of Orthopsychiatry*, 1978, *48*, 580–593.

Green, A. H., Gaines, R. W., and Sandgrund, A. Child Abuse: Pathological Syndrome of Family Reaction. *American Journal of Psychiatry*, 1974, *131*, 882–886.

Harlow, H. F., and Harlow, M. K. Learning to Love. *American Scientist*, 1966, *54*, 244–272.

Harper, L. V., and Huie, K. S. The Effects of Prior Group Experience, Age, and Familiarity on the Quality and Organization of Preschoolers' Social Relationships. *Child Development*, 1985, *56*, 707–714.

Hart, S. N., and Brassard, M. R. A Major Threat to Children's Mental Health: Psychological Maltreatment. *American Psychologist*, 1987, *42*, 160–166.

Hartup, W. W. Peer Interaction and Social Organization. In P. H. Mussen (ed.), *Carmichael's Manual of Child Development* (3rd ed.). New York: Wiley, 1970.

Hetherington, E. M. The Effects of Familial Variables on Sex Typing, on Parent-Child Similarity, and on Imitation in Children (1967). In P. H. Mussen, J. Conger, and J. Kagan (eds.), *Basic and Contemporary Issues in Child Development.* New York: Harper and Row, 1977.

Hoffman, L. Effects of Maternal Employment on the Child: A Review of the Research. *Developmental Psychology*, 1974, *10*, 204–228.

Horney, K. *Feminine Psychology.* New York: Norton, 1967.

———. *New Ways in Psychoanalysis.* New York: Norton, 1939.

Howes, C. Sharing Fantasy: Social Pretend Play in Toddlers. *Child Development*, 1985, *5*, 1253–1259.

Hyde, J. S. How Large Are Gender Differences in Aggression: A Developmental Meta-Analysis. *Developmental Psychology*, 1984, *20*, 722–736.

Jones, C. O. Development of Children from Abusive Families. In A. W. Franklin (ed.), *Child Abuse*, 61–71. Edinburgh: Churchill-Livingston, 1977.

Jossselyn, W. D. Androgen-Induced Social Dominance in Infant Rhesus Monkeys. *Journal of Child Psychology and Psychiatry*, 1973, *14*, 137–145.

Karen, R. L. *An Introduction to Behavior Therapy and Its Application.* New York: Harper and Row, 1974.

Kaufman, J., and Zigler, E. Do Abused Children Become Abusive Parents. *American Journal of Orthopsychiatry*, 1987, *57*, 186–192.

Kazdin, A. E. *Behavior Modification in Applied Settings* (3rd ed.). Homewood, Ill.: Dorsey, 1984.

Kempe, R. S., and Kempe, C. H. *Child Abuse.* Cambridge, Mass.: Harvard University Press, 1978.

Kendrick, C., and Dunn, J. Sibling Quarrels and Maternal Responses. *Developmental Psychology*, 1983, *19*, 62–71.

Kinard, E. M., and Klerman, L. V. Teenage Parenting and Child Abuse: Are They Related? *American Journal of Orthopsychiatry*, 1980, *50*, 481–488.

Kline, P. *Fact and Fantasy in Freudian Theory.* London: Methuen, 1972.

Langois, J. H., and Downs, A. C. Mothers, Fathers, and Peers as Socialization Agents of Sex-Typed Play Behavior in Young Children. *Child Development*, 1980, *51*, 1237–1247.

Levy-Shiff, R., and Hoffman, M. A. Social Behavior of Urban and Preschool Children in Israel. *Developmental Psychology*, 1985, *21*, 1204–1205.

Lystad, M. H. Violence at Home: A Review of the Literature. *American Journal of Orthopsychiatry*, 1975, *46*, 328–345.

Maccoby, E., and Jacklin, C. *The Psychology of Sex Differences.* Stanford, Calif.: Stanford University Press, 1974.

Maccoby, E. E., and Martin, J. A. Socialization in the Context of the Family: Parent-Child Interaction. In P. H. Mussen (ed.), *Handbook of Child Development* (4th ed.), vol. 4, 1–103. New York: Wiley, 1983.

Martin, B. Parent-Child Relationships. In F. D. Horowitz (ed.), *Review of Child Development Research*, vol. 4, 463–540. Chicago: University of Chicago Press, 1975.

Martin, H. A. Child-Oriented Approach to Prevention of Abuse. In A. W. Franklin (ed.), *Child Abuse*, 9–20. London: Churchill-Livingston, 1978.

McGuinness, D. How Schools Discriminate Against Boys (1977). In S. Hochman and P. Kaplan (eds.), *Readings in Psychology: A Soft Approach* (rev. ed.), 74–79. Lexington, Mass.: Ginn, 1979.

———. Sex Differences in the Organization of Perception and Cognition. In B. Lloyd and J. Archer (eds.), *Exploring Sex Differences*, 123–157. London: Academic Press, 1976.

McLaughlin, B. Child Compliance to Parental Control Techniques. *Developmental Psychology*, 1983, *19*, 667–674.

Mead, M. On Freud's View of Female Psychology. In J. Strouse (ed.), *Women and Analysis*. New York: Grossman, 1974.

Melton, G. B., and Davidson, H. A. Child Protection and Society: When Should the State Intervene? *American Psychologist*, 1987, *42*, 172–176.

Minton, H. L., and Schneider, F. W. *Differential Psychology*. Monterey, Calif.: Brooks/Cole, 1980.

Mischel, W. *Introduction to Personality* (2nd ed.). New York: Holt, Rinehart, and Winston, 1976.

———. Sex-Typing and Socialization. In P. H. Mussen (ed.), *Carmichael's Manual of Child Psychology* (3rd ed.). New York: Wiley, 1970.

Money, J., and Ehrhardt, A. *Man and Woman, Boy and Girl*. Baltimore: Johns Hopkins University Press, 1972.

Mullahy, P. *Oedipus: Myth and Complex*. New York: Hermitage, 1948.

Parke, R. D., and Collmer, C. W. Child Abuse: An Interdisciplinary Analysis. In E. M. Hetherington (ed.), *Review of Child Development Research*, vol. 5. Chicago: University of Chicago Press, 1975.

Parten, M. B. Social Play Among Preschool Children. *Journal of Abnormal and Social Psychology*, 1932, *27*, 243–269.

Plomin, R., and Foch, T. T. Sex Differences and Individual Differences. *Child Development*, 1981, *52*, 383–385.

Queens Bench Foundation. Sexual Abuse of Children: A Guide for Parents (1977). In *Sexual Abuse of Children: Selected Readings*. Washington, D.C.: Department of Health and Human Services, pub. no. (OHDS) 78–30161, November 1980, 173–181.

Rheingold, H., and Cook, K. The Contents of Boys' and Girls' Rooms as an Index of Parents' Behavior. *Child Development*, 1975, *46*, 459–463.

Richmond-Abbott, M. *Masculine and Feminine*. Reading, Mass.: Addison-Wesley, 1983.

Rogers, L. Male Hormones and Behaviour. In B. B. Lloyd and J. Archer (eds.), *Exploring Sex Differences*, 185–213. London: Academic Press, 1976.

Rosenberg, M. S. New Directions for Research on the Psychological Maltreatment of Children. *American Psychologist*, 1987, *42*, 166–172.

Rubin, K. H., Fein, G. G., and Vandenberg, B. Play. In P. H. Mussen (ed.), *Handbook of Child Psychology* (4th ed.), vol. 4, 693–775. New York: Wiley, 1983.

Russell, G. The Father's Role and Its Relation to Masculinity, Femininity, and Androgyny. *Child Development*, 1978, *49*, 1174–1181.

Sarafino, E. P. An Estimate of Nationwide Incidence of Sexual Offenses Against Children. *Child Welfare*, February, 1979, 127–135.

Schaffer, K. F. *Sex Roles and Human Behavior*. Cambridge, Mass.: Winthrop, 1981.

Schultz, L. G., and Jones, P. Sexual Abuse of Children: Issues for Social and Health Professionals. *Child Welfare*, March–April 1983, *62*, 99–109.

Sears, R. R., Rae, L., and Alpert, R. *Identification and Child Rearing*. Stanford, Calif.: Stanford University Press, 1965.

Smetana, J. G. Preschool Children's Conceptions of Sex-Role Transgressions. *Child Development*, 1986, *57*, 862–871.

Smith, P. K. A Longitudinal Study of Social Participation in Preschool Children: Solitary and Parallel Play Reexamined. *Developmental Psychology*, 1978, *14*, 517–523.

Smith, P. K., and Vollstedt, R. On Defining Play: An Empirical Study of the Relationship Between Play and Various Play Criteria. *Child Development*, 1985, *56*, 1042–1050.

Spence, J. H., Helmreich, R., and Stapp, J. Ratings of Self and Peers on Sex-Role Attribution and Their Relationship to Self-Esteem and Concept of Masculinity and Femininity. *Journal of Personality and Social Psychology*, 1975, *32*, 29–39.

Starr, R. Y. Child Abuse. *American Psychologist*, 1979, *34*, 872–878.

Steinberg, L. D., Catalano, R., and Dooley, D. Economic Antecedents of Child Abuse. *Child Development*, 1981, *52*, 975–985.

Stewart, R. B. Sibling Attachment Relationships: Child-Infant Interactions in Infancy. *Developmental Psychology*, 1983, *19*, 192–200.

Sutton-Smith, B., and Roberts, J. M. Play, Games, and Sports. In H. C. Triandis and A. Heron (eds.), *Handbook of Cross-Cultural Psychology*, vol. 4. Boston: Allyn and Bacon, 1981.

Sutton-Smith, B., and Rosenberg, B. G. *The Sibling*. New York: Holt, Rinehart, and Winston, 1970.

Vandenberg, B. Play and Development from an Ethological Perspective. *American Psychologist*, 1978, *33*, 724–739.

Vandenberg, S. G., and Kuse, A. R. Spatial Ability: A Critical Review of the Sex-Linked Major-Gene Hypothesis. In M. Whittig and A. Petersen (eds.), *Determinants of Sex Related Differences in Cognitive Functioning*. New York: Academic Press, 1979.

Weitzman, N., Birns, B., and Friend, R. Traditional and Nontraditional Mothers' Communication with Their Daughters and Sons. *Child Development*, 1985, *56*, 894–898.

Williams, J. E., Bennett, S. M., and Best, D. L. Awareness and Expression of Sex Stereotypes in Young Children. *Developmental Psychology*, 1975, *11*, 635–642.

Chapter 9

Adelman, H. S., and Taylor, L. *An Introduction to Learning Disabilities*. Glenview, Ill.: Scott, Foresman, 1986.

American Dental Association. *Your Child's Teeth*. Chicago: American Dental Association.

Ames, L. B. Ready or Not. *American Educator*, Summer 1986, *10*, 30–34.

Anderson, R. C., and Faust, G. W. *Educational Psychology: The Science of Instruction and Learning*. New York: Dodd, Mead, 1973.

Ault, R. *Children's Cognitive Development*. New York: Oxford University Press, 1977.

Austin, A. B., and Draper, D. C. Peer Relationships of the Academically Gifted: A Review. *Gifted Child Quarterly*, 1981, *25*, 129–133.

Becker, D. J., and Drash, A. L. Endocrinology. In J. D. Noshpitz (ed.), *Basic Handbook of Child Psychiatry*, vol. 1, 601–621. New York: Basic Books, 1979.

Bersoff, D. N. Test Bias: The Judicial Report Card. *New York University Educational Quarterly*, 1981a, *13*, 2–9.

———. Testing and the Law. *American Psychologist*, 1981b, *36*, 1047–1057.

Biehler, R. F., and Snowman, J. *Psychology Applied to Teaching* (4th ed.). Boston: Houghton Mifflin, 1982.

Blank, M. Intelligence Testing. In C. B. Kopp and J. B. Krakow (eds.), *The Child: Development in a Social Context*, 708–715. Reading, Mass.: Addison-Wesley, 1982.

Blank, M., and Klig, S. The Child and the School Experience. In C. B. Kopp and J. B. Krakow (eds.), *The Child: Development in a Social Context*, 456–508. Reading, Mass.: Addision-Wesley, 1982.

Bloom, B. S. *Human Characteristics and School Learning*. New York: McGraw-Hill, 1976.

Borkowski, J. G., Peck, V. A., Reid, M. K., and Kurtz, B. E. Impulsivity and Strategy Transfer: Metamemory as Mediator. *Child Development*, 1983, *54*, 459–473.

Brickey, M., and Campbell, K. Fast Food Employment for Moderately and Mildly Mentally Retarded Adults. *Mental Retardation*, 1981, *19*, 113–116.

Bringuier, J. C. *Conversations with Jean Piaget.* Chicago: University of Chicago Press, 1980.

Brophy, J. Successful Teaching Strategies for the Inner-City Child. *Phi Delta Kappan*, April 1982, 527–530.

Brown, A. L., Bransford, J. D., Ferrara, R. A., and Campione, J. C. Learning, Remembering, and Understanding. In P. H. Mussen (ed.), *Handbook of Child Psychology* (4th ed.), vol. 3. New York: Wiley, 1983.

Brown, A. L., and Smiley, S. S. Rating the Importance of Structural Units of Prose Passages: A Problem of Metacognitive Development. *Child Development*, 1977, *48*, 1–8.

Brown, F. G. *Principles of Educational and Psychological Testing.* New York: Holt, Rinehart, and Winston, 1983.

Buchanan, M., and Wolf, J. A Comprehensive Study of Learning Disabled Adults. *Journal of Learning Disabilities*, 1986, *19*, 34–38.

Bullen, B. A., Read, R. B., and Mayer, J. Physical Activity of Obese and Non-Obese Adolescent Girls Appraised by Motion Picture Sampling. *American Journal of Clinical Nutrition*, 1964, 211–215.

Burstein, B., Bank, L., and Jarvik, L. F. Sex Differences in Cognitive Functioning: Evidence, Determinants, Implications. *Human Development*, 1980, *23*, 289–313.

Busch-Rossnagel, N. A., and Vance, A. K. The Impact of the Schools on Social and Emotional Development. In B. B. Wolman (ed.), *Handbook of Developmental Psychology*, 452–471. Englewood Cliffs, N.J.: Prentice-Hall, 1982.

Cataldo, C. B., and Whitney, E. N. *Nutrition and Diet Therapy: Principles and Practices.* St. Paul: West, 1986.

Centra, J. A., and Potter, D. A. School and Teacher Effects: An Interrelational Model. *Review of Educational Research*, 1980, *50*, 273–290.

Cohen, M. Effective Schools: Accumulating Research Findings. *American Education*, January 1982, 13–16.

Cohen, R. L. Reading Disabled Children Are Aware of Their Cognitive Deficits. *Journal of Learning Disabilities*, 1983, *16*, 286–289.

Cole, N. S. Bias in Testing. *American Psychologist*, 1981, *36*, 1067–1078.

Coleman, J. S., et al. *Equality of Educational Opportunity Survey.* Washington, D.C.: U.S. Government Printing Office, 1966.

Corbin, C. B. Childhood Obesity. In C. B. Corbin (ed.), *A Textbook of Motor Development.* Dubuque, Iowa: Brown, 1980a, 121–128.

———. The Physical Fitness of Children: A Discussion and Point of View. In C. B. Corbin (ed.), *A Textbook of Motor Development*, 100–107. Dubuque, Iowa: Brown, 1980b.

Cratty, B. J. *Perceptual and Motor Development in Infants and Children* (2nd ed.). Englewood Cliffs, N.J.: Prentice-Hall, 1978.

Dasen, P., and Heron, A. Cross-Cultural Tests of Piaget's Theory. In H. C. Triandis and A. Heron (eds.), *Handbook of Cross-Cultural Psychology: Developmental Psychology*, vol. 4. Boston: Allyn and Bacon, 1981.

Davis, G. A. *Educational Psychology: Theory and Practice.* Reading, Mass.: Addison-Wesley, 1983.

Dembo, M. H. *Teaching for Learning: Applying Educational Psychology in the Classroom* (2nd ed.). Santa Monica, Calif.: Goodyear, 1981.

DeOreo, K., and Keough, J. Performance of Fundamental Motor Tasks. In C. B. Corbin (ed.), *A Textbook of Motor Development* (2nd ed.), 76–91. Dubuque, Iowa: Brown, 1980.

Diamond, N. Cognitive Theory. In B. B. Wolman (ed.), *Handbook of Developmental Psychology*, 3–23. Englewood Cliffs, N.J.: Prentice-Hall, 1982.

Dirks, J., and Neisser, U. Memory for Objects in Real Scenes: The Development of Recognition and Recall. *Journal of Experimental Child Psychology*, 1977, *23*, 315–328.

Durkin, D. Confusion and Misconceptions in the Controversy About Kindergarten Reading (1970). In S. Coopersmith and R. Feldman (eds.), *The Formative Years: Principles of Early Childhood Education*, 228–235. San Francisco: Albion, 1974.

Entwisle, D. R., and Baker, D. P. Gender and Young Children's Expectations for Performance in Arithmetic. *Developmental Psychology*, 1983, *19*, 100–209.

Espenschade, A. S. Science and Medicine of Exercise and Sport. In W. R. Johnson, *Motor Development*, 419–439. New York: Harper and Row, 1960.

Etaugh, C., and Hughes, V. Teachers' Evaluations of Sex-Typed Behaviors in Children: The Role of Teacher Sex and School Setting. *Developmental Psychology*, 1975, *11*, 394–395.

Federal Register. Education of Handicapped Children, U.S. Office of Education. *Federal Register*, 1977, *42*, 65082–65085.

Feingold, B. F. Hyperkinesis and Learning Disabilities Linked to Artificial Food Flavors and Colors. *American Journal of Nursing*, 1975, *75*, 797–803.

Flavell, J. H. *Cognitive Development.* Englewood Cliffs, N.J.: Prentice-Hall, 1977. Second edition 1985.

Flavell, J. H., Beach, D. H., and Clinsky, J. M. Spontaneous Verbal Rehearsal in Memory Tasks as a Function of Age. *Child Development*, 1966, *37*, 283–299.

Flavell, J. H., Friedrichs, A. G., and Hoyt, J. D. Developmental Changes in Memorization Processes. *Cognitive Psychology*, 1970, *1*, 324–340.

Forman, G. E., and Kuschner, D. S. *The Child's Construction of Knowledge: Piaget for Teaching Children.* Monterey, Calif.: Brooks/Cole, 1977.

Frederiksen, N. Toward a Broader Conception of Human Intelligence. *American Psychologist*, 1986, *41*, 445–452.

Fulkerson, K. F., Furr, S., and Brown, D. Expectations and Achievement Among Third-, Sixth-, and Ninth-Grade Black and White Males and Females. *Developmental Psychology*, 1983, *19*, 231–236.

Gadow, K. D. Effects of Stimulant Drugs on Academic Hyperactive and Learning Disabled Children. *Journal of Learning Disabilities*, 1983, *16*, 290–299.

Gardner, H. *Frames of Mind: The Theory of Multiple Intelligences.* New York: Basic Books, 1983.

Gearheart, B. R., and Weishahn, M. W. *The Exceptional Student in the Regular Classroom* (3rd ed.). St. Louis: Times Mirror/Mosby, 1984.

Gelfand, D. M., Jenson, W. R., and Drew, C. J. *Understanding Child Behavior Disorders.* New York: Holt, Rinehart, and Winston, 1982.

Gifted and Talented Children's Act of 1978, P.L. 95–561, Section 902.

Goetzels, J. W., and Jackson, P. W. *Creativity and Intelligence.* New York: Wiley, 1962.

Gresham, F. M. Misguided Mainstreaming: The Case for Social Skills Training with Handicapped Children. *Exceptional Children*, 1982, *48*, 422–430.

Grossman, H. J. (ed.), *Manual on Terminology and Classification in Mental Retardation.* Washington, D.C.: American Association on Mental Deficiency, 1973 and 1977 editions.

Guilford, J. P. *The Nature of Human Intelligence.* New York: McGraw-Hill, 1967.

Hamachek, D. E. Characteristics of Good Teachers and Implications for Teacher Education. *Phi Delta Kappan*, 1969, *50*, 341–345.

Hamill, D. D., Leigh, J. E., McNutt, G., and Larsen, S. C. A New Definition of Learning

Disabilities. *Learning Disability Quarterly*, 1981, *4*, 372–382.

Hamill, P. V. V. *NCHS Growth Curves for Children*. Vital Health Statistics: Series 11, Data from the National Health Survey, no. 165. Washington, D.C.: U.S. Government Printing Office (DHEW no. 78–1650), 1977.

Hamilton, E. M. N.,and Whitney, E. N. *Nutrition: Concepts and Controversies* (2nd ed.). St. Paul: West, 1982.

Haring, N. G. Introduction. In N. G. Haring and L. McCormick (eds.), *Exceptional Children and Youth* (4th ed.), 2–39. Columbus, Ohio: Merrill, 1986.

Harter, S. Developmental Perspective on the Self-System. In P. H. Mussen (ed.), *Handbook of Child Psychology* (4th ed.), vol. 4, 275–387. New York: Wiley, 1983.

Hartsough, C. S., and Lambert, N. M. Medical Factors in Hyperactive and Normal Children: Prenatal, Developmental, and Health History Findings. *Journal of Orthopsychiatry*, 1985, *55*, 190–201.

Heilman, A. W. *Principles and Practices of Teaching Reading* (2nd ed.). Columbus, Ohio: Merrill, 1967.

Heward, W. L., and Orlansky, M. D. *Exceptional Children* (2nd ed.). Columbus, Ohio: Merrill, 1984.

Hirst, M. A. Young People with Disabilities: What Happens After 16? *Child Care, Health, and Development*, 1983, *9*, 273–284.

Holborow, P., Elkins, J., and Berry, P. The Effect of the Feingold Diet on "Normal" School Children. *Journal of Learning Disabilities*, 1981, *14*, 143–147.

Holt, J. *How Children Fail*. New York: Pitman, 1964.

Humphreys, L. G., Rich, S. A., and Davey, T. C. A Piagetian Test of General Intelligence. *Developmental Psychology*, 1985, *21*, 872–877.

Hyde, J. S. How Large Are Cognitive Gender Differences? *American Psychologist*, 1981, *36*, 892–901.

Ilg, F. L., and Ames, L. B. *School Readiness*. New York: Harper and Row, 1972.

Johnson, D. W., and Johnson, R. T. Integrating Handicapped Students into the Mainstream. *Exceptional Children*, October 1980, *47*, 335–343.

Johnson, J. A. The Etiology of Hyperactivity. *Exceptional Children*, 1981, *47*, 348–354.

Johnson, R. T. Integrating Severely Adaptively Handicapped Seventh-Grade Students into Constructive Relationships with Nonhandicapped Peers in Science Class. *American Journal of Mental Deficiency*, 1983, *87*, 611–618.

Juntune, J. Myth: The Gifted Constitutes a Single Homogeneous Group! *Gifted Child Quarterly*, 1982, *26*, 9–10.

Justice, E. Categorization as a Preferred Memory Strategy: Developmental Changes During Elementary School. *Developmental Psychology*, 1985, *21*, 1105–1110.

Kagan, J. Reflectivity-Impulsivity and Reading Ability in Primary Grade Children. *Child Development*, 1965, *36*, 609–628.

Kail, R., and Hagen, J. W. Memory in Childhood. In B. B. Wolman (ed.), *Handbook of Developmental Psychology*, 350–367. Englewood Cliffs, N.J.: Prentice-Hall, 1982.

Kail, R., and Pellegrino, J. W. *Human Intelligence: Perspectives and Prospects*. New York: Freeman, 1985.

Kaplan, P. S. It's the I.Q. Tests That Flunk. *New York Times*, March 13, 1977, p. 26.

Kavale, K. The Efficacy of Stimulant Drug Treatment for Hyperactivity: A Meta-Analysis. *Journal of Learning Disabilities*, 1982, *15*, 280–289.

Kavale, K. A., and Forness, S. R. Hyperactivity and Diet Treatment: A Meta-Analysis of the Feingold Hypothesis. *Journal of Learning Disabilities*, 1983, *16*, 324–330.

Kegan, R. *The Evolving Self: Problem and Process in Human Development*. Cambridge, Mass.: Harvard University Press, 1982.

Kirk, S. A., and Gallagher, J. J. *Educating Exceptional Children* (5th ed.). Boston: Houghton Mifflin, 1986.

Kogan, N. Stylistic Variation in Childhood and Adolescence: Creativity, Metaphor, and Cognitive Style. In P. H. Mussen (ed.), *Handbook of Child Psychology* (4th ed.). New York: Wiley, 1983.

Kohen-Raz, R. *Psychophysiological Aspects of Cognitive Growth*. New York: Academic Press, 1977.

Krogman, W. M. *Child Growth*. Ann Arbor: University of Michigan Press, 1980.

Laboratory of Comparative Human Cognition, Culture, and Cognitive Development. In P. H. Mussen (ed.), *Handbook of Child Development* (4th ed.), vol. 1, 295–357. New York: Wiley, 1983.

Landesman-Dwyer, S. Living in the Community. *American Journal of Mental Deficiency*, 1981, *86*, 223–234.

Leal, L., Crays, N., and Moely, B. E. Training Children to Use Self-Monitoring Study Strategy in Preparation for Recall: Maintenance and Generalization Effects. *Child Development*, 1985, *56*, 643–653.

Lezotte, L. W. Characteristics of Effective Schools and Programs for Realizing Them. *Education Digest*, November 1982, 27–29.

Lockhart, A. S. Motor Learning and Motor Development During Infancy and Childhood. In C. B. Corbin (ed.), *A Textbook of Motor Development* (2nd ed.), 246–253. Dubuque, Iowa: Brown, 1980.

MacKinnon, D. *In Search of Human Effectiveness*. Buffalo: Creative Education Foundation, 1978.

Maddux, C. D., Scheiber, L. M., and Bass, J. E. Self-Concept and Social Distance in Gifted Children. *Gifted Child Quarterly*, 1982, *26*, 77–81.

Mandell, C. J., and Fiscus, E. *Understanding Exceptional People*. St. Paul: West, 1981.

Markman, E. M. Realizing That You Don't Understand: A Preliminary Investigation. *Child Development*, 1977, *46*, 986–992.

———. Facilitation of Part-Whole Comparisons by Use of the Collective Noun "Family." *Child Development*, 1973, *44*, 837–840.

Masters, J. C. Developmental Psychology. In M. R. Rosenzweig and L. W. Porter (eds.), *Annual Review of Psychology*, 1981, *32*, 117–153.

Mattes, J. A. The Feingold Diet: A Current Reappraisal. *Journal of Learning Disabilities*, 1983, *16*, 319–323.

McCallum, R. S., Karnes, F. A., and Edwards, R. P. The Test of Choice for Assessment of Gifted Children: A Comparison of the K-ABC and WISC-R and Stanford-Binet. *Journal of Psychoeducational Assessment*, 1984, *2*, 57–63.

McConaughty, S. H., and Ritter, D. R. Social Competence and Behavioral Problems of Learning Disabled Boys Aged 6–11. *Journal of Learning Disabilities*, 1985, *18*, 547–553.

McGuinness, D. How Schools Discriminate Against Boys. In S. Hochman and P. S. Kaplan (eds.), *Readings in Psychology: A Soft Approach* (rev. ed.), 74–79. Lexington, Mass.: Ginn, 1979.

Meichenbaum, D. H., and Goodman, J. Training Impulsive Children to Talk to Themselves: A Means of Developing Self-Control. *Journal of Abnormal Psychology*, 1971, *77*, 115–126.

Mendelson, B. K., and White, D. R. Development of Self-Body-Esteem in Overweight Youngsters. *Developmental Psychology*, 1985, *21*, 90–97.

Mercer, C. D., Hughes, C., and Mercer, A. R. Learning Disabilities Definitions Used by State Education Departments. *Learning Disability Quarterly*, 1985, *8*, 45–55.

Messer, S. Reflection-Impulsivity: Stability and School Failure. *Journal of Educational Psychology*, 1970, *61*, 487–490.

Miller, S. A. Parents' Beliefs About Their Children's Cognitive Abilities. *Developmental Psychology*, 1986, *22*, 276–284.

Moore, R. S., and Moore, D. R. How Early Should They Go to School? *Childhood Education*, June 1976, 13–18.

New York Times. Allen on Fitness Gap. *New York Times*, September 24, 1986, D27.

Paulsen, K., and Johnson, M. Sex Role Attitudes and Mathematical Ability in 4th-, 8th-, and 11th-Grade Students from a High Socioeconomic Area. *Developmental Psychology*, 1983, *19*, 210–214.

Perkins, H. V. Human Development. Belmont, Calif.: Wadsworth, 1975.

Piaget, J. *Six Psychological Studies.* New York: Vintage, 1967.

————. *The Child's Conception of the World.* Totowa, N.J.: Littlefield, 1965.

————. *The Origins of Intelligence in Children.* New York: International Universities Press, 1952.

————. *Judgment and Reasoning in the Young Child.* New York: Harcourt, Brace, and World, 1928.

Piaget, J., and Inhelder, B. *The Psychology of the Child.* New York: Basic Books, 1969.

Polloway, E. A., and Patton, J. R. Psychosocial Causes of Mental Retardation, cited in J. M. Patton and J. S. Payne, Mild Mental Retardation. In N. G. Haring (ed.), *Exceptional Children and Youth*, 111–143. Columbus, Ohio: Merrill, 1982.

President's Commission on Mental Retardation. *Mental Retardation: Past and Present.* Washington, D.C.: U.S. Government Printing Office, 1977.

Pulaski, M. A. S. *Understanding Piaget: An Introduction to Children's Cognitive Development* (rev. ed.). New York: Harper and Row, 1980.

Report of the Commission on Reading: What We Know About Learning to Read. *American Educator*, Winter 1986, 9, 24–30.

Reschly, D. J. Psychological Testing in Educational Classification and Placement. *American Psychologist*, 1981, *36*, 1094–1103.

Richardson, S. A., Goodman, U., Hastoff, A. H., and Dornbusch, S. A. Cultural Uniformity in Reaction to Physical Disabilities. *American Sociological Review*, 1961, *26*, 241–247.

Rickert, E. S. Media Mirrors of the Gifted: E. Susanne Richert's Review of the Film "Simon." *Gifted Child Quarterly*, 1981, *25*, 3–4.

Rimland, B. The Feingold Diet: An Assessment of the Reviews by Mattes, by Kavale and Forness and others. *Journal of Learning Disabilities*, 1983, *16*, 331–333.

Rogoff, B., Newcombe, N., and Kagan, J. Planfulness and Recognition Memory. *Child Development*, 1974, *45*, 972–977.

Ross, D. M., and Ross, S. A. *Hyperactivity: Research, Theory, and Action.* New York: Wiley, 1976.

Rusalem, H., and Malikin, D. *Contemporary Vocational Rehabilitation.* New York: New York University Press, 1976.

Rutter, M. School Effects on Pupil Progress: Research Findings and Policy Implications. *Child Development*, 1983, *54*, 1–29.

Salend, S. J. Factors Contributing to the Development of a Successful Mainstreaming Program. *Exceptional Child*, 1984, *50*, 409–416.

Schofield, H. L. Sex, Grade Level, and the Relationship Between Mathematics Attitude and Achievement in Children. *Journal of Educational Research*, 1982, *75*, 280–284.

Smart, M. S., and Smart, R. C. *School-Age Children: Development and Relationships* (2nd ed.). New York: Macmillan, 1978.

Sobel, D. Hyperactive Children Suffer as Adults. *New York Times*, December 4, 1979, C1.

Spearman, C. "General Intelligence" Objectively Determined and Measured. *American Journal of Psychology*, 1904, *15*, 201–293.

Staffieri, R. J. A Study of Social Stereotype of Body Image in Children. *Journal of Personality and Social Psychology*, 1967, *7*, 101–104.

Sternberg, R. J. General Intellectual Ability. In R. J. Sternberg (ed.), *Human Abilities: An Information Processing Approach*, 5–31. New York: Freeman, 1985.

————. Mechanisms of Cognitive Development: A Componential Approach. In R. J. Sternberg (ed.), *Mechanisms of Cognitive Development*, 163–187. New York: Freeman, 1984.

————. Who's Intelligent? *Psychology Today*, April 1982, 30–39.

Stevenson, H. W., and Newman, R. Long-Term Prediction of Achievement and Attitudes in Mathematics and Reading. *Child Development*, 1986, *57*, 646–659.

Stevenson, H. W., Parke, T., Wilkinson, A., Hegion, A., and Fish, E. Longitudinal Study of Individual Differences in Cognitive Development and Scholastic Achievement. *Journal of Educational Psychology*, 1976, *68*, 377–400.

Stevenson, H. W., Stigler, J. W., Lee, S., Lucker, G. W., Kitamura, S., and Hsu, C. Cognitive Performance and Academic Achievement of Japanese, Chinese, and American Children. *Child Development*, 1985, *56*, 718–734.

Stewart, O., and Tei, E. Some Implications of Metacognition for Reading Instruction. *Journal of Reading*, 1983, *26*, 36–42.

Stigler, A. E., Shin-Ying, L., Lucker, G. W., and Stevenson, H. W. Curriculum and Achievement in Mathematics: A Study of Elementary School Children in Japan, Taiwan, and the United States. *Journal of Educational Psychology*, 1982, *73*, 315–322.

Stigler, J. W., Shin-Ying, L., and Stevenson, H. W. Mathematics Classrooms in Japan, Taiwan, and the United States. *Child Development*, 1987, *58*, 1272–1286.

Tanner, J. M. *Foetus into Man: Physical Growth from Conception to Maturity.* Cambridge, Mass.: Harvard University Press, 1978.

Tarver-Behring, S., Barkley, R. A., and Karlsson, J. The Mother-Child Interactions of Hyperactive Boys and Their Normal Siblings. *Journal of Orthopsychiatry*, 1985, *55*, 202–209.

Telford, C. W., and Sawrey, J. M. *The Exceptional Individual* (4th ed.). Englewood Cliffs, N.J.: Prentice-Hall, 1981.

Terman, L. M., and Oden, M. H. *Genetic Studies of Genius, 1: Mental and Physical Traits of a Thousand Gifted Children.* Stanford, Calif.: Stanford University Press, 1959.

Terman, L. M. *Mental and Physical Traits of a Thousand Gifted Children.* Stanford, Calif.: Stanford University Press, 1925.

Thurstone, L. L. Primary Mental Abilities. *Psychometric Monographs*, 1938, no. 1.

Tolkoff, E. Mainstreaming: A Promise Gone Awry. Albany: New York State United Teachers, 1981.

Torrance, E. P. Psychology of Gifted Children and Youth. In W. M. Cruickshank (ed.), *Psychology of Exceptional Children and Youth* (4th ed.), 469–497. Englewood Cliffs, N.J.: Prentice-Hall, 1980.

Treffinger, D. J. Demythologizing Gifted Education: An Editorial Essay. *Gifted Child Quarterly*, 1982, *26*, 3–8.

Varley, C., and Trupin, E. W. Double-Blind Assessment of Stimulant Medication for Attention Deficit Disorder: A Model for Clinical Application. *American Journal of Orthopsychiatry*, 1983, *53*, 542–547.

Vaughn, S. Why Teach Social Skills to Learning Disabled Students? *Journal of Learning Disabilities*, 1985, *18*, 588–591.

Wadsworth, B. Misinterpretations of Piaget's Theory. *Educational Digest*, September 1981, 56–58.

————. *Piaget's Theory of Cognitive Development.* New York: McKay, 1971.

Walden, E. L., and Thompson, S. A. A Review of Some Alternative Approaches to Drug Management of Hyperactivity in Children. *Journal of Learning Disabilities*, 1981, *4*, 213–217.

Wanat, P. E. Social Skills: An Awareness Program with Learning Disabled Adolescents. *Journal of Learning Disabilities*, 1983, *16*, 35–38.

Wheeler, T. C. *The Great American Writing Block: Causes and Cures of the New Illiteracy.* New York: Viking, 1979.

White, K. R. The Relation Between Socioeconomic Status and Academic Achievement. *Psychological Bulletin*, 1982, *91*, 461–481.

Whitney, E. N., and Hamilton, E. M. N. *Understanding Nutrition* (4th ed.). St. Paul: West, 1987.

Williams, J. W., and Stith, M. *Middle Childhood: Behavior and Development* (2nd ed.). New York: Macmillan, 1980.

Winick, M. Introduction. In M. Winick (ed.), *Childhood Obesity*, 1–12. New York: Wiley, 1975.

Wolf, J. S., and Stephens, T. M. Gifted and Talented. In N. G. Haring and L. McCormick (eds.), *Exceptional Children and Youth* (4th ed.), 431–473. Columbus, Ohio: Merrill, 1986.

Yap, J. N. K., and DeV. Peters, R. An Evaluation of Two Hypotheses Concerning the Dynamics of Cognitive Impulsivity: Anxiety-Over-Errors or Anxiety-Over-Competence? *Developmental Psychology*, 1985, *21*, 1055–1064.

Zigler, E., and Berman, W. Discerning the Future of Early Childhood Intervention. *American Psychologist*, 1983, *38*, 894–907.

Chapter 10

Abarbanel, A. Shared Parenting After Separation and Divorce: A Study of Joint Custody. *American Journal of Orthopsychiatry*, 1979, *49*, 320–329.

Asher, S., and Gottman, J. *The Development of Children's Friendships*. New York: Cambridge University Press, 1981.

Asher, S. R., Oden, S. L., and Gottman, J. M. Children's Friendship in School Settings (1977), cited in M. Putallaz and J. M. Gottman, Social Skills and Group Acceptance in School Setting. In S. R. Asher and J. M. Gottman (eds.), 116–149. *The Development of Children's Friendships.* Cambridge, Cambridge University Press, 1981.

Asher, S. R., and Renshaw, P. D. Children Without Friends: Social Knowledge and Social Skill Training. In S. R. Asher and J. M. Gottman (eds.), *The Development of Children's Friendships*, 273–297. Cambridge: Cambridge University Press, 1981.

Bandura, A. *Social Foundations of Thought and Action: A Social Cognitive Theory.* Englewood Cliffs, N.J.: Prentice-Hall, 1986.

———. *Social Learning Theory.* Englewood Cliffs, N.J.: Prentice-Hall, 1977.

Bandura, A., Ross, D., and Ross, S. A. Transmission of Aggression Through Imitation of Aggressive Models. *Journal of Abnormal and Social Psychology*, 1961, *63*, 575–582.

Barker, R. G., and Wright, H. F. *The Midwest and Its Children.* New York: Harper and Row, 1955.

Baumrind, D. Sex Differences in Moral Reasoning: Response to Walker's (1984) Conclusion That There Are None. *Child Development*, 1986, *57*, 511–521.

———. Current Patterns of Parental Authority. *Developmental Psychology Monographs*, 1979, *41*, 1, part 2.

———. Child Care Practices Anteceding Three Patterns of Preschool Behavior. *Genetic Psychology Monographs*, 1967, *75*, 43–88.

Bell, R. J., and Chapman, M. Child Effects in Studies Using Experimental or Brief Longitudinal Approaches to Socialization. *Developmental Psychology*, 1986, *22*, 595–603.

Benson, C. S., and Gottman, J. M. Children's Popularity and Peer Social Interaction (1975), cited in M. Putallaz and J. M. Gottman, Social Skills and the Group Acceptance. In S. R. Asher and J. M. Gottman (eds.), *The Development of Children's Friendships*, 116–150. New York: Cambridge University Press, 1981.

Berndt, T. J. Relations Between Social Cognition, Nonsocial Cognition, and Social Behavior: The Case of Friendship. In J. H. Flavell and L. Ross (eds.), *Social Cognitive Development.* Cambridge: Cambridge University Press, 1981.

Berndt, T. J., and Hoyle, S. G. Stability and Change in Childhood and Adolescent Friendship. *Developmental Psychology*, 1985, *21*, 1007–1015.

Berndt, T. J., and Perry, T. B. Children's Perceptions of Friendships as Supportive Relationships. *Developmental Psychology*, 1986, *22*, 640–648.

Bierman, K. L., and Furman, W. The Effects of Social Skills Training and Peer Involvement on the Social Adjustment of Preadolescents. *Child Development*, 1984, *55*, 151–162.

Bigelow, B. J. Children's Friendship Expectations: A Cognitive-Developmental Study. *Child Development*, 1977, *48*, 246–253.

Blasi, A. Bridging Moral Cognition and Moral Action: A Critical Review of the Literature. *Psychological Bulletin*, 1980, *88*, 1–45.

Blatt, M., and Kohlberg, L. The Effects of Classroom Moral Discussion upon Children's Level of Moral Judgment. *Journal of Moral Education*, 1975, *4*, 129–161.

Block, J. H., Block, J., and Gjerde, P. F. The Personality of Children Prior to Divorce: A Prospective Study. *Child Development*, 1986, *57*, 827–840.

Bower, E. M. School-Age Issues of Prevention. In J. D. Noshpitz (ed.), *Basic Handbook of Child Psychiatry*, vol. 4, 139–149. New York: Basic Books, 1979.

Brody, G. H., Pillegrini, A. D., and Sigel, I. E. Marital Quality and Mother-Child and Father-Child Interactions with School-Aged Children. *Developmental Psychology*, 1986, *22*, 291–296.

Bukowski, W. M., and Newcomb, A. F. Stability and Determinants of Sociometric Status and Friendship Choice: A Longitudinal Perspective. *Developmental Psychology*, 1984, *20*, 941–953.

Burns, R. B. *The Self-Concept: Theory, Management, Development, and Behaviour.* London: Longman, 1979.

Burton, R. V. Generality of Honesty Reconsidered. *Psychological Review*, 1963, *70*, 481–499.

Busch-Rossnagel, and Vance, A. K. The Impact of the Schools on Social and Emotional Development. In B. B. Wolman (ed.), *Handbook of Developmental Psychology*, 452–471. Englewood Cliffs, N.J.: Prentice-Hall, 1982.

Cairns, R. B. *Social Development: The Origins and Plasticity of Interchanges.* San Francisco: Freeman, 1979.

Carroll, J. L., and Rest, J. R. Moral Development. In B. B. Wolman (ed.), *Handbook of Developmental Psychology*, 434–452. Englewood Cliffs, N.J.: Prentice-Hall, 1982.

Carter, D. B., and Patterson, C. J. Sex Roles as Social Conventions: The Development of Children's Conceptions of Sex-Role Stereotypes. *Developmental Psychology*, 1982, *18*, 812–825.

Chandler, M., and Boyes, M. Social-Cognitive Development. In B. B. Wolman (ed.), *Handbook of Developmental Psychology*, 387–400. Englewood Cliffs, N.J.: Prentice-Hall, 1982.

Cherlin, A. The Trends: Marriage, Divorce, Remarriage (1981). In A. S. Skolnick and J. H. Skolnick. *Family in Transition* (4th ed.), 128–137. Boston: Little, Brown, 1983.

———. Remarriage as an Incomplete Institution (1978). In A. S. Skolnick and J. H. Skolnick, *Family in Transition* (4th ed.), 388–402. Boston: Little, Brown, 1983.

Chivian, E., Mack, J., Waletzky, J. P., Lazaroff, C., Dotor, R., and Goldenring, J. M. Soviet Children and the Threat of Nuclear War: A Preliminary Study. *American Journal of Orthopsychiatry*, 1985, *55*, 484–501.

Clarizio, H. F., and McCoy, G. F. *Behavior Disorders in Children* (3rd ed.). New York: Harper and Row, 1983.

Cline, V. B., Croft, R. G., and Courrier, S. Desensitization of Children to Television Violence. *Journal of Personality and Social Psychology*, 1973, *27*, 360–365.

Clingempeel, W. G., and Segal, S. Stepparent-Stepchild Relationships and the Psychological Adjustment of Children in Stepmother and Stepfather Families. *Child Development*, 1986, *57*, 474–484.

Coopersmith, S. *The Antecedents of Self-Esteem.* San Francisco: Freeman, 1967.

Corsaro, W. A. Friendship in the Nursery School: Social Organization in a Peer Environment. In S. R. Asher and J. M. Gottman (eds.), *The Development of Children's Friendships*, 207–242. Cambridge, Mass.: Cambridge University Press, 1981.

Cullinan, D., and Epstein, M. H. Behavior Disorders. In N. G. Haring (ed.), *Exceptional Children and Youth* (3rd ed.), 207–239. Columbus, Ohio: Merrill, 1982.

Damon, W. *Social and Personality Development.* New York: Norton, 1983.

Damon, W., and Hart, D. The Development of Self-Understanding from Infancy Through Adolescence. *Child Development*, 1982, *53*, 841–864.

Dion, K. K. Young Children's Stereotyping of Facial Attractiveness. *Developmental Psychology*, 1973, *9*, 183–188.

Dodge, K. A. Social Cognition and Children's Aggressive Behavior. *Child Development*, 1980, *51*, 162–170.

Dodge, K. A., and Frame, C. L. Social Cognitive Biases and Deficits in Aggressive Boys. *Child Development*, 1982, *53*, 620–635.

Drabman, R. S., and Thomas, M. H. Does TV Violence Breed Indifference? *Journal of Communication*, 1975, *25*, 86–89.

Edwards, C. P. The Comparative Study of the Development of Moral Judgment and Reasoning. In R. Monroe and B. B. Whiting (eds.), *Handbook of Cross-Cultural Human Development.* New York: Garland, 1977.

Edwards, C. P., and Lewis, M. Young Children's Concepts of Social Relations: Social Functions and Social Objects. In M. Lewis and L. A. Rosenblum (eds.), *The Child and Its Family Genesis of Behavior*, vol. 2. New York: Plenum, 1979.

Eidelberg, L. (ed.). *Encyclopedia of Psychoanalysis.* New York: Free Press, 1968.

Eisenberg-Berg, N. Development of Children's Prosocial Moral Judgment. *Developmental Psychology*, 1979, *15*, 128–138.

Eisenberg-Berg, N., and Neal, C. Children's Moral Reasoning About Their Own Spontaneous Prosocial Behavior. *Developmental Psychology*, 1979, *15*, 228–230.

Emery, R. E. Interparental Conflict and the Children of Discord and Divorce. *Psychological Bulletin*, 1982, *92*, 310–330.

Erikson, E. H. *Childhood and Society.* New York: Norton, 1963, 1950.

Eron, L. D. Parent-Child Interaction, Television Violence, and Aggression of Children. *American Psychologist*, 1982, *37*, 197–212.

Eron, L. D., Huesmann, L. R., Brice, P., Fischer, P., and Mermelstein, R. Age Trends in the Development of Aggression, Sex Typing, and Related Television Habits. *Developmental Psychology*, 1983, *19*, 71–78.

Eron, L. D., Walder, L. O., and Lefkowitz, M. M. *Learning of Aggression in Children.* Boston: Little, Brown, 1971.

Etzioni, A. Can Schools Teach Kids Moral Values? *New York University Education Quarterly*, 1977, *9*, 2–8.

Ferguson, T. J., and Rule, B. G. Influence of Inferential Set, Outcome Intent, and Outcome Severity on Children's Moral Judgments. *Developmental Psychology*, 1982, *18*, 843–851.

Fine, M. A., Moreland, J. R., and Schwebel, A. I. Long-Term Effects of Divorce on Parent-Child Relationships. *Developmental Psychology*, 1983, *5*, 703–714.

Freud, S. *New Introductory Lectures on Psychoanalysis.* New York: Norton, 1965, 1933.

Froming, W. J., Allen, L., and Jensen, R. Altruism, Role-Taking, and Self-Awareness: The Acquisition of Norms Governing Altruistic Behavior. *Child Development*, 1985, *56*, 1223–1228.

Furman, W., and Bierman, K. L. Children's Conceptions of Friendship: A Multimethod Study of Developmental Changes. *Developmental Psychology*, 1984, *20*, 925–932.

————. Developmental Changes in Young Children's Conception of Friendship. *Child Development*, 1981, *54*, 549–556.

Furman, W., and Buhrmester, D. Children's Perceptions of the Personal Relationships in Their Social Networks. *Developmental Psychology*, 1985, *21*, 1016–1024.

Gerbner, G., and Gross, L. The Violent Face of Television and Its Lessons. In E. L. Palmer and A. Dorr (eds.), *Children and the Faces of Television: Teaching, Violence, Selling*, 149–162. New York: Academic Press, 1980.

Gilligan, C. *In a Different Voice.* Cambridge, Mass.: Harvard University Press, 1982.

————. In a Different Voice: Women's Conceptions of Self and of Morality. *Harvard Educational Review*, 1977, *47*, 481–517.

Glick, P. C. Marriage, Divorce, and Living Arrangements: Prospective Changes. *Journal of Family Issues*, 1984, *5*, 7–26.

Greif, J. B. Fathers, Children, and Joint Custody. *American Journal of Orthopsychiatry*, 1979, *49*, 311–320.

Gronlund, N. E. *Sociometry in the Classroom.* New York: Harper, 1959.

Hallinan, M. T. Recent Advances in Sociometry. In S. R. Asher and J. M. Gottman (eds.), *The Development of Children's Friendships*, 91–116. New York: Cambridge University Press, 1981.

Harter, S. Developmental Perspectives on the Self-System. In E. M. Hetherington (ed.), *Handbook of Child Psychology*, 103–197. New York: Wiley, 1983.

Hartshorne, H., and May, M. A. *Studies in the Nature of Character*, vol. 1. New York: Macmillan, 1928.

Hartup, W. W. Peer Relations. In P. H. Mussen (ed.), *Handbook of Child Psychology: Socialization, Personality, and Social Development*, vol. 4 (4th ed.), 103–197. New York: Wiley, 1983.

————. The Social Worlds of Childhood. *American Psychologist*, 1979, *34*, 944–951.

————. Aggression in Childhood: Developmental Perspectives. *American Psychologist*, 1974, *29*, 336–341.

————. Aggression in Childhood: Developmental Perspectives. In P. Mussen (ed.), *Carmichael's Manual of Child Psychology* (3rd ed.). New York: Wiley, 1970.

Hay, D. F., and Ross, H. S. The Social Nature of Early Conflict. *Child Development*, 1982, *53*, 105–113.

Hayes, D. Cognitive Bases for Liking and Disliking Among Preschool Children. *Child Development*, 1978, *49*, 906–909.

Hess, R. D., and Camara, K. A. Post-Divorce Family Relationships as Mediating Variables in the Consequences of Divorce for Children. *Journal of Social Issues*, 1979, *35*, 4.

Hetherington, E. M. Divorce: A Child's Perspective. *American Psychologist*, 1979, *34*, 851–859.

————. Effects of Father Absence on Personality: Development in Adolescent Daughters. *Developmental Psychology*, 1972, *7*, 313–321.

Hetherington, E. M., Cox, M., and Cox, R. The Aftermath of Divorce. In J. H. Stevens and M. Mathews (eds.), *Mother-Child/Father-Child Relations.* Washington, D.C.: National

Association for the Education of Young Children, 1978.

Hoffman, M. L. Development of Moral Thought, Feeling, and Behavior. *American Psychologist,* 1979, *34,* 958–967.

———. Empathy, Its Development and Prosocial Implications. In C. B. Keasey (ed.), *Nebraska Symposium on Motivation,* vol. 25. Lincoln: University of Nebraska Press, 1978.

Huesmann, L. R., Lagerspetz, K., and Eron, L. D. Intervening Variables in TV Violence-Aggression Relation: Evidence from Two Countries. *Developmental Psychology,* 1984, *20,* 746–776.

Huston, A. C. Sex-Typing. In E. H. Hetherington (ed.), *Handbook of Child Psychology* (4th ed.), vol. 4, 387–469. New York: Wiley, 1983.

Jensen, L. C. *Adolescence: Theories, Research, Applications.* St. Paul: West, 1985.

Kaplan, P. S., and Stein, J. *Psychology of Adjustment.* Belmont, Calif.: Wadsworth, 1984.

Kazden, A. E. *Behavior Modification in Applied Settings* (3rd ed.). Homewood, Ill.: Dorsey, 1984.

Kelly, J. B., and Wallerstein, J. S. The Effects of Parental Divorce: Experiences of the Child in Early Latency. *American Journal of Orthopsychiatry,* 1976, *46,* 20–33.

Kline, P. *Fact and Fantasy in Freudian Theory.* London: Methuen, 1972.

Kohlberg, L. The Development of Moral Judgment and Moral Action in L. Kohlberg (ed.). *Child Psychology* and *Childhood Education: A Cognitive-Developmental View.* New York: Longman, 1987, 259–329.

Kohlberg, L. Moral Stages and Moralization: The Cognitive-Developmental Approach. In T. Lickona (ed.), *Moral Development and Behavior.* New York: Holt, Rinehart, and Winston, 1976.

———. Stage and Sequence: The Cognitive-Developmental Approach to Socialization. In D. Goslin (ed.), *Handbook of Socialization Theory and Research.* Skokie, Ill.: Rand-McNally, 1969.

Kohlberg, L., Colby, A., Gibbs, J., Speicher-Dubin, B., and Powers, C. *Assessing Moral Development Stages: A Manual.* Cambridge, Mass.: Center for Moral Education, 1978.

Kohlberg, L., and Kramer, R. Continuities and Discontinuities in Childhood and Adult Moral Development. *Human Development,* 1969, *12,* 83–120.

Kohlberg, L and Lichona T. R. Moral Discussion and the Class Meeting in DeVries and L. Kohlberg (eds.), *Programs of Early Education: The Constructivist View.* New York: Longman, 1987, 143–181.

Kurdek, L. A. An Integrative Perspective on Children's Divorce Adjustment. *American Psychologist,* 1981, *36,* 856–866.

Kurdek, L. A. Blisk, D., and Siesky, A. E. Correlates of Children's Long-Term Adjustment to Their Parents' Divorce. *Developmental Psychology,* 1981, *17,* 565–580.

Laupa, M., and Turiel, E. Children's Conceptions of Adult and Peer Authority. *Child Development,* 1986, *57,* 405–412.

Lefkowitz, M. M., and Tesiny, E. P. Dejection and Depression: Prospective and Contemporaneous Analyses. *Developmental Psychology,* 1984, *20,* 776–786.

Liebert, R. M. Effects of Television on Children and Adolescents. *Journal of Developmental and Behavioral Pediatrics,* 1986, *7,* 43–48.

Livesley, W. J., and Bromley, D. C. *Person Perception in Childhood and Adolescence.* London: Wiley, 1973.

Loeb, R. C., Horst, L., and Horton, P. J. Family Interaction Patterns Associated with Self-Esteem in Preadolescent Girls and Boys. *Merrill-Palmer Quarterly,* 1980, *26,* 203–217.

Maccoby, E. E. *Social Development: Psychological Growth and the Parent-Child Relationship.* New York: Harcourt Brace Jovanovich, 1980.

Maccoby, E. E., and Jacklin, C. N. Sex Differences in Aggression: A Rejoinder and Reprise. *Child Development,* 1980, *51,* 964–980.

———. *The Psychology of Sex Differences.* Stanford, Calif.: Stanford University Press, 1974.

Maccoby, E. E., and Martin, J. A. Socialization in the Context for Social Development. In E. M. Hetherington (ed.), *Handbook of Child Development,* vol. 4, 1–103. New York: Wiley, 1983.

Malinowski, C. I., and Smith, C. P. Moral Reasoning and Moral Conduct: An Investigation Prompted by Kohlberg's Theory. *Journal of Personality and Social Psychology,* 1985, *49,* 1016–1027.

Miller, P. M., Danaher, D. L., and Forbes, D. Sex-Related Strategies for Coping with Interpersonal Conflict in Children Aged Five and Seven. *Developmental Psychology,* 1986, *22,* 543–548.

Mink, I. T., and Nihira, K. Family Life-Styles and Child Behaviors: A Study of Direction of Effects. *Developmental Psychology,* 1986, *22,* 610–616.

Minuchin, P. P., and Shapiro, E. K. The School as a Context for Social Development. In E. M. Hetherington (ed.), *Handbook of Child Psychology: Socialization, Personality, and Social Development* (4th ed.), vol. 4, 197–275. New York: Wiley, 1983.

Mussen, P. H., and Eisenberg-Berg, N. *Roots of Caring, Sharing, and Helping.* San Francisco: Freeman 1977.

Nadelman, L. Sex Identity in American Children: Memory, Knowledge, and Preference Tests. *Developmental Psychology,* 1974, *10,* 413–417.

National Coalition on TV Violence. *Newsletter,* March–April 1984.

Nelson, J., and Aboud, F. E. The Resolution of Social Conflict Between Friends. *Child Development,* 1985, *56,* 1009–1017.

Newman, P. R. The Peer Group. In B. B. Wolman (ed.), *Handbook of Developmental Psychology,* 526–536. Englewood Cliffs, N.J.: Prentice-Hall, 1982.

Newson, J., and Newson, E. Seven Years Old in the Home Environment (1976), cited in A. C. Huston, Sex-Typing. In E. M. Hetherington (ed.), *Handbook of Child Psychology* (4th ed.), vol. 4, 387–467. New York: Wiley, 1983.

Nisan, M., and Kohlberg, L. Universality and Variation in Moral Judgment: A Longitudinal and Cross-Sectional Study in Turkey. *Child Development,* 1982, *53,* 865–876.

Olweus, D. Development of Stable Aggressive Reaction Patterns in Males. In R. Blanchard and C. Blanchard, *Advances in the Study of Aggression,* vol. 1. New York: Academic Press, 1982.

———. Stability and Aggressive Reaction Patterns in Males: A Review. *Psychological Bulletin,* 1979, *86,* 852–875.

———. Aggression and Peer Acceptance in Adolescent Boys: Two Short-Term Longitudinal Studies of Ratings. *Child Development,* 1977, *48,* 1301–1313.

Oshman, H. P., and Manosevitz, M. Father Absence: Effects of Stepfathers upon Psychosocial Development in Males. *Developmental Psychology,* 1976, *12,* 479–480.

Parke, R. D., and Slaby, R. G. The Development of Aggression. In E. M. Hetherington (ed.), *Handbook of Child Psychology: Socialization, Personality, and Social Development* (4th ed.), vol. 4, 547–643. New York: Wiley, 1983.

Patterson, G. R. A. Performance Theory for Coercive Family Interaction. In R. Cairns (ed.), *Social Interaction: Methods, Analysis, and Evaluations.* Hillsdale, N.J.: Erlbaum, 1979.

Patterson, G. R., and Cobb, J. A. A Dyadic Analysis of "Aggressive" Behaviors. In J. P. Hill (eds.), *Minnesota Symposium on Child Psychology,* vol. 5. Minneapolis: University of Minnesota Press, 1971.

Pearl, D. Violence and Aggression. *Society,* 1984, *21,* 17–22.

Perry, D. G., Perry, L. C., and Rasmussen, P. Cognitive Social Learning Mediators of Aggression. *Child Development*, 1986, *57*, 700–711.

Peterson, L. Influence of Age, Task Competence, and Responsibility Focus on Children's Altruism. *Developmental Psychology*, 1983, *19*, 141–148.

Piaget, J. *The Moral Judgment of the Child* (M. Gabain, trans.). New York: Free Press, 1965 (originally published 1932).

Putallaz, M., and Gottman, J. M., Social Skills and Group Acceptance. In S. R. Asher and J. M. Gottman (eds.), *The Development of Children's Friendships*, 116–149. Cambridge: Cambridge University Press, 1981.

Rest, J. R. Morality. In P. H. Mussen (ed.), *Handbook of Child Psychology: Cognitive Development*, vol. 3 (4th ed.), 556–630. New York: Wiley, 1983.

Rubin, Z. *Children's Friendships*. Cambridge, Mass.: Harvard University Press, 1980.

Rubinstein, E. A. Television Violence: A Historical Perspective. In E. L. Palmer and A. Dorr (eds.), *Children and The Faces of Television: Teaching, Violence, Selling*, 113–125. New York: Academic Press, 1980.

Santrock, J. W. Relation of Type and Onset of Father Absence to Cognitive Development. *Child Development*, 1972, *43*, 455–469.

Schofield, J. W. Complementary and Conflicting Identities: Images and Interaction in an Interracial School. In S. R. Asher and J. M. Gottman (eds.), *The Development of Children's Friendships*, 53–91. Cambridge: Cambridge University Press, 1981.

Sears, R. R., Maccoby, E. E., and Lewin, H. *Patterns of Child Rearing*. Evanston, Ill.: Row and Peterson, 1957.

Selman, R. L. The Child as a Friendship Philosopher. In S. R. Asher and J. M. Gottman (eds.), *The Development of Children's Friendships*, 242–273. Cambridge: Cambridge University Press, 1981.

Serbin, L. A., O'Leary, K. D., Kent, R. N., and Tonick, I. J. A Comparison of Teacher Response to the Preacademic and Problem Behavior of Boys and Girls. *Child Development*, 1973, *44*, 796–804.

Shantz, C. U. Social Cognition. In P. H. Mussen (ed.), *Handbook of Child Psychology: Cognitive Development*, vol. 4 (4th ed.), 495–556. New York: Wiley, 1983.

Shantz, D. W., and Voydanoff, D. A. Situational Effects on Retaliatory Aggression at Three Age Levels. *Child Development*, 1973, *44*, 149–153.

Shepherd-Look, D. L. Sex Differentiation and the Development of Sex Roles. In B. B. Wolman (ed.), in *Handbook of Developmental Psychology*, 403–434. Englewood Cliffs, N.J.: Prentice-Hall.

Singer, J. L., and Singer, D. G. Psychologists Look at Television: Cognitive, Developmental, Personality, and Social Policy Implications. *American Psychologist*, 1983, *38*, 826–835.

Skolnick, A. S., and Skolnick, J. H. *Family in Transition* (4th ed.). Boston: Little, Brown, 1983.

Snarey, J. R., Reimer, J., and Kohlberg, L. Development of Social-Moral Reasoning Among Kibbutz Adolescents: A Longitudinal Cross-Cultural Study. *Developmental Psychology*, 1985, *21*, 3–18.

Solnit, A. J., Call, J. D., and Feinstein, C. B. Psychosexual Development: Five to Ten Years. In J. D. Noshpitz (ed.), *Basic Handbook of Child Psychiatry*, 184–190. New York: Basic Books, 1979.

Spurlock, J., and Lawrence, L. E. The Black Child. In J. D. Noshpitz (ed.), *Basic Handbook of Child Psychiatry*, vol. 1, 248–256. New York: Basic Books, 1979.

Thomas, M. H., Horton, R. W., Lippincott, E. C., and Drabman, R. S. Desensitization to Portrayals of Real-Life Aggression as a Function of Exposure to Television Violence. *Journal of Personality and Social Psychology*, 1977, *35*, 450–458.

Tieger, T. On the Biological Basis of Sex Differences in Aggression. *Child Development*, 1980, *51*, 943–963.

Tisak, M. S. Children's Conceptions of Parental Authority. *Child Development*, 1986, *57*, 166–176.

Tuma, N., and Hallinan, M. T. The Effects of Sex, Race, and Achievement in School Children's Friendships. *Social Forces*, 1979, *57*, 1265–1285.

Visher, J. S., and Visher, E. B. Stepfamilies and Stepchildren. In J. D. Noshpitz (ed.), *Handbook of Child Psychiatry*, 347–354. New York: Basic Books, 1979.

Vosk, B., Forehand, R., Parker, J. B., and Richard, K. A. Multimethod Comparison of Popular and Unpopular Children. *Developmental Psychology*, 1982, *18*, 571–575.

Walker, L. J. Sex Differences in the Development of Moral Reasoning: A Rejoinder to Baumrind. *Child Development*, 1986, *57*, 522–526.

———. Sex Differences in the Development of Moral Reasoning: A Critical Review. *Child Development*, 1984, *55*, 677–691.

———. The Sequentiality of Kohlberg's Stages of Moral Development. *Child Development*, 1982, *53*, 1330–1336.

Wallerstein, J. S. Children of Divorce: The Psychological Tasks of the Child. *American Journal of Orthopsychiatry*, 1983, *53*, 230–243.

Wallerstein, J. S., and Kelly, J. Effects of Divorce on the Visiting Father-Child Relationship. *American Journal of Psychiatry*, 1980, *137*, 1534–1539.

———. Divorce and Children. In J. D. Noshpitz (ed.), *Basic Handbook of Child Psychiatry*, vol. 4, 339–347. New York: Basic Books, 1979.

Whiting, B. B., and Whiting, J. W. M. *Children of Six Cultures*. Cambridge, Mass.: Harvard University Press, 1975.

Williams, J. W., and Stith, M. *Middle Childhood: Behavior and Development* (2nd ed.). New York: Macmillan, 1980.

Yarrow, M. R., Waxler, C. Z., and Chapman, M. Children's Prosocial Dispositions and Behavior. In P. H. Mussen (ed.), *Handbook of Child Psychology*, vol. 4 (4th ed.), 469–547. New York: Wiley, 1983.

Chapter 11

Adelson, J. The Political Imagination of the Young Adolescent. In J. Kagan and R. Coles (ed.), *Twelve to Sixteen: Early Adolescence*, 106–144. New York: Norton, 1972.

Adelson, J., and O'Neil, R. P. Growth of Political Ideas in Adolescence: The Sense of Community. *Journal of Personality and Social Psychology*, 1966, *4*, 295–306.

Allgeier, E. R., and Allgeier, A. R. *Sexual Interactions*. Lexington, Mass., D. C. Health, 1984.

American Psychiatric Association. *Diagnostic and Statistical Manual of the American Psychiatric Association, 111*. Washington, D.C.: American Psychiatric Association, 1980.

Ames, R. Physical Maturing Among Boys as Related to Adult Social Behavior: A Longitudinal Study. *California Journal of Educational Research*, 1957, *8*, 69–75.

Astin, A. W. *The American Freshman: Twenty Year Trends, 1966–1985*. Los Angeles: Higher Education Research Institute, U.C.L.A., 1986.

Ault, R. *Children's Cognitive Development*. New York: Oxford University Press, 1977.

Bachman, J. G., and Johnston, L. D. The Freshmen. *Psychology Today*, September 1979, 78–87.

Barret, R. L, and Robinson, B. E. Teenage Fathers: A Profile. *Personnel and Guidance Journal*, 1981, *60*, 226–228.

Brandt, G., Maschoff, T., and Chandler, N. S. A Residential Camp Experience as an Approach to Adolescent Weight Management. *Adolescence*, 1980, *60*, 807–822.

Breit, E. B., and Ferrandino, M. M. Social Dimensions of the Menstrual Taboo and the Effects on Female Sexuality. In J. H. Williams (ed.), *Psychology of Women: Selected Readings*, 228–241. New York: Norton, 1979.

Brooks-Gunn, J., and Ruble, D. N. The Development of Menstrual-Related Beliefs and Behavior During Adolescence. *Child Development*, 1982, *53*, 1567–1577.

Bruch, H. *The Golden Cage: The Enigma of Anorexia Nervosa*. Cambridge, Mass.: Harvard University Press, 1978.

Bullough, V. Age at Menarche: A Misunderstanding. *Science*, 1981, *213*, 365–366.

Burns, R. B. *The Self Concept*. London: Longman, 1979.

Card, J. J., and Wise, L. L. Teenage Mothers and Teenage Fathers: The Impact of Early Childbearing on the Parents' Personal and Professional Lives. *Family Planning Perspectives*, 1978, *10*, 199–205.

Carroll, J. L., and Rest, J. R. Moral Development. In B. B. Wolman (ed.), *Handbook of Human Development*, 434–452. Englewood Cliffs, N.J.: Prentice-Hall, 1982.

Chess, S., Thomas, A., and Cameron, M. Sexual Attitudes and Behavior Patterns in a Middle-Class Population. *American Journal of Orthopsychiatry*, 1976, *46*, 689–702.

Chilman, C. S. *Adolescent Sexuality in a Changing American Society* (2nd ed.). New York: Wiley, 1983.

Chumlea, W. C. Physical Growth in Adolescence. In B. B. Wolman (ed.), *Handbook of Developmental Psychology*, 471–486. Englewood-Cliffs, N.J.: Prentice-Hall, 1982.

Conger, J. J., and Petersen, A. C. *Adolescence and Youth: Psychological Development in a Changing World* (3rd ed.). New York: Harper and Row, 1984.

Connolly, L. Boy Fathers. *Human Behavior*, January 1978, 40–43.

Dale, G., and Chamis, G. C. (1971), cited in P. Scales, Sex Education and the Prevention of Teenage Pregnancy: An Overview of Policies and Programs in the United States. In T. Ooms (ed.), *Teenage Pregnancy in a Family Context: Implications for Policy*, 2133–2153. Philadelphia: Temple University Press, 1981.

Danner, F. W., and Day, M. C. Eliciting Formal Operations. *Child Development*, 1977, *48*, 1600–1606.

Dason, P., and Heron, A. Cross-Cultural Tests of Piaget's Theory. In H. C. Triandis and A. Heron (ed.), *Handbook of Cross-Cultural Psychology: Developmental Psychology*, vol. 4, 295–343. Boston: Allyn and Bacon, 1981.

DeLora, J. S., Warren, C. A. B., and Ellison, C. R. *Understanding Sexual Interaction* (2nd ed.). Boston: Houghton Mifflin, 1981.

Dreyer, P. H. Sexuality During Adolescence. In B. B. Wolman (ed.), *Handbook of Developmental Psychology*, 559–602. Englewood Cliffs, N.J.: Prentice-Hall, 1982.

Earls, F., and Siegel, B. Precocious Fathers. *American Journal of Orthopsychiatry*, 1980, *50*, 469–480.

Eisele, J., Hertsgaard, D., and Light, H. K. Factors Related to Eating Disorders in Young Adolescent Girls. *Adolescence*, 1986, *21*, 283–290.

Elkind, D. Egocentrism in Adolescence. *Child Development*, 1967, *38*, 1025–1034.

Elkind, D., and Bowen, R. Imaginary Audience Behavior in Children and Adolescence. *Developmental Psychology*, 1979, *15*, 38–44.

Faust, M. S. Developmental Maturation as a Determinant in Prestige of Adolescent Girls. *Child Development*, 1960, *31*, 173–184.

Fischer, K. W. A Theory of Cognitive Development: The Control and Construction of Hierarchies of Skills. *Psychological Review*, 1980, *87*, 477–531.

Flavell, J. H. *Cognitive Development*. Englewood Cliffs, N.J.: Prentice-Hall, 1977. Second edition, 1985.

Flavell, J. H., and Wohlwill, J. F. Formal and Functional Aspects of Cognitive Development. In D. Elkind and J. H. Flavell (eds.), *Studies in Cognitive Development*, 67–120. New York: Oxford University Press, 1969.

Forbush, J. B. Adolescent Parent Programs and Family Involvement. In T. Ooms (ed.), *Teenage Pregnancy in a Family Context: Implications for Policy*, 254–277. Philadelphia: Temple University Press, 1981.

Forisha-Kovach, B. *The Experience of Adolescence: Development in Context*. Glenview, Ill.: Scott, Foresman, 1983.

Foster, C. D., and Miller, G. M. Adolescent Pregnancy: A Challenge for Counselors. *Personnel and Guidance Journal*, 1980, *59*, 236–241.

Freedman, S. G. New Focus Placed on Young Unwed Fathers. *New York Times*, December 2, 1986, p. 1.

Freud, S. Three Essays on the Theory of Sexuality. London: Hogarth, 1925, 1953.

Furstenberg, F., Jr. The Social Consequences of Teenage Parenthood. *Family Planning Perspectives*, 1976, *8*, 148–164.

Furstenberg, F. F. Implicating the Family: Teenage Parenthood and Kinship Involvements. In T. Ooms (ed.), *Teenage Pregnancy in a Family Context: Implications for Policy*, 131–165. Philadelphia: Temple University Press, 1981.

———. Premarital Pregnancy and Marital Instability. In G. Levinger and O. Moles (eds.), *Divorce and Separation: Context, Causes, and Consequences*. New York: Basic Books, 1979.

Gallatin, J., and Adelson, J. Legal Guarantees of Individual Freedom: A Cross-National Study of the Development of Political Thought. *Journal of Social Issues*, 1971, *27*, 93–108.

Garner, D. M., and Garfinkel, P. E. Body Image in Anorexia Nervosa, Measurement, Theory, and Clinical Implications. *International Journal of Psychiatry in Medicine*, 1981, *11*, 263–284.

Gordon, S. and Dickman, I. R. Sex Education Promotes Responsible Sexual Behavior (1980) in B. Leone and M. T. O'Neill (eds.), *Sexual Values: Opposing Viewpoints*. St. Paul, Minn.: Greenhaven Press, 1983, 50–53.

Grant, C. L, and Fodor, I. G. Adolescent Attitudes Toward Body Image and Anorexic Behavior. *Adolescence*, 1986, *21*, 269–281.

Greene, E. Shifts in Students' Attitudes Seen Threat to Liberal Arts. *The Chronicles of Higher Education*, November 5, 1986, pp. 32–35.

Guttmacher Institute. *11 Million Teenagers: What Can Be Done About the Epidemic of Adolescent Pregnancies in the United States*. New York: Planned Parenthood Federation, 1976.

Halmi, K. A. Anorexia Nervosa: Recent Investigations. *Annual Review of Medicine*, 1978, *29*, 37–149.

Hamill, P. V. V. *NCHS Growth Curves for Children*. Vital and Health Statistics, Series 11, Data from the National Health Survey, no. 165. Washington, D.C.: U.S. Government Printing Office (DHEW no. 78–1650), 1977.

Hamilton, E. M., and Whitney, E. *Nutrition: Concepts and Controversies*. St. Paul: West, 1979.

Hass, A. *Teenage Sexuality: A Survey of Teenage Sexual Behavior*. New York: Macmillan, 1979.

Holstein, C. B. Irreversible, Stepwise Sequence in the Development of Moral Judgement: A Longitudinal Study of Males and Females. *Child Development*, 1976, *47*, 51–61.

Hubble, J., Wilder, R., and Kennedy, C. E. The Student as Physical Being. *Personnel and Guidance Journal*, 1969, *48*, 229–233.

Inhelder, B., and Piaget, J. *The Growth of Logical Thinking*. New York: Basic Books, 1958.

Jones, M. C. Psychological Correlates of Somatic Development. *Child Development*, 1965, *36*, 899–911.

———. The Later Careers of Boys Who Are Early and Late Maturers. *Child Development*, 1957, *28*, 113–128.

————. Adolescence in Our Society: Anniversary Papers of the Community Service Society of New York. In *The Family in a Democratic Society*, 70–82. New York: Columbia University Press, 1949.

Jones, M. C., and Bayley, N. Physical Maturing Among Boys as Related to Behavior. *Journal of Educational Psychology*, 1950, *41*, 129–148.

Jones, M. C., and Mussen, P. H. Self-Conceptions, Motivations, and Interpersonal Attitudes of Early- and Late-Maturing Girls. *Child Development*, 1958, *29*, 491–501.

Kalat, J. W. *Biological Psychology*. Belmont, Calif.: Wadsworth, 1981.

Kantner, J., and Zelnik, M. Sexual Experiences of Young Unmarried Women. In *U.S. Family Planning Perspectives*, 1972, *4*, 9–17.

Katchadourian, H. *The Biology of Adolescence*. San Francisco: Freeman, 1977.

Kelly, J. B. Divorce: The Adult Perspective. In B. B. Wolman (ed.), *Handbook of Developmental Psychology*, 734–750. Englewood Cliffs, N.J.: Prentice-Hall, 1982.

Kohlberg, L. The Development of Moral Judgment and Moral Action. In L. Kohlberg (ed.), *Child Psychology and Childhood Education*. New York: Longman, 1987, 259–328.

Kohlberg, L. Stage and Sequence: The Cognitive-Developmental Approach to Socialization. In D. A. Goslin (ed.), *Handbook of Socialization Theory and Research*. Chicago: Rand-McNally, 1969.

Kohlberg, L., and Turiel, E. Moral Development and Moral Education. In G. Lesser (ed.), *Moral Development and Moral Education*. Chicago: Scott, Foresman, 1971.

Krogman, W. M. *Child Growth*. Ann Arbor: University of Michigan Press, 1980.

Kuhn, D. Short-Term Longitudinal Evidence for the Sequentiality of Kohlberg's Early Stages of Moral Development. *Developmental Psychology*, 1976, *12*, 162–166.

Kuhn, D., Ho, V., and Adams, C. Formal Reasoning Among Pre and Late Adolescents. *Child Development*, 1979, *50*, 1149–1152.

Lerner, R. M., and Spanier, G. B. *Adolescent Development: A Life-Span Perspective*. New York: McGraw-Hill, 1980.

Libby, R. Parental Attitudes Towards High School Sex Education Programs. *The Family Coordinator*, 1970, *19*, 234–247.

Logan, D. D. The Menarche Experience in Twenty-Three Foreign Countries. *Adolescence*, 1980, *58*, 247–257.

Luker, K. C. (1975), cited in P. H. Dreyer. Sexuality During Adolescence. In B. B. Wolman (ed.), *Handbook of Developmental Psychology*, 559–601. Englewood Cliffs, N.J.: Prentice-Hall, 1982.

Marin, G. Perceiving Justice Across Culture: Equity vs. Equality in Colombia and in the United States. *International Journal of Psychology*, 1981, *16*, 153–159.

Martorano, C. S. A Developmental Analysis of Performance on Piaget's Formal Operations Tasks. *Developmental Psychology*, 1977, *13*, 666–672.

McKinney, J. P., Fitzgerald, H. E., and Strommen, E. A. *Developmental Psychology: The Adolescent and Young Adult* (rev. ed.). Homewood, Ill.: Dorsey, 1982.

McKinney, J. P., and Moore, D. Attitudes and Values During Adolescence. In B. B. Wolman (ed.). *Handbook of Human Development*, 549–559. Englewood Cliffs, N.J.: Prentice-Hall, 1982.

Merelman, R. M. The Adolescence of Political Socialization. *Sociology of Education*, 1972, *45*, 134–166.

————. The Development of Policy Thinking in Adolescence. *American Political Science Review*, 1971, *65*, 1033–1047.

Milgram, S. Some Conditions of Obedience to Authority (1968). In R. Flacks (ed.), *Conformity Resistance and Self-Determination: The Individual and Authority*, 225–239. Boston: Little, Brown, 1973.

Miller, D. C. Industry and the Worker. In H. Borow (ed.), *Man in a World at Work*. Boston: Houghton Mifflin, 1964.

Moore, K. A., and Waite, L. F. Early Childbearing and Educational Attainment. *Family Planning Perspectives*, 1977, *9*, 220–225.

Morrison, D. M. Adolescent Contraceptive Behavior: A Review. *Psychological Bulletin*, 1985, *98*, 538–568.

Mussen, P. H., and Jones, M. C. Some Conceptions, Motivations, and Interpersonal Attitudes of Late- and Early-Maturing Boys. *Child Development*, 1957, *28*, 242–256.

Muuss, R. E. Adolescent Eating Disorder: Bulimia. *Adolescence*, 1986, *21*, 257–267.

————. Adolescent Eating Disorder: Anorexia Nervosa. *Adolescence*, 1985, *20*, 525–536.

————. *Theories of Adolescence* (4th ed.). New York: Random House, 1982.

Neimark, E. D. Adolescent Thought: Transition to Formal Operations. In B. B. Wolman (ed.), *Handbook of Human Development*, 486–503. Englewood Cliffs, N.J.: Prentice-Hall, 1982.

————. Intellectual Development During Adolescence. In F. D. Horowitz (ed.), *Review of Child Development Research*, vol. 4. Chicago: University of Chicago Press, 1975.

New York Times. Reflections on School Birth Control. *New York Times*, November 8, 1986, p. 30.

Peel, E. A. Intellectual Growth During Adolescence. In R. E. Grinder (ed.), *Studies in Adolescence* (2nd ed.), 486–497. New York: Macmillan, 1969.

Perlez, J. Children with Children: Coping with a Crisis. *New York Times*, December 1, 1986, p. 1.

Peskin, H. Influences of the Development Schedule on Learning and Ego Functioning. *Journal of Youth and Adolescence*, 1973, *2*, 273–290.

————. Pubertal Onset and Ego Functioning. *Journal of Abnormal Psychology*, 1967, *72*, 1–15.

Pestrak, V. A., and Martin, D. Cognitive Development and Aspects of Adolescent Sexuality. *Adolescence*, 1985, *20*, 981–987.

Piaget, J. Intellectual Evolution from Adolescence to Adulthood. *Human Development*, 1972, *15*, 1–12.

Pulaski, M. A. S. *Understanding Piaget*. New York: Harper and Row, 1980.

Reichelt, P. (1976). Cited in P. H. Dreyer, Sexuality During Adolescence. In B. B. Wolman (ed.), *Handbook of Developmental Psychology*, 559–601. Englewood Cliffs, N.J.: Prentice-Hall, 1982.

Rierdan, J., and Koff, E. The Psychological Impact of Menarche: Integrative Versus Disruptive Changes. *Journal of Youth and Adolescence*, 1980, *9*, 49–58.

Rinck, C., Rudolph, J. A., and Simkins, L. A Survey of Attitudes Concerning Contraception and the Resolution of Teenage Pregnancy. *Adolescence*, 1983, *72*, 923–929.

Roberge, J. R., and Flexer, B. K. Further Examination of Formal Operational Reasoning Abilities. *Child Development*, 1979, *50*, 478–484.

Robinson, I. E., and Jedlicka, D. Change in Sexual Attitudes and Behavior of College Students from 1965 to 1980: A Research Note. *Journal of Marriage and the Family*, 1982, *44*, 237–240.

Roche, A. F. Secular Trends in Stature, Weight, and Maturation. In A. F. Roche (ed.), Secular Trends in Growth, Maturation, and Development of Children. *Monographs of the Society for Research in Child Development*, 1979, *44*, 3–27.

Roche, J. P. Premarital Sex: Attitudes and Behavior by Dating Stage. *Adolescence*, 1986, *21*, 107–121.

Rogoff, B. Schooling and the Development of Cognitive Skills. In H. C. Triandis and

A. Heron, *Handbook of Cross-Cultural Psychology*, vol. 4: *Developmental Psychology*, 233–295. Boston: Allyn and Bacon, 1981.

Rokeach, M. *The Nature of Human Values.* New York: Free Press, 1973.

Rosenhan, D. L., and Seligman, M. E. P. *Abnormal Psychology.* New York: Norton, 1984.

Ruble, D. N., and Brooks-Gunn, J. The Experience of Menarche. *Child Development*, 1982, 53, 1557–1566.

Salkind, N. J. *Theories of Human Development.* New York: Van Nostrand, 1981.

Savin-Williams, R. C., and Small, S. A. The Timing of Puberty and Its Relationship to Adolescent and Parent Perceptions of Family Interactions. *Developmental Psychology*, 1986, 22, 342–348.

Scales, P. Adolescent Sexuality and Education: Principles, Approaches, and Resources. In C. S. Chilman (ed.), *Adolescent Sexuality in a Changing American Society*, 207–230. New York: Wiley, 1983.

————. Sex Education and the Prevention of Teenage Pregnancy: An Overview of Policies and Programs in the United States. In T. Ooms (ed.), *Teenage Pregnancy in Family Context: Implications for Policy*, 213–254. Philadelphia: Temple University Press, 1981.

————. *Sex Education Policies and the Primary Prevention of Teenage Pregnancy* (1978), cited in E. R. Allgeier and A. R. Allgeier, *Sexual Interactions.* Lexington, Mass.: D. C. Heath, 1984.

Schafer, R. The Self-Concept as a Factor in Diet Selection and Quality. *Journal of Nutrition Education*, 1979, 11, 37–39.

Shaver, J. P., and Strong, W. *Facing Value Decisions: Rationale-Building for Teachers.* Belmont, Calif.: Wadsworth, 1976.

Shestowsky, B. Ego Identity Development and Obesity in Adolescent Girls. *Adolescence*, 1983, 71, 550–559.

Shope, D. F. *Interpersonal Sexuality.* Philadelphia: Saunders, 1975.

Smart, D. E., Beumont, P. J., and George, G. C. Some Personality Characteristics of Patients with Anorexia Nervosa. *British Journal of Psychiatry*, 1976, 128, 57–60.

Sobesky, W. E. The Effects of Situational Factors on Moral Judgments. *Child Development*, 1983, 54, 575–584.

Sommer, B. B. *Puberty and Adolescence.* New York: Oxford University Press, 1978.

Sorenson, R. C. *The Sorenson Report: Adolescent Sexuality in Contemporary America.* New York: World, 1973.

Sprintall, N. A., and Collins, W. A. *Adolescent Psychology: A Developmental Approach.* New York: Random House, 1984.

Staffieri, J. R. Body Build and Behavioral Expectancies in Young Females. *Developmental Psychology*, 1972, 6, 125–127.

Steinberg, L. *Adolescence.* New York: Knopf, 1985.

Stolz, H. R., and Stolz, L. M. *Somatic Development of Adolescent Boys.* New York: Macmillan, 1951.

Tanner, J. M. Physical Growth. In P. H. Mussen (ed.), *Carmichael's Manual of Child Development* (3rd ed.), 77–155. New York: Wiley, 1970.

————. Early Maturation in Man. *Scientific American*, 1968, 218, 21–27.

————. *Growth at Adolescence.* Oxford: Blackwell, 1962.

Voget, F. X. Bulimia. *Adolescence*, 1985, 20, 46–50.

Weatherley, D. Self-Perceived Rate of Physical Maturation and Personality in Late Adolescence. *Child Development*, 1964, 35, 1197–1210.

Weiss, R. J. Understanding Moral Thought: Effects on Moral Reasoning and Decision Making. *Developmental Psychology*, 1982, 18, 852–861.

Wenar, C. *Psychopathology from Infancy Through Adolescence.* New York: Random House, 1982.

Whisnant, L., and Zegans, L. A Study of Attitudes Towards Menarche in White Middle-Class American Adolescent Girls. *American Journal of Psychiatry*, 1975, 132, 809–814.

Whitney, E. N., and Hamilton, E. M. N. *Understanding Nutrition* (3rd ed.). St. Paul: West, 1984.

Williams, J. H. *Psychology of Women: Behavior in a Biosocial Context.* New York: Norton, 1977.

Wonderly, D. M., and Kupfersmid, J. H. Promoting Postconventional Morality: The Adequacy of Kohlberg's Aim. *Adolescence*, 1980, 15, 609–631.

Zabin, L. S., Kantner, J. L, and Zelnik, M. The Risk of Adolescent Pregnancy in the First Months of Intercourse. *Family Planning Perspectives*, 1979, 4, 215–222.

Zakus, G., Chin, M. L., Yeown, M., Herbert, F., and Held, M. A Group Behavior Modification Approach to Adolescent Obesity. *Adolescence*, 1979, 55, 481–491.

Zelnik, M., and Kantner, J. F. Sexual Activity, Contraceptive Use, and Pregnancy Among Metropolitan-Area Teenagers: 1971–1979. *Family Planning Perspectives*, 1980, 12, 230–237.

————. First Pregnancies to Women Aged 15–19; 1976 and 1971. *Family Planning Perspectives*, 1978, 10, 11–20.

————. Sexual and Contraceptive Experience of Young Unmarried Women in the United States, 1976 and 1971. *Family Planning Perspectives*, 1977, 9, 115–134.

Zelnik, M., and Kim, Y. J. Sex Education and Its Association with Teenage Sexual Activity, Pregnancy, and Contraceptive Use. *Family Planning Perspectives*, May–June 1982, 14, 117–126.

Zougher, C. E. The Self-Concept of Adolescent Girls. *Adolescence*, 1977, 12, 477–488.

Chapter 12

Adams, G. R., Abraham, K. G., and Markstrom, C. A. The Relations Among Identity Development, Self-Consciousness, and Self-Focusing During Middle and Late Adolescence. *Developmental Psychology*, 1987, 23, 292–298.

Archer, J., and Lopata, A. Marijuana Revisited. *American Personnel and Guidance Journal*, 1979, 57, 244–252.

Archer, S. L. The Lower Boundaries of Identity Development. *Child Development*, 1982, 53, 1555–1556.

Astin, A. W. *The American Freshman: Twenty Year Trends, 1966–1985.* Los Angeles: Higher Education Research Institute, U.C.L.A., 1986.

Auster, C. J., and Auster, D. Factors Influencing Women's Choice of Nontraditional Careers: The Role of Family, Peers, and Counselors. *Vocational Guidance Quarterly*, 1981, 29, 253–265.

Bachman, J., Green, S., and Wirtanen, I. *Youth in Transition*, vol. 3: *Dropping-Out—Problem or Symptom?* Ann Arbor: Institute for Social Research, University of Michigan, 1972.

Bachman, J. G., O'Malley, P. M., and Johnston, J. *Adolescence to Adulthood: Change and Stability in the Lives of Young Men*, vol. 6 of *Youth in Transition.* Ann Arbor: University of Michigan Institute for Social Research, 1978.

Barnes, H. L., and Olson, D. H. Parent-Adolescent Communication and the Circumplex Model. *Child Development*, 1985, 56, 438–447.

Barton, J., Chassin, L., Presson, C. C., and Sherman, T. J. Social Image Factors as Motivators of Smoking Initiation in Early and Middle Adolescence. *Child Development*, 1982, 53, 1499–1511.

Bernard, H. S. Identity Formation During Late Adolescence: A Review of Some Empirical Findings. *Adolescence*, 1981, 16, 349–356.

Berndt, T. Developmental Changes in Conformity to Peers and Parents. *Developmental Psychology*, 1979, 15, 608–617.

Bloom, D. E. Women and Work. *American Demographics*, September 1986, 8, 25–30.

Blum, R. H., et al. *Society and Drugs*, vol. 1. San Francisco: Jossey-Bass, 1970.

Boyer, E. L. *High School: A Report on Secondary Education in America*. New York: Harper and Row, 1983.

Braucht, G. N., Brakarsh, D., Follingstad, D., and Berry, K. L. Deviant Drug Use in Adolescence: A Review of Psychosocial Correlates. *Psychological Bulletin*, 1973, 79, 92–106.

Brinkley, J. Drug Use Held Mostly Stable or Lower. *New York Times*, October 10, 1986, A14.

——. Drug Use in High Schools Down. *New York Times*, January 8, 1985, B5.

Brittain, C. V. A Comparison of Rural and Urban Adolescents with Respect to Peer vs. Parent Compliance. *Adolescence*, 1969, 13, 59–68.

——. Adolescent Choices and Parent-Peer Cross-Pressures. *American Sociological Review*, 1963, 28, 385–391.

Brook, J. S., Lukoff, I. F., and Whiteman, M. Family Socialization and Adolescent Personality and Their Association with Adolescent Use of Marijuana. *Journal of Genetic Psychology*, 1978, 133, 261–271.

Brook, J. S., Whiteman, M., Brook, D. W., and Gordon, A. S. Paternal Determinants of Male Adolescent Marijuana Use. *Developmental Psychology*, 1981, 17, 841–847.

Brook, J. S., Whiteman, M., Gordon, A. S., and Brook, D. W. Identification with Parental Attributes and Its Relationship to the Son's Personality and Drug Use. *Developmental Psychology*, 1984, 20, 1111–1119.

Brook, J. S., Whiteman, M., and Gordon, A. S. Stages of Drug Use in Adolescence: Personality, Peer, and Family Correlates. *Developmental Psychology*, 1983, 19, 269–277.

Brown, B. B., Clasen, D. R., and Eicher, S. A. Perceptions of Peer Pressure, Peer Conformity Dispositions, and Self-Reported Behavior Among Adolescents. *Developmental Psychology*, 1986, 22, 521–530.

Campbell, A. *Girl Delinquents*. New York: St. Martin's Press, 1981.

Chand, I. P., Crider, D. M., and Willets, F. K. Parent-Youth Disagreement as Perceived by Youth: A Longitudinal Study. *Youth and Society*, 1975, 6, 365–375.

Chassin, L., Presson, C. C., Sherman, S. J., Montello, D., and McGrew, J. Changes in Peer and Parent Influence During Adolescence: Longitudinal Versus Cross-Sectional Perspectives on Smoking Initiation. *Developmental Psychology*, 1986, 22, 327–334.

Clarey, J. H., and Sanford, A. Female Career Preference and Androgyny. *Vocational Guidance Quarterly*, 1982, 20, 258–265.

Clarizio, H. F., and McCoy, G. F. *Behavior Disorders in Children* (3rd ed.). New York: Harper and Row, 1983.

Coleman, E. Counseling Adolescent Males. *American Personnel and Guidance Journal*, 1981, 60, 215–219.

Colt, G. H. Suicide. *Harvard Magazine*, September–October 1983, 46–53, 63–66.

Conger, J. J., and Petersen, A. C. *Adolescence and Youth* (3rd ed.). New York: Harper and Row, 1984.

Conye, R. K. Primary Prevention Through a Campus Alcohol Education Project. *Personnel and Guidance Journal*, May 1984, 62, 524–529.

Cooper, C. R., Grotevant, H. D., and Condon, S. M. Methodological Challenges of Selectivity in Family Interaction: Assessing Temporal Patterns of Individuation. *Journal of Marriage and the Family*, 1982, 44, 749–754.

Cross, H. J., and Allen, J. G. Ego Identity Status, Adjustment, and Academic Achievement. *Journal of Consulting and Clinical Psychology*, 1970, 34, 288.

Dawkins, R. L, and Dawkins, M. P. Alcohol Use and Delinquency Among Black, White, Hispanic Adolescent Offenders. *Adolescence*, 1983, 18, 799–809.

deVaus, D. A. The Relative Importance of Parents and Peers for Adolescent Religious Orientation: An Australian Study. *Adolescence*, 1983, 18, 147–158.

Donovan, J. M. Identity Status and Interpersonal Style. *Journal of Youth and Adolescence*, 1975, 4, 37–55.

Dornbusch, S. M., Carlsmith, J. M., Bushwall, S. J., Ritter, P. L., Leiderman, H., Hastorf, A. H., and Gross, R. T. Single Parents, Extended Households, and the Control of Adolescence. *Child Development*, 1985, 56, 326–341.

Douvan, E., and Adelson, J. *The Adolescent Experience*. New York: Wiley, 1966.

Eagly, A. H. Sex Differences in Influenceability. *Psychological Bulletin*, 1978, 85, 86–116.

Erikson, E. H. *Identity, Youth, and Crisis*. New York: Norton, 1968.

——. The Problem of Ego Identity. In *Identity and the Life Cycle* (1959). New York: Norton, 1980.

Farberow, N. L. Youth Suicide: A Summary. In M. L. Peck, N. L. Farberow, and R. E. Litman (eds.), *Youth Suicide*, 191–205. New York: Springer, 1985.

Farmer, H. S. Career Counseling Implications for the Lower Social Class and Women. *Personnel and Guidance Journal*, 1978, 56, 467–472.

Federal Bureau of Investigation (FBI). *Uniform Crime Reports for the United States, 1985*. Washington, D.C.: U.S. Department of Justice, July 1986.

Finckenauer, J. Scared Straight. *Psychology Today*, 1979, 13, 6–11.

Fitch, S. A., and Adams, G. R. Ego Identity and Intimacy: Replication and Extension. *Developmental Psychology*, 1983, 19, 839–845.

Fitzgerald, L. F., and Betz, N. E. Issues in the Vocational Psychology of Women. In W. B. Walsh and S. H. Osipow (eds.), *Handbook of Vocational Psychology*, 83–161. Hillsdale, N.J.: Erlbaum, 1983.

Fox, V. *Introduction to Criminology* (2nd ed.). Englewood Cliffs, N.J.: Prentice-Hall, 1985.

Frederick, C. J. An Introduction and Overview of Youth Suicide. In M. L. Peck, N. L. Farberow, and R. E. Litman (eds.), *Youth Suicide*, 1–19. New York: Springer, 1985.

Gibbons, D. C. *Society, Crime, and Criminal Behavior* (4th ed.). Englewood Cliffs, N.J.: Prentice-Hall, 1982.

Ginott, H. G. *Between Parent and Teenager*. New York: Macmillan, 1969.

Gispert, M., Wheeler, K., Marsh, L., and Davis, M. S. Suicidal Adolescents: Factors in Evaluations. *Adolescence*, 1985, 20, 753–762.

Greenglass, E. R., and Devins, R. Factors Related to Marriage and Career Plans in Unmarried Women. *Sex Roles*, 1982, 8, 57–72.

Grinder, R. L. *Adolescence*. New York: Wiley, 1973.

Grotevant, H. D., and Cooper, C. R. Individuation in Family Relationships. *Human Development*, 1986, 29, 82–100.

——. Patterns of Interaction in Family Relationships and the Development of Identity Exploration in Adolescence. *Child Development*, 1985, 56, 415–428.

Hardert, R. A., Gordon, L., Laner, M. R., and Reader, M. *Confronting Social Problems*. St. Paul: West, 1984.

Harmon, L. W., and Farmer, H. S. Current Theoretical Issues in Vocational Psychology. In W. B. Walsh and S. H. Osipow (eds.), *Handbook of Vocational Psychology*, vol. 1: *Foundations*, 39–83. Hillsdale, N.J.: Erlbaum, 1983.

Hendin, H. Suicide Among the Young: Psychodynamics and Demography. In M. L. Peck, N. L. Farberow, and R. E. Litman (eds.), *Youth Suicide*, 19–39. New York: Springer, 1985.

Hendin, H., Pollinger, A., Ulman, R., and Carr, A. C. *Adolescent Marijuana Abusers and Their Families.* NIDA Research Monograph 40. Washington, D.C.: Department of Health and Human Services, 1981.

Henggeler, S. W., Rodick, J. D., Borduin, C. M., Hanson, C. L., Watson, S. M., and Urey, J. R. Multisystemic Treatment of Juvenile Offenders: Effects on Adolescent Behavior and Family Interaction. *Developmental Psychology,* 1986, *22,* 132–141.

Hobart, T. Y. Helping the Young Defeat the Scourges of Drugs, Alcohol, Suicide. *New York Teacher,* October 13, 1986, *28,* p. 10.

Hunter, F. T. Adolescents' Perception of Discussions with Parents and Friends. *Developmental Psychology,* 1985, *21,* 443–440.

————. Socializing Procedures in Parent-Child and Friendship Relations During Adolescence. *Developmental Psychology,* 1984, *20,* 1092–1100.

Hunter, F. T., and Youniss, J. Changes in Functions of Three Relations During Adolescence. *Developmental Psychology,* 1982, *18,* 806–812.

Hyde, J. S. *Half the Human Experience: The Psychology of Women* (3rd ed.). Lexington, Mass.: D.C. Heath, 1985.

Jarvik, M. E., Cullen, J. W., Gritz, E. R., Vogt, T. M., and West, L. J. (eds.). *Research on Smoking Behavior.* U.S. Department of Health, Education and Welfare, NIDA Research Monograph 17. Washington, D.C.: U.S. Government Printing Office, 1977.

Jensen, L. C. *Adolescence: Theories, Research, Applications.* St. Paul: West, 1985.

Kandel, D., and Lesser, G. S. Parent-Adolescent Relationships and Adolescent Independence in the United States and Denmark. *Journal of Marriage and the Family,* 1969, *31,* 348–358.

Keith, P. M. Sex-Role Attitudes, Family Plans, and Career Orientations: Implications for Counseling. *Vocational Guidance Quarterly,* 1981, *29,* 244–253.

Kerr, P. High-School Marijuana Use Still Declining, U.S. Survey Shows. *New York Times,* February 24, 1987, A21.

————. Anatomy of the Drug Issue: How, After Years, It Erupted. *New York Times,* November 17, 1986, A1 and B6.

Lerner, R. M, Karson, M., Meisels, M., and Knapp, J. R. Actual and Perceived Attitudes of Late Adolescents and Their Parents: The Phenomenon of the Generation Gap. *Journal of Genetic Psychology,* 1975, *126,* 195–207.

Lerner, R. M., and Spanier, G. B. *Adolescent Development: A Life-Span Perspective.* New York: McGraw-Hill, 1980.

Levanthal, H., and Cleary, P. The Smoking Problem: A Review of the Research and Theory in Behavioral Risk Modification. *Psychological Bulletin,* 1980, *88,* 370–405.

Lloyd, D. Prediction of School Failure from Third-Grade Data. *Educational and Psychological Measurement,* 1978, *38,* 1193–1200.

Lowney, J., Winslow, R. W., and Winslow, V. *Deviant Reality: Alternative World Views* (2nd ed.). Boston: Allyn and Bacon, 1981.

Lueptow, L. B. Sex-Typing and Change in the Occupational Choices of High School Seniors, 1964–1975. *Sociology of Education,* 1981, *54,* 16–24.

Marcia, J. Identity in Adolescence. In J. Adelson (ed.), *Handbook of Adolescent Psychology.* New York: Wiley, 1980.

————. Ego Identity Status: Relationship to Change in Self-Esteem, "General Maladjustment," and Authoritarianism. *Journal of Personality,* 1967, *35,* 118–133.

————. Development and Validation of Ego-Identity Status. *Journal of Personality and Social Psychology,* 1966, *3,* 551–558.

Marcia, J. E., and Friedman, M. L. Ego Identity Status in College Women. *Journal of Personality,* 1970, *38,* 249–263.

McDermitt, D. The Relationship of Parental Drug Use and Parents' Attitude Concerning Adolescent Drug Use. *Adolescence,* 1984, *73,* 89–97.

Meilman, P. W. Cross-Sectional Age Changes in Ego Identity Status During Adolescence. *Developmental Psychology,* 1979, *15,* 230–231.

Montemayor, R. The Relationship Between Parent-Adolescent Conflict and the Amount of Time Adolescents Spend Alone and with Parents and Peers. *Child Development,* 1982, *53,* 1512–1519.

Munley, P. H. Erikson's Theory of Psychosocial Development and Career Development. *Journal of Vocational Behavior,* 1977, *10,* 261–269.

————. Erik Erikson's Theory of Psychosocial Development and Career Development. *Journal of Counseling Psychology,* 1975, *22,* 314–319.

Muuss, R. E. *Theories of Adolescence* (4th ed.). New York: Random House, 1982.

Nassi, A. J. Survivors of the Sixties: Comparative Psychosocial and Political Development of Former Berkeley Student Activists. *American Psychologist,* 1981, *36,* 753–762.

Nathan, P. E. Failures in Prevention: Why We Can't Prevent the Devastating Effects of Alcoholism and Drug Abuse? *American Psychologist,* 1983, *38,* 459–468.

National Institute on Drug Abuse. *Drugs and American High School Students, 1975–1983.* Washington, D.C.: National Institute on Drug Abuse, 1983.

New York State Division of Alcohol and Alcohol Abuse. *Alcohol Abuse.* New York State Division of Alcohol and Alcohol Abuse, 1986.

New York State Division of Substance Abuse Services. *Crack Down on Crack: What You Should Know.* New York State Division of Substance Abuse Services, 1986.

Norem-Hebeisen, A., and Hedin, D. Influences on Adolescent Problem Behavior: Causes, Connections, and Contexts. In *Adolescent Peer Pressure,* 21–47. Washington, D.C.: U.S. Department of Health and Human Services, 1984.

O'Donnell, J. A., and Andersen, D. G. Factors Influencing Choice of Major and Career of Capable Women. *Vocational Guidance Journal,* 1978, *26,* 214–222.

Olson, L. Broader Approach to Dropouts Urged. *Education Week,* March 18, 1987, p. 5.

Orlofsky, J. L, Marcia, J. E., and Lesser, T. M. Ego Identity Status and the Intimacy Versus Isolation Crisis of Young Adulthood. *Journal of Personality and Social Psychology,* 1973, *27,* 211–219.

Oshman, H., and Manosevitz, M. The Impact of the Identity Crisis on the Adjustment of Late Adolescent Males. *Journal of Youth and Adolescence,* 1974, *3,* 207–217.

Petitpas, A. Identity Foreclosure: A Unique Challenge. *American Personnel and Guidance Journal,* 1978, *56,* 558–562.

Richards, L. G. (ed.), *Demographic Trends and Drug Abuse, 1980–1985.* NIDA Research Monograph 35. Washington, D.C.: Department of Health and Human Services, 1981.

Rosenberg, J. S., and Berberian, R. M. A Report on the Dropout Study, Yale University School of Medicine (1975). In G. A. Austin and M. L. Prendergast, *Drug Use and Abuse: A Guide to Research Findings,* vol. 2, 560–562. Santa Barbara, Calif.: ABC-Clio Information Services, 1984.

Ruittenbeck, H. M. *The Individual and the Crowd: A Study of Identity in America.* New York: New American Library, 1964.

Schiedel, D. G., and Marcia, J. E. Ego Identity, Intimacy, Sex Role Orientation, and Gender. *Developmental Psychology,* 1985, *21,* 149–160.

Scott, G. J. Career Search, Selection, and Entry. In W. B. Walsh and S. H. Osipow (eds.), *Handbook of Vocational Psychology,* vol. 2: *Applications,* 77–99. Hillsdale, N.J.: Erlbaum, 1983.

Sharabany, R., Gershoni, R., and Hofman, J. E. Girlfriend, Boyfriend: Age and Sex Differences in Intimate Friendship. *Developmental Psychology,* 1981, *17,* 800–809.

Sheppard, M. A., Wright, D.,and Goodstadt, M. S. Peer Pressure and Drug Use: Exploding the Myth. *Adolescence,* 1985, 20, 949–958.

Shneidman, E. S., Farberow, N. L., and Litman, R. E. *The Psychology of Suicide.* New York: Science House, 1970.

Siegel, O. Personality Development in Adolescence. In B. B. Wolman (ed.), *Handbook of Developmental Psychology,* 537–549. Englewood Cliffs, N.J.: Prentice-Hall, 1982.

Silverstein, B., Feld, S., and Kozlowski, L. T. The Availability of Low-Nicotine Cigarettes as a Cause of Cigarette Smoking Among Teenage Females. *Journal of Health and Social Behavior,* 1980, 21, 383–388.

Silverstein, B., Kelley, E., Swan, J., and Kozlowski, L. T. Physiological Predisposition Toward Becoming a Cigarette Smoker: Experimental Evidence for a Sex Difference. *Addictive Behaviors,* 1982, 7, 83–86.

Smith, E. J. Issues in Racial Minorities' Career Behavior. In W. B. Walsh and S. H. Osipow (eds.), *Handbook of Vocational Psychology,* vol. 1: *Foundations,* 161–223. Hillsdale, N.J.: Erlbaum, 1983.

Smith, G. M. Relations Between Personality and Smoking Behavior in Preadult Subjects. *Journal of Consulting and Clinical Psychology,* 1969, 33, 710–715.

Snider, W. Study Finds Rise in Cocaine Smoking. *Education Week,* March 4, 1987, p. 9.

Sorosiak, F. M., Thomas, L. E., and Balet, F. N. Adolescent Drug Use: An Analysis. *Psychological Reports,* 1976, 38, 211–221.

Sprintall, N. A., and Collins, W. A. *Adolescent Psychology: A Developmental View.* New York: Random House, 1984.

Steinberg, L. *Adolescence.* New York: Random House, 1985.

Steinberg, L., and Silverberg, S. B. The Vicissitudes of Autonomy in Early Adolescence. *Child Development,* 1986, 57, 841–851.

Super, D. A Theory of Vocational Development. *American Psychologist,* 1953, 8, 185–190.

Supple, T. S. The Coming Labor Shortage. *American Demographics,* September 1986, 9, 32–38.

Toffler, A. *Future Shock.* New York: Random House, 1970.

Treiman, D., and Terrell, K. Sex and the Process of Status Attainment: A Comparison of Working Women and Men. *American Sociological Review,* 1975, 40, 174–200.

U.S. Bureau of the Census. *Statistical Abstract of the United States, 1986.* Washington, D.C., 1986.

U.S. Department of Health, Education, and Welfare. *Smoking and Health: A Report of the Surgeon General.* Washington, D.C.: U.S. Government Printing Office, 1978.

U.S. Department of Labor. *Employment in Perspective: Women in the Labor Force* (second quarter, 1986). Bureau of Labor Statistics Report no. 730. Washington, D.C., 1986a.

————. *Employment in Perspective: Minority Workers* (second quarter 1986b). Bureau of Labor Statistics Report no. 731. Washington, D.C.: U.S. Department of Labor, 1986.

U.S. Office of Drug Abuse Policy. Report Prepared by the White House Committee on Drug Abuse for the President, 1978.

Varenhorst, B. The Adolescent Society. In *Adolescent Peer Pressure,* 1–21. Washington, D.C.: U.S. Department of Health and Human Services, 1984.

Voss, H. L., Wendling, A., and Elliott, D. S. Some Types of High-School Dropouts. *Journal of Educational Research,* 1966, 59, 363–368.

Waterman, A. S. Identity Development from Adolescence to Adulthood: An Extension of Theory and a Review of the Literature. *Developmental Psychology,* 1982, 18, 341–359.

Waterman, A. S., and Waterman, C. K. A Longitudinal Study of Changes in Ego Identity Status During the Freshman Year at College. *Developmental Psychology,* 1971, 5, 167–173.

Wenar, C. *Psychopathology from Infancy through Adolescence.* New York: Random House, 1982.

Wilson, J. Q., and Herrnstein, R. J. *Crime and Human Nature.* New York: Simon and Schuster, 1985.

Wilson, J., Weikel, W. J., and Rose, H. A. A Comparison of Nontraditional and Traditional Career Women. *Vocational Guidance Quarterly,* 1982, 31, 109–117.

Chapter 13

Cohler, B. J. Personal Narrative and Life Course. In P. B. Baltes and O. G. Brim, *Life-Span Development and Behavior,* vol. 4, 205–241. New York: Academic Press, 1982.

Erikson, E. H. *Childhood and Society.* New York: Norton, 1950 (rev. ed. 1963).

Giele, J. Z. Adulthood as Transcendence of Age and Sex. In N. J. Smelser and E. H. Erikson (eds.), *Themes of Work and Love in Adulthood,* 151–174. Cambridge, Mass.: Harvard University Press, 1980.

Gilligan, C. *In a Different Voice.* Cambridge, Mass.: Harvard University Press, 1982.

Gould, R. L. Transformations During Early and Middle Adult Years. In N. J. Smelser and E. H. Erikson (eds.), *Themes of Work and Love in Adulthood,* 213–238. Cambridge, Mass.: Harvard University Press, 1980.

————. *Transformations: Growth and Change in Adult Life.* New York: Simon and Schuster, 1978.

————. Adult Life Stages: Growth Toward Self-Tolerance. *Psychology Today,* February 1975, 74–78.

Hall, G. S. *Senescence: The Last Half of Life.* New York: Appleton, 1922.

Havighurst, R. J. The World of Work. In B. B. Wolman (ed.), *Handbook of Developmental Psychology,* 771–787. Englewood Cliffs, N.J.: Prentice-Hall, 1982.

Honzik, M. P. Life-Span Development. In M. R. Rosenzweig and L. W. Porter (eds.), *Annual Review of Psychology,* 1984, 35, 309–331.

Katchadourian, H. A. Medical Perspectives on Adulthood. In E. H. Erikson (ed.), *Adulthood,* 33–60. New York: Norton, 1978.

Levinson, D. J. Toward a Conception of the Adult Life Course. In N. J. Smelser and E. H. Erikson (eds.), *Themes of Work and Love in Adulthood,* 265–291. Cambridge, Mass.: Harvard University Press, 1980.

————. *The Seasons of a Man's Life.* New York: Knopf, 1978.

Neugarten, B. L. Personality and Aging. In J. Birren and K. Warner Schaie (eds.), *Handbook of the Psychology of Aging,* 626–649.

————. The Future and the Young-Old. *The Gerontologist,* 1975, 15, 4–9.

Neugarten, B. L., and Datan, N. The Middle Years. In S. Arieti (ed.), *American Handbook of Psychiatry,* 592–608. New York: Basic Books, 1973.

Neugarten, B. L., and Moore, J. W. The Changing Age-Status System. In B. L. Neugarten (ed.), *Middle Age and Aging.* Chicago: University of Chicago Press, 1968.

Neugarten, B. L., Moore, J. W., and Lowe, J. C. Age Norms, Age Constraints, and Adult Socialization. *American Journal of Sociology,* 1965, 70, 710–717.

Pearlin, L. I. Life Strains and Psychological Distress Among Adults. In N. J. Smelser and E. H. Erikson (eds.), *Themes of Work and Love in Adulthood,* 174–193. Cambridge, Mass.: Harvard University Press, 1980.

Peck, R. C. Psychological Developments in the Second Half of Life. In B. L. Neugarten (ed.), *Middle Age and Aging.* Chicago: University of Chicago Press, 1968.

Perlmutter, M., and Hall, E. *Adult Development and Aging.* New York: Wiley, 1985.

Piaget, J. Intellectual Evolution from Adolescence to Adulthood. *Human Development,* 1972, 15, 1–12.

Rubin, Z. Does Personality Really Change After 20? *Psychology Today*, May 1981, 18.

Salkind, N. J. *Theories of Human Development.* New York: Van Nostrand, 1981.

Schlossberg, N. K. Exploring the Adult Years. In A. M. Rogers and C. J. Scheirer (eds.), *The G. Stanley Hall Lecture Series*, vol. 4, 101–155. Washington, D.C.: American Psychological Association, 1984.

Thomas, M. L., and Kuh, G. D. Understanding Development During the Early Adult Years: A Composite Framework. *Personnel and Guidance Journal*, 1982, 61, 14–17.

Thomas, R. M. *Comparing Theories of Child Development.* Belmont, Calif.: Wadsworth, 1979.

Vaillant, G. E. *Adaptation to Life.* Boston: Little, Brown, 1977.

Vaupel, J. W., and Gowan, A. E. Passage to Methuselah: Some Demographic Consequences of Continued Progress Against Mortality. *American Journal of Public Health*, 1986, 76, 430–433.

Chapter 14

Abraham, S. *Weight and Height of Adults 17–74 Years of Age in U.S., 1971–1974.* Vital and Health Statistics, serial no. 211, DHEW pub no. PHS 76–1659. Washington, D.C.: U.S. Government Printing Office, 1979.

Altman, D. *AIDS in the Mind of America.* Garden City N.Y.: Anchor/Doubleday, 1986.

Arlin, P. K. Piagetian Operators in Problem-Solving. *Developmental Psychology*, 1977, 13, 297–298.

———. Cognitive Development in Adulthood: A Fifth Stage? *Developmental Psychology*, 1975, 11, 602–606.

Bachman, J. G., O'Malley, P. M., and Johnston, L. D. Drug Use Among Young Adults: The Impacts of Role Status and Social Environment. *Journal of Personality and Social Psychology*, 1984, 47, 629–645.

Bardwick, J. M. *Psychology of Women: A Study of Biocultural Conflicts.* New York: Harper and Row, 1971.

Bayley, N. Cognition and Aging. In K. W. Schaie (ed.), *Theory and Methods of Research on Aging.* Morgantown: West Virginia University, 1968a.

———. Behavioral Correlates of Mental Growth: Birth to Thirty-Six Years. *American Psychologist*, 1968b, 23, 1–17.

———. Learning in Adulthood: The Role of Intelligence. In H. J. Klaus and C. W. Harris (eds.), *Analyses of Concept Learning.* New York: Academic Press, 1966.

Birren, J. E. (ed.), *Relations of Development and Aging.* Springfield, Ill.: Thomas, 1964.

Bocknek, G. *The Young Adult: Development After Adolescence.* Belmont, Calif.: Wadsworth, 1980.

Botwinick, J. *Aging and Behavior* (3rd ed.). New York: Springer, 1984.

———. Intellectual Abilities. In J. E. Birren and K. W. Schaie (eds.), *Handbook of the Psychology of Aging.* New York: Van Nostrand Reinhold, 1977.

Brand, R. J. Coronary Prone Behavior as an Independent Risk Factor for Coronary Heart Disease. In T. M. Dembroski, S. M. Weiss, S. G. Haynes, and M. Feinlab (eds.), *Coronary Prone Behavior.* New York: Springer-Verlag, 1978.

Brim, O. G., and Kagan, J. Constancy and Change: A View of the Issues. In O. G. Brim and J. Kagan (eds.), *Constancy and Change in Human Development*, 1–26. Cambridge, Mass.: Harvard University Press, 1980.

Bromley, D. B. *The Psychology of Human Aging* (2nd ed.). Baltimore: Penguin, 1974.

Brooks, J., Ruble, D. N., and Clarke, A. E. College Women's Attitudes and Expectations Concerning Menstrual-Related Changes. *Psychosomatic Medicine*, 1977, 39, 288–298.

Burke, R. J., Weir, T. W., and DuWors, R. E., Jr. Type A Behavior of Administrators and Wives' Reports of Marital Satisfaction. *Journal of Applied Psychology*, 1979, 64, 57–65.

Burns, R. B. *The Self Concept.* London: Longman, 1979.

Business Week. The Sobering of America: The Push to Put Drinking in Its Place. *Business Week*, September 13, 1983, pp. 112–113.

Carlsson, G., and Karlsson, K. Age, Cohorts, and the Generation of Generations. *American Sociological Review*, 1970, 35, 710–718.

Cattell, R. B. Theory of Fluid and Crystallized Intelligence: A Critical Experiment. *Journal of Educational Psychology*, 1963, 54, 1–22.

Chiriboga, D., and Cutler, L. Stress and Adaptation: Life Span Perspectives. In L. W. Poon (ed.), *Aging in the 1980s: Psychological Issues*, 347–362. Washington, D.C.: American Psychological Association, 1980.

Colby, A., Kohlberg, L., Gibbs, J., and Lieberman, M. A Longitudinal Study of Moral Judgment. Unpublished manuscript, Harvard University, 1980.

Commons, M. L., Richards, F. A., and Kuhn, D. Systematic and Metasystematic Reasoning: A Case for Levels of Reasoning Beyond Piaget's Stage of Formal Operations. *Child Development*, 1982, 53, 1058–1070.

Corso, J. F. *Aging Sensory Systems and Perception.* New York: Praeger, 1981.

Curfman, G. D., Gregory, T. S., and Paffenbarger, R. S. Physical Activity and Primary Prevention of Cardiovascular Disease. *Cardiology Clinics*, May 1985, 3, 203–222.

Dalton, K. Cyclical Criminal Acts in Premenstrual Syndrome. *The Lancet*, 1980, 2, 1070–1071.

DeLongis, A., Coyne, J. C., Dakof, G., Folkman, S., and Lazarus, R. S. Relationship of Daily Hassles, Uplifts, and Major Life Events to Health Status. *Health Psychology*, 1982, 1, 119–136.

deVries, H. A. Physiology of Exercise and Aging. In D. S. Woodruff and J. E. Birren (eds.), *Aging: Scientific Perspectives and Social Issues*, 257–278. New York: Van Nostrand, 1975.

Diekelmann, N. *Primary Health Care of the Well Adult.* New York: McGraw-Hill, 1977.

Doering, C. H. The Endocrine System. In O. G. Brim and J. Kagan (eds.), *Constancy and Change in Human Development*, 229–272. Cambridge, Mass.: Harvard University Press, 1980.

Doyle, J. A. *Sex and Gender: The Human Experience.* Dubuque, Iowa: Brown, 1985.

Fischer, K. W., and Silvern, L. Stages and Individual Differences in Cognitive Development. In M. R. Rosenzweig and L. W. Porter, *Annual Review of Psychology*, 1985, 36, 613–649.

Foege, W. The National Pattern of AIDS. In K. M. Cahill (ed.), *The AIDS Epidemic*, 7–18. New York: St. Martin's Press, 1983.

Folkins, C. H., and Sime, W. E. Physical Fitness Training and Mental Health. *American Psychologist*, 1981, 36, 373–389.

Friedland, G. H., Saltzman, B. R., Rogers, M. F., et al. Lack of Transmission of HTLV–111/LAV Infection to Household Contacts of Patients with AIDS or AIDS-Related Complex with Oral Candidiasis. *New England Journal of Medicine*, 1986, 314, 344–349.

Friedman, M., and Rosenman, R. H. *Type A Behavior and Your Heart.* New York: Knopf, 1975.

Gadpaille, W. J. *The Cycles of Sex.* New York: Scribner's, 1975.

Gardner, H. *Frames of Mind: The Theory of Multiple Intelligences.* New York: Basic Books, 1983.

Gillagan, C. *In a Different Voice.* Cambridge, Mass.: Harvard University Press, 1982.

Glass, D. C. *Behavior Patterns, Stress, and Coronary Heart Disease.* Hillsdale, N.J.: Erlbaum, 1977.

Glenn, N. D. Values, Attitudes, and Beliefs. In O. G. Brim and J. Kagan (eds.), *Constancy and Change in Human Development*, 596–641. Cambridge, Mass.: Harvard University Press, 1980.

Golub, S. The Effect of Premenstrual Anxiety and Depression on Cognitive Function. *Journal of Personality and Social Psychology*, 1976, 34, 99–104.

Gong, V. Signs and Symptoms of AIDS. In V. Gong (ed.), *Understanding AIDS*, 36–40. New Brunswick, N.J.: Rutgers University Press, 1985a.

———. AIDS—Defining the Syndrome. In V. Gong (ed.), Understanding AIDS, 1–10. New Brunswick, N.J.: Rutgers University Press, 1985b.

Hammar, S. L., and Owens, J. W. M. (1973) cited in J. Stevens-Long. *Adult Life*, 2nd ed. Palo Alto: Mayfield, 1984.

Hershey, D. *Life Span and Factors Affecting It.* Springfield, Ill.: Thomas, 1974.

Hilyer, J., and Mitchell, W. Effect of Systematic Physical Fitness Training Combined with Counseling on the Self-Concept of College Students. *Journal of Counseling Psychology*, 1979, 26, 427–436.

Hirsch, R. Hemophiliacs, Blood Transfusions, and AIDS. In V. Gong (ed.), *Understanding AIDS*, 100–112. New Brunswick, N.J.: Rutgers University Press, 1985.

Hoge, D. R., and Bender, I. E. Factors Influencing Value Change Among College Graduates in Adult Life. *Journal of Personality and Social Psychology*, 1974, 29, 572–585.

Holmes, T. H., and Rahe, R. H. The Social Readjustment Rating Scale. *Journal of Psychosomatic Research*, 1967, 11, 213–218.

Hongladarom, G., McCorkle, R., and Woods, N. F. *The Complete Book of Women's Health.* Englewood Cliffs, N.J.: Prentice-Hall, 1982.

Honzik, M. P. Life-Span Development. In M. R. Rosenzweig and L. W. Porter (eds.), *Annual Review of Psychology*, 1984, 35, 309–331.

Horn, J. L. Organization of Data on Life-Span Development of Human Abilities. In L. R. Goulet and P. B. Baltes (eds.), *Life-Span Developmental Psychology: Research and Theory*, vol. 1. New York: Academic Press, 1970.

Horn, J. L., and Donaldson, G. Cognitive Development in Adulthood. In O. G. Brim and J. Kagan (eds.), *Constancy and Change in Human Development*, 445–530. Cambridge, Mass.: Harvard University Press, 1980.

Hyde, J. S. *Half the Human Experience: The Psychology of Women.* Lexington, Mass.: D. C. Heath, 1985.

Kaplan, P. S., and Stein, J. *The Psychology of Adjustment.* Belmont, Calif.: Wadsworth, 1984.

Keating, D. P., and Clark, L. V. Development of Physical and Social Reasoning in Adolescents. *Developmental Psychology*, 1980, 16, 23–30.

Kerr, C. H., and Scully, A. L. *The American Medical Association Book of Woman Care.* New York: Random House, 1982.

Knox, D. *Human Sexuality: The Search for Understanding.* St. Paul: West, 1984.

Kohn, R. R. Heart and Cardiovascular System. In C. Finch and L. Hayflick (eds.), *Handbook of the Physiology of Aging*, 281–317. New York: Van Nostrand, 1977.

Koop, C. E. Report of the Surgeon General of the United States on Acquired Immune Deficiency Syndrome. Washington, D.C.: DHEW, 1987.

Krantz, D. S., Grunberg, N. E., and Baum, A. Health Psychology. In M. R. Rosenzweig and L. W. Porter, *Annual Review of Psychology*, 1985, 36, 349–383.

Kuhn, D., Langer, J., Kohlberg, L., and Haan, N. S. The Development of Formal Operations in Logical and Moral Judgment. *Genetic Psychology Monographs*, 1977, 95, 97–188.

Kuhn, D. Pennington, N., and Leadbeater, B. Adult Thinking in Developmental Perspective. In P. B. Baltes and O. G. Brim (eds.), *Life-Span Development and Behavior*, vol. 5, 158–193. New York: Academic Press, 1983.

Labouvie-Vief, G. Growth and Aging in Life-Span Perspective. *Human Development*, 1982, 25, 65–78.

———. Beyond Formal Operations: Uses and Limits of Pure Logic in Life-Span Development. *Human Development*, 1980, 23, 141–161.

Landesman, S. H. The Haitian Connection. In K. M. Cahill (ed.), *The AIDS Epidemic*, 28–41. New York: St. Martin's Press, 1983.

Lehman, V., and Russell, N. Psychological and Social Issues of AIDS and Strategies for Survival. In V. Gong (ed.), *Understanding AIDS*, 175–190. New Brunswick, N.J.: Rutgers University Press, 1985.

Matthews, K. A. Psychological Perspectives on the Type A Behavior Pattern. *Psychological Bulletin*, 1982, 91, 293–323.

Metropolitan Life Insurance Co. *Ideal Weights.* New York: Metropolitan Life Insurance Co., 1983.

Milsum, J. H. *Health, Stress, and Illness: A Systems Approach.* New York: Praeger, 1984.

Morris, J. N., Everitt, M. G., Pollard, R., et al. Vigorous Exercise in Leisure-Time: Protection Against Coronary Heart-Disease. *The Lancet*, 1980, 2, 1207.

Murphy, J. M., and Gilligan, C. Moral Development in Late Adolescence and Adulthood: A Critique and Reconstruction of Kohlberg's Theory. *Human Development*, 1980, 23, 77–104.

Neugarten, B. L. Adaptation and the Life Cycle. *Journal of Geriatric Psychiatry*, 1970, 4, 71–87.

Newman, B. M. Mid-Life Development. In B. B. Wolman (ed.), *Handbook of Developmental Psychology*, 617–634. Englewood Cliffs, N.J.: Prentice-Hall, 1982.

Oskamp, S. *Applied Social Psychology.* Englewood Cliffs, N.J.: Prentice-Hall, 1984.

Paffenbarger, R. S., Jr., Wing, A. L., Hyde, R. T., et al. Chronic Disease in Former College Students: Physical Activity as an Index of Heart Attack Risk in College Alumni. *American Journal of Epidemiology*, 1978, 108, 151.

Paige, K. E. Women Learn to Sing the Menstrual Blues. *Psychology Today*, April 1973, 41–46.

———. Effects of Oral Contraceptives on Affective Fluctuations Associated with the Menstrual Cycle. *Psychosomatic Medicine*, 1971, 33, 515–537.

Parlee, M. B. The Premenstrual Syndrome. *Psychological Bulletin*, 1973, 80, 454–465.

Pelletier, K. R. Mind as Healer, Mind as Slayer. *Psychology Today*, 1977, 10, 35.

Perry, W. *Forms of Intellectual and Ethical Development in the College Years.* New York: Holt, Rinehart, and Winston, 1970.

Piaget, J. Piaget's Theory (1970). In P. H. Mussen (ed.), *Handbook of Child Psychology* (4th ed.). New York: Wiley, 1983.

———. Intellectual Evolution from Adolescence to Adulthood. *Human Development*, 1972, 15, 1–12.

Princeton Religious Research Center. *Religion in America, 1979–1980.* Princeton, 1980.

Quayle, D. American Productivity: The Devastating Effect of Alcoholism and Drug Abuse. *American Psychologist*, 1983, 38, 454–458.

Ramey, E. Men's Cycles. MS. Spring 1972, 8–14.

Roche, A. F., and Davila, G. H., Late Adolescent Growth in Stature. *Pediatrics*, 1972, 50, 874–880.

Rosen, R., and Rosen, L. R. *Human Sexuality.* New York: Knopf, 1981.

Rosenman, R. H., Brand, R. J., Jenkins, C. D., Friedman, M., Straus, R., et al. Coronary Heart Disease in the Western Collaborative Group Study Final Follow-up Experience of 8½ Years. *Journal of the American Medical Association*, 1975, 223, 872–877.

Rosenman, R. H., Friedman, M., Straus, R., Jenkins, C. D., Zyzanski, S., Wurm, M., Kositchek, R., Hahn, W., and Werthessen, N. T. Coronary Heart Disease in the Western Collaborative Study: A Follow-up Experience of

4½ years. *Journal of Chronic Diseases*, 1970, 23, 173–190.

Rosenman, R. H., Friedman, M., Straus, R., Wurm, M., Kositchek, R., Hahn, W., and Werthessen, N. T. A Predictive Study of Coronary Heart Disease: The Western Collaborative Group Study. *Journal of the American Medical Association*, 1964, 189, 15–22.

Rosentsweig, J. Motor Development Through Life. In C. B. Corbin (ed.), *A Textbook of Motor Development* (2nd ed.), 283–290. Dubuque, Iowa: Brown, 1980.

Ruble, D. N. Premenstrual Symptoms: A Reinterpretation. *Science*, 1977, 197, 291–292.

Sande, M. A. Transmission of AIDS: The Case Against Casual Contagion. *New England Journal of Medicine*, February 6, 1986, 314, 380–382.

Sattler, J. M. *Assessment of Children's Intelligence* (rev. ed.). Philadelphia: Saunders, 1974.

Schaie, K. W. Age Changes in Adult Intelligence. In D. S. Woodruff and J. E. Birren (eds.), *Aging: Scientific Perspectives and Social Issues* (2nd ed.), 137–148. Monterey, Calif.: Brooks/Cole, 1983.

Schaie, K. W., and Hertzog, C. Longitudinal Methods. In B. B. Wolman (ed.), *Handbook of Developmental Psychology*, 91–116. Englewood Cliffs, N.J.: Prentice-Hall, 1982.

Schram, N. R. AIDS: 1991. *Los Angeles Times Magazine*, August 10, 1986, pp. 10–16.

Sensakovic, J. W., and Greer, B. Preventing AIDS. In *Understanding AIDS*, 166–175. New Brunswick, N.J.: Rutgers University Press, 1985.

Sherif, C. A Social Psychological Perspective on the Menstrual Cycle. In J. Parson (ed.), *The Psychology of Sex Differences and Sex Roles*, 245–268. New York: McGraw-Hill, 1980.

Siscovick, D. S., Weiss, N. S., Fletcher, R. H., et al. The Incidence of Primary Cardiac Arrest During Vigorous Exercise. *New England Journal of Medicine*, 1984, 311, 874.

Solomon, H. A. *The Exercise Myth*. San Diego: Harcourt Brace Jovanovich, 1984.

Sommer, B. PMS in the Courts: Are All Women on Trial? *Psychology Today*, August 1984, 36–38.

Spilka, B., Hood, R. W., and Gorsuch, R. L. *The Psychology of Religion: An Empirical Approach*. Englewood Cliffs, N.J.: Prentice-Hall, 1985.

Spotts, J. V., and Shontz, F. C. Cocaine Users: A Representative Case Approach, summarized in G. A. Austin and M. L. Prendergast (reviewers), *Drug Use and Abuse: A Guide to Research Findings*, vol. 1, *Adults*. Santa Bar-

bara, Calif.: ABC-Clio Information Services, 1980.

Starfield, B., and Pless, I. B. Physical Health. In O. G. Brim and J. Kagan (eds.), *Constancy and Change in Human Development*, 272–325. Cambridge, Mass.: Harvard University Press, 1980.

Stevens-Long, J. *Adult Life* (2nd ed.). Palo Alto: Mayfield, 1984.

Strand, F. L. *Physiology* (2nd ed.). New York: Macmillan, 1983.

Suinn, R. M. Intervention with Type A Behaviors. *Journal of Consulting and Clinical Psychology*, 1982, 50, 797–803.

Tanner, J. M. The Adolescent Growth-Spurt and Developmental Age in G. A. Harrison, J. S. Werner, J. M. Tannert, and N. A. Barnicot (eds.), *Human Biology: An Introduction to Human Evolution, Variation, and Growth*, 321–339. Oxford: Carendoin Press, 1964.

Tietjen, A. M., and Walker, L. J. Moral Reasoning and Leadership Among Men in a Papua New Guinea Society. *Developmental Psychology*, 1985, 21, 982–992.

Timiras, P. S. *Developmental Physiology and Aging*. New York: Macmillan, 1972.

Troll, L. E. *Early and Middle Adulthood* (2nd ed.). Monterey, Calif.: Wadsworth, 1985.

Tyler, S. (M.D.) Personal communication, 1986.

U.S. Bureau of the Census. *Statistical Abstract of the United States*, 107th ed. Washington, D.C., 1985.

———. *Statistical Abstract of the United States*, 100th ed. Washington, D.C., 1979.

U.S. Department of Health and Human Services. *The Health Consequences of Smoking: The Changing Cigarette: A Report of the Surgeon General*. Washington, D.C., 1981.

———. *The Health Consequences of Smoking for Women: A Report of the Surgeon General*. Washington, D.C., 1980.

U.S. Department of Health, Education, and Welfare. *Health, United States, 1975*. DHEW Pub. 76-1232. Washington, D.C., 1976.

U.S. National Center for Health Statistics. Reported in *Statistical Abstracts of the United States, 1986*. Washington, D.C., 1986.

U.S. News & World Report. AIDS: At the Dawn of Fear. *U.S. News & World Report*, January 12, 1987, pp. 60–70.

Wechsler, D. *The Measurement and Appraisal of Adult Intelligence* (4th ed.). Baltimore: Williams and Wilkins, 1958.

Whitbourne, S. K., and Weinstock, C. S. *Adult Development: The Differentiation of Experience*. New York: Holt, Rinehart, and Winston, 1979.

White, R. *Lives in Progress* (3rd ed.). New York: Holt, Rinehart, and Winston, 1975 (first published 1952).

Whitney, E. N., and Hamilton, E. M. N. *Understanding Nutrition* (3rd ed.). St. Paul: West, 1984.

Willis, S. L, and Baltes, P. B. Intelligence in Adulthood and Aging: Contemporary Issues. In L. W. Poon (ed.), *Aging in the 1980s: Psychological Issues*. Washington, D.C.: American Psychological Association, 1980.

Wynder, E. L., Hertzberg, S., and Parker, E. *The Book of Health*. New York: Watts, 1981.

Chapter 15

Albanese, R., and Van Fleet, D. D. *Organizational Behavior: A Managerial Viewpoint*. Chicago: Dryden, 1983.

Albrecht, S. Reactions and Adjustments to Divorce: Differences in the Experiences of Males and Females. *Family Relations*, January 1980, 59–68.

Alvarez, W. F. The Meaning of Maternal Employment for Mothers and Their Perceptions of Their Three-Year-Old Children. *Child Development*, 1985, 56, 350–361.

American Council of Life Insurance. *The Economic Value of a Housewife*. Washington, D.C., 1983.

———. *Datatrack*. Washington, D.C., 1980.

Anderson, S. A., Russell, C. S., and Schumm, W. R. Perceived Marital Quality and Family Life-Cycle Categories: A Further Analysis. *Journal of Marriage and the Family*, 1983, 45, 127–139.

Athanasion, R., and Yushioka, G. A. The Special Character of Friendship Formation. *Environment and Behavior*, 1973, 5, 143–165.

Bane, M. J. *Here to Stay: American Families in the Twentieth Century*. New York: Basic Books, 1976.

Belsky, J., Lang, M. E., and Rovine, M. Stability and Change in Marriage Across the Transition to Parenthood: A Second Study. *Journal of Marriage and the Family*, 1985, 47, 855–865.

Bentler, P. M., and Newcomb, M. D. Longitudinal Study of Marital Success and Failure. *Journal of Consulting and Clinical Psychology*, 1978, 46, 1053–1070.

Bernard, J. *Remarriage: A Study of Marriage*. New York: Dryden, 1956.

Biller, H. B. Fatherhood: Implications for Child and Adult Development. In B. B. Wolman (ed.), *Handbook of Developmental Psychology*, 702–726. Englewood Cliffs, N.J.: Prentice-Hall, 1982.

———. *Paternal Deprivation*. Lexington, Mass.: D. C. Heath, 1974.

Bloom, B. L, Asher, S. J., and White, S. W. Marital Disruption as a Stressor: A Review and Analysis. *Psychological Bulletin*, 1978, 85, 867–894.

Brehm, S. S. *Intimate Relationships*. New York: Random House, 1985.

Brody, J. E. Personal Health. *New York Times*, November 27, 1985, C7.

Caldwell, M. A., and Peplau, L. A. Sex Differences in Same-Sex Relationships. *Sex Roles*, 1982, 8, 721–721.

Campbell, A. The American Way of Mating: Marriage Si, Children Only Maybe. *Psychology Today*, 1975, 8, 37–43.

Cate, R. M., Henton, J. M., Koval, J., Christopher, F. S., and Lloyd, S. Premarital Abuse: A Social-Psychological Perspective. *Journal of Family Issues*, 1982, 3, 79–90.

Cherlin, A. *Marriage, Divorce, Remarriage*. Cambridge, Mass.: Harvard University Press, 1981.

———. Remarriage as an Incomplete Institution. *American Journal of Sociology*, 1978, 84, 634–650.

Cherlin, A., and Walters, P. Trends in United States Men's and Women's Attitudes: 1972 and 1978. *American Sociological Review*, 1981, 46, 453–460.

Chodorow, N. *The Reproduction of Mothering*. Berkeley: University of California Press, 1978.

Cleek, M. G., and Pearson, T. A. Perceived Causes of Divorce: An Analysis of Interrelationships. *Journal of Marriage and the Family*, 1985, 47, 179–183.

Cohler, B. Personal Narrative and Life Course. In P. B. Baltes and O. G. Brim (eds.), *Life-Span Development and Behavior*, 206–229. New York: Academic Press, 1982.

Coleman, K. H. Conjugal Violence: What 33 Men Report. *Journal of Marital and Family Therapy*, 1980, 6, 207–213.

Coombs, L. C., and Zumeta, Z. Correlates of Marital Dissolution in a Prospective Fertility Study: A Research Note. *Social Problems*, 1970, 18, 92–101.

Cox, F. D. *Human Intimacy: Marriage, the Family, and Its Meaning*. St. Paul: West, 1984.

Cuber, J. F., and Harroff, P. B. *Sex and the Significant Americans*. Baltimore: Penguin, 1965.

DeMaris, A., and Leslie, G. R. Cohabitation with the Future Spouse: Its Influence upon Marital Satisfaction and Communication. *Journal of Marriage and the Family*, 1984, 46, 77–83.

Doherty, W. J., and Jacobson, N. S. Marriage and the Family. In B. B. Wolman (ed,), *Handbook of Developmental Psychology*, 667–681. Englewood Cliffs, N.J.: Prentice-Hall, 1982.

Duberman, L. Step-Kin Relationships. *Journal of Marriage and the Family*, 1973, 35, 283–292.

Edwards, M. Coupling and Re-Coupling vs. the Challenge of Being Single. *Personnel and Guidance Journal*, 1977, 55, 542–545.

Featherman, D. L. Schooling and Occupational Careers: Constancy and Change in Worldly Success. In O. G. Brim and J. Kagan (eds.), *Constancy and Change in Human Development*, 675–739. Cambridge, Mass.: Harvard University Press, 1980.

Fein, M. Motivation for Work. In R. Dubin (ed.), *Handbook of Work, Organization, and Society*. Chicago: Rand-McNally, 1976.

Fein, R. A. Research on Fathering: Social Policy and an Emergent Perspective. *Journal of Social Issues*, 1978, 34, 122–135.

———. Men's Entrance to Parenthood. *The Family Coordinator*, 1976, 25, 341–350.

Field, T. M. Early Development of Infants Born to Teenage Mothers. In K. Scott, T. Field, and E. Robertson (eds.), *Teenage Parents and Their Offspring*. New York: Grune and Stratton, 1980.

Field, T. M., and Widmayer, S. M. Motherhood. In B. B. Wolman (ed.), *Handbook of Developmental Psychology*, 681–702. Englewood Cliffs, N.J.: Prentice-Hall, 1982.

Fine, M. A. Perceptions of Stepparents: Variation in Stereotypes as a Function of Current Family Structure. *Journal of Marriage and the Family*, 1986, 48, 537–543.

Frank, E., Anderson, C., and Rubinstein, D. Marital Role Strain and Sexual Satisfaction. *Journal of Consulting and Clinical Psychology*, 1979, 217, 1096–1103.

Freedman, J. *Happy People: What Happiness Is, Who Has It, and Why*. New York: Harcourt Brace Jovanovich, 1978.

Furstenberg, F. F. Conjugal Succession: Reentering Marriage and Divorce. In P. B. Baltes and O. G. Brim, *Life-Span Development and Behavior*, vol. 4, 107–146. New York: Academic Press, 1982.

———. Recycling the Family: Perspectives for Researching a Neglected Family Form. *Marriage and Family Review*, 1979, Haworth Press, 2.

Ganong, L. H., and Coleman, M. A Comparison of Clinical and Empirical Literature on Children in Stepfamilies. *Journal of Marriage and the Family*, 1986, 48, 309–318.

Gelles, R. J. Violence in the Family: A Review of Research in the Family. *Journal of Marriage and the Family*, 1980, 42, 873–885.

Gigy, L. L Self-Concept of Single Women. *Psychology of Women Quarterly*, 1980, 5, 321–340.

Glenn, N. Psychological Well-Being in the Post Parental Stage: Some Evidence from National Surveys. *Journal of Marriage and the Family*, 1975, 37, 105–111.

Glenn, N. D., and Supancic, M. The Social and Demographic Correlates of Divorce and Separation in the United States: An Update and Reconsideration. *Journal of Marriage and the Family*, 1984, 46, 563–570.

Glenn, N. D., and Weaver, C. N. Age, Cohort, and Reported Job Satisfaction in the United States. In Z. S. Blau (ed.), *Current Perspectives on Aging and the Life Cycle*, 1985, vol. 1, 89–109. Greenwich, Conn.: Jai, 1985.

Glick, P. C. How American Families Are Changing. *American Demographics*, 1984a, 6, 20–25.

———. Marriage, Divorce, and Living Arrangements: Prospective Changes. *Journal of Family Issues*, 1984b, 5, 7–26.

———. Remarriage: Some Recent Changes and Variations. *Journal of Family Issues*, 1980, 1, 455–579.

———. Updating the Life Cycle of the Family. *Journal of Marriage and the Family*, 1977, 39, 5–13.

Glick, P. C., and Ling-Lin, S. Recent Changes in Divorce and Remarriage. *Journal of Marriage and the Family*, 1986, 48, 737–747.

Glick, P. C., and Norton, A. J. Marrying, Divorcing, and Living Together in the U.S. Today. *Population Bulletin*, 1977, 32, 1–53.

Glick, P. C., and Spanier, G. B. Married and Unmarried Cohabitation in the United States. *Journal of Marriage and the Family*, 1980, 42, 19–31.

Goetting, A. Divorce Outcome Research: Issues and Perspective (1981). In A. S. Skolnick and J. H. Skolnick (eds.), *Family in Transition* (4th ed.), 367–387. Boston: Little, Brown, 1983.

Golanty, E., and Harris, B. B. *Marriage and Family Life*. Boston: Houghton Mifflin, 1982.

Goleman, D. Marriage: Research Reveals Ingredients of Happiness. *New York Times*, April 16, 1985, C1, C4.

Greenblatt, C. S. The Salience of Sexuality in the Early Years of Marriage. *Journal of Marriage and the Family*, 1983, 45, 289–299.

Haller, M., and Rosenmayr, L. The Pluridimensionality of Work Commitment: A Study of Young Married Women in Different Social Contexts of Occupational and Family Life. *Human Relations*, 1971, 24, 501–508.

Havighurst, R. J. The World of Work. In B. B. Wolman (ed.), *Handbook of Developmental Psychology*, 771–786. Englewood Cliffs, N.J.: Prentice-Hall, 1982.

Herzberg, F., Mausner, B., and Snyderman, B. B. *The Motivation to Work* (2nd ed.). New York: Wiley, 1959.

Hetherington, E. M. Divorce: A Child's Perspective. *American Psychologist*, 1979, *34*, 851–865.

Hetherington, E. M., Cox, M., and Cox, R. The Development of Children in Mother Headed Families. In H. Hoffman and D. Reiss (eds.), *The American Family: Dying and Developing*. New York: Plenum, 1978.

Hetherington, E. M., Cox. M., and Cox, R. The Aftermath of Divorce. In J. H. Stevens and M. Matthews (eds.), *Mother-Child, Father-Child Relations*. Washington, D.C.: National Association of the Education of Young Children, 1977.

———. Divorced Fathers. *Family Coordinator*, 1976, *25*, 417–428.

Hobbs, D. F., and Cole, S. P. Transition to Parenthood: A Decade Replication. *Journal of Marriage and the Family*, 1976, *38*, 723–731.

Hoffman, L. W. Social Change and Its Effects on Parents and Children: Limitations to Knowledge. In P. W. Berman and E. R. Ramey (eds.), *Women: A Developmental Perspective*. Washington, D.C.: U.S. Department of Health and Human Services, Public Health Services, NIH pub. no. 82–2298, April 1982.

Hoffman, W., and Manis, J. D. The Value of Children in the United States: A New Approach to the Study of Fertility. *Journal of Marriage and the Family*, 1979, *41*, 583–596.

———. Influences of Children on Marital Interaction and Parental Satisfactions and Dissatisfactions. In R. M. Lerner and G. B. Spanier, *Child Influences and Family Interaction: A Life-Span Perspective*. New York: Academic Press, 1978.

Hopkins, J., Marcus, M., and Campbell, S. R. Postpartum Depression: A Critical Review. *Psychological Bulletin*, 1984, *95*, 498–515.

Houseknecht, S. Childlessness and Marital Adjustment. *Journal of Marriage and the Family*, 1979, *41*, 259–265.

Hunt, M. *Sexual Behavior in the 1970s*. Chicago: Playboy Press, 1974.

Hyde, J. S. *Half the Human Experience: The Psychology of Women* (3rd ed.). Lexington, Mass.: D. C. Heath, 1985.

Iaffaldano, M. T., and Muchinsky, P. M. Job Satisfaction and Job Performance: A Meta-Analysis. *Psychological Bulletin*, 1985, *97*, 251–273.

James, B. E. The Honeymoon Effect on Marital Coitus. *Journal of Sex Research*, 1981, *17*, 114–123.

Johnston, M. W., and Eklund S. J. Life-Adjustment of the Never-Married: A Review with Implications for Counseling. *Journal of Counseling and Development*, 1984, *63*, 230–237.

Kahn, A. S. (ed.). *Social Psychology*. Dubuque, Iowa: Brown, 1984.

Kalmuus, D. The Intergenerational Transmission of Marital Aggression. *Journal of Marriage and the Family*, 1984, *46*, 11–20.

Kaplan, P. S. *A Child's Odyssey*. St. Paul: West, 1986.

Kaplan, P. S., and Stein, J. *Psychology of Adjustment*. Belmont, Calif.: Wadsworth, 1984.

Kelly, J. B. Divorce: The Adult Perspective. In B. B. Wolman (ed.), *Handbook of Developmental Psychology*, 734–750. Englewood Cliffs, N.J.: Prentice-Hall, 1982.

Kennedy, C. E. *Human Development: The Adult Years and Aging*. New York: Macmillan, 1978.

Knox, D. *Choices in Relationships*. St. Paul: West, 1985.

Kosinski, F. Improving Relationships in Stepfamilies. *Elementary School Guidance and Counseling*, 1983, *17*, 200–217.

Kossen, S. *The Human Side of Organizations* (3rd ed.). New York: Harper and Row, 1983.

Krausz, M. Policies of Organizational Choice at Different Vocational Life Stages. *Vocational Guidance Quarterly*, 1982, *31*, 60–68.

Lawler, E. E. *Pay and Organizational Effectiveness: A Psychological View*. New York: McGraw-Hill, 1971.

Levinger, G. Sources of Marital Dissatisfaction Among Applicants for Divorce. *American Journal of Orthopsychiatry*. 1966, *36*, 803–807.

Linn, M. W., Sandifer, R., and Stein, S. Effects of Unemployment on Mental and Physical Health. *American Journal of Public Health*, 1985, *75*, 502–506.

———. Lopata, H. Z. *Occupation: Housewife*. New York: Oxford University Press, 1971.

Lowenthal, M. F., Thurnher, M., and Chiriboga, D., et al. *Four Stages of Life*. San Francisco: Jossey-Bass, 1975.

Macklin, E. Nonmarital Heterosexual Cohabitation: An Overview. In E. Macklin and R. Rubin, *Shared Intimacies*. New York: Harper and Row, 1983.

———. Nonmarital Heterosexual Cohabitation. *Marriage and Family Review*, 1978, *1*, 1–12.

Manion, J. A Study of Fathers and Infant Caretaking. *Birth and the Family Journal*, 1977, *4*, 174–179.

Maples, M. F. Dual Career Marriages: Elements for Potential Success. *The Personnel and Guidance Journal*, 1981, *60*, 19–25.

Markman, H. J. Prediction of Marital Distress: A Five-Year Follow-up. *Journal of Consulting and Clinical Psychology*, 1981, *49*, 760–762.

Marshall, J. Reducing the Effects of Work Oriented Values on the Lives of Male American Workers. *Vocational and Guidance Journal*, 1983, *32*, 109–115.

Masters, W. H., and Johnson, V. E. *Human Sexual Response*. Boston: Little, Brown, 1966.

Maymi, C. R. Women in the Labor Force. In P. W. Berman and E. R. Ramey (eds.), *Women: A Developmental Perspective*. Washington, D.C.: U.S. Department of Health and Human Services, Public Health Services, NIH pub. no. 82–2298, April 1982.

Meyers, L. Battered Wives, Dead Husbands (1978). In A. S. Skolnick and J. H. Skolnick (eds.). *Family in Transition* (4th ed.), 345–352. Boston: Little, Brown, 1983.

Miller, D. C. Industry and the Worker. In H. Borow (ed.), *Man in a World at Work*. Boston: Houghton Mifflin, 1964.

Mueller, K. H. Educating Women for a Changing World (1954), cited in Havighurst, The World of Work. In B. B. Wolman (ed.), *Handbook of Developmental Psychology*, 771–787. Englewood Cliffs, N.J.: Prentice-Hall, 1982.

Murstein, B. I. Marital Choice. In B. B. Wolman (ed.), *Handbook of Developmental Psychology*, 652–667. Englewood Cliffs, N.J.: Prentice-Hall, 1982.

———. *Who Will Marry Whom? Theories and Research in Marital Choice*. New York: Springer, 1976.

———. *Theories of Attraction and Love*. New York: Springer, 1971.

———. Stimulus-Value-Role: A Theory of Marital Choice. *Journal of Marriage and the Family*, 1970, *32*, 465–481.

National Center for Health Statistics. *Advance Report of Final Marriage Statistics, 1983: NCHS Monthly Vital Statistics Report*, May 2, 1986, 35.

———. *Advance Report of Final Divorce Statistics, 1981: NCHS Monthly Vital Statistics Report*. DHHS pub. no. (PHS) 84–1120. Hyattsville, Md.: U.S. Public Health Service, January 17, 1984.

National Opinion Research Center. *General Social Surveys, 1972–1978*. New Haven, Conn.: Roper Public Opinion Research Center of Yale University, 1978.

Nord, W. R. Job Satisfaction Reconsidered. *American Psychologist*, 1977, *32*, 1026–1036.

Norton, A. J., and Glick, P. C. Marital Instability in America: Past, Present, and Future. In G. Levinger and O. C. Moles (eds.), *Divorce and Separation*. New York: Basic Books, 1979.

———. Marital Instability: Past, Present, Future. *Journal of Social Issues*, 1976, *32*, 6–7.

Notarius, C. I., and Johnson, J. S. Emotional Expression in Husbands and Wives. *Journal of Marriage and the Family*, 1982, *44*, 483–489.

Oshman, H., and Manosevitz, M. Father-Absence: Effects of Stepfathers Upon Psychosocial Development in Males. *Developmental Psychology*, 1976, *12*, 477–480.

Parish, T. S. Locus of Control as a Function of Father Loss and the Presence of Stepfather. *Journal of Genetic Psychology*, 1982, *140*, 321–322.

Parker, M., Peltier, S., and Wolleat, P. Understanding Dual Career Couples. *Personnel and Guidance Journal*, 1981, *60*, 14–19.

Parlee, M. B. The Friendship Bond. *Psychology Today*, October 1979, 43–54.

Parsons, T., and Bales, R. F. *Family, Socialization, and Interaction Process*. Glencoe, Ill.: Free Press, 1955.

Perfetti, L. J., and Bingham, W. C. Unemployment and Self- Esteem in Metal Refinery Workers. *Vocational Guidance Quarterly*, 1983, *31*, 195–203.

Peterman, D. J., Ridley, C. A., and Anderson, S. M. A Comparison of Cohabiting and Non-Cohabiting College Students. *Journal of Marriage and the Family*, 1974, *36*, 344–354.

Ponzetti, J. H., Cate, R. M., and Doval, J. E. Violence Between Couples: Profiling the Male Abuser. *Personnel and Guidance Journal*, 1982, *61*, 222–224.

Prosen, S., and Farmer, J. Understanding Stepfamilies: Issues and Importance for Counselors. *Personnel and Guidance Journal*, 1982, *60*, 393–397.

Quinn, R. P., and Staines, G. L. *The 1977 Quality of Employment Survey: Descriptive Statistics, with Comparison Data From the 1969–1970 and the 1972–1973 Surveys*. Ann Arbor: Institute for Social Research, University of Michigan, 1979.

Rallings, E. M. The Special Role of Stepfather. *The Family Coordinator*, 1976, *25*, 445–450.

Reedy, M. N., Birren, J. E., and Schaie, K. W. Age and Sex Differences in Satisfying Love Relationships Across the Life- Span. *Human Development*, 1982, *24*, 52–66.

Reiss, I. L. *Family Systems in America* (3rd ed.). New York: Holt, Rinehart, and Winston, 1980.

Renwick, P. A., and Lawler, E. E. What Do You Really Want from a Job? *Psychology Today*, May 1978, *11*, 53–65.

Rhodes, S. R. Age-Related Differences in Work Attitudes and Behavior: A Review and Conceptual Analysis. *Psychological Bulletin*, 1983, *93*, 328–367.

Rhyne, D. Bases of Marital Satisfaction Among Men and Women. *Journal of Marriage and the Family*, 1981, *43*, 941–955.

Richmond-Abbott, M. *Masculine and Feminine*. Reading, Mass.: Addison-Wesley, 1983.

Riegle, D. W. The Psychological and Social Effects of Unemployment. *American Psychologist*, 1982, *37*, 1113–1116.

Risman, B., Hill, C. T., Rubin, Z., and Peplau, L. A. Living Together in College: Implications for Courtship. *Journal of Marriage and the Family*, 1981, *42*, 77–117.

Robey, B., and Russell, C. How America Is Changing. *American Demographics*, July–August 1982, 16–22.

Rollins, B., and Cannon, K. Marital Satisfaction over the Family Life Cycle: A Reevaluation. *Journal of Marriage and the Family*, 1974, *36*, 271–281.

Rollins, B., and Feldman, H. Marital Satisfaction over the Life Span. *Journal of Marriage and the Family*, 1970, *32*, 20–28.

Rossi, A. Gender and Parenthood. *American Sociological Review*, 1984, *49*, 1–19.

———. Transition to Parenthood. *Journal of Marriage and the Family*, 1968, *30*, 26–39.

Rubin, L. B. *Worlds of Pain*. New York: Basic Books, 1976.

Rubin, Z. Are Working Wives Hazardous to Their Husband's Mental Health? *Psychology Today*, May 1983, 70–72.

Russo, N. F. Overview: Sex Roles, Fertility, and the Motherhood Mandate. *Psychology of Women Quarterly*, 1979, *4*, 7–15.

Rutter, M. Social-Emotional Consequences of Day Care for Preschool Children. *American Journal of Orthopsychiatry*, 1981, *51*, 4–29.

Ryder, R. G. Longitudinal Data Relating Marriage Satisfaction to Having a Child. *Journal of Marriage and the Family*, 1973, *46*, 604–606.

Santrock, J. W. Relation of Type and Onset of Father Absence to Cognitive Development. *Child Development*, 1972, *43*, 455–469.

Schneider, B. Organizational Behavior. In M. R. Rosenzweig and L. W. Porter (eds.), *Annual Review of Psychology* (Palo Alto, Calif.), 1985, *36*, 573–611.

Schultz, D. P. *Psychology and Industry Today* (2nd ed.). New York: Macmillan, 1978.

Schultz, D. A. *Human Sexuality*. Englewood Cliffs, N.J.: Prentice-Hall, 1984.

Schultz, D. A., and Rodgers, S. F. *Marriage, the Family, and Personal Fulfillment*. Englewood Cliffs, N.J.: Prentice-Hall, 1975.

Schumm, W. R., and Bugaighis, M. A. Marital Quality over the Marital Career: Alternative Explanations. *Journal of Marriage and the Family*, 1986, *48*, 165–168.

Shamir, B. Sex Differences in Psychological Adjustment to Unemployment and Reemployment: A Question of Commitment, Alternatives or Finance? *Social Problems*, 1985, *33*, 67–78.

Sherman, M. A., and Haas, A. Man to Man, Woman to Woman. *Psychology Today*, June 1984, 72–73.

Skolnick, A. S., and Skolnick, J. H. *Family in Transition* (4th ed.). Boston: Little, Brown, 1983.

Spanier, G. B., and Margolis, R. L. Marital Separation and Extramarital Sexual Behavior. *Journal of Sex Research*, 1983, *19*, 23–48.

Spanier, G. B., Roos, P. A., and Shockey, J. Marital Trajectories of American Women: Variations in the Life Course. *Journal of Marriage and the Family*, 1985, *47*, 993–1003.

Stein, P. J. *Single*. Englewood Cliffs, N.J.: Prentice-Hall, 1976.

Steinmetz, S. K. Violence Between Family Members. *Marriage and Family Review*, 1978, *1*, 1–16.

Steinmetz, S., and Strauss, M. The Family as a Cradle of Violence. *Society*, 1973, *10*, 55–56.

Straus, M. A. "Wife-Beating": How Common and Why. In M. A. Straus and G. T. Hotaling (eds.), *The Social Causes of Husband-Wife Violence*. Minneapolis: University of Minnesota Press, 1980.

Straus, M., Gelles, R., and Steinmetz, S. K. *Behind Closed Doors: Violence in the American Family*. New York: Doubleday, 1980.

Strube, M. J., and Barbour, L. S. The Decision to Leave an Abusive Relationship: Economic Dependence and Psychological Commitment. *Journal of Marriage and the Family*, 1983, *45*, 785–794.

Thayer, P. W. Industrial/Organizational Psychology: Science and Application. In C. J. Scheirer and A. M. Rogers, *The G. Stanley Hall Lecture Series*, vol. 3, 9–32. Washington, D.C.: American Psychological Association, 1983.

Thompson, A. P. Extramarital Sex: A Review of the Research Literature. *Journal of Sex Research*, 1983, *19*, 1–22.

Thornton, A., and Freedman, D. Changing Attitudes Toward Marriage and Single Life (1982), cited in S. S. Brehm, *Intimate Relationships*. New York: Random House, 1985.

Tiggle, R. B., Peters, M. D., Kelley, H. H., and Vincent, J. Correlational and Discrepancy Indices of Understanding and Their Relation to Marital Satisfaction. *Journal of Marriage and the Family*, 1982, *44*, 209–216.

Tokuno, K. A. Friendship and Transition in Early Adulthood. *Journal of Genetic Psychology*, 1983, *143*, 207–216.

Troll, L. E. *Early and Middle Adulthood* (2nd ed.). Monterey: Brooks/Cole, 1985.

Trussell, J., and Westoff, C. F. Contraceptive Practice and Trends in Coital Frequency. *Family Planning Perspectives*, 1980, *12*, 246–249.

U.S. Bureau of Labor Statistics. *Employment in Perspective: Women in the Labor Force, First Quarter, 1987*. Report 740. Washington, D.C., 1987.

U.S. Bureau of Labor Statistics. *Working Women and Public Policy*. Washington, D.C.: U.S. Department of Labor, 1984.

U.S. Bureau of the Census. *Statistical Abstract of the United States, 1986*. Washington, D.C., 1986.

———. *Statistical Abstract of the United States, 1985*. Washington, D.C., 1985.

———. *Statistical Abstract of the United States, 1984*. Washington, D.C., 1984.

———. *Statistical Abstract of the United States, 1979*. Washington, D.C., 1979.

U.S. Department of Health and Human Services, *Births, Marriages, Divorces, and Deaths for 1986*. DHHS pub. no. (PHS) 87–1120. Washington, D.C.: National Center for Health Statistics, 1987.

U.S. Department of Labor. *United States Department of Labor News*. Washington, D.C., 1987, 87–345 (August 1987).

———. *Labor Force Activity of Mothers of Young Children Continues at a Record Pace*. Washington, D.C.: Bureau of Labor Statistics, 1985a.

———. *Employment in Perspective: Women in the Labor Force*, Third Quarter. Report 725. Washington, D.C., 1985b.

———. *News* (USDL 85–381). Washington, D.C.: Bureau of Labor Statistics, September 19, 1985.

———. *The Female-Male Earnings Gap: A Review of Employment and Earnings Issues*. Washington, D.C.: Bureau of Labor Statistics, September 1982.

U.S. Department of Labor. Women's Bureau, *Legislative Issues on Battered Women*, February 1978, p. 1.

Vanek, J. Household Work, Wage Work, and Sexual Equality. In S. F. Berk (ed.), *Women and Household Labor*, 275–291. Beverly Hills, Calif.: Sage, 1980.

Van Hoose, W. H., and Worth, M. R. *Adulthood in the Life Cycle*. Dubuque, Iowa: Brown, 1982.

Veroff, J., and Field, S. *Marriage and Work in America: A Study of Motives and Roles*. New York: Van Nostrand Reinhold.

Vigderhous, G., and Fishman, G. The Impact of Unemployment and Familial Integration on Changing Suicide Rates in the U.S.A., 1920–1969. *Social Psychiatry*, 1978, *13*, 239–248.

Wagenaar, T. C. High School Seniors' Views of Themselves and Their Schools: A Trend Analysis. *Phi Delta Kappan*, 1981, *63*, 29–32.

Wallerstein, J. S. Women After Divorce: Preliminary Report from a Ten-Year Follow-up. *American Journal of Orthopsychiatry*, 1986, *56*, 65–77.

Wallerstein, J. S., and Kelly, J. B. *Surviving the Breakup: How Children and Parents Cope with Divorce*. New York: Basic Books, 1980.

———. Divorce and Children. In J. P. Noshpitz (ed.), *Basic Handbook of Child Psychiatry*, 339–346. New York: Basic Books, 1979.

Watson, R. E. L. Premarital Cohabitation vs. Traditional Courtship: Their Effects on Subsequent Marital Adjustment. *Family Relations*, 1983, *32*, 139–147.

Weed, J. A. National Estimates of Marriage Dissolution and Survivorship: United States. *Vital and Health Statistics*, ser. 3, Analytical Studies, no. 19, DHHJ pub. no. (PHS) 81–1403. Hyattsville, Md.: National Center for Health Statistics, Office of Health Research, U.S. Department of Health and Human Services, 1980.

Weiss, L., and Lowenthal, M. Life-Course Perspectives on Friendship. In M. Lowenthal, M. Thurnher, and D. Chiriboga (eds.), *Four Stages of Life*. San Francisco, Calif.: Jossey-Bass, 1975.

Williams, J. H. *Psychology of Women*. New York: Norton, 1977.

Wilson, K., Zurcher, L., McAdams, D., and Curtis, R. Stepfamilies and Stepchildren: An Exploratory Analysis from Two National Surveys. *Journal of Marriage and the Family*, 1975, *37*, 526–536.

Winch, R. F. *Mate Selection: A Study of Complementary Needs*. New York: Harper and Row, 1958.

Yankelovich, D. New Rules in American Life: Searching for Self-Fulfillment in a World Turned Upside Down. *Psychology Today*, April 1981, 35–91.

Yarrow, M. R., Waxler, C. Z., and Scott, P. M. Child Effects on Adult Behavior. *Developmental Psychology*, 1971, *5*, 300–311.

Yilo, K., and Straus, M. A. Interpersonal Violence Among Married and Cohabiting Couples. *Family Relations*, 1981, *30*, 339–347.

Youngblood, S. A., Mobley, W. H., and Meglino, B. M. A Longitudinal Analysis of the Turnover Process. *Journal of Applied Psychology*, 1983, *68*, 507–516.

Chapter 16

Anders, T. R., and Fozard, J. L. Effects of Age upon Retrieval from Primary and Secondary Memory. *Developmental Psychology*, 1973, *9*, 411–415.

Arenberg, D., and Robertson-Tchabo, E. A. Learning and Aging. In J. E. Birren and K. W. Schaie (eds.), *Handbook of the Psychology of Aging*, 421–450. New York: Van Nostrand, 1977.

Bahrick, H. P., Bahrick, P. O., and Wittlinger, R. P. Fifty Years of Memory for Names and Faces: A Cross-Sectional Approach. *Journal of Experimental Psychology: General*, 1975, *104*, 54–75.

Baltes, P. B., Reese, H. W., and Lipsitt, L. P. Life-Span Development Psychology. *Annual Review of Psychology*, 1980, *31*, 65–110.

Barrow, G. M., and Smith, P. A. *Aging, The Individual, and Society* (2nd ed.). St. Paul: West, 1983.

Bayley, N. Development of Mental Abilities. In P. H. Mussen (ed.). *Carmichael's Manual of Child Psychology*. New York: Wiley, 1970.

Bischof, L. J. *Adult Psychology* (2nd ed.). New York: Harper and Row, 1976.

Botwinick, J. *Aging and Behavior* (3rd ed.). New York: Springer, 1984.

———. Intellectual Abilities. In J. E. Birren and K. W. Schaie (eds.), *Handbook of the Psychology of Aging*, 580–603. New York: Van Nostrand, 1977.

———. *Aging and Behavior*. New York: Springer, 1973.

Botwinick, J., and Thompson, L. W. Age Differences in Reaction Time: An Artifact? *The Gerontologist*, 1968, *8*, 25–28.

Breslow, L., and Enstrom, J. E. Persistence of Health Habits and Their Relationship to Mortality. *Preventive Medicine*, 1980, *9*, 469–483.

Brim, O. G., and Kagan, J. *Constancy and Change in Human Development*. Cambridge, Mass.: Harvard University Press, 1980.

Burkitt, D. P. Colonal-Rectal Cancer: Fiber and Other Dietary Factors. *American Journal of Clinical Nutrition*, 1978, *31*, 58–64.

Cameron, P. The Generation Gap: Beliefs About Sexuality and Self-Reported Sexuality. In W. R. Looft (ed.), *Developmental Psychology: A Book of Readings*. New York: Holt, Rinehart, and Winston, 1972.

Chew, P. *The Inner World of the Middle-Aged Man*. New York: Macmillan, 1976.

Chown, S. M. Profiles of Abilities. In J. E. Birren et al. (eds.), *Aging: Challenge to Science and Society*, 264–276. New York: Oxford, 1983.

———. Morale, Careers, and Personal Potentials. In J. E. Birren and K. W. Schaie (eds.),

Handbook of the Psychology of Aging, 672–692. New York: Van Nostrand, 1977.

Cole, S. Age and Scientific Performance. *American Journal of Sociology*, 1979, 84, 958–977.

Coren, S., Porac, C., and Ward, L. M. *Sensation and Perception*. New York: Academic Press, 1979.

Cornelius, S. W. Classic Pattern of Intellectual Aging: Test Familiarity, Difficulty, and Performance. *Journal of Gerontology*, 1984, 39, 201–206.

Corso, J. F. Sensory Processes and Age Effects in Normal Adults. *Journal of Gerontology*, 1971, 26, 90–105.

Curtis, H. *Biology* (2nd ed.). New York: Worth, 1975.

Danziger, W. L. Measurement of Response Bias in Aging Research. In L. W. Poon (ed.), *Aging in the 1980s*, 552–557. Washington, D.C.: American Psychological Association, 1980.

Denney, N. W. Aging and Cognitive Changes. In B. B. Wolman (ed.), *Handbook of Developmental Psychology*, 807–822. Englewood Cliffs, N.J.: Prentice-Hall, 1982.

Denney, N. W., and Palmer, A. M. Adult Age Differences in Traditional and Practical Problem Solving Measures (1980), cited in N. W. Denney, Aging and Cognitive Changes. In B. B. Wolman (ed.), *Handbook of Developmental Psychology*, 807–827. Englewood Cliffs, N.J.: Prentice-Hall, 1982.

Dennis, W. Creative Production Between Ages of 20 and 80 Years. *Journal of Gerontology*, 1966, 21, 1–8.

Diamond, A. M. The Life-Cycle Research Productivity of Mathematicians and Scientists. *Journal of Gerontology*, 1986, 41, 520–525.

Diekelmann, N. *Primary Health Care of the Well Adult*. New York: McGraw-Hill, 1977.

Doering, C. H. The Endocrine System. In O. G. Brim and J. Kagan (eds.), *Constancy and Change in Human Development*, 229–272. Cambridge, Mass.: Harvard University Press, 1980.

Ebersole, P. B., and Hess, P. *Toward Healthy Aging*. St. Louis: Mosby, 1981.

Engen, T. Taste and Smell. In J. E. Birren and K. W. Schaie (eds.), *Handbook of the Psychology of Aging*, 544–562. New York: Van Nostrand, 1977.

"Fending off the Leading Killers." *U.S. News & World Report*, August 17, 1987, pp. 56–58.

Fozard, J. L., Wolf, E., Bell, B., McFarland, R. A., and Podolsky, S. Visual Perception and Communication. In J. E. Birren and K. W. Schaie (eds.), *Handbook of the Psychology of Aging*, 499–535. New York: Van Nostrand, 1977.

Gasner, D, and McCleary, E. H. *The American Medical Association's Book of Heart Care*. New York: Random House, 1982.

Griffen, J. A Cross-Cultural Investigation of Behavioral Changes at Menopause. *Social Science Journal*, 1977, 14, 49–55.

Grzegorczyk, P. B., Jones, S. W., and Mistretta, C. M. Age-Related Differences in Salt Taste Acuity. *Journal of Gerontology*, 1979, 34, 834–840.

Hamilton, E. M. N., and Whitney, E. N. *Concepts and Controversies in Nutrition* (2nd ed.). St. Paul: West, 1982.

Haponski, W. C., and McCabe, A. L. *Back to School: The College Guide for Adults*. Princeton: Peterson's Guides, 1982.

Harbin, T. J., and Blumenthal, J. A. Relationships Among Age, Sex, and Type-A Behavior Pattern, and Cardiovascular Reactivity. *Journal of Gerontology*, 1985, 40, 714–720.

Heimbach, J. T. Cardiovascular Disease and Diet: The Public View. *Public Health Reports*, January–February 1985, 100, 5–12.

Hellman, L. M. The Medical Status of Women. In P. W. Berman and E. R. Ramey (eds.), *Women: A Developmental Perspective*, 13–23. Washington, D.C.: U.S. Department of Health and Human Services, NIH pub. no. 82–2298, April 1982.

Hongladarom, G., McCorkle, R., and Woods, N. F. *The Complete Book of Women's Health*. Englewood Cliffs, N.J.: Prentice-Hall, 1982.

Honzik, M. P. Life-Span Psychology. *Annual Review of Psychology*, 1984, 35, 309–333.

Horn, J. L. and Cattell, R. B. Age Differences in Primary Mental Ability Factors. *Journal of Gerontology*, 1966, 21, 210–222.

Horn, J. L., and Donaldson, G. Cognitive Development in Adulthood. In O. G. Brim and J. Kagan (eds.), *Constancy and Change in Human Development*, 445–530. Cambridge, Mass.: Harvard University Press, 1980.

Hultsch, D. Adult Age Differences in Retrieval: Trace Development and Cue Dependent Forgetting. *Developmental Psychology*, 1975, 11, 197–201.

———. Learning to Learn in Adulthood. *Journal of Geronotology*, 1974, 29, 302–308.

Hunt, M. *Sexual Behavior in the 1970s*. Chicago: Playboy Press, 1974.

Jackson, D. Advanced Age Adults' Reflections of Middle Age. *The Gerontologist*, 1974, 14, 255.

Knox, D. *Choices in Relationships*. St. Paul: West, 1985.

Krantz, D. S., Grunberg, N. E., and Baum, A. Health Psychology *Annual Review of Psychology*, 1985, 36, 349–385.

Lair, C. V., and Moon, W. H. The Effects of Praise and Reproof on the Performance of Middle Aged and Older Subjects. *Aging and Human Development*, 1972, 3, 279–284.

Lehman, H. C. The Production of Master's Work Prior to Age 30. *The Gerontologist*, 1965, 5, 24–30.

———. Chronological Age Versus Present-Day Contribution to Medical Progress. *The Gerontologist*, 1963, 3, 71–75.

———. The Influence of Longevity upon Curves Showing Man's Creative Production Rate at Successive Age Levels. *Journal of Gerontology*, 1958, 13, 187–191.

———. *Age and Achievement*. Princeton: Princeton University Press, 1953.

Levinson, D. J. *The Seasons of a Man's Life*. New York: Knopf, 1978.

Lidz, T. *The Person* (rev. ed.). New York: Basic Books, 1976.

Long, P. J., and Shannon, B. *Nutrition: An Inquiry into the Issues*. Englewood Cliffs, N.J.: Prentice-Hall, 1983.

Lowenthal, M. F., et al. *Four Stages of Life: A Comparative Study of Women and Men Facing Transitions*. San Francisco: Jossey-Bass, 1975.

Marsh, G. R., and Thompson, L. W. Psychophysiology of Aging. In J. E. Birren and K. W. Schaie (eds.), *Handbook of the Psychology of Aging*, 219–241. New York: Van Nostrand, 1977.

Mason, S. E., and Smith, A. D. Imagery in the Aged. *Experimental Aging Research*, 1977, 3, 17–32.

Masters, W., and Johnson, V. E. *Human Sexual Response*. Boston: Little, Brown, 1966.

McCarthy, B. W. Sexual Dysfunctions and Dissatisfactions Among Middle-Years Couples. *Journal of Sex Education and Therapy*, 1982, 8, 9–12.

McKinlay, S. M., and Jeffreys, M. The Menopausal Syndrome. *British Journal of Preventive and Social Medicine*, 1974, 28, 108.

Metropolitan Life Insurance Co. Variations in Mortality from Cancer. *Statistical Bulletin*, January–March 1986, 22–27.

———. Slight Gains in U.S. Longevity. *Statistical Bulletin*, July–September 1985, 20–23.

Monge, R., and Hultsch, D. Paired Associate Learning as a Function of Adult Age and Length of Anticipation and Inspection Intervals. *Journal of Gerontology*, 1971, 26, 157–162.

Moore, L. M., Nielsen, C. R., and Mistretta, C. M. Sucrose Taste Thresholds: Age Related Differences. *Journal of Gerontology*, 1982, 37, 64–69.

Napoli, M. *Health Facts: A Critical Evaluation of the Major Problems, Treatments, and Alterna-*

tives Facing Medical Consumers. Westock, N.Y.: Overlook, 1982.

Neugarten, B. L. Adaptation and the Life Cycle. In N. K. Schlossberg and A. D. Entine, Counseling Adults, 34–47. Monterey, Calif.: Brooks/Cole, 1977.

———. Dynamics of Transition of Middle Age to Old Age. Journal of Geriatric Psychiatry, 1970, 4, 71–87.

Neugarten, B. L, and Kraines, R. J. Menopausal Symptoms in Women of Various Ages. Psychosomatic Medicine, 1965, 27, 266–273.

Neugarten, B. L., Wood, V., Kraines, R. J., and Loomis, B. Women's Attitudes Toward the Menopause. Vita Humana, 1963, 6, 140–151.

Newman, B. M. Mid-Life Development. In B. B. Wolman (ed.), Handbook of Developmental Psychology, 617–636. Englewood Cliffs, N.J.: Prentice-Hall, 1982.

New York Times. Two New Studies Link High Cholesterol to Risk of Colon Cancer. New York Times, December 25, 1986, p. 14.

Notelovitz, M., and Ware, M. Stand Tall: The Informed Woman's Guide to Preventing Osteoporosis. Gainesville, Fla.: Triad Co., 1982.

Nowak, C. Does Youthfulness Equal Attractiveness? In E. Troll, J. Israel, and K. Israel, Looking Ahead: A Woman's Guide to the Problems and Joys of Growing Older, 59–64. Englewood Cliffs, N.J.: Prentice-Hall, 1977.

Ochsner, A. The Health Menace of Tobacco. American Scientist, 1972, 59, 2346–2352.

Pacovsky, V., and Hermanova, H. Aging and the Worker. In J. E. Birren et al. (eds.), Aging: A Challenge to Science and Society, 186–192. New York: Oxford, University Press, 1983.

Palmore, E. B. Social Class, Sex Differences, and Longevity. In J. E. Birren et al. (eds.), Aging: A Challenge to Science and Society, 41–49. New York: Oxford University Press, 1983.

Peck, R. C. Psychological Developments in the Second Half of Life. In B. L. Neugarten (ed.), Middle Age and Aging. Chicago: University of Chicago Press, 1968.

Pfeiffer, E. Health, Sexuality, and Aging. In J. E. Birren et al. (eds.), Aging: A Challenge to Science and Society, vol. 3, 67–73. New York: Oxford University Press, 1983.

Pfeiffer, E., and Davis, G. C. Determinants of Sexual Behavior in Middle and Old Age. Journal of the American Geriatric Society, 1972, 20, 151–158.

Pocs, O., and Godow, A. Can Students View Parents as Sexual Beings? The Family Coordinator, 1976, 26, 31–36.

Prohaska, T. R., Leventhal, E. A., Leventhal, H., and Keller, M. L. Health Practices and Illness Cognition in Young Middle Aged and Elderly Adults. Journal of Gerontology, 1985, 40, 569–578.

Riege, W. H., and Inman, V. Age Differences in Nonverbal Memory Tasks. Journal of Gerontology, 1981, 36, 51–58.

Riesman, D. On Higher Education. San Francisco: Jossey-Bass, 1980.

Robey, B., and Russell, C. How America Is Changing. American Demographics, July–August 1982, 16–22.

Rosen, R., and Rosen, L. R. Human Sexuality. New York: Knopf, 1981.

Rowe, E. J., and Schnore, M. M. Item Concreteness and Reported Strategies in Pared-Associate Learning as a Function of Age. Journal of Gerontology, 1971, 26, 470–475.

Salthouse, T. A. Speed of Behavior and Its Implications for Cognition. In J. E. Birren and K. W. Schaie (eds.), Handbook of the Psychology of Aging (2nd ed.). New York: Van Nostrand, 1984.

Salthouse, T. A., and Kail, R. Memory Development Throughout the Life Span: The Role of Processing Rate. In P. B. Baltes and O. G. Brim (eds.), Life-Span Development and Behavior, vol. 5, 90–113. New York: Academic Press, 1983.

Saxon, S. V., and Etten, M. J. Physical Change and Aging. New York: Tiresias, 1978.

Schaffer, K. F. Sex Roles and Human Behavior. Cambridge, Mass.: Winthrop, 1981.

Schaie, K. W., and Geitwitz, J. Adult Development and Aging. Boston: Little, Brown, 1982.

Schaie, K. W., and Hertzog, C. Fourteen-Year Cohort-Sequential Analyses of Adult Intellectual Development. Developmental Psychology, 1983, 19, 531–544.

Schaie, K. W., and Parham, I. A. Cohort-Sequential Analyses of Adult Intellectual Development. Developmental Psychology, 1977, 13, 649–653.

Schonfield, D., and Robertson, E. A. Memory Storage and Aging. Canadian Journal of Psychology, 1966, 20, 228–236.

Shanan, J. Transitional Phases of Human Development in Transient Society. In J. E. Birren et al. (eds.), Aging: A Challenge to Science and Society, 112–125. New York: Oxford University Press, 1983.

Sheehy, G. Pathfinders. New York: Morrow, 1981.

Shock, N. W., and Norris, H. H. Neuromuscular Coordination as a Factor in Age Changes in Muscular Exercise. In D. Brunner and E. Joki, Physical Activity and Aging. Baltimore: University Park Press, 1970.

Simons, G. Coping with Crisis. New York: Macmillan, 1972.

Simonton, D. K. Creative Productivity, Age, and Stress: A Biological Time-Series Analysis of Ten Classical Composers. Journal of Personality and Social Psychology, 1977, 35, 791–804.

Smallwood, K. B., and Van Dyck, D. G. Menopause Counseling: Coping with Realities. Journal of Sex Education and Therapy, 1979, 1, 72–76.

Smith, A. D. Adult Age Differences in Cued Recall. Developmental Psychology, 1977, 13, 326–331.

Sontag, S. The Double Standard of Aging. In J. H. Williams (ed.), Psychology of Women: Selected Readings, 462–478. New York: Norton, 1977.

———. The Double Standard of Aging. Saturday Review, 1972, 50, 29–38.

Stevens-Long, J. Adult Life (2nd ed.). Palo Alto, Calif.: Mayfield, 1984.

Strand, F. L. Psysiology (2nd ed.). New York: Macmillan, 1983.

Szafran, J. Psychophysiological Studies of Aging in Pilots (1968), cited in R. Walk, Perceptual Development. Monterey, Calif.: Brooks/Cole, 1981.

Tierney, J. The Aging Body. Esquire, May 1982.

Time. Stress: Can We Cope? Time, April 3, 1983.

Timiras, P. S., and Meisami, E. Changes in Gonadal Function. In P. S. Timiras (ed.), Developmental Physiology and Aging, 527–542. New York: Macmillan, 1972.

U.S. Bureau of the Census. Statistical Abstract of the United States, 1985. Washington, D.C., 1985.

———. Statistical Abstract of the United States, 1984. Washington, D.C., 1984.

U.S. Department of Health and Human Services. The Health Consequences of Smoking: Cardiovascular Disease. Rockville, Md.: Public Health Service pub. no. PHS 84–50204, 1983.

Vaillant, G. E. Adaptation to Life. Boston: Little, Brown, 1977.

Verwoerdt, A., Pfeiffer, E., and Wang, H. S. Sexual Behavior in Senescence, 2: Patterns of Change in Sexual Activity and Interest. Geriatrics, 1969, 24, 137–154.

Walk, R. D. Perceptual Development. Monterey, Calif.: Brooks/Cole, 1981.

Warrington, E. K., and Silberstein, M. A. A Questionnaire Technique for Investigating Very Long Term Memory. Quarterly Journal of Experimental Psychology, 1970, 12, 508–512.

Welford, A. T. Motor Performance. In J. E. Birren and K. W. Schaie (eds.), Handbook of the Psychology of Aging, 450–497. New York: Van Nostrand, 1977.

Wetzler, H. P., and Cruess, D. F. Self-Reported Physical Health Practices and Health Care Utilization: Findings from the National Health Interview Survey. *American Journal of Public Health*, 1985, 75, 1329–1330.

Wigdor, B. T. Mental Health and Social Conditions. In J. E. Birren et al. (eds.), *Aging: A Challenge to Science and Society*, 49–57. New York: Oxford University Press, 1983.

Williams, J. H. *Psychology of Women*. New York: Norton, 1977.

Wingfield, A., and Byrnes, D. E. *The Psychology of Human Memory*. New York: Academic Press, 1981.

Zivian, M. T., and Darjes, M. T. Free Recall by In-School and Out-of-School Adults: Performance and Metamemory. *Developmental Psychology*, 1983, 19, 513–520.

Chapter 17

Alpert, J. L., and Richardson, M. S. Parenting. In L. W. Poon (ed.), *Aging in the 1980s*, 441–455. Washington, D.C.: American Psychological Association, 1980.

Anderson, S. A., Russell, C. S., and Schumm, W. R. Perceived Marital Quality and Family Life-Cycle Categories: A Further Analysis. *Journal of Marriage and the Family*, 1983, 45, 127–139.

Argyle, M., and Furnham, A. Sources of Satisfaction and Conflict in Long-Term Relationships. *Journal of Marriage and the Family*, 1983, 45, 481–493.

Armstrong, J. C. Decision Behavior and Outcome of Midlife Career Changers. *Vocational Guidance Quarterly*, 1981, 29, 205–213.

Bachman, J. G. *Youth in Transition*, vol. 2. The Impact of Family Background and Intelligence on Tenth-Grade Boys. Ann Arbor: Institute for Social Research, University of Michigan, 1970.

Bart, P. Depression in Middle-Aged Women. In V. Gornick and B. K. Moran (eds.), *Woman in Sexist Society: Studies in Power and Powerlessness*. New York: Basic Books, 1971.

Baruch, G., and Barnett, R. Adult Daughters' Relationships with Their Mothers. *Journal of Marriage and the Family*, 1983, 45, 601–606.

Beck, S. H., and Beck, R. W. The Formation of Extended Households During Middle Age. *Journal of Marriage and the Family*, 1984, 46, 277–286.

Benin, M. H., and Nienstedt, B. C. Happiness in Single- and Dual-Earner Families: The Effects of Marital Happiness, Job Satisfaction, and Life Cycle. *Journal of Marriage and the Family*, 1985, 47, 975–984.

Birren, J. E., and Renner, V. J. Research on the Psychology of Aging. In J. E. Birren and K. W. Schaie (eds.), *Handbook of the Psychology of Aging* (2nd ed.), 3–39. New York: Van Nostrand, 1977.

Block, J. *Lives Through Time*. Berkeley, Calif.: Bancroft, 1971.

Botwinick, J. *Aging and Behavior* (3rd ed.). New York: Springer, 1984.

Bozett, F. W. Male Development and Fathering Throughout the Life Cycle. *American Behavioral Scientist*, 1985, 29, 41–54.

Braiker, H. B., and Kelley, H. H. Conflict in the Development of Close Relationships. In R. L Burgess and T. I. Huston (eds.), *Social Exchange in Developing Relationships*, 135–168. New York: Academic Press, 1979.

Brim, O. G. Theories of Male Midlife Crisis. *Counseling Psychologist*, 1976, 1, 21–25.

Brody, E. M., Johnsen, P. T., and Fulcomer, M. C. What Should Adult Children Do for Elderly Parents? Opinions and Preferences of Three Generations of Women. *Journal of Gerontology*, 1984, 39, 736–746.

Bronson, W. C. Adult Derivatives of Emotional Experiences and Reactivity-Control Developmental Continuities from Childhood to Adulthood. *Child Development*, 1967, 38, 801–878.

———. Central Orientations: A Study of Behavior Organization from Childhood to Adolescence. *Child Development*, 1966, 37, 125–155.

Campbell, D. P., and Klein, K. L. Job Satisfaction and Vocational Interests. *Vocational Guidance Quarterly*, 1975, 24, 125–132.

Cherrington, D. J. The Work Ethic: Working Values and Values That Work, cited in R. Albanese and D. D. Van Fleet, *Organizational Behavior: A Managerial Viewpoint*. Chicago: Dryden, 1983.

Chown, S. M. Personality and Aging. In J. E. Birren and K. W. Schaie, *Handbook of the Psychology of Aging*, 672–692. New York: Van Nostrand, 1977.

Coleman, L. M., and Antonucci, T. C. Impact of Work on Women at Midlife. *Developmental Psychology*, 1983, 19, 290–294.

Conley, J. J. Longitudinal Stability of Personality Traits: A Multitrait-Multioccasion Analysis. *Journal of Personality and Social Psychology*, 1985, 49, 1266–1281.

———. Longitudinal Consistency of Adult Personality: Self- Reported Psychological Characteristics Across 45 Years. *Journal of Personality and Social Psychology*, 1984, 47, 1325–1333.

Costa, P. T., and McCrae, R. R. Still Stable After All These Years: Personality as a Key

to Some Issues in Aging. In P. B. Baltes and O. G. Brim (eds.), *Life-Span Development and Behavior*, vol. 3. New York: Academic Press, 1980.

Costa, P. T., McCrae, R., and Arenberg, D. Enduring Dispositions in Adult Males. *Journal of Personality and Social Psychology*, 1980, 38, 793–800.

Cuber, J. F., and Haroff, P. B. Five Types of Marriage (1965). In A. S. Skolnick and J. H. Skolnick (ed.), *Family in Transition* (4th ed.), 318–329. Boston: Little, Brown, 1983.

Cytrynbaum, S., Blum, L., Patrick, R., Stein, J., Wadner, D., and Wilk, C. Midlife Development: A Personality and Social Systems Perspective. In L. W. Poon (ed.), *Aging in the 1980s*, 463–475. Washington, D.C.: American Psychological Association, 1980.

Danielson, K., and Cytrynbaum, S. Midlife Development for Blue- Collar Working Men. In Cytrynbaum S. et al. Midlife Development: A Personality and Social Systems Perspective in L. W. Poon (ed.), *Aging in the 1980s*, 463–475. Washington, D.C.: American Psychological Association, 1980.

Draughn, P. S. Perception of Competence in Work and Marriage of Middle-Age Men. *Journal of Marriage and the Family*, 1984, 46, 403–409.

Ellenburg, F. C. More Than a Bandaid for Burnout. *Clearing House*, 1981, 55, 153–154.

Erikson, E. H. *Childhood and Society* (rev. ed.). New York: Norton, 1963.

Etzion, D. Moderating Effect of Social Support on the Stress-Burnout Relationship. *Journal of Applied Psychology*, 1984, 69, 615–622.

Feshbach, S., and Weiner, B. *Personality*. Lexington, Mass.: D. C. Heath, 1982.

Field, T. M., and Widmayer, S. M. Marriage and the Family. In B. B. Wolman (ed.), *Handbook of the Psychology of Aging*, 681–697. Englewood Cliffs, N.J.: Prentice-Hall, 1982.

Fincham, F., and O'Leary, K. D. Causal Inferences for Spouse Behavior in Maritally Distressed and Nondistressed Couples. *Journal of Clinical and Social Psychology*, 1983, 1, 42–57.

Fiske, M., and Weiss, L. Intimacy and Crises in Adulthood. In N. K. Schlossberg and A. D. Entine, *Counseling Adults*, 19–34. Monterey, Calif.: Brooks/Cole, 1977.

Frederickson, R. H., Macy, F. U., and Vickers, D. Barriers to Adult Career Change. *Personnel and Guidance Journal*, 1978, 57, 166–169.

Freudenberger, H. J. Staff Burnout. *Journal of Social Issues*, 1974, 30, 159–165.

Freudiger, P. Life Satisfaction Among Three Categories of Married Women. *Journal of Marriage and the Family*, 1983, 45, 213–219.

Gannon, M. J. *Management: An Integrated Framework* (2nd ed.). Boston: Little, Brown, 1982.

Gilmer, B. H., and Deci, E. L. *Industrial and Organizational Psychology* (4th ed.). New York: McGraw-Hill, 1977.

Glenn, M. D. Psychological Well-Being in the Post-Parental Stage: Some Evidence from National Surveys. *Journal of Marriage and the Family*, 1975, *32*, 105–110.

Gould, R. *Transformations: Growth and Changes in Adult Life*. New York: Simon and Schuster, 1978.

————. Growth Toward Self-Tolerance. *Psychology Today*, February 1975.

Gurin, G., Veroff, J., and Feld, S. *Americans View Their Mental Health*. Joint Commission on Mental Illness and Health, Monograph Series no. 4. New York: Basic Books, 1960.

Guttman, D. The Cross-Cultural Perspective: Notes Toward a Comparative Psychology of Aging. In J. E. Birren and K. W. Schaie (eds.), *Handbook of the Psychology of Aging*. New York: Van Nostrand, 1977.

Harkins, E. B. Effects of Empty Nest Transition on Self-Report of Psychological and Physical Well-Being. *Journal of Marriage and the Family*, 1978, *40*, 549–558.

Havighurst, R. J. The World of Work. In B. B. Wolman (ed.), *Handbook of Developmental Psychology*, 771–786. Englewood Cliffs, N.J.: Prentice-Hall, 1982.

Hedlund, B., and Ebersole, P. A Test of Levinson's Mid-Life Reevaluation. Journal of Genetic Psychology, 1983, *143*, 189–192.

Huesmann, L. R., Eron, L. D., and Lefkowitz, M. M. Stability of Aggression over Time and Generations. *Developmental Psychology*, 1984, *20*, 1120–1134.

Hunter, F. T. Adolescents' Perception of Discussions with Parents and Friends. *Developmental Psychology*, 1985, *21*, 443–450.

Isaacson, L. E. Counseling Male Midlife Career Changes. *Vocational Guidance Quarterly*, 1981, *29*, 324–332.

Jacob, T., Feiring, C., and Anderson, C. Factor Analysis of Data on the Barrett-Leonard Relationship Inventory from Married Couples. *Psychological Reports*, 1980, *47*, 619–626.

Kagan, J., and Moss, H. A. *Birth to Maturity: A Study in Psychological Development*. New York: Wiley, 1962.

Kossen, S. *The Human Side of Organizations* (3rd ed.). New York: Harper and Row, 1983.

Levinson, D. J. *The Seasons of a Man's Life*. New York: Ballantine, 1978.

Linn, M. W., Sandifer, R., and Stein, S. Effects of Unemployment on Mental and Physical Health. *American Journal of Public Health*, 1985, *75*, 502–506.

Lowenthal, M. F., and Chiriboga, D. Transition to the Empty Nest. *Archives of General Psychiatry*, 1972, *26*, 8–14.

Maher, E. L. Burnout and Commitment: A Theoretical Alternative. *Personnel and Guidance Journal*, 1983, *61*, 390–394.

Marks, S. R. Multiple Roles and Role Strain: Some Notes on Human Energy, Time, and Commitment. *American Sociological Review*, 1977, *42*, 921–936.

McIlroy, J. H. Midlife in the 1980s: Philosophy, Economy, and Psychology. *Personnel and Guidance Journal*, 1984, *62*, 623–628.

Meltzer, H. Attitudes of Workers Before and After Forty. *Geriatrics*, 1965, *20*, 425–443.

Miller, J., Slomczynski, K. M., and Kohn, M. L. Continuity of Learning-Generalization: The Effect of Job on Men's Intellective Process in the United States and Poland. *American Journal of Sociology*, 1985, *91*, 593–615.

Moss, H. A., and Susman, E. J. Longitudinal Study of Personality Development. In O. G. Brim and J. Kagan, *Constancy and Change in Human Development*, 530–596. Cambridge, Mass.: Harvard University Press, 1980.

Neugarten, B. L. Personality and Aging. In J. E. Birren and K. W. Schaie (eds.), *Handbook of the Psychology of Aging*, 626–644. New York: Van Nostrand, 1977.

————. Adaptation and the Life Cycle. *Counseling Psychologist*, 1976, *6*, 16–20.

————. The Roles We Play. In American Medical Association. *Quality of Life: The Middle Years*. Acton, Mass.: Publishing Sciences Group, 1974.

————. Dynamics of Transition of Middle Age to Old Age. *Journal of Geriatric Psychiatry*, 1970, *4*, 71–87.

————. Adult Personality: Toward a Psychology of the Life Cycle. In B. L. Neugarten (ed.), *Middle Age and Aging*. Chicago: University of Chicago Press, 1968a.

————. The Awareness of Middle Age. In B. L. Neugarten (ed.), *Middle Age and Aging*, 93–99. Chicago: University of Chicago Press, 1968b.

————. *Personality in Middle and Later Life*. New York: Atherton, 1964.

Neugarten, B. L., and Datan, N. Sociological Perspectives on the Life Cycle. In P. B. Baltes and K. W. Schaie (eds.), *Life-Span Developmental Psychology*. New York: Academic Press, 1973.

Neugarten, B. L., and Peterson, W. A. A Study of the American Age-Grade System (1957), cited in B. L. Neugarten (ed.), *Middle Age and Aging*. Chicago: University of Chicago Press, 1968.

Newsday. Ex-Teachers Happier in New Jobs. *Newsday*, March 14, 1986, p. 15.

Palmore, E., Cleveland, W. P., Nowlin, J. B., Ramm, D., and Siegler, I. Stress and Adaptation in Later Life. *Journal of Gerontology*, 1979, *34*, 841–851.

Peck, R. C. Psychological Developments in the Second Half of Life. In B. L. Neugarten (ed.), *Middle Age and Aging*. Chicago: University of Chicago Press, 1968.

Pineo, P. C. Disenchantment in the Later Years of Marriage. *Marriage and Family Living*, 1961, *23*, 3–11.

Powell, B. The Empty Nest, Employment, and Psychiatric Symptoms in College-Educated Women. *Psychology of Women Quarterly*, 1977, *2*, 253–265.

Pritchard, R. D., Maxwell, S. E., and Jordan, W. C. Interpreting Relationships Between Age and Promotion in Age-Discrimination Cases. *Journal of Applied Psychology*, 1984, *69*, 199–206.

Rhodes, S. R. Age-Related Differences in Work Attitudes and Behavior: A Review and Conceptual Analysis. *Psychological Bulletin*, 1983, *93*, 328–367.

Riley, M. W., Johnson, M. E., and Foner, A. (eds.), *Aging and Society: A Sociology of Age Stratification*. New York: Russell Sage Foundation, 1972.

Rollins, B. C., and Feldman, H. Marital Satisfaction over the Life Cycle. *Journal of Marriage and the Family*, 1970, *32*, 20–28.

Rollins, B. C., and Galligan, R. The Developing Child and Marital Satisfactions of Parents. In R. M. Lerner and G. B. Spanier (eds.), *Child Influences on Marital and Family Interaction*. New York: Academic Press, 1982.

Rosenberg, S. D., and Farrell, M. P. Identity and Crisis in Middle-Age Men. *International Journal of Aging and Human Development*, 1976, *7*, 153–170.

Rubin, L. *Women of a Certain Age*. New York: Harper and Row, 1979.

Saleh, S. D., and Otis, J. L. Age and Level of Job Satisfaction. *Personnel Psychology*, 1964, *17*, 425–430.

Salthouse, T. A. *Adult Cognition: An Experimental Psychology of Human Aging*. New York: Springer, 1982.

Scanzoni, J. Social Exchange and Behavioral Interdependence. In R. L. Burgess and T. L. Huston (eds.), *Social Exchange in Developing Relationships*, 61–98. New York: Academic Press, 1979a.

————. Social Processes and Power in Families. In W. R. Burr, Hill, R., Nye, F. I., and Reiss, I. L. (eds.), *Contemporary Theories about the Family: Research Based Theories*, vol. 1. New York: Free Press, 1979b.

Schaie, K. W., and Parham, I. A. Stability of Adult Personality: Fact or Fable? *Journal of Personality and Social Psychology*, 1976, 36, 146–158.

Shaie, K. W., and Parr, J. Concepts and Criteria for Functional Age. In J. E. Birren et al. (eds.), *Aging: A Challenge to Science and Society*, vol. 3, 249–264. Oxford, Eng.: Oxford University Press, 1983.

Shanas, E. Social Myth as Hypothesis: The Case of the Family Relations of Old People. *The Gerontologist*, 1979a, 19, 3–20.

————. The Family as a Social Support System in Old Age. *The Gerontologist*, 1979b, 19, 169–174.

————. Family-Kin Networks and Aging: A Cross-Cultural Perspective. *Journal of Marriage and the Family*, 1973, 35, 505–511.

Sheppard, H. L. The Emerging Pattern of Second Careers. *Vocational Guidance Quarterly*, 1971, 20, 89–96.

Siegler, I. C., George, L. K., and Okun, M. A. Cross-Sequential Analysis of Adult Personality. *Developmental Psychology*, 1979, 15, 350–351.

Skovholt, T. M., and Morgan, J. E. Career Development: An Outline of Issues for Men. *Personnel and Guidance Journal*, 1981, 60, 231–237.

Spanier, G. B., Roos, P. A., and Shockey, J. Marital Trajectories of American Women: Variations in the Life Course. *Journal of Marriage and the Family*, 1985, 47, 993–1003.

Spanier, G. B., Sauer, W., and Larzelere, R. An Empirical Evaluation of the Family Life Cycle. *Journal of Marriage and the Family*, 1979, 41, 27–38.

Stagner, R. Aging in Industry. In J. E. Birren and K. W. Schaie (eds.), *Handbook of the Psychology of Aging* (2nd ed.), 789–818. New York: Van Nostrand, 1985.

Staw, B. M., and Ross, J. Stability in the Midst of Change: A Dispositional Approach to Job Attributes. *Journal of Applied Psychology*, 1985, 70, 469–480.

Steinberg, L. Early Temperamental Antecedents of Adult Type A Behaviors. *Developmental Psychology*, 1985, 21, 1171–1180.

Stevens, D. P., and Truss, C. V. Stability and Change in Adult Personality over 12 and 20 Years. *Developmental Psychology*, 1985, 21, 568–584.

Stinnett, N., Sanders, G., DeFrain, J., and Parkhurst, A. A Nationwide Study of Families Who Perceive Themselves as Strong. *Family Perspective*, 1982, 16, 15–22.

Taffel, S. *Trends in Fertility in the United States*, Vital and Health Statistics, Series 21: Data from the National Vital Statistics System, no. 28. Hyattsville, Md.: National Center for Health Statistics, 1977, table 13.

Thomas, L. E. A Typology of Mid-Life Career Changes. *Journal of Vocational Behavior*, 1980, 16, 173–182.

Thurnher, M., Spence, D., and Lowenthal, M. F. Value Conflict and Behavioral Conflict in Intergenerational Relations. *Journal of Marriage and the Family*, 1974, 36, 308–319.

Ullmann, C. A. Second Careers for Military Retirees. *Vocational Guidance Quarterly*, 1971, 20, 96–103.

U.S. Bureau of the Census. *Statistical Abstract of the United States, 1979*, table 82.

U.S. Bureau of the Census, *Population Profile of the United States: 1978*, Current Population Reports, Series P-20, no. 336, table 3.

U.S. Department of Labor. *Employment in Perspective: Women in the Labor Force*, Report no. 721. Washington, D.C.: Bureau of Labor Statistics, 1985.

U.S. News & World Report. When a Generation Turns Forty. March 10, 1986, pp. 60–64.

Vaillant, G. E. *Adaptation to Life*. Boston: Little, Brown, 1977.

Van Velsor, E., and O'Rand, A. M. Family Life Cycle, Work Career Patterns, and Women's Wages at Midlife. *Journal of Marriage and the Family*, 1984, 46, 365–373.

Veroff, J., Reuman, D., and Feld, S. Motives in American Men and Women Across the Adult Life Cycle. *Developmental Psychology*, 1984, 20, 995–1003.

Waldman, D. A., and Avolio, B. J. A Meta-Analysis of Age Differences in Job Performance. *Journal of Applied Psychology*, 1986, 71, 33–38.

Weaver, C. N. Job Satisfaction in the United States in the 1970s. *Journal of Applied Psychology*, 1980, 65, 364–367.

Wilson, M. R., and Filsinger, E. E. Religiosity and Marital Adjustment: Multidimensional Interrelationships. *Journal of Marriage and the Family*, 1986, 48, 147–151.

Woodruff, D. S., and Birren, J. E. Age Changes and Cohort Differences in Personality. *Developmental Psychology*, 1972, 6, 252–259.

Chapter 18

Altrocchi, J. *Abnormal Psychology*. New York: Harcourt Brace Jovanovich, 1980.

American Psychiatric Association. *Diagnostic and Statistical Manual of Mental Disorders* (3rd ed.). Washington, D.C.: American Psychiatric Association, 1980.

Balazs, E. A. Intercellular Matrix of Connective Tissue. In C. E. Finch and L. Hayflick (eds.), *Handbook of the Biology of Aging*, 222–241. New York: Van Nostrand, 1977.

Baltes, P. B. Functional Age and Social Policy in Aging. In J. E. Birren et al. (eds.). *Aging: A Challenge to Science and Society*, vol. 3, 435–439. New York: Oxford University Press, 1983.

Barrow, G. M., and Smith, P. A. *Aging, the Individual, and Society* (2nd ed.). St. Paul: West, 1983.

Barrows, C. H., and Roeder, L. M. Nutrition. In C. E. Finch and L. Hayflick (eds.), *Handbook of the Biology of Aging*, 561–582. New York: Van Nostrand, 1977.

Bernard, A. Accidents and the Elderly (1969). In R. A. Kalish (ed.), *The Later Years: Social Applications of Gerontology*, 183–189. Monterey, Calif.: Brooks/Cole, 1977.

Birren, J. E. *The Psychology of Aging*. Englewood Cliffs, N.J.: Prentice-Hall, 1964.

Birren, J. E., and Cunningham, W. Research on the Psychology of Aging: Principles, Concepts, and Theory. In J. E. Birren and K. W. Schaie (eds.), *Handbook of the Psychology of Aging* (2nd ed.), 3–20. New York: Van Nostrand Reinhold, 1985.

Birren, J. E., and Renner, V. J. Health, Behaviour, and Aging. In J. E. Birren et al. (eds.), *Aging: A Challenge to Science and Society*, vol. 3, 9–35. New York: Oxford University Press, 1983.

Bjorksten, J. The Crosslinkage Theory of Aging. *Journal of the American Geriatric Society*, 1968, 16, 408–427.

Bondareff, W. The Neural Basis of Aging. In J. E. Birren and K. W. Schaie, *Handbook of the Psychology of Aging* (2nd ed.), 95–108. New York: Van Nostrand Reinhold, 1985.

Botwinick, J. *Aging and Behavior* (3rd ed.). New York: Springer, 1984.

Burnside, I. M. Mental Health and Mental Illness in Later Life. In B. M. Steffl (ed.), *Handbook of Gerontological Nursing*, 91–106. New York: Van Nostrand Reinhold, 1984.

————. Mental Health and the Aged. In I. M. Burnside (ed.), *Nursing and the Aged* (2nd ed.), 70–85. New York: McGraw-Hill, 1981.

Burrus-Bammel, L. L., and Bammel, G. Leisure and Recreation. In J. E. Birren and K. W. Schaie (eds.), *Handbook of the Psychology of Aging* (2nd ed.), 848–864. New York: Van Nostrand Reinhold, 1985.

Cameron, P. Mood as an Indicant of Happiness: Age, Sex, Social Class, and Situational Differences. *Journal of Gerontology*, 1975, *30*, 216–224.

Chiriboga, D. A. Stress and Coping (introduction to section 6). In L. W. Poon (ed.), *Aging in the 1980s*, 343–345. Washington, D.C.: American Psychological Association, 1980.

Chiriboga, D. A., and Cutler, L. Stress and Adaptation: Life Span Perspectives. In L. W. Poon (ed.), *Aging in the 1980s*, 347–363. Washington, D.C.: American Psychological Association, 1980.

Chiriboga, D. A., and Dean, H. Dimensions of Stress: Perspectives from a Longitudinal Study. *Journal of Psychosomatic Research*, 1978, *22*, 47–55.

Clarke, H. H. Exercise and Aging. In *Physical Fitness Research Digest*. Washington, D.C.: President's Council on Physical Fitness and Sports, April 1977.

Cockerman, W. C., Sharp, K., and Wilcox, J. A. Aging and Perceived Health Status. *Journal of Gerontology*, 1983, *38*, 349–355.

Cohen, F. Coping with Surgery: Information, Psychological Preparation, and Recovery. In L. W. Poon (ed.), *Aging in the 1980s*, 375–383. Washington, D.C.: American Psychological Association, 1980.

Coleman, P. G. Cognitive Functioning and Health. In J. E. Birren et al. (eds.), *Aging: A Challenge to Science and Society*, 57–67. New York: Oxford University Press, 1983.

Corso, J. F. Auditory Perception and Communication. In J. E. Birren and K. W. Schaie (eds.), *Handbook of the Psychology of Aging*, 535–553. New York: Van Nostrand Reinhold, 1977.

Costa, P. T., and McCrae, R. R. Still Stable After All These Years: Personality as a Key to Some Issues in Adulthood and Old Age. In P. B. Baltes and O. G. Brim (eds.), *Life-Span Development and Behavior*, 65–102. New York: Academic Press, 1980.

Coyle, J. T., Price, D. L., and DeLong, M. R. Alzheimer's Disease: A Disorder of Cortical Cholinergic Innervation. *Science*, 1983, *219*, 1184–1190.

Crook, T. H., and Miller, N. E. The Challenge of Alzheimer's Disease. *American Psychologist*, 1985, *40*, 1245–1251.

Curtis, H. J., and Miller, K. Chromosome Aberrations in Liver Cells of Guinea Pigs. *Journal of Gerontology*, 1971, *26*, 292–294.

Dean, L. Aging and the Decline of Affect. *Journal of Gerontology*, 1962, *17*, 440–446.

Diekelmann, N. *Primary Health Care of the Well Adult*. New York: McGraw-Hill, 1977.

Ebersole, P., and Hess, P. *Toward Healthy Aging: Human Needs and Nursing Response*. St. Louis: Mosby, 1981.

Eisdorfer, C., and Wilkie, F. Stress, Disease, Aging, and Behavior. In J. E. Birren and K. W. Schaie (eds.), *Handbook of the Psychology of Aging*, 251–276. New York: Van Nostrand Reinhold, 1977.

Engen, T. Taste and Smell. In J. E. Birren and K. W. Schaie (eds.), *Handbook of the Psychology of Aging*, 554–562. New York: Van Nostrand Reinhold, 1977.

Ferraro, K. F. Self-Ratings of Health Among the Old and Old-Old. *Journal of Health and Social Behavior*, 1980, *21*, 377–383.

Friedman, M., and Rosenman, R. H. *Type A Behavior and Your Heart*. New York: Fawcett, 1974.

Fries, J. A., and Crapo, L. M. *Vitality and Aging: Implications of the Rectangular Curve*. San Francisco: Freeman, 1981.

Fry, C. L. Culture, Behavior, and Aging in Comparative Perspective. In J. E. Birren and K. W. Schaie (eds.), *Handbook of the Psychology of Aging* (2nd ed.), 216–245. New York: Van Nostrand Reinhold, 1985.

Gatz, M., Smyer, M. A., and Lawton, M. P. The Mental Health System and the Older Adult. In L. W. Poon (ed.), *Aging in the 1980s*, 5–19. Washington, D.C.: American Psychological Association, 1980.

Goble, F. C., and Konopka, E. A. Sex as a Factor in Infectious Disease. *Transactions of the New York Academy of Science*, 1973, *35*, 325.

Hamilton, E. M. N., and Whitney, E. N. *Nutrition: Concepts and Controversies* (2nd ed.). St. Paul: West, 1982.

Harman, D. The Aging Process. *Proceedings of the National Academy of Science*, 1981, *78*, 7124.

Hayflick, L. The Cellular Basis for Biological Aging. In C. E. Finch and L. Hayflick (eds.), *Handbook of the Psychology of Aging*, 159–179. New York: Van Nostrand, 1977.

———. The Cell Biology of Human Aging. *New England Journal of Medicine*, 1976, *295*, 1302–1308.

———. The Strategy of Senescence. *Journal of Gerontology*, 1974, *14*, 37–43.

Haynes, S. G., Feinleib, M., Levine, S., Scotch, N., and Kannel, W. B. The Relationship of Psychosocial Factors to Coronary Heart Disease in the Framingham Study, 2: Prevalence of Coronary Heart Disease. *American Journal of Epidemiology*, 1978, *107*, 382–402.

Heckler, M. M. The Fight Against Alzheimer's Disease. *American Psychologist*, 1985, *40*, 1240–1245.

Holmes, T. H., and Rahe, R. H. The Social Readjustment Rating Scale. *Journal of Psychosomatic Research*, 1967, *11*, 213–218.

Hongladarom, G., McCorkle, R., and Woods, N. F. The Complete Book of Women's Health. Englewood Cliffs, N.J.: Prentice-Hall, 1982.

Hull, R. H. Talking to the Hearing-Impaired Older Person (1980). In J. Botwinick, *Aging and Behavior* (3rd ed.). New York: Springer, 1984.

Jackson, J. J. *Minorities and Aging*. Belmont, Calif.: Wadsworth, 1980.

Jarvik, L. F., and Falek, A. Comparative Data on Cancer in Aging Twins. *Cancer*, 1962, *15*, 1009–1018.

Kalish, R. A. *The Later Years: Social Applications of Gerontology*. Monterey, Calif.: Brooks/Cole, 1977.

———. *Late Adulthood: Perspectives on Human Development*. Monterey, Calif.: Brooks/Cole, 1975.

Kallman, F. J., and Jarvik, L. F. Individual Differences in Constitution and Genetic Background. In J. E. Birren (ed.), *Handbook of Aging and the Individual*, 216–263. Chicago: University of Chicago Press, 1959.

Kastenbaum, R. Dying and Death: A Life-Span Approach. In J. E. Birren and K. W. Schaie (eds.), *Handbook of the Psychology of Aging* (2nd ed.), 619–647. New York: Van Nostrand Reinhold, 1985.

Kenshalo, D. R. Age Changes in Touch, Vibration, Temperature, Kinesthesis, and Pain. In J. E. Birren and K. W. Schaie (eds.), *Handbook of the Psychology of Aging*, 562–580. New York: Van Nostrand Reinhold, 1977.

Kermis, M. D. *The Psychology of Aging: Theory, Research, and Practice*. Boston: Allyn and Bacon, 1984.

Khachaturian, Z. S. Progress of Research on Alzheimer's Disease: Research Opportunities for Behavioral Scientists. *American Psychologist*, 1985, *40*, 1251–1256.

Kline, D. W., and Schieber, F. Vision and Aging. In J. E. Birren and K. W. Schaie (eds.), *Handbook of the Psychology of Aging*, 296–332. New York: Van Nostrand Reinhold, 1985.

Larson, R. Thirty Years of Research on the Subjective Well-Being of Older Americans. *Journal of Gerontology*, 1978, *33*, 109–125.

LaRue, A., Dessonville, C., and Jarvik, L. F. Aging and Mental Disorders. In J. E. Birren and K. W. Schaie (eds.), *Handbook of the Psychology of Aging* (2nd ed.), 664–703. New York: Van Nostrand Reinhold, 1985.

Leaf, A. Every Day Is a Gift When You Are over 100. *National Geographic*, 1973, *143*, 93–118.

Levin, J., and Levin, W. C. *Ageism: Prejudice and Discrimination Against the Elderly*. Belmont, Calif.: Wadsworth, 1980.

Levy, S. M., Derogatis, L. R., Gallagher, D., and Gatz, M. Intervention with Older Adults and the Evaluation of Outcome. In L. W. Poon (ed.), *Aging in the 1980s*, 41–65. Washington, D.C.: American Psychological Association, 1980.

Long, P. J., and Shannon, B. *Nutrition: An Inquiry into the Issues*. Englewood Cliffs, N.J.: Prentice-Hall, 1983.

Makinodan, T. Immunity and Aging. In C. E. Finch and L. Hayflick, *Handbook of the Biology of Aging*, 379–409. New York: Van Nostrand, 1977.

Mazess, R. B., and Foreman, S. H. Longevity and Age Exaggeration in Vilcabamba, Ecuador. *Journal of Gerontology*, 1979, *34*, 94–98.

McCay, C. M., Crowell, M. F., and Maynard, L. A. The Effect of Retarded Growth upon the Length of Life Span and upon the Ultimate Body Size. *Journal of Nutrition*, 1935, *10*, 63–79.

McClearn, G., and Foch, T. T. Behavioral Genetics. In J. E. Birren and K. W. Schaie (eds.), *Handbook of the Psychology of Aging* (2nd ed.), 113–138. New York: Van Nostrand Reinhold, 1985.

McCrae, R. R. Age Differences in the Use of Coping Mechanisms. *Journal of Gerontology*, 1982, *37*, 454–460.

Medvedev, Z. A. Caucasus and Altay Longevity: A Biological or Social Problem? *The Gerontologist*, 1974, *14*, 381–387.

Metropolitan Life Insurance Co. Recent International Changes in Longevity. *Statistical Bulletin*, January–March 1986, 16–21.

———. Slight Gains in U.S. Longevity. *Statistical Bulletin*, July–September 1985, 20–23.

———. Projections of Population Growth at the Older Ages. *Statistical Bulletin*, April–June 1984, 8–12.

Miller, F. T. Measurement and Monitoring of Stress in Communities. In L. W. Poon (ed.), *Aging in the 1980s*. Washington, D.C.: American Psychological Association, 1980, 383–391.

Miller, M. Geriatric Suicide: The Arizona Study. *The Gerontologist*, 1978, *18*, 488–495.

Moore, L. M., Nielsen, C. R., and Mistretta, C. M. Sucrose Taste Thresholds: Age Related Differences. *Journal of Gerontology*, 1982, *37*, 64–69.

Murphy, C. Cognitive and Chemosensory Influences on Age- Related Changes in the Ability to Identify Blended Foods. *Journal of Gerontology*, 1985, *40*, 47–52.

Murphy, C., and Withee, J. Age-Related Differences in the Pleasantness of Chemosensory Stimuli. *Psychology and Aging*, 1986, *4*, 312–318.

National Center for Health Statistics. *Prevalence, Impact, and Demography of Known Diabetes in the United States*. U.S. Department of Health and Human Services (Advanced Data), no. 114. Washington, D.C., February 12, 1986.

———. Health in the Later Years of Life: Selected Data from the National Center for Health Statistics (1971). In R. A. Kalish (ed.), *The Later Years: Social Applications of Gerontology*, 166–174. Monterey, Calif.: Brooks/Cole, 1977.

National Safety Council. *Accident Facts, 1986 Edition*. Chicago, Illinois: National Safety Council, 1986.

National Safety Council. *Accident Facts*. Chicago: National Safety Council, 1981.

Nebes, R. D., Boller, F., and Holland, D. Use of Semantic Context by Patients with Alzheimer's Disease. *Psychology and Aging*, 1986, *1*, 261–269.

Newsday. Oldest Known Man Dies at 120. *Newsday*, February 22, 1986, p. 8.

Notelovitz, M., and Ware, M. Stand Tall! The Informed Woman's Guide to Preventing Osteoporosis. Gainesville, Fla.: Triad, 1982.

Ochs, A. L., Newberry, J., Lenhardt, M. L., and Harkins, S. W. Neural and Vestibular Aging Associated with Falls. In J. E. Birren and K. W. Schaie (eds.), *Handbook of the Psychology of Aging*, 378–400. New York: Van Nostrand Reinhold, 1985.

Olsho, L. W., Harkins, S. W., and Lenhardt, M. I. Aging and268the Auditory System. In J. E. Birren and K. W. Schaie (eds.), *Handbook of the Psychology of Aging*, 332–378. New York: Van Nostrand Reinhold, 1985.

Palmore, E. B. Social Class, Sex Differences, and Longevity. In J. E. Birren et al. (eds.), *Aging: A Challenge to Science and Society*, vol. 3, 41–48. New York: Oxford University Press, 1983.

Peck, R. C. Psychological Developments in the Second Half of Life. In B. L. Neugarten (ed.), *Middle Age and Aging*. Chicago: University of Chicago Press, 1968.

Pelizza, J. Suicide in the Elderly: Can It Be Prevented? (1979), cited in P. Ebersole and P. Hess. *Towards Health Aging: Human Needs and Nursing Response*. St. Louis: Mosby, 1981.

Pfeiffer, E. Psychopathology and Social Pathology. In J. E. Birren and K. W. Schaie (eds.), *Handbook of the Psychology of Aging*. New York: Van Nostrand Reinhold, 1977.

Poon, L. W., Powell, L. S., and Courtice, K. *Alzheimer's Disease: A Guide for Families*. Reading, Mass.: Addison-Wesley, 1983.

Remnet, V. L. The Home Assessment. In I. M. Burnside (ed.), *Nursing and the Aged*, 437–450. New York: McGraw-Hill, 1981.

Rickards, L. D., Zuckerman, D. M., and West, P. R. Alzheimer's Disease: Current Congressional Response. *American Psychologist*, 1985, *40*, 1256–1262.

Rockstein, M., and Sussman, M. *Biology of Aging*. Belmont, Calif.: Wadsworth, 1979.

Ron, M. A., Toone, B. K., Gerralda, M. E., and Lishman, W. A. Diagnostic Accuracy and Senile Dementia. *British Journal of Psychiatry*, 1979, *124*, 161–167.

Rosenhan, D. L., and Seligman, M. E. *Abnormal Psychology*. New York: Norton, 1984.

Rossman, I. Human Aging Changes. In I. M. Burnside (ed.), *Nursing and the Aged* (2nd ed.), 30–41. New York: McGraw-Hill, 1981.

Sacher, G. A. Life Table Modification and Life Prolongation. In C. E. Finch and L. Hayflick, *Handbook of the Biology of Aging*, 582–638. New York: Van Nostrand, 1977.

Sachuk, N. N., and Moskalets, G. Sociological Study of the Relationship Between Mode of Life and State of Health in Pensioners of a Large Town. In J. E. Birren et al. (eds.), *Aging: A Challenge to Science and Society*, vol. 3, 192–202. New York: Oxford University Press, 1983.

Salthouse, T. A. Speed of Behavior and Its Implications for Cognition. In J. E. Birren and K. W. Schaie (eds.), *Handbook of the Psychology of Aging* (2nd ed.), 400–427. New York: Van Nostrand Reinhold, 1985.

———. *Adult Cognition: An Experimental Psychology of Human Aging*. New York: Springer-Verlag, 1982.

Saxon, S. V., and Etten, M. J. *Physical Change and Aging*. New York: Tiresias, 1978.

Schaie, K. W. Psychological Changes from Midlife to Early Old Age: Implications for the Maintenance of Mental Health. *American Journal of Orthopsychiatry*, 1981, *51*, 199–218.

Schanck, A. H. Musculoskeletal Problems in Aging. In I. M. Burnside (ed.), *Nursing and the Aged*, 282–295. New York: McGraw-Hill, 1981.

Schiffman, S. S. Food Recognition by the Elderly. *Journal of Gerontology*, 1977, *32*, 586–592.

Schmitz-Scherzer, R. Medical and Psychological Determinants of Development in Aged Persons. In J. E. Birren et al. (eds.), *Aging: A Challenge to Science and Society*, 35–41. New York: Oxford University Press, 1983.

Schulz, R. D. Emotionality and Aging: A Theoretical and Empirical Analysis. *Journal of Gerontology*, 1982, *37*, 42–51.

Shiffman, S., and Pasternak, M. Decreased Discrimination of Food Odors in the Elderly. *Journal of Gerontology*, 1979, *34*, 73–79.

Shock, N. W. Effects of Environmental Factors and Life Patterns on Life Span. In J. E. Birren et al. (eds.), *Aging: A Challenge to Science and Society*, vol. 3, 413–415. New York: Oxford University Press, 1983.

———. System Integration. In C. E. Finch and L. Hayflick (eds.), *Handbook of the Biology of Aging*, 639–666. New York: Van Nostrand, 1977.

Steffl, B. M. Assessment of Safety Factors. In I. M. Burnside (ed.), *Nursing and the Aged*. New York: McGraw-Hill, 1981.

Sterns, H. L., Barrett, G. V., and Alexander, R. A. Accidents and the Aging Individual. In J. E. Birren and K. W. Schaie (eds.), *Handbook of the Psychology of Aging* (2nd ed.), 703–725. New York: Van Nostrand Reinhold, 1985.

Thornbury, J., and Mistretta, C. M. Tactile Sensitivity as a Function of Age. *Journal of Gerontology*, 1981, *36*, 34–39.

Turkington, C. Alzheimer's and Aluminum. *The APA Monitor*, January 1987, 13.

Turner, B. F. Sex-Related Differences in Aging. In B. B. Wolman (ed.), *Handbook of Developmental Psychology*, 912–936. Englewood Cliffs, N.J.: Prentice-Hall, 1982.

U.S. Bureau of the Census, *Statistical Abstract of the United States, 1985*. Washington, D.C., 1985.

Upton, A. C. Pathobiology. In C. E. Finch and L. Hayflick (eds.), *Handbook of the Biology of Aging*, 513–536. New York: Van Nostrand Reinhold, 1977.

Vaillant, G. E. *Adaptation to Life*. Boston: Little, Brown, 1977.

Van der Plaats, M. Health. In J. E. Birren et al. (eds.), *Aging: A Challenge to Science and Society*, vol. 3, 397–398. New York: Oxford University Press, 1983.

Vitaliano, P. P., Russo, J., Breen, A. R., Vitiello, M. J., and Prinz, P. N. Functional Decline in the Early Stages of Alzheimer's Disease. *Psychology and Aging*, 1986, *1*, 41–47.

Waldron, J. Why Do Women Live Longer Than Men? *Social Science and Medicine*, 1976, *20*, 349–362.

Walford, R. L. *Maximum Life Span*. New York: Norton, 1983.

Walk, R. D. *Perceptual Development*. Monterey, Calif.: Brooks/Cole, 1981.

Watkin, D. M. *Handbook of Nutrition, Health, and Aging*. Park Ridge, N.J.: Noyes, 1983.

Welford, A. T. Motor Performance. In J. E. Birren and K. W. Schaie (eds.), *Handbook of the Psychology of Aging*, 450–497. New York: Van Nostrand Reinhold, 1977.

Whitney, E. N., and Hamilton, E. M. N. *Understanding Nutrition* (3rd ed.). St. Paul: West, 1984.

Wigdor, B. T. Mental Health and Social Conditions. In J. E. Birren et al. (eds.), *Aging: A Challenge to Science and Society*, 49–57. New York: Oxford University Press, 1983.

Wolanin, M. O. The Nursing Assessment. In I. M. Burnside (ed.), *Nursing and the Aged*, 384–403. New York: McGraw-Hill, 1981.

Woodruff, D. S. Arousal, Sleep, and Aging. In J. E. Birren and K. W. Schaie (eds.), *Handbook of the Psychology of Aging* (2nd ed.), 261–296. New York: Van Nostrand Reinhold, 1985.

Chapter 19

Arenberg, D. Memory and Learning Do Decline Late in Life. In J. E. Birren et al. (eds.), *Aging: A Challenge to Science and Society*, vol. 3, 312–322. New York: Oxford University Press, 1983.

———. Concept Problem Solving in Young and Old Adults. *Journal of Gerontology*, 1968, *23*, 279–282.

Baltes, P. B., Dittmann-Kohli, F., and Kliegl, R. Reserve Capacity of the Elderly in Aging-Sensitive Tests of Fluid Intelligence: Replication and Extension. *Psychology and Aging*, 1986, *1*, 172–177.

Barrow, G. M. *Aging, the Individual, and Society* (3rd ed.). St. Paul: West, 1986.

Best, J. B. *Cognitive Psychology*. St. Paul: West, 1986.

Birkhill, W. R., and Schaie, K. W. The Effect of Differential Reinforcement of Cautiousness in Intellectual Performance Among the Elderly. *Journal of Gerontology*, 1975, *30*, 578–583.

Birren, J. E., Cunningham, W. R., and Yamamoto, K. Psychology of Adult Development and Aging. In M. R. Rosenzweig and L. W. Porter (eds.), *Annual Review of Psychology*, 1983, *34*, 543–577.

Botwinick, J. *Aging and Behavior* (3rd ed.). New York: Springer, 1984.

———. Intellectual Abilities. In J. E. Birren and K. W. Schaie (eds.), *Handbook of the Psychology of Aging*, 580–605. New York: Van Nostrand Reinhold, 1977.

———. *Aging and Behavior: A Comprehensive Integration of Research Findings*. New York: Springer, 1973.

———. Disinclination to Venture Response Versus Cautiousness in Responding: Age Differences. *Journal of Genetic Psychology*, 1969, *115*, 55–62.

———. *Cognitive Processes in Maturity and Old Age*. New York: Springer, 1967.

Botwinick, J., and Storandt, M. *Memory, Related Functions, and Age*. Springfield, Ill.: Thomas, 1974.

Botwinick, J., West, R., and Storandt, M. Predicting Death from Behavior Test Performance. *Journal of Gerontology*, 1978, *33*, 755–762.

Bransford, J. D. *Human Cognition: Learning, Understanding, and Remembering*. Belmont, Calif.: Wadsworth, 1979.

Cavanaugh, J. C., Grady, J. G., and Perlmutter, M. P. Forgetting and Use of Memory Aids in 20- and 70-Year Olds' Everyday Life. *International Journal of Aging and Human Development*, 1983, *18*, 457–490.

Cerella, J., Poon, L. W., and Fozard, J. L. Age and Iconic Read-Out. *Journal of Gerontology*, 1982, *37*, 197–202.

Cicirelli, V. G. Categorization Behaviors in Aging Subjects. *Journal of Gerontology*, 1976, *31*, 676–680.

Coleman, P. G. Cognitive Functioning and Health. In J. E. Birren et al. (eds.), *Aging: A Challenge to Science and Society*, vol. 3, 57–67. New York: Oxford University Press, 1983.

Craik, F. I. M. Age Differences in Human Memory. In J. E. Birren and K. W. Schaie (eds.), *Handbook of the Psychology of Aging*, 384–421. New York: Van Nostrand Reinhold, 1977.

Daniel, D. E., Templin, R. G., and Shearon, R. W. The Value Orientation of Older Adults Towards Education. *Educational Gerontology*, 1977, *2*, 33–42.

Denney, D. R., and Denney, N. W. The Use of Classification for Problem Solving: A Comparison of Middle and Old Age. *Developmental Psychology*, 1973, *9*, 275–278.

Denney, N. W. Aging and Cognitive Changes. In B. B. Wolman (ed.), *Handbook of Developmental Psychology*, 807–824. Englewood Cliffs, N.J.: Prentice-Hall, 1982.

———. Classification Abilities in the Elderly. *Journal of Gerontology*, 1974, *29*, 309–314.

Denney, N., and Cornelius, S. Class Inclusion and Multiple Classification in Middle and Old Age. *Developmental Psychology*, 1975, *11*, 521–522.

Denney, N., and Denney, D. The Relationship Between Classification and Questioning Strategies Among Adults. *Journal of Gerontology*, 1982, *37*, 190–196.

———. The Relationship Between Classification and Questioning Strategies Among Adults. *Journal of Gerontology*, 1974, *10*, 458.

Denney, N., Jones, F., and Krigel, S. Modifying the Questioning Strategies of Young Children and Elderly Adults with Strategy- Modeling Techniques. *Human Development*, 1979, *22*, 23–36.

Denney, N., and Palmer, A. Adult Age Differences on Traditional and Practical Problem-Solving Measures. *Journal of Gerontology*, 1981, *36*, 323–328.

Duchek, J. M. Encoding and Retrieval Differences Between Young and Old: The Impact of Attentional Capacity Usage. *Developmental Psychology*, 1984, *20*, 1173–1181.

Ebersole, P., and Hess, P. *Toward Healthy Aging: Human Needs and Nursing Response*. St. Louis: Mosby, 1981.

Eisdorfer, C. E. Functional Age-Cognitive Change. In J. E. Birren et al. (eds.), *Aging: A Challenge to Science and Society*, vol. 3, 433–434. New York: Oxford University Press, 1983.

Elder, G. Military Times and Turning Points in Men's Lives. *Developmental Psychology*, 1986, *22*, 233–246.

Gardner, H. *Frames of Mind: The Theory of Multiple Intelligences*. New York: Basic Books, 1983.

Giambra, L. M., and Arenberg, D. Problem Solving, Concept Learning, and Aging. In L. W. Poon (ed.), *Aging in the 1980s*, 253–260. Washington, D.C.: American Psychological Association, 1980.

Green, R. F. Age-Intelligence Relationship Between Ages Sixteen and Sixty-Four. *Developmental Psychology*, 1969, *1*, 618–627.

Hartley, A. A. Adult Age Differences in Deductive Reasoning Processes. *Journal of Gerontology*, 1981, *36*, 700–706.

Hartley, J. T., Harker, J. O., and Walsh, D. A. Contemporary Issues and New Directions in Adult Development of Learning and Memory. In L. W. Poon (ed.), *Aging in the 1980s*, 239–253. Washington, D.C.: American Psychological Association, 1980.

Hayslip, B., and Sterns, H. L. Age Differences in Relationships Between Crystallized and Fluid Intelligences and Problem Solving. *Journal of Gerontology*, 1979, *34*, 404–414.

Heglin, H. J. Problem Solving Set in Different Age Groups. *Journal of Gerontology*, 1956, *11*, 310–317.

Heyn, J. E., Barry, J. R., and Pollack, R. H. Problem Solving as a Function of Age, Sex, and Role Appropriateness of the Problem Context. *Experimental Aging Research*, 1978, *5*, 505–519.

Hofland, B. F., Willis, S. L., and Baltes, P. B. Fluid Intelligence Performance in the Elderly: Intraindividual Variability and Conditions of Assessment. *Journal of Educational Psychology*, 1981, *73*, 573–587.

Hooper, F. H., Fitzgerald, J., and Papalia, D. Piagetian Theory and the Aging Process: Extensions and Speculations. *Aging and Human Development*, 1971, *2*, 3–20.

Horn, J. L. The Aging of Human Abilities. In B. B. Wolman (ed.), *Handbook of Developmental Psychology*, 847–871. Englewood Cliffs, N.J.: Prentice-Hall, 1982.

Horn, J. L, and Donaldson, G. Cognitive Development in Adulthood. In O. G. Brim and J. Kagan (eds.), *Constancy and Change in Human Development*, 445–530. Cambridge, Mass.: Harvard University Press, 1980.

House, A. E., and Lewis, M. L., Wechsler Adult Intelligence Scale—Revised. In C. S. Newmark (ed.), *Major Psychological Assessment Instruments*, 323–379. Boston: Allyn and Bacon, 1985.

Hoyer, W. J., Rebok, G. W., and Sved, S. M. Effects of Varying Irrelevant Information in Adult Age Differences in Problem Solving. *Journal of Gerontology*, 1979, *34*, 553–560.

Hultsch, D. F. Adult Age Differences in the Organization of Free Recall. *Developmental Psychology*, 1969, *1*, 673–678.

Hultsch, D. F., Hertzog, C., and Dixon, R. Text Recall in Adulthood: The Role of Intellectual Abilities. *Developmental Psychology*, 1984, *20*, 1193–1210.

Kausler, D. H., Lichty, W., and Davis, R. T. Temporal Memory for Performed Activities: Intentionality and Adult Age Differences. *Developmental Psychology*, 1985, *21*, 1132–1139.

Kleemeier, R. W. Intellectual Change in the Senium, or Death and the I.Q. (1961), cited in J. Botwinick, *Aging and Behavior* (3rd ed.). New York: Springer, 1984.

Labouvier-Vief, G. Intelligence and Cognition. In J. E. Birren and K. W. Schaie (eds.), *Handbook of the Psychology of Aging* (2nd ed.), 500–531. New York: Van Nostrand Reinhold, 1985.

———. Growth and Aging in Life-Span Perspective. *Human Development*, 1982, *25*, 65–79.

———. Adult Cognitive Development: In Search of Alternative Interpretations. *Merrill-Palmer Quarterly*, 1977, *23*, 227–263.

Labouvier-Vief, G., and Gonda, J. N. Cognitive Strategy Training and Intellectual Performance in the Elderly. *Journal of Gerontology*, 1976, *31*, 327–332.

Labouvier-Vief, G., and Schell, D. A. Learning and Memory in Later Life. In B. B. Wolman (ed.), *Handbook of Developmental Psychology*, 828–847. Englewood Cliffs, N.J.: Prentice-Hall, 1982.

Lachman, J. L., Lachman, R., and Threnesbery, C. Metamemory Through the Adult Life Span. *Developmental Psychology*, 1979, *15*, 543–551.

Lair, C. V., and Moon, H. W. The Effects of Praise and Reproof on Performance of Middle-Aged and Older Subjects. *Aging and Human Development*, 1972, *3*, 279–284.

LaRue, A., and Jarvik, L. F. Old Age and Biobehavioral Changes. In B. B. Wolman (ed.), *Handbook of Developmental Psychology*, 791–807. Englewood Cliffs, N.J.: Prentice-Hall, 1982.

Lieberman, M. A. Studies of Terminal Decline: Implications for a Developmental Theory of Personality. In J. E. Birren et al. (eds.), *Aging: A Challenge to Science and Society*, vol. 3, 73–79. New York: Oxford University Press, 1983.

———. Psychological Correlates of Impending Death: Some Preliminary Observations. *Journal of Gerontology*, 1965, *20*, 181–190.

List, J. A. Age and Schematic Differences in the Reliability of Eyewitness Testimony. *Developmental Psychology*, 1986, *22*, 50–58.

Lowenthal, M. F., Berkman, P. L., Beuhler, J. A., Pierce, R. C., Robinson, B. C., and Trier, M. L. *Aging and Mental Disorder in San Francisco*. San Francisco: Jossey-Bass, 1967.

Murphy, M. D., Sanders, R. E., Gabriesheski, A. S., and Schmitt, F. A. Metamemory in the Aged. *Journal of Gerontology*, 1981, *36*, 185–193.

Newmark, C. S. *Major Psychological Assessment Instruments*. Boston: Allyn and Bacon, 1985.

Obler, L. K., and Albert, M. L. Language Skills Across Adulthood. In J. E. Birren and K. W. Schaie (eds.), *Handbook of the Psychology of Aging* (2nd ed.), 463–474. New York: Van Nostrand Reinhold, 1985.

Okun, M. A. Adult Age and Cautiousness in Decision: A Review of the Literature. *Human Development*, 1976, *19*, 220–233.

Papalia, D. E. The Status of Several Conservation Abilities Across the Life-Span. *Human Development*, 1972, *15*, 229–243.

Perlmutter, M. What Is Memory Aging the Aging Of? *Developmental Psychology*, 1978, *14*, 330–345.

Petros, T., Tabor, L., Cooney, T., and Chabot, R. J. Adult Age Differences in Sensitivity to Semantic Structure of Pose. *Developmental Psychology*, 1983, *19*, 907–915.

Piaget, J. Intellectual Evolution from Adolescence to Adulthood. *Human Development*, 1972, *15*, 1–12.

Poon, L. W. Differences in Human Memory with Aging: Nature, Causes, and Clinical Implications. In J. E. Birren and K. W. Schaie (eds.), *Handbook of the Psychology of Aging* (2nd ed.), 427–463. New York: Van Nostrand Reinhold, 1985.

Powell, R. R. Psychological Effects of Exercise Therapy upon Institutionalized Geriatric Mental Patients. *Journal of Gerontology*, 1974, *29*, 157–161.

Reese, H. W., and Rodeheaver, D. Problem Solving and Complex Decision Making. In J. E. Birren and K. W. Schaie (eds.), *Handbook of the Psychology of Aging* (2nd ed.), 474–500. New York: Van Nostrand Reinhold, 1985.

Ribot, T. (1882), cited in G. Labouvier-Vief and D. A. Schell, Learning and Memory in Later Life. In B. B. Wolman (ed.), *Handbook of Developmental Psychology*, 427–462. New York: Van Nostrand Reinhold, 1985.

Riegel, K. F., and Riegel, R. M. Development, Drop, and Death. *Developmental Psychology*, 1972, *6*, 306–319.

Salthouse, T. A. Speed of Behavior and Its Implications for Cognition. In J. E. Birren and K. W. Schaie (eds.), *Handbook of the Psychology of Aging* (2nd ed.), 400–427. New York: Van Nostrand Reinhold, 1985.

———. *Adult Cognition: An Experimental Psychology of Aging.* New York: Springer-Verlag, 1982.

Salthouse, T. A., and Kail, R. Memory Development Throughout the Life Span. In P. B. Baltes and O. G. Brim (eds.), *Life-Span Development and Behavior*, vol. 5, 90–118. New York: Academic Press, 1983.

Sanders, J. A. C., Sterns, H. L., Smith, M., and Sanders, R. E. Modification of Concept Identification Performance in Older Adults. *Developmental Psychology*, 1975, *11*, 824–829.

Sanders, R. E., and Sanders, J. A. Long-Term Durability and Transfer of Enhanced Conceptual Performance in the Elderly. *Journal of Gerontology*, 1978, *33*, 408–412.

Schaie, K. W. The Seattle Longitudinal Study: A Twenty-One-Year Exploration of Psychometric Intelligence in Adulthood. In K. W. Schaie (ed.), *Longitudinal Studies of Adult Psychological Development.* New York: Guilford, 1982.

———. Psychological Changes from Midlife to Early Old Age: Implications for the Maintenance of Mental Health. *American Journal of Orthopsychiatry*, 1981, *51*, 199–219.

———. External Validity in Assessment of Intellectual Development in Adulthood. *Journal of Gerontology*, 1978, *33*, 696–701.

Schaie, K. W., and Hertzog, C. Fourteen-Year Cohort-Sequential Analyses of Adult Intellectual Development. *Developmental Psychology*, 1983, *19*, 531–544.

Schaie, K. W., and Labouvier-Vief, G. Generational Versus Ontogenetic Components of Change in Adult Cognitive Behavior: A Fourteen-Year Cross-Sequential Study. *Developmental Psychology*, 1974, *10*, 305–420.

Schaie, K. W., and Willis, S. L. Can Decline in Adult Intellectual Functioning Be Reversed? *Developmental Psychology*, 1986, *22*, 223–233.

Siegler, I. C., McCarty, S. M., and Logue, P. E. Wechsler Memory Scale Scores, Selective Attribution, and Distance from Death. *Journal of Gerontology*, 1982, *37*, 176–181.

Sinnott, J. D. Prospective/Intentional and Incidental Everyday Memory: Effects of Age and Passage of Time. *Psychology and Aging*, 1986, *1*, 110–116.

Skinner, B. F. Intellectual Self-Management in Old Age. *American Psychologist*, 1983, *38*, 239–245.

Smith, A. D. Age Differences in Encoding, Storage, and Retrieval. In L. W. Poon, J. L Fozard, L. S. Cermak, D. Arenberg, and L. W. Thompson (eds.), *New Directions in Memory and Aging.* Hillsdale, N.J.: Erlbaum, 1980.

Storandt, M. Age, Ability Level, and Method of Administering and Scoring the WAIS. *Journal of Gerontology*, 1977, *32*, 175–178.

Storck, P. A., Looft, W. R., and Hooper, F. H. Interrelationships Among Piagetian Tasks and Traditional Measures of Cognitive Abilities in Mature and Aged Adults. *Journal of Gerontology*, 1972, *27*, 461–465.

U.S. Bureau of the Census. *Statistical Abstract of the United States, 1986.* Washington, D.C., 1986.

Wallach, M. A., and Kogan, N. Aspects of Judgment and Decision Making: Interrelationships and Changes with Age. *Behavioral Science*, 1961, *6*, 23–36.

Walsh, D. A. Age Differences in Learning and Memory. In D. S. Woodruff and J. E. Birren (eds.), *Aging: Scientific Perspectives and Social Issues* (2nd ed.), 149–177. Monterey, Calif.: Brooks/Cole, 1983.

Warrington, E. K., and Silberstein, M. A. Questionnaire Technique for Investigating Very Long Term Memory. *Quarterly Journal of Experimental Psychology*, 1970, *22*, 508–512.

Waugh, N. C., Thomas, J. C., and Fozard, J. L. Retrieval Time from Different Memory Stores. *Journal of Gerontology*, 1978, *33*, 718–724.

Wechsler, D. *WAIS-R Manual.* New York: Psychological Corp., 1981.

———. *The Measurement and Appraisal of Adult Intelligence* (4th ed.). Baltimore: Williams and Wilkins, 1958.

West, R. L., Odom, R. D., and Aschkenasy, J. R. Perceptual Sensitivity and Conceptual Coordination in Children and Younger and Older Adults. *Human Development*, 1978, *21*, 334–345.

Wetherick, N. E. A Comparison of the Problem-Solving Ability of Young, Middle-Aged, and Old Subjects. *Gerontologia*, 1964, *9*, 164–178.

Willis, S. L. Towards an Educational Psychology of the Older Adult Learner: Intellectual and Cognitive Bases. In J. E. Birren and K. W. Schaie (eds.), *Handbook of the Psychology of Aging* (2nd ed.), 818–848. New York: Van Nostrand Reinhold, 1985.

Willis, S. L, and Baltes, P. B. Intelligence in Adulthood and Aging: Contemporary Issues. In L. W. Poon (ed.), *Aging in the 1980s*, 260–273. Washington, D.C.: American Psychological Association, 1980.

Willis, S. L., Blieszner, R., and Baltes, P. B. Intellectual Training Research in Aging: Modification of Performance on the Fluid Ability of Figural Relations. *Journal of Educational Psychology*, 1981, *73*, 41–51.

Wingfield, A., and Byrnes, D. L. *The Psychology of Human Memory.* New York: Academic Press, 1981.

Zelinski, E. M., Light, L. L., and Gilewski, M. J. Adult Age Differences in Memory for Prose: The Question of Sensitivity to Passage Structure. *Developmental Psychology*, 1984, *20*, 1181–1192.

Chapter 20

Ager, C. L., White, L. W., Mayberry, W. L., Crist, P. A., and Conrad, M. E. Creative Aging. *International Journal of Aging and Human Development*, 1980, *14*, 361–367.

Aizenberg, R., and Treas, J. The Family in Later Life. In J. E. Birren and K. W. Schaie (eds.), *Handbook of the Psychology of Aging* (2nd ed.), 169–190. New York: Van Nostrand Reinhold, 1985.

American Association of Retired Persons. *The Challenge of Retirement* (Retirement Planning Seminar material). Washington, D.C.: Action for Independent Maturity, 1977.

Ansell, E. F. Age and Ageism in Children's First Literature. *Educational Gerontology*, 1977, *2*, 255–274.

Arens, D. A. Well-Being and Widowhood: Interpreting Sex Differences. In B. F. Turner, *Sex-Related Differences in Aging*, 912–936. Englewood Cliffs, N.J.: Prentice-Hall, 1982.

Atchley, R. C. *The Social Forces in Later Life* (3rd ed.). Belmont, Calif.: Wadsworth, 1980.

———. *The Social Forces in Later Life* (2nd ed.). Belmont, Calif.: Wadsworth, 1977.

———. *The Sociology of Retirement.* Cambridge, Mass.: Schenkman, 1976.

Baker, P. M. The Status of Age: Preliminary Results. *Journal of Gerontology*, 1985, *40*, 506–508.

Barfield, R., and Morgan, J. Trends in Satisfaction with Retirement. *The Gerontologist*, 1978, *18*, 19–23.

Barnum, P. W. Discrimination Against the Aged in Young Children's Literature. *Elementary School Journal*, 1977, *4*, 301–306.

Barrow, G. M. *Aging, the Individual, and Society* (3rd ed.). St. Paul: West, 1986.

———. Personal Reactions to Growing Old (1976) (unpublished study), cited in G. M. Barrow. *Aging, the Individual, and Society* (3rd ed.). St. Paul: West, 1986.

Beck, S. H. Adjustment to and Satisfaction with Retirement. *Journal of Gerontology*, 1982, *37*, 616–624.

Belbin, R. M. The Implications of Gerontology for New Work Roles in Later Life. In J. E. Birren et al. (eds.), *Aging: A Challenge to Science and Society*, vol. 3, 214–225. New York: Oxford University Press, 1983.

Bengtson, V. L., and DeTerre, E. Aging and Family Relations. *Marriage and Family Review*, 1980, *3*, 51–76.

Bengtson, V. L., Kasschau, P. L., and Ragan, P. K. The Impact of Social Structure on Aging Individuals. In J. E. Birren and K. W. Schaie (eds.), *Handbook of the Psychology of Aging*, 327–355. New York: Van Nostrand Reinhold, 1977.

Bengtson, V. L., Reedy, M. N., and Gordon, C. Aging and Self-Conceptions: Personality Processes and Social Contexts. In J. E. Birren and K. W. Schaie (eds.), *Handbook of the Psychology of Aging* (2nd ed.), 544–585. New York: Van Nostrand Reinhold, 1985.

Bernardo, F. M. Widowhood Status in the United States: Perspectives on a Neglected Aspect of the Famiy Cycle. *Family Coordinator*, 1968, *17*, 191–203.

Bild, B. R., and Havighurst, R. J. Life Satisfaction. *The Gerontologist*, 1976, *16*, 70–75.

Blank, R. C. A Changing Worklife and Retirement Pattern: An Historical Perspective. In M. H. Morrison (ed.), *Economics of Aging: The Future of Retirement*, 1–60. New York: Van Nostrand Reinhold, 1982.

Blau, Z. *Old Age in a Changing Society*. New York: Watts, 1982.

Blazer, D., and Palmore, E. Religion and Aging in a Longitudinal Panel. *The Gerontologist*, 1976, *16*, 82–85.

Borges, M. A., and Dutton, C. Attitudes Towards Aging: Increasing Optimism Found with Age. *The Gerontologist*, 1976, *16*, 220–224.

Botwinick, J. *Aging and Behavior* (3rd ed.). New York: Springer, 1984.

Brown, A. S. Satisfying Relationships for Elderly and Their Patterns of Disengagement. *The Gerontologist*, 1974, *14*, 258–262.

Burkhauser, R. V., and Quinn, J. P. Planned and Actual Retirement: An Empirical Analysis. In Z. S. Blau (ed.), *Current Perspectives on Aging and the Life Cycle*, vol. 1, 147–169. Greenwich, Conn.: Jai, 1985.

Burns, G. Cited in R. N. Butler, Ageism. In H. Cox (ed.), *Aging*. Guilford, Conn.: Dushkin, 1985.

Burns, R. R. *The Self-Concept: Theory, Measurement, Development, and Behaviour*. New York: Longman, 1979.

Burrus-Bammel, L. L., and Bammel, G. Leisure and Recreation. In J. E. Birren and K. W. Schaie (eds.), *Handbook of the Psychology of Aging* (2nd ed.), 848–864. New York: Van Nostrand Reinhold, 1985.

Butler, R. N. The Life Review: An Interpretation of Reminiscence in the Aged. *Psychiatry*, 1963, *26*, 65–76.

California Association of Health Facilities. *Facts About California Nursing Homes*. Sacramento, Calif.: November 1985.

Cameron, P. Mood as an Indicant of Happiness: Age, Sex, Social Class, and Situational Differences. *Journal of Gerontology*, 1975, *30*, 216–224.

Carp, F. M. Background and Statement of Purpose. In F. M. Carp (ed.), *The Retirement Process*. Public Health Service pub. no. 1778. Washington, D.C.: U.S. Government Printing Office, 1968a.

———. Some Components of Disengagement. *Journal of Gerontology*, 1968b, *23*, 383–386.

Caspi, A., and Elder, G. H. Life Satisfaction in Old Age: Linking Social Psychology and History. *Psychology and Aging*, 1986, *1*, 18–27.

Cicirelli, V. G. Sibling Relationships in Adulthood. In L. W. Poon (ed.), *Aging in the 1980s*, 455–463. Washington, D.C.: American Psychological Association, 1980.

———. Social Services for Elderly in Relation to the Kin Network. *Report to the NRTA-AARP* (1979), cited in V. G. Cicirelli. Sibling Relationships in Adulthood. In L. W. Poon (ed.), *Aging in the 1980s*, 455–463. Washington, D.C.: American Psychological Association, 1980.

Clark, M. Cultural Values and Dependency in Later Life (1969), cited in L. E. Troll and V. L. Bengtson, Intergenerational Relations Throughout the Life Span. In B. B. Wolman (ed.), *Handbook of Developmental Psychology*, 890–911. Englewood Cliffs, N.J.: Prentice-Hall, 1982.

Clark, M. M., and Anderson, B. G. *Culture and Aging: An Anthropological Study of Older Americans*. Springfield, Ill.: Thomas, 1967.

Clark, R. L., and Spengler, J. J. *The Economics of Individual and Population Aging*. New York: Cambridge University Press, 1980.

Clark, R. L, and Sumner, D. A. Inflation and the Real Income of the Elderly: Recent Evidence and Expectations for the Future. *The Gerontologist*, 1985, *25*, 146–152.

Coberly, S., and Newquist, D. Hiring Older Workers: Employment Concerns. *Aging*. February–March 1984, 18–21.

Colson, E., and Scudder, T. Old Age in Guemb District, Zambia (1981), cited in C. L. Fry. Culture, Behavior, and Aging in the Comparative Perspective. In J. E. Birren and K. W. Schaie (eds.), *Handbook of the Psychology of Aging* (2nd ed.), 216–244. New York: Van Nostrand Reinhold, 1985.

Costa, P. T., McCrae, R. R., Zonderman, A. B., Barbano, H. E., Lebowitz, B., and Larson, D. M. Cross-Sectional Studies of Personality in a National Sample: Stability in Neuroticism, Extroversion, and Openness. *Psychology and Aging*, 1986, *1*, 144–150.

Cottrell, F., and Atchley, R. C. *Women in Retirement: A Preliminary Report*. Oxford, Ohio: Scripps Foundation, 1969.

Cowgill, D. O., and Holmes, L. *Aging and Modernization*. New York: Appleton Century-Croft, 1972.

Craft, J. A., Doctors, S. I., Shkop, Y. M., and Benecki, T. J. Simulated Management Perceptions, Hiring Decisions, and Age. *Aging and Work*, 1979, *2*, 95–102.

Cumming, E., and Henry, W. *Growing Old*. New York: Basic Books, 1961.

Cutler, N. E. Age Variations in the Dimensionality of Life Satisfaction. *Journal of Gerontology*, 1979, *34*, 573–578.

Donovan, R. Planning for an Aging Work Force. *Aging*, February–March 1984, 4–7.

Ebersole, P., and Hess, P. *Toward Healthy Aging: Human Needs and Nursing Response*. St. Louis: Mosby, 1981.

Eisdorfer, C. Conceptual Models of Aging. *American Psychologist*, 1983, *38*, 197–202.

Ekerdt, D. J., Bosse, R., and Levkoff, S. An Empirical Test for Phases of Retirement: Findings from the Normative Aging Study. *Journal of Gerontology*, 1985, *40*, 95–101.

Ekerdt, D. J., Bosse, R., and LoCastro, J. S. Claims That Retirement Improves Health. *Journal of Gerontology*, 1983, *38*, 231–236.

Erikson, E. *Youth and Society*. New York: Norton, 1963.

Evans, L., Ekerdt, D. J., and Bosse, R. Proximity to Retirement and Anticipatory Involvement: Findings from the Normative Aging Study. *Journal of Gerontology*, 1985, 40, 368–374.

Fenwick, R., and Baresi, C. Health Consequences of Marital-Status Change Among the Elderly: A Comparison of Cross-Sectional and Longitudinal Analyses. *Journal of Health and Social Behavior*, 1981, 22, 106–116.

Fillenbaum, G., et al. Determinants and Consequences of Retirement. *Journal of Gerontology*, 1985, 40, 85–94.

Flynn, C. B., Longino, Co F., Wiseman, R. F., and Biggar, J. C. The Redistribution of America's Older Population: Major National Migration Patterns for Three Census Decades, 1960–1980. *The Gerontologist*, 1985, 25, 292–296.

Foner, A., and Schwab, K. *Aging and Retirement.* Monterey, Calif.: Brooks/Cole, 1981.

Fry, C. L. Culture, Behavior, and Aging in the Comparative Perspective. In J. E. Birren and K. W. Schaie (eds.), *Handbook of the Psychology of Aging* (2nd ed.), 216–245. New York: Van Nostrand Reinhold, 1985.

George, L. K. *Role Transitions in Later Life.* Monterey, Calif.: Brooks/Cole, 1980.

Gerbner, G., Gross, L., Signorielli, N., and Morgan, M. Aging with Television: Images in Television Drama and Conceptions of Social Reality. *Journal of Communication*, 1980, 30, 37–47.

Gilford, R., and Bengtson, V. Measuring Marital Satisfaction in Three Generations: Positive and Negative Dimensions. *Journal of Marriage and the Family*, 1979, 41, 387–398.

Gilford, R., and Black, D. The Grandchild-Grandparent Dyad: Ritual or Relationship (1972), cited in L. E. Troll and V. L. Bengtson, Intergenerational Relations Throughout the Life Span. In B. B. Wolman (ed.), *Handbook of Developmental Psychology*, 890–911. Englewood Cliffs, N.J.: Prentice-Hall, 1982.

Gilgoff, H. How Old Is Too Old? Age Discrimination, Public Safety, and the Law. *Newsday*, February 23, 1986, p. 8.

Glenn, N. D., and McLanahan, S. The Effects of Offspring on the Psychological Well-Being of Older Adults. *Journal of Marriage and the Family*, 1981, 43, 409–421.

Glenn, N. D., and Weaver, C. N. Age, Cohort, and Reported Job Satisfaction in the United States. In Z. S. Blau (ed.), *Current Perspectives on Aging and the Life Cycle*, vol. 1, 89–111. Greenwich, Conn.: Jai, 1985.

Goldstein, M. C., Schuler, S., and Ross, J. L. Social and Economic Forces Affecting Inter-generational Relations in Extended Families in a Third World Country: A Cautionary Tale from South Asia. *Journal of Gerontology*, 1983, 38, 716–724.

Gordon, C., and Gaitz, C. M. Leisure Activities Late in the Life Span. In J. E. Birren et al. (eds.), *Aging: A Challenge to Science and Society*, vol. 3, 169–186. New York: Oxford University Press, 1983.

Gottesman, L., and Bourestom, N. Why Nursing Homes Do What They Do. *The Gerontologist*, 1974, 14, 501–506.

Granick, S., and Patterson, R. D. *Human Aging, 2: Age 11-up, Follow-up Biomedical and Behavioral Study.* Rockville, Md.: Public Health Service, 1971, pub. no. (HSM) 71–9037.

Grant, D. P. An Architect Discovers the Aged. *The Gerontologist*, 1970, 10, 275.

Guttman, D. The Cross-Cultural Perspective: Notes Toward a Comparative Psychology of Aging. In J. E. Birren and K. W. Schaie (eds.), *Handbook of the Psychology of Aging*, 302–326. New York: Van Nostrand Reinhold, 1977.

Harris, L., et al. *The Myth and Reality of Aging in America.* Washington, D.C.: National Council on the Aging, 1975.

Havighurst, R. J. *Ageing in Western Societies.* In D. Hobman (ed.). *The Social Challenge of Ageing.* New York: St. Martin's Press, 1978, 15–45.

Havighurst, R. J. Successful Aging. *The Gerontologist*, 1961, 1, 8–13.

Havighurst, R. J., and Albrecht, R. *Older People.* New York: Longmans, Green, 1953.

Havighurst, R. J., Neugarten, B., and Tobin, S. Disengagement and Patterns of Aging. In B. Neugarten (ed.), *Middle Age and Aging.* Chicago: University of Chicago Press, 1968.

Haviland, W. A. *Cultural Anthropology.* New York: Holt, Rinehart, and Winston, 1975.

Hellebrandt, F. Aging Among the Advantaged: A New Look at the Stereotype of the Elderly. *The Gerontologist*, 1980, 20, 404–414.

Hill, E. A., and Dorfman, L. T. Reaction of Housewives to the Retirement of Their Husbands. *Family Relations*, 1982, 31, 195–200.

Holmes, T., and Rahe, R. The Social Readjustment Rating Scale. *Journal of Psychosomatic Research*, 1967, 11, 213–218.

Holtzman, J. M., and Akiyama, H. What Children See: The Aged on Television in Japan and the United States. *The Gerontologist*, 1985, 25, 62–68.

Hoyt, D. R., et al. Life Satisfaction and Activity Theory: A Multidimensional Approach. *Journal of Gerontology*, 1980, 35, 935–941.

Jacobsohn, D. Attitudes Towards Work and Retirement Among Older Industrial Workers in Three Firms (1972), cited in R. M. Belbin. The Implications of Gerontology for New Work Roles in Later Life. In J. E. Birren et al. (eds.), *Aging: A Challenge to Science and Society*, vol. 3, 214–224. New York: Oxford University Press, 1983.

Jaslow, P. Employment, Retirement, and Morale Among Older Women. *Journal of Gerontology*, 1976, 31, 212–218.

Johnson, E. S., and Bursk, B. J. Relationships Between the Elderly and Their Adult Children. *The Gerontologist*, 1977, 17, 90–95.

Kahana, B. Social Behavior and Aging. In B. B. Wolman (ed.), *Handbook of Developmental Psychology*, 871–889. Englewood Cliffs, N.J.: Prentice-Hall, 1982.

———. The Young and Old View Each Other. *Geriatric Focus*, 1970, 9, no. 10.

Kahana, B., Kahana, E., and McLenigan, P. (1980), cited in B. Kahana, Social Behavior and Aging. In B. B. Wolman (ed.), *Handbook of Developmental Psychology*, 871–889. Englewood Cliffs, N.J.: Prentice-Hall, 1982.

Kahn, D. A Fresh Young Market Seen in Affluent Over-50s. *Newsday*, March 3, 1986, part 3, p. 9.

Keating, N., and Marshall, J. The Process of Retirement: The Rural Self-Employed. *The Gerontologist*, 1980, 20, 437–443.

Keating, N. C., and Cole, P. What Do I Do with Him 24 Hours a Day? Changes in the Housewife Role After Retirement. *The Gerontologist*, 1980, 20, 804–809.

Keating-Groen, N. Marital Satisfaction (1977), cited in B. F. Turner, Sex-Related Differences in Aging. In B. B. Wolman (ed.), *Handbook of Developmental Psychology*, 912–936. Englewood Cliffs, N.J.: Prentice-Hall, 1982.

Keith, P. M. Work, Retirement, and Well-Being Among Unmarried Men and Women. *The Gerontologist*, 1985, 25, 410–416.

Lowenthal, M., and Haven, C. Interaction and Adaptation: Intimacy as a Critical Variable. In B. Neugarten (ed.), *Middle Age and Aging.* Chicago: University of Chicago Press, 1968.

Kleiber, D. A., and Kelly, J. R. Leisure, Socialization, and the Life Cycle (1980), cited in L. L. Burrus-Bammel and G. Bammel, Leisure and Recreation. In J. E. Birren and K. W. Schaie (eds.), *Handbook of the Psychology of Aging* (2nd ed.), 848–863. New York: Van Nostrand Reinhold, 1985.

Kozma, A., and Stones, M. J. Predictors of Happiness. *Journal of Gerontology*, 1983, 38, 626–628.

Kutza, E. A. Towards an Aging Policy. *Social Policy*, May–June 1981.

La Greca, A. J., Steib, G. F., and Folts, W. E. Retirement Communities and Their Life Stages. *Journal of Gerontology*, 1985, *40*, 211–218.

Langer, E. J., and Rodin, J. The Effects of Choice and Enhanced Personal Responsibility for the Aged: A Field Experiment in an Institutional Setting. *Journal of Personality and Social Psychology*, 1976, *34*, 191–198.

Larson, R. Thirty Years of Research on the Subjective Well-Being of Older Americans. *Journal of Gerontology*, 1978, *33*, 109–125.

LaRue; A., Dessonville, C. and Jarvik, L. F. Aging and Mental Disorders. In J. E. Birren and K. W. Schaie (eds.), *Handbook of the Psychology of Aging* (2nd ed.), 664–703. New York: Van Nostrand Reinhold, 1985.

Lehr, U. Stereotypes of Aging and Age Norms. In J. E. Birren et al. (eds.), *Aging: A Challenge to Science and Society*, vol. 3, 101–112. New York: Oxford University Press, 1983.

Lemon, B. W., Bengtson, V. L., and Peterson, J. A. An Explanation of the Activity Theory of Aging: Activity Types and Life Satisfaction Among In-Movers to a Retirement Community. *Journal of Gerontology*, 1972, *27*, 511–523.

Levin, J., and Levin, W. C. *Ageism: Prejudice and Discrimination Against the Elderly*. Belmont, Calif.: Wadsworth, 1980.

LeVine, R. Adulthood and Aging. In Cross-Cultural Perspective (1978), cited in C. L. Fry in Culture, Behavior, and Aging in the Comparative Perspective. In J. E. Birren and K. W. Schaie (eds.), *Handbook of the Psychology of Aging* (2nd ed.), 216–245. New York: Van Nostrand Reinhold, 1985.

Liang, J. Sex Differences in Life Satisfaction Among the Elderly. *Journal of Gerontology*, 1982, *37*, 100–108.

Lieberman, M. A. Symposium—Long Term Care: Research, Policy, and Practice. *The Gerontologist*, 1974, *14*, 494–501.

Linn, M. W., Giurel, L., and Linn, B. S. Patient Outcome as a Measure of Quality of Nursing Home Care. *American Journal of Public Health*, 1977, *67*, 337–344.

Loeb, M. B., and Wasow, M. Sexuality in Nursing Homes. In I. Burnside (ed.), *Sexuality and Aging*, 35–41. Los Angeles: University of Southern California Press, 1985.

Lopata, H. Z. Widowhood: Social Norms and Social Integration. In J. E. Birren et al. (eds.), *Aging: A Challenge to Science and Society*, vol. 3, 155–169. New York: Oxford University Press, 1983.

———. *Women as Widows: Support Systems*. New York: Elsevier, 1979.

———. *Widowhood in an American City*. Cambridge, Mass.: Schenkman, 1973.

Lowenthal, M., and Haven, C. Interaction and Adaptation: Intimacy as a Critical Variable. *American Sociological Review*, 1968, *33*, 20–31.

Lowenthal, M. Thurnher, M., and Chiriboga, D. *Four Stages of Life*. San Francisco: Jossey-Bass, 1975.

Ludeman, K. The Sexuality of the Older Person: Review of the Literature. *The Gerontologist*, 1981, *21*, 203–208.

Maas, H. S., and Kuypers, J. A. *From Thirty to Seventy: A Forty-Year Longitudinal Study of Adult Life Styles and Personality*. San Francisco: Jossey-Bass, 1974.

Maddox, G. Fact and Artifact: Evidence Bearing On Disengagement Theory. In E. Palmore (ed.), *Normal Aging*. Durham, N.C.: Duke University Press, 1970.

———. Persistence of Life Style Among the Elderly: A Longitudinal Study of Patterns of Social Activity in Relation to Life Satisfaction (1966). In B. L. Neugarten (ed.), *Middle Age and Aging*. Chicago: University of Chicago Press, 1968.

Maeda, D. Ageing in Eastern Society. In D. Hobman (ed.), *The Social Challenge of Ageing*, 45–73. New York: St. Martin's Press, 1978.

Mancini, J. A. Family Relationships and Morale Among People 65 Years of Age and Older. *American Journal of Orthopsychiatry*, 1981, *49*, 292–300.

Manney, J. D. *Aging*. Washington, D.C.: Department of Health, Education, and Welfare, 1975.

Markides, K. S. Aging, Religiosity, and Adjustment: A Longitudinal Analysis. *Journal of Gerontology*, 1983, *38*, 621–625.

Markides, K. S., and Martin, H. W. A Causal Model of Life Satisfaction Among the Elderly. *Journal of Gerontology*, 1979, *34*, 36–93.

Masters, W. H., and Johnson, V. E. *Human Sexual Response*. Boston: Little, Brown, 1966.

Matthews, S. H., and Sprey, J. Adolescents' Relationships with Grandparents: An Empirical Contribution to Conceptual Clarification. *Journal of Gerontology*, 1985, *40*, 621–626.

Maxwell, R. J., and Silverman, P. Information and Esteem. *Aging and Human Development*, 1970, *1*, 127–146.

McAuley, W., and Blieszner, R. Selection of Long-Term Care Arrangements. *The Gerontologist*, 1985, *25*, 188–193.

McAvoy, L. The Leisure Preferences, Problems, and Needs of the Elderly. *Journal of Leisure Research*, 1979, *11*, 40–47.

McCrae, R. R., and Costa, P. T. Psychological Maturity and Subjective Well-Being: Toward a New Synthesis. *Developmental Psychology*, 1983, *19*, 243–248.

McPherson, B., and Guppy, N. Pre-Retirement Life-Style and the Degree of Planning for Retirement. *Journal of Gerontology*, 1979, *34*, 254–263.

McTavish, D. G. Perceptions of Old People: A Review of Research, Methodologies, and Findings. *The Gerontologist*, 1971, *11*, 90–101.

Mercer, W. M. Employer Attitudes: Implications of an Aging Work Force (1981), cited in R. Stagner, *Aging in Industry*. In J. E. Birren and K. W. Schaie (eds.), *Handbook of the Psychology of Aging* (2nd ed.), 789–817. New York: Van Nostrand Reinhold, 1985.

Metropolitan Life Insurance Co. Projections of Population Growth at the Older Ages. *Statistical Bulletin*, April–June 1984, 8–10.

Mindel, C. H., and Vaughn, C. E. A Multidimensional Approach to Religiosity and Disengagement. *Journal of Gerontology*, 1978, *33*, 103–308.

Missinne, L. E. Aging in Bakongo Culture. *International Journal of Aging and Human Development*, 1980, *11*, 283–295.

Mitchell, J., Wilson, K., Revicki, D., and Parker, L. Children's Perceptions of Aging: A Multidimensional Approach to Differences by Age, Sex, and Race. *The Gerontologist*, 1985, *25*, 182–187.

Moberg, D. O. Religion and the Aging Family. *Family Coordinator*, 1972, *21*, 47–60.

Montgomery, R. Impact of Institutional Care Policies on Family Integration. *The Gerontologist*, 1982, *22*, 54–58.

Moos, R. H., and Lemke, S. Specialized Living Environments for Older People. In J. E. Birren and K. W. Schaie (eds.), *Handbook of the Psychology of Aging* (2nd ed.), 864–891. New York: Van Nostrand Reinhold, 1985.

Morrison, M. H. *Economics of Aging: The Future of Retirement*. New York: Van Nostrand Reinhold, 1982.

Moss, H. A., and Susman, E. J. Longitudinal Study of Personality Development. In O. G. Brim and J. Kagan (eds.), *Constancy and Change in Human Development*. Cambridge, Mass.: Harvard University Press, 1980.

Mussen, P., Honzik, M. P., and Eichorn, D. H. Early Adult Antecedents of Life Satisfaction at Age 70. *Journal of Gerontology*, 1982, *37*, 316–322.

Myles, J. F. Institutionalization and Sick Role Identification Among the Elderly. *American Sociological Review*, 1978, *43*, 508–521.

National Council on the Aging. *Fact Book on Aging: A Profile on America's Older Population.*

Washington, D.C.: National Council on the Aging, 1978.

———. *The Myth and Reality of Aging in America*. Washington, D.C.: National Council on the Aging, 1975.

Neugarten, B. L. Personality and Aging. In J. E. Birren and K. W. Schaie (eds.), *Handbook of the Psychology of Aging*. New York: Van Nostrand Reinhold, 1977.

———. A Developmental View of Adult Personality. In J. E. Birren (ed.), *Relations of Development and Aging*, 176–208. Springfield, Ill.: Thomas, 1964.

Neugarten, B. L., Havighurst, R. J., and Tobin, S. S. Personality and Patterns of Aging. In B. L. Neugarten (ed.), *Middle Age and Aging*. Chicago: University of Chicago Press, 1968.

Neugarten, B. L., and Weinstein, K. The Changing American Grandparent. *Journal of Marriage and the Family*, 1964, *26*, 199–204.

Neugarten, B. L., Havighurst, R. J., and Tobin, S. S. The Measurement of Life Satisfaction. *Journal of Gerontology*, 1961, *16*, 134–143.

Pacovski, V., and Hermanova, H. Aging and the Worker. In J. E. Birren et al. (eds.), *Aging: A Challenge to Science and Society*, vol. 3, 186–192. New York: Oxford University Press, 1983.

Palmore, E., Cleveland, W. P., Nowlin, J. G., Ramm, D., and Siegler, I. C. Stress and Adaptation in Later Life. *Journal of Gerontology*, 1979, *34*, 841–851.

Palmore, E. B., George, L. K., and Fillenbaum, G. G. Predictors of Retirement. *Journal of Gerontology*, 1982, *37*, 733–742.

Palmore, E., and Kivett, V. Change in Life Satisfaction: A Longitudinal Study of Persons Aged 46–70. *Journal of Gerontology*, 1977, *32*, 311–316.

Palmore, E., and Manton, K. Modernization and the Status of the Aged: International Correlations. *Journal of Gerontology*, 1974, *29*, 205–210.

Pampel, F. C. Determinants of Labor Force Participation Rates of Aged Males in Developed and Developing Nations, 1965–1975. In Z. S. Blau (ed.), *Current Perspectives on Aging and the Life Cycle*, vol. 1, 243–275. Greenwich, Conn.: Jai, 1985.

Parnes, H. (ed.). *Work and Retirement*. Cambridge, Mass.: M.I.T. Press, 1981.

Parnes, H., and Less, L. Variation in Selected Forms of Leisure Activity Among Elderly Males. In Z. S. Blau (ed.), *Current Perspectives on Aging and the Life Cycle*, vol. 1, 223–243. Greenwich, Conn.: Jai, 1985.

Passuth, P. M., and Cook, F. L. Effects of Television Viewing on Knowledge and Attitudes About Older Adults: A Critical Reexamination. *The Gerontologist*, 1985, *25*, 69–77.

Peck, R. C. Psychological Developments in the Second Half of Life. In B. L. Neugarten (ed.), *Middle Age and Aging*. Chicago: University of Chicago Press, 1968.

Pfeiffer, E. Health, Sexuality, and Aging. In J. E. Birren et al. (eds.), *Aging: A Challenge to Science and Society*, vol. 3, 67–73. New York: Oxford University Press, 1983.

———. Sexual Behavior in Old Age. In E. Pfeiffer and E. W. Busse (eds.), *Behavior and Adaptation in Late Life*. Boston: Little, Brown, 1969.

Pfeiffer, E., and Davis, G. Determinants of Sexual Behavior in Middle and Old Age. *Journal of the American Geriatrics Society*, 1972, *20*, 151–158.

Pfeiffer, E., Verwoerdt, A., and Davis, G. Sexual Behavior in Middle Life. *American Journal of Psychiatry*, 1972, *128*, 1262–1267.

Pihlblad, C. T., and Adams, D. Widowhood, Social Participation, and Life Satisfaction. *Aging and Human Development*, 1972, *3*, 323–330.

Poon, L. W. (ed.). Introduction. In *Aging in the 1980s*, 3–4. Washington, D.C.: American Psychological Association, 1980.

Powers, E. A., Keith, P., and Goudy, W. H. Family Relationships and Friendships (1975), cited in R. C. Atchley, *The Social Forces in Later Life*. Belmont, Calif.: Wadsworth, 1977.

Regnier, V., and Gelwicks, L. E. Preferred Supportive Services for Middle to Higher Income Retirement Housing. *The Gerontologist*, 1981, *21*, 54–58.

Richman, J. The Foolishness and Wisdom of Age: Attitudes Toward the Elderly as Reflected in Jokes. *The Gerontologist*, 1977, *17*, 210–219.

Riley, M. W., and Foner, A. *Aging and Society: An Inventory of Research Findings*, vol. 1. New York: Russell Sage Foundation, 1968.

Robertson, J. F. Grandmotherhood: A Study of Role Conceptions. *Journal of Marriage and the Family*, 1977, *33*, 165–174.

———. Significance of Grandparents: Perceptions of Young Adult Grandchildren. *The Gerontologist*, 1976, *16*, 137–140.

———. Interaction in Three-Generation Families, Parents as Mediators: Towards a Theoretical Perspective. *International Journal of Aging and Human Development*, 1975, *6*, 103–110.

Robinson, J. P., and Shaper, P. R. *Measures of Social Psychological Attitudes*. Ann Arbor: Institute for Social Research, University of Michigan, 1973.

Rodin, J., and Langer, E. J. Long-Term Effects of a Control-Relevant Intervention with the Institutionalized Aged. *Journal of Personality and Social Psychology*, 1977, *35*, 897–902.

Rogers, G. T. Nonmarried Women Approaching Retirement: Who Are They and When Do They Retire? In Z. S. Blau (ed.), *Current Perspectives on Aging and the Life Cycle*, 169–193. Greenwich, Conn.: Jai, 1985.

Rosen, B. Management Perception of Older Employees. *Monthly Labor Review*, 1978, *101*, 33–35.

Rosenberg, G. S. and Anspach, D. F. Sibling Solidarity in the Working Class. *Journal of Marriage and the Family*, 1973, *35*, 108–113.

Rosenmayr, L. Changing Values and Positions of Aging in Western Culture. In J. E. Birren and K. W. Schaie (eds.), *Handbook of the Psychology of Aging* (2nd ed.), 190–216. New York: Van Nostrand Reinhold, 1985.

Rubenstein, C. V., and Shaver, P. *In Search of Intimacy*. New York: Delacorte, 1982.

Rubenstein, C. V., Shaver, P., and Peplau, L. A. Loneliness. *Human Nature*, 1979, *2*, 58–65.

Runback, R. B., and Carr, T. S. Schema Guided Information Search in Stereotyping of the Elderly. *Journal of Applied Social Psychology*, 1984, *14*, 57–68.

Schaie, K. W. Psychological Changes from Midlife to Early Old Age: Implications for the Maintenance of Mental Health. *American Journal of Orthopsychiatry*, 1981, *51*, 199–219.

Schaie, K. W., and Parham, I. A. Stability of Adult Personality: Fact or Fable? *Journal of Personality and Social Psychology*, 1976, *34*, 146–158.

Schlossberg, N. K. Older Adults and the Media. *National Forum*, Fall 1982.

Schulz, R. Emotion and Affect. In J. E. Birren and K. W. Schaie (eds.), *Handbook of the Psychology of Aging* (2nd ed.), 531–544. New York: Van Nostrand Reinhold, 1985.

Scott, J. Siblings and Other Kin. In T. Brubaker (ed.), *Family Relationships in Later Life*, 47–62. Beverly Hills, Calif.: Sage Publications, 1983.

Shanas, E. The Family as a Social Support System in Old Age (1979). In S. H. Zarit (ed.), *Readings in Aging and Death: Contemporary Perspectives* (2nd ed.), 139–144. New York: Harper and Row, 1982.

———. Family Relations of Older People (1961), cited in P. Ebersole and P. Hess. *Toward Healthy Aging: Human Needs and Nursing Response*. St. Louis: Mosby, 1981.

————. *A National Survey of the Aged: Final Report to the Administration on Aging.* Washington, D.C.: U.S. Department of Health, Education, and Welfare, 1978.

Shanas, E., Townsend, P., Wedderburn, D., Friis, H., Milhoj, P., and Stehouwer, J. *Old People in Three Industrial Societies.* New York: Atherton, 1968.

Shuttlesworth, G., Rubin, A., and Duffy, M. Families vs. Institutions: Incongruent Role Expectations in the Nursing Home. *The Gerontologist,* 1982, *22,* 200–207.

Siegler, I. C., George, L. K, and Okun, M. A. Cross-Sequential Analysis of Adult Personality. *Developmental Psychology,* 1979, *15,* 350–351.

Simpson, I. H., Back, K. W., and McKinney, J. C. Continuity of Work and Retirement Activities and Self-Evaluation. In I. H. Simpson and J. C. McKinney (eds.), *Social Aspects of Aging.* Durham, N.C.: Duke University Press, 1966.

Smith, K. F., and Bengtson, V. L. Positive Consequences of Institutionalization: Solidarity Between Elderly Parents and Their Middle-Aged Children. *The Gerontologist,* 1979, *19,* 238–247.

Spencer, D. G., and Steers, R. M. The Influence of Personal Factors and Perceived Work Experiences on Employee Turnover and Absenteeism (1980), cited in J. E. Birren and K. W. Schaie (eds.), *Handbook of the Psychology of Aging* (2nd ed.), 789–817. New York: Van Nostrand Reinhold, 1985.

Spilka, B., Hood, R. W., and Gorsuch, R. L. *The Psychology of Religion: An Empirical Approach.* Englewood Cliffs, N.J.: Prentice-Hall, 1985.

Stagner, R. Aging in Industry. In J. E. Birren and K. W. Schaie (eds.), *Handbook of the Psychology of Aging* (2nd ed.), 789–818. New York: Van Nostrand Reinhold, 1985.

Starr, B. D., and Weiner, M. B. The Starr-Weiner Report on Sex and Sexuality in the Mature Years. New York: McGraw-Hill, 1982.

Stevens-Long, J. *Adult Life* (2nd ed.). Palo Alto, Calif.: Mayfield, 1984.

Stimson, A., Wase, J., and Stimson, J. Sexuality and Self-Esteem Among the Aged. *Research on Aging,* 1981, *3,* 228–239.

Streib, G., and Schneider, C. *Retirement in American Society.* Ithaca, N.Y.: Cornell University Press, 1971.

Stroebe, M. S., and Stroebe, W. Who Suffers More? Sex Differences in Health Risks of the Widowed. *Psychological Bulletin,* 1983, *93,* 279–301.

Szinovacz, M. Introduction: Research on Women's Retirement. In M. Szinovacz (ed.), *Women's Retirement.* Beverly Hills, Calif.: Sage, 1982.

Tallmer, M., and Kutner, B. Disengagement and Morale. *The Gerontologist,* 1970, *10,* 317–320.

Thomae, H. Is There a Functional Age for Personality? In J. E. Birren et al. (eds.), *Aging: A Challenge to Science and Society,* vol. 3, 329–338. New York: Oxford University Press, 1983.

Tobin, S., and Lieberman, M. (1976). Last Home for the Aged, cited in P. Ebersole and P. Hess, *Toward Healthy Aging: Human Needs and Nursing Response.* St. Louis: Mosby, 1981.

Troll, L. E. Grandparenting. In L. W. Poon (ed.), *Aging in the 1980s,* 475–481. Washington, D.C.: American Psychological Association, 1980.

Troll, L. E., and Bengtson, V. Intergenerational Relations Throughout the Life Span. In B. B. Wolman (ed.), *Handbook of Developmental Psychology,* 890–912. Englewood Cliffs, N.J.: Prentice-Hall, 1982.

Turner, B. F. Sex-Related Differences in Aging. In B. B. Wolman (ed.), *Handbook of Developmental Psychology,* 912–931. Englewood Cliffs, N.J.: Prentice-Hall, 1982.

U.S. Bureau of the Census. *Statistical Abstracts of the United States, 1985.* Washington, D.C., 1985.

Ward, R. A. *The Aging Experience: An Introduction to Social Gerontology* (2nd ed.). New York: Harper and Row, 1984.

Warner, R. A., and McDonald, L. Ageism in the Labor Market: Estimating Earnings Discrimination Against Older Workers. *Journal of Gerontology,* 1983, *38,* 738–745.

Watson, W. H. *Aging and Social Behavior.* Monterey, Calif.: Wadsworth, 1982.

Wentowski, G. J. Older Women's Perceptions of Great-Grandmotherhood: A Research Note. *The Gerontologist,* 1985, *25,* 593–596.

Winn, R. L., and Newton, N. Sexuality in Aging: A Study of 106 Cultures. *Archives of Sexual Behavior,* 1982, *11,* 283–299.

Wood, V., and Robertson, J. F. The Significance of Grandparenthood. In J. Gubrium (ed.), *Time, Roles, and Self in Old Age.* New York: Behavioral Publications, 1976.

Woodruff, D. S., and Birren, J. E. Age Changes and Cohort Differences in Personality. *Developmental Psychology,* 1972, *6,* 252–259.

Wright, J. D., and Hamilton, F. F. Work Satisfaction and Age: Some Evidence for "Job Change" Hypothesis. *Social Forces,* 1978, *56,* 1140–1158.

Chapter 21

Albert, M. V. L., and Steffl, B. M. Loss, Grief, and Death in Old Age. In B. M. Steffl (ed.), *Handbook of Gerontological Nursing,* 73–87. New York: Van Nostrand Reinhold, 1984.

Barrow, G. M. *Aging, the Individual, and Society* (3rd ed.). St. Paul: West, 1986.

Bengtson, V. L, Cuellar, J. B., and Regan, P. K. Stratum Contrasts and Similarities in Attitudes Towards Death. *Journal of Gerontology,* 1977, *32,* 76–88.

Bluebond-Langner, M. The Meanings of Death to Children. In H. Feifel (ed.), *New Meanings of Death.* New York: McGraw-Hill, 1977.

Botwinick, J. *Aging and Behavior* (3rd ed.). New York: Springer, 1984.

Bryer, K. B. The Amish Way of Death. *American Psychologist,* 1979, *34,* 255–261.

Bugen, L. A. (ed.). *Death and Dying,* 291–298. Dubuque, Iowa: Brown, 1979.

Bugen, L. A. Death Education: Perspectives for Schools and Communities. In L. A. Bugen (ed.), *Death and Dying,* 237–249. Dubuque, Iowa: Brown, 1979.

————. Human Grief: A Model for Prediction and Intervention. *American Journal of Orthopsychiatry,* 1977, *2,* 196–206.

Burnside, I. M. Depression and Grief in the Aged Person. In I. M. Burnside (ed.), *Nursing and the Aged,* 122–136. New York: McGraw-Hill, 1981.

Butler, R. N. Successful Aging and the Role of the Life Review (1974). In *Aging* (3rd ed.), 15–21. Guilford, Conn.: Dushkin, 1983.

————. *Why Survive? Being Old in America.* New York: Harper and Row, 1975.

————. The Life Review: An Interpretation of Reminiscence in the Aged. *Psychiatry,* 1963, *26,* 65–76.

Callahan, E. J., Brasted, W. S., and Granados, J. L. Fetal Loss and Sudden Infant Death: Grieving and Adjustment for Families. In E. J. Callahan and K. A. McCluskey (eds.), *Life-Span Developmental Psychology: Nonnormative Events,* 145–166. New York: Academic Press, 1983.

Carey, R. G. Living Until Death: A Program of Service and Research for the Terminally Ill. In E. Kübler-Ross (ed.), *Death: The Final Stages of Growth,* 75–86. Englewood Cliffs, N.J.: Prentice-Hall, 1975.

Carey, R. G., and Posavac, E. J. Attitudes of Physicians on Disclosing Information to and Maintaining Life for Terminal Patients. *Omega,* 1978, *9,* 66–77.

Cassell, E. J. Dying in a Technological Society (1974). In L. A. Bugen and D. S. Davenport. A Closer Look at the "Healthy" Grieving Process. *Personnel and Guidance Journal,* 1981, *59,* 332–335.

Childers, P., and Wimmer, M. The Concept of Death in Early Childhood. *Child Development*, 1971, *42*, 705–715.

Clayton, P. J., Halikes, J. A., and Maurice, W. L., The Bereavement of the Widowed. *Diseases of the Nervous System*, 1971, *32*, 597–604.

Cytrynbaum, S., Blum, L., Patrick, R., Stein, J., Wasdner, D., and Wilk, C. Midlife Development: A Personality and Social Systems Perspective. In L. W. Poon (ed.), *Aging in the 1980s*, 463–475. Washington, D.C.: American Psychological Association, 1980.

Diekelmann, N. *Primary Health Care of the Well Adult*. New York: McGraw-Hill, 1977.

Ebersole, P., and Hess, P. *Toward Healthy Aging*. St. Louis: Mosby, 1981.

Epstein, G., Weitz, L., Roback, H., and McKee, E. Research on Bereavement: A Selective and Critical Review (1975). In L. A. Bugen (ed.), *Death and Dying*, 55–65. Dubuque, Iowa: Brown, 1979.

Farley, F. H. The Hypostatization of Death in Adolescence. *Adolescence*, 1979, *14*, 341–351.

Fry, C. L. Culture, Behavior, and Aging in Comparative Perspective. In J. E. Birren and K. W. Schaie (eds.), *Handbook of the Psychology of Aging* (2nd ed.), 216–235. New York: Van Nostrand Reinhold, 1985.

Glaser, B. G., and Strauss, A. *Time for Dying*. New York: Macmillan, 1968.

Hardt, D. V. *Death: The Final Frontier*. Englewood Cliffs, N.J.: Prentice-Hall, 1979.

Hinton, J. Speaking of Death with the Dying. In E. Shneidman (ed.), *Death: Current Perspectives*. Palo Alto, Calif.: Mayfield, 1976.

———. *Dying*. Baltimore: Penguin, 1972.

Holden, C. Hospices: For the Dying, Relief from Pain and Fear. *Science*, July 30, 1976.

Ingram, D., and Barry, J. National Statistics on Deaths in Nursing Homes: Interpretations and Implications. *The Gerontologist*, 1977, *17*, 303–308.

Kalish, R. *Death, Grief, and Caring Relationships*. Monterey, Calif.: Brooks/Cole, 1981.

———. The Elderly Confront Death (1976). In R. A. Kalish, *The Later Years: Social Applications of Gerontology*, 83–90. Monterey, Calif.: Brooks/Cole, 1977.

Kalish, R., and Reynolds, D. *Death and Ethnicity: A Psychocultural Study*. Los Angeles: University of Southern California Press, 1976.

Kastenbaum, R. Dying and Death: A Life-Span Approach. In J. E. Birren and K. W. Schaie (eds.), *Handbook of the Psychology of Aging* (2nd ed.), 619–639. New York: Van Nostrand Reinhold, 1985.

———. Death, Dying, and Bereavement in Old Age. *Aged Care and Services Review*, May–June, 1978.

———. *Death, Society, and Human Experience*. St. Louis: Mosby, 1977.

———. Time and Death in Adolescence. In H. Feifel (ed.), *The Meaning of Death*, 99–113. New York: McGraw-Hill, 1959.

Kastenbaum, R., and Aisenberg, R. *The Psychology of Death*. New York: Springer, 1976.

Kastenbaum, R., and Costa, P. T. Psychological Perspectives on Death. *Annual Review of Psychology*, 1977, *28*, 225–249.

Kieffer, G. H. Ethical Issues in the Life Sciences. Unpublished manuscript. 1977.

Koocher, G. Childhood, Death, and Cognitive Development. *Developmental Psychology*, 1973, *9*, 369–375.

Koza, P. E. Euthanasia: Some Legal Considerations (1977). In L. A. Bugen (ed.), *Death and Dying*, 311–323. Dubuque, Iowa: Brown, 1979.

Kübler-Ross, E. *Death: The Final Stage of Growth*. Englewood Cliffs, N.J.: Prentice-Hall, 1975.

———. *Questions and Answers on Death and Dying*. New York: Macmillan, 1974.

———. On Death and Dying. *Journal of the American Medical Association*, February 1972.

———. *On Death and Dying*. New York: Macmillan, 1969.

Kübler-Ross, E., and Goleman, D. The Child Will Always Be There: Real Love Doesn't Die. *Psychology Today*, 1976, *10*, 48–52.

LaRue, A., Dessonville, C., and Jarvik, L. F. Aging and Mental Disorders. In J. E. Birren and K. W. Schaie (eds.), *Handbook of the Psychology of Aging* (2nd ed.), 664–703. New York: Van Nostrand Reinhold, 1985.

Lindemann, E. Symptomatology and Management of Acute Grief (1944). In L. A. Bugen (ed.), *Death and Dying*, 7–17. Dubuque, Iowa: Brown, 1979.

Maddison, D. C., and Walker, W. L. Factors Affecting the Outcome of Conjugal Bereavement. *British Journal of Psychiatry*, 1967, *113*, 1057–1067.

Marshall, V. *Last Chapters: A Sociology of Aging and Dying*. Monterey, Calif.: Brooks/Cole, 1980.

McCrae, R. R., Bartone, P. T., and Costa, P. T. Age, Personality, and Self-Reported Health. *International Journal of Aging and Human Development*, 1976, *6*, 49–58.

Mullins, L. C., and Lopez, M. A. Death Anxiety Among Nursing Home Residents: A Comparison of the Young-Old and Old-Old. *Death Education*, Spring 1982, *6*, 75–86.

Nagy, M. The Child's View of Death. In H. Feifel (ed.), *The Meaning of Death*. New York: McGraw-Hill, 1959.

———. The Child's Theories Concerning Death. *Journal of Genetic Psychology*, 1948, *73*, 3–27.

New York Times. Death of a Character Is "Sesame Street" Topic. *New York Times*, August 31, 1983.

Parkes, C. M. *Bereavement: Studies of Grief in Later Life*. New York: International Universities Press, 1972.

Pattison, E. *The Experience of Dying*. Englewood Cliffs, N.J.: Prentice-Hall, 1977.

Ross, K., Braga, J., and Braga, L. Z. Omega. In E. Kübler-Ross (ed.), *Death: The Final Stage of Growth*, 164–166. Englewood Cliffs, N.J.: Prentice-Hall, 1975.

Rubin, S. A Two-Track Model of Bereavement: Theory and Application in Research. *American Journal of Orthopsychiatry*, 1981, *51*, 101–109.

Ryder, C. F., and Ross, D. M. Terminal Care: Issues and Alternatives. *Public Health Reports*, 1977, *92*, 20–29.

Saunders, C. St. Christopher's Hospice. In E. Schniedman (ed.), *Death: Current Perspectives*. Palo Alto, Calif.: Mayfield, 1977.

Saxon, S. V., and Etten, M. J. *Physical Change and Aging*. New York: Tiresias, 1978.

———. *Death: Current Perspectives*. Palo Alto, Calif.: Mayfield, 1973.

Schoenberg, B., Carr, A. C., Jutscher, A. H., Peretz, D., and Goldberg, I. K. (eds.). *Anticipatory Grief*. New York: Columbia University Press, 1974.

Schulz, R. *The Psychology of Death, Dying, and Bereavement*. Reading, Mass.: Addison-Wesley, 1978.

Schulz, R., and Aderman, D. How the Medical Staff Copes with Dying Patients: A Critical Review (1976). In L. A. Bugen (ed.), *Death and Dying*, 179–188. Dubuque, Iowa: Brown, 1979.

———. Clinical Research and the Stages of Dying. *Omega: Journal of Death and Dying*, 1974, *5*, 137–143.

Shneidman, E. The College Student and Death. In H. Feifel (ed.), *New Meanings of Death*, 67–88. New York: McGraw-Hill, 1977.

Spilka, B., Hood, R. W., and Goresuch, R. L. *The Psychology of Religion: An Empirical Approach*. Englewood Cliffs, N.J.: Prentice-Hall, 1985.

Steele, R. L. Dying, Death, and Bereavement Among the Maya Indians of Mesoamerica. *American Psychologist*, 1977, *32*, 1060–1068.

U.S. News & World Report. A New Understanding About Dying. *U.S. News & World Report*, July 11, 1983, 62–65.

Ward, R. A. *The Aging Experience: An Introduction to Gerontology* (2nd ed.). New York: Harper and Row, 1984.

———. Age and Acceptance of Euthanasia. *Journal of Gerontology,* 1980, *35,* 421–431.

Wass, H., and Myers, J. E. Psychosocial Aspects of Death Among the Elderly: A Review of the Literature. *Personnel and Guidance Journal,* 1982, *61,* 131–137.

Weisman, A. D. *On Dying and Denying: A Psychiatric Study of Terminality.* New York: Behavioral Publications, 1972.

Weisman, A. D., and Kastenbaum, R. *The Psychological Autopsy: A Study of the Terminal Phase of Life.* Community Mental Health Journal Monograph. New York: Behavioral Publications, 1968.

Winget, C., Kapp, F. T., and Yeaworth, R. C. Attitudes Toward Euthanasia. *Journal of Medical Ethics,* 1977, *3,* 18–25.

T A B L E S

TABLE 1

Major Genetic and Chromosomal Disorders

Disorder	Description/ Identification	Incidence	Cause
Cleft Palate and Cleft Lip	Two sides of upper lip or palate fail to close	One in 700 births or about 5,000 per year	Multifactorial; multiple causes including genetic, prenatal insults, malnutrition, and drugs
Club Foot	Ankle and foot deformities; foot twisted in and down	One in 400 births or about 9,000 cases per year; twice as frequent in boys	Multifactorial
Congenital Heart Defects	Heart defects of varying degrees of severity	20,000 cases per year or one in 175 births	Multifactorial; often cause is unknown
Cystic Fibrosis	Enzyme deficiency causes mucus obstructions and problems in controlling production of mucus, saliva and sweat; often diagnosed through analysis of perspiration which contains high salt content	One in 1,000 births	Two abnormal recessive genes on chromosome 7
Diabetes I (Juvenile-onset)	Pancreatic problem brought on by lack of insulin	Ten percent of all cases; one child in 2,500	Multifactorial; 20 to 50 percent concordance in monozygotic twins; associated with certain virus and infections
Diabetes II (Adult-onset)	Pancratic problem brought on by lack of insulin receptors or defective insulin	About 90 percent of all cases; five million Americans with disease	Multifactorial; nearly 100 percent concordance in monozygotic twins; associated with diet and obesity
Down's Syndrome	Distinctive physical appearance allows for early identification	One in 600 births increasing with age of parents, especially mother; one in 30 for women in early 40s	Chromosomal abnormality; extra chromosome #21
Hemophilia	Lack of blood clotting	One in 10,000 births	Sex linked disorder
Huntington's Chorea	Deterioration of central nervous system and body during middle age	Extremely rare	Dominant gene on chromosome 4

Problems	Treatment	Prenatal Detection	Carrier Detection
Speech and cosmetic problems	Surgery	No	No
Walking difficulties	Casts and/or surgery	No	Possible
Depends upon severity of disorder; can be fatal	surgery	Sometimes through ultrasound	No
Respiratory and digestive problems; most die in adolescence or early adulthood	Advances in medical care have raised hopes for a more normal life span	Yes*	Yes*
Depending upon severity, diabetes may lead to serious medical problems, blindness, and death	Administration of insulin, dietary restrictions	No	No
Depending upon severity, diabetes may lead to serious medical problems, blindness, and death	Administration of insulin, dietary restrictions	No	No
Moderate to severe retardation and physical problems especially involving circulatory and respiratory systems	Good medical care and surgery to correct structural heart problems; special education and help for parents to enable them to care for child at home	Yes	Possible in 5 percent of cases.**
Potential life threatening crises whenever injured	Blood transfusions and administration of "clotting factor"	Yes*†	Yes*
Disorder is fatal		Yes*	Yes*

*A new method that requires only routine amniocentesis uses sophisticated chemical techniques to study variations in DNA called polymorphisms. The polymorphisms are compared with those signifying a particular genetic disorder thus allowing for detection of the abnormal gene signifying the disorder. This method has been used in the detection of hemophilia, cystic fibrosis, muscular dystrophy, phenylketonuria, sickle cell anemia, and thalasemia among others. Carrier detection is found through testing tissue from adults. Both prenatal and carrier detection require the genetic evaluation of close relatives as well.

**About five percent of Down's Syndrome incidence is due to an unblanced translocation (chromosomal rearrangement). Such cases are independent of maternal age. If one of the parents is known to "carry" this chromosome rearrangement (translocation) in a balanced fashion, then all pregnancies should be monitored by prenatal diagnosis. Carriers of chromosomal translocations are identified by performing a chromosomal analysis of their blood.

†Fetal blood may be sampled by a process called fetoscopy. This has a risk of miscarriage of 3 to 5 percent as compared to the ½ of 1 percent risk associated with amniocentesis.

TABLE 1

Major Genetic and Chromosomal Disorders (Continued)

Disorder	Description/ Identification	Incidence	Cause
Hydroencephalus	Excess fluid buildup in brain	One in 500 births	Multifactorial
Kleinfelter's Syndrome	Abnormal sexual development, sterility, absence of secondary sex characteristics: about half are mentally retarded: Identification in adolescence	One in every 600 male births	Chromosomal abnormality: XXY configuration on 23rd chromosome
Muscular Dystrophy (Duchenne)	Progressive muscular deterioration; there are many diseases which fall under this title; the most common form, called Duchenne, begins in childhood	One in 4,000 males have Duchenne	Duchenne is a recessive X-linked (almost always boys are affected); other forms follow other patterns
Phenylketonuria (PKU)	Inability to process phenylalanine prevents brain development; blood test can identify disorder two days after birth	One in 10,000 births; more often found among North Europeans	Two abnormal recessive genes
Pyloric Stenosis	Digestive difficulties caused by an overgrowth of muscle in the lower stomache; identification early in infancy since infants cannot keep food down and do not gain weight	One in every 200 boys and one in every 1000 girls	Multifactorial
Rh Disease	Blood disorder	7000 babies per year	If mother is Rh negative and baby is Rh positive some of mother's antibodies may kill baby's red blood cells
Sickle Cell Anemia Anemia	Blood disorder causes damage to vital organs; diagnosed through blood test	One in every 400–600 Blacks; one in every 1000–1500 Hispanics	Two abnormal recessive genes
Spina Bifida	Spine fails to close; noticeable at birth	One in 1,000 births	Multifactorial

Problems	Treatment	Prenatal Detection	Carrier Detection
Brain damage; can be fatal	Surgery	Sometimes	No
Mental retardation, emotional problems	Administration of testosterone	Yes	No
Weakening and wasting away of muscles leads to physical incapabilities and death	Physical therapy and surgery	Yes*	Yes*
If left untreated condition leads to mental retardation, restlessness, and irritability	Low phenylalanine diet; no cow's milk	Yes*	Yes*
Can be fatal if not corrected	Surgery	No	No
Blood problems, multiple medical difficulties; can be fatal	Transfusions; prevention possible if mother receives shot of Rh immune globulin after birth, miscarriage, or after prenatal diagnosis	Yes	Yes
Problems vary depending upon severity of disorder; can be fatal	Medical care to reduce pain and severity of disorder	Yes*	Yes*
May lead to paralysis and problems in bladder and bowel control	Surgery, physical therapy, and training in personal hygiene	Yes	No

*A new method that requires only routine amniocentesis uses sophisticated chemical techniques to study variations in DNA called polymorphisms. The polymorphisms are compared with those signifying a particular genetic disorder thus allowing for detection of the abnormal gene signifying the disorder. This method has been used in the detection of hemophilia, cystic fibrosis, muscular dystrophy, phenylketonuria, sickle cell anemia, and thalasemia among others. Carrier detection is found through testing tissue from adults. Both prenatal and carrier detection require the genetic evaluation of close relatives as well.

T A B L E 1

Major Genetic and Chromosomal Disorders (Continued)

Disorder	Description/ Identification	Incidence	Cause
Tay Sachs Disease	Enzyme deficiency causes buildup of fat in nerve cells; leads to retardation, blindness, and convulsions; identification through exaggerated startle response and psychomotor retardation in infancy	One in every 25 American Jews is a carrier	Abnormal recessive gene
Thalasemia (Cooley's Anemia)	Severe anemia and listlessness; identified through blood test	3 to 10 percent of Greeks and Italians are carriers; about 1,000 cases per year	Abnormal recessive gene
Turner's Syndrome	Short stature, delayed sexual development, infantile genitalia, swelling of feet, hands, and neck, heart abnormalities	One in every 2,000–3,000 live births	Chromosomal problems: Forty-five chromosomes, single X on 23rd chromosome

Problems	Treatment	Prenatal Detection	Carrier Detection
Disease is fatal in all cases; death occurs usually between the ages of three to five years	Not available	Yes	Yes
Severe anemia causes many physical problems	Blood transfusions and bone marrow transplants	Yes*	Yes*
Child has normal intelligence although perceptual deficits are common; physical stature and sexual problems may lead to social problems	Hormone therapy, counseling	Yes	No

*A new method that requires only routine amniocentesis uses sophisticated chemical techniques to study variations in DNA called polymorphisms. The polymorphisms are compared with those signifying a particular genetic disorder thus allowing for detection of the abnormal gene signifying the disorder. This method has been used in the detection of hemophilia, cystic fibrosis, muscular dystrophy, phenylketonuria, sickle cell anemia, and thalasemia among others. Carrier detection is found through testing tissue from adults. Both prenatal and carrier detection require the genetic evaluation of close relatives as well.

Sources: L. F. Annis, 1978; V. Apgar and J. Beck, 1973; D. Bergsma, 1979; R. M. Goodman and R. J. Gorlin, 1983; N. J. Karagan, 1979; A. P. Mange and E. J. Mange, 1980; March of Dimes, FACTS, 1984; S. Sassower, 1985; D. W. Smith, 1982; R. Thompson and A. P. Thompson, 1980; Cahill, 1987; J. S. Colome, 1987; J. Stone, 1987.

Summary of Developmental Theories

Theory	Basic Premises	Values and Strengths	Criticisms and Weaknesses
Freud's Psychoanalytic Theory	1. Behavior is motivated by unconscious thoughts, memories, and feelings 2. Life is the unfolding of the sex instinct. 3. The child's early experience is crucial to his later personality. The manner in which the mother satisfies the child's basic needs is important to later mental health. 4. Children develop through a sequence of stages called psychosexual stages. 5. People protect themselves from anxiety and other negative emotions through unconscious and automatic reactions called defense mechanisms.	1. Encourages developmental specialists to look beyond the obvious visible behavior and seek insights into the unconscious. 2. Emphasizes the importance of the child's early experience and relationships which in turn focuses our attention on the caregiver-infant relationship. The idea that later problems may be due to disturbed early relationships is challenging. 3. The concept of stages in Freudian theory has become a popular way of viewing the development of children. 4. Emphasis on sexuality, while debatable, still alerts us to the existence of sexuality at all ages. 5. Serves as a focal point for other theorists.	1. Since theory is based upon clinical experiences with troubled people it may have more to say about unhealthy than healthy development. 2. Hypotheses are very difficult to test. 3. Failure to appreciate the importance of culture.
Erik Erikson's Psychosocial Theory	1. Explains development in terms of the epigenetic principle. Personality develops according to predetermined steps which are maturationally set. Society is structured to encourage the challenges which arise at these times in a person's life. 2. Describes development in terms of eight stages from cradle to grave. Each has positive and negative outcomes. 3. Emphasizes the importance of culture and the historical period in which the individual is living.	1. Sees development as continuing over the life span. 2. Importance of culture and historical period adds to our appreciation of factors that affect children's development. 3. Provides a good general overview of crises that occur at each stage of a child's life. Some of these crises such as identity versus role confusion have become important in understanding specific periods in a child's life.	1. Difficult to test experimentally. 2. Theory is rather general.

Summary of Developmental Theories (Continued)

Theory	Basic Premises	Values and Strengths	Criticisms and Weaknesses
Piaget's Theory of Cognitive Psychology	1. Children do not think or solve problems in the same manner as adults. 2. Emphasizes the importance of the child's active interaction with the environment. 3. Sees maturation and experience as more important than formal learning in the child's cognitive development. 4. Views cognitive development as occurring in four stages. Each stage shows a qualitative leap forward in the child's ability to solve problems and reason logically. 5. Most complete description of cognitive development from infancy through childhood available.	1. Emphasizes the importance of active experience in child's development. Leads to a view of young children as little scientists sifting through information and actively coping with the world. 2. Descriptions of the way in which children think and approach problems very helpful in understanding their behavior. 3. Many of the sequences for understanding specific concepts are very challenging.	1. May underestimate the influence of learning on cognitive development and the nature of task on the child's performance. 2. Piaget's style of research has been criticized. He presented children with a problem and sought to discover how they reasoned and tried to solve the problem. His experiments were not controlled.
Information Processing	1. Emphasizes the importance of the manner in which children take in information, process it, and then act upon it. 2. Such processes as attention, perception memory, and processing strategies are studied.	1. Yields a detailed look at the processes involved in taking in and processing information. 2. May serve as a diagnostic aid in discovering where people have difficulties in solving problems.	1. It is not a unified field. A number of models have been advanced. 2. It still awaits adequate testing.

TABLE 2

Summary of Developmental Theories (Continued)

Theory	Basic Premises	Values and Strengths	Criticisms and Weaknesses
Radical Behavioral Approach	1. Human behavior may be explained by the processes of learning including classical and operant conditioning. 2. The behavioral approach has been successful in modifying the behavior of people in many situations. 3. The behavioral approach does not deny consciousness and mental processes like thinking, but rather deals with behavior and development in a different manner. 4. Development is seen as continuous with no stages posited to explain progress.	1. Learning theories are clear, precise, and laboratory tested. 2. The emphasis on the environment is important.	1. Some consider it too mechanical. Its avoidance of mental processes such as consciousness and thinking may yield only a partial picture of behavior. 2. Sees little qualitative difference between humans and animals.
Social Learning Theory	1. Human behavior is partially explained through the process of imitation and observation learning. 2. The process of imitation may be explained using a four step process involving attention, encoding and memory, behavioral reproduction, and, finally, reinforcement.	1. Is useful in understanding certain behaviors such as altruism and aggression. 2. Encourages us to look at the models in the person's environment.	1. Lacks a developmental framework. The process of imitation is viewed as the same no matter who is observing. 2. Does not explain age related changes.

TABLE 3

Growth in Infancy and Toddlerhood

All data is presented in centimeters. To convert to inches multiply by .39.

Sex and Age	Percentile						
	5th	10th	25th	50th	75th	90th	95th
Male	*Recumbent length in centimeters*						
Birth	46.4	47.5	49.0	50.5	51.8	53.5	54.4
1 month	50.4	51.3	53.0	54.6	56.2	57.7	58.6
3 months	56.7	57.7	59.4	61.1	63.0	64.5	65.4
6 months	63.4	64.4	66.1	67.8	69.7	71.3	72.3
9 months	68.0	69.1	70.6	72.3	74.0	75.9	77.1
12 months	71.7	72.8	74.3	76.1	77.7	79.8	81.2
18 months	77.5	78.7	80.5	82.4	84.3	86.6	88.1
24 months	82.3	83.5	85.6	87.6	89.9	92.2	93.8
30 months	87.0	88.2	90.1	92.3	94.6	97.0	98.7
36 months	91.2	92.4	94.2	96.5	98.9	101.4	103.1
Female							
Birth	45.4	46.5	48.2	49.9	51.0	52.0	52.9
1 month	49.2	50.2	51.9	53.5	54.9	56.1	56.9
3 months	55.4	56.2	57.8	59.5	61.2	62.7	63.4
6 months	61.8	62.6	64.2	65.9	67.8	69.4	70.2
9 months	66.1	67.0	68.7	70.4	72.4	74.0	75.0
12 months	69.8	70.8	72.4	74.3	76.3	78.0	79.1
18 months	76.0	77.2	78.8	80.9	83.0	85.0	86.1
24 months	81.3	82.5	84.2	86.5	88.7	90.8	92.0
30 months	86.0	87.0	88.9	91.3	93.7	95.6	96.9
36 months	90.0	91.0	93.1	95.6	98.1	100.0	101.5

Source: P. V. V. Hamill, et al. 1977.

TABLE 4

Weight Gain in Infancy and Toddlerhood

All data is given in kilograms. To convert to pounds multiply by 2.2.

	Percentile						
Sex and Age	5th	10th	25th	50th	75th	90th	95th
Male	*Weight in kilograms*						
Birth	2.54	2.78	3.00	3.27	3.64	3.82	4.15
1 month	3.16	3.43	3.82	4.29	4.75	5.14	5.28
3 months	4.43	4.78	5.32	5.98	6.56	7.14	7.37
6 months	6.20	6.61	7.20	7.85	8.49	9.10	9.46
9 months	7.52	7.95	8.56	9.18	9.88	10.49	10.93
12 months	8.43	8.84	9.49	10.15	10.91	11.54	11.99
18 months	9.59	9.92	10.67	11.47	12.31	13.05	13.44
24 months	10.54	10.85	11.65	12.59	13.44	14.29	14.70
30 months	11.44	11.80	12.63	13.67	14.51	15.47	15.97
36 months	12.26	12.69	13.58	14.69	15.59	16.66	17.28
Female							
Birth	2.36	2.58	2.93	3.23	3.52	3.64	3.81
1 month	2.97	3.22	3.59	3.98	4.36	4.65	4.92
3 months	4.18	4.47	4.88	5.40	5.90	6.39	6.74
6 months	5.79	6.12	6.60	7.21	7.83	8.38	8.73
9 months	7.00	7.34	7.89	8.56	9.24	9.83	10.17
12 months	7.84	8.19	8.81	9.53	10.23	10.87	11.24
18 months	8.92	9.30	10.04	10.82	11.55	12.30	12.76
24 months	9.87	10.26	11.10	11.90	12.74	13.57	14.08
30 months	10.78	11.21	12.11	12.93	13.93	14.81	15.35
36 months	11.60	12.07	12.99	13.93	15.03	15.97	16.54

Source: P. V. V. Hamill, et al. 1977.

T A B L E 5

Growth in Early Childhood

The slowing rate of growth during early childhood is shown in this table. The data is given in centimeters. To convert to inches, multiply by .39.

Sex and Age	Percentile						
	5th	10th	25th	50th	75th	90th	95th
Male	Stature in centimeters						
3.0 years	89.0	90.3	92.6	94.9	97.5	100.1	102.0
3.5 years	92.5	93.9	96.4	99.1	101.7	104.3	106.1
4.0 years	95.8	97.3	100.0	102.9	105.7	108.2	109.9
4.5 years	98.9	100.6	103.4	106.6	109.4	111.9	113.5
5.0 years	102.0	103.7	106.5	109.9	112.8	115.4	117.0
5.5 years	104.9	106.7	109.6	113.1	116.1	118.7	120.3
6.0 years	107.7	109.6	112.5	116.1	119.2	121.9	123.5
Female							
3.0 years	88.3	89.3	91.4	94.1	96.6;	99.0	100.6
3.5 years	91.7	93.0	95.2	97.9	100.5	102.8	104.5
4.0 years	95.0	96.4	98.8	101.6	104.3	106.6	108.3
4.5 years	98.1	99.7	102.2	105.0	107.9	110.2	112.0
5.0 years	101.1	102.7	105.4	108.4	111.4	113.8	115.6
5.5 years	103.9	105.6	108.4	111.6	114.8	117.4	119.2
6.0 years	106.6	108.4	111.3	114.6	118.1	120.8	122.7

Source: P. V. V. Hamill, et al., 1977.

T A B L E 6

Weight Gain in Early Childhood

The data is given in kilograms. To convert to pounds, multiply by 2.2.

Sex and Age	Percentile						
	5th	10th	25th	50th	75th	90th	95th
Male	Weight in kilograms						
3.0 years	12.05	12.58	13.52	14.62	15.78	16.95	17.77
3.5 years	12.84	13.41	14.46	15.68	16.90	18.15	18.98
4.0 years	13.64	14.24	15.39	16.69	17.99	19.32	20.27
4.5 years	14.45	15.10	16.30	17.69	19.06	20.50	21.63
5.0 years	15.27	15.96	17.22	18.67	20.14	21.70	23.09
5.5 years	16.09	16.83	18.14	19.67	21.25	22.96	24.66
6.0 years	16.93	17.72	19.07	20.69	27.40	24.31	26.34
Female							
3.0 years	11.61	12.26	13.11	14.10	15.50	16.54	17.22
3.5 years	12.37	13.08	14.00	15.07	16.59	17.77	18.59
4.0 years	13.11	13.84	14.80	15.96	17.56	18.93	19.91
4.5 years	13.83	14.56	15.55	16.81	18.48	20.06	21.24
5.0 years	14.55	15.26	16.29	17.66	19.39	21.23	22.62
5.5 years	15.29	15.97	17.05	18.56	20.36	22.48	24.11
6.0 years	16.05	16.72	17.86	19.52	21.44	23.89	25.75

Source: P. V. V. Hamill, et al., 1977.

TABLE 7

Growth in Middle Childhood

Stature is noted in centimeters. To convert to inches multiply by .39.

Sex and Age	5th	10th	25th	50th	75th	90th	95th
				Percentile			
Male				Stature in centimeters			
6.0 years	107.7	109.6	112.5	116.1	119.2	121.9	123.5
6.5 years	110.4	112.3	115.3	119.0	122.2	124.9	126.6
7.0 years	113.0	115.0	118.0	121.7	125.0	127.9	129.7
7.5 years	115.6	117.6	120.6	124.4	127.8	130.8	132.7
8.0 years	118.1	120.2	123.2	127.0	130.5	133.6	135.7
8.5 years	120.5	122.7	125.7	129.6	133.2	136.5	138.8
9.0 years	122.9	125.2	128.2	132.2	136.0	139.4	141.8
9.5 years	125.3	127.6	130.8	134.8	138.8	142.4	144.9
10.0 years	127.7	130.1	133.4	137.5	141.6	145.5	148.1
10.5 years	130.1	132.6	136.0	140.3	144.6	148.7	151.5
11.0 years	132.6	135.1	138.7	143.3	147.8	152.1	154.9
11.5 years	135.0	137.7	141.5	146.4	151.1	155.6	158.5
12.0 years	137.6	140.3	144.4	149.7	154.6	159.4	162.3
Female							
6.0 years	106.6	108.4	111.3	114.6	118.1	120.8	122.7
6.5 years	109.2	111.0	114.1	117.6	121.3	124.2	126.1
7.0 years	111.8	113.6	116.8	120.6	124.4	127.6	129.5
7.5 years	114.4	116.2	119.5	123.5	127.5	130.9	132.9
8.0 years	116.9	118.7	122.2	126.4	130.6	134.2	136.2
8.5 years	119.5	121.3	124.9	129.3	133.6	137.4	139.6
9.0 years	122.1	123.9	127.7	132.2	136.7	140.7	142.9
9.5 years	124.8	126.6	130.6	135.2	139.8	143.9	146.2
10.0 years	127.5	129.5	133.6	138.3	142.9	147.2	149.5
10.5 years	130.4	132.5	136.7	141.5	146.1	150.4	152.8
11.0 years	133.5	135.6	140.0	144.8	149.3	153.7	156.2
11.5 years	136.6	139.0	143.5	148.2	152.6	156.9	159.5
12.0 years	139.8	142.3	147.0	151.5	155.8	160.0	162.7

Source: P. V. V. Hamill, et al., 1977.

TABLE 8

Weight Gain in Middle Childhood

All data is given in kilograms. To convert to pounds multiply by 2.2.

Sex and Age	Percentile						
	5th	10th	25th	50th	75th	90th	95th
Male	*Weight in kilograms*						
6.0 years	16.93	17.72	19.07	20.69	22.40	24.31	26.34
6.5 years	17.78	18.62	20.02	21.74	23.62	25.76	28.16
7.0 years	18.64	19.53	21.00	22.85	24.94	27.36	30.12
7.5 years	19.52	20.45	22.02	24.03	26.36	29.11	32.73
8.0 years	20.40	21.39	23.09	25.30	27.91	31.06	34.51
8.5 years	21.31	22.34	24.21	26.66	29.61	33.22	36.96
9.0 years	22.25	23.33	25.40	28.13	31.46	35.57	39.58
9.5 years	23.25	24.38	26.68	29.73	33.46	38.11	42.35
10.0 years	24.33	25.52	28.07	31.44	35.61	40.80	45.27
10.5 years	25.51	26.78	29.59	33.30	37.92	43.63	48.31
11.0 years	26.80	28.17	31.25	35.30	40.38	46.57	51.47
11.5 years	28.24	29.72	33.08	37.46	43.00	49.61	54.73
12.0 years	29.85	31.46	35.09	39.78	45.77	52.73	58.09
Female							
6.0 years	16.05	16.72	17.86	19.52	21.44	23.89	25.75
6.5 years	16.85	17.51	18.76	20.61	22.68	25.50	27.59
7.0 years	17.71	18.39	19.78	21.84	24.16	27.39	29.68
7.5 years	18.62	19.37	20.95	23.26	25.90	29.57	32.07
8.0 years	19.62	20.45	22.26	24.84	27.88	32.04	34.71
8.5 years	20.68	21.64	23.70	26.58	30.08	34.73	37.58
9.0 years	21.82	22.92	25.27	28.46	32.44	37.60	40.64
9.5 years	23.05	24.29	26.94	30.45	34.94	40.61	43.85
10.0 years	24.36	25.76	28.71	32.55	37.53	43.70	47.17
10.5 years	25.75	27.32	30.57	34.72	40.17	45.84	50.57
11.0 years	27.24	28.97	32.49	36.95	42.84	49.96	54.00
11.5 years	28.83	30.71	34.48	39.23	45.58	53.03	57.42
12.0 years	30.52	32.53	36.52	41.53	48.07	55.99	60.81

Source: P. V. V. Hamill, et al., 1977.

TABLE 9

Growth in Adolescence

Stature is given in centimeters. To convert to inches multiply by .39.

Sex and Age	5th	10th	25th	50th	75th	90th	95th
				Percentile			
Male				*Stature in centimeters*			
12.0 years	137.6	140.3	144.4	149.7	154.6	159.4	162.3
12.5 years	140.2	143.0	147.4	153.0	158.2	163.2	166.1
13.0 years	142.9	145.8	150.5	156.5	161.8	167.0	169.8
13.5 years	145.7	148.7	153.6	159.9	165.3	170.5	173.4
14.0 years	148.8	151.8	156.9	163.1	168.5	173.8	176.7
14.5 years	152.0	155.0	160.1	166.2	171.5	176.6	179.5
15.0 years	155.2	158.2	163.3	169.0	174.1	178.9	181.9
15.5 years	158.3	161.2	166.2	171.5	176.3	180.8	183.9
16.0 years	161.1	163.9	168.7	173.5	178.1	182.4	185.4
16.5 years	163.4	166.1	170.6	175.2	179.5	183.6	186.6
17.0 years	164.9	167.7	171.9	176.2	180.5	184.4	187.3
17.5 years	165.6	168.5	172.4	176.7	181.0	185.0	187.6
18.0 years	165.7	168.7	172.3	176.8	181.2	185.3	187.6
Female							
12.0 years	139.8	142.3	147.0	151.5	155.8	160.0	162.7
12.5 years	142.7	145.4	150.1	154.6	158.8	162.9	165.6
13.0 years	145.2	148.0	152.8	157.1	161.3	165.3	168.1
13.5 years	147.2	150.0	154.7	159.0	163.2	167.3	170.0
14.0 years	148.7	151.5	155.9	160.4	164.6	168.7	171.3
14.5 years	149.7	152.5	156.8	161.2	165.6	169.8	172.2
15.0 years	150.5	153.2	157.2	161.8	166.3	170.5	172.8
15.5 years	151.1	153.6	157.5	162.1	166.7	170.9	173.1
16.0 years	151.6	154.1	157.8	162.4	166.9	171.1	173.3
16.5 years	152.2	154.6	158.2	162.7	167.1	171.2	173.4
17.0 years	152.7	155.1	158.7	163.1	167.3	171.2	173.5
17.5 years	153.2	155.6	159.1	163.4	167.5	171.1	173.5
18.0 years	153.6	156.0	159.6	163.7	167.6	171.0	173.6

Source: P. V. V. Hamill, et al., 1977.

TABLE 10

Weight Gain in Adolescence

All data is given in kilograms. To convert to pounds multiply by 2.2.

Sex and Age	Percentile						
	5th	10th	25th	50th	75th	90th	95th
Male	Weight in kilograms						
12.0 years	29.85	31.46	35.09	39.78	45.77	52.73	58.09
12.5 years	31.64	33.41	37.31	42.27	48.70	55.91	61.52
13.0 years	33.64	35.60	39.74	44.95	51.79	59.12	65.02
13.5 years	35.85	38.03	42.40	47.81	55.02	62.35	68.51
14.0 years	38.22	40.64	45.21	50.77	58.31	65.57	72.13
14.5 years	40.66	43.34	48.08	53.76	61.58	68.76	75.66
15.0 years	43.11	46.06	50.92	56.71	64.72	71.91	79.12
15.5 years	45.50	48.69	53.64	59.51	67.64	74.98	82.45
16.0 years	47.74	51.16	56.16	62.10	70.26	77.97	85.62
16.5 years	49.76	53.39	58.38	64.39	72.46	80.84	88.59
17.0 years	51.50	55.28	60.22	66.31	74.17	83.58	91.31
17.5 years	52.89	56.78	61.61	67.78	75.32	86.14	93.73
18.0 years	53.97	57.89	62.61	68.88	76.04	88.41	95.76
Female							
12.0 years	30.52	32.53	36.52	41.53	48.07	55.99	60.81
12.5 years	32.30	34.42	38.59	43.84	50.56	58.81	64.12
13.0 years	34.14	36.35	40.65	46.10	52.91	61.45	67.30
13.5 years	35.98	38.26	42.65	48.26	55.11	63.87	70.30
14.0 years	37.76	40.11	44.54	50.28	57.09	66.04	73.08
14.5 years	39.45	41.83	46.28	52.10	58.84	67.95	75.59
15.0 years	40.99	43.38	47.82	53.68	60.32	69.54	77.78
15.5 years	42.32	44.72	49.10	54.96	61.48	70.79	79.59
16.0 years	43.41	45.78	50.09	55.89	62.29	71.68	80.99
16.5 years	44.20	46.54	50.75	56.44	62.75	72.18	81.93
17.0 years	44.74	47.04	51.14	56.69	62.91	72.38	82.46
17.5 years	45.08	47.33	51.33	56.71	62.89	72.37	82.62
18.0 years	45.26	47.47	51.39	56.62	62.78	72.25	82.47

Source: P. V. V. Hamill, et al., 1977.

TABLE 11

Metropolitan Height and Weight Tables for Men and Women
(According to frame, ages 25–29)

Height (In Shoes)†		Weight in Pounds (In Indoor Clothing)*		
		Small Frame	Medium Frame	Large Frame
Feet	Inches		Men	
5	2	128–134	131–141	138–150
5	3	130–136	133–143	140–153
5	4	132–138	135–145	142–156
5	5	134–140	137–148	144–160
5	6	136–142	139–151	146–164
5	7	138–145	142–154	149–168
5	8	140–148	145–157	152–172
5	9	142–151	148–160	155–176
5	10	144–154	151–163	158–180
5	11	146–157	154–166	161–184
6	0	149–160	157–170	164–188
6	1	152–164	160–174	168–192
6	2	155–168	164–178	172–197
6	3	158–172	167–182	176–202
6	4	162–176	171–187	181–207
			Women	
4	10	102–111	109–121	118–131
4	11	103–113	111–123	120–134
5	0	104–115	113–126	122–137
5	1	106–118	115–129	125–140
5	2	108–121	118–132	128–143
5	3	111–124	121–135	131–147
5	4	114–127	124–138	134–151
5	5	117–130	127–141	137–155
5	6	120–133	130–144	140–159
5	7	123–136	133–147	143–163
5	8	126–139	136–150	146–167
5	9	129–142	139–153	149–170
5	10	132–145	142–156	152–173
5	11	135–148	145–159	155–176
6	0	138–151	148–162	158–179

*Indoor clothing weighing 5 pounds for men and 3 pounds for women.
†Shoes with 1-inch heels.

Source of basic data: *Build Study, 1979.* Society of Actuaries and Association of Life Insurance Medical Directors of America, 1980. Copyright 1983 Metropolitan Life Insurance Company. Used by permission.

T A B L E 12

Average Heights and Weights for Men and Women, Selected Time Periods, 1960–1980

Sex, Period, and Height	Weight (lb.)					
	18–24 years	25–34 years	35–44 years	45–54 years	55–64 years	65–74 years
Men						
1960–1962, total	158	169	170	170	164	158
1971–1974, total	165	176	178	175	171	164
1976–1980, total	163	173	178	178	174	165
5'2"	130	139	146	148	147	143
5'3"	135	145	149	154	151	148
5'4"	139	151	155	158	156	152
5'5"	143	155	159	163	160	156
5'6"	148	150	164	167	165	161
5'7"	152	164	169	171	170	165
5'8"	157	168	174	176	174	169
5'9"	162	173	178	180	178	174
5'10"	166	177	183	185	183	178
5'11"	171	182	188	190	187	182
6'	175	186	192	194	192	187
6'1"	180	191	197	196	197	192
6'2"	185	196	202	204	201	195
Women						
1960–1962, total	127	134	142	145	150	144
1971–1974, total	132	140	148	149	149	148
1876–1980, total	134	142	148	150	150	147
4'9"	111	120	131	129	132	132
4'10"	114	123	133	132	135	135
4'11"	118	126	136	136	138	138
5'	121	130	139	139	142	142
5'1"	124	133	141	143	145	145
5'2"	128	136	144	146	148	148
5'3"	131	139	146	150	151	151
5'4"	134	142	149	153	154	154
5'5"	137	146	151	157	157	157
5'6"	141	149	154	160	161	160
5'7"	144	152	156	164	164	163
5'8"	147	155	159	168	167	186

Source: U.S. National Center for Health Statistics, *Vital and Health Statistics*, series 11, and unpublished data, 1985.

T A B L E 13

Expectation of Life and Mortality Rates at Single Years of Age by Race and Sex, United States, 1983

| | | Expectation of Life in Years | | | |
| | | White | | All Other | |
Age	Total Persons	Male	Female	Male	Female
0	74.6	71.5	78.8	66.8	75.0
1	74.4	71.3	78.5	67.1	75.2
2	73.5	70.4	77.5	66.2	74.3
3	72.5	69.4	76.5	65.2	73.3
4	71.6	68.4	75.6	64.3	72.4
5	70.6	67.5	74.6	63.3	71.4
6	69.6	66.6	73.6	62.3	70.5
7	68.6	65.5	72.6	61.4	69.5
8	67.7	64.5	71.7	60.4	68.5
9	66.7	63.6	70.7	59.4	67.5
10	65.7	62.6	69.7	58.4	66.5
11	64.7	61.6	68.7	57.4	65.6
12	63.7	60.6	67.7	56.5	64.6
13	62.7	59.6	66.7	55.5	63.6
14	61.7	58.6	65.7	54.5	62.6
15	60.8	57.7	64.7	53.5	61.6
16	59.8	56.7	63.8	52.6	60.6
17	58.9	55.8	62.8	51.6	59.7
18	57.9	54.9	61.8	50.7	58.7
19	57.0	53.9	60.9	49.8	57.7
20	56.0	53.0	59.9	48.8	56.8
21	55.1	52.1	58.9	47.9	55.8
22	54.1	51.2	58.0	47.0	54.8
23	53.2	50.3	57.0	46.1	53.9
24	52.3	49.4	56.0	45.2	52.9
25	51.3	48.4	55.0	44.4	52.0
26	50.4	47.5	54.1	43.5	51.0
27	49.5	46.6	53.1	42.6	50.1
28	48.5	45.7	52.1	41.7	49.1
29	47.6	44.7	51.2	40.8	48.2
30	46.6	43.8	50.2	39.9	47.2
31	45.7	42.9	49.2	39.1	46.3
32	44.7	41.9	48.2	38.2	45.3
33	43.8	41.0	47.3	37.3	44.4
34	42.9	40.1	46.3	36.5	43.5
35	41.9	39.1	45.3	35.6	42.5
36	41.0	38.2	44.4	34.7	41.6
37	40.0	37.3	43.4	33.9	40.7
38	39.1	36.3	42.5	33.0	39.7
39	38.2	35.4	41.5	32.2	38.8
40	37.2	34.5	40.6	31.3	37.9
41	36.3	33.6	39.6	30.5	37.0
42	35.4	32.7	38.7	29.7	36.1
43	34.5	31.8	37.7	28.8	35.2

T A B L E 13

Expectation of Life and Mortality Rates at Single Years of Age by Race and Sex, United States, 1983 (Continued)

| Age | Total Persons | Expectation of Life in Years | | | |
| | | White | | All Other | |
		Male	Female	Male	Female
44	33.6	30.9	36.8	28;0	34.3
45	32.7	30.0	35.9	27.2	33.5
46	31.8	29.1	34.9	26.4	32.6
47	30.9	28.2	34.0	25.6	31.7
48	30.1	27.3	33.1	24.9	30.9
49	29.2	26.5	32.2	24.1	30.0
50	28.3	25.6	31.3	23.4	29.2
51	27.5	24.8	30.4	22.7	28.4
52	26.7	24.0	29.6	22.0	27.6
53	25.8	23.2	28.7	21.3	26.8
54	25.0	22.4	27.8	20.6	26.0
55	24.2	21.6	27.0	20.0	25.2
56	23.4	20.8	26.1	19.3	24.5
57	22.6	20.1	25.3	18.7	23.7
58	21.9	19.3	24.4	18.0	23.0
59	21.1	18.6	23.6	17.4	22.3
60	20.4	17.9	22.8	16.8	21.5
61	19.6	17.2	22.0	16.3	20.8
62	18.9	16.5	21.2	15.7	20.2
63	18.2	15.8	20.4	15.2	19.5
64	17.5	15.2	19.6	14.6	18.8
65	16.8	14.5	18.9	14.1	18.2
66	16.2	13.9	18.1	13.6	17.5
67	15.5	13.3	17.4	13.1	16.9
68	14.9	12.7	16.7	12.6	16.2
69	14.3	12.2	16.0	12.2	15.6
70	13.7	11.6	15.3	11.7	15.0
71	13.1	11.1	14.6	11.2	14.4
72	12.5	10.6	13.9	10.8	13.8
73	11.9	10.0	13.2	10.4	13.3
74	11.3	9.6	12.6	9.9	12.7
75	10.8	9.1	12.0	9.5	12.1
76	10.3	8.6	11.3	9.1	11.6
77	9.8	8.2	10.7	8.7	11.1
78	9.3	7.8	10.2	8.3	10.5
79	8.8	7.4	9.6	7.9	10.0
80	8.3	7.0	9.0	7.5	9.5
81	7.9	6.6	8.5	7.1	9.1
82	7.4	6.3	8.0	6.7	8.6
83	7.0	5.9	7.6	6.4	8.2
84	6.6	5.6	7.1	6.1	7.8
85	6.3	5.3	6.7	5.8	7.5

Source: Statistical Bulletin, July-September, 1985, Metropolitan Life Insurance Company. Used by permission.

NAME INDEX

Bertis, A.E., 185
Best, J.B., 496
Betz, N.E., 328
Beyer, N.R., 182
Biehler, R.F., 240
Bierman, K.L., 268
Bigelow, B.J., 268
Bild, B.R., 521
Biller, H.B., 141, 394
Bingham, W.C., 405
Birch, H.G., 73, 75
Birch, L.L., 182
Birkhill, W.R., 492
Birren, J.E., 29, 369, 444, 473, 496, 498, 528
Bischof, L.J., 417
Bjorksten, J., 464
Black, D., 520
Blackeslee, S., 77
Blackhurst, A.E., 41
Blakemore, J.E., 220
Blank, I.D., 29
Blank, M., 234, 244
Blasi, A., 275
Blass, E.M., 97
Blatt, M., 276
Blazer, D., 528
Blehar, M.C., 144
Blieszner, R., 510
Block, J.H., 219, 221, 267, 449
Bloom, B.S., 160, 239
Bloom, D.E., 327, 328
Bluebond-Langner, M., 537
Blum, R.H., 332
Blumenthal, J.A., 419
Bocknek, G., 378
Bogatz, G., 197
Bohannon, J.N., 164
Bombi, A.S., 185
Bond, E., 94
Bondareff, W., 468
Borges, M.A., 527
Boriskin, J.A., 218
Borkowski, J.G., 243–44
Bornstein, M.H., 94, 119
Bottoms, S.F., 79
Botwinick, J., 5, 6, 361, 369, 374, 421, 422, 423, 425, 427, 442, 452, 466, 467, 473, 476, 478, 488, 490, 491, 496, 498, 499, 509, 523, 527, 540
Bouchard, T.J., 56
Bowen, D., 300
Bower, G.H., 194, 262
Bower, T.G.R., 6, 94, 116, 117
Bowerman, M., 163
Bowlby, J., 130, 132, 133
Boyer, E.L., 329
Boyes, M., 275
Brackbill, Y., 81, 97

Bradbard, M.R., 145
Bradley, R.H., 120
Brand, G., 372
Brandt, G., 296
Bransford, J.D., 496
Brassard, M.R., 217
Braucht, G.N., 332
Brazelton, T.B., 70, 91, 137
Brehm, S.S., 384, 385, 397
Breit, E.B., 290
Brickley, M., 253
Bridges, F.A., 51
Bridges, K.A., 129
Brierly, J., 96, 99, 101
Briggs, C., 195
Brim, O.G., 376
Bringuier, J.C., 237
Brinkley, J., 332
Brislin, R.W., 29
Brittain, C.V., 323
Brody, E.M., 441
Brody, G.H., 196, 212, 263
Brody, J., 59, 402
Brody, L.R., 118
Bromley, D., 262, 368
Bronfenbrenner, U., 9
Bronson, G., 129
Bronson, W.C., 450
Bronstein, P., 24
Brook, J.S., 333, 334
Brooks, J., 373
Brooks-Gunn, J., 129, 290
Brophy, J., 240
Brown, A.L., 5, 189, 193, 238
Brown, A.S., 529
Brown, B.B., 322
Brown, F.G., 246
Brown, R., 159, 165
Bruch, H., 296
Bruner, J., 166
Buchanon, M., 250
Bugaighis, M.A., 389
Bugen, L.A., 548, 549
Buhrmester, D., 267
Bukatko, D., 191
Bukowski, W.M., 268
Bullen, B.A., 231
Bullock, M., 188
Bullough, V., 219
Burkitt, D.P., 421
Burns, G., 512
Burns, R.B., 262, 295, 369, 512
Burnside, I.M., 473, 474, 475, 548
Burrus-Bammel, L.L., 476, 521, 526
Bursk, B.J., 519
Burton, R.V., 277
Busch-Roissnagel, N.A., 199, 241, 271
Business Week, 365

Butler, N., 69
Butler, R., 528, 540
Butterfield, E.C., 98
Byrnes, D., 117, 426, 496

C

Cairns, R.B., 14, 23, 277, 280
Caldwell, M.A., 120, 391
Callahan, E.J., 549
Campbell, A., 393
Campbell, K., 253
Campos, J., 94, 141
Canavan, J.W., 216
Caputo, D.V., 84
Card, J.J., 310
Carew, J.V., 120
Carey, R.G., 542, 543, 546
Carp, F.M., 529
Carpenter, G.C., 99
Carper, L., 206
Carr, T.S., 511
Carroll, J.L., 274
Carter, C.P., 48
Carter, D.B., 271
Caspi, A., 9, 527
Cassell, E.J., 544
Cassidy, J., 136
Cataldo, C.B., 231
Cate, R.M., 397
Cattell, R.B., 376, 425
Cavanaugh, J.C., 497
Cavanaugh, P.J., 98
Cave, V.G., 72
Cazden, C.B., 167
Centra, J.A., 240
Cerella, J., 496
Cernoch, J.M., 96
Chafetz, J.S., 221
Chamis, G.C., 310
Chand, I.P., 324
Chandler, M.J., 83, 275
Chapman, M., 262
Charles, A.G., 82
Chasoff, I.J., 70
Chassin, L., 333
Chazan, M., 195
Cherlin, A., 267, 403
Chervenak, F.A., 77
Chess, S., 144, 150
Chew, P., 418, 419
Chi, M.T.H., 194, 195
Chibucos, T.R., 140
Childers, P., 537
Chilman, C.S., 306, 307
Chiriboga, D., 369, 442, 472
Chivian, E., 279
Chodorow, N., 13, 393
Chomsky, N., 166

Hubble, J., 295
Huei, K.S., 209
Huesmann, L.R., 282
Hughes, V., 241
Hultsch, D.F., 427, 496
Hummel, R., 318
Humphreys, L.G., 246
Hunt, J.McV., 121
Hunt, M., 388, 415
Hunter, F.T., 325, 440
Huston, A.C., 192
Hutchins, F.L., 73, 75
Hutt, C.R., 101
Hutt, S.J., 101
Hyde, J.S., 45, 220, 241, 321, 372, 373, 392, 397
Hynes, S.G., 467

I

Iaffaldino, M.I., 402
Ilg, F.L., 234
Illingworth, R.S., 99
Ingram, D., 543
Inhelder, B., 16, 17, 182, 184, 185, 189, 235, 237, 298
Inman, V., 426
Intons-Peterson, M.J., 112
Isaacson, L.E., 447
Istomina, Z.M., 194

J

Jacklin, C.N., 169, 219, 222, 280
Jackson, D., 414
Jackson, J.J., 467
Jackson, P.W., 254
Jacobson, A.L., 136
Jacobson, J.L., 72, 86
Jacobson, N.S., 387
James, B.E., 388
Janes, C., 363
Jarvik, L.F., 55, 463, 493
Jarvik, M.E., 332
Jaslow, P., 524
Jedlicka, D., 306
Jeffreys, M., 416
Jeffries, D., 71
Jencks, C., 56
Jensen, A.R., 56, 57
Jensen, K., 96
Jensen, L.C., 273, 330
Joffe, L.S., 135
Johnson, D.W., 415
Johnson, E.S., 519
Johnson, J.A., 252
Johnson, M., 241, 242
Johnson, N., 190, 195
Johnson, V.E., 518

Johnston, L.D., 302, 331
Jones, K.L., 70
Jones, M.C., 294, 295
Jones, P., 216, 219
Juntune, J., 255
Justice, E., 238

K

Kadushin, A., 7
Kagan, J., 7, 58, 118, 119, 130, 243, 376, 448
Kahana, B., 511, 512, 529
Kahana, E., 529
Kahn, A.S., 391
Kahn, D., 509
Kahn, M.D., 149
Kail, R., 5, 20, 193, 194, 244, 426, 499
Kalat, J.W., 51, 97, 101, 112, 293
Kalish, R.A., 469, 476, 539, 550, 551
Kallman, F.J., 463
Kalmuus, D., 397, 400
Kamin, L.J., 56
Kammerman, S.B., 144
Kandel, D., 325
Kang, J.K., 393
Kantner, J.F., 307
Kaplan, P.S., 261, 246, 371
Karen, R.L., 215
Kastenbaum, R., 474, 537, 538, 541, 542, 543, 547
Katchadourian, H., 291, 343
Katz, L.G., 195
Kauffman, J., 218
Kausler, D.H., 497
Kavale, K., 251, 252
Kaye, H., 97
Kazdin, A.E., 215, 282
Kearsley, R.B., 95
Keating, D.P., 374
Keating-Groen, N., 516
Keeney, T.J., 193
Kegan, R., 237
Keiffer, G.H., 546
Keith, P.M., 328, 524
Kellogg, R., 181
Kelly, J.B., 266, 309, 395, 396, 398
Kelly, J.R., 529
Kempe, C.H., 216
Kempe, R.S., 216
Kendrick, C., 212
Kennedy, C.E., 400
Kennell, J.H., 139, 140
Keogh, J., 232
Kermis, M.D., 45
Kerr, C.H., 373
Key, M.A., 77
Khachaturian, Z.S., 475
Kidd, K.K., 43, 52, 56

Kim, Y.J., 310
Kirk, S.A., 253
Kisilevsky, B.S., 99
Kivett, V., 527
Klaus, M.H., 139
Klaus, R.A., 200
Kleiber, D.A., 529
Klein, R.E., 7
Klein, R.P., 144
Klerman, L.V., 218
Klig, S., 234
Kline, D.W., 478
Kline, J., 70
Kline, P., 10, 13, 223, 276
Klorman, R.C., 97
Knothe, H., 67
Knox, D., 71, 372, 388, 390, 397, 398, 415
Koff, E., 290
Kogan, N., 244, 254, 499
Kohen-Raz, R., 234
Kohlberg, L., 271, 272, 274, 275, 276, 301, 302
Kohn, R.R., 368
Koocher, G., 537
Kopp, C.B., 84
Korner, A.F., 112
Kosinski, F., 400
Koslowski, B., 189
Kossen, S., 401, 405, 445
Kotelchuk, M., 140, 141
Kowles, R.V., 39, 50
Koza, P.E., 545
Kozma, A., 527
Kraines, J.J., 416
Kramer, J., 116
Kramer, R., 274
Krantz, D.S., 371, 426
Krausz, M., 401
Kreminitzer, J.P., 95
Kroeger, E., 29, 31
Krogman, W.M., 230, 288, 292
Kübler-Ross, E., 540, 541, 543, 549
Kuhn, D., 299, 374, 375
Kuhn, G., 352
Kupfersmid, J.H., 302
Kurdek, L.A., 264, 265, 266
Kuschner, D.S., 234
Kuse, A.R., 221
Kutner, B., 529
Kutza, E.A., 509

L

Laboratory of Comparative Human Cognition, 237
Labouvier-Vief, G., 375, 487, 490, 491, 493, 496, 497, 498, 499, 500
Labov, W., 169
Lachman, M.E., 54
Lair, C.V., 498

Lamaze, F., 82
Lamb, M.E., 140, 141, 218
Landesman, S.H., 367
Landesman-Dwyer, S., 69, 252
Langer, E.J., 511
Lappy, M., 59
Larson, R., 473, 527
La Rue, A., 473, 474, 493, 517, 518, 549
Laughlin, H.P., 11
Lawler, E.E., 401, 402
Lawrence, L.E., 260
Lazar, I., 9, 57, 200
Leaf, A., 460
Leal, L., 239
Leavitt, F., 69
Leboyer, F., 82
Lehman, H.C., 429
Lehman, V., 367
Lehr, U., 512, 513
Lemke, S., 510
Lemon, B.W., 530
Lempers, J.D., 190
Lenneberg, E.H., 162
Lenz, W., 73
Lerner, R.M., 324, 325
Leslie, G.R., 390
Less, L., 526
Lesser, G.S., 197, 325
Lester, B.M., 81, 85
Leventhal, H., 333
Levin, J., 467, 526
Levin, S.R., 192, 197
Levin, W.C., 467, 526
Levine, R., 513
Levinger, G., 388
Levinson, D.J., 347, 348, 349, 353, 413, 439, 447, 451
Levy, N., 96
Levy, S.M., 474
Levy-Shiff, R., 211
Lewis, M., 85, 122, 129, 144, 168, 267
Lewontin, R.C., 55
Lezotte, L.W., 240
Lickona, T.R., 276
Lidz, T., 413
Lieberman, M.A., 491, 510, 511
Liebert, R.M., 191, 281
Lightbourne, R., 105
Lindauer, B.K., 193
Lindberg, M., 194
Lindeman, E., 547
Lindzey, G., 13
Lingle, K.M., 116
Lingle, T.H., 116
Ling-Lin, S., 399
Linn, M., 45, 405
Linn, M.W., 445, 511
Lipsitt, L., 21, 95, 96, 103

List, J.A., 496
Livesly, W.J., 262
Lloyd, B., 112
Loeb, M.B., 518
Loeb, R.C., 263
Logan, D.D., 289, 290
Londerville, S., 136
Long, P.J., 420, 477
Longstreth, L.E., 56
Lopata, A., 337
Lopata, H., 518
Lopez, M.A., 540
Lorch, E.P., 192
Lorenz, K., 139
Los Angeles Times, 178
Lowenthal, 391, 442, 495, 521
Lowney, J., 332
Ludeman, K., 517
Lueptow, L.B., 322
Luker, K.C., 308
Lutkenhaus, P., 136
Lyle, J., 196
Lystad, M.H., 216

M

Maccoby, E.E., 130, 137, 138, 141, 169, 214, 219, 222, 263, 264, 275, 280
MacFarlane, A., 96
MacKinnon, D., 254
Macklin, E., 389, 390
MacNamara, J., 163
Maddox, G.L., 529, 530
Maeda, D., 512
Maher, E.L., 445, 446
Main, M., 136, 137, 138, 141
Makinodan, T., 463
Malinowski, C.I., 275
Mancini, J.A., 516
Mandell, C.J., 240
Mandell, W., 84
Mandler, J.M., 183, 190, 195
Mange, A.P., 44
Mange, E.J., 44
Manion, J., 395
Mann, M.J., 200
Manney, J.D., 521
Manosevitz, M., 267, 318, 400
Manton, K., 513
Maples, M.F., 405
March of Dimes, 46, 48, 67, 69, 70, 71
Marcia, J.E., 317, 318, 319, 321
Marin, G., 303
Markides, K.S., 528, 529
Markman, E.M., 238, 389
Markman, H.J., 389
Marks, S.R., 446
Marquis, A.L., 164
Marsh, G.R., 422

Marshall, J., 401
Marshall, V., 539, 549
Martin, B., 216
Martin, D., 308
Martin, G.B., 117
Martin, J.C., 69, 73, 214, 264
Martorano, C.S., 299
Martz, E., 50
Mascola, L., 71
Mason, S.E., 427
Masters, J.C., 239
Masters, W., 415, 518
Matas, L., 135, 136
Matheny, A.P., 54
Matthews, K.A., 372
Maurer, D., 92, 117
Maxwell, R.J., 513
May, M.A., 277
Maymi, C.R., 403
Mazess, R.B., 472
McBroom, P., 38
McCall, R.B., 4, 119
McCallum, R.S., 254
McCanaughty, S.H., 251
McCarthy, B.V., 425
McCarthy, D.A., 168
McCartney, K., 162
McCauley, E., 51
McCauley, W., 510
McCay, C.M., 464
McClearn, G., 463
McCleary, E.H., 417, 418
McClintock, B.S., 199
McCluskey, K., 137
McCoy, G.F., 280, 282, 330, 331
McCrae, R.R., 28, 472, 540
McDermitt, D., 332
McDonald, L., 524
McGhee, P.E., 28
McGowan, R.J., 119
McGraw, M.B., 111
McGue, M., 56
McGuinness, D., 221, 241
McGurk, D.J., 122
McIlroy, J.H., 436, 438, 448
McKee, J.S., 18
McKinlay, S.M., 416
McKinney, J.P., 298, 302
McLaughlin, B., 182, 215
McNeill, D., 162
McPherson, B., 522
McTavish, D.G., 511
Mead, M., 223
Medvedev, Z.A., 460
Mehler, J., 95
Meichenbaum, D.H., 244
Meier, B.G., 199
Meilman, P.W., 321

Meisami, E., 416
Melton, G.B., 215
Meltzer, H., 443
Meltzoff, A.N., 98
Melzack, R., 82
Mendelson, B.K., 231
Mercer, C.P., 250
Mercer, W.M., 524
Merrelman, R.M., 314
Messer, S., 243
Metcalf, D.R., 129
Metropolitan Life Insurance Company, 361, 420, 465, 466, 469, 508
Meyers, L., 397
Milewski, A.E., 92
Milgram, N.A., 5
Milgram, S., 32, 307
Miller, D.C., 401
Miller, D.J., 119
Miller, G.M., 295
Miller, J., 425
Miller, R., 72
Miller, S.A., 241
Mills, J.L., 70
Milsum, J.H., 369
Minard, J., 96
Mink, I.T., 263
Minton, H.L., 219
Minuchin, P.P., 199, 266
Miranda, S.B., 92
Mirsky, A.F., 52
Mischel, W., 55, 220, 222
Missinne, L.E., 513
Mitchell, W., 363
Moles, O., 311
Molfese, D.L., 156, 164
Mollnow, E., 67
Money, J., 220
Monge, R., 427
Montemayor, R., 325
Montgomery, R., 511
Moon, H.W., 498
Moore, D., 196, 234, 302
Moore, J.W., 351
Moore, K.A., 309
Moore, L.M., 422
Moore, M.K., 98
Moore, R.S., 196, 234
Moore, T., 147
Moos, R.H., 510
Morell, P., 101
Morgan, J., 447, 522, 523
Morris, D., 92
Morris, J.N., 365
Morris, P.M., 182
Morrison, D.M., 307, 308
Morrison, M.H., 508, 509
Moskalets, G., 476

Moskowitz, B.A., 161
Moss, H.A., 448, 528
Most, R.K., 114
Muchinsky, P.M., 402
Mueller, E., 140, 149, 150
Mueller, K.H., 403
Mullahy, P., 13, 223
Mullins, L.C., 540
Munley, P.H., 326
Murphy, J.M., 380
Murray, S.E., 81
Murstein, B.I., 384, 386, 390
Mussen, P.H., 23, 277, 294
Muuss, R.E., 297, 299, 320
Myers, J.E., 548
Myers, N.A., 192

N

Nadelman, L., 270
Nagy, M., 536
Najarian, P., 105
Napoli, M., 418
Nassi, A.J., 319
Nathan, P.E., 332
National Center for Clinical Infant Programs, 74, 75
National Center for Health Statistics, 74, 384, 473, 510
National Council on the Aging, 519, 521, 526
National Institute on Drug Abuse, 333
National Safety Council, 471
Navarick, D.J., 23
Nebes, R.D., 475
Neimark, E.D., 299
Neisworth, J.T., 40, 159
Nelson, K., 158, 160, 163, 167
Nelson, N.M., 82, 194, 195
Neugarten, B.L., 148, 350, 351, 352, 416, 417, 438, 442, 447, 449, 488, 519, 520, 528, 530
Newcomb, A.F., 268
Newman, B.M., 361, 368, 369, 417, 421, 422, 429
Newman, P.R., 268
Newmark, C.S., 488
Newport, E.L., 163
Newquist, D., 525
Newsday, 145, 446, 460
Newson, E., 270
Newson, J., 270
Newton, N., 517
New York State Council on Alcoholism, 332
New York State Department of Health, 69
New York State Department of Substance Abuse, 334
New York Times, 334, 538
Nienstedt, B.C., 440

Nieser, U., 238
Nihira, K., 263
Noam, G.G., 11
Nord, W.R., 402
Norem-Hebeisen, A., 334
Norris, H.H., 413
Norton, A.J., 395
Norton, W., 101
Notelovitz, M., 421, 470, 471
Nowak, C., 414
Nunnally, J.C., 28
Nye, R.D., 13
Nyhan, W.L., 59
Nyiti, R.M., 116

O

Obler, L.K., 502
O'Bryan, K.G., 197
Obstetrics and Gynecological Survey, 79
Ochs, A.L., 471
Ochsner, A., 420
Oden, M.H., 118, 254
O'Donnell, J.A., 328
Okun, M.A., 499
O'Leary, K.D., 439
Olim, E.G., 167
Olness, K.N., 31
Olsho, L.W., 478
Olweus, D., 280
O'Neil, R.P., 304
Orenberg, C.L., 69
Orlansky, M.D., 246
Orlofsky, J.L., 318, 320
Ortho Diagnostics, 72
Oshman, H., 267, 318, 400
Oshman, J.A., 318
Oskamp, S., 365, 371
Osofsky, J.D., 139
Otis, J.L., 443
Ounsted, M., 84
Owens, J.W.M., 361
Oyemade, V.J., 200

P

Pacovsky, V., 417
Paffenbarger, R.S., 364
Pai, A.C., 38
Paige, K.E., 372, 373
Palmer, A.M., 427, 500
Palmer, F.H., 200
Palmore, E.B., 417, 476, 513, 522, 524, 527, 528
Pampel, F.C., 524
Papalia, D.E., 493
Parham, I.A., 424
Paris, S.G., 193
Parish, T.S., 400

Parke, R.D., 140, 141, 196, 218, 280, 281
Parker, M., 405
Parkes, C.M., 548
Parlee, M.B., 373, 391
Parmellee, A.H., 84, 96, 97
Parnes, H., 524, 526
Parr, J., 444
Parten, M.B., 208
Passuth, P.M., 511
Pastor, D., 136
Patterson, G.R., 6, 270
Patterson, R.D., 529
Pattison, E., 542
Paulsen, K., 241, 242
Pawson, I.G., 363
Pearl, D., 281
Pecheux, A., 99
Peck, R.C., 344, 413, 439, 473, 516
Pelizza, J., 474
Pelletier, K.R., 371
Pelligrino, J.W., 244
Penner, S.G., 162
Peplau, L.A., 391
Perfetti, L.J., 405
Perkins, H.V., 234
Perlez, J., 308, 309
Perlmutter, M., 192, 352
Perry, D.G., 268
Perry, T.B., 277
Peskin, H., 294
Pestrak, V.A., 308
Peterman, D.J., 389
Peters, D.L., 197
Petersen, A.C., 45, 289, 291, 329, 330
Peterson, G.H., 82
Peterson, L., 277
Petitpas, A., 319
Petros, T., 496
Pfeiffer, E., 415, 416, 472, 517, 518
Phillips, J.L., 113, 144, 145, 183, 187
Piaget, J., 16, 17, 26, 113, 114, 115, 117,
    182, 183, 184, 185, 186, 187, 188, 189,
    235, 236, 237, 271, 272, 298, 299, 342,
    374, 493
Pihlblad, C.T., 518
Pinching, A.J., 71
Pineo, P.C., 440
Planned Parenthood, 69
Pless, I.B., 361
Plomin, R., 54, 56, 220
Pocs, O., 415
Ponzetti, J.H., 397
Poon, L.W., 496, 509
Porter, J.N., 96
Posavac, E.J., 546
Potter, D.A., 240
Powell, B., 442
Powell, R.R., 492

Power, T., 140
Powers, E.A., 521
Pratt, K.C., 96
Princeton Religion Research Center, 378, 379
Prohaska, T.R., 419
Prosen, S., 399
Pulaski, M.A.S., 187, 188, 235, 299
Putallaz, M., 268

Q

Quayle, D., 365
Quinn, R.P., 401

R

Rachlin, H., 6
Rader, N., 116
Ragozin, A.S., 137
Rahe, R.H., 369, 370
Rainer, J.D., 49
Rallings, E.M., 400
Raloff, J., 170
Ramey, C.T., 119
Ramey, E., 372
Ransom, J.W., 25
Raspberry, W., 169
Reddell, M., 112
Reed, E., 49
Reese, H.W., 21, 493
Regnier, V., 509
Reichelt, P., 308
Reiss, I.L., 398
Renner, V.J., 444, 473
Renshaw, P.D., 268
Renwick, P.A., 401, 402
Report on the Commission on Reading, 248
Reschley, D.J., 246
Rest, J.R., 272, 274, 275, 276
Restak, R.M., 118
Reynolds, D.K., 539, 550, 551
Rheingold, H.L., 129, 149, 221
Rhodes, A.J., 73
Rhodes, S.R., 407, 444
Rhyne, D., 389
Ribot, T., 498
Ricciuti, H.N., 75, 111, 144
Rice, R.D., 9, 84
Richardson, M.S., 440
Richardson, S.A., 111, 231
Richman, J., 511
Richmond-Abbott, M., 45, 221, 393, 394
Rickert, E.S., 254
Ridenauer, M.V., 105
Riebe, M.H., 426
Riegle, D.W., 405
Rierdan, S., 290
Riley, M.W., 522
Rimland, B., 252

Rinck, C., 310
Risman, B., 390
Ritter, B.R., 251
Rizzo, J.V., 253
Roberge, J.R., 299
Roberts, J.M., 207
Robertson, E.A., 426
Robertson, J., 130
Robertson, J.F., 520
Robertson-Tchabo, E.A., 427
Robinson, B.E., 306
Robinson, I.E., 310
Roche, A.F., 291, 361
Roche, J.P., 25
Rodeheaver, D., 493
Rodgers, S.F., 385
Rodin, J., 511
Roe, K.V., 168, 169
Roeder, L.M., 464
Roffwarg, H.P., 96
Rogers, C.R., 23
Rogers, G.T., 524
Rogers, L., 220
Rogoff, B., 238, 299
Rokeach, M., 302
Rollins, B.C., 440
Ron, M.A., 474
Rose, R.J., 55
Rose, S.A., 117, 119, 122
Roselli, L.L., 318
Rosen, B., 524
Rosen, L.R., 40, 415
Rosen, R., 40, 415
Rosenberg, G., 521
Rosenberg, J.S., 332
Rosenberg, L., 69
Rosenberg, S.D., 452
Rosenblum, L.A., 129
Rosenhan, D.L., 298
Rosenman, R.H., 371, 372, 467
Rosenmayr, L., 513
Rosentsweig, J., 363, 368
Rosenzweig, M.R., 101
Ross, D.B., 355
Ross, D.M., 251, 543
Ross, H.S., 149, 281
Ross, J., 445
Ross, K., 540
Ross, S.A., 251
Rossiter, J.R., 197
Rossman, R.H., 468
Rowe, E.J., 427
Rubin, K.H., 208, 209
Rubin, J., 112
Rubin, L.B., 401
Rubin, R.A., 119
Rubin, Z., 267, 268, 342
Rubinstein, E., 196, 197, 281

Vaughn, B.E., 135, 144
Vernon, P.E., 122, 196
Veroff, J., 450
Vigderhous, G., 405
Vinci, G.A., 25
Vinter, A., 98
Visher, E.B., 267
Visher, J.S., 267
Vitaliano, P.P., 475
Voget, F.X., 297
Vollstedt, R., 206
Volpe, E.P., 78
Vorhees, C.V., 67
Vosk, B., 268
Voss, H.L., 329
Vurpillot, E., 192

W

Wachs, M., 518
Wachs, T.D., 120
Wackman, D., 197
Waddington, C.H., 104
Wade, N., 105
Wadsworth, B., 234, 237
Wagenaar, T.C., 403
Waite, L.F., 309
Walden, E.L., 252
Waldman, D.A., 444
Waldron, J., 466
Walk, L., 95
Walk, R.D., 94, 95, 421, 422, 478
Walker, A., 222
Walker, E., 56
Walker, L.J., 274, 275
Wallace, I.F., 117
Wallach, M.A., 496
Wallerstein, J.S., 265, 266, 395, 396, 398
Walsh, D.A., 498
Walters, P., 403
Walters, R.H., 23
Walzer, S., 58
Wanat, P.E., 249
Ward, R.A., 510, 518, 519, 528, 536, 546
Ward, S., 197
Ware, M., 421, 470, 471
Warner, R.A., 524
Warrington, E.K., 426, 498
Washington, V., 199, 200
Wass, H., 539
Waterhouse, J.A., 78
Waterman, A.S., 318, 320, 322
Waterman, C.K., 320
Waters, E., 132, 133, 135, 136, 141

Watkin, D.M., 462, 464
Watkins, B.A., 197
Watkins, H.D., 144, 145
Watson, J.B., 21
Watson, R.E., 390
Watson, W.H., 521
Waugh, N.C., 496
Weatherly, P., 294
Weaver, C.N., 443, 524
Webster, R.L., 95
Wechsler, D., 374, 488
Weed, J.A., 395
Weinberg, R.A., 57, 199
Weiner, M.B., 517
Weinstein, K., 148, 519, 520
Weinstock, C.S., 374, 375
Weisenfeld, A.R., 97
Weisfeld, G.E., 52
Weishahn, M.W., 247
Weisman, A.D., 541, 543
Weiss, L., 442
Weiss, R.J., 301
Weitzman, N., 222
Welford, A.T., 422, 423, 463, 480
Wellman, H.M., 193
Wells, B.W.P., 54
Wenar, C., 83, 296, 335
Wentowski, G.J., 521
Wertheimer, M., 95
West, R.L., 500
Westinghouse Learning Corporation, 199
Westoff, C.F., 388
Weston, D.R., 141
Wetherick, N.E., 500
Wheeler, T.C., 240
Whisnant, L., 290
Whitbourne, S.K., 374, 375
White, B.L., 121
White, D.R., 231
White, K.R., 196, 241
White, M.A., 196
White, R., 378
Whitehurst, G.J., 104, 167
Whitely, R.J., 71
Whiting, B.B., 277
Whiting, J.W.M., 277
Whitney, E.N., 182, 231, 295, 297, 361, 364, 464, 470
Whitten, B., 58
Wickelgren, L.W., 92
Widmayer, S.M., 393, 440
Wiesel, T.N., 101
Wigdor, B.T., 473
Wilkie, F., 472

Willerman, L., 56
Williams, J.E., 222
Williams, J.H., 289, 416, 417
Williams, J.W., 238
Willis, S.L., 374, 487, 489, 490, 493, 502
Wilson, J.G., 78
Wilson, L.M., 78
Wilson, M.R., 439
Wimmer, H., 195
Wimmer, M., 537, 548
Winch, R., 386
Winget, C., 547
Wingfield, A., 117, 426, 496
Winick, M., 75, 110, 111, 231
Winn, R.L., 517
Wishart, J.G., 116
Wolanin, M.O., 469
Wolf, J., 250, 254, 255
Wolff, P.H., 96, 97, 160
Wolins, M., 134
Wonderly, D.M., 302
Wood, G., 27
Wood, V., 520
Woodruff, D.S., 468, 528
Wright, H.F., 267
Wright, J.C., 191, 192, 198
Wright, R.L.D., 27
Wynder, E.L., 366

Y

Yankelovich, D., 401
Yarrow, M.R., 129, 145, 277, 394
Yilo, K., 390
Young, D., 79, 83
Youngblood, S.A., 402
Youniss, J.S., 325
Yushioka, G.A., 391

Z

Zabin, L.B., 307
Zakus, G., 295
Zegans, L.A., 290
Zelazo, P.R., 105
Zelinski, E.M., 496
Zelnik, M., 307, 310
Ziegler, D.J., 15, 199, 200
Zigler, E., 144, 218
Zinchenko, V.P., 192
Zinsser, C., 121, 196, 200
Zivian, M.T., 427
Zougher, C.E., 309
Zumeta, Z., 395

Classic pattern of aging, 488–89
Classification (Piagetian), 183, 237
Climacteric, 416
Clinical method of research, 26
Cocaine, 70, 324
Cognitive development and change
    in adolescence, 298–301
    and contraception, 308
    in early adulthood, 373–77
    environmental effects, 195–99, 240–42
    in infancy and toddlerhood, 113–19
    in later adulthood, 487–93
    in middle adulthood, 423–26
    in middle childhood, 234–40
    and moral development, 301–2
    in preschool stage, 182–92. See also
        Intelligence, Memory, Information
        processing
Cognitive style, 242–43
Cognitive theory and language development,
    163
Cohabitation, 389–90
Cohort effect, 8–9, 375
Color blindness, 45
Combinational logic, 298
Communication. See also Marriage, Child-
    rearing, Discipline
    with children about death, 538–39
    and language, 154
    with parents and peers during adolescence,
        324–26
Companionate love, 387–88
Comparable worth, 404–5
Compensatory education, 199–200
Competency-performance argument, 116, 487
Complementary theory of mate selection,
    386–87
Comprehension, 160
Concordance rate, 52
Concrete operations, 19, 234–37
Conditioned response, 21
Conditioned stimulus, 21
Conflict-habituated marriage, 388
Conscience, 276
Consciousness, 10
Conservation
    in early childhood, 184–85
    in middle childhood, 235–36
Contact comfort, 134
Contraceptive use, 307–8
Control group, 27
Convergent thinking, 254
Cooperative play, 208
Correlations, 27–28
Creativity, 254, 429–30
Critical period, 773
Cross-cultural research in human development
    and achievement differences, 242–43

and adult development, 354–55
on aging and life expectancy, 458–61, 460–
    63, 512–16
on birth, 80
and burnout, 448–49
and child-rearing environments, 211–12
on child-rearing practices, 392–93
and cognitive abilities of elderly, 494–95
on death and dying, 550–51
on early experience, 7–8
and fathering, 141–43
on feeding practices, 108–9
genetics and, 47–48
and infant mortality, 86
and interactions with children, 24
on job structure, 424–25
and language development, 164–65
on money, the concept of, 184–85
on medical and social problems, 30–31
on motor development, 104–5
and moving to new countries, 362–63
in Piagetian experimentation, 347
problems and opportunities, 29–30
on religion, 323–24
on rewards, concept of, 303–4
on temperament, 54
and views of nuclear war, 278–79
Cross-sectional studies, 28–29, 426, 489–90
Crowning, 79
Crying, 97
Crystallized intelligence
    in early adulthood, 376–77
    in later adulthood, 489
    in middle adulthood, 425
    as theoretical approach, 376
Cystic fibrosis, 40, 41, 42

D

Day care
    and attachment, 144
    checklist for evaluation of, 145
    and intellectual development, 144
    quality of, 145
    and social development, 144–45
Death
    adolescent and adult understanding of, 539–
        40
    bereavement and grief, 547–49
    children's understanding of, 536–38
    culture and, 550–51
    helping children deal with, 538–39
    new interest in, 536
    phases of, 542–43
    place of, 543–45
    "right to die," 545–47
    stages in acceptance of own, 540–42
Death education, 549
Deception, 32

Deductive reasoning, 183
Defense mechanisms, 11–12
Deferred imitation, 183
Delinquency, 330–31
Delivery of the placenta, 79
Dentition, 232–33
Dependent variable, 27
Depression, 473–74
Despair, 130
Detachment, 130
Devitalized marriage, 388
Diethylstilbestrol, 69
Difficult temperament, 53–54
Dilation, 78
Discipline, 213–15
Discrimination, 21
Disenchantment phase of retirement, 523
Disengagement theory, 524
Distant figure style of grandparenting, 148
Divergent thinking, 254
Divorce
    adult view and experience, 395–97
        causes of, 396
        consequences of, 396
        predictors of, 395
    children's view
        experience, 264
        immediate reactions to, 265
        long-term effects, 266
        sex differences, 266
Dizygotic twins, 39–40, 65
Dominant traits, 40, 43
Down's Syndrome, 50–51
Dramatic play, 209
"Dream," the, 348
Dropout, school, 329–30
Drug-nutrient reactions, 477
Drug use
    in adolescence, 331–34
    in adulthood, 365–66
Dual-career marriages, 405

E

Early adulthood. See Young adulthood
Early childhood
    cognitive development in, 182–96
    growth, 178–79
    home influences on cognitive development,
        195–96
    information processing in, 190–95
    motor skills, 179–81
    nursery and preschools, 198–200
    nutrition in, 181–82
    peer group relationships, 209–11
    play in, 206–9
    preoperational stage, 182–90
    relations with parents, 213–15
    television's influence in, 196–98

Physical development
  in adolescence, 288–94
  in early adulthood, 360–69
  in infancy, 92–97
  in middle age, 412–17
  in middle childhood, 230–34
  in preschool period, 178–80
Piaget. *See also* Sensorimotor, Preoperational,
    Concrete, Formal operational stages
  abilities in later adulthood, 493–94
  in early adulthood, 374
  in middle adulthood, 234–37
  theory of cognitive development, 15–19
  theory of moral development, 271–72
Play, 206–9
Political philosophy, 304
Pollution and fetus, 72
Polygenic inheritance, 43
Popularity of children, 268
Power-assertive discipline, 214
Pragmatics, 156
Preconscious, 10
Pregnancy, 67, 72, 76–77, 393–94
  adolescent, 308–10
Prematurity, 83–84
Premenstrual syndrome (PMS), 374
Prenatal development, 64–71
Preoperational stage, 17–18, 182–90
Preschoolers. *See* Early childhood
Pressure and pain
  in infancy, 96
  in later maturity, 479
Preterm infants, 84
Primary process, 11
Primary sex characteristics, 288
Problem solving
  in later adulthood, 499–501
  in middle adulthood, 427–28
Production of language, 160
Progeria, 460–61
Project Head Start, 57, 199–200
Prosocial behavior, 277–79
Protest, 130
Proto-conversations, 156
Proximodistal principle, 104
Psychoanalytic theory. *See also* Freud's
    psychoanalytic theory, Psychosexual stages
  and moral development, 276
  and sex-role development, 223
Psycholinguistics, 162
Psychosexual stages, 11–14
Psychosocial dwarfism, 44
Puberty, 288, 292–93
Punishment, 213–16

Q

Qualitative change, 5
Quantitative change, 6

R

Racial differences in life expectancy, 466
Radiation, 72
Reaction time, 422–23
Readiness for school, 234
Reading, 55, 195, 239–40
Realistic love, 387–88
Reality process, 11
Recall, 117, 237–38
Recessive traits, 40–42
Reciprocal interaction, 22–23
Recognition, 117, 238
Rectangular curve of survival, 428
Referential children, 158
Reflective cognitive style, 243–44
Reflexes in the neonate, 99–100
Reinforcement and language development,
    160–61. *See also* Operant conditioning
Religion
  in early adulthood, 378–79
  and euthanasia, 546
  in later adulthood, 528–29
  in middle adulthood, 439
  peer and parental influence, 323–24
REM, 96–97
Remarriage, 399
Reorientation phase of retirement, 523
Research methods, 23–32
Reservoir of family wisdom grandparenting
    style, 148
Retirement
  attitudes towards, 522
  consequences of, 523–24
  phases of, 522–23
  women and, 524
Retrolental fibroplasia, 84
Reversibility, 235
Rh factor, 72
Role models and imitation, 222–23. *See also*
    Social learning theory
Romantic love, 387–88
Rooting reflex, 99
Rubella, 71

S

Safety, 181
Satisfaction in life, 527–28
Schizophrenia, 51–52
School experience, 240–44. *See also* Nursery
    school, Learning, Reading
Scripts, 194–95
Secondary process, 11
Secondary sex characteristics, 288
Secular trend, 291–92
Secure attachment, 135–36
Self-concept, 261–62, 294–95
Self-esteem, 261

Self-fulfilling prophecy, 217
Selman's model of friendship, 268–70
Semantics, 155
Senile dementia, 474–75
Sensorimotor stage, 12, 113–17
Sensory development and functioning
  in early adulthood, 369
  in infancy, 92–96
  in later adulthood, 477–80, 495–96
  in middle adulthood, 421–23
Separation anxiety, 129–30
Seriation, 183, 237
Sesame Street, 197–98, 538–39
Sex. *See also* Contraception
  in adolescence, 304–8
  and elderly, 517–18
  and marriage in early adulthood, 388
  in middle age, 415–16
Sex chromosomes, 40
Sex determination, 40, 41
Sex differences
  in aging, 413–14
  at birth and during infancy, 84–85, 112–13
  in career choice, 327
  in friendship in middle childhood, 270–71
  identity formation, 321
  in language acquisition, 168–69
  in life expectancy, 465–67
  Maccoby and Jacklin's research on, 219
  in maturation, 220
  in moral development, 274–75
  in motor skills, 179, 232–33
  orientation towards social experiences, 353
  in play, 209
  in reaction to divorce, 266–67
  in school achievement, 241
Sex education, 310–11
Sex-limited inheritance, 45
Sex-linked traits, 44–45
Sex-role acquisition, 219–25
Sex stereotypes, 270–71
Sex typing, 220
Sexual abuse, 216–17
Siamese twins, 65
Sibling relationships
  in childhood, 212–13
  and elderly, 521
  in infancy and toddlerhood, 149
Sickle cell anemia, 49
Similarity theory of mate selection, 385–86
Simple reaction time, 422
Single lifestlye, 390–91
Single parenting, 398–99
Sleeping-waking cycle, 96–97
Slow to warm up temperament, 53
Small-for-date babies, 84
Smell, 95–96, 369, 422
Smoking, 69, 332–33

Social clocks, 351–52
Social learning theory, 23, 222–23
Social readjustment rating scale, 370
Socioeconomic status
  and career choice, 327–28
  and cognitive development, 119
  as unsatisfactory variable, 119
Solitary play, 208
Sonogram, 77
Spatial perception, 45
Spouse abuse, 397
Stability and change during the life span, 9
Stability phase of retirement, 523
Stage theories, 9–10
Stanford-Binet Intelligence Test, 245
State (infant), 97
Stepchildren, 267
Stepparenting, 399–401
Stepping reflex, 99
Stimulus discrimination, 134
Stimulus generalization, 21
Stimulus-value-role theory of mate selection,
  386–87
Strange situation, 135–36
Stress
  in early adulthood, 369–72
  in later adulthood, 471–73
  in middle adulthood, 419–20
  during pregnancy, 76–77
    See also Type A personality
Stroke, 469
Sucking reflex, 99
Sudden Infant Death Syndrome, 102–3
Suicide, 334–35, 474
Superego, 11, 276
Surrogate parent grandparenting style, 148
Survey method, 25–26
Symbolic function, 183
Synchrony, 139
Syntax, 155
Syphilis, 71

T

Taste, 96, 422
Tay-Sachs disease, 46–47, 48
Telegraphic speech, 158
Television
  advertising, 196
  aggression and, 281–82
  early childhood and, 196–98
  extent of viewing in childhood, 196

Temperament, 52–54
Teratogen, 67
Terminal drop, 491–92
Termination phase of retirement, 523
Tetracycline, 67
Thalidomide, 67
Theories. *See also* Freud, Erikson, Piaget,
  Information processing, Behaviorism,
  Levinson, Gould, Vaillant, Neugarten
  of adulthood, 342–54
  of aging, 461–64
  of development, 9–23
Time out, 282
Toddlerhood. *See also* Infancy
  cognitive development, 114
  communication with, 158–59
  interactions with peers and siblings, 149–50
  memory, 117
  psychosocial challenges in, 134
  sex differences in treatment, 112–13
Toilet training, 111–12
Total marriage, 388
Touch, 369
Traffic accidents, 471
Transductive reasoning, 183
Transformations, 186–87
Transition, 79
Transitive inferences, 184
Triarchic theory of human intelligence, 244–
  45
Trust vs. mistrust, 15, 134–35
Turner's Syndrome, 51
Twins, 167. *See also* Monozygotic, Dizygotic
Type A and Type B personality patterns, 54,
  371–72, 419–20, 467

U

Ultrasound, 77–78
Unconditioned response, 21
Unconditioned stimulus, 21
Unconscious, 10
Underextensions, 159
Unemployment, 405–6
Unintegrated personality, 530

V

Vaillant's (George) theory, 345–47, 384, 452
Values, 302–4
Values clarification course, 276
Vernix caseosa, 92

Vision
  in early adulthood, 369
  in infancy, 92–95
  in later adulthood, 477–78
  in middle adulthood, 421–22
Visual cliff, 94
Vital marriage, 388
Vocational development, 401–6, 442–47

W

Wechsler Intelligence Tests, 245–46, 488–89
Weight, 231, 361
Wernicke's area, 162
Widowhood, 518–19
Women. *See also* Sex differences, Mothers,
  Working mothers
  and careers, 327–28
  and lifestyle patterns, 403
  and retirement, 524
Workers
  characteristics of modern, 401
  elderly, 524–26
Working mothers, 145–48
Writing, 240

Y

Young adulthood
  cognitive functioning in, 373–77
  divorce in, 395–97
  drug use in, 365–66
  dual career marriages, 405
  exercise in, 362–65
  friendships in, 391
  health in, 360
  height and weight, 361–62
  marriage in, 384–89
  morals and ethics in, 378–80
  parenting in, 393–95
  physical abilities in, 367–69
  religion in, 378
  sensory functioning in, 369
  being single, 390–91
  single parenting, 398
  stress in, 369–72
  unemployment in, 405
  vocational development in, 401–5
Young-old, 353

Z

Zygote, 64

Acknowledgments—Continued

Pages 142–3, cross-cultural current. From "The Father's Role and Its Relation to Masculinity, Femininity, and Androgyny," by G. Russell. In *Child Development*, 1978, 49, 1177–1181. Copyright © The Society for Research in Child Development, Inc. Used by permission of the Society and the author.

Pages 146–47, Fig. 5.2. Adapted from "A Day-Care Checklist," by Joyce P. Stines, 1983. Used by permission of J. P. Stines.

Page 161, Fig. 6.1. From *The Acquisition of Language*, by B. A. Moskowitz. Copyright © 1978 by Scientific American, Inc. All rights reserved.

Pages 180–81, Table 7.1. From *A Textbook of Motor Development*, 2nd Edition, by Charles B. Corbin. Copyright © 1973, 1980, Wm. C. Brown Publishers, Dubuque, Iowa. All rights reserved. Reprinted by permission.

Page 233, Fig. 9.1. Copyright by the American Dental Association. Reprinted by permission.

Page 247, Table 9.1. From *The Exceptional Student in the Regular Classroom*, by Bill R. Gearheart and Mel W. Weishahn. Copyright © 1984 Times Mirror/Mosby College Publishing. Copyright © 1985 Merrill Publishing Company, Columbus, Ohio. Reprinted by permission of Merrill Publishing Company.

Page 248, Table 9.2. From *Exceptional Children: Introduction to Special Education*, 3rd Edition, by D. P. Hallahan and J. M. Kauffman. Copyright © 1986. Reprinted by permission of Prentice-Hall, Inc., Englewood Cliffs, New Jersey.

Page 249, Fig. 9.2. From "Instructional Alternatives for Exceptional Children," by E. Deno. Copyright © Council for Exceptional Children, 1973.

Page 253, Table 9.3. From *Special Children*, by B. G. Suran and J. V. Rizzo. Copyright © 1983 by Scott, Foresman and Company. Reprinted by permission.

Page 269, Table 10.1. Excerpt from *The Development of Children's Friendships*, by Steven Asher and John Gottman, eds. Copyright © 1981 Cambridge University Press. Reprinted with permission of Cambridge University Press.

Page 273, Table 10.2. From "Definition of Moral Stages: Kohlberg's Stages" in *Cognitive Development and Epistemology*, T. Mischel, ed. Copyright © 1971 by Academic Press, Inc.

Pages 278–79, cross-cultural current. From "Soviet Children and the Threat of Nuclear War: A Preliminary Study," by E. Chivian et al. In *American Journal of Orthopsychiatry 55*, 497. Copyright © 1985 the American Orthopsychiatric Association, Inc. Reproduced by permission.

Page 289, Table 11.1. From *Adolescence and Youth*, 3rd Edition, by John Janeway Conger and Anne C. Petersen. Copyright © 1984 by John Janeway Conger and Anne C. Petersen. Reprinted by permission of Harper & Row, Publishers, Inc.

Page 291, Table 11.2. From *Adolescence and Youth*, 3rd Edition, by John Janeway Conger and Anne C. Petersen. Copyright © 1984 by John Janeway Conger and Anne C. Petersen. Reprinted by permission of Harper & Row, Publishers, Inc.

Page 293, Fig. 11.1. Reprinted by permission from *Adolescence: Theories, Research and Applications*, by L. C. Jensen. Copyright © 1985 by West Publishing Company. All rights reserved.

Page 305, Fig.11.2. From "Shifts in Students' Attitudes Seen as Threat to Liberal Arts," by E. Green. In *The Chronicle of Higher Education*, November 5, 1986. Copyright © 1986 The Chronicle of Higher Education. Reprinted with permission.

Page 318, Table 12.1. From "Identity Status and Academic Achievement in Female Adolescents," by R. Hummel and L. L. Roselli. In *Adolescence 18*, 1983. Copyright © 1983. Reprinted by permission.

Page 351, Table 13.1. From "Consensus in a Middle-Class, Middle-Aged Sample Regarding Various Age-Related Characteristics from Age Norms, Age Constraints, and Adult Socialization," by Bernice L. Neugarten et al. In *American Journal of Sociology 70*, 1965. Reprinted by permission of the author and The University of Chicago Press.

Page 370, Table 14.2. Reprinted with permission from "The Social Readjustment Rating Scle," by T. Holmes and R. H. Rahe in *Journal of Psychosomatic Research 11*. Copyright © 1967, Pergamon Journals, Ltd.

Page 376, Fig. 14.1. Reprinted by permission from *Constancy and Change in Human Development*, by J. L Horn and G. Donaldson. Copyright © 1980 by Harvard University Press.

Page 377, Fig. 14.2. Reprinted by permission from *Constancy and Change in Human Development*, by J. L. Horn and G. Donaldson. Copyright © 1980 by Harvard University Press.

Page 390, Table 15.1. Reprinted by permission from *Choices in Relationships*, by D. Knox. Copyright © 1985 by West Publishing Company. All rights reserved.

Page 429, Fig. 16.3. From "Aging and Cognitive Changes," by Nancy W. Denney, in *Handbook of Developmental Psychology* by Benjamin B. Wolman, ed. Copyright © 1982. Reprinted by permission of Prentice-Hall, Inc. Englewood Cliffs, New Jersey.

Page 412, quotation. Reprinted by permission from *Pathfinders*, by G. Sheehy. Copyright © 1981 William Morrow Company. All rights reserved.

Page 430, Figs. 16.4–5. From *Aging and Behavior*, 3rd Edition, by J. Botwinick. Copyright © 1984 by Springer Publishing Company, Inc., New York. Used by permission.

Page 437, Fig. 17.1. From "America's Baby Boom Generation: The Fateful Bulge," by L. F. Bouvier, In *Population Bulletin, 35*, 1. Population Reference Bureau, Inc. Washington, D.C., 1980.

Page 453, Fig. 17.2. From *Midlife Development in Aging in the 1980's*, by S. Cytrynbaum et al. Copyright © 1980 by the American Psychological Association. Adapted by permission of the author.

Page 465, Table 18.1. Courtesy of Statistical Bulletin, the Metropolitan Life Insurance Company.

Page 470, Fig. 18.2. From *Stand Tall! The Informed Woman's Guide to Preventing Osteoporosis*, by Morris Notelovitz and Marsha Ware. Copyright © 1982 by Triad Publishing Co.

Page 480, Fig. 18.3. From *Vitality and Aging*, by James F. Fries and Lawrence M. Crapo. Copyright © 1981 by W. H. Freeman and Company. Used by permission.

Page 489, Table 19.1. From *Principles of Educational and Psychological Testing*, 3rd Edition, by F. G. Brown. Copyright © 1983 by Holt, Rinehart and Winston. Reprinted by permission of Holt,

Rinehart and Winston, Inc.

Page 494–95, cross-cultural current. From *Adult Development: The Differentiation of Experience,* by Susan Krauss Whitbourne and Comilda S. Weinstock. Copyright © 1979 by Holt, Rinehart and Winston. Reprinted by permission of Holt, Rinehart and Winston, Inc.

Page 510, Table 20.1. From *The Myth and Reality of Aging in America,* by L. Harris and Associates, 1975. Courtesy of The National Council on Aging.

Page 522, Fig. 20.1. From *The Social Forces in Later Life,* 2nd Edition, by Robert C. Atchley. Copyright © 1977 by Wadsworth Publishing Company, Inc. Reprinted by permission of the publisher.

Page 547, Table 21.1. From "Attitudes Toward Euthanasia," by Carolyn Winget, M.A., Assoc. Prof. Dept. of Psychiatry, University of Cincinnati. In *Journal of Medical Ethics 3,* 1977. Reprinted by permission of the author and publisher.

Page 549, Table 21.2. From "Human Grief: A Model for Prediction and Intervention," by Larry Bugen. In *American Journal of Orthopsychiatry,* April 1977. Copyright © 1977 the American Orthopsychiatric Association. Reprinted by permission of the author and publisher.

Page 551, Table A. *Death and Ethnicity: A Psychological Study,* by R. A. Kalish and D. K. Reynolds. Copyright © 1976 by Lexington Books. Reprinted by permission.

Page 552, Fig. 21.1. From "The Bereavement of the Widowed," by P. J. Clayton, J. A. Halikes, and W. L. Maurice. In *Diseases of the Nervous System 32,* 1971. Reprinted by permission.

Page T-18, Table 11. Courtesy *Statistical Bulletin,* Metropolitan Life Insurance Company.

Pages T-20 to T-21, Table 13. Courtesy *Statistical Bulletin,* Metropolitan Life Insurance Company.

Credits for Part-opening Fine Art

1 Grandma Moses: *Bringing in the Maple Sugar.* Copyright © 1982 Grandma Moses Properties Co., N.Y. Anna Mary Robertson (1860–1961) began painting in old age and became internationally known as "Grandma Moses."

89 Richard C. Woodville: *Return of the Cavalier.* Courtesy of The New York Historical Society, New York City.

175 Pablo Picasso, (Spanish, 1881–1973): *Mother and Child,* 1922. Oil on canvas; 39⅜ × 31⅞ in. The Baltimore Museum of Art; The Cone Collection, formed by Dr. Claribel Cone and Miss Etta Cone of Baltimore, Maryland.

227 Winslow Homer (1836–1910): *Snap the Whip,* 1872. Oil on canvas, 12 × 20 in. Reproduced with permission. The Metropolitan Museum of Art, Gift of Christian A. Zabriskie, 1950.

285 Paul Gauguin: *Le Repas des Jeunes Tahitiens,* 1891. Oil on canvas; 28⅛ × 35¼ in. Louvre, Paris. Collection, Mr. and Mrs. André Meyer.

339 Mary Cassatt: *The Boating Party,* 1893–94. Oil on canvas. The National Gallery of Art, Washington, D.C., The Chester Dale Collection.

409 Pierre Auguste Renoir: *Le Cabaret de la mère Anthony,* 1866. Oil on canvas; 194 × 131 cm. National Museum, Stockholm, Sweden.

457 L.L. Kern H.: *The Fruit Peddler,* 1880. Oil on wood panel; 18⁹⁄₁₆ × 12¼ in. Milwaukee Art Museum Collection, Gift of Rene von Schleinitz Foundation.

Photo Credits

2 Jane Scherr, Jeroboam; **4** Barbara Kirk, The Stock Market; **7** Elizabeth Crews, Stock, Boston; **8** Paula Weight, Black Star; **10** National Archives, Photo Researchers, Inc.; **14** Courtesy of the Harvard University News Office; **17** Bill Anderson, Monkmeyer; **20** Elizabeth Crews; **22** Elizabeth Crews, Stock, Boston; **24** Michael Weisbrot, Stock, Boston; **25** Hazel Hankin, Stock, Boston; **26** Gabe Palmer, The Stock Market; **36** Joe Skipper, AP/Wide World Photos; **39** Courtesy of Dr. Fred Hecht, The Genetics Center for Southwest Biomedical Research Institute; **40** Alice Kandell, Photo Researchers, Inc.; **45** Don Causey, Black Star; **49** David Farr, Imagesmythe, Inc.; **50** Sybil Shelton, Peter Arnold, Inc.; **56** Charles Gatewood, Stock, Boston; **59** Catherine Ursillo, Photo Researchers, Inc.; **62** Joel Gordon, Design Conceptions; **64** Donald Dietz, Stock, Boston; **70** Stock, Boston; **75** Elizabeth Crews; **78, 79** Mimi Cotter, International Stock Photography, Ltd.; **81** Freda Leinwand, Monkmeyer; **83** David Powers, Stock, Boston; **90** Elizabeth Crews; **94** William Vandivert, *Scientific American,* April 1960. Used by permission; **98** From A. N. Meltzoff and M. K. Moore in *Science,* 1979, 198, 75–78. Copyright © 1977 by the AAAS; **101** (left) Elizabeth Crews; **101** (right) Ellis Herwig, Stock, Boston; **102** (left) Lew Merrim, Monkmeyer; **102** (right) Ray Ellis, Photo Researchers, Inc.; **103** (left) Ed Lettau, Photo Researchers, Inc.; **103** (right) Mimi Forsyth, Monkmeyer; **115** George Zimbel, Monkmeyer; **116** Hazel Hankin, Stock, Boston; **122** Elizabeth Crews; **126** Elizabeth Crews, Stock, Boston; **132** Frank Keillor, Jeroboam; **135** Courtesy of the University of Wisconsin Primate Laboratory; **136** Mimi Cotter, International Stock Photography, Ltd.; **139** Thomas McAvoy, *Life Magazine* © Time Inc.; **140** Elizabeth Crews; **149** Elizabeth Crews; **152** Joel Gordon, Design Conceptions; **155** Elizabeth Crews; **160** Rick Smolan, Stock, Boston; **166** Elizabeth Crews; **168** David Strickler, Monkmeyer; **171** Elizabeth Crews; **172** Culver Pictures; **176** Mel DiGiacomo, The Image Bank; **178** Michael Grecco, AP/Wide World Photos; **190** Mimi Forsyth, Monkmeyer; **193** Elizabeth Crews; **194** Peter Menzel, Stock, Boston; **198** Michael Weisbrot, International Stock Photography, Ltd.; **204** Deborah Kahn-Kalas, Stock, Boston; **207** Jean-Claude Lejeune, Stock, Boston; **210** Elizabeth Crews, Stock, Boston; **212** Elizabeth Crews; **214** Laimute Druskis, Taurus Photos; **222** Shirley Zeiberg, Taurus Photos; **224** Mimi Cotter, International Stock Photography, Ltd.; **228** Jim Anderson, Woodfin Camp & Associates; **235** Marty Heitner, Taurus Photos; **236** Marion Faller, Monkmeyer; **239** Mimi Forsyth, Monkmeyer; **245** James R. Holland, Stock, Boston; **250** David Strickler, Monkmeyer; **254** Elizabeth Crews; **258** Tom Ballard, EKM-Nepenthe; **261** Eric Neurath, Stock,